P9-CEX-444

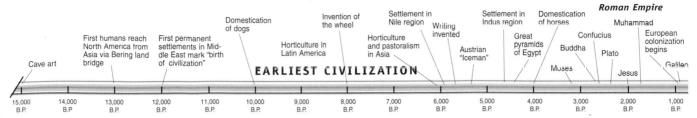

Earliest horticultural and pastoral societies

Rise of agriculture and bureaucracy

European Middle Ages

Roman Empire

Cave art

First humans reach North America from Asia via Bering land bridge

First permanent settlements in Middle East mark "birth of civilization"

Domestication of dogs

Horticulture In Latin America

Invention of the wheel

Settlement in Nile region

Horticulture and pastoralism in Asia

Writing invented

Settlement in Indus region

Austrian "Iceman"

Domestication of horses

Great pyramids of Egypt

Muhammad

Confucius

Buddha

Plato

European colonization begins

Muses

Jesus

Galileo

EARLIEST CIVILIZATION

| 15,000 B.P. | 14,000 B.P | 13,000 B.P. | 12,000 B.P. | 11,000 B.P. | 10,000 B.P. | 9,000 B.P. | 8,000 B.P. | 7,000 B.P. | 6,000 B.P. | 5,000 B.P. | 4,000 B.P. | 3,000 B.P. | 2,000 B.P. | 1,000 B.P. |

"Baby bust"

Women's movement intensifies

U.S. life expectancy 77 years

Movement

1974 Punk begins

1960 Rise of folk era and Motown

1981 MTV debuts

1997 Backstreet Boys lead revival of pop

1979 SugarHill Gang popularizes rap

1991 Nirvana takes grunge mainstream

1999 Eminem merges musical styles

1969 Woodstock

1977 Disco peaks

1964 British music invasion (The Beatles)

1988 Last U.S. Playboy Club closes

1970 First Earth Day

1980 Women earn majority of college degrees

2000 60% of U.S. women in labor force

1965 Foreign-born Japanese eligible for citizenship

1969 Stonewall riot begins gay rights movement

1975 First women's shelter

1987 Rhode Island enacts statewide recycling law

1981 First AIDS cases reported

Sept. 11, 2001 Terrorist attacks

1961 European colonization of Africa ends

1968 First interracial kiss on TV (Star Trek)

1977 First gay TV character

2001 War on Terrorism

1973 Roe v. Wade

Revolutions in USSR and Eastern Europe 1989–1990

Persian Gulf War 1991

P R E S E N T

Vietnam War 1963–1975

Iraq War 2003

1975

2000

1981 Space shuttle

1990 Human Genome Project

1957 Sputnik launched

1975 Microsoft founded

1983 Laptop computers hit the market

2002 Birth control patch invented

1969 First human on moon

1993 First cloned cells

1960 Birth control pill invented

1973 First cell phone call

1982 Modern Internet opens

1965 Compact disc invented

1971 E-mail invented

1968 First heart transplant

1977 First computerized arcade game

1990s Expansion of the Internet

2000 First hybrid cars sold in U.S.

jobs

Postindustrial era

Information Revolution

| 3 billion | 4 billion | 5 billion | 6 billion |

292.2 million

1959 Goffman debuts "dramaturgical analysis"

1981 Bernard nurtures gender studies

Piaget probes how we learn

This book is offered to teachers of sociology
in the hope that it will help our students understand
their place in today's society and in tomorrow's world.

John J. Macionis

SOCIETY THE BASICS

8

EIGHTH EDITION

JOHN J. MACIONIS

Kenyon College

PEARSON
Prentice Hall

Upper Saddle River, New Jersey 07458

Library of Congress Cataloging-in-Publication Data

Macionis, John J.
    Society: the basics / John J. Macionis. — 8th ed.
        p. cm.
    Includes bibliographical references and index.
    ISBN 0-13-192244-0 (alk. paper)
    1. Sociology.   I. Title
HM586.M1657 2005
301—dc222001057794

2004052940

Editorial Director: *Leah Jewell*
AVP, Publisher: *Nancy Roberts*
Executive Editor: *Christopher DeJohn*
Editor in Chief of Development: *Rocbelle Diogenes*
Development Editor: *Karen Trost*
VP, Director of Production and Manufacturing: *Barbara Kittle*
Production Editor: *Barbara Reilly*
Copyeditors: *Bruce Emmer, Amy Macionis*
Supplements Editor: *Erin Katchmar*
Proofreaders: *Alison Lorber, Beatrice Marcks*
Editorial Assistant: *Kristin Haegele*
Prepress and Manufacturing Manager: *Nick Sklitsis*
Prepress and Manufacturing Buyer: *Mary Ann Gloriande*
Senior Marketing Manager: *Marissa Feliberty*

Marketing Assistant: *Jennifer Lang*
Creative Design Director: *Leslie Osher*
Interior and Cover Designer: *Anne DeMarinis*
Line Art Illustrations: *Mirella Signoretto*
Director, Image Resource Center: *Melinda Reo*
Manager, Rights and Permissions: *Zina Arabia*
Manager, Visual Research: *Beth Brenzel*
Image Permissions Coordinator: *Debra Hewitson*
Photo Researcher: *Julie Tesser*
Manager, Cover Visual Research and Permissions: *Karen Sanatar*
Media Editor: *Kate Ramunda*
Media Project Manager: *Raegan Keida*
Manager of Media Production: *Lynn Pearlman*

This book was set in 10/12 Minion by Lithokraft and was printed and bound by Webcrafters, Inc. The cover was printed by Coral Graphics.

For permission to use copyrighted material, grateful acknowledgment is made to the copyright holders listed on pages 503–4, which are considered an extension of this copyright page.

Copyright © 2006, 2004, 2002, 2000, 1998, 1996, 1994, 1992 by Pearson Education, Inc. Upper Saddle River, New Jersey 07458

Pearson Prentice Hall. All rights reserved. Printed in the United States of America. This publication is protected by copyright, and permission should be obtained from the publisher prior to any prohibited reproduction, storage in a retrieval system, or transmission in any form or by any means, electronic, mechanical, photocopying, recording, or likewise. For information regarding permission(s), write to: Rights and Permissions Department.

Pearson Prentice Hall™ is a trademark of Pearson Education, Inc.
Pearson® is a registered trademark of Pearson plc
Prentice Hall® is a registered trademark of Pearson Education, Inc.

Pearson Education LTD.
Pearson Education Singapore, Pte. Ltd
Pearson Education, Canada, Ltd
Pearson Education—Japan
Pearson Education Australia PTY, Limited

Pearson Education North Asia Ltd
Pearson Educación de Mexico, S.A. de C.V.
Pearson Education Malaysia, Pte. Ltd
Pearson Education, Upper Saddle River, New Jersey

10 9 8 7 6 5 4 3 2 1
ISBN 0-13-192244-0

BRIEF CONTENTS

CONTENTS

Sociology: Perspective, Theory, and Method   1

Culture   34

Socialization: From Infancy to Old Age   62

Social Interaction in Everyday Life   86

Groups and Organizations   108

Sexuality and Society   134

Deviance   160

Social Stratification   190

Are Those Leaving Welfare Better Off Now? Yes and No   223

Global Stratification   224

 *Brazilian Slums Seen as Pawns in Political Games   249*

Gender Stratification   250

Race and Ethnicity 278

Economics and Politics 308

Family and Religion   344

Education and Medicine 380

Population, Urbanization, and Environment 416

Social Change: Modern and Postmodern Societies 448

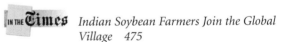 *Indian Soybean Farmers Join the Global Village 475*

MAPS

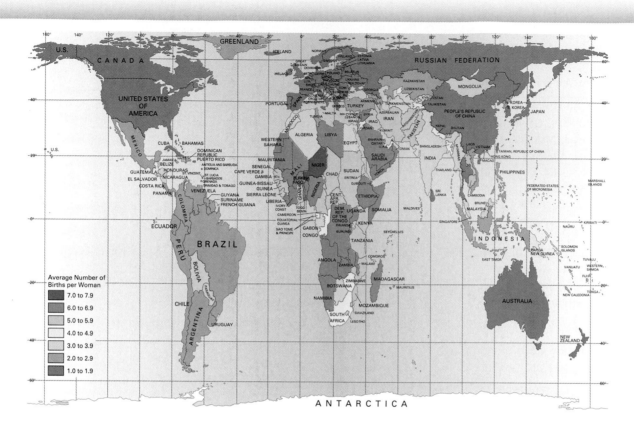

Average Number of Births per Woman
- 7.0 to 7.9
- 6.0 to 6.9
- 5.0 to 5.9
- 4.0 to 4.9
- 3.0 to 3.9
- 2.0 to 2.9
- 1.0 to 1.9

GLOBAL MAPS:
WINDOW ON THE WORLD

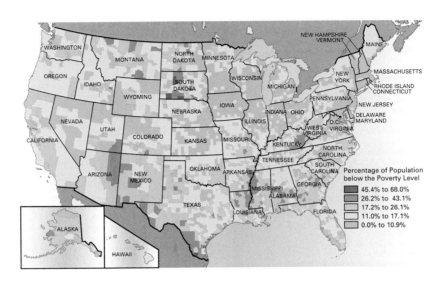

NATIONAL MAPS:
SEEING OURSELVES

BOXES

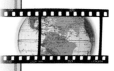

CRITICAL THINKING

CONTROVERSY & DEBATE

APPLYING SOCIOLOGY

The New York Times

IN THE **Times**

PREFACE

An Invitation to Students; A Welcome to Instructors

I did not start out to become a sociologist. Guided by teachers and counselors who pointed to my good grades in mathematics and physics, I applied to and entered engineering school. The first year went well enough. Early in my sophomore year, however, I realized that I had lost my interest in engineering. To be honest, my school was also quickly losing its interest in me, and my engineering career came to a crashing halt soon after I posted a grade point average of 1.3 for the fall semester.

The personal crisis that followed caused me to take a hard look at other fields of study, and the following spring, I enrolled in my first sociology course. This one course would truly change my life. From the very beginning, sociology helped me make sense of the world, and just as important, sociology was *fun*. Thirty-five years later, I can still say the same thing.

The importance of one person's story lies in the fact that countless people have been turned on to sociology in much the same way. Thousands of students have discovered the excitement of sociology in an introductory class, and many have gone on to make it their life's work.

If you are a student, I invite you to open this book, to enjoy it, and to find a new and very useful way of looking at the world. If you are an instructor, I stand with you in knowing the deep satisfaction that comes from making a difference in the lives of our students. There is surely no greater reward for our work and, in my case, no better reason for striving for ever-better revisions of *Society: The Basics*, which, along with the longer, hardcover version, *Sociology*, stands out as the discipline's most popular text.

The new eighth edition of *Society: The Basics* is exciting, covers it all, and—as students' e-mail messages testify—is plain fun to read. This major revision elevates sociology's most popular text to a still higher standard of excellence and is an unparalleled resource to help today's students learn about our diverse and changing world.

This book is just one part of a complete learning package. Found in the back of every new copy of *Society: The Basics, Eighth Edition*, is a CD-ROM, included *at no additional cost to the student*. This CD-ROM is the best of its kind, a fully interactive window into others' lives—both in the United States and around the world. The CD includes relevant *ABC News* video clips and a library of sixteen short "author's tip" videos—one for each chapter—that brings to life key themes. All of the maps from the text become interactive on the CD-ROM, and students can review key terms using a flashcard feature. Simply put, no other CD-ROM offers as much support to make students eager to learn.

In addition, students using *Society: The Basics, Eighth Edition*, can log on to a free, full-featured Web site at http://www.prenhall.com/macionis. From the main page, simply click on the cover of *Society: The Basics, Eighth Edition*, to find chapter overviews and learning objectives, suggested essay questions and paper topics, multiple-choice and true-false questions that the server will grade, and chapter-relevant Web destinations with learning questions.

Instructors and students will benefit from our other technology innovation. OneKey—a "one-stop shop" for teaching and learning materials—will transform both the classroom and the learning experience. Pulling together the many resources available with this textbook, OneKey has the power to make instructors more effective and students more engaged.

Textbook, CD-ROM, Web site, and One-Key: A multimedia package that is the foundation for sound learning in this new information age. We invite you to examine these important pieces of the learning process!

Organization of This Text

Society: The Basics carries students through sociology's basic ideas, research, and insights in sixteen logically organized chapters. Chapter 1 ("Sociology: Perspective, Theory, and Method") explains how the discipline's distinctive point of view illuminates the world in a new and exciting way. In addition, the first chapter introduces major theoretical approaches and explains the methods sociologists use to test and refine their knowledge.

The next six chapters examine core sociological concepts. Chapter 2 ("Culture") explores the fascinating diversity of human living that marks our world. Chapter 3 ("Socialization: From Infancy to Old Age") investigates how people everywhere develop their humanity as they learn to participate in society. While highlighting the importance of the early years to the socialization process, this chapter describes significant transformations that occur over the entire life course, including old age. Chapter 4 ("Social Interaction in Everyday Life") takes a micro-level look at how people construct the daily realities that we often take for granted. Chapter 5 ("Groups and Organizations") focuses on social groups, within which we have many of our most meaningful experiences. It also highlights the expansion of formal organizations and points up some of the problems of living in a bureaucratic age. Chapter 6 ("Sexuality and Society") explains the social foundation of human sexuality. Based on recent research, this chapter surveys sexual patterns in the United States and also explores variations in sexual practices through history and around the world today.

Chapter 7 ("Deviance") analyzes how the routine operation of society promotes deviance as well as conformity.

The next four chapters provide more coverage of social inequality than is found in any other brief text. Chapter 8 ("Social Stratification") introduces basic concepts that describe social hierarchy throughout history and around the world. The chapter then highlights dimensions of social difference in the United States today. Chapter 9 ("Global Stratification") extends this text's commitment to global education by analyzing the social ranking of nations themselves. Why, in other words, do people in some societies have abundant wealth while in others people struggle every day just to survive? *Society: The Basics* also provides full-chapter coverage of two additional dimensions of social difference. Chapter 10 ("Gender Stratification") describes how gender is a central element of social stratification in the United States, as it is worldwide. Chapter 11 ("Race and Ethnicity") explores racial and ethnic diversity in the United States, explaining how societies use physical and cultural traits to construct and rank categories of people in a hierarchy.

Next are three chapters that survey all the major social institutions. Chapter 12 ("Economics and Politics") examines the political economy of U.S. society in global context. Beginning with a historical look at how the Industrial Revolution transformed the Western world, this chapter contrasts capitalist and socialist economic models and investigates how economic systems are linked to a society's distribution of power. It also contains coverage of the military, issues of war and peace, and a much-expanded discussion of terrorism.

Chapter 13 ("Family and Religion") spotlights two institutions central to the symbolic organization of social life. The chapter begins by focusing on the variety of families in the United States, making frequent comparisons to kinship systems in other parts of the world. Basic elements of religious life follow, with an overview of recent religious trends.

Chapter 14 ("Education and Medicine") examines two institutions with special importance in the modern world. The chapter looks first at the historical expansion of schooling, noting many ways in which the scope and kind of education in any society are linked to other social institutions. Next, we look at medicine, which also has become a central institution during the last century and a half. The chapter concludes by explaining the distinctive strategies various countries—including the United States—employ to promote public health.

The final two chapters of the text focus on dimensions of social change. Chapter 15 ("Population, Urbanization, and Environment") is a synthesis that begins by spotlighting the growth of population in the world. Then, our attention turns to the rise of cities in the United States and to the urban explosion now taking place in poor nations of the world. Finally, the chapter explains how the state of the natural environment reflects social organization. Chapter 16 ("Social Change: Modern and Postmodern Societies") concludes the text with summaries of major theories of social change, a look at how people forge social movements to encourage or resist change, and analysis of the various benefits and liabilities of modern social patterns as well as the emergence of a "postmodern" way of life.

Continuity: Established Features of *Society: The Basics*

Society: The Basics is no ordinary textbook: In sociology, it represents *the* standard of excellence, which explains why this book is selected by far more faculty than any other. The extraordinary strength of *Society: The Basics* results from a combination of the following features.

The best writing style. Most important, this text offers a writing style widely praised by students and faculty alike as elegant and inviting. *Society: The Basics* is an enjoyable text that encourages students to read—even beyond their assignments. No one says it better than the students themselves, whose recent e-mail includes testimonials such as these:

> I just want to tell you this is the best text I have ever used.

> I want to thank you for providing us with such a comprehensive, easy-to-read, and engaging book. . . . In fact, my instructor thought it was so interesting and well done, she read the book from cover to cover. Your work has been a great service to us all. My sociology book is the only textbook that I currently own that I actually enjoy reading. Thank you!

> I'm a college student in California and my sociology class used your book. It was by far the best textbook I have ever used. I actually liked to read it for pleasure as well as to study. I just wanted to say it was great.

> My sociology class used your book [and] it was by far the best textbook I have ever used. I actually liked to read it for pleasure as well as to study. I just want to say it was great.

> I am taking a Sociology 101 class using your text, a book that I have told my professor is the best textbook that I have ever seen, bar none. I've told her as well that I will be more than happy to take more sociology classes as long as there is a Macionis text to go with them.

> I am fascinated by the contents of this textbook. In contrast to texts in my other classes, I actually enjoy the reading. Thank you for such a thought-provoking, well-written textbook.

> Dude, your book *rocks!*

A global perspective. *Society: The Basics* has taken a leading role in expanding the horizons of our discipline beyond the United States. It was the first brief text to mainstream global content, the first to introduce global maps, and the first to offer comprehensive coverage of global topics such as stratification and the natural environment. It is no wonder that *Sociology* and *Society: The Basics* have been adapted and translated into half a dozen languages for use around the world. Each chapter explores the world's social diversity and explains why social trends in the United States—from musical tastes to the price of wheat to the growing disparity of income—are influenced by what happens elsewhere. Just as important, students will learn ways in which social patterns and policies in the United States affect poor nations around the world.

A celebration of social diversity. *Society: The Basics* invites students from all social backgrounds to discover a fresh and exciting way to see themselves within the larger social world. Readers will discover in this text the diversity of U.S. society—people of African, Asian, European, and Latino ancestry, as well as women and men of various class positions and at all points in the life course. Just as important, without ignoring the problems that marginalized people face, this text does not treat minorities as social problems but notes their achievements. A scholarly analysis of sociology texts published in the American Sociological Association's journal *Teaching Sociology* evaluated Macionis's *Sociology* (the hardcover companion to this text) as the best of all the leading texts in terms of integrating racial and ethnic material throughout (Stone, 1996).

Emphasis on critical thinking. Critical-thinking skills include the ability to challenge common assumptions by formulating questions, to identify and weigh appropriate evidence, and to reach reasoned conclusions. This text not only teaches but encourages students to discover on their own.

Engaging and instructive chapter openings. One of the most popular features of earlier editions of *Society: The Basics* has been the engaging vignettes that begin each chapter. These openings—for instance, using the tragic sinking of the *Titanic* to illustrate the life and death consequences of social inequality, describing one California neighborhood to illustrate the increasing social diversity of the United States, or recounting how a fire in a Bangladesh sweatshop that manufactures clothing for sale in the United States left dozens of low-paid workers dead—spark the interest of readers as they introduce important themes. While keeping seven of the best chapter-opening vignettes from earlier editions, this revision offers nine that are new.

Inclusive focus on women and men. Beyond devoting two full chapters to the important concepts of sex and gender, *Society: The Basics* mainstreams gender into *every* chapter, showing how the topic at hand affects women and men differently and explaining how gender operates as a basic part of social organization.

Theoretically clear and balanced. This text makes theory easy. The discipline's major theoretical approaches are introduced in Chapter 1 and are carried through later chapters. The text highlights the social-conflict, structural-functional, and symbolic-interaction approaches and also introduces social-exchange analysis, ethnomethodology, cultural ecology, and sociobiology.

Recent research and the latest data. *Society: The Basics, Eighth Edition,* blends classic sociological statements with the latest research as reported in the leading publications in the field. While some texts ignore new work in sociology journals, *Society: The Basics* reflects recent research in a dozen of the discipline's top publications. Almost 1,000 research citations support this revision, with most published since 1995. Using the latest sources ensures that the text's content and statistical data are the most recent available.

Learning aids. This text has many features to help students learn. In each chapter, **Key Concepts** are identified by bold-faced type, and following each appears *a precise, italicized definition.* A listing of key concepts with their definitions appears at the end of each chapter, and a complete **Glossary** is found at the end of the book. Each chapter also contains a numbered **Summary** and four **Critical-Thinking Questions** that help students review material and assess their understanding. Following these are **Applications and Exercises,** which provide students with activities to do on or near the campus. Each chapter ends with an annotated list of worthwhile **Sites to See** on the Internet and a suggestion for how to use **Research Navigator™** to pursue further research.

Outstanding images: Photography and fine art. *Society: The Basics, Eighth Edition,* offers the finest and most extensive program of photography and artwork available in any comparable book. The author searches extensively to obtain the finest images of the human condition and presents them with insightful captions, often in the form of thought-provoking questions. Moreover, both photographs and artwork present people of various social backgrounds and historical periods. For example, alongside art by Europeans such as Pieter Breughel the Elder and U.S. artists including George Tooker, this edition has paintings by celebrated African American artists Henry Ossawa Tanner and Jonathan Green, outstanding Latino artist Carmen Lomas Garza, Navajo painter Harrison Begay, renowned folk artists including Anna Bell Lee Washington, and the engaging Australian painter and feminist Sally Swain.

Thought-provoking theme boxes. Although boxed material is common to introductory texts, *Society: The Basics, Eighth Edition,* provides a wealth of uncommonly good boxes. Each chapter typically contains three or four boxes, which fall into five types that amplify central themes of the text. **Global Sociology** boxes provoke readers to think about their own way of life by examining the fascinating social diversity that characterizes our world. **Diversity: Race, Class, & Gender** boxes, which have been expanded for this revision, focus on multicultural issues and present the voices of women and people of color. **Critical Thinking** boxes teach students to ask sociological questions about their surroundings, and help them evaluate important, controversial issues. Each Global Sociology, Diversity, and Critical Thinking box is followed by three "What do you think?" questions. **Controversy & Debate** boxes present several points of view on hotly debated issues and conclude with "Continue the debate . . ." questions to stimulate thought and generate spirited class discussion. Finally, **Applying Sociology** boxes, new to this revision, show readers how to apply the perspective, theory, and methods of sociology to greatest advantage; they, too, are followed by three "What do you think?" questions.

Society: The Basics, Eighth Edition, contains fifty-four boxes in all, including thirteen that are new to this edition. A complete listing of all the boxes appears after the table of contents.

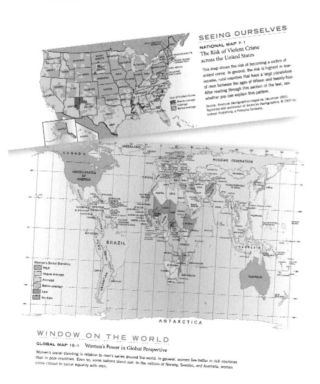

SEEING OURSELVES

NATIONAL MAP 7-1
The Risk of Violent Crime
across the United States

This map shows the risk of becoming a victim of violent crime. In general, the risk is highest in low-income, rural counties that have a large population of men between the ages of fifteen and twenty-four. After reading through this section of the text, see whether you can explain this pattern.

Source: American Demographics magazine, December 2003. Reprinted with permission of American Demographics, © 2003 by Primedia Business Magazines and Media, a Primedia Company.

WINDOW ON THE WORLD

GLOBAL MAP 10-1 Women's Power in Global Perspective

Women's social standing in relation to men's varies around the world. In general, women live better in rich countries than in poor countries. Even so, some nations stand out. In the nations of Norway, Sweden, and Australia, women come closest to social equality with men.

An unparalleled program of forty-six global and national maps. Another popular feature of *Society: The Basics* is the program of global and national maps. Window on the World global maps—twenty-three in all with one new

to this edition—are truly sociological maps offering a comparative look at income disparity, favored languages, the extent of prostitution, permitted marriage forms, the degree of political freedom, the incidence of HIV infection, and a host of other issues. The global maps use the non-Eurocentric projection devised by cartographer Arno Peters that accurately portrays the relative size of all the continents.

Seeing Ourselves national maps—twenty-three in all with three new to this edition—help to illuminate the social diversity of the United States. Most of these maps offer a close-up look at all 3,141 U.S. counties, highlighting suicide rates, teen pregnancy, risk of violent crime, poverty, racially mixed people, most widespread religious affiliation, and, as measures of popular culture, where people play golf or where households drink wine or beer. Each national map includes an explanatory caption that poses a question to stimulate students' thinking about social forces. A complete listing of the Seeing Ourselves national maps as well as the Window on the World global maps follows the table of contents.

An annotated instructor's edition. This is the only brief text available in an instructor's edition with a full program of helpful annotations—written by the author—on every page. These annotations provide additional data, notable quotations, and comments about maps and end-of-chapter study questions.

Innovation: Changes in the Eighth Edition

Each new edition of *Society: The Basics* and *Sociology* has broken new ground, one reason that some 5 million students have learned from these sociological best-sellers. In fact, one reason this book has always been the best-seller is that it never stands still. A revision raises high expectations, but after two years of planning and hard work, we are pleased to offer a major revision that sets a new standard for brief texts. Here is an overview of the innovations that define *Society: The Basics, Eighth Edition.*

Student friendly: A new look. As instructors understand, today's students are visually oriented—in a world of rapid-fire images, they respond to what they see. Just as important, the photographs that we see in newspapers, on television, and online are more sociological than ever. As a result, this new edition of *Society: The Basics* offers more and better images, and the text has an exciting new look that is clean, attractive, and sure to boost student interest.

Society: The Basics encourages students to use images to learn. Bold, vibrant, and colorful photos pull students into

the chapter material and become teaching opportunities, not just elements that add visual appeal. Combined with the chapter-opening stories that follow, students will be inspired by the visuals and educated by the context.

Student friendly: New chapter-opening questions. Each chapter of this new edition begins with three questions—a "what," a "how," and a "why" question—that alert students to key themes discussed in the chapter.

Student friendly: A new feel. A new look also calls for a new feel to the text. Our goal in this new edition can be stated in the form of a promise: Every student in every class will be able to immediately understand the material on every page of the text. This promise does not mean that we have left out any of the content you expect. What it does mean is that the author has prepared this revision with the greatest care and with an eye toward making language and arguments as clear as they can be. Student tested—student friendly!

Student friendly: A greater focus on careers. Most students who enroll in a sociology course hope to find something useful for their future careers. They will. *Society: The Basics, Eighth Edition,* reflects the discipline's *career relevance* more than ever before. Many chapters now apply sociological insights to careers—for example, read how today's marketing is learning to be more multicultural (Chapter 2, "Culture") and why physicians should understand the social dynamics of an office visit or a medical examination (Chapter 4, "Social Interaction in Everyday Life"). In addition, there is greatly expanded coverage of the entire criminal justice system (Chapter 7, "Deviance"), as well as a new discussion of nursing as part of the medical establishment (Chapter 14, "Health and Medicine").

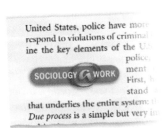

For additional connections between sociology and careers, look for the Sociology@Work icon. Found in most chapters, these icons draw student attention to discussion that has particular importance to the world of work.

Student friendly: More applied sociology. The value of sociology depends on students' ability to apply what they learn to their own lives. This revision illustrates concepts in ways that encourage students to see these connections. In addition, there is a new box theme: Applying Sociology. Ten of these boxed features show sociology at work in people's everyday lives.

Student friendly: Encouraging active reading. This book encourages students to be active readers. Of course, the lively and easy-to-understand writing style and current examples are important. In addition, all of the boxes in this revision now include three follow-up questions that invite students to think critically and to apply what they have learned to new situations.

Student friendly: A better way to teach theory. Sociological theory is important, but it is sometimes challenging to students. To ensure that students learn the important lessons, all theoretical discussions are followed by a "Critical review" section. In this revision, we have also added new "Applying Theory" tables, which summarize, at a glance, how the various theoretical approaches view the topic at hand.

APPLYING THEORY
FAMILY

	Structural-Functional Approach	Social-Conflict Approach	Symbolic-Interaction Approach
What is the level of analysis?	Macro-level	Macro-level	Micro-level
What is the importance of the family for society?	The family performs vital tasks, including socializing the young and providing emotional and financial support for members. The family helps regulate sexual activity.	The family perpetuates social inequality by handing down wealth from one generation to the next. The family supports patriarchy as well as racial and ethnic inequality.	The reality of family life is constructed by members in their interaction. Courtship typically brings together people who offer the same level of advantages.

Student friendly: *In the Times* readings. What better way to bring sociology to life than to provide students with brief, well-written news articles that apply sociology to today's world! After twelve of the chapters —including after *every* social institution chapter—you will find a one-page reading on U.S. society that recently appeared in *The New York Times*. These readings present important and current issues that are sure to engage student readers:

Chapter 1 ("Sociology: Perspective, Theory, and Method")
  Military Mirrors Working-Class America
Chapter 2 ("Culture") *Cultural Divide over Parental Discipline*
Chapter 3 ("Socialization: From Infancy to Old Age") *Elderly Immigrants Embrace Nursing Homes*

Chapter 5 ("Groups and Organizations") *Snoop Software Gains Power and Raises Privacy Concerns*

Chapter 6 ("Sexuality and Society") *The Skin Wars Start Earlier and Earlier*

Chapter 8 ("Social Stratification") *Are Those Leaving Welfare Better Off Now? Yes and No*

Chapter 9 ("Global Stratification") *Brazilian Slums Seen as Pawns in Political Games*

Chapter 10 ("Gender Stratification") *Still a Gender Wage Gap*

Chapter 12 ("Economics and Politics") *Rewards of a 90-Hour Week: Poverty and Dirty Laundry*

Chapter 13 ("Family and Religion") *Putting the American in "American Muslim"*

Chapter 14 ("Education and Medicine") *Good and Bad Marriage: Boon and Bane to Health*

Chapter 16 ("Social Change: Modern and Postmodern Societies") *Indian Soybean Farmers Join the Global Village*

Student friendly: Student Snapshots. Among the popular features of *Society* are the Global Snapshots (colorful graphs that compare social patterns in the United States with those in other nations) and Diversity Snapshots (figures that illustrate differences by race, ethnicity, class, or gender). For this revision, we have added twelve Student Snapshots, which document trends in the behavior and opinions of college students and are based on the surveys conducted by the Higher Education Research Institute at the University of California at Los Angeles since 1968.

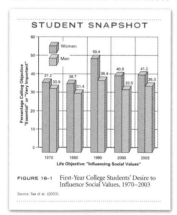

FIGURE 16–1   First-Year College Students' Desire to Influence Social Values, 1970–2003

Source: Sax et al. (2003).

Student friendly: Expanded and improved timeline. An easy way to help students put their lives in historical perspective is the timeline, an exclusive feature found inside the front cover of *Society: The Basics, Eighth Edition*. For this revision, we have expanded the timeline to three pages, adding more material about popular culture and social diversity, as well as a number of color images.

Student friendly: Improved high-tech! For this edition, the CD-ROM includes a video library, presenting short clips that illustrate important concepts and ideas. The video material, drawn from the archives of *ABC News*, takes learning to a whole new level.

Students will also have open access to the Companion Website™ at http://www.prenhall.com/macionis. Begin by clicking on the cover of this book and follow the easy-to-use menus. At the site, students will find a full range of study materials, including computer-graded practice tests. In addition, all users of this book are invited to make use of videos, sociologists' biographies, and dozens of links found at the author's personal Web site: http://www.TheSociologyPage.com or http://www.macionis.com.

Both students and faculty benefit from the following innovations:

New and updated maps. The only way to improve on our colorful sociological maps is to ensure that they are as up-to-date as possible. This edition features forty-six global and national maps, many updated and four new to this edition.

New chapter-opening vignettes. This revision keeps the best of the popular chapter-opening vignettes and adds nine new ones. In all, more than half of the openings are new.

Many new boxes. A total of fifty-four boxes supports five themes of the text: Global Sociology, Diversity: Race, Class, & Gender, Critical Thinking, Controversy & Debate, and—new to this edition—Applying Sociology. Many boxes are revised and updated; thirteen boxes are new to this edition.

A small change in chapter ordering. In this revision, "Sexuality and Society" is moved up one spot to fall before, rather than after, the chapter on "Deviance." This small change results in a more logical flow of topics.

The latest statistical data. Instructors count on this text to include the very latest statistical data. The eighth edition comes through again, making use of the latest data from various government agencies and private organizations. The author and Amy Marsh Macionis have worked together to ensure that the newest statistics are used throughout the text—in most cases for 2003 or even 2004. In addition, instructors will find dozens of new research citations as well as many familiar current events that raise the interest of students.

Keeping up with the field. As surprising as it may seem, some textbooks do not reflect new work in the field, making few references to sociology's journals and taking little notice of new books. In preparing this revision, the author has reviewed new publications—including *American Journal of Sociology, American Sociological Review, Rural Sociology, Social Forces, Sociological Focus, Sociological Forum, Society, The Public Interest, Social Problems, Population Bulletin, Teaching Sociology,*

Contemporary Sociology, and *Social Science Quarterly*—as well as popular press publications that keep us abreast of current trends and events. Of course, material selected for inclusion in an introductory textbook must be both interesting and relevant to the lives of students.

New topics. The eighth edition of *Society: The Basics* is completely updated with new and expanded discussions in every chapter. Here is a partial listing, by chapter.

- **Chapter 1 Sociology: Perspective, Theory, and Method:** New data on suicide by gender and race also show the power of society; there are updates on race and sports; a new Applying Theory table helps students understand the three main sociological theories; the methods discussion has been greatly expanded and now includes discussion of real-life studies to illustrate each of the major methods; a new Critical Thinking box gives students tips on reading tables; and there is new discussion of institutional review boards.

- **Chapter 2 Culture:** A new chapter opening points out the gains businesses can make by better understanding cultural diversity; a new Applying Sociology box looks at the new cyber-symbols found in our computer culture; there is an expanded, more critical discussion of the Sapir-Whorf thesis; there are statistical updates on the increasing number of foreign-born people in the United States; the new Student Snapshot series begins with a look at the changing life objectives of college students; and a new Applying Theory table helps students use theory to understand culture.

- **Chapter 3 Socialization:** This chapter offers expanded discussion of the role of the family (including the concept of cultural capital) in socialization; there is an update on the political content of television; a new Student Snapshot asks whom U.S. teens trust the most; and look for a new Critical Thinking box on the social transitions that define "adulthood" in the United States.

- **Chapter 4 Social Interaction in Everyday Life:** A new Critical Thinking box describes how anyone can detect lying.

- **Chapter 5 Groups and Organizations:** An update applies the concept of groupthink to the invasion of Iraq; a new Student Snapshot shows the extent of volunteer work among college women and men; find a new global map on Internet users around the world; there is an update on bureaucratic ritualism, new material on changes in Japanese organizations in light of that nation's economic downturn, and an update on the gradual loss of privacy, including the passage of the USA PATRIOT Act.

- **Chapter 6 Sexuality and Society:** A new chapter opening discusses the pressures and problems linked to becoming sexually active at a young age; there is a new discussion of intersexual people; a new national map shows where in the United States the law permits or forbids marriage between first cousins; there is an update on where gay marriages began to be performed in 2004; a new Diversity Snapshot identifies four

sexual orientations; there is expanded discussion of teen pregnancy; also find a new Applying Theory table that helps students use theory to study sexuality, a new Student Snapshot showing changing student views of homosexual relationships, and a new Applying Sociology box on the campus culture of "hooking up."

- **Chapter 7 Deviance:** A new chapter opening highlights one of the corporate scandals that has changed the look of "criminals" in the United States; a new Critical Thinking box asks whether cheating has become more common today in the United States; a new Diversity box examines arguments for and against hate crime laws; there is an update on the controversy surrounding the use of the death penalty in the United States, as well as the number of prisoners on death row by state; a new Applying Theory table helps students use theory to understand deviance; a new Student Snapshot shows trends in student opinion on the death penalty; and there is more applied material on criminal justice, including new discussions of due process and community-based corrections, such as probation and parole.

- **Chapter 8 Social Stratification:** This chapter now includes a new discussion of emerging social classes in China, a new Applying Theory table helps students apply theory to stratification issues; the global map showing income inequality is updated; find an expanded discussion of the link between social class and political participation; there is updated discussion of how income changes over the life course; a new Applying Sociology box describes the return of the super-rich and the new great mansions they are building; and a new national map shows the poverty rates for all counties of the United States.

- **Chapter 9 Global Stratification:** A new chapter opening describes a deadly fire that ended the lives of fifty-two people in a Bangladesh sweatshop; a new Diversity box profiles the "Third World poverty" found along the southwestern border of the United States; a new Applying Theory table helps students apply theory to the issue of global poverty; find new data showing which global regions are prospering and which are not.

- **Chapter 10 Gender Stratification:** This chapter contains updates on the share of women in the U.S. labor force as well as the gender composition of jobs and government leaders; find the latest income data for working women and men; there is a new Student Snapshot charting student opinion about feminism over time; find a new Global Sociology box describing the practice of female genital mutilation; a new Applying Theory table helps students use theory to understand gender.

- **Chapter 11 Race and Ethnicity:** A new chapter opening highlights the increasing racial and ethnic diversity of U.S. society; there is expanded discussion of the social construction of race and ethnicity; an expanded discussion of prejudice contains new research findings showing patterns of prejudice among today's college students; find updates on the social standing of all U.S. minority categories; the chapter includes the latest on the affirmative action debate, including discussion of the U.S. Supreme Court decision in the recent University of Michigan case.

- **Chapter 12 Economics and Politics**: A new chapter opening highlights the economic power of Wal-Mart, the nation's largest employer; a new Student Snapshot shows the career plans of college students; find an update on the extent of political freedom in the world; a new national map shows the county-by-county results of the presidential election of 2004; a new discussion points out the political consequences of laws barring convicted criminals from voting; another new Student Snapshot shows the political leanings of students over time; a new Applying Theory table helps students use theory to understand politics; there are updates on the War in Iraq and the global war against terror; the chapter includes a new discussion of the role of the mass media in war; a new Controversy & Debate box examines the link between Islam and political freedom.

- **Chapter 13 Family and Religion**: A new chapter-opening story points to the diversity of families in the United States; a new Applying Theory table helps students use theory to understand the family; the chapter offers statistical updates on marital infidelity as well as family size, the cost of raising children, singlehood, single parenting, patterns of child care, divorce, and domestic violence; there is a new discussion of American Indian families; find statistical updates on religiosity in the United States; another new Applying Theory table is found in the religion discussion; and a new Student Snapshot shows the increasing share of students who claim no religious affiliation.

- **Chapter 14 Education and Medicine**: A new chapter opening highlights the rising number of U.S. children being home-schooled; there are statistical updates for educational achievement in the United States; a new Diversity Snapshot shows the dramatic link between family income and college attendance; there is a new discussion of how community colleges have expanded educational opportunity in the United States; a new Diversity box asks whether school discipline operates as a type of racial profiling; there are new suggestions for increasing student participation in the classroom; find a new section on home schooling; the chapter includes a new discussion—and a new Student Snapshot—focusing on grade inflation; find an update on national school reform; the health section includes a new national map showing health by county across the United States; there is an update on income and health; find a new Global Sociology box dealing with culture and eating disorders; there is an update on AIDS around the world and HIV infection in the United States; a new Student Snapshot shows the declining share of college women and men who rate their health as above average; and a new discussion explores our country's shortage of nurses.

- **Chapter 15 Population, Urbanization, and Environment**: A new chapter opening describes the loss of population in one dying town of North Dakota; find updates on all the demographic indicators for the United States and the world; there is a new discussion of the $I = PAT$ formula of environmental impact, as well as updates on the composition of community solid waste and the state of the global environment.

- **Chapter 16 Social Change: Modern and Postmodern Societies**: A new discussion of political-economy theory rounds out six theories explaining the rise of social movements; a substantially revised Critical Thinking box asks whether "progress" is good for traditional people in Brazil and also in Hog Hammock, a traditional Gullah community off the coast of Georgia that is being drawn into modern ways of life with good and bad consequences; also, find updates from the National Opinion Research Center on people's attitudes toward social change and modernity and a new Student Snapshot showing young people's desire to influence social values.

A Word about Language

This text's commitment to describing the social diversity of the United States as well as the world carries with it the responsibility to use language thoughtfully. In most cases, we prefer the terms *African American* and *person of color* to the word *black*. We use the terms *Hispanic* and *Latino* to refer to people of Spanish descent. Most tables and figures refer to "Hispanics" because this is the term the Census Bureau uses when collecting statistical data about our population.

Students should realize, however, that many individuals do not describe themselves using these terms. Although the word "Hispanic" is commonly used in the eastern part of the United States, and "Latino" and the feminine form "Latina" are widely heard in the West, across the United States people of Spanish descent identify with a particular ancestral nation, whether it be Argentina, Mexico, some other Latin American country, or Spain or Portugal in Europe.

The same holds for Asian Americans. Although this term is a useful shorthand in sociological analysis, most people of Asian descent think of themselves in terms of a specific country of origin (say, Japan, the Philippines, Taiwan, or Vietnam).

In this text, the term "Native American" refers to all the inhabitants of the Americas (including Alaska and the Hawaiian Islands) whose ancestors lived here prior to the arrival of Europeans. Here again, however, most people in this broad category identify with their historical society (for example, Cherokee, Hopi, Seneca, or Zuni). The term "American Indian" refers to only those Native Americans who live in the continental United States, not including Native peoples living in Alaska or Hawaii.

On a global level, we avoid the word "American"—which literally designates two continents—to refer to just the United States. For example, referring to this country, the term "U.S. economy" is more correct than the "American economy." This convention may seem a small point, but it implies the significant recognition that we in this country represent only one society (albeit a very important one) in the Americas.

A Word about Web Sites

Because of the increasing importance of the Internet, each chapter of this new edition of *Society: The Basics* ends with an annotated list of Sites to See. The goal is to provide sites that are current, informative, and, above all, relevant to the topic at hand.

However, students should be mindful of several potential problems. First, Web sites change all the time. Prior to publication, we make every effort to ensure that the sites listed meet our high standards. But readers may find that sites have changed quite a bit, and some may have gone away entirely. Obviously, this problem is beyond our control.

Second, sites have been selected in order to provide different points of view on various issues. The listing of a site does not imply that the author or publisher agrees with everything—or even anything—on the site. For this reason, we urge students to examine all sites with a critical eye.

Supplements

Society: The Basics, Eighth Edition, is the heart of an unprecedented multimedia learning package that includes a wide range of proven instructional aids as well as several new ones. As the author of the text, I maintain a keen interest in all the supplements to ensure their quality and integration with the text. The supplements for this revision have been thoroughly updated, improved, and expanded.

FOR THE INSTRUCTOR

Annotated Instructor's Edition (0-13-192247-5). The AIE is a complete student text annotated on every page by the author. Annotations—which have been thoroughly revised for this edition—have won praise from instructors for enriching class presentations. Margin notes include summaries of research findings, statistics from the United States or other nations, insightful quotations, information highlighting patterns of social diversity in the United States, and high-quality survey data from the National Opinion Research Center's (NORC) General Social Survey and the World Values Survey data from the Inter-University Consortium for Political and Social Research (ICPSR).

Instructor's Manual (0-13-192250-5). Formerly called the *Data File*, this is the "instructor's manual" that is of interest even to those who have never used one before. Providing far more than detailed chapter outlines and discussion questions, it contains statistical profiles of the United States and other nations, summaries of important developments, recent articles from *Teaching Sociology* that are relevant to the classroom, and supplemental lecture material for every chapter of the text.

Test Item File (0-13-192245-9). Written by the text author, John Macionis, this key supplement better reflects the material in the textbook—both in content and in language—than any other introductory sociology textbook. The file contains over 2000 items—at least 100 per chapter—in multiple-choice, true-false, and essay formats, plus new questions based on the supplemental items that allow you to assess a student's use of these important tools.

TestGEN-EQ (0-13-192249-1). This computerized software allows instructors to create their own personalized exams, to edit any or all of the existing test questions, and to add new questions. Other special features of this program include random generation of test questions, creation of alternate versions of the same test, scrambling question sequence, and test preview before printing.

Instructor Resource CD-ROM (0-13-154737-2). Pulling together all of the media assets available to instructors, this interactive CD allows instructors to insert media—video, PowerPoint, graphs, charts, maps—into their interactive classroom presentations.

Prentice Hall Film and Video Guide: Introductory Sociology, Seventh Edition (0-13-154744-5). Newly updated by Peter Remender of the University of Wisconsin-Osh Kosh, this guide links important concepts in the text directly to compelling, student-focused feature films and documentaries. Each film is summarized, and critical thinking questions allow the instructor to highlight the relevance of each film or video to concepts in sociology.

ABCNEWS /Prentice Hall Video Library for Sociology. Few will dispute that video is the most dynamic supplement you can use to enhance a class. However, the quality of the video material and how well it relates to your course still make all the difference. Prentice Hall and *ABC News* are working together to bring to you the best and most comprehensive video material available in the college market. Through its wide variety of award-winning programs—*Nightline, This Week, World News Tonight,* and *20/20*—ABC News offers a resource for feature and documentary-style videos related to the chapters in *Society: The Basics, Eighth Edition*. The programs have high production quality, present substantial content, and are hosted by well-versed, well-known anchors. The author, working with editors at Prentice Hall, has carefully selected videos on topics that complement *Society: The Basics*, and included notes on how to use them in the classroom. An excellent instructor's guide carefully and completely integrates the videos into your lecture. The guide has a synopsis of each video showing its relation to the chapter and discussion questions to help students focus on how concepts and theories apply to real-life situations.

Volume I: Social Stratification (0-13-466228-8)
Volume II: Marriage/Families (0-13-209537-8)
Volume III: Race/Ethnic Relations (0-13-458506-2)
Volume IV: Criminology (0-13-375163-5)
Volume V: Social Problems (0-13-437823-7)
Volume VI: Intro to Sociology I (0-13-095066-1)
Volume VII: Intro to Sociology II (0-13-095060-2)
Volume VIII: Intro to Sociology III (0-13-095773-9)
Volume IX: Social Problems (0-13-095774-7)
Volume X: Marriage/Families II (0-13-095775-5)
Volume XI: Race and Ethnic Relations II (0-13-021134-6)
Volume XII: Institutions (0-13-021133-8)
Volume XIII: Introductory Sociology IV (0-13-018507-8)
Volume XIV: Introductory Sociology V (0-13-018509-4)

Prentice Hall Introductory Sociology PowerPoint™ Transparencies. These PowerPoint™ slides combine graphics and text in a colorful format to help you convey sociological principles in a new and exciting way. Each chapter of the textbook has 15 to 25 slides that communicate the key concepts within that chapter. For easy access, they are available on the Instructor Resource CD-ROM or within the instructor portion of OneKey for *Society: The Basics, Eighth Edition.*

Prentice Hall Color Transparencies: Sociology Series VIII (0-13-154736-4). Full color illustrations, charts, and other visual materials from the text as well as outside sources have been selected to make up this useful in-class tool. An instructor's guide is also available that offers suggestions on how to use the transparencies in the classroom.

Media Supplements

OneKey. To accompany *Society: The Basics, Eighth Edition,* this innovative resource pulls together the teaching and learning materials available with the text into one easy-to-access location. For students, OneKey offers video, animations, interactive exercises, assignments, and a customized study plan with supporting e-book. For instructors, OneKey offers presentation materials, assessment materials, and communication tools. Students access OneKey using an access code packaged with a new textbook. For a preview of OneKey or for more on ordering information, please visit http://www.prenhall.com/macionis.

Interactive CD-ROM. Using video as a window to the world outside of the classroom, this innovative CD-ROM offers students videos and animations to reinforce the material covered in each chapter. Arranged by the themes of the book within each chapter, students can watch relevant *ABC News* clips, view "author's tip" videos, interact with the global and national maps, as well as review sociological concepts through the many assignments available to instructors. The CD-ROM is available free with all new copies of *Society: The Basics, Eighth Edition.*

Census 2000 Interactive CD-ROM. Capturing the rich picture of our nation drawn by Census2000, this CD-ROM brings related Census data into your classroom in a rich, multimedia format. It uses files taken directly from the Census Bureau Web site—even recently released Census Briefs—organizes them around your course, and offers teaching aids to support student learning. This updated CD-ROM is free when packaged with *Society: The Basics, Eighth Edition.*

Companion Website™. In tandem with the text, students and professors can now take full advantage of the Internet to enrich their study of sociology. The Macionis Companion Website™ continues to lead the way in providing students with avenues for delving deeper into the topics covered in the text. Features of the Web site include chapter objectives, study questions, as well as links to interesting material and information from other sites on the Web that will reinforce and enhance the content of each chapter. Free to both students and instructors, please visit the site at http://www.prenhall.com/macionis and click on the cover of *Society: The Basics, Eighth Edition.*

Research Navigator™. Research Navigator™ can help students confidently and efficiently complete research assignments. Research Navigator™ does this by providing students and faculty with three exclusive databases of high-quality scholarly and popular articles and search engines to select what they want. Gain access to Research Navigator™ through an access code found in the front of the *OneSearch with Research Navigator™: Sociology* guide. This guide can be packaged with *Society: The Basics, Eighth Edition,* at no additional cost.

- **EBSCO's ContentSelect™ Academic Journal Database,** organized by subject, contains 50 to 100 of the leading academic journals for that discipline. Instructors and students can search the online journals by keyword, topic, or multiple topics. Articles include abstract and citation information and can be cut, pasted, e-mailed, or saved for later use.

- *The New York Times* **Search-by-Subject™ Archive** provides articles specific to sociology and is searchable by keyword or multiple keywords. Instructors and students can view full-text articles from the world's leading journalists writing for *The New York Times*.

- **Link Library** offers editorially selected "Best of the Web" sites for *Society: The Basics*. Link Libraries are continually scanned and kept up to date, providing the most relevant and accurate links for research assignments.

OneSearch with Research Navigator™: Sociology. This guide focuses on developing the critical thinking skills necessary to evaluate and use online sources. Encouraging students to become critical consumers of online sources, this guide walks students through the process of selecting and citing their online sources properly. It also includes a section on using Research Navigator™—Prentice Hall's own gateway to academically sound and current sources. This supplementary book along with the Research Navigator™ access code is free to students when packaged with *Society: The Basics, Eighth Edition*. Please contact your Prentice Hall representative for more information.

Distance Learning Solutions. Prentice Hall is committed to providing our leading content to the growing number of courses being delivered over the Internet by developing relationships with the leading vendors—Blackboard™, Web CT™, and CourseCompass™—Prentice Hall's own easy-to-use course management system powered by Blackboard™. Please visit our technology solutions site at http://www.prenhall.com/demo.

FOR THE STUDENT

Study Guide (0-13-154616-3). This complete guide helps students to review and reflect on the material presented in *Society: The Basics, Eighth Edition*. Each of the sixteen chapters in the Study Guide provides an overview of the corresponding chapter in the student text, summarizes its major topics and concepts, offers applied exercises, and features end-of-chapter tests with solutions.

SocNotes (0-13-192256-4). Designed to help students study more effectively for tests, this study resource allows students to better organize their course materials. Formatted like a study guide, each chapter has 12 to 15 Power-Point™ slides on each page that summarize major points for the students. Lines for in-class note-taking are next to the PowerPoint™ slides. This can be wrapped for free with all new copies of *Society: The Basics, Eighth Edition*.

TIME **Special Edition.** Showing how the popular media write with a sociological eye, this special edition of *TIME* magazine pulls together the best articles of the past two years that cover sociological topics. This can be wrapped for free with all new copies of *Society: The Basics, Eighth Edition*.

"10 Ways to Fight Hate" brochure (0-13-028146-8). Produced by the Southern Poverty Law Center, the leading hate-crime and crime-watch organization in the United States, this free supplement walks students through ten steps that they can take on their own campus or in their own neighborhood to fight hate every day.

In Appreciation

The usual practice of listing a single author hides the efforts of dozens of women and men that have resulted in *Society: The Basics, Eighth Edition*. I would like to express my thanks to the Prentice Hall editorial team, including Yolanda de Rooy, division president, Leah Jewell, editorial director, Nancy Roberts, publisher, and Chris DeJohn, executive editor for sociology, for their steady enthusiasm, and for pursuing both innovation and excellence. Day-to-day work on the book is shared by the author and the production team. Barbara Reilly, production editor at Prentice Hall, is a key member of the team who is responsible for the attractive page layout of the book; indeed, if anyone "sweats the details" more than the author, it is Barbara! Amy Marsh Macionis, the text's "in house" editor, checks virtually everything, untangling awkward phrases and catching errors and inconsistencies in all the statistical data. Amy is a most talented editor who is relentless in her pursuit of quality. My debt to her is great, indeed.

I also have a large debt to the members of the Prentice Hall sales staff, the men and women who have given this text such remarkable support over the years. Thanks, especially, to Marissa Feliberty, who directs our marketing campaign.

Thanks, too, to Anne DeMarinis for providing the interior design of the book, which was coordinated in-house by creative director Leslie Osher. Developmental and copy editing of the manuscript was provided by Karen Trost, Bruce Emmer, and Amy Marsh Macionis.

It goes without saying that every colleague knows more about some topics covered in this book than the author does. For that reason, I am grateful to the hundreds of faculty and students who have written to me to offer comments and suggestions. More formally, I am grateful to the following people who have reviewed some or all of this manuscript:

William Dowell, Heartland Community College
Dona Fletcher, Sinclair Community College
Patricia L. Gibbs, Foothill College
Audra Kallimanis, Mt. Olive College
Kooros Mahmoudi, Northern Arizona University
Peter B. Morrill, Bronx Community College

Dina B. Neal, Vernon College
Therese Nemec, Fox Valley Technical College
Joong-Hwan Oh, Hunter College (CUNY)
Michael Ryan, Dodge City Community College
Thomas Soltis, Westmoreland Community College

I also wish to thank the following colleagues for sharing their wisdom in ways that have improved this book:

Doug Adams (The Ohio State University), Francis O. Adeola (University of New Orleans), Arfa Aflatooni (Linn-Benton Community College), Kip Armstrong (Bloomsburg University), Rose Arnault (Fort Hays State University), Scott Beck (Eastern Tennessee State University), Lois Benjamin (Hampton University), Philip Berg (University of Wisconsin, La Crosse), Janet Carlisle Bogdan (LeMoyne College), Alessandro Bonanno (Sam Houston State University), Charlotte Brauchle (Southwest Texas Junior College and Saint Mary's University), Bill Brindle (Monroe Community College), John R. Brouillette (Colorado State University), Cathryn Brubaker (Georgia Perimeter College), Brent Bruton (Iowa State University), Richard Bucher (Baltimore City Community College), Karen Campbell (Vanderbilt University), Cecilia Cantrell (Georgia State University), Harold Conway (Blinn College), Gerry Cox (Fort Hays State University), Lovberta Cross (Southwest Tennessee Community College), James A. Davis (Harvard University), Sumati Devadutt (Monroe Community College), Mary Donaghy (Arkansas State University), Keith Doubt (Northeast Missouri State University), Denny Dubbs (Harrisburg Area Community College), Travis Eaton (Northeast Louisiana State University), Helen Rose Fuchs Ebaugh (University of Houston), John Ehle (Northern Virginia Community College), Roger Eich (Hawkeye Community College), Tracy Elliott (Collin County Community College), Kevin Everett (Radford University), Heather Fitz Gibbon (The College of Wooster), Kevin Fitzpatrick (University of Alabama-Birmingham), Charles Frazier (University of Florida), Karen Lynch Frederick (St. Anselm College), Patricia Gagné (University of Kentucky, Louisville), Pam Gaiter (Collin County Community College), Jarvis Gamble (Owen's Technical College), Steven Goldberg (City College, City University of New York), Charlotte Gotwald (York College of Pennsylvania), Norma B. Gray (Bishop State Community College), Rhoda Greenstone (DeVry Institute), Jeffrey Hahn (Mount Union College), Harry Hale (Northeast Louisiana State University), Dean Haledjian (Northern Virginia Community College), Dick Haltin (Jefferson Community College), Marvin Hannah (Milwaukee Area Technical College), Charles Harper (Creighton University), Michael Hart (Broward Community College), Adonna Helmig (Pittsburgh State University), Gary Hodge (Collin County Community College), Elizabeth A. Hoisington (Heartland Community College), Sara Horsfall (Stephen F. Austin State University), Peter Hruschka (Ohio Northern University), Glenna Huls (Camden County College), Jeanne Humble (Lexington Community College), James Hunter (Indiana-Purdue University at Indianapolis), Richard Hutchinson (Weber State University), Cynthia Imanaka (Seattle Central Community College), Miles Jackson (Clark College), Patricia Johnson (Houston Community College), Ed Kain (Southwestern University), Paul Kamolnick (Eastern Tennessee State University), Irwin Kantor (Middlesex County College), Douglas B. Kennard (Mount Vernon Nazarene University), Thomas Korllos (Kent State University), Rita Krasnow (Virginia Western Community College), Donald Kraybill (Elizabethtown College), Michael Lacy (Colorado State University), Michael Levine (Kenyon College), George Lowe (Texas Tech University), Don Luidens (Hope College), Larry Lyon (Baylor University), Li-Chen Ma (Lamar University), Karen E. B. McCue (University of New Mexico, Albuquerque), Ronald McGriff (College of the Sequoias), Meredith McGuire (Trinity College), Lisa McMinn (Wheaton College), Setma Maddox (Texas Wesleyan University), Errol Magidson (Richard J. Daley College), Jean-Louis Marchand (Chesapeake College), Allan Mazur (Syracuse University), Jack Melhorn (Emporia State University), Ken Miller (Drake University), Richard Miller (Navarro College), Jessica Kelley-Moore (Purdue University), Joe Morolla (Virginia Commonwealth University), Craig Nauman (Madison Area Technical College), Toby Parcel (The Ohio State University), Fernando Parra (California State Polytechnic University, Pomona), Anne Peterson (Columbus State Community College), Marvin Pippert (Roanoke College), Lauren Pivnik (Monroe Community College), Nevel Razak (Fort Hays State College), Jim Rebstock (Broward Community College), George Reim (Cheltenham High School), Virginia Reynolds (Indiana University of Pennsylvania), Laurel Richardson (The Ohio State University), Keith Roberts (Hanover College), Ellen Rosengarten (Sinclair Community College), Howard Schneiderman (Lafayette College), Marvin Scott (Butler University), Ray Scupin (Lindenwood College), Steve Severin (Kellogg Community College), Harry Sherer (Irvine Valley College), Walt Shirley (Sinclair Community College), Anson Shupe (Indiana University-Purdue University at Fort Wayne), Ree Simpkins (Missouri Southern State University), Glen Sims (Glendale Community College), Paula Snyder (Columbus Community College), Nancy Sonleitner (University of Oklahoma), Larry Stern (Collin County Community College), Randy Ston (Oakland Community College), Verta Taylor (University of California-Santa Barbara), Vickie H. Taylor (Danville Community College), Mark J. Thomas (Madison Area Technical College), Len Tompos (Lorain County Community College), Christopher Vanderpool (Michigan State University), Phyllis Watts (Tiffin University), Murray Webster (University of North Carolina, Charlotte), Debbie White (Collin County Community College), Marilyn Wilmeth (Iowa University), Stuart Wright (Lamar University), William Yoels (University of Alabama, Birmingham), Dan Yutze (Taylor University), Wayne Zapatek (Tarrant County Community College), Assata Zerai (Syracuse University), and Frank Zulke (Harold Washington College).

Finally, I would like to dedicate this edition of the book to all the students who, as they open this book, accept our invitation to learn about sociology, to enjoy it, and to make it part of their daily lives.

Jan J. Macionis

Make the Most of Your Study Time!

SOCIETY: THE BASICS

EIGHTH EDITION

INTERACTIVE CD-ROM

John Macionis and Prentice Hall offer you an invitation to think sociologically about the world around you. This innovative CD-ROM is filled with great media resources and interactive study material for every chapter of *Society: The Basics, Eighth Edition*. Organized around the concepts of **seeing, thinking,** and **doing,** the CD-ROM challenges you to think critically about the topics covered in each chapter and uses interesting videos and animations to guide you through the finer theoretical points.

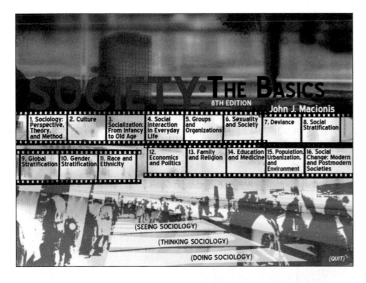

This great resource comes FREE in the back of every new copy of *Society: The Basics, Eighth Edition*. Its features include:

ABC News Videos   Imagine using the power and depth of the *ABC News* archives to bring to life sociological concepts. These high-quality actual news videos are tied to topics in the text and include study questions that underscore the relevance of sociological concepts to real life. They literally pull you from your seat to explore sociologically the world outside the classroom.

Author's Tip Videos   The textbook author, John J. Macionis, offers a personal insight on each chapter's topic. These clips will motivate you to reflect on key points from the chapter and strengthen your knowledge of sociological concepts. A very valuable tool!

Map Animations   Every map in the textbook becomes interactive on the CD-ROM. Roll-over graphics allow you to focus in on the sociological relevance of each of the forty-six Window on the World global maps and Seeing Ourselves national maps.

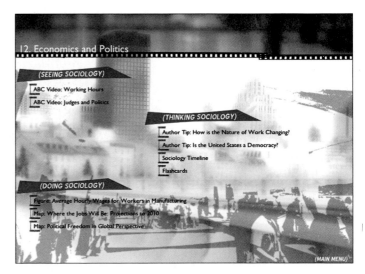

Flashcards   All key terms from the text are available for review in our innovative flashcard feature. Hear the more difficult terms pronounced, study their definitions, and discard terms as you master them.

ABOUT THE AUTHOR

John J. Macionis (pronounced ma-SHOW-nis) was born and raised in Philadelphia, Pennsylvania. He earned a bachelor's degree from Cornell University and a doctorate in sociology from the University of Pennsylvania.

His publications are wide-ranging, focusing on community life in the United States, interpersonal intimacy in families, effective teaching, humor, new information technology, and the importance of global education. He and Nijole V. Benokraitis have edited the anthology *Seeing Ourselves: Classic, Contemporary, and Cross-Cultural Readings in Sociology.* Macionis has also authored *Sociology,* the leading comprehensive text in the field, and he collaborates on international editions of the texts: *Sociology: Canadian Edition; Society: The Basics, Canadian Edition; Seeing Ourselves, Canadian Edition; and Sociology: A Global Introduction. Sociology* is also available for high school students and in various foreign language editions. In addition, Macionis and Vincent Parrillo have written the urban studies text *Cities and Urban Life* (Prentice Hall). Macionis's most recent textbook is *Social Problems* (Prentice Hall). The latest on all the Macionis textbooks, as well as information and dozens of Internet links of interest to students and faculty in sociology, are found at the author's personal Web site: http://www.macionis.com or http://www.TheSociologyPage. com. Additional information, instructor resources, and online student study guides for the texts are found at the Prentice Hall site: http://www.prenhall.com/macionis.

John Macionis is Professor and Distinguished Scholar of Sociology at Kenyon College in Gambier, Ohio. In 2003, he received the Philander Chase Medal for completing twenty-five years of teaching at Kenyon. During that time, he has chaired the Sociology Department, directed the college's multidisciplinary program in humane studies, presided over the campus senate and the college's faculty, and most importantly, taught sociology to thousands of students.

In 2002, the American Sociological Association named Macionis recipient of the Award for Distinguished Contributions to Teaching, citing his innovative use of global material as well as introduction of new teaching technology in the development of his textbooks.

Professor Macionis has been active in academic programs in other countries, having traveled to some fifty nations. During his last study tour, he directed the global education course for the University of Pittsburgh's Semester at Sea program, teaching 400 students on a floating campus that visited twelve countries as it circled the globe.

Macionis writes, "I am an ambitious traveler, eager to learn and, through the texts, to share much of what I discover with students, many of whom know little about the rest of the world. For me, traveling and writing are all dimensions of teaching. First, and foremost, I am a teacher—a passion for teaching animates everything I do." At Kenyon, Macionis offers a wide range of upper-level courses, but his favorite course is Introduction to Sociology, which he teaches every year. He enjoys extensive contact with students and each term invites members of his classes to enjoy a home-cooked meal.

The Macionis family—John, Amy, and children McLean and Whitney—live on a farm in rural Ohio. In his free time, John plays tennis and enjoys swimming and bicycling through the Ohio countryside. During the summer he is a competitive sailor, and year-round he enjoys performing oldies rock and roll and playing the Scottish bagpipes.

Professor Macionis welcomes (and responds to) comments and suggestions about this book from faculty and students. Write to the Sociology Department, Palme House, Kenyon College, Gambier, Ohio 43022, or direct e-mail to MACIONIS@ KENYON.EDU.

For thirty-five years, John Macionis has made the classroom the center of his life.

COMPANION WEBSITE™

http://www.prenhall.com/macionis

Updated and enhanced to accompany the eighth edition of *Society: The Basics*, this full-featured site adds an exciting interactive element to your study both in and out of the classroom. The Macionis **Companion Website™** provides review and assessment tools for each chapter of the text as well as offering a direct gateway to the wealth of resources available on the World Wide Web.

Companion Website™ features:

• **Chapter Overview:** Focuses on the most important sociological points made in each chapter.

• **Study Guide:** Offers multiple-choice, true/false, and essay questions and line art essays that can be graded immediately and e-mailed to your instructor.

• **Applications and Exercises:** Brings to life the exercises at the end of each chapter by linking you directly to related Internet sites.

• **Boxed Material:** Links to relevant Internet sites so you can delve more deeply into topics covered in the text's boxed features.

• **Keyword Search:** Encourages you to search the Internet using keywords provided for each chapter.

RESEARCH NAVIGATOR™

Offering premium research resources online!

http://www.researchnavigator.com

Prentice Hall's Research Navigator™ is the easiest way for you to start a research assignment. Review the information on the research process itself, and then explore the three exclusive databases of source material—EBSCO's ContentSelect™ Academic Journal Database, *The New York Times* Search-by-Subject Archive, and "Best of the Web" Link Library.

Research Navigator™ is accessed by students and faculty using a free access code printed on the inside front cover of *OneSearch with Research Navigator™: Sociology*.

Research Navigator™ includes three databases of credible and reliable source material:

EBSCO's
ContentSelect Academic Journal Database

EBSCO's ContentSelect™ Academic Journal Database, organized by subject, contains more than 100 of the leading academic journals for each discipline. Instructors and students can search these online journals by keyword, topic, or multiple topics.

The New York Times
ON THE WEB

The New York Times Search-by-Subject Archive is organized by academic subject and can be searched using single or multiple keywords. Search results yield the full text of relevant articles from *The New York Times* written by the world's leading journalists.

L i n k
L I B R A R Y

Link Library, organized by subject, offers editorially selected "Best of the Web" sites. Link Libraries are continually scanned and updated in order to provide the most relevant and accurate links for research assignments.

Give yourself the tools you need to excel in sociology!

CHAPTER ONE

Sociology: Perspective, Theory, and Method

What sets human beings apart
from all other forms of life?

Why is sociology an important tool for your future?

How should you respond to people whose
way of life differs from your own?

The sociological perspective shows us patterns of behavior common within a society. ▶
Here, a member of Brazil's Pataxo tribe offers a traditional greeting to a visitor.

I f you were to ask 100 people, "Why do couples marry?" it is a safe bet that at least ninety would reply, "People marry because they fall in love." Indeed, it is hard for us to imagine a happy marriage without love; likewise, when people fall in love, we expect them to think about marriage.

But is the decision about whom to marry really so simple and so personal? There is plenty of evidence that if love is the key to marriage, Cupid's arrow is carefully aimed by the society around us.

In short, society has a number of "rules" about whom we should marry. What are they? Right off the bat, society rules out half the population because U.S. laws (despite recent actions in cities such as San Francisco and likely change in Massachusetts) do not allow people to marry someone of the same sex even if the couple is deeply in love. But there are other rules as well. Sociologists have found that people—especially when they are young—are very likely to marry someone close in age, and men and women of all ages typically marry someone of the same race, of a similar social class background, of much the same level of education, and who is about equal in physical attractiveness (Chapter 13 gives details). Although it may be true that we make choices about whom to marry, society certainly narrows the field (Gardyn, 2002; Zipp, 2002).

When it comes to love and most other dimensions of our lives, the decisions we make do not result from what philosophers call "free will." The essential wisdom we gain from sociology is that our social world guides our actions and life choices in much the same way that the seasons influence our clothing and activities.

The Sociological Perspective

Sociology is *the systematic study of human society*. At the heart of this discipline is a distinctive point of view called "the sociological perspective."

SEEING THE GENERAL IN THE PARTICULAR

Peter Berger (1963) described the sociological perspective as *seeing the general in the particular*. That is, sociology helps us see *general* patterns in the behavior of *particular* people. Although every individual is unique, society shapes the lives of people in various *categories* (such as children and adults, women and men, the rich and the poor) very differently. We begin to think sociologically by realizing how the general categories into which we fall shape our particular life experiences.

This text explores the power of society to guide our actions, thoughts, and feelings. We may think of marriage as the simple product of personal feelings. Yet the sociological perspective shows us that patterns involving our sex, age, race, and social class guide our selection of a partner. Indeed, it might be more accurate to think of "love" as a feeling we have for others who match up with what society teaches us to want in a mate.

SEEING THE STRANGE IN THE FAMILIAR

At first, using the sociological perspective amounts to *seeing the strange in the familiar*. Consider how you would react if someone were to say to you, "You fit all the right categories; you would make a wonderful wife. Let's get married!" Looking at life sociologically requires giving up the *familiar* idea that we live our lives only in terms of what we decide, in favor of the initially *strange* notion that society shapes these decisions, as it does all our experiences.

For individualistic North Americans, learning to see how society affects us may take a bit of practice. Consider the decision by women to bear children. Like the selection of a mate, the choice of how many children to have would seem to be a personal one. Yet there are social patterns here

WINDOW ON THE WORLD

GLOBAL MAP 1–1   Women's Childbearing in Global Perspective

Is childbearing simply a matter of personal choice? A look around the world shows that it is not. In general, women living in poor countries have many more children than women in rich nations. Can you point to some of the reasons for this global disparity? In simple terms, such differences mean that if you had been born into another society (whether you are female or male), your life might be quite different from what it is now.

Source: Data from Mackay (2000). Map projection from *Peters Atlas of the World* (1990).

as well. As shown in Global Map 1–1, the average woman in the United States and Canada has slightly fewer than two children during her lifetime. In India, however, the "choice" is about three; in South Africa, about four; in Cambodia, about five; in Saudi Arabia, about six; and in Niger, about seven.

What accounts for these striking differences? As later chapters explain, women in poor countries have less schooling and fewer economic opportunities, are more likely to remain in the home, and are less likely to use contraception. Clearly, society has much to do with the decisions women and men make about childbearing.

We can easily see the power of society over the individual by imagining how different our lives would be had we been born in place of any of these children from, respectively, Bolivia, Ethiopia, Thailand, Botswana, South Korea, and El Salvador.

SEEING INDIVIDUALITY IN SOCIAL CONTEXT

What could be a more lonely, personal act than taking your own life? Emile Durkheim (1858–1917), one of sociology's pioneers, showed that social forces are at work even in such an intensely personal action as suicide, providing strong evidence of how social forces affect individual behavior.

Examining official records in and around his native France, Durkheim (1966, orig. 1897) found that some categories of people were more likely than others to take their own lives. He found that men, Protestants, wealthy people, and the unmarried each had much higher suicide rates than women, Catholics and Jews, the poor, and married people. Thinking over these differences, Durkheim realized the key to the pattern was *social integration:* Categories of people with strong social ties had low suicide rates, and more individualistic people had high suicide rates.

In the male-dominated societies Durkheim studied, men certainly had more freedom than women. But despite its advantages, freedom also contributes to social isolation and a higher suicide rate. Likewise, self-reliant Protestants were more prone to suicide than traditional Catholics and Jews, whose rituals foster stronger social ties. The wealthy, too, have more freedom than the poor but, once again, at the cost of a higher suicide rate. Finally, can you see why single people are at greater risk than married people?

A century later, Durkheim's analysis still holds true. Figure 1–1 shows suicide rates for four categories of the U.S. population. In 2001, there were 11.9 recorded suicides for every 100,000 white people, which is more than twice the rate for African Americans (5.3). For both races, suicide was more common among men than among women. White men (19.5) are more than four times as likely as white women (4.6) to take their own lives. Among African Americans, the rate for men (9.2) was more than five times that for women (1.7). Following Durkheim's logic, the higher suicide rate among white people and men reflects their greater wealth and freedom. Conversely, the lower rate among women and people of color follows from their limited social choices. Just as in Durkheim's day, then, we can see general sociological patterns in the personal actions of individuals.

Some situations can stimulate sociological insights for everyone. Observing the diversity of people in our own society, we might wonder why others think and act differently than we do. As we continue to interact with people from social backgrounds that initially seem strange to us, we grasp the power of society to shape our lives and find ourselves easing into the use of the sociological perspective. The ability to think sociologically comes more quickly to people our society labels as "different." Those who routinely experience *social marginality*—that is, being set apart as "outsiders"—rapidly sense the power of society. For example, most African Americans are keenly aware of how much race affects our lives. Being the dominant majority, many whites think about race only from time to time and may imagine that race affects only people of color rather than themselves as well.

Finally, the U.S. sociologist C. Wright Mills (1959) pointed out that periods of social crisis also spark sociological thinking. For example, when the Great Depression of the 1930s threw one-third of the labor force out of work, unemployed workers could not help but see general social forces at work in their particular lives. Rather than thinking,

 For a look at how society has shaped celebrity names, click on the "Play 'The Name Game'" link at http://www.TheSociologyPage.com

"There must be something wrong with me; I can't find a job," they were likely to say, "We're all out of work because the economy has collapsed!" Of course, just as change stimulates sociological thinking, thinking sociologically suggests possibilities for change. The 1930s was a period of activism, resulting in many new programs, such as Social Security, aimed at increasing the well-being of the U.S. population.

BENEFITS OF THE SOCIOLOGICAL PERSPECTIVE

Applying the sociological perspective to our daily lives benefits us in four ways:

1. **The sociological perspective helps us critically assess "commonsense" ideas.** Ideas we take for granted are not always true. One good example, noted earlier, is the notion that we are free individuals personally responsible for our lives. If we think that people decide their own fate, we may be quick to praise successful people as superior and consider people with

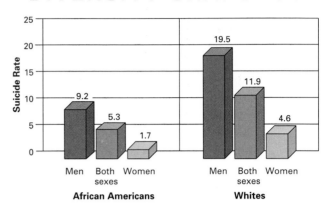

DIVERSITY SNAPSHOT

FIGURE 1–1   Rate of Death by Suicide, by Race and Sex, for the United States

Rates indicate the number of deaths by suicide for every 100,000 people in each category for 2001.

Source: Arias et al. (2003).

fewer achievements as personally lacking. A sociological approach encourages us to ask how factors outside the control of individuals shape their successes and failures.

2. **The sociological perspective helps us see the opportunities and constraints in our lives.** Sociological thinking leads us to see that, in the game of life, we

 To see how family income affects college attendance, go to http://www.census.gov/population/socdemo/school/cps2002/tab15-1.pdf

may have a say in how to play our cards, but it is society that deals us the hand. The more we understand the game, the better players we will be. Sociology helps us size up the world around us so that we can more effectively pursue our goals.

3. **The sociological perspective empowers us to be active participants in our society.** The better we understand how society operates, the more effective citizens we become. For some, this may mean supporting society as it is; others may attempt to change the world in some way. Whatever your goal, evaluating any aspect of social life includes identifying social forces and understanding their consequences.

4. **The sociological perspective helps us live in a diverse world.** North Americans make up just 5 percent of the world's population, and as this book's remaining chapters explain, much of the other 95 percent lead

One important reason to gain a global understanding is that, living in a high-income nation, we hardly can appreciate the suffering that goes on in much of the world. This boy is growing up in the African nation of Ghana, where he carries water for cooking and drinking from a public faucet and sewerage flows freely over unpaved streets. In poor nations like this, children have only a fifty-fifty chance to grow to adulthood.

lives very different from our own. Still, like people everywhere, we tend to view our own way of life as "right," "natural," and "better." The sociological perspective prompts us to think critically about the strengths and weaknesses of all ways of life, including our own.

APPLIED SOCIOLOGY

The benefits of sociology go well beyond our personal growth. As you read this text, you will learn that sociologists have helped shape public policy and law in countless ways involving issues such as school desegregation and busing, divorce law, and social welfare. Family researcher Lenore Weitzman reports that the research she did focusing on the financial hardships women face after divorce "had a real impact on public policy and resulted in the passage of fourteen new laws in California" (1996:538).

Training in sociology is also good preparation for the working world. According to the American Sociological Association (ASA), sociologists  are hired for hundreds of jobs in fields such as advertising, banking, criminal justice, education, government, health care, public relations, and research.

Most men and women who pursue advanced degrees in sociology go on to careers in teaching and research. But professional sociologists also work in many applied fields.

 In a short video, the author offers a personal response to the question, "Why would someone want to be a sociologist?" See the Video Gallery at http://www.TheSociologyPage.com

For example, clinical sociologists work with troubled clients much as clinical psychologists do, focusing on a person's web of social relationships rather than on the individual. Another type of applied sociology is evaluation research. In today's cost-conscious political climate, administrators must evaluate the effectiveness of virtually every program and policy. Sociologists, especially those with advanced research skills, are in high demand for this kind of work.

THE IMPORTANCE OF A GLOBAL PERSPECTIVE

As new communication technology draws even the farthest reaches of the Earth closer together, many academic disciplines take a **global perspective,** *the study of the larger world and our society's place in it.* What is the importance of a global perspective for sociology?

First, global awareness is a logical extension of the sociological perspective. Sociology shows us that our place in society profoundly affects our life experiences. It stands to reason, then, that the position of our society in the larger world system affects everyone in the United States.

Global Map 1–2 shows the relative economic development of the world's countries. **High-income countries** are *the richest nations with the highest overall standards of living.* High-income countries include the United States and Canada, Argentina, the nations of Western Europe, Israel, Saudi Arabia, South Africa, Japan, and Australia. Taken together, these fifty nations generate most of the world's goods and services and control most of its wealth. On average, individuals in these countries live well, not because they are smarter than anyone else, but because they had the good luck to be born in a wealthy region of the world.

The world's **middle-income countries** are *nations with a standard of living about average for the world as a whole.* Individuals living in any of these roughly eighty nations— many of the countries of Eastern Europe, some of Africa, and almost all of Latin America and Asia—are as likely to

WINDOW ON THE WORLD

GLOBAL MAP 1-2 Economic Development in Global Perspective

In high-income countries—including the United States, Canada, Argentina, the nations of Western Europe, South Africa, Israel, Saudi Arabia, Australia, and Japan—a highly productive economy provides people, on average, with material plenty. Middle-income countries—including most of Latin America and Asia—are less economically productive, with a standard of living about average for the world as a whole but far below that of the United States. These nations also have a significant share of poor people who are barely able to feed and house themselves. In the low-income countries of the world, poverty is severe and widespread. Although small numbers of elites live very well in the poorest nations, most people struggle to survive on a small fraction of the income common in the United States.

Note: Data for this map are provided by the United Nations. Each country's economic productivity is measured in terms of its gross domestic product (GDP), which is the total value of all goods and services produced each year. Dividing each country's GDP by the country's population gives us the per capita (per person) GDP and allows us to compare the economic performance of countries of different population sizes. High-income countries have a per capita GDP of more than $10,000. Many are far richer than this, however; the figure for the United States exceeds $35,000. Middle-income countries have a per capita GDP ranging from $2,500 to $10,000. Low-income countries have a per capita GDP of less than $2,500. Figures used here reflect the United Nations "purchasing power parities" system, which is an estimate of what people can buy using their income in the local economy.

Source: Prepared by the author using data from United Nations Development Programme (2004). Map projection from *Peters Atlas of the World* (1990).

live in villages as in cities and to walk or ride animals, bicycles, scooters, or tractors as they are to drive cars, and they generally receive only a few years of schooling. Like high-income countries, middle-income countries are marked by pronounced social inequality, meaning that some people are extremely rich, but many more lack safe housing and adequate nutrition.

Finally, about half the world's people live in the sixty **low-income countries,** *nations with a low standard of living in which most people are poor.* As Global Map 1–2 shows, most of the poorest societies in the world are in Africa. In these nations, a small number of people are rich, but the majority struggle to get by with unclean water, too little food, little or no sanitation, and perhaps worst of all, little chance to improve their lives.

Chapter 9 ("Global Stratification") discusses the causes and consequences of global wealth and poverty. But every chapter highlights life in the world beyond our own borders for four reasons:

1. **Where we live makes a great deal of difference in shaping our lives.** As we saw in Global Map 1–1, women who live in rich and poor nations lead strikingly different lives. To understand ourselves and appreciate the situation of others, we must grasp the social landscape of the world—one good reason to pay attention to the dozens of global maps found in this text.

2. **Societies throughout the world are increasingly interconnected.** Historically, the United States has paid little attention to the countries beyond its own borders. In recent decades, however, the United States and the rest of the world have become linked as never before. Electronic technology now transmits pictures, sounds, and written documents around the globe in a matter of seconds.

   One consequence of new technology, as later chapters will explain, is that people all over the world now share many tastes in music, clothing, and food. With their economic power, high-income countries such as the United States influence other nations, whose people eagerly gobble up our hamburgers, dance to our music, and more and more, speak the English language.

   We are spreading our way of life around the world, but the larger world also has an impact on us. Almost 1 million documented immigrants enter the United States each year, and we are quick to adopt many of their favorite sounds, tastes, and customs as our own, which greatly increases the cultural diversity of this country.

Business across national borders has also created a global economy. Corporations make and market goods worldwide, just as global financial centers linked by satellite now operate around the clock. Stock traders in New York follow the financial markets in Tokyo and Hong Kong, just as wheat farmers in Kansas watch the price of grain in the former Soviet republic of Georgia. With eight out of ten new U.S. jobs involving international trade, gaining greater global understanding has never been more important.

3. **Many social problems that we face in the United States are far more serious elsewhere.** Poverty is a serious problem in this country, but as Chapter 9 ("Global Stratification") explains, poverty in Latin America, Africa, and Asia is both more widespread and more severe. Similarly, although women have lower social standing than men in the United States, gender inequality is much greater in the world's poor countries.

4. **Thinking globally is a good way to learn more about ourselves.** We cannot walk the streets of a foreign city without becoming keenly aware of what it means to live in the United States. Making these comparisons often leads to unexpected lessons. For instance, in Chapter 9, we visit a squatter settlement in Madras, India. There, despite a desperate lack of basic material goods, people thrive in the love and support of family members. Why, then, does poverty in the United States lead to isolation and anger? Are material goods, so central to our definition of a "rich" life, the best way to measure human well-being?

In sum, in an increasingly interconnected world, we can understand ourselves only to the extent that we understand others.

The Origins of Sociology

Like the "choices" made by individuals, major historical events rarely just "happen." Sociology was born as the result of powerful and complex social forces.

SOCIAL CHANGE AND SOCIOLOGY

Striking changes in eighteenth- and nineteenth-century Europe caused the social ground to tremble under people's feet. Understandably, people focused their attention on society, leading to the rise of the new science of sociology.

Industrial technology. In the Middle Ages, most people in Europe farmed near their homes or engaged in small-scale

Here we see Galileo, one of the great pioneers of the scientific revolution, defending himself before church officials, who were greatly threatened by his claims that science could explain the operation of the universe. Just as Galileo challenged the common sense of his day, pioneering sociologists such as Auguste Comte later argued that society is neither rigidly fixed by God's will nor set by human nature. On the contrary, Comte claimed, society is a system we can study scientifically, and based on what we learn, we can act intentionally to improve our lives.

North Wind Picture Archives

manufacturing (derived from Latin, meaning "to make by hand"). By the end of the eighteenth century, inventors had harnessed new sources of energy—the power of moving water and then steam—to operate large machines in mills and factories. As a result, instead of laboring at home or in tightly knit groups, workers became part of a large and anonymous labor force, toiling for strangers who owned the large factories. This change in the system of production separated families and weakened traditions that had guided members of small communities for centuries.

The growth of cities. Across Europe, factories drew people in need of work. Along with this "pull" came the "push" of the enclosure movement. Landowners fenced off more and more land, turning farms into grazing land for sheep, the source of wool for the thriving textile mills. Deprived of their land, countless tenant farmers left the countryside in search of work in the new factories.

Cities grew to enormous size, and streets churned with strangers. Widespread social problems—including pollution, crime, and homelessness—further stimulated development of the sociological perspective.

Political change. Economic development and the growth of cities also brought new ways of thinking. In the writings of Thomas Hobbes (1588–1679), John Locke (1632–1704), and Adam Smith (1723–1790), we find less concern with people's moral duties to God and to political rulers and more focus on the pursuit of self-interest. Indeed, the key phrases in the new political climate were *individual liberty*

and *individual rights*. Echoing the thoughts of Locke, our own Declaration of Independence clearly states that each citizen has "certain unalienable rights," including "life, liberty, and the pursuit of happiness."

The political revolution in France that began in 1789 symbolized the Western world's break with the old political and social traditions. As the French social analyst Alexis de Tocqueville (1805–1859) declared after the French Revolution, the change in society amounted to "nothing short of the regeneration of the whole human race" (1955:13, orig. 1856). As the new industrial economy, enormous cities, and fresh political ideas combined to draw attention to society, sociology flowered in France, Germany, and England, the countries experiencing the greatest changes.

SCIENCE AND SOCIOLOGY

The nature of society has fascinated people since ancient times, including the brilliant philosophers K'ung Fu-tzu, or Confucius (551–479 B.C.E.), in China and Plato (427–347 B.C.E.) and Aristotle (384–322 B.C.E.) in Greece.[1] Later, the Roman emperor Marcus Aurelius (121–180), the medieval thinkers Saint Thomas Aquinas (c. 1225–1274) and Christine de Pizan (c. 1363–1431), and the great English playwright William Shakespeare (1564–1616) took up the question.

---

[1]This text uses the abbreviation B.C.E. ("before the common era.") rather than B.C. ("before Christ") to respect the religious diversity of U.S. society. Similarly, we use the abbreviation C.E. ("common era") in place of A.D. (*anno Domini*, "in the year of our Lord").

During the nineteenth century, women and people of color lived at the margins of social life. In recent decades, however, several of sociology's founders have been recognized for the important contributions they made to the development of the discipline. Harriet Martineau (in England) and Jane Addams and W. E. B. Du Bois (in the United States) all took an active part in debating the social issues of their day.

Yet these men and women were more interested in envisioning the ideal society than they were in analyzing society as it really was. In creating their new discipline, sociology's pioneers certainly cared how society could be improved, but their major goal was to understand how it operates. It was the French social thinker Auguste Comte (1798–1857) who coined the term *sociology* in 1838 to describe this new way of thinking. Thus, sociology is among the youngest of the academic disciplines—far newer than history, physics, or economics, for example.

 For a biographical sketch of Comte, go to the Gallery of Sociologists at http://www. TheSociologyPage.com

Comte (1975, orig. 1851–54) saw sociology as the product of three stages of historical development. During the earliest *theological stage,* up to the end of the European Middle Ages, people took a religious view that society expressed God's will. With the Renaissance, this theological approach gradually gave way to a *metaphysical stage* in which people saw society as a natural rather than supernatural phenomenon. The English philosopher Thomas Hobbes, for example, suggested that society reflected not the perfection of God as much as the failings of a selfish human nature.

What Comte called the *scientific stage* began with the work of early scientists such as the Polish astronomer Nicolaus Copernicus (1473–1543), the Italian astronomer and physicist Galileo (1564–1642), and the English physicist and mathematician Isaac Newton (1642–1727). Comte's contribution came in applying the scientific approach—first used to analyze the physical world—to the study of society.

Comte thus favored **positivism,** *a way of understanding based on science.* As a positivist, Comte believed that society operates according to certain laws, just as the physical world operates according to gravity and other laws of nature.

At the beginning of the twentieth century, sociology took hold as an academic discipline in the United States, strongly influenced by Comte's ideas. Today, most sociologists still consider science a crucial element of sociology. But we now realize that human behavior is far more complex than the movement of planets or even the actions of other living things. We are creatures of imagination and spontaneity, so human behavior can never be explained by any rigid "laws of society." In addition, early sociologists such as Karl Marx (1818–1883) were deeply troubled by the striking inequality of the new industrial society. They wanted the new discipline of sociology not just to understand society but also to bring about change toward social justice.

GENDER AND RACE: MARGINAL VOICES

Auguste Comte and Karl Marx stand among the giants of sociology. But in recent years, we have come to see the important contributions made by others who were pushed to the margins of society because of their sex or race.

This map shows which states have high, average, and low suicide rates. Look for patterns. By and large, high suicide rates occur where people live far apart from one another. More densely populated states have low suicide rates. Do these data support or contradict Durkheim's theory of suicide? Why?

Source: Arias et al. (2003).

Number of Suicides per 100,000 People

- Above average: 14.1 or more
- Average: 10.0 to 14.0
- Below average: 9.9 or fewer

Harriet Martineau (1802–1876), who is regarded as the first woman sociologist, was born to a wealthy English family. She first made her mark in 1853 by translating the writings of Auguste Comte from French into English. Later, she became a noted scholar in her own right, documenting the evils of slavery and arguing for laws to protect factory workers and to advance the standing of women.

In the United States, Jane Addams (1860–1935) was a sociological pioneer whose contribution began in 1889 when she helped found Hull House, a Chicago settlement house that provided help to immigrant families. Although widely published (she wrote eleven books and hundreds of articles), Addams chose the life of a public activist over that of a university sociologist, conducting research and speaking out on issues involving immigration and the pursuit of peace. Despite controversy caused by her pacifism during World War I, she was awarded the Nobel Peace Prize in 1931.

An important contribution to understanding race in the United States was made by another sociological pioneer, William Edward Burghardt Du Bois (1868–1963). Born to a poor Massachusetts family, Du Bois enrolled at Fisk University in Nashville, Tennessee, and then at Harvard University, where he earned the first doctorate awarded by that university to a person of color. Like Martineau and Addams, Du Bois believed that sociologists should try to solve contemporary problems. He therefore studied the black community (1967, orig. 1899), spoke out against racial inequality, and served as a founding member of the National Association for the Advancement of Colored People (NAACP).

The fact that women and African Americans were second-class citizens reduced the attention paid to the work of Martineau, Addams, and Du Bois. Today, however, sociologists are bringing their accomplishments to new generations of students.

Sociological Theory

Weaving observations into understanding brings us to another aspect of sociology: theory. A **theory** is *a statement of how and why specific facts are related.* To illustrate, recall Emile Durkheim's theory that categories of people with low social integration (men, Protestants, the wealthy, and the unmarried) are at higher risk of suicide.

Like all scientists, sociologists conduct research to test and refine their theories. National Map 1–1, which shows the suicide rates for the fifty states, gives you a chance to do some theorizing of your own.

In building theory, sociologists face two basic questions: What issues should we study? How should we connect the facts? In answering these questions, sociologists look to one or more theoretical approaches or "road maps." Think of a **theoretical approach** as *a basic image of society that guides thinking and research.* Sociologists make use of the *structural-functional approach,* the *social-conflict approach,* and the *symbolic-interaction approach.*

THE STRUCTURAL-FUNCTIONAL APPROACH

The **structural-functional approach** is *a framework for building theory that sees society as a complex system whose parts work together to promote solidarity and stability.* As its name suggests, this approach points to the importance of **social structure,** *any relatively stable pattern of social behavior.* Social structure gives our lives shape in families,

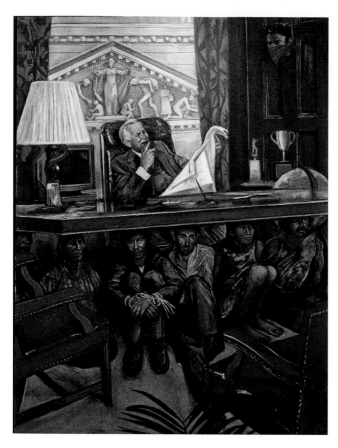

The painting *Furnishings,* by Paul Marcus, presents the essential wisdom of social-conflict theory: Society operates in a way that conveys wealth, power, and privilege to some at the expense of others. What categories of people does the artist suggest are advantaged and disadvantaged?

Paul Marcus, *Furnishings,* oil painting on canvas, 64 in. × 48 in., Studio SPM, Inc.

the workplace, or the college classroom. Second, this approach looks for any structure's **social functions,** *the consequences of any social pattern for the operation of society as a whole.* All social patterns—from a simple handshake to complex religious rituals—function to keep society going, at least in its present form.

The structural-functional approach owes much to Auguste Comte, who pointed out the need for social integration during a time of rapid change. Emile Durkheim, who helped establish sociology in French universities, also based his work on this view. A third structural-functional pioneer was the English sociologist Herbert Spencer (1820–1903). Spencer compared society to the human body: Just as the structural parts of the human

Find biographical sketches of Durkheim and Spencer in the Gallery of Sociologists at http://www.TheSociologyPage.com

body—the skeleton, muscles, and various internal organs—function together to help the entire organism survive, social structures work together to preserve society. The structural-functional approach, then, leads sociologists to identify various structures of society and investigate their functions.

The U.S. sociologist Robert K. Merton (1910–2003) expanded our understanding of social function by pointing out that any social structure probably has many functions, some more obvious than others. He distinguished between **manifest functions,** *the recognized and intended consequences of any social pattern,* and **latent functions,** *the unrecognized and unintended consequences of any social pattern.* To illustrate, the obvious function of this country's system of higher education is to give young people the information and skills they will need to perform jobs after graduation. Perhaps just as important, although less often acknowledged, is college's function as a "marriage broker," bringing together young people of similar social backgrounds. Another latent function of higher education is to limit unemployment by keeping millions of people out of the labor market, where many of them may not easily find jobs.

But Merton also recognized that the effects of social structure are not all good and certainly not good for everybody. Thus, a **social dysfunction** is *any social pattern that may disrupt the operation of society.* People usually disagree on what is helpful and what is harmful. Moreover, what is functional for one category of people (say, high profits for factory owners or landlords) may well be dysfunctional for another category of people (say, low wages for factory workers or high rents for tenants).

Critical review. The main idea of the structural-functional approach is its vision of society as stable and orderly. The main goal of sociologists who use this approach, then, is to figure out "what makes society tick."

In the mid-1900s, most sociologists favored the structural-functional approach. In recent decades, however, its influence has declined. By focusing attention on social stability and unity, critics point out, structural-functionalism ignores inequalities of social class, race, ethnicity, and gender, which can generate tension and conflict. In general, its focus on stability at the expense of conflict makes this approach somewhat conservative. As a critical response, sociologists developed the social-conflict approach.

THE SOCIAL-CONFLICT APPROACH

The **social-conflict approach** is *a framework for building theory that sees society as an arena of inequality that generates conflict and change.* Unlike the structural-functional emphasis on solidarity, this approach highlights conflict. Guided by this approach, sociologists investigate how factors such as class, race, ethnicity, gender, and age are linked to the unequal distribution of money, power, education, and social prestige. A conflict analysis rejects the idea that social structure promotes the operation of society as a whole, focusing instead on how any social pattern benefits some people while hurting others.

Sociologists use the social-conflict approach to look at ongoing conflict between dominant and disadvantaged categories of people: the rich in relation to the poor, white people in relation to people of color, or men in relation to women. They find that, typically, people in advantaged positions try to protect their privileges while the disadvantaged try to gain more for themselves.

A conflict analysis of our educational system shows how schooling reproduces class inequality in every new generation. For example, secondary schools assign students to either college preparatory or vocational training programs. From a structural-functional point of view, such "tracking" benefits everyone by providing schooling that fits students' abilities. But conflict analysis counters that tracking often has less to do with talent than with social background, so that well-to-do students are placed in higher tracks and poor children end up in lower tracks.

In this way, young people from privileged families get the best schooling and later pursue high-income careers. The children of poor families, on the other hand, are not prepared for college and, like their parents before them, typically enter low-paying jobs. In both cases, the social standing of one generation is passed on to the next, with schools justifying the practice in terms of individual merit (Bowles & Gintis, 1976; Oakes, 1982, 1985).

Many sociologists who use social-conflict analysis try not just to understand society but also to reduce inequality. This was the goal of W. E. B. Du Bois, who was guided by the social-conflict approach to raise the standing of people of color. Likewise, Karl Marx championed the workers against those who owned the factories. In a well-known statement (inscribed on his monument in London's Highgate Cemetery), Marx declared, "The philosophers have only interpreted the world, in various ways; the point, however, is to change it."

Critical review.   The social-conflict approach has gained a large following in recent decades, but like other approaches, it has met with its share of criticism. Because this analysis focuses on inequality, it largely ignores how shared values and interdependence can unify members of a society. In addition, to the extent that it pursues political goals, the social-conflict approach cannot claim scientific objectivity. Supporters of social-conflict analysis respond that *all* theoretical approaches have political consequences.

To understand how the symbolic-interaction approach views society, consider Sherry Karver's painting, *Faces in the Crowd III.* Just as the images seem to flow together in new and never quite predictable ways, society is never at rest; it is an ongoing process by which interacting people define and redefine reality.

Sherry Karver, *Faces in the Crowd III*, 2001, oil and photography on panel, 24 in. × 19 in. Courtesy of Lisa Harris Gallery, Seattle, Washington.

A final criticism of both the structural-functional and social-conflict approaches is that they paint society in broad strokes—in terms of "family," "social class," "race," and so on. A third theoretical approach views society less in general terms and more as the specific, everyday experiences of individual people.

THE SYMBOLIC-INTERACTION APPROACH

The structural-functional and social-conflict approaches share a **macro-level orientation,** meaning *a broad focus on social structures that shape society as a whole.* Macro-level sociology takes in the big picture, rather like observing a city from a helicopter and seeing how highways help people move from place to place or how housing differs from rich to poor neighborhoods. Sociology also uses a **micro-level orientation,** *a close-up focus on social interaction in specific*

APPLYING THEORY

MAJOR THEORETICAL APPROACHES

	Structural-Functional Approach	Social-Conflict Approach	Symbolic-Interaction Approach
What is the level of analysis?	Macro-level	Macro-level	Micro-level
What image of society does the approach have?	Society is a system of interrelated parts that is relatively stable. Each part works to keep society operating in an orderly way. Members have general agreement about what is morally right.	Society is a system of social inequality. Society operates to benefit some categories of people and harm others. Social inequality causes conflict that leads to social change.	Society is an ongoing process. People interact in countless settings using symbolic communications. The reality people experience is variable and changing.
What core questions does the approach ask?	How is society held together? What are the major parts of society? How are these parts linked? What does each part do to help society work?	How does society divide a population? How do advantaged people protect their privileges? How do disadvantaged people challenge the system seeking change?	How do people experience society? How do people shape the reality they experience? How do behavior and meaning change from person to person and from one situation to another?

situations. Exploring city life in this way occurs at street level, where you might watch how children invent games on a school playground or observe how pedestrians respond to homeless people. The **symbolic-interaction approach,** then, is *a framework for building theory that sees society as the product of the everyday interactions of individuals.*

How does "society" result from the ongoing experiences of tens of millions of people? One answer, detailed in Chapter 4 ("Social Interaction in Everyday Life"), is that society is nothing more than the reality people construct for themselves as they interact with one another. That is, human beings are creatures who live in a world of symbols, attaching *meaning* to virtually everything. "Reality," therefore, is simply how we define our surroundings, our duties toward others, and even our own identities.

The symbolic-interaction approach has roots in the thinking of Max Weber (1864–1920), a German sociologist who emphasized understanding a particular setting from the point of view of the people in it. Since Weber's time, sociologists have taken micro-level sociology in a number of directions. Chapter 3 ("Socialization: From Infancy to Old Age") discusses the ideas of George Herbert Mead (1863–1931), who explored how we create our personalities from social experience. Chapter 4 ("Social Interaction in Everyday Life") presents the work of Erving Goffman (1922–1982), whose *dramaturgical analysis* describes how

we resemble actors on a stage as we play out our various roles. Other contemporary sociologists, including George Homans and Peter Blau, have developed *social-exchange analysis,* the idea that interaction is guided by what each person stands to gain and lose from others. In the ritual of courtship, for example, people seek mates who can offer them at least as much—in terms of physical attractiveness, intelligence, and social background—as they offer in return.

Critical review. Without denying the existence of macro-level social structures such as "the family" and "social class," the symbolic-interaction approach reminds us that society basically amounts to *people interacting.* That is, micro-level sociology tries to show how individuals actually experience society. But on the other side of the coin, by emphasizing what is unique in each social scene, this approach risks overlooking the widespread influence of culture, as well as factors such as class, gender, and race.

The Applying Theory table summarizes the features of the structural-functional approach, the social-conflict approach, and the symbolic-interaction approach. As you read the chapters in this book, keep in mind that each is helpful in answering particular types of questions. As the Applying Sociology box about sports on pages 16–17 shows, the fullest understanding of society comes from using all three approaches.

Three Ways to Do Sociology

All sociologists want to learn about the social world. But, in the same way that they may prefer one theoretical approach to another, so they may prefer one methodological orientation. The following sections describe three ways to do sociological research.

SCIENTIFIC SOCIOLOGY

The first, and probably most popular, way to do sociological research is based on **science,** *a logical system that bases knowledge on direct, systematic observation.* Scientific knowledge is based on *empirical evidence,* information we can verify with our senses.

A scientific orientation often challenges what we accept as "common sense." Here are three examples of widely held beliefs that are contradicted by scientific evidence:

1. **"Differences in the behavior of females and males reflect 'human nature'."** Wrong. Much of what we call human nature is constructed by the society in which we live. We know this because researchers have documented how definitions of "feminine" and "masculine" change over time and vary from one society to another (see Chapter 10, "Gender Stratification").

2. **"The United States is a middle-class society in which most people are more-or-less equal."** Not true. As Chapter 8 ("Social Stratification") explains, the richest 5 percent of U.S. families control more than half of the country's wealth, while almost half of all families have scarcely any wealth at all.

3. **"People marry because they are in love."** Not exactly. In our own society, as we have already explained, various social rules guide the selection of mates. Around the world, research indicates that marriages in most societies have little to do with love. Chapter 13 ("Family and Religion") explains why.

These examples confirm the old saying that "it's not what we don't know that gets us into trouble as much as the things we *do* know that just aren't so." Scientific sociology is a useful way to assess many kinds of information.

Concepts, variables, and measurement. A basic element of science is the **concept,** *a mental construct that represents some part of the world in a simplified form.* Sociologists use concepts to label aspects of social life, including "the family" and "the economy," and to categorize people in terms of their "gender" or "social class."

A **variable** is *a concept whose value changes from case to case.* The familiar variable "price," for example, changes from item to item in a supermarket. Similarly, people use the concept "social class" to size up others as "upper class," "middle class," "working class," or "lower class."

The use of variables depends on **measurement,** *a procedure for determining the value of a variable in a specific case.* Some variables are easy to measure, as when a checkout clerk adds up the cost of our groceries. But measuring sociological variables can be far more difficult. For example, how would you measure a person's social class? You might be tempted to look at clothing, listen to patterns of speech, or note a home address. Or, trying to be more precise, you might ask about income, occupation, and education. Because there are many ways to measure almost anything, researchers must *operationalize* their variables; that is, they must specify exactly what they are measuring in each case.

Sociologists also face the problem of dealing with large numbers of people. For example, how do you report income for thousands or even millions of individuals? Listing streams of numbers would carry little meaning and tell us nothing about the people as a whole. Therefore, sociologists use *descriptive statistics* to state what is "average" for a large population. Most commonly used are the *mean* (the arithmetic average of all measures, obtained by adding them up and dividing by the number of cases), the *median* (the middle score that divides a set of numbers in half), and the *mode* (the single score that appears most often).

Reliability and validity. Beyond carefully operationalizing variables, useful measurement must be reliable and valid. **Reliability** is *consistency in measurement.* For measurement to be reliable, in other words, the process must yield the same results when repeated. However, even consistent results may not be valid. **Validity** is *actually measuring exactly what you intend to measure.* Valid measurement means more than hitting the same spot somewhere on a target again and again; it means hitting the precise target, the bull's-eye.

Say you want to know just how religious people are. You might ask how often your subjects attend religious services. But is going to a church or temple or mosque really the same thing as being religious? Maybe not, because people take part in religious rituals for many reasons, not all of them religious, and some strong believers avoid organized religion altogether. Thus, even when a measure yields consistent results (making it reliable), it can still miss the real, intended target (and lack validity). In sum, sociological research depends on careful measurement, which is always a challenge to researchers.

Correlation and cause. The real payoff in scientific research is determining how variables are related. **Correlation** means

APPLYING SOCIOLOGY

Sports: Playing the Theory Game

Who among us doesn't enjoy sports? Children as young as six or seven may play as many as two or three organized sports at a time. For adults who don't participate themselves, weekend television is filled with sporting events, and whole sections of our newspapers report the scores. What can we learn by applying sociology's three theoretical approaches to this familiar element of life in the United States?

According to the structural-functional approach, the manifest functions of sports include recreation, getting in shape, and a relatively harmless way to let off steam. Sports have important latent functions as well, from fostering social relationships to creating countless jobs. Perhaps the most important latent function of sports is to encourage competition, which is central to this nation's way of life (Coakley, 1990).

Of course, sports also have dysfunctional consequences. For example, colleges and universities intent on fielding winning teams sometimes recruit students for their athletic ability rather than their academic aptitude. This practice not only pulls down a school's academic standards but also shortchanges athletes, who have little time to devote to academic work.

A social-conflict analysis points out how sports are linked to social inequality. Some sports—tennis,

swimming, golf, skiing—are expensive, so participation is largely limited to the well-to-do. By contrast, football, baseball, and basketball are accessible to people of almost all income levels. Thus, the games people play are not simply a matter of choice but also a reflection of their social standing.

Moreover, men dominate sports. The first modern Olympic Games, held in 1896, excluded women from competition. In the United States through most of the twentieth century, Little League teams barred girls from the playing field on the unfounded ideas that girls lack the strength and the stamina to play sports and that they risk losing their femininity if they do. Both the Olympics and the Little League are now open to females as well as males. But in the world of sports, women still take a back seat to men, particularly in sports that yield the greatest earnings and social prestige.

Although our society long excluded people of color from professional sports, opportunities have expanded in recent decades. In 1947, Jackie Robinson broke through the "color line" to become the first African American player in Major League Baseball. More than fifty years later, professional baseball retired the legendary Robinson's number 42 on *all* teams, and in 2002, African Americans (12 percent of the U.S. population) accounted for

10 percent of Major League Baseball players, 65 percent of National Foot-

 For a sociological look at sports, see the research reports at http://www.aafla.org

ball League (NFL) players, and 78 percent of National Basketball Association (NBA) players (Lapchick, 2003).

One reason for the increasing share of African Americans in professional sports is the fact that athletic performance—in terms of batting average or number of points scored per game—is measured objectively and is not influenced by racial prejudice. It is also true that some people of color make a special effort to excel in athletics, where they see more opportunity than in other careers (Steele, 1990; Edwards, 2000). In recent years, in fact, African American athletes have earned higher salaries, on average, than white players.

But racial discrimination still taints professional sports in the United States. For one thing, race is linked to the positions athletes play on the field, a pattern called "stacking." The figure shows the results of a study of race in football. Notice that white players dominate the offense and also play the central positions on both sides of the line. More broadly, African Americans figure prominently in only five major sports: basketball, football, baseball, boxing, and track. And across all professional

a relationship in which two (or more) variables change together. But sociologists want to know not just *how* variables change but *why.* The scientific ideal, then, is mapping out **cause and effect,** which means *a relationship in which change in one variable causes change in another.* As we noted earlier, Emile Durkheim found that the degree of social

integration (the cause) affected the suicide rate (the effect) among categories of people. Scientists refer to the causal factor as the *independent variable* and call the effect the *dependent variable.* Understanding cause and effect is valuable because it allows researchers to *predict* how one pattern of behavior will produce another.

sports, the vast majority of managers, head coaches, and team owners are still white (Lapchick, 2003).

Overall, who benefits most from professional sports? Although individual players may get sky-high salaries, and millions of fans love following their teams, the vast profits sports generate are controlled by a small number of people (predominantly white men). In sum, sports in the United States are bound up with inequalities based on gender, race, and wealth.

At a micro-level, a sporting event is a complex drama of face-to-face interaction. In part, play is guided by assigned positions and, of course, by the rules of the game. But players are also spontaneous and unpredictable. According to the symbolic-interaction approach, sports are less a system than an ongoing process. Also, we expect each player to understand the game a little differently. Some enjoy stiff competition, whereas for others love of the game may be greater than the need to win.

Team members also shape their particular realities according to the prejudices, jealousies, and ambitions they bring to the field. Moreover, the behavior of any single player changes

over time. A rookie in professional baseball, for example, typically feels self-conscious during the first few games in the big leagues but goes on to develop a comfortable sense of fitting in with the team. Coming to feel at

home on the field was especially difficult for Jackie Robinson in 1947. At first, he was painfully aware that many white players and millions of white fans resented his presence. In time, however, his outstanding ability and his confident, cooperative manner won him the respect of the entire nation.

The three theoretical approaches differ in how they view sports, and none is entirely correct. Each generates its own insights; to fully appreciate the power of the sociological perspective, you should try to apply all three to any given issue.

WHAT DO YOU THINK?

1. Describe how a macro-level approach to sports differs from a micro-level approach. Which theoretical approaches are macro-level, and which one is micro-level?

2. Make up three questions about sports, one that reflects the focus of each of the three theoretical approaches.

3. How might you apply the three approaches to other social patterns, such as the workplace or family life?

Offense | **Defense**

Wide Receiver — Cornerback
Tackle — Linebacker
Defensive End
Guard — Safety
Defensive Tackle
Running Back — Quarterback — Center — Linebacker
Defensive Tackle
Guard — Safety
Running Back
Defensive End
Tackle — Linebacker
Tight End
Wide Receiver — Cornerback

☐ White Players   ☐ African American Players

Race and Sport: "Stacking" in Professional Football

Source: Lapchick (2003).

Just because two variables change together does not necessarily mean that they have a cause-and-effect relationship. For instance, the marriage rate in the United States falls to its lowest point in January, exactly the same month in which the national death rate is highest. This hardly means that people drop dead if they decide not to marry (or that they don't marry because they die). More likely, it is the dreary weather across much of the country during January (perhaps combined with the postholiday "blahs") that causes both the low marriage rate and the high death rate.

When two variables change together but neither one causes the other, sociologists describe the relationship as a

Myths are an important dimension of human existence. In his painting, *Creation of North Sacred Mountain,* Navajo artist Harrison Begay offers a mythic account of creation. A myth (from the Greek, meaning "story" or "word") may or may not be factual in the literal sense. Yet it conveys some basic truth about the meaning and purpose of life. It is the meanings that shape social behavior that the interpretive sociologist seeks to understand.

35464/13 *Creation of North Sacred Mountain* by Harrison Begay, Haskey-Yah-Ne-Yah, Navajo. In the Collections of the Museum of Indian Arts and Culture/Laboratory of Anthropology, Museum of New Mexico. Photograph by Blair Clark.

spurious, or false, correlation. A spurious correlation between two variables usually results from some third factor. For example, delinquency rates are high where young people live in crowded housing, but both of these factors result from being poor. To be sure of a real cause-and-effect relationship, we must show that (1) the two variables are correlated, (2) the independent (or causal) variable occurs before the dependent variable, and (3) there is no evidence that the correlation is spurious because of some third variable.

The ideal of objectivity.   A guiding principle of scientific study is *objectivity,* or personal neutrality, in conducting research. The ideal of objective research is to allow the facts to speak for themselves and not become colored by the personal values and biases of the researcher. In reality, of course, achieving total neutrality is impossible for anyone. But carefully observing the rules of scientific research will maximize objectivity.

The German sociologist Max Weber noted that people usually choose *value-relevant* research topics—topics they care about. But, he cautioned, once their work is underway, researchers should try to be *value-free.* That is, we must be dedicated to finding truth as it *is* rather than as we think it

should be. For Weber, this difference sets science apart from politics. Researchers (unlike politicians) must try to stay open-minded and be willing to accept whatever results come from their work, whether they like them or not.

Weber's argument still carries much weight in sociology, although most researchers admit that we can never be completely value-free or even aware of all our biases (Demerath, 1996). Moreover, sociologists are not "average" people: Most are white people who are highly educated and more politically liberal than the population as a whole. Sociologists need to remember that they, too, are influenced by their social backgrounds.

INTERPRETIVE SOCIOLOGY

Not all sociologists agree that the scientific orientation is the best way to study human society. Unlike planets or other elements of the natural world, humans do not simply move about; we engage in *meaningful* action. A second type of research is **interpretive sociology,** *the study of society that focuses on the meanings people attach to their social world.* Max Weber, the pioneer of this framework, argued that the proper focus of sociology is *interpretation,* or understanding the meaning people create in their everyday lives.

The importance of meaning.   Interpretive sociology differs from scientific, or positivist, sociology in three ways. First, scientific sociology focuses on action, what people do; interpretive sociology, by contrast, focuses on the meaning people attach to behavior. Second, whereas scientific sociology sees an objective reality "out there," interpretive sociology sees reality constructed by people themselves in the course of their everyday lives. Third, whereas scientific sociology tends to favor *quantitative* data—numerical measurements of social behavior—interpretive sociology favors *qualitative* data, researchers' perceptions of how people understand their surroundings. In sum, the scientific orientation is well suited for research in a laboratory, where investigators stand back and take careful measurements. The interpretive orientation is better suited for research in a natural setting, where investigators interact with people to learn how they make sense of their everyday lives.

Weber's concept of *Verstehen.*   Max Weber claimed that the key to interpretive sociology lies in *Verstehen,* the German word for "understanding." It is the interpretive sociologist's job not just to observe *what* people do but also to share in their world of meaning, coming to appreciate *why* they act as they do. Subjective thoughts and feelings—which science tends to dismiss as "bias"—now move to the center of the researcher's attention.

Three Methodological Orientations in Sociology

	Scientific	Interpretive	Critical
What is reality?	Society is an orderly system. There is an objective reality "out there."	Society is ongoing interaction. People construct reality as they attach meanings to their behavior.	Society is patterns of inequality. Reality is that some categories of people dominate others.
How do we conduct research?	Researcher gathers empirical, ideally quantitative, data. Researcher tries to be a neutral observer.	Researcher develops a qualitative account of the subjective sense people make of their world. Researcher is a participant.	Research is a strategy to bring about desired social change. Researcher is an activist.
Corresponding theoretical approach	Structural-functional approach	Symbolic-interaction approach	Social-conflict approach

CRITICAL SOCIOLOGY

Like the interpretive orientation, critical sociology developed in reaction to the limitations of scientific sociology. In the case of this third way to do research, however, the problem was the foremost principle of scientific research: objectivity.

Scientific sociology holds that reality is "out there," and the researcher's job is to study and document this reality. But Karl Marx, who founded the critical orientation, rejected the idea that society exists as a "natural" system with a fixed order. Assuming this, he claimed, amounts to saying that society cannot be changed. Scientific sociology, in his view, ends up supporting the status quo.

The importance of change. **Critical sociology,** then, is *the study of society that focuses on the need for social change.* Rather than asking the scientific question, "How does society work?" critical sociologists ask moral and political questions, especially, "Should society exist in its present form?" Their answer, typically, is that it should not. The point, said Marx (1972:109, orig. 1845), is not just to study the world as it is but to *change* it. In making value judgments about how society should be improved, critical sociology rejects the scientific claim that research should be value-free.

Sociologists using the critical orientation seek to change not only society but also the character of research itself. They consider their research subjects as equals and encourage their participation in deciding what to study and how to do the work. Often researchers and subjects use their findings to provide a voice for less powerful people and advance the political goal of a more equal society (Wolf, 1996; Hess, 1999).

Sociology as politics. Scientific sociologists object to taking sides in this way, charging that critical sociology (whether feminist, Marxist, or some other critical orientation) is political and gives up any claim to objectivity. Critical sociologists respond that *all* research is political in that either it calls for change or it does not; sociologists thus have no choice about their work being political, but they can choose which positions to support. Critical sociology, therefore, is an activist approach tying knowledge to action and seeks not just to understand the world but also to improve it. Generally speaking, scientific sociology tends to appeal to researchers with more conservative political views; critical sociology appeals to those with liberal and radical-left politics.

METHODS AND THEORY

What about the link between methodological orientations and theory? In general, each of the three ways to do sociology is related to one of the theoretical approaches presented earlier in this chapter. The scientific orientation corresponds to the structural-functional approach, the interpretive orientation to the symbolic-interaction approach, and the critical orientation to the social-conflict approach. The Summing Up table reviews the differences among the three ways to do sociology. Keep in mind that, although sociologists may favor one orientation over another, most make use of all three.

Research Ethics

Like all other scientific investigators, sociologists must remember that their work can harm as well as help subjects and communities. For this reason, the American Sociological Association, the professional organization of U.S. sociologists, provides formal guidelines for conducting research (1997).

Sociologists must try to be both technically competent and fair-minded in their work. They must report their findings without omitting significant data, and they are ethically bound to share their work with other sociologists who may want to conduct the same study.

Sociologists must also ensure the safety of subjects taking part in a research project and must stop work immediately if they suspect that a subject is at risk of any harm. Researchers are also required to protect the privacy of individuals involved in a research project, even if they come under pressure from authorities, such as the police or the courts, to release confidential information. Researchers must also get the *informed consent* of participants, which means that the subjects understand their responsibilities and risks and agree—before the work begins—to take part in the study.

Another guideline concerns funding. Sociologists must reveal all sources of financial support in their published results. Furthermore, sociologists are required to avoid conflicts of interest (or even the appearance of such conflicts) that may call their results into question. For example, researchers must never accept funding from any organization that seeks to influence the research results for its own purposes.

The federal government, as well, plays a part in research ethics. Every college and university that seeks federal funding for research involving human subjects must have an *institutional review board* (IRB) that reviews grant applications and ensures that research will not violate ethical standards.

There are also global dimensions to research ethics. Before beginning work in another nation, investigators must become familiar enough with that society to understand what people *there* are likely to regard as a violation of privacy or a source of personal danger. In a diverse society such as our own, the same rule applies to studying people with different backgrounds. The Diversity box offers tips on the sensitivity outsiders should apply when studying Hispanic communities.

GENDER AND RESEARCH

In trying to be ethical in their research, sociologists must pay special attention to **gender**, *the personal traits and social positions that members of a society attach to being female or male.* Margrit Eichler (1988) identifies four ways in which gender can influence research, to which can be added a fifth:

1. **Androcentricity.** *Androcentricity* (*andro* is the Greek word for "male"; *centricity* refers to "being centered

on") means acting as if only the actions of men are important, ignoring what women do. The parallel concept of *gynocentricity*—seeing the world from a female perspective—is a problem, too, but one that is far less common in our male-dominated society.

2. **Overgeneralizing.** This problem occurs when sociologists use data obtained from men to make conclusions about all people. For example, a researcher might gather information from a handful of male public officials and draw conclusions about an entire community.

3. **Gender blindness.** Failing to consider gender at all is called "gender blindness." A study of growing old in the United States that overlooks the fact that most elderly men live with spouses while elderly women generally live alone would be limited by gender blindness.

4. **Double standards.** Researchers must be careful not to judge men and women differently. For example, a family researcher who labels a couple "man and wife" (rather than "husband and wife") implies that the marital status of one sex is more significant than that of the other.

5. **Interference.** We can add to Eichler's list the problem of subjects reacting to the sex of the investigator in ways that interfere with the research project. For instance, while conducting research in Sicily, Maureen Giovannini (1992) found that many men reacted to her as a *woman* rather than as a *researcher*. Gender dynamics also kept her from certain activities, such as private conversations with men, that were considered inappropriate for single women.

There is nothing wrong with focusing research on people of one sex or the other. But all sociologists, as well as people who read their work, should be mindful of how gender can affect an investigation.

Research Methods

A **research method** is *a systematic plan for doing research.* Here we examine four widely used methods of sociological investigation: experiments, surveys, participant observation, and use of existing sources. None is better or worse than any other. Rather, just as a carpenter selects a particular tool for a particular job, researchers choose a method according to whom they want to study and what they want to learn.

TESTING A HYPOTHESIS: THE EXPERIMENT

The **experiment** is *a research method for investigating cause and effect under highly controlled conditions.* Experiments

DIVERSITY: RACE, CLASS, & GENDER
Studying the Lives of Hispanics

Sociological investigators often study people who differ from themselves. Learning—in advance—the cultural traits of research subjects will both speed the work and ensure that no hard feelings arise along the way.

Gerardo Marín and Barbara Van Oss Marín have identified five areas of concern when conducting research with Hispanics:

1. **Be careful with terms.** The Maríns point out that "Hispanic" is a label of convenience used by the U.S. Census Bureau. Some people of Spanish descent think of themselves as "Hispanic," and others prefer the term "Latino"; however, most identify with a particular country, such as Cuba, Argentina, or Spain.

2. **Be culturally aware.** By and large, the U.S. population is individualistic and competitive. Many Hispanics, by contrast, are more group oriented. An outsider may judge the behavior of a Hispanic subject as conformist or overly trusting when in fact the person is simply trying to be courteous. Hispanic respondents might agree with a researcher's statement out of politeness rather than belief.

3. **Anticipate family dynamics.** Hispanic cultures have strong family loyalties. Asking subjects to reveal information about another family member may make them uncomfortable or even angry. The Maríns add that a researcher's request to speak privately with a Hispanic woman in the home may provoke suspicion or outright disapproval from her husband or father.

4. **Take your time.** Hispanics, the Maríns explain, tend to be more concerned with the quality of relationships than with simply getting a job done. A non-Hispanic researcher who tries to hurry an interview with a Hispanic family, perhaps not wanting to delay their dinner, may be thought rude for not proceeding at a more sociable and relaxed pace.

5. **Think about personal space.** Finally, the Maríns point out that people of Spanish descent typically maintain closer physical contact than many non-Hispanics. Therefore, researchers who seat themselves across the room from their subjects may come across as "stand-offish." Conversely, researchers may inaccurately label Hispanics "pushy" when they move closer than a non-Hispanic researcher may find comfortable.

Of course, Hispanics differ among themselves just as people in any category do, and these generalizations apply to some more than to others. But investigators should be aware of cultural dynamics when carrying out any research, especially in the United States, where hundreds of distinctive categories of people make up this diverse society.

WHAT DO YOU THINK?

1. What are some likely consequences of researchers' not being sensitive to the culture of their subjects?
2. What do researchers need to do to avoid these problems?
3. Discuss the research process with classmates from various cultural backgrounds. What similar or different concerns would be raised by these people when taking part in research?

Source: Marín & Marín (1991).

test a specific *hypothesis,* a statement of a possible relationship between two (or more) variables. A hypothesis is really an educated guess about how variables are linked. An experimenter gathers the evidence needed to accept or reject the hypothesis in three steps: (1) measuring the dependent variable (the "effect"), (2) exposing the dependent variable to the independent variable (the "cause" or "treatment"), and (3) measuring the dependent variable again to see whether the predicted change took place. If the expected change took place, the experiment supports the hypothesis; if not, the hypothesis must be modified.

Successful experiments depend on careful control of all factors that might affect what the experiment is trying to measure. Control is easiest in a research laboratory. But experiments in an everyday location—"in the field," as sociologists say—have the advantage of letting researchers observe subjects in their natural settings.

An illustration: The "Stanford County Prison" experiment. Prisons can be violent settings, but is this due simply to the "bad" people who end up there? Or, as Philip Zimbardo suspected, does prison itself somehow create violent behavior?

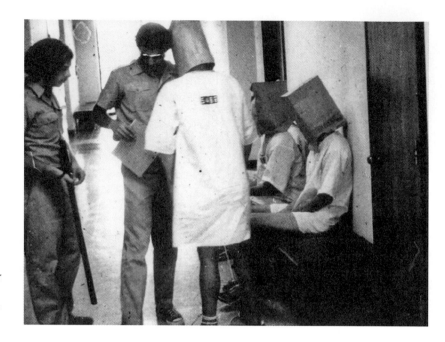

Philip Zimbardo's research helps to explain why violence is a common element in our society's prisons. At the same time, his work demonstrates the dangers that sociological investigation poses for subjects and the need for investigators to observe ethical standards that protect the welfare of people who participate in research.

To answer this question, Zimbardo devised a fascinating experiment, which he called the "Stanford County Prison" (Zimbardo, 1972; Haney, Banks, & Zimbardo, 1973).

Zimbardo thought that once inside a prison, even emotionally healthy people are prone to violence. Thus, Zimbardo treated the *prison setting* as the independent variable capable of causing *violence,* the dependent variable.

To test this hypothesis, Zimbardo's research team first constructed a realistic-looking "prison" in the basement of the psychology building on the campus of Stanford University. Then they placed an ad in a Palo Alto newspaper, offering to pay young men to help with a two-week research project. To each of the seventy who responded they administered a series of physical and psychological tests and then selected the healthiest twenty-four.

The next step was to assign randomly half the men to be "prisoners" and half to be "guards." The plan called for the guards and prisoners to spend the next two weeks in the mock prison. The prisoners began their part of the experiment soon afterward when the Palo Alto police "arrested" them at their homes. After searching and handcuffing the men, the police drove them to the local police station, where they were fingerprinted. Then police transported their captives to the Stanford prison, where the guards locked them up. Zimbardo started his video camera rolling and watched to see what would happen next.

The experiment turned into more than anyone had bargained for. Both guards and prisoners soon became embittered and hostile toward one another. Guards humiliated the

prisoners by giving them jobs such as cleaning out toilets with their bare hands. The prisoners, for their part, resisted and insulted the guards. Within four days, the researchers removed five prisoners who displayed "extreme emotional depression, crying, rage and acute anxiety" (Hanley, Banks, & Zimbardo, 1973:81). Before the end of the first week, the situation had become so bad that the researchers had to cancel the experiment.

The events that unfolded at the "Stanford County Prison" supported Zimbardo's hypothesis that prison violence is rooted in the social character of jails themselves, not in the personalities of guards and prisoners. This finding raises questions about our society's prisons, suggesting the need for basic reform. Zimbardo was not surprised by the recent scandal over the abuse of prisoners in Iraq (Schwartz, 2004).

But also note that Zimbardo's experiment reveals the potential of research to threaten the physical and mental well-being of subjects. Such dangers are not always as obvious as they were in this case. Therefore, researchers must consider carefully the potential harm to subjects at all stages of their work and end any study, as Zimbardo did, if subjects may suffer harm of any kind.

ASKING QUESTIONS: THE SURVEY

A **survey** is *a research method in which subjects respond to a series of statements or questions in a questionnaire or an interview.* The most widely used of all research methods, the survey is well suited to studying what cannot be observed directly, such as political attitudes or religious beliefs.

A survey targets some *population,* such as unmarried mothers or adults living in rural counties in Wisconsin. Sometimes every adult in the country is the survey population, as in polls taken during national political campaigns. Of course, contacting a vast number of people is all but impossible, so researchers usually study a *sample,* a much smaller number of subjects selected to represent the entire population. Surveys commonly give accurate estimates of national opinions based on samples of only 1,500 people.

Beyond selecting subjects, the survey must have a specific plan for asking questions and recording answers. The most common way to do this is to give subjects a *questionnaire* with a series of written statements or questions. Often the researcher lets subjects choose possible responses to each item, as in a multiple-choice examination. Sometimes, though, a researcher may want subjects to respond freely, to permit all opinions to be included. Of course, this free-form approach means that the researcher later has to make sense out of what can be a bewildering array of answers.

In an *interview,* a researcher personally asks subjects a series of questions, thereby solving one problem common to the questionnaire method: the failure of some subjects to return the questionnaire to the researcher. A further difference is that interviews give participants freedom to respond as they wish. Researchers often ask follow-up questions to clarify an answer or to probe a bit more deeply. In doing this, however, a researcher must avoid influencing the subject even in subtle ways, such as by raising an eyebrow as the subject offers an answer.

An illustration: Surveying the African American elite.
Do very successful African Americans escape the sting of racism? The sociologist Lois Benjamin—herself a successful college professor who had become the first black faculty member at the University of Tampa—thought the answer was no. To investigate the effects of racism on talented African American men and women, Benjamin set out to conduct survey research.

Benjamin chose to interview subjects rather than distribute a questionnaire because, first, she wanted to enter into a conversation with her subjects, to ask follow-up questions, and to pursue topics that she could not anticipate. A second reason Benjamin favored interviews over questionnaires is that racism is a sensitive topic. A supportive researcher can make it easier for subjects to answer painful questions.

As the first African American professor at the University of Tampa, Lois Benjamin knew that race can be a barrier to personal achievement in U.S. society. Interviewing 100 other African American women and men—all high achievers—she confirmed that they all had experienced the pain of racism in their own careers.

Because conducting interviews take a great deal of time, Benjamin had to limit the number of people in her study. She settled for 100 men and women. Even this small number kept Benjamin busy for more than two years of scheduling, traveling, and meeting with respondents. She spent two more years transcribing the tapes of her interviews, sorting out what the hours of talk told her about racism, and writing up her results.

Benjamin began by interviewing people she knew and asking them to suggest others. This strategy is called *snowball sampling* because the number of individuals included grows rapidly over time. Snowball sampling is appealing because it is an easy way to do research—we begin with familiar people, who provide introductions to their friends and colleagues. The drawback, however, is that snowball sampling rarely produces a sample that is representative of the larger population. Benjamin's sample probably contained many like-minded individuals, and it was certainly biased toward people willing to talk openly about race. She understood these problems and did try to make her sample as varied as she could in terms of sex, age, and region of the country. The Critical Thinking box on page 24 presents a statistical profile of Benjamin's respondents and some tips on how to read tables.

Benjamin based all her interviews on a series of questions and allowed her subjects to answer however they wished. As usually happens, the interviews took place in a wide range of settings. She met subjects in offices (hers or theirs), in hotel rooms, and in cars. In each case, Benjamin

CRITICAL THINKING
Reading Tables: An Important Skill

A table provides a lot of information in a small amount of space, so learning to read tables can increase your reading efficiency. When you spot a table, look first at the title to see what information it contains. The title tells you that the table presents a profile of the 100 subjects participating in Lois Benjamin's research. Across the top of the table, you will see eight variables that define these men and women. Reading down each column, note the categories within each variable; the percentages in each column add up to 100.

Starting at the top left, we see that Benjamin's sample was mostly men (63 percent, versus 37 percent women). In terms of age, most of the respondents (68 percent) were in the middle stage of life, and most grew up in a predominantly black community in the South or in the North or Central region of the United States.

These individuals are indeed a professional elite. Notice that half have earned either a doctorate (32 percent) or a medical or law degree (17 percent). Given their extensive education (and Benjamin's own position as a professor), we should not be surprised that the largest share (35 percent) work in academic institutions. In terms of income, these are wealthy individuals, with most (64 percent) earning more than $50,000 annually during the 1980s (a salary that only 20 percent of all U.S. workers make even today).

Finally, we see that these 100 individuals are generally left-of-center in their political views. In part, this reflects their extensive schooling (which encourages progressive thinking) and the tendency of academics to fall on the liberal side of the political spectrum.

WHAT DO YOU THINK?

1. Statistical data, such as those in this table, are an efficient way to convey lots of information. Can you explain why?
2. Looking at the table, can you determine how long it took most people to become part of this elite? Explain.
3. Do you see any ways in which this African American elite might differ from a comparable white elite? What are they?

The Talented 100: Lois Benjamin's African American Elite

Sex	Age	Childhood Racial Setting	Childhood Region	Highest Educational Degree	Job Sector	Income	Political Orientation
Male 63%	35 or younger 6%	Mostly black 71%	West 6%	Doctorate 32%	College or university 35%	More than $50,000 64%	Radical left 13%
Female 37%	36 to 54 68%	Mostly white 15%	North or Central 32%	Medical or law 17%	Private, profit 17%	$35,000 to $50,000 18%	Liberal 38%
	55 or older 26%	Racially mixed 14%	South 38%	Master's 27%	Private, nonprofit 9%	$20,000 to $34,999 12%	Moderate 28%
			Northeast 12%	Bachelor's 13%	Government 22%	Less than $20,000 6%	Conservative 5%
			Other 12%	Less 11%	Self-employed 14%		Depends on issue 14%
					Retired 3%		Unknown 2%
100%	100%	100%	100%	100%	100%	100%	100%

Source: Adapted from Lois Benjamin, *The Black Elite: Facing the Color Line in the Twilight of the Twentieth Century* (Chicago: Nelson-Hall, 1991), p. 276.

tape-recorded the conversation, which lasted from two-and-one-half to three hours, so that she would not be distracted by taking notes.

As research ethics demand, Benjamin offered full anonymity to participants. Even so, many—including notables such as Vernon E. Jordan Jr. (former president of the National Urban League) and Yvonne Walker-Taylor (first woman president of Wilberforce University)—were accustomed to being in the public eye and permitted Benjamin to use their names.

What surprised Benjamin most about her research was how eagerly many subjects responded to her request for an interview. These normally busy men and women appeared to go out of their way to contribute to her project. Furthermore, once the interviews were underway, many became very emotional. Benjamin reports that at some point in the conversation, about 40 of her 100 subjects cried. For them, apparently, the research provided an opportunity to release feelings and share experiences never revealed before. How did Benjamin respond to such sentiments? She reports that she laughed and cried along with her respondents.

Benjamin's research is less scientific and more interpretive sociology (she wanted to find out what race meant to her subjects) and critical sociology (she undertook the study partly to show that racial prejudice still exists). Indeed, many subjects reported fearing that race might someday undermine their success, and others spoke of a race-based "glass ceiling" preventing them from reaching the highest positions in our society. Summarizing her findings, Benjamin concluded that despite the improving social standing of African Americans, black people in the United States still suffer the effects of racial hostility.

IN THE FIELD: PARTICIPANT OBSERVATION

Participant observation is *a research method in which investigators systematically observe people while joining them in their routine activities.* This method lets researchers study social life in any natural setting, from a motorcycle club to a religious seminary. Cultural anthropologists use participant observation to study other societies, calling this method "fieldwork."

Researchers may begin with few specific hypotheses, unsure of what the important questions will turn out to be. Compared with experiments and surveys, participant observation has few hard-and-fast rules. Flexibility can be an advantage, however, because investigators often must adapt to unexpected circumstances in an unfamiliar environment.

Participant observers try to gain entry into a setting without disturbing the routine behavior of others. Their role is a dual one: To gain an insider's viewpoint, they must become participants in the setting, "hanging out" for months or even years, trying to act, think, and even feel the same way as the people they are observing; at the same time, they must remain observers, standing back from the action and applying the sociological perspective to social patterns that others take for granted.

Because the personal impressions of a researcher play such a central role, critics claim that participant observation lacks scientific rigor. Yet its personal approach is also a strength: Where a high-profile team of sociologists administering a formal survey might disrupt a setting, a sensitive participant-observer often can gain profound insight into people's behavior.

An illustration: Participant observation in "Cornerville." Did you ever wonder what life was like on the busy streets of an unfamiliar neighborhood? In the late 1930s, a young graduate student at Harvard University named William Foote Whyte (1914–2000) set out to study social life in a nearby, rather rundown section of Boston. His curiosity ultimately led him to carry out four years of participant observation in this neighborhood, which he called "Cornerville."

At the time, Cornerville was home to first- and second-generation Italian immigrants. Many were poor, and many people in other parts of Boston considered Cornerville a place to avoid: a slum inhabited by criminals. Unwilling to accept easy stereotypes, Whyte set out to discover for himself exactly what kind of life went on inside this community. His celebrated book, *Street Corner Society* (1981, orig. 1943), describes Cornerville as a community with its own code of values, complex social patterns, and particular social conflicts.

To start, Whyte considered a range of research methods. He could have taken questionnaires to one of Cornerville's community centers and asked local people to fill them out. Or he could have invited members of the community to come to his Harvard office for interviews. But it is easy to see that such formal strategies would have prompted little cooperation from the local people and yielded few insights. Whyte decided, therefore, to ease into Cornerville life and patiently build an understanding of this rather mysterious place.

Soon enough, Whyte discovered the challenges of even getting started in field research. After all, an upper-middle-class WASP graduate student from Harvard did not exactly fit into Cornerville life. He soon found out, for example, that even an outsider's friendly overture could seem pushy and rude. Early on, Whyte dropped in at a local bar, hoping to buy a woman a drink and encourage her to talk about Cornerville. But looking around the room, he could find no woman alone. Presently, he thought he might have an opportunity when a fellow sat down with two women. He gamely asked, "Pardon me. Would you mind if I joined you?" Instantly, he realized his mistake:

> There was a moment of silence while the man stared at me. Then he offered to throw me down the stairs. I assured him that this would not be necessary, and demonstrated as much by walking right out of there without any assistance. (1981:289)

As this incident suggests, gaining entry to a community is the vital—and sometimes hazardous—first step in field research. "Breaking in" requires patience, ingenuity, and a little luck. Whyte's big break came in the form of a young man named "Doc," whom he met in a local social service agency. Listening to Whyte's account of his bungled efforts to make friends in Cornerville, Doc was sympathetic and decided to take Whyte under his wing and introduce him to others in the community. With Doc's help, Whyte soon became a neighborhood regular.

Whyte's friendship with Doc illustrates the importance of a *key informant* in field research. Such people not only introduce a researcher to a community but often remain a source of information and help. But using a key informant also has its risks. Because any person has a particular circle of friends, a key informant's guidance is certain to "spin" the study in one way or another. Moreover, in the eyes of others, the reputation of the key informant—for better or worse—usually rubs off on the investigator. In sum, a key informant is helpful at the outset, but a participant-observer soon must seek a broad range of contacts.

Having entered the Cornerville world, Whyte began his work in earnest. But he soon realized that a field researcher needs to know when to speak up and when simply to look, listen, and learn. One evening, he joined a group discussing neighborhood gambling. Wanting to get the facts straight, Whyte asked innocently, "I suppose the cops were all paid off?"

> The gambler's jaw dropped. He glared at me. Then he denied vehemently that any policeman had been paid off and immediately switched the conversation to another subject. For the rest of that evening I felt very uncomfortable.

The next day, Doc offered some sound advice:

> "Go easy on that 'who,' 'what,' 'why,' 'when,' 'where' stuff, Bill. You ask those questions and people will clam up on you. If people accept you, you can just hang around, and you'll learn the answers in the long run without even having to ask the questions." (1981:303)

In the months and years that followed, Whyte became familiar with life in Cornerville and married a local woman with whom he would spend the rest of his life. In the

process, he learned that this neighborhood was hardly the stereotypical slum. On the contrary, most immigrants worked hard, many were quite successful, and some even boasted of sending children to college. In short, Whyte's book makes for fascinating reading about the deeds, dreams, and disappointments of people living in one ethnic community, and it contains a richness of detail that can only come from long-term participant observation.

Whyte's work shows that participant observation is a method based on tensions and contrasts. Its flexibility allows a researcher to respond to the unexpected but makes repeating the study difficult. Participation means getting close to people, but observation depends on keeping some distance. Because no special equipment or laboratory is needed, little expense is involved. But this method is costly in terms of time—most studies take a year or more, which probably explains why participant observation is used less often than the other methods described in this chapter. Yet the depth of understanding gained through interpretive research of this kind greatly enriches our knowledge of many types of human communities.

USING AVAILABLE DATA: EXISTING SOURCES

Not all research involves collecting new data. In many cases, sociologists save time and money by analyzing existing sources, data collected by others.

The most widely used data are gathered by government agencies such as the U.S. Census Bureau. Data about other nations in the world are found in various publications of the United Nations and the World Bank.

Drawing on available data is appealing to sociologists with little money, and the data are often better than what researchers could hope to get on their own. However, data

 For easy access to many data links, visit the author's Web site at http://www.TheSociologyPage.com

may not be available in the specific form a researcher may want, and it may be difficult to know how accurate the data are. In his nineteenth-century study of suicide, described earlier, Emile Durkheim used official records. But Durkheim knew that some recorded suicides probably were really accidents, just as some true suicides were never recorded as such.

An illustration of the use of existing sources: A tale of two cities. Why might one city's history include many more famous people than another's? To those of us living in the present, historical data offer a key to unlocking secrets of the past. The award-winning study *Puritan Boston and Quaker Philadelphia*, by E. Digby Baltzell (1979), illustrates the clever use of existing data.

The story begins with a chance visit to Bowdoin College in Maine. Entering the college library, Baltzell gazed on portraits of the celebrated author Nathaniel Hawthorne, the famous poet Henry Wadsworth Longfellow, and Franklin Pierce, the fourteenth U.S. president. He was startled to learn that all three of these great men were members of a single class at Bowdoin, graduating in 1825. How could it be, Baltzell wondered, that this small college had graduated more famous people in a single year than his own, much bigger University of Pennsylvania had graduated in its entire history? To answer this question, Baltzell was soon poring over historical documents to see if New England had indeed produced more famous people than his native Pennsylvania.

For data, Baltzell turned to the *Dictionary of American Biography*, twenty volumes profiling more than 13,000 outstanding men and women in fields such as politics, law, and the arts. The *Dictionary* told Baltzell *who* was great, but he also wanted some way to measure *how* great people were. He decided to base his ranking on the *Dictionary*'s statement that the more impressive the person's achievements, the longer the biography. So counting the number of lines in a biography yielded a reasonable measure of "greatness."

By the time Baltzell had identified the seventy-five individuals with the longest biographies, he saw a striking pattern. Massachusetts had the most by far, with twenty-one of the seventy-five top achievers. The New England states, combined, claimed thirty-one of the entries. By contrast, Pennsylvania could boast of only two, and all the states in the Middle Atlantic region had just twelve. Looking more closely, Baltzell discovered that most of New England's great achievers had grown up in and around the city of Boston. Again, in stark contrast, almost no one of comparable standing came from his own Philadelphia, a city with many more people than Boston.

What could explain this remarkable pattern? Baltzell drew inspiration from the German sociologist Max Weber (1958, orig. 1904–5), who linked achievement to religious beliefs (see Chapter 13, "Family and Religion"). In the religious differences that set Boston apart from Philadelphia, Baltzell found the answer to his puzzle. Boston was a Puritan settlement, founded by people who were determined in their pursuit of excellence and public achievement. Philadelphia, by contrast, was settled by Quakers, who were equally determined to avoid public notice.

Both the Puritans and the Quakers were fleeing religious persecution in England, but the two religious traditions produced quite different cultural patterns. Convinced of humanity's innate sinfulness, Boston Puritans built a rigid society in which family, church, and school regulated people's behavior. They celebrated hard work as a means of glorifying God and viewed public success as a reassuring

The U.S. Census Bureau collects a vast amount of information about the population of this country. Data are available in Census Bureau publications found in your local library or on the Internet at http://www.census.gov

sign of God's blessing. In other words, Puritanism fostered a disciplined life in which people both sought and respected achievement.

Philadelphia's Quakers, by contrast, built their way of life on the belief that all human beings are basically good. They saw little need for strong social institutions to "save" people from sinfulness. They believed in equality, so that even those who became rich considered themselves no better than anyone else. Thus, rich and poor alike lived modestly and discouraged one other from standing out by seeking fame or even public office.

In Baltzell's sociological imagination, Boston and Philadelphia took the form of two social "test tubes": Puritanism was poured into one, Quakerism into the other. Centuries later, we can see that different "chemical reactions" occurred in each case. The two belief systems apparently led to different attitudes toward personal achievement, which in turn shaped the history of each region. Moreover, we can see the results of these cultural differences even today. Boston's Kennedys (despite being Catholic) are but one of that city's families that exemplify the Puritan pursuit of recognition and leadership, but there has *never* been a family with such public stature in the entire history of Philadelphia.

Baltzell's study uses scientific logic, but it also illustrates the interpretive approach by showing how people understood their world. His research reminds us that sociological investigation often involves mixing methodological orientations and a lively sociological imagination.

Four Research Methods

	Experiment	Survey	Participant Observation	Existing Sources
Application	For explanatory research that specifies relationships between variables Generates quantitative data	For gathering information about issues that cannot be directly observed, such as attitudes and values Useful for descriptive and explanatory research Generates quantitative or qualitative data	For exploratory and descriptive study of people in a "natural" setting Generates qualitative data	For exploratory, descriptive, or explanatory research whenever suitable data are available
Advantages	Provides the greatest opportunity to specify cause-and-effect relationships Replication of research is relatively easy	Sampling, using questionnaires, allows surveys of large populations Interviews provide in-depth responses	Allows study of "natural" behavior Usually inexpensive	Saves time and expense of data collection Makes historical research possible
Limitations	Laboratory settings have an artificial quality Unless the research environment is carefully controlled, results may be biased	Questionnaires must be carefully prepared and may yield a low return rate Interviews are expensive and time-consuming	Time-consuming Replication of research is difficult Researcher must balance roles of participant and observer	Researcher has no control over possible biases in data Data may only partially fit current research needs

Characteristics of the four major methods of sociological investigation we have introduced are found in the Summing Up table.

Putting It All Together: Ten Steps in Sociological Research

The following ten questions will guide you through a research project in sociology:

1. **What is your topic?** Being curious and using the sociological perspective can generate ideas for social research at any time and in any place. Pick a topic you find important to study.

2. **What have others already learned?** You are probably not the first person with an interest in some issue. Visit the library to see what theories and methods other researchers have applied to your topic. In reviewing the existing research, note problems that have come up.

3. **What, exactly, are your questions?** Are you seeking to explore an unfamiliar setting? To describe some

category of people? Or to investigate cause and effect between variables? Clearly state the goals of your research and operationalize all variables.

4. **What will you need to carry out research?** How much time and money are available to you? What special equipment or skills does the research require? Can you do all the work yourself?

5. **Are there ethical concerns?** Can the research harm anyone? How can you minimize the chances for injury? Will you promise your subjects anonymity? If so, how will you ensure that anonymity will be maintained?

6. **What method will you use?** Consider all major research strategies and combinations of approaches. The best method depends on the kinds of questions you are asking and the resources available to you.

7. **How will you record the data?** The research method you use guides your data collection. Be sure to record information accurately and in a way that will make sense later on (it may be months before you write up the results of your work). Watch out for any bias that may creep into your work.

CONTROVERSY & DEBATE

Is Sociology Nothing More than Stereotypes?

"Protestants are the ones who kill themselves!"

"People in the United States? They're rich, they love to marry, and they love to divorce!"

"Everybody knows that you have to be black to play professional basketball!"

Everyone—including sociologists—makes generalizations. But many beginning students of sociology may wonder how sociological generalizations differ from simple stereotypes.

Each of the preceding three statements is an example of a **stereotype,** *an exaggerated description applied to every person in some category.* First, rather than describing averages, each statement describes every person in some category in exactly the same way; second, each ignores facts and distorts reality (even though many stereotypes do contain an element of truth); third, each sounds more like a put-down than a fair-minded observation.

Good sociology involves generalizations with three conditions: First, sociologists do not carelessly apply any generalization to all individuals. Second, sociologists make sure that a generalization squares with available facts. Third, sociologists offer generalizations fair-mindedly, with an interest in getting at the truth.

Earlier in this chapter, we noted that the suicide rate among Protestants is higher than the rate among Catholics or Jews. However, the statement "Protestants are the ones who kill themselves" is not a reasonable generalization because most Protestants do no such thing. Furthermore, it would be wrong to assume that a particular friend, because he is a Protestant male, is on the verge of self-destruction. (Imagine refusing to lend some money to him, explaining, "Well, given your risk of suicide, I might never get paid back!")

Second, sociologists adapt their generalizations to available facts. A more factual version of the second statement is that by world standards, the U.S. population, on average, has a very high standard of living. It is also true that our marriage rate is one of the highest in the world, and although few people take pleasure in divorcing, so is our divorce rate.

Third, sociologists try to be fair-minded, and they have a passion for truth. The last of the box-opening statements, about African Americans and professional basketball, is not good sociology for two reasons. First, it is simply not true, and second, it seems motivated by bias rather than truth-seeking.

Good sociology, then, stands apart from harmful stereotyping. But a sociology course is an excellent setting for talking about common stereotypes. The classroom encourages discussion and offers the factual information you need to determine whether a particular belief is a valid sociological generalization or just a stereotype.

CONTINUE THE DEBATE . . .

1. Do people in the United States have stereotypes of sociologists? What are they? Are they valid? How would you know?
2. Do you think taking a sociology course challenges people's stereotypes? Why or why not?
3. Can you think of other stereotypes that sociology challenges?

8. **What do the data tell you?** Determine what the data say about your initial questions. If your study involves a specific hypothesis, you should be able to confirm, reject, or modify it based on your findings. Keep in mind that there will be several ways to interpret your results, depending on the theoretical approach you apply, and you should consider them all.

9. **What are your conclusions?** Prepare a final report indicating what you have learned. Also, evaluate your own work. What problems arose during the research process? What questions were left unanswered?

10. **How can you share what you have learned?** Consider making a presentation to a class or maybe even to a meeting of professional sociologists. The important point is to share what you have learned with others and to let them respond to your work.

To review many of the issues raised in this chapter, the final Controversy & Debate box examines how sociological generalizations differ from common stereotypes.

Summary

1. The sociological perspective shows that the general operation of society affects the experiences of particular people. In this way, sociology helps us better understand barriers and opportunities in our lives.

2. Early social thinkers focused on what society *ought to be*. Sociology, named by Auguste Comte in 1838, uses scientific methods to understand society *as it is*.

3. The development of sociology was triggered by rapid change in Europe in the eighteenth and nineteenth centuries. The rise of an industrial economy, the explosive growth of cities, and the emergence of new political ideas combined to weaken tradition and make people more aware of their social world.

4. Theory is the process of linking facts to create meaning. Sociologists use theoretical approaches to guide theory building.

5. The structural-functional approach is a framework for exploring how social structures work together to promote the overall operation of society.

6. The social-conflict approach highlights dimensions of social inequality that generate conflict and promote change.

7. In contrast to these macro-level orientations, the symbolic-interaction approach is a micro-level framework for studying how people, in everyday interaction, construct reality.

8. Scientific sociology uses the logic of science, based on empirical evidence we confirm with our senses.

9. Measurement is the process of giving a value to a variable in a specific case. Sound measurement is both reliable and valid.

10. Scientific research seeks to determine how variables are related. Ideally, researchers try to identify how one (independent) variable causes change in another (dependent) variable.

11. Although researchers select topics according to their personal interests, the scientific ideal of objectivity demands that they try to suspend personal values and biases as they conduct research.

12. Interpretive sociology is a methodological orientation that focuses on the meanings that people attach to behavior. Reality is not "out there" (as scientific sociology claims) but is constructed by people in their everyday interaction.

13. Critical sociology is a methodological orientation that uses research to bring about social change. It rejects the scientific principle of objectivity, claiming that all research has a political character.

14. Because their work can harm subjects, professional sociologists must observe ethical guidelines when doing research.

15. Scientific research is most clearly expressed in the experiment, which investigates cause-and-effect relationships between two (or more) variables under controlled laboratory conditions.

16. A survey uses either a questionnaire or an interview to gather subjects' responses to a series of questions.

17. Participant observation involves joining with people in a social setting for an extended period of time.

18. Often sociologists use existing sources rather than collect their own data; doing so is common among researchers with limited research budgets.

19. Sociologists make generalizations about categories of people. Unlike stereotypes, these sociological statements (1) are not applied indiscriminately to all individuals, (2) are supported by research-based facts, and (3) are put forward in the fair-minded pursuit of truth.

Key Concepts

sociology (p. 2) the systematic study of human society

global perspective (p. 6) the study of the larger world and our society's place in it

high-income countries (p. 6) the richest nations with the highest overall standards of living

middle-income countries (p. 6) nations with a standard of living about average for the world as a whole

low-income countries (p. 8) nations with a low standard of living in which most people are poor

positivism (p. 10) a way of understanding based on science

theory (p. 11) a statement of how and why specific facts are related

theoretical approach (p. 11) a basic image of society that guides thinking and research

structural-functional approach (p. 11) a framework for building theory that sees society as a complex system whose parts work together to promote solidarity and stability

social structure (p. 11) any relatively stable pattern of social behavior

social functions (p. 12) the consequences of any social pattern for the operation of society as a whole

manifest functions (p. 12) the recognized and intended consequences of any social pattern

latent functions (p. 12) the unrecognized and unintended consequences of any social pattern

social dysfunction (p. 12) any social pattern that may disrupt the operation of society

social-conflict approach (p. 12) a framework for building theory that sees society as an arena of inequality that generates conflict and change

macro-level orientation (p. 13) a broad focus on social structures that shape society as a whole

micro-level orientation (p. 13) a close-up focus on social interaction in specific situations

symbolic-interaction approach (p. 14) a framework for building theory that sees society as the product of the everyday interactions of individuals

science (p. 15) a logical system that bases knowledge on direct, systematic observation

concept (p. 15) a mental construct that represents some part of the world in a simplified form

variable (p. 15) a concept whose value changes from case to case

measurement (p. 15) a procedure for determining the value of a variable in a specific case

reliability (p. 15) consistency in measurement

validity (p. 15) actually measuring exactly what you intend to measure

correlation (p. 15) a relationship in which two (or more) variables change together

cause and effect (p. 16) a relationship in which change in one variable (the independent variable) causes change in another (the dependent variable)

interpretive sociology (p. 18) the study of society that focuses on the meanings people attach to their social world

critical sociology (p. 19) the study of society that focuses on the need for social change

gender (p. 20) the personal traits and social positions that members of a society attach to being female or male

research method (p. 20) a systematic plan for doing research

experiment (p. 20) a research method for investigating cause and effect under highly controlled conditions

survey (p. 22) a research method in which subjects respond to a series of statements or questions in a questionnaire or an interview

participant observation (p. 25) a research method in which investigators systematically observe people while joining them in their routine activities

stereotype (p. 29) an exaggerated description applied to every person in some category

CRITICAL-THINKING QUESTIONS

1. In what ways does using the sociological perspective make us seem less in control of our lives? In what ways does it give us greater power over our surroundings?

2. "Sociology would not have arisen if human behavior resulted only from biological instincts (like, say, the highly predictable behavior of ants), nor would sociology exist if human behavior were totally random. Sociology thrives because humans are partly guided by social structure and partly free." Do you agree or disagree with this argument? Why?

3. What factors explain why sociology developed where and when it did?

4. Guided by sociology's three major theoretical approaches, what types of questions might a sociologist ask about (a) television, (b) war, (c) humor, and (d) colleges and universities?

APPLICATIONS AND EXERCISES

1. Packaged in the back of this new textbook is an interactive CD-ROM that offers a variety of video and interactive review materials intended to help you better understand the material covered in this chapter. For this chapter, the CD-ROM contains a relevant clip from *ABC News,* an author's tip video, interactive map animations, an interactive timeline, and flashcards with audio pronunciations of the more difficult words.

2. Spend several hours exploring your local area on foot, by bicycle, or by car so that you can draw a sociological map of the community. This map might show the categories of people and types of buildings found in various places ("big, single-family homes," "run-down business district," "new office buildings," "student apartments," and so on). What patterns do you see?

3. Look ahead to Figure 13–3 on page 357, which shows the U.S. divorce rate over the past century. What societal factors pushed the divorce rate down after 1930, up after 1940, down in 1950, up after 1960, and down again after 1980?

4. During a class, carefully observe the behavior of the instructor and other students. What patterns do you see in how people use space? Regarding who speaks? What categories of people are taking the class in the first place?

5. Say you were going to observe your sociology teacher to grade that individual's teaching skills. How would you operationalize the concept "good teaching"? What, exactly, would you look for? Do you think students are the best judges of good and bad teaching? Why or why not?

6. Conduct a practice interview with a roommate or friend on the topic "What is the value of a college education?" Before the actual interview, prepare a list of specific questions or issues you think are important. Afterward, give some thought to why conducting a good interview is much harder than it initially may seem.

SITES TO SEE

http://www.prenhall.com/macionis

The author and publisher of this book invite you to visit the interactive Companion Website™ that accompanies this text. Begin by clicking on the cover of your book. You will find a chapter-by-chapter study guide, practice tests, suggested Web links, and links to other relevant material.

http://www.TheSociologyPage.com (or **http://www.macionis.com**)

The author maintains this Web site (use either address), where you will find information about sociology, short videos, biographies of important sociologists, and a Links Library that will connect you to dozens of other interesting sites.

http://www.asanet.org/members/ecointro.html

Read the Professional Code of Ethics at the Web site of the American Sociological Association.

http://quickfacts.census.gov/qfd/
http://www.countrywatch.com

The first of these sites provides statistical data and other information about the United States, your own state, and your own county. The second offers a range of data about all 192 nations in the world.

http://plasma.nationalgeographic.com/mapmachine/
http://www.nationalatlas.gov

These two sites provide a number of maps showing patterns and trends of interest to sociologists.

http://www.bus.ucf.edu/sport/public/downloads/media/ides/release_05.pdf

Are you interested in learning more about race and gender in sports? Read the 2003 Racial and Gender Report Card for U.S. professional sports, prepared at the University of Central Florida.

 ## INVESTIGATE WITH RESEARCH NAVIGATOR™

To access the full resources of Research Navigator™, please find the access code printed on the inside cover of the *OneSearch with Research Navigator™: Sociology* guide. You may have received this booklet if your instructor recommended this guide be packaged with new textbooks. (If your book did not come with this printed guide, you can purchase one through your college bookstore.) Visit our Research Navigator™ site at **http://www.researchnavigator.com**

Once at this site, click on "Register" under "New Users" and enter your access code to create a personal Login Name and Password. (When revisiting the site, use the same Login Name and Password to enter.) Browse the features of the Research Navigator™ Web site and search the databases of academic journals, newspapers, magazines, and Web links using keywords such as "sociology," "suicide," and "sports."

Introducing . . . In the Times

The articles featured at the end of selected chapters throughout this text originally appeared in the pages of one of the world's leading newspapers: *The New York Times*.

Founded in 1851, *The New York Times* is commonly accepted as the paper-of-record in the United States. It is the leader among news organizations in winning the Pulitzer Prize, journalism's top award.

We chose these particular articles because they look at current events through a sociological lens and because they raise deeper issues related to topics covered in this text. Please keep in mind that these articles were originally published in a daily newspaper and, as such, each one is a snapshot of an issue at a particular point in time; however, great care was taken to ensure that the selections are of lasting interest.

These *New York Times* articles illustrate how sociology is a part of our everyday lives. Watching your favorite television show, reading the daily newspaper, or surfing the Internet can all be exercises in using your sociological imagination. Enjoy reading all twelve *In the Times* features and use the questions at the end of each article to analyze the issues with a sociological eye!

March 30, 2003

Military Mirrors Working-Class America

By DAVID M. HALBFINGER
and STEVEN A. HOLMES

They left small towns and inner cities, looking for a way out and up, or fled the anonymity of the suburbs, hoping to find themselves. They joined the all-volunteer military, gaining a free education or a marketable skill or just the discipline they knew they would need to get through life.

As the United States engages in its first major land war in a decade, the soldiers, sailors, pilots and others who are risking, and now giving, their lives in Iraq represent a slice of a broad swath of American society but by no means all of it.

Of the 28 servicemen killed who have been identified so far, 20 were white, 5 black, and 3 Hispanic—proportions that neatly mirror those of the military as a whole. But just one was from a well-to-do family, and with the exception of a Naval Academy alumnus, just one had graduated from an elite college.*

A survey of the American military's . . . demographics paints a picture of a fighting force that is anything but a cross section of America. With minorities overrepresented and the wealthy and the underclass essentially absent, with political conservatism ascendant in the officer corps and Northeasterners fading from the ranks, America's 1.4 million-strong military seems to resemble the makeup of a two-year commuter or trade school outside Birmingham or Biloxi far more than that of a ghetto or barrio or four-year university in Boston.

*[As of September 4, 2004, of the 979 service men and women killed who have been identified, 678 were white (69.3 percent), 125 were black (12.8 percent), and 122 Hispanic (12.4 percent)—proportions that mirror those of the country as a whole. But just a handful were from elite families or graduated from elite colleges (cnn.com).]

Today's servicemen and women may not be Ivy Leaguers, but in fact they are better educated than the population at large: Reading scores are a full grade higher for enlisted personnel than for their civilian counterparts of the same age. While whites account for three of five soldiers, the military has become a powerful magnet for blacks, and black women in particular, who now outnumber white women in the Army. . . .

Sgt. Annette Acevedo, 22, a radio operator from Atlanta, could have gone to college but chose the Army because of all the benefits it offered: travel, health coverage, work experience and independence from her parents. The Army seemed a better opportunity to get started with her life and be a more independent person, she said. . . .

Though Hispanics are underrepresented in the military, their numbers are growing rapidly. Even as the total number of military personnel dropped 23 percent over the last decade, the number of Hispanics in uniform grew to 118,000 from 90,600, a jump of about 30 percent.

While blacks tend to be more heavily represented in administrative and support functions, a new study shows that Hispanics, like whites, are much more likely to serve in combat operations. But those Hispanics in combat jobs tend to be infantry grunts, particularly in the Marine Corps, rather than fighter or bomber pilots. . . .

Confronted by images of the hardships of overseas deployment and by the stark reality of casualties in Iraq, some have raised questions about the composition of the fighting force and about requiring what is, in essence, a working-class military to fight and die for an affluent America.

"It's just not fair that the people that we ask to fight our wars are people who join the military because of economic conditions, because they have fewer options," said Representative Charles B. Rangel, a Democrat from Manhattan and a Korean War veteran who is calling for restoring the draft.

Some scholars have noted that since the draft was abolished in 1973, the country has begun developing what could be called a warrior class or caste, often perpetuating itself from father or uncle to son or niece, whose political and cultural attitudes do not reflect the diversity found in civilian society, potentially foreshadowing a social schism between those who fight and those who ask them to.

It is an issue that today's soldiers grapple with increasingly as they watch their comrades, even their spouses, deploy to the combat zone. "As it stands right now, the country is riding on the soldiers who volunteer," said Sgt. Barry Perkins, 39, a career military policeman at Fort Benning, Ga. "Everybody else is taking a free ride."

WHAT DO YOU THINK?

1. What are some of the reasons people may give for joining the military? How are these reasons different from the reasons sociologists would give for why people join the military?

2. In the article, Charles Rangel states that it is not fair to have people fighting our wars who joined the military because they had fewer options than other people. Do you agree with his position? Why or why not?

Adapted from the original article by David M. Halbfinger and Steven A. Holmes published in *The New York Times* on March 30, 2003. Copyright © 2003 by The New York Times Company. Reprinted with permission.

CHAPTER TWO

Culture

What is culture?

How does technology affect people's ways of life?

Why is it so important to understand
people's cultural differences?

Music and dress are among the many cultural elements ▶ that define a way of life. Accordion players at a street festival strike up tunes familiar to people in the Dordogne region of France.

Back in 1990, a group of executives of Charles Schwab & Co., a large investment brokerage corporation, gathered in a conference room at the company's headquarters in San Francisco to discuss strategies to expand the company's business. One conclusion was that the company would profit by giving greater attention to the increasing racial and ethnic diversity of the United States. In particular, the company's officers noted, Census Bureau data showed the number of Asian Americans was rising very rapidly, not only in San Francisco but throughout the country. The data also showed (then as now) that Asian Americans are not only much more numerous, they are also, on average, wealthy, with more than one-third of households earning more than $75,000 a year (in today's dollars).

As a result of this meeting, Schwab launched a diversity initiative, assigning three executives to work exclusively on building awareness of the company among Asian Americans. In the years since then, the scope of the initiative has grown rapidly: Today, Schwab employs more than 300 people who are fluent in Chinese, Japanese, Korean, Vietnamese, or another Asian language. This is important because research shows that most Asian Americans who come to the United States prefer to communicate in their first language. In addition, the company has launched Web sites using Chinese and other Asian languages. Finally, the company has opened branch offices in many predominantly Asian American neighborhoods in cities on the East and West Coasts.

What has been the result of this diversity initiative? Schwab claims a substantial increase in its share of business with Asian Americans. Because estimates place the annual buying power of Asian Americans at more than $300 billion, any company would do well  to follow Schwab's lead. Indeed, businesses can gain an advantage by learning to attract the interest of not only Asian Americans but also African Americans (who spend more than $600 billion each year), Hispanics ($580 billion), and other segments of the U.S. population (Fattah, 2002; Karrfalt, 2003).

The United States is the most *multicultural* of all the world's nations, reflecting its long history of welcoming immigrants from around the world. Worldwide, cultural differences are truly astounding, involving not only musical tastes and preferred foods but also family patterns and beliefs about right and wrong. Some of the world's people have many children, while other have few; some honor the elderly, while others are obsessed with youth. Some societies are peaceful, others warlike; and segments of humanity embrace a thousand different religious beliefs as well as particular ideas about what is polite and rude, beautiful and ugly, pleasant and repulsive. This amazing human capacity for so many different ways of life is a matter of human culture.

What Is Culture?

Culture is *the values, beliefs, behavior, and material objects that together form a people's way of life.* When studying culture, sociologists often distinguish between thoughts and things. *Nonmaterial culture* includes symbolic human creations ranging from art to Zen; *material culture* refers to physical creations of a society, everything from armaments to zippers. The terms "culture" and "society" obviously go hand in hand, but their precise meanings differ. Culture is a shared way of life or social heritage; **society** refers to *people who interact in a defined territory and share a culture.* Neither society nor culture could exist without the other.

Human beings around the globe create diverse ways of life. Such differences begin with outward appearance: Contrast the women shown here from Brazil, Kenya, New Guinea, and South Yemen, and the men from Taiwan (Republic of China), India, Canada, and New Guinea. Less obvious, but of even greater importance, are internal differences, since culture also shapes our goals in life, our sense of justice, and even our innermost personal feelings.

Culture not only shapes what we do but also what we think and how we feel—elements of what we commonly but inaccurately describe as "human nature." The warlike Yąnomamö of the Brazilian rain forest think aggressiveness is natural, but halfway around the world, the Semai of Malaysia live in peace and cooperation with one another. The cultures of the United States and Japan both stress achievement and hard work, but members of our society value individualism, whereas the Japanese value collective harmony.

Behavior that people in one society consider routine can be chilling to members of another culture. In the Russian city of St. Petersburg, this young mother and her six-week-old son brave the 17°F temperatures for a dip in a nearby lake. To Russians, this is something of a national pastime. To some members of our society, however, this practice may seem cruel or even dangerous.

Given the cultural differences in the world and people's tendency to view their own way of life as "natural," it is no wonder that travelers may suffer **culture shock,** *personal disorientation when experiencing an unfamiliar way of life.* People can experience culture shock right here in the United States, when, say, African Americans explore an Iranian neighborhood in Los Angeles, college students venture into the Amish countryside in Ohio, or New Yorkers travel through small towns in the Deep South. But culture shock is most intense when we travel abroad: The Global Sociology box tells the story of a U.S. researcher making his first visit to the home of the Yąnomamö people living in the Amazon region of South America.

December 1, Istanbul, Turkey. Harbors everywhere, it seems, have two things in common: ships and cats. Istanbul, the tenth port on our voyage, is awash with felines, prowling about in search of an easy meal. People certainly change from place to place—but not cats.

No way of life is "natural" to humanity, even though most people around the world view their own behavior that way.

What is natural to human beings is the capacity to create culture. Every other form of life, from ants to zebras, behaves in fixed, species-specific ways. To a world traveler, the enormous diversity of human life stands out in contrast to the behavior of, say, cats, which is pretty much the same everywhere. This uniformity follows from the fact that most living creatures are guided by *instincts,* biological programming over which animals have no control. A few animals, notably chimpanzees and related primates, have a limited capacity for culture, and researchers have observed them using tools and teaching simple skills to their offspring. But the creative power of humans far exceeds that of any other form of life. In short, *only humans rely on culture rather than instinct to ensure their survival* (Harris, 1987). To understand how human culture came to be, we need to look back at the history of our species.

CULTURE AND HUMAN INTELLIGENCE

In a universe 15 billion years old, our planet is a much younger 4.5 billion years of age (see the timeline inside the front cover of this text). Life appeared about 1 billion years later. Fast-forward another 2 to 3 billion years, and we find dinosaurs ruling the Earth. It was when these giant creatures disappeared, some 65 million years ago, that our history took a crucial turn with the appearance of the animals we call primates.

What sets primates apart is their intelligence: They have the largest brains relative to body size of all living creatures. About 12 million years ago, primates began to develop along two different lines, setting apart humans from the great apes, our closest relatives. But our common ancestry is evident in traits that humans share with chimpanzees, gorillas, and orangutans: great sociability, affectionate and long-lasting bonds that form the basis for child rearing and mutual protection, and the abilities to walk upright (normal in humans but less common among other primates) and to precisely manipulate objects with our hands.

Fossil records show that some 3 million years ago, our distant human ancestors learned cultural basics, such as the use of fire, tools, and weapons, and were able to build simple shelters and fashion basic clothing. These Stone Age achievements may seem modest, but they mark the point at which our ancestors embarked on a distinct evolutionary course, making culture their primary strategy for survival.

Culture, then, is a relatively recent development that was a long time in the making. As culture became a strategy for survival, our ancestors descended from the trees into the tall grasses of Central Africa. There they learned the advantages of hunting in groups. As mental capacity expanded, some 250,000 years ago our species emerged as *Homo sapiens,* Latin for "thinking person." Humans became the only

Confronting the Yąnomamö: The Experience of Culture Shock

A small aluminum motorboat chugged steadily along the muddy Orinoco River, deep within South America's vast tropical rain forest. Anthropologist Napoleon Chagnon was nearing the end of a three-day journey to the home territory of the Yąnomamö, one of the most technologically simple societies on Earth.

Some 12,000 Yąnomamö live in villages scattered along the border of Venezuela and Brazil. Their way of life could hardly be more different from our own. The Yąnomamö wear little clothing and live without electricity, cars, or other conveniences most people in the United States take for granted. They use bows and arrows for hunting and warfare, as they have for centuries. Many of the Yąnomamö have had little contact with the outside world, so Chagnon would be as strange to them as they would be to him.

By 2:00 in the afternoon, Chagnon had almost reached his destination. The hot sun and humid air were becoming unbearable. Chagnon's clothes were soaked with sweat, and his face and hands were swollen from the bites of gnats swarming around him. But he scarcely noticed, so focused was he on the fact that in just a few moments he would be face to face with people unlike any he had ever known.

Chagnon's heart pounded as the boat slid onto the riverbank. He and his guide climbed from the boat and walked toward the Yąnomamö village, stooping as they pushed their way through the dense undergrowth. Chagnon describes what happened next:

> I looked up and gasped when I saw a dozen burly, naked, sweaty, hideous men staring at us down the shafts of their drawn arrows! Immense wads of green tobacco were stuck between their lower teeth and lips, making them look even more hideous, and strands of dark green slime dripped or hung from their nostrils—strands so long that they clung to their [chests] or drizzled down their chins.
>
> My next discovery was that there were a dozen or so vicious, underfed dogs snapping at my legs, circling me as if I were to be their next meal. I just stood there holding my notebook, helpless and pathetic. Then the stench of the decaying vegetation and filth hit me and I almost got sick. I was horrified. What kind of welcome was this for the person who came here to live with you and learn your way of life, to become friends with you? (1992:11–12)

Fortunately for Chagnon, the Yąnomamö villagers recognized his guide and lowered their weapons. Reassured that he would survive the afternoon, Chagnon still was shaken by his inability to make any sense of these people. And this was to be his home for a year and a half! He wondered why he had given up physics to study human culture in the first place.

WHAT DO YOU THINK?

1. As they came to know Chagnon, might the Yąnomamö, too, have experienced culture shock? Why?
2. Can you think of an experience you had that is similar to the one described here?
3. Can studying sociology help reduce the experience of culture shock? How?

Source: Chagnon (1992).

species that names itself, and the biological forces we call instincts gave way to a more efficient survival scheme: *Human beings developed the mental power to fashion the natural environment for themselves.* Ever since, humans have made and remade their world in countless ways, which explains today's fascinating cultural diversity.

The Components of Culture

Although cultures vary greatly, they all have common components, including symbols, language, values, and norms. We shall begin with the component that is the basis for all the others: symbols.

People throughout the world communicate not just with spoken words but also with bodily gestures. Because gestures vary from culture to culture, they can occasionally be the cause for misunderstandings. For instance, the commonplace "thumbs up" gesture we use to express "Good job!" can get a person from the United States into trouble in Australia, where people take it to mean "Up yours!"

SYMBOLS

Like all other creatures, human beings sense the surrounding world, but unlike others, we also create a reality of *meaning*. Humans transform the elements of the world into **symbols,** *anything that carries a particular meaning recognized by people who share a culture.* A word, a whistle, a wall of graffiti, a flashing red light, a raised fist—all serve as symbols. We see the human capacity to create and manipulate symbols reflected in the variety of meanings associated with the simple act of winking the eye, which can convey interest, understanding, or insult.

We are so dependent on our culture's symbols that we often take them for granted. We become keenly aware of the importance of a symbol, however, when it is used in an unconventional way, as when someone burns a U.S. flag during a political demonstration. Entering an unfamiliar culture also reminds us of the power of symbols; culture shock is really the inability to "read" meaning in new surroundings. Not understanding the symbols of a culture leaves a person feeling lost and isolated, unsure of how to act, and sometimes frightened.

Culture shock is a two-way process. On one hand, the traveler *experiences* culture shock when meeting people whose way of life is different. For example, North Americans who

consider dogs beloved household pets might be put off by the Masai of eastern Africa, who pay no attention to dogs and never feed them. The same travelers might be horrified to find that in parts of Indonesia and in the northern regions of the People's Republic of China, people *roast* dogs for dinner.

On the other hand, a traveler can *inflict* culture shock on others by acting in ways that offend them. The North American who asks for a cheeseburger in an Indian restaurant offends Hindus, who consider cows sacred and never to be eaten. Indeed, global travel provides endless opportunities for misunderstanding. When in an unfamiliar setting, we need to remember that even behavior that seems innocent and normal to us can offend others, as the photo caption explains.

Symbolic meanings can also vary within a single society. In the recent debate about flying the Confederate flag over the South Carolina state house, some saw the flag as a symbol of regional pride, while others saw it as a symbol of racial oppression.

Finally, societies create new symbols all the time. The Applying Sociology box offers a case in point, describing some of the cyber-symbols that have developed along with our increasing use of computers for communication.

LANGUAGE

The heart of a symbolic system is **language,** *a system of symbols that allows people to communicate with one another.* Humans have created many alphabets to express the hundreds of languages we speak. Several examples are shown in Figure 2–1. Even rules for writing differ: Most people in Western societies write from left to right, people in

Arabic	**Read** English	독서 Korean
Armenian	διαβαζω Greek	Persian
Cambodian	Hebrew	читать Russian
閱讀 Chinese	पढ़ना Hindi	Ven a leer! Spanish

FIGURE 2–1   Human Languages: A Variety of Symbols

Here is a single word written in twelve of the hundreds of languages humans use to communicate with each other.

APPLYING SOCIOLOGY

The New Cyber-Symbols

It all started with the "smiley" figure that means a person is happy or telling a joke. Now a new language of symbols is emerging as creative people use computer keystrokes to create *emoticons,* symbols that convey thoughts and emotions. Here is a sampling of the new cyber-language. (Rotate this page 90° to the right to appreciate the emoticon faces.)

: -)	I'm smiling at you.
:'-)	I'm so happy (laughing so hard) that I'm starting to cry.
:-O	Wow!
:-x	My lips are sealed!
:-ll	I'm angry with you!
:-P	I'm sticking my tongue out at you!
:-(	I feel sad.
:-l	Things look grim.
%-}	I think I've had too much to drink.

-:(	Somebody cut my hair into a mohawk!
+O:-)	I've just been elected pope!
@}———>———	Here's a rose for you!

Computers are as popular in Japan as they are in the United States. The Japanese have their own emoticons:

(^_^)	I'm smiling at you.
(*^o^*)	This is exciting!
(^o^)	I am happy.
\(^o^)/	Banzai! This is wonderful!

How far will this new keyboard language go? If you're creative enough, anything is possible. Here's a routine that has been making the rounds on the Internet. It's called "Mr. Asciihead learns the Macarena"! To see Mr. Asciihead in action, go to the link at http://www.TheSociologyPage.com

```
o         o         o         o
.l.       \l.       \l/       //
/\        >\        /<        >\

o         <o        <o>       o>        o
X         \         l         <l        <l>
/<        >\        /<        >\        /<
```

WHAT DO YOU THINK?

1. What does the creation of symbols such as these suggest about culture?
2. Do you think such symbols convey meaning as well as facial expressions do? Why or why not?
3. What other recently created symbols of this kind can you point to?

Sources: Pollack (1996) and Krantz (1997).

"Mr. Asciihead" is the creation of Leow Yee Ling.

---

northern Africa and western Asia write from right to left, and people in eastern Asia write from top to bottom. Global Map 2–1 on page 42 shows where in the world we find the three most widely spoken languages.

Language not only allows communication but also ensures the continuity of culture. Whether spoken or written, language is a cultural heritage in coded form, the key to **cultural transmission,** *the process by which one generation passes culture to the next.* Just as our bodies contain the genes of our ancestors, our cultural heritage contains countless symbols of those who came before us. Language is the key that unlocks centuries of accumulated wisdom.

Language skills may link us to the past, but they also spark the human imagination to connect symbols in new ways, creating an almost limitless range of future possibilities. Language sets apart human beings as the only creatures who are self-conscious, aware of our limitations

Can animals use language? To learn more, go to http://www. newscientist.com/news/news. jsp?id=ns99993218

and ultimate mortality, yet able to dream and hope for a better future.

The Sapir-Whorf thesis. Does someone who speaks Cherokee, an American Indian language, experience the world differently from North Americans who think in English or Spanish? The answer is "yes"—each language has its own distinct symbols that serve as the building blocks of reality.

Edward Sapir and Benjamin Whorf proposed that languages are not just different sets of labels for the same reality (Sapir, 1929, 1949; Whorf, 1956, orig. 1941). Rather, each symbolic system is at least partly unique, with words or expressions that have no precise counterpart in another symbolic system. As multilingual people know, a single idea may "feel" different if spoken in Spanish rather than in English or Chinese (Falk, 1987).

Formally, the **Sapir-Whorf thesis** holds that *people perceive the world through the cultural lens of language.* In the

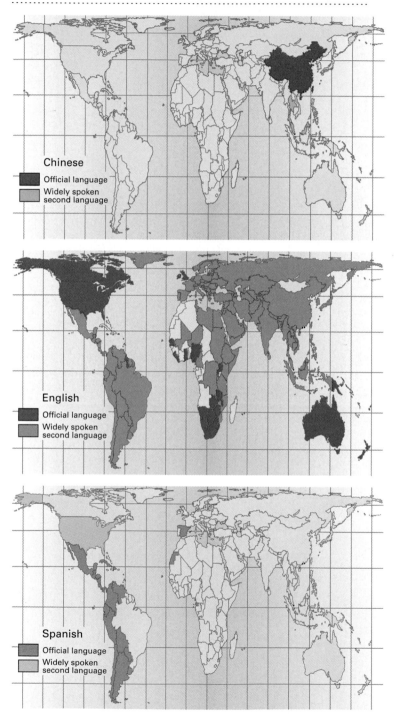

GLOBAL MAP 2–1

Language in Global Perspective

Chinese (including Mandarin, Cantonese, and dozens of other dialects) is the native tongue of one-fifth of the world's people, almost all of whom live in Asia. Although all Chinese people read and write with the same characters, they use several dozen dialects. The "official" dialect, taught in schools throughout the People's Republic of China and the Republic of Taiwan, is Mandarin (the dialect of Beijing, China's historic capital city). Cantonese, the language of Canton, is the second most common Chinese dialect; it differs in sound from Mandarin roughly the way French differs from Spanish.

English is the native tongue or official language in several world regions (spoken by one-tenth of humanity) and has become the preferred second language in most of the world.

The largest concentration of Spanish speakers is in Latin America and, of course, Spain. Spanish is also the second most widely spoken language in the United States.

Source: *Peters Atlas of the World* (1990); updated by the author.

decades since Sapir and Whorf published their work, however, scholars have taken issue with this idea. Current thinking is that while we do fashion reality out of our symbols, evidence does not support the notion that language *determines* reality the way Sapir and Whorf claimed. For example, we know that children understand the idea of "family" long before they learn that word; similarly, adults can imagine new ideas or things before devising a name for them (Kay & Kempton, 1984; Pinker, 1994).

VALUES AND BELIEFS

What accounts for the popularity of movie characters such as James Bond, Dirty Harry, Rambo, and Erin Brockovich? Each is ruggedly individualistic, relying on personal skill and know-how to challenge "the system." In admiring such characters, we are supporting certain **values,** *culturally defined standards that people use to assess desirability, goodness, and beauty and that serve as broad guidelines for social living.* Values are statements, from the standpoint of a culture, of what *ought to be.*

Values are broad principles that underlie **beliefs,** *specific statements that people hold to be true.* That is, values are *abstract standards* of goodness, whereas beliefs are *particular matters* that people hold to be true or false. For example, because most U.S. adults share the value of equal opportunity for all, they believe that a qualified woman could be president (NORC, 2003).

U.S. values. The sociologist Robin Williams (1970) points to the following ten values as central to our way of life:

1. **Equal opportunity.** People in the United States believe in not *equality of condition* but *equality of opportunity.* This means that society should provide everyone with the chance to get ahead according to individual talents and efforts.

2. **Achievement and success.** Our way of life encourages competition so that each person's rewards should reflect personal merit. Moreover, success confers worthiness on a person—the label of being a "winner."

3. **Material comfort.** Success in the United States generally means making money and enjoying what it will buy. Although people sometimes remark that "money won't buy happiness," most pursue wealth all the same.

4. **Activity and work.** Our heroes, from film's famed archaeologist Indiana Jones to golf champion Tiger Woods, are "doers" who get the job done. Our culture values *action* over *reflection* and taking control of events over passively accepting our fate.

Australian artist and feminist Sally Swain alters famous artists' paintings to make fun of our culture's tendency to ignore the everyday lives of women. This spoof is entitled *Mrs. Matisse Polishes the Goldfish.*

Mrs. Matisse Polishes the Goldfish from *Great Housewives of Art* by Sally Swain, copyright © 1988, 1989 by Sally Swain. Used by permission of Viking Penguin, a division of Penguin Group (USA) Inc.

5. **Practicality and efficiency.** People in the United States value the practical over the theoretical— "doing" over "dreaming." "Major in something that will help you get a job!" parents say to their college-age children.

6. **Progress.** We are an optimistic people who, despite waves of nostalgia, believe that the present is better than the past. We celebrate progress by equating the "very latest" with the "very best."

7. **Science.** We expect scientists to solve problems and to improve our lives. We believe that we are rational people, which probably explains our cultural tendency (especially among men) to devalue emotion and intuition as sources of knowledge.

8. **Democracy and free enterprise.** Members of our society recognize numerous individual rights that cannot be overridden by government. We believe that a just political system is based on free elections in which people select their leaders and on an economy that responds to the desires of individual consumers.

9. **Freedom.** Our culture favors individual initiative over group conformity. We believe that individuals should be free to pursue personal goals with minimal interference from anyone else.

10. **Racism and group superiority.** Despite strong ideas about individualism and freedom, most people in the United States still judge others according to gender, race, ethnicity, and social class. U.S. culture values males over females, whites over people of color, people with northwestern European backgrounds over those whose ancestors came from other lands, and rich over poor. Although we describe ourselves as a nation of equals, there is little doubt that some of us are "more equal" than others.

Values: Sometimes in conflict. Looking over Williams's list, we see that some of our core cultural values contradict others. For example, people may believe in equality of opportunity, yet they may also put down others because of their sex or race. Such value conflict inevitably causes strain, leading to awkward balancing acts in our beliefs. Sometimes we decide that one value is more important than another; for example, we may support equal opportunity while at the same time oppose acceptance of gays into the U.S. military. In these cases, we simply learn to live with inconsistencies.

NORMS

Most people in the United States are eager to gossip about "who's hot" and "who's not." Members of American Indian societies, however, typically condemn such behavior as rude and divisive. Both patterns illustrate the operation of **norms,** *rules and expectations by which a society guides the behavior of its members.*

William Graham Sumner (1959, orig. 1906), an early U.S. sociologist, coined the term **mores** (pronounced "MORE-ayz") to refer to *norms that are widely observed and have great moral significance.* Mores, or *taboos,* include our society's insistence that adults not engage in sexual relations with children.

People are more casual about **folkways,** *norms for routine or casual interaction.* Examples include ideas about what are acceptable greetings and proper dress. A man who does not wear a tie to a formal dinner party may raise an eyebrow for violating folkways or "etiquette." Were he to

arrive at the dinner party wearing *only* a tie, however, he would invite more serious punishment for violating cultural mores. Although we sometimes bristle when others pressure us to conform, norms make our encounters with others more orderly and predictable.

As we learn cultural norms, we gain the capacity to evaluate our own behavior. Doing wrong (say, downloading a term paper from the Internet) can cause not only *shame*—the painful sense that others disapprove of our actions—but also *guilt*—a negative judgment we make of ourselves. Only cultural creatures can experience shame and guilt. This is what writer Mark Twain had in mind when he remarked that people "are the only animals that blush—or need to."

IDEAL AND REAL CULTURE

Values and norms suggest how we *should* behave more than they describe actual behavior. We must remember that *ideal culture* always differs from the *real culture* that actually occurs in everyday life. To illustrate, most men and women agree on the importance of sexual faithfulness in marriage. Even so, in one study, 25 percent of married men and 10 percent of married women reported having been sexually unfaithful to their spouses at some point in the marriage (Laumann et al., 1994). But a culture's moral standards are important all the same, calling to mind the old saying, "Do as I say, not as I do."

Technology and Culture

In addition to symbolic elements such as values and norms, every culture includes a wide range of physical human creations called *artifacts.* The Chinese eat with chopsticks rather than knives and forks, the Japanese place mats rather than rugs on the floor, and many men and women in India prefer flowing robes to the close-fitting clothing common in the United States. The material culture of a people can seem as strange to outsiders as their language, values, and norms.

A society's artifacts partly reflect underlying cultural values. The warlike Yąnomamö carefully craft their weapons and prize the poison tips on their arrows. U.S. society's embrace of individuality and independence goes a long way to explain our high regard for the automobile: We own about 220 million motor vehicles, more than one for every licensed driver. Figure 2–2 shows that the United States stands out as one of the most car-loving nations.

In addition to reflecting values, material culture also indicates a society's level of **technology,** *knowledge that people use to make a way of life in their surroundings.* The more complex a society's technology, the easier it is for members of a society to shape the world for themselves.

Gerhard Lenski (Nolan & Lenski, 2004) argues that a society's level of technology is crucial in determining what cultural ideas and artifacts emerge or are even possible. Thus, he sees *sociocultural evolution*—the historical change in culture caused by new technology—in terms of four major levels of development: hunting and gathering, horticulture and pastoralism, agriculture, and industry.

HUNTING AND GATHERING

The oldest and most basic way of living is **hunting and gathering,** *the use of simple tools to hunt animals and gather vegetation for food.* From the time of our earliest human ancestors 3 million years ago until about 1800, most people in the world lived as hunters and gatherers. Today, however, this technology describes only a few societies, including the Kaska Indians of northwest Canada, the Pygmies of Central Africa, the Bushmen of southwestern Africa, the Aborigines of Australia, and the Semai of Malaysia. In most cases, hunters and gatherers spend most of their time searching for game and edible plants. Their societies stay small, generally with several dozen people living in a nomadic, family-like group, moving on as they use up an area's vegetation or follow migratory animals.

Everyone participates in searching for food, with the very young and the very old helping as they can. Women usually gather vegetation—the primary food source for these people—while men do most of the hunting. Despite having different roles, the two sexes have about the same social importance (Leacock, 1978).

Hunters and gatherers have few formal leaders. They may look to one person as a *shaman,* or priest, but this position does not excuse the person from the daily work of finding food. Overall, hunting and gathering stands as a simple and egalitarian way of life.

Limited technology leaves hunters and gatherers vulnerable to the forces of nature. Storms and droughts can easily destroy their food supply, and they have few effective ways to respond to accident or disease. Not surprisingly, then, many children die in childhood, and only half live to the age of twenty.

As people with powerful technology steadily close in on them, hunters and gatherers are fast vanishing from the Earth. Fortunately, studying their way of life has already produced valuable information about our sociocultural history and our fundamental ties to the natural environment.

HORTICULTURE AND PASTORALISM

Horticulture, *the use of hand tools to raise crops,* first appeared 10,000 years ago. The hoe and the digging stick (used to punch holes in the ground for seeds) first appeared

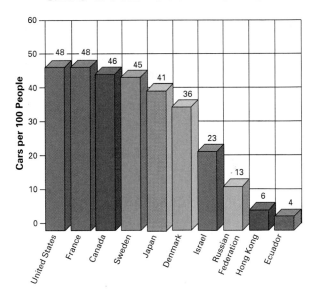

FIGURE 2-2 Car Ownership in Global Perspective

Source: World Bank (2004).

in fertile regions of the Middle East and Southeast Asia, and by 6,000 years ago, these tools were in use from Western Europe to China. Central and South Americans also learned to cultivate plants, but rocky soil and mountainous land forced members of many societies to continue to hunt and gather even as they adopted this new technology (Fisher, 1979; Chagnon, 1992).

In especially dry regions, societies turned not to raising crops but to **pastoralism,** *the domestication of animals.* Throughout the Americas, Africa, the Middle East, and Asia, many societies blend horticulture and pastoralism.

Growing plants and raising animals allows societies to feed hundreds of members. Whereas pastoral peoples remain nomadic, horticulturalists make permanent settlements. In a horticultural society, a material surplus means that not everyone is needed to produce food; some people are free to make crafts, become traders, or serve as full-time priests. Compared with hunters and gatherers, pastoral and horticultural societies are also more unequal, with some families operating as a ruling elite.

Because hunters and gatherers have little control over nature, they generally believe that the world is inhabited by spirits. As they gain the power to raise plants and animals, however, people come to believe in God as the creator of the world. The pastoral roots of Judaism and Christianity are evident in the term "pastor" and the common view of God as a "shepherd" who stands watch over all.

AGRICULTURE

Five thousand years ago, further technological advances led to **agriculture,** *large-scale cultivation using plows harnessed to animals or more powerful energy sources.* Agrarian technology first appeared in the Middle East and gradually spread throughout the world. The invention of the animal-drawn plow, the wheel, writing, numbers, and new metals were so important that historians call this era "the dawn of civilization."

By turning the soil, plows allow land to be farmed for decades, so agrarian people live in permanent settlements. With large food surpluses that can be transported by animal-powered wagons, populations easily grow into the millions. As members of agrarian societies become more and more specialized in their work, money is used as a form of common exchange, replacing the earlier system of barter. Although the development of agrarian technology expands human choices and fuels urban growth, it also makes social life more individualistic and impersonal.

Agriculture also brings about a dramatic increase in social inequality. Most people live as serfs or slaves, but a few elites are freed from labor to cultivate a "refined" way of life based on the study of philosophy, art, and literature. At all levels of such a society, men gain pronounced power over women.

People with only simple technology live much the same the world over, with minor differences caused by regional variations in climate. But, Lenski explains, agrarian technology gives people enough control over the world that cultural diversity increases.

INDUSTRY

Industrialization occurred as societies replaced the muscles of animals and humans with new forms of power. Formally, **industry** is *the production of goods using advanced sources of energy to drive large machinery.* The introduction of steam power, starting in England about 1775, greatly boosted productivity and transformed culture in the process.

Whereas agrarian people work in or near the home, most people in industrial societies work in large factories, under the supervision of strangers. Thus, industrialization pushes aside traditional cultural values that guided family-centered agrarian life for centuries.

Industry also made the world seem smaller. In the nineteenth century, railroads and steamships carried people across land and sea faster and farther than ever before.

In the twentieth century, this process continued with the invention of the automobile, the airplane, radio, television, and computers.

Industrial technology also raises living standards and extends the human life span. Schooling becomes the rule because industrial jobs demand more and more skills. Furthermore, industrial societies reduce economic inequality and steadily extend political rights.

It is easy to see industrial societies as more "advanced" than those relying on simpler technology. After all, industry raises living standards and stretches life expectancy to the seventies and beyond—about twice that of the Yąnomamö. Even so, industry intensifies individualism, which expands personal freedom but weakens human community. Also, industry has led people to abuse the natural environment—at our peril. And although advanced technology gives us work-saving machines and miraculous forms of medical treatment, it also contributes to unhealthy levels of stress and has created weapons capable of destroying in a flash everything that our species has achieved.

POSTINDUSTRIAL INFORMATION TECHNOLOGY

Going beyond the four categories discussed by Lenski, we see that many industrial societies, including the United States, have now entered a postindustrial era in which more and more economic production makes use of *new information technology.* Production in industrial societies centers on factories that make *things,* whereas postindustrial production centers on computers and other electronic devices that create, process, store, and apply *ideas and information.*

The emergence of an information economy thus changes the skills that define a way of life. No longer are mechanical abilities the only key to success. People find that they must learn to work with symbols by speaking, writing, computing, and creating images and sounds. The overall effect of this change is that our society now has the capacity to create symbolic culture on an unprecedented scale. The Critical Thinking box takes a closer look.

Cultural Diversity

In the United States, we are aware of our cultural diversity when we hear the distinctive accents of people who have lived for many years in New England, the Midwest, or the Deep South. Ours is also a nation of religious pluralism, a land of class differences, and a home to individualists who try to be like no one else. Over the centuries, heavy immigration has made the United States the most *multicultural* of all high-income countries. By contrast, historic isolation makes Japan the most *monocultural* of all high-income nations.

CRITICAL THINKING

Virtual Culture: Is It Good for Us?

January 16, Orlando, Florida. Walt Disney World is a delight to the kids but a little disturbing to the sociologist. It is ready-made culture: Streets, stores, and events re-create a nineteenth-century small town, populated with Disney characters. Here, life is carefully controlled to ensure a good time, with the ultimate purpose of relieving us of whatever cash we have.

The Information Revolution is now generating symbols—words, sounds, and images—faster than ever before and rapidly spreading them across the nation and around the world. What does this new information technology mean for our way of life?

In centuries past, culture was a way of life passed down from generation to generation. It was a heritage—a society's collective memory—that was authentically our own because it belonged to our ancestors (Schwartz, 1996). But in our emerging cyber-society, more and more cultural symbols are new, intentionally *created* by a small cultural elite of composers, writers, filmmakers, and others who work in the expanding information economy.

To illustrate, consider the changing character of cultural heroes, people who serve as role models and represent cultural ideals. A century ago, our heroes were real men and women who made a difference in the life of this nation: George Washington, Abigail Adams, Betsy Ross, Davy Crockett, Daniel Boone, Abraham Lincoln, Harriet Tubman. Of course, when a society makes a hero of someone (almost always well after the person has died), it "cleans up" the person's biography, highlighting the successes and overlooking the shortcomings.

Culture used to be a way of life passed across many generations. Today, large corporations and the mass media create culture to entertain—and to make money.

Even so, these people were authentic parts of our history.

Today's children, by contrast, are fed a steady diet of *virtual culture,* images that spring from the minds of contemporary culture makers and that reach them through television, movie, or computer screen. Today's "heroes" are Aragorn, Anakin Skywalker, Rug Rats, Scooby Doo, Batman, Barbie, and Powerpuff Girls, a continuous flow of Disney characters, and the ever-smiling Ronald McDonald. Some of these cultural icons embody values that shape our way of life. But few of them have any historical reality, and almost all have been created for a single purpose: to make money.

WHAT DO YOU THINK?

1. Over the course of the twenty-first century, do you think virtual culture will become more or less important? Why?
2. Does virtual culture weaken or strengthen our cultural traditions? Is that good or bad?
3. What image of this country do U.S. movies and television shows give to people abroad?

Source: I thank Roland Johnson for the basic idea for this box.

Between 1820 (when the government began keeping track of immigration) and 2003, some 69 million people have added their ways of life to the mix of cultures in the United States. A century ago, as shown in Figure 2–3 on page 48, most immigrants hailed from Europe; today, the majority of newcomers arrive from Latin America and Asia. To understand the reality of life in the United States, we must move beyond shared cultural patterns to consider the importance of cultural diversity.

HIGH CULTURE AND POPULAR CULTURE

Cultural diversity often involves social class. In fact, in everyday conversation, we usually reserve the term "culture" for

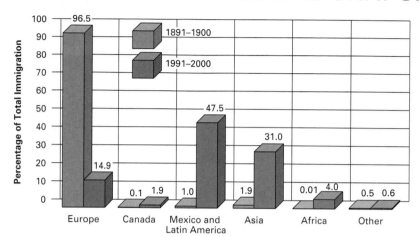

GLOBAL SNAPSHOT

FIGURE 2-3

Recorded Immigration to the United States, by Region of Birth, 1891–1900 and 1991–2000

Sources: U.S. Department of Commerce (1930) and U.S. Citizenship and Immigration Services (2004).

art forms such as literature, music, dance, and painting. We describe people who attend the opera or the theater as "cultured," thinking that they appreciate the "finer things in life."

We speak less well of ordinary people, assuming that their everyday culture is somehow less worthy. So we are tempted to judge the music of Beethoven as "more cultured" than the blues, croissants as better than cornbread, and polo as more polished than Ping-Pong.

In short, many cultural patterns are readily accessible to only some members of a society (Hall & Neitz, 1993). Sociologists use the shorthand term **high culture**[1] to refer to *cultural patterns that distinguish a society's elite* and **popular culture** to designate *cultural patterns that are widespread among a society's population.* National Map 2–1 looks at preferred alcoholic beverages to show the distribution of high and popular culture across the United States.

Common sense may suggest that high culture is superior to popular culture. But we should resist quick judgments about the merits of high culture over popular culture for two main reasons. First, neither elites nor ordinary people have uniform tastes and interests; people in both categories differ in numerous ways. Second, do we praise high culture because it is inherently better than popular culture or simply because its supporters have more money, power, and prestige? For example, there is no difference between a

violin and a fiddle; however, we name the instrument one way when it is used to produce a type of music typically enjoyed by a person of higher position and the other way when it produces music appreciated by people with lower social standing. Therefore, sociologists are uneasy with distinctions between high and popular culture, preferring the term "culture" to refer to *all* elements of a society's way of life, including patterns of rich and poor alike.

SUBCULTURE

The term **subculture** refers to *cultural patterns that set apart some segment of a society's population.* People who ride "chopper" motorcycles, Polish Americans, New England "Yankees," Colorado cowboys, the southern California "beach crowd," campus poets, computer "nerds," and wilderness campers all display subcultural patterns.

It is easy but often inaccurate to put people in subcultural categories because almost everyone participates in many subcultures without having much commitment to any one of them. In some cases, ethnicity and religion set people apart from one another with tragic results. Consider the former nation of Yugoslavia in southeastern Europe. The recent civil war there was fueled by astounding cultural diversity. This *one* small country with a population about equal to the Los Angeles metropolitan area made use of *two* alphabets, embraced *three* major religions, spoke *four* major languages, contained *five* major nationalities, was divided into *six* separate republics, and reflected the cultural influences of *seven* surrounding countries. The cultural conflict that plunged this nation into civil war

---

[1]The term "high culture" is derived from the term "highbrow." A century ago, people believed that personality was affected by the shape of the human skull and praised the tastes of those they called "highbrows" while dismissing the interests of others they derided as "lowbrows."

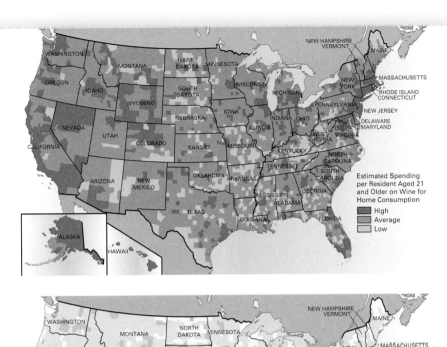

SEEING OURSELVES

NATIONAL MAP 2-1

What'll Ya Have? Popular Beverages across the United States

What people consume is one mark of their status as a "highbrow" or "lowbrow." Drinking wine at home is an indicator of highbrow standing. Well-to-do people not only enjoy a glass of wine with dinner but drink water from bottles rather than the tap, prefer Grey Poupon to Gulden's mustard, and favor Häagen-Dazs over the local Tastee-Freeze. Drinking beer, on the other hand, marks a person as a "lowbrow." Such a person has a low to moderate income, consumes a good deal of snack food, and frequents fast-food restaurants. On the maps, where have the "highbrows" and the "lowbrows" created centers of "high culture" and "popular culture"?

Source: *American Demographics* magazine, March 1998, p. 19. Copyright © 1998 by Primedia. Reprinted with permission of Primedia Business Magazines & Media.

shows that subcultures are a source not only of pleasing variety but also of tension and outright violence.

Today, as in decades past, we view the United States as a melting pot where many nationalities blend into a single "American" culture (Gardyn, 2002). But given our cultural diversity, how accurate is the melting pot image? For one thing, subcultures involve not just *difference* but *hierarchy.* Too often, what we view as dominant or "mainstream" culture are patterns favored by powerful segments of the population, whereas we view the lives of disadvantaged people as "subculture." For example, are the cultural patterns of rich skiers in Aspen, Colorado, any less a "subculture" than the cultural patterns of street gangs in Los Angeles? Some researchers therefore prefer to level the playing field of society by emphasizing multiculturalism.

MULTICULTURALISM

Multiculturalism is *an educational program recognizing the cultural diversity of the United States and promoting the equality of all cultural traditions.* Multiculturalism represents a sharp change from the past, when our society downplayed cultural diversity, defining itself in terms of its European (and especially English) immigrants. Today, a spirited debate asks whether or not we should focus on historical traditions or contemporary diversity (Orwin, 1996; Rabkin, 1996).

E pluribus unum, the Latin phrase that appears on each U.S. coin, means "out of many, one." This motto symbolizes not only our national political union but also the idea that the varied experiences of immigrants from around the

Source: U.S. Census Bureau (2003).

NATIONAL MAP 2-2

Language Diversity
across the United States

Of more than 262 million people over the age
of five in the United States, the 2000 Census
reports that 47 million (18 percent) typically speak
a language other than English at home. Of these
people, 60 percent speak Spanish, 15 percent use
an Asian language, and the remaining 25 percent
communicate with some other tongue (the Census
Bureau lists 25 languages, each of which is
favored by more than 100,000 people in the
United States). The map shows that non-English-
speakers are concentrated in certain regions of the
country. Which ones? What do you think accounts
for this pattern?

world come together to form a new way of life. But from the outset, the many cultures did not melt together as much as harden into a hierarchy. At the top were the English, who formed a majority and established English as the nation's dominant language. Further down, people of other backgrounds were advised to model themselves after "their betters" so that the "melting" was more accurately a process of Anglicization—adoption of English ways. Thus, early in its history, U.S. society set up the English way of life as an ideal to which all should aspire and by which all should be judged.

Ever since, historians have chronicled events from the point of view of the English and others of European ancestry, paying little attention to the perspectives and accomplishments of Native Americans and people of African and Asian descent. Multiculturalists call this view **Eurocentrism,** *the dominance of European (especially English) cultural patterns.* Molefi Kete Asante, a supporter of multiculturalism, argues that like "the fifteenth-century Europeans who could not cease believing that the Earth was the center of the universe, many . . . find it difficult to cease viewing European culture as the center of the social universe" (1988:7).

One hotly contested issue involves language. Some people believe that English should be the official language of the United States; by 2004, legislatures in twenty-seven states had enacted such laws. Others point out that almost 50 million U.S. adults—nearly one in six—speak a language other than English in their homes. Spanish is the second most commonly spoken language in the United States, and

several hundred other tongues are heard across the country, including Italian, German, French, Filipino, Japanese, Korean, Vietnamese, Russian, and a host of Native American languages. National Map 2–2 shows where in the United States large numbers of people speak a language other than English at home.

Supporters also paint multiculturalism as a way of coming to terms with our country's increasing social diversity. With the Asian and Hispanic populations increasing rapidly, some analysts predict that our young children will live to see people of African, Asian, and Hispanic ancestry become the *majority* of this country's population.

Supporters also claim that multiculturalism is a good way to strengthen the academic achievement of African American children. To offset Eurocentrism, some multicultural educators are calling for **Afrocentrism,** *emphasizing and promoting African cultural patterns,* which they see as a strategy for correcting centuries of ignoring the achievements of African societies and African Americans.

Although multiculturalism has found favor in recent years, it has drawn criticism as well. Opponents say it encourages divisiveness rather than unity because it urges people to identify with only their own category rather than with the nation as a whole. Moreover, critics doubt that multiculturalism actually benefits minorities as its supporters claim. Some multicultural policies (from African American studies departments to all-black dorms) seem to support precisely the kind of racial separation that our nation has struggled so long to end. Furthermore, an Afrocentric curriculum may deny children important knowledge and skills by forcing them to study only certain topics from a single point of view.

Almost everyone agrees that we need greater appreciation of our nation's cultural diversity. But precisely where the balance is to be struck—between the *pluribus* and the *unum*—is likely to remain an issue for some time to come.

COUNTERCULTURE

Cultural diversity also includes outright rejection of conventional ideas or behavior. **Counterculture** refers to *cultural patterns that strongly oppose those widely accepted within a society.*

In many societies, counterculture is linked to youth (Spates, 1976, 1983; Spates & Perkins, 1982). The youth-oriented counterculture of the 1960s, for example, rejected mainstream culture as too competitive, self-centered, and materialistic. Instead, hippies and other counterculturalists favored a collective and cooperative lifestyle in which "being" took precedence over "doing," and personal growth—or "expanded consciousness"—was prized over material possessions such as homes and cars. Such differences led some people to "drop out" of the larger society.

Countercultures are still flourishing today. At the extreme, small bands of religious militants exist in the United States, some of them engaging in violence intended to threaten our way of life. Members of al-Qaeda, one such group under the leadership of Osama bin Laden, lived for years in this country before carrying out the September 11, 2001, attacks on the World Trade Center and the Pentagon.

CULTURAL CHANGE

Perhaps the most basic human truth is that "all things shall pass." Even the dinosaurs, which thrived on this planet for 160 million years (see the timeline), exist today only as fossils. Will humanity survive for millions of years to come? All we can say with certainty is that given our reliance on culture, the human record will be one of continuous change.

Figure 2–4 shows changes in student attitudes between 1969 (the height of the 1960s counterculture) and 2003. Some things have changed only slightly: Today, as a generation ago, most men and women look forward to raising a family. But today's students are much less concerned than those of the 1960s with developing a philosophy of life and much more interested in making money.

Change in one dimension of a cultural system usually sparks changes in others. For example, women's increased participation in the labor force is linked to changing family patterns, including later first marriages and a rising divorce

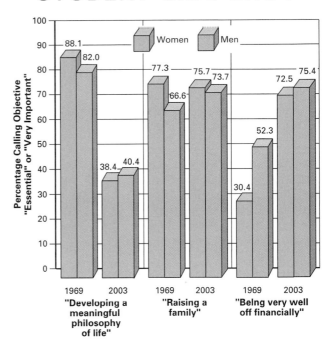

STUDENT SNAPSHOT

FIGURE 2–4 Life Objectives of First-Year College Students, 1969–2003

Sources: Astin et al. (2002) and Sax et al. (2003).

rate. Such connections illustrate the principle of **cultural integration,** *the close relationships among various elements of a cultural system.*

Some parts of a cultural system change more quickly than others. William Ogburn (1964) observed that technology moves quickly, generating new elements of material culture (such as test-tube babies) faster than nonmaterial culture (such as ideas about parenthood) can keep up with them. Ogburn called this inconsistency **cultural lag,** *the fact that some cultural elements change more quickly than others, disrupting a cultural system.* How are we to apply traditional ideas about motherhood and fatherhood in a culture where one woman now can give birth to a child by using another woman's egg, which has been fertilized in a laboratory with the sperm of a total stranger?

Cultural changes are set in motion in three ways. The first is *invention,* the process of creating new cultural elements, such as the telephone (1876), the airplane (1903), and the computer (late 1940s). The process of invention goes on constantly, as indicated by the thousands of applications submitted annually to the U.S. Patent Office. The

In the world's low-income countries, most children must work to provide their families with needed income. This young child in Dhaka, Bangladesh, is sorting discarded materials in a factory that makes recycled lead batteries. Is it ethnocentric for people living in high-income nations to condemn the practice of child labor because we think youngsters belong in school? Why or why not?

timeline inside the front cover of this text shows other inventions that have helped change our way of life.

Discovery, a second cause of change, involves recognizing and better understanding something already in existence, from a distant star to the foods of a foreign culture to the athletic abilities of women. Many discoveries result from painstaking scientific research, and others happen by a stroke of luck, as when Marie Curie unintentionally left a rock on a piece of photographic paper in 1898 and discovered radium.

The third cause of cultural change is *diffusion,* the spread of objects or ideas from one society to another. The ability of new information technology to send information around the world in seconds means that the extent of cultural diffusion has never been greater than it is today.

Certainly, U.S. society has contributed many significant cultural elements to the world, ranging from computers to jazz music. Sometimes, though, we forget that diffusion works the other way, so that much of what we assume is "American" actually comes from elsewhere. Most clothing, furniture, clocks, newspapers, money, and even the English language are derived from other cultures around the world (Linton, 1937a).

ETHNOCENTRISM AND CULTURAL RELATIVISM

December 10, a small village in rural Morocco. Watching many of our shipmates browsing through this tiny ceramic factory, one can hardly doubt that North Americans are among the world's greatest shoppers. They delight in surveying hand-woven carpets in China or India,

inspecting finely crafted metals in Turkey, or collecting beautifully colored porcelain tiles here in Morocco. And of course, all these items are wonderful bargains. But the major reason for the low prices is unsettling: Many products from the world's low- and middle-income countries are produced by children—some as young as five or six—who work long days for pennies per hour.

We think of childhood as a time of innocence and freedom from adult burdens such as work. In poor countries throughout the world, however, families depend on income earned by children. Child labor is one example of a practice that people in one society think of as right and natural and people elsewhere find puzzling and even immoral. Perhaps the Chinese philosopher Confucius had it right when he noted, "All people are the same; it's only their habits that are different."

Just about every imaginable idea or behavior is common somewhere in the world, and this cultural variation causes travelers equal measures of excitement and distress. The Australians flip light switches down to turn them on, whereas North Americans flip them up; the Japanese name city blocks rather than streets, a practice that regularly confuses North Americans, who do the opposite; Egyptians move very close to others in conversation, which irritates North Americans, used to maintaining several feet of personal space. Bathrooms lack toilet paper in much of rural Morocco, causing concern among Westerners unaccustomed to using the left hand for bathroom hygiene.

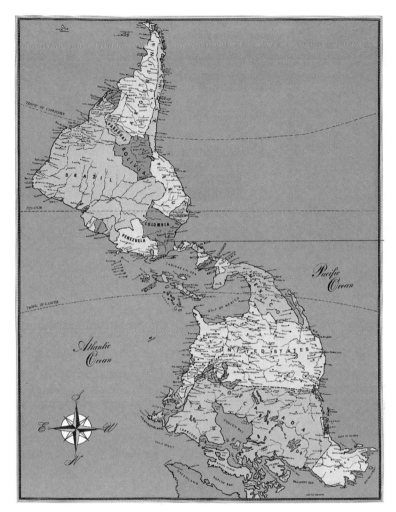

The View from "Down Under"
North America should be "up" and South America "down," or so we think. But because we live on a globe, "up" and "down" have no meaning at all. The reason this map of the Western Hemisphere looks wrong to us is not that it is geographically inaccurate; it simply violates our ethnocentric assumption that the United States should be "above" the rest of
the Americas.

Given that a particular culture is the basis for everyone's reality, it is no wonder that people throughout the world exhibit **ethnocentrism,** *the practice of judging another culture by the standards of one's own culture.* Some ethnocentrism is necessary if people are to be emotionally attached to their own cultural system. But ethnocentrism also generates misunderstanding and conflict.

Even our language is culturally biased. People in North America or Europe call China the "Far East." Such a term, which has little meaning to the Chinese, is an ethnocentric expression for a region that is far east *of us.* For their part, the Chinese name their country using a word translated as "Central Kingdom," suggesting that they see their society as the center of the world. The map above challenges our ethnocentrism by presenting a "down under" view of the Western Hemisphere.

The logical alternative to ethnocentrism is **cultural relativism,** *the practice of evaluating a culture by its own*

standards. Cultural relativism is a difficult attitude to adopt because it requires an understanding of unfamiliar values and norms and the suspension of lifelong cultural standards. But as people of the world increasingly come into contact with one another, the importance of understanding other cultures becomes even greater.

As noted in the opening to this chapter, businesses in the United States are realizing that success in the global economy depends on cultural sophistication. IBM, for example, now provides technical  support for its products using Web sites in twenty-two languages (Fonda, 2001). In the past, companies paid little attention to cultural differences, sometime with negative consequences. General Motors learned the hard way that its Nova wasn't selling well in Spanish-speaking nations because the name in Spanish means "no go." Coors's phrase "Turn It Loose" startled

Spanish-speaking customers by proclaiming that the beer would cause diarrhea. Braniff Airlines translated its slogan "Fly in Leather" into Spanish so clumsily that it read "Fly Naked"; similarly, Eastern Airlines's slogan "We Earn Our Wings Daily" became "We Fly Every Day to Heaven," discouraging timid air travelers. Even poultry giant Frank Perdue fell victim to poor marketing when his pitch "It Takes a Tough Man to Make a Tender Chicken" was transformed into the Spanish phrase "A Sexually Excited Man Makes a Chicken Affectionate" (Helin, 1992).

But cultural relativism introduces problems of its own. If almost any behavior is the

 In two brief videos, the author considers issues of cultural relativism at http://www. TheSociologyPage.com

norm *somewhere* in the world, does that mean everything is equally right? Does the fact that some Indian and Moroccan families benefit from their children working long hours justify child labor?

Because we are all members of a single human species, surely there must be some universal standards of proper conduct. But what are they? And in trying to identify them, how can we avoid imposing our own standards on others? There are no simple answers. But when confronting an unfamiliar cultural practice, resist making judgments before learning what the people in that culture think and why. Remember also to think about your own way of life as others might see it. After all, what we gain most from studying others is better insight into ourselves.

A GLOBAL CULTURE?

Today, more than ever before, we see many of the same cultural patterns the world over. Walking the streets of Seoul (South Korea), Kuala Lumpur (Malaysia), Madras (India), Cairo (Egypt), and Casablanca (Morocco), we find jeans, hear well-known pop music, and see advertising for many of the same products we use at home. Recall, too, from Global Map 2–1 that English is rapidly becoming the second language of most of the world. Are we witnessing the birth of a single global culture?

Societies around the world now have more contact with one another than ever before, thanks to the flow of goods, information, and people:

1. **The global economy: The flow of goods.** There has never been more international trade. The global economy has spread many consumer goods (from cars and TV shows to music and fashion) throughout the world.

2. **Global communication: The flow of information.** Satellite-based communication enables people throughout the world to experience the sights and sounds of events taking place thousands of miles away, often as they are happening.

3. **Global migration: The flow of people.** Knowing about the rest of the world motivates people to move where they imagine life will be better. Moreover, today's transportation technology, especially air travel, makes moving about faster than ever before. As a result, in most nations, significant numbers of people have been born elsewhere (including some 34 million people in the United States—12 percent of the population).

These global links have made the cultures of the world more similar. But there are three important limitations to the global culture thesis. First, the flow of information, goods, and people is uneven. Generally speaking, urban areas (centers of commerce, communication, and people) have stronger ties to one another, and rural villages remain more isolated. In addition, the greater economic and military power of North America and Western Europe means that nations in these regions influence the rest of the world more than happens the other way around.

Second, the global culture thesis assumes that people everywhere are able to afford the new goods and services. As Chapter 9 ("Global Stratification") explains, desperate poverty in much of the world deprives people of even the basic necessities of a safe and secure life.

Third, although many cultural elements have spread throughout the world, people everywhere do not attach the same meanings to them. Do teenagers in Tokyo understand hip-hop the way young people in New York or Los Angeles do? Similarly, although we may enjoy foods from around the world, we probably know little or nothing about the lives of the people who created them. In short, people everywhere look at the world through their own cultural lenses.

Theoretical Analysis of Culture

Sociologists have the special task of investigating how culture helps us make sense of ourselves and the surrounding world. Here we present several macro-level theoretical approaches to understanding culture; a micro-level approach to the personal experience of culture is the focus of Chapter 4 ("Social Interaction in Everyday Life").

STRUCTURAL-FUNCTIONAL ANALYSIS

The structural-functional approach explains culture as a complex strategy for meeting human needs. Drawing from the philosophical doctrine of *idealism,* this approach considers values to be the core of a culture (Parsons, 1966; Williams, 1970). In other words, cultural values direct our lives, give meaning to what we do, and bind people together.

Following the structural-functional approach, what do you make of the Amish practice of "barn raising," by which everyone in a community joins together to raise a family's new barn in a day? Why is such a ritual almost unknown in rural areas outside of Amish communities?

Countless other cultural traits have various functions that support the operation of society.

Thinking functionally helps us make sense of an unfamiliar way of life. Consider the Amish farmer in Ohio plowing hundreds of acres with a team of horses. His methods may violate the U.S. cultural value of efficiency, but from the Amish point of view, hard work functions to develop the discipline necessary for a highly religious way of life. Long days of working together not only make the Amish self-sufficient but also strengthen family ties and unify local communities.

Of course, Amish practices have dysfunctions as well. The hard work and strict religious discipline are too demanding for some, who end up leaving the community. Also, religious devotion sometimes prevents compromise, resulting in lasting divisions within the Amish world (Kraybill, 1989; Kraybill & Olshan, 1994).

If cultures are strategies for meeting human needs, we would expect to find many common patterns around the world. **Cultural universals** are *traits that are part of every known culture.* Comparing hundreds of cultures, George Murdock (1945) identified dozens of cultural universals. One common element is the family, which functions everywhere to control sexual reproduction and to oversee the care and upbringing of children. Funeral rites are also found everywhere because all human communities cope with death. Jokes are another cultural universal, serving as a safe means of releasing social tensions.

Critical review. The strength of structural-functional analysis lies in showing how culture operates to meet human needs. Yet by emphasizing a society's dominant cultural patterns, this approach overlooks cultural diversity. In addition, because this approach emphasizes cultural stability, it downplays the importance of change. In short, cultural systems are neither as stable nor a matter of as much agreement as structural-functional analysis leads us to believe.

SOCIAL-CONFLICT ANALYSIS

The social-conflict approach draws attention to the link between culture and inequality. From this point of view, any cultural trait benefits some members of society at the expense of others.

Why do certain values dominate a society in the first place? Many conflict theorists, especially Marxists, argue that culture is shaped by a society's system of economic production. Social-conflict theory, then, is rooted in the philosophical doctrine of *materialism*, which holds that a society's system of material production (such as our own capitalist economy) has a powerful effect on the rest of a culture. This materialist approach contrasts with the idealist leanings of structural-functionalism.

Social-conflict analysis ties the competitive values of the United States to the capitalist economy, which serves the interests of the nation's wealthy elite. The culture of capitalism further teaches us that rich and powerful people have more energy and talent than others and therefore deserve their wealth and privilege. Viewing capitalism as somehow "natural" also discourages efforts to reduce economic inequality in the United States.

Using an evolutionary perspective, sociobiologists explain that different reproductive strategies give rise to a double standard: Men treat women as sexual objects more than women treat men that way. While this may be so, many sociologists counter that behavior—such as that shown in Ruth Orkin's photograph, *American Girl in Italy*—is more correctly understood as resulting from a culture of male domination.

Copyright 1952, 1980 Ruth Orkin.

Eventually, however, the strains of inequality erupt into movements for social change. Two recent examples in the United States are the civil rights movement and the women's movement. Both seek greater equality, and both encounter opposition from defenders of the status quo.

Critical review. The social-conflict approach points out that cultural systems do not address human needs equally; rather, they allow some people to dominate others. This inequality, in turn, generates pressure toward change.

Yet by stressing the divisiveness of culture, this approach understates ways in which cultural patterns integrate members of a society. Thus, we should consider both social-conflict and structural-functional insights for a fuller understanding of culture.

SOCIOBIOLOGY

Does our biological existence influence how humans create culture? A third theoretical approach, standing with one leg in biology and the other in sociology, is **sociobiology,** *a theoretical approach that explores ways in which human biology affects how we create culture.*

Sociobiology rests on the theory of evolution proposed by Charles Darwin in his book *On the Origin of Species* (1859). Darwin asserted that living organisms change over long periods of time as a result of *natural selection,* a matter of four simple principles. First, all living things live to reproduce themselves. Second, the blueprint for reproduction is in the genes, the basic units of life that carry traits of

one generation into the next. Third, some random variation in genes allows each species to "try out" new life patterns in a particular environment. This variation enables some organisms to survive better than others and to pass on their advantageous genes to their offspring. Fourth and finally, over thousands of generations, the genes that promote reproduction survive and become dominant. In this way, as biologists say, a species *adapts* to its environment, and dominant traits emerge as the "nature" of the organism.

Sociobiologists claim that the large number of cultural universals reflects the fact that all humans are members of a single biological species. It is our common biology that underlies, for example, the apparently universal "double standard." As sex researcher Alfred Kinsey put it, "Among all people everywhere in the world, the male is more likely than the female to desire sex with a variety of partners" (quoted in Barash, 1981:49). But why?

We all know that a child results from joining a woman's egg with a man's sperm. But the biological significance of a single sperm is very different from that of a single egg. For healthy men, sperm is a "renewable resource" produced by the testes throughout most of the life course. A man releases hundreds of millions of sperm in a single ejaculation, technically enough to fertilize every woman in North America (Barash, 1981:47). However, a newborn girl's ovaries contain her entire lifetime supply of immature eggs. A woman releases a single egg cell from the ovaries each month. So whereas men are biologically capable of fathering thousands of offspring, a woman is able to bear a much smaller number of children.

APPLYING THEORY
CULTURE

	Structural-Functional Approach	Social-Conflict Approach	Sociobiology Approach
What is the level of analysis?	Macro-level	Macro-level	Macro-level
What is culture?	Culture is a system of behavior by which members of societies cooperate to meet their needs.	Culture is a system that benefits some people and disadvantages others.	Culture is a system of behavior that is partly shaped by human biology.
What is the foundation of culture?	Cultural patterns are rooted in a society's core values and beliefs.	Cultural patterns are rooted in a society's system of economic production.	Cultural patterns are rooted in humanity's biological evolution.
What core questions does the approach ask?	How does a cultural pattern help society to operate? What cultural patterns are found in all societies?	How does a cultural pattern benefit some people and harm others? How does a cultural pattern support social inequality?	How does a cultural pattern help a species adapt to its environment?

Given this biological difference, the two sexes have distinctive strategies for reproduction. Men reproduce their genes most efficiently by being promiscuous, engaging in sex readily and often. But this scheme opposes the reproductive interests of women. Each of a woman's pregnancies demands that she carry the child, give birth, and provide care for some time afterward. Thus, efficient reproduction on the part of the woman depends on selecting a man whose qualities (beginning with the likelihood that he will simply stay around) will contribute to her child's survival and, later, successful reproduction.

The "double standard" certainly involves more than biology; it is also a product of the historical domination of women by men. But sociobiology suggests that this cultural pattern, like many others, has an underlying "bio-logic." Simply put, the "double standard" exists around the world because women and men everywhere tend toward distinctive reproductive strategies.

Critical review. Sociobiology provides intriguing insights into the biological roots of some cultural patterns. But this approach remains controversial for two main reasons.

First, some critics fear that sociobiology may revive the biological arguments of a century ago that claimed the superiority of one race or sex. But defenders counter that sociobiology rejects the past pseudoscience of racial superiority. In fact, sociobiology unites all humanity because all people share a single evolutionary history. Sociobiology does assert that men and women differ biologically in some ways that culture may not overcome. But far from claiming that males are somehow more important than females,

sociobiology emphasizes that both sexes are vital to human survival.

Second, sociobiologists have little evidence to support their theories. Research to date suggests that biological forces do not *determine* human behavior in any rigid sense. Rather, humans *learn* behavior within a culture. The contribution of sociobiology, then, lies in explaining why some cultural patterns seem easier to learn than others (Barash, 1981).

The Applying Theory table summarizes the main lessons of each theoretical approach to an understanding of culture. Note that because any analysis of culture requires a broad focus on the workings of society, all these approaches are macro-level in scope. The symbolic-interaction approach, with its micro-level focus on people's behavior in specific situations, will be explored in Chapter 4, "Social Interaction in Everyday Life."

Culture and Human Freedom

Underlying the discussion throughout this chapter is an important question: To what extent are human beings, as cultural creatures, free? Does culture bind us to each other and force us to relive the past? Or does it enhance our capacity for individual thought and independent choice?

Humans cannot live without culture. But living as symbolic creatures does have some drawbacks. We may be the only animals able to name ourselves, but living in a symbolic world means that we are also the only creatures who experience alienation. Culture is largely a matter of habit, which limits our choices and drives us to repeat

The United States and Canada: Are They Culturally Different?

The United States and Canada are two of the largest high-income nations in the world, and they share a common border of about 4,000 miles. But do the United States and Canada share the same culture?

One important point to make right away is that both nations are *multicultural.* Not only do both countries have hundreds of Native American societies, but immigration has brought people to both Canada and the United States from all over the world. Most early immigrants to Canada and the United States came from Europe; more recent immigrants have come from nations in Asia and Latin America. The Canadian city of Vancouver, for example, has a Chinese community almost as large as the Latino community in Los Angeles.

Canada differs from the United States in one important respect. Historically, it has had *two* dominant cultures: French (about 25 percent of the population) and British (roughly 40 percent). People of French ancestry are a large majority of the province of Quebec (where French is the official language) and a large minority of New Brunswick (which is officially bilingual).

Are the dominant values of Canada much the same as those we have described for the United States? Seymour Martin Lipset (1985) found some important differences. The United States declared independence from Great Britain in 1776; Canada formally separated from Great Britain only in 1982. For this reason, Lipset concludes, the dominant culture of Canada lies between that of the United States and Great Britain.

One difference is that the culture of the United States is more individualistic, whereas Canada's is more collective. In the United States, individualism is seen in the historical importance of the cowboy, a self-sufficient type of person, and even outlaws such as Jesse James and Billy the Kid are regarded as heroes because they challenged authority. In Canada, it is the Mountie—Canada's well-known police officer on horseback—who is looked on with great respect.

Politically, people in the United States tend to think that individuals ought to do things for themselves. In Canada, as in Great Britain, there is a strong sense that government should look after the interests of everyone. This is one reason that Canada has a much broader social welfare system (including universal health care) than the United States (the only high-income nation without universal health care). About half of all U.S. households own one or more guns, and the belief that individuals are entitled to own a gun is strongly held by many in this country. In Canada, few households have guns, and government greatly restricts gun ownership, as in Great Britain.

WHAT DO YOU THINK?

1. Why do some Canadians feel that their way of life is overshadowed by that of the United States?
2. Ask your professor to see how many people in your class know the capital city of Canada. Are you surprised by the results of this poll? Why or why not?
3. Why do many people in the United States have little interest in our neighbor nations to the north and south?

Sources: Lipset (1985) and Macionis & Gerber (2005).

troubling patterns, such as racial prejudice and sex discrimination, in each new generation. In addition, in this age of new information technology, business-dominated mass media have the power to manipulate our culture in pursuit of profits.

Our insistence on competitive achievement urges us toward excellence, yet often at the cost of isolating us from one another. Material comforts do make life easy but divert us from close relationships and spiritual strength.

For better and worse, human beings are cultural creatures, just as ants and bees are prisoners of their biology. But there is a crucial difference. Biological instincts create a ready-made world; culture forces us to make choices as we create and re-create our world. No better evidence of this freedom exists than the cultural diversity of our own society and the even greater human diversity around the world.

Learning about this cultural diversity is one goal of sociology; as an example, the Global Sociology box offers some contrasts between the cultures of the United States and Canada. Wherever we may live, the better we understand the workings of the surrounding culture, the better prepared we will be to use the freedom it offers us.

Summary

1. Culture is a way of life shared by members of a society. Several species display limited capacity for culture, but only human beings rely on culture for survival.

2. As the human brain evolved, the first elements of culture appeared some 3 million years ago; culture replaced biological instincts as our species' primary strategy for survival.

3. Culture is built using symbols. Language is the symbolic system by which one generation passes on culture to the next.

4. Values are culturally defined standards of what ought to be; beliefs are statements that people who share a culture hold to be true. Norms, which guide human behavior, are of two kinds: mores, which have great moral significance, and folkways, which are everyday matters of politeness.

5. Culture is shaped by technology. We understand technological development in terms of stages of sociocultural evolution: hunting and gathering, horticulture and pastoralism, agriculture, industry, and the postindustrial information age.

6. High culture refers to patterns that distinguish a society's elites; popular culture includes patterns widespread in a society.

7. There are many dimensions of cultural diversity in the United States. Immigration has brought cultural traits from nations around the world. Our ways of life also include distinctive subcultures as well as countercultures strongly at odds with a conventional way of life. Multiculturalism is an effort to enhance appreciation of cultural diversity.

8. Invention, discovery, and diffusion all generate cultural change. Cultural lag results when some parts of a cultural system change faster than others.

9. Ethnocentrism involves judging others using standards of one's own culture. Cultural relativism is the evaluation of another culture according to its own standards.

10. Global cultural patterns result from the worldwide flow of goods, information, and people.

11. The structural-functional approach views culture as a relatively stable system built on core values. All cultural traits play some part in the ongoing operation of society.

12. The social-conflict approach envisions culture as a dynamic arena of inequality and conflict. Cultural traits benefit some categories of people more than others.

13. Sociobiology studies how evolution shapes the human creation of culture.

14. Culture can limit social possibilities, yet as cultural creatures, we have the capacity to shape and reshape our world to meet our needs and pursue our dreams.

Key Concepts

culture (p. 36) the values, beliefs, behavior, and material objects that together form a people's way of life

society (p. 36) people who interact in a defined territory and share a culture

culture shock (p. 38) personal disorientation when experiencing an unfamiliar way of life

symbol (p. 40) anything that carries a particular meaning recognized by people who share a culture

language (p. 40) a system of symbols that allows people to communicate with one another

cultural transmission (p. 41) the process by which one generation passes culture to the next

Sapir-Whorf thesis (p. 41) the idea that people perceive the world through the cultural lens of language

values (p. 43) culturally defined standards that people use to assess desirability, goodness, and beauty and that serve as broad guidelines for social living

beliefs (p. 43) specific statements that people hold to be true

norms (p. 44) rules and expectations by which a society guides the behavior of its members

mores (p. 44) norms that are widely observed and have great moral significance

folkways (p. 44) norms for routine or casual interaction

technology (p. 44) knowledge that people use to make a way of life in their surroundings

hunting and gathering (p. 45) the use of simple tools to hunt animals and gather vegetation for food

horticulture (p. 45) the use of hand tools to raise crops

pastoralism (p. 45) the domestication of animals

agriculture (p. 46) large-scale cultivation using plows harnessed to animals or more powerful energy sources

industry (p. 46) the production of goods using advanced sources of energy to drive large machinery

high culture (p. 48) cultural patterns that distinguish a society's elite

popular culture (p. 48) cultural patterns that are widespread among a society's population

subculture (p. 48) cultural patterns that set apart some segment of a society's population

multiculturalism (p. 49) an educational program recognizing the cultural diversity of the United States and promoting the equality of all cultural traditions

Eurocentrism (p. 50) the dominance of European (especially English) cultural patterns

Afrocentrism (p. 50) emphasizing and promoting African cultural patterns

counterculture (p. 51) cultural patterns that strongly oppose those widely accepted within a society

cultural integration (p. 51) the close relationships among various elements of a cultural system

cultural lag (p. 51) the fact that some cultural elements change more quickly than others, disrupting a cultural system

ethnocentrism (p. 53) the practice of judging another culture by the standards of one's own culture

cultural relativism (p. 53) the practice of evaluating a culture by its own standards

cultural universals (p. 55) traits that are part of every known culture

sociobiology (p. 56) a theoretical approach that explores ways in which human biology affects how we create culture

CRITICAL-THINKING QUESTIONS

1. In the United States, hot dogs, hamburgers, French fries, and ice cream have long been considered national favorites. What cultural patterns help explain the widespread popularity of these kinds of foods?

2. What cultural lessons do games such as king of the mountain, tag, or keep-away teach our children? What about a schoolroom spelling bee? What cultural values are expressed by children's stories such as *The Little Engine That Could* and popular board games such as Chutes and Ladders, Monopoly, and Risk?

3. To what extent, in your opinion, is a global culture emerging? Do you consider the possibility of a global culture as positive or negative? Why?

4. Do you identify with one or more subcultures? If so, describe each one, pointing out how it differs from the dominant culture.

APPLICATIONS AND EXERCISES

1. Talk to someone who grew up in another country. Discuss how the culture of that society differs from the way of life here. How does the person see U.S. culture differently than you do?

2. Make a list of words with the prefix *self-* ("self-service," "self-esteem," "self-destructive," and so on); there are hundreds of them. What does this fact suggest about our way of life?

3. Watch a Disney video such as *The Little Mermaid, Aladdin, Pocahontas,* or *Mulan.* All of these films share cultural themes, which is one reason for their popularity. In these films, what do young people strive for? What conflicts do they have with their parents? What makes these films especially "American"?

4. Packaged in the back of this textbook is an interactive CD-ROM that offers a variety of video and interactive review materials intended to help you better understand the material covered in this chapter. For this chapter, the CD-ROM contains a relevant clip from *ABC News,* an author's tip video, interactive map animations, an interactive timeline, and flashcards with audio pronunciations of the more difficult words.

 ## SITES TO SEE

http://www.prenhall.com/macionis

Visit the interactive Companion Website™ that accompanies this text. Begin by clicking on the cover of your book. You will find a chapter-by-chapter study guide, practice tests, suggested Web links, and links to other relevant material.

http://www.aaanet.org

Anthropologists study cultures all over the world. This is the Web site for the American Anthropological Association, where you can find out more about this discipline, which is closely related to sociology.

http://www.TheSociologyPage.com (or **http://www.macionis.com**)

View several short videos in which the author describes the excitement and challenges of experiencing other cultures.

http://www.nationalgeographic.com

The National Geographic Society offers information on world cultures, including search engines and a library of maps.

http://www.gorilla.org

What does a 450-pound gorilla say? Anything she wants! The Gorilla Foundation offers a look at the sign language used by a 450-pound gorilla named Koko.

 ## INVESTIGATE WITH RESEARCH NAVIGATOR™

Follow the instructions on page 32 of this text to access the features of **Research Navigator™.** Once at the Web site, enter your Login Name and Password. Then, to use the **Content Select™** database, enter keywords such as "ethnocentrism," "multiculturalism," and "immigration," and the search engine will supply relevant and recent scholarly and popular press publications. Use the *New York Times* **Search-by-Subject Archive** to find recent news articles related to sociology and the **Link Library** feature to find relevant Web links organized by the key terms associated with this chapter.

May 29, 2002

Cultural Divide Over Parental Discipline

By YILU ZHAO

When a Chinese immigrant mother beat her 8-year-old son with a broomstick last month because he had not been doing his homework, she thought she was acting within the bounds of traditional Chinese disciplinary practices. . . .

The next day, when the boy's reddish welts were seen by his teachers, his school in Rego Park, Queens, reported the incident to the Administration for Children's Services, the city agency that protects children. That evening, the police went to the home in Rego Park, and her three children, 6 to 8, were put in foster care. The parents were investigated for child abuse.

. . . The handling of the case touched a nerve in immigrant communities, where many parents have disciplinary ideas that differ from mainstream American views.

"It's something cultural," said David Chen, the executive director of the Chinese-American Planning Council, a nonprofit organization, referring to corporal punishment among Chinese immigrants. "The Chinese believe I hit you because I love you. The harder I hit you, the more I love you."

As more such incidents involving immigrant families occur and are reported in New York's ethnic media, from Korean newspapers to Spanish TV, advocacy groups are joining with public schools to educate immigrants about America's child welfare laws. . . .

When the Coalition for Asian American Children and Families, an advocacy group, printed a brochure to advise parents on child abuse issues, it addressed fundamental cultural beliefs.

"In the Chinese culture, the family is most important," it said. "A Chinese family might expect their child to support the family by doing well in school and obeying his parents.

"In America, the individual is the most important. American society might consider the family's discipline to be too strong, especially if the child is hurt physically or emotionally."

The clash about how to discipline a child is not new in New York City, where half of the population are immigrants and their children. Many immigrant parents have said for years that American parents are too permissive, and that children are disrespectful to elders. . . .

Well-meaning advice can put parents in a predicament, said social workers, since many parents know no other way to discipline children.

Mrs. Liu, a Chinatown resident who would give only her last name, said she had been at a loss after she learned about local laws. "I don't even dare to touch him," said Mrs. Liu, referring to her mischievous 11-year-old son. "Every time I want to hit him, he threatens to call 911 and have me arrested."

Joe Semidei, a director of the Committee for Hispanic Children and Families, said his organization teaches parents other ways to discipline children.

Mr. Semidei said: "Here are some examples: You are not going to the baseball game this weekend if you do this. But you are going to have a new toy if you do that. You negotiate with the kids and lay the boundaries. Here in America, you reinforce good discipline by rewards."

But many immigrant parents see this as bribery. . . . They grow more antagonistic toward the child welfare system when their children encounter negligent foster parents or guardians.

"Some Chinese kids have become addicted to drugs in foster care, and a few teenage girls got pregnant," said Xuejun Chi, who was a university professor in China and is now a social worker at the Y.M.C.A. in Chinatown. "When their parents eventually get them back, they

are so messed up. The parents ask, 'How has the system cared for them any better than I did?'"

Children's Services is willing to become more sensitive to cultural differences. "Our goal is to keep families together, not to break them up," said Kathleen Walsh, a spokeswoman. "But our ultimate goal is to keep the children safe." The agency has formed an immigrant issues group, which meets once every three months, when officials are briefed by immigrant community leaders about their groups' cultural practices.

WHAT DO YOU THINK?

1. Do you think it is ethnocentric to expect the Chinese families described in this article to discipline their children according to cultural norms common in the United States? Or would you support a culturally relativist approach to letting these parents do what seems right to them?

2. Can you cite other cultural patterns brought by immigrants that have come into conflict with established cultural norms? What about such patterns changing U.S. culture?

Adapted from the original article by Yilu Zhao published in *The New York Times* on May 29, 2002. Copyright © 2002 by The New York Times Company. Reprinted with permission.

CHAPTER THREE

Socialization: From Infancy to Old Age

Why is social experience considered
the key to human personality?

What familiar social settings have special importance
to socialization?

How do people's experiences change over the life course?

Socialization is the process by which older members of a society teach ▶ their ways of life to the young. In the south Asian nation of Brunei, these Muslim fathers pass their traditional beliefs on to their sons.

On a cold winter day in 1938, a social worker knocked on the door of a rural Pennsylvania farmhouse. Investigating a case of possible child abuse, the social worker soon discovered a five-year-old girl hidden in a second-floor storage room. The child, whose name was Anna, was wedged into an old chair with her arms tied above her head so she couldn't move. Her clothes were filthy, and her arms and legs were as thin as matchsticks (Davis, 1940:554).

Anna's situation can only be described as tragic. She was born in 1932 to an unmarried, mentally impaired woman of twenty-six who lived with her strict father. Enraged by his daughter's "illegitimate" motherhood, the grandfather did not even want the child in his house. For her first six months, Anna was shuttled among various welfare agencies. But when her mother was no longer able to pay for care, Anna returned to the hostile home of her grandfather.

To lessen the grandfather's anger, Anna's mother kept the child in the storage room. She gave the child just enough milk to keep her alive, but she gave her no loving attention, no smiles, no hugs, no play. There in the dark and lonely world of the storage room she stayed, day after day, month after month, with almost no human contact, for five long years.

When he heard about the discovery of Anna, sociologist Kingsley Davis (1940) immediately went to see the child. He found her being cared for by local authorities at a county home. Davis was appalled by the sight of the emaciated girl, who could not laugh, speak, or even smile. Anna was completely unresponsive, as if alone in an empty world.

Social Experience: The Key to Our Humanity

Here is a horrible case of a child who was completely deprived of social contact. Although physically alive, Anna hardly seemed human. Her plight reveals that without social experience, a human being is incapable of thought, emotion, or meaningful action, seeming more an object than a person.

Sociologists use the term **socialization** to refer to *the lifelong social experience by which individuals develop their human potential and learn culture.* Unlike other living species, whose behavior is biologically set, humans need social experience to learn their culture and survive. Social experience is also the basis of **personality,** *a person's fairly consistent patterns of acting, thinking, and feeling.* We build a personality by internalizing—taking in—our surroundings. But without social experience, as Anna's case shows, personality simply does not develop at all.

HUMAN DEVELOPMENT: NATURE AND NURTURE

Anna's case makes clear the fact that humans depend on others to provide the care needed not only for physical growth but for personality to develop. A century ago, however, people mistakenly believed that humans were born with instincts that determined their personality and behavior.

Charles Darwin's groundbreaking study of evolution, described in Chapter 2 ("Culture"), led people to think that human behavior was instinctive, simply our "nature." Such ideas led to claims that the U.S. economic system reflects "instinctive human competitiveness," that some people are "born criminals," or that women are "naturally" emotional and men are "naturally" more rational (Witkin-Lanoil, 1984).

People trying to understand cultural diversity also misunderstood Darwin's thinking. Centuries of world exploration had taught Western Europeans that people around the world display very different behavior. But Europeans linked these differences to biology rather than culture. It was an easy, although incorrect and very damaging, step to

The personalities we develop depend largely on the environment in which we live. As William Kurelek shows in this painting, *Prairie Childhood*, based on his childhood in the Alberta, Canada, prairies, a young person's life on a farm is often characterized by periods of social isolation and backbreaking work. How would such a boy's personality be likely to differ from that of his wealthy cousin raised in a large city, such as Montreal?

William Kurelek, *Prairie Childhood*. The Estate of William Kurelek and the Isaacs Gallery, Toronto.

claim that members of technologically simple societies were biologically less evolved and therefore less human than their Western counterparts. But this ethnocentric view helped justify colonialism: Why not take advantage of others if they seem not to be as human as you are?

Biological explanations of human behavior came under fire in the twentieth century. Psychologist John B. Watson (1878–1958) developed a theory called *behaviorism,* which held that behavior is not instinctive but learned. People everywhere are equally human, differing only in their cultural patterns. In short, Watson rooted human behavior not in nature but in *nurture.*

Today, social scientists are cautious about describing *any* human behavior as instinctive. This does not mean that biology plays no part in human behavior. Human life, after all, depends on the functioning of the body. We also know that children often share biological traits (such as height and hair color) with their parents and that heredity plays a part in intelligence, musical and artistic aptitude, and personality (such as how one reacts to frustration). However, whether you *realize* an inherited potential depends on your chance to develop it. In fact, unless children use their brains early in life, the brain itself does not fully develop (Goldsmith, 1983; Begley, 1995).

Without denying the importance of nature, then, nurture matters more in shaping human behavior. More precisely, *nurture is our nature.*

SOCIAL ISOLATION

As the opening to this chapter suggests, cutting people off from the social world can be harmful indeed. Researchers can never place human beings in total isolation to study this process. But in the past, they have studied the effects of social isolation on nonhuman primates.

Research with monkeys. In a classic study, psychologists Harry and Margaret Harlow (1962) placed rhesus monkeys, whose behavior is in some ways surprisingly similar to human behavior, in various conditions of social isolation. They found that complete isolation (with adequate nutrition) for even six months seriously disturbed the monkeys' development. When returned to their group, these monkeys were passive, anxious, and fearful.

The Harlows then placed infant rhesus monkeys in cages with an artificial "mother" made of wire mesh with a wooden head and the nipple of a feeding tube where the breast would be. These monkeys also survived but were unable to interact with others when placed in a group.

But monkeys isolated with an artificial "mother" covered with soft terry cloth did better, clinging to her more closely than those with "mothers" of just wire mesh. Because these monkeys showed less developmental damage than the earlier groups, the Harlows concluded that the monkeys benefited from the contact. The experiment confirmed how important it is that adults cradle infants lovingly.

Finally, the Harlows discovered that infant monkeys could recover from as much as three months of isolation. But by about six months, isolation caused irreversible emotional and behavioral damage.

Isolated children.   The rest of Anna's story squares with the Harlows' findings. After her discovery, Anna received extensive social contact and soon showed improvement. When Kingsley Davis (1940) revisited her after ten days, he found her more alert and even smiling with obvious pleasure. Over the next year, Anna made slow but steady progress, showing more interest in other people and gradually learning to walk. After a year and a half, she could feed herself and play with toys.

As the Harlows might have predicted, however, Anna's five years of social isolation had caused permanent damage. At age eight, her mental development was still less than that of a two-year-old. Not until she was almost ten did she begin to use words. Because Anna's mother was mentally retarded, perhaps Anna was similarly challenged. The riddle was never solved, however, because Anna died at age ten of a blood disorder, possibly related to the years of abuse she suffered (Davis, 1940, 1947).

A more recent case of childhood isolation involves a California girl abused by her parents (Curtiss, 1977; Rymer, 1994). From the time she was two, Genie was tied to a potty chair in a dark garage. In 1970, when she was rescued at age thirteen, Genie weighed only fifty-nine pounds and had the

 Learn more about the life of Genie at http://www.pbs.org/wgbh/nova/transcripts/2112gchild.html

mental development of a one-year-old. With intensive treatment, she became physically healthy, but her language ability remains that of a young child. Today Genie lives in a home for developmentally disabled adults.

All evidence points to the crucial role of social experience in forming personality. Human beings can sometimes recover from abuse and isolation. Although it is unclear exactly when, there is a point at which isolation in infancy causes permanent developmental damage.

Understanding Socialization

Socialization is a complex, lifelong process. The following sections highlight the work of six researchers who made lasting contributions to our understanding of human development.

SIGMUND FREUD'S ELEMENTS OF PERSONALITY

 For a biographical sketch of Freud, see the Gallery of Sociologists at http://www.TheSociologyPage.com

Sigmund Freud (1856–1939) lived in Vienna at a time when most Europeans considered human behavior biologically fixed. Trained as a physician, Freud soon turned to the analysis of personality and eventually developed the celebrated theory of psychoanalysis.

Basic needs.   Freud claimed that biology plays a major part in human development, although not in terms of specific instincts as in other species. He theorized that humans have two basic needs or drives. First is a need for bonding, which he called the life instinct, or *eros* (from the Greek god of love). Second, we share an aggressive drive he called the death instinct, or *thanatos* (derived from the Greek word for "death"). According to Freud, these opposing forces, operating at an unconscious level, generate deep inner tension.

Freud's personality model.   Freud combined basic drives and the influence of society into a model of personality with three parts: id, ego, and superego. The **id** (Latin for "it") is *the human being's basic drives,* which are unconscious and demand immediate satisfaction. Rooted in biology, the id is present at birth, making a newborn a bundle of demands for attention, touching, and food. But society opposes the self-centered id, which is why one of the first words a child usually learns is "no."

To avoid frustration, a child must learn to approach the world realistically. This is done through the **ego** (Latin for "I"), which is *a person's conscious efforts to balance innate pleasure-seeking drives with the demands of society.* The ego arises as we gain awareness of our distinct existence and face the fact that we cannot have everything we want.

In the human personality, **superego** (Latin for "above or beyond the ego") is *the cultural values and norms internalized by an individual.* The superego operates as our conscience, telling us *why* we cannot have everything we want. The superego begins to form as a child becomes aware of parental demands and matures as the child comes to understand that everyone's behavior should take account of cultural norms.

To the id-centered child, the world is a bewildering array of physical sensations that bring either pleasure or pain. As the superego develops, however, the child learns the moral concepts of right and wrong. In other words, initially children can feel good only in a physical way, but after three or four years of age, they feel good or bad as they judge their behavior against cultural norms.

The id and the superego remain in conflict, but in a well-adjusted person, the ego manages these opposing forces. If conflicts are not resolved during childhood, they may surface as personality disorders later on.

Culture, in the form of superego, *represses* selfish demands, forcing people to look beyond their own desires. Often the competing demands of self and society result in a compromise Freud called *sublimation,* which changes selfish drives into socially acceptable behavior. For example, marriage makes the satisfaction of sexual urges socially acceptable, and competitive sports are an outlet for aggression.

Critical review. In Freud's time, few people were ready to accept sex as a basic drive. More recent critics charge that Freud's work presents humans in male terms and devalues women (Donovan & Littenberg, 1982). But Freud influenced everyone who later studied human personality. Of special importance to sociology are his ideas that we internalize social norms and that childhood experiences have a lasting impact on our personalities.

JEAN PIAGET'S THEORY OF COGNITIVE DEVELOPMENT

The Swiss psychologist Jean Piaget (1896–1980) studied human *cognition:* how people think and understand. As

To learn more about Piaget and his work, visit http://www. piaget.org

Piaget watched his own three children grow, he wondered not only *what* they knew but *how* they made sense of the world; he went on to identify four stages of cognitive development.

The sensorimotor stage. Stage one is the **sensorimotor stage,** *the level of human development at which individuals experience the world only through their senses.* For about the first two years of life, infants know the world only by touching, tasting, smelling, looking, and listening. "Knowing" to young children amounts to sensory experience.

The preoperational stage. About age two, children enter the **preoperational stage,** *the level of human development at which individuals first use language and other symbols.* Now children begin to think about the world using their imagination. But "pre-op" children attach meanings only to specific experiences and objects. They can identify a special toy, for example, but they cannot describe what *kinds* of toys they like.

Lacking abstract concepts, a child cannot judge size, weight, or volume. In one of his best-known experiments, Piaget placed two identical glasses containing equal amounts of water on a table. He asked several five- and six-year-olds whether the amount in each was the same. They nodded that it was. The children then watched Piaget take one of the glasses and pour its contents into a taller, narrower glass, raising the level of the water. He asked again whether each glass held the same amount. The typical five- or six-year-old now insisted that the taller glass held more water. By about

Why is it that one of the first words children come to understand is "no!"? Sigmund Freud's model of personality suggests that socialization is the process of internalizing cultural values and norms, by which society controls our innate, selfish desires.

age seven, children are able to think more abstractly and realize that the amount of water stays the same.

The concrete operational stage. Next comes the **concrete operational stage,** *the level of human development at which individuals first see causal connections in their surroundings.* Between the ages of seven and eleven, children focus on how and why things happen. In addition, they attach more than one symbol to an event or object. For example, if you say to a child of five, "Today is Wednesday," she might respond, "No, it's my birthday," indicating that she can use just one symbol at a time. But an older child at the concrete operational stage would be able to respond, "Yes, and it's also my birthday."

The formal operational stage. The last step in Piaget's model is the **formal operational stage,** *the level of human development at which individuals think abstractly and critically.* At about age twelve, young people begin to reason abstractly rather than think only of concrete situations. For example, if you ask a child of seven, "What would you like to be when you grow up?" you will get a concrete response such as "a teacher." But most teenagers can consider the question more abstractly and might respond,

"I would like a job that helps others." As they gain the capacity for abstract thought, young people also learn to understand metaphors. Hearing the phrase "A penny for your thoughts" might lead a child to ask for a coin, but a teenager will recognize a gentle invitation to intimacy.

Critical review.   Whereas Freud saw human beings passively torn by opposing forces of biology and culture, Piaget saw the mind as active and creative. In his view, the ability to engage the world unfolded in stages and was the result of both biological maturation and social experience.

But do people in all societies pass through all four of Piaget's stages? In fact, living in a traditional society that changes slowly probably limits the capacity for abstract, critical thought. Even in the United States, perhaps 30 percent of people never reach the formal operational stage (Kohlberg & Gilligan, 1971).

LAWRENCE KOHLBERG'S THEORY OF MORAL DEVELOPMENT

Lawrence Kohlberg (1981) built on Piaget's work to study moral reasoning, that is, how people come to judge situations as right or wrong. Here, again, development of this skill occurs in stages.

Young children who experience the world in terms of pain and pleasure (Piaget's sensorimotor stage) are at the *preconventional* level of moral development. At first, "rightness" amounts to "what feels good to me."

The *conventional* level, Kohlberg's second stage, appears by the teens (corresponding to Piaget's final, formal operational stage). At this point, young people lose some of their selfishness as they learn to define right and wrong in terms of what pleases parents and conforms to cultural norms.

In the final stage of moral development, the *postconventional* level, people move beyond their society's norms to consider abstract ethical principles. As they think about ideas such as liberty, freedom, or justice, they may argue that what is lawful still may not be right.

Critical review.   Like the work of Piaget, Kohlberg's model explains moral development in terms of distinct stages. But whether this model applies to people in all societies remains unclear. Furthermore, many people in the United States apparently never reach the postconventional level of moral reasoning, although exactly why is still an open question.

Another problem with Kohlberg's research is that all his subjects were boys. He committed a common research error, described in Chapter 1 ("Sociology: Perspective, Theory, and Method"), by generalizing the results of male subjects to all people. This problem led a colleague, Carol Gilligan, to investigate how gender affects moral reasoning.

CAROL GILLIGAN'S THEORY OF GENDER AND MORAL DEVELOPMENT

Carol Gilligan (1982) set out to compare the moral development of girls and boys and concluded that the two sexes use different standards of rightness. Males, she claims, have a *justice perspective,* relying on formal rules to define right and wrong. Girls, by contrast, have a *care and responsibility perspective,* judging a situation with an eye toward personal relationships and loyalties. For example, as boys see it, stealing is wrong because it breaks the law. However, girls are more likely to wonder why someone would steal and to be sympathetic toward someone who steals, say, to feed a hungry child.

Kohlberg treats rule-based male reasoning as morally superior to the person-based female perspective. But Gilligan notes that impersonal rules have long governed men's lives in the workplace, whereas personal relationships are more relevant to women's lives as mothers and caregivers. Why, then, Gilligan asks, should we set up male patterns as the standard by which we judge everyone?

Critical review.   Gilligan's work sharpens our understanding of both human development and gender issues in research. Yet the question remains: Does nature or nurture account for the differences between females and males? In Gilligan's view, cultural conditioning is at work. Therefore, we might predict that as more women organize their lives around the workplace, the moral reasoning of women and men will become more similar.

GEORGE HERBERT MEAD'S THEORY OF THE SOCIAL SELF

George Herbert Mead (1863–1931) developed a theory of *social behaviorism* to explain how social experience develops an individual's personality (1962, orig. 1934).

Mead is featured in the Gallery of Sociologists at http://www. TheSociologyPage.com

The self.   Mead's central concept is the **self,** *the part of an individual's personality composed of self-awareness and self-image.* Mead's genius lay in seeing the self as the product of social experience.

First, said Mead, *the self develops only with social experience.* The self is not part of the body and does not exist at birth. Mead rejected the idea that personality is guided by biological drives (as Freud asserted) or even biological maturation (as Piaget claimed). For Mead, self develops only as the individual interacts with others. Without interaction— as we know from isolated children—the body grows, but no self emerges.

Second, Mead explained, *social experience is the exchange of symbols.* Only people use words, a wave of the hand, or a smile to create meaning. We can train a dog using reward and punishment, but the dog attaches no meaning to its actions. By contrast, human beings find meaning in action by imagining people's underlying intentions. In short, a dog responds to *what you do,* but a human responds to *what you have in mind* as you do it. Thus you can train a dog to go to the hallway and bring back an umbrella. But without understanding intention, if the dog cannot find the umbrella, it is incapable of the *human* response: to look for a raincoat instead.

Third, Mead continues, *to understand intention, you must imagine a situation from the other's point of view.* Using symbols, we imagine ourselves in another person's shoes and see ourselves as that person does. This capacity lets us anticipate how others will respond to us even before we act. A simple toss of a ball, for example, requires stepping outside yourself to imagine how the other person will catch your throw. All symbolic interaction, then, involves seeing ourselves as others see us, a process Mead called *taking the role of the other.*

The looking-glass self. In effect, others are a mirror (which people used to call a looking glass) in which we see ourselves. What we think of ourselves, then, depends on how we think others view us. In other words, if we think others see us as clever, we will think of ourselves in the same way. But if we think others see us as clumsy, then that is how we will see ourselves. Charles Horton Cooley (1864–1929) used the phrase **looking-glass self** to mean *a self-image based on how we think others see us.*

The I and the me. Mead's fourth point is that *by taking the role of another, we become self-aware.* The self, then, has two parts. As subject, the self is active and spontaneous. Mead called the subjective side of the self the *I* (the subjective form of the personal pronoun). But the self is also an object, as we imagine ourselves as others see us. Mead called the objective side of the self the *me* (the objective form of the personal pronoun). All social experience has both components: We initiate action (the I-phase of the self), and we continue the action based on how others respond to us (the me-phase of the self).

Stages of development. The key to developing the self, then, is learning to take the role of the other. Infants, with their limited social experience, cannot do this and respond to others only through *imitation.* That is, they mimic behavior without understanding underlying intention, and thus have no self.

George Herbert Mead wrote: "No hard-and-fast line can be drawn between our own selves and the selves of others." The painting *Manyness* by Rimma Gerlovina and Valeriy Gerlovin conveys this important truth. Although we tend to think of ourselves as unique individuals, each person's characteristics develop in an ongoing process of interaction with others.

Rimma Gerlovina and Valeriy Gerlovin, *Manyness,* 1990. © the artists, New City, N.Y.

As children learn to use language and other symbols, the self emerges in the form of *play.* Play involves assuming roles modeled on **significant others,** *people—such as parents—who have special importance for socialization.* Playing "mommy" or "daddy" (often putting themselves, literally, in the shoes of a parent) begins to teach children to imagine the world from a parent's point of view.

Gradually, children learn to take the roles of several others at once. This skill lets them move from simple play (say, playing catch) involving one other person to complex *games* (such as baseball) involving many others. By about age seven, most children have the social experience needed to engage in team sports.

Figure 3–1 on page 70 charts the progression from imitation to play to games. But a final stage in the development of self remains. Games involve dealing with a limited number of other people in one specific situation, but social life demands that we see ourselves in terms of cultural norms as *anyone* else might. Mead used the term **generalized other** to refer to *widespread cultural norms and values we use as a reference in evaluating ourselves.*

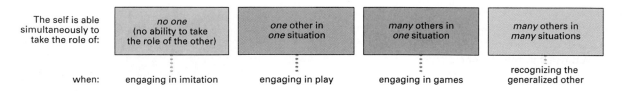

The self is able simultaneously to take the role of:	*no one* (no ability to take the role of the other)	*one* other in *one* situation	*many* others in *one* situation	*many* others in *many* situations
when:	engaging in imitation	engaging in play	engaging in games	recognizing the generalized other

FIGURE 3-1   Building on Social Experience

George Herbert Mead described the development of the self as a process of gaining social experience. That is, the self develops as we expand our capacity to take the role of the other.

As life goes on, the self continues to change along with our social experiences. But no matter how much events change us, we remain creative beings. Thus, Mead concluded, we play a key role in our own socialization.

Critical review.   Mead's work explores the character of social experience itself. In the symbolic interaction of human beings, Mead found the root of both self and society.

Some critics say Mead's view is completely social, allowing no biological element at all. In this, he stands apart from Freud (who identified general human drives) and Piaget (whose stages of development are tied to biological maturation).

Be careful not to confuse Mead's concepts of the *I* and the *me* with Freud's terms *id* and *superego*. Freud rooted the id in the biological organism, whereas Mead rejected any biological element of self (although he never clearly spelled out the origin of the I). Moreover, whereas the superego and id are locked in continual combat, the I and the me work cooperatively together (Meltzer, 1978).

ERIK H. ERIKSON'S EIGHT STAGES OF DEVELOPMENT

Although some analysts (including Freud) point to childhood as the crucial time when personality takes shape, Erik H. Erikson (1902–1994) took a broader view of socialization. He explained that we face challenges throughout the life course (1963, orig. 1950).

Stage 1—Infancy: the challenge of trust (versus mistrust).   Between birth and about eighteen months, infants face the first of life's challenges: to gain a sense of trust that their world is a safe place. Family members play a key role in how any infant meets this challenge.

Stage 2—Toddlerhood: the challenge of autonomy (versus doubt and shame).   The next challenge, up to age three, is to learn skills to cope with the world in a confident way. Failure to gain self-control leads children to doubt their abilities.

Stage 3—Preschool: the challenge of initiative (versus guilt).   Four- and five-year-olds must learn to engage their surroundings—including people outside the family—or experience guilt at having failed to meet the expectations of parents and others.

Stage 4—Preadolescence: the challenge of industriousness (versus inferiority).   Between ages six and thirteen, children enter school, make friends, and strike out on their own more and more. They feel proud of their accomplishments or, at times, fear that they do not measure up.

Stage 5—Adolescence: the challenge of gaining identity (versus confusion).   During the teenage years, young people struggle to establish their own identity. In part, teens identify with others close to them, but they also see themselves as unique. Almost all teens experience some confusion as they struggle to establish an identity.

Stage 6—Young adulthood: the challenge of intimacy (versus isolation).   The challenge for young adults is to form and keep intimate relationships with others. Falling in love (as well as making close friendships) involves balancing the need to bond with the need to have a separate identity.

Stage 7—Middle adulthood: the challenge of making a difference (versus self-absorption).   The challenge of middle age is to contribute to the lives of others in the family, at work, and in the larger world. Failing at this, people become stagnant, trapped in their own limited concerns (think of Scrooge in Dickens's classic novel *A Christmas Carol*).

Stage 8—Old age: the challenge of integrity (versus despair).   Near the end of their lives, people hope to look back on what they have accomplished with a sense of integrity and satisfaction. For those who have been self-absorbed, old age brings only a sense of despair over missed opportunities.

Critical review. Erikson's theory views personality formation as a lifelong process, with success at one stage (say, an infant gaining trust) preparing us to meet the next challenge. However, not everyone faces these challenges in the exact order presented by Erikson. Nor is it clear that failure to meet a challenge at one stage of life means that a person is doomed to fail later on. A broader question, raised earlier in our discussion of Piaget's ideas, is whether people in other cultures and at other times in history would define a successful life in Erikson's terms.

In sum, Erikson's model points out how many factors—including the family and school—shape our personalities. We now take a closer look at these important agents of socialization.

Agents of Socialization

Every social experience we have affects us in some way, large or small. However, several familiar settings have special importance to the socialization process.

THE FAMILY

The family has the greatest impact on socialization. The responsibility for the care of infants, who are totally dependent on others, typically falls on parents and other family members. In addition, at least until children begin school, the family has the job of teaching children skills, values, and beliefs. Even teenagers continue to place their greatest trust in their parents, according to the results of a survey shown in Figure 3–2. Overall, research suggests, nothing is more likely to produce a happy, well-adjusted child than a loving family (Gibbs, 2001b).

Not all family learning results from intentional teaching by parents. Children also learn from the type of environment adults create. Whether children learn to see themselves as strong or weak, smart or stupid, loved or simply tolerated, and, as Erik Erikson suggests, whether they see the world as trustworthy or dangerous, depends largely on their surroundings.

The family also gives children a social position in terms of race, religion, ethnicity, and class. In time, all these elements become part of the child's self-concept.

Research in the United States shows that the class position of parents influences how they raise their children (Ellison, Bartowski, & Segal, 1996). Social class affects not only the amount of money parents have to spend but also what they expect of their children. When asked to pick from a list of traits that are most desirable in a child, lower-class people favor obedience and conformity, whereas well-to-do

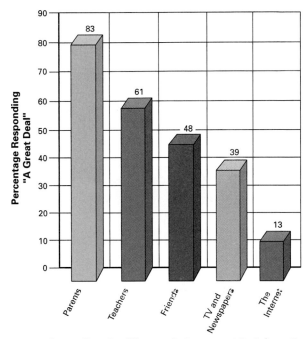

Survey Question: "How much do you trust the information you get from...?"

FIGURE 3-2 Trust among U.S. Teenagers

Source: Data from Okrent (1999).

people select qualities such as good judgment and creativity (NORC, 2003).

Why the difference? Melvin Kohn (1977) explains that people of lower social standing usually have limited education and perform routine jobs under close supervision. Expecting that their children will hold similar positions, they encourage obedience and may even use physical punishment such as spanking to get it. Well-off parents, with more schooling, usually have jobs that demand imagination and provide more personal freedom, and they try to inspire the same qualities in their children. Consciously or not, all parents act in ways that encourage their children to follow in their footsteps.

More well-off parents typically provide their children with an extensive program of leisure activities, including sports, travel, and music lessons. These enrichment activities—far less available to children growing up in low-income families—represent important *cultural capital* that advances learning and creates a sense of confidence that they will succeed later in life (Lareau, 2002).

Sociological research indicates that affluent parents tend to encourage creativity in their children while poor parents tend to foster conformity. While this general difference may be valid, parents at all class levels can and do provide loving support and guidance by simply involving themselves in their children's lives. Henry Ossawa Tanner's painting *The Banjo Lesson* stands as a lasting testament to this process.

Henry Ossawa Tanner, *The Banjo Lesson*, 1893. Oil on canvas. 49" × 35½". Hampton University Museum, Hampton, Virginia.

THE SCHOOL

Schooling enlarges children's social world to include people with different backgrounds. In the process, they learn the importance that society attaches to race and gender. Studies document that at play, children tend to cluster in groups made up of one race and gender. In class, boys are more aggressive, engage in more physical activities, and spend more time outdoors, while girls are more well behaved and often volunteer to help teachers with various housekeeping chores (Lever, 1978; Best, 1983; Jordan & Cowan, 1995). Gender differences continue in college as women tend toward majoring in the arts or humanities and men lean toward economics, the physical sciences, and computing.

Schooling teaches children a wide range of knowledge and skills. But schools informally convey other value lessons, known as the *hidden curriculum.* Activities such as spelling bees and sports, for example, encourage the values of competition and success. Children also receive countless subtle lessons that their own society's way of life is morally good.

School is also most children's first experience with bureaucracy. The school day is based on impersonal rules and a strict time schedule. Not surprisingly, these are also the traits of the large organizations that will employ them later in life.

THE PEER GROUP

By the time they enter school, children have also discovered the **peer group,** *a social group whose members have interests, social position, and age in common.* Unlike the family and the school, the peer group allows children to escape the direct supervision of adults. Among their peers, children learn how to form relationships on their own. Peer groups also offer the chance to discuss interests that adults may not share (such as clothes and popular music) or permit (such as drugs and sex).

It is not surprising, then, that parents express concern about who their children's friends are. In a rapidly changing society, peer groups have great influence, and the attitudes of young and old may be different enough to form a "generation gap." The importance of peer groups typically peaks during adolescence, when young people begin to break away from their families and think of themselves as adults.

Even during adolescence, however, parental influence on children remains strong. Peers may guide short-term choices in dress and music, but parents shape long-term goals such as going to college (Davies & Kandel, 1981).

Finally, any neighborhood or school is a social mosaic of many peer groups. As Chapter 5 ("Groups and Organizations") explains, individuals tend to view their own group in positive terms and put down other groups. Moreover, people are also influenced by peer groups they would like to join, a process sociologists call **anticipatory socialization,** *learning that helps a person achieve a desired position.* In school, for example, young people may copy the styles and slang of a group they hope will accept them. Later in life, a young lawyer may conform to the attitudes and behavior of the firm's partners in order to win approval.

THE MASS MEDIA

 September 29, the Pacific Ocean, nearing Japan. We have been out of sight of land for two weeks now, which makes this ship

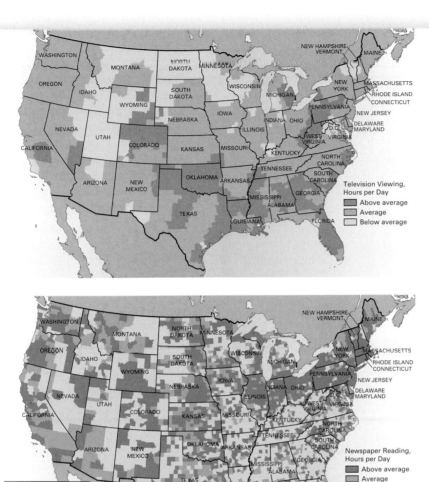

Television Viewing and Newspaper Reading across the United States

The upper map identifies U.S. counties where television watching is above average, average, and below average. The lower map provides comparable information for time devoted to reading newspapers. What do you think accounts for the high level of television viewing across much of the South and in rural West Virginia? Does your theory also account for patterns of newspaper reading?

Sources: *American Demographics* magazine, August 1993, p. 64; *American Demographics* magazine, November 1998, p. 46. Copyright © 1993, 1998 by Primedia. Reprinted with permission of Primedia Business Magazines & Media.

our entire social world. But more than land, many of the students miss television! Tapes of Dawson's Creek are a hot item.

The **mass media** are *the means for delivering impersonal communications to a vast audience.* The term "media" comes from the Latin word for "middle" or "between," suggesting that media connect people. *Mass* media resulted as communication technology (first newspapers, then radio and television) spread information on a mass scale.

In the United States, the mass media have an enormous effect on our attitudes and behavior. Television, introduced in the 1930s, soon became the dominant medium, and 98 percent of U.S. households now have at least one set (by

comparison, just 95 percent of households have telephones). Two of three households also have cable television. As Figure 3–3 on page 74 indicates, the United States has one of the highest rates of television ownership in the world. Some categories of people, including those with lower incomes, spend more time watching TV than others do. National Map 3–1 shows where in the country people are likely to be television watchers and where they are likely to spend their leisure time reading newspapers.

Just how "glued to the tube" are we? Government statistics show that the average household has at least one set turned on for seven hours each day, and people spend almost half their free time watching television. One recent study found that youngsters between the ages of two and

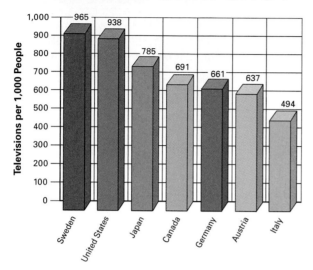

GLOBAL SNAPSHOT

Televisions per 1,000 People

Sweden	965
United States	938
Japan	785
Canada	691
Germany	661
Austria	637
Italy	494

FIGURE 3-3 Television Ownership in Global Perspective

Source: International Telecommunication Union (2003).

eighteen average five-and-one-half hours per day "consuming media," including almost three hours a day watching television and the rest divided between watching videotapes and playing video games (MacPherson, 1999; Cornell, 2000).

Years before children learn to read, television watching is a regular part of their daily routine. As they grow, children spend as many hours in front of a television as they do in school or interacting with their parents. This continues to be so despite research that suggests that television makes children more passive and less likely to use their imaginations (American Psychological Association, 1993; Fellman, 1995).

Comedian Fred Allen once quipped that we call television a "medium" because it is "rarely well done." For a variety of reasons, television (like other media) provokes plenty of criticism. Some liberal critics argue that television shows mirror our society's patterns of social inequality and rarely challenge the status quo. They point out that for most of television's history, racial and ethnic minorities have been invisible or have been included only in stereotypical roles (such as African Americans playing butlers, Asian Americans playing gardeners, or Hispanics playing new immigrants). In recent years, however, minorities have moved

closer to center stage on television. For example, the fall 2002 television lineup featured ten times as many Hispanic actors as ten years before, and those men and women played a far broader range of characters (Lichter & Amundson, 1997; Fetto, 2003).

On the other side of the fence, conservative critics charge that the television and film industries are dominated by a liberal "cultural elite." In recent years, they claim, "politically correct" media have advanced liberal causes including feminism and gay rights (Rothman, Powers, & Rothman, 1993; Goldberg, 2002). On the other hand, the popularity of the Fox Network, which includes Bill O'Reilly, Sean Hannity, Brit Hume, and other more conservative commentators, suggests that people can now find programming consistent with political "spin" from both sides of the political spectrum.

A final issue concerns violence and the mass media. In 1996, the American Medical Association (AMA) declared that violence in the mass media, especially television and films, has reached such a high level that it poses a hazard to the health of this country's people. More recently, a study found a link between aggressive behavior and the amount of time elementary school children spend watching television and using video games (Robinson et al., 2001). The public seems concerned about this issue: Three-fourths of U.S. adults have either walked out of a movie or turned off television because of too much violence. Almost two-thirds of television programs contain violence, and in most scenes, violent characters show no remorse and are not punished (Wilson, 1998).

In 1997, the television industry adopted a rating system for programs. But larger questions remain: Does viewing violent programming hurt people as much as critics say it does? More important, why do the mass media contain so much violence in the first place?

In sum, television and other mass media have enriched our lives with entertaining and educational programming. The media also increase our exposure to other cultures and provoke discussion of current issues. At the same time, the power of the media—especially television—to shape how we think remains highly controversial.

Other spheres of life beyond family, school, peer group, and the media also play a part in social learning. For most people in the United States, these include religious organizations, the workplace, the military, and social clubs. In the end, socialization is not a simple learning process but a complex balancing act as we absorb different information from different sources. In the process of sorting and weighing all the information we encounter, we form our own distinctive personalities and worldviews.

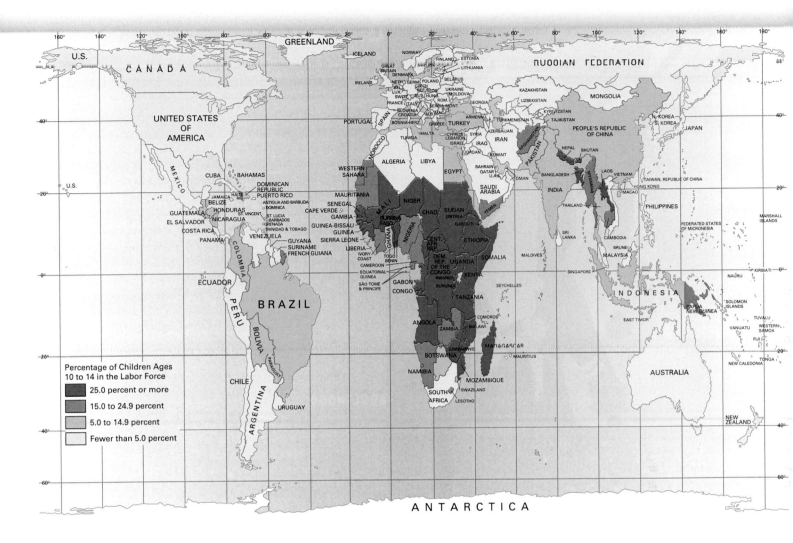

WINDOW ON THE WORLD

GLOBAL MAP 3-1   Child Labor in Global Perspective

Industrialization extends childhood and discourages children from work and other activities considered suitable only for adults. Thus, child labor is uncommon in the United States and other high-income countries. In less economically developed nations of the world, however, children are a vital economic asset, and they typically begin working as soon as they are able.

Source: World Bank (2004) and author estimates; map projection from *Peters Atlas of the World* (1990).

Socialization and the Life Course

Although childhood has special importance to socialization, this process continues throughout our lives. An overview of the life course reveals that our society organizes human experience according to age: childhood, adolescence, adulthood, and old age.

CHILDHOOD

A few years ago, the Nike corporation, maker of popular athletic shoes, came under fire. The company's shoes are made in Taiwan and Indonesia, in many cases by young children who work in factories rather than go to school. In fact, some 250 million of the world's children work, half of them full time, earning about 50 cents an hour (Human Rights Watch, 2004). Global Map 3–1

In recent decades, some people have become concerned that U.S. society is shortening childhood, pushing children to grow up faster and faster. Do films such as *Thirteen,* which show young girls dressing and behaving as if they were much older, encourage a "hurried childhood"? Do you see this as a problem or not?

shows that child labor is most common in the nations of Africa and Asia.

Criticism of Nike springs from the fact that most North Americans think of *childhood*—roughly the first twelve years of life—as a carefree time of learning and play. In fact, explains historian Philippe Ariès (1965), the whole idea of "childhood" is fairly new. In the Middle Ages, children of four or five were treated like adults and expected to take care of themselves.

A Web site that reports on the state of children working as soldiers around the world is http://www.hrw.org/campaigns/crp/index.htm

We defend our idea of childhood because youngsters are biologically immature. But a look back in time and around the world shows that the concept of childhood is grounded not in biology but in culture (LaRossa & Reitzes, 2001). In rich countries, not everyone has to work. In addition, societies such as our own extend childhood to allow time for young people to learn the skills they will need in a high-technology workplace.

ADOLESCENCE

At the same time industrialization created childhood as a distinct stage of life, adolescence emerged as a buffer between childhood and adulthood. We generally link *adolescence,* or the teenage years, with emotional and social turmoil as young people develop their own identities. Again, we are tempted to attribute teenage turbulence to the biological changes of puberty. But this turmoil more correctly reflects cultural inconsistency. For example, the mass media glorify sex, and schools hand out condoms, even as parents urge restraint. Consider, too, that an eighteen-year-old may face the adult duty of going to war but lacks the adult right to drink alcohol. In short, adolescence is a time of social contradictions, when people are no longer children but not yet adults.

As is true of all stages of life, adolescence varies according to social background. Most young people from working-class families move right from high school to the adult world of work and parenting. However, wealthier teens have the resources to attend college and perhaps graduate school, thereby stretching adolescence to the late twenties and even the thirties.

ADULTHOOD

If stages of the life course were based on biological changes, there would be widespread agreement about the timing of *adulthood.* However, as the Critical Thinking box explains, the definition of "growing up" turns out to be quite complex.

Regardless of exactly when it begins, adulthood is the time of life when most accomplishments occur, such as pursuing careers and raising families. Personalities are largely formed, although marked change in a person's environment—such as unemployment, divorce, or serious illness—may result in significant change to the self.

During early adulthood—until about age forty—young adults learn to manage day-to-day affairs for themselves, often juggling conflicting priorities: parents, partner, children, schooling, and work. Women especially try to "do it all," because our culture gives them major responsibility for child rearing and household chores even if they have demanding jobs outside the home.

In middle adulthood—roughly between ages forty and sixty—people sense that their life circumstances are pretty well set. They also become more aware of the fragility of health, which the young typically take for granted. Women who have devoted many years to raising a family can find middle adulthood emotionally trying. As children grow up, they need less attention, and husbands become absorbed in their careers, leaving some women with spaces in their lives that are difficult to fill. Many women who divorce during middle adulthood

CRITICAL THINKING
Are We Grown Up Yet? Defining Adulthood

Are you an adult or still an adolescent? In the United States, when can young people expect to be treated by others as grown up? According to sociologist Tom Smith (2003), there is no one factor that announces the onset of "adulthood." On the contrary, the results of his survey—using a representative sample of 1,398 people over the age of eighteen—suggest that becoming an adult is a gradual process that involves a number of transitions.

According to the survey, the single most important transition in claiming adult standing is the completion of schooling. But other transitions are also important: Smith's respondents linked adult standing to taking on a full-time job, gaining the ability to

support a family financially, no longer living with parents, and finally, marrying and becoming a parent. In other words, almost everyone in the United States regards a person who has done *all* these things as an adult.

At what age are these transitions likely to be completed? On average, according to the respondents in this study, by age twenty-six. But this number masks an important difference based on social class. People who do not attend college (more common among people growing up in lower-income families) typically finish school by about age twenty, and a full-time job, independent living, marriage, and parenthood may follow in a year or two. Those from more privileged backgrounds are likely to attend college

and may even go on to graduate or professional school, delaying the process of becoming an adult for as long as ten years, past the age of thirty.

WHAT DO YOU THINK?

1. Do you consider yourself an adult? At what age did your adulthood begin?
2. Which of the transitions noted here do you consider the most important in becoming an adult? Why?
3. How does this research show that "adulthood" is a socially defined concept rather than a biological stage of life?

Source: Smith (2003).

---

also face serious financial problems (Weitzman, 1985, 1996). For all these reasons, an increasing number of women in middle adulthood return to school and seek new careers.

For everyone, growing older means facing physical decline, a prospect our culture makes more painful for women. Because good looks are considered more important for women, the appearance of wrinkles and graying hair can be traumatic. Men have their own particular difficulties as they grow older. Some must admit that they are never going to reach their career goals. Others realize that the price of career success has been neglect of family or personal health.

OLD AGE

Old age—the later years of adulthood and the final stage of life—begins about the mid-sixties. With people living longer, the elderly population is growing nearly as fast as the U.S. population as a whole. As Figure 3–4 on page 78 shows, about one in eight people is over age sixty-five, and the elderly now outnumber teenagers. By 2030, the number of seniors will double to 71 million, and almost half the country's people will be over forty (U.S. Census Bureau, 2001, 2003).

We can only begin to imagine the full consequences of the "graying of the United States." As more and more people retire from the labor force, the share of nonworking adults—already ten times greater than in 1900—will go up, increasing demand for health care and other social resources. But perhaps most important, elderly people will be more visible in everyday life. In the twenty-first century, the young and the old will interact far more.

The aging of the U.S. population is one focus of **gerontology** (from the Greek word *geron,* meaning "old person"), *the study of aging and the elderly.* Gerontologists study both the physical and social dimensions of growing old.

Aging and biology. For most of our population, gray hair, wrinkles, and declining energy begin in middle age. After about age fifty, bones become more brittle, injuries take longer to heal, and the risks of chronic illnesses (such as arthritis and diabetes) and life-threatening conditions (such as heart disease and cancer) rise steadily. Sensory abilities—taste, sight, touch, smell, and especially hearing—become less sharp with age (Treas, 1995; Metz & Miner, 1998).

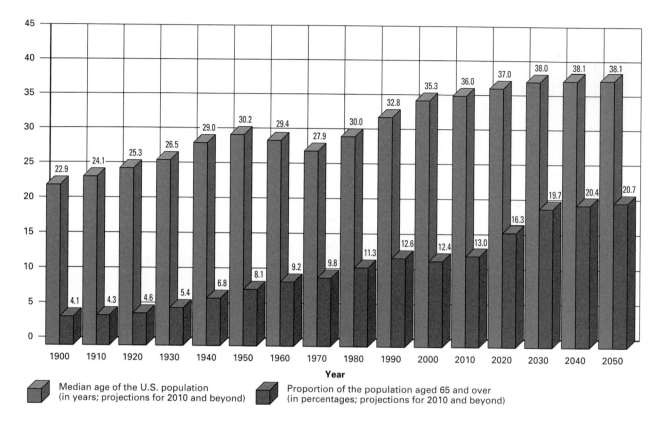

FIGURE 3-4 The Graying of U.S. Society

Source: U.S. Census Bureau (2003).

Even so, most older people are neither disabled nor discouraged by their physical condition. Only one in ten seniors reports trouble walking, and fewer than one in twenty needs care in a hospital or nursing home. Overall, although 27 percent of people over age sixty-five characterize their health as "fair" or "poor," 73 percent consider their overall condition "good" to "excellent." On average, the health of U.S. seniors is steadily improving (Lethbridge-Cejku, Schiller, & Bernadel, 2004).

Aging and culture. Culture shapes how we understand growing old. In low-income countries, old age confers great

For data and graphics on aging around the world, visit http://www.un.org/esa/population/publications/worldageing19502050/

influence and respect because elders control the most land and possess wisdom gained over the course of a lifetime. A preindustrial society, then, usually takes the form of a **gerontocracy,** *a form of social organization in which the elderly have the most wealth, power, and prestige.*

Industrialization lessens the social standing of the elderly. In a more affluent, industrial society, older people typically live apart from their grown children, and rapid social change renders much of what seniors know obsolete, at least from the point of view of the young. A problem of technologically advanced societies, then, is **ageism,** *prejudice and discrimination against older people.*

November 1, approaching Kandy, Sri Lanka. Our little van struggles up the steep mountain incline. Breaks in the lush vegetation offer spectacular views that interrupt our conversation about growing old. "Then there are no old-age homes in your country?" I ask. "In Colombo and other cities, I am sure," our driver responds, "but not many. We are not like you Americans." "And how is that?" I ask, stiffening a bit. His eyes remain fixed on the road: "We would not leave our fathers and mothers to live alone."

The reality of old age is as much a matter of culture as it is of biology. In the United States, being elderly often means being inactive; yet in many other countries of the world, elders often continue many familiar and productive routines.

Not surprisingly, growing old in the United States is challenging. Early in life, advancing in years means taking on new roles and responsibilities. In old age, by contrast, aging means leaving behind roles that have provided social identity and prestige. Removed from familiar work routines, some people view retirement as restful recreation, but others lose their self-worth and suffer outright boredom.

Reaching old age also means living with less income. But today the U.S. elderly population is doing better than ever. In 1960, some 35 percent of the elderly were poor; in 2003, this figure fell to 10.2 percent—less than the poverty rate of 12.5 percent for the population as a whole (U.S. Census Bureau, 2004). A generation ago, old age carried the highest risk of poverty; today, that is true of childhood.

Why the change? Incomes are up over the life course, which helps people save more. In addition, better health allows older people to continue to work for income, and retirees receive more generous pensions. Government programs also help out, with almost half of all government spending now assisting the elderly even as spending on children has remained more or less flat.

Since 1980, on average, seniors have posted a 33 percent increase in income (in constant dollars), whereas the income of people under thirty-five has increased by only 15 percent (U.S. Census Bureau, 2004). A reasonable question, then, is whether we should continue to favor the oldest members of our society and risk slighting the youngest, who now suffer most from poverty.

DEATH AND DYING

Throughout most of human history, low living standards and limited medical technology meant that death, caused most often by disease or accident, came at any stage of life. Today, however, 85 percent of people in the United States die after age fifty-five (Arias et al., 2003).

After observing many dying people, the psychologist Elisabeth Kübler-Ross (1969) described death as an orderly transition involving five distinct stages. Typically, a person first reacts to the prospect of dying with *denial*. The second phase is *anger*, as the person facing death sees it as a gross injustice. Third, anger gives way to *negotiation*, as the person imagines it might be possible to avoid death by striking a bargain with God. The fourth stage, *resignation*, often is accompanied by psychological depression. Finally, a complete adjustment to death requires *acceptance*. At this point, no longer paralyzed by fear and anxiety, the person whose life is ending sets out to make the most of whatever time remains.

As the share of women and men in old age steadily increases, we can expect our culture to become more comfortable with the idea of death. In recent years, for example, people in the United States and elsewhere have been discussing death more openly, and the trend is toward viewing dying as preferable to painful or prolonged suffering. More married couples are taking steps to prepare for death with legal and financial planning; this

DIVERSITY: RACE, CLASS, & GENDER

The Development of Self among High School Students

Adolescence is a time when people are concerned about identity, trying to answer questions such as "Who am I?" and "What should I try to become?" Depending on their race and ethnicity, young people come up with very different answers to these questions.

Grace Kao (2000) investigated the identity and goals of students enrolled in Johnstown High School, a large (3,000-student) school in a Chicago suburb. Johnstown High is considered a good school, with above-average test scores. It is also racially and ethnically diverse: 47 percent of the students are white, 43 percent are African American, 7 percent are Hispanic, and 3 percent are of Asian descent.

Kao interviewed sixty-three Johnstown students, female and male, both individually and in small groups with others of the same race and ethnicity. From these interviews, she documented the importance of racial and ethnic stereotypes in a student's developing sense of self. Kao found wide agreement about these stereotypes.

What are they? White students are seen as hardworking and studious,

motivated by a desire for high grades. African American students are thought to be less studious, either because they are less intelligent or because they don't try as hard. In any case, students see African Americans as at high risk of failure in school. Hispanics are seen as destined for manual occupations—as gardeners or laborers—so doing well in school is less important. Finally, Asian American students are seen as hardworking high achievers, either because they are smarter or because they focus on academics rather than, say, sports.

From her interviews, Kao concludes that most students take these stereotypes very personally. That is, they assume that these beliefs are true and that they will perform in school more or less as the stereotype predicts. One reason for this, Kao explains, is that white, black, Hispanic, and Asian students tend to socialize, both in and out of school, with others like themselves. Another reason is that although students of all racial and ethnic categories say they want to do well in school, they measure success *only in relation to their own category*. To African American

students, in other words, "success" means doing as well as other black students and not flunking out. To Hispanics, "success" means avoiding manual labor and ending up with any job in an office. Whites and Asians define "success" as earning high grades and living up to the high achievement embodied in the stereotype. For all these young people, then, self develops through the lens of how U.S. society defines race and ethnicity.

WHAT DO YOU THINK?

1. Were you aware of racial and ethnic stereotypes, similar to those described here, in your high school? What about your college?
2. Do widespread gender stereotypes affect the performance of women and men in school? What are these stereotypes?
3. What steps can be taken to reduce the damaging effects of racial and ethnic stereotypes?

Source: Kao (2000).

---

openness may ease somewhat the pain of the surviving spouse, a consideration for women who, more often than not, outlive their husbands.

THE LIFE COURSE: PATTERNS AND VARIATIONS

This brief examination of the life course points to two major conclusions. First, although each stage of life reflects the biological process of aging, the life course is largely a social construction. For this reason, people in various societies may experience a stage of life quite differently or, for that matter, not at all. Second, in any society, the stages of

the life course present certain problems and transitions that involve learning something new and, in many cases, unlearning familiar routines.

Societies organize the life course according to age, but other forces such as class, race, ethnicity, and gender also shape people's lives. Thus, the general patterns described in this chapter apply somewhat differently to various categories of people. The Diversity box provides an example of how race and ethnicity can shape the academic performance of high school students.

Finally, people's life experiences also vary depending on when, historically, they are born. A **cohort** is *a category of* *people with a common characteristic, usually their age.* Because members of a particular age cohort generally are influenced by the same economic and cultural trends, they tend to have similar attitudes and values. Women and men born in the late 1940s and 1950s grew up during a period of economic expansion that gave them a sense of optimism. Today's college students, who have grown up in an age of economic uncertainty, are less confident about the future.

Resocialization: Total Institutions

A final type of socialization, experienced by more than 2 million people in the United States at any one time, involves being confined, often against their will, in prisons or mental hospitals. This is the special world of the **total institution,** *a setting in which people are isolated from the rest of society and manipulated by an administrative staff.*

According to Erving Goffman (1961), total institutions have three distinctive characteristics. First, staff members supervise all aspects of daily life, including where residents (often called "inmates") eat, sleep, and work. Second, the environment of a total institution is highly standardized, with institutional food, uniforms, and one set of activities for everyone. Third, rules and schedules dictate when, where, and how inmates perform their daily routines.

The purpose of such rigid routines is **resocialization,** *radically changing an inmate's personality by carefully controlling the environment.* Prisons and mental hospitals physically isolate inmates behind fences, barred windows, and locked doors and control their access to the telephone, mail, and visitors. The institution is the inmate's entire world, making it easier for the staff to bring about lasting change—or at least immediate compliance—in the inmate.

Resocialization is a two-part process. First, the staff breaks down a new inmate's existing identity. For example, an inmate must surrender personal possessions, including clothing and grooming articles used to maintain a distinctive appearance. Instead, the staff provides standard-issue clothes so that everyone looks alike. The staff subjects new inmates to "mortifications of self," which can include searches, medical examinations, head shaving, fingerprinting, and assignment of a serial number. Once inside the walls, individuals also give up their privacy as guards routinely monitor their living quarters.

In the second part of the resocialization process, the staff tries to build a new self in the inmate through a system of rewards and punishments. Having a book to read, watching television, or accessing the Internet may seem like minor pleasures to the outsider, but in the rigid environment

Prisons are one example of a total institution in which inmates dress alike and carry out daily routines under the direct supervision and control of the institutional staff. What do we expect prison to do to young people convicted of crimes? How well do you think prisons do what people expect them to?

of the total institution, gaining these simple privileges can be a powerful motivation to conform. The length of incarceration typically depends on how well the inmate cooperates with the staff.

Total institutions affect people in different ways. Whereas some inmates are considered "rehabilitated" or "recovered," others may change little, and still others may become hostile and bitter. Over a long period of time, living in a rigidly controlled environment can leave some *institutionalized,* without the capacity for independent living.

But what about the rest of us? Does socialization crush our individuality or empower us? The Controversy & Debate box on page 82 takes a closer look at this vital question.

CONTROVERSY & DEBATE

Are We Free within Society?

This chapter stresses one key theme: Society shapes how we think, feel, and act. If this is so, then in what sense are we free? To answer this important question, consider the Muppets, puppet stars of television and film. Watching the antics of Kermit the Frog, Miss Piggy, and the rest of the troupe, we almost believe they are real, not objects animated from backstage. As the sociological perspective points out, human beings are like puppets in that we, too, respond to backstage forces. Society gives us a culture and shapes our lives according to class, race, and gender. In the face of such social constraints, are we puppets, too?

Sociologists speak with many voices when addressing this question. The politically liberal response is that individuals are *not* free of society; in fact, as social creatures, we never could be. But if we are condemned to live in a society with power over us, it is important to do what we can to make our home as just as possible. The right actions would include working to lessen class differences and other barriers to opportunity for minorities, including women. Conservatives argue that we *are* free because society can never dictate our dreams. Our history as a nation, right from the revolutionary act that led to its founding, is one story after another of individuals pursuing and achieving personal goals despite great odds.

Both attitudes are included in George Herbert Mead's analysis of socialization. Mead recognized that society makes demands on us, sometimes setting itself before us and limiting our options. But he also reminded us that human beings are spontaneous and creative, capable of acting on society and bringing about change. Mead noted the power of society while still affirming the human capacity to evaluate, criticize, and ultimately choose and change.

In the end, we may resemble puppets, but only on the surface. A crucial difference is that we can stop and look up at the "strings" that animate much of our action, and even yank on them defiantly (Berger, 1963:176). If our pull is persistent and powerful enough, we may accomplish more than we might imagine. As anthropologist Margaret Mead once mused, "Do not make the mistake of thinking that concerned people cannot change the world; it's the only thing that ever has."

CONTINUE THE DEBATE . . .

1. Do you think our society offers more freedom to males than to females? Why or why not?
2. Are some of the world's people more free than others? Compare modern, high-income countries with traditional, low-income nations.
3. How does an understanding of sociology increase your freedom?

SUMMARY

1. Socialization is the way individuals develop their humanity and particular identities. Through socialization, one generation passes on culture to the next.

2. A century ago, people thought that most human behavior was guided by biological instinct. Today, we recognize that human behavior results mostly from nurture rather than nature.

3. The permanently damaging effects of social isolation reveal that social experience is essential to human development.

4. Sigmund Freud's model of human personality has three parts. The id expresses innate human needs or drives (the life and death instincts); the superego represents internalized cultural values and norms; the ego resolves competition between the demands of the id and the restraints of the superego.

5. Jean Piaget believed that human development reflects both biological maturation and increasing social experience. He

identified four stages of cognitive development: sensorimotor, preoperational, concrete operational, and formal operational.

6. Lawrence Kohlberg applied Piaget's approach to moral development. Individuals first judge rightness in preconventional terms, according to their individual needs. Next, conventional moral reasoning takes account of parents' attitudes and cultural norms. Finally, postconventional moral reasoning allows people to criticize society itself.

7. Carol Gilligan discovered that males rely on abstract standards of rightness, whereas females look at the effect of decisions on interpersonal relationships.

8. To George Herbert Mead, social experience generates the self, which he characterized as partly autonomous (the I) and partly guided by society (the me). Infants engage in imitation; children engage in play and games and eventually recognize the "generalized other."

9. Charles Horton Cooley used the term "looking-glass self" to explain that we see ourselves as we imagine others see us.

10. Erik H. Erikson identified challenges that individuals face at eight stages of life from infancy to old age.

11. Usually the first setting of socialization, the family is the greatest influence on a child's attitudes and behavior.

12. Schools expose children to greater social diversity and introduce them to impersonal performance evaluations in the form of testing.

13. Peer groups free children from adult supervision and take on special significance during adolescence.

14. The mass media, especially television, also shape the socialization process. The average U.S. child spends as much time watching television as attending school or interacting with parents.

15. Each stage of the life course, from childhood to old age, is socially constructed in ways that vary from society to society.

16. People in high-income countries typically fend off death until old age. Accepting death is part of socialization for older adults.

17. Total institutions such as prisons and mental hospitals try to resocialize inmates—that is, to radically change their personalities.

18. Socialization demonstrates the power of society to shape our thoughts, feelings, and actions. Yet as humans, we have the ability to act back, shaping both ourselves and our social world.

KEY CONCEPTS

socialization (p. 64) the lifelong social experience by which individuals develop their human potential and learn culture

personality (p. 64) a person's fairly consistent patterns of acting, thinking, and feeling

id (p. 66) Freud's term for the human being's basic drives

ego (p. 66) Freud's term for a person's conscious efforts to balance innate pleasure-seeking drives with the demands of society

superego (p. 66) Freud's term for the cultural values and norms internalized by an individual

sensorimotor stage (p. 67) Piaget's term for the level of human development at which individuals experience the world only through their senses

preoperational stage (p. 67) Piaget's term for the level of human development at which individuals first use language and other symbols

concrete operational stage (p. 67) Piaget's term for the level of human development at which individuals first see causal connections in their surroundings

formal operational stage (p. 67) Piaget's term for the level of human development at which individuals think abstractly and critically

self (p. 68) George Herbert Mead's term for the part of an individual's personality composed of self-awareness and self-image

looking-glass self (p. 69) Charles Horton Cooley's term for a self-image based on how we think others see us

significant others (p. 69) people—such as parents—who have special importance for socialization

generalized other (p. 69) Mead's term for widespread cultural norms and values we use as a reference in evaluating ourselves

peer group (p. 72) a social group whose members have interests, social position, and age in common

anticipatory socialization (p. 72) learning that helps a person achieve a desired position

mass media (p. 73) the means for delivering impersonal communications to a vast audience

gerontology (p. 77) the study of aging and the elderly

gerontocracy (p. 78) a form of social organization in which the elderly have the most wealth, power, and prestige

ageism (p. 78) prejudice and discrimination against older people

cohort (p. 80) a category of people with a common characteristic, usually their age

total institution (p. 81) a setting in which people are isolated from the rest of society and manipulated by an administrative staff

resocialization (p. 81) radically changing an inmate's personality by carefully controlling the environment

CRITICAL-THINKING QUESTIONS

1. What do cases of social isolation teach us about the importance of social experience to human beings?

2. State the two sides of the "nature-nurture" debate. In what sense are human nature and nurture not opposed to each other?

3. We have all seen very young children place their hands in front of their faces and exclaim, "You can't see me!" They assume that if they cannot see you, you cannot see them. What does this behavior suggest about a young child's ability to "take the role of the other"? Should a parent expect a young child to "see things from *my* point of view"?

4. What are the common themes in the ideas of Freud, Piaget, Kohlberg, Gilligan, Mead, and Erikson? In what ways do their theories differ?

APPLICATIONS AND EXERCISES

1. Working with several members of your sociology class, gather data by asking several classmates and friends to name traits they consider elements of "human nature." Then compare notes and discuss the extent to which these traits are the product of nature or nurture.

2. Find a copy of the book or film *Lord of the Flies*, a tale by William Golding based on a Freudian model of personality. Jack (and his hunters) represent the power of the id; Piggy consistently opposes them as the superego; Ralph stands between the two as the ego, the voice of reason. Golding was inspired to write the book after participating in the bloody D-Day landing in France during World War II. Do you agree with his belief that violence is part of human nature?

3. Make a list of the personality traits you think characterize you. If you have the courage, ask several others who know you well to make similar lists about you, and compare them. Can you explain the origin of the traits on these lists?

4. Watch several hours of prime-time programming on network or cable television. Keep track of all the violence you see. Assign each program a "YIP rating," for the number of *years in prison* a person would serve for committing all the violent acts you witness (Fobes, 1996). On the basis of observing this small and unrepresentative sample of programs, what are your conclusions?

5. Packaged in the back of this new textbook is an interactive CD-ROM that offers a variety of video and interactive review materials intended to help you better understand the material covered in this chapter. For this chapter, the CD-ROM contains a relevant clip from *ABC News*, an author's tip video, interactive map animations, an interactive timeline, and flashcards with audio pronunciations of the more difficult words.

 ## SITES TO SEE

http://www.prenhall.com/macionis

Visit the interactive Companion Website™ that accompanies this text. Begin by clicking on the cover of your book. You will find a chapter-by-chapter study guide, practice tests, suggested Web links, and links to other relevant material.

http://www.TheSociologyPage.com (or **http://www.macionis.com**)

At the author's Web site, you can find brief biographies of George Herbert Mead, Charles Horton Cooley, and other sociologists.

http://www.freud-museum.at/

Visit the Sigmund Freud museum of Vienna, Austria, at this site.

http://www.nd.edu/~rbarger/kohlberg.html

This Web site is dedicated to the ideas and research of Lawrence Kohlberg.

http://www.prenticehall.ca/macionis/massmedia.html

An online chapter on the mass media is available at the Web site for Macionis Canadian texts.

 ## INVESTIGATE WITH RESEARCH NAVIGATOR™

Follow the instructions on page 32 of this text to access the features of **Research Navigator™.** Once at the Web site, enter your Login Name and Password. Then, to use the **Content Select™** database, enter keywords such as "Sigmund Freud," "childhood," and "mass media," and the search engine will supply relevant and recent scholarly and popular press publications. Use the *New York Times* **Search-by-Subject Archive** to find recent news articles related to sociology and the **Link Library** feature to find relevant Web links organized by the key terms associated with this chapter.

October 20, 2003

Elderly Immigrants Embrace Nursing Homes

SEATTLE, Wash.—The weekly activities at a retirement home here include bingo, shuffleboard and "ice cream social with shoulder massage." But also listed on the crowded schedule are Howa Kai (a Japanese Buddhist church service), rummi kub (a Japanese version of gin rummy played with plastic tiles), shuji (calligraphy) and kokoro kai (a program held three times a week and loosely translated as "a meeting of hearts and minds").

Nikkei Manor, where 46 Japanese-Americans are spending their old age, is one of a growing number of assisted-living facilities and nursing homes across the nation that cater to first- and second-generation elderly immigrants. It is a fast-growing population that has begun to embrace the very American tradition of living the last years with peers, not family. That phenomenon is driven by two-career families that have little time to care for their parents, increasing wealth for some immigrant populations and gradual acceptance of a lifestyle that was unheard of a generation ago. . . .

For many immigrants, and their children, the move into nursing homes or assisted-living facilities runs counter to deeply held beliefs about elders and family. And for some, experts on elderly immigrants say, the decision to send a parent away is clouded with shame and ambivalence.

Still, places like Nikkei Manor, where miso soup, soba noodles, red ginger and dark-roasted tea are staples of the daily lunch and dinner menus, are sprouting up at a rapid pace, from Seattle to the Lower East Side of Manhattan, signaling a major shift in how immigrants in this country care for their elders. . . .

Immigrant groups that have been here the longest, like the Japanese, are the most likely to accept living in an assisted-living facility, according to Namkee G. Choi, a gerontologist and professor of social work at the University of Texas, who specializes in elderly immigrants. . . .

Dr. Choi. . . said that . . . Hispanic immigrants have been more [reluctant]. . . . "Latinos tend to hold on and avoid doing that," said Maria Martinez-Montes, outreach coordinator for On Lok Senior Health Services, a federally financed program in San Francisco that provides medical care and social services to elderly immigrants, allowing them to remain in their homes.

"In my eyes, I would never put my mom in a nursing home, ever," Ms. Martinez-Montes said. "It would kill me. It would totally kill me. I would not sleep, and it was the same with my grandmother."

There is also the question of what the elderly and their children can afford. Experts say Asian immigrants, particularly those who have been here longest, tend to have a stronger financial base than newer immigrants.

The newer Hispanic immigrants are likely to be among the working poor, so they and their children may not be able to afford the high cost . . ., Dr. Choi said.

While many of the assisted-living facilities accept Medicaid clients, and under federal law cannot discriminate based on race if they do accept them, some immigrants who do not have legal status or who face language barriers or other obstacles to enrolling in Medicaid would probably not seek out an assisted-living facility or a nursing home, even if it were culturally acceptable.

The type of care provided at assisted-living facilities like Nikkei Manor is expensive. At Nikkei Manor, where the residents live in either studio or one-bedroom apartments, the cost is $2,700 monthly. That is relatively inexpensive compared with some other assisted-living facilities, which can run residents as much as $10,000 a month. . . .

As much as many children feel pressure to take care of their parents, many elderly parents fear being a burden on their busy children and spending too much time alone. . . .

Helen Kubo, 92, . . . moved into Nikkei Manor soon after it opened in 1998, with her husband, Frank, who died two months ago. She was born in the United States but spent much of her childhood in Japan, where . . . sending elderly parents into either an assisted-living center or a nursing home was unheard of, she said.

"We were taught to look after the parents," Mrs. Kubo said. . . . "We were taught to be good to our parents. But I like it here. Better than with family. It's more free."

She added: "We're all getting old together, anyway. We're lucky this place exists."

WHAT DO YOU THINK?

1. Why are more elderly immigrants spending their old age in nursing homes or other assisted living facilities? Do you consider this trend to be good or bad? Why?

2. What are advantages and disadvantages of spending old age in the company of peers rather than family? Who is advantaged and disadvantaged?

Adapted from the original article published in *The New York Times* on October 20, 2003. Copyright ©2003 by The New York Times Company. Reprinted with permission.

CHAPTER FOUR

Social Interaction in Everyday Life

How do we create reality in our face-to-face interactions?

Why do employers try to control their workers' feelings as well as their on-the-job behavior?

What are the elements that make something funny?

Sociology points to the many rules that guide behavior in everyday situations. This waiter ▶ respectfully presents food to first-class passengers traveling on the Orient Express railroad train.

arold and Sybil are late for their visit to another couple's home in an unfamiliar area near Fort Lauderdale, Florida. For the last twenty minutes, they have traveled in circles, searching in vain for Coconut Palm Road. Harold, gripping the wheel ever more tightly, is doing a slow burn. Sybil, sitting next to him, looks straight ahead, afraid to utter a word (Tannen, 1990:62).

Harold and Sybil are lost in more ways than one: They are unable to understand why they are growing angry at their situation and at each other. Like most men, Harold cannot tolerate getting lost, and the longer he drives around, the more incompetent he feels. Sybil cannot understand why Harold does not pull over and ask someone where Coconut Palm Road is. If she were driving, she thinks to herself, they would already have arrived and would now be comfortably settled in with their friends.

Why don't men like to ask for directions? Because men value their independence, they are uncomfortable asking for help (and also reluctant to accept it). To ask someone for assistance is the same as saying, "You know something I don't." If it takes Harold a few more minutes to find Coconut Palm Road on his own—and keep his self-respect in the process—he thinks it's a good bargain.

Women are more attuned to others and strive for connectedness. From Sybil's point of view, asking for help is right because sharing information reinforces social bonds. Asking for directions seems as natural to her as searching on his own is to Harold. Obviously, getting lost is sure to create conflict as long as neither one understands the other's point of view.

Such everyday social patterns are the focus of this chapter. The central concept is **social interaction,** *the process by which people act and react in relation to others.* We begin by presenting the rules and building blocks of common experience and then explore the almost magical way in which face-to-face interaction creates the reality in which we live.

Social Structure: A Guide to Everyday Living

October 21, Ho Chi Minh City, Vietnam. This morning we leave the ship and make our way along the docks toward the center of Ho Chi Minh City, known to an earlier generation as Saigon. Government security officers wave us through the heavy iron gates. Pressed against the fence are dozens of men who operate cyclos (bicycles that push a small carriage attached to the front), the Vietnamese version of taxicabs. We wave them off but spend the next twenty minutes shaking our heads at several persistent drivers who pedal alongside, pleading for our business. The pressure is uncomfortable. We decide to cross the street but realize suddenly that there are no stop signs or signal lights, and the street is an unbroken stream of bicycles, cyclos, motorbikes, and small trucks. The locals don't bat an eye; they just walk at a steady pace across the street, parting waves of vehicles that immediately close in again behind them. Walk right into traffic? With our small children on our backs? Yup, we did it; that's the way it works in Vietnam.

Members of every society rely on social structure to make sense out of daily situations. As one family's introduction to the streets of Vietnam suggests, the world can be disorienting—even frightening—when society's rules are unclear. We turn now to other building blocks of our daily lives.

 For a short video ("Sociology and Cultural Relativism") on the difficulty of traveling to unfamiliar places, go to http://www.TheSociologyPage.com

Status

One building block of social organization is **status,** *a social position that a person holds.* In everyday use, the word "status" generally refers to "prestige," as when a college president is said to have more "status" than a newly hired assistant professor. But sociologically speaking, both "president" and "professor" are statuses, or positions, within the collegiate organization.

Status is part of our social identity and defines our relationships to others. In the college classroom, for example, professors and students have distinct, well-defined responsibilities. As George Simmel (1950:307, orig. 1902), one of sociology's founders, put it, "The first condition of having to deal with somebody . . . is knowing with *whom* one has to deal."

Each of us holds many statuses at once. The term **status set** refers to *all the statuses a person holds at a given time.* A teenage girl is a daughter to her parents, a sister to her brother, a student at her school, and a goalie on her hockey team.

Status sets also change over the life course. A child turns into a parent, a student becomes a lawyer, and people marry to become husbands and wives, sometimes becoming single again as a result of divorce or death. Joining an organization or finding a job enlarges our status set; retirement or withdrawing from activities makes it smaller. Over a lifetime, people gain and lose dozens of statuses.

ASCRIBED AND ACHIEVED STATUS

Sociologists analyze statuses in terms of how people attain them. An **ascribed status** is *a social position a person receives at birth or takes on involuntarily later in life.* Examples of ascribed statuses are being a daughter, a Cuban, a teenager, or a widower. Ascribed statuses are matters about which people have little or no choice.

By contrast, an **achieved status** refers to *a social position a person takes on voluntarily that reflects personal ability and effort.* Examples of achieved statuses are being an honor student, an Olympic athlete, a spouse, a computer programmer, or a thief.

In practice, of course, most statuses involve a combination of ascription and achievement. That is, people's ascribed statuses influence the statuses they achieve. People who achieve the status of lawyer, for example, are likely to share the ascribed trait of having been born into well-off families. By the same token, many less desirable statuses, such as criminal, drug addict, or unemployed worker, are more easily achieved by people born into poverty.

In any rigidly ranked setting, no interaction can proceed until people assess each other's social standing. Thus, military personnel wear clear insignia to designate their level of authority. Don't we size up one another in much the same way in routine interactions, noting a person's rough age, quality of clothing, and manner for clues about social position?

MASTER STATUS

Some statuses matter more than others. A **master status** is *a status that has special importance for social identity, often shaping a person's entire life.* For most people, a job is a master status because it reveals a great deal about social background, education, and income. In a few cases, a person's name is a master status; being a "Bush" or a "Kennedy" attracts attention and creates opportunities.

A master status can be negative as well as positive. Consider serious illness. Sometimes people, even lifelong friends, avoid cancer patients or people with acquired immune deficiency syndrome (AIDS) because of their illness. Most societies of the world also limit opportunities for women, whatever their abilities, making gender a master status (Webster & Hysom, 1998).

If people see an individual in terms of a physical disability, it can become a master status. As one young woman living in Oklahoma, who is a wife and a mother and is blind, puts it, "Most people don't expect handicapped people to grow up, they are always supposed to be children. . . . You aren't supposed to date, you aren't supposed to have a job, somehow you're just supposed to disappear" (Orlansky & Heward, 1981).

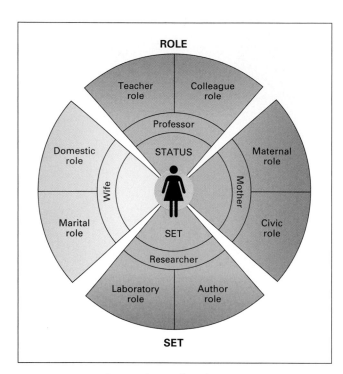

ROLE

Teacher role

Colleague role

Professor

Domestic role

STATUS

Wife

Maternal role

Marital role

Mother

Civic role

SET

Researcher

Laboratory role

Author role

SET

FIGURE 4–1 Status Set and Role Set

Role

A second building block of social interaction is **role,** *behavior expected of someone who holds a particular status.* A person *holds* a status and *performs* a role (Linton, 1937b). For example, holding the status of student leads you to perform the role of attending classes and completing assignments and, more broadly, devoting much of your time to personal growth through academic study.

Both statuses and roles vary by culture. In the United States, the status "uncle" refers to a brother of either mother or father; in Vietnam, however, the word for "uncle" is different when referring to the mother's or father's side of the family, and the two men have different responsibilities. In every society, actual role performance varies according to a person's unique personality, although some societies permit more individual expression than others.

Robert Merton (1968) introduced the term **role set** to identify *a number of roles attached to a single status.* Because we hold more than one status at a time—a status set—everyday life is a mix of many roles.

Figure 4–1 shows four statuses of one person, with each status linked to a different role set. First, as a professor, this woman interacts with students (the teacher role) and other

academics (the colleague role). Second, as a researcher, she gathers data (the laboratory role) that lead to publications (the author role). Third, the woman holds the status of "wife," with a marital role (such as confidante and sexual partner) toward her husband, with whom she shares a domestic role toward the household. Fourth, she holds the status of "mother," with routine responsibilities for her children (the maternal role) as well as their school and other organizations (the civic role).

A global perspective shows us that the roles people use to define their lives differ from society to society. In low-income countries, most people work in farming or factories; high-income nations offer a far greater range of job choices. Another dimension of difference is housework. As Global Map 4–1 shows, especially in poor nations of the world, housework falls heavily on women.

ROLE CONFLICT AND ROLE STRAIN

People in modern, high-income countries juggle many responsibilities demanded by their various statuses and roles. As most mothers can testify, both parenting and working outside the home are physically and emotionally draining. Sociologists thus recognize **role conflict** as *conflict among the roles corresponding to two or more statuses.*

Even roles linked to a single status can make competing demands on us. **Role strain** is *tension among the roles connected to a single status.* A plant supervisor may enjoy being friendly with other workers. At the same time, however, he has production goals and must maintain the personal distance needed to evaluate his staff. In short, performing the roles of even a single status can be a balancing act (Gigliotti & Huff, 1995).

One strategy for minimizing role conflict is separating parts of our lives so that we perform roles for one status at one time and place and carry out roles for another status in a completely different setting. A familiar example of this is deciding to "leave the job at work" before heading home to the family.

ROLE EXIT

After she left the life of a Catholic nun to become a university sociologist, Helen Rose Fuchs Ebaugh (1988) began to study *role exit,* the process by which people disengage from important social roles. In studying a range of "exes," including ex-nuns, ex-doctors, ex-husbands, and ex-alcoholics, Ebaugh saw a pattern in the process of becoming an "ex."

According to Ebaugh, the process begins as people come to doubt their ability to continue in a certain role. As

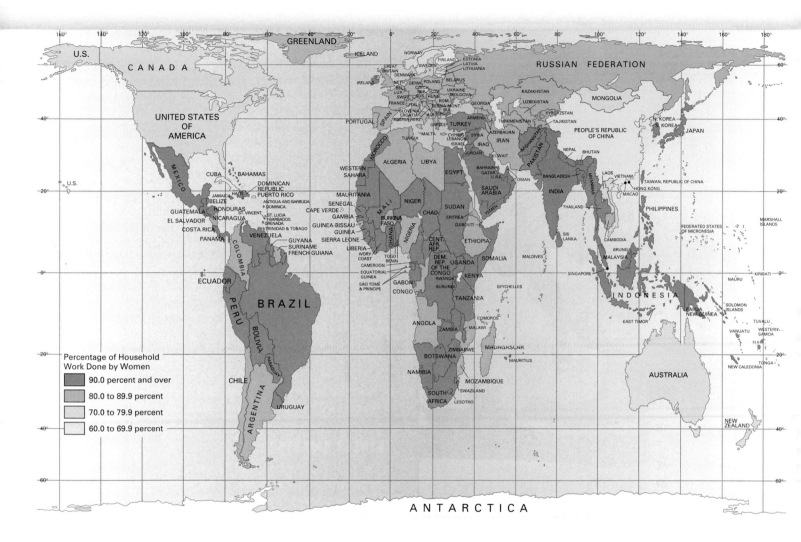

Percentage of Household Work Done by Women	
	90.0 percent and over
	80.0 to 89.9 percent
	70.0 to 79.9 percent
	60.0 to 69.9 percent

WINDOW ON THE WORLD

GLOBAL MAP 4–1 Housework in Global Perspective

Throughout the world, housework is a major part of women's routines and identities. This is especially true in poor societies of Latin America, Africa, and Asia, where women are not generally in the paid labor force. But our society also defines housework and child care as "feminine" activities, even though a majority of U.S. women work outside the home.

Source: *Peters Atlas of the World* (1990); updated by the author.

they imagine alternative roles, they ultimately reach a tipping point when they decide to pursue a new life. Even at this point, however, a past role can continue to influence their lives. "Exes" carry with them a self-image shaped by an earlier role, which can interfere with building a new sense of self. For example, an ex-nun may hesitate to wear stylish clothing and makeup.

"Exes" must also rebuild relationships with people who knew them in their earlier life. Learning new social skills is another challenge. For example, Ebaugh reports, ex-nuns who enter the dating scene after decades devoted to religious life are often startled to learn that today's sexual norms are vastly different from those they knew when they were teenagers.

Flirting is an everyday experience in reality construction. Each person offers information to the other and hints at romantic interest. Yet the interaction proceeds with a tentative and often humorous air so that either individual can withdraw at any time without further obligation.

The Social Construction of Reality

In 1917, the Italian playwright Luigi Pirandello wrote a play titled *The Pleasure of Honesty,* about a character named Angelo Baldovino, a brilliant man with a checkered past. Baldovino enters the fashionable home of the Renni family and introduces himself in a peculiar way:

> Inevitably we construct ourselves. Let me explain. I enter this house and immediately I become what I have to become, what I can become: I construct myself. That is, I present myself to you in a form suitable to the

relationship I wish to achieve with you. And, of course, you do the same with me. (1962:157–58)

Baldovino suggests that although behavior is guided by status and role, we have considerable ability to shape what happens from moment to moment. In other words, "reality" is not as fixed as we may think.

The phrase **social construction of reality** describes *the process by which people creatively shape reality through social interaction.* This idea is the familiar foundation of the symbolic-interaction approach, described in Chapter 1 ("Sociology: Perspective, Theory, and Method"). As Baldovino's remark suggests, quite a bit of "reality" remains unclear in everyone's minds, especially in unfamiliar situations. As we present ourselves in terms that suit the setting and our purposes, and as others do the same, reality emerges.

Social interaction, then, is a complex negotiation of reality. Most everyday situations involve at least some agreement about what's going on, but participants' perceptions of events are based on their different interests and intentions.

Our very choice of words is one way we put a "spin" on events. The Applying Sociology box provides examples of language used by the military to create (or conceal?) reality.

"STREET SMARTS"

What people commonly call "street smarts" is actually a form of constructing reality. In his autobiography, *Down These Mean Streets,* Piri Thomas remembers moving to a new apartment in Spanish Harlem. Returning home one evening, young Piri found himself cut off by Waneko, the leader of the local street gang, who was flanked by a dozen others.

> "Whatta ya say, Mr. Johnny Gringo," drawled Waneko.
> *Think man,* I told myself, *think your way out of a stomping. Make it good.* "I hear you 104th Street coolies are supposed to have heart," I said. "I don't know this for sure. You know there's a lot of streets where a whole 'click' is made out of punks who can't fight one guy unless they all jump him for the stomp." I hoped this would push Waneko into giving me a fair one. His expression didn't change.
> "Maybe we don't look at it that way."
> *Crazy, man,* I cheer inwardly, *the* cabron *is falling into my setup.* . . . "I wasn't talking to you," I said. "Where I come from, the pres is president 'cause he got heart when it comes to dealing."
> Waneko was starting to look uneasy. He had bit on my worm and felt like a sucker fish. His boys were now light on me. They were no longer so much interested in stomping me as seeing the outcome between Waneko and me. "Yeah," was his reply. . . .

APPLYING SOCIOLOGY

The "Spin" Game: Choosing Our Words Carefully

Military organizations choose words carefully to hide the horrors of war and make military action seem necessary and good. William Lutz, an English professor at Rutgers University, collected examples of language used by U.S. military officers. Read the military terminology and the straight-talk translations in the shaded box. How do these terms put a "spin" on reality?

Military Language	Everyday Meaning
Incontinent ordnance	Bombs or shells that miss their targets and hit civilians
Area denial weapons	Cluster bombs that kill or destroy everything within a particular area
Collateral damage	Unintended death, injury, and destruction
Coercive potential	The capacity of bombs and shells to kill or injure the enemy
Suppressing assets	Reducing the enemy's ability to fight by killing people and destroying equipment
Ballistically induced aperture	Bullet hole
Scenario-dependent postcrisis environment	Whether we win or lose

WHAT DO YOU THINK?

1. Why, in your opinion, does the military "spin" reality in this way? Do you approve of this practice?
2. What does this example suggest about the role of power in the construction of reality? Do large organizations have the power to shape the reality experienced by individuals?
3. Can you think of another organization that shapes the reality we experience? How does it do so?

I knew I'd won. Sure, I'd have to fight; but one guy, not ten or fifteen. If I lost, I might still get stomped, and if I won I might get stomped. I took care of this with my next sentence. "I don't know you or your boys," I said, "but they look cool to me. They don't feature as punks."

I had left him out purposely when I said "they." Now his boys were in a separate class. I had cut him off. He would have to fight me on his own, to prove his heart to himself, to his boys, and most important, to his turf. He got away from the stoop and asked, "Fair one, Gringo?" (1967:56–57)

This situation reveals the drama—sometimes subtle, sometimes savage—by which human beings creatively build reality. Of course, not everyone enters a situation with equal power. Should a police officer have come upon the fight that took place between Piri and Waneko, both young men might have ended up in jail.

THE THOMAS THEOREM

By using his wits and boxing with Waneko until they both tired, Piri Thomas won acceptance by the gang. What took place that evening in Spanish Harlem is an example of the **Thomas theorem,** named after W. I. Thomas (1966:301, orig. 1931): *Situations that are defined as real are real in their consequences.*

Applied to social interaction, the Thomas theorem means that although reality is "soft" as it is being shaped, it can become "hard" in its effects. In the case just described, local gang members saw Piri Thomas act in a worthy way, so in their eyes, he *became* worthy.

ETHNOMETHODOLOGY

How can we become more aware of the social reality in which we play a part? Harold Garfinkel (1967) helped answer this question when he devised **ethnomethodology,** *the study of the way people make sense of their everyday surroundings.* This approach begins by pointing out that everyday behavior rests on a number of assumptions, usually taken for granted. When you ask someone the simple question "How are you?" you might be wondering how the person is physically,

People build reality from their surrounding culture. Yet, because cultural systems are marked by diversity and even outright conflict, reality construction always involves tensions and choices. Turkey is a nation with a mostly Muslim population, but it is also a country that has embraced Western culture. Here, women confront starkly different definitions of what is "feminine."

Staton R. Winter, *The New York Times.*

mentally, spiritually, or financially. The person, however, assumes that you are really not interested in details about any of these things; rather, you are "just being polite."

One good way to discover the assumptions we make about reality is to purposely break the rules. To test the assumption made above, for example, the next time someone asks, "How're you doing?" offer details from your last physical examination or explain all the good and bad things that have happened since you woke up that morning, and see how the person reacts. To test assumptions about how far apart people should stand while talking, slowly move closer to the other person during the conversation.

The results are predictable, because we all have certain ideas about the "rules" of everyday interaction. When people become confused or irritated by unexpected behavior, it helps us to see what the rules are and how important our everyday reality is.

REALITY BUILDING: CLASS AND CULTURE

People do not build everyday experience from nothing. In part, how we act or what we see in our surroundings

 You can interact with all the maps found in this text at the Companion Website™: http://www.prenhall.com/macionis

depends on our interests. Scanning the sky on a starry night, for example, lovers discover romance, whereas scientists see hydrogen atoms fusing into helium. Social background also directs what we see, so that residents

of, say, Spanish Harlem experience the world somewhat differently than people living on Manhattan's high-income Upper East Side.

In truth, the reality construction that goes on across the United States is quite diverse. The activities people choose in one part of the country differ from those common in another. Take golf, a popular sport among some segments of the population. National Map 4–1 shows where people are—and are not—likely to tee off.

In global perspective, the construction of reality is even more variable. Consider these everyday situations: People waiting for a bus in London typically "queue up" in a straight line; people in New York City, on the other hand, are rarely so orderly. The law in Saudi Arabia forbids women to drive cars, a constraint unheard of in the United States. Significant events also shape reality: Consider the heightened level of fear and anxiety and changes in behavior that followed the September 11 terrorist attacks in 2001.

The general conclusion is that people build reality from the surrounding culture. Chapter 2 ("Culture") explained how people the world over find different meanings in specific gestures, so travelers can find themselves building an unexpected reality. Similarly, what we see in a book or a film also depends on the assumptions we make about the world. In a study of popular culture, JoEllen Shively (1992) screened western films to men of European descent and to Native American men. The men in both categories claimed to enjoy the films but for different reasons. White men

NATIONAL MAP 4–1

Teeing Off across the United States

The map shows the popularity of the game of golf in all 3,141 counties in the United States in 2000. More than 25 million people across the country enjoy golf, but they are not typical in a number of respects. Looking at the map, what patterns can you see? As a hint, serious golfers tend to be white men who are somewhat older than the national average and who have incomes much higher than average.

Source: *American Demographics* magazine, August 2000, p. 50. Copyright © 2000 by Primedia. Reprinted with permission of Primedia Business Magazines and Media.

interpreted the films as praising rugged people striking out for the West and imposing their will on nature. Native American men saw in the same films a celebration of land and nature apart from any human ambitions.

Dramaturgical Analysis: "The Presentation of Self"

Erving Goffman (1922–1982) was another sociologist who analyzed social interaction, explaining how people in their everyday behavior are very much like actors performing on a stage. If we imagine ourselves observing what goes on in the theater of everyday life, we are doing what Goffman called **dramaturgical analysis,** *the study of social interaction in terms of theatrical performance.*

Dramaturgical analysis offers a fresh look at the concepts of status and role. A status is like a part in a play, and a role is a script, supplying dialogue and action for the characters. Goffman described each person's performance as the **presentation of self,** *a person's efforts to create specific impressions in the minds of others.* This process, sometimes called *impression management,* begins with the idea of personal performance (Goffman, 1959, 1967).

PERFORMANCES

As we present ourselves in everyday situations, we reveal information—consciously and unconsciously—to others. Our performances include the way we dress (costume), the objects we carry (props), and our tone of voice and gestures (manner). In addition, we craft our performances according to the setting. We may joke loudly in a restaurant, for example, but lower our voices when entering a church. People design settings, such as homes or offices, to bring about desired reactions in others.

An application: The doctor's office. Consider how a doctor's office conveys information to an audience of patients. The fact that medical doctors enjoy high prestige and power in the United States is clear upon entering one of their offices. First, the doctor is nowhere to be seen. Instead, in  what Goffman describes as the "front region" of the setting, the patient encounters a receptionist, or gatekeeper, who decides whether and when the patient can see the doctor. A simple survey of the doctor's waiting room, with patients (often impatiently) waiting to gain entry to the "back region," leaves little doubt that the doctor and his staff are in control.

The back region is composed of the examination rooms as well as the doctor's private office. In the office, the patient can see a wide range of props, such as medical books and framed degrees, that give the impression that the doctor has the specialized knowledge necessary to call the shots. The doctor usually is seated behind a desk—the larger and grander the desk, the greater the statement of power—and the patient is given only a chair.

The doctor's appearance and manner offer still more information. The usual white lab coat (costume) may have the practical function of keeping clothes from becoming

© 2002 David Sipress from cartoonbank.com. All Rights Reserved.

dirty, but its social function is to let others know at a glance the doctor's status. A stethoscope around the neck and a black medical bag in hand (more props) have the same purpose. The doctor uses highly technical language that is often mystifying to the patient, again emphasizing that the doctor is in charge. Finally, patients use the title "doctor," but they, in turn, often are addressed only by their first names, which further shows the doctor's dominant position. The overall message of a doctor's performance is clear: "I will help you, but you must allow me to take charge."

NONVERBAL COMMUNICATION

The novelist William Sansom describes the performance of a character named Mr. Preedy, an English vacationer on a beach in Spain:

> He took care to avoid catching anyone's eye. First, he had to make it clear to those potential companions of his holiday that they were of no concern to him whatsoever. He stared through them, round them, over them—eyes lost in space. The beach might have been empty. If by chance a ball was thrown his way, he looked surprised; then let a smile of amusement light his face (Kindly Preedy), looked around dazed to see that there were people on the beach, tossed it back with a smile to himself and not a smile *at* the people. . . .

[He] then gathered together his beach-wrap and bag into a neat sand-resistant pile (Methodical and Sensible Preedy), rose slowly to stretch his huge frame (Big-Cat Preedy), and tossed aside his sandals (Carefree Preedy, after all). (1956; quoted in Goffman, 1959:4–5)

Without saying a single word, Mr. Preedy offers a great deal of information about himself to anyone observing him. This illustrates the process of **nonverbal communication,** *communication using body movements, gestures, and facial expressions rather than speech.*

Many parts of the body can be used to generate *body language,* that is, to convey information to others. Facial expressions are the most significant form of body language. Smiling, for example, shows pleasure, although we can tell the difference between the deliberate smile of Kindly Preedy on the beach, a spontaneous smile of joy at seeing a friend, a pained smile of embarrassment, and the full, unrestrained smile of self-satisfaction we often associate with winning some important contest.

Eye contact is another crucial element of nonverbal communication. Generally, we use eye contact to invite social interaction. Someone across the room "catches our eye," sparking a conversation. Avoiding another's eyes, by contrast, discourages communication. Hands also speak for us. Common hand gestures within our culture can convey, among other things, an insult, a request for a ride, an invitation for someone to join us, or a demand that others stop in their tracks. Gestures also supplement spoken words. For example, pointing in a threatening way gives greater emphasis to a word of warning, shrugging the shoulders adds an air of indifference to the phrase "I don't know," and rapidly waving the arms lends urgency to the single word "Hurry!"

Body language and deception. As any actor knows, it is very difficult to pull off a perfect performance in front of others. In everyday performances, unintended body language can contradict our planned meaning: A teenage boy explains why he is getting home so late, for example, but his mother doubts his words because he avoids looking her in the eye; the movie star on a television talk show claims that her recent flop at the box office is "no big deal," but the nervous swing of her leg suggests otherwise. Because nonverbal communication is hard to control, it provides clues to deception, in much the same way that a lie detector records the changes in breathing, pulse rate, perspiration, and blood pressure that suggest a person is lying.

Look at the two faces in the Critical Thinking box. Can you tell which one is the honest smile and which one is the deception? Uncovering phony performances is difficult,

CRITICAL THINKING
Spotting Lies: What Are the Clues?

Deception is a common element of everyday social life. There may be no way to rid the world of dishonesty, but researchers have learned a great deal about how to tell when someone is lying. According to Paul Ekman, a specialist in analyzing social interaction, clues to deception can be found in four elements of a performance: words, voice, body language, and facial expressions.

- **Words.** People who are good liars mentally go over their lines, but they cannot always avoid inconsistencies that suggest deception. In addition, a simple slip of the tongue—something the person did not mean to say in quite that way—can occur in even the most carefully prepared performance. Any such "leak" might indicate that the person is hiding information.

- **Voice.** Tone and patterns of speech contain clues to deception because they are hard to control. A person cannot easily prevent the voice from trembling or breaking when trying to hide a powerful emotion. Speed

provides another clue; an individual may speak more quickly than normal, suggesting anger, or more slowly, indicating sadness.

- **Body language.** A "leak" conveyed through body language, which is also difficult to control, may tip off an observer to deception. Subtle body movements, sudden swallowing, or rapid breathing give the impression of nervousness. Powerful emotions that flash through a performance and change body language—what Ekman calls a "hot spot"—are good clues to deception.

- **Facial expressions.** Because there are forty-three distinct muscles in the face that humans use to create expressions, facial expressions are

even more difficult to control than other body language. Look at the two faces in the photos. Can you tell which is the lying face? It's the one on the left. A real smile usually has a relaxed expression and lots of "laugh lines" around the eyes; a phony smile seems forced and unnatural, with fewer wrinkles around the mouth and eyes.

We all try to fake emotions—some of us more successfully than others.

 For more on detecting deception, visit http://www. sciencenews.org/articles/ 20040731/bob8.asp

Obviously, the more powerful the emotion, the more difficult it is to deceive others.

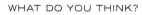

WHAT DO YOU THINK?

1. Why can parents tell if their children are not being entirely truthful?
2. Might Ekman's research be useful in the war against terror? How?
3. Are there "good liars" and "bad liars"? Explain.

Sources: Ekman (1985), Golden (1999b), and Kaufman (2002).

because no one bodily gesture tells us that someone is lying. But because any performance involves so many forms of body language, few people can keep up a lie without some slip-up, raising the suspicions of a careful observer. Therefore, the key to detecting lies is to view the whole performance with an eye for inconsistencies.

GENDER AND PERFORMANCES

Because women are socialized to respond to others, they tend to be more sensitive than men to nonverbal communication. In fact, as we now explain, gender is a central element in personal performances.

Demeanor. Demeanor—the way we act and carry ourselves—is a clue to social power. Simply put, powerful people enjoy more personal freedom in how they act. Off-color remarks, swearing, or removing shoes and putting one's feet up on a desk may be acceptable for the boss but rarely for employees. Similarly, powerful people can interrupt others, whereas less-powerful people are expected to show respect through silence (Smith-Lovin & Brody, 1989; Henley, Hamilton, & Thorne, 1992).

Because women generally occupy positions of lesser power, demeanor is a gender issue as well. As Chapter 10 ("Gender Stratification") explains, 43 percent of all working women in the United States hold secretarial or service jobs under the control of supervisors who are usually men. Women, then, learn to craft their personal performances more carefully than men and defer to them more often in everyday interaction.

Use of space.   How much space does a personal performance take? Power plays a key role here; the more power you have, the more space you use. Men typically command more space than women, whether pacing back and forth before an audience or casually sitting on a bench. Why? Our culture has traditionally measured femininity by how *little* space women occupy—the standard of "daintiness"—and masculinity by how *much* territory a man controls—the standard of "turf" (Henley, Hamilton, & Thorne, 1992).

For both sexes, **personal space** is *the surrounding area over which a person makes some claim to privacy.* In the United States, people generally stay several feet apart when speaking; throughout the Middle East, by contrast, people stand much closer. But just about everywhere, men (with their greater social power) often intrude into women's personal space. If a woman moves into a man's personal space, however, he is likely to take it as a sign of sexual interest.

Staring, smiling, and touching.   Eye contact encourages interaction. In conversations, women hold eye contact more than men. But men have their own brand of eye contact: staring. When men stare at women, they are claiming social dominance and defining women as sexual objects.

Although often showing pleasure, smiling is also a symbol of appeasement or submission. In a male-dominated world, it is not surprising that women smile more than men (Henley, Hamilton, & Thorne, 1992).

Finally, mutual touching conveys intimacy and caring. Apart from close relationships, however, touching is generally something men do to women (and rarely, in our culture, to other men). A male doctor touches the shoulder of his female nurse as they examine a report, a young man touches the back of his woman friend as he guides her across the street, or a male instructor touches the arms of young women as he teaches them to ski. In such examples, the intent of the touching may be harmless and may bring little response, but it amounts to a subtle ritual by which men claim dominance over women.

IDEALIZATION

Complex motives underlie human behavior. Even so, Goffman suggests, we construct performances to *idealize* our intentions. That is, we try to convince others (and perhaps ourselves) that our actions reflect ideal cultural standards rather than selfish motives.

Idealization is easily illustrated by returning to the world of doctors and patients. In a hospital, doctors engage in a performance known as "making rounds." Upon entering a patient's room, the doctor often stops at the foot of the bed and silently examines the patient's chart. Afterward, doctor and patient talk briefly. In ideal terms, this routine represents a personal visit to check on a patient's condition.

In reality, the picture is not so perfect. A doctor may see dozens of patients a day and remember little about many of them. Reading the chart is a chance to recall the patient's name and medical problems, but revealing the impersonality of the patient's care would undermine the cultural ideal of the doctor as deeply concerned about the welfare of others.

Doctors, college professors, and other professionals typically idealize their motives for entering their chosen careers. They describe their work as "making a contribution to science," perhaps "serving the community," or even "answering a call from God." Rarely do people admit the more common, less honorable motives: the income, power, prestige, and leisure that these careers provide.

We all use idealization to some degree. When was the last time you smiled and made polite remarks to someone you did not like? Such little lies ease our way through social interactions. Even when we suspect that others are putting on an act, we are unlikely to challenge their performance, for reasons that we shall examine next.

EMBARRASSMENT AND TACT

The famous professor keeps mispronouncing the dean's name; the visiting ambassador rises from the table to speak, unaware of the napkin that still hangs from his neck; the president becomes ill at a state dinner. As carefully as people may craft their performances, slip-ups of all kinds happen. The result is *embarrassment,* or discomfort after a spoiled performance. Goffman describes embarrassment as "losing face."

Embarrassment is an ever-present danger because idealized performances typically contain some deception. In

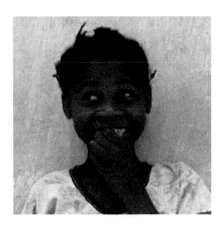

Hand gestures vary widely from one culture to another. Yet people everywhere define a chuckle, grin, or smirk in response to someone's performance as an indication that one does not take another person seriously. Therefore, the world over, people who cannot restrain their mirth tactfully cover their faces.

addition, most performances involve juggling so many elements that one thoughtless moment can shatter the intended impression.

A curious fact is that an audience often overlooks flaws in a performance, allowing the actor to avoid embarrassment. If we do point out a misstep ("Excuse me, but do you know your fly is open?"), we do it quietly and only to help someone avoid even greater loss of face. In Hans Christian Andersen's classic fable "The Emperor's New Clothes," the child who blurts out that the emperor is naked tells the truth but is scolded for being rude.

Often members of an audience actually help the performer recover from a flawed performance. *Tact* is helping someone "save face." After hearing a supposed expert make an embarrassingly inaccurate remark, for example, we might ignore the comment, as if it had never been spoken. Or with mild laughter we could treat what was said as a joke. Or we could simply respond, "I'm sure you didn't mean that," noting the statement but not allowing it to destroy the actor's performance. With these options in mind, it is easier to understand Abraham Lincoln's comment, "Tact is the ability to describe others the way they see themselves."

Why is tact so common? Embarrassment creates discomfort not only for the actor but for everyone. Just as the entire audience feels uneasy when an actor forgets a line, people who observe awkward behavior are reminded of how fragile their own performances often are. Socially constructed reality thus functions like a dam holding back a sea of chaos. Should one person's performance spring a leak, others tactfully help make repairs. After all, everyone lends a hand in building reality, and no one wants it to be suddenly swept away.

In sum, Goffman's research shows that although behavior is spontaneous in some respects, it is more patterned than we like to think. Almost 400 years ago, William Shakespeare captured this idea in lines that still ring true:

> All the world's a stage,
> And all the men and women merely players:
> They have their exits and their entrances;
> And one man in his time plays many parts.
> (*As You Like It*, act 2, scene 7)

Interaction in Everyday Life: Three Applications

We have now examined the major elements of social interaction. The final sections of this chapter illustrate these lessons by focusing on three important dimensions of everyday life: emotions, language, and humor.

EMOTIONS: THE SOCIAL CONSTRUCTION OF FEELING

Emotions, more commonly called *feelings,* are an important dimension of everyday life. Indeed, what we *do* often matters less than how we *feel* about it. Emotions seem very personal because they are "inside." Even so, just as society guides our behavior, it guides our emotional life.

The biological side of emotions. Studying people all over the world, Paul Ekman (1980a, 1980b) reported that people everywhere express six basic emotions: happiness, sadness, anger, fear, disgust, and surprise (see also Lutz & White, 1986;

To most people in the United States, these expressions convey anger, fear, disgust, happiness, surprise, and sadness. But do people elsewhere in the world define them in the same way? Research suggests that all human beings experience the same basic emotions and display them to others in the same basic ways. But culture plays a part by specifying the situations that trigger one emotion or another.

Lutz, 1988). Ekman also found that all people use much the same facial expressions to show these emotions. Indeed, he argues, some emotional responses seem to be "wired" into human beings, that is, biologically programmed in our facial features, muscles, and central nervous system.

Why? Complex emotions arose over the course of our species' evolution, but despite this biological root, the purpose of emotions is social: supporting group life. Emotions are powerful forces that allow us to overcome our individualism and build connections with others. Thus, the capacity for emotion arose in our ancestors along with the capacity for culture (Turner, 2000).

The cultural side of emotions. But culture does play an important role in guiding human emotions. First, Ekman explains, culture defines *what triggers* an emotion. Whether people define the departure of an old friend as joyous (causing happiness), insulting (arousing anger), a loss (creating sadness), or a mystical event (causing surprise and awe) has a lot to do with the culture. Second, culture provides rules for the *display* of emotions. For example, most people in the United States express emotions more freely with family members than with co-workers. Similarly, we expect children to express emotions to parents, although parents tend to hide their emotions from their children. Third, culture guides how we *value* emotions. Some societies encourage the expression of emotion, whereas others expect members to control their feelings and maintain a "stiff upper lip." Gender also plays a part; traditionally at least, many cultures expect women to show emotions while condemning emotional expression by men as a sign of weakness. In some cultures, of course, this pattern is less pronounced or even reversed.

Many of us think emotions are simply part of our biological makeup. While there is a biological foundation to human emotion, sociologists have demonstrated that what triggers an emotion—as well as when, where, and to whom the emotion is displayed—is shaped by culture. For example, many jobs not only regulate a worker's behavior, but also expect workers to display a particular emotion, as in the case of the always-smiling airline flight attendant. Can you think of other jobs that regulate emotions in this way?

Emotions on the job. In the United States most people are freer to express their feelings at home than on the job. This is because, as Arlie Russell Hochschild (1979, 1983) explains, the typical company does indeed try to control not only the behavior but also the emotions of its employ-ees. Take the case of an airline flight attendant who offers passengers a pillow, a drink, and a smile. Although this smile might convey real pleasure at serving the customer, Hochschild's study of flight attendants points to a different conclusion: The smile is an emotional script demanded by the airline as the right way to do the job. Therefore, we see that the "presentation of self" described by Erving Goffman can involve not just surface acting but also the "deep acting" of emotions.

With these patterns in mind, it is easy to see that we socially construct our emotions as part of our everyday reality, a process sociologists call *emotion management.* The Diversity box on page 102 tells the story of how women who decide to have an abortion display emotions according to emotional scripts called "feeling rules."

---

[1]The following sections draw primarily on Henley, Hamilton, & Thorne (1992). Additional material is drawn from Thorne, Kramarae, & Henley (1983) and other sources as noted.

LANGUAGE: THE SOCIAL CONSTRUCTION OF GENDER

As Chapter 2 ("Culture") explained, language is the thread that connects members of a society in the symbolic web we call culture. Language conveys not only a surface message but also deeper levels of meaning. One level involves gender. Language defines men and women differently in terms of both power and value.[1]

Language and power. A young man proudly rides his new motorcycle up his friend's driveway and asks, "Isn't she a beauty?" On the surface, the question has little to do with gender. Yet why does he use the pronoun "she" rather than "he" to refer to his prized possession?

The answer is that language helps men establish control over their surroundings. That is, a man attaches a female pronoun to a motorcycle (or car, boat, or other object) because it reflects *ownership*. Perhaps this is also why, in the United States and elsewhere, traditionally a woman who marries takes the last name of her husband. Because many of today's women in the United States value their independence, an increasing share (about 15 percent) now keep their own name or combine the two family names.

Language and value. Typically, the English language treats as masculine whatever has greater value, force, or significance. For instance, the adjective "virtuous," meaning "morally worthy" or "excellent," is derived from the Latin word *vir*, meaning "man." On the other hand, the adjective

DIVERSITY: RACE, CLASS, & GENDER

Managing Feelings: The Case of Women's Abortion Experiences

Few issues today generate as much emotion as abortion. In a study of women's abortion experiences, sociologist Jennifer Keys (2002) discovered emotional scripts or "feeling rules" that guided how women felt about ending a pregnancy.

Keys begins by explaining that emotional scripts arise from the political controversy surrounding abortion. The antiabortion movement defines abortion as a personal tragedy: the "killing of an unborn child." Given this definition, women who end a pregnancy through abortion are doing something very wrong and can expect to feel significant grief, guilt, and regret. Indeed, so intense are these feelings, according to supporters of this position, that such women often suffer from "postabortion syndrome."

Those who take the pro-choice position have an opposing view of abortion. From this point of view, the woman's problem is the *unwanted pregnancy*; abortion is a medical solution. Therefore, the emotion common to women who end a pregnancy is not guilt but relief.

In her research, Keys conducted in-depth interviews with forty women who had recently had abortions and found that all of them activated scripts as they "framed" their situation in an antiabortion or pro-choice manner. In part, this construction of reality reflects the woman's own attitude about abortion. In addition, however, women's partners and friends typically encouraged specific feelings about the event. Ivy, one young woman in the study, had a close friend who was also pregnant. "Congratulations!" she exclaimed when she learned of Ivy's condition. "We're going to be having babies together!" Such a statement established one "feeling rule": having a baby is *good,* which sent the message to Ivy that her planned abortion should trigger guilt. Working in the other direction, Jo's partner was horrified at the news that she was pregnant. Doubting his own ability to be a father, he blurted out, "I would rather put a gun to my head than have this baby!" His panic not only defined having the child as a mistake but alarmed Jo as well. Clearly, her partner's reaction made the decision to end the pregnancy a matter of relief from a terrible problem.

Medical personnel play a part in the process of reality construction by using specific terms. Nurses and doctors who talk about "the baby" encourage the antiabortion framing of abortion and provoke grief and guilt. On the other hand, those who use language such as "pregnancy tissue," "fetus," or "the contents of the uterus" encourage the pro-choice framing of abortion as a simple medical procedure leading to relief. Olivia began using the phrase "products of conception," which she picked up from her doctor. Denise spoke of her procedure as "taking the extra cells out of my body. Yeah, I did feel some guilt when I thought that this was the beginning of life, but my body is full of life—you have lots of cells in you."

After the procedure, most women reported actively trying to manage their feelings. Explained Ivy, "I never used the word 'baby.' I kept saying to myself that it was not formed yet. There was nothing there yet. I kept that in my mind." On the other hand, Keys found that all of the women in her study who had undergone abortions but nevertheless leaned toward the antiabortion position did use the term "baby." When interviewed, Gina explained, "I do think of it as a baby. The truth is that I ended my baby's life and I should not have done that. Thinking that makes me feel guilty. But—considering what I did—maybe I *should* feel guilty." Believing that what she had done was wrong, in other words, Gina actively called out the feeling of guilt—in part, Keys concluded, to punish herself.

WHAT DO YOU THINK?

1. In your own words, what are "emotional scripts" or "feeling rules"?
2. Can you apply the idea of "scripting feelings" to the experience of getting married?
3. In light of this discussion, to what extent is it correct to say that our feelings are not as personal as we might have thought?

Sources: McCaffrey & Keys (2000) and Keys (2002).

"hysterical," meaning uncontrollable emotion, comes from the Greek word *hyster,* meaning "uterus."

In many familiar ways, language also confers a different value on the two sexes. Traditional masculine terms such as "king" or "lord" have a positive meaning, whereas comparable terms such as "queen," "madam," or "dame" have a negative meaning. Similarly, the use of the suffixes "-ess" and "-ette" to indicate femininity usually devalues the words to which they are added. For example, a "major" has higher standing than a "majorette," as does a "host" in relation to a "hostess." Thus, language both mirrors social attitudes and helps perpetuate them.

Given the importance of gender in everyday life, perhaps we should not be surprised that women and men sometimes have trouble communicating clearly. In the Diversity box on page 104, Harold and Sybil, whose misadventures finding their friends' home opened this chapter, return to illustrate how the two sexes often seem to be speaking different languages.

REALITY PLAY: THE SOCIAL CONSTRUCTION OF HUMOR

Humor plays a vital part in everyday life. But although everyone laughs at a joke, few people think about what makes something funny or why humor is a part of people's lives all around the world. We can apply many of the ideas developed in this chapter to explain how, when we use humor, we "play with reality."[2]

The foundation of humor. Humor is produced by the social construction of reality; specifically, it arises as people create and contrast two different realities. Generally, one reality is *conventional,* that is, what people expect in some situation. The other reality is *unconventional,* an unexpected violation of cultural patterns. In short, humor arises from contradiction, ambiguity, and double meanings found in differing definitions of the same situation.

There are countless ways to mix realities and thereby generate humor. Contrasting realities emerge from statements that contradict themselves, such as "Nostalgia is not what it used to be." Switching words also can create humor, as in Oscar Wilde's line, "Work is the curse of the drinking class"; even reordering syllables does the trick, as in the case of the country song "I'd Rather Have a Bottle in Front of Me than a Frontal Lobotomy."

Of course, a joke can be built the other way around, so that the comic leads the audience to expect an unconventional answer and then delivers a very ordinary one. When a reporter asked the famous criminal Willy Sutton why he robbed banks, for example, he replied dryly, "Because that's where the money is." However a joke is constructed, the greater the opposition or difference between the two definitions of reality, the greater the humor.

When telling jokes, the comedian can strengthen this opposition in various ways. One common technique used

on the stage is to present the first, conventional remark in conversation with another actor, then turn toward the audience (or the camera) to deliver the second, unexpected line. In a Marx Brothers movie, Groucho remarks, "Outside of a dog, a book is a man's best friend." Then, dropping his voice and turning to the camera, he adds, "And *inside* of a dog, it's too dark to read!" Such "changing channels" emphasizes the difference between the conventional and unconventional realities. Following the same logic, many stand-up comedians also "reset" the audience to conventional expectations by adding "But seriously, folks, . . ." between jokes.

To construct the strongest contrast in meaning, comedians pay careful attention to their performances—the precise words they use and the timing of their delivery. A joke is well told if the comic creates the sharpest possible opposition between the realities; in a careless performance, the humor falls flat. Because the key to humor lies in the collision of realities, we can see why the climax of a joke is termed the "*punch* line."

The dynamics of humor: "Getting it." Someone who does not understand either the expected or the unexpected reality in a joke may complain, "I don't get it." To "get" humor, members of an audience must understand the two realities involved well enough to appreciate their difference.

But comics may make getting the joke harder still by leaving out some important information. In other words, the audience must pay attention to the *stated* elements of the joke and fill in the missing pieces on their own. As a simple example, consider the comment of movie producer Hal Roach upon reaching his hundredth birthday: "If I had known I would live to be one hundred, I would have taken better care of myself!" Here, getting the joke depends on realizing the unstated fact that Roach *must* have taken pretty good care of himself because he did make it to one hundred. Or take one of W. C. Fields's lines: "Some weasel took the cork out of my lunch!" "Some lunch!" we think to ourselves to "finish" the joke.

Here is an even more complex joke: What do you get if you cross an insomniac, a dyslexic, and an agnostic? Answer: A person who stays up all night wondering if there is a dog. To get this one, you must know that insomnia is an inability to sleep, that dyslexia causes a person to reverse letters in words, and that an agnostic doubts the existence of God.

Why would an audience be required to make this kind of effort to understand a joke? Simply because our enjoyment of a joke is increased by the pleasure of having completed the puzzle necessary to "get it." In addition, "getting" the joke confers a special insider status. We can also understand the frustration of *not* getting a joke: fear of being

---

[2]The ideas contained in this discussion are based on Macionis (1987), except as otherwise noted. The general approach draws on work presented earlier in this chapter, especially the ideas of Erving Goffman.

DIVERSITY: RACE, CLASS, & GENDER

Gender and Language: "You Just Don't Understand!"

In the story that opened this chapter, Harold and Sybil faced a situation that rings all too true to many people: When they are lost, men grumble to themselves and perhaps blame their partners but avoid asking for directions. For their part, women can't understand why.

Deborah Tannen explains that men typically define most everyday encounters as competitive. Therefore, getting lost is bad enough without asking for help and thereby letting someone else get "one up." By contrast, because women traditionally have had a subordinate position, they find it easy to ask for help. Sometimes, Tannen points out, women ask for assistance even when they don't need it.

A similar gender-linked pattern involves what women consider "trying to be helpful" and men call "nagging." Consider the following exchange (adapted from Adler, 1990:74):

SYBIL: What's wrong, honey?
HAROLD: Nothing.
SYBIL: Something is bothering you. I can tell.
HAROLD: I told you nothing is bothering me. Leave me alone.
SYBIL: But I can see that something is wrong.
HAROLD: OK. Just why do you think something is bothering me?

SYBIL: Well, for one thing, you're bleeding all over your shirt.
HAROLD (*now irritated*): Yeah, well, it doesn't bother me.
SYBIL (*losing her temper*): WELL, IT SURE IS BOTHERING ME!
HAROLD: Fine. I'll go change my shirt.

The problem couples face in communicating is that what one partner *intends* by a comment is not always what the other *hears* in the words. To Sybil, her opening question is an effort at cooperative problem solving. She can see that something is wrong with Harold (who has cut himself while doing yard work), and she wants to help him. But Harold interprets her pointing out his problem as belittling him and tries to close off the discussion. Sybil, confident that Harold would be more positive toward her if

he just understood that she only wants to be helpful, repeats herself. This sets in motion a vicious circle in which Harold, thinking his wife is trying to make him feel incapable of looking after himself, responds by digging in his heels. This, in turn, makes his wife all the more sure that she needs to do something. And around it goes until somebody loses patience.

In the end, Harold agrees to change his shirt but still refuses to discuss the original problem. Mistaking his wife's concern for nagging, Harold just wants Sybil to leave him alone. For her part, Sybil fails to understand her husband's view of the situation and walks away convinced that he is a stubborn grouch.

WHAT DO YOU THINK?

1. Based on this box, how would you describe the basic difference between the way men and women talk?
2. In your opinion, what is the reason for any gender differences in language?
3. Do you think that understanding Tannen's conclusions would help female-male couples communicate better? Why?

Sources: Adler (1990) and Tannen (1990).

judged stupid, coupled with a sense of being excluded from the pleasure shared by others. Not surprisingly, outsiders in such a situation sometimes fake "getting" the joke.

Sometimes someone may tactfully explain a joke so the other person doesn't feel left out. But as the old saying goes, if a joke has to be explained, it won't be very funny. Besides taking the edge off the language and timing on which the "punch" depends, an explanation removes the mental involvement and greatly reduces the listener's pleasure.

The topics of humor. People throughout the world smile and laugh, making humor a universal human trait. But the world's people use different languages and live in different cultures. As a result, they differ in what they find funny, and that is why humor rarely travels well.

October 1, Kobe, Japan. Can you share a joke with people who live halfway around the world? At dinner, I ask two Japanese college women to tell me a joke. "You know 'crayon'?" Asako asks. I nod. "How do you ask for a crayon in Japanese?" I respond that I have no idea. She laughs out loud as she says what sounds like "crayon crayon." Her companion Mayumi laughs, too. My wife and I sit awkwardly straight-faced. Asako relieves some of our embarrassment by explaining that the Japanese word for "give me" is kureyo, which sounds like "crayon." I force a smile.

What is humorous to the Japanese, then, may be lost on the Chinese, Iraqis, or people in the United States. To some degree, too, the social diversity of our own country means that people will find humor in different situations. New Englanders, southerners, and westerners have their own brands of humor, as do Latinos and Anglos, fifteen- and fifty-year-olds, Wall Street bankers and southwestern rodeo riders.

But for everyone, topics that lend themselves to double meanings or controversy generate humor. For example, in the United States, the first jokes many of us learned as children concerned bodily functions kids are not supposed to talk about. The mere mention of "unmentionable acts" or certain parts of the body can dissolve young faces in laughter.

Are there jokes that can break through the cultural barrier? Yes, but they must touch upon universal human experiences such as, say, turning on a friend.

I think of a number of jokes, but none seems to work. Understanding jokes about the United States is difficult for people who have never been there. Is there something more universal? Inspiration: "Two fellows are walking in the woods and come upon a huge bear. One guy leans over and tightens up the laces on his running shoes. 'Jake,' says the other, 'what are you doing? You can't outrun that bear!' 'I don't have to outrun the bear,' responds Jake. 'I just have to outrun you!'" Smiles all around.

The controversy found in humor often walks a fine line between what is funny and what is considered "sick." During the Middle Ages, the word "humors" (derived from the Latin *humidus,* meaning "moist") referred to a balance of bodily fluids that regulated a person's health. Researchers today document the power of humor to reduce stress and improve health, confirming the old saying, "Laughter is the best medicine" (Robinson, 1983; Haig, 1988). At the extreme, however, people who always take conventional reality lightly risk being defined as deviant or even mentally ill (a common stereotype shows insane people laughing uncontrollably, and we have long dubbed mental hospitals "funny farms").

Then, too, every social group considers certain topics too sensitive for humorous treatment. If you joke about such things, you risk criticism for telling a "sick" joke (and being called "sick"). People's religious beliefs, tragic accidents, or appalling crimes are some of the subjects of "sick" jokes or no jokes at all. Even years later, there have been no jokes about the September 11, 2001, terrorist attacks.

The functions of humor. Humor is found everywhere because it acts as a safety valve to vent potentially disruptive sentiments. Put another way, humor provides a way to discuss an opinion on a sensitive topic without being serious. Having said something controversial, people often use humor to defuse a situation by simply stating, "I didn't mean anything by what I said—it was just a joke!"

Similarly, people use humor to relieve tension in uncomfortable situations. One study of medical examinations found that most patients begin to joke with doctors to ease their own nervousness (Baker et al., 1997).

Humor and conflict. Humor holds the potential to liberate those who laugh, but it can also be used to put down others. Men who tell jokes about women, for example, typically are voicing hostility toward them (Powell & Paton, 1988; Benokraitis & Feagin, 1995). Similarly, jokes at the expense of gay people reveal tensions about sexual orientation. Humor often is a sign of real conflict in situations in which one or both parties choose not to bring the conflict out into the open (Primeggia & Varacalli, 1990).

"Put-down" jokes make one category of people feel good at the expense of another. After analyzing jokes from many societies, Christie Davies (1990) confirmed that ethnic conflict is a driving force behind humor almost everywhere. The typical ethnic joke makes fun of some disadvantaged category of people, thereby making the jokester and the audience feel superior. Given the Anglo-Saxon traditions of U.S. society, Poles and other ethnic and racial minorities have long been the butt of jokes, as have Newfoundlanders ("Newfies") in eastern Canada, Scots in England, Irish in Scotland, Sikhs in India, Turks in Germany, Hausas in Nigeria, Tasmanians in Australia, and Kurds in Iraq.

Of course, disadvantaged people also make fun of the powerful, although usually with some care. Women in the

United States joke about men, just as African Americans find humor in white people's ways and poor people poke fun at the rich. Throughout the world, people target their leaders with humor, and officials in some countries take such jokes seriously enough to arrest those who do not show proper respect (Speier, 1998).

In sum, the significance of humor is much greater than we may think. Humor amounts to a means of mental escape from a conventional world that is not entirely to our liking (Flaherty, 1984, 1990; Yoels & Clair, 1995). Indeed, this idea would explain why so many of our nation's comedians come from the ranks of historically marginalized peoples, including Jews and African Americans. As long as we maintain a sense of humor, we assert our freedom and are never prisoners of reality. By putting a smile on our faces, we change ourselves and the world just a little.

SUMMARY

1. Social structure provides guidelines for behavior, making everyday life understandable and predictable.

2. A major component of social structure is status. Within a person's status set, a master status has special importance for the person's identity.

3. Ascribed statuses are involuntary, whereas achieved statuses are earned. In practice, most statuses are both ascribed and achieved.

4. Role is the active expression of a status. Tension among the roles corresponding to two or more statuses generates role conflict. Likewise, tension among the roles linked to a single status causes role strain.

5. The "social construction of reality" is the idea that we build the social world through our interactions with others.

6. The Thomas theorem states that situations defined as real are real in their consequences.

7. Ethnomethodology seeks to reveal the assumptions and understandings people have of their social world.

8. Dramaturgical analysis views everyday life as theatrical performance, noting how people try to create particular impressions in the minds of others.

9. Social power affects performances, which is one reason that men's behavior typically differs from women's.

10. Everyday behavior carries the ever-present danger of embarrassment. People use tact to prevent others' performances from breaking down.

11. Although the same basic emotions appear to be biologically programmed into human beings, culture guides what triggers emotions, how we display emotions, and what value we attach to emotion. In everyday life, presentations of self involve managing emotions as well as behavior.

12. Language is vital to the process of socially constructing reality. In various ways, language defines women and men differently, generally to the advantage of men.

13. Humor stems from the difference between conventional and unconventional definitions of a situation. Because humor is an element of culture, people throughout the world find different situations funny.

KEY CONCEPTS

social interaction (p. 88) the process by which people act and react in relation to others

status (p. 89) a social position that a person holds

status set (p. 89) all the statuses a person holds at a given time

ascribed status (p. 89) a social position a person receives at birth or takes on involuntarily later in life

achieved status (p. 89) a social position a person takes on voluntarily that reflects personal ability and effort

master status (p. 89) a status that has special importance for social identity, often shaping a person's entire life

role (p. 90) behavior expected of someone who holds a particular status

role set (p. 90) a number of roles attached to a single status

role conflict (p. 90) conflict among the roles corresponding to two or more statuses

role strain (p. 90) tension among the roles connected to a single status

social construction of reality (p. 92) the process by which people creatively shape reality through social interaction

Thomas theorem (p. 93) W. I. Thomas's statement that situations defined as real are real in their consequences

ethnomethodology (p. 93) Harold Garfinkel's term for the study of the way people make sense of their everyday surroundings

dramaturgical analysis (p. 95) Erving Goffman's term for the study of social interaction in terms of theatrical performance

presentation of self (p. 95) Goffman's term for a person's efforts to create specific impressions in the minds of others

nonverbal communication (p. 96) communication using body movements, gestures, and facial expressions rather than speech

personal space (p. 98) the surrounding area over which a person makes some claim to privacy

CRITICAL-THINKING QUESTIONS

1. Consider ways in which a physical disability can be a master status. What assumptions do people commonly make about the mental ability of someone with a physical disability such as cerebral palsy? What assumptions are made about the person's sexuality?

2. The word "conversation" has the same root as the religious term "convert," suggesting that we engage one another with the expectation of change on the part of everyone involved. In what sense, then, does a conversation require being open-minded?

3. George Jean Nathan once remarked, "I only drink to make other people interesting." What does this mean in terms of reality construction? Can you identify the elements of humor in this comment?

4. Here is a joke about sociologists: Question: How many sociologists does it take to change a light bulb? Answer: None. There is nothing wrong with the light bulb; it's *the system* that needs to be changed! What makes this joke funny? What sort of people are likely to get it? What kind of people probably won't? Why?

APPLICATIONS AND EXERCISES

1. Write down as many of your own statuses as you can. Do you consider any of them to be a master status? To what extent is each of your statuses ascribed or achieved?

2. During the next twenty-four hours, every time people ask "How are you?" stop and actually give a full and truthful answer. What happens when you respond to a polite question in an unexpected way? (Notice people's body language as well as their words.) What does this experience suggest about everyday interactions?

3. This chapter illustrated Erving Goffman's ideas with a description of a doctor's office. Investigate the offices of several professors in the same way. What furniture is there, and how is it arranged? What props do professors use? How are the offices of doctors and professors different? Which are tidier? Why?

4. Spend an hour or two walking around the businesses of your town (or shops at a local mall). Observe the number of women and men in each business. Based on your observations, would you conclude that physical space is "gendered"? Why or why not?

5. Packaged in the back of this new textbook is an interactive CD-ROM that offers a variety of video and interactive review materials intended to help you better understand the material covered in this chapter. For this chapter, the CD-ROM contains a relevant clip from *ABC News,* an author's tip video, interactive map animations, an interactive timeline, and flashcards with audio pronunciations of the more difficult words.

SITES TO SEE

http://www.prenhall.com/macionis

Visit the interactive Companion Website™ that accompanies this text. Begin by clicking on the cover of your book. You will find a chapter-by-chapter study guide, practice tests, suggested Web links, and links to other relevant material.

http://www.census.gov/genealogy/www/namesearch.html

Many interesting patterns of everyday life involve names. This Census Bureau Web site has a search engine for names. Study how often different last names (or first names) appear in the U.S.

population. What patterns can you find? How many others share your own name?

http://www.ai.mit.edu/projects/humanoid-robotics-group/

Is it possible to build a machine capable of human interaction? That is the goal of robotics engineers at the Massachusetts Institute of Technology; this Web site provides details and photographs. Look over their work and think about issues raised in this chapter. In what ways are machines able, and unable, to imitate human behavior?

 INVESTIGATE WITH RESEARCH NAVIGATOR™

Follow the instructions on page 32 of this text to access the features of **Research Navigator™.** Once at the Web site, enter your Login Name and Password. Then, to use the **Content Select™** database, enter keywords such as "humor," "ethnomethodology," and "emotions," and the search engine will supply relevant and

recent scholarly and popular press publications. Use the *New York Times* **Search-by-Subject Archive** to find recent news articles related to sociology and the **Link Library** feature to find relevant Web links organized by the key terms associated with this chapter.

Amnesty International USA
Member

Mr. Charles Reilly

Member ID#: 00499644

Member Since 1988

CHAPTER FIVE

Groups
and Organizations

How do groups affect the behavior of members?

Why can "who you know" be as important
as "what you know"?

In what ways have large business organizations
changed in recent decades?

We carry out much of our daily lives as members of groups and organizations. ▶
The Canadian synchronized swimming team spends long hours together training for the Olympics.

Back in 1948, people in Pasadena, California, paid little attention to the opening of a new restaurant by brothers Maurice and Richard McDonald. Yet this one small business would not only transform the restaurant industry but also introduce a new organizational model copied by countless businesses of all kinds.

The McDonald brothers' basic concept, which was soon called "fast food," was to serve meals quickly and cheaply to large numbers of people. The brothers trained employees to do highly specialized jobs: One person grilled hamburgers while others "dressed" them, made French fries, whipped up milkshakes, and handed the food to the customers in assembly-line fashion.

As the years went by, the McDonald brothers prospered, and they decided to move their restaurant to San Bernardino. It was there, in 1954, that Ray Kroc, a traveling blender and mixer salesman, paid them a visit.

Kroc was fascinated by the efficiency of the brothers' system and saw the potential for a whole chain of fast-food restaurants. The three launched the plan as partners. Soon Kroc bought out the McDonalds (who went back to running their original restaurant) and went on to become one of the greatest success stories of all time. More than 30,000 McDonald's restaurants now serve almost 50 million people every day throughout the United States and in 118 nations around the world.

The success of McDonald's represents more than the popularity of hamburgers and French fries. The organizational principles that guide this company are coming to dominate social life in the United States and elsewhere.

We begin this chapter with an examination of *social groups*, the clusters of people with whom we interact in our daily lives. As you will learn, the scope of group life expanded greatly during the twentieth century. From a world of families, local neighborhoods, and small businesses, our society now turns on the operation of huge businesses and other bureaucracies that sociologists describe as *formal organizations*. Understanding this expansion of social life and appreciating what it means for us as individuals are the main objectives of this chapter.

Social Groups

Almost everyone wants a sense of belonging, which is the essence of group life. A **social group** is *two or more people who identify and interact with one another.* Human beings come together as couples, families, circles of friends, churches, clubs, businesses, neighborhoods, and large organizations.

Whatever the form, groups contain people with shared experiences, loyalties, and interests. While keeping their individuality, members of social groups also think of themselves as a special "we."

Not every collection of individuals forms a group. People with a status in common, such as women, homeowners, soldiers, millionaires, college graduates, and Roman Catholics, are not a group but a *category*. They know that others hold the same status, but most are strangers to one another. Similarly, students sitting in a large lecture hall interact to a very limited extent. Such a loosely formed collection of people is a *crowd* rather than a group.

However, the right circumstances can quickly turn a crowd into a group. Events from power failures to terrorist attacks can make people bond quickly with strangers.

PRIMARY AND SECONDARY GROUPS

Friends often greet one another with a smile and the simple phrase "Hi! How are you?" The response usually is, "Fine, thanks. How about you?" This answer is often more scripted than truthful. Explaining how you *really* are doing might make people feel so awkward that they would beat a hasty retreat.

As human beings, we live our lives as members of groups. Such groups may be large or small, temporary or long-lasting, and can be based on kinship, cultural heritage, or some shared interest.

Social groups fall into one of two types, based on their members' degree of genuine personal concern for one another. According to Charles Horton Cooley

 To learn more about Cooley, see the Gallery of Sociologists at http://www.TheSociologyPage.com

(1864–1929), a **primary group** is *a small social group whose members share personal and lasting relationships*. Joined by *primary relationships*, people spend a great deal of time together, engage in a wide range of activities, and feel that they know one another pretty well. In short, they show real concern for one another. The family is every society's most important primary group.

Cooley called personal and tightly integrated groups "primary" because they are among the first groups we experience in life. In addition, family and friends have primary importance in the socialization process, shaping our attitudes, behavior, and social identity.

Members of primary groups help one another in many ways, but they generally think of their group as an end in itself rather than as a means to other ends. In other words, we tend to think that family and friendship link people who "belong together." Members of a primary group also tend to view each other as unique and irreplaceable. Especially in the family, we are bound to others by emotion and loyalty. Brothers and sisters may not always get along, but they always remain siblings.

In contrast to the primary group, the **secondary group** is *a large and impersonal social group whose members pursue a specific goal or activity*. In most respects, secondary groups have characteristics precisely opposite to those of primary groups. *Secondary relationships* involve weak emotional ties and little personal knowledge of one another. Many secondary groups exist for only a short time, beginning and ending with no particular significance. Students in a college course, who may or may not see one another after the semester ends, are one example of a secondary group.

Secondary groups include many more people than primary groups. For example, dozens or even hundreds of people may work in the same company, yet most of them pay only passing attention to one another. Sometimes the passage of time transforms a group from secondary to primary, as with co-workers who share an office for many years and develop closer relationships. But generally, members of a secondary group do not think of themselves as "we." Secondary ties need not be hostile or cold, of course. Interactions among students, co-workers, and business associates are often quite pleasant even if they are impersonal.

Unlike members of primary groups, who display a *personal orientation*, people in secondary groups have a *goal orientation*. Whereas primary group members define each other according to *who* they are in terms of family ties or personal qualities, people in secondary groups look to one another for *what* they are, that is, what they can do for each other. In secondary groups, we tend to "keep score," aware of what we give others and what we receive in return. This goal orientation means that secondary group members usually remain formal and polite. It is in a secondary relationship, therefore, that we ask the question "How are you?" without expecting a truthful answer.

SUMMING UP

Primary Groups and Secondary Groups

	Primary Group ⟷	Secondary Group
Quality of relationships	Personal orientation	Goal orientation
Duration of relationships	Usually long-term	Variable; often short-term
Breadth of relationships	Broad; usually involving many activities	Narrow; usually involving few activities
Perception of relationships	As ends in themselves	As means to an end
Examples	Families, circles of friends	Co-workers, political organizations

The Summing Up table reviews the characteristics of primary and secondary groups. Keep in mind that these traits define two ideal types of groups; most real groups contain elements of both. But placing these concepts at opposite ends of a continuum helps us describe and analyze group life.

Many people think that small towns and rural areas emphasize primary relationships and that large cities are characterized by secondary ties. This generalization holds some truth, but some urban neighborhoods, especially those populated by people of a single ethnic or religious category, can be very tightly knit.

GROUP LEADERSHIP

How do groups operate? One important element of group dynamics is leadership. Although a small circle of friends may have no leader at all, most large secondary groups place leaders in a formal chain of command.

Instrumental and expressive leaders. Groups typically benefit from two kinds of leadership. **Instrumental leadership** refers to *group leadership that focuses on the completion of tasks*. Members look to instrumental leaders to get things done. **Expressive leadership,** by contrast, is *group leadership that focuses on the group's well-being*. Expressive leaders take less of an interest in achieving goals than in promoting the well-being of members and minimizing tension and conflict among members.

Because they concentrate on performance, instrumental leaders usually have formal, secondary relationships with other members. These leaders give orders and reward or punish people according to how much they contribute to the group's efforts. Expressive leaders build more personal, primary ties. They offer sympathy to members going through tough times, keep the group united, and lighten serious moments with humor. Whereas successful instrumental leaders enjoy more *respect* from members, expressive leaders generally receive more personal *affection*.

In the traditional North American family, the two types of leadership are linked to gender. Historically, cultural norms gave instrumental leadership to men who, as fathers and husbands, assumed primary responsibility for earning income and making major family decisions. Traditionally, women exercised expressive leadership: As mothers and wives, they encouraged supportive and peaceful relationships between family members. One result of this division of labor was that many children had greater respect for their fathers but closer personal ties with their mothers (Parsons & Bales, 1955; Macionis, 1978a).

Greater equality between men and women has blended the gender-based distinction between instrumental and expressive leadership. In most group settings, women and men now take on both leadership roles.

Leadership styles. Sociologists also describe leadership in terms of its decision-making style. *Authoritarian leadership* focuses on instrumental concerns, takes personal charge of decision making, and demands that group members obey orders. Although this leadership style may win little affection from the group, a fast-acting authoritarian leader is appreciated in a crisis.

Democratic leadership is more expressive, making a point of including everyone in the decision-making process. Although less successful in a crisis situation, where there is little time for discussion, democratic leaders generally draw on the ideas of all members to develop creative solutions to problems.

Laissez-faire leadership (a French phrase meaning roughly "to leave alone") allows the group to function more or less on its own. This style typically is the least effective in promoting group goals (White & Lippitt, 1953; Ridgeway, 1983).

GROUP CONFORMITY

Groups influence the behavior of their members, often promoting conformity. "Fitting in" provides a secure feeling of belonging, but at the extreme, group pressure can be unpleasant and even dangerous. Interestingly, as experiments by Solomon Asch and Stanley Milgram showed, even strangers can encourage conformity.

Asch's research. Asch (1952) recruited students supposedly to study visual perception. Before the experiment began, he explained to all but one member of a small group that their real purpose was to put pressure on the remaining person. Placing six to eight students around a table, Asch showed them a "standard" line, as drawn on Card 1 in Figure 5–1, and asked them to match it to one of the three lines on Card 2.

Anyone with normal vision can see that the line marked "A" on Card 2 is the correct choice. Initially, as planned, everyone made the correct matches. But then Asch's accomplices began answering incorrectly, leaving the naive subject (seated at the table so as to answer next to last) bewildered and uncomfortable.

What happened? Asch found that one-third of all subjects chose to conform by answering incorrectly. Apparently, many of us are willing to compromise our own judgment to avoid the discomfort of being different, even from people we do not know.

Milgram's research. Stanley Milgram, a former student of Solomon Asch's, conducted conformity experiments of his own. In Milgram's controversial study (Milgram, 1963, 1965; Miller, 1986), a researcher explained to male recruits that they would be taking part in a study of how punishment affects learning. One by one, he assigned them to the role of teacher and placed another person—actually an accomplice of Milgram's—in a connecting room to pose as a learner.

The teacher watched the learner sit down in a contraption resembling an electric chair. As the teacher looked on, the researcher applied electrode paste to the learner's wrist, explaining that this would "prevent blisters and burns." The researcher then attached an electrode to the learner's wrist and fastened the leather straps, explaining that they would "prevent excessive movement while the learner was being shocked." Although the shocks would be painful, the

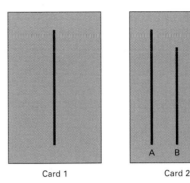

Source: Asch (1952).

FIGURE 5-1 Cards Used in Asch's Experiment in Group Conformity

researcher reassured the teacher, they would cause "no permanent tissue damage."

The researcher then led the teacher back into the adjoining room, pointing out that the "electric chair" was connected to a "shock generator," actually a phony but realistic-looking piece of equipment with a label that read "Shock Generator, Type ZLB, Dyson Instrument Company, Waltham, Mass." On the front was a dial that supposedly regulated electric current from 15 volts (labeled "Slight Shock") to 300 volts ("Intense Shock") to 450 volts ("Danger: Severe Shock").

Seated in front of the "shock generator," the teacher was told to read aloud pairs of words. Then the teacher was to repeat the first word of each pair and wait for the learner to recall the second word. Whenever the learner failed to answer correctly, the teacher was told to apply an electric shock.

The researcher directed the teacher to begin at the lowest level (15 volts) and to increase the shock by another 15 volts every time the learner made a mistake. And so the teacher did. At 75, 90, and 105 volts, the teacher heard moans from the learner; at 120 volts, shouts of pain; by 270 volts, screams; at 315 volts, pounding on the wall; after that, deadly silence. None of the forty subjects assigned to the role of teacher during the initial research even questioned the procedure before reaching 300 volts, and twenty-six of the subjects—almost two-thirds—went all the way to 450 volts. Even Milgram was surprised at how readily people obeyed authority figures.

Milgram (1964) then modified his research to see whether Solomon Asch had documented such a high degree of group conformity only because the task—matching lines—was a trivial one. What if groups could also pressure people to administer electrical shocks?

We form attitudes and plan our actions imagining how others will respond to us. Often, researchers have found, people in specific groups—called reference groups—have special importance to us. Reference groups may be groups we are already a member of or groups we would like to accept us.

This time, Milgram formed a group of three teachers, two of whom were his accomplices. Each of the teachers was to suggest a shock level when the learner made an error; the rule was that the group would then administer the lowest of the three suggested levels. This arrangement gave the naive subject the power to deliver a lesser shock regardless of what the others proposed.

The accomplices suggested increasing the shock level with each error, putting pressure on the subject to do the same. The subjects in these groups applied voltages three to four times higher than other subjects acting alone. Thus, Milgram's research suggests that people are surprisingly likely to follow the directions not only of legitimate authority figures but also of groups of ordinary individuals, even when it means harming another person.

Janis's research. Experts also cave in to group pressure, says Irving L. Janis (1972, 1989). Janis argues that a number of U.S. foreign policy blunders, including the failure to foresee the Japanese attack on Pearl Harbor during World War II and our ill-fated involvement in the Vietnam War, resulted from group conformity among our highest-ranking political leaders.

Common sense tells us that group discussion improves decision making. Janis counters that group members often seek agreement that closes off other points of view. Janis called this process **groupthink,** *the tendency of group members to conform, resulting in a narrow view of some issue.*

A classic example of groupthink resulted in the disastrous 1961 invasion of the Bay of Pigs in Cuba. Looking back, Arthur Schlesinger Jr., an adviser to President Kennedy, confessed feeling guilty "for having kept so quiet during those crucial discussions in the Cabinet Room," adding that the group discouraged anyone from challenging what, in hindsight, Schlesinger considered "nonsense" (quoted in Janis, 1972:30, 40). It may be that groupthink was also at work in 2003 when U.S. leaders went to war assuming that Iraq had stockpiles of weapons of mass destruction.

REFERENCE GROUPS

How do we assess our own attitudes and behavior? Often we use a **reference group,** *a social group that serves as a point of reference in making evaluations and decisions.*

A young man who imagines his family's reaction to a woman he is dating is using his family as a reference group. A supervisor who tries to predict her employees' reaction to a new vacation policy is using them in the same way. As these examples suggest, reference groups can be primary or secondary. In either case, our need to conform shows how others' attitudes affect us.

We also use groups we do *not* belong to for reference. Being well prepared for a job interview means showing up dressed the way people in that company dress for work. Conforming to groups we do not belong to is a strategy to win acceptance and illustrates the process of *anticipatory socialization*, discussed in Chapter 3 ("Socialization: From Infancy to Old Age").

Stouffer's research. Samuel A. Stouffer and his colleagues conducted a classic study of reference groups during World War II. Researchers asked soldiers to rate their own, or any competent soldier's, chances of promotion in their branch of the Army. One might guess that soldiers serving in outfits with high promotion rates would be optimistic about advancement. Yet Stouffer's research pointed to the opposite conclusion: Soldiers in Army units with low promotion rates were actually more positive about their chances to move ahead (Stouffer et al., 1949).

The key to understanding Stouffer's results lies in the groups against which soldiers measured themselves. Those assigned to units with lower promotion rates looked around them and saw people making no more headway than they were. Although they had not been promoted, neither had many others, so they did not feel deprived. However, soldiers in units with higher promotion rates could think of many people who had been promoted sooner or more often than they had. With such people in mind, even soldiers who had been promoted themselves were likely to feel shortchanged.

The point is that we do not make judgments about ourselves in isolation, nor do we compare ourselves with just anyone. Regardless of our situation in *absolute* terms, we form a subjective sense of our well-being by looking at ourselves *relative* to specific reference groups (Merton, 1968; Mirowsky, 1987).

IN-GROUPS AND OUT-GROUPS

Everyone favors some groups over others, whether because of political outlook, social prestige, or manner of dress. On the college campus, for example, left-leaning student activists may look down on fraternity members, whom they view as conservative; fraternity members, in turn, may snub the computer "nerds" and "grinds," who work too hard. People in virtually every social setting make similar positive and negative evaluations about members of other groups.

Such judgments illustrate another key element of group dynamics: the opposition of in-groups and out-groups. An **in-group** is *a social group toward which a member feels respect and commitment.* An **out-group,** by contrast, is *a social group toward which a person feels a sense of competition or opposition.* In-groups and out-groups are based on the idea that "we" have valued traits that "they" lack.

Tensions between groups sharpen the groups' boundaries and give people a clearer social identity. However, members of in-groups generally hold overly positive views of themselves and unfairly negative views of various out-groups (Tajfel, 1982; Bobo & Hutchings, 1996).

Power also shapes intergroup relations. A powerful in-group can define others as a lower-status out-group. Historically, for example, white people viewed people of color as an out-group and subordinated them socially, politically, and economically. Internalizing these negative attitudes, minorities often struggle to overcome negative self-images. In this way, in-groups and out-groups foster loyalty but also generate conflict (Bobo & Hutchings, 1996).

GROUP SIZE

The next time you go to a party, try to arrive first. If you do, you will be in a position to observe some fascinating group

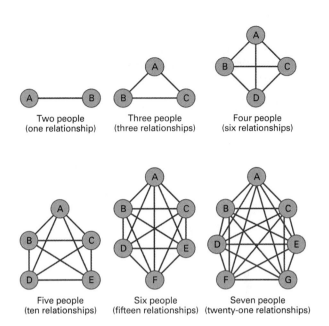

FIGURE 5-2 Group Size and Relationships

dynamics. Until about six people enter the room, everyone generally shares a single conversation. But as more people arrive, the group soon divides into two or more clusters. Group size plays a crucial role in how group members interact.

To understand why, note the mathematical number of relationships possible among two to seven people. As shown in Figure 5–2, two people form a single relationship; adding a third person results in three relationships; a fourth person yields six. Increasing the number of people further boosts the number of relationships much more rapidly because every new individual can interact with everyone already there. Thus, by the time seven people join one conversation, twenty-one "channels" connect them. With so many open channels, at this point the group usually divides.

German sociologist Georg Simmel (1858–1918) explored the dynamics of the smallest social groups. Simmel (1950, orig. 1902) used the term **dyad** (from the Greek word for "pair") to describe *a social group with two members.*

Simmel explained that social interaction in a dyad typically is more intense than in larger groups because neither member shares the other's attention with anyone else. In the United States, love affairs, marriages, and the closest friendships are dyadic.

But like a stool with only two legs, dyads are unstable. Both members of a dyad must work to keep the relationship going; if either withdraws, the group collapses. Because

The triad, illustrated by Jonathan Green's painting *Friends,* includes three people. A triad is more stable than a dyad because conflict between any two persons can be mediated by the third member. Even so, should the relationship between any two become more intense in a positive sense, those two are likely to exclude the third.

Jonathan Green, *Friends,* 1992. Oil on masonite, 14 in. × 11 in. © Jonathan Green, Naples, Florida. Collection of Patric McCoy.

stable marriages are important to society, the marital dyad is supported with legal, economic, and often religious ties.

A **triad,** *a social group with three members,* contains three relationships, each uniting two of the three people. A triad is more stable than a dyad because one member can act as a mediator if relations between the other two become strained. This bit of group dynamics explains why members of a dyad (say, a married couple) often seek out a third person (such as a counselor) to discuss tensions between them.

On the other hand, two of the three can pair up to press their views on the third, or two may intensify their relationship, leaving the other feeling left out. For example, when two of the three members of a triad develop a romantic interest in each other, they discover the meaning of the old saying, "Two's company, three's a crowd."

As groups grow beyond three people, they become more stable and capable of withstanding the loss of one or more members. At the same time, increases in group size reduce the intense interaction possible in only the smallest groups. This is why larger groups are based less on personal attachments and more on formal rules and regulations. Such formality helps the group persist over time, although it may also undergo change. The greater the number of members, the more contact there is with the outside world, opening the door to new attitudes and behaviors (Carley, 1991).

SOCIAL DIVERSITY: RACE, CLASS, AND GENDER

Race, ethnicity, class, and gender each affect group dynamics. Peter Blau (1977; Blau, Blum, & Schwartz, 1982; South & Messner, 1986) points out three ways in which social diversity influences intergroup contact:

1. **Large groups turn inward.** Blau explains that the larger a group is, the more likely its members are to concentrate relationships among themselves. Say a college is trying to enhance social diversity by increasing the number of international students. These students may add a dimension of difference, but as their numbers rise, they become more likely to form their own social group. Thus, efforts to promote social diversity may have the unintended effect of promoting separatism.

2. **Heterogeneous groups turn outward.** The more socially diverse a group is, the more likely its members are to interact with outsiders. Campus groups that recruit people of both sexes and various social backgrounds typically have more intergroup contact than those with members of one social type.

3. **Physical boundaries create social boundaries.** To the extent that a social group is physically segregated from others (by having its own dorm or dining area, for example), its members are less likely to interact with other people.

NETWORKS

A **network** is *a web of weak social ties.* Think of a network as a "fuzzy" group containing people who come into occasional contact but lack a sense of boundaries and belonging. If you think of a group as a "circle of friends," think of a network as a "social web" expanding outward, often reaching great distances and including large numbers of people.

Some networks come close to being groups, as in the case of college friends who stay in touch years after graduation by e-mail and telephone. More commonly, however, a network includes people we *know of*—or who *know of us*—but with whom we interact rarely, if at all. As one woman known as a

The Internet: A Global Network

Its beginnings seem right out of the 1960s Cold War film *Dr. Strangelove*. Back then, government officials and scientists were trying to figure out how to run the country after an atomic attack, which, they assumed, would knock out telephones and television. The solution was brilliant: Create a communication system with no central headquarters, no one in charge, and no main power switch—in short, an electronic web that would link the country in one vast network.

By 1985, the federal government began installing high-speed data lines around the country, and the Internet was born. Today, thousands of colleges and universities, as well tens of thousands of government offices, are joined by the Internet and share in the cost of its operation. Home computers can be connected to the "information superhighway" using a cable connection or a telephone line modem and a subscription to an Internet service provider.

How many people use the Internet? A rough estimate is that as of 2004, about 700 million people in 180 (of 192) countries around the world are connected, forming the largest network in history.

What is available on the Internet? Popular search engines such as Google (http://www.google.com) allow you to find Web sites for just about any topic you can imagine. The Internet also allows you to send e-mail: You can start a cyber-romance with a pen pal, write to your textbook author (macionis@kenyon.edu), or even send a message to the president of the United States (president@whitehouse.gov). Through the Internet, you can join in discussion groups, visit museums through "virtual tours," access data from government agencies (a good starting point is http://www.census.gov), explore sites of sociological interest (try the author's Web site at http://www.TheSociologyPage.com), or review for exams in this course (http://www.prenhall.com/macionis). With no formal rules for its use, the Internet's potential is limited only by our own imaginations.

Ironically, perhaps, it is precisely this freedom that disturbs some people. Critics claim that "electronic democracy" threatens our political system, parents fear that their children will access sexually explicit "adult sites," and purists are angered as the Internet becomes flooded with advertising.

In its "anything goes" character, the Internet is very much like the real world. Not surprisingly, then, a recent trend is that more and more users now use passwords, fees, and other "gates" to create subnetworks limited to people like themselves. From one vast network, then, is emerging many social groups.

WHAT DO YOU THINK?

1. How much of your contact with other people is over the Internet?
2. How do you feel about the "anything goes" character of the Internet?
3. Can you point to both advantages and disadvantages of Internet communication?

Sources: Based on Hafner (1994) and O'Connor (1997).

community organizer puts it, "I get calls at home, [and] someone says, 'Are you Roseann Navarro? Somebody told me to call you. I have this problem . . .'" (Kaminer, 1984:94).

Network ties may be weak, but they can be a powerful resource. For immigrants trying to become established in a new community, businesspeople seeking to expand their operations, or anyone looking for a job, *whom* you know often is just as important as *what* you know (Luo, 1997; Hagan, 1998; Petersen, Saporta, & Seidel, 2000).

Networks are based on people's colleges, clubs, neighborhoods, political parties, and personal interests. Obviously, some networks are made up of people with more wealth, power, and prestige than others; that explains the importance of being "well connected." The networks of more privileged categories of people—such as the members of a country club—are a valuable form of "social capital," which is more likely to lead people in these categories to higher-paying jobs (Green, Tigges, & Diaz, 1999; Lin, Cook, & Burt, 2001).

Some people also have denser networks than others; that is, they are connected to more people. Typically, the largest social networks include people who are young, well-educated, and living in large cities (Fernandez & Weinberg, 1997; Podolny & Baron, 1997).

Gender also shapes networks. Although the networks of men and women are typically of the same size, women include more relatives (and women) in their networks, whereas men include more co-workers (and more men). Women's ties, therefore, may not be quite as powerful as the "old boy" networks. Even so, research suggests that the networks of men and women are becoming more alike as gender inequality in the United States decreases (Mencken & Winfield, 1999; Reskin & McBrier, 2000; Torres & Huffman, 2002).

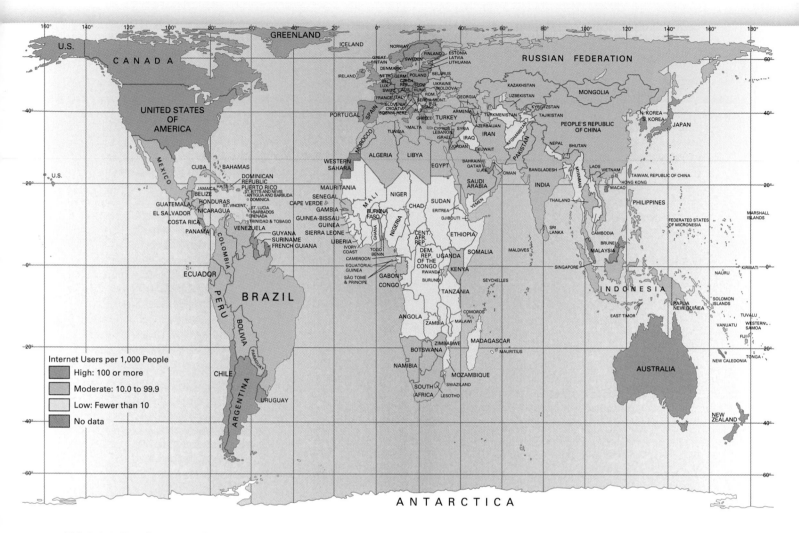

WINDOW ON THE WORLD

GLOBAL MAP 5-1   Internet Users in Global Perspective

This map shows how the Information Revolution has affected countries around the world. In most high-income nations, at least one-third of the population uses the Internet. By contrast, only a small share of people in low-income nations does so. What effect does this have on people's access to information? What does this mean for the future in terms of global inequality?

Sources: International Telecommunication Union (2003) and United Nations Development Programme (2004).

Finally, new information technology has generated a global network of unprecedented size in the form of the Internet. The Global Sociology box on page 117 takes a closer look at the history and development of this twenty-first-century form of communication. Global Map 5–1 shows that Internet use around the world is linked to income levels.

Formal Organizations

As noted earlier, a century ago, most people lived in small groups of family, friends, and neighbors. Today, our lives revolve more and more around **formal organizations,** *large secondary groups organized to achieve their goals efficiently.* Formal organizations such as corporations and government agencies differ from small primary groups in their impersonality and their formally planned atmosphere.

When you think about it, organizing almost 300 million members of U.S. society is a remarkable operation, involving countless jobs, from collecting taxes to delivering the mail. To carry out most of these tasks, we rely on large formal organizations, which develop lives and cultures of their own so that as members come and go, their operation can stay much the same over many years.

TYPES OF FORMAL ORGANIZATIONS

Amitai Etzioni (1975) identified three types of formal organizations, distinguished by the reasons people participate in them. Just about everyone who works for income belongs to a *utilitarian organization*. Joining a utilitarian organization usually is a matter of individual choice, although most people must join one or another such organization to make a living.

People join *normative organizations* not for income but to pursue some goal they think is morally worthwhile. Sometimes called *voluntary associations*, these include community service groups (such as the PTA, the Lions Club, the League of Women Voters, and the Red Cross), political parties, and religious organizations. In global perspective, people in the United States are more likely than those in the rest of the world to be members of voluntary associations (Curtis, Grabb, & Baer, 1992; Curtis, Baer, & Grabb, 2001; Schofer & Fourcade-Gourinchas, 2001). Figure 5–3 shows the extent of volunteer work among first-year college students, which has risen in recent years.

Coercive organizations have involuntary memberships. People are forced to join these organizations as a form of punishment (prisons) or treatment (psychiatric hospitals). Coercive organizations have special physical features, such as locked doors and barred windows, and are supervised by security personnel. They isolate people (whom they label "inmates" or "patients") for a period of time in order to radically change their attitudes and behavior (Goffman, 1961).

It is possible for a single formal organization to fall into *all* of these categories. For example, a mental hospital serves as a coercive organization for a patient, a utilitarian organization for a psychiatrist, and a normative organization for a hospital volunteer.

ORIGINS OF BUREAUCRACY

Formal organizations date back thousands of years. Elites who governed early empires relied on government officials to collect taxes, undertake military campaigns, and build monumental structures, from the Great Wall of China to the pyramids of Egypt.

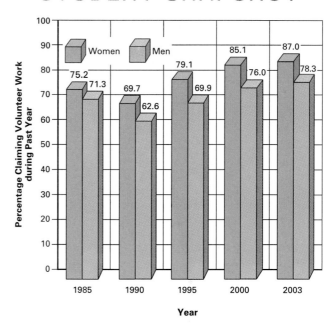

STUDENT SNAPSHOT

FIGURE 5-3   Volunteer Work among First-Year College Students, 1985–2003

Sources: Astin et al. (2002) and Sax et al. (2003).

However, early organizations had two limitations. First, they lacked the technology to travel over large distances, to communicate quickly, and to collect and store information. Second, the preindustrial societies they were trying to rule had a traditional culture. **Tradition,** according to German sociologist Max Weber, consists of *values and beliefs passed from generation to generation.* Tradition makes a society conservative, Weber explained, because it limits an organization's efficiency and ability to change.

By contrast, Weber described the modern worldview as **rationality,** *a way of thinking that emphasizes deliberate, matter-of-fact calculation of the most efficient means to accomplish a particular task.* A rational worldview pays little attention to the past and is open to any changes that might get the job done better or more quickly.

The rise of the "organizational society" rests on what Weber called the **rationalization of society,** *the historical change from tradition to rationality as the dominant mode of human thought.* Modern society, he claimed, becomes "disenchanted" as sentimental ties give way to a rational focus on science, complex technology, and the organizational structure called bureaucracy.

Although formal organization is vital to modern, high-income nations, it is far from new. Twenty-five centuries ago, the Chinese philosopher and teacher K'ung Fu-Tzu (known to Westerners as Confucius) endorsed the idea that government offices should be filled by the most talented young men. This led to what was probably the world's first system of civil service examinations. Here, would-be bureaucrats compose essays to demonstrate their knowledge of Confucian texts.

CHARACTERISTICS OF BUREAUCRACY

Bureaucracy is *an organizational model rationally designed to perform tasks efficiently.* Bureaucratic officials regularly create and revise policy to increase efficiency. To appreciate the power and scope of bureaucratic organization, consider that any one of some 300 million phones in the United States can connect you within seconds to any other phone in a home, business, automobile, or even a hiker's backpack on a remote trail in the Rocky Mountains. Such instant communication is beyond the imagination of people who lived in the ancient world.

Of course, the telephone system depends on technology such as electricity, fiber optics, and computers. But the system could not exist without the organizational capacity

to keep track of every telephone call—recording which phone called which other phone, when, and for how long—and presenting all this information to more than 100 million telephone users in the form of monthly bills.

What specific traits promote organizational efficiency? Max Weber (1978, orig. 1921) identified six key elements of the ideal bureaucratic organization:

1. **Specialization.** Our ancestors spent most of their time looking for food and finding shelter. Bureaucracy, by contrast, assigns individuals highly specialized jobs.

2. **Hierarchy of offices.** Bureaucracies arrange workers in a vertical ranking of offices. Each person is thus supervised by "higher-ups" in the organization while in turn supervising others in lower positions. Usually, with few people at the top and many at the bottom, bureaucratic organizations take the form of a pyramid.

3. **Rules and regulations.** Rationally enacted rules and regulations guide a bureaucracy's operation. Ideally, a bureaucracy seeks to operate in a completely predictable fashion.

4. **Technical competence.** Bureaucratic officials have the technical competence to carry out their duties. Bureaucracies typically hire new members according to set standards and then monitor their performance. Such impersonal evaluation contrasts with the ancient custom of favoring relatives, whatever their talents, over strangers.

5. **Impersonality.** Bureaucracy puts rules ahead of personal whim so that both clients and workers are all treated the same. From this impersonal approach comes the idea of the "faceless bureaucrat."

6. **Formal, written communications.** Someone once said that the heart of bureaucracy is not people but To learn more about Max Weber, visit the Gallery of Sociologists at http://www. TheSociologyPage.com paperwork. Rather than casual, face-to-face talk, bureaucracy depends on formal, written memos and reports, which accumulate in vast files.

Bureaucratic organization promotes efficiency by carefully hiring workers and limiting the unpredictable effects of personal taste and opinion. The Summing Up table reviews the differences between small social groups and large formal organizations.

ORGANIZATIONAL ENVIRONMENT

No organization operates in a vacuum. How any organization performs depends not only on its own goals and policies

SUMMING UP

Small Groups and Formal Organizations

	Small Groups	Formal Organizations
Activities	Much the same for all members	Distinct and highly specialized
Hierarchy	Often informal or nonexistent	Clearly defined, corresponding to offices
Norms	General norms, informally applied	Clearly defined rules and regulations
Membership criteria	Variable; often based on personal affection or kinship	Technical competence to carry out assigned tasks
Relationships	Variable and typically primary	Typically secondary, with selective primary ties
Communications	Typically casual and face to face	Typically formal and in writing
Focus	Person-oriented	Task-oriented

but also on the **organizational environment,** *factors outside an organization that affect its operation.* These factors include technology, economic and political trends, and the available workforce, as well as other organizations.

Modern organizations are shaped by the *technology* of computers, telephone systems, and copiers. Computers give employees access to more information and people than ever before. At the same time, computer technology allows managers to closely monitor the activities of workers (Markoff, 1991).

Economic and political trends affect organizations. All organizations are helped or hurt by periodic economic growth or recession. Most industries also face competition from abroad as well as changes in law—such as new environmental standards—at home.

Population patterns, such as the size and composition of the surrounding population, also affect organizations. The average age, typical education, and social diversity of a local community determine the available workforce and sometimes the market for an organization's products or services.

Other organizations also contribute to the organizational environment. To be competitive, a hospital must be responsive to the insurance industry and organizations representing doctors, nurses, and other workers. It must also be aware of the equipment and procedures available at nearby facilities, as well as their prices.

THE INFORMAL SIDE OF BUREAUCRACY

Weber's ideal bureaucracy deliberately regulates every activity. In actual organizations, however, human beings are creative (and stubborn) enough to resist bureaucratic regulation. Informality may amount to simply cutting corners on the job, but it also can provide the flexibility necessary for an organization to survive and prosper (Scott, 1981).

In part, informality comes from the varying personalities of organizational leaders. Studies of U.S. corporations show that the qualities and quirks of individuals—including personal charisma and interpersonal skills—greatly affect organizational success or failure (Halberstam, 1986; Baron, Hannan, & Burton, 1999).

Authoritarian, democratic, and laissez-faire types of leadership (described earlier in this chapter) reflect individual personality as much as any organizational plan. Then, too, in the "real world" of organizations, leaders sometimes seek to benefit personally through abuse of organizational power. Perhaps even more commonly, leaders take credit for the efforts of those who work for them. For example, many secretaries have far more authority and responsibility than their official job titles and salaries suggest.

Communication offers another example of organizational informality. Memos and other written documents are the formal way to spread information through the organization. Typically, however, people create informal networks, or "grapevines," that spread information quickly, if not always accurately. Grapevines, using word of mouth and e-mail, are particularly important to rank-and-file workers because higher-ups often attempt to keep important information from them.

The spread of e-mail has "flattened" organizations somewhat, allowing even the lowest-ranking employee to bypass immediate superiors to communicate directly with

George Tooker's painting *Government Bureau* is a powerful statement about the human costs of bureaucracy. The artist paints members of the public in a drab sameness—reduced from human beings to mere "cases" to be disposed of as quickly as possible. Set apart from others by their positions, officials are "faceless bureaucrats" concerned more with numbers than with providing genuine assistance (notice that the artist places the fingers of the officials on calculators).

George Tooker, *Government Bureau*, 1956. Egg tempera on gesso panel, 19⅝ × 29⅝ inches. The Metropolitan Museum of Art, George A. Hearn Fund, 1956 (56.78). Photograph © 1984 The Metropolitan Museum of Art.

the organization's leader or all fellow employees at once. Some organizations consider such "open channel" communication unwelcome and limit the use of e-mail. Leaders also may seek to protect themselves from a flood of messages each day. Microsoft Corporation (whose leader, Bill Gates, has an "unlisted" address yet still receives hundreds of e-mail messages a day) has developed screens that filter out all messages except those from approved people (Gwynne & Dickerson, 1997).

Despite the highly regulated nature of bureaucracy, members of formal organizations still find ways to personalize their work and surroundings. Such efforts suggest that we now take a closer look at some of the problems of bureaucracy.

PROBLEMS OF BUREAUCRACY

We rely on bureaucracy to manage countless dimensions of everyday life, but many people are uneasy about large organizations. Bureaucracy can dehumanize and manipulate us, and some say it poses a threat to political democracy.

Bureaucratic alienation. Max Weber held up bureaucracy as a model of productivity. Yet Weber was keenly aware of bureaucracy's potential to *dehumanize* the people it is supposed to serve. The same impersonality that fosters efficiency at the same time keeps officials and clients from responding to each other's unique personal needs. Typically, officials treat each client impersonally as a standard "case."

Formal organizations create *alienation*, according to Weber, by reducing the human being to "a small cog in a ceaselessly moving mechanism" (1978:988, orig. 1921). Although formal organizations are designed to serve humanity, Weber feared that people might well end up serving formal organizations.

Bureaucratic inefficiency and ritualism. *Inefficiency*, the failure of a formal organization to carry out the work it exists to perform, is a familiar problem. According to one report, the General Services Administration, the government agency that buys equipment for federal workers, takes up to three years to process a request for a new computer. This ensures that by the time the computer arrives, it is already out of date (Gwynne & Dickerson, 1997).

The problem of inefficiency is captured in the concept of *red tape*, a term derived from the ribbon used by eighteenth-century English administrators to wrap official parcels and records (Shipley, 1985). To Robert Merton (1968), red tape amounts to a new twist on the familiar concept of group conformity. He coined the term **bureaucratic ritualism** to describe *a focus on rules and regulations to the point of undermining an organization's goals.* After the terrorist attacks in 2001, for example, the post office continued to deliver mail addressed to Osama bin Laden to a post office in Afghanistan, despite the objections of the FBI. It took an act of Congress to change the policy (Bedard, 2002).

Bureaucratic inertia. If bureaucrats sometimes have little reason to work efficiently, they have every reason to protect their jobs. Thus, officials typically work to keep their organization going even when its goal has been realized. As Weber put it, "Once fully established, bureaucracy is among the social structures which are hardest to destroy" (1978:987, orig. 1921).

Bureaucratic inertia refers to *the tendency of bureaucratic organizations to perpetuate themselves.* Formal organizations tend to take on a life of their own beyond their formal objectives. For example, the U.S. Department of Agriculture still has offices in nearly every county in all states, even though only about one county in ten has any working farms. Usually, an organization stays in business by redefining its goals; for example, the Agriculture Department now performs a broad range of work not directly related to farming, including nutritional and environmental research.

Oligarchy.   Early in the twentieth century, Robert Michels (1876–1936) pointed out the link between bureaucracy and political **oligarchy,** *the rule of the many by the few* (1949, orig. 1911). According to what Michels called "the iron law of oligarchy," the pyramid shape of bureaucracy places a few leaders in charge of organizational resources.

Max Weber credited a strict hierarchy of responsibility with superior organizational efficiency. But Michels countered that hierarchy also undermines democracy because officials can—and often do—use their access to information, resources, and the media to promote their personal interests.

Furthermore, bureaucracy helps distance officials from the public, as in the case of the corporate president or public official who is "unavailable for comment" to the local press or the national president who claims "executive privilege" when withholding documents from Congress. Oligarchy, then, thrives in the hierarchical structure of bureaucracy and reduces the accountability of leaders to the people (Tolson, 1995).

Political competition, term limits, and a system of checks and balances prevent the U.S. government from becoming an out-and-out oligarchy. Even so, those in office enjoy a significant advantage in U.S. politics. In the 2000 congressional elections, only 15 of 437 congressional officeholders running for reelection were defeated by their challengers (Giroux, 2000; Pierce, 2000).

The Evolution of Formal Organizations

The problems of bureaucracy—especially the alienation it produces and its tendency toward oligarchy—stem from two organizational traits: hierarchy and rigidity. To Weber, bureaucracy is a top-down system: Rules and regulations made at the top guide every part of people's work down the

According to Max Weber, bureaucracy is an organizational strategy that promotes efficiency. Impersonality, however, also fosters alienation among employees, who may become indifferent to the formal goals of the organization. The behavior of this municipal employee in Bombay, India, is understandable to members of formal organizations almost anywhere in the world.

chain of command. A century ago in the United States, Weber's ideas took hold in an organizational model called *scientific management.* We begin with a look at this model and then examine three challenges over the course of the twentieth century that gradually led to a new model: the *flexible organization.*

SCIENTIFIC MANAGEMENT

Frederick Winslow Taylor (1911) had a simple message: Most businesses in the United States were sadly inefficient. Most managers had little idea of how to increase output, and workers relied on the same tired skills of earlier generations.

To increase efficiency, Taylor explained, business should apply the principles of science. **Scientific management** is *the application of scientific principles to the operation of a business or other large organization.*

Scientific management involves three steps. First, managers carefully observe the job performed by each worker, identifying all the operations involved and measuring the time needed for each. Second, managers then analyze their data, trying to discover ways for workers to perform each job more efficiently. For example, managers might decide to give

The ideas of scientific management were most successfully applied by Henry Ford, who pioneered the automobile assembly line. As shown in this 1928 photograph of the Dearborn, Michigan, plant, Ford divided up the job of building cars into hundreds of different tasks, each performed by a worker as the cars moved along an assembly line. The result was that new cars could be produced so cheaply that most of these autoworkers could afford to buy one.

workers different tools or reposition various work operations within the factory. Third, management provides guidance and incentives for workers to do their jobs more efficiently. If a factory worker moves 20 tons of pig iron in one day, for example, management would show the worker how to do the job more efficiently and then provide higher wages as the worker's productivity rises. Applying scientific principles in this way, Taylor concluded, companies become more profitable, workers earn higher wages, and in the end, consumers end up paying lower prices. Auto pioneer Henry Ford, who was enthusiastic in his support of scientific management, put it this way: "Save ten steps a day for each of 12,000 employees, and you will have saved fifty miles of wasted motion and misspent energy" (Allen & Hyman, 1999:209).

In the early 1900s, the Ford Motor Company and many other businesses followed Taylor's lead and made dramatic improvements in efficiency. As time went on, however, formal organizations faced three new challenges, involving race and gender, rising competition from abroad, and changes in the nature of work itself. Let us take a brief look at each of these challenges.

THE FIRST CHALLENGE: RACE AND GENDER

In the 1960s, critics pointed out that big businesses and other organizations were inefficient—and also unfair—in their hiring practices. Rather than hiring on the basis of competence, as Weber had proposed, they routinely excluded women and other minorities. As a result, most managers were white men.

Patterns of privilege and exclusion. Even by the early twenty-first century, as shown in Figure 5–4, white men in the United States (35 percent of the working-age population) still held 56 percent of management jobs. White women made up 35 percent of the population, but they held just 28 percent of managerial positions (U.S. Equal Employment Opportunity Commission, 2004). The members of other minorities lagged further behind.

Rosabeth Moss Kanter (1977; Kanter & Stein, 1979) points out that excluding women and minorities from the workplace ignores the talents of more than half the population. Furthermore, underrepresented people in an organization often feel like socially isolated out-groups: uncomfortably visible, taken less seriously, and given fewer chances for promotion.

Opening up an organization, Kanter claims, improves everyone's on-the-job performance by motivating employees to become "fast-trackers" who work harder and are more committed to the company. By contrast, an organization with many dead-end jobs turns workers into unproductive "zombies." An open organization also encourages leaders to seek out the ideas of everyone, which benefits the whole organization. It is officials in rigid organizations—those who have little reason themselves to be creative—who jealously guard their privileges and closely supervise their employees.

The "female advantage." Some organizational researchers argue that including more women, in particular, brings specialized management skills that strengthen an organization. According to Deborah Tannen (1994), women have a greater "information focus" and more readily ask questions in order to understand an issue. Men, by contrast, have an "image focus" that makes them wonder how asking questions in a particular situation will affect their reputation.

In another study of women executives, Sally Helgesen (1990) found three additional gender-linked patterns. First, women place greater value on communication skills and share information more than men do. Second, women are more flexible leaders who typically give their employees greater freedom. Third, women place greater emphasis on the interconnectedness of all organizational operations.

She coined the term *female advantage* for these patterns, which help companies that are trying to be more flexible and democratic.

In sum, one challenge to conventional bureaucracy is increased openness and flexibility that can take advantage of everyone's experience, ideas, and creativity. The result goes right to the bottom line: greater profits.

THE SECOND CHALLENGE: THE JAPANESE WORK ORGANIZATION

In 1980, the corporate world in the United States was shaken to discover that the most popular automobile model sold in this country was not a Chevrolet, Ford, or Plymouth but the Honda Accord, made in Japan. To people old enough to remember the 1950s, the words "made in Japan" generally meant a cheap, poorly made product. But times had changed. The success of the Japanese auto industry (and shortly thereafter, companies making electronics, cameras, and other products) soon had analysts buzzing about the "Japanese organization." How else could so small a country challenge the world's economic powerhouse?

Japanese organizations reflect that nation's strong collective spirit. In contrast to the U.S. emphasis on rugged individualism, the Japanese value cooperation. In effect, formal organizations in Japan are like very large primary groups. A generation ago, William Ouchi (1981) highlighted differences between formal organizations in Japan and in the United States. First, Japanese companies hired new workers in groups, giving everyone the same salary and responsibilities. Second, many Japanese companies hired workers for life, fostering strong loyalties. Third, many Japanese organizations trained workers in all phases of operations, again with the idea that employees will remain with the company for life. Fourth, although Japanese corporate leaders took ultimate responsibility for their organization's performance, they involved workers in "quality circles" to discuss decisions that affect them. Fifth, Japanese companies played a large role in the lives of workers, providing home mortgages, sponsoring recreational activities, and scheduling social events. These characteristics encourage loyalty among members of Japanese organizations—much more than is typically the case in the United States.

For decades, people around the world marveled at the economic "miracle" of Japanese organizations. But the praise was premature. Around 1990, the Japanese economy entered a downward trend that is only now showing signs of ending. As a result of this downturn, most Japanese companies no longer offer workers jobs for life or many of the other benefits that Ouchi noted.

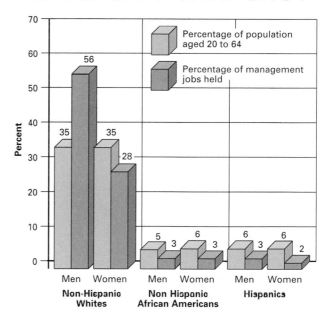

DIVERSITY SNAPSHOT

FIGURE 5-4 U.S. Managers in Private Industry by Race, Sex, and Ethnicity, 2002

Sources: U.S. Census Bureau (2002) and U.S. Equal Employment Opportunity Commission (2004).

THE THIRD CHALLENGE: THE CHANGING NATURE OF WORK

Beyond rising global competition and the need to provide equal opportunity for all, pressure to modify conventional organizations is also coming from changes in the nature of work itself. In recent decades, the U.S. economy has moved from industrial to postindustrial production. In other words, rather than working in factories using heavy machinery to make *things*, more people are using computers and other electronic technology to create or process *information*. A postindustrial society, then, is characterized by information-based organizations.

Frederick Taylor developed his concept of scientific management at a time when most jobs involved tasks that, though often backbreaking, were routine. Workers shoveled coal, poured liquid iron into molds, welded body panels to automobiles on an assembly line, or shot hot rivets into steel girders to build skyscrapers. In addition, a large part of the U.S. labor force in Taylor's day was immigrants, most of whom had little schooling and many of whom knew little English. The routine nature of industrial jobs, coupled with

FIGURE 5-5 Two Organizational Models

The conventional model of bureaucratic organizations has a pyramid shape, with a clear chain of command. Orders flow from the top down, and reports of performance flow from the bottom up. Such organizations have extensive rules and regulations, and their workers have highly specialized jobs. More open and flexible organizations have a flatter shape, more like a football. With fewer levels in the hierarchy, responsibility for generating ideas and making decisions is shared throughout the organization. Many workers do their jobs in teams and have a broad knowledge of the entire organization's operation.

Source: Created by the author.

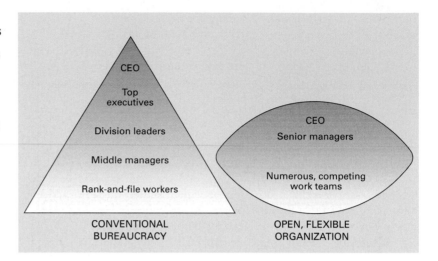

the limited skills of the labor force, led Taylor to treat work as a series of fixed tasks set down by management and followed by employees.

Many of today's information age jobs are very different: The work of designers, artists, consultants, writers, editors, composers, programmers, business owners, and others now demands creativity and imagination. What does this mean for formal organizations? Here are several ways in which today's organizations differ from those of a century ago:

1. **Creative freedom.** As one Hewlett-Packard executive put it, "From their first day of work here, people are given important responsibilities and are encouraged to grow" (cited in Brooks, 2000:128). Today's organizations treat employees with information age skills as a vital resource. Executives can set production goals but cannot dictate how to accomplish tasks involving imagination and discovery. This gives highly skilled workers *creative freedom*, which means they are subject to less day-to-day supervision as long as they generate good ideas in the long run.

2. **Competitive work teams.** Many organizations give several groups of employees the freedom to work on a problem, at the same time offering the greatest rewards to the group that comes up with the best solution. Competitive work teams—a strategy first used by Japanese organizations—draw out the creative contributions of everyone and at the same time reduce the alienation often found in conventional organizations (Maddox, 1994; Yeatts, 1994).

3. **A flatter organization.** By spreading responsibility for creative problem solving throughout the workforce,

organizations take on a flatter shape. That is, the pyramid shape of conventional bureaucracy is replaced by an organizational form with fewer levels in the chain of command, as shown in Figure 5–5.

4. **Greater flexibility.** The typical industrial age organization was a rigid structure guided from the top. Such organizations may accomplish a good deal of work, but they are not especially creative or able to respond quickly to changes in their larger environment. The ideal model in the information age is a *more open, flexible* organization, one that both generates new ideas and, in a rapidly changing global marketplace, adapts quickly.

As David Brooks puts it, "The machine is no longer held up as the standard that healthy organizations should emulate. Now, it's the ecosystem" (2000:128). Today's "smart" companies seek out intelligent, creative people (America Online's main building is called "Creative Center One") and encourage the growth of their talents.

Keep in mind, however, that many of today's jobs do not involve creative work at all. In reality, the postindustrial economy has created two very different types of work: highly skilled creative work and low-skilled service work. The work in the fast-food industry, for example, is routine and highly supervised and thus has much more in common with factory work of a century ago than with the creative teamwork typical of today's information organizations. Therefore, at the same time that some organizations have taken on a flatter, more flexible form, others continue to use a rigid chain of command, as the next section explains.

The best of today's "information-age jobs"—including working at the popular search-engine Web site Google—allow people lots of personal freedom as long as they produce good ideas. At the same time, many other jobs—such as working the counter at McDonald's—involve the same routines and strict supervision found in factories a century ago.

THE "MCDONALDIZATION" OF SOCIETY[1]

As noted in the opening to this chapter, McDonald's has enjoyed enormous success, now operating more than 30,000 restaurants in the United States and around the world. Japan now has more than 2,400 sets of Golden Arches, and the world's largest McDonald's is found in China's capital city of Beijing.

> October 9, Macao. Here we are, halfway around the world, in the Portuguese colony of Macao, a little nub jutting from the Chinese coast. Few people speak English, and life on the streets seems a world apart from the urban rhythms of New York, Chicago, or Los Angeles. Then I turn the corner and stand face to face with (who else?) Ronald McDonald! After eating who-knows-what for many days, forgive me for giving in to the lure of the Big Mac. But the most amazing thing is that the food—the burger, fries, and drinks—looks, smells, and tastes exactly the same as it does back home 10,000 miles away!

McDonald's is far more than a restaurant chain; it is a symbol of U.S. culture. Not only do people around the world associate McDonald's with the United States, but here at home, one poll found that 98 percent of schoolchildren could identify Ronald McDonald, making him as well known as Santa Claus.

Even more important, the organizational principles that underlie McDonald's are coming to dominate our entire society. Our culture is becoming "McDonaldized," an awkward way of saying that many aspects of life are modeled on the famous restaurant chain. Parents buy toys at worldwide chain stores such as Toys 'R' Us; we drive in to Jiffy Lube for a ten-minute oil change; face-to-face communication is being replaced more and more with voice mail, e-mail, and junk mail; more vacations take the form of resort and tour packages; television presents news in the form of ten-second sound bites; college admissions officers size up students they have never met by glancing at their GPA and SAT scores; and professors assign ghostwritten textbooks[2] and evaluate students by giving tests mass-produced for them by publishing companies. The list goes on and on.

---

[1]The term "McDonaldization" was coined by Jim Hightower (1975); much of the material in this section is based on Ritzer (1993, 1998, 2000) and Schlosser (2002).

[2]A number of popular sociology texts were not written by the person whose name appears on the cover. This book is not one of them.

Computer Technology, Large Organizations, and the Assault on Privacy

Late for a meeting with a new client, Sarah drives her car through a yellow light just as it turns red. A computer notes the violation, and a camera snaps a picture of the rear of the car, showing the license plate. At the same moment, another camera photographs the side of the car, showing Sarah behind the wheel. In seven days, she receives a summons to appear in court.

Joe dials a toll-free number to check the pollen count. As he listens to a recorded message, a Caller ID computer identifies Joe and pulls up his profile from a public records database. The fact that Joe suffers from allergies is added to his profile, which is sold to a drug company, prompting the company to send Joe a free sample of a new allergy medication.

At a local department store, Nina uses her American Express card to buy an expensive new watch and some sleepwear. The store's computer adds Nina's name to its databases of "buyers of expensive jewelry" and "buyers of sexy lingerie." The store trades these databases with other companies, and within a month, Nina receives four jewelry catalogues and an adult video brochure (Bernstein, 1997; Hamilton, 2001).

Are these cases of serving the public, or are they violations of people's privacy? The answer, of course, is both: The same systems that help organizations operate efficiently also allow them to invade our lives and manipulate us. As bureaucracy has expanded in the United States, privacy has declined.

People had little privacy in the small-town life of the past, but at least if people knew something about you, you were just as likely to know something about them. Today, unknown people "out there" can access information about any of us at any time.

In part, the loss of privacy is a result of increasingly complex computer technology. Are you aware that every time you send an e-mail or visit a Web site, you leave a record in one or more computers? Most of these records can be seen by people you don't know, as well as by employers and even by police and other public officials.

Another part of today's loss of privacy reflects the increasing number and size of formal organizations. As explained in this chapter, large organizations tend to treat people impersonally, and they have a huge appetite for information. Mix large organizations with ever more complex computer technology, and it is no wonder that most people in the United States are concerned about who knows what about them—and what is being done with this information.

Basic principles. What do all these developments have in common? According to George Ritzer (1993), the McDonaldization of society involves four basic organizational principles:

1. **Efficiency.** Ray Kroc, the marketing genius behind McDonald's, set out with one goal: to serve a hamburger, French fries, and a milkshake to every customer in fifty seconds or less. Today, one of the company's most popular items is the Egg McMuffin, an entire breakfast in a single sandwich. In the restaurant, customers bus their own trays or, better still, drive away from the pickup window, taking whatever mess they make with them. Such efficiency is now central to our way of life. We tend to think that anything done quickly is, for that reason alone, good.

2. **Standardization.** The first McDonald's operating manual declared the weight of a regular raw hamburger to be 1.6 ounces, its size to be 3.875 inches across, and its fat content to be 19 percent. A slice of cheese weighs exactly half an ounce, and French fries are cut precisely 9/32 of an inch thick.

   Think about how many objects around the home, the workplace, and the campus are designed and mass-produced uniformly according to a standard plan. Not just our environment but our life experiences—from traveling the nation's interstate highways

For decades, the level of personal privacy in the United States has been declining. Early in the twentieth century, when state agencies began issuing driver's licenses, they generated files for every licensed driver. Today, officials can send this information at the touch of a button to other organizations, including the police. Similarly, the Internal Revenue Service, the Social Security Administration, and government agencies that benefit veterans, students, the unemployed, and the poor all collect extensive information.

Business organizations now do much the same thing, although, as the examples show, people may not be aware that their choices and activities end up in a company's database. Most people find credit cards a great convenience—the U.S. population now holds more than 1 billion of them, averaging more than five per adult—but one price we pay for the convenience of credit card purchases is automatic creation of records that can end up almost anywhere.

Then there are the small cameras that are found in stores, public buildings, parking garages, and college campuses. The number of surveillance cameras that monitor our movements is rapidly increasing with each passing year. Such cameras may increase public safety in some ways—say, by discouraging a mugger or even a terrorist—but only at the cost of the little privacy we have left.

After the September 11, 2001, terrorist attacks, the federal government took steps (including passage of the USA Patriot Act) to strengthen national security. Now government officials more closely monitor not just who enters the country but the activities of all members of U.S. society. National security and privacy do not go well together.

Of course, some legal protections remain. All the states have enacted laws giving citizens rights to examine some records about themselves kept by employers, banks, and credit bureaus. The U.S. Privacy Act of 1974 also limits the exchange of personal information among government agencies and permits citizens to examine and correct most government files. But so many organizations (both public and private) now have information about us—experts estimate that 90 percent of U.S. households are profiled in databases somewhere—that current laws simply do not address the extent of the privacy problem. In the past decade, the Internet revolution has made the safeguarding of personal privacy more difficult than ever. Yet there are still no national standards that protect public privacy.

CONTINUE THE DEBATE . . .

1. Do you believe that the concern over national security is eroding privacy? Which is more important? Explain your position.

2. Internet search engines such as Yahoo! (http://www.yahoo.com) have "people search" programs that let you locate almost anyone. Do you think such programs pose a threat to personal privacy?

3. In your opinion, will personal privacy continue to decline in the United States in years to come? Why or why not?

Sources: Wright (1998), "Online Privacy" (2000), Rosen (2000), Hamilton (2001), and Heymann (2002).

to sitting at home viewing national TV shows—are now more standardized than ever before.

3. **Uniformity and predictability.** A person can walk into a McDonald's restaurant almost anywhere and buy the same sandwiches, drinks, and desserts prepared in precisely the same way.[3] Uniformity results from a highly rational system that specifies every action and leaves nothing to chance.

4. **Control through automation.** The most unreliable element in the McDonald's system is human beings. After all, people have good and bad days, sometimes let their minds wander, or decide to try something a different way. To minimize the unpredictable human element, McDonald's has automated its equipment to cook food at a fixed temperature for a set length of time. Even the cash register at McDonald's is keyed to pictures of the items so that ringing up a customer's order is as simple as possible.

---

[3]As McDonald's has "gone global," a few products have been added or changed according to local tastes. For example, in Uruguay, customers enjoy the McHuevo (hamburger with poached egg on top); Norwegians can buy McLaks (grilled salmon sandwiches); the Dutch favor the Groenteburger (vegetable burger); in Thailand, McDonald's serves Samurai pork burgers; the Japanese can purchase Chicken Tatsuta Sandwich (chicken seasoned with soy and ginger); Filipinos eat McSpaghetti (spaghetti with tomato sauce and bits of hot dog); and in India, where Hindus eat no beef, McDonald's sells a vegetarian Maharaja Mac (Sullivan, 1995).

Similarly, automatic teller machines are replacing banks, highly automated bakeries produce bread with scarcely any human intervention, and chickens and eggs (or is it eggs and chickens?) emerge from automated hatcheries. In supermarkets, laser scanners at self-checkouts are phasing out human checkers. Most of our shopping now occurs in malls, where everything from temperature and humidity to the kinds of stores and products are subject to continuous control and supervision (Ide & Cordell, 1994).

Can rationality be irrational? There can be no argument about the popularity or efficiency of McDonald's. But there is another side to the story.

Max Weber was alarmed at the increasing rationalization of the world, fearing that formal organizations would cage our imaginations and crush the human spirit. As he saw it, rational systems were efficient but dehumanizing. McDonaldization bears him out. Each of the four principles just discussed limits human creativity, choice, and freedom. Echoing Weber, Ritzer states that "the ultimate irrationality of McDonaldization is that people could lose control over the system and it would come to control us" (1993:145). Not surprisingly, perhaps, McDonald's itself now owns a large stake in more upscale restaurants, such as Chipotle's and Pret-à-Manger, that offer food that is more sophisticated, fresh, and healthful (Philadelphia, 2002).

The Future of Organizations: Opposing Trends

Early in the twentieth century, ever-larger organizations arose in the United States, most taking on the bureaucratic form described by Max Weber. In many respects, these organizations were like armies led by powerful generals who passed down orders to their captains and lieutenants. Foot soldiers, working in the factories, did what they were told.

With the emergence of a postindustrial economy after 1950, as well as rising competition from abroad, many organizations evolved toward the flatter, more flexible model that encourages communication and creativity. Such "intelligent organizations" (Pinchot & Pinchot, 1993; Brooks, 2000) have become more productive than ever. Just as important, for highly skilled people who enjoy creative freedom, these organizations create less of the alienation that so worried Max Weber.

But this is only half the story. Although the postindustrial economy created many highly skilled jobs, it created even more routine service jobs, such as those offered by McDonald's. Fast-food companies now represent the largest pool of low-wage labor aside from migrant workers (Schlosser, 2002). Work of this kind—commonly called "McJobs"—offers few of the benefits that today's highly skilled workers enjoy. On the contrary, the automated routines that define work in the fast-food industry, telemarketing, and similar fields are very much the same as those that Frederick Taylor described a century ago.

Moreover, the organizational flexibility that gives better-off workers more freedom carries, for rank-and-file employees, the ever-present threat of "downsizing" (Sennett, 1998). Organizations facing global competition are eager to attract creative employees, but they are just as eager to cut costs by eliminating as many routine jobs as possible. The net result is that some people are better off than ever while others worry about holding their jobs and struggle to make ends meet, a trend that Chapter 8 ("Social Stratification") explores in detail.

U.S. organizations remain the envy of the world for their productive efficiency. Indeed, there are few places on Earth where the mail arrives as quickly and dependably as it does in the United States. But we should remember that the future is far brighter for some than for others. In addition, as the Controversy & Debate box on pages 128–29 explains, formal organizations pose a mounting threat to our privacy, something to keep in mind as we envision our organizational future.

Summary

1. Social groups, large and small, link members of society and perform various tasks.

2. Primary groups tend to be small and person-oriented; secondary groups typically are large and goal-oriented.

3. Instrumental leadership is concerned with realizing a group's goals; expressive leadership focuses on members' morale and well-being.

4. Because group members often seek agreement, groups can pressure members toward conformity.

5. Individuals use reference groups—both in-groups and out-groups—to evaluate situations and make decisions.

6. Georg Simmel described the dyad, a group with just two members, as intense but unstable; the three-member triad is more stable but can easily turn into a dyad with the loss of one member.

7. Peter Blau explored how group size, social diversity, and physical segregation of groups affect members' behavior.

8. Social networks are relational webs that link people who have little common identity and limited interaction. The Internet is a vast electronic network linking millions of people worldwide.

9. Formal organizations are large secondary groups that try to perform complex tasks efficiently. They are classified as normative, coercive, or utilitarian, based on their members' reasons for joining.

10. Bureaucratic organization expands in modern societies to perform many complex tasks efficiently. Bureaucracy is based on specialization, hierarchy, rules and regulations, technical competence, impersonal interaction, and formal, written communication.

11. Technology, economic and political trends, population patterns, and other organizations are all part of the organizational environment in which a particular organization operates.

12. Ideally, bureaucracy promotes efficiency, but bureaucracy may also generate alienation and oligarchy and contribute to the erosion of personal privacy.

13. Frederick Taylor's theory of scientific management shaped U.S. organizations a century ago. Since then, organizations have evolved toward a more open and flexible form as they have included a larger share of women and minorities; responded to global competition, especially from Japan; and shifted their focus from industrial production to postindustrial information processing.

14. Reflecting the collective spirit of Japanese culture, formal organizations in Japan are based more on personal ties than their U.S. counterparts.

15. The "McDonaldization" of society involves increasing automation and impersonality.

16. The future of organizations probably will involve opposing trends: increasing creative freedom for highly skilled information workers and increasing supervision and discipline of less-skilled service workers.

KEY CONCEPTS

social group (p. 110) two or more people who identify and interact with one another

primary group (p. 111) a small social group whose members share personal and lasting relationships

secondary group (p. 111) a large and impersonal social group whose members pursue a specific goal or activity

instrumental leadership (p. 112) group leadership that focuses on the completion of tasks

expressive leadership (p. 112) group leadership that focuses on the group's well-being

groupthink (p. 114) the tendency of group members to conform, resulting in a narrow view of some issue

reference group (p. 114) a social group that serves as a point of reference in making evaluations and decisions

in-group (p. 115) a social group toward which a member feels respect and commitment

out-group (p. 115) a social group toward which a person feels a sense of competition or opposition

dyad (p. 115) a social group with two members

triad (p. 116) a social group with three members

network (p. 116) a web of weak social ties

formal organization (p. 118) a large secondary group organized to achieve its goals efficiently

tradition (p. 119) values and beliefs passed from generation to generation

rationality (p. 119) a way of thinking that emphasizes deliberate, matter-of-fact calculation of the most efficient means to accomplish a particular task

rationalization of society (p. 119) Weber's term for the historical change from tradition to rationality as the dominant mode of human thought

bureaucracy (p. 120) an organizational model rationally designed to perform tasks efficiently

organizational environment (p. 121) factors outside an organization that affect its operation

bureaucratic ritualism (p. 122) a focus on rules and regulations to the point of undermining an organization's goals

bureaucratic inertia (p. 122) the tendency of bureaucratic organizations to perpetuate themselves

oligarchy (p. 123) the rule of the many by the few

scientific management (p. 123) Frederick Taylor's term for the application of scientific principles to the operation of a business or other large organization

CRITICAL-THINKING QUESTIONS

1. How do primary groups differ from secondary groups? Identify examples of each in your own life.

2. According to Max Weber, what are the six characteristics of bureaucracy? In what ways do new, more flexible organizations differ from his model?

3. George Ritzer (1996:1), a critic of McDonaldization, suggests that fast-food restaurants should carry the following label:

"Sociologists warn us that habitual use of McDonald's systems are destructive to our physical and psychological well-being as well as to society as a whole." Do you agree? Why or why not?

4. The twentieth century saw the widespread use of initials, such as IRS, IRA, IMF, IBM, WPA, CIA, PLO, FBI, NATO, CNN, and CDC. What does this trend suggest about our future?

APPLICATIONS AND EXERCISES

1. Spend several hours observing customers at a fast-food restaurant. Think about ways in which customers as well as employees are trained to behave in certain ways. For example, customer norms include lining up to order and finding a table. Who is supposed to place trash in waste containers? What other such norms are at work?

2. Visit a large public building with an elevator. Observe groups of people as they approach the elevator, and enter the elevator with them. Watch their behavior: What happens to the conversations? Where do people fix their eyes? Can you account for these patterns?

3. Make a list of in-groups and out-groups on your campus. What traits account for a group's falling into each category? Ask several other people if they agree with your classifications.

4. Using available publications (and some assistance from an instructor), try to draw an "organizational pyramid" for your college or university, showing the key officials and how they supervise and report to one another.

5. Packaged in the back of this new textbook is an interactive CD-ROM that offers a variety of video and interactive review materials intended to help you better understand the material covered in this chapter. For this chapter, the CD-ROM contains a relevant clip from *ABC News*, an author's tip video, interactive map animations, an interactive timeline, and flashcards with audio pronunciations of the more difficult words.

 SITES TO SEE

http://www.prenhall.com/macionis

Visit the interactive Companion Website™ that accompanies this text. Begin by clicking on the cover of your book. You will find a chapter-by-chapter study guide, practice tests, suggested Web links, and links to other relevant material.

http://www.saturn.com

Visit the Saturn car company Web site to learn about Saturn's flattened organizational structure.

http://www.riotmanhattan.com/riotmanhattan/webcam.html

This site connects you to a camera placed at New York City's Fifth Avenue at Forty-Fifth Street. Do you think new Internet technology of this kind threatens people's privacy? Why or why not?

http://groups.yahoo.com

At this site, people build their own social groups to chat and exchange personal information. Take a look and see what you think about "virtual groups."

 INVESTIGATE WITH RESEARCH NAVIGATOR™

Follow the instructions on page 32 of this text to access the features of **Research Navigator™**. Once at the Web site, enter your Login Name and Password. Then, to use the **Content Select™** database, enter keywords such as "Max Weber," "bureaucracy," "social network," and "McDonald's," and the search engine will supply relevant and recent scholarly and popular press publications. Use the *New York Times* **Search-by-Subject Archive** to find recent news articles related to sociology and the **Link Library** feature to find relevant Web links organized by the key terms associated with this chapter.

October 10, 2003

Snoop Software Gains Power and Raises Privacy Concerns

By JOHN SCHWARTZ

Earlier this year, Rick Eaton did something unusual in the world of high technology: he made his product weaker.

Mr. Eaton is the founder of True-Active, which makes a computer program that buyers can install on a target computer and monitor everything that the machine's user does on the PC.

Spying with software has been around for several years but Mr. Eaton decided that one new feature in his program crossed a line between monitoring and snooping.

That feature, . . . called "silent deploy," . . . allows the buyer to place the program on someone else's computer secretly via e-mail, without having physical access to the machine. To Mr. Eaton, that constituted an invitation to install unethical and even illegal wiretaps. He made the change, he said, "so we could live with ourselves."

Such principles seem almost quaint in a market where the products seem to grow more powerful and intrusive all the time. Other makers of "snoopware". . . enthusiastically pitch their products' ability to be installed remotely. They typically skirt the ethical and legal issues with fig-leaf disclaimers and check-off boxes where buyers promise not to violate the law.

Privacy experts are not buying such arguments. Marc Rotenberg, who heads the Electronic Privacy Information Center in Washington, contended that selling software that can tap people's communications without their knowledge violated the Electronic Communications Privacy Act. "I don't think there's any question that they are violating the federal law," he said. The disclaimers, he said, "fail the straight-face test."

Law enforcement officials seem to agree. . . . [T]he F.B.I. recently began an investigation in California into the maker of one program, LoverSpy, that advertises heavily via junk e-mail, or spam.

LoverSpy promises to let buyers "Spy on anyone by sending them an e-mail greeting card!" Federal officials note that federal laws on wiretapping make it illegal even to advertise illegal wiretap products, and a little-noted change to the law last year expanded its scope explicitly to include advertising on the Internet.

There are more than a dozen snooping programs on the market, and their makers say they are used legally by employers to monitor workers' Internet use, by parents to follow their children's online wanderings, and by husbands and wives to catch cheating mates.

Mr. Eaton's program has even been used by the F.B.I., with approval of the courts, to capture hackers. . . .

[A] new market has emerged: criminals are using such programs on public computer terminals at copy shops and libraries to harvest credit card numbers, computer passwords and personal financial information. . . .

Last year the Secret Service warned colleges and universities that key-logger systems had been found on public computers in schools in Arizona, Texas, Florida and California. . . . "Anybody who routinely uses a computer that isn't their own ought to be thinking, 'who's looking over my shoulder?'" said Ross Stapleton-Gray, a computer consultant who has worked for the University of California system. . . .

The companies that say they make products for legitimate uses bristle at the suggestion that their products are used illegally, except in a few exceptional cases.

Doug Fowler, the president of Spectorsoft, makes three snooping programs, including eBlaster, which can be installed remotely. He said the product was used legitimately by parents whose children were away at school, and by companies with far-flung field offices. The product can be used for nefarious purposes, he admits, but he added: "A car can run somebody over. That doesn't mean you design a car to run over somebody."

He says he has no respect for the company that puts out LoverSpy and advertises its remote-spying abilities online. "Lines have to be drawn somewhere in this world," he said. . . .

Mr. Eaton, the TrueActive founder, said that while he had worked closely with law enforcement, the decision to hamstring his program. . . was not based on worries about possible liability. "It was an ethical problem," he said. Mr. Eaton also noted that the feature demanded a disproportionate amount of attention from his technical support staff. . . .

[A]t least one program. . . may not pose a real threat, of spying, at least. . . . [One] company's security researchers, working with the Justice Department, were unable to find any actual working software that could be downloaded from the LoverSpy site after paying the fee. . . .

WHAT DO YOU THINK?

1. Do you think employers have the right to monitor the use of company computers by employees? Explain your position.
2. Overall, are you concerned about losing personal privacy? Why or why not?

Adapted from the original article by John Schwartz published in *The New York Times* on October 10, 2003. Copyright © 2003 by The New York Times Company. Reprinted with permission.

CHAPTER SIX

Sexuality and Society

How did the sexual revolution change U.S. society?

Why do societies control people's sexual behavior?

What part does sexuality play in social inequality?

This kind of street dancing, common in Buenos Aires, Brazil, ►
would probably never be seen in a city in, say, China.

K ate, Emily, and Tara stream through the door of the pizza shop a few blocks from their Princeton, New Jersey, high school, where they have just started their sophomore year. They check out the room to see who is there while pushing their bookbags beneath their favorite table and then walk to the counter to place their order (three plain slices, three Diet Cokes). Minutes later, food in hand, the girls slide into the booth to talk about their favorite topic: sex.

Tara begins, "Now that we've had sex, Tom says I'm being a tease if we get together and I say I just want to kiss." "Me, too," Kate interrupts, scarcely waiting for her friend to finish. "It's like once you do it, you have to do it all the time! I don't know how it's supposed to be—he has a temper, and sometimes, if I don't feel like doing anything, he gets really mad." Emily, who has been listening while finishing her pizza, has not yet had sex. But listening to her friends, she is glad, although she would never say so (based on Mulrine, 2002).

There is nothing new about young people being interested in sex. But more of today's teens are doing more than talk—they are having sex, and at younger and younger ages. According to the federal government's Centers for Disease Control and Prevention, about 10 percent of young people in the United States report losing their virginity by age thirteen, and half do so before age sixteen. Among high school sophomores like the girls in our chapter-opening story, one in six has already had at least four sexual partners.

Is more and earlier sexual activity a cause for concern? Yes, for a number of reasons. As this chapter explains, the United States has a high rate of pregnancy among teenagers. In addition, a surprisingly high number of young women are victims of sexual violence. All sexually active people (especially those with multiple partners) run the risk of infection with a sexually transmitted disease. It is also true that many young people—and a number of their parents—understand too little about sexuality to make the best choices.

This chapter presents what researchers have learned about patterns of sexual behavior to challenge some of the popular myths you may have heard in the local pizza shop or elsewhere. We shall examine the various ways societies define sex, the diverse ways in which people express themselves sexually, and a number of the social issues that involve sexuality, including gay rights, prostitution, and date rape.

Understanding Sexuality

How much of your day does *not* involve thoughts about sexuality? If you are like most people, the answer is "not very much," because sexuality is not just about having sex. Sexuality is a theme found throughout society—it is apparent on campus, in the workplace, and especially in the mass media. The sex industry, including pornography and prostitution, is a multibillion-dollar business in its own right. Sexuality is also an important part of how we think about ourselves as well as how others evaluate us. In truth, there are few areas of social life in which sexuality does *not* play some part.

Despite its importance, for much of our history sex has been a cultural taboo; at least in polite conversation, people usually do not even talk about it. As a result, although sex can produce much pleasure, it also causes confusion, anxiety, and sometimes outright fear. Even scientists long considered sex off limits as a topic of research. Not until the middle of the twentieth century did researchers turn their attention to this important element of social life. Since then, as you will learn shortly, we have discovered a great deal about human sexuality.

SEX: A BIOLOGICAL ISSUE

Sex refers to *the biological distinction between females and males.* From a biological point of view, sex is the means by which humans reproduce. A female ovum and a male

We claim that beauty is in the eye of the beholder, which suggests the importance of culture in setting standards of attractiveness. All of the people pictured here—from Morocco, South Africa, Nigeria, Myanmar, Japan, and Ecuador—are beautiful to members of their own society. At the same time, sociobiologists point out that, in every society on Earth, people are attracted to youthfulness. The reason is that, as sociobiologists see it, attractiveness underlies our choices about reproduction, which is most readily accomplished in early adulthood.

sperm, each containing twenty-three chromosomes (biological codes that guide physical development), combine to form a fertilized embryo. To one of these pairs of chromosomes, which determines the child's sex, the mother contributes an X chromosome and the father contributes either an X or a Y. An X from the father produces a female (XX) embryo; a Y from the father produces a male (XY) embryo. A child's sex is determined biologically at the moment of conception.

Within weeks, the sex of an embryo starts to guide its development. If the embryo is male, testicular tissue starts to produce testosterone, a hormone that triggers the development of male genitals (sex organs). If little testosterone is present, the embryo develops female genitals. In the United States, about 105 boys are born for every 100 girls, but a

higher death rate among males makes females a slight majority by the time people reach their mid-thirties (U.S. Census Bureau, 2003).

SEX AND THE BODY

What sets females and males apart are differences in their bodies. Right from birth, the two sexes have different **primary sex characteristics,** namely, *the genitals, organs used for reproduction.* At puberty, as people reach sexual maturity, additional sex differentiation takes place. At this point, people develop **secondary sex characteristics,** *bodily development, apart from the genitals, that distinguishes biologically mature females and males.* Mature females have wider hips for giving birth, milk-producing breasts for nurturing

Practices for showing affection to one another vary from one culture to another. The French kiss on both cheeks; the Belgians kiss three times, alternating cheeks; the Chinese almost never kiss in public; and the Maori of New Zealand rub noses.

infants, and soft, fatty tissue that provides a reserve supply of nutrition during pregnancy and breast feeding. Mature males typically develop more muscle in the upper body, more extensive body hair, and deeper voices. Of course, these are general differences; some males are smaller and have less body hair and higher voices than some females.

Keep in mind that *sex* refers to biological traits that distinguish females and males. *Gender,* by contrast, is an element of culture and refers to the personal traits and patterns of behavior (including social opportunities and privileges) that a culture attaches to being female or male. Chapter 10 ("Gender Stratification") describes the importance of gender in social life.

Intersexual people. Sex is not always as clear-cut as we have just described. The term **intersexual people** refers to *people whose bodies (including genitals) have both female and male characteristics.* An older term for intersexual people is *hermaphrodite* (a word derived from Hermaphroditus, the child of the mythological Greek gods Hermes and Aphrodite, who embodied both sexes). A true hermaphrodite has both a female ovary and a male testis. Tens of thousands of intersexual people are born in the United States with some combination of male and female genitals, and no specific pattern applies to all (Miracle, Miracle, & Baumeister, 2003).

But our culture wants sex to be clear-cut, a fact evident in the demand that parents record at birth the sex of their new child as either female or male. It is also true that in the United States, some people respond to hermaphrodites with confusion or even disgust. But in other cultures, people respond quite differently: The Pokot of eastern Africa pay little attention to what they consider a simple biological error, and the Navajo look on intersexual people with awe, seeing in them the full potential of both the female and the male (Geertz, 1975).

Transsexuals. **Transsexuals** are *people who feel they are one sex even though biologically they are the other.* Tens of thousands of people in the United States experience the feeling of being trapped in a body of the wrong sex and a desire to be the other sex. Most become *transgendered,* meaning that they ignore conventional ideas about how females and males should look and behave. Many go one step further and undergo *gender reassignment,* surgical alteration of their genitals, usually with hormone treatment. This medical process is complex and takes months or even years, but it helps many people gain a joyful sense of becoming on the outside who they feel they are on the inside (Tewksbury & Gagné, 1996; Gagné, Tewksbury, & McGaughey, 1997).

SEX: A CULTURAL ISSUE

Sexuality has a biological foundation. But like all other elements of human behavior, sexuality is also very much a cultural issue. Biology may explain some animals' mating rituals, but humans have no similar biological program. Although there is a biological "sex drive" in the sense that people find sex pleasurable and may seek to engage in sexual activity, our biology does not dictate any specific ways of being sexual any more than our desire to eat dictates any particular foods or table manners.

First-Cousin Marriage Laws across the United States

There is no single view on first-cousin marriages in the United States: Twenty-four states forbid such unions, nineteen allow them, and seven allow them with restrictions.* In general, states that permit first-cousin marriages are found in New England, the Southeast, and the Southwest.

*Of the seven states that allow first-cousin marriages with restrictions, six states permit them only when couples are past childbearing age.

Source: "Cousin Couples" (2004).

First-Cousin Marriages
- Allowed
- Allowed with Restrictions
- Not Allowed

Cultural variation. Almost every sexual practice varies from one society to another. In his pioneering study of sexuality in the United States, Alfred Kinsey (1948) found that most couples reported having intercourse in a single position: face to face, with the woman on the bottom and the man on top. Halfway around the world, in the South Seas, most couples *never* have sex in this way. In fact, when the people of the South Seas learned of this practice from Western missionaries, they poked fun at it as the strange "missionary position."

Even the simple practice of displaying affection shows extensive cultural variation. Most people in the United States kiss in public, but the Chinese kiss only in private. The French kiss publicly, often twice (once on each cheek), and Belgians kiss three times (starting on either cheek). The Maoris of New Zealand rub noses, and most people in Nigeria don't kiss at all.

Modesty, too, is culturally variable. If a woman stepping into a bath is disturbed, what body parts does she cover? Helen Colton (1983) reports that an Islamic woman covers her face, a Laotian woman covers her breasts, a Samoan woman covers her navel, a Sumatran woman covers her knees, and a European woman covers her breasts with one hand and her genital area with the other.

Around the world, some societies restrict sexuality, and others are more permissive. In China, for example, societal norms so closely regulate sexuality that few people have sexual intercourse before they marry. The traditional cultures of many countries condemn women, but not men, who have sex before marriage. In the United States, at least in recent decades, intercourse before marriage has become the norm, and some people choose to have sex even without strong commitment.

THE INCEST TABOO

When it comes to sex, do all societies agree on anything? The answer is yes. One cultural universal—an element found in every society the world over—is the **incest taboo,** *a norm forbidding sexual relations or marriage between certain relatives.* In the United States, the law, reflecting cultural mores, prohibits close relatives (including brothers and sisters, parents and children) from having sex or marrying. But in another example of cultural variation, exactly which family members are included in a society's incest taboo varies from place to place, even within our own country. National Map 6–1 shows that twenty-four states outlaw marriage between first cousins; twenty-six states do not.

Some societies (such as the North American Navajo) apply incest taboos only to the mother and others on her side of the family. There are also societies on record (including ancient Peru and Egypt) that have approved brother-sister marriages among the nobility to keep power within a single family (Murdock, 1965, orig. 1949).

Why does some form of incest taboo exist everywhere? Part of the reason is biology: Reproduction between close relatives of any species raises the odds of producing offspring with mental or physical problems. But why, of all living species, do only humans observe an incest taboo? This fact suggests that controlling sexuality between close relatives is a necessary element of *social* organization. For one thing, the incest taboo limits sexual competition in families

In 1925, women in Chicago were charged with indecent exposure and trucked off to the police station for wearing these "revealing" bathing suits. Today, attitudes in the United States have become much more relaxed regarding matters of human sexuality.

by allowing sex only between spouses (ruling out, for example, sex between parent and child). Second, because family ties define people's rights and obligations toward one another, reproduction between close relatives would hopelessly confuse kinship; if a mother and son had a daughter, would the child consider the male a father or a brother? Third, by requiring people to marry outside their immediate families, the incest taboo integrates the larger society as people look beyond their close kin when seeking to form new families.

The incest taboo has long been a sexual norm in the United States and throughout the world. But in this country, many other sexual norms have changed over time. In the twentieth century, as the next section explains, our society experienced both a sexual revolution and a sexual counterrevolution.

Sexual Attitudes in the United States

What do people in the United States think about sex? Our culture's attitudes toward sexuality have always been something of a contradiction. On one hand, most European immigrants arrived with rigid ideas about "correct" sexuality, typically limiting sex to reproduction within marriage. The early Puritan settlers of New England demanded strict conformity in attitudes and behavior, and they imposed severe penalties for any misconduct, even if the sexual "misconduct" took place in the privacy of the home. Efforts to

regulate sexuality continued well into the twentieth century: As late as the 1960s, for example, some states legally banned the sale of condoms in stores. Until 2003, when the Supreme Court struck them down, laws in thirteen states banned sexual acts between people of the same sex, and "fornication" laws remain in eleven states that could be used to punish heterosexual intercourse among unmarried couples.

But this is just one side of the story. As Chapter 2 ("Culture") explained, because U.S. culture is individualistic, many believe in giving people freedom to do pretty much as they wish, as long as they cause no direct harm to others. The idea that what people do in the privacy of their own homes is *their* business makes sex a matter of individual freedom and personal choice.

So is the United States a restrictive society or a permissive society when it comes to sexuality? The answer is both. On one hand, many people in the United States still view sexual conduct as an important sign of personal morality. On the other, sex is exploited and glorified everywhere in our culture—and strongly promoted in the mass media—as if to say "anything goes." Within this general and rather confusing framework, we turn now to changes in sexual attitudes and behavior over the course of the twentieth century.

THE SEXUAL REVOLUTION

Over the past century, people witnessed profound changes in sexual attitudes and practices. The first indications of this change came in the 1920s as millions of people from farms and small towns migrated to the rapidly growing cities. There, living apart from their families and meeting in the workplace, young men and women enjoyed greater sexual freedom, one reason the decade became known as the "Roaring Twenties."

In the 1930s and 1940s, the Great Depression and World War II slowed the rate of change. But in the postwar period, after 1945, Alfred Kinsey set the stage for what later came to be known as the *sexual revolution.* In 1948, Kinsey and his colleagues published their first study of sexuality in the United States, and it raised eyebrows everywhere. Although Kinsey did present some surprising results, the national uproar resulted not so much from what he said about sexual behavior as from the fact that scientists were actually *studying sex,* a topic many people were uneasy talking about even in the privacy of their own homes.

Kinsey's two books (1948, 1953) became best-sellers because they revealed that people in the United States, on average, were far less conventional in sexual matters than most had thought. These books encouraged a new openness toward sexuality, which helped set in motion the sexual revolution.

In the late 1960s, the sexual revolution truly came of age. Youth culture dominated public life, and expressions such as "if it feels good, do it" and "sex, drugs, and rock 'n' roll" summed up the new, freer attitude toward sex. Some people were turned off by the idea of "turning on," of course, but the baby boom generation, born between 1946 and 1964, became the first cohort in U.S. history to grow up with the idea that sex was part of people's lives, whether they were married or not.

Technology also played a part in the sexual revolution. The birth control pill, usually referred to simply as "the pill," introduced in 1960, not only prevented pregnancy but also made sex more convenient. Unlike a condom or a diaphragm, which has to be used at the time of intercourse, the pill could be taken anytime during the day. Now women as well as men could engage in sex without any special preparation.

The sexual revolution has special meaning for women because historically women were subject to greater sexual regulation than men. According to the *double standard,* society allows (and even encourages) men to be sexually active but expects women to be virgins until marriage and faithful to their husbands afterward. Survey data (shown in Figure 6–1) support this conclusion. Among people born in the United States between 1933 and 1942 (that is, people in their sixties and seventies today), 56 percent of men but just 16 percent of women report having had two or more sexual partners by age twenty. Compare this wide gap with the pattern among those born between 1953 and 1962

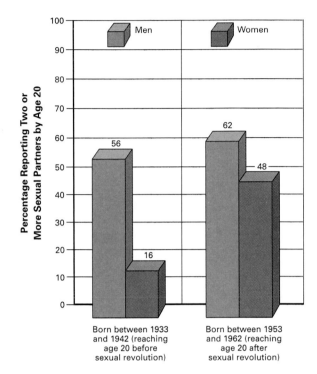

DIVERSITY SNAPSHOT

FIGURE 6–1 The Sexual Revolution: Closing the Double Standard

Source: Laumann et al. (1994:198).

(people now in their forties and fifties), who came of age after the sexual revolution. In this category, 62 percent of men and 48 percent of women say they had two or more sexual partners by age twenty (Laumann et al., 1994:198). The sexual revolution increased sexual activity overall, but it changed behavior among women more than among men.

Greater openness about sexuality develops as societies become richer and the opportunities for women increase. With this in mind, try to find a pattern in the global use of birth control shown in Global Map 6–1 on page 142.

THE SEXUAL COUNTERREVOLUTION

The sexual revolution made sex a topic of everyday discussion and sexual activity more a matter of individual choice. However, by 1980, the climate of sexual freedom that had marked the late 1960s and 1970s was criticized by some as evidence of our country's moral decline, and the *sexual counterrevolution* began.

GLOBAL MAP 6–1   Contraceptive Use in Global Perspective

The map shows the percentage of married women using modern contraception methods (such as barrier methods, contraceptive pill, implants, injectables, intrauterine contraceptive devices [IUDs], or sterilization). In general, how do high-income nations differ from low-income nations? Can you explain this difference?

Source: Data from Mackay (2000).

Politically speaking, the sexual counterrevolution was a conservative call for a return to "family values" and a change from sexual freedom back toward the sexual responsibility that had been valued by earlier generations. There was a strong push to limit sex to married couples. Critics of the sexual revolution objected not just to the idea of "free love" but to trends such as cohabitation (living together) and unmarried couples having children.

Looking back, we can see that the sexual counterrevolution did not greatly change the opinion among the majority that individuals should decide for themselves when and with whom to have a sexual relationship. But whether for moral reasons or concerns about sexually transmitted diseases, more people began limiting the number of sexual partners or choosing not to have sex at all.

PREMARITAL SEX

In light of the sexual revolution and the sexual counterrevolution, how much has sexual behavior in the United States really changed? One interesting trend, discussed in the opening to this chapter, involves premarital sex—sexual intercourse before marriage—among young people.

Consider, first, what U.S. adults *say* about premarital intercourse. Table 6–1 shows that about 35 percent characterize sexual relations before marriage as "always wrong" or "almost always wrong." Another 20 percent consider premarital sex "wrong only sometimes," and more than 40 percent say premarital sex is "not wrong at all." Public opinion is more accepting of premarital sex today than a generation ago, but our society clearly remains divided on this issue.

Now let's look at what people actually *do*. For women, there has been marked change over time. The Kinsey studies (1948, 1953; see also Laumann et al., 1994) reported that for people born in the early 1900s, about 50 percent of men but just 6 percent of women had premarital sexual intercourse before age nineteen. Studies of baby boomers born after World War II show a slight increase in premarital sex among men but a large increase—to about one-third—among women. The most recent studies, targeting men and women born in the 1970s, show that 76 percent of men and 66 percent of women had premarital sexual intercourse by their senior year in high school (Laumann et al., 1994:323–24). Thus, although general public attitudes remain divided, premarital sex is largely accepted among young people.

SEX BETWEEN ADULTS

Judging from the mass media, people in the United States are very active sexually. But do popular images exaggerate reality? The Laumann study (1994), the largest study of sexuality since Kinsey's groundbreaking research, found that frequency of sexual activity varies widely in the U.S. population. One-third of adults report having sex with a partner a few times a year or not at all, another one-third have sex once or several times a month, and the remaining one-third have sex with a partner two or more times a week. In short, no single stereotype accurately describes sexual activity in the United States.

Moreover, despite the widespread image of "swinging singles" promoted on television shows such as *Sex and the City*, it is married people who have sex with partners the most. In addition, married people report the highest level of satisfaction—both emotional and physical—with their partners (Laumann et al., 1994).

TABLE 6–1

How We View Premarital and Extramarital Sex

Survey Question: "There's been a lot of discussion about the way morals and attitudes about sex are changing in this country. If a man and a woman have sexual relations before marriage, do you think it is always wrong, almost always wrong, wrong only sometimes, or not wrong at all? What about a married person having sexual relations with someone other than the marriage partner?"

	Premarital Sex	Extramarital Sex
"Always wrong"	26.7%	78.5%
"Almost always wrong"	8.0	13.4
"Wrong only sometimes"	19.4	4.2
"Not wrong at all"	43.4	2.1
"Don't know"/No answer	2.5	1.8

Source: *General Social Surveys, 1972–2002: Cumulative Codebook* (Chicago; National Opinion Research Center, 2003), pp. 233–34.

EXTRAMARITAL SEX

What about married people having sex with someone other than their marriage partner? What people commonly call "adultery" (sociologists prefer the more neutral term "extramarital sex") is widely condemned. Table 6–1 shows that more than 90 percent of U.S. adults consider a married person having sex with someone other than the marital partner to be "always wrong" or "almost always wrong." The norm of sexual fidelity within marriage has been and remains a strong element of U.S. culture.

But actual behavior falls short of the cultural ideal. The Laumann study reports that about 25 percent of married men and 10 percent of married women have had at least one extramarital sexual experience. Put the other way around, 75 percent of men and 90 percent of women have remained sexually faithful to their partners (Laumann et al., 1994:214; NORC, 2003:1227).

Sexual Orientation

In recent decades, public opinion about sexual orientation has shown a remarkable change. **Sexual orientation** is *a person's romantic and emotional attraction to another person.* The norm in all human societies is **heterosexuality** (*hetero* is a Greek word meaning "the other of two"), *sexual attraction to someone of the other sex.* Yet in every society, a significant share of people experience **homosexuality** (*homo* is the Greek word for "the same"), *sexual attraction to someone*

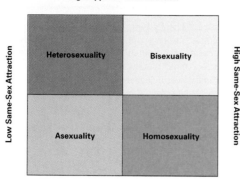

High Opposite-Sex Attraction

Heterosexuality	Bisexuality
Asexuality	Homosexuality

Low Same-Sex Attraction

High Same-Sex Attraction

Low Opposite-Sex Attraction

FIGURE 6–2 Four Sexual Orientations

Source: Adapted from Storms (1980).

of the same sex. Keep in mind that people do not necessarily fall into one category or the other but may have varying degrees of sexual orientation.

The idea that sexual orientation is often not clear-cut is confirmed by the existence of a third category: **bisexuality,** *sexual attraction to people of both sexes.* Some bisexual people are attracted equally to males and females; many others are attracted more strongly to one sex than the other. Finally, **asexuality** is *no sexual attraction to people of either sex.* Figure 6–2 places each of these sexual orientations in relation to the others.

It is important to remember that sexual *attraction* is not the same thing as sexual *behavior.* Many people have experienced some attraction to someone of the same sex, but far fewer ever actually engage in same-sex behavior. This is in large part because our culture discourages such actions.

Cultural systems do not value all sexual orientations equally. Throughout the world, heterosexuality is the

For a summary of recent research on sexual orientation, go to http://www.davidmyers. org/sexorient/accepting.html

norm because heterosexual relations permit human reproduction. Even so, most societies tolerate homosexuality. Among the ancient Greeks, upper-class men considered homosexuality the highest form of relationship, partly because they looked down on women as intellectually inferior. As men saw it, heterosexuality was necessary only so they could have children; "real" men preferred homosexual relations (Kluck-hohn, 1948; Ford & Beach, 1951; Greenberg, 1988).

WHAT GIVES US A SEXUAL ORIENTATION?

The question of *how* people come to have a particular sexual orientation is strongly debated. But the arguments fall into two general categories: that sexual orientation is a product of society and that sexual orientation is a product of biology.

Sexual orientation: A product of society. This approach argues that people in any society construct a set of meanings that lets them make sense of sexuality. Therefore, an understanding of sexuality can differ from place to place and over time. As Michel Foucault (1990, orig. 1978) points out, for example, there was no distinct category of people called "homosexuals" until a century ago, when scientists and eventually the public as a whole began labeling people that way. Throughout history, many people no doubt had what we would call "homosexual experiences." But neither they nor others saw in this behavior the basis for any special identity.

Anthropological studies show that patterns of homosexuality differ greatly from one society to another. In Siberia, for example, the Chukchee Eskimo perform a ritual during which one man dresses like a woman and does a woman's work. The Sambia, who dwell in the Eastern Highlands of New Guinea, have a ritual in which young boys perform oral sex on older men in the belief that eating semen will make them more masculine. The existence of such diverse patterns in societies around the world seems to indicate that for human beings, sexual expression is socially constructed (Herdt, 1993; Blackwood & Wieringa, 1999; Murray & Roscoe, 1999).

Sexual orientation: A product of biology. A growing body of research suggests that sexual orientation is innate, or rooted in human biology in much the same way that people are born right-handed or left-handed. Arguing this position,

The American Psychological Association posts answers to commonly asked questions about sexual orientation at http://www.apa.org/pubinfo/ answers.html

Simon LeVay (1993) links sexual orientation to the structure of a person's brain. LeVay studied the brains of both homosexual and heterosexual men and found a small but important difference in the size of the hypothalamus, a part of the brain that regulates hormones. Such an anatomical difference, he claims, plays a part in shaping sexual orientation.

Genetics, too, may influence sexual orientation. One study of forty-four pairs of brothers, all homosexual, found that thirty-three pairs had a distinctive genetic pattern involving the X chromosome. Moreover, the gay brothers had an unusually high number of gay male relatives, but only on their mother's side. Such evidence leads some researchers to think there may be a "gay gene" located on the X chromosome (Hamer & Copeland, 1994).

Critical review.   Mounting evidence supports the conclusion that sexual orientation is rooted in biology, although the best guess at present is that both nature and nurture play a part. Remember that sexual orientation is not a matter of neat categories: Most people who think of themselves as homosexual have had one or more heterosexual experiences, just as many people who think of themselves as heterosexual have had one or more homosexual experiences. Explaining sexual orientation, then, is a difficult job.

There is also a political issue here with great importance for gay men and lesbians. To the extent that sexual orientation is based in biology, homosexuals have no more choice about their sexual orientation than they do about their skin color. If this is so, shouldn't gay men and lesbians expect the same legal protection from discrimination as African Americans? (Herek, 1991)

HOW MANY GAY PEOPLE ARE THERE?

What share of our population is gay? This is a hard question to answer because, as we have explained, sexual orientation is not a matter of neat categories. In addition, people are not always willing to discuss their sexuality with strangers. Pioneering sex researcher Alfred Kinsey (1948, 1953) estimated that about 4 percent of males and 2 percent of females have an exclusively same-sex orientation, although his research suggested that at least one-third of men and one-eighth of women have had at least one homosexual experience leading to orgasm.

In light of the Kinsey studies, many social scientists put the gay share of the population at 10 percent. But the Laumann survey shows that how homosexuality is defined makes a big difference in the results (Laumann et al., 1994). As part (a) of Figure 6–3 shows, around 9 percent of men and 4 percent of women between the ages of eighteen and fifty-nine reported engaging in homosexual activity at some time in their lives. The second set of numbers in the bar graph shows that fewer men (and even fewer women) had a homosexual experience during childhood but not after puberty. And 2.8 percent of men and 1.4 percent of women defined themselves as "partly" or "entirely" homosexual.

Finally, Kinsey treated sexual orientation as an "either-or" trait: To be homosexual was, by definition, not to be heterosexual. But same-sex and other-sex attractions can operate independently, as shown in Figure 6–2. Bisexual people feel a strong attraction to people of both sexes; by contrast, asexual people experience little sexual attraction to people of either sex.

FIGURE 6-3   Sexual Orientation in the United States: Survey Data

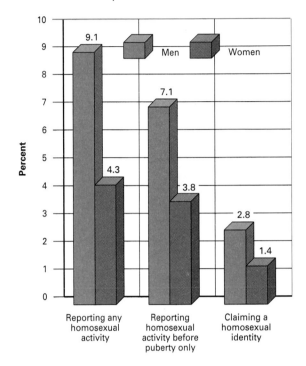

(a) How Many Gay People?

Source: Adapted from Laumann et al. (1994).

(b) Attitudes toward Homosexual Relations, 1973–2002

Source: NORC (2003).

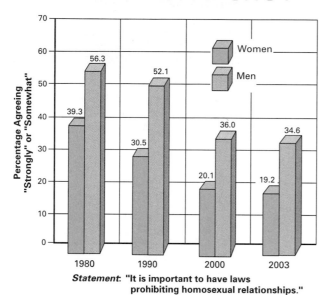

FIGURE 6-4 Opposition to Homosexual Relationships: Attitudes of First-Year College Students, 1980–2003

Sources: Astin et al. (2002) and Sax et al. (2003).

In the Laumann survey, less than 1 percent of U.S. adults described themselves as bisexual. But bisexual experiences appear to be fairly common (at least for a time) among younger people, especially on college and university campuses (Laumann et al., 1994; Leland, 1995). Many bisexuals do not think of themselves as either gay or straight, and their behavior reflects elements of both gay and straight living.

THE GAY RIGHTS MOVEMENT

The public's attitude toward homosexuality has been moving toward greater acceptance. Back in 1973, as shown in part (b) of Figure 6–3, about three-fourths of U.S. adults claimed that homosexual relations were "always wrong" or "almost always wrong." Although that percentage changed little in the 1970s and 1980s, by 2002 it had dropped to less than 60 percent (NORC, 2003:234). Among college students, whose acceptance of homosexual relationships has been significantly greater than that of the population as a whole, we see a similar trend. Approximately half of college students in 1980 were in favor of laws prohibiting

homosexual relationships; by 2003, only one-quarter felt the same way, as Figure 6–4 shows (Astin et al., 2002; Sax et al., 2003).

In large measure, this change of thinking came about as a result of the gay rights movement, which arose in the middle of the twentieth century. Up to that time, most people in this country did not discuss homosexuality, and it was common for companies (including the federal government and the armed forces) to fire anyone who was accused of being gay. Mental health professionals also took a hard line, describing homosexuals as "sick" and sometimes placing them in mental hospitals where, it was hoped, they might be "cured." It is no surprise that most lesbians and gay men remained "in the closet," closely guarding the secret of their sexual orientation. But the gay rights movement gained strength during the 1960s. One early milestone for the movement occurred in 1973 when the American Psychiatric Association declared that homosexuality was not an illness but simply "a form of sexual behavior."

The gay rights movement also began using the term **homophobia** to describe *discomfort over close personal interaction with people thought to be gay, lesbian, or bisexual* (Weinberg, 1973). The concept of homophobia, "fear of sameness," turns the tables on society: Instead of asking "What's wrong with gay people?" the question becomes "What's wrong with people who can't accept a different sexual orientation?" In 2004, a number of cities and towns and the state of Massachusetts issued marriage licenses and performed ceremonies for gay and lesbian couples, but eleven states reacted by passing constitutional bans on gay marriages.

Sexual Controversies

Sexuality lies at the heart of a number of controversies in the United States today. Here we take a look at four key issues: teen pregnancy, pornography, prostitution, and sexual violence.

TEEN PREGNANCY

Because it carries the risk of pregnancy, being sexually active—especially having intercourse—demands a high

 Read a report from the Alan Guttmacher Institute on teenage pregnancy statistics: http://www.agi-usa.org/pubs/state_pregnancy_trends.pdf

level of responsibility. Teenagers may be biologically mature enough to conceive, but many are not emotionally mature enough to appreciate the consequences of their actions. Indeed, surveys indicate that

SEEING OURSELVES

NATIONAL MAP 6-2

Teenage Pregnancy Rates
across the United States

The map shows pregnancy rates for 2000 for
women aged fifteen to nineteen. In what regions
of the country are rates high? Where are they
low? What explanation can you offer for these
patterns?

Source: Alan Guttmacher Institute (2004).

Pregnancies per
1,000 Women
Aged 15 to 19

Above average
Average
Below average

although nearly 1 million U.S. teens become pregnant each
year, most of them do not intend to. This country's rate of
births to teens is higher than that of other high-income
countries and is twice as high, for example, as in Canada
(Darroch et al., 2001).

For young women of all racial and ethnic categories,
weak families and low income sharply raise the risk of
becoming sexually active and having an unplanned child.
To make matters worse, having unplanned children raises
the risk that young women (as well as young fathers-to-be)
will face numerous disadvantages in life, including not finishing school and becoming poor (Alan Guttmacher Institute, 2002).

Did the sexual revolution raise the rate of teenage pregnancy? Perhaps surprisingly, the answer is no. The rate of
pregnancy among teens in 1950 was higher than it is today,
partly because people back then married at a younger age.
In fact, many pregnancies led to quick marriages. As a
result, there were many pregnant teenagers, but almost
90 percent were married. Today, by contrast, the number of
pregnant teens has fallen, but about 80 percent are unmarried women. In a slight majority (57 percent) of such cases,
these women keep their babies; in the remainder, they have
abortions (29 percent) or miscarriages (14 percent) (Alan
Guttmacher Institute, 2004). National Map 6–2 shows pregnancy rates for women between the ages of fifteen and nineteen throughout the United States.

Concern about the high rate of teenage pregnancy has
led to sex education programs in schools. The ongoing controversy over such programs is outlined in the Critical
Thinking box on page 148.

PORNOGRAPHY

In general terms, **pornography** is *sexually explicit material
intended to cause sexual arousal.* But what is and is not
pornographic has long been a matter of debate. Recognizing
that different people view portrayals of sexuality differently,
the U.S. Supreme Court gives local communities the power
to decide for themselves what type of material violates
"community standards" of decency and lacks "redeeming
social value."

Definitions aside, pornography is certainly popular in
the United States: X-rated videos, telephone "sex lines," and
a wide assortment of sexually explicit movies and magazines make up a thriving industry that takes in almost
$10 billion each year. And that figure is rising as people buy
more and more pornography from thousands of sites on
the Internet.

Traditionally, people have criticized pornography on
moral grounds. National surveys confirm the concern of
60 percent of U.S. adults that "sexual materials lead to a
breakdown of morals" (NORC, 2003:235). Today, however,
pornography is also seen as a *political* issue because most of
it degrades women, portraying them as the sexual playthings of men.

Some critics also claim that pornography is a cause of
violence against women. Although it is difficult to prove a
scientific cause-and-effect relationship between what people view and how they act, the public shares a concern about
pornography and violence, with almost half of adults holding the opinion that pornography encourages people to
commit rape (NORC, 2003:235).

CRITICAL THINKING

Sex Education: Solution or Problem?

Most schools today have sex education programs that teach the basics of sexuality. Instructors explain to young people how their bodies grow and change, how reproduction occurs, and how to avoid pregnancy by using birth control or abstaining from sex.

Half of U.S. teenage boys report having sex before they reach sixteen, and half of girls report doing so by seventeen. "Sex ed" programs, then, seem to make sense. But critics point out that as sex education programs spread across the country, the level of teenage sexual activity actually went *up*. This trend seems to suggest that sex education may not be discouraging sex among teens and possibly that

learning more about sex actually encourages young people to become sexually active sooner. Critics also say that parents, not schools, should be responsible for teaching their children about sex.

Supporters of sex education counter that sexual activity among today's young people is a reality and that the sensible strategy is to make sure they understand what they are doing and take reasonable steps to protect themselves from unwanted pregnancy and sexually transmitted diseases.

WHAT DO YOU THINK?

1. Schools can teach the facts about sexuality, but do you think they can

address the emotional issues that often accompany sex? What about the moral issues? Why or why not?

2. Are parents doing their job in teaching children about sex? Ask members of your class how many received instruction in sexual matters from their parents.

3. Overall, do you think young people know too little about sexuality? Do you think they know too much? What specific changes would you suggest to address the problem of unwanted pregnancy among teens?

Sources: Stodghill (1998), Alan Guttmacher Institute (2001), and Voss & Kogan (2001).

Although people everywhere object to sexual material they find offensive, many also value the principle of free speech and the protection of artistic expression. Nevertheless, pressure to restrict pornography is building from an unlikely coalition of conservatives (who oppose pornography on moral grounds) and liberals (who condemn it for political reasons).

PROSTITUTION

Prostitution is *the selling of sexual services*. Often called "the world's oldest profession," prostitution has been widespread throughout recorded history; about one in five adult men in the United States reports having paid for sex at some time (NORC, 2003:1226). Because most people think of sex as an expression of intimacy between two people, they find the idea of sex for money disturbing. As a result, prostitution is against the law everywhere in the United States except for parts of Nevada.

Around the world, prostitution is greatest in poor countries where patriarchy is strong and traditional cultural norms limit women's ability to earn a living.

Global Map 6–2 shows where in the world prostitution is most widespread.

Types of prostitution. Most prostitutes (many prefer the morally neutral term "sex workers") are women, but they fall into different categories. *Call girls* are elite prostitutes, typically young, attractive, and well educated women who arrange their own "dates" with clients by telephone. The classified pages of any large city newspaper contain numerous ads for "escort services," by which women (and sometimes men) offer both companionship and sex for a fee.

In the middle are prostitutes who work in "massage parlors" or brothels under the control of managers. These sex workers have less choice about their clients, receive less money for their services, and get to keep no more than half of what they make.

At the bottom of the sex worker hierarchy are *streetwalkers*, women and men who "work the streets" of large cities. Typically, female streetwalkers are under the control of male pimps who take most of their earnings. Many streetwalkers fall victim to violence, from pimps as well as clients (Davidson, 1998; Estes, 2001).

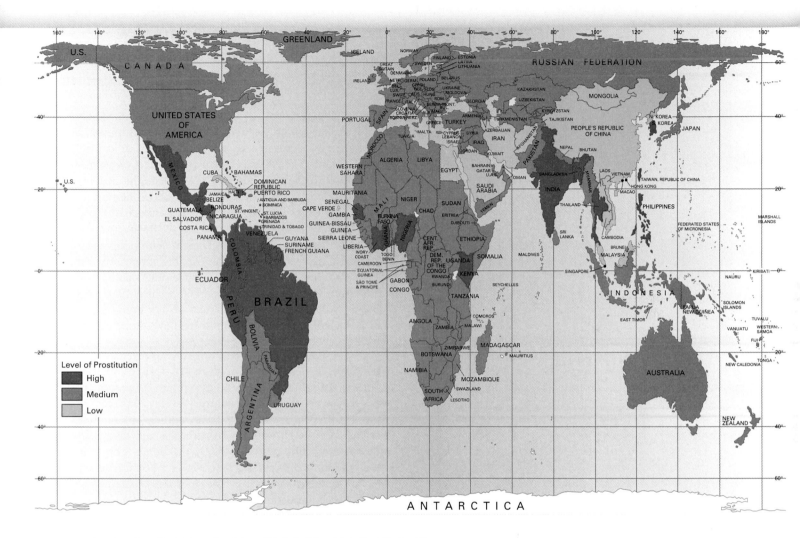

WINDOW ON THE WORLD

GLOBAL MAP 6-2   Prostitution in Global Perspective

Generally speaking, prostitution is widespread in societies where women have low standing. Officially, at least, the People's Republic of China boasts of gender equality, including the elimination of "vice" such as prostitution, which oppresses women. By contrast, in much of Latin America, where patriarchy is strong, prostitution is common. In many Islamic societies, patriarchy is also strong, but religion is a counterbalance, so prostitution is limited. Western, high-income nations have a moderate amount of prostitution.

Sources: *Peters Atlas of the World* (1990) and Mackay (2000).

Most prostitutes offer heterosexual services. However, gay prostitutes also trade sex for money. Researchers report that many gay prostitutes have suffered rejection by family and friends because of their sexual orientation (Weisberg, 1985; Boyer, 1989; Kruks, 1991).

A victimless crime?   As noted earlier, prostitution is against the law almost everywhere. Many people consider it a victimless crime (defined in Chapter 7, "Deviance," as a crime in which there are no obvious victims). Consequently, instead of consistently and aggressively enforcing

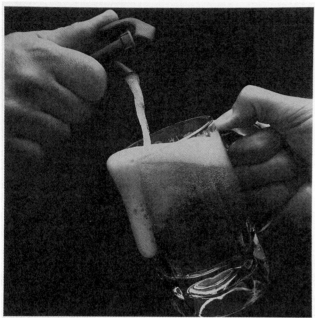

A lot of campus rapes start here.

Whenever there's drinking or drugs, things can get out of hand.
So it's no surprise that many campus rapes involve alcohol.
But you should know that under any circumstances, sex without
the other person's consent is considered rape. A felony, punishable
by prison. And drinking is no excuse.
That's why, when you party, it's good to know what your limits are.
You see, a little sobering thought now can save you from a big
problem later.

© 1990 Rape Treatment Center, Santa Monica Hospital

Experts agree that one factor that contributes to the problem of sexual violence on the college campus is the widespread use of alcoholic beverages. What policies are in force on your campus to discourage the kind of drinking that leads to one person imposing sex on another?

prostitution laws, police stage only occasional crackdowns. This policy reflects a desire to control prostitution while acknowledging that it is impossible to totally eliminate it.

Like the police, many people take a "live and let live" attitude about the world's oldest profession. But prostitution subjects many women to abuse and outright violence and plays a part in spreading sexually transmitted diseases, including AIDS. In addition, many poor women become trapped in a life of selling sex, especially in low-income nations. Thailand, in Southeast Asia, has 2 million prostitutes; about 10 percent of all women work in the country's thriving sex tourism industry, many of whom suffer abuse and half of whom are infected with HIV (Wonders & Michalowski, 2001).

SEXUAL VIOLENCE: RAPE AND DATE RAPE

Ideally, sexual activity occurs within a loving relationship, but sex can sometimes be twisted by hatred and violence. Here we consider two types of sexual violence: rape and date rape.

Rape. Although some people think rape is motivated only by a desire for sex, it is actually an expression of power, a violent act that uses sex to hurt, humiliate, or control another person. The Federal Bureau of Investigation reports that about 95,000 women are raped each year. This number reflects only the reported cases, and the actual number of rapes is likely several times higher (Federal Bureau of Investigation, 2003).

According to the official government definition, rape is "the carnal knowledge of a female forcibly and against her will." Thus, official rape statistics include only victims who are women. But men also are raped—in perhaps 10 percent of all cases. Most men who rape men are not homosexual; they are heterosexuals who are motivated by a desire not for sex but to dominate another person.

Date rape. A common myth is that rape involves strangers. In reality, however, only about 30 percent of rapes fit this pattern. On the contrary, about 70 percent of rapes involve people who know one another—more often than not, pretty well—and these crimes usually take place in familiar surroundings, especially the home. The term "date rape" or "acquaintance rape" refers to forcible sexual violence against women by men they know (Laumann et al., 1994; U.S. Bureau of Justice Statistics, 2004).

A second myth, often linked specifically to date rape, is the idea that a woman who has been raped must have done something to encourage the man and make him think she wanted to have sex. Perhaps the victim agreed to go out with the offender. Maybe she even invited him into her room. But of course, acting in this way no more justifies rape than it would any other kind of physical assault.

Rape is a physical assault, but it also leaves emotional and psychological scars. Beyond the brutality of being physically violated, rape by an acquaintance also undermines a victim's sense of trust. Psychological scars are especially serious among the 50 percent of rape victims who are under eighteen; one-third of these young victims are attacked by their own fathers or stepfathers (Greenfield, 1996).

How common is date rape? One recent study found that about 20 percent of a sample of high school girls in the United States reported being victims of sexual or physical violence inflicted by the boys they were dating (Dickinson, 2001).

Nowhere has the issue of date rape been more widely discussed than on college campuses, where the danger of

APPLYING SOCIOLOGY

When Sex Is Only Sex: The Campus Culture of "Hooking Up"

Have you ever been in a sexual situation and not been sure of the right thing to do? What are the social norms on campus for sexual relationships? Most colleges and universities highlight two important rules. First, sexual activity must take place only when both participants have given clear statements of consent. The consent principle provides a clear distinction between having sex and date rape. Second, because sexual activity can spread disease, no one should knowingly expose a partner to a sexually transmitted disease, especially when that partner is unaware of the danger.

These rules are very important; yet they say little about the larger issue of what sex *means*. For example, when is it appropriate to have a sexual relationship? Does agreeing to have sex with someone mean you really like that person? Are you obligated to see the person again?

Two generations ago, there were informal rules for campus sex. In ideal terms, dating was considered part of the courtship process. That is, "going out" was a way in which women and men evaluated each other as possible marriage partners while they sharpened their own sense of what they wanted in a mate. Because, on average, marriage took place at a younger age, a number of college students became engaged and married while they were still in school. Having "honorable intentions" meant that sex

was a sign of a serious—potentially marital—interest in the other person.

Of course, not all sexual activity fell under the umbrella of courtship. A fair share of men (and some women, too) have always looked for sex where they could find it. But in an era that linked sex and courtship, casual sex could easily lead to one partner feeling "used."

Today, the sexual culture of the campus is very different. Partly because people now marry much later, the culture of courtship has declined dramatically. About three-fourths of women in a recent national survey point to a new campus pattern, the culture of "hooking up." What is "hooking up"? Most describe it in words like these: "When a girl and a guy get together for a physical encounter—anything from kissing to having sex—and don't necessarily expect anything further."

Student responses to the survey suggest that "hookups" have three characteristics. First, most couples who hook up know little about each other. Second, a typical hookup involves people who have been drinking alcohol, usually at a campus party. Third, most women are critical of the culture of hooking up and express little satisfaction with these encounters. Certainly, some women (and men) who hook up simply walk away, happy to have enjoyed a sexual experience free of further obligation. But given the

powerful emotions that sex can unleash, hooking up often leaves at least one of the partners wondering what to expect next. "Will you call me tomorrow?" "Will I see you again?"

The survey asked women who had experienced a recent hookup to report how they felt, a day later, about the experience. A majority of respondents said they felt "awkward," while about half felt "disappointed" and "confused," and one in four said she felt "exploited." Clearly, for many people, sex involves something more than a physical encounter. Further, because today's campus is very sensitive to charges of sexual exploitation, there is a definite need for clearer standards of fair play.

WHAT DO YOU THINK?

1. How extensive is hooking up on your campus? Are you aware of differences between heterosexual and homosexual encounters in this regard?
2. What are the advantages of sex without commitment? What are the disadvantages of this kind of relationship? Do you think your answers depend in part on whether you are male or female? Why or why not?
3. Do you think college students need more guidance about sexual issues? If so, who should provide this guidance?

Source: Based in part on Marquardt & Glenn (2001).

date rape is high. The collegiate environment promotes easy friendships and encourages trust. At the same time, many

A government report on the sexual victimization of college women is available at http://www.ojp.usdoj.gov/bjs/abstract/svcw.htm

young students have much to learn about relationships and about themselves. Yet as the

Applying Sociology box explains, while college life encourages communication, it also provides few social norms that help guide young people's sexual experiences. To counter the problem, many schools now actively address myths about rape. In addition, greater attention is now focused on the use of alcohol, which increases the likelihood of sexual violence.

APPLYING THEORY

SEXUALITY

	Structural-Functional Approach	Symbolic-Interaction Approach	Social-Conflict Approach
What is the level of analysis?	Macro-level	Micro-level	Macro-level
What is the importance of sexuality for society?	Society depends on sexuality for reproduction. Society uses the incest taboo and other norms to control sexuality in order to maintain social order.	Sexual practices vary among the many cultures of the world. Some societies allow individuals more freedom than others in matters of sexual behavior.	Sexuality is linked to social inequality. U.S. society regulates women's sexuality more than men's, which is part of the larger pattern of men dominating women.
Has sexuality changed over time? How?	Yes. As advances in birth control technology separate sex from reproduction, societies relax some controls on sexuality.	Yes. The meanings people attach to virginity and other sexual matters are all socially constructed and subject to change.	Yes and no. Some sexual standards have relaxed, but society still defines women in sexual terms, just as homosexual people are harmed by society's heterosexual bias.

Theoretical Analysis of Sexuality

Applying sociology's various theoretical approaches gives us a better understanding of human sexuality. The following sections discuss the three major approaches. The Applying Theory table highlights the key insights of each approach.

STRUCTURAL-FUNCTIONAL ANALYSIS

The structural-functional approach emphasizes the contribution of any social pattern to the overall operation of society. Because sexuality is an important element of social life, society must regulate sexual behavior.

The need to regulate sexuality. From a biological point of view, sex allows our species to reproduce. But culture and social institutions regulate *with whom* and *when* people reproduce. For example, as you have already learned, most societies condemn married people who have sex with someone other than their spouses. To do otherwise—to allow the forces of sexual passion to go unchecked—would threaten family life and, especially, the raising of children.

The fact that the incest taboo exists everywhere shows clearly that no society is willing to permit completely free choice in sexual partners. Reproduction resulting from sex between family members other than married partners would break down the system of kinship and hopelessly confuse human relationships.

Historically, the social control of sexuality was strong, mostly because sex inevitably led to childbirth. We see this in the old-fashioned distinction between "legitimate" reproduction (within marriage) and "illegitimate" reproduction (outside marriage, or "out of wedlock"). But once a society develops the technology to control births, its sexual norms become more permissive. This occurred in the United States, where, over the course of the twentieth century, sex moved beyond its basic reproductive function and became a form of intimacy and even recreation (Giddens, 1992).

Latent functions: The case of prostitution. It is easy to see that prostitution is harmful because it spreads disease and exploits women. But are there latent functions that help explain why prostitution is so widespread? According to Kingsley Davis (1971), prostitution performs several useful functions. It is one way to meet the sexual needs of a large number of people who do not have ready access to sex, including soldiers, travelers, and people who are not physically attractive or who have trouble establishing relationships. Some people favor prostitution because they want sex without the "trouble" of a relationship. As one analyst said of prostitution, "Men don't pay for sex; they pay so they can leave" (Miracle, Miracle, & Baumeister, 2003:421).

Critical review. The structural-functional approach helps us appreciate the important role sexuality plays in the organization of society. The incest taboo and other cultural norms also suggest that society has always paid attention to who has sex with whom, especially who reproduces with whom.

At the same time, this approach pays little attention to the great diversity of sexual ideas and practices found within every society. In addition, the fact that sexual patterns change over time, just as they differ in remarkable ways around the world, is ignored by this perspective. To appreciate the varied and changeable character of sexuality, let us turn to the symbolic-interaction approach.

SYMBOLIC-INTERACTION ANALYSIS

The symbolic-interaction approach highlights how, as people interact, they construct everyday reality. As explained in Chapter 4 ("Social Interaction in Everyday Life"), reality construction is a highly variable process, so the views of one group or society may well differ from those of another. In the same way, our understanding of sexuality can and does change over time.

The social construction of sexuality. Almost all social patterns involving sexuality have changed over the course of the twentieth century. One good illustration is the changing importance of virginity. A century ago, our society's norm—for women, at least—was virginity until marriage. This norm was strong because there was no effective means of birth control, and virginity was the only assurance a man had that his bride-to-be was not carrying another man's child. Today, because we have gone a long way toward separating sex from reproduction, the virginity norm has weakened considerably. In the United States, among people born between 1963 and 1974, just 16.3 percent of men and 20.1 percent of women report being virgins at first marriage (Laumann et al., 1994:503).

Another example of our society's construction of sexuality involves young people's awareness of sex. A century ago, childhood was a time of innocence in sexual matters. In recent decades, however, thinking has changed. Although few people encourage sexual activity between children, most people believe children should be educated about sex so that they can make intelligent choices about their behavior as they grow older.

Global comparisons. Around the world, different societies attach different meanings to sexuality. For example, the anthropologist Ruth Benedict (1938), who spent years learning the ways of life of the Melanesian people of southeastern New Guinea, reported that adults paid little attention when young children engaged in sexual experimentation with one another. Parents in Melanesia shrugged off such activity because before puberty, sex cannot lead to reproduction. Is it likely that most parents in the United States would respond the same way?

Sexual practices also vary from culture to culture. Male circumcision of infant boys (the practice of removing all or

The control of women's sexuality is a common theme in human history. During the Middle Ages, Europeans devised the "chastity belt"—a metal device locked about a woman's groin that prevented sexual intercourse (and probably interfered with other bodily functions as well). While such devices are all but unknown today, the social control of sexuality continues. Can you point to examples?

part of the foreskin of the penis) is common in the United States but rare in most other parts of the world. A practice sometimes referred to as female circumcision (the removal of the clitoris) is rare in the United States but common in parts of Africa and the Middle East (Crosette, 1995; Huffman, 2000). (For more about this practice, more accurately referred to as "female genital mutilation," see the box on page 267).

Critical review. The strength of the symbolic-interaction approach lies in revealing the constructed character of familiar social patterns. Understanding that people "construct" sexuality, we can better appreciate the variety of sexual attitudes and practices found over the course of history and around the world.

One limitation of this approach is that not everything is so variable. Throughout our own history—and around the

The Abortion Controversy

A black van pulls up to a storefront in a busy section of the city. Two women get out of the front seat and cautiously scan the sidewalk. After a moment, one nods to the other, and they open the rear door to let a third young woman out of the van. Standing to the right and left of the woman, the two quickly whisk her inside the building.

This might describe two federal marshals escorting a convict to a police station, but it is actually an account of two clinic workers escorting a young woman who has decided to have an abortion. Why must they be so cautious? Anyone who has read the papers in recent years knows about the angry confrontations at abortion clinics across North America. Some opponents have even targeted and killed doctors who carry out abortions. Although abortion is one of the most hotly debated issues in the nation today, more than 1.3 million such procedures are performed each year in the United States.

Abortion has not always been so controversial. In colonial times, midwives and other healers performed abortions with little community opposition and with full approval of the law. But controversy arose about 1850, when early medical doctors wanted to eliminate the competition they faced from midwives and other traditional health providers, whose income came largely from ending pregnancies. By 1900, medical doctors succeeded in getting every state to pass a law banning abortion.

Such laws did not end abortion, but they greatly reduced their number. In addition, these laws drove abortion underground so that many women, especially those who were poor, had little choice but to seek help from unlicensed "back alley" abortionists, sometimes with tragic results.

By the 1960s, opposition to antiabortion laws was rising. In 1973, the U.S. Supreme Court rendered a landmark decision (in the cases of *Roe* v. *Wade* and *Doe* v. *Bolton*), striking down all state laws banning abortion. In effect, this action by the Supreme Court established a woman's legal access to abortion nationwide.

Even so, the abortion controversy continues. On one side of the issue are people who describe themselves as "pro-choice," supporting a woman's right to choose abortion. On the other side are those who call themselves "pro-life," opposing abortion as morally wrong; these people would like to see the Supreme Court reverse its 1973 decision.

How strong is the support for each side of the abortion controversy? A recent national survey asked the question, "Should it be possible for a pregnant woman to obtain a legal abortion if the woman wants it for any reason?" In response, 41.9 percent said yes (placing them in the pro-choice camp), and 55.5 percent said no (the pro-life position); the remaining 2.6 percent offered no opinion (NORC, 2003:227).

A closer look shows that particular circumstances make a big difference in

---

world—men are more likely to see women in sexual terms than the other way around. If this pattern is widespread, some broader social structure must be at work, as we shall see in the following section on the social-conflict approach.

SOCIAL-CONFLICT ANALYSIS

As you have seen in previous chapters, the social-conflict approach highlights dimensions of inequality. Therefore, this approach shows how sexuality reflects patterns of social inequality and also how it helps perpetuate them.

Sexuality: Reflecting social inequality. Recall our discussion of prostitution, a practice outlawed almost everywhere.

Enforcement is uneven at best, especially when it comes to who is and is not likely to be arrested. Although two people are involved, the record shows that police are far more likely to arrest (less powerful) female prostitutes than (more powerful) male clients. Of all women engaged in prostitution, it is streetwalkers—women with the least income and those most likely to be minorities—who face the highest risk of arrest (COYOTE, 2000). Furthermore, would so many women be involved in prostitution at all if they had economic opportunities equal to those of men?

Sexuality: Creating social inequality. Social-conflict theorists, especially feminists, point to sexuality as the root of inequality between women and men. Defining women in

154 CHAPTER 6 SEXUALITY AND SOCIETY

how people see this issue. The figure shows that most U.S. adults favor legal abortion if a pregnancy seriously threatens a woman's health, if the woman became pregnant as a result of rape, or if the fetus is very likely to have a serious defect. The bottom line is that about 42 percent support access to abortion under *any* circumstances, but nearly 90 percent support access to abortion under *some* circumstances.

Many of those who take the pro-life position feel strongly that abortion is nothing other than the killing of unborn children, some 40 million since *Roe* v. *Wade* was passed in 1973. To them, people never have the right to end innocent life in this way. But pro-choice people are no less committed to their position, that women must have control over their own bodies. If pregnancy decides the course of women's lives, women will never be able to compete with men on equal terms, whether it is on campus or in the workplace. Therefore, the pro-choice position concludes, women must have access to legal, safe abortion as a necessary condition to full participation in society.

CONTINUE THE DEBATE . . .

1. The more conservative, pro-life people see abortion as a moral issue, and more liberal, pro-choice people see abortion as a power issue. Compare these positions to how conservatives and liberals view the issue of pornography.
2. Surveys show that men and women have almost the same opinions about abortion. Does this surprise you? Why or why not?
3. Why do you think the abortion controversy is often so bitter? Do you think our nation can find a middle ground on this issue?

Sources: Based in part on Tannahill (1992), NORC (2003), and various news reports.

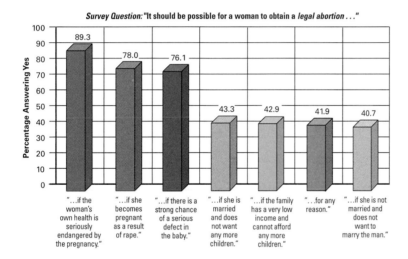

Survey Question: "It should be possible for a woman to obtain a *legal abortion* . . ."

When Should the Law Allow a Woman to Choose Abortion?

Source: NORC (2003).

sexual terms amounts to devaluing them from full human beings to objects of men's interest and attention. Is it any wonder that the word "pornography" comes from the Greek word *porne,* meaning "a man's sexual slave"?

If men define women in sexual terms, it is easy to see pornography, almost all of which is consumed by males, as a power issue. Because pornography typically shows women focused on pleasing men, it supports the idea that men have power over women.

Some radical critics doubt that this element of power can ever be removed from heterosexual relations (Dworkin, 1987). Most social-conflict theorists do not reject heterosexuality, but they do agree that sexuality can and does degrade women. Our culture often describes sexuality in terms of sport (men "scoring" with women) and violence ("slamming," "banging," and "hitting on," for example, are verbs used for both fighting and sex).

Queer theory. Finally, social-conflict theory has taken aim not only at men dominating women but also at heterosexuals dominating homosexuals. In recent years, as many lesbians and gay men have sought public acceptance, some sociologists have tried to add a gay voice to their discipline. The term **queer theory** refers to *a growing body of research findings that challenges the heterosexual bias in U.S. society.*

Queer theory begins with the claim that our society is characterized by **heterosexism,** *a view that labels anyone who is not heterosexual as "queer."* Our heterosexual culture victimizes a wide range of people, including gay men, lesbians, bisexuals, transsexuals, and even asexual people. Furthermore, although most people agree that bias against women (sexism) and people of color (racism) is wrong, heterosexism is widely tolerated and sometimes well within the law. For example, U.S. military forces cannot legally discharge a female soldier for "acting like a woman" because that would be a clear case of gender discrimination. But the military forces can discharge her for homosexuality if she is a sexually active lesbian.

Heterosexism also exists at a more subtle level in our everyday understanding of the world. When we describe something as "sexy," for example, don't we really mean attractive to *heterosexuals?*

Critical review. The social-conflict approach shows how sexuality is both a cause and an effect of inequality. In particular, it helps us understand men's power over women and heterosexual people's domination of homosexual people.

At the same time, this approach overlooks the fact that sexuality is not always a power issue: Many couples enjoy a vital sexual relationship that deepens their commitment to one another. In addition, the social-conflict approach pays little attention to steps our society has made toward reducing inequality. In polite company at least, men today are less likely to describe women as sex objects than a few decades ago; moreover, our rising public concern about sexual harassment (see Chapter 10, "Gender Stratification") has reduced the abuse of sexuality in the workplace. There is also much evidence that the gay rights movement has secured greater opportunities and social acceptance for gay people.

This chapter closes with a look at what is perhaps the most divisive sexuality-related issue of all: **abortion,** *the deliberate termination of a pregnancy.* There seems to be no middle ground in the debate over this controversial issue, as described in the Controversy & Debate box on pages 154–55.

SUMMARY

1. U.S. culture has long defined sex as a taboo topic. The Kinsey studies, among the first publications by social scientists on human sexuality, were highly controversial when they were published in 1948 and 1953.

2. Sex is the biological distinction between females and males, which is determined at conception as a male sperm joins a female ovum.

3. Males and females are distinguished not only by their genitals (primary sex characteristics) but also by bodily development as they mature (secondary sex characteristics). Intersexual people have some combination of both male and female genitalia. Transsexuals are people who feel they are one sex although, biologically, they are the other.

4. For most species, sex is rigidly directed by biology; for human beings, sex is a matter of cultural definition and personal choice. Patterns of kissing, modesty, and standards of beauty all vary around the world, revealing the cultural foundation of sexual practices.

5. Historically, U.S. society rigidly controlled sexual behavior. Social attitudes toward sex have become more permissive over time.

6. The sexual revolution, which came of age in the 1960s and 1970s, brought a far greater openness in matters of sexuality. Research shows that changes in sexuality were greater for women than for men. By 1980, a sexual counterrevolution was taking form, condemning permissiveness and urging a return to more conservative "family values."

7. The share of people in the United States who have premarital sexual intercourse increased over the course of the twentieth century. Research shows that about three-fourths of young men and two-thirds of young women have intercourse by their senior year in high school.

8. The level of sexual activity varies within the population of U.S. adults: One-third report having sex with a partner a few times a year or not at all, another one-third have sex once or several times a month, and the remaining one-third have sex with a partner two or more times a week.

9. Although extramarital sex is widely condemned, about 25 percent of married men and 10 percent of married women report being sexually unfaithful to their spouses at some time.

10. Sexual orientation refers to a person's romantic and emotional attraction to another person. Four major orientations are heterosexuality, homosexuality, bisexuality, and asexuality. Sexual orientation reflects both biological and cultural factors.

11. The share of the population that is homosexual depends on how researchers define homosexuality. About 9 percent of adult men and 4 percent of adult women report having had one or more homosexual experiences; 2.8 percent of men and 1.4 percent of women consider themselves to be homosexual.

12. The gay rights movement has gained greater acceptance for gay people. Largely because of this movement, the percentage of the U.S. population condemning homosexuality as

morally wrong has steadily decreased and stands now at about half.

13. Nearly 1 million teenagers become pregnant each year in the United States. The rate of teenage pregnancy has dropped since 1950, when many teens married and had children. Today, most pregnant teens are not married and, especially if they drop out of school, are at high risk of poverty.

14. With no universal definition of pornography, the law allows local communities to set standards of decency. Conservatives condemn pornography as immoral; liberals condemn it as demeaning to women.

15. Prostitution, the selling of sexual services, is illegal almost everywhere in the United States. Although many people think of prostitution as a victimless crime, others point out that it victimizes women and spreads sexually transmitted diseases.

16. Some 95,000 rapes are reported each year, but the actual number is likely several times greater. Although many people think of rape as a sexual act, rape is really a violent expression of power. Most rapes involve people who know one another.

17. Structural-functional theory highlights society's need to regulate sexual activity. A universal norm in this regard is the incest taboo, which keeps family relations clear.

18. The symbolic-interaction approach notes how people attach various meanings to sexuality. Societies differ from one another in terms of sexual attitudes and practices, and sexual patterns can change within any one society over time.

19. According to the social-conflict approach, one way in which men dominate women is by devaluing them as sexual objects.

KEY CONCEPTS

sex (p. 136) the biological distinction between females and males

primary sex characteristics (p. 137) the genitals, organs used for reproduction

secondary sex characteristics (p. 137) bodily development, apart from the genitals, that distinguishes biologically mature females and males

intersexual people (p. 138) people whose bodies (including genitals) have both female and male characteristics

transsexuals (p. 138) people who feel they are one sex even though biologically they are the other

incest taboo (p. 139) a norm forbidding sexual relations or marriage between certain relatives

sexual orientation (p. 143) a person's romantic and emotional attraction to another person

heterosexuality (p. 143) sexual attraction to someone of the other sex

homosexuality (p. 143) sexual attraction to someone of the same sex

bisexuality (p. 144) sexual attraction to people of both sexes

asexuality (p. 144) no sexual attraction to people of either sex

homophobia (p. 146) discomfort over close personal interaction with people thought to be gay, lesbian, or bisexual

pornography (p. 147) sexually explicit material intended to cause sexual arousal

prostitution (p. 148) the selling of sexual services

queer theory (p. 155) a growing body of research findings that challenges the heterosexual bias in U.S. society

heterosexism (p. 155) a view that labels anyone who is not heterosexual as "queer"

abortion (p. 156) the deliberate termination of a pregnancy

CRITICAL-THINKING QUESTIONS

1. What do sociologists mean by the *sexual revolution?* What did the sexual revolution change? Can you suggest some of the reasons these changes occurred?

2. What is sexual orientation? Why is this characteristic difficult for researchers to measure?

3. What evidence can you point to that supports the view of U.S. society as permissive about sexuality? In what ways does U.S. society try to control sexuality?

4. What do you think is the most important sexuality-related issue facing U.S. society today? Give reasons for your choice.

APPLICATIONS AND EXERCISES

1. The most complete study of sexual patterns in the United States to date is the 1994 study *The Social Organization of Sexuality: Sexual Practices in the United States,* by Edward Laumann and others. You can find this book in your campus or community library. Get a copy, and browse through some of the chapters you find most interesting. As you read, think about ways in which sexuality is shaped by society.

2. Contact your school's student services office, and ask for information about the extent of sexual violence on your campus. Do people report such crimes? What policies and procedures does your school have to respond to sexual violence?

3. Sex is not always a simple matter of being female or male. Do you think that health care policies should cover gender reassignment surgery for adults who want it? Why or why not?

4. Packaged in the back of this new textbook is an interactive CD-ROM that offers a variety of video and interactive review materials intended to help you better understand the material covered in this chapter. For this chapter, the CD-ROM contains a relevant clip from *ABC News,* an author's tip video, interactive map animations, an interactive timeline, and flashcards with audio pronunciations of the more difficult words.

 ## SITES TO SEE

http://www.prenhall.com/macionis

Visit the interactive Companion Website™ that accompanies this text. Begin by clicking on the cover of your book. You will find a chapter-by-chapter study guide, practice tests, suggested Web links, and links to other relevant material.

http://www.teenpregnancy.org

Visit the Web site of the National Campaign to Prevent Teen Pregnancy, an organization formed to guide teens toward responsible sexual behavior. You can find data for your state at this site. What are the key parts of this organization's program? How effective do you imagine it is? Why?

http://www.qrd.org/qrd/

This Web site, the Queer Resources Directory, looks at a wide range of issues—including family, religion, education, and health—from a queer theory perspective. Visit this site to see in what ways various social institutions can be considered "heterosexist." Do you agree or disagree? Why?

http://www.gay.com

This is a search engine for all sorts of information highlighting issues involving homosexuality.

 ## INVESTIGATE WITH RESEARCH NAVIGATOR™

Follow the instructions on page 32 of this textbook to access the features of **Research Navigator™.** Once at the Web site, enter your Login Name and Password. Then, to use the **Content Select**™ database, enter keywords such as "sexuality," "incest," "transgender," and "abortion," and the search engine will supply relevant and recent scholarly and popular press publications. Use the *New York Times* **Search-by-Subject Archive** to find recent news articles related to sociology and the **Link Library** feature to find relevant Web links organized by the key terms found in this chapter.

September 2, 2003

The Skin Wars Start Earlier and Earlier

By GUY TREBAY

The front lines are drawn in the cool nonspace of every suburban mall. Here, at the Abercrombie & Fitch store in Westchester . . . pictures of half-nude models hang coyly above registers, and shoppers skirmish amiably over cropped miniskirts and skimpy tank tops against an aural backdrop of the White Stripes.

The combatants, if they can be called that, are parents and their daughters, and the fraught territory they are contesting is adolescent sexuality. When *The Washington Post* reported last summer that fashions for girls in the "tween" years were "long on skin, short on modesty," it was noting a reality that many parents of teenagers know only too well. . . .

"The 'whore wars' are a big issue," said Donna Cristen, who was shopping for back-to-school clothing on Thursday with her daughter, Tess, 13. Ms. Cristen's reference was to a term that arose on the Internet, where commentators like Betsy Hart of CNN complained that stores as mainstream as J. C. Penney, Target, and The Limited Too were increasingly carrying clothing that could seem designed to suit the needs of women who work the Lincoln Tunnel on-ramp. . . .

"Everything in stores now is so provocative, you have to keep a close watch," Ms. Cristen said, referring to the plethora of spaghetti strap blouses, midriff-baring tank tops, platform shoes, thongs, T-shirts emblazoned with double-entendre slogans and camisoles with built-in bras, all pitched by retailers at girls who have barely crossed the threshold of puberty. . . .

Randi Cardia, who lives in Manhattan and has two teenage daughters, described a majority of the clothes offered for them as "hooker wear." "There are a lot of us out there that are just appalled that someone hasn't taken a stand," Ms. Cardia said. . . .

"It's normal now to see these 12-year-old or younger girls trying to be Britney and Christina, with their pierced bellybuttons, their tiny little tube tops, their strappy shoes and their shorts showing the tops of their buttocks," said Ms. Cardia, who, discouraged by the current run of back-to-school offerings, shops with her daughters at stores that cater to boys. . . .

Many schools have been forced to modify dress codes to address concerns that are as much practical as moral. "If you can't sit on the floor in a discussion group about a piece of literature without calling attention to yourself," said John Fierro, the principal of Dorchester Elementary School in Woodcliff Lake, N.J., referring to the micro-miniskirts now popular among middle-school girls, "you're not appropriately dressed." . . .

"In marketing circles, they talk about K.G.O.Y.," an abbreviation for Kids Getting Older Younger, said Alissa Quart, the author of *Branded: The Buying and Selling of Teenagers* (Perseus Books, 2003). "You want to get them younger, so they're full of aspiration not only to look older but to spend older."

That this strategy works seemed clear at Delia's, an apparel store in the Westchester mall, which was packed on Thursday with young shoppers pawing through racks of $22 T-shirts imprinted with phrases like "Parental Guidance Suggested." It is by no means obvious how well such guidance is heard. . . . "You'll never hear a mother say, 'You can't wear that to school,'" she said. . . .

"You don't want to sound censorious or reactionary," Ms. Quart said. "But kids watch HBO. They see late-night TV. They see the 200 channels teeming with quasi-pornographic imagery." . . .

"Parents have to think about a life of commerce these kids are caught up in and teach them some media literacy," Ms. Quart suggested. Kimora Lee Simmons, designer of the hugely popular Baby Phat line, said they also "have to sit their kids down and take some major responsibility when they start wearing clothes that make them look like hootchie mamas, stuff that was never designed with children in mind."

WHAT DO YOU THINK?

1. Why are today's clothing manufacturers encouraging adult patterns of sexuality among young girls? What about teen stars such as Britney Spears and Christina Aguilera—how important is sexuality to their performances?

2. Does the pattern described in this article apply only to girls or does it also apply to boys? Explain your answer.

Adapted from the original article by Guy Trebay published in *The New York Times* on September 2, 2003. Copyright © 2003 by The New York Times Company. Reprinted with permission.

CHAPTER SEVEN

Deviance

Why is deviance found in all societies?

How does *who* and *what* are defined as deviant reflect social inequality?

What effect has punishment had in reducing crime in the United States?

Societies have a variety of ways to control the behavior of their members. After being convicted ▶ of serious crimes, these women in Arizona have been assigned to a work gang.

Dennis Kozlowski was on a roll. As the chief executive officer of Tyco International, a large Bermuda-based manufacturing corporation, Kozlowski was buying new companies so fast he had earned the nickname "Deal-a-Month Dennis." Kozlowski also played the part of a frugal and level-headed business leader: "We don't believe in perks," he stated in a business magazine interview.

On the face of it, Tyco appeared to be a highly successful and responsibly run corporation. But all that was to change in 2002: As it became clear that Tyco had misreported its profits, the company suddenly collapsed, causing great harm to Tyco employees and stockholders alike. As the person in charge, Kozlowski stood accused of grand larceny, enterprise corruption, and falsifying business records—in short, of looting the company of more than $600 million for his own benefit.

The details of the alleged crimes are staggering. Prosecutors claim Kozlowski used company money for one extravagant purchase after another, including a $30 million New York apartment (with expensive furnishings that included a $6,000 shower curtain), paintings by the likes of Monet and Renoir, and a 130-foot yacht. He even charged more than $1 million to the company to cover half the cost of a fortieth birthday party for his wife, Angie (some seventy-five guests were whisked by jet to the Mediterranean island of Sardinia, where Jimmy Buffet joined them to sing "Margaritaville" to the guest of honor). In short, Kozlowski lived very well—on other people's money.

Kozlowski was indicted by a criminal court. In 2004, his first trial ended without a verdict, and a new trial is pending. In the wake of jail terms handed down to other top executives in the recent series of corporate scandals, it is likely that he, too, will spend time behind bars (Lavelle, 2003; Smart, 2003).

This chapter explores the issue of crime and criminals, showing that individuals accused of wrongdoing do not always fit the common stereotype of the "street" criminal. More broadly, it also tackles the larger question of why societies develop standards of right and wrong in the first place. As we shall see, law is simply one part of a complex system of social control: Society teaches us all to conform, at least most of the time, to countless rules. We begin our investigation by defining several basic concepts.

What Is Deviance?

Deviance is *the recognized violation of cultural norms.* Norms guide virtually all human activities, so the concept of deviance is quite broad. One category of deviance is **crime,** *the violation of a society's formally enacted criminal*
law. Even criminal deviance spans a wide range, from minor traffic violations to sexual assault to murder.

Most familiar examples of nonconformity are negative instances of rule breaking, such as stealing from a convenience store, abusing a child, or driving while drunk. But we also define especially good people—students who volunteer too much in class or people who are overly enthusiastic about new computer technology—as deviant, even if we give them a measure of respect. What all deviant actions or attitudes have in common is some element of *difference* that causes us to think of another person as an "outsider" (Becker, 1966).

Not all deviance involves action or even choice. The very *existence* of some categories of people can be troublesome to others. To the young, elderly people may seem hopelessly "out of it," and to some whites, the mere presence of people of color may cause discomfort. Able-bodied people often view people with disabilities as an out-group, just as rich people may avoid the poor, who appear to fall short of their standards.

All of us are subject to **social control,** *attempts by society to regulate people's thoughts and behavior.* Often this process is informal, as when parents praise or scold their children or when friends make fun of someone's musical taste. Cases of serious deviance, however, may bring action by the **criminal justice system,** *a formal response by police, courts, and prison officials to alleged violations of the law.*

 Learn more about juvenile delinquency at http://www. ojjdp.ncjrs.org/

How a society defines deviance, *who* is branded as deviant, and *what* people decide to do about deviance are all issues of social organization. Only gradually, however, have people recognized that deviance is much more than a matter of individual choice or personal failing, as the chapter now explains.

THE BIOLOGICAL CONTEXT

Chapter 3 ("Socialization: From Infancy to Old Age") explained that a century ago most people understood—or more correctly, misunderstood—human behavior to be the result of biological instincts. Early interest in criminality thus focused on biological causes. In 1876, Cesare Lombroso (1835–1909), an Italian physician who worked in prisons, theorized that criminals stand out physically, with low foreheads, prominent jaws and cheekbones, protruding ears, hairiness, and unusually long arms. All in all, Lombroso claimed that criminals look like our apelike ancestors.

Had Lombroso looked more carefully, he would have found the physical features he linked to criminality throughout the entire population. We now know that no physical traits distinguish criminals from noncriminals (Goring, 1972, orig. 1913).

At mid-century, William Sheldon (Sheldon, Hartl, & McDermott, 1949) took a different approach, suggesting that body structure might predict criminality. He crosschecked hundreds of young men for body type and criminal history and concluded that delinquency was most common among boys with muscular, athletic builds. Sheldon Glueck and Eleanor Glueck (1950) confirmed Sheldon's conclusion but cautioned that a powerful build does not necessarily *cause* or even predict criminality. Parents, they suggested, tend to be more distant from powerfully built sons, who in turn grow up to show less sensitivity toward others. Moreover, in a self-fulfilling prophecy, people who expect muscular boys to be bullies may act in ways that bring about the aggressive behavior they expect.

Deviance is always a matter of difference. Deviance emerges in everyday life as we encounter people whose appearance or behavior differs from what we consider to be "right." Who is the "deviant" in this photograph? From whose point of view?

Today, genetics research seeks possible links between biology and crime. Although no conclusive evidence connects criminality to any specific genetic trait, people's overall genetic composition, in combination with social influences, probably accounts for some tendency toward criminality. In other words, biological factors may have a real but small effect on whether a person becomes a criminal (Wilson & Herrnstein, 1985; Jencks, 1987; Pallone & Hennessy, 1998).

Critical review. At best, biological theories offer a very limited explanation of crime. Recent sociobiological research—noting, for example, that violent crime is overwhelmingly male and that parents are more likely to abuse foster children than natural children—is promising, but we know too little about the links between genes and human behavior to draw firm conclusions (Daly & Wilson, 1988).

Furthermore, because a biological approach looks at the individual, it offers no insight into how some kinds of behaviors come to be defined as deviant in the first place. Therefore, although there is much to learn about how human biology may affect behavior, research currently places far greater emphasis on social influences.

PERSONALITY FACTORS

Like biological theories, psychological explanations of deviance focus on individual abnormality. Some personality traits are inherited, but most psychologists think personality is shaped primarily by social experience. Deviance, then, is viewed as the result of "unsuccessful" socialization.

Research by Walter Reckless and Simon Dinitz (1967) illustrates the psychological approach. Reckless and Dinitz began by asking teachers to categorize twelve-year-old male students as either likely or unlikely to get into trouble with the law. They then interviewed both the boys and their mothers to assess each boy's self-concept and how he related to others. Analyzing their results, the researchers found that the "good boys" displayed a strong conscience (or superego, in Freud's terminology), could handle frustration, and identified with cultural norms and values. The "bad boys," by contrast, had a weaker conscience, displayed little tolerance for frustration, and felt out of step with conventional culture.

As we might expect, the "good boys" went on to have fewer run-ins with the police than the "bad boys." Because all the boys lived in areas where delinquency was widespread, the investigators attributed staying out of trouble to a personality that controlled deviant impulses. Based on this conclusion, Reckless and Dinitz called their analysis *containment theory*.

Critical review. Psychologists have shown that personality patterns have some connection to deviance. However, most serious crimes are committed by people whose psychological profiles are normal.

Overall, both biological and psychological research views deviance as an individual trait, without exploring how ideas of right and wrong initially arise, why people define some rule breakers but not others as deviant, and what role power plays in shaping a society's system of social control. To explore these issues, we now turn to a sociological analysis of deviance.

THE SOCIAL FOUNDATIONS OF DEVIANCE

Although we tend to view deviance as the free choice or personal failings of individuals, all behavior—deviance as well as conformity—is shaped by society. Three social foundations of deviance identified here will be detailed later in this chapter:

1. **Deviance varies according to cultural norms.** No thought or action is inherently deviant; it becomes deviant only in relation to particular norms. State law permits prostitution in rural areas of Nevada, although the practice is outlawed in the rest of the United States. Eleven states have gambling casinos; twenty-eight have casinos on Indian reservations. In all other states, casino gambling is illegal.

   Furthermore, most cities and towns have at least one unique law. For example, Mobile, Alabama, outlaws the wearing of stiletto-heeled shoes; Amityville, New York, bans building a home with more than one front door; Mount Prospect, Illinois, has a law against keeping pigeons or bees; Los Angeles bans gas-powered leaf blowers; Hoover, South Dakota, does not allow fishing with a kerosene lantern; and Beverly Hills, California, regulates the number of tennis balls allowed on the court at one time (Sanders & Horn, 1998; Steele, 2000).

   Around the world, deviance is even more diverse. Albania outlaws any public display of religious faith, such as "crossing" oneself; Cuba and Vietnam can prosecute citizens for meeting with foreigners; Malaysia does not allow tight-fitting jeans for women; police in Iran can arrest a woman simply for wearing makeup.

2. **People become deviant as others define them that way.** Everyone violates cultural norms at one time or another. For example, have you ever walked around talking to yourself or "borrowed" a pen from your workplace? Whether such behavior defines us as criminal or mentally ill depends on how others perceive, define, and respond to it.

3. **Both norms and the way people define situations involve social power.** According to Karl Marx, the law is the means by which powerful people protect their interests. A homeless person who stands on a street corner speaking out against the government risks arrest for disturbing the peace; a mayoral candidate during an election campaign does exactly the same thing and gets police protection. In short, norms and how we apply them reflect social inequality.

The Functions of Deviance: Structural-Functional Analysis

The key insight of the structural-functional approach is that deviance is a necessary element of social organization. This point was made a century ago by Emile Durkheim.

Art can be used to push the boundaries of a cultural system, sometimes becoming controversial in the process. This painting by Honore D. Sharrer, *Tribute to the American Working People,* was painted in 1951, when, in many parts of the United States, black and white children did not attend classes in school together. What do you think the artist was trying to do in this painting?

Tribute to the American Working People (Panel from five-part painting, *Classroom Scene*). © Smithsonian American Art Museum, Washington, D.C. / Art Resource. 1986.6.97

DURKHEIM'S BASIC INSIGHT

In his pioneering study of deviance, Emile Durkheim (1964a, orig. 1893; 1964b, orig. 1895) made the surprising statement that there is nothing abnormal about deviance. In fact, it performs four essential functions:

1. **Deviance affirms cultural values and norms.** As moral creatures, people must prefer some attitudes and behaviors to others. But any definition of virtue rests on an opposing idea of vice: There can be no good without evil and no justice without crime. Deviance is needed to define and sustain morality.

2. **Responding to deviance clarifies moral boundaries.** By defining some individuals as deviant, people draw a boundary between right and wrong. For example, a college marks the line between academic honesty and deviance by disciplining students who cheat on exams.

3. **Responding to deviance brings people together.** People typically react to serious deviance with shared outrage. In doing so, Durkheim explained, they reaffirm the moral ties that bind them. For example, after the September 11, 2001, terrorist attacks, people across the United States were joined by a common desire to protect the country and bring those responsible to justice.

4. **Deviance encourages social change.** Deviant people push a society's moral boundaries; their lives suggest alternatives to the status quo and may encourage

change. Today's deviance, declared Durkheim, can become tomorrow's morality (1964b:71, orig. 1895). For example, rock 'n' roll, condemned as immoral in the 1950s, became a mainstream, multibillion-dollar industry just a few years later; in recent decades, hip-hop music followed the same path.

MERTON'S STRAIN THEORY

Some deviance may be necessary for a society to function, but Robert Merton (1938, 1968) argued that excessive deviance arises from particular social arrangements. Specifically, the extent and kind of deviance depend on whether a society provides the *means* (such as schooling and job opportunities) to achieve cultural *goals* (such as financial success).

Conformity lies in pursuing cultural goals through approved means. Thus, the U.S. "success story" is someone who gains wealth and prestige through talent, schooling, and hard work. But not everyone who wants conventional success has the opportunity to attain it. For example, people living in poverty may see little hope of becoming successful if they play by the rules. According to Merton, the strain between our culture's emphasis on wealth and the lack of opportunities to get rich gives rise, especially among the poor, to stealing, the sale of illegal drugs, and other forms of street crime. Merton called this type of deviance *innovation:* using unconventional means (street crime) to

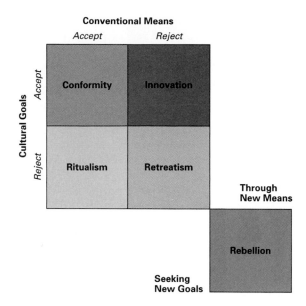

Conventional Means

	Accept	Reject
Cultural Goals *Accept*	Conformity	Innovation
Reject	Ritualism	Retreatism

Through
New Means

Rebellion

Seeking
New Goals

FIGURE 7-1   Merton's Strain Theory of Deviance

Source: Merton (1968).

achieve a culturally approved goal (wealth). Figure 7–1 shows that innovation involves accepting the cultural goal (financial success) but rejecting the conventional means (hard work at a "straight" job) in favor of unconventional means (street crime).

The inability to reach a cultural goal may also prompt another type of deviance that Merton calls *ritualism* (see Figure 7–1). For example, many people may believe they cannot achieve the cultural goal of becoming rich; therefore, they obsessively stick to the rules (the conventional means) in order to at least feel respectable.

A third response to the inability to succeed is *retreatism:* rejecting both cultural goals and means so that one, in effect, "drops out." Some alcoholics, drug addicts, and street people are retreatists. The deviance of retreatists lies in their unconventional lifestyles and, perhaps more seriously, in what seems to be their willingness to live that way.

The fourth response to failure is *rebellion.* Like retreatists, rebels such as radical "survivalists" reject both the cultural definition of success and the conventional means of achieving it but go one step further by forming a counterculture and advocating alternatives to the existing social order.

DEVIANT SUBCULTURES

Richard Cloward and Lloyd Ohlin (1966) extended Merton's theory, proposing that crime results not simply from

limited legitimate (legal) opportunity but also from readily accessible illegitimate (illegal) opportunity. In short, deviance or conformity depends on the *relative opportunity structure* that frames a person's life.

The life of Al Capone, a notorious gangster, illustrates Cloward and Ohlin's theory. As a son of poor immigrants, Capone faced barriers of poverty and ethnic prejudice, which lowered his odds of achieving success in conventional terms. Yet as a young man during the Prohibition era (when alcoholic beverages were banned in the United States, from 1920 to 1933), Capone found in his neighborhood people who could teach him how to sell alcohol illegally—a source of illegitimate opportunity. Where the structure of opportunity favors criminal activity, Cloward and Ohlin predict the development of *criminal subcultures,* such as street gangs.

But what happens when people are unable to find *any* opportunities, legal or illegal? Then deviance may take one of two forms: *conflict subcultures* (armed street gangs), where violence is ignited by frustration and a desire for respect, or *retreatist subcultures,* in which deviants drop out and abuse alcohol or other drugs.

Albert Cohen (1971, orig. 1955) suggests that criminality is most common among lower-class youths because they have the least opportunity to achieve conventional success. Neglected by society, they seek self-respect by creating a deviant subculture that defines as worthy the traits these youths do have. Being feared on the street may win few points with society as a whole, but it may satisfy a youth's desire to "be somebody" in a local neighborhood.

Walter Miller (1970, orig. 1958) adds that deviant subcultures are characterized by (1) *trouble,* arising from frequent conflict with teachers and police; (2) *toughness,* the value placed on physical size, strength, and agility, especially among males; (3) *smartness,* the ability to succeed on the streets, to outsmart or "con" others; (4) *a need for excitement,* the search for thrills, risk, or danger; (5) *a belief in fate,* a sense that people lack control over their own lives; and (6) *a desire for freedom,* often expressed as anger toward all authority figures.

Finally, Elijah Anderson (1994, 2002) explains that in poor urban neighborhoods, most people manage to conform to conventional ("decent") values. Yet faced daily with the dangers of crime and violence, hostility from police, and sometimes even neglect from their own parents, some young men decide to live by the "street code." To show that he can survive on the street, a young man displays "nerve," a willingness to stand up to any threat. Following this street code, the young man believes that even a violent death is better than being "dissed" (disrespected) by others. Some manage to escape the dangers,

Young people cut off from legitimate opportunity often form subcultures that many people view as deviant. Gang subcultures, including tattoos on the fingers, are one way young people gain the sense of belonging and respect denied to them by the larger culture.

but the risk of ending up in jail—or worse—is very high for these young men, who have been pushed to the margins of our society.

Critical review.   Durkheim made an important contribution by pointing out the functions of deviance. However, there is evidence that a community does not always come together in reaction to crime; sometimes fear of crime drives people to withdraw from public life (Liska & Warner, 1991; Warr & Ellison, 2000).

Merton's strain theory also has been criticized for explaining some kinds of deviance (stealing, for example) better than others (crimes of passion or mental illness). Furthermore, not everyone seeks success in conventional terms of wealth, as strain theory suggests.

The general argument of Cloward and Ohlin, Cohen, and Miller—that deviance reflects the opportunity structure of society—has been confirmed by subsequent research (Allan & Steffensmeier, 1989; Uggen, 1999). However, these theories fall short by assuming that everyone shares the same cultural standards for judging right and wrong. If we define crime as including not just street theft but the insider trading for which Martha Stewart was convicted in 2004 or the kind of corporate fraud described in the opening to this chapter, then more high-income people will be counted among criminals. There is evidence that people of all social backgrounds have become more casual about breaking the rules, as the Critical Thinking box on page 168 explains.

Finally, all structural-functional theories suggest that everyone who breaks the rules will be labeled deviant. However, becoming deviant is actually a highly complex process, as the next section explains.

Labeling Deviance: Symbolic-Interaction Analysis

The symbolic-interaction approach explains how people define deviance in everyday situations. From this point of view, definitions of deviance and conformity are surprisingly flexible.

LABELING THEORY

The central contribution of symbolic-interaction analysis is **labeling theory,** *the assertion that deviance and conformity result not so much from what people do as from how others respond to those actions.* Labeling theory stresses the relativity of deviance, meaning that people may define the same behavior in any number of ways. Howard Becker claims that deviance is nothing more than behavior that people define as deviant (1966).

Consider these situations: A college student takes an article of clothing from a roommate's drawer, a married woman at a convention in a distant city has sex with an old boyfriend, and a mayor gives a big city contract to a major campaign contributor. We might define the first situation as carelessness, borrowing, or theft. The consequences of the second situation depend largely on whether the woman's behavior becomes known back home. In the third situation, is the mayor choosing the best contractor or paying off a political debt? The social construction of reality is a highly variable process of detection, definition, and response.

PRIMARY AND SECONDARY DEVIANCE

Edwin Lemert (1951, 1972) observed that some norm violations—say, skipping school or underage drinking—

CRITICAL THINKING
Deviant (Sub)Culture: Has It Become Okay to Do Wrong?

It's been a couple of bad years for the idea of playing by the rules. First we learn that the executives of not just one but many U.S. corporations are guilty of fraud and outright stealing. Then Martha Stewart, the country's lifestyle guru, is convicted of crimes linked to an illegal stock deal. Perhaps worst of all, the Catholic church, which we hold up as a model of moral behavior, has become embroiled in a scandal of its own. In this case, hundreds of priests are said to have sexually abused parishioners (most of them teens and children) over many decades while church officials busied themselves covering up the crimes. By the beginning of 2004, more than 300 priests in the United States had been removed from their duties pending investigations of abuse.

Plenty of people are offering explanations for this widespread pattern of wrongdoing. Some suggest that the pressure to win in the highly competitive corporate world—by whatever means necessary—can be overwhelming. As one analyst put it, "You can get away with your embezzlements and your

lies, but you can never get away with *failing*."

Such thinking helps explain the wrongdoing among many CEOs in the corporate world, but it offers little insight into the problem of abusive priests. In some ways at least, wrongdoing seems to have become a way of life for just about everybody. For example, the Internal Revenue Service reports that U.S. taxpayers cheat on their taxes, failing to pay an estimated $200 billion each year (an average of about $1,600 per taxpayer). The music industry claims that it has lost

a vast amount of money due to illegal piracy of recordings, a practice especially common among young people. And surveys of high school students reveal that three-fourths admit to having cheated on a test at least once during the past year.

Emile Durkheim considered society to be a moral system, built on a set of rules about what people should and should not do. Years earlier, another French thinker named Blaise Pascal made the opposite claim that "cheating is the foundation of society." Today, which of the two statements is closer to the truth?

WHAT DO YOU THINK?

1. In your opinion, how widespread is wrongdoing in U.S. society today?
2. Do you think the people whose actions are described in this box consider what they are doing as wrong? Why or why not?
3. What are the reasons for this apparent increase in dishonesty?

Do you consider cheating in school to be wrong? Would you turn in someone you saw cheat? Why or why not?

Source: Based on "Our Cheating Hearts" (2002).

provoke slight reaction from others and have little effect on a person's self-concept. Lemert calls such passing episodes *primary deviance.*

But what happens if people take notice of someone's deviance and make something of it? For example, if people begin to describe a young man as an "alcohol abuser" and exclude him from their friendship network, he may become bitter, drink even more, and seek the company of those who approve of his behavior. The response to primary deviance can set in motion *secondary deviance,* by which a person repeatedly violates a norm and begins to take on a deviant

identity. The development of secondary deviance is one application of the Thomas theorem (see Chapter 4, "Social Interaction in Everyday Life"), which states that situations people define as real become real in their consequences.

STIGMA

Secondary deviance marks the start of what Erving Goffman (1963) called a *deviant career.* As people develop a stronger commitment to deviant behavior, they typically acquire a **stigma,** *a powerfully negative label that greatly* changes a person's self-concept and social identity. Stigma operates as a master status (see Chapter 4), overpowering other dimensions of identity so that a person is discredited in the minds of others and consequently becomes socially isolated. Sometimes an entire community stigmatizes a person through what Harold Garfinkel (1956) calls a *degradation ceremony*. A criminal prosecution is one example, operating much like a high school graduation ceremony in reverse: A person stands before the community to be labeled in a negative rather than a positive way.

Once people stigmatize a person, they may engage in *retrospective labeling*, a reinterpretation of the person's past in light of some present deviance (Scheff, 1984). For example, after discovering that a priest has sexually molested a child, others rethink his past, perhaps musing, "He always did want to be around young children." Retrospective labeling distorts a person's biography by being highly selective, a process that can deepen a deviant identity.

Similarly, people may engage in *projective labeling* of a stigmatized person. That is, people use a deviant identity to predict a person's future actions. Regarding the priest, people might say, "He's going to keep at it until he's caught." The more people in someone's social world think such things, of course, the greater the chance that they will come true.

LABELING DIFFERENCE AS DEVIANCE

Is a homeless man who refuses to allow police to take him to a city shelter on a cold night simply trying to live independently, or is he "crazy"? People have a tendency to treat behavior that irritates or threatens them not simply as "difference" but as deviance or even mental illness.

The psychiatrist Thomas Szasz charges that people are too quick to apply the label of mental illness to conditions that simply amount to a difference we don't like. The only way to avoid this troubling practice, Szasz concludes, is to abandon the idea of mental illness entirely (1961, 1970, 1994, 1995). As he sees it, illness is physical; therefore, mental illness is a myth. The world is full of people whose differences in thought or action may irritate others, but such differences are not grounds for defining someone as sick. Such labeling, Szasz claims, simply enforces conformity to the standards created by people powerful enough to impose their will on others.

Most mental health professionals reject the idea that there is no such thing as mental illness. But they do agree that it is important to think critically about how we define "difference." First, people who are mentally ill are no more to blame for their condition than people who suffer from cancer or some other physical problem. In other words,

having a mental or physical illness is not grounds for being labeled "deviant" or "crazy." Second, ordinary people without the knowledge to diagnose mental illness should avoid applying such labels just to make people conform to our own standards of behavior.

THE MEDICALIZATION OF DEVIANCE

Labeling theory, particularly the ideas of Szasz and Goffman, helps explain an important shift in the way our society understands deviance. Over the past fifty years, the growing influence of psychiatry and medicine has led to the **medicalization of deviance,** *the transformation of moral and legal deviance into a medical condition.*

Medicalization amounts to swapping one set of labels for another. In moral terms, we judge people or their behavior as "bad" or "good." However, the scientific objectivity of medicine passes no moral judgment, instead using clinical diagnoses such as "sick" or "well."

To illustrate, until the mid-twentieth century, most people viewed alcoholics as morally weak people easily tempted by the pleasure of drink. Gradually, however, medical specialists redefined alcoholism so that most people now consider it a disease, making people "sick" rather than "bad." In the same way, obesity, drug addiction, child abuse, promiscuity, and other behaviors that used to be strictly moral matters are widely defined today as illnesses for which people need help rather than punishment.

Whether we define deviance as a moral or medical issue has three consequences. First, it affects *who responds* to deviance. An offense against common morality typically brings a reaction from members of the community or the police. However, applying medical labels transfers the situation to the control of clinical specialists, including counselors, psychiatrists, and physicians.

A second issue is *how people respond*. A moral approach defines deviants as offenders subject to punishment. Medically, however, they are patients who need treatment. Whereas punishment is designed to fit the crime, treatment programs are tailored to the patient and may involve virtually any therapy that a specialist thinks might prevent future illness.

Third, and most important, the two labels differ on the issue of *the personal competence of the deviant person*. From a moral standpoint, whether we are right or wrong, at least we take responsibility for our own behavior. Once defined as sick, however, we are seen as unable to control (or, if "mentally ill," even understand) our actions. People who are incompetent are in turn subject to treatment, often against their will. For this reason alone, defining deviance in medical terms should be done with extreme caution.

In some gangs, young people learn attitudes and skills that promote violence. Gangs offer their members a sense of belonging and social importance, but the price of membership is often high. This graffiti memorial to a fallen gang member is found in Bridgeport, Connecticut.

SUTHERLAND'S DIFFERENTIAL ASSOCIATION THEORY

Learning any social pattern, whether conventional or deviant, is a process that takes place in groups. Therefore, according to Edwin Sutherland (1940), a person's tendency toward conformity or deviance depends on the amount of contact with others who encourage—or reject—conventional behavior. This is Sutherland's theory of *differential association*.

A number of studies confirm the idea that young people are more likely to engage in delinquency if they believe that members of their peer group encourage such activity (Akers et al., 1979; Miller & Matthews, 2001). One recent investigation focused on sexual activity among eighth-grade students. Two strong predictors of such behavior in young girls were having a boyfriend who, presumably, encouraged sexual relations and having girlfriends they believed would approve of such activity. Similarly, boys were encouraged to become sexually active by friends who rewarded them with high status in the peer group (Little & Rankin, 2001).

HIRSCHI'S CONTROL THEORY

The sociologist Travis Hirschi (1969; Gottfredson & Hirschi, 1995) developed *control theory*, which states that social control depends on anticipating the consequences of one's behavior. Hirschi assumes that everyone finds at least some deviance tempting. But the thought of a ruined career keeps most people from breaking the rules; for some, just imagining the reactions of family and friends is enough. On the other hand, people who think that they have little to lose from deviance are likely to become rule-breakers.

Specifically, Hirschi links conformity to four different types of social control:

1. **Attachment.** Strong social attachments encourage conformity. Weak family, peer, and school relationships leave people freer to engage in deviance.

2. **Opportunity.** The greater a person's access to legitimate opportunity, the greater the advantages of conformity. By contrast, someone with little confidence in future success is freer to drift toward deviance.

3. **Involvement.** Extensive involvement in legitimate activities—such as holding a job, going to school, or playing sports—inhibits deviance (Langbein & Bess, 2002). By contrast, people who simply "hang out" waiting for something to happen have the time and energy to engage in deviant activity.

4. **Belief.** Strong beliefs in conventional morality and respect for authority figures restrain tendencies toward deviance. By contrast, people with a weak conscience (and who are left unsupervised) are more open to temptation (Stack, Wasserman, & Kern, 2004).

Hirschi's analysis combines a number of earlier ideas about the causes of deviant behavior. Note that a person's relative social privilege and strength of moral character are crucial in generating a stake in conformity to conventional norms (Sampson & Laub, 1990; Free, 1992).

Critical review. The various symbolic-interaction theories all see deviance as a process. Labeling theory links deviance not to *action* but to the *reaction* of others. Thus, some people are defined as deviant whereas others who think or behave in the same way are not. The concepts of secondary deviance, deviant career, and stigma show how being labeled deviant can become a lasting self-concept.

Yet labeling theory has several limitations. First, because it takes a highly relative view of deviance, labeling theory ignores the fact that some kinds of behavior—such as murder—are condemned virtually everywhere. Therefore, labeling theory is most usefully applied to less serious issues, such as sexual promiscuity or mental illness. Second, research on the consequences of deviant labeling is inconclusive (Smith & Gartin, 1989; Sherman & Smith, 1992). Does deviant labeling produce further deviance or discourage it? Third, not everyone resists being labeled as deviant; some people actually seek it (Vold & Bernard, 1986). For example, people engage in civil disobedience and willingly subject themselves to arrest in order to call attention to social injustice.

Both Sutherland's differential association theory and Hirschi's control theory have had considerable influence in sociology. But why do society's norms and laws define certain kinds of activities as deviant in the first place? This important question is addressed by social-conflict analysis, the focus of the next section.

Deviance and Inequality: Social-Conflict Analysis

The social-conflict approach links deviance to social inequality. That is, *who* or *what* is labeled "deviant" depends on which categories of people hold power in a society.

DEVIANCE AND POWER

Alexander Liazos (1972) points out that the people we tend to define as deviants—those we dismiss as "nuts" and "sluts"—are typically those who share the trait of powerlessness. Bag ladies (not corporate polluters) and unemployed men on street corners (not international arms dealers) carry the stigma of deviance.

Social-conflict theory explains this pattern in three ways. First, all norms and especially the laws of any society generally reflect the interests of the rich and powerful. People who threaten the wealthy, either by taking their property or by pushing for a more egalitarian society, are labeled "common thieves" or "political radicals." Karl Marx, a major architect of the social-conflict approach, argued that the law (and all social institutions) supports the interests of the rich. Or as Richard Quinney puts it, "Capitalist justice is by the capitalist class, for the capitalist class, and against the working class" (1977:3).

Second, even if their behavior is called into question, the powerful have the resources to resist deviant labels. The majority of the corporate executives involved in recent scandals have yet to be arrested; very few have gone to jail.

Third, the widespread belief that norms and laws are natural and good masks their political character. For this reason, although we may condemn the *unequal application* of the law, most of us give little thought to whether the *laws themselves* are inherently unfair (Quinney, 1977).

DEVIANCE AND CAPITALISM

In the Marxist tradition, Steven Spitzer (1980) argues that deviant labels are applied to people who interfere with the operation of capitalism. First, because capitalism is based on private control of property, people who threaten the property of others—especially the poor who steal from the rich—are prime candidates for being labeled deviant. Conversely, the rich who take advantage of the poor are less likely to be labeled deviant. For example, landlords who charge poor tenants high rents and evict those who cannot pay are not considered a threat to anyone; they are simply "doing business."

Second, because capitalism depends on productive labor, people who cannot or will not work risk being labeled deviant. Many members of our society think of unemployed people as deviant, even if they lost their jobs through no fault of their own.

Third, capitalism depends on respect for authority figures, causing people who resist authority to be labeled deviant. Examples are children who skip school or talk back to parents and teachers, and adults who do not cooperate with employers or police.

Fourth, anyone who directly challenges the capitalist status quo is likely to be defined as deviant. Such has been the case with antiwar activists, radical environmentalists, and labor organizers.

On the other side of the coin, society positively labels whatever supports the operation of capitalism. For example, winning athletes enjoy celebrity status because they make money and express the values of individual achievement and competition, both vital to capitalism. Also, Spitzer notes, we condemn using drugs of escape (marijuana, psychedelics, heroin, crack) as deviant but promote drugs (such as alcohol and caffeine) that encourage adjustment to the status quo.

The capitalist system also tries to control people who don't fit into the system. The elderly, people with mental or physical disabilities, and Robert Merton's "retreatists" (including people addicted to alcohol or other drugs) represent a "costly yet relatively harmless burden" to society. Such people, claims Spitzer, are subject to control by social welfare agencies. But people who directly challenge the capitalist system, including the inner-city "underclass" and revolutionaries—Merton's "innovators" and "rebels"—are controlled by the criminal justice system or, in times of crisis, military forces such as the National Guard.

Note that both the social welfare and criminal justice systems blame individuals, not the system, for social problems. Welfare recipients are considered unworthy freeloaders, poor people who rage at their plight are labeled rioters, anyone who actively challenges the government is branded

After the recent collapse of many large corporations due to fraud and other illegal activities, some corporate executives are facing criminal charges. Here, Andrew S. Fastow, chief financial officer of Enron Corporation, is escorted to a court appearance by FBI agents. In your opinion, what share of the executives involved in corporate crime will ever serve jail time?

a radical or a Communist, and those who attempt to gain illegally what they will never acquire legally are rounded up as common criminals.

WHITE-COLLAR CRIME

In a sign of things to come, a Wall Street stockbroker named Michael Milken made headlines back in 1987 when he was jailed for business fraud. Milken attracted attention because not since the days of Al Capone had anyone made so much money in one year: $550 million—*about $1.5 million a day* (Swartz, 1989).

Milken committed a **white-collar crime,** defined by Edwin Sutherland in 1940 as *crime committed by people of high social position in the course of their occupations.* White-collar crimes do not involve violence and rarely bring police with guns drawn to the scene. Rather, white-collar criminals use their powerful offices to illegally enrich themselves or others, often causing significant public harm in the process (Hagan & Parker, 1985; Vold & Bernard, 1986). For this reason, sociologists sometimes call white-collar offenses *crime in the suites* as opposed to *crime in the streets.*

The most common white-collar crimes are bank embezzlement, business fraud, bribery, and antitrust violations. Sutherland (1940) explains that such white-collar offenses typically end up in a civil hearing rather than a criminal courtroom. *Civil law* regulates business dealings between private parties; *criminal law* defines a person's moral responsibilities to society. In practice, someone who loses a civil case pays for damage or injury but is not labeled a criminal. Furthermore, corporate officials are protected by the fact that most charges of white-collar crime target the organization rather than individuals.

In the rare cases that white-collar criminals are charged and convicted, they have only a fifty-fifty chance of going to jail. One accounting shows that just 55 percent of the embezzlers convicted in the U.S. federal courts served prison sentences; the rest were put on probation and/or paid a fine (U.S. Bureau of Justice Statistics, 2004).

CORPORATE CRIME

Sometimes whole companies, not just individuals, break the law. **Corporate crime** consists of *the illegal actions of a corporation or people acting on its behalf.*

Corporate crime ranges from knowingly selling faulty or dangerous products to deliberately polluting the environment (Benson & Cullen, 1998). The collapse of Enron Corporation in 2001 following a number of alleged violations of business and accounting practices appears to be a very serious case of corporate crime. Estimates of the loss to stockholders and others exceed $50 billion, which is four times the annual loss in the United States due to common theft (Lavella, 2002).

As with white-collar crime, most cases of corporate crime go unpunished, and many never even become a matter of public record. Furthermore, the cost of corporate crime goes beyond dollars. The collapse of Enron, Global Crossing, Tyco International, and other corporations in recent years cost tens of thousands of people their jobs and their pensions. Even more seriously, for decades, coal mining companies have put miners at risk from inhaling coal dust, so that hundreds of people die annually from "black lung" disease. The death toll from all job-related hazards that are known to companies probably exceeds 100,000 annually (Carroll, 1999; Jones, 1999).

ORGANIZED CRIME

Organized crime is *a business supplying illegal goods or services.* Sometimes crime organizations force people to do business with them, as when a gang extorts money from shopkeepers for "protection." In most cases, however, organized crime involves selling illegal goods and services—including sex, drugs, or gambling—to a willing public.

APPLYING THEORY

DEVIANCE

	Structural-Functional Approach	Symbolic-Interaction Approach	Social-Conflict Approach
What is the level of analysis?	Macro-level	Micro-level	Macro-level
What is deviance? What part does it play in society?	Deviance is a basic part of social organization. By defining deviance, society sets its moral boundaries.	Deviance is part of socially constructed reality that emerges in interaction. Deviance comes into being as individuals label something as such.	Deviance results from social inequality. Norms, including laws, reflect the interests of powerful members of society.
What is important about deviance?	Deviance is universal: All societies contain deviance.	Deviance is variable: Any act or person may or may not be labeled as deviant.	Deviance is political: People with little power are at high risk for becoming deviant.

Organized crime has flourished in the United States for more than a century. The scope of its operations expanded among immigrants who found that this society was not willing to share its opportunities with them. Thus, some ambitious minorities (such as Al Capone, mentioned earlier) made their own success, especially during Prohibition (1920–1933), when the government banned the sale of alcohol.

The Italian Mafia is a well-known example of organized crime. But other criminal organizations involve African Americans, Chinese, Colombians, Cubans, Haitians, and Russians, as well as others of almost every racial and ethnic category. Organized crime today involves a wide range of activities, from selling illegal drugs to prostitution to credit card fraud and selling false identification papers to illegal immigrants (Valdez, 1997).

Critical review. According to social-conflict theory, a capitalist society's inequality in wealth and power guides the creation and application of laws and other norms. The criminal justice and social welfare systems thus act as political agents, controlling categories of people who threaten the capitalist system.

Like other approaches to deviance, social-conflict theory has its critics. First, this approach suggests that laws and other cultural norms are created directly by the rich and powerful. At the very least, this is an oversimplification because the law also protects workers, consumers, and the environment, sometimes opposing the interests of corporations and the rich.

Second, social-conflict analysis argues that criminality springs up only to the extent that a society treats its members unequally. However, as Durkheim noted, deviance exists in all societies, whatever their economic system.

The sociological explanations for crime and other types of deviance are summarized in the Applying Theory table.

Deviance, Race, and Gender

What people consider deviant reflects the relative power and privilege of different categories of people. The following sections offer two examples: how racial and ethnic hostility motivates hate crimes and how gender is linked to deviance.

HATE CRIMES

The term **hate crime** refers to *a criminal act against a person or a person's property by an offender motivated by racial or other bias.* A hate crime may express hostility toward someone based on race, religion, ancestry, sexual orientation, or physical disability. The federal government records about 9,000 incidents of hate crimes each year.

Most people were stunned by the brutal killing in 1998 of Matthew Shepard, a gay student at the University of Wyoming, by two men filled with hatred toward homosexuals. The National Gay and Lesbian Task Force reports that one in five lesbians and gay men has been physically assaulted and more than 90 percent have been verbally abused because of their sexual orientation (cited in Berrill, 1992:19–20). Victims of hate-motivated violence are especially likely to be people who deal with multiple stigmas, such as gay men of color. Yet anyone can be a victim: A recent study found that about 25 percent of the hate crimes based on race targeted white people (Jenness & Grattet, 2001).

By 2004, forty-six states and the federal government had enacted legislation that raises penalties for crimes

DIVERSITY: RACE, CLASS, & GENDER

Hate Crime Laws: Do They Punish Actions or Attitudes?

On a cool October evening, Todd Mitchell, an African American teenager, was standing with some friends in front of their apartment complex in Kenosha, Wisconsin. They had just seen the film *Mississippi Burning* and were fuming over a scene that showed a white man beating a young black boy kneeling in prayer.

"Do you feel hyped up to move on some white people?" asked Mitchell. Minutes later, they saw a young white boy walking toward them on the other side of the street. Mitchell commanded: "There goes a white boy. Go get him!" The group swarmed around the youngster, beating him bloody and leaving him on the ground in a coma. The attackers took the boy's tennis shoes as a trophy.

Police soon arrested the boys and charged them with the beating. Todd Mitchell went to trial as the ringleader, where the jury found him guilty of aggravated battery *motivated by racial*

Read one critic's ideas about hate crimes at http://www.andrewsullivan.com/politics.php

hatred. Instead of the usual two-year prison sentence, Mitchell went to jail for four years.

As this case illustrates, hate crime laws punish a crime more severely if the offender is motivated by bias against some category of people. Supporters make three arguments in favor of hate crime legislation. First, the offender's intentions are always important in weighing criminal responsibility, so considering hatred as an intention is nothing new. Second, a crime motivated by racial or other bias inflames the public mood more than a crime carried out, say, for money. Third, victims of hate crimes typically suffer more serious injuries than victims of crimes with other motives.

Critics counter that while some hate crime cases involve hard-core racism, most are impulsive acts by young people. Even more important, critics maintain, hate crime laws are a threat to First Amendment guarantees of free speech. Hate crime laws allow courts to sentence offenders not just for actions but also for their attitudes.

As the Harvard University law professor Alan Dershowitz cautions, "As much as I hate bigotry, I fear much more the Court attempting to control the minds of citizens." In short, according to critics, hate crime laws open the door to punishing beliefs rather than behavior.

In 1993, the U.S. Supreme Court upheld the sentence handed down to Todd Mitchell. In a unanimous decision, the justices reaffirmed that the government should not punish an individual's beliefs. But, they reasoned, a belief is no longer protected when it becomes the motive for a crime.

WHAT DO YOU THINK?

1. Do you think crimes motivated by hate are more harmful than those motivated by, say, greed? Why or why not?
2. Do you think minorities such as African Americans should be subject to hate crime laws just as white people are? Why or why not?
3. On balance, do you favor or oppose hate crime laws? Why?

Sources: Terry (1993) and Sullivan (2002).

---

motivated by hatred. Supporters are gratified, but opponents charge that such laws, which increase the penalty for a crime based on the attitudes of the offender, amount to punishing "politically incorrect" thoughts. The Diversity box takes a closer look at the issue of hate crime laws.

DEVIANCE AND GENDER

Virtually every society in the world applies stricter normative controls to women than to men. Historically, our own society has centered women's lives around the home. In the United States even today, women's opportunities in the workplace, in politics, and in the military are limited. Elsewhere in the world, the constraints on women are greater still. In Saudi Arabia, women cannot vote or legally operate motor vehicles; in Iran, women who expose their hair or wear makeup in public can be whipped; and a Nigerian court recently convicted a divorced woman of bearing a child out of wedlock and sentenced her to death by stoning (Eboh, 2002; her life was later spared out of concern for her child).

Gender also figures into the theories about deviance noted earlier. For example, Robert Merton's strain theory defines cultural goals in terms of financial success. Traditionally at least, this goal has had more to do with the lives of men, because women have been socialized to define success in terms of relationships, particularly marriage and motherhood (Leonard, 1982). A more woman-focused theory might recognize the "strain" that results from the

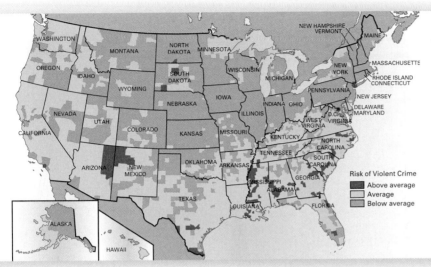

SEEING OURSELVES

NATIONAL MAP 7-1

The Risk of Violent Crime across the United States

This map shows the risk of becoming a victim of violent crime. In general, the risk is highest in low-income, rural counties that have a large population of men between the ages of fifteen and twenty-four. After reading through this section of the text, see whether you can explain this pattern.

Risk of Violent Crime
- ▉ Above average
- ▢ Average
- ▨ Below average

Source: *American Demographics* magazine, December 2000. Copyright © 2000 by Primedia. Reprinted with permission of Primedia Business Magazines & Media.

cultural ideal of equality clashing with the reality of gender-based inequality.

According to labeling theory, gender influences how we define deviance, because people commonly use different standards to judge the behavior of females and males. Furthermore, because society puts men in positions of power over women, men often escape direct responsibility for actions that victimize women. In the past, at least, men who sexually harassed or assaulted women were labeled only mildly deviant and sometimes escaped punishment entirely.

By contrast, women who are victimized may have to convince others—even members of a jury—that they are not to blame for their own sexual harassment or assault. Research confirms an important truth: Whether people define a situation as deviant—and, if they do, who the deviant party is—depends on the sex of both the audience and the actors (King & Clayson, 1988).

Finally, despite its focus on inequality, much social-conflict analysis does not address the issue of gender. If, as conflict theory suggests, poverty is a primary cause of crime, why do women (who are more likely to be poor than men) commit far *fewer* crimes than men?

Crime

Crime is the violation of criminal laws enacted by a locality, state, or the federal government. Technically, all crimes are composed of two distinct elements: an *act* (or in some cases, a failure to act) and *criminal intent* (in legal terminology, *mens rea,* or "guilty mind"). Intent is a matter of degree, ranging from willful conduct to negligence. Someone who is negligent does not set out deliberately to hurt anyone but acts (or fails

to act) in such a way that results in harm. Prosecutors weigh the degree of intent in determining whether, for example, to charge someone with first-degree murder, second-degree murder, or negligent manslaughter. Alternatively, they may consider a killing justifiable, as in self-defense.

TYPES OF CRIME

In the United States, the Federal Bureau of Investigation (FBI) gathers information on criminal offenses and regularly reports the results in a publication called *Crime in the United States.* Two major types of crimes make up the FBI "crime index."

Crimes against the person, also referred to as *violent crimes,* are *crimes that direct violence or the threat of violence against others.* Violent crimes include murder and manslaughter (legally defined as "the willful killing of one human being by another"), aggravated assault ("an unlawful attack by one person on another for the purpose of inflicting severe or aggravated bodily injury"), forcible rape ("the carnal knowledge of a female forcibly and against her will"), and robbery ("taking or attempting to take anything of value from the care, custody, or control of a person or persons, by force or threat of force or violence and/or putting the victim in fear"). National Map 7–1 shows the risk of violent crime for all the counties in the United States.

Crimes against property, also called *property crimes,* are *crimes that involve theft of property belonging to others.* Property crimes include burglary ("the unlawful entry of a

Find a report on the violent victimization of college students at http://www.ojp.usdoj.gov/bjs/pub/pdf/vvcs00.pdf

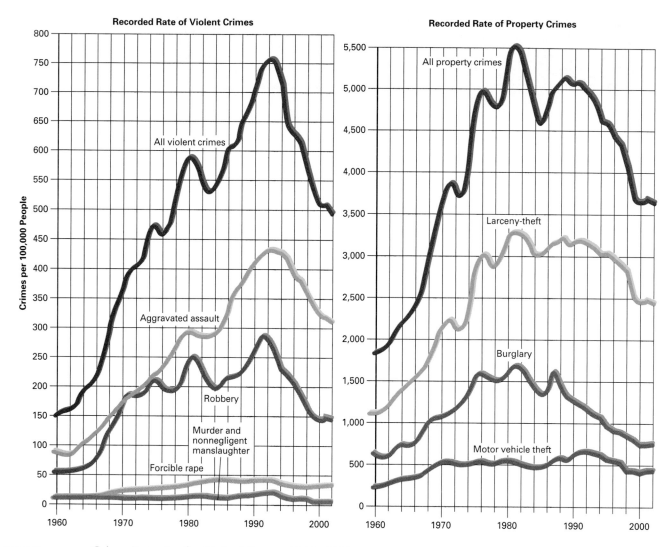

FIGURE 7-2 Crime Rates in the United States, 1960–2002

The graphs represent crime rates for various violent crimes and property crimes during recent decades.

Source: Federal Bureau of Investigation (2003).

structure to commit a [serious crime] or a theft"), larceny-theft ("the unlawful taking, carrying, leading, or riding away of property from the possession of another"), auto theft ("the theft or attempted theft of a motor vehicle"), and arson ("any willful or malicious burning or attempt to burn the personal property of another").

A third category of offenses, not included in major crime indexes, is **victimless crimes,** *violations of law in which there are no obvious victims.* Also called *crimes without complaint,* they include illegal drug use, prostitution, and gambling. The term "victimless crime" is misleading,

however. How victimless is a crime when young drug users embark on a life of crime to support their drug habit? What about a pregnant woman who, by smoking crack, permanently harms her baby? Perhaps it is more correct to say that people who commit such crimes are themselves both offenders and victims.

Because public views of victimless crime vary greatly, laws differ from place to place. Although gambling and prostitution are legal in very limited areas, both activities are common across the country. Homosexual (and some heterosexual) behavior between consenting adults is legally restricted in about half the states; however, where such laws exist, enforcement is light and selective.

CRIMINAL STATISTICS

Statistics gathered by the FBI show crime rates rising from 1960 to 1990, declining through 2000, and rising slightly thereafter. Even so, police still count nearly 12 million serious crimes each year. Figure 7–2 shows the trends for various serious crimes.

You should always read crime statistics with caution, however, because they include only crimes known to the police. Almost all murders are reported, but other assaults, especially between acquaintances, often are not. Police records include an even smaller proportion of property crimes, especially when the losses are small.

Researchers check official crime statistics by conducting *victimization surveys,* in which they ask a representative sample of people about their experiences with crime. According to these surveys, the overall crime rate is about three times higher than official reports indicate (Russell, 1995b).

THE STREET CRIMINAL: A PROFILE

Using government crime reports, we can draw a general description of the categories of people most likely to be arrested for violent and property crimes.

Age. Official crime rates rise sharply during adolescence and peak in the late teens, falling thereafter. People between the ages of fifteen and twenty-four represent just 14 percent of the U.S. population, but in 2002, they accounted for 38.9 percent of all arrests for violent crimes and 47.2 percent of arrests for property crimes.

Gender. Although each sex makes up roughly half the population, police collared males in 69.3 percent of all property crime arrests in 2002; the other 30.7 percent of arrests involved women. In other words, men are arrested more than twice as often as women for property crimes. In the case of violent crimes, the difference is even greater, with 82.6 percent of arrests involving males and just 17.4 percent females (a five-to-one ratio).

It may be that law enforcement officials are reluctant to define women as criminals. In global perspective, the greatest gender difference in crime rates occurs in societies that most severely limit the opportunities of women. In the United States, the difference in arrest rates for women and men has been narrowing, which probably indicates increasing gender equality in our society. Between 1993 and 2002, there was a

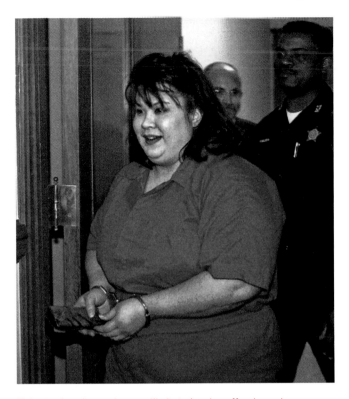

Violent crime is much more likely to involve offenders who are males than females. Of more than 800 people executed for serious crimes since 1977, only ten have been women. Here, Christina Riggs, the only woman on death row in Arkansas, leaves a courtroom in Pulaski County. Why, in your opinion, are men much more likely to be involved in serious, violent crime?

14.1 percent *increase* in arrests of women and a *drop* of 5.9 percent in arrests of men (Federal Bureau of Investigation, 2003).

Social class. The FBI does not assess the social class of arrested persons, so no statistical data of the kind given for age and gender are available. But research has long indicated that criminality is more widespread among people of lower social position (Thornberry & Farnsworth, 1982; Wolfgang, Thornberry, & Figlio, 1987).

Yet the connection between class and crime is more complicated than it appears on the surface. For one thing, many people look upon the poor as less worthy than the rich, whose wealth and power confer "respectability" (Tittle, Villemez, & Smith, 1978; Elias, 1986). And although crime—especially violent crime—is a serious problem in the poorest inner-city communities of the United States, most of these crimes are committed by a few hard-core offenders. The majority of people in inner-city neighborhoods have no

"You look like this sketch of someone who's thinking about committing a crime."

© The New Yorker Collection 2000, David Sipress from cartoonbank.com. All rights reserved.

criminal record at all (Wolfgang, Figlio, & Sellin, 1972; Elliott & Ageton, 1980; Harries, 1990).

The connection between social standing and criminality also depends on the type of crime (Braithwaite, 1981). If we expand our definition of crime beyond street offenses to include white-collar crime, the "common criminal" suddenly looks much more affluent and, like the executive involved in the corporate scandal described in the opening to this chapter, may live in a $100 million home.

Race and ethnicity. Both race and ethnicity are strongly linked to crime rates, although the reasons are many and complex. Official statistics indicate that 65.5 percent of arrests for index crimes in 2002 involved white people. However, arrests of African Americans are higher in proportion to their share of the general population. African Americans represent 12.3 percent of the population of the United States but 29.6 percent of the arrests for property crimes (versus 67.7 percent for whites) and 38.0 percent of arrests for violent crimes (versus 59.7 percent for whites) (Federal Bureau of Investigation, 2003).

There are several reasons for the disproportionate number of arrests among African Americans. First, prejudice prompts white police to arrest black people more readily and leads citizens to report African Americans more willingly, so people of color are overly criminalized (Covington, 1995;

Chiricos, McEntire, & Gertz, 2001; Quillian & Pager, 2001).

Second, race in the United States closely relates to social standing, which, as we have already explained, affects the likelihood of engaging in street crimes. Poor people living in the midst of wealth come to see society as unjust and therefore are more likely to turn to crime to get what they feel is their share (Blau & Blau, 1982; Anderson, 1994; Martinez, 1996).

Third, black and white family patterns differ: Two-thirds of non-Hispanic black children (compared with one-fourth of non-Hispanic white children) are born to single mothers. There are two risks associated with single parenting: children get less supervision and experience a higher risk of poverty. With one-third of African American children growing up in poor families (compared with one in eight white children), no one should be surprised at proportionately higher crime rates for African Americans (Courtwright, 1996; Jacobs & Helms, 1996; U.S. Census Bureau, 2004).

Fourth, remember that the official crime index does not include arrests for offenses ranging from drunk driving to white-collar violations. This omission contributes to the view of the typical criminal as a person of color. If we broaden our definition of crime to include drunk driving, business fraud, embezzlement, stock swindles, and cheating on income tax returns, the proportion of white criminals rises dramatically.

Keep in mind, too, that categories of people with high arrest rates are also at higher risk for being victims of crime. In the United States, for example, African Americans are almost six times as likely to die as a result of homicide as white people (Murphy, 2000; Rogers et al., 2001).

Finally, some categories of the population have unusually low rates of arrest. People of Asian descent, who account for about 4 percent of the population, figure in only 1.4 percent of all arrests. As Chapter 11 ("Race and Ethnicity") explains, Asian Americans enjoy higher than average educational achievement and income. Also, Asian American culture emphasizes family solidarity and discipline, both of which keep criminality down.

CRIME IN GLOBAL PERSPECTIVE

By world standards, the U.S. crime rate is high. Although recent crime trends are downward, there were 16,204 murders in the United States in 2002, which amounts to one every half hour around the clock. In large cities such as New York, rarely does a day pass with no murder; in fact, more

New Yorkers are hit with stray bullets than are deliberately gunned down in most large cities elsewhere in the world.

The rate of violent crime (but not property crime) in the United States is several times higher than in Europe. The contrast is even greater between our country and the nations of Asia, including India and Japan, where violent and property crime rates are among the lowest in the world.

Elliott Currie (1985) suggests that crime arises from our culture's emphasis on individual economic success, often at the expense of strong families and neighborhoods. The United States also has extraordinary cultural diversity, a result of centuries of immigration. Moreover, economic inequality is higher in this country than in most other high-income nations. Thus, our society's relatively weak social fabric, combined with considerable frustration among the poor, generates widespread criminal behavior.

Another factor contributing to violence in the United States is extensive private ownership of guns. About two-thirds of murder victims in the United States die from shootings. Since the early 1990s, in Texas and several other southern states, shooting deaths have exceeded automobile-related fatalities. The U.S. rate of handgun deaths is about seven times higher than in Canada, a country that strictly limits handgun ownership.

Surveys suggest that almost half of U.S. households have at least one gun (J. Wright, 1995; NORC, 2003). Put differently, there are more guns than adults in this country, and one-third of these weapons are handguns that figure in violent crime. In large part, gun ownership reflects people's fear of crime, yet easy availability of guns in this country makes crime more deadly.

But as critics of gun control point out, waiting periods and background checks at retail gun stores do not keep guns out of the hands of criminals, who almost always obtain guns illegally (J. Wright, 1995). And gun control is not a magic bullet in the war on crime. For example, Currie (1985) notes that the number of Californians killed each year by knives alone exceeds the number of Canadians killed by weapons of all kinds. However, most experts think that stricter gun control laws would reduce the level of deadly violence.

Crime rates are soaring in some of the largest cities of the world, such as Manila, the Philippines, and São Paulo, Brazil, which have rapid population growth and millions of desperately poor people. Outside of big cities, however, the traditional character of low-income societies and their strong family structure allow local communities to control crime informally.

Some types of crime have always been multinational, such as terrorism, espionage, and arms dealing (Martin & Romano, 1992). But today, the globalization also extends to other types of crime. Consider the illegal drug trade. The problem of illegal drugs in the United States is partly a *demand* issue; the demand for cocaine and other drugs in this country is high, and many young people are willing to risk arrest or even violent death for a chance to get rich in the drug trade. But the *supply* side of the issue is just as important. In the South American nation of Colombia, at least 20 percent of the people depend on cocaine production for their livelihood. Not only is cocaine Colombia's most profitable export, but it outsells all other exports—including coffee—combined. Clearly, then, drug dealing and many other crimes are closely related to social conditions both in this country and elsewhere.

Different countries have different strategies for dealing with crime. The use of capital punishment (the death penalty) is a case in point. According to Amnesty International (2003), three nations account for 81 percent of the world's executions carried out by governments. Global Map 7–1 on page 180 shows which countries currently use capital punishment. The global trend is toward abolishing the death penalty: Amnesty International (2004) reports that since 1985, more than fifty nations have ended this practice.

The U.S. Criminal Justice System

December 10, Casablanca, Morocco. Casablanca! An exciting mix of African, European, and Middle Eastern cultures. Returning from a stroll through the medina, the medieval section of this coastal North African city, we confront lines of police along a boulevard, standing between us and our ship in the harbor. The police are providing security for many important leaders attending an Islamic conference at a nearby hotel. Are the streets closed? No one asks, but people stop short of an invisible line some fifty feet from the police officers. I play the brash North American and start across the street to inquire (in broken French) if we can pass by, but I stop cold as several officers draw a bead on me with their eyes. Their fingers nervously tap at the grips on their automatic weapons. This is no time to strike up a conversation.

The criminal justice system is a society's formal response to crime. In some countries, military police keep a tight rein on people's behavior; in others, including the

WINDOW ON THE WORLD

GLOBAL MAP 7–1   Capital Punishment in Global Perspective

The map identifies seventy-eight countries and territories in which the law allows the death penalty for ordinary crimes; in fifteen more, the death penalty is reserved for exceptional crimes under military law or during times of war. The death penalty does not exist in eighty countries and territories; in twenty-three more, although the death penalty remains in law, no execution has taken place in more than ten years. Compare rich and poor nations: What general pattern do you see? In what way do the United States and Japan stand out?

Source: Amnesty International (2004).

United States, police have more limited powers and only respond to violations of criminal law. We shall briefly examine the key elements of the U.S. criminal justice system: police, courts, and the punishment of convicted offenders. First, however, we must understand an important principle that underlies the entire system: the idea of due process.

DUE PROCESS

Due process is a simple but very important idea: The criminal justice system must operate within the bounds of law. This principle is grounded in the first ten amendments to the U.S. Constitution—known as the Bill of Rights—adopted by Congress in 1791. The Constitution offers various protections to any person charged with a crime,

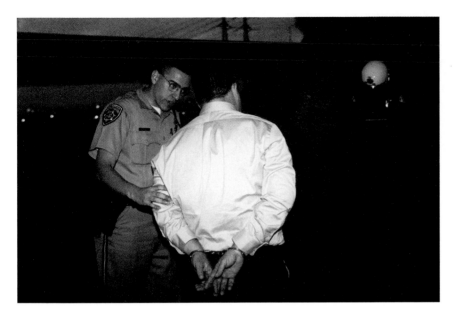

Police must be allowed discretion if they are to handle effectively the many different situations they face every day. At the same time, it is important to treat people fairly. Here, we see a police officer deciding whether or not to charge a motorist for driving while drunk. What factors do you think enter into this decision?

including the right to counsel, the right to refuse to testify against oneself, the right to confront one's accusers, freedom from being tried twice for the same crime, and freedom from being "deprived of life, liberty, or property without due process of law." Furthermore, the Constitution gives all people the right to a speedy and public trial, with a jury if desired, and freedom from excessive bail as well as cruel and unusual punishment.

 To read the Bill of Rights, go to http://www.archives.gov/national_archives_experience/bill_of_rights.html

In general terms, the concept of due process means that anyone charged with a crime must receive (1) fair notice of the proceedings, (2) a hearing on the charges conducted according to law and with the ability to present a defense, and (3) a judge or jury that weighs evidence in an impartial way (Inciardi, 2000).

Due process limits the power of government, with an eye toward this nation's cultural support of individual rights and freedoms. Of course, deciding exactly how far government can go makes up much of the work of the judicial system, especially the U.S. Supreme Court.

POLICE

The police generally serve as the point of contact between a population and the criminal justice system. In principle, the police maintain public order by enforcing the law. Of course, there is only so much that 665,555 full-time police officers in the United States can do to monitor the activities of 291 million people. As a result, the police use a great deal of personal judgment in deciding which situations require their attention and how to handle them.

How do police carry out their duties? In a study of police behavior in five cities, Douglas Smith and Christy Visher (1981; Smith, 1987) concluded that because they must act swiftly, police quickly size up situations in terms of six factors. First, the more serious they think the situation is, the more likely they are to make an arrest. Second, police take account of the victim's wishes in deciding whether to make an arrest. Third, the odds of arrest go up the more uncooperative a suspect is. Fourth, police are more likely to take into custody someone they have arrested before, presumably because this suggests guilt. Fifth, the presence of bystanders increases the chances of arrest. According to Smith and Visher, the presence of observers prompts police to take stronger control of a situation, if only to move the encounter from the street (the suspect's turf) to the police department (where law officers have the edge). Sixth, all else being equal, police are more likely to arrest people of color than whites, perceiving people of African or Latino descent as either more dangerous or more likely to be guilty.

COURTS

After arrest, a court determines a suspect's guilt or innocence. In principle, U.S. courts rely on an adversarial process involving attorneys—one representing the defendant and another the state—in the presence of a judge who monitors legal procedures.

SUMMING UP

Four Justifications for Punishment

Retribution	The oldest justification for punishment. Punishment is society's revenge for a moral wrong. In principle, punishment should be equal in severity to the deviance itself.
Deterrence	An early modern approach. Deviance is considered social disruption, which society acts to control. People are viewed as rational and self-interested; deterrence works because the pain of punishment outweighs the pleasure of deviance.
Rehabilitation	A modern strategy linked to the development of social sciences. Deviance is viewed as the result of social problems (such as poverty) or personal problems (such as mental illness). Social conditions are improved; treatment is tailored to the offender's condition.
Societal protection	A modern approach easier to carry out than rehabilitation. If society is unable or unwilling to rehabilitate offenders or reform social conditions, people are protected by the imprisonment or execution of the offender.

In practice, however, about 90 percent of criminal cases are resolved before court appearance through **plea bargaining,** *a legal negotiation in which a prosecutor reduces a charge in exchange for a defendant's guilty plea.* For example, the state may offer a defendant charged with burglary a lesser charge, perhaps possession of burglary tools, in exchange for a guilty plea.

Plea bargaining is widespread because it spares the system the time and expense of trials. A trial is usually unnecessary if there is little disagreement as to the facts of the case. Moreover, because the number of cases entering the system has doubled over the past decade, prosecutors cannot possibly bring every one to trial. By quickly resolving most of their work, then, the courts devote most of their resources to the most important cases.

But plea bargaining pressures defendants (who are presumed innocent) to plead guilty. A person can exercise the right to a trial, but only at the risk of receiving a more severe sentence if found guilty. Furthermore, low-income defendants often must rely on a public defender—typically an overworked and underpaid attorney who may devote little time to even the most serious cases (Novak, 1999). Plea bargaining may be efficient, but it undercuts the adversarial process as well as the rights of defendants.

PUNISHMENT

When a young man is shot dead on the street after leaving a restaurant, some people may wonder why it happened, but almost everyone believes that someone should have to "pay" for the crime. Indeed, sometimes the desire to punish is so great that in the end justice may not be done.

Such cases force us to ask *why* a society should punish its wrongdoers. Scholars answer with four basic reasons: retribution, deterrence, rehabilitation, and societal protection.

Retribution. The oldest justification for punishment is to satisfy a society's need for **retribution,** *an act of moral vengeance by which society makes the offender suffer as much as the suffering caused by the crime.* Retribution rests on a view of society as being in moral balance. When criminality upsets this balance, punishment in equal measure restores the moral order, as suggested by the biblical saying, "an eye for an eye."

In the Middle Ages, most people viewed crime as sin—an offense against God as well as society—that required a harsh response. Although critics point out that retribution does little to reform the offender, many people today still consider vengeance reason enough for punishment.

Deterrence. A second justification for punishment is **deterrence,** *the attempt to discourage criminality through the use of punishment.* Deterrence is based on the eighteenth-century Enlightenment idea that as calculating and rational creatures, humans will not break the law if they think that the pains of punishment outweigh the pleasures of crime.

Deterrence emerged as a reform measure in response to harsh punishments based on retribution. Why put someone

To increase the power of punishment to deter crime, capital punishment was long carried out in public. Here is a photograph from the last public execution in the United States, with twenty-two-year-old Rainey Bethea standing on the scaffold moments from death in Owensboro, Kentucky, on August 16, 1937. Children as well as adults were in the crowd. Now that the mass media report the story of executions across the country, states carry out capital punishment behind closed doors.

to death for stealing if theft can be discouraged by a prison sentence? As the concept of deterrence gained acceptance in industrial societies, execution and physical mutilation of criminals were replaced by milder forms of punishment such as imprisonment.

Punishment may deter crime in two ways. *Specific deterrence* convinces an individual offender that crime does not pay. Through *general deterrence,* punishing one person serves as an example to others.

Rehabilitation. The third justification for punishment, **rehabilitation,** is *a program for reforming the offender to prevent later offenses.* Rehabilitation arose along with the social sciences in the nineteenth century. Since then, sociologists have claimed that crime and other deviance spring from a social environment marked by poverty or lack of parental supervision. Logically, then, if offenders learn to be deviant, they can also learn to obey the rules; the key is controlling the environment. *Reformatories* or *houses of correction* provided a controlled setting where people could learn proper behavior (recall the description of total institutions in Chapter 3, "Socialization: From Infancy to Old Age").

Like deterrence, rehabilitation motivates the offender to conform. But rehabilitation emphasizes constructive improvement, whereas deterrence and retribution simply make the offender suffer. In addition, retribution demands that the punishment fit the crime, but rehabilitation tailors

treatment to each offender. Thus, identical crimes would prompt similar acts of retribution but different rehabilitation programs.

Societal protection. A final justification for punishment is **societal protection,** *rendering an offender incapable of further offenses temporarily through imprisonment or permanently by execution.* Like deterrence, societal protection is a rational approach to punishment intended to protect society from crime.

Currently, 2 million people are imprisoned in the United States. In response to tougher public attitudes and an increasing number of drug-related arrests, the U.S. prison population has tripled since 1980. The size of the inmate population is going up in most other high-income nations as well. Yet the United States imprisons a larger share of its population than any other country in the world (Sutton, 2000; Sentencing Project, 2004).

Critical review. The Summing Up table reviews the four justifications for punishment. However, an accurate assessment of the actual consequences of punishment is no simple task.

The value of retribution lies in Durkheim's claim that punishing the deviant person increases society's moral awareness. For this reason, punishment traditionally was a public event. Although the last public execution in the United States took place in Kentucky nearly 70 years ago,

The United States and Japan are the only high-income nations in which the government imposes the death penalty. Yet within the United States, the fifty states differ in their capital punishment laws: Half of the 3,557 prisoners on death row are in five states. What regional pattern do you see in the map? Can you explain this pattern?

Source: U.S. Bureau of Justice Statistics (2003).

Number of Prisoners on Death Row

- Very high: 300 or more
- High: 125 to 299
- Average: 60 to 124
- Low: 15 to 59
- Very low: 0 to 14
- No death penalty

today's mass media ensure public awareness of executions carried out inside prison walls (Kittrie, 1971).

Certainly, punishment deters some crime. Yet our society has a high rate of **criminal recidivism,** *later offenses by people previously convicted of crimes.* About three-fourths of state prisoners have been jailed before, and about half will be back within a few years after release (Petersilia, 1997; DeFina & Arvanites, 2002). So does punishment really deter crime? Only about one-third of all crimes are known to police; of these, only about one in five results in an arrest. The old saying "crime doesn't pay" rings hollow when we consider these statistics.

General deterrence is even more difficult to investigate scientifically because we have no way of knowing how people might act if they were unaware of punishments handed down to others. Opponents of capital punishment point to research suggesting that the death penalty has limited value as a general deterrent and note that the United States is the only Western, high-income nation that routinely executes serious offenders. A troubling fact is that some death sentences have been pronounced against innocent people. Between 1973 and 2003, almost 100 people were released from death row after new evidence established their innocence, which means that innocent people may have been put to death. Before leaving office in January 2003, Illinois Governor George Ryan claimed his state's judicial system was flawed and commuted the sentences of all 157 of the state's death row inmates to life in prison (Levine, 2003). National Map 7–2 identifies the thirty-eight states that have the death penalty and the three states that stand out with the most prisoners on death row.

Despite the growing controversy over the use of the death penalty, a majority of adults in the United States (63 percent) say they support capital punishment for people convicted of murder (NORC, 2003:121). Figure 7–3 shows that among students, opposition to the death penalty dropped between 1970 and 1990 and has been on the rise since then.

Prisons provide short-term societal protection by keeping offenders off the streets, but they do little to reshape attitudes or behavior in the long term (Carlson, 1976; Wright, 1994). Perhaps rehabilitation is an unrealistic expectation

 Human Rights Watch has issued a report on rape in prison: http://www.hrw.org/reports/2001/prison/

because, according to Sutherland's theory of differential association, locking up criminals together for years probably strengthens criminal attitudes and skills. Imprisonment also breaks whatever social ties inmates may have in the outside world, which, following Hirschi's control theory, makes inmates likely to commit more crimes upon release.

COMMUNITY-BASED CORRECTIONS

Prisons keep convicted criminals off the streets. But the evidence suggests that locking people up does little to rehabilitate most offenders. Furthermore, prisons are expensive, costing our society at least $25,000 per year to support each inmate, in addition to the initial costs of building the prison facilities.

One recent alternative to the traditional prison that has been adopted by many cities and states across the country is

community-based corrections, *correctional programs operating within society at large rather than behind prison walls.* Community-based corrections have a number of advantages: They reduce the overcrowding in prisons, handle convicts at a lower cost than prisons, and allow for supervision of convicts while eliminating the hardships of prison life as well as the stigma that accompanies being imprisoned. In general, the idea of community-based corrections is not so much to punish as to reform; such programs are therefore usually offered to individuals who have committed less serious offenses and who appear to be good prospects for avoiding future criminal violations (Inciardi, 2000).

Probation.   One form of community-based corrections is *probation*, a policy of permitting a convicted offender to remain in the community under conditions imposed by a court, including regular supervision. Courts may require that a probationer receive counseling, attend a drug treatment program, hold a job, avoid associating with "known criminals," or anything else deemed appropriate. Typically, a probationer must check in with an officer of the court (the "probation officer") on a regular schedule to make sure the guidelines are being followed. Should the probationer fail to live up to the conditions set by the court or commit a new offense, the court may revoke probation in favor of imprisonment.

Shock Probation.   A related strategy is *shock probation*, a policy by which a judge orders a convicted offender to prison for a short time and then suspends the remainder of the sentence in favor of probation. Shock probation is thus a mix of prison and probation that is used to impress on the offender the seriousness of the situation while still withholding full-scale imprisonment. In some cases, shock probation takes place in a special "boot camp" facility where offenders might spend one to three months in a military-style setting intended to teach discipline and respect for authority (Cole & Smith, 2002).

Parole.   *Parole* is a policy of releasing inmates from prison to serve the remainder of their sentences under the supervision of a parole officer in the local community. Although some sentences specifically deny the possibility of parole, most inmates become eligible for parole after serving a certain portion of their sentence. At this time, a parole board evaluates the risks and benefits of an inmate's early release from prison. If parole is granted, the parole board monitors the offender's conduct until the sentence is completed. Should the offender not comply with the conditions of parole or be arrested for another crime, the board can

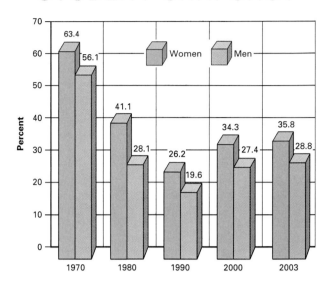

STUDENT SNAPSHOT

FIGURE 7-3   Opposition to the Death Penalty among First-Year College Students, 1970–2003

Sources: Astin et al. (2002) and Sax et al. (2003).

revoke parole, returning the offender to prison to complete the sentence.

Critical review.   Evaluations of community-based corrections are mixed. There is little question that probation and parole programs are much less expensive than conventional imprisonment; they also free up room in prisons for people who commit more serious crimes. Yet research suggests that although probation and shock probation do seem to work for some people, they do not significantly reduce criminal recidivism. Similarly, parole is useful to prison officials as a means to encourage good behavior among inmates who hope for early release. Yet levels of crime among individuals who have been released on parole are high. Indeed, recidivism among parolees is so high that a number of states have ended their parole programs entirely (Inciardi, 2000).

Evaluations of all aspects of the criminal justice system point to a sobering truth: The criminal justice system cannot eliminate crime. As the Applying Sociology box on pages 186–87 explains, while police, courts, and prisons do affect crime rates, crime and other deviance are not just the acts of "bad people" but reflect the operation of society itself.

Violent Crime Is Down—but Why?

During the 1980s, crime rates shot upward. Just about everyone lived in fear of violent crime, and in many larger cities, the numbers of people killed and wounded made whole neighborhoods seem like war zones. There seemed to be no solution to the problem.

In the 1990s, something good and unexpected happened: Serious crime rates began to fall until by 2000, they were at levels not seen in more than a generation. Why? Researchers point to several reasons:

1. **A reduction in the youth population.** We have already noted that young people (particularly males) are responsible for much violent crime. Between 1990 and 2000, the share of the population aged fifteen to twenty-four dropped by about 5 percent (in part because of the legalization of abortion in 1973).

2. **Changes in policing.** Much of the drop in crime (as well as the earlier rise in crime) has taken place in large cities. New York City, where the number of murders fell from 2,245 in 1990 to just 587 in 2002, has adopted a policy of *community policing,* which means that police are concerned not just with making arrests but in preventing crime before it happens. Officers get to know the areas they patrol and frequently stop young men for jaywalking or other minor infractions so they can check them for concealed weapons (the word has gotten around that you can be arrested for carrying a gun). In addition, there are more police at work in large cities. For example, Los Angeles added more than 2,000 police in the 1990s, and it, too, saw its violent crime rate fall during that period.

3. **More prisons.** From 1985 to 2002, the number of inmates in U.S. jails and prisons soared from 750,000 to 2 million. The main reason for this increase is tough new laws that demand prison time for many crimes, especially drug offenses.

As one analyst put it, "When you lock up an extra million people, it's got to have some effect on the crime rate" (Franklin Zimring, cited in Witkin, 1998:31).

4. **A better economy.** The U.S. economy boomed during the 1990s. With unemployment down, more people were working, reducing the likelihood that some would turn to crime out of economic desperation. The logic here is simple: More jobs, fewer crimes. By the same token, the economic downturn of the early 2000s may well push crime rates up again.

5. **The declining drug trade.** Many analysts think that the most important factor in reducing rates of violent crime is the decline of crack cocaine. Crack came on the scene around 1985, and violence spread as young people—especially in the inner cities and increasingly armed with guns—became part of a booming drug trade. Facing few

SUMMARY

1. Deviance refers to norm violations, ranging from bad manners to serious violence.

2. Biological research, from Lombroso's nineteenth-century observations of convicts to recent genetic studies, has yet to offer much insight into the causes of deviance.

3. Psychological studies link deviance to a person's abnormal personality resulting from biological causes or unsuccessful socialization. Psychological theories help explain some types of deviance.

4. The roots of deviance lie in society rather than individuals because deviance varies according to cultural norms, is socially defined, and reflects patterns of social power.

5. Taking a structural-functional approach, Durkheim explained that deviance affirms norms and values, clarifies moral boundaries, brings people together, and encourages social change.

6. The symbolic-interaction approach is the basis of labeling theory, which holds that deviance lies in people's reaction to a person's behavior, not in the behavior itself. Acquiring the stigma of deviance can lead to secondary deviance and a deviant career.

7. Based on Karl Marx's ideas, social-conflict theory holds that laws and other norms reflect the interests of powerful members of society. Although white-collar and corporate crimes cause extensive social harm, offenders are rarely branded as criminals.

8. Official statistics indicate that arrest rates peak in late adolescence and drop steadily thereafter. About 70 percent of

legitimate job opportunities but increasing opportunities to make money illegally, a generation of young people became part of a wave of violence. Widespread crack cocaine use also explains the trend, noted earlier, of the younger age of violent criminals.

By the early 1990s, however, the popularity of crack had begun to fall as people saw the damage the drug was causing to entire communities. This realization, coupled with steady economic improvement and stiffer sentences for drug offenses, brought the turnaround in violent crime.

The current picture looks better relative to what it was a decade ago. The crime problem, says one researcher, "looks better, but only because the early 1990s were so bad. So let's not fool ourselves into thinking everything is resolved. It's not."

WHAT DO YOU THINK?

1. Do you support the policy of community policing? Why or why not?
2. What do you see as the pros and cons of building more prisons?
3. Of all the factors mentioned here, which do you think is the most important in crime control? Which is least important? Why?

Sources: Based on Fagan, Zimring, & Kim (1998), Witkin (1998), Winship & Berrien (1999), Donahue & Levitt (2000), and Rosenfeld (2002).

One reason that crime has gone down is that there are 2 million people incarcerated in this country. This has caused severe overcrowding of facilities such as this Maricopa County, Arizona, prison.

people arrested for property crimes and 83 percent of those arrested for violent crimes are male.

9. Poorer people commit more street crime than those with greater wealth. When white-collar crimes are included among criminal offenses, however, this difference in criminal activity becomes smaller.

10. More whites than African Americans are arrested for street crimes. However, African Americans are arrested more often than whites in proportion to their respective numbers in the population. Asian Americans have lower than average rates of arrest.

11. The idea of due process, which is based in the U.S. Constitution (Bill of Rights), guides the operation of the U.S. criminal justice system.

12. Police use a great deal of personal judgment in their work. Arrest is more likely if the offense is serious, bystanders are present, or the accused is African American or Hispanic.

13. Although set up as an adversarial system, U.S. courts resolve most cases through plea bargaining. Though efficient, this method puts less powerful people at a disadvantage.

14. Justifications of punishment include retribution, deterrence, rehabilitation, and societal protection. Because its consequences are difficult to evaluate scientifically, punishment—like deviance itself—sparks controversy.

15. Community-based corrections include probation and parole. Such policies reduce the cost of supervising people convicted of crimes as well as prison overcrowding but have not been shown to greatly reduce recidivism.

KEY CONCEPTS

deviance (p. 162) the recognized violation of cultural norms

crime (p. 162) the violation of a society's formally enacted criminal law

social control (p. 163) attempts by society to regulate people's thoughts and behavior

criminal justice system (p. 163) a formal response by police, courts, and prison officials to alleged violations of the law

labeling theory (p. 167) the assertion that deviance and conformity result not so much from what people do as from how others respond to those actions

stigma (p. 168) a powerfully negative label that greatly changes a person's self-concept and social identity

medicalization of deviance (p. 169) the transformation of moral and legal deviance into a medical condition

white-collar crime (p. 172) crime committed by people of high social position in the course of their occupations

corporate crime (p. 172) the illegal actions of a corporation or people acting on its behalf

organized crime (p. 172) a business supplying illegal goods or services

hate crime (p. 173) a criminal act against a person or a person's property by an offender motivated by racial or other bias

crimes against the person (violent crimes) (p. 175) crimes that direct violence or the threat of violence against others

crimes against property (property crimes) (p. 175) crimes that involve theft of property belonging to others

victimless crimes (crimes without complaint) (p. 176) violations of law in which there are no obvious victims

plea bargaining (p. 182) a legal negotiation in which a prosecutor reduces a charge in exchange for a defendant's guilty plea

retribution (p. 182) an act of moral vengeance by which society makes the offender suffer as much as the suffering caused by the crime

deterrence (p. 182) the attempt to discourage criminality through the use of punishment

rehabilitation (p. 183) a program for reforming the offender to prevent later offenses

societal protection (p. 183) rendering an offender incapable of further offenses temporarily through imprisonment or permanently by execution

criminal recidivism (p. 184) later offenses by people previously convicted of crimes

community-based corrections (p. 185) correctional programs operating within society at large rather than behind prison walls

CRITICAL-THINKING QUESTIONS

1. How does a sociological view of deviance differ from the commonsense idea that bad people do bad things?

2. List Durkheim's functions of deviance. From his point of view, can society ever be free from deviance? Why or why not?

3. An old saying is "sticks and stones can break my bones, but names can never hurt me." Explain how labeling theory challenges this statement.

4. A recent study found that one in three African American men between the ages of twenty and twenty-nine is in jail, on probation, or on parole (Mauer, 1999). What factors, noted in this chapter, help explain this pattern?

APPLICATIONS AND EXERCISES

1. Research computer crime. What new kinds of crime are emerging in the information age? Is computer technology also creating new ways to track down lawbreakers?

2. Rent a wheelchair (check with a local pharmacy or medical supply store), and use it as much as possible for a day or two. Not only will you gain a firsthand understanding of the physical barriers to getting around, but you will discover that people respond to you in many new ways.

3. Watch an episode of the real-action police show *COPS*. Based on this program, how would you describe the people who commit crimes?

4. Packaged in the back of this new textbook is an interactive CD-ROM that offers a variety of video and interactive review materials intended to help you better understand the material covered in this chapter. For this chapter, the CD-ROM contains a relevant clip from *ABC News*, an author's tip video, interactive map animations, an interactive timeline, and flashcards with audio pronunciations of the more difficult words.

 SITES TO SEE

http://www.prenhall.com/macionis

Visit the interactive Companion Website™ that accompanies this text. Begin by clicking on the cover of your book. You will find a chapter-by-chapter study guide, practice tests, suggested Web links, and links to other relevant material.

http://www.civilrights.org

The Leadership Conference on Civil Rights maintains this site dealing with hate crimes and other civil rights issues.

http://www.spr.org

The organization Stop Prisoner Rape hosts this site to increase awareness of the problem of rape in U.S. prisons.

http://www.ncadp.org
http://justice.uaa.alaska.edu/death/intl.html

These sites provide information on the death penalty. The first presents the views of the National Coalition to Abolish the Death Penalty. The second looks at the death penalty in global perspective.

http://www.cybercrime.gov

This site, operated by the U.S. Department of Justice, provides a great deal of information on computer crime and protecting intellectual property.

http://www.unodc.org/unodc/crime_cicip_survey_seventh.html

The United Nations's Office on Drugs and Crime conducts a survey of crime trends and the operation of the criminal justice system in individual countries around the world.

 INVESTIGATE WITH RESEARCH NAVIGATOR™

Follow the instructions on page 32 of this text to access the features of **Research Navigator™**. Once at the Web site, enter your Login Name and Password. Then, to use the **Content Select™** database, enter keywords such as "crime," "rape," and "prison," and the search engine will supply relevant and recent scholarly and popular press publications. Use the *New York Times* **Search-by-Subject Archive** to find recent news articles related to sociology and the **Link Library** feature to find relevant Web links organized by the key terms associated with this chapter.

CHAPTER EIGHT

Social Stratification

What is social stratification?

Why does social inequality exist?

How do social classes in the United States differ from one another?

All societies give far more to some categories of people than to others. Though officially outlawed, ▶ the traditional caste system in India still defines some people, including this woman, as Dalits or "Untouchables"; these people remain socially scorned and very poor.

On April 10, 1912, the ocean liner *Titanic* slipped away from the docks of Southampton, England, on its first voyage across the North Atlantic to New York. A proud symbol of the new industrial age, the towering ship carried 2,300 passengers, some enjoying more luxury than most travelers today could imagine. Poor people crowded the lower decks, journeying to what they hoped would be a better life in the United States.

Two days out, the crew received reports of icebergs in the area but paid little notice. Then, near midnight, as the ship steamed swiftly westward, a stunned lookout reported a massive shape rising out of the dark ocean directly ahead. Moments later, the *Titanic* collided with a huge iceberg, as tall as the ship itself, that split open its side as if the grand vessel were a giant tin can.

Seawater flooded into the ship's lower levels, pulling the ship down by the bow. Within twenty-five minutes of impact, people were rushing for the lifeboats. By 2:00 A.M., the bow was completely submerged, and the stern rose high above the water. Clinging to the deck, quietly observed by those in lifeboats, hundreds of helpless passengers and crew solemnly passed their final minutes before the ship disappeared into the frigid Atlantic (Lord, 1976).

The tragic loss of more than 1,600 lives made news around the world. Looking back on this terrible event with a sociological eye, we see that some categories of passengers had much better odds of survival than others. During this more traditional time, women and children boarded the lifeboats first, with the result that 80 percent of those who died were men. Class was also a factor. More than 60 percent of the passengers traveling on first-class tickets were saved because they were on the upper decks, where warnings were sounded first and lifeboats were accessible. Only 36 percent of the second-class passengers survived, and of the third-class passengers on the lower decks, only 24 percent escaped drowning. On board the *Titanic,* class meant more than the quality of accommodations—it was a matter of life or death.

The fate of the passengers on the *Titanic* dramatically illustrates how social inequality affects the way people live and, sometimes, whether they live at all. This chapter explores the important concept of social stratification and examines social inequality in the United States.

What Is Social Stratification?

Every society is marked by inequality, with some people having more money, schooling, health, and power than others. **Social stratification,** defined as *a system by which a society ranks categories of people in a hierarchy,* involves four basic principles:

1. **Social stratification is a trait of society, not simply a reflection of individual differences.** Many of us think of social standing in terms of personal talent and effort, exaggerating the extent to which we control our own destinies. Did a higher percentage of the first-class passengers on the *Titanic* survive because they were better swimmers than second- and third-class passengers? Hardly. They did better because of their privileged position on the ship. Similarly, children born into wealthy families are more likely than children born into poverty to enjoy good health, do well in school, succeed in a career, and live a long life. Neither the rich nor the poor are responsible for creating social stratification, yet this system shapes the lives of us all.

2. **Social stratification carries over from generation to generation.** We have only to look at how parents pass their social position on to their children to see that stratification is a trait of societies rather than individuals.

   Some individuals, especially in industrial societies, do experience **social mobility,** *a change in position within the social hierarchy.* Social mobility may be upward or downward. We celebrate the achievements of rare individuals such as Britney Spears and Michael Jordan, both of whom rose from modest beginnings to fame and fortune. Some people move downward in the social hierarchy because of business setbacks, unemployment, or illness. More often people move horizontally, when, say, they switch one job for another at about the same social level. The social standing of most people remains much the same over their lifetime.

3. **Social stratification is universal but variable.** Social stratification is found everywhere. Yet *what* is unequal and *how* unequal it is vary from one society to another. In some societies inequality is mostly a matter of prestige; in others, wealth or power is the key element of difference. Furthermore, some societies contain more inequality than others.

4. **Social stratification involves not just inequality but beliefs.** Any system of inequality not only gives some people more than others, but it also defines these arrangements as fair. Like the *what* of social inequality, the explanation of *why* people should be unequal differs from society to society.

Caste and Class Systems

Sociologists distinguish between *closed systems,* which allow little change in social position, and *open systems,* which permit some social mobility (Tumin, 1985). The caste system is an example of a closed system, and the class system is a more open system.

THE CASTE SYSTEM

A **caste system** amounts to *social stratification based on ascription, or birth.* A pure caste system is closed because birth alone decides a person's future, with little or no social mobility based on individual effort. People are ranked in rigid categories, in which they live out their lives.

An illustration: India. Many of the world's societies, most of them agrarian, are caste systems. One example is India's traditional villages, where most of the country's people still live. The Indian system identifies four major castes (or *varna,* a Sanskrit word that means "color"): Brahmin, Kshatriya, Vaishya, and Shudra. On the local level, however, each of these is composed of hundreds of subcaste (or *jati*) groups.

From birth, caste position determines the direction of a person's life. First, with the exception of farming, which is open to all, families in each caste perform one type of work, as priests, soldiers, barbers, leather workers, sweepers, and so on.

The personal experience of poverty is captured in Sebastiao Salgado's photograph, which shows how social standing is passed on from one generation to the next. The essential sociological insight is that, however strongly individuals feel its effects, our social standing is largely a consequence of the way in which a society (or a world of societies) structures opportunity and reward. To the core of our being, then, we are all the products of social stratification.

Second, a caste system demands that people marry others of the same ranking. If people were to have "mixed" marriages with members of other castes, what rank would their children hold? Sociologists call this pattern of marrying within a social category *endogamous* marriage (*endo-* stems from the Greek word meaning "within"). According to tradition, Indian parents select their children's marriage partners, often before the children reach their teens.

Third, caste systems shape members' beliefs. Indian culture is built on the Hindu tradition that accepting an arranged marriage and doing the caste's life work is a moral duty.

Fourth, caste guides everyday life by keeping people in the company of "their own kind." Norms reinforce this practice by teaching, for instance, that a more "pure" person of a higher caste position is "polluted" by contact with someone of lower standing.

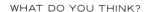

GLOBAL SOCIOLOGY
Race as Caste: A Report from South Africa

At the southern tip of the African continent lies South Africa, a country about the size of Alaska with a population of about 47 million. The native Africans were joined by Dutch traders and farmers in the mid-seventeenth century. Early in the nineteenth century, a second wave of British colonization pushed the Dutch inland. By the early 1900s, the British had taken over the country, proclaiming it the Union of South Africa. In 1961, the nation declared its independence as the Republic of South Africa.

But freedom was a reality only for the white minority. To ensure their control over the black majority, whites used a policy of *apartheid,* or racial separation. Apartheid, written into law in 1948, denied blacks citizenship, ownership of land, and any voice in the government. As a lower caste, blacks received little schooling and performed menial, low-paying jobs. White people of even moderate wealth had at least one black household servant.

The white minority claimed apartheid protected their cultural traditions, and many believed blacks were inferior beings. Resistance to apartheid prompted whites to use brutal military repression to maintain their power.

Nevertheless, steady resistance—especially from younger blacks impatient for political and economic opportunity—gradually

forced change. Adding to the internal pressure was criticism from other industrial nations. By the mid-1980s, the tide began to turn as the South African government granted limited rights to people of mixed race and Asian ancestry. This was followed by the rights for all people to form labor unions, to enter various occupations once limited to whites, and to own property. Officials also repealed laws that separated the races in public places.

The pace of change increased in 1990 with the release from prison of Nelson Mandela, a revered resistance leader. In 1994, the first national election open to all races made Mandela president, ending centuries of white minority rule.

Despite this dramatic political change, social position in South Africa is still based on race. About one-third of black South Africans have no work,

and the majority remain dirt poor. The worst off are the 7 million *ukuhleleleka,* which means "marginal people" in the Xhosa language. Soweto-by-the-Sea may sound like a summer getaway, but it is home to thousands of people crammed into shacks made from packing cases, corrugated metal, cardboard, and other discarded materials. There is no electricity for lights or refrigeration. Without plumbing, people use buckets to haul sewerage; women line up to take a turn at a single water tap that serves more than 1,000 people. Jobs are hard to come by, and those who do find work are lucky to earn $250 a month.

South Africa's current president, Thabo Mbeki, elected in 1999, leads a nation still crippled by its history of racial caste. Tourism is up and holds out promise of an economic boom in years to come, but the country can shed its past only by providing real opportunity to all its people.

WHAT DO YOU THINK?

1. How has race been a form of caste in South Africa?
2. Do you think racial caste will eventually break down in South Africa? In how long?
3. Does race operate as caste in the United States? Explain your answer.

Sources: Fredrickson (1981), Wren (1991), Hawthorne (1999), and Mabry & Masland (1999).

Caste systems are typical of agrarian societies because agriculture demands a lifelong routine of hard work; by teaching a sense of moral duty, a caste system ensures that people are disciplined for a lifetime of work and are willing to perform the same jobs as their parents. Thus, caste hangs on in rural India more than half a century after being

formally outlawed. People living in the industrial cities of India have many more choices about work and marriage partners than people in rural areas.

Another country dominated by caste is South Africa, although the racial system of *apartheid* is now in decline. The Global Sociology box takes a closer look.

THE CLASS SYSTEM

A modern economy, which depends on developing people's talents rather than the lifelong discipline required for farming, gives rise to a **class system**, *social stratification based on both birth and individual achievement.*

Class systems are more open than caste systems, so people who gain schooling and skills may be socially mobile in relation to their parents and siblings. Such mobility blurs class boundaries, so even blood relatives may have different social standing. Categorizing people according to their color, sex, or social background comes to be seen as wrong in modern societies as all people gain political rights and, in principle, equal standing before the law. Furthermore, work is no longer fixed at birth but involves some personal choice. Greater individuality also translates into more freedom in selecting a marital partner.

Meritocracy. The concept of **meritocracy** refers to *social stratification based on personal merit*. Because industrial societies need to develop a broad range of abilities (beyond farming), stratification is based not just on the accident of birth but also on *merit* (from a Latin word meaning "worthy of praise")—in this case, the type of job held and how well it is performed. To advance meritocracy, industrial societies expand equality of opportunity, although people expect inequality of outcomes.

In a pure meritocracy, social position would depend entirely on a person's ability and effort. Such a system would have ongoing social mobility, blurring social categories as individuals continuously move up or down in the system depending on their latest performance.

Caste societies define merit in terms of loyalty to the system—that is, dutifully performing whatever job comes with a person's birth. Caste systems waste human potential, but they are very orderly. And here lies the answer to an important question: Why do modern, industrial societies keep some elements of caste—such as letting wealth pass from generation to generation—rather than becoming complete meritocracies? Simply because a pure meritocracy weakens families and other social groupings. Economic performance is not everything, after all. Would we want to evaluate our family members solely on their jobs? Probably not. Therefore, class systems in industrial societies move toward meritocracy to promote productivity and efficiency but retain some caste elements, such as family, to maintain order and social unity.

Status consistency. **Status consistency** is *the degree of consistency in a person's social standing across various dimensions of social inequality*. A caste system has little social mobility and high status consistency, so the typical person has the same relative standing with regard to wealth, power, and prestige. However, the greater mobility of class systems produces less status consistency. In the United States, a college professor with an advanced degree might enjoy high social prestige but earn only a modest income. Low status consistency means that *classes* are less well defined than *castes*.

An illustration: The United Kingdom. The mix of meritocracy and caste in class systems is well illustrated by the United Kingdom (Great Britain—composed of England, Wales, and Scotland—and Northern Ireland), an industrial nation with a long agrarian history.

In the Middle Ages, England had a castelike system of three *estates*. The *first estate* was a hereditary nobility, making up perhaps 5 percent of the population, who controlled most of the land, which was the chief form of wealth (Laslett, 1984). Most nobles had no occupation at all, and they considered engaging in trade or doing other work for income "beneath" them. Well attended by servants, nobles used their leisure time to develop refined tastes in art, music, and literature.

To prevent vast landholdings from being divided by heirs, the law of *primogeniture* (from Latin, meaning "first born") stated that all landholdings passed to the oldest son or other male relation. Younger sons had to find other means of support. Some entered the clergy—the *second estate*—where spiritual power was supported by the church's extensive landholdings. Other men of high birth became military officers or lawyers, professions considered honorable for gentlemen. In an age when no woman could inherit her father's property and few women had the chance to earn a living on their own, a noble daughter depended for her security on marrying well.

Below the nobility and the clergy, most men and women formed the *third estate,* or commoners. Most commoners were serfs, who worked the land owned by nobles. Unlike members of the first and second estates, most commoners had little schooling and were illiterate.

As the Industrial Revolution expanded England's economy, some commoners living in cities made enough money to challenge the nobility. More emphasis on meritocracy, the growing importance of money, and the expansion of schooling and legal rights eventually blurred social rankings and gave rise to a class system.

Perhaps it is a sign of the times that these days, traditional titles are put up for sale by British nobles who need money. In 1996, for example, Earl Spencer—the brother of Princess Diana—sold his title, Lord of Wimbledon, to raise the $300,000 he needed to redo the plumbing in one of his large homes (McKee, 1996).

Yet the caste elements of England's past can still be seen today. A small cluster of British families still holds

In 2002, Queen Elizabeth II celebrated her silver jubilee, marking fifty years on the throne as England's monarch. Perhaps it is a sign of more egalitarian times that the event was not a performance of the London Philharmonic but a rock and roll concert—a popular culture ritual—intended to appeal to ordinary people both in England and around the world.

considerable inherited wealth and enjoys the highest prestige, the best schooling at elite universities, and political influence. A traditional monarch, Queen Elizabeth II, stands as head of state, and Parliament's House of Lords is composed of "peers," about half of whom are of noble birth. However, control of government has passed to the House of Commons, where the prime minister and other ministers typically reach their positions by achievement—winning an election—rather than by birth.

London's *Sunday Times* recently published a list of the richest people in Great Britain and other countries. Find the "Rich List" at http://www. sunday-times.co.uk.richlist/

Further down in the hierarchy, roughly one-fourth of the British people fall into the middle class. Some earn comfortable incomes from professions and businesses and are likely to have investments in the form of stocks and bonds. Below the middle class, perhaps half of all Britons consider themselves "working-class," earning modest incomes through manual labor. The remaining one-fourth of the British people make up the lower class, the poor who lack steady work. Most live in the nation's northern and western regions, which are plagued by closings of mines and factories.

Today's British class system has a mix of caste elements and meritocracy, producing a highly stratified society with some opportunity to move upward or downward. One consequence of the historical estate system is that social mobility occurs less often in the United Kingdom than in the United States (Kerckhoff, Campbell, & Winfield-Laird, 1985). This more rigid system of inequality in the United Kingdom is reflected in the importance attached to accent. Distinctive patterns of speech develop when people are set off from one another over many generations. In the United States, accent is a clue to where a person lives or grew up (there is no mistaking a midwestern "twang" or a southern "drawl"). In the United Kingdom, however, accent is a mark of social class (upper-class people speak the "King's English," but most people speak like "commoners"). So different are these two accents that the British seem to be, as the saying goes, "a single people divided by a common language."

CLASSLESS SOCIETIES?

Nowhere in the world do we find a society without some degree of social inequality. Yet some nations have claimed to be classless.

An illustration: The former Soviet Union. The Union of Soviet Socialist Republics (USSR), which rivaled the United States as a military superpower in the mid- to late twentieth century, was born out of a revolution in Russia in 1917. The Russian Revolution ended the feudal estate system ruled by a hereditary nobility and transferred most farms, factories, and other productive property from private ownership to state control. Following the lead of Karl Marx, who believed that private ownership of property was the basis for social classes, Soviet leaders boasted of becoming a classless society.

Yet just 6 percent of the population belonged to the Communist Party, which ran the country. High government officials, or *apparatchiks,* ranked highest in the social order, followed by intellectuals and other professionals, manual workers, and, at the lowest level, the rural peasantry. The fact that the members of these rankings had very different standards of living shows that the former Soviet Union never really became classless.

In 1985, Mikhail Gorbachev came to power with a new economic program known as *perestroika,* meaning "restructuring." Gorbachev saw that although the Soviet system had reduced economic inequality, living standards lagged far behind those of other industrial nations. Gorbachev tried to generate economic expansion by reducing inefficient centralized government control of the economy.

Gorbachev's reforms turned into one of the most dramatic social movements in history. People throughout

Eastern Europe toppled their socialist governments, and in 1991, the Soviet Union itself collapsed, remaking itself as the Russian Federation. People blamed their poverty and their lack of basic freedoms on the repressive ruling class of Communist Party officials.

The Soviet story shows that social inequality involves more than economic resources. Soviet society may not have had the extremes of wealth and poverty found in the United Kingdom and the United States, but it did have an elite class, based on power rather than wealth.

What about social mobility in so-called classless societies? In the twentieth century, there was as much upward social mobility in the Soviet Union as in the United Kingdom or the United States. Rapidly expanding industry and government drew many poor rural peasants into factories and offices. This trend illustrates what sociologists call **structural social mobility**, *a shift in the social position of large numbers of people due more to changes in society than to individual efforts.*

November 24, Odessa, Ukraine. The first snow of our voyage flies over the decks as our ship puts in at Odessa, the former Soviet Union's southern port on the Black Sea. Not far from the dock, we gaze up at the Potemkin Steps, the steep stairway up to the city, where the first shots of the Russian Revolution rang out. It has been six years since our last visit, and much has changed; indeed, the Soviet Union itself has collapsed. Has life improved? For some people, certainly. There are now chic boutiques in which well-dressed shoppers buy fine wines, designer clothes, and imported perfumes. Outside, shiny new Volvos, Mercedes, and even a few Cadillacs stand out against the small Ladas from the "old days." But for most people, life seems much worse. Flea markets line the curbs as families sell their home furnishings. When meat sells for $4 a pound and the average person earns just $30 a month, people become desperate. Even the city has to save money by turning off street lights after 8:00 P.M. The spirits of most people seem as dim as Odessa's streets.

During the 1990s, structural social mobility in the Russian Federation turned downward. One indicator is that the average life span for men dropped by eight years and for women by two years. Many factors are involved, including Russia's poor health care system, but the Russian people clearly have suffered in the turbulent period of economic

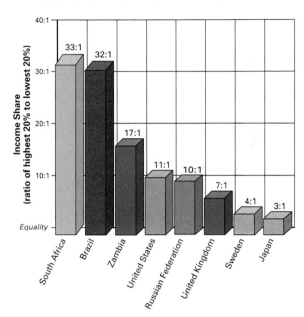

GLOBAL SNAPSHOT

Income Share (ratio of highest 20% to lowest 20%)

40:1
33:1 — South Africa
32:1 — Brazil
30:1
17:1 — Zambia
20:1
11:1 — United States
10:1 — Russian Federation
10:1
7:1 — United Kingdom
4:1 — Sweden
3:1 — Japan
Equality

FIGURE 8-1   Economic Inequality in Selected Countries

These data are the most recent available, representing income share for various years between 1993 and 2001.

Sources: U.S. Census Bureau (2003) and World Bank (2004).

change that began in 1991 (Bohlen, 1998; Gerber & Hout, 1998).

In the long run, closing inefficient state industries may improve the Russian Federation's economic performance. But in the short run, most citizens face hard times as living standards fall. As businesses have returned to private ownership, the gulf between rich and poor has grown to about the same level as in the United States, as shown in Figure 8–1. Today, some Russians praise the recent changes while others hang on, patiently hoping for better times.

An illustration: China.   Sweeping political and economic change has affected not just the Russian Federation but also the People's Republic of China. After the Communist revolution in 1949, the state took control of all farms, factories, and other productive property. Communist Party leader Mao Zedong declared all work to be equally important, so officially, social classes no longer existed.

The new program greatly reduced economic inequality. But as in the Soviet Union, social differences remained. The country was ruled by a political elite with enormous power

In recent decades, the government of China has permitted a market economy to operate in limited areas of the country. The result has been increased production and also the emergence of a new business class with a lifestyle similar to that of wealthy people in the United States.

and considerable privilege; below them were managers of large factories and skilled professionals; next came industrial workers; at the bottom were rural peasants, who were not even allowed to leave their villages to migrate to cities.

Further economic change came in 1978, when Mao died and Deng Xiaoping became China's leader. The state gradually loosened its hold on the economy, allowing a new class of business owners to emerge. Communist Party leaders remain in control of the country, and some have prospered as they have joined the ranks of the small but wealthy elite who control new, privately run industries. Much of this new economic growth has been concentrated in coastal areas where living standards have soared far above those in China's rural interior.

Today, a new class system is emerging with a mix of the old political hierarchy and a new business hierarchy. At this early stage, scholars point to its complexity and debate its likely future. But the lesson of China is clear: With new patterns of inequality emerging over time, social stratification is highly dynamic (Bian, 2002).

IDEOLOGY: THE POWER BEHIND STRATIFICATION

How do societies persist without sharing their resources more equally? The British estate system lasted for centuries, and for 2,000 years people in India accepted the idea that they should be privileged or poor based on the accident of birth.

A major reason that social hierarchies endure is **ideology,** *cultural beliefs that justify particular social arrangements, including patterns of inequality*. Any beliefs, such as the idea that the rich are smart and the poor are lazy, are ideological to the extent that they define elites as worthy and suggest that those less well off deserve their plight.

According to the ancient Greek philosopher Plato (427–347 B.C.E.), every culture considers some type of inequality fair. Although Karl Marx understood this, he was far more critical of inequality than Plato. Marx criticized capitalist societies for defending wealth and power in the hands of a few as a "law of the marketplace." Capitalist law, he continued, defines the right to own property and ensures that money stays within the same families from one generation to the next. In short, Marx concluded, culture and institutions combine to support a society's elite, which is why established hierarchies last a long time.

Ideology changes along with a society's economy and technology. Because agrarian societies depend on the routine labor of their people, they develop caste systems that make performing the duties of a person's "station" a moral responsibility. With the rise of industrial capitalism, an ideology of meritocracy arises, defining wealth and power as prizes to be won by those who perform the best. This change means that the poor—often the targets of charity and sympathy in feudal societies—are looked down upon under industrial capitalism as personally undeserving. This harsh view is linked to the work of Herbert Spencer, as explained in the Critical Thinking box.

History shows how difficult it is to change social stratification. However, challenges to the status quo always arise. Traditional ideas about "a woman's place," for example, have given way to economic opportunity for women. The continuing struggle for racial equality in South Africa is another case of widespread rejection of the ideology of apartheid.

The Functions of Social Stratification

Why does social stratification exist at all? According to the structural-functional approach, social stratification plays a vital part in the operation of society. This argument was presented sixty years ago by Kingsley Davis and Wilbert Moore (1945).

Is Getting Rich "the Survival of the Fittest"?

"The survival of the fittest"—we have all heard these words used to describe society as a competitive jungle. The phrase was coined by one of sociology's pioneers, Herbert Spencer (1820–1903), whose ideas about social inequality are still widespread today.

Spencer, who lived in England, eagerly followed the work of the natural scientist Charles Darwin (1809–1882). Darwin's theory of biological evolution held that a species changes physically over many generations as it adapts to the natural environment. Spencer distorted Darwin's theory, applying it to the operation of society: Society became the "jungle," with the "fittest" people rising to wealth and the "failures" sinking into miserable poverty.

It is no surprise that Spencer's views were popular among the rising U.S. industrialists of the day. John D. Rockefeller (1839–1937), who made a vast fortune building the oil industry, recited Spencer's "social gospel" to young children in Sunday school. As Rockefeller saw it, the growth of giant corporations—and the astounding wealth of their owners—was merely the result of "the survival of the fittest," a basic fact of nature. Neither Spencer nor Rockefeller had much sympathy for the poor, seeing poverty as evidence of individuals' failing to measure up in a competitive world. Spencer opposed social welfare programs because he thought they penalized society's "best" people (through taxes) and rewarded its "worst" members (through welfare benefits).

Today's sociologists are quick to point out that society is far from a meritocracy, as Spencer claimed. Moreover, it is not the case that companies or individuals who generate lots of money necessarily benefit society. Yet Spencer's view that people get what they deserve in life remains part of our individualistic culture.

WHAT DO YOU THINK?

1. What did Herbert Spencer mean when he said that society encourages "the survival of the fittest"?
2. Why do you think Spencer's ideas are still popular in the United States today?
3. In what sense do highly paid people benefit society? In what ways do they not?

THE DAVIS-MOORE THESIS

The **Davis-Moore thesis** states that *social stratification has beneficial consequences for the operation of a society*. How else, ask Davis and Moore, can we explain the fact that some form of social stratification has been found in every society?

Davis and Moore note that modern societies have hundreds of occupational positions of varying importance. Certain jobs—say, washing windows or answering a telephone—are fairly easy and can be performed by almost anyone. Other jobs—such as designing new generations of computers or transplanting human organs—are very difficult and demand the scarce talents of people with extensive (and expensive) training.

Therefore, Davis and Moore explain, the greater the functional importance of a position, the more rewards a society attaches to it. This strategy promotes productivity and efficiency because rewarding important work with income, prestige, power, or leisure encourages people to do these things and to work better, longer, and harder. In short, unequal rewards (which is what social stratification is) benefit society as a whole.

Davis and Moore admit that any society could be egalitarian, but only to the extent that people are willing to let *anyone* perform *any* job. Equality also demands that someone who does a job poorly be rewarded just as much as someone who performs well. Such a system clearly offers little incentive for people to try their best and thereby reduces a society's productive efficiency.

The Davis-Moore thesis suggests why some form of stratification exists everywhere; it does not state exactly what rewards a society should give to any occupational position or how unequal rewards should be. It merely points out that positions a society considers crucial must offer enough rewards to draw talented people away from less important work.

Critical review. Although the Davis-Moore thesis is an important contribution to sociological analysis, it has provoked criticism. Melvin Tumin (1953) wondered, first, how we assess the importance of a particular occupation. Perhaps the high rewards our society gives to physicians result partly from deliberate efforts by medical schools to limit the supply of physicians and thereby increase the demand for their services. Furthermore, do rewards actually reflect the contribution someone makes to society? With income approaching $100 million per year, television personality Oprah Winfrey earns more in two days than the U.S. president earns all year. Would anyone argue that hosting a talk show is more important than leading a country? Then there is the case of Larry Ellison, the chief executive officer of Oracle, who earned more than $700 million even as the value of the company slid downward—an amount it would take a college teacher 10,000 years to earn (Benjamin, 2002; Broder, 2002). Do corporate executives deserve such megasalaries for their "contributions to society"?

Second, Tumin claimed that Davis and Moore ignore how the caste elements of social stratification can *prevent* the development of individual talent. Born to privilege, rich children may develop their abilities, something many gifted poor children may never have the opportunity to do.

Third, living in a society that places so much importance on money, we tend to overestimate the importance of high-paying work; beyond making money, how do stockbrokers or people who trade international currencies really contribute to society? For the same reason, it is difficult for us to see the importance of work not oriented toward making money, such as parenting, creative writing, playing music in a symphony, or just being a good friend to someone in need (Packard, 2002).

Finally, by suggesting that social stratification benefits all of society, the Davis-Moore thesis ignores how social inequality promotes conflict and even outright revolution. This criticism leads to the social-conflict approach, which provides a very different explanation for social hierarchy.

Stratification and Conflict

Social-conflict analysis argues that rather than benefiting society as a whole, stratification provides some people with advantages over others. This analysis draws heavily on the ideas of Karl Marx, with contributions from Max Weber.

KARL MARX: CLASS CONFLICT

As Marx saw it, the Industrial Revolution promised humanity a society free from want. Yet during Marx's lifetime, the capitalist economy had done little to improve the lives of most people. Marx set out to explain a glaring contradiction: how, in a society so rich, so many could be so poor.

In Marx's view, social stratification is rooted in people's relationship to the means of production. Individuals either own productive property (such as factories and businesses) or they labor for others. In feudal Europe, the nobility and the church owned the productive land; the peasants toiled as farmers. Under industrial capitalism, the nobility was replaced by **capitalists** (sometimes called the *bourgeoisie,* a French word meaning "town dwellers"), *people who own and operate factories and other businesses in pursuit of profits.* Peasants became the **proletarians,** *people who sell their productive labor for wages.* Capitalists and proletarians have opposing interests and are separated by a vast gulf of wealth and power, making class conflict inevitable.

Marx's analysis reflects the capitalism he observed in the nineteenth century, when industry had raised some individuals to great wealth while most made do with low wages. In this era, wealthy U.S. capitalists such as Andrew Carnegie, J. P. Morgan, and John Jacob Astor (one of the few rich passengers to drown on the *Titanic*) lived in fabulous mansions that were filled with priceless works of art and staffed by dozens of servants. Even by today's standards, their incomes were staggering. For example, Carnegie earned more than $20 million in 1900 (more than $100 million in today's dollars), when the average worker's wages totaled perhaps $500 a year (Baltzell, 1964; Pessen, 1990).

In time, Marx believed, the working majority would overthrow the capitalists once and for all. Capitalism would bring about its own downfall, Marx reasoned, by making workers poorer and poorer and giving them little control over what they made or how they made it. Under capitalism, work produces only **alienation,** *the experience of isolation and misery resulting from powerlessness.*

To replace capitalism, Marx imagined a *socialist* system that would meet the needs of all rather than just the few: "The proletarians have nothing to lose but their chains. They have a world to win" (Marx & Engels, 1972:362, orig. 1848).

Critical review. Marx has had enormous influence on sociological thinking. But his revolutionary ideas—calling for the overthrow of capitalist society—also make his work highly controversial.

One of the strongest criticisms of the Marxist approach is that it ignores a central idea of the Davis-Moore thesis: that a system of unequal rewards is needed to motivate people to do their work well. Marx separated reward from performance; his egalitarian ideal was based on the principle "from each according to ability, to each according to need" (Marx & Engels, 1972:388, orig. 1848). However, failure to reward individual performance may be precisely what caused the low productivity of the former Soviet Union and other socialist economies around the world. Defenders respond to such criticism by asking why we assume that humanity is inherently selfish rather than social; individual rewards are not the only way to motivate people to perform their social roles (Clark, 1991; Fiske, 1991).

APPLYING THEORY

SOCIAL STRATIFICATION

	Structural-Functional Approach	Social-Conflict Approach
What is the level of analysis?	Macro-level	Macro-level
Who benefits from social inequality?	Stratification benefits society as a whole.	Stratification benefits some people and harms others.
Are unequal rewards fair?	Yes. Linking greater rewards to more important work is widely accepted by people. Unequal rewards boost economic productivity by encouraging people to work harder and try new ideas.	No. There is widespread opposition to existing social inequality. Unequal rewards only serve to divide society.
Is stratification stable?	Yes. Stratification typically lasts for generations.	No. Opposition causes ongoing social change.

A second problem is that the revolutionary change Marx predicted has failed to happen, at least in advanced capitalist societies. The next section explores this issue.

WHY NO MARXIST REVOLUTION?

Despite Marx's prediction, capitalism is still thriving. Why have industrial workers not overthrown capitalism? Ralf Dahrendorf (1959) proposed four reasons:

1. **The fragmentation of the capitalist class.** Today, tens of millions of stockholders rather than single families own most large companies. Day-to-day corporate operations are in the hands of a large class of managers, who may or may not be major stockholders. With stock so widely held—about 45 percent of U.S. adults are in the market—more and more people have a direct stake in the capitalist system.

2. **A higher standard of living.** As Chapter 12 ("Economics and Politics") explains, a century ago, most U.S. workers were in factories or on farms in **blue-collar occupations,** *lower-prestige jobs that involve mostly manual labor*. Today, most workers are in **white-collar occupations,** *higher-prestige jobs that involve mostly mental activity*. These jobs are in sales, management, and other service fields. Most of today's white-collar workers do not think of themselves as an "industrial proletariat." Just as important, the average income in the United States rose almost tenfold over the course of the twentieth century, even allowing for inflation, and the number of hours in the workweek decreased. As a result, most workers today are far better off than

workers were a century ago, an example of structural social mobility helping people accept the status quo.

3. **More worker organizations.** Workers today have the right to form labor unions that make demands of management, backed by threats of work slowdowns and strikes. Consequently, labor disputes are settled without threatening the capitalist system.

4. **Greater legal protections.** Over the past century, new laws made the workplace safer, and unemployment insurance, disability protection, and Social Security now provide workers with greater financial security.

A counterpoint. These developments suggest that our society has smoothed many of capitalism's rough edges. Yet many observers claim that Marx's analysis of capitalism is still largely valid (Domhoff, 1983; Stephens, 1986; Boswell & Dixon, 1993; Hout, Brooks, & Manza, 1993). First, wealth remains highly concentrated, with 40 percent of all privately owned property in the hands of 1 percent of the U.S. population (Keister, 2000). Second, many of today's white-collar jobs offer no more income, security, or satisfaction than factory work did a century ago. Third, many benefits enjoyed by today's workers came about through the class conflict Marx described, and workers still struggle to hold on to what they have. Fourth, although workers have gained legal protections, the law has not helped ordinary people use the legal system as effectively as the rich. Therefore, social-conflict theorists conclude, the absence of a socialist revolution in the United States does not disprove Marx's analysis of capitalism.

The Applying Theory table summarizes the two contrasting explanations of social stratification.

The extent of social inequality in agrarian systems is greater than that found in industrial societies. One indication of the unchallenged power of rulers is the monumental structures built over years with the unpaid labor of common people. Although the Taj Mahal in India is among the world's most beautiful buildings, it is merely a tomb for a single individual.

MAX WEBER: CLASS, STATUS, AND POWER

Max Weber agreed with Karl Marx that social stratification causes social conflict, but he viewed Marx's two-class model as simplistic. Instead, he viewed social stratification as involving three distinct types of inequality.

The first dimension is economic inequality—the issue so important to Marx—which Weber called *class* position. Weber did not think of classes as well-defined categories but as a continuum ranging from high to low. Weber's second dimension is *status,* or social prestige, and the third is *power*.

The socioeconomic status hierarchy. Marx viewed prestige and power as simple reflections of economic position and did not treat them as distinct dimensions of inequality. But Weber noted that status consistency in modern societies often is quite low: A local official might exercise great power yet have little wealth or social prestige.

Weber, then, characterizes stratification in industrial societies as a multidimensional ranking rather than a hierarchy of clearly defined classes. In line with Weber's thinking, sociologists use the term **socioeconomic status (SES)** to refer to *a composite ranking based on various dimensions of social inequality*.

Inequality in history. Weber observed that each of his three dimensions of social inequality stands out at a different time in the evolution of human societies. Status or social prestige is the main dimension of difference in agrarian societies, taking the form of honor. Members of these societies gain prestige by carrying out the duties the culture gives to people born to a given rank.

Industrialization and the development of capitalism level traditional rankings based on birth but generate striking financial inequality. Thus, Weber argued, in an industrial society, the crucial difference between people is the economic dimension of class.

Over time, industrial societies witness the growth of a bureaucratic state. Bigger government and the spread of all types of other organizations make power more important in the stratification system. Especially in socialist societies, where government regulates many aspects of life, high-ranking officials become the new ruling elite.

This historical analysis points to a final difference between Weber and Marx. Marx thought societies could eliminate social stratification by abolishing private ownership of productive property. Weber doubted that overthrowing capitalism would significantly lessen social stratification. It might lessen economic differences, he reasoned, but socialism would increase inequality by expanding government and concentrating power in the hands of a political elite. Popular uprisings against entrenched socialist bureaucracies in Eastern Europe and the former Soviet Union support Weber's position.

Critical review. Weber's multidimensional view of social stratification has enormously influenced sociologists. But critics (particularly those who favor Marx's ideas) argue that although social class boundaries may have blurred, industrial and postindustrial nations still show striking patterns of social inequality. Moreover, as we shall see, economic inequality has increased recently in the United States. Thus, whereas some people favor Weber's multidimensional hierarchy, others think that Marx's view of the rich versus the poor is closer to the mark.

Stratification and Technology: A Global Perspective

We can weave together a number of observations made in this chapter by considering the relationship between a society's technology and its type of social stratification. This analysis draws on Gerhard Lenski's model of sociocultural evolution discussed in Chapter 2 ("Culture").

With simple technology, hunters and gatherers produce only what is necessary for day-to-day living. Some people may produce more than others, but the group's survival depends on all sharing what they have. Thus, no categories of people are better off than others.

As technological advances generate a surplus, social inequality increases. In horticultural and pastoral societies, a small elite controls most of the surplus. Larger-scale agriculture is more productive still, and striking inequality—as great as at any time in history—places the nobility in an almost godlike position over the masses.

Industrialization turns the tide, nudging inequality downward. Prompted by the need to develop people's talents, meritocracy takes hold and weakens the power of traditional elites. Industrial productivity also raises the living standards of the historically poor majority. Specialized work demands schooling for all, sharply reducing illiteracy. A literate population, in turn, presses for a greater voice in political decision making, reducing social inequality and lessening men's domination of women.

Over time, even wealth becomes somewhat less concentrated (countering the trend predicted by Marx). In the 1920s, the richest 1 percent of U.S. families owned about 40 percent of all wealth, a figure that fell to 30 percent by the 1980s (Williamson & Lindert, 1980; Beeghley, 1989; U.S. House of Representatives, 1991). Such trends help explain why Marxist revolutions occurred in *agrarian* societies, such as Russia (1917), Cuba (1959), and Nicaragua (1979), where social inequality is most pronounced, rather than in *industrial* societies as Marx predicted. However, wealth inequality turned upward again after 1990 and is once again about the same as it was in the 1920s (Keister, 2000).

In human history, then, technological advances first increase but then moderate the intensity of social

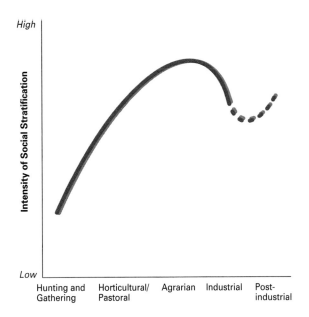

FIGURE 8-2 Social Stratification and Technological Development: The Kuznets Curve

The Kuznets curve shows that greater technological sophistication generally is accompanied by more pronounced social stratification. The trend reverses itself as industrial societies relax rigid, castelike distinctions in favor of greater opportunity and equality under the law. Political rights are more widely extended, and there is even some leveling of economic differences. However, the emergence of postindustrial society has brought an upturn in economic inequality, as indicated by the broken line added by the author.

Source: Created by the author, based on Kuznets (1955) and Lenski (1966).

stratification. Greater inequality is functional for agrarian societies, but industrial societies benefit from a less unequal system. This historical pattern was first recognized fifty years ago by the Nobel Prize–winning economist Simon Kuznets (1955, 1966) and is illustrated by the Kuznets curve, shown in Figure 8–2.

Patterns of global inequality follow the Kuznets curve. Global Map 8–1 on page 204 shows that high-income nations that have passed through the industrial era (including the United States, Canada, and the nations of Western Europe) have somewhat less income inequality than nations in which agriculture remains a major part of the economy (as is common in Latin America and Africa). Of course, income inequality reflects not just technological development but also a society's political and economic priorities. Of all high-income nations, the United States has the greatest income inequality.

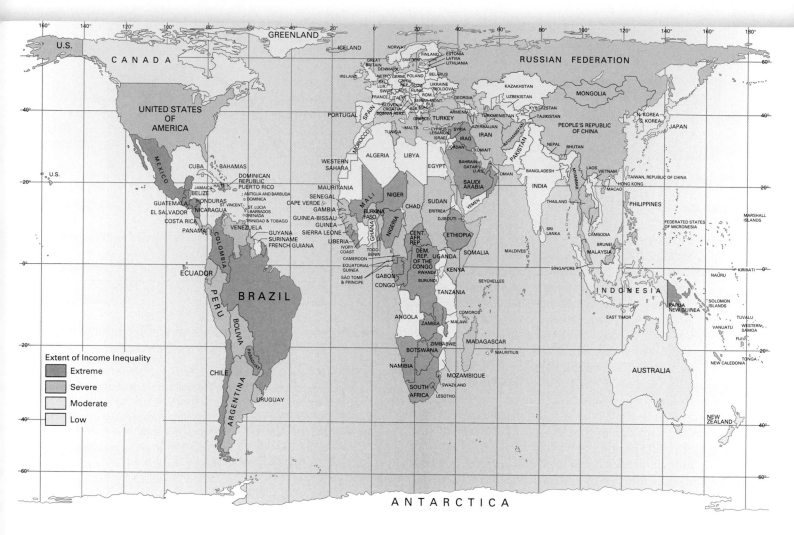

WINDOW ON THE WORLD

GLOBAL MAP 8–1   Income Inequality in Global Perspective

Societies throughout the world differ in the rigidity and extent of their social stratification and in overall standard of living. This map highlights income inequality. Generally speaking, the United States stands out among high-income nations, such as Great Britain, Sweden, Japan, and Australia, as having greater income inequality. The less economically developed countries of Latin America and Africa, including Colombia, Brazil, and the Central African Republic, as well as much of the Arab world, exhibit the most pronounced inequality of income. Is this pattern consistent with the Kuznets curve?

Source: Based on Gini coefficients obtained from World Bank (2004).

And what of the future? Notice that in Figure 8–2, the trend described by Kuznets has been extended to the postindustrial era (the broken line) to show social inequality increasing once again. As the Information Revolution moves ahead, U.S. society is experiencing greater economic inequality, suggesting that the long-term trend may differ from the one Kuznets observed half a century ago (Nielsen & Alderson, 1997).

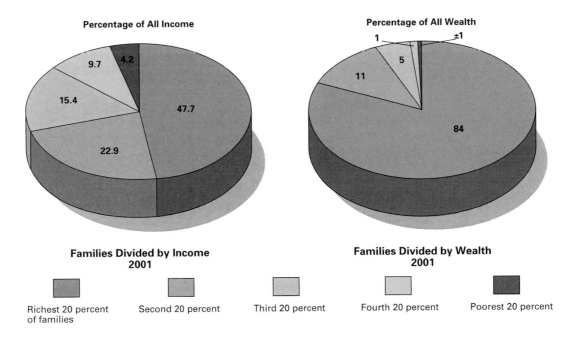

Percentage of All Income

9.7 4.2
15.4
47.7
22.9

**Families Divided by Income
2001**

Percentage of All Wealth

1   ±1
5
11
84

**Families Divided by Wealth
2001**

Richest 20 percent of families	Second 20 percent	Third 20 percent	Fourth 20 percent	Poorest 20 percent

FIGURE 8-3 Distribution of Income and Wealth in the United States

Sources: Income data from U.S. Census Bureau (2004); wealth data are author estimates based on Keister (2000) and Russell & Mogelonsky (2000).

Inequality in the United States

The United States stands apart from most European nations in never having had a titled nobility. With the significant exception of our racial history, we have never known a caste system that rigidly ranks categories of people.

Even so, U.S. society is highly stratified. Not only do the rich have most of the money, but they also receive the most schooling, enjoy the best health, and consume the most goods and services. Such privilege contrasts sharply with the poverty of millions of women and men who worry about paying next month's rent or a doctor's bill if a child becomes ill. Many people think the United States is a middle-class society, but is this really the case?

Read a government report on U.S. wealth inequality at http://www.census.gov/hhes/www/wealth/1998_2000/wealth98_00.html

INCOME, WEALTH, AND POWER

One important dimension of economic inequality is **income,** *wages or salary from work and earnings from investments.* The Census Bureau reports that the median U.S. family income in 2003 was $52,680. The left side of Figure 8–3 shows the distribution of income among all U.S.

families.[1] The richest 20 percent of families (earning at least $98,200 annually, with a mean of about $165,000) received 47.7 percent of all income, and the bottom 20 percent (earning less than $24,000, with a mean of about $14,000) received only 4.2 percent.

Table 8–1 on page 206 takes a closer look at income distribution. In 2003, the highest-paid 5 percent of U.S. families earned at least $170,000 (averaging almost $300,000), or 21.0 percent of all income, more than the total earnings of the lowest-paid 40 percent. At the very top of the pyramid, the richest half of 1 percent earned at least $1.5 million. In short, while a small number of people earn very high incomes, the majority make do with far less.

Income is only one part of a person's or family's **wealth,** *the total value of money and other assets, minus*

---

[1] The Census Bureau reports both mean and median incomes for families ("two or more persons related by blood, marriage, or adoption") and households ("two or more persons sharing a living unit"). In 2003, mean family income was $68,563, higher than the median because high-income families pull up the mean but not the median. For households, these figures are somewhat lower—a mean of $59,067 and a median of $43,318—largely because families average 3.1 people and households average 2.6.

TABLE 8-1	
U.S. Family Income, 2003	

Highest paid . . .	Annually earns at least . . .
0.5%	$1,500,000
1	347,000
5	170,000
10	116,000
20	98,000
30	76,500
40	65,000
50	54,500
60	42,000
70	31,500
80	24,000
90	10,000

Source: U.S. Census Bureau (2004) and author calculations.

outstanding debts. Wealth—including stocks, bonds, and real estate—is distributed even more unequally than income.

The right side of Figure 8–3 shows the approximate distribution of wealth in the United States. The richest 20 percent of U.S. families own roughly 84 percent of the country's entire wealth. High up in this privileged category are the top 5 percent of families, the "very rich," who own 60 percent of all private property. Richer still, with wealth into the tens of millions, are the 1 percent of families that qualify as "super-rich" and possess about 40 percent of this nation's privately held resources (Keister, 2000; Keister & Moller, 2000). At the top of the wealth pyramid, the ten richest U.S. families have a combined net worth of more than $240 billion (Kroll & Goldman, 2004). This equals the total property of 3.1 million average families, including enough people to fill the cities of Chula Vista, California; Chicago, Illinois; Chattanooga, Tennessee; and Clearwater, Florida.

The wealth of the average U.S. household, currently about $71,600, rose throughout the 1990s and fell somewhat during the economic downturn beginning in 2000. Household wealth reflects the total value of homes, cars, investments, insurance policies, retirement pensions, furniture, clothing, and all other personal property, minus a home mortgage and other debts. The wealth of average people is not only less than that of the rich but also different in kind. Most people's wealth centers on a home and a car—property that generates no income—but the greater wealth of the rich is mostly in the form of stocks and other income-producing investments.

When financial assets are balanced against debits, the lowest-ranking 40 percent of families have virtually no wealth at all. The negative percentage shown in Figure 8–3 for the poorest 20 percent means that these families actually live in debt.

In the United States, wealth is an important source of power. The small proportion of families that controls most of the wealth also has the ability to shape the agenda of the entire society. As explained in Chapter 12 ("Economics and Politics"), some sociologists argue that such concentrated wealth weakens democracy because the political system serves the interests of the super-rich.

OCCUPATIONAL PRESTIGE

In addition to generating income, work is also an important source of prestige. We commonly evaluate one another according to the kind of work we do, giving greater respect to those who do what we consider important work and less to others with more modest jobs.

Sociologists measure the relative social prestige of various occupations (Counts, 1925; Hodge, Treiman, & Rossi, 1966; NORC, 2003). Table 8–2 shows that people give high prestige  to occupations, such as medicine, law, and engineering, that require extensive training and generate high income. By contrast, less prestigious work—as a waitress or janitor, for example—not only pays less but requires less ability and schooling. Occupational prestige rankings are much the same in all high-income nations (Lin & Xie, 1988).

In any society, high-prestige occupations go to privileged categories of people. In Table 8–2, for example, the highest-ranking occupations are dominated by men. Only thirteen jobs down the list do we find "registered nurse," most of whom are women. Similarly, many of the lowest-prestige jobs are commonly performed by people of color.

SCHOOLING

Industrial societies expand opportunities for schooling, but some people still receive much more than others. Table 8–3 on page 208 shows the schooling for women and men aged twenty-five and over in the United States. In 2003, although 85 percent had completed high school, only about 27 percent were college graduates.

Schooling affects both occupation and income because most (but not all) of the better-paying, white-collar jobs shown in Table 8–2 require a college degree or other advanced study. By contrast, most blue-collar jobs, which bring lower income and less social prestige, require less schooling.

TABLE 8–2

The Relative Social Prestige of Selected Occupations in the United States

White-Collar Occupations	Prestige Score	Blue-Collar Occupations	White-Collar Occupations	Prestige Score	Blue-Collar Occupations
Physician	86		Funeral director	49	
Lawyer	75		Realtor	49	
College/university professor	74		Bookkeeper	47	
Architect	73			47	Machinist
Chemist	73			47	Mail carrier
Physicist/astronomer	73		Musician/composer	47	
Aerospace engineer	72			46	Secretary
Dentist	72		Photographer	45	
Member of the clergy	69		Bank teller	43	
Psychologist	69			42	Tailor
Pharmacist	68			42	Welder
Optometrist	67			40	Farmer
Registered nurse	66			40	Telephone operator
Secondary school teacher	66			39	Carpenter
Accountant	65			36	Brick/stone mason
Athlete	65			36	Child-care worker
Electrical engineer	64		File clerk	36	
Elementary school teacher	64			36	Hairdresser
Economist	63			35	Baker
Veterinarian	62			34	Bulldozer operator
Airplane pilot	61			31	Auto body repairperson
Computer programmer	61		Retail apparel salesperson	30	
Sociologist	61			30	Truck driver
Editor/reporter	60		Cashier	29	
	60	Police officer		28	Elevator operator
Actor	58			28	Garbage collector
Radio/TV announcer	55			28	Taxi driver
Librarian	54			28	Waiter/waitress
	53	Aircraft mechanic		27	Bellhop
	53	Firefighter		25	Bartender
Dental hygienist	52			23	Farm laborer
Painter/sculptor	52			23	Household laborer
Social worker	52			22	Door-to-door salesperson
	51	Electrician		22	Janitor
Computer operator	50			09	Shoe shiner

Source: Adapted from *General Social Surveys, 1972–2002: Cumulative Codebook* (Chicago: National Opinion Research Center, 2003), pp. 1488–1506.

ANCESTRY, RACE, AND GENDER

A class system rewards individual talent and effort. But nothing affects social standing as much as birth into a particular family, which has a strong bearing on future schooling, occupation, and income. Research suggests that almost half of our country's richest people—those with hundreds of millions of dollars in wealth—derived their fortunes mostly from inheritance (Kroll & Goldman, 2004). Inherited poverty shapes the future of a much larger share of the population.

Also closely linked to social position in the United States is race. White people have a higher overall occupational standing than African Americans and they also receive more schooling. The median African American family income was $34,369 in 2003, just 57 percent of the $59,937 earned by non-Hispanic white families. This difference in income makes a real difference in people's lives. For example, non-Hispanic white families are more likely to own their homes (75 percent do) than black families (47 percent) (U.S. Census Bureau, 2004).

TABLE 8-3

Schooling of U.S. Adults, 2003 (aged 25 and over)

	Women	Men
Not a high school graduate	**15.0%**	**15.9%**
8 years or less	6.4	6.8
9–11 years	8.6	9.1
High school graduate	**85.0**	**84.1**
High school only	33.1	30.9
1–3 years college	26.2	24.3
College graduate or more	25.7	28.9

Source: U.S. Census Bureau (2004).

Some of the racial difference in income results from the larger proportion of single-parent families among African Americans. Comparing only families that include a married couple, African American families earned 79 percent as much as non-Hispanic white families.

Over time, this income difference builds into a huge wealth gap (Altonji, Doraszelski, & Segal, 2000). A recent survey of households by the Federal Reserve found that median wealth for all minorities, including African Americans, Hispanics, and Asian Americans ($17,100), is just 14 percent of the median ($120,900) for non-Hispanic whites (Aizcorbe, Kennickell, & Moore, 2003).

Social ranking involves ethnicity as well. Historically, people of English ancestry have enjoyed the most wealth and wielded the greatest power in the United States. The rapidly growing Latino population, by contrast, has long been disadvantaged. In 2003, median income among Hispanic families was $34,272, which is 57 percent of the median income for non-Hispanic white families. A detailed examination of how race and ethnicity affect social standing is presented in Chapter 11 ("Race and Ethnicity").

Of course, both men and women are found in families at every social level. Yet on average, women have less income, wealth, and occupational prestige than men. Among single-parent families, those headed by a woman are six times more likely to be poor than those headed by a man. Chapter 10 ("Gender Stratification") examines the link between gender and social stratification.

Social Class in the United States

As we have explained, rankings in a caste system are rigid and obvious to all. Defining the social categories in a more fluid class system is not so easy. Followers of Karl Marx see two major social classes: capitalists and proletariat. Other sociologists find as many as six classes (Warner & Lunt, 1941) or even seven (Coleman & Rainwater, 1978). Still others side with Max Weber, believing that people form not clear-cut classes but a multidimensional status hierarchy.

Defining classes in the United States is difficult because of the relatively low level of status consistency. Especially toward the middle of the hierarchy, people's social position on one dimension may contradict their standing on another. For example, a government official may have the power to administer a multimillion-dollar budget yet earn a modest personal income. Similarly, many members of the clergy enjoy ample prestige but only moderate power and low pay. Or consider a lucky day trader in the stock market who wins no special respect but makes a lot of money.

Finally, the social mobility characteristic of class systems—again, most pronounced near the middle—means that social position may change during a person's lifetime, further blurring class boundaries. With these problems in mind, we can describe four general rankings: the upper class, the middle class, the working class, and the lower class.

THE UPPER CLASS

Families in the upper class—the top 5 percent of the U.S. population—earn at least $170,000, and some earn ten times that much. As a general rule, the more a family's income comes from inherited wealth in the form of stocks and bonds, real estate, and other investments, the stronger a family's claim to being upper-class.

In 2004, *Forbes* magazine identified 277 people in the United States who are worth at least $1 billion (and as much as $47 billion) (Kroll & Goldman, 2004). These people form the core of the upper class or Karl Marx's "capitalists"—the owners of the means of production and thus of most of the nation's private wealth. Many upper-class people are business owners, top executives in large corporations, or senior government officials. Historically, though less so today, the upper class has been composed of white Anglo-Saxon Protestants (WASPs) (Baltzell, 1964, 1976, 1988).

Upper-uppers. The *upper-upper class*, sometimes called "blue bloods" or simply "society," includes less than 1 percent of the U.S. population (Coleman & Neugarten, 1971; Baltzell, 1995). Membership is almost always the result of birth, as suggested by the joke that the easiest way to become an upper-upper is to be born one. Most of these families possess enormous wealth that is mostly inherited. For this reason, members of the upper-upper class are said to have "old money."

Set apart by their wealth, upper-uppers live in exclusive neighborhoods such as Beacon Hill in Boston, the Rittenhouse Square section of Philadelphia, the Gold Coast of Chicago, and Nob Hill in San Francisco. Their children typically attend private schools with others of similar background and complete their formal education at high-prestige colleges and universities. In the historical pattern of European aristocrats, they study liberal arts rather than vocational skills. Women of the upper-upper class often do volunteer work for charitable organizations; while helping the larger community, these activities also build networks that increase this elite's power (Ostrander, 1980, 1984).

Lower-uppers. Most upper-class people actually fall into the *lower-upper class.* The Queen of England is in the upper-upper class based not on her fortune of $660 million but on her family tree. J. K. Rowling, author of the Harry Potter books, is worth even more—about $1 billion—but this woman (who was once on welfare) is a member of the lower-upper class. The major difference is that members of the lower-upper class are the "working rich": The primary source of their income is earnings, not inherited wealth. Although these "new rich" families—who make up 3 or 4 percent of the U.S. population—generally live in expensive neighborhoods, most do not gain entry into the clubs and associations of "old money" families.

THE MIDDLE CLASS

Made up of 40 to 45 percent of the U.S. population, the large middle class has a tremendous influence on our culture. Television and movies usually show middle-class people, and most commercial advertising is directed at these average consumers. The middle class contains far more ethnic and racial diversity than the upper class.

Upper-middles. The people in the top half of this category are referred to as the *upper-middle class,* based on their above-average income, in the range of $80,000 to $170,000 a year. Such income allows upper-middle-class families to accumulate property: a comfortable house in a fairly expensive area, several automobiles, and investments. Two-thirds of upper-middle-class children receive college education, and postgraduate degrees are common. Many go on to high-prestige occupations as physicians, engineers, lawyers, accountants, or business executives. Lacking the power of the richest people to influence national or international events, upper-middles often play an important role in local political affairs.

Average-middles. The rest of the middle class falls close to the center of the U.S. class structure. *Average-middles*

For decades, farm families who worked hard could expect to fall within the U.S. middle class. But the trend toward large-scale agribusiness has put the future of the small family farm in doubt. Although many young people in rural areas are turning away from farming toward other careers, some carry on, incorporating high technology into their farm management in their determined efforts to succeed.

typically work in less prestigious white-collar occupations as bank tellers, middle managers, or sales clerks or in highly skilled blue-collar jobs such as electrical work and carpentry. Family income falls between $40,000 and $80,000 a year, which is roughly the national average.

Average-middle-class people generally build up a small amount of wealth over the course of their working lives, mostly in the form of a house and a retirement account. Most average-middle-class men and women are likely to be high school graduates, but the odds are just fifty-fifty that they will complete a college degree, usually at a less expensive, state-supported school.

THE WORKING CLASS

About one-third of the population is in the working class (sometimes called the *lower-middle class*). In Marxist terms, the working class forms the core of the industrial proletariat. The blue-collar jobs held by members of the working class generally yield a family income of between $25,000 and $40,000 a year, somewhat below the national average. Working-class families have little or no wealth and are vulnerable to financial problems caused by unemployment or illness.

Compared to high-income people, low-income people are half as likely to report good health and, on average, live about seven fewer years. The toll of low income—played out in inadequate nutrition, little medical care, and high stress—is easy to see on the faces of the poor, who look old before their time.

Many working-class jobs provide little personal satisfaction—they require discipline but rarely imagination—and place workers under constant supervision. These jobs also offer fewer benefits, such as medical insurance and pension plans. About half of working-class families own their homes, usually in lower-cost neighborhoods. College becomes a reality for only about one-third of working-class children.

THE LOWER CLASS

The remaining 20 percent of our population make up the lower class. Low income makes their lives insecure and difficult. In 2003, the federal government classified 35.9 million people (12.5 percent of the population) as poor. Millions more, called the "working poor," are just slightly better off, holding low-prestige jobs that provide little satisfaction and minimal income. Barely half manage to complete high school, and only one in four ever reaches college.

Society segregates the lower class, especially when the poor are racial or ethnic minorities. About 40 percent of lower-class families own their own home, typically in the least desirable neighborhoods. Although poor neighborhoods are found in inner cities, lower-class families also live in rural areas, especially across the South.

The Difference Class Makes

Social stratification affects nearly every dimension of our lives. We will briefly examine some of the ways social standing is linked to our health, values, politics, and family life.

HEALTH

Health is closely related to social standing. Children born into poor families are three times more likely to die from disease, neglect, accidents, or violence during their first year of life than children born into privileged families. Among adults, people with above-average incomes are twice as likely as low-income people to describe their health as excellent. Moreover, on average, richer people live seven years longer because they eat more nutritious food, live in safer and less stressful environments, and receive better medical care (Lethbridge-Cejku, Schiller, & Bernadel, 2004).

VALUES AND ATTITUDES

Some cultural values vary from class to class. The "old rich" have an unusually strong sense of family history because their position is based on wealth passed down from generation to generation. Secure in their birthright privileges, upper-uppers also favor understated manners and tastes, whereas many "new rich" people practice *conspicuous consumption,* using homes, cars, and even airplanes as *status symbols* to make a statement about their social position.

Affluent people with greater education and financial security are also more tolerant of controversial behavior such as homosexuality. Working-class people, who grow up in an atmosphere of greater supervision and discipline and are less likely to attend college, tend to be less tolerant (Baltzell, 1979a, orig. 1958; Lareau, 2002; NORC, 2003).

POLITICS

Do political attitudes follow class lines? The answer is yes, but the pattern is complex. A desire to protect wealth prompts well-off people to take a more conservative approach to *economic* issues, favoring, for example, lower taxes. But on *social* matters—such as abortion and gay rights—highly educated, more affluent people are more liberal. People of lower social standing, on the other hand, tend to be economic liberals, favoring government social programs, but typically have more conservative values (NORC, 2003).

A clearer pattern emerges when it comes to political involvement. Higher-income people, who are better served by the system, are more likely to vote and to join political organizations than people with low incomes. In the 2000 presidential election, about half of adults with family incomes of $35,000 voted, compared to three-fourths of those with family incomes of $75,000 (Samuelson, 2003).

FAMILY AND GENDER

Social class also shapes family life. Generally, lower-class families are somewhat larger than middle-class families because of earlier marriage and less use of birth control. Another family pattern is that working-class parents encourage children to conform to conventional norms and respect authority figures. Parents of higher social standing pass on a different "cultural capital" to their children, teaching them to express their individuality and imagination more freely (Kohn, 1977; McLeod, 1995; Lareau, 2002).

Of course, the more money a family has, the better parents can develop their children's talents and abilities. An affluent family earning $100,000 a year will spend $261,270 raising a child born in 2003 to the age of eighteen. Middle-class people, with an average income of $54,100 a year, will spend $178,590, and a lower-class family earning less than $40,700 will spend $130,290 (Lino, 2004). Privilege leads to privilege as family life reproduces the class structure in each generation.

Class also shapes our world of relationships. Elizabeth Bott (1971, orig. 1957) found that most working-class couples divide their responsibilities according to gender roles; middle-class couples, by contrast, are more egalitarian, sharing more activities and expressing greater intimacy. More recently, Karen Walker (1995) discovered that working-class friendships typically serve as sources of material assistance; middle-class friendships are likely to involve shared interests and leisure pursuits.

Social Mobility

Ours is a dynamic society marked by significant social movement. Earning a college degree, landing a higher-paying job, or marrying someone who earns a high income contributes to *upward social mobility*; dropping out of school, losing a job, or becoming divorced (especially for women) may result in *downward social mobility*.

"So long, Bill. This is my club. You can't come in."

© The New Yorker Collection 1979, Robert Weber from cartoonbank.com. All rights reserved.

Over the long term, though, social mobility is not so much a matter of individual changes as changes in society itself. In the first half of the twentieth century, for example, industrialization expanded the U.S. economy, pushing up living standards. Even people who were not good swimmers rode the rising tide of prosperity. More recently, downward structural social mobility has dealt economic setbacks to many people.

Sociologists distinguish between shorter- and longer-term changes in social position. **Intragenerational social mobility** is *a change in social position occurring during a person's lifetime.* **Intergenerational social mobility,** *upward or downward social mobility of children in relation to their parents,* is important because it reveals long-term changes in society that affect almost everyone.

MYTH VERSUS REALITY

In few societies do people think about "getting ahead" as much as in the United States. Moving up, after all, is the American dream. But is there as much social mobility in our country as we like to think?

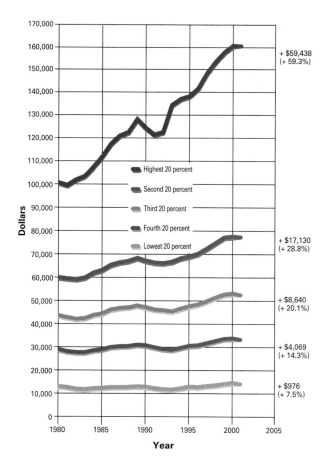

FIGURE 8-4 Mean Income, U.S. Families, 1980–2001 (in 2001 dollars, adjusted for inflation)

Source: U.S. Census Bureau (2004).

Studies of intergenerational mobility (almost all of which, unfortunately, have focused only on men) show that almost 40 percent of the sons of blue-collar workers take white-collar jobs and about 30 percent of sons born into white-collar families end up doing blue-collar work. *Horizontal social mobility*—changing jobs at the same class level—is even more common; overall, about 80 percent of sons showed some type of social mobility in relation to their fathers (Blau & Duncan, 1967; Featherman & Hauser, 1978; Hout, 1998).

Research points to four general conclusions about social mobility in the United States:

1. **Social mobility over the course of the past century has been fairly high.** Mobility is what we would expect in an industrial class system.

2. **The long-term trend in social mobility has been upward.** Industrialization, which greatly expanded the U.S. economy, and the growth of white-collar work over the course of the twentieth century have raised living standards.

3. **Within a single generation, social mobility usually is small.** Most young families increase their income over time as they gain education and skills. A typical family headed by a thirty-year-old earned about $51,000 in 2003; a typical family headed by a fifty-year-old earned $71,000 (U.S. Census Bureau, 2004). Yet only a few people move from "rags to riches" (the way J. K. Rowling did) or lose a lot of money (a number of highly paid rock stars had little money a few years after their records stopped selling). Most social mobility involves small movement *within* one class level rather than large movement *between* classes.

4. **Social mobility since the 1970s has been uneven.** Real income (adjusted for inflation) rose during the twentieth century until the 1970s. Between 1975 and 1985, gains were far smaller. During the 1980s, real income changed little for many people, rising slowly during the 1990s and falling again after 2000. But general trends do not show the experiences of different categories of people, as the next section explains.

MOBILITY BY INCOME LEVEL

In Figure 8–4, we see how U.S. families at different income levels made out between 1980 and 2001. Well-to-do families (the highest 20 percent, but not exactly the same families over the entire period) saw their incomes jump 59 percent, from an average $100,206 in 1980 to $159,644 in 2001. People in the middle of the population also had gains, but more modest ones. The lowest-income 20 percent saw only a 7.5 percent increase in earnings.

For families at the top of the income scale (the highest 5 percent), recent decades have brought a windfall. These families, with average income of almost $150,000 in 1980, were making $280,000 in 2001—almost twice as much (U.S. Census Bureau, 2004).

MOBILITY: RACE, ETHNICITY, AND GENDER

White people in the United States have always been in a more privileged position than people of African or Hispanic descent. Through the economic expansion of the 1980s and 1990s, more African Americans entered the ranks of the wealthy. But overall, the real income of African Americans has changed little in three decades. African American family income as a percentage of white family income was only

Some 1.4 million people in the United States work full time and yet do not earn enough to escape poverty. This hotel worker washes windows to earn $7 an hour or about $14,500 per year. Do you think such workers still have the opportunity to realize the American dream? Why or why not?

slightly higher (62 percent) in 2003 as it was in 1970 (61 percent). Compared with white families, Latino families lost ground between 1975 (when their average income was 67 percent of that of white families) and 2003 (when it had slipped to 61 percent) (Featherman & Hauser, 1978; Pomer, 1986; U.S. Census Bureau, 2004).

Historically, women have had less chance for upward mobility than men because most working women hold clerical jobs (such as secretary) and service positions (such as food server) that offer few opportunities for advancement. When marriages end in divorce (as almost half do), women commonly experience downward social mobility because they may lose not only income but also many benefits, including health care and insurance coverage (Weitzman, 1996).

Over time, the earnings gap between women and men has been narrowing. Women working full time in 1980 earned 60 percent as much as men working full time; by 2003, women earned 76 percent as much. Unfortunately, much of this change resulted from a drop in men's earnings through the 1980s, while the income of women stayed about the same (U.S. Census Bureau, 2004).

THE AMERICAN DREAM: STILL A REALITY?

The expectation of upward social mobility is deeply rooted in U.S. culture. Through much of our history, economic expansion fulfilled this promise by raising living standards. Research shows that for some people, the American dream is still alive and well. In 1967, for example, just 3 percent of U.S. families earned $100,000 or more (in 2001 dollars, to control for inflation); by 2001, this share approached

18 percent. There are now at least 5 million millionaires in the United States, four times the number a decade ago (D'Souza, 1999; Rank & Hirschl, 2001; U.S. Census Bureau, 2004).

Yet not all indicators are so positive. Note these disturbing trends:

1. **For many workers, earnings have stalled.** The annual income of a fifty-year-old man working full time climbed by 49 percent between 1958 and 1974 (from $25,671 to $38,190 in constant 2001 dollars). But between 1974 and 2001, this worker's income rose only slightly, even as the number of hours worked increased and the cost of necessities such as housing, education, and medical care went up substantially (Russell, 1995a; U.S. Census Bureau, 2004).

2. **Multiple job holding is up.** According to the Bureau of Labor Statistics, 4.7 percent of the U.S. labor force worked at two or more jobs in 1975; by 2003, the share had risen to 5.3 percent.

3. **More jobs offer little income.** In 1979, the Census Bureau classified 12 percent of full-time workers as "low-income earners" because they earned less than $6,905; by 1998, 15.4 percent of workers fell into this category, earning less than $15,208 (comparable to the 1979 level when adjusted for inflation).

4. **Young people are remaining at home.** Fully 48 percent of young people aged eighteen to twenty-four are living with their parents. Since 1975, the average age at marriage has moved upward three years (to 25.3 years for women and 27.1 years for men).

As CEOs Get Richer, the Great Mansions Return

I grew up in Elkins Park, Pennsylvania, an older suburban community just to the north of Philadelphia. Elkins Park was and still is a mostly middle-class community, although like most of suburbia, some neighborhoods boast bigger houses than others.

What made Elkins Park special was that scattered over the area were a handful of great mansions, built a century ago by early Philadelphia industrialists. At that time, all there was to the town was these great "estates," along with fields and meadows. By about 1940, however, most of this land had been split off into lots for the homes of newer middle-class suburbanites. The great mansions suddenly seemed out of place, with heirs disagreeing over who should live there and how to pay the rising taxes. As a result, many of the great mansions were sold, the buildings taken down, and the land subdivided.

In the 1960s, when I was a teenager, a short bike ride could take me past the Breyer estate (built by the founder of the ice-cream company, now the township police building), the Curtis estate (built by a magazine publisher and transformed into a community park), and the Wanamaker estate (built by the founder of a large Philadelphia department store, now gone entirely). Probably the grandest of them all was the Wiedner estate, modeled after a French chateau, complete with door knobs and window pulls covered in gold; it now stands empty.

In their day, these structures were not just home to a family and many servants; they were also monuments to a time when the rich were, well, *really* rich. By contrast, the community that emerged on the grounds once owned by

these rich families is middle-class, with homes built on quarter-acre lots.

But did the so-called Gilded Age of great wealth disappear forever? Hardly. By the 1980s, a new wave of great mansions was being built in the United States. Take the architect Thierry Despont, who designs huge houses for the super-rich. One of Despont's "smaller" homes might be 20,000 square feet (about ten times the size of the average U.S. house), and they go all the way up to 60,000 square feet (as big as any of the Elkins Park mansions built a century ago and almost the size of the White House). These megahomes have kitchens as large as a college classroom, exercise rooms, indoor swimming pools, and even indoor tennis courts.

Megahouses are being built by newly rich chief executive officers (CEOs) of large corporations. Although CEOs have always made more money than most people, recent years have seen soaring executive compensation. Between 1970 and 2001, the average U.S. family saw only a modest increase in income (about 10 percent after inflation). According to *Fortune* magazine, during the same period, the

average compensation for the 100 highest-paid CEOs soared from $1.3 million (about 40 times the earnings of an average worker) to $37.5 million, an increase of roughly 2,500 percent (equal to 1,000 times the salary of today's average worker). Some CEOs, of course, earn far more: In the year before Enron collapsed, for example, Kenneth Lay earned about $150 million. Assuming that Lay worked forty-eight hours per week for fifty weeks that year, that amounts to more than $60,000 *per day*.

Some analysts argue that in today's competitive global economy, many CEOs are true "superstars" who build profits and deserve what they earn. Some take a less generous view, suggesting that CEOs have stacked their corporate boards of directors with friends whose "payback" includes approving enormous paychecks and bonuses. In any case, executive pay has become a national scandal. In light of the harm that this pay scandal has done to the corporate world (not to mention cases of outright executive fraud and theft such as those allegedly committed by Kenneth Lay), it appears that we have been living in an era of uncontrolled greed. The question is whether or not this era is coming to an end.

WHAT DO YOU THINK?

1. Do you consider increasing economic inequality a problem? Why or why not?
2. How many times more than an average worker should a CEO earn? Why?
3. Do you think very high CEO pay hurts stockholders? The general public? Why or why not?

Source: Written by the author, with material from Myers (2000) and Krugman (2002).

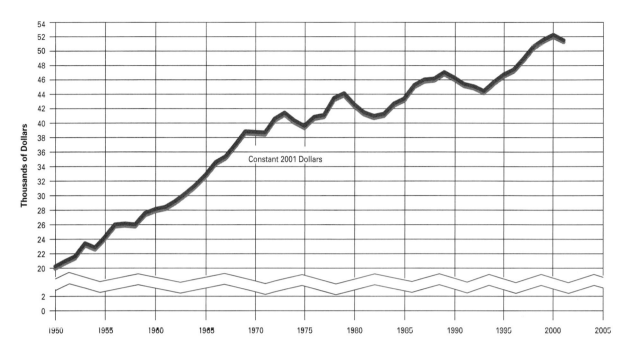

FIGURE 8-5 Median Income, U.S. Families, 1950–2001

Source: U.S. Census Bureau (2004).

Over the last generation, more people have become rich, and the rich have become richer; as the Applying Sociology box explains, the highest-paid corporate executives have enjoyed a runaway rise in their earnings. Yet the rising share of low-paying jobs has also brought downward mobility for millions of families, creating widespread fear that the chance for a middle-class life is slipping away. As Figure 8–5 shows, although median family income doubled between 1950 and 1973, it has grown by only 25 percent since then (Newman, 1993; U.S. Census Bureau, 2004).

THE GLOBAL ECONOMY AND THE U.S. CLASS STRUCTURE

Underlying the shifts in U.S. class structure is global economic change. Much of the industrial production that gave U.S. workers high-paying jobs a generation ago has moved overseas. With less industry at home, the United States now serves as a vast market for industrial goods such as cars, stereos, cameras, and computers made in Japan, South Korea, and elsewhere.

High-paying jobs in manufacturing, held by 26 percent of U.S. workers in 1960, support only 12 percent of workers today. In their place, the economy offers service work, which pays far less. Traditionally high-paying corporations such as USX (formerly United States Steel) now employ fewer people than the expanding McDonald's chain, and fast-food clerks make only a fraction of what steelworkers earn.

The global reorganization of work has not been bad news for everyone. On the contrary, the global economy is driving upward social mobility for educated people who specialize in law, finance, marketing, and computer technology. In addition, global economic expansion has helped push up the stock market (even with the recent declines) almost eightfold between 1980 and 2004, reaping profits for families with money to invest.

But the same trend has hurt many average workers, who have seen their factory jobs move overseas. Many companies have also downsized—cutting the ranks of their workforce—to stay competitive in world markets. As a result, although 60 percent of all families contain two or more workers—more than twice the share in 1950—many families are working harder simply to hold on to what they have (Nelson, 1998; Schlesinger, 1998; Sennett, 1998).

Poverty in the United States

Social stratification creates both "haves" and "have-nots." Thus, all systems of social inequality generate poverty, or at

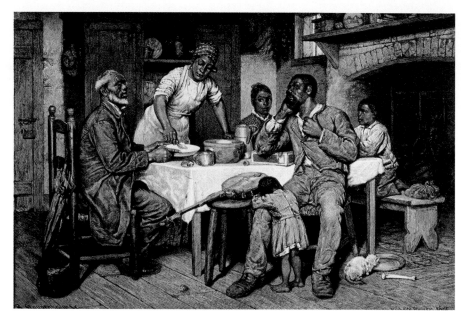

This woodcut from the 1880s showing a family sharing a meal with a visiting pastor captures the humanity and humility of impoverished people. This message—that the poor are human beings, most doing the best they can to get by—is important to remember in a society that tends to define poor people as morally unworthy and deserving of their bitter plight.

North Wind Picture Archives

least **relative poverty,** *the deprivation of some people in relation to those who have more.* A more serious but preventable problem is **absolute poverty,** *a deprivation of resources that is life-threatening.*

As Chapter 9 ("Global Stratification") explains, almost 1 billion human beings around the world—one person in six—are at risk of absolute poverty. Even in the affluent United States, families go hungry, live in inadequate housing, and suffer poor health because of wrenching poverty.

THE EXTENT OF POVERTY

In 2003, the government classified 35.9 million men, women, and children—12.5 percent of the U.S. population—as poor. This count of relative poverty refers to families with income below an official poverty line, which, for a family of four, was set that year at $18,810. The poverty line is about three times what the government estimates a family will spend for food. But the income of the average poor family was just 64 percent of this amount. This means that the typical poor family had to get by on about $12,109 in 2003 (U.S. Census Bureau, 2004).

WHO ARE THE POOR?

Although no single description fits all poor people, poverty is greater among certain categories of our population. Where these categories overlap, the problem is especially serious.

Age. A generation ago, the elderly were at greatest risk for poverty. But thanks to better retirement programs offered today by private employers and government, the poverty rate for people over age sixty-five fell from 30 percent in 1967 to 10.2 percent—well below the national average—in 2003. Looking at it from another angle, about 10 percent (3.6 million) of the poor are elderly people.

Today, the burden of poverty falls most heavily on children. In 2003, 17.6 percent of people under age eighteen (12.9 million children) were poor. Put another way, 36 percent of the U.S. poor are children.

Race and ethnicity. Two-thirds of all poor people are white; 24 percent are African American. But in relation to their overall numbers, African Americans are about three times as likely as non-Hispanic whites to be poor. In 2003, 24.4 percent of African Americans (8.8 million people) lived in poverty, compared with 22.5 percent of Hispanics (9.1 million), 11.8 percent of Asians and Pacific Islanders (1.4 million), and 8.2 percent of non-Hispanic whites (15.9 million). The poverty gap between whites and minorities has changed little since 1975 (U.S. Census Bureau, 2004).

Gender and family patterns. Of all poor people age eighteen or older, 60 percent are women and 40 percent are men. This difference reflects the fact that women who head households are at high risk of poverty. Of all poor families, 51 percent are headed by women with no husband present, and just 8 percent are headed by single men.

This map shows that the poorest counties in the United States—where the poverty rate is more than twice the national average—are in Appalachia, spread across the Deep South, along the border with Mexico, near the Four Corners region of the southwest, and in the Dakotas. Can you suggest some reasons for this pattern?

Source: U.S. Census Bureau (2001).

Percentage of Population below the Poverty Level

- 45.4% to 68.0%
- 26.2% to 43.1%
- 17.2% to 26.1%
- 11.0% to 17.1%
- 0.0% to 10.9%

The term **feminization of poverty** describes *the trend of women making up an increasing proportion of the poor.* In 1960, only 25 percent of all poor households were headed by women; the majority of poor families had both wives and husbands in the home. By 2003, however, the proportion of poor households headed by single women had doubled.

The feminization of poverty is one result of a larger trend: the rapidly increasing number of households at all class levels headed by single women. When this trend is coupled with the fact that households headed by women are at high risk of poverty, it is easy to see why women (and their children) now represent a larger share of the poor in the United States.

Urban and rural poverty. The greatest concentration of poverty is found in central cities, where the 2003 poverty rate stood at 17.5 percent. The poverty rate in suburbs is 9.1 percent. Thus, the poverty rate for urban areas as a whole is 12.1 percent, lower than the 14.2 percent found in rural areas. National Map 8–1 shows the areas of the United States where poverty is most pronounced.

EXPLAINING POVERTY

For the richest nation on Earth to contain tens of millions of poor people raises serious questions. It is true, as some analysts remind us, that most poor people in the United States are far better off than the poor in other countries: For example, 41 percent of U.S. poor families own their home, 70 percent own a car, and only a few percent report often going without food (Rector, 1998; Gallagher, 1999). Nevertheless, poverty harms the overall well-being of millions of people in this country.

What, then, are the causes of poverty? One view holds that *the poor are primarily responsible for their own poverty.* Throughout our history, people in the United States have placed a high value on self-reliance, convinced that social standing is mostly a matter of a person's individual talent and effort. According to this view, society offers plenty of opportunities to anyone able and willing to take advantage of them, and the poor are those who cannot or will not work, women and men with fewer skills, less schooling, and little motivation.

In his study of Latin American cities, the anthropologist Oscar Lewis (1961) concluded that the poor become trapped in a *culture of poverty,* a lower-class subculture that can destroy people's ambition to improve their lives. Socialized in poor families, children become resigned to their situation, producing a self-perpetuating cycle of poverty.

In 1996, hoping to free people from the culture of poverty in the United States, Congress changed the welfare system, which had provided a federal guarantee of financial assistance to poor people since 1935. The federal government continues to send money to the states to distribute to needy people, but benefits carry strict limits—in most cases, no more than two years at a stretch and a total of five years if a person moves in and out of the welfare system. The purpose of this reform is to force people to be self-supporting and move them away from dependence on government.

 A report on food scarcity in the United States is found at this Internet address: http://www.ers.usda.gov/publications/fanrr35/

A different position, argued by William Julius Wilson (1996a, 1996b), holds that *society is primarily responsible for*

CONTROVERSY & DEBATE

The Welfare Dilemma

In 1996, Congress ended federal public assistance, which guaranteed some income to all poor people. The new state-run programs require people who receive aid to get training or find work—or have the benefits cut off.

Almost no one likes welfare. Liberals criticize welfare for doing too little to help the poor, conservatives charge that it hurts the people it is supposed to help, and the poor themselves find welfare a complex and often degrading program.

So what, exactly, is welfare? The term "welfare" refers to an assortment of policies and programs designed to improve the well-being of some of the U.S. population. Until the welfare reform of 1996, most people used the term to refer to one part of the overall system: Aid to Families with Dependent Children (AFDC), a program of monthly financial support to parents (mostly single women) to care for themselves and their children. In 1996, some 5 million households received AFDC for some part of the year.

Did AFDC help or hurt the poor? Conservative critics charge that rather than reducing child poverty, AFDC actually made the problem worse, in two ways. First, they claim that this form of welfare weakened families, because for years after the program began, public assistance regulations provided benefits to poor mothers only if no husband lived in the home. As conservatives see it, AFDC operated as an economic incentive to women to have children outside of marriage, and they blame it for the rapid rise in out-of-wedlock births among poor people. To conservatives, the connection between being poor and not being married is clear: Fewer than one in ten married-couple families were poor, and more than nine out of ten AFDC families were headed by an unmarried woman.

Second, conservatives believe that welfare encouraged poor people to become dependent on government handouts, the main reason that eight out of ten poor heads of households did not have full-time jobs. Furthermore, more than half of nonpoor single mothers worked full time, compared with only 5 percent of single mothers receiving AFDC. Conservatives thus claim that welfare strayed far from its original purpose of short-term help to nonworking women with children (typically, after the death or divorce of a husband) and became a way of life. Once trapped in dependency, poor women are likely to raise children who will themselves be poor as adults.

Liberals charge that their opponents use a double standard in evaluating government programs. Why, they ask, do so many object to the government giving money to poor mothers and their children when most "welfare" actually goes to richer people? The AFDC budget amounted to around $25 billion annually—no small sum, to be sure, but just half of the $50 billion in home mortgage deductions that homeowners pocket each year. And it pales in comparison to the $300 billion in annual Social Security benefits Uncle Sam provides to senior citizens, most of whom are not poor. And what about "corporate welfare" to big companies? Their tax write-offs and other benefits run into hundreds of billions of dollars per year. As liberals see it, "wealthfare" is far more expensive than welfare.

Liberals also claim that conservatives have a distorted picture of public assistance. The popular images of do-nothing "welfare queens" mask the fact that most poor families who turn to public assistance are truly needy. Moreover, the typical household receiving AFDC received barely $400 per month, hardly enough to attract people to a life of welfare dependency. In constant dollars, in fact, AFDC payments actually declined over the years. Liberals therefore fault public assistance as a "Band-Aid approach" to the serious social problems of too few

poverty. Wilson points to the loss of jobs in our inner cities as the primary cause of poverty, claiming that there is simply not enough work to support families. Hence, Wilson sees any apparent lack of trying on the part of the poor as a *result* of little opportunity rather than as a *cause* of poverty. From his point of view, Lewis's analysis amounts to blaming the victims for their own suffering (Ryan, 1976). To combat poverty and reduce the need for welfare, Wilson argues, the government should fund jobs and provide affordable child care for low-income mothers and fathers.

Critical review. The U.S. public is evenly divided over whether government or people themselves should take responsibility for reducing poverty (NORC, 2003), and both sides have evidence to support their positions. Government statistics show that 39 percent of the heads of poor families

jobs and too much income inequality in the United States.

As for the charge that public assistance undermines families, liberals admit that the proportion of single-parent families has risen, but they dispute that AFDC was to blame. Rather, they see single parenting as a broad cultural trend found at all class levels in many countries.

Thus, liberals conclude, programs such as AFDC were attacked not because they have failed but because they benefited a part of the population many consider undeserving. Our cultural tradition of equating wealth with virtue and poverty with vice allows rich people to display privilege as a badge of ability, whereas poverty is a sign of personal failure. According to Richard Sennett and Jonathan Cobb (1973), the negative stigma of poverty is the "hidden injury of class."

The figure at the right shows that people in the United States, more than people in other industrial nations, tend to see poverty as a mark of laziness and personal failure. It should not be surprising, then, that Congress replaced the federal AFDC program with state-run programs called Temporary Assistance for

Needy Families (TANF). States set their own qualification requirements and benefits, but they must limit benefits to two consecutive years, with a lifetime limit of five years.

By 2002, TANF had moved about half of single parents on welfare into jobs or job training. President Bush and other supporters of welfare reform declared the reforms successful. However, opponents point out that

many of the "success stories"—that is, people who are now working—earn so little pay that they are hardly better off than before (and half of these jobs provide no health insurance). In other words, welfare reform has slashed the number of people receiving welfare, but it has done far less to reduce poverty. In addition, say the critics, many of these working women now spend less time with their children. In sum, the welfare debate goes on.

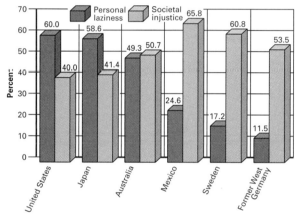

GLOBAL SNAPSHOT

Assessing the Causes of Poverty

Survey Question: "Why are there people in this country who live in need?" Percentages reflect respondents' identification of either "personal laziness" or "societal injustice" as the primary cause of poverty.

Note: Percentages for each country may not add up to 100 because less frequently identified causes of poverty were omitted from this figure.

Source: Inglehart et al. (2000).

CONTINUE THE DEBATE . . .

1. How does our cultural emphasis on self-reliance help explain the controversy surrounding public assistance? Why do people not criticize benefits (such as home mortgage deductions) for more well-to-do people?

2. Do you approve of the benefit time limits built into the TANF program? Why or why not?

3. Why do you think the welfare reforms have done little to reduce poverty?

Sources: Corcoran et al. (2000), U.S. Department of Health and Human Services (2000), Rogers-Dillon (2001), Lichter & Crowley (2002), and Lichter & Jayakody (2002).

did not work at all during 2003, and an additional 31 percent worked only part time (U.S. Census Bureau, 2004). Such facts seem to support the "blame the poor" position because a major cause of poverty is *not holding a job.*

But the *reasons* that people do not work are more in step with the "blame society" position. Middle-class women may be able to combine working and child rearing, but this is much harder for poor women who cannot afford child care,

and few employers provide child care programs. As William Julius Wilson explains, many people are jobless not because they are avoiding work but because there are not enough jobs to go around. In short, most poor people in the United States find few opportunities to improve their lives (Edin & Lein, 1996; Wilson, 1996a; Pease & Martin, 1997; Duncan, 1999).

But not all poor people are jobless, and the *working poor* command the sympathy and support of people on both sides of the poverty debate. In 2003, 19 percent of heads of poor families (1.4 million women and men) worked at least fifty weeks of the year and yet could not escape poverty. Another 31 percent of these heads of families (2.3 million people) remained poor despite part-time employment. Put differently, about 5 percent of full-time workers earn so little that they remain poor (U.S. Census Bureau, 2004). A key cause of working poverty is the fact that a full-time worker earning $6 per hour—above the 2004 minimum wage of $5.15 per hour—cannot lift an urban family of four above the poverty line.

 For a profile of the working poor, visit http://www.bls.gov/cps/cpswp2000.htm

Individual ability and personal initiative do play a part in shaping social position. However, the weight of sociological evidence points toward society—not individual character traits—as the primary source of poverty, because entire *categories* of people—female heads of families, people of color, people in inner-city neighborhoods isolated from the larger society—face special barriers and limited opportunities.

HOMELESSNESS

We have no precise count of homeless people. Fanning out across the United States on the night of March 27, 2000, Census Bureau officials counted 170,706 people at emergency and homeless shelters. But experts estimate that a full count of the homeless would probably reach 500,000 *on any given night,* rising to perhaps three times that number—1.5 million people—*at some time during the course of a year* (U.S. Census Bureau, 2000; Wickham, 2000; Marks, 2001).

The familiar stereotypes of homeless people—men sleeping in doorways and women carrying everything they own in shopping bags—have been replaced by the "new homeless": people thrown out of work because of factory closings, people forced out of apartments by rent increases, and others who cannot meet mortgage or rent payments because of low wages or no work at all. Today, no stereotype paints a complete picture of the homeless.

The majority of homeless people report that they do not work, but 44 percent say they work at least part time (U.S. Department of Housing and Urban Development, 1999). Working or not, all homeless people have one thing in common: poverty. For that reason, the explanations of poverty just presented also apply to homelessness. Some people blame the *personal traits* of the homeless. One-third of homeless people are substance

 Find the HUD report on homelessness at http://www.huduser.org/publications/homeless/homelessness/contents.html

abusers, and one-fourth are mentally ill. More broadly, a fraction of 1 percent of our population, for one reason or another, seems unable to cope with our complex and highly competitive society (Bassuk, 1984; Whitman, 1989).

Others see homelessness resulting from *societal factors,* including low wages and a lack of low-income housing (Kozol, 1988; Schutt, 1989; Bohannan, 1991). Supporters of this position point out that one-third of the homeless consist of entire families, and children are the fastest-growing category of the homeless.

No one disputes that a large proportion of homeless people are personally impaired to some degree, although how much is cause and how much is effect is difficult to untangle. But structural changes in the U.S. economy, reduced aid to low-income people, and a real estate market that puts housing out of reach of the poorest members of U.S. society all contribute to homelessness.

CLASS, WELFARE, POLITICS, AND VALUES

We have reviewed many facts about social inequality. In the end, however, our opinions about wealth and poverty depend not just on facts but also on our politics and values. As we might expect, the idea that social standing reflects personal merit is popular among well-off people; the opposing idea, that society should spread wealth more equally, finds favor among those who are less well off (NORC, 2003).

In the United States, our cultural emphasis on individual responsibility encourages us to see successful people as personally worthy and to view poor people as personally lacking. Such attitudes go a long way toward explaining why our society spends much more than other high-income nations on education (to promote opportunity) but much less on public assistance programs (which directly support the poor).

Most members of our society are willing to accept a high level of income inequality, and many hold a harsh view of the poor. To the extent that we define poor people as undeserving, we look on public assistance programs as at best a waste of money and at worst a threat to personal initiative. The Controversy & Debate box on pages 218–19 takes a closer look at recent welfare reforms.

Finally, the drama of social stratification extends far beyond the borders of the United States. The most striking social inequality is found not by looking inside one country but by comparing living standards in various parts of the world. In Chapter 9, we broaden our focus by investigating global stratification.

SUMMARY

1. Social stratification refers to categories of people ranked in a hierarchy. Caste systems, common in agrarian societies, are based on ascription (birth) and permit little or no social mobility. Class systems are found in industrial societies and allow social mobility based on individual achievement.

2. The Davis-Moore thesis states that social stratification is universal because it is useful to a society. In class systems, unequal rewards attract the ablest people to the most important jobs.

3. According to Karl Marx, conflict in industrial societies places the capitalists, who own the means of production and seek profits, in opposition to the proletariat, who provide labor in exchange for wages.

4. Max Weber identified three distinct dimensions of social stratification: economic class, social status or prestige, and power. Together, these form a multidimensional hierarchy of socioeconomic status (SES).

5. Gerhard Lenski explained that historically, advancing technology tends to increase social inequality. Some reversal of this trend occurs in industrial societies, as represented by the Kuznets curve; even so, the new postindustrial society shows an increase in economic inequality.

6. The upper class (5 percent of the population) includes this country's richest, most powerful individuals. Those in the upper-upper class (the "old rich") typically inherit wealth; those in the lower-upper class ("new rich") work for their income.

7. The middle class (40 to 45 percent) enjoys reasonable financial security, but only some of these people (the upper-middle class) have significant wealth. With below-average incomes, members of the working class or lower-middle class (33 percent) typically perform blue-collar work, and only one-third of their children attend college.

8. About one-fifth of the U.S. population belongs to the lower class, defined as people living at or below the government's poverty line. People of African and Hispanic descent, as well as women, are disproportionately represented in the lower class.

9. Social mobility is common in the United States, as it is in other industrial societies; typically, however, there are only small changes from one generation to the next.

10. The growing global economy has increased the wealth of rich families in the United States but stalled or even lowered the standard of living of low-income families.

11. The government classifies 35.9 million people as poor. About 36 percent of the poor are under age eighteen.

12. The "culture of poverty" thesis suggests that poverty is caused by shortcomings in the poor themselves. An alternative approach claims that poverty is caused by a society's unequal distribution of income and wealth.

13. The U.S. cultural emphasis on individual responsibility helps explain why public assistance for the poor is controversial.

KEY CONCEPTS

social stratification (p. 192) a system by which a society ranks categories of people in a hierarchy

social mobility (p. 192) a change in position within the social hierarchy

caste system (p. 193) social stratification based on ascription, or birth

class system (p. 195) social stratification based on both birth and individual achievement

meritocracy (p. 195) social stratification based on personal merit

status consistency (p. 195) the degree of consistency in a person's social standing across various dimensions of social inequality

structural social mobility (p. 197) a shift in the social position of large numbers of people due more to changes in society than to individual efforts

ideology (p. 198) cultural beliefs that justify particular social arrangements, including patterns of inequality

Davis-Moore thesis (p. 199) the assertion that social stratification exists in every society because it has beneficial consequences for the operation of society

capitalists (p. 200) people who own and operate factories and other businesses in pursuit of profits

proletarians (p. 200) people who sell their productive labor for wages

alienation (p. 200) the experience of isolation and misery resulting from powerlessness

blue-collar occupations (p. 201) lower-prestige jobs that involve mostly manual labor

white-collar occupations (p. 201) higher-prestige jobs that involve mostly mental activity

socioeconomic status (SES) (p. 202) a composite ranking based on various dimensions of social inequality

income (p. 205) wages or salary from work and earnings from investments

wealth (p. 205) the total value of money and other assets, minus outstanding debts

intragenerational social mobility (p. 211) a change in social position occurring during a person's lifetime

intergenerational social mobility (p. 211) upward or downward social mobility of children in relation to their parents

relative poverty (p. 216) the deprivation of some people in relation to those who have more

absolute poverty (p. 216) a deprivation of resources that is life-threatening

feminization of poverty (p. 217) the trend of women making up an increasing proportion of the poor

CRITICAL-THINKING QUESTIONS

1. How is social stratification a creation of society rather than simply an expression of individual differences?

2. How do caste and class systems differ? What do they have in common? In what ways does industrialization introduce a measure of meritocracy to social stratification?

3. Would you be in favor of class-based affirmative action? That is, should U.S. society give people born to lower-class families an advantage in college admissions and company hiring? Why or why not?

4. Our society is always ready to assist the "worthy" poor, including elderly people, whom we do not expect to take care of themselves. At the same time, we are less generous toward the "unworthy poor," healthy people who, we think, could take care of themselves but apparently do not. If this is so, why has U.S. society not done more to reduce poverty among children, who surely fall into the "worthy" category?

APPLICATIONS AND EXERCISES

1. Sit down with parents, grandparents, or other relatives, and assess the social position of your family over the last three generations. Has social mobility taken place? How much? Why?

2. Develop several simple questions that, taken together, would let you measure someone's social class position. The trick is to decide exactly what you think social class really means. Then try your questions on several adults, refining the questions as you proceed.

3. During an evening of television viewing, assess the social class of the characters you see on various shows. In each case,

explain why you assign someone a specific social class position. What patterns do you find?

4. Packaged in the back of this new textbook is an interactive CD-ROM that offers a variety of video and interactive review materials intended to help you better understand the material covered in this chapter. For this chapter, the CD-ROM contains a relevant clip from *ABC News*, an author's tip video, interactive map animations, an interactive timeline, and flashcards with audio pronunciations of the more difficult words.

 SITES TO SEE

http://www.prenhall.com/macionis

Visit the interactive Companion Website™ that accompanies this text. Begin by clicking on the cover of your book. You will find a chapter-by-chapter study guide, practice tests, suggested Web links, and links to other relevant material.

http://www.bea.doc.gov

This site, run by the U.S. government's Bureau of Economic Analysis, provides income data by county and many other statistics about economic inequality. See what you can learn about social standing in your part of the country.

http://www.usmayors.org/uscm/news/press_releases/documents/hunger_121803.asp

This is a recent report on hunger in the United States.

http://www.iwpr.org

The Institute for Women's Policy Research investigates the links between gender and poverty.

http://www.ssc.wisc.edu/irp
http://www.jcpr.org
http://www.nber.org

Here are three Web sites that are worth a visit to learn more about poverty in the United States. The first is operated by the Institute for Research on Poverty, the second by the Joint Center for Poverty Research, and the third by the National Bureau of Economic Research.

http://www.researchforum.org
http://www.childrensdefense.org/

In the United States, children are at high risk of poverty. The two sites noted here introduce you to the Research Forum at the National Center for Children in Poverty and the Children's Defense Fund, organizations concerned with child poverty.

http://www.journalofpoverty.org

This site describes a journal that focuses on poverty issues.

 INVESTIGATE WITH RESEARCH NAVIGATOR™

Follow the instructions on page 32 of this text to access the features of **Research Navigator™.** Once at the Web site, enter your Login Name and Password. Then, to use the **ContentSelect™** database, enter keywords such as "social class," "poverty," "apartheid," and "homelessness," and the search engine will supply relevant and

recent scholarly and popular press publications. Use the *New York Times* **Search-by-Subject Archive** to find recent news articles related to sociology and the **Link Library** feature to find relevant Web links organized by key terms associated with this chapter.

October 20, 2003

Are Those Leaving Welfare Better Off Now? Yes and No

By LESLIE KAUFMAN

By many measures, the overhaul of welfare has been a success. Seven years after Congress rewrote the rules in an effort to end long-term dependency on benefits, hundreds of thousands of Americans have moved from welfare to work, many of them substantially raising their incomes. . . .

But several recent studies by state governments and urban-policy researchers point to a result that has been less obvious and slower to emerge: a significant number of those who have left the welfare rolls have no jobs, and are sinking deeper into poverty. . . .

There are 2.4 million fewer American families on the federal welfare rolls than in 1996, when there were 4.4 million.

More than half have left welfare for work, although many who left for jobs did not keep them. Others have gone off welfare voluntarily, possibly because they chafed under the new rules or turned to other sources of support. And roughly a third have been forced out because they failed to comply with stricter state requirements or reached the five-year lifetime limit on federal benefits. . . .

Many urban-policy researchers and advocates for the poor . . . argue that the deepening poverty among former welfare recipients reflects flaws in the legislation that were entirely predictable and need to be corrected.

They say the people who are losing ground face all sorts of obstacles that keep them from work . . . like learning disabilities, depression, minor illnesses or a lack of transportation. Families with more obvious handicaps are frequently exempted from the work rules under the 1996 law. . . .

Census Bureau figures for 2002 showed the number of people living in severe poverty with incomes less than half of the poverty rate had grown by 600,000 over the previous year. . . . Researchers say they suspect many of the new severely poor are people who left welfare, because benefits automatically lift families out of this lowest category.

Tracy Lawrence, 34, a single mother in Hartford, was cut off from benefits two years ago after she reached her lifetime limit. Ms. Lawrence insists her chronic stomach problems make her too sick to work, but has not been able to provide adequate proof to state authorities to be exempted from the work rules. Welfare was not her only income. She also received and still receives food stamps, gifts from her mother and small child-support payments from the father of her 6-year-old daughter. Perhaps most important, she pays only $77 a month for rent in state housing.

Still, she says life is much harder without the federal check. "I can't buy shampoo or personal care items because they are not covered by food stamps," she said. Clothing is not covered, either, and she said she had been unable to find her daughter a winter coat or snow boots at local charities. She has received a notice of eviction because she is months behind on her rent, and fears her phone will be cut off as well. . . .

Cynthia Brown of New Haven is also feeling the pinch. Ms. Brown, 31, who says she is healthy, has spent most of her life on welfare. . . . In 2001, Connecticut denied her benefits, saying she had already hit her lifetime limit. Ms. Brown and her three children did not cope well. They lived with an aunt in public housing until she made them leave, fearing the overcrowding would cause her to lose her lease. They lived in a park for a week and then in a homeless shelter for three months, until Ms. Brown obtained subsidized housing and a year's extension on welfare. . . .

Two months before the extension will expire, Ms. Brown says she is earnestly looking for work but has not found any. She was briefly employed at Yale as a cook, but says she lost the job after her cutting skills were found wanting. Now, she says, her only chance is that something in her life will go so wrong that she will be exempted from the state's rules.

"I am hoping for a disaster," she said.

WHAT DO YOU THINK?

1. Do you think people on welfare should be required to look for work? What role should the government play in helping them find work?

2. Do you consider the 1996 welfare reform to be a success or not? Explain.

Adapted from the original article by Leslie Kaufman published in *The New York Times* on October 20, 2003. Copyright © 2003 by The New York Times Company. Reprinted with permission.

CHAPTER NINE

Global Stratification

What share of the world's people live in absolute poverty?

Why are some of the world's countries so rich
and others so poor?

Are rich nations making global poverty
better or worse? How?

Around the world, tens of millions of children grow up in severe poverty. This eight-year-old boy ▶ lives and works in a garbage dump in Manila, capital city of the Philippines.

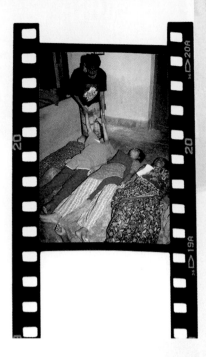

More than 1,000 workers were busily sewing together polo shirts on the fourth floor of the garment factory in Narsingdi, a small town about thirty miles northeast of Bangladesh's capital city of Dhaka. The thumping of hundreds of sewing machines produced a steady roar throughout the long working day.

But in an instant everything changed when an electric gun used to shoot spot remover onto stained fabric gave off a spark, which ignited the cloth soaked in flammable liquid. Suddenly, a whole work table burst into flames. Nearby workers rushed to smother the fire with shirts, but there was no stopping the blaze: In a room filled with combustible materials, the flames spread quickly.

The workers scrambled toward the narrow staircase that led to the street. At the bottom, however, the human wave pouring down the steep steps collided with a folding metal gate, stretched across the doorway and locked to keep workers from leaving. Panicked, the people at the front turned, only to be pushed back by the hundreds behind them. In a single terrifying minute of screaming voices, thrusting legs, and pounding hearts, dozens were crushed and trampled. By the time the gates were opened and the fire put out, fifty-two garment workers lay dead.

Garment factories like this one are big business in Bangladesh, where clothing accounts for 75 percent of the country's total economic exports. Half of these garments end up in clothing stores in the United States. The reason so much of the clothing we buy is made in poor countries like Bangladesh is simple economics—Bangladeshi garment workers labor for close to twelve hours a day, typically every day of the week, and yet earn only $400 to $500 a year, which is just a few percent of what a garment worker makes in the United States.

Tanveer Chowdhury manages this garment factory, which is owned by his family. He complained bitterly to reporters about the tragedy. "This fire has cost me $586,373, and that does not include $70,000 for machinery and $20,000 for furniture. I made commitments to meet deadlines, and I still have the deadlines. I am now paying for air freight at $10 a dozen when I should be shipping by sea at 87 cents a dozen."

There was one other cost Mr. Chowdhury did not mention. To compensate families for the loss of their loved ones in the fire, the factory eventually agreed to pay $1,952 per person. In Bangladesh, life—like labor—is cheap (based on Bearak, 2001).

These garment workers in Bangladesh are part of the roughly 1 billion of the world's people who work hard every day and yet remain poor. As this chapter explains, although poverty is a reality in the United States and other nations, the greatest social inequality is not *within* nations but *between* them (Goesling, 2001). We can understand the full dimensions of poverty only by exploring **global stratification**, *patterns of social inequality in the world as a whole.*

Global Stratification: An Overview

Chapter 8 ("Social Stratification") described inequality in the United States. In global perspective, however, social stratification is far greater. Figure 9–1 divides the world's total income by fifths of the population. Recall from Chapter 8 that the richest 20 percent of the U.S. population earns about 48 percent of the national income (see Figure 8–3 on page 205). However, the richest 20 percent of the global population receives about 80 percent of world income. At the other extreme, the poorest 20 percent of the U.S. population earns 4 percent of our national income; the poorest fifth of the world's people, by contrast, struggles to survive on just 1 percent of global income.

Because global income is so concentrated, even people in the United States with income below the government's poverty line live far better than the majority of the Earth's people. The average person in a rich nation such as the United States is extremely well-off by world standards. At the top of the pyramid, the world's richest person (Bill Gates in the United States, who was worth about $47 billion in 2004) has more wealth than the world's forty-six poorest *countries* (United Nations Development Programme, 2004; Kroll & Goldman, 2004).

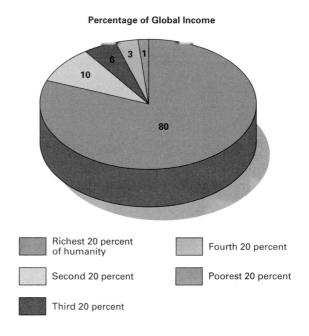

Percentage of Global Income

- Richest 20 percent of humanity
- Second 20 percent
- Third 20 percent
- Fourth 20 percent
- Poorest 20 percent

FIGURE 9-1   Distribution of World Income

Sources: Calculated by the author based on United Nations Development Programme (2000) and World Bank (2001).

A WORD ABOUT TERMINOLOGY

Classifying the 192 nations on Earth into categories ignores many striking differences. These nations have rich and varied histories, speak different languages, and take pride in their distinctive cultures. However, models have been developed that help distinguish countries on the basis of global stratification.

One such model, developed after World War II, labeled the rich, industrial countries the "First World"; the less industrialized, socialist countries the "Second World"; and the nonindustrialized, poor countries the "Third World." But the "three worlds" model is less useful today. For one thing, it grew out of Cold War politics, when the capitalist West (the First World) faced off against the socialist East (the Second World) while other nations (the Third World) remained more or less on the sidelines. But the sweeping changes in Eastern Europe and the collapse of the former Soviet Union means that a distinctive Second World no longer exists.

A second problem is that the "three worlds" model lumped together more than 100 countries as the Third World. In reality, some better-off nations of the Third World (such as Chile in South America) have thirteen times the per-person productivity seen in the poorest countries of the world (including Ethiopia in eastern Africa).

These facts call for a modestly revised system of classification. Here, we define the fifty **high-income countries** as *the richest nations with the highest overall standards of living*. The world's eighty **middle-income countries** are somewhat poorer; they are *nations with a standard of living about average for the world as a whole*. The remaining sixty **low-income countries** are *nations with a low standard of living in which most people are poor*.

This model has two advantages over the "three worlds" system. First, it focuses on economic development rather than whether societies are capitalist or socialist. Second, it gives a better picture of the relative economic development of various countries because it does not lump together all lower-income nations into a single "Third World" category.

Keep in mind that every country is also a stratified society. In Bangladesh, members of the Chowdhury family, who own the garment factory described in the opening vignette, earn as much as $1 million per year, which is several thousand times more than one of their workers earns. Worldwide, the full extent of global inequality is even greater than national comparisons suggest because the most well-off people in rich countries (such as the United States) live worlds apart from the poorest people in low-income countries (such as Bangladesh, Haiti, and Sudan).

Japan represents the world's high-income countries, in which industrial technology and economic expansion have produced material prosperity. The presence of market forces is evident in this view of downtown Tokyo (above, left). The Russian Federation represents the middle-income countries of the world. Industrial development and economic performance were sluggish under socialism; as a result, Moscow residents had to wait in long lines for their daily needs (above, right). The hope is that the introduction of a market system will raise living standards, although in the short run, Russian citizens must adjust to increasing economic inequality. Bangladesh (left) represents the world's low-income countries. As the photograph suggests, these nations have limited economic development and rapidly increasing populations. The result is widespread poverty.

HIGH-INCOME COUNTRIES

In nations where the Industrial Revolution first took place more than two centuries ago, productivity increased more than one-hundredfold. Industrial technology—and the even newer technology that is part of the Information Revolution—is extremely powerful: The small European nation of the Netherlands is more productive than the vast continent of Africa south of the Sahara, and tiny South Korea outproduces all of India.

Look back at Global Map 1–2 on page 7, which identifies the fifty high-income countries of the world. They include the United States and Canada, Argentina, the nations of Western Europe, Israel, Saudi Arabia, South Africa, Singapore, Hong Kong (now part of the People's Republic of China), Japan, South Korea, Australia, and New Zealand.

These countries cover roughly 25 percent of the Earth's land area, including parts of five continents, and lie mostly in the Northern Hemisphere. In 2004, the population of these nations was about 1 billion, or about 18 percent of the Earth's people. About three-fourths of the people in high-income countries live in or near cities.

Significant cultural differences exist among high-income countries; for example, the nations of Europe recognize more than thirty official languages. But these societies have something in common: They all produce enough economic goods to enable their people to lead a comfortable material life. Per capita annual income—that is, average income per person in a year—ranges from about $10,000 annually (in Lithuania and South Africa) to more than $35,000 annually (in the United States and Norway).[1] In fact, people in high-income countries enjoy 79 percent of the world's total income.

Production in rich nations is capital-intensive; that is, it is based on factories, big machinery, and advanced technology. Most of the largest corporations that design and market computers, as well as most of the world's computer

---

[1]High-income countries have per capita annual incomes of more than $10,000. For middle-income countries, per capita annual income is $2,500–$10,000 and for low-income countries, less than $2,500. All data reflect the United Nations' concept of purchasing power parities, which is an estimate of what people can buy using their income in the local economy.

When natural disasters strike high income countries, property loss is great but loss of life is low. In low-income countries, the converse is true: Poor people have less property to lose, but many die.

users, are located in high-income countries. High-income countries also control the world's financial markets, so that daily events on the stock exchanges of New York, London, and Tokyo affect people throughout the world.

MIDDLE-INCOME COUNTRIES

Middle-income countries have per capita annual incomes ranging from $2,500 to $10,000. Note that these figures are average for the world's *nations* but above that for the world's *people* because most people live in the poorest countries. Two-thirds of the people in middle-income countries live in cities, and industrial jobs are common. The remaining one-third of the people live in rural areas, where most are poor and lack access to schools, medical care, adequate housing, and even safe drinking water.

Looking back at Global Map 1–2 (page 7), we see that more than eighty of the world's nations fall in the middle-income category. At the high end are Chile (Latin America), Latvia (Europe), and Malaysia (Asia), where annual income is about $9,000. At the low end are Ecuador (Latin America), Morocco (Africa), and Indonesia (Asia), with roughly $3,000 annually in per capita income.

One cluster of middle-income countries includes the countries that once made up the Soviet Union and the nations of Eastern Europe (formerly known as the Second World). These countries had mostly socialist economies until popular revolts between 1989 and 1991 swept their governments aside. Since then, these nations have begun to introduce free-market systems, but so far the results have been uneven. Some (including Poland) have improving economies, but living standards in others (including Russia) have fallen.

The remaining middle-income nations include Chile and Brazil in South America, as well as Namibia and Botswana in Africa. Recently, both India and the People's Republic of China entered the middle-income category, which now includes most of Asia.

Taken together, middle-income countries span roughly 55 percent of the Earth's land area and are home to about 4.5 billion people, or about 70 percent of humanity. Some countries (such as Russia) are far less crowded than others (such as El Salvador), but compared with high-income countries, these societies on the whole are densely populated.

LOW-INCOME COUNTRIES

Low-income countries, where most people are very poor, are mostly agrarian societies with some industry. Most of these sixty nations, identified in Global Map 1–2, are found in Central and East Africa as well as Asia. Low-income countries cover 20 percent of the planet's land area and are home to 12 percent of its people. Population density is generally high, although it is greater in Asian countries (such as Bangladesh and Pakistan) than in Central African nations (such as Chad and the Democratic Republic of the Congo).

In poor countries, one-third of the people live in cities; most inhabit villages and farms as their ancestors have done

DIVERSITY: RACE, CLASS, & GENDER

Las Colonias: "America's Third World"

"We wanted to have something for ourselves," explains Olga Ruiz, who has lived in the border community of College Park, Texas, for eleven years. There is no college in College Park, nor does this dusty stretch of rural land even have water or sewer lines. Yet this town is one of some 1,800 settlements that have sprouted up in southern Texas along the 1,200-mile border with Mexico that runs from El Paso down to Brownsville; these towns are home to between 500,000 and 700,000 people, numbers expected to pass 1 million within five years.

Many people speak of *las colonias* (Spanish for "the colonies") as "America's Third World" because these desperately poor communities look much like their counterparts in Mexico or many other middle- or low-income nations. But almost all of the people living in the *colonias* are Hispanic Americans, 85 percent of them are legal residents, and more than half are U.S. citizens.

Anastacia Ledsema, now 72 years old, moved to a *colonia* called Sparks more than forty years ago. Born in Mexico, Ledsema married a Texas man, and together they paid $200 for

a one-quarter-acre lot in a new border community. For months, they camped out on their land. Step by step, however, they invested their labor and their money to build a modest house. But only seven years ago did their small community get running water—a service promised by developers years before. After the water line came, things changed more than they expected. "When we got water," recalls Ledsema, "that's when so many people came in." The population of Sparks quickly doubled to about 3,000, overwhelming the water supply.

The residents of all the *colonias* know that they are poor. Indeed, the Census Bureau recently declared one

colonia to be the poorest county in the entire United States. Concerned over the lack of basic services in so many of these communities, Texas officials have banned any new settlements. But most of the people who move here—even those who start off sleeping in their cars or trucks—see these communities as the first step on the path to the "American dream." Oscar Solis, a neighborhood leader in Panorama Village, with a population of about 150, is proud to show visitors around the small but growing town. "All of this work we have done ourselves," he says with a smile, "to make our dream come true."

WHAT DO YOU THINK?

1. Are you surprised that such poverty exists in the United States?
2. Why do you think such communities get little attention in the mass media?
3. What special challenges do people living in these communities face in trying to improve their lives?

Source: Based on Schaffer (2002).

for centuries. In fact, half the world's people are farmers, most of whom follow cultural traditions. With limited industrial technology, they are not very productive—one reason that many endure severe poverty. Hunger, disease, and unsafe housing frame the lives of the world's poorest people.

People living in rich nations such as the United States find it hard to grasp the extent of human poverty in much

of the world. From time to time, televised pictures of famine in very poor countries such as Ethiopia and Bangladesh give us shocking glimpses into the poverty that makes every day a life-and-death struggle for many in low-income nations. Behind these images lie cultural, historical, and economic forces that we shall explore in the remainder of this chapter.

Global Wealth and Poverty

October 14, Manila, the Philippines. What caught my eye was how clean she was: a girl no more than seven or eight years old, wearing a freshly washed dress and with her hair carefully combed. She followed us with her eyes: Camera-toting Americans stand out in this, one of the poorest neighborhoods in the entire world.

Fed by methane from the decomposing garbage, the fires never go out on Smokey Mountain, the vast garbage dump on the north side of Manila that is home to thousands of people. The smoke envelops the hills of refuse like a thick fog. It is hard to imagine a setting more hostile to human life. Amid the smoke and the squalor, men and women do what they can to survive. They pick plastic bags from the garbage and wash them in the river and collect cardboard boxes or anything else they can sell. What chance do their children have, in families that earn a few hundred dollars a year? With barely any opportunity for schooling? Year after year, breathing this air? Against this backdrop of human tragedy, one lovely little girl has put on a fresh dress and gone out to play.

Now our taxi driver threads his way through heavy traffic as we head for the other side of Manila. The change is amazing: The smoke and smell of the dump give way to neighborhoods that could be in Miami or Los Angeles. In the distance, a cluster of yachts floats on the bay. No more rutted streets; now we glide quietly along wide, tree-lined boulevards filled with expensive Japanese cars. We pass shopping plazas, upscale hotels, and high-rise office buildings. Every block or so we see the gated entrance to an exclusive residential enclave with security guards standing watch. Here, in air-conditioned homes, the rich of Manila live and many of the poor work.

Low-income nations are home to some rich and many poor people. The fact that most people live with incomes of a few hundred dollars a year means the burden of poverty is far greater than among the poor of the United States. This does not mean that poverty here is a minor problem. In so rich a country, too little food, substandard housing, and no medical care for tens of millions of people—almost half of them children—amount to a national tragedy. The Diversity box profiles the striking poverty that exists along the southwestern border of the United States. Yet poverty in

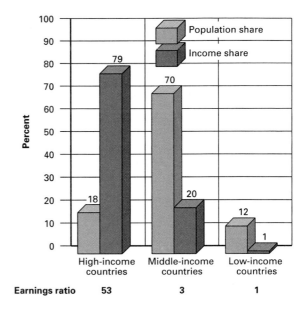

FIGURE 9-2 The Relative Share of Income and Population by Level of Economic Development

Sources: Calculated by the author based on United Nations Development Programme (2000) and World Bank (2001).

poor countries is both more severe and more widespread than in the United States.

THE SEVERITY OF POVERTY

Poverty in poor countries is more severe than it is in rich countries. A key reason that quality of life differs so much around the world is that economic productivity is lowest in precisely the regions where population growth is highest. Figure 9–2 shows the proportion of global population and global income for countries at each level of economic development. High-income countries are by far the most advantaged, with 79 percent of global income supporting just 18 percent of humanity. In middle-income nations, 70 percent of the world's people earn 20 percent of global income. This leaves 12 percent of the planet's population with just 1 percent of global income. For every dollar received by an individual in a low-income country, someone in a high-income nation takes home $53.

Table 9–1 on page 232 shows the extent of wealth and well-being in specific countries around the world. The first column of figures gives gross domestic product (GDP) for a number of high-, middle-, and low-income countries.[2] The

---

[2]Gross domestic product (GDP) is the value of all the goods and services produced by a country's economy in a given year within its borders.

TABLE 9-1

Wealth and Well-Being in Global Perspective, 2002

Country	Gross Domestic Product (US$ billions)	GDP per Capita (PPP US$)*	Quality of Life Index
High Income			
Norway	191	36,600	.956
Sweden	240	26,050	.946
Australia	409	28,260	.946
Canada	714	29,480	.943
United States	10,383	35,750	.939
Japan	3,993	26,940	.938
United Kingdom	1,566	26,150	.936
France	1,431	26,920	.932
South Korea	477	16,950	.888
Middle Income			
Eastern Europe			
Latvia	8	9,210	.823
Russian Federation	347	8,230	.795
Romania	46	6,560	.778
Ukraine	42	4,870	.777
Latin America			
Mexico	637	8,970	.802
Venezuela	94	5,380	.778
Brazil	452	7,770	.775
Asia			
Malaysia	95	9,120	.793
Thailand	127	7,010	.768
People's Republic of China	1,266	4,580	.745
Middle East			
Iran	108	6,690	.732
Syria	21	3,620	.710
Africa			
Algeria	56	5,760	.704
Botswana	5	8,170	.589
Low Income			
Latin America			
Bolivia	8	2,460	.681
Haiti	3	1,610	.463
Asia			
Bangladesh	48	1,700	.509
Pakistan	59	1,940	.497
Africa			
Guinea	3	2,100	.425
Democratic Republic of the Congo	6	650	.365
Ethiopia	6	780	.359
Sierra Leone	1	520	.273

*These data are the United Nations' purchasing power parity (PPP) calculations, which avoid currency rate distortion by showing the local purchasing power of each domestic currency.

Source: United Nations Development Programme, *Human Development Report 2004* (New York: United Nations Development Programme, 2004).

United States, a large industrial nation, had a 2002 GDP of about $10 trillion; Japan's GDP that same year was about $4 trillion. The world's richest nations are thousands of times more productive than the poorest countries.

The second column of figures in Table 9–1 divides GDP by the entire population size to give an estimate of what people can buy using their income in the local economy. The per capita GDP for the richest high-income countries, including the United States, Sweden, and Canada, is very high, exceeding $26,000. For middle-income countries, such as Botswana and the Russian Federation, the figures are in the $8,000 range. In the world's low-income countries, per capita GDP is just a few hundred dollars. In the Democratic Republic of the Congo, a typical person labors all year to make what the average worker in the United States earns in a week.

The last column of Table 9–1 is a measure of quality of life in the various nations. This index, calculated by the United Nations, combines income, education (extent of adult literacy and average years of schooling), and longevity (how long people typically live). Index values are decimals that fall between extremes of one (highest) and zero (lowest). By this calculation, Norwegians enjoy the highest quality of life (.956), with residents of the United States close behind (.939). At the other extreme, people in the African nation of Sierra Leone have the lowest quality of life (.273).

Relative versus absolute poverty. The distinction between relative and absolute poverty, made in Chapter 8, has an

 Find a report by the World Bank on strategies to reduce global poverty at http://www1.worldbank.org/publications/pdfs/14978frontmat.pdf

important application to global inequality. People living in rich countries generally focus on *relative poverty*, meaning that some people lack resources that are taken for granted by others. By definition, relative poverty exists in every society, rich or poor.

More important in global perspective, however, is *absolute poverty*, a lack of resources that is life-threatening. Human beings in absolute poverty lack the nutrition necessary for health and long-term survival. To be sure, some absolute poverty exists in the United States. But such immediately life-threatening poverty strikes only a small proportion of the U.S. population; in low-income countries, by contrast, one-third or more of the people are in desperate need.

Because absolute poverty is deadly, one global indicator of this problem is the median age at death. Global Map 9–1 identifies the age by which half of all people born in a nation die. In rich countries, most people die after the age of seventy-five, but in poor countries, half of all deaths occur among children under the age of ten.

WINDOW ON THE WORLD

GLOBAL MAP 9–1 Median Age at Death in Global Perspective

This map identifies the age below which half of all deaths occur in any year. In the high-income countries of the world, including the United States, it is mostly the elderly who face death, that is, people aged seventy-five or older. In middle-income countries, including most of Latin America, most people die years or even decades earlier. In low-income countries, especially in Africa and parts of Asia, it is children who die, half of them never reaching their tenth birthday.

Sources: World Bank (1993), with updates by the author; map projection from *Peters Atlas of the World* (1990).

THE EXTENT OF POVERTY

Poverty in poor countries is more widespread than it is in rich nations such as the United States. Chapter 8 ("Social Stratification") indicated that the U.S. government officially classifies about 12 percent of the population as poor. In low-income countries, however, most people live no better than the poor in the United States, and many are far worse off. As Global Map 9–1 shows, the high death rates among children in Africa indicate that absolute poverty is greatest there, where half the population is malnourished. In the world as a whole, at any given time, 15 percent of the people—about 1 billion—suffer from chronic hunger, which leaves them less able to work and puts them at high risk of

Tens of millions of children fend for themselves on the streets of Latin America, where many fall victim to disease, drug abuse, and outright violence. What do you think must be done to put an end to scenes like this one in San Salvador, the capital city of El Salvador?

disease (Kates, 1996; United Nations Development Programme, 2001).

The typical adult in a rich nation such as the United States consumes about 3,500 calories a day, an excess that contributes to obesity and related health problems. The typical adult in a low-income country not only does more physical labor but consumes just 2,000 calories a day. The result is undernourishment: too little food or not enough of the right kinds of food.

In the ten minutes it takes to read through this section of the chapter, about 300 people in the world who are sick and weakened from hunger will die. This amounts to about 40,000 people a day, or 15 million people each year. Clearly, easing world hunger is one of the most serious challenges facing humanity today.

POVERTY AND CHILDREN

Death comes early in poor societies, where families lack adequate food, safe drinking water, secure housing, and access to medical care. Organizations fighting child poverty estimate that at least 100 million city children in poor countries beg, steal, sell sex, or work for drug gangs to provide income for their families. Such a life almost always means dropping out of school and places children at high risk of disease and violence. Many girls, with little or no access to medical assistance, become pregnant, a case of children who cannot support themselves having children of their own.

Analysts estimate that another 100 million of the world's children leave their families altogether, sleeping and living on the streets as best they can or perhaps trying to migrate to the United States. Roughly half of all street children are found in Latin American cities such as Mexico City and Rio de Janeiro, where perhaps half of all children grow up in poverty. Many people in the United States know these cities as exotic travel destinations, but they are also home to thousands of children living in makeshift huts, under bridges, or in alleyways (Ross, 1996; United Nations Development Programme, 2000; Collymore, 2002).

POVERTY AND WOMEN

In rich societies, the work women do typically is undervalued, underpaid, or overlooked entirely. In poor societies, women face even greater disadvantages. For example, most of the people who work in sweatshops like the one described in the opening to this chapter are women.

To make matters worse, tradition keeps women out of many jobs in low-income nations; in Bangladesh, women work in garment factories because that nation's conservative Muslim religious norms bar them from most other paid work and limit their opportunities for advanced schooling (Bearak, 2001). At the same time, traditional norms give women primary responsibility for raising children and maintaining the household. The

 To learn more about women laboring in sweatshops, visit http://www.globalexchange.org/campaigns/sweatshops/

GLOBAL SOCIOLOGY

"God Made Me to Be a Slave"

Fatma Mint Mamadou is a young woman living in North Africa's Islamic Republic of Mauritania. When asked her age, she pauses and smiles. She has no idea when she was born. Nor can she read or write. What she knows is tending camels, herding sheep, hauling bags of water, sweeping, and serving tea to her owners. This young woman is one of perhaps 90,000 slaves in Mauritania.

In the central region of this nation, having very dark skin almost always means being a slave to an Arab owner. Fatma accepts her situation, because she knows nothing else. She explains in a matter-of-fact voice that she is a slave, like her mother before her and her grandmother before that. "Just as God created a camel to be a camel," she shrugs, "he created me to be a slave."

Fatma, her mother, and her brothers and sisters live together in a squatter settlement on the edge of Nouak-chott, Mauritania's capital city. Their home is a nine-by-twelve-foot hut they built from wood

scraps and other building materials taken from construction sites. The roof is nothing more than a piece of cloth; there is no plumbing or furniture. The nearest water comes from a well a mile down the road.

In this region, slavery began 500 years ago, about the time Columbus sailed west toward the New World. As Arab and Berber tribes moved across the continent spreading Islam, they raided local villages and made slaves of the people, a practice that was continued for dozens of generations. In 1905, the French colonial

Human slavery continues to exist in the twenty-first century.

rulers of Mauritania banned slavery. After the nation gained independence in 1961, the new government reaffirmed the ban. But such proclamations have done little to change strong traditions. Indeed, people like Fatma have no idea what freedom means.

The next question is more personal: "Are you and other girls ever raped?" Again, Fatma hesitates. With no hint of emotion, she responds, "Of course, in the night the men come to breed us. Is that what you mean by rape?"

WHAT DO YOU THINK?

1. How does tradition play a part in keeping people in slavery?
2. Why do you think the world still tolerates slavery?
3. Do you think this practice will still be found a century from now? Why or why not?

Source: Based on Burkett (1997).

United Nations estimates that in poor countries, men own 90 percent of the land, a far greater gender disparity in wealth than is found in high-income nations. It is no surprise, then, that about 70 percent of the world's 1 billion people living near absolute poverty are women (Hymowitz, 1995).

Finally, the fact that women in poor countries generally do not have access to birth control raises the birth rate and keeps women at home with their children. In addition, the world's poorest women typically give birth without help from trained health workers. Figure 9–3 on page 236 shows the stark contrast between high- and low-income countries in this regard.

SLAVERY

Poor societies have many problems in addition to hunger, including illiteracy, warfare, and even slavery. The British Empire banned slavery in 1833, followed by the United States in 1865. But according to Anti-Slavery International (ASI), as many as 400 million men, women, and children (almost 7 percent of humanity) live today in conditions that amount to slavery.

ASI describes four types of slavery. First is *chattel slavery,* in which one person owns another. The number of chattel slaves is difficult to estimate because this practice is

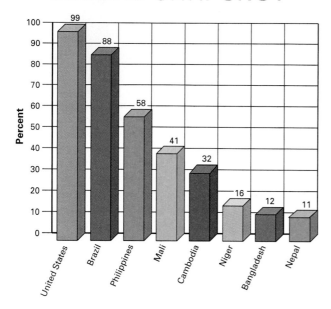

GLOBAL SNAPSHOT

FIGURE 9-3 Percentage of Births Attended by Skilled Health Staff

Source: World Bank (2004).

against the law almost everywhere. But the buying and selling of slaves still takes place in many countries in Asia, the Middle East, and especially Africa. The Global Sociology box on page 235 describes the reality of one slave's life in the African nation of Mauritania.

A second, more common form of bondage is *child slavery,* in which desperately poor families let their children take to the streets to do what they can to survive. Perhaps 100 million children—many in poor countries of Latin America—fall into this category.

Third, *debt bondage* is the practice by which employers hold workers captive by paying them too little to meet their debts. In this case, workers receive a wage, but it is too small to cover the food and housing provided by the employer; for practical purposes, they are enslaved. Many sweatshop workers in low-income nations fall into this category.

Fourth, *servile forms of marriage* may also amount to slavery. In India, Thailand, and some African nations, families marry off women against their will. Many end up as slaves to their husband's family; some are forced into prostitution.

Finally, one additional form of slavery is *human trafficking,* the movement of men, women, and children from

one place to another for the purpose of performing forced labor. Women or men brought to a new country on the promise of a job and then forced to become prostitutes or farm laborers, or "parents" who adopt children from another country and then force them to work in sweatshops are examples of trafficking in human beings. Such activity is big business: Next to trading in guns and drugs, trading in people brings the greatest profits to organized crime around the world (Orhant, 2002).

In 1948, the United Nations issued the Universal Declaration of Human Rights, which states, "No one shall be held in slavery or servitude; slavery and the slave trade shall be prohibited in all their forms." Unfortunately, nearly six decades later, this social evil persists.

 Read the UN's Universal Declaration of Human Rights at http://www.un.org/rights/50/decla.htm

CORRELATES OF GLOBAL POVERTY

What accounts for the severe and widespread poverty throughout much of the world? The rest of this chapter provides answers to this question using the following facts about poor nations:

1. **Technology.** About one-quarter of people in low-income countries farm the land using human muscles or animal power. With limited energy sources, agricultural production is modest.

2. **Population growth.** As Chapter 15 ("Population, Urbanization, and Environment") explains, the poorest countries have the world's highest birth rates. Despite the death toll from poverty, the populations of poor countries in Africa double every twenty-five years. In these countries, half the people are teenagers or younger. With such a large share of the population just entering the childbearing years, the wave of population growth will continue to roll into the future. In recent years, for example, the population of Chad has swelled by 3.3 percent annually, so that even with economic development, living standards have fallen.

3. **Cultural patterns.** Poor societies are usually traditional. People who hold to long-established ways of life resist change—even changes that promise a richer material life. The Global Sociology box on page 237 explains why traditional people in India respond to their poverty differently than poor people in the United States.

4. **Social stratification.** Low-income nations distribute their wealth very unequally. Chapter 8 ("Social Stratification") explained that social inequality is greater in agrarian societies than in industrial

A Different Kind of Poverty: A Report from India

Although India has become a middle-income nation, its per capita GDP is only $2,670, less than one-tenth that in the United States. For this reason, India is home to one-fourth of the world's hungry people.

But most North Americans do not easily understand the reality of poverty in India. Many of the country's 1.1 billion people live in conditions far worse than those our society labels "poor." A traveler's first experience of Indian life can be shocking. Madras, one of India's largest cities with 7 million inhabitants, seems chaotic to the outsider, with streets choked by motorbikes, trucks, carts pulled by oxen, and waves of people. Along the roadway, vendors sit on burlap cloths selling fruits, vegetables, and cooked food while people a few yards away work, talk, bathe, and sleep.

Although some people live well, Madras is dotted by more than a thousand shanty settlements, home to half a million people from rural villages who have come in search of a better life. Shantytowns are clusters of huts built with branches, leaves, and pieces of discarded cardboard and tin. These dwellings offer little privacy and lack refrigeration, running water, and bathrooms.

A visitor from the United States may feel uneasy in such an area, knowing that the poorest sections of our own inner cities seethe with frustration and sometimes explode with violence.

But India's people understand poverty differently than we do. No restless young men hang out at the corner, no drug dealers work the streets, and there is little danger of violence. In the United States, poverty often means anger and isolation; in India, even shantytowns are organized around strong families—children, parents, and often grandparents—who offer a smile of welcome to a stranger.

For traditional people in India, life is shaped by *dharma*, the Hindu concept of duty and destiny that teaches people to accept their fate, whatever it may be. Mother Teresa, who worked among the poorest of India's people, goes to the heart of the cultural differences: "Americans have angry poverty," she explains. "In India, there is worse poverty, but it is a happy poverty." Perhaps we should not describe anyone who clings to the edge of survival as happy. But poverty in India is eased by the strength and support of families and communities, a sense that life has a purpose, and a worldview that encourages each person to accept whatever life offers. As a result, a visitor may come away from a first encounter with Indian poverty rather confused: "How can people be so poor and yet seem content, active, and *joyful*?"

WHAT DO YOU THINK?

1. What did Mother Teresa mean when she said that in India there is "happy poverty"?
2. How might an experience like this change the way you think about the meaning of "rich"?
3. Are there poor people in regions of the United States who behave like these people in India? Explain.

Source: Based on the author's research in Madras, India, November 1988.

---

societies. In some low-income countries, half of all farmland is owned by just 1 percent of the people (Bergamo & Camarotti, 1996).

5. **Gender inequality.** Extreme gender inequality in poor societies keeps women from holding jobs, which typically means they have many children. An expanding population, in turn, slows economic development. Many analysts conclude that raising living standards in much of the world depends on improving the social standing of women.

6. **Global power relationships.** A final cause of global poverty lies in the relationships between the nations

of the world. Historically, wealth flowed from poor societies to rich nations through **colonialism,** *the process by which some nations enrich themselves through political and economic control of other nations.* The countries of Western Europe colonized much of Latin America beginning roughly 500 years ago. Such global exploitation allowed some nations to develop economically at the expense of others.

Although 130 former colonies gained their independence during the twentieth century, exploitation continues through **neocolonialism** (*neo* is the Greek word for "new"), *a new form of global power relationships that involves not direct political control but economic exploitation by multinational corporations.* A **multinational corporation** is *a large business that operates in many countries.* Corporate leaders can impose their will on countries in which they do business to create favorable economic conditions, just as colonizers did in the past.

Global Stratification: Theoretical Analysis

There are two major explanations for the unequal distribution of the world's wealth and power: *modernization theory* and *dependency theory.* Each theory suggests a different solution to the suffering of hungry people in much of the world.

MODERNIZATION THEORY

Modernization theory is *a model of economic and social development that explains global inequality in terms of technological and cultural differences between nations.* Modernization theory emerged in the 1950s, a time when U.S. society was fascinated with new technology. To counter the growing influence of the Soviet Union and socialism in much of the world, U.S. policymakers drafted a foreign policy that supported capitalism and free markets. This general policy has been with us ever since.[3]

Historical perspective. Until a few centuries ago, the entire world was poor. Because poverty has been the norm throughout human history, modernization theory proposes that it is *affluence* that demands an explanation.

---

[3]The following discussion of modernization theory draws primarily on Rostow (1960, 1978), Bauer (1981), Berger (1986), Firebaugh (1996), and Firebaugh & Sandu (1998).

Affluence came within reach of a growing share of people in Western Europe during the late Middle Ages as world exploration and trade expanded. Soon the Industrial Revolution was underway, transforming first Western Europe and then North America. Industrial technology, together with the spirit of capitalism, created new wealth as never before. At first, this new wealth benefited only a few. But industrial technology was so productive that gradually the living standards of even the poorest people began to improve. Absolute poverty, which had plagued humanity throughout history, was finally in decline.

During the twentieth century, the standard of living in high-income countries, where the Industrial Revolution began, jumped at least fourfold. Many middle-income nations in Asia and Latin America have now industrialized, and they, too, have become richer. But with limited industrial technology, low-income countries have changed much less.

The importance of culture. Why didn't the Industrial Revolution sweep away poverty the world over? Modernization theory points out that not every society wants to adopt new technology. Doing so takes a cultural environment that emphasizes the benefits of material wealth and new ideas.

Modernization theory identifies *tradition* as the greatest barrier to economic development. A reverence for the past may discourage people from adopting new technologies that would raise their living standards. Even today, many people—from the North American Amish to traditional Islamic people in the Middle East to the Semai of Malaysia—oppose new technology as a threat to their family relationships, customs, and religious beliefs.

Max Weber (1958, orig. 1904–5) found that at the end of the Middle Ages, Western Europe's cultural environment favored change. As Chapter 13 ("Family and Religion") explains, the Protestant Reformation reshaped traditional Catholic beliefs to generate a progress-oriented way of life. Wealth, looked on with suspicion by the Catholic church, became a sign of personal virtue, and the growing importance of individualism steadily replaced the traditional emphasis on family and community. These new cultural patterns nurtured the Industrial Revolution.

Rostow's stages of modernization. Modernization theory holds that the door to affluence is open to all. Indeed, as technological advances spread around the world, all societies should gradually industrialize. According to W. W. Rostow (1960, 1978), modernization occurs in four stages:

1. **Traditional stage.** Socialized to honor the past, people in traditional societies cannot easily imagine how

In rich nations such as the United States, most parents expect their children to enjoy years of childhood, largely free from the responsibilities of adult life. This is not the case in poor nations across Latin America, Africa, and Asia. Poor families depend on whatever income their children can earn, and many children as young as six or seven work full days weaving or performing other kinds of manual labor. Child labor lies behind the low prices of many products imported for sale in this country.

life can be very different. Therefore, they build their lives around families and local communities, following well-worn paths that allow little individual freedom or change. Life is often spiritually rich but lacking in material goods.

A century ago, much of the world was in this initial stage of economic development. Nations such as Bangladesh, Niger, and Somalia are still at the traditional stage and remain poor.

2. **Take-off stage.** As a society shakes off the grip of tradition, people start to use their talents and imagination, sparking economic growth. A market emerges as people produce goods not just for their own use but to trade with others for profit. Greater individualism, a willingness to take risks, and a desire for material goods also take hold, often at the expense of family ties and time-honored norms and values.

Great Britain reached take-off by about 1800, the United States by 1820. Thailand, a middle-income country in eastern Asia, is now in this stage. Such development typically is speeded by progressive influences from rich nations, including foreign aid, the availability of advanced technology and investment capital, and opportunities for schooling abroad.

3. **Drive to technological maturity.** As this stage begins, "growth" is a widely accepted idea that fuels a society's pursuit of higher living standards. A diversified economy drives a population eager to enjoy the benefits of industrial technology. At the same time, people begin

to realize (and sometimes regret) that industrialization is weakening traditional family and local community life. Great Britain entered this stage by about 1840, the United States by 1860. Today, Mexico, the U.S. territory of Puerto Rico, and South Korea are among the nations driving to technological maturity.

Absolute poverty is greatly reduced in nations in stage three. Cities swell with people who have left rural villages in search of economic opportunity; job specialization makes relationships less personal, and growing individualism generates social movements demanding greater political rights. Societies approaching technological maturity also provide basic schooling to all their people and advanced training for some. The newly educated consider tradition "backward," opening the door to further change. In addition, the social position of women steadily approaches that of men.

4. **High mass consumption.** Economic development driven by industrial technology steadily raises living standards as mass production stimulates mass consumption. Simply put, people soon learn to "need" the expanding selection of goods that their society produces.

The United States, Japan, and other rich nations entered this stage of development by 1900. Approaching this level of economic prosperity today are two former British colonies in eastern Asia: Hong Kong (now part of the People's Republic of China) and Singapore (independent since 1965).

Although the world continues to grow richer, billions of people are being left behind. The shantytown of Cité Soleil ("City of the Sun") near Port-au-Prince, the capital of Haiti, is built around an open sewer. What would you estimate life expectancy to be in such a place?

The role of rich nations. Modernization theory claims that high-income countries play four important roles in global economic development:

1. **Controlling population.** Because population growth is greatest in the poorest societies, rising population can overtake economic advances. Rich nations can help limit population growth by exporting birth control technology and promoting its use. Once economic development is underway, birth rates should decline, as they have in industrialized nations, because children are no longer an economic asset.

2. **Increasing food production.** Rich nations can export high-tech farming methods to poor nations to help raise agricultural yields. Such techniques, collectively referred to as the "Green Revolution," include new hybrid seeds, modern irrigation methods, chemical fertilizers, and pesticides for insect control.

3. **Introducing industrial technology.** Rich nations can encourage economic growth in poor societies by introducing machinery and information technology, which raise productivity. Industrialization also shifts the labor force from farming to skilled industrial and service jobs.

4. **Providing foreign aid.** Investment capital from rich nations can boost the prospects of poor societies striving to reach Rostow's take-off stage. Foreign aid can help raise agricultural productivity by enabling poor countries to purchase more fertilizer and build irrigation systems. In addition, financial and technical assistance to build power plants and factories improves industrial output.

Critical review. Modernization theory has many influential supporters among social scientists (Parsons, 1966; Moore, 1977, 1979; Bauer, 1981; Berger, 1986; Firebaugh & Beck, 1994; Firebaugh, 1996; Firebaugh & Sandu, 1998). For decades it has shaped the foreign policy of the United States and other rich nations. Supporters point to rapid economic development in Asia—including South Korea, Taiwan, Singapore, and Hong Kong—as proof that the affluence created in Western Europe and North America is within the reach of all countries.

But modernization theory faces criticism from socialist countries (and left-leaning analysts in the West) as little more than a defense of capitalism. Its most serious flaw, according to critics, is that modernization simply has not occurred in many poor countries. The United Nations reported that living standards in a number of nations, including Haiti and Nicaragua in Latin America and Sudan, Ghana, and Rwanda in Africa, are actually lower today than they were in 1960 (United Nations Development Programme, 1996).

A second criticism of modernization theory is that it fails to recognize how rich nations, which benefit from the status quo, often block the path to development for poor countries. Centuries ago, rich countries industrialized from a position of global *strength*. Can we expect poor countries today to do so from a position of global *weakness*?

Third, modernization theory treats rich and poor societies as separate worlds, ignoring how international relations have affected all nations. Countries in Latin America and Asia are still struggling from the effects of their colonization, which boosted the fortunes of Europe.

Fourth, modernization theory holds up the world's most developed countries as the standard for judging the rest of humanity, revealing an ethnocentric bias. We need to remember that our Western idea of "progress" has caused us to rush headlong into a competitive, materialistic way of life, which uses up the world's scarce resources and pollutes the natural environment.

Fifth, and finally, modernization theory suggests that the causes of global poverty lie almost entirely within the poor societies themselves. Critics see this analysis as little more than blaming the victims for their own problems. Instead, they argue, an analysis of global inequality should focus just as much on the behavior of rich nations as it does on the behavior of poor ones.

Concerns such as these reflect a second major approach to understanding global inequality: dependency theory.

DEPENDENCY THEORY

Dependency theory is *a model of economic and social development that explains global inequality in terms of the historical exploitation of poor nations by rich ones.* This analysis puts primary responsibility for global poverty on rich nations, which for centuries have systematically impoverished low-income countries and made them *dependent* on the rich ones. This destructive process continues today.

Historical perspective. Everyone agrees that before the Industrial Revolution, there was little affluence in the world. However, dependency theory asserts that people living in poor countries were actually better off economically in the past than their descendants are now. André Gunder Frank (1975), a noted supporter of this theory, argues that the colonial process that helped develop rich nations also *underdeveloped* poor societies.

Dependency theory is based on the idea that the economic positions of the rich and poor nations of the world are linked and cannot be understood apart from one another. Poor nations are not simply lagging behind rich ones on the "path of progress"; rather, the prosperity of the most developed countries came largely at the expense of less developed ones. In short, some nations became rich only because others became poor. Both are the result of the expansion of global commerce five centuries ago.

The importance of colonialism. Late in the fifteenth century, Europeans began surveying the Americas to the west,

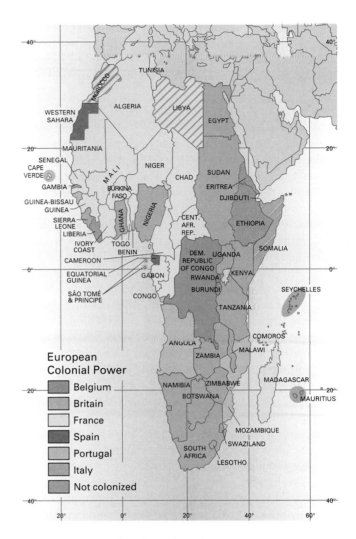

FIGURE 9–4 Africa's Colonial History

Africa to the south, and Asia to the east in order to establish colonies. They were so successful that a century ago, Great Britain controlled about one-fourth of the world's land, boasting, "The sun never sets on the British Empire." The United States, itself originally thirteen small British colonies on the eastern seaboard, soon expanded across the North American continent, purchased Alaska, and gained control of Haiti, Puerto Rico, Guam, the Philippines, the Hawaiian Islands, and part of Cuba.

Meanwhile, Europeans and Africans engaged in a brutal form of human exploitation—the slave trade—from about 1500 until 1850. Even as the world was rejecting slavery, Europeans took control of Africa itself, as Figure 9–4 shows. European powers dominated most of the continent until the early 1960s.

Formal colonialism has almost disappeared from the world. However, according to dependency theory, political liberation has not meant economic independence. Far from it: The economic relationship between poor and rich nations continues the colonial pattern of domination. This *neocolonialism* is the heart of the capitalist world economy.

Wallerstein's capitalist world economy. Immanuel Wallerstein (1974, 1979, 1983, 1984) explains global stratification using a model of the "capitalist world economy." Wallerstein's term "world economy" suggests that the prosperity or poverty of any country is the result of a global economic system. He traces the roots of the global economy to the beginning of colonization more than 500 years ago when Europeans began gathering wealth from the rest of the world. Because the global economy is based in high-income countries, it is capitalist in character.[4]

Wallerstein calls the rich nations the *core* of the world economy. Colonialism enriched this core by funneling raw materials from around the world to Western Europe, where they fueled the Industrial Revolution. Today, multinational corporations operate profitably worldwide, bringing wealth to North America, Western Europe, Australia, and Japan.

Low-income countries are the *periphery* of the world economy. Drawn into the world economy by colonial exploitation, poor nations continue to support rich ones by providing low-cost labor and a vast market for industrial products. The remaining countries are the *semiperiphery* of the world economy. They include middle-income countries such as Mexico and Brazil that have closer ties to the global economic core.

According to Wallerstein, the world economy benefits rich societies (by generating profits) and harms the rest of the world (by causing poverty). The world economy thus makes poor nations dependent on rich ones. This dependency involves three factors:

1. **Narrow, export-oriented economies.** Poor nations produce only a few crops for export to rich countries. Examples include coffee and fruits from Latin American nations, oil from Nigeria, hardwoods from the Philippines, and palm oil from Malaysia.

   Today's multinational corporations buy raw materials cheaply in poor societies and transport them to core nations, where factories process them for profitable sale. Thus, poor nations develop few industries of their own.

2. **Lack of industrial capacity.** Without an industrial base, poor societies depend on rich nations to buy their inexpensive raw materials and try to buy from them whatever expensive manufactured goods they can afford. In a classic example of this dependency, British colonialists encouraged the people of India to raise cotton but prevented them from weaving their own cloth. Instead, the British shipped Indian cotton to English textile mills in Birmingham and Manchester, manufactured the cloth, and shipped finished goods back to India, where the very people who harvested the cotton bought the garments.

   Dependency theorists claim the Green Revolution—widely praised by modernization theorists—works the same way. Poor countries sell cheap raw materials to rich nations and then try to buy expensive fertilizers, pesticides, and machinery in return. Typically, rich countries profit from this exchange more than poor nations.

3. **Foreign debt.** Unequal trade patterns have plunged poor countries into debt. Collectively, the poor nations of the world owe rich countries $2.3 trillion; hundreds of billions of dollars are owed to the United States alone. Such staggering debt paralyzes a country, causing high unemployment and rampant inflation (World Bank, 2004).

The role of rich nations. Modernization theory and dependency theory assign rich nations very different roles. Modernization theory holds that rich societies *produce wealth* through capital investment and new technology. Dependency theory views global inequality in terms of how countries *distribute wealth,* arguing that rich nations have *over*developed themselves as they have *under*developed the rest of the world.

Dependency theorists do not believe that strategies by rich countries to control population and increase agricultural and industrial output will help raise living standards in poor countries. Instead, they claim, such programs actually benefit rich nations and the ruling elites, not the poor majority, in low-income countries (Kentor, 2001).

Hunger activists Frances Moore Lappé and Joseph Collins (1986) maintain that the capitalist culture of the United States encourages people to think of poverty as somehow inevitable. Following this line of reasoning, poverty results from "natural" processes, including having too many children, and from natural disasters such as droughts. But according to dependency theory, global poverty is far from inevitable; it results from deliberate policies. Lappé and Collins point out that the world already produces enough food to allow every person on the planet to

---

[4]Though based on Wallerstein's ideas, this section also reflects the work of Frank (1980, 1981), Delacroix & Ragin (1981), Bergesen (1983), Dixon & Boswell (1996), and Kentor (1998).

APPLYING THEORY
GLOBAL POVERTY

	Modernization Theory	Dependency Theory
Which theoretical approach is applied?	Structural functional approach	Social conflict approach
How did global poverty come about?	The whole world was poor until some countries developed industrial technology, which allowed mass production and created affluence.	Colonialism moved wealth from some countries to others, making some nations poor as it made other nations rich.
What are the main causes of global poverty today?	Traditional culture and a lack of productive technology.	Neocolonialism—the operation of multinational corporations in the global, capitalist economy.
Are rich countries part of the problem or part of the solution?	Rich countries are part of the solution, contributing new technology, advanced schooling, and foreign aid.	Rich countries are part of the problem, making poor countries economically dependent and in debt.

become quite fat. India and most of Africa actually *export* food, even though many of their own people go hungry.

According to Lappé and Collins, the existence of poverty amid plenty stems from the rich nations' policy of producing food for profits, not people. That is, corporations in rich nations work with elites in poor countries to grow and export profitable crops such as coffee, which means using land that could otherwise produce basics such as beans and corn for local families. Governments of poor countries support the practice of growing for export because they need food profits to help pay off huge foreign debt. According to Lappé and Collins, the capitalist corporate structure of the global economy is at the core of this vicious cycle.

Critical review. The main idea of dependency theory is that no nation develops (or fails to develop) in isolation, because the global economy shapes the future of all nations. Pointing to Latin America and other poor regions of the world, dependency theorists claim that development simply cannot proceed under the constraints imposed by rich countries. Rather, they call for radical reform of the entire world economy so that it operates in the interests of the majority of people.

Critics charge that dependency theory wrongly treats wealth as if no one gets richer without someone else getting poorer. Corporations, small business owners, and farmers can and do create new wealth through their drive and imaginative use of new technology. After all, they point out, the entire world's wealth has increased sixfold since 1950.

Second, dependency theory is wrong in blaming rich nations for global poverty, because many of the world's poorest countries (such as Ethiopia) have had little contact with rich nations. On the contrary, a long history of trade with rich countries has dramatically improved the economies of nations including Sri Lanka, Singapore, and Hong Kong (all former British colonies), as well as South Korea and Japan. In short, say the critics, most evidence shows that foreign investment by rich nations encourages economic growth, as modernization theory claims, not economic decline, as dependency theory says (Vogel, 1991; Firebaugh, 1992).

Third, critics call dependency theory simplistic for pointing the finger at a single factor—world capitalism—as the cause of global inequality (Worsley, 1990). Dependency theory views poor societies as passive victims and ignores factors inside these countries that contribute to their economic problems. Sociologists have long recognized the vital role of culture in shaping people's willingness to accept or resist change. Under the rule of the ultratraditional Muslim Taliban, for example, Afghanistan became economically isolated, and its living standards sank to among the lowest in the world. Is it reasonable to blame capitalist societies for that country's stagnation?

Nor can rich societies be held responsible for the reckless behavior of foreign leaders whose corruption and militaristic campaigns impoverish their countries. Examples include the regimes of Ferdinand Marcos in the Philippines, François Duvalier in Haiti, Manuel Noriega in Panama, Mobutu Sese Seko in Zaire (today's Democratic Republic of the Congo), and Saddam Hussein in Iraq. Some leaders even use food supplies as a weapon in internal political struggles, leaving the people starving in the African nations of Ethiopia, Sudan, and Somalia. Likewise, many countries throughout the world have done little to improve the status of women or control population growth.

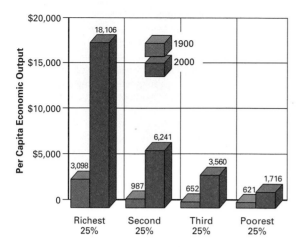

FIGURE 9-5 The World's Increasing Economic Inequality

Source: International Monetary Fund (2000).

Fourth, critics say dependency theory focuses on capitalist countries including the United States but downplays the economic dependency created by the former Soviet Union. The Soviet army seized control of most of Eastern Europe during World War II and then politically and economically dominated these countries. Many see the uprisings between 1989 and 1991 as a wholesale rejection of the Soviet Union's socialist colonial system.

Fifth, critics fault dependency theory for offering only vague solutions to global poverty. Most dependency theorists urge poor nations to end all contact with rich countries, and some call for nationalizing foreign-owned industries. In other words, dependency theory is really an argument for some sort of world socialism. Given the difficulties socialist societies (even richer socialist countries such as Russia) have had in meeting the needs of their own people, critics ask, should we really expect such a system to rescue the entire world from poverty?

The Applying Theory table on page 243 summarizes the main arguments of modernization theory and dependency theory.

Global Stratification: Looking Ahead

Among the most important trends of recent decades is the development of a global economy. Increased production and sales abroad have brought huge profits to many corporations and their stockholders. At the same time, the global economy has cut factory jobs in this country, hurting many average workers. The net result: economic polarization in the United States.

As this chapter has explained, social inequality is far more striking in global perspective. The concentration of wealth among high-income countries, coupled with grinding poverty in low-income nations, may well be the biggest problem facing humanity in the twenty-first century.

Finding answers to questions about global poverty is urgent. Both modernization theory and dependency theory have their strengths and their limitations. In searching for truth, we must consider empirical evidence. Over the course of the twentieth century, living standards rose in most of the world. Even the economic output of the poorest 25 percent of the world's people almost tripled over the course of the twentieth century. However, the economic output of the other 75 percent of the world's people increased about sixfold. By this measure, although all people are better off in *absolute* terms, there was almost twice as much *relative* economic inequality in the world in 2000 as there was in 1900. Therefore, as shown in Figure 9–5, the poorest of the world's people are being left behind.

Most of this economic polarization took place between 1900 and 1970. Since 1970, the degree of economic inequality worldwide has declined. In addition, the ranks of the world's poorest people—those living on less than $1 per day—have fallen from about 600 million in 1970 to about 350 million in 2000 (Schultz, 1998; Firebaugh, 1999, 2000; Sala-i-Martin, 2002).

The greatest reduction in poverty has taken place in Asia, a region generally seen as an economic success story. Back in 1970, 75 percent of global $1-per-day poverty was found in Asia; by 2000, that figure had fallen to 15 percent (Sala-i-Martin, 2002).

Latin America represents a mixed case. During the 1970s, this world region enjoyed significant economic growth; during the 1980s and 1990s, however, there was little overall improvement. The share of global $1-per-day poverty was the same in 2000 (3 percent) as it was in 1970 (Sala-i-Martin, 2002).

Africa, specifically the countries south of the Sahara Desert, represents a region of economic decline. There, the extent of extreme poverty has become worse. In 1970, sub-Saharan Africa accounted for 11 percent of $1-per-day poverty; by 2000, this share had risen to 66 percent (Sala-i-Martin, 2002). Global Map 9–2 provides a visual picture of prosperity and stagnation around the world.

These trends in economic performance have caused both modernization and dependency theorists to revise their views. Governments have played a large role in the economic growth that has occurred in Asia and elsewhere;

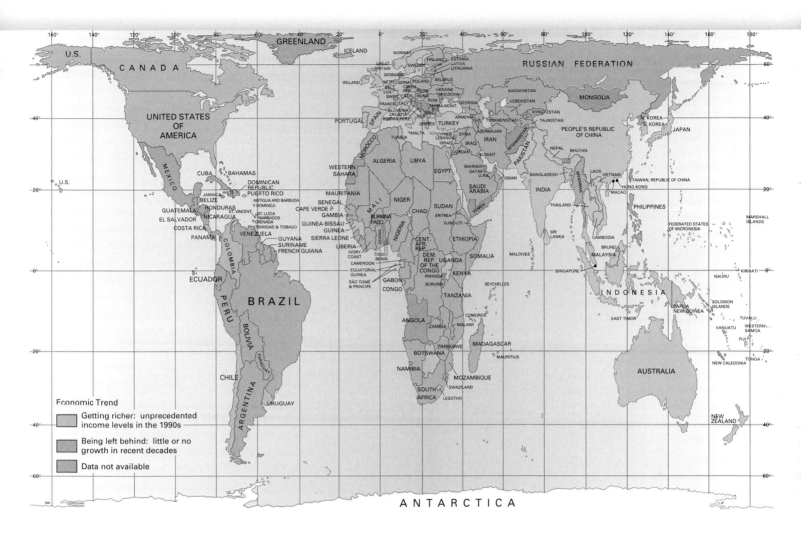

WINDOW ON THE WORLD

GLOBAL MAP 9-2   Prosperity and Stagnation in Global Perspective

In about sixty nations of the world, people are enjoying a higher standard of living than ever before. These prospering countries include some rich nations (such as the United States and the countries of Western Europe) and some poor nations (especially in Asia). For most countries, however, living standards have remained steady or even slipped in recent decades. Especially in Eastern Europe and the Middle East, some nations have experienced economic setbacks since the 1980s. And in sub-Saharan Africa, some nations are no better off than they were in 1960. The overall pattern is economic polarization, with an increasing gap between rich and poor nations.

Source: United Nations Development Programme (1996); updates by the author.

no nation has a market economy completely free of government involvement. This fact challenges modernization theory and its free-market approach to development. On the other hand, since the upheavals in the former Soviet Union and Eastern Europe, a global reevaluation of socialism has been underway. Because these uprisings follow decades of poor economic performance and political repression, many poor nations are unwilling to follow the advice of dependency theory and place economic development entirely under government control.

In the end, reducing hunger around the world is a matter not just of policy but of commitment. As the Controversy

Will the World Starve?

The animals' feet leave their prints
on the desert's face.
Hunger is so real, so very real, that
it can make you walk around a
barren tree looking for
nourishment.
Not once,
Not twice,
Not thrice . . .

These lines, by Indian poet Amit Jayaram, describe the appalling hunger found in Rajasthan, in northwestern India. As this chapter has explained, hunger casts a menacing shadow over many regions of the world. Hundreds of millions of adults do not eat enough food to enable them to work. Most tragically, some 10 million children die each year because of hunger. As we begin the twenty-first century, what are the prospects for ending the wretched misery of daily hunger?

Pessimists point out that the population of poor countries is currently increasing by 73 million people annually, equivalent to adding another Egypt to the world every year. Poor countries can hardly feed the people they have now; how will they ever feed *twice* as many people a generation in the future?

In addition, hunger forces poor people to exploit the Earth's resources by using short-term strategies for food production that lead to long-term disaster. For example, farmers are cutting rain forests in order to increase their farmland; without the protective canopy of trees, it is only a matter of time before much of this land turns to desert. Rising populations and short-sighted policies raise the possibility of even greater hunger and human misery.

But there are also grounds for optimism. Thanks to the Green Revolution, food production the world over has increased sharply over the last fifty years, well outpacing the growth in population. The world's economic productivity has risen steadily, so that the average person on the planet has more income now to purchase food and other necessities than ever before. This growth has increased daily caloric intake, life expectancy, access to safe water, and adult literacy; around the world, infant mortality is half what it was in 1960.

What are the prospects for ending world hunger? Overall, we see less hunger in both rich and poor countries, and a smaller *share* of the world's people are hungry now than in 1960. But as global population increases, with 98 percent of children born in middle- and low-income countries, the *number of lives* at risk is as great today as ever before. Many low-income countries have made solid gains, but many more are stagnating or even losing ground.

The best-case region of the world is eastern Asia, where incomes controlled for inflation have tripled over the last generation. Optimists point to Asia for evidence that poor countries can raise living standards and reduce hunger. The worst-case region is sub-Saharan Africa, where living standards have fallen over the last decade, high technology is least evident, and birth rates are highest. Pessimists typically look to Africa when they argue that poor countries are losing ground in the struggle to feed their people.

Television brings home the tragedy of hunger when news cameras focus on starving people in places such as Ethiopia and Somalia. But hunger—and early death from illness—is the plight of millions all year round. The world has the technical means to feed everyone; the question is, do we have the moral determination?

CONTINUE THE DEBATE . . .

1. In your opinion, what are the primary causes of global hunger?
2. Do you place more responsibility for solving this problem on poor countries or rich ones? Why?
3. Do you consider yourself an optimist or a pessimist about the problem of global hunger? Why?

Sources: United Nations Development Programme (2000, 2001, 2002, 2003, 2004).

& Debate box explains, many analysts wonder whether humanity has the determination to provide for everyone on the planet.

Although the world's future is uncertain, we have learned a great deal about global stratification. One major insight, offered by modernization theory, is that poverty is partly a *problem of technology*. A higher standard of living for a growing world population depends on raising agricultural and industrial productivity. A second insight, derived from dependency theory, is that global inequality is also a *political issue*. Even with higher productivity, the human community must address crucial questions concerning the distribution of resources, both within societies and around the globe.

Although economic development raises living standards, it also places greater strains on the natural environment. As nations such as India and China—with a combined population of 2.4 billion—become more affluent, their people will consume more energy and other natural resources and produce more solid waste and other forms of pollution.

Finally, the vast gulf that separates the world's richest and poorest people puts everyone at greater risk of war as the poorest people challenge the social arrangements that threaten their existence. In the long run, we can achieve peace on this planet only by ensuring that all people enjoy a significant measure of dignity and security.

SUMMARY

1. Around the world, social stratification is more pronounced than in the United States. About 18 percent of the world's people live in industrialized, high-income countries such as the United States and receive 79 percent of all income. Another 70 percent of humanity live in middle-income countries with significant industrialization, receiving about 20 percent of all income. Twelve percent of the world's population live in low-income countries with limited industrialization and earn only 1 percent of global income.

2. Although relative poverty is found everywhere, poor societies struggle with widespread, absolute poverty. Worldwide, the lives of some 1 billion people are at risk because of poor nutrition. About 15 million people, most of them children, die annually from diseases caused by poor nutrition.

3. Women are more likely than men to be poor nearly everywhere in the world. Gender bias against women is greatest in poor, agrarian societies.

4. The poverty found in much of the world is a complex problem reflecting limited industrial technology, rapid population growth, traditional cultural patterns, internal social stratification, male domination, and global power relationships.

5. Modernization theory maintains that successful development requires giving up traditional cultural patterns in favor of advanced technology.

6. Modernization theorist W. W. Rostow identifies four stages of development: traditional, take-off, drive to technological maturity, and high mass consumption.

7. Arguing that rich societies hold the keys to creating wealth, modernization theory claims that rich nations can help poor nations by providing population control programs, agricultural technology such as hybrid seeds and fertilizers to increase food production, industrial technology including machinery and information technology, and foreign aid to help pay for power plants and factories.

8. Critics of modernization theory say that rich nations do not spread economic development around the world and that poor nations cannot follow the path to development taken by rich nations centuries ago.

9. Dependency theory claims that global wealth and poverty are the historical products of the capitalist world economy because of colonialism and, more recently, the operation of multinational corporations.

10. Immanuel Wallerstein views the high-income countries as the advantaged "core" of the capitalist world economy; middle-income nations are the "semiperiphery," and poor societies form the global "periphery."

11. According to dependency theory, three key factors—export-oriented economies, a lack of industrial capacity, and foreign debt—are responsible for poor countries' dependency on rich nations.

12. Critics of dependency theory argue that this approach overlooks the sixfold increase in the world's wealth since 1950 and note that the world's poorest societies are not those with the strongest ties to rich countries.

13. Both the modernization and dependency approaches offer useful insights into the development of global inequality. The theories agree that there is an urgent need to address the various problems caused by worldwide poverty.

KEY CONCEPTS

global stratification (p. 226) patterns of social inequality in the world as a whole

high-income countries (p. 227) the richest nations with the highest overall standards of living

middle-income countries (p. 227) nations with a standard of living about average for the world as a whole

low-income countries (p. 227) nations with a low standard of living in which most people are poor

colonialism (p. 238) the process by which some nations enrich themselves through political and economic control of other nations

neocolonialism (p. 238) a new form of global power relationships that involves not direct political control but economic exploitation by multinational corporations

multinational corporation (p. 238) a large business that operates in many countries

modernization theory (p. 238) a model of economic and social development that explains global inequality in terms of technological and cultural differences between nations

dependency theory (p. 241) a model of economic and social development that explains global inequality in terms of the historical exploitation of poor nations by rich ones

CRITICAL-THINKING QUESTIONS

1. Based on what you have read here and elsewhere, what is your prediction about the extent of global hunger fifty years from now? Will the problem be more or less serious? Why?

2. What is the difference between relative and absolute poverty? Use these two concepts to describe social stratification in the United States and around the world.

3. Why do many analysts argue that economic development in low-income countries depends on raising the social standing of women?

4. State the basic ideas of modernization theory and dependency theory. What are several criticisms of each approach?

APPLICATIONS AND EXERCISES

1. Keep a log book of mass media advertising mentioning low-income countries (selling, say, coffee from Colombia or exotic vacations to a Caribbean island). What image of life in low-income countries does the advertising present? In light of this chapter, do you think this image is accurate?

2. Millions of students from abroad study on U.S. campuses. Find a woman and a man on your campus raised in a poor country. Approach them, explain that you have been studying global stratification, and ask if they are willing to share what life is like back home. You may learn quite a bit from them.

3. Use the global maps in this text (or the animated maps on the CD-ROM) to identify social traits associated with the world's

richest and poorest nations. Try to use both modernization theory and dependency theory to build theoretical explanations of the patterns you find.

4. Packaged in the back of this new textbook is an interactive CD-ROM that offers a variety of video and interactive review materials intended to help you better understand the material covered in this chapter. For this chapter, the CD-ROM contains a relevant clip from *ABC News*, an author's tip video, interactive map animations, video matching, an interactive time line, and flashcards with audio pronunciations of the more difficult words.

 # SITES TO SEE

http://www.prenhall.com/macionis

View the interactive Companion Website™ that accompanies this text. Begin by clicking on the cover of your book. You will find a chapter-by-chapter study guide, practice tests, suggested Web links, and links to other relevant material.

http://members.aol.com/casmasalc

This is the Web site for the Coalition against Slavery in Mauritania and Sudan. This site provides information about the problem of slavery and links to similar organizations.

http://www.worldbank.org/data/

This site, operated by the World Bank, provides data and analyses of global poverty.

http://www.census.gov/ipc/www/idbnew.html
http://www.prb.org

These two sites, operated by the U.S. Census Bureau and the Population Reference Bureau, offer a statistical profile of world nations.

http://www.fh.org
http://www.worldconcern.org
http://www.worldvision.org
http://www.care.org

Here are four additional Web sites that address global inequality. The first is operated by Food for the Hungry, the second takes you to the home page for World Concern, the third organization is World Vision, and the fourth is CARE. Visit them all, and watch for differences in their focus and strategies.

 # INVESTIGATE WITH RESEARCH NAVIGATOR™

Follow the instructions found on page 32 of this textbook to access the features of **Research Navigator™**. Once at the Web site, enter your Login Name and Password. Then, to use the **Content Select™** database, enter keywords such as "colonialism," "world hunger," and "slavery," and the search engine will supply relevant and recent

scholarly and popular press publications. Use the *New York Times* **Search-by-Subject Archive** to find recent news articles related to sociology and the **Links Library** feature to find relevant Web links organized by the key terms used in this chapter.

January 18, 2004

Brazilian Slums Seen as Pawns in Political Games

By CELIA W. DUGGER

ESTRUTURAL, Brazil–Izailde Souza, nine months pregnant with her sixth child, is a prisoner in her two-room shack. She says she is so afraid that thieves roaming the slum will steal her meager possessions that she never leaves her cramped quarters—not to look for work, go to market or walk her children to school. The last time she remembers going out was more than a year ago. . . .

Estrutural is a sprawling slum where the shanties look like collages of scrap lumber, rusted metal and chicken wire. It is part of an illegal housing development, one that its critics say is highly organized. Vote-hungry politicians encouraged the poor to settle on public land, then provided them with a school, a clinic and other services to attract more people, environmentalists and prosecutors say.

Estrutural fits a pattern of squatter settlements across Asia and Africa, where explosive growth is expected to nearly double the population of many large cities in the next 15 years, according to the United Nations. Already, a third of the world's urban population—almost a billion people—live in slums. . . .

Estrutural itself is a half-hour drive from Brasília, the nation's futuristic capital, built in the 1950's in the shape of an airplane, symbolically taking the country off into a bright future. But as the carefully planned capital has grown, so has Estrutural, with its haphazard maze of jerry-built shanties. The yawning gap between the prosperous capital city and the impoverished slum mirrors the deeper disparities in Brazil, one of the world's most unequal nations.

Squatter settlements like Estrutural have filled a crying need, urban planners say. Government and the market economy have failed to create affordable housing for millions of poor Brazilians who have streamed from the countryside to the cities.

"What you see in Estrutural is structural," said Edesio Fernandes, a professor of urban planning at the University of London who spent last year as director of land affairs in the Ministry of Cities, created by President Luiz Inácio Lula da Silva of Brazil. "It's not an exception. This is the main characteristic of our urbanization process and it needs to be recognized before we can change it." . . .

The slum, which hovers over a water basin, has no sewage system. Residents dig holes in their dirt floors and put a toilet on top. The raw waste seeps into the ground, contaminating the water. The cost of installing underground sewer pipes with a city already in place would be high.

"These people . . . stimulated the poor to settle in open areas owned by the government," said Paulo Salles, a professor of ecology at the University of Brasília. "They create problems for the whole city without any consideration for the environment or sustainability. These words don't mean anything for them. They're just interested in votes and making money for themselves." . . .

In Estrutural, everything, from peoples' homes to their clothes to their very skin, seems to be stained with the reddish brown clay the city is built on. Children splash in dirty puddles left by the seasonal rains.

Ms. Souza, 32, . . . does not romanticize life here. She describes it as a level of hell a notch higher than the rural life she left at age 14. In the countryside, the poverty was so deep and medical care so distant that people often died of sickness and hunger.

In Estrutural, her husband can sometimes find work as a day laborer. Churches donate food and clothes. A school and clinic are nearby. But crime is a curse. Her every waking hour is devoted to guarding her family's tenuous hold on a ramshackle shanty that leaks buckets of water when it rains.

"The bandits come out on the streets," she said, rolling up her T-shirt, looking for respite from the searing heat. "They boast about people they've ripped off. They have no shame, and the law of silence rules. They'll come get you, your kids or your husband if you talk."

She put her hand up to shield her face, trying to hide the tears that slipped off the tip of her nose.

"The boys and men can leave, but not me," she said. "The women have to bear it. We need this place to live."

WHAT DO YOU THINK?

1. Why are squatter settlements like the one described here so common in poor nations around the world? Why do so many people come to live in places that seem so terrible?

2. Why is so little progress being made to solve the problems of squatter settlements? Can you offer some ideas about how to improve life for the people who live in them?

Adapted from the original article by Celia W. Dugger published in *The New York Times* on January 18, 2004. Copyright © 2004 by The New York Times Company. Reprinted with permission.

CHAPTER TEN

Gender Stratification

How is gender a creation of society?

What differences does gender make in people's lives?

Why is gender an important dimension
of social stratification?

In societies around the world, men have higher social standing than women. In this traditional ▶ Japanese teahouse, a woman in geisha costume politely serves businessmen.

At first we traveled quite alone . . . but before we had gone many miles, we came on other wagon-loads of women, bound in the same direction. As we reached different cross-roads, we saw wagons coming from every part of the country and, long before we reached Seneca Falls, we were a procession.

So wrote Charlotte Woodward in her journal as she made her way in a horse-drawn wagon along the rutted dirt roads leading to Seneca Falls, a small town in upstate New York. The year was 1848, a time when slavery was legal in much of the United States and the social standing of all women, regardless of color, was far below that of men. Back then, in much of the country, women could not own property, keep their own wages if they were married, draft a will, file lawsuits in a court (including lawsuits seeking custody of their own children), or attend college, and husbands were widely viewed as having unquestioned authority over their wives and children.

Some 300 women gathered at Wesleyan Chapel in Seneca Falls to challenge this second-class citizenship. They listened as their leader, Elizabeth Cady Stanton, called for expanding women's rights and opportunities, including the right to vote. At that time, most people considered such a proposal absurd and outrageous. Even many of those attending the conference were shocked by the idea: Stanton's husband, Henry, rode out of town in protest (Gurnett, 1998).

Much has changed in the century and a half since the Seneca Falls convention, and many of the "outrageous" proposals made by Stanton are now accepted as matters of basic fairness. But as this chapter explains, women and men still lead different lives in the United States and elsewhere in the world, and in most respects, men are still in charge. This chapter explores the importance of gender and explains how, like class position, gender is a major dimension of social stratification.

Gender and Inequality

Chapter 6 ("Sexuality and Society") explained that biological differences divide the human population into categories of female and male. **Gender** refers to *the personal traits and social positions that members of a society attach to being female or male.* Gender, then, is a dimension of social organization, shaping how we interact with others and even how

we think about ourselves. More important, gender also involves *hierarchy,* placing men and women in different positions in terms of power, wealth, and other resources. This is why sociologists speak of **gender stratification,** *the unequal distribution of wealth, power, and privilege between men and women.* In short, gender affects the opportunities and limitations each of us faces throughout our lives.

MALE-FEMALE DIFFERENCES

Many people think there is something "natural" about gender distinctions because biology does make one sex different from the other. But we must be careful not to think of social differences in biological terms. In 1848, for example, women were not allowed to vote because many people assumed that women did not have enough intelligence or interest in politics. Such attitudes had nothing to do with biology; they reflected the *cultural patterns* of that time and place.

Another example is athletic performance. In 1925, most people—both women and men—believed that the best women runners could never compete with men in a marathon. Today, as Figure 10–1 on page 254 shows, the best women routinely post better times than the fastest men of decades past, and the performance gap between the sexes has narrowed greatly. Here, again, most of the differences between men and women turn out to be socially created.

There are some differences in physical ability between the sexes. On average, males are 10 percent taller than women, 20 percent heavier, and 30 percent stronger, especially in the upper body (Ehrenreich, 1999). On the other hand, women outperform men in the ultimate game of life itself: Life expectancy for men is 74.4 years, and women can expect to live 79.8 years (Arias, 2004).

In adolescence, males show greater mathematical ability, whereas adolescent females excel in verbal skills, a difference that reflects both biology and socialization (Maccoby & Jacklin, 1974; Baker et al., 1980; Lengermann & Wallace, 1985). However, research does not point to any overall differences in intelligence between males and females. Biologically, then, men and women differ in limited ways, with neither one naturally superior. But culture can define the two sexes differently, as the global study of gender described in the next section shows.

GENDER IN GLOBAL PERSPECTIVE

The best way to see how gender is based in culture is by comparing one society to another. Three important studies highlight just how different "masculine" and "feminine" can be.

The Israeli kibbutzim. In Israel, collective Jewish settlements are called *kibbutzim.* The kibbutz (the singular form of the word) is an important setting for gender research because gender equality is one of its stated goals; men and women share in both work and decision making.

In kibbutzim, both sexes share most everyday jobs. Both men and women take care of children, cook and clean, repair buildings, and make day-to-day decisions concerning life in the kibbutz. Girls and boys are raised in the same way, and from the first weeks of life, children live together in dormitories. Women and men in the kibbutzim have achieved remarkable (although not complete) social equality, evidence of the wide range that cultures have in defining what is feminine and what is masculine.

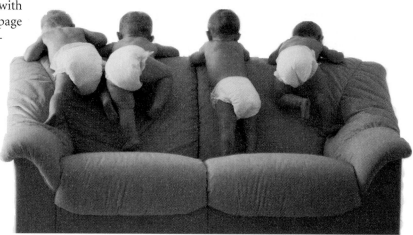

Sex is a biological distinction that develops prior to birth. Gender is the meaning that a society attaches to being female or male. Gender differences are a matter of power, as what is masculine typically has social priority over what is feminine. The importance of gender is not evident among infants, of course, but the ways in which we think of boys and girls set in motion patterns that will continue for a lifetime.

Margaret Mead's research. The anthropologist Margaret Mead carried out groundbreaking research on gender. If gender is based in the biological differences between men and women, she reasoned, people everywhere should define "feminine" and "masculine" in the same way; if gender is cultural, these concepts should vary.

Mead studied three societies in New Guinea (1963, orig. 1935). In the mountainous home of the Arapesh, Mead observed men and women with remarkably similar attitudes and behavior. Both sexes, she reported, were cooperative and sensitive to others—in short, what our culture would label "feminine."

Moving south, Mead studied the Mundugumor, whose headhunting and cannibalism stood in striking contrast to the gentle ways of the Arapesh. Both sexes were typically selfish and aggressive, traits we define as more "masculine."

Finally, traveling west to the Tchambuli, Mead discovered a culture that, like our own, defined females and males differently. But, Mead reported, the Tchambuli *reversed* many of our ideas of gender: Females were dominant and rational, whereas males were submissive, emotional, and nurturing toward children. Based on her observations, Mead concluded that culture is the key to gender distinctions because what one society defines as masculine another may see as feminine.

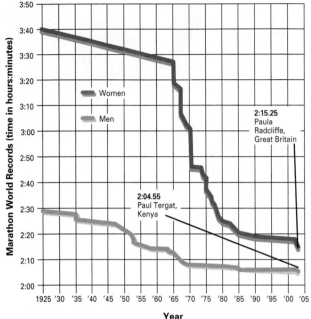

DIVERSITY SNAPSHOT

FIGURE 10-1   Men's and Women's Athletic
Performance

Do men naturally outperform women in athletic competition? The
answer is not obvious. Early in the twentieth century, men
outdistanced women by many miles in marathon races. But as
opportunities for women in athletics have increased, women have
been closing the performance gap. Only ten minutes separate the
current world marathon records for women (set in 2003) and for
men (set in 2003).

Sources: *The Christian Science Monitor,* © 1995 The Christian Science Monitor
(www.csmonitor.com) and Marathonguide.com (2004). Adapted with permission of the
Christian Science Monitor.

Some critics consider Mead's findings "too neat," as if
she saw in these societies just the patterns she was looking
for. Deborah Gewertz (1981) challenged what she called
Mead's "reversal hypothesis," pointing out that Tchambuli
males are really the more aggressive sex. Gewertz explains
that Mead visited the Tchambuli (who actually call themselves the Chambri) during the 1930s, after they had lost
much of their property in tribal wars, and observed men
rebuilding their homes, a temporary role for Chambri
men.

George Murdock's research.   In a broader study of more
than 200 preindustrial societies, George Murdock (1937)

found some global agreement on which tasks are feminine
and which are masculine. Hunting and warfare, Murdock
observed, generally fall to men, and home-centered tasks
such as cooking and child care tend to be women's work.
With their simple technology, preindustrial societies apparently assign roles reflecting men's and women's physical
characteristics. With their greater size and strength, men
hunt game and protect the group; because women bear
children, they do most work in the home.

Beyond this general pattern, Murdock found much
variety. Consider agriculture: Women did the farming in
about the same number of societies as men; in most societies, the two sexes divided this work. When it came to many
other tasks, from building shelters to tattooing the body,
Murdock found that preindustrial societies were as likely to
turn to one sex as the other.

In sum: Gender and culture.   Global comparisons show
that overall, societies do not consistently define tasks as
feminine or masculine. With industrialization, the importance of muscle power declines, further reducing gender
differences (Nolan & Lenski, 2004). In sum, gender is too
variable to be a simple expression of biology; what it means
to be female and male is mostly a creation of society.

PATRIARCHY AND SEXISM

Although conceptions of gender vary, everywhere in the
world we find some degree of **patriarchy** (literally, "the rule
of fathers"), *a form of social organization in which males
dominate females.* Despite mythical tales of societies run by
female "Amazons," **matriarchy,** *a form of social organization
in which females dominate males,* has never been documented in human history (Gough, 1971; Harris, 1977;
Lengermann & Wallace, 1985).

Although some degree of patriarchy may be universal,
Global Map 10–1 shows the great variation in the relative
power and privilege of women that exists from country to
country. According to the United Nations' gender development index, Norway, Sweden, and Australia give women the
highest social standing; by contrast, women in the African
nations of Niger, Burkina Faso, Mali, Guinea-Bissau, and
Burundi have the lowest social standing compared with
men. Of the world's nations, the United States ranked
eighth in terms of gender equality (United Nations Development Programme, 2004).

Sexism, *the belief that one sex is innately superior to the
other,* is the ideological basis of patriarchy. Sexism is not just
a matter of individual attitudes; it is built into the institutions of our society. *Institutional sexism* is found throughout the economy, with women highly concentrated in

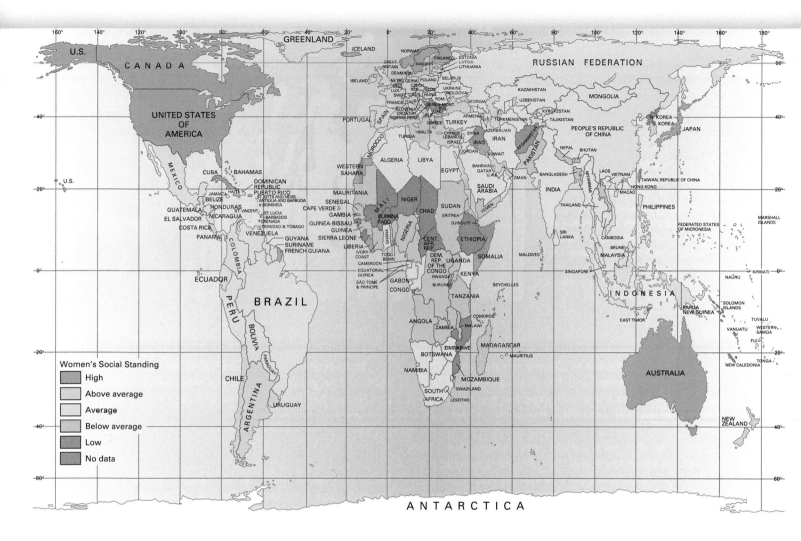

GLOBAL MAP 10–1   Women's Power in Global Perspective

Women's social standing in relation to men's varies around the world. In general, women live better in rich countries than in poor countries. Even so, some nations stand out: In the nations of Norway, Sweden, and Australia, women come closest to social equality with men.

Source: Data from Seager (2003).

Women's Social Standing
- High
- Above average
- Average
- Below average
- Low
- No data

low-paying jobs. Similarly, the legal system has long excused violence against women, especially on the part of boyfriends, husbands, and fathers.

The costs of sexism.   Sexism limits the talents and the ambitions of half the population. Although men benefit in some respects from sexism, their privilege comes at a high price. Masculinity in our culture calls for men to engage in many high-risk behaviors: using tobacco and alcohol, playing dangerous sports, and even driving recklessly. As Marilyn French (1985) argues, patriarchy drives men to relentlessly seek control, not only of women but also of themselves and their world. Thus, masculinity is linked not only to accidents but also to suicide, violence, and stress-related diseases. The

In every society, people assume certain jobs, patterns of behavior, and ways of dressing are "naturally" feminine while others are just as obviously masculine. But in global perspective, we see remarkable variety in such social definitions. These men, Wodaabe pastoral nomads who live in the African nation of Niger, are proud to engage in a display of beauty most people in our society would consider feminine.

Type A personality—marked by chronic impatience, driving ambition, competitiveness, and free-floating hostility—is a recipe for heart disease and an almost perfect match with the behavior our culture considers masculine (Ehrenreich, 1983).

Finally, as men seek control over others, they lose opportunities for intimacy and trust. As one researcher put it, competition is supposed to separate "the men from the boys," but in practice it separates men from men and everyone else (Raphael, 1988).

Is patriarchy inevitable? In preindustrial societies, women have little control over pregnancy and childbirth, which limits the scope of their lives. In those same societies, men's greater height and physical strength are valued resources. But industrialization, including birth control technology, gives people choices about how to live. In societies like our own, biological differences offer little justification for patriarchy.

But males are dominant in the United States and elsewhere. Does this mean that patriarchy is inevitable? Some sociologists claim that biological factors "wire" the sexes with different motivations and behaviors—especially aggressiveness in males—making patriarchy difficult, perhaps even impossible, to eliminate (Goldberg, 1974; Rossi, 1985; Popenoe, 1993b; Udry, 2000). However, most sociologists believe that gender is socially constructed and *can* be changed. Just because no society has yet eliminated patriarchy does not mean that we must stay prisoners of the past.

To understand the persistence of patriarchy, we next examine how gender is rooted and reproduced in society, a process that begins in childhood and continues throughout our lives.

Gender and Socialization

From birth until death, gender shapes human feelings, thoughts, and actions. Children quickly learn that their society defines females and males as different kinds of people; by about age three, they begin to apply gender standards to each other and to themselves.

Table 10–1 presents traits that people in the United States traditionally link to "feminine" and "masculine" behavior. Note that the traits in each column are direct opposites, even though research shows that most people do not develop consistently feminine or masculine personalities (Bem, 1993).

Just as gender affects how we think of ourselves, so it teaches us to act in normative ways. **Gender roles** (or **sex roles**) are *attitudes and activities that a society links to each sex.* Insofar as our culture defines males as ambitious and competitive, we expect them to play team sports and seek out positions of leadership. To the extent that we define females as deferential and emotional, we expect them to be supportive helpers and quick to show their feelings.

GENDER AND THE FAMILY

The first question people usually ask about a newborn—"Is it a boy or a girl?"—has great importance because the answer involves not just sex but the likely direction of a child's life.

In fact, gender is at work even before a child is born because, especially in lower-income nations, parents hope their firstborn will be a boy rather than a girl. Soon after birth, family members welcome infants into the "pink world" of girls or the "blue world" of boys (Bernard, 1981). People even send gender messages in the way they handle infants. One researcher at an English university presented an infant dressed as either a boy or a girl to a number of women; her subjects handled the "female" child tenderly, with frequent hugs and caresses, while treating the "male" child more aggressively, often lifting him up high in the air or bouncing him on the knee (Bonner, 1984; Tavris & Wade, 2001). The lesson is clear: The female world revolves around cooperation and emotion, and the male world puts a premium on independence and action.

GENDER AND THE PEER GROUP

About the time they enter school, children move outside the family, making friends with others of the same age. Considerable research points to the fact that young children tend to form single-sex play groups (Martin & Fabes, 2001).

Peer groups teach additional lessons about gender. After spending a year watching children at play, Janet Lever (1978) concluded that boys favor team sports with complex rules and clear objectives such as scoring runs or touchdowns. Such games nearly always involve winners and losers, reinforcing masculine traits of aggression and control.

Girls, too, play team sports. But, Lever explains, girls also play hopscotch or jump rope or simply talk, sing, or dance. These activities have few rules, and rarely is "victory" the ultimate goal. Instead of teaching girls to be competitive, Lever explains, female peer groups encourage interpersonal skills of communication and cooperation, presumably the basis for girls' future roles as wives and mothers.

Lever's observations recall Carol Gilligan's gender-based theory of moral reasoning, which was introduced in Chapter 3, ("Socialization"). According to Gilligan (1982), boys reason according to abstract principles. For them, "rightness" amounts to "playing by the rules." By contrast, girls consider morality a matter of responsibility to others. Thus, the games we play have serious implications for our later lives.

GENDER AND SCHOOLING

Gender shapes our interests and beliefs about our own abilities, guiding areas of study and, eventually, career choices (Correll, 2001). In high school, more girls than boys learn secretarial skills and take vocational classes such as

TABLE 10-1

A Traditional View of Gender Identity

Feminine Traits	Masculine Traits
Submissive	Dominant
Dependent	Independent
Unintelligent and incapable	Intelligent and competent
Emotional	Rational
Receptive	Assertive
Intuitive	Analytical
Weak	Strong
Timid	Brave
Content	Ambitious
Passive	Active
Cooperative	Competitive
Sensitive	Insensitive
Sex object	Sexually aggressive
Attractive because of physical appearance	Attractive because of achievement

cosmetology and food services. Classes in woodworking and auto mechanics attract mostly young men.

In college, the pattern continues, with men overly represented in mathematics and the natural sciences, including physics, chemistry, and biology. Women cluster in the humanities (such as English), the fine arts (painting, music, dance, and drama), and the social sciences (including anthropology and sociology). Newer areas of study are also gender-typed: computer science enrolls mostly men, and courses in gender studies enroll mostly women.

GENDER AND THE MASS MEDIA

Since television first captured the public imagination in the 1950s, white males have held center stage; racial and ethnic minorities were all but absent from television until the early 1970s. Even when both sexes appear on camera, men generally play the brilliant detectives, fearless explorers, and skilled surgeons. Women play the less capable characters, who are often unnecessary except for the sexual interest they add to the story.

Historically, ads have shown women in the home, cheerfully using cleaning products, serving food, trying out appliances, and modeling clothes. Men predominate in ads for cars, travel, banking services, industrial companies, and alcoholic beverages. The authoritative voiceover—the faceless voice that describes a product in television and radio advertising—is almost always male (Davis, 1993).

Further, a careful look at advertising in the print media reveals that men usually appear taller than women,

DIVERSITY: RACE, CLASS, & GENDER
The Beauty Myth

The Duchess of Windsor once remarked, "A woman cannot be too rich or too thin." The first half of her observation might apply to men as well, but certainly not the second. After all, most ads placed by the $20-billion-a-year U.S. cosmetics industry and the $40-billion diet industry target women.

According to Naomi Wolf (1990), certain cultural patterns create a "beauty myth" that is damaging to women. The beauty myth arises, first, because society teaches women to measure themselves in terms of physical appearance (Backman & Adams, 1991). Yet the standards of beauty embodied by the *Playboy* centerfold or the 100-pound New York fashion model are out of reach of most women.

The way society teaches women to prize relationships with men, whom they presumably attract with their beauty, also contributes to the beauty myth. Striving for beauty not only drives women to be extremely disciplined but also forces them to be highly attentive and responsive to men. In short, beauty-minded women try to please men and avoid challenging male power.

The beauty myth affects males as well: Men should want to possess

beautiful women. Thus, our ideas about beauty reduce women to objects and motivate men to possess women as if they were dolls rather than human beings.

In sum, there can be little doubt that the idea of beauty is important in everyday life. According to Wolf, the question is whether beauty is about how we look or how we act.

WHAT DO YOU THINK?

1. What, exactly, is the myth surrounding beauty?
2. How does the beauty myth apply differently to men and women?
3. Do you agree that the great importance attached to beauty for women is a problem? Why or why not?

Source: Based on Wolf (1990).

---

implying male superiority. Women, by contrast, are more frequently presented lying down (on sofas and beds) or, like children, seated on the floor. Men's facial expressions and behavior give off an air of competence and imply dominance, whereas women often appear childlike, submissive, and sexual. Men focus on the products being advertised; women often focus on the men (Goffman, 1979; Cortese, 1999).

Finally, advertising perpetuates what Naomi Wolf (1990) calls the "beauty myth." The Diversity box takes a closer look at how this myth affects women.

Gender and Social Stratification

Gender involves more than how people think and act. It is also about social hierarchy. The reality of gender stratification can be seen, first, in the world of work.

WORKING WOMEN AND MEN

Back in 1900, just one-fifth of women were in the U.S. labor force. Today, 60 percent of women aged sixteen and over work for income, and 70 percent of working women do so full time. The traditional view that earning an income is a man's role no longer holds true, as Figure 10–2 shows.

Factors that have changed the U.S. labor force include the decline of farming, the growth of cities, shrinking family size, and a rising divorce rate. The United States, along with most other nations of the world, considers women working for income to be the rule rather than the exception. In fact, more than half of U.S. married couples now depend on two incomes. As Global Map 10–2 on page 260 shows, women represent almost half the labor force in the United States; however, this is not the case in many of the poorer societies of the world.

SOCIOLOGY WORK

A century ago, most younger women in the labor force were childless. But today, 61 percent of married women with children under age six work for income, as do 77 percent of married women with children between six and seventeen years of age. For widowed, divorced, or separated women with children, the comparable figures are 78 percent of women with younger children and 84 percent of women with older children (U.S. Census Bureau, 2003).

Gender and occupations. Although women are closing the gap with men as far as working for income is concerned, the work done by the two sexes remains very different. The U.S. Department of Labor (2004) reports a high concentration of women in two job types. Administrative support work draws 23 percent of working women, most of whom hold positions as secretaries or other office workers. These are often called "pink collar" jobs because 76 percent are filled by women. Another 20 percent of employed women perform service work. Most of these jobs are in the food service industries, child care, and health care.

Table 10–2 shows the ten occupations with the highest concentrations of women. Overall, although more women now work for pay, they remain segregated in the labor force in jobs at the low end of the pay scale; advancement opportunities are limited, and they are usually supervised by men (U.S. Department of Labor, 2004).

Men dominate most other job categories, including the building trades, where 99 percent of brickmasons, stonemasons, and heavy-equipment mechanics are men. Likewise, men make up 88 percent of police officers, 86 percent of engineers, 72 percent of lawyers, 70 percent of physicians and surgeons, and 63 percent of corporate managers. According to a recent survey, the top earners in *Fortune* 500 companies include 2,141 men (95 percent of the total) and 118 women (5 percent). Just 17 of the 1,000 largest corporations in the United States have a woman as their chief executive officer (Catalyst, 2003, 2004; U.S. Department of Labor, 2004).

See a report on women in corporate leadership positions in Europe and the U.S. at http://www.catalystwomen.org/press_room/factsheets/WICL-US_and_EU_comparisons.pdf

Gender stratification in the workplace is easy to see: Female nurses assist male doctors, female secretaries serve male executives, and female flight attendants are under the command of male airline pilots. In any field, the greater a job's income and prestige, the more likely it is to be held by a man. For example, women represent 98 percent of kindergarten teachers, 81 percent of elementary and middle school teachers, 55 percent of secondary school educators, 45 percent of professors in colleges and universities, and 21 percent of college and university presidents (Chronicle of Higher Education, 2004; U.S. Department of Labor, 2004).

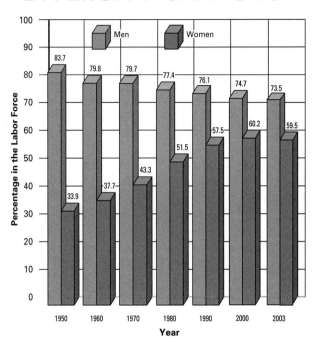

DIVERSITY SNAPSHOT

FIGURE 10-2 Men and Women in the U.S. Labor Force

Source: U.S. Department of Labor (2004).

TABLE 10-2

Jobs with the Highest Concentrations of Women, 2003

Occupation	Number of Women Employed	Percentage in Occupation Who Are Women
1. Dental hygienist	125,000	98.9%
2. Preschool and kindergarten teacher	650,000	97.8
3. Secretary and administrative assistant	3,509,000	96.6
4. Child care worker	1,221,000	95.1
5. Dental assistant	238,000	95.0
6. Licensed practical and licensed vocational nurse	503,000	94.8
7. Speech-language pathologist	88,000	94.5
8. Hairdresser, hairstylist, and cosmetologist	673,000	93.7
9. Word processor and typist	339,000	93.6
10. Receptionist and information clerk	1,282,000	93.2

Source: U.S. Department of Labor (2004).

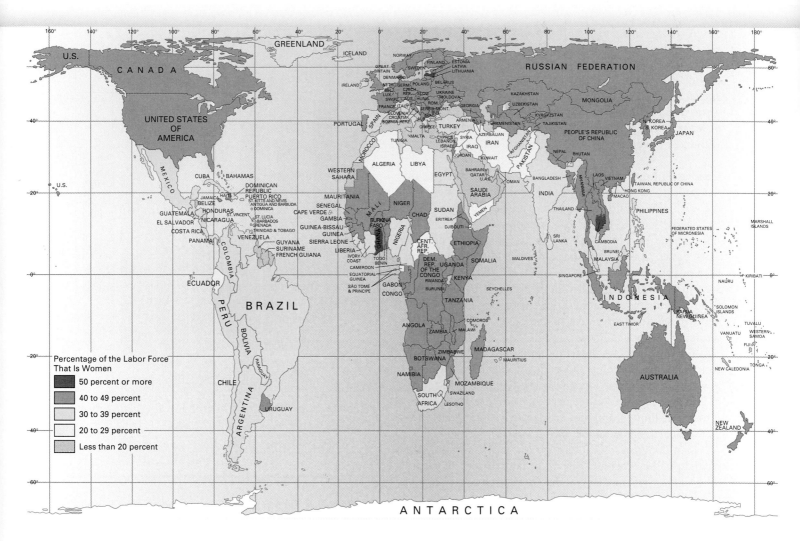

WINDOW ON THE WORLD

GLOBAL MAP 10-2 Women's Paid Employment in Global Perspective

This map shows the percentage of the labor force made up of women. A country's level of technological development plays an important part here. In 2003, women were 47 percent of the labor force in the United States, up almost 10 percent over the preceding generation. In high-income nations, overall, nearly one-half of the labor force is made up of women. In poor societies, however, women work even harder than in this country, but they are less likely to be paid for their efforts. In Latin America, for example, women represent about one-third of the paid labor force; in Islamic societies of northern Africa and the Middle East, the figure is significantly lower. One exception to this rule is central and southern Africa, where, traditionally, women make up a large share of farmers.

Sources: *Peters Atlas of the World* (1990); updated by the author from World Bank (2004).

How are women kept out of certain jobs? By defining some kinds of work as "masculine," companies define women as unsuitable workers. In a study of coal mining in southern West Virginia, Suzanne Tallichet (2000) found that most men considered it "unnatural" for women to work in the mines. Consequently, women who did so were defined as "unnatural" and subject to labeling as "sexually loose" or as lesbians. Such labeling made these women

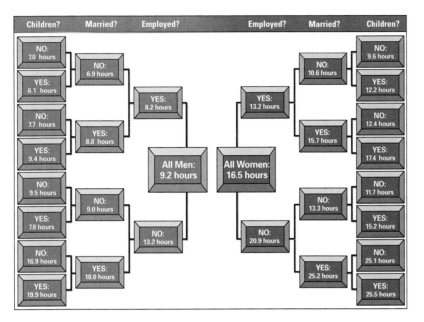

| Children? | Married? | Employed? | | Employed? | Married? | Children? |

FIGURE 10-3 Housework: Who Does How Much?

Overall, women average 16.5 hours of housework per week, compared with 9.2 hours for men. This pattern holds whether people are employed or not, married or not, and parenting or not.

Source: Adapted from Stapinski (1998).

outcasts, presented a challenge to holding the job, and made advancement all but impossible.

One challenge to male domination in the workplace comes from women who are entrepreneurs. Women now own more than 9 million small businesses, twice the number of a decade ago and more than one-third of the total. Although the large majority of these businesses are one-person operations, women-owned businesses employ one-fourth of the entire labor force. Women have shown they can make opportunities for themselves apart from large, male-dominated companies (U.S. Small Business Administration, 2001b).

HOUSEWORK: WOMEN'S "SECOND SHIFT"

Global Map 4–1 on page 91 shows that housework—maintaining the home and caring for children—is mainly the responsibility of women throughout the world. In the United States, housework has always presented a cultural contradiction: We claim that it is essential for family life, but housework carries little prestige or reward (Bernard, 1981).

The amount of housework performed by women has declined with their rapid entry into the labor force; nevertheless, the *share* of it that women do has stayed about the same. Figure 10–3 shows that overall, women average 16.5 hours of housework per week, compared with 9.2 hours for men. As the figure shows, women in all categories do significantly more housework than men (Stapinski, 1998).

Men do support the idea of women entering the paid labor force, and most count on the money they earn. But many men resist taking on an equal share of household duties (Heath & Bourne, 1995; Harpster & Monk-Turner, 1998; Stratton, 2001).

GENDER, INCOME, AND WEALTH

In 2003, the median earnings for women working full time were $30,724, and men working full time earned $40,668. This means that for every dollar earned by men, women earned about 76 cents. These earning differences are greatest among older workers because older working women typically have less education and seniority than older working men. Earning differences are smaller among younger workers because younger men and women tend to have similar schooling and job experience.

Among full-time workers of all ages, 35 percent of women earned less than $25,000 in 2003, compared with 23 percent of comparable men. At the upper end of the income scale, men were nearly three times more likely than women (17.7 percent versus 6.7 percent) to earn more than $75,000 (U.S. Census Bureau, 2004).

The main reason women earn less is the *kind* of work they do: largely clerical and service jobs. In effect, jobs and gender interact. People still think of less important jobs as "women's work," just as people devalue work simply because it is performed by women (England, 1992; Bellas, 1994; Huffman, Velasco, & Bielby, 1996; England, Hermsen, & Cotter, 2000).

TABLE 10-3

Significant "Firsts" for Women in U.S. Politics

1869   Law allows women to vote in Wyoming territory.

1872   First woman to run for the presidency (Victoria Wood-hull) represents the Equal Rights party.

1917   First woman elected to the House of Representatives (Jeannette Rankin of Montana).

1924   First women elected state governors (Nellie Taylor Ross of Wyoming and Miriam "Ma" Ferguson of Texas); both followed their husbands into office. First woman to have her name placed in nomination for vice-presidency at the convention of a major political party (Lena Jones Springs, a Democrat).

1931   First woman to serve in the Senate (Hattie Caraway of Arkansas); completed the term of her husband upon his death and won reelection in 1932.

1932   First woman appointed to the presidential cabinet (Frances Perkins, secretary of labor in the cabinet of President Franklin D. Roosevelt).

1964   First woman to have her name placed in nomination for the presidency at the convention of a major political party (Margaret Chase Smith, a Republican).

1972   First African American woman to have her name placed in nomination for the presidency at the convention of a major political party (Shirley Chisholm, a Democrat).

1981   First woman appointed to the U.S. Supreme Court (Sandra Day O'Connor).

1984   First woman to be successfully nominated for the vice-presidency (Geraldine Ferraro, a Democrat).

1988   First woman chief executive to be elected to a consecutive third term (Madeleine Kunin, governor of Vermont).

1992   Political "Year of the Woman" yields record number of women in the Senate (six) and the House (forty-eight), as well as (1) first African American woman to win election to U.S. Senate (Carol Moseley-Braun of Illinois), (2) first state (California) to be served by two women senators (Barbara Boxer and Dianne Feinstein), and (3) first woman of Puerto Rican descent elected to the House (Nydia Velazquez of New York).

1996   First woman appointed secretary of state (Madeleine Albright).

2000   Record number of women in the House (sixty).

2000   First First Lady to win elected political office (Hillary Rodham Clinton, senator from New York).

2001   First woman to serve as National Security Advisor (Condoleezza Rice).

2001   First Asian American woman to serve in a presidential cabinet (Elaine Chao).

2002   Record number of women in the Senate (fourteen).

Source: Compiled by the author.

In recent decades, supporters of gender equality have proposed a policy of "comparable worth," paying people not according to the historical double standard but according to the value of what they do. Several nations, including Great Britain and Australia, have adopted comparable worth policies, but these policies have found limited acceptance in the United States. As a result, critics claim, women in this country lose as much as $1 billion in income annually.

A second cause of gender-based income inequality has to do with society's view of the family. Both men and women have children, of course, but our culture gives more of the responsibility of parenting to women. Pregnancy and raising small children keep many younger women out of the labor force at a time when their male peers are making significant career advancements. When women workers return to the labor force, they have less job experience and seniority than their male counterparts (Stier, 1996; Waldfogel, 1997).

In addition, women who choose to have children may be unable or unwilling to take on fast-paced jobs that tie up their evenings and weekends. To avoid role strain, they may take jobs that offer shorter commuting distances, more flexible hours, and employer child care services. Women pursuing both a career and a family are torn between their dual responsibilities in ways that men are not.

 The *Monthly Labor Review* reports on the gender earnings gap at http://www.bls.gov/opub/mlr/2003/03/art2full.pdf

Consider this: At age forty, 90 percent of men but only 35 percent of women in executive positions have at least one child (Schwartz, 1989). This pattern is also found on the campus: A recent study of college and university teachers found that young women with at least one child were at least 20 percent less likely to have tenure than comparable men in the same field (Shea, 2002).

The two factors noted so far—type of work and family responsibilities—account for about two-thirds of the earnings difference between women and men. A third factor—discrimination against women—accounts for most of the remainder (Fuller & Schoenberger, 1991). Because discrimination is illegal, it is practiced in subtle ways. Women on their way up the corporate ladder often run into a *glass ceiling*, an invisible barrier, denied to exist by company officials, that effectively prevents women from rising above middle management (Benokraitis & Feagin, 1995; Yamagata et al., 1997).

For all these reasons, women earn less than men in all major occupational categories. Even so, many people think that women own most of the country's wealth, perhaps because they typically outlive men. Government statistics tell a different story: Sixty-one percent of people with $1 million or more in assets are men, although widows are highly represented in this elite club (Internal Revenue Service, 2003). Just 10 percent of the people identified in 2004 by *Forbes* magazine as the richest people in the United States are women (Kroll & Goldman, 2004).

NATIONAL MAP 10-1

Women in State Government across the United States

Although women make up half of U.S. adults, just 23 percent of the seats in state legislatures are held by women. Look at the state-by-state variation in the map. In which regions of the country have women gained the greatest political power? What do you think accounts for this pattern?

Source: Center for American Women and Politics (2004).

Share of State Legislative Seats Held by Women

- High: 30.0% and over
- Above average: 25.0% to 29.9%
- Average: 20.0% to 24.9%
- Below average: 15.0% to 19.9%
- Low: 14.9% and under

U.S. average: 22.5%

GENDER AND EDUCATION

In the past, our society considered schooling unnecessary for women because women's lives focused on the home. But times have changed. By 1980, women earned a majority of all associate and bachelor's degrees; in 2001, their share was 58 percent (National Center for Education Statistics, 2003).

College doors have opened to women, and differences in men's and women's majors are becoming smaller. In 1970, for example, women earned just 17 percent of bachelor's degrees in the natural sciences, computer science, and engineering; by 2001, the proportion had doubled to 35 percent.

In 1992, for the first time, women earned a majority of postgraduate degrees, which are often a springboard to high-prestige jobs. In all areas of study in 2001, women A report on trends in equal education for girls and women can be found at http://nces.ed.gov/programs/quarterly/vol_2/2_2/q6-1.asp earned 59 percent of all master's degrees and 45 percent of all doctorates (including 58 percent of all Ph.D. degrees in sociology). Women have also broken into many graduate fields that used to be almost all male. For example, in 1970, only a few hundred women received a master's of business administration (M.B.A.) degree, compared to more than 47,000 in 2001 (41 percent of all such degrees) (National Center for Education Statistics, 2003).

Despite this progress, men continue to dominate some professional fields. In 2001, men received 53 percent of law degrees (LL.B. and J.D.), 57 percent of medical degrees (M.D.), and 61 percent of dental degrees (D.D.S. and D.M.D.) (National Center for Education Statistics, 2003). Our society still defines high-paying professions (and the

drive and competitiveness needed to succeed in them) as masculine. Nevertheless, the proportion of women in all these professions is rising steadily: For example, the American Bar Association reported that the law school class of 2007 across the United States was about evenly split between women and men (American Bar Association, 2004).

GENDER AND POLITICS

A century ago, almost no women held elected office in the United States. In fact, women were legally barred from voting in national elections until the passage of the Nineteenth Amendment to the Constitution in 1920. However, a few women were candidates for political office even before they could vote. The Equal Rights party supported Victoria Woodhull for the U.S. presidency in 1872; perhaps it was a sign of the times that she spent election day in a New York City jail. Table 10–3 identifies milestones in women's gradual movement into political life.

Today, thousands of women serve as mayors of cities and towns across the United States, and tens of thousands more  For the latest on women in national politics, visit http://www.cawp.rutgers.edu hold responsible administrative jobs in the federal government. At the state level, 23 percent of state legislators in 2004 were women (up from just 6 percent in 1970). National Map 10–1 shows where in the United States women have made the greatest political gains.

Less change has occurred at the highest levels of power, although a majority of U.S. adults claim they would support a qualified woman for any office, including the presidency.

The basic insight of intersection theory is that various dimensions of social stratification—including race and gender—can add up to great disadvantages for some categories of people. Just as African Americans earn less than whites, women earn less than men. Thus, African American women confront a "double disadvantage," earning just 60 cents for every dollar earned by non-Hispanic white men. How would you explain the fact that some categories of people are much more likely to end up in low-paying jobs like this one?

As of mid-2004, 9 of the 50 state governors were women (18 percent), and in Congress, women held 60 of the 435 seats in the House of Representatives (14 percent) and 14 of the 100 seats in the Senate (14 percent).

In global perspective, although women make up half the Earth's population, they hold just 15.4 percent of seats in the world's 183 parliaments. Although this represents a rise from 3 percent fifty years ago, only in the Nordic nations of Norway, Sweden, Finland, and Denmark (ranging from 45.3 to 36.4 percent) does the share of parliamentary seats held by women approach their share of the population (Inter-Parliamentary Union, 2004).

GENDER AND THE MILITARY

Since colonial times, women have served in the U.S. armed forces. Yet in 1940, at the outset of World War II, just 2 percent of armed forces personnel were women. By the time of the 2003 War in Iraq, women represented about 7 percent of

all deployed U.S. troops and 15 percent of all people in the armed forces.

Clearly, women make up a growing share of the U.S. military, and almost all military assignments are now open to women. But some people object to women's taking part in the military, claiming that women lack the physical strength of men. Others reply that military women are better educated and score higher on intelligence tests than military men. But the heart of the issue is our society's deeply held view of women as *nurturers*—people who give life and help others—which clashes with the image of women trained to kill.

Although integrating women into military culture has been difficult, women in all branches of the armed forces are taking on more and more assignments. One reason is that high technology blurs the distinction between combat and noncombat personnel. A combat pilot can fire missiles at a target miles away, but nonfighting medical evacuation teams must travel directly into the line of fire (Segal & Hansen, 1992; Wilcox, 1992; Kaminer, 1997).

ARE WOMEN A MINORITY?

A **minority** is *any category of people distinguished by physical or cultural difference that a society sets apart and subordinates*. Given the clear economic disadvantage of being a woman in our society, it seems reasonable to say that women are a minority in the United States even though they outnumber men.[1]

Even so, most white women do not think of themselves this way (Hacker, 1951; Lengermann & Wallace, 1985). This is partly because, unlike racial minorities (including African Americans) and ethnic minorities (say, Hispanics), white women are well represented at all levels of the class structure, including the very top.

Bear in mind, however, that at every class level, women typically have less income, wealth, education, and power than men. In fact, patriarchy makes women depend on men—first their fathers and later their husbands—for their social standing (Bernard, 1981).

MINORITY WOMEN: INTERSECTION THEORY

If women are defined as a minority, what about minority women? Are they doubly handicapped? This question lies at

---

[1]The term "minority" is used instead of "minority group" because, as explained in Chapter 5 ("Groups and Organizations"), women make up a *category,* not a group. Members of a category share a status or identity but generally do not know one another.

the heart of **intersection theory,** *the investigation of the interplay of race, class, and gender, often resulting in multiple dimensions of disadvantage.* Research shows that disadvantages linked to race and gender often combine to produce especially low social standing (Ovadia, 2001).

Income data illustrate the value of this approach. Looking first at race and ethnicity, the median income in 2003 for African American women working full time was $27,622, which is 81 percent as much as the $34,037 earned by non-Hispanic white women; Hispanic women earned $23,062, just 68 percent as much as non-Hispanic white women. Looking at gender, African American women earned 83 percent as much as African American men, and Hispanic women earned 87 percent as much as Hispanic men.

Combining these disadvantages, African American women earned 60 percent as much as non-Hispanic white men, and Hispanic women earned 50 percent as much (U.S. Census Bureau, 2004). These differences reflect minority women's lower positions in the occupational and educational hierarchies compared with white women. These data confirm that although gender has a powerful effect on our lives, it does not operate alone. Class position, race and ethnicity, and gender form a multilayered system that provides disadvantages for some and privileges for others (St. Jean & Feagin, 1998).

VIOLENCE AGAINST WOMEN

As noted in the opening to this chapter, about 150 years ago, men claimed the right to rule their households, even to the point of using physical discipline against their wives. Even today, a great deal of "manly" violence is still directed

Here is a United Nations report on violence against women and girls around the world: http://www.unicef-icdc.org/ publications/pdf/digest6e.pdf

against women. A government report estimates that 413,000 aggravated assaults against women occur annually. To this number can be added 179,000 rapes or sexual assaults and perhaps 1.5 million simple assaults (Goetting, 1999; U.S. Bureau of Justice Statistics, 2004).

Gender violence is also an issue on college and university campuses. A report from the U.S. Department of Justice (2000) states that in 2000, 1.7 percent of female college students were victims of rape, and another 1.1 percent were victims of attempted rape. In 90 percent of all campus cases, the victims knew the offenders, and most of the assaults took place in the woman's living quarters.

Off the campus as well, most gender-linked violence occurs where men and women interact most: in the home. Richard Gelles (cited in Roesch, 1984) argues that with the exception of the police and the military, the family is the most violent organization in the United States. Both sexes

suffer from family violence, although, by and large, women receive more serious injuries than men (Gelles & Cornell, 1990; Smolowe, 1994).

Violence toward women also occurs in casual relationships. As noted in Chapter 7 ("Deviance"), most rapes involve men known, and often trusted, by their victims. Dianne Herman (2001) argues that the extent of sexual abuse shows that the tendency toward sexual violence is built into our way of life. All forms of violence against women—from the catcalls that intimidate women on city streets to a pinch in a crowded subway to physical assaults that occur at home—express what she calls a "rape culture" of men trying to dominate women. In fact, sexual violence is fundamentally about *power,* not sex, and therefore should be understood as a dimension of gender stratification.

In global perspective, violence against women is built into other cultures in many different ways. One case in point is the practice of female genital mutilation, a painful and often dangerous surgical procedure performed in more

For information on female genital mutilation, see http://www.amnesty.org/ailib/intcam/femgen/fgm1.htm

than forty countries and known to occur in the United States, as shown in Global Map 10–3 on page 266. The Global Sociology box on page 267 presents a case of female genital mutilation that took place recently in California.

Sexual harassment. The term **sexual harassment** refers to *comments, gestures, or physical contact of a sexual nature that are deliberate, repeated, and unwelcome.* In the 1990s, sexual harassment became a national issue that rewrote the rules for workplace interaction between women and men.

Most (but not all) victims of sexual harassment are women. First, our culture encourages men to be sexually assertive and to see women in sexual terms. As a result, social interaction in the workplace, on campus, and elsewhere can easily take on sexual overtones. Second, most people in positions of power—including business executives, doctors, bureau chiefs, assembly line supervisors, professors, and military officers—are men who oversee the work of women. Surveys carried out in widely different work settings show that half of women respondents receive unwanted sexual attention (NORC, 2003).

Sexual harassment is sometimes obvious and direct: A supervisor may ask for sexual favors from an employee and make threats if the advances are refused. Courts have declared such *quid pro quo* sexual harassment (the Latin phrase means "one thing in return for another") to be a violation of civil rights.

More often, however, the problem of unwelcome sexual attention is a matter of subtle behavior—sexual teasing,

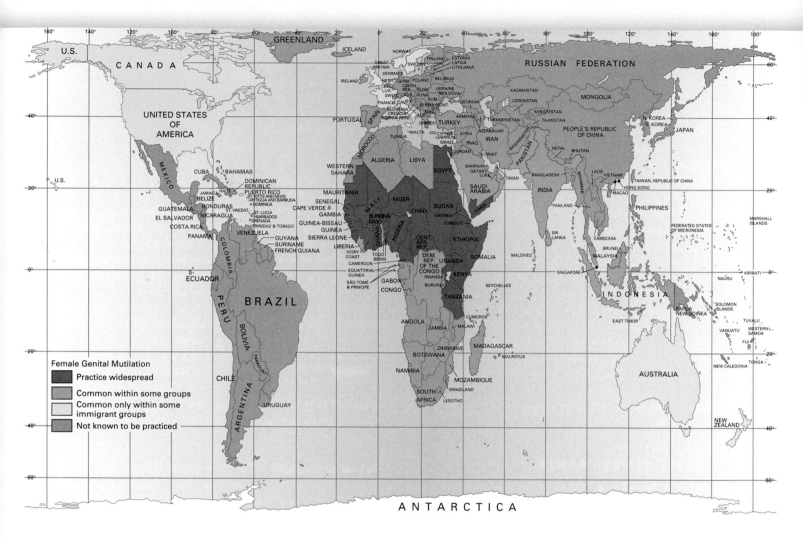

WINDOW ON THE WORLD

GLOBAL MAP 10-3 Female Genital Mutilation in Global Perspective

Female genital mutilation, sometimes called female circumcision, is known to be performed in more than forty countries around the world. Across Africa, the practice is common and affects a majority of girls in the eastern African nations of Sudan, Ethiopia, and Somalia. In several Asian nations, including India, the practice is limited to a few ethnic minorities. In the United States, Canada, several European nations, and Australia, there are reports of the practice among some immigrants.

Source: Data from Seager (2003).

off-color jokes, pin-ups displayed in the workplace—that may not even be *intended* to harass anyone. But based on the *effect* standard, favored by many feminists, such actions add up to creating a *hostile environment* (Cohen, 1991; Paul, 1991). Incidents of this kind are far more complex because they involve very different understandings of the same behavior. For example, a man may think that repeatedly complimenting a co-worker on her appearance is simply being friendly. The co-worker may believe the man is thinking of her in sexual terms and is not taking her work seriously, an attitude that could harm her job performance and prospects for advancement.

Female Genital Mutilation: Violence in the Name of Morality

Meserak Ramsey, a woman born in Ethiopia and now working as a nurse in California, paid a visit to an old friend's home. Soon after arriving, she noticed her friend's eighteen-month-old daughter huddled in the corner of a room in obvious pain. "What's wrong?" she asked.

Ramsey was shocked when the woman said her daughter had recently had a clitoridectomy, the surgical removal of the clitoris. This type of female genital mutilation—performed by a midwife, a tribal practitioner, or a doctor and typically without anesthesia—is common in Nigeria, Togo, Somalia, and Egypt and is known to exist in certain cultural groups in other nations around the world. It is illegal in the United States.

Among members of highly patriarchal societies, husbands demand that their wives be virgins at marriage and remain sexually faithful thereafter. The point of female genital mutilation is to eliminate sexual feeling, which, people assume, makes the girl less likely to violate sexual norms and thus be more desirable to men. In about one-fifth of all cases, an even more severe procedure, called infibulation, is performed, in which the entire external genital area is removed and the surfaces are stitched together, leaving only a small hole for urination. Before marriage, a husband has the right to open the wound and ensure himself of his bride's virginity.

How many women have undergone female genital mutilation? Worldwide, estimates place the number at more than 130 million. In the United States, hundreds and probably thousands of such procedures are performed every year. In most cases, immigrant mothers and grandmothers who have themselves been mutilated insist that young girls in their family follow their example. Indeed, many immigrant women demand the procedure *because* their daughters now live in the United States, where sexual mores are less rigid. "I don't have to worry about her now," the girl's mother explained to Meserak Ramsey. "She'll be a good girl."

Medically, the consequences of female genital mutilation include more than loss of sexual pleasure. Pain is intense and can persist for years. There is also danger of infection, infertility, and even death. Ramsey knows this all too well: She herself underwent genital mutilation as a young girl. She is one of the lucky ones who has had few medical problems since. But the extent of her suffering is suggested by this story: She had invited a young U.S. couple to stay at her home. Late at night, she heard the woman's cries and burst into their room to investigate, only to learn that the couple was making love and the woman had just had an orgasm. "I didn't understand," Ramsey recalls. "I thought that there must be something wrong with American girls. But now I know that there is something wrong with me." Or with a system that inflicts such injury in the name of traditional morality.

WHAT DO YOU THINK?

1. Is female genital mutilation a medical procedure or a means of social control? Why?
2. Can you think of other examples of physical mutilation imposed on women?
3. What do you think should be done about the practice of female genital mutilation?

These young women have just undergone female genital mutilation. What do you think should be done about this practice?

Sources: Based on Crossette (1995) and Boyle, Songora, & Foss (2001).

Pornography. Chapter 6 ("Sexuality and Society") defined *pornography* as sexually explicit material that causes sexual arousal. However, people take different views of exactly what is or is not pornographic; the law gives local communities the power to define whether sexually explicit material violates "community standards of decency" and lacks "any redeeming social value."

Traditionally, U.S. society has raised concerns about pornography on *moral* grounds. But pornography also plays a part in gender stratification. From this point of view,

In the 1950s, Talcott Parsons proposed that sociologists interpret gender as a matter of *differences*. As he saw it, masculine men and feminine women formed strong families and made for an orderly society. In recent decades, however, social-conflict theory has reinterpreted gender as a matter of *inequality*. From this point of view, U.S. society places men in a position of dominance over women.

pornography is really a *power* issue because most pornography dehumanizes women, treating them as the playthings of men. It is based on the belief that both sexuality and women should fall under the control of men. Worth noting in this context is that the term "pornography" is derived from the Greek word *porne,* meaning a woman kept as a man's sexual slave.

In addition, there is widespread concern that pornography encourages violence against women. Portraying them as merely the playthings of men amounts to defining women as weak and undeserving of respect. Men show contempt for women defined in this way by striking out against them. National surveys show that about half of U.S. adults think that pornography encourages people to commit rape (NORC, 2003:235).

Like sexual harassment, pornography raises complex and sometimes conflicting concerns. Although everyone may find some material offensive, many also support rights of free speech and artistic expression. Nevertheless, pressure to restrict pornography has increased in recent years, reflecting both the long-standing concern that pornography weakens morality and the more recent concern that it is demeaning and threatening to women.

Theoretical Analysis of Gender

Sociology's two macro-level approaches, summarized in the Applying Theory table, address the central place of gender in social organization.

STRUCTURAL-FUNCTIONAL ANALYSIS

The structural-functional approach views society as a complex system of many separate but integrated parts. From this point of view, gender serves as a means to organize social life.

As Chapter 2 ("Culture") explained, the earliest hunting and gathering societies had little power over the forces of biology. Lacking effective birth control, women were frequently pregnant, and the responsibilities of child care kept them close to home. At the same time, men's greater strength made them better suited for warfare and hunting. Over the centuries, this sex-based division of labor became institutionalized and largely taken for granted (Lengermann & Wallace, 1985; Freedman, 2002).

Industrial technology opens up a much greater range of cultural possibilities. With human muscle power no longer the main energy source, the physical strength of men becomes less significant. In addition, the ability to control reproduction gives women greater choices about how to live. Modern societies relax traditional gender roles as people come to recognize the enormous amount of human talent they waste; yet change comes slowly because gender is deeply rooted in culture.

Talcott Parsons: Gender and complementarity. As Talcott Parsons (1942, 1951, 1954) observed, gender helps integrate society, at least in its traditional form. Gender forms a *complementary* set of roles that links women and

APPLYING THEORY

GENDER

	Structural-Functional Approach	Social-Conflict Approach
What is the level of analysis?	Macro-level	Macro-level
What does gender mean?	Parsons described gender in terms of two complementary patterns of behavior: masculine and feminine.	Engels described gender in terms of the power of one sex over the other.
Is gender helpful or harmful?	Helpful. Gender gives men and women distinctive roles and responsibilities that help society operate smoothly. Gender builds social unity as men and women come together to form families.	Harmful. Gender limits people's personal development. Gender divides society by giving power to men to control the lives of women. Capitalism makes patriarchy stronger.

men into family units for the purpose of carrying out various important tasks. Women take primary responsibility for managing the household and raising children. Men connect the family to the larger world as they participate in the labor force.

Parsons further argued that distinctive socialization teaches the two sexes their appropriate gender identities and skills needed for adult life. Society teaches boys—presumably destined for the labor force—to be rational, self-assured, and competitive. Parsons called this complex of traits *instrumental* qualities. To prepare girls for child rearing, socialization stresses *expressive* qualities, such as emotional responsiveness and sensitivity to others.

Society encourages gender conformity by instilling fear in men and women that straying too far from accepted standards of masculinity or femininity will cause rejection by the opposite sex. In simple terms, women learn to reject nonmasculine men as sexually unattractive, and men learn to reject unfeminine women. In sum, gender integrates society both structurally (in terms of what people do) and morally (in terms of what they believe).

Critical review. Influential a half century ago, this approach has lost much of its standing today. First, functionalism assumes a singular vision of society that is not shared by everyone. For example, historically, many women have worked outside the home because of economic need, a fact not reflected in Parsons's conventional, middle-class view of social life. Second, Parsons's analysis ignores the personal strains and social costs of rigid gender roles. Third, in the eyes of those seeking sexual equality, Parsons's gender "complementarity" amounts to little more than women submitting to male domination.

SOCIAL-CONFLICT ANALYSIS

From a social-conflict point of view, gender involves differences not just in behavior but in power as well. Consider the striking similarity between how traditional ideas about gender benefit men and the ways oppression of racial and ethnic minorities benefits white people. Conventional ideas about gender do not contribute to the smooth operation of society; instead, they create division and tension, with men seeking to protect their privileges as women challenge the status quo.

As earlier chapters noted, the social-conflict approach draws heavily on the ideas of Karl Marx. Yet as far as gender is concerned, Marx was a product of his times, and his writings focused almost entirely on men. However, his friend and collaborator Friedrich Engels did develop a theory of gender stratification.

Friedrich Engels: Gender and class. Looking back through history, Engels saw that in hunting and gathering societies, the activities of women and men, though different, had the same importance. A successful hunt brought men great prestige, but the vegetation gathered by women provided most of a group's food supply. As technological advances led to a productive surplus, social equality and communal sharing gave way to private property and, ultimately, a class hierarchy. At this point, men gained pronounced power over women. With surplus wealth to pass on to heirs, upper-class men needed to be sure who their sons were, which led them to control the sexuality of women. The desire to control property brought about monogamous marriage and the family. Women were taught to remain virgins until marriage, to remain faithful to their husbands thereafter, and to build their lives around bearing and raising one man's children.

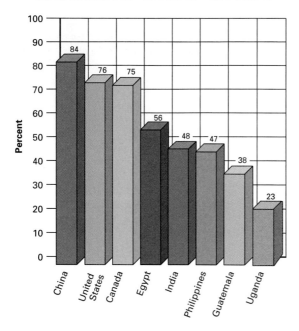

FIGURE 10–4 Use of Contraception by Married Women of Childbearing Age

Source: United Nations Development Programme (2004).

According to Engels (1902, orig. 1884), capitalism intensifies this male domination. First, capitalism creates more wealth, which gives greater power to men as owners of property and as primary wage earners. Second, an expanding capitalist economy depends on turning people, especially women, into consumers who seek personal fulfillment by buying and using products. Third, society assigns women the task of maintaining the home to free men to work in factories. The double exploitation of capitalism, as Engels saw it, lies in paying low wages for male labor and paying women no wages at all.

Critical review. Social-conflict analysis is strongly critical of conventional ideas about gender, claiming that society would be better off if we minimized or even did away with this dimension of social structure. One problem with this approach is that it sees conventional families—supported by traditionalists as morally good—as a social evil. Second, social-conflict analysis minimizes the extent to which women and men live together cooperatively, and often happily, in families. A third problem with this approach lies in its

claim that capitalism is the root of gender stratification. In fact, agrarian societies typically are more patriarchal than industrial-capitalist societies, and socialist nations—including the People's Republic of China and the former Soviet Union—did move women into the labor force but, by and large, provided women with very low pay in sex-segregated jobs (Moore, 1992; Rosendahl, 1997; Haney, 2002).

Feminism

Feminism is *the advocacy of social equality for men and women, in opposition to patriarchy and sexism.* The "first wave" of the feminist movement in the United States began in the 1840s as women opposed to slavery, including Elizabeth Cady Stanton and Lucretia Mott, showed the similarities between the oppression of African Americans and the oppression of women. Their main objective was obtaining the right to vote, which was finally achieved in 1920. But other disadvantages persisted, causing a "second wave" of feminism to arise in the 1960s that continues today.

BASIC FEMINIST IDEAS

Feminism views the personal experiences of women and men through the lens of gender. How we think of ourselves (gender identity), how we act (gender roles), and our sex's social standing (gender stratification) are all rooted in the operation of society.

Although people who consider themselves feminists disagree about many things, most support five general principles:

1. **Working to increase equality.** Feminist thinking is strongly political; it relates ideas to action. Feminism is critical of the status quo, pushing for change toward social equality for women and men.

2. **Expanding human choice.** Feminists argue that cultural ideas about gender divide the full range of human qualities into two opposing and limiting spheres: the female world of emotion and cooperation and the male world of rationality and competition. As an alternative, feminists propose a "reintegration of humanity" by which all individuals develop all human traits (French, 1985).

3. **Eliminating gender stratification.** Feminism opposes laws and cultural norms that limit the education, income, and job opportunities of women. For this reason, feminists have long supported passage of the Equal Rights Amendment (ERA) to the U.S. Constitution, which states, "Equality of rights under the law shall not be denied or abridged by the United States

or any State on account of sex." The ERA was first proposed in Congress in 1923. Although it has widespread support, it has yet to become law.

4. **Ending sexual violence.** Today's women's movement seeks to eliminate sexual violence. Feminists argue that patriarchy distorts relationships between women and men, encouraging violence against women in the form of rape, domestic abuse, sexual harassment, and pornography (Dworkin, 1987; Freedman, 2002).

5. **Promoting sexual freedom.** Finally, feminism advocates women's control over their sexuality and reproduction. Feminists support the free availability of birth control information. As Figure 10–4 shows, contraceptives are much less available in most of the world than in the United States. Most feminists also support a woman's right to choose whether to have children or to end a pregnancy, rather than allowing men—as fathers, husbands, doctors, and legislators—to control their reproduction. Many feminists also support gay people's efforts to overcome prejudice and discrimination in a predominantly heterosexual culture (Jagger, 1983; Ferree & Hess, 1995; Armstrong, 2002).

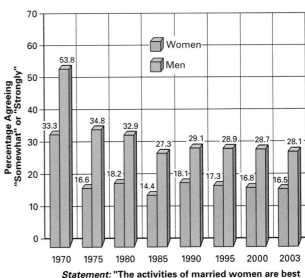

STUDENT SNAPSHOT

Statement: "The activities of married women are best confined to the home and family."

FIGURE 10-5 Opposition to Feminism among First-Year College Students, 1970–2003

Sources: Astin et al. (2002) and Sax et al. (2003).

TYPES OF FEMINISM

Although feminists agree on the importance of gender equality, they disagree on how to achieve it: through liberal feminism, socialist feminism, or radical feminism (Stacey, 1983; Vogel, 1983; Ferree & Hess, 1995; Freedman, 2002).

Liberal feminism is rooted in classic liberal thinking that individuals should be free to develop their own talents and pursue their own interests. Liberal feminism accepts the basic organization of our society but seeks to expand the rights and opportunities of women, in part by passage of the Equal Rights Amendment.

Liberal feminists support reproductive freedom for all women. They respect the family as a social institution but seek changes in society, including more widely available maternity and paternity leave and child care for parents who work.

Socialist feminism evolved from the ideas of Karl Marx and Friedrich Engels, in part as a critical response to Marx's inattention to gender. From this point of view, capitalism increases patriarchy by concentrating wealth and power in the hands of a small number of men. Socialist feminists do not think the reforms supported by liberal feminists go far enough. The family form fostered by capitalism must change in order to replace "domestic slavery" with some collective means of carrying out housework and child care.

Replacing the traditional family can come about only through a socialist revolution that creates a state-centered economy to meet the needs of all.

Like socialist feminism, *radical feminism* finds liberal feminism inadequate. Radical feminists believe that patriarchy is so firmly entrenched that even a socialist revolution would not end it. Instead, reaching the goal of gender equality means that society must eliminate gender itself. One possible way to achieve this goal is to use new reproductive technology (see Chapter 13, "Family and Religion") to separate women's bodies from the process of childbearing. With an end to motherhood, society could leave behind the entire family system, liberating women, men, and children from the oppression of family, gender, and sex itself (Dworkin, 1987). Radical feminism seeks an egalitarian and gender-free society, a revolution much more sweeping than that sought by Marx.

OPPOSITION TO FEMINISM

Today, just 20 percent of U.S. adults express attitudes in opposition to feminism, a share that has declined over time (NORC, 2003). Figure 10–5 shows a similar downward

A Closer Look: Are Men *Really* So Privileged?

When Hanover High School in Massachusetts held its graduation in June, it was the ninth year in a row that a female student sat at center stage as the class valedictorian. Almost all of the school's academic prizes—even the science prize—went to young women.

It is no surprise to college students that women outnumber men on the campus. But is this evidence that men are not quite as privileged as we tend to think? This chapter argues that men dominate society. They enjoy higher earnings, control more wealth, exercise more power, get more respect, and do less housework than women. But a closer look reveals that the male world is less privileged in a number of ways.

If men are so privileged in our society, why do they turn to crime more often than women? And the criminal justice system certainly does not

give men any special privileges. Most people would probably not be surprised to learn that police hesitate to arrest a woman, especially if she has children. This fact helps explain why 83 percent of arrests for serious crime put the handcuffs on a male. Nor do men get a break from the courts: Males make up 93 percent of the U.S. prison population. And even though women can and do kill, all but ten of more than 800 offenders executed since 1977 have been men.

Culture is not always generous to men either. "Real men" work and play hard; they typically drink, smoke, and speed on the highways. Given this view of maleness, is it any wonder that men are nearly twice as likely as women to suffer serious assault, three times more likely to fall victim to homicide, and four times more likely to commit suicide? In light of these statistics,

how do we explain our society's attention to violence against *women*? Perhaps, critics suggest, we are in the grip of a cultural double standard: We accept harm that comes to men while showing sympathy for the far fewer cases of violence against women. It is this same double standard, the argument continues, that moves women and children out of harm's way and expects men to "go down with the ship" or die defending their country on the battlefield.

Across the United States, more boys than girls flunk out, drop out, or are kicked out of school. Girls are the majority in high school advanced placement courses; boys are more likely to be diagnosed with a learning disability. Boys are less likely than girls to go to college, and those who do go on to higher education earn lower grades while women claim most

trend in opposition to feminism among college students after 1970; note, however, little change in recent years and a continuing gender gap by which a larger share of men than women express antifeminist attitudes.

Feminism provokes criticism and resistance from both men and women who hold conventional ideas about gender. Some men oppose sexual equality for the same reasons that many white people have historically opposed social equality for people of color: They do not want to give up their privileges. Other men and women, including those who are neither rich nor powerful, distrust a social movement (especially its radical expressions) that attacks the traditional family and rejects patterns that have guided male-female relations for centuries.

Men who have been socialized to value strength and dominance may feel uneasy about feminist ideals of men as gentle and warm (Doyle, 1983). Similarly, women who have

built their lives around husbands and children think feminism does not value the social roles that give meaning to their lives. In general, opposition to feminism is greatest among women who have the least education and those who do not work outside the home (Marshall, 1985; Ferree & Hess, 1995).

Race and ethnicity play some part in shaping people's attitudes toward feminism. In general, African Americans (especially African American women) express the greatest support of feminist goals, followed by whites, with Hispanic Americans holding somewhat more traditional attitudes when it comes to gender (Kane, 2000).

Resistance to feminism also comes from academic circles. Some sociologists charge that feminism ignores a growing body of evidence that men and women do think and act in somewhat different ways, which may make complete gender equality impossible. Furthermore, say critics,

of the academic awards. This pattern holds for just about all segments of society and for new immigrants as well as for children born in the United States.

Child custody is another sore point from the perspective of many men. Despite decades of "consciousness raising" in pursuit of gender fairness and clear evidence that men earn more than women, divorce courts across the United States routinely award primary care of children to mothers. To make matters worse, men separated from their children by the courts are often stigmatized as "runaway fathers" or "deadbeat dads," even though government statistics show that *women* are more likely to refuse to pay court-ordered child support (in 33 percent of cases) than men (25 percent).

Finally, male advocates point out that affirmative action laws now cover three-fourths of the population but notably exclude white males. Therefore, in today's affirmative action climate, women have the inside track to

college (where they now outnumber men) and often in the workforce (where businesses expect they will have to justify their hiring practices).

Even nature seems to plot against men, as women live an average of five years longer. The controversial question is this: When society plays favorites, who is favored?

CONTINUE THE DEBATE . . .

1. Do you think the criminal justice system favors women over men? Or do men simply get what they deserve? Why, in your opinion, are so many more men than women in prison?
2. On your campus, do male organizations (such as fraternities and athletic teams) enjoy special privileges? What about women's organizations? Why do you think this is the case?
3. Overall, are men advantaged over women? Provide specific evidence to support your position.

Sources: Based on Scanlon (1992), Rosenfeld (1998), Kleinfeld (1999), Campo-Flores (2002), and CBS News (2002).

with its drive to increase women's presence in the workplace, feminism undervalues the crucial and unique contribution women make to the development of children, especially in the first years of life (Baydar & Brooks-Gunn, 1991; Popenoe, 1993b; Gibbs, 2001b).

Finally, there is the question of *how* women should go about improving their social standing. A large majority of U.S. adults think that women should have equal rights, but 70 percent also say women should advance individually, according to their training and abilities; only 10 percent favor women's rights groups or collective action (NORC, 2003:345).

In sum, most opposition to feminism is directed toward its socialist and radical forms; support for liberal feminism is widespread. In addition, we are seeing an unmistakable trend toward gender equality. In 1977, 65 percent of all adults endorsed the statement "It is much better

for everyone involved if the man is the achiever outside the home and the woman takes care of the home and family." By 2002, however, the share supporting this statement had dropped sharply, to 38 percent (NORC, 2003:253).

Looking Ahead: Gender in the Twenty-First Century

At best, predictions about the future are no more than educated guesses. Just as economists disagree about the likely inflation rate a year from now, sociologists can offer only general observations about the likely future of gender and society.

Change so far has been remarkable. A century ago, women held a position of striking subordination. Husbands

As a general rule, patriarchy is strongest in nations with traditional cultures and limited economic development. Here we see a man in Eritrea traveling to a wedding with his three wives walking alongside him. Although gender stratification in the United States is not always so obvious, it remains a reality in this country as well.

controlled property in marriage, and laws barred women from most jobs, from holding political office, and from voting. Although women remain socially disadvantaged, the movement toward equality has surged ahead. Two-thirds of people entering the workforce in the 1990s were women, and in 2000, for the first time, a majority of families had both husband and wife in the paid labor force. Clearly, today's economy depends a great deal on the earnings of women.

Many factors have contributed to this transformation. Perhaps most important, industrialization and the more recent technological advances that have resulted from the Information Revolution have shifted the nature of work from physically demanding tasks that favored male strength to jobs that require thought and imagination. This change puts women and men on a more even footing. Also, because birth control technology has given us greater control over reproduction, women's lives are less constrained by pregnancy and the demands of childrearing.

Many women and men have deliberately pursued social equality. For example, sexual harassment complaints in the workplace are taken much more seriously today than they were a generation ago. As more women assume positions of power in the corporate and political worlds, social changes in the twenty-first century may be as great as what we have already witnessed.

Gender is woven into the fabric of social life. Efforts to change deeply rooted ideas about the roles of women and men will continue to spark debate and opposition, as the Controversy & Debate box on pages 272–73 illustrates. On balance, however, although change may occur slowly, we are seeing steady movement toward a society in which women and men enjoy equal rights and opportunities.

SUMMARY

1. Gender is the meaning a culture attaches to being female or male. Because society gives men more power and resources than women, gender is an important dimension of social stratification.

2. Although some degree of patriarchy exists everywhere, gender varies throughout history and across cultures.

3. Through the socialization process, people build gender into their personalities (gender identity) as well as their actions (gender roles). The major agents of socialization—family, peer groups, schools, and the mass media—reinforce cultural definitions of femininity and masculinity.

4. Gender stratification shapes the workplace. Although a majority of women are now in the paid labor force, most hold clerical or service jobs. Unpaid housework remains a task performed mostly by women, whether or not they hold jobs outside the home.

5. On average, women earn 76 percent as much as men. This disparity stems from differences in jobs and family responsibilities, as well as from discrimination on the part of employers.

6. Women now earn a majority of all bachelor's and master's degrees. Men still earn a majority of doctorates and professional degrees.

7. The number of women in politics has increased sharply in recent decades. Still, most elected officials, especially at the national level, are men. Women make up only 15 percent of U.S. military personnel.

8. Intersection theory investigates the intersection of race, class, and gender, which often results in multiple disadvantages.

9. Because women have a distinctive social identity and are disadvantaged, they are a minority, although most white women do not think of themselves that way. Minority women encounter greater social disadvantages than white women and earn much less than white men.

10. Violence against women is a widespread problem in the United States. Our society is also dealing with issues of sexual harassment and pornography.

11. Structural-functional analysis suggests that in preindustrial societies, distinct roles for females and males reflect biological differences between the sexes. In industrial societies, marked gender inequality becomes dysfunctional and gradually decreases. Talcott Parsons claimed that complementary gender roles promote the social integration of families and society as a whole.

12. Social-conflict analysis views gender as a dimension of social inequality and conflict. Friedrich Engels tied gender stratification to the development of private property.

13. Feminism supports the social equality of the sexes and opposes patriarchy and sexism. Feminism also seeks to end violence against women and give women control over their sexuality and reproduction.

14. There are three variations of feminist thinking. Liberal feminism seeks equal opportunity for both sexes within current social arrangements, socialist feminism advocates abolishing private property as the means to social equality, and radical feminism seeks to create a gender-free society.

15. Although a majority of U.S. adults support the Equal Rights Amendment, this legislation, first proposed in Congress in 1923, has yet to become part of the U.S. Constitution.

KEY CONCEPTS

gender (p. 252) the personal traits and social positions that members of a society attach to being female or male

gender stratification (p. 252) the unequal distribution of wealth, power, and privilege between men and women

patriarchy (p. 254) a form of social organization in which males dominate females

matriarchy (p. 254) a form of social organization in which females dominate males

sexism (p. 254) the belief that one sex is innately superior to the other

gender roles (sex roles) (p. 256) attitudes and activities that a society links to each sex

minority (p. 264) any category of people distinguished by physical or cultural difference that a society sets apart and subordinates

intersection theory (p. 265) the investigation of the interplay of race, class, and gender, often resulting in multiple dimensions of disadvantage

sexual harassment (p. 265) comments, gestures, or physical contact of a sexual nature that are deliberate, repeated, and unwelcome

feminism (p. 270) the advocacy of social equality for men and women, in opposition to patriarchy and sexism

CRITICAL-THINKING QUESTIONS

1. In what ways are sex and gender related? In what ways are they distinct?

2. What techniques do the mass media use to "sell" conventional ideas about gender to women and men?

3. Why is gender a dimension of social stratification? How does gender intersect other dimensions of inequality such as class, race, and ethnicity?

4. Consider the following two statements: "He fathered the child" and "She mothered the child." Describe the differences in meaning. How do you account for these differences?

5. A number of European nations, including Great Britain, Norway, Denmark, and Finland, require that at least 25 percent of candidates for national offices be women. Because just 14 percent of the people in Congress are women, should the United States adopt a similar policy? Is such a policy likely?

APPLICATIONS AND EXERCISES

1. Take a walk through a business area of your local community. Which businesses are frequented almost entirely by women? By men? By both men and women? Try to explain the patterns you find.

2. Watch several hours of children's television programming on a Saturday morning. Notice the advertising, which sells mostly toys and breakfast cereal. Keep track of what share of toys are "gendered," that is, aimed at one sex or the other. What traits do you associate with toys intended for boys and those intended for girls?

3. Do some research on the history of women's issues in your state. When was the first woman sent to Congress? What laws have existed restricting the work women could do? Are any such laws in effect today? Did your state support the passage of the Equal Rights Amendment or not? What percentage of political officials in your state are women?

4. Packaged in the back of this new textbook is an interactive CD-ROM that offers a variety of video and interactive review materials intended to help you better understand the material covered in this chapter. For this chapter, the CD-ROM contains a relevant clip from *ABC News,* an author's tip video, interactive map animations, an interactive timeline, and flashcards with audio pronunciations of the more difficult words.

 ## SITES TO SEE

http://www.prenhall.com/macionis

Visit the interactive Companion Website™ that accompanies this text. Begin by clicking on the cover of your book. You will find a chapter-by-chapter study guide, practice tests, suggested Web links, and links to other relevant material.

http://www.now.org

Visit the Web site for the National Organization for Women to discover the goals and strategies of this organization.

http://www.iwpr.org

Another informative site is run by the Institute for Women's Policy Research. Identify the issues this organization finds most important. Would you characterize this site as feminist? Why or why not?

http://www.wwwomen.com

This site provides a search engine to locate all sorts of information concerning women.

http://www.educationindex.com/women/

This site provides numerous and widely varied links to sites concerned with women's issues.

http://www.feminist.org

The Feminist Majority Foundation Online offers news and information about the women's movement.

http://www.un.org/womenwatch/

Here is the United Nations Internet gateway on the advancement and empowerment of women.

 ## INVESTIGATE WITH RESEARCH NAVIGATOR™

Follow the instructions found on page 32 of this textbook to access the features of **Research Navigator™.** Once at the Web site, enter your Login Name and Password. Then, to use the **Content Select™** database, enter keywords such as "gender," "feminism," and "sexual harassment," and the search engine will supply relevant and recent scholarly and popular press publications. Use the *New York Times* **Search-by-Subject Archive** to find recent news articles related to sociology and the **Links Library** feature to find relevant Web links organized by the key terms associated with this chapter.

June 10, 2004

Still a Gender Wage Gap

By JEFF MADRICK

The great defense against stagnating male wages in America over the last few decades has been the two-worker family. . . . [C]onsider the monetary advantages. The latest data show that the median income of two-worker families was nearly $71,000. If only the husband worked, the median family income was $41,000.

. . .[W]omen's wages have been rising substantially. . . . Forty years ago, the Census Bureau reports, women made . . . 59 percent of what men made. Now they make 77 percent. . . . Small wonder the proportion of two-worker families has soared in America, to 62 percent of all married couples, from 39 percent in 1970.

But valuable new research by two economists. . . shows that such measures substantially overstate what women earn over time. A big reason, almost always overlooked, is that women work far fewer hours than men on average and often drop out of the work force for years at a time. Usually they do so for child-rearing and to tend to the family. The traditional, widely trumpeted measures of the gender wage gap track only those women who work full time for a full year—at most about half of working women in any single year.

So . . . [Stephen J.] Rose, senior research economist at ORC Macro, . . . and . . .[Heidi] Hartmann, president of the Institute for Women's Policy Research, decided to study actual earnings histories of men and women over 15 years. They . . . found . . . that. . . women on average earned only 38 percent of what men did. Adding it up, the researchers found that the average woman earned $273,592 over 15 years, compared with $722,693 for men (in 1999 dollars).

Fewer work hours account for much of the difference. . . .[F]ewer than half of women earned income in all 15 years but 85 percent of men did. About 30 percent of women did not work at all for four or more years. By contrast, only one man in 27 was out of work so much. . . .

But hours alone do not account for the discrepancy in pay over time. A far higher proportion of females have had jobs that pay at the bottom of the income scale, and fewer of them climb to jobs of higher quality. Even when they are well educated, women predominantly take different kinds of jobs from those men do—jobs that usually pay less. . . .

Ms. Hartmann and Mr. Rose argue, most disturbingly, that these tendencies are self-reinforcing. Because wives usually earn less, they are more likely to give up their jobs to do child care.

Women also often take low-paying temporary or part-time jobs that provide few benefits so they can be home for the family. This in turn creates a labor pool that business can consistently exploit, encouraging companies to orient their operations to use such low-paid workers rather than create better jobs. . . .

There are encouraging trends. Women are increasingly better educated. Government policies against discrimination have had success. And a service economy reduces the advantage men once had doing heavy labor in a manufacturing economy.

Yet problems persist. . . . and effective public policies are called for.

First, stronger government programs to encourage paid family leave and more flexible hours will enable women to maintain long-term careers.

Second, the nation needs a serious commitment to quality day care for all as well as to the high-level personnel required for such work.

Third, . . . more federal support for discrimination oversight agencies . . . and . . . regular audits of large corporations for discrimination against women would be valuable.

Such policies are often seen as costs to the nation. . . . But they would be likely to raise the nation's productivity by fully exploiting and enhancing the talents of women, and improving family life and the development of children. There is evidence they do just that in Europe and Scandinavia.

Fourth, . . . research is required into correcting subtle forms of prejudice in the early school years that encourage women to take jobs that pay less.

Given the self-reinforcing nature of the problem, one would think that such issues would be red meat for a presidential election year. But the presidential candidates address these matters only in passing. Perhaps we also need more research into why this is so—a place to begin might be to take note that the presidential candidates are men.

WHAT DO YOU THINK?

1. Based on the article, cite several reasons that, in the United States, working women earn a good deal less than working men. Why do you think only about half of working women work full time all year long?
2. If the goal is to give women the same economic opportunities and rewards as men, how might U.S. family life have to change?

Adapted from the original article by Jeff Madrick published in *The New York Times* on June 10, 2004. Copyright © 2004 by The New York Times Company. Reprinted with permission.

CHAPTER ELEVEN

Race and Ethnicity

What are race and ethnicity,
and how are they created by society?

Why is the United States known
as a nation of immigrants?

How are race and ethnicity important dimensions
of social inequality today?

Race is an important basis of social inequality. In Johannesburg, South Africa, as in the United States, ▶ the lowest-paying jobs are commonly performed by people of color.

equoia Way, running through an average-looking neighborhood on the south side of Sacramento, California, is a winding road lined with one-story frame houses set on small patches of lawn. Most of the people who live there think of themselves as middle class. If such a thing as a "typical American neighborhood" exists at all, this may well be it.

Try to imagine the people who live here. The facts may surprise you. Residents of Sequoia Way include Tom and Debra Burruss, who moved in three years ago; Tom is African American, and Debra, his wife, is white. Next door live Ken Wong and Binh Lam, a Vietnamese couple. Across the street live the Cardonas, who are Mexican American. Next to the Cardonas are the Farrys: He is white, and she is Japanese. The elementary school a few blocks away enrolls 347 students, 189 of whom speak a language other than English at home. You get the idea—this "all-American neighborhood" comes in more flavors than you find at Baskin Robbins (adapted from Stodghill & Bower, 2002).

Sacramento may well be the most integrated city in the United States. Non-Hispanic whites make up only 41 percent of the city's population. What we find in Sacramento is starting to happen throughout the United States, because everywhere racial and ethnic diversity is increasing rapidly.

This chapter examines the meaning of race and ethnicity, explains how these social constructs have shaped our history, and suggests why they will play an even greater part in social life as we move through the twenty-first century.

The Social Meaning of Race and Ethnicity

People often confuse the terms "race" and "ethnicity." For this reason, we begin with some definitions.

RACE

A **race** is *a socially constructed category composed of people who share biologically transmitted traits that members of a society consider important.* People may classify one another racially based on physical characteristics such as skin color, facial features, hair texture, and body shape.

Racial diversity appeared among our human ancestors as the result of living in different regions of the world. In regions of intense heat, people developed darker skin (from the natural pigment melanin) that offers protection from the sun; in moderate climates, people developed lighter skin. Such traits are literally only skin deep because human beings the world over are members of a single biological species.

The striking variety of racial traits found today is also the product of migration; genetic characteristics once common to a single place are now found in many lands. Especially pronounced is the racial mix in the Middle East (that is, western Asia), historically a crossroads of migration. Greater racial uniformity characterizes more isolated peoples such as the island-dwelling Japanese. But every population has some genetic mixture, and increasing contact ensures even more racial blending in the future.

Although we often think of race in terms of biological traits, race is a socially constructed concept. At one level, research shows that white people rate black people as darker in skin tone than black people do (Hill, 2002). Also, a number of people—especially biracial and multiracial people—define themselves and are defined by others differently, depending on the setting (Harris & Sim, 2002). More broadly, entire societies define physical traits differently. Typically, people in the United States "see" fewer racial categories (commonly, black, white, and Asian) than people in

The range of biological variation in human beings is far greater than any system of racial classification allows. This fact is made obvious by trying to place all of the people pictured here into simple racial categories.

Brazil, who distinguish between *branca* (white), *parda* (brown), *morena* (brunette), *mulata* (mulatto), *preta* (black), and *amarela* (yellow) (Inciardi, Surratt, & Telles, 2000). In countries such as the United States, people consider racial differences more important; the people of other countries, such as Brazil, consider them less important.

In any society, definitions and meanings concerning race change over time. For example, in 1900, many people in the United States viewed individuals of Irish and Italian ancestry as racially different, a practice that was far less common by 1950 (Loveman, 1999). Today, the Census Bureau allows people to describe themselves using more than one racial category (offering a total of sixty-three racial options), thus recognizing a wide range of multiracial people (Porter, 2001).

Racial types.   Scientists invented the concept of race more than a century ago as they tried to organize the world's physical diversity using three racial types. They called people with light skin and fine hair *Caucasoid,* people with dark skin and coarse hair *Negroid,* and people with yellow or brown skin and distinctive folds on the eyelids *Mongoloid.*

Sociologists consider such terms misleading at best and harmful at worst. For one thing, no society contains biologically "pure" people. The skin color of people we might call "Caucasoid" (or "Indo-European," "Caucasian," or more commonly, "white") ranges from very light (typical in Scandinavia) to very dark (in southern India). The same variation exists among so-called "Negroids" ("Africans" or, more commonly, "black" people) and "Mongoloids" (that is, "Asians"). In fact, many "white" people (say, in southern India) actually have darker skin than many "black" people (such as the Negroid aborigines of Australia). Overall, the three racial categories differ in about 6 percent of their genes, less than the genetic variation *within* each category (Boza, 2002; Harris & Sim, 2002).

Why, then, do people make so much of race? Such categories allow societies to rank people in a hierarchy, allowing some people to feel that they are by nature "better" than others. Because racial ranking shapes access to wealth and prestige, societies may construct racial categories in extreme ways. Throughout much of the twentieth century, for example, many southern states labeled as "colored" anyone with as little as one thirty-second African ancestry (that is, one

Fifty years ago, in some states, marrying someone of another race violated the law. Since then, the number of multiracial couples has risen steadily, and the number of recorded interracial births has tripled since the mid-1980s. The result is that more and more people consider themselves to be multiracial. What effect will this trend have on the use of traditional racial categories?

African American great-great-great-grandparent). Today, the law allows parents to declare the race of a child as they wish. Even so, most members of our society are still very sensitive to people's racial backgrounds.

A trend toward mixture. Over many generations and throughout the Americas, the genetic traits from around the world have become mixed. Many "black" people have a significant Caucasoid ancestry, just as "white" people have some Negroid genes. Whatever people may think, race is no black-and-white issue.

Today, people are more willing to define themselves as multiracial. When completing their 2000 census forms, almost 7 million people described themselves by checking two or more racial categories. The official number of interracial births tripled over the past twenty years to 172,000 annually, about 5 percent of all births.

ETHNICITY

Ethnicity is *a shared cultural heritage.* People define themselves—or others—as members of an *ethnic category* based on common ancestors, language, and religion that give

them a distinctive social identity. The United States is a multiethnic society that favors the English language; even so, more than 47 million people (18 percent of the U.S. population) speak Spanish, Italian, German, French, Chinese, or some other language in their homes. In California, more than one-third of the population speaks a language other than English at home. Similarly, the United States is a predominantly Protestant nation, but most people of Spanish, Italian, and Polish ancestry are Roman Catholic, and many others of Greek, Ukrainian, and Russian descent belong to the Eastern Orthodox Church. More than 6 million Jewish Americans have ancestral ties to various nations around the world. And more than 7 million Muslim men and women now outnumber Episcopalians in the United States.

Like the reality of race, the reality of ethnicity is socially constructed. This means it becomes important only because society defines it that way. For example, U.S. society defines people of Spanish descent as "Latin," even though Italy probably has a more "Latin" culture than Spain. People of Italian descent are viewed not as Latin but as "European" and thus less "different" (Camara, 2000; Brodkin, 2001). Like racial differences, the importance of ethnic differences can change over time. A century ago, Catholics and Jews were considered "different" in the predominantly Protestant United States. This is far less the case today.

Keep in mind that race highlights *biological* traits and ethnicity emphasizes *cultural* traits. Of course, the two may go hand in hand. For example, Japanese Americans have distinctive physical traits and, for those who maintain a traditional way of life, a distinctive culture as well. Table 11–1 presents the range of racial and ethnic diversity in the United States as recorded by the 2000 census.

On an individual level, people play up or play down their ethnicity, depending on whether they want to fit in or stand apart from the surrounding society: Immigrants may drop their cultural traditions over time or, like many people of Native American descent in recent years, try to revive their heritage. For most people, ethnicity is a more complex issue than race, because they identify with several ethnic backgrounds. The golf star Tiger Woods describes himself as one-eighth American Indian, one-fourth Thai, and one-fourth Chinese—as well as one-eighth white and one-fourth black (White, 1997).

MINORITIES

March 3, Dallas, Texas. Sitting in the lobby of just about any hotel in a major U.S. city presents a lesson in contrasts: The majority of the guests checking in and out are white; the majority of the employees who carry the luggage, serve the food, and clean the rooms are people of color.

As Chapter 10 ("Gender Stratification") described, a **minority** is *any category of people distinguished by physical or cultural difference that a society sets apart and subordinates.* Minority standing can be based on race, ethnicity, or both. As shown in Table 11–1, white people of non-Hispanic background (71 percent of the total) continue to predominate numerically. But the share of minorities is increasing. Today, minorities are a numerical majority in three states and half of the country's 100 largest cities (Schmitt, 2001). By about 2050, minorities are likely to form a majority of the entire U.S. population. National Map 11–1 on page 284 shows where a minority-majority already exists.

Minorities have two important characteristics. First, they share a *distinct identity,* which may be based on physical or cultural traits. Second, minorities experience *subordination.* As the rest of this chapter shows, U.S. minorities typically have lower income, lower occupational prestige, and limited schooling. Class, race, and ethnicity, as well as gender, are overlapping and reinforcing dimensions of social stratification. The Diversity box on page 285 describes the struggles of recent Latin American immigrants to the United States.

Of course, not all members of a minority category are disadvantaged. For example, some Latinos are quite wealthy, certain Chinese Americans are celebrated business leaders, and African Americans are among our nation's leading scholars. But even job success rarely allows individuals to escape their minority standing (Benjamin, 1991). As described in Chapter 4 ("Social Interaction in Everyday Life"), race or ethnicity often serves as a *master status* that overshadows personal accomplishments.

As noted, minorities usually—but not always—make up a small proportion of a society's population. For example, black South Africans are disadvantaged even though they are a numerical majority in their country. In the United States, women are slightly more than half the population but are still struggling for the opportunities and privileges enjoyed by men.

PREJUDICE AND STEREOTYPES

November 19, Jerusalem, Israel. We are driving along the edge of this historic city, a holy place to Jews, Christians, and Muslims, when Razi, our taxi driver, spots a small group of

TABLE 11–1

Racial and Ethnic Categories in the United States, 2000

Racial or Ethnic Classification*	Approximate U.S. Population	Percentage of Total Population
Hispanic descent	**35,305,818**	**12.5%**
Mexican	20,640,711	7.3
Puerto Rican	3,406,178	1.2
Cuban	1,241,685	0.4
Other Hispanic	10,017,244	3.6
African descent	**34,658,190**	**12.3**
Nigerian	165,481	0.1
Ethiopian	86,918	<
Cape Verdean	77,103	<
Ghanaian	49,944	<
South African	45,569	<
Native American descent	**2,475,956**	**0.9**
American Indian	1,815,653	0.6
Eskimo	45,919	<
Other Native American	614,384	0.2
Asian or Pacific Island descent	**10,641,833**	**3.8**
Chinese	2,432,585	0.9
Filipino	1,850,314	0.7
Asian Indian	1,678,765	0.6
Vietnamese	1,122,528	0.4
Korean	1,076,872	0.4
Japanese	796,700	0.3
Cambodian	171,937	<
Hmong	169,428	<
Laotian	168,707	<
Other Asian or Pacific Islander	1,173,997	0.4
West Indian descent	**1,869,504**	**0.7**
Arab descent	**1,202,871**	**0.4**
Non-Hispanic European descent	**194,552,774**	**70.9**
German	42,885,162	15.2
Irish	30,528,492	10.8
English	24,515,138	8.7
Italian	15,723,555	5.6
Polish	8,977,444	3.2
French	8,309,908	3.0
Scottish	4,890,581	1.7
Dutch	4,542,494	1.6
Norwegian	4,477,725	1.6
Two or more races	**6,826,228**	**2.4**

*People of Hispanic descent may be of any race. Many people also identify with more than one ethnic category. Therefore, figures total more than 100 percent.
< Indicates less than 1/10 of 1 percent.

Sources: U.S. Census Bureau (2001, 2002, 2004).

Falasha—Ethiopian Jews—on a street corner. "Those people over there," he begins, "they are different. They don't drive cars. They don't want to improve

SEEING OURSELVES

NATIONAL MAP 11–1

Where the Minority-Majority Already Exists

By 2000, minorities had become a majority in three states—Hawaii, California, and New Mexico—and the District of Columbia. With a 45 percent minority population, Texas is approaching a minority-majority. At the other extreme, Vermont and Maine have the lowest share of racial and ethnic minorities (about 2 percent). Why are states with high minority populations in the South and Southwest?

Source: "America 2000: A Map of the Mix," *Newsweek,* September 18, 2000, p. 48. Copyright © 2000 Newsweek, Inc. All rights reserved. Reprinted by permission.

themselves. Even when our country offers them schooling, they don't take it." He shakes his head at the Ethiopians and drives on.

Prejudice is *a rigid and unfair generalization about an entire category of people.* Prejudice is unfair because such attitudes are supported by little or no direct evidence. Prejudice may target people of a particular social class, sex, sexual orientation, age, political affiliation, race, or ethnicity.

Prejudices are *prejudgments* that can be either positive or negative. Our positive prejudices exaggerate the virtues of people like ourselves, and our negative prejudices condemn those who are different from us. Negative prejudice can be expressed as anything from mild dislike to outright hostility. Because such attitudes are rooted in culture, everyone has at least some measure of prejudice.

 Take a test for prejudice at http://www.tolerance.org/ hidden_bias/index.html

Prejudice often takes the form of *stereotypes* (*stereo* is derived from the Greek word for "hard" or "solid"), which are exaggerated descriptions applied to every person in some category. Many white people hold stereotypical views of minorities. Stereotyping is especially harmful to minorities in the workplace. If company officials see minority workers only in terms of a stereotype, they will make assumptions about their abilities, steer them toward certain jobs, and limit their access to better opportunities (Kaufman, 2002).

Minorities, too, stereotype whites and also other minorities (Smith, 1996; Cummings & Lambert, 1997). For example, recent surveys show that more African Americans than whites express the belief that Asians engage in unfair business practices and that more Asians than whites criticize Hispanics for having too many children (Perlmutter, 2002).

MEASURING PREJUDICE: THE SOCIAL DISTANCE SCALE

One measure of prejudice is *social distance,* which refers to how closely people are willing to interact with members of some category. Eighty years ago, the sociologist Emory Bogardus developed the *social distance scale* shown in Figure 11–1 on page 286. Bogardus asked students at colleges and universities in the United States how closely they were willing to interact with people in thirty racial and ethnic categories. People express the greatest social distance (most negative prejudice) by declaring that some category of people should be barred from the country entirely (point 7 in the figure); at the other extreme, people express the least social distance (most social acceptance) by saying they would accept a member of some category into their family through marriage.

Bogardus (1925, 1967; Owen, Elsner, & McFaul, 1977) found that people felt much more social distance toward some categories than they did toward others. In general, students in his surveys expressed the most social distance

Hard Work: The Immigrant Life in the United States

Early in the morning, it is already hot in Houston as a line of pickup trucks snakes slowly into a dusty yard, where 200 laborers have been gathered since dawn, hoping for a day's work. The driver of the first truck opens his window and tells the foreman that he is looking for a crew to spread boiling tar on a roof. The foreman turns to the crowd, and after a few minutes, three workers step forward and climb into the back of the truck. The next driver is looking for two experienced house painters. The scene is repeated over and over as men and a few women leave to dig ditches, spread cement, hang drywall, open clogged septic tanks, and even crawl under houses to poison rats.

As each driver enters, the foreman, Abdonel Cespedes, asks, "How much?" Most of the people in the trucks offer $5 an hour. Cespedes automatically responds, "$6.50; the going rate is $6.50 for an hour's hard work." Sometimes he convinces people to pay that much, but usually not. The workers, who come from Mexico, El Salvador, and Guatemala, know that dozens of them will end up with no work at all this day. Most jump at the offer of $5 an hour because they know, when the day is over, they will have earned $50.

Labor markets like this one are common in large cities, especially across the southwestern United States. The surge in immigration in recent years has brought millions of people to this country in search of work, and most have little schooling and speak little English.

Manuel Barrera has taken a day's work moving the entire contents of a store to a storage site as part of a repossession. He arrives at the boarded-up store and gazes at the mountains of heavy furniture that he must carry out to a moving van, drive across town, and then carry again. He sighs when he realizes how hot it is outside and that it is even hotter in the building. He will have no break for lunch. No one says anything about toilets. Barrera shakes his head. "I will

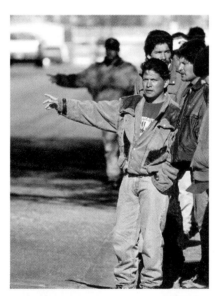

do this kind of work because it puts food on the table. But I did not foresee it would turn out like this."

The hard truth is that immigrants to the United States do the jobs that no one else wants. Immigrants represent the bottom level of the national economy, working in restaurants and hotels, on construction crews, and in private homes cooking, cleaning, and caring for children. Across the United States, about half of all housekeepers, household cooks, tailors, and restaurant waiters are men or women born abroad. Few immigrants make much more than the minimum wage ($5.15 per hour), and it is rare that an immigrant worker receives any health or pension benefits. Many wealthy families take the labor of immigrants for granted as much as they do their sport utility vehicles and cell phones.

WHAT DO YOU THINK?

1. In what ways do you or members of your family depend on the low-paid labor of immigrants?
2. Do you think there is anything wrong with paying someone the current minimum wage for hard work? Why or why not?
3. Why has there always been opposition to large numbers of immigrants entering the United States?

Source: Based on Booth (1998).

toward Hispanics, African Americans, Asians, and Turks by indicating that they would accept such people as co-workers but did not welcome them as neighbors, close friends, or family members. People expressed the least social distance toward those from northern and western Europe, including English and Scottish people, and also Canadians, indicating that they were willing to include them in their families by marriage.

What patterns of social distance do we find among college students today? A recent study using the same social

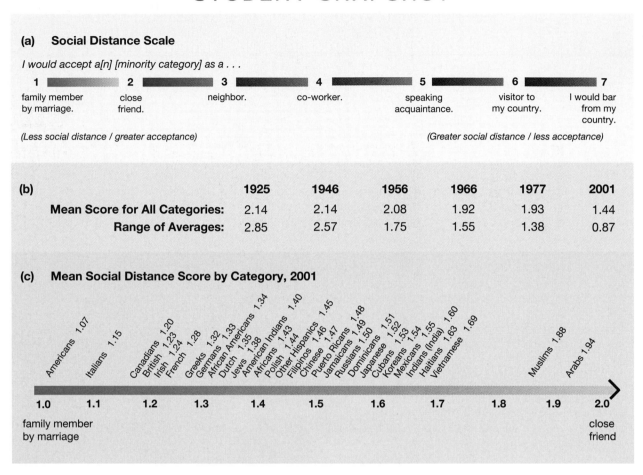

(a) Social Distance Scale

I would accept a[n] [minority category] as a . . .

1	2	3	4	5	6	7
family member by marriage.	close friend.	neighbor.	co-worker.	speaking acquaintance.	visitor to my country.	I would bar from my country.

(Less social distance / greater acceptance)   *(Greater social distance / less acceptance)*

(b)

	1925	1946	1956	1966	1977	2001
Mean Score for All Categories:	2.14	2.14	2.08	1.92	1.93	1.44
Range of Averages:	2.85	2.57	1.75	1.55	1.38	0.87

(c) Mean Social Distance Score by Category, 2001

Americans 1.07, Italians 1.15, Canadians 1.20, British 1.23, Irish 1.24, French 1.28, Greeks 1.32, Germans 1.33, African Americans 1.34, Dutch 1.35, Jews 1.38, American Indians 1.40, Africans 1.43, Polish 1.44, Other Hispanics 1.45, Filipinos 1.46, Chinese 1.47, Puerto Ricans 1.48, Jamaicans 1.49, Russians 1.50, Dominicans 1.51, Japanese 1.52, Cubans 1.53, Koreans 1.54, Mexicans 1.55, Indians (India) 1.60, Haitians 1.63, Vietnamese 1.69, Muslims 1.88, Arabs 1.94

1.0	1.1	1.2	1.3	1.4	1.5	1.6	1.7	1.8	1.9	2.0

family member by marriage   close friend

FIGURE 11–1   Bogardus Social Distance Research

Source: Parrillo (2003b).

distance scale reported three major findings (Parrillo, 2003b):[1]

1. **Student opinions show a trend toward greater acceptance.** Today's students express less social distance toward all minorities than students did decades ago. Figure 11–1 shows that the average (mean) score on the social distance scale declined from 2.14 in 1925 to 1.93 in 1977 to 1.44 in 2001. Respondents (81 percent of whom were white) showed notably greater acceptance of African Americans, a category of people that moved up from near the bottom in 1925 to the top one-third in 2001.

2. **People see less difference among various minorities.** The earliest studies found the difference between the highest- and lowest-ranked minorities equal to almost three points on the scale. As the figure shows, the most recent research produced a range of averages less than one point.

---

[1]Parrillo dropped seven of the categories used by Bogardus (Armenians, Czechs, Finns, Norwegians, Scots, Swedes, and Turks), claiming they were no longer visible minorities. He added nine new categories (Africans, Arabs, Cubans, Dominicans, Haitians, Jamaicans, Muslims, Puerto Ricans, and Vietnamese), claiming that these are visible minorities today. This change probably encouraged higher social distance scores, making the trend toward decreasing social distance all the more significant.

Racial and ethnic stereotypes are deeply embedded in our culture and language. Many people speak of someone "gypping" another without realizing that this word insults European Gypsies, a category of people long pushed to the margins of European societies. What about terms such as "Dutch treat," "French kiss," or "Indian giver"?

3. **The terrorist attacks of September 11, 2001, may have reduced social acceptance of Arabs and Muslims.** The most recent study was conducted just a few weeks after September 11, 2001. Perhaps the fact that the nineteen men who attacked the World Trade Center and the Pentagon were Arabs and Muslims is part of the reason that students ranked these categories last on the social distance scale. However, not a single student gave Arabs or Muslims a 7, indicating that they should be barred from the country. On the contrary, the 2001 scores (1.94 for Arabs and 1.88 for Muslims) show higher social acceptance than students in 1977 expressed toward eighteen of the thirty categories of people.

RACISM

A powerful and destructive form of prejudice, **racism** is *the belief that one racial category is innately superior or inferior to another.* Racism has existed throughout world history. Despite their many achievements, the ancient Greeks, the peoples of India, and the Chinese were all quick to consider people unlike themselves inferior.

Racism has also been widespread in the United States, where for centuries ideas about racial inferiority supported slavery. Today, overt racism in this country has decreased to some extent because our cultural belief in equality encourages us to evaluate people, in

 Racism can give rise to hate crimes. For more information, go to http://www.civilrights.org/issues/hate/

Dr. Martin Luther King's words, "not by the color of their skin but by the content of their character."

Even so, racism remains a serious social problem, as some people still argue that certain racial and ethnic categories are smarter or better than others. As the Applying Sociology box on pages 288–89 explains, however, racial differences in mental abilities result from environment rather than biology.

THEORIES OF PREJUDICE

Where does prejudice come from? Social scientists provide several answers to this vexing question, focusing on frustration, personality, culture, and social conflict.

Scapegoat theory. *Scapegoat theory* holds that prejudice springs from frustration among people who are themselves disadvantaged (Dollard, 1939). Take the case of a white woman who is frustrated by her low-paying job in a textile factory. Directing her hostility at the powerful factory owners carries the obvious risk of being fired; therefore, she may blame her low pay on the presence of minority coworkers. Her prejudice does not improve her situation, but it is a relatively safe way to express anger, and it may give her the comforting feeling that at least she is superior to someone.

A **scapegoat,** then, is *a person or category of people, typically with little power, whom people unfairly blame for their own troubles.* Because they are usually "safe targets," minorities often are used as scapegoats.

Does Race Affect Intelligence?

Are Asian Americans smarter than white people? Is the typical white person more intelligent than the average African American? Throughout the history of the United States, we have painted one category of people as intellectually more gifted than another. People have used such thinking to justify the privileges of the allegedly superior category and even to bar supposedly inferior people from entering this country.

Scientists know that the distribution of the intelligence of individuals forms a bell-shaped curve, as shown in the figure. Average performance is defined as an *intelligence quotient* (IQ) score of 100 (technically, an IQ score is mental age as measured by a test divided by age in years, with the result multiplied by 100; thus, an eight-year-old who performs like a

ten-year-old has an IQ of 10 ÷ 8 = 1.25 × 100 = 125).

In a controversial study of intelligence and social inequality, Richard Herrnstein and Charles Murray (1994) claim that overwhelming evidence shows that race is related to measures of intelligence. More specifically, they say the average IQ of people with European ancestry is 100, the average for

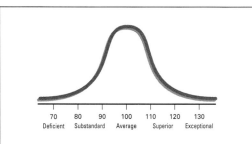

| 70 | 80 | 90 | 100 | 110 | 120 | 130 |
| Deficient | Substandard | | Average | | Superior | Exceptional |

IQ: The Distribution of Intelligence

people of East Asian ancestry is 103, and for people of African descent, the average is 90.

Statements like this go against our democratic and egalitarian beliefs that no racial type is naturally better than another. Some critics argue that intelligence tests are not valid and even that the concept of intelligence has little real meaning.

Most social scientists believe that IQ tests do measure something important that we think of as intelligence, and they agree that *individuals* vary in intellectual aptitude. But they reject the idea that any *category* of people, on average, is naturally smarter than any other. So how do we explain the overall differences in IQ scores by race?

Thomas Sowell (1994, 1995) explains that most of the

Authoritarian personality theory. Theodor Adorno and others (Adorno et al., 1950) considered extreme prejudice a personality trait of certain individuals. This conclusion is supported by research indicating that people who show strong prejudice toward one minority usually are intolerant of all minorities. These *authoritarian personalities* rigidly conform to conventional cultural values, see moral issues as clear-cut matters of right and wrong, and look upon society as naturally competitive with "better" people (like themselves) dominating those who are weaker (including all minorities).

Adorno also found that people tolerant toward one minority are likely to be accepting of all. They tend to be more flexible in their moral judgments and treat all people as equals.

Adorno thought that people with little education and those raised by cold and demanding parents tend to develop authoritarian personalities. Filled with anger and anxiety as

children, they grow into hostile and aggressive adults, seeking scapegoats whom they consider inferior.

Culture theory. A third theory claims that although extreme prejudice is found in certain people, some prejudice is found in everyone. Why? Because prejudice is rooted in culture, as the Bogardus social distance studies illustrate. Bogardus found that students across the country had mostly the same attitudes toward specific racial and ethnic categories, feeling closer to some and more distant from others.

Finally, we know that prejudice is rooted in culture because minorities tend to express the same attitudes as white people toward categories other than their own. Such patterns suggest that individuals hold prejudices because we live in a "culture of prejudice" that has taught us to view certain categories of people as "better" or "worse" than others.

documented differences in intelligence result not from biology but from environment. In some skillful sociological detective work, Sowell traced IQ scores for various racial and ethnic categories throughout the twentieth century. He found that on average, early-twentieth-century immigrants from European nations such as Poland, Lithuania, Italy, and Greece, as well as Asian countries including China and Japan, scored 10 to 15 points below the U.S. average, but by the end of the twentieth century, people in these same categories had IQ scores that were average or above average. Among Italian Americans, for example, average IQ jumped almost 10 points; among Polish and Chinese Americans, the increase was almost 20 points.

Because genetic changes occur over thousands of years and most people in the various categories married others like themselves, biological factors cannot explain such a rapid rise in IQ scores. The only reasonable explanation is changing cultural patterns.

The descendants of early immigrants improved their intellectual performance as their standard of living rose and their opportunity for schooling increased.

Sowell found that much the same was true of African Americans. Historically, the average IQ score of African Americans living in the North has been about 10 points higher than the average score of those living in the South. Among the descendants of African Americans who migrated from the South to the North after 1940, IQ scores went up just as they did for descendants of European and Asian immigrants. Thus, environmental factors appear to be critical in explaining differences in IQ among various categories of people.

According to Sowell, these test score differences tell us that *cultural patterns* matter. Asians who score high on tests are no smarter than other people, but they have been raised to value learning and pursue excellence. For their part, African Americans are no

less intelligent than anyone else, but they carry a legacy of disadvantage that can undermine self-confidence and discourage achievement.

WHAT DO YOU THINK?

1. If IQ scores reflect people's environment, are they valid measures of intelligence? Might they be harmful?
2. According to Thomas Sowell, why do some racial and ethnic categories show dramatic short-term gains in average IQ scores?
3. Do you think parents and schools influence a child's IQ score? If so, how?

Conflict theory. A fourth explanation proposes that prejudice is used as a tool by powerful people to oppress others. Anglos who look down on Latino immigrants in the Southwest, for example, can get away with paying the immigrants low wages for hard work. Similarly, all elites benefit when prejudice divides workers along racial and ethnic lines and discourages them from working together to advance their common interests (Geschwender, 1978; Olzak, 1989).

According to another conflict-based argument, made by Shelby Steele (1990), minorities themselves encourage *race consciousness* to win greater power and privileges. Because of their historic disadvantage, minorities claim that they are victims entitled to special consideration based on their race. Although this strategy may bring short-term gains, Steele cautions that such thinking often sparks a backlash from whites or others who oppose "special treatment" on the basis of race or ethnicity.

DISCRIMINATION

Closely related to prejudice is **discrimination,** *treating various categories of people unequally.* Whereas prejudice refers to *attitudes,* discrimination is a matter of *action.* Like prejudice, discrimination can be either positive (providing special advantages) or negative (creating obstacles) and ranges from subtle to blatant.

INSTITUTIONAL PREJUDICE AND DISCRIMINATION

We typically think of prejudice and discrimination as the hateful ideas or actions of specific people. But Stokely

 Do banks unfairly refuse loans to African American applicants? Go to http://www.hud.gov/library/bookshelf18/pressrel/subprime.html

Carmichael and Charles Hamilton (1967) pointed out that far greater harm results from **institutional**

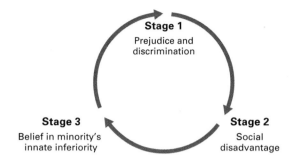

Stage 1
Prejudice and
discrimination

Stage 3
Belief in minority's
innate inferiority

Stage 2
Social
disadvantage

Stage 1: Prejudice and discrimination begin, often as an
expression of ethnocentrism or an attempt to justify
economic exploitation.

Stage 2: As a result of prejudice and discrimination, a
minority is socially disadvantaged, occupying a low
position in the system of social stratification.

Stage 3: This social disadvantage is then interpreted not as
the result of earlier prejudice and discrimination
but as evidence that the minority is innately
inferior, unleashing renewed prejudice and
discrimination by which the cycle repeats itself.

FIGURE 11-2   Prejudice and Discrimination:
The Vicious Circle

Prejudice and discrimination can form a vicious circle,
perpetuating themselves.

prejudice and discrimination, *bias built into the operation
of society's institutions,* including schools, hospitals, the
police, and the workplace. For example, researchers have
shown that banks reject home mortgage applications from
minorities at a higher rate than those from white people,
even when income and quality of neighborhood are held
constant (Gotham, 1998).

According to Carmichael and Hamilton, people are
slow to condemn or even recognize institutional prejudice
and discrimination because it often involves respected public officials and long-established traditions. A case in point
is *Brown* v. *Board of Education of Topeka,* the 1954 Supreme
Court decision that ended legally segregated schools. The
principle of "separate but equal" facilities had been the law
of the land, supporting racial inequality by allowing school
segregation. Despite the change in the law, fifty years later,
most U.S. students still attend schools that are overwhelmingly one race or the other (Barnes, 2004). Indeed, in 1991,
the courts declared that neighborhood schools will never
provide equal education as long as our population is segregated, with most African Americans living in central cities
and most white people (and Asian Americans) living
beyond the city limits in suburbs.

PREJUDICE AND DISCRIMINATION: THE VICIOUS CIRCLE

Prejudice and discrimination reinforce each other. The
Thomas theorem, discussed in Chapter 4 ("Social Interaction in Everyday Life"), offers a simple explanation of this
fact: *Situations that are defined as real become real in their
consequences* (Thomas, 1966:301, orig. 1931).

As Thomas recognized, stereotypes become real to people who believe them, sometimes even to those victimized
by them. For example, prejudice on the part of white people
toward people of color does not produce *innate* inferiority,
but it can produce *social* inferiority, pushing minorities into
low-paying jobs, inferior schools, and racially segregated
housing. Then, as white people see social disadvantage as
evidence that minorities are inferior, they unleash a new
round of prejudice and discrimination, creating a vicious
circle in which each perpetuates the other, as shown in
Figure 11–2.

Majority and Minority: Patterns of Interaction

Social scientists describe interaction between majority and
minority members of a society in terms of four models: pluralism, assimilation, segregation, and genocide.

PLURALISM

Pluralism is *a state in which people of all races and ethnicities are distinct but have equal social standing.* In other
words, people who differ in appearance or social heritage all
share resources roughly equally.

The United States is pluralistic to the extent that all
people have equal standing under the law. In addition, large
cities contain countless "ethnic villages" where people
proudly display the traditions of their immigrant ancestors.
These include New York's Spanish Harlem, Little Italy, and
Chinatown; Philadelphia's Italian "South Philly"; Chicago's
"Little Saigon"; and Latino East Los Angeles. New York City
alone has 189 different ethnic newspapers (Paul, 2001;
Logan, Alba, & Zhang, 2002).

But the United States is not really pluralistic, for three
reasons. First, although many people appreciate their cultural heritage, only a small proportion want to live with
others exactly like themselves (NORC, 2003). Second, our
tolerance for social diversity goes only so far. One reaction
to the growing proportion of minorities in the United States
is a social movement to make English the nation's official
language. Third, as we shall see later in this chapter, it is

In an effort to force assimilation, the U.S. Bureau of Indian Affairs took American Indian children from their families and placed them in boarding schools like this one—Oklahoma's Riverside Indian School. There, they were taught the English language by non-Indian teachers with the goal of making them into "Americans." As this photo from about 1890 suggests, discipline in these schools was strict.

simply a fact that people of various colors and cultures do not have equal social standing.

ASSIMILATION

Many people think of the United States as a "melting pot" in which different nationalities blend together. In truth, however, rather than everyone "melting" into some new cultural pattern, most minorities have adopted the dominant culture established by the earliest settlers. Why? Because doing so is both the avenue to upward social mobility and a way to escape the prejudice and discrimination directed against more visible foreigners. Sociologists use the term **assimilation** to describe *the process by which minorities gradually adopt patterns of the dominant culture.* Assimilation involves changing styles of dress, values, religion, language, and friends.

The amount of assimilation varies by category. For example, Canadians have "melted" more than Cubans, the Dutch more than Dominicans, Germans more than the Japanese. Multiculturalists oppose making assimilation a goal, because it suggests that minorities are "the problem" and defines them (rather than majority people) as the ones who need to do all the changing.

Note that assimilation involves changes in ethnicity but not in race. For example, many descendants of Japanese immigrants have discarded their ethnic traditions but retain their racial identity. In order for racial traits to diminish over generations, **miscegenation,** or *biological reproduction by partners of different racial categories*, must occur. Although interracial marriage is becoming more common, it still amounts to only 3 percent of all marriages (U.S. Census Bureau, 2004).

SEGREGATION

Segregation is *the physical and social separation of categories of people.* Sometimes minorities, especially religious orders such as the Amish, voluntarily segregate themselves from the larger world by forming their own isolated communities. However, majorities usually segregate minorities by excluding them. Neighborhoods, schools, occupations, hospitals, and even cemeteries can be segregated. Whereas pluralism encourages cultural distinctiveness without disadvantage, segregation enforces separation that harms members of a minority.

Racial segregation has a long history in the United States, beginning with slavery and evolving into racially separate housing, schooling, buses, and trains. Decisions such as the 1954 *Brown* case have reduced *de jure* (Latin, "by law") discrimination in the United States. However, *de facto* ("in fact") segregation continues in the form of countless neighborhoods that are home to people of a single race.

In the years following the founding of the National League in 1876, a handful of talented African American players joined a number of professional baseball teams. By the 1890s, however, a "color line" had been drawn, racially segregating professional baseball and giving rise to the "Negro leagues," which reached their greatest popularity in the 1930s and 1940s. After professional baseball was once again integrated in 1947 (first by Jackie Robinson of the Brooklyn Dodgers and, months later, by Larry Dobie of the Cleveland Indians), the "Negro leagues" faded away in the 1950s.

Despite some recent decline, segregation continues in the United States. For example, Livonia, Michigan, is 96 percent white, while neighboring Detroit is 83 percent African American. Kurt Metzger (2001) explains, "Livonia was pretty much created by white flight [from Detroit]." Further, research shows that across the country, whites (especially those with young children) continue to avoid neighborhoods where African Americans live (Emerson, Yancey, & Chai, 2001; Krysan, 2002). At the extreme, Douglas Massey and Nancy Denton (1989) documented the *hypersegregation* of poor African Americans in some inner cities. Hypersegregation means having little contact of any kind with people beyond the local community. Hypersegregation is the daily experience of about 20 percent of poor African Americans.

GENOCIDE

Genocide is *the systematic killing of one category of people by another*. This deadly form of racism and ethnocentrism violates nearly every recognized moral standard, yet it has occurred time and again in human history.

Genocide was common in the history of contact between Europeans and the original inhabitants of the Americas. From the sixteenth century on, the Spanish, Portuguese, English, French, and Dutch forcibly colonized vast empires. Although most native people died from diseases brought by Europeans, to which they had no natural defenses, many were killed deliberately (Matthiessen, 1984; Sale, 1990).

Genocide also occurred in the twentieth century. Unimaginable horror befell European Jews in the 1930s and 1940s during Adolf Hitler's reign of terror, known as the Holocaust. The Nazis murdered more than 6 million Jewish men, women, and children (along with gay people, gypsies, and people with handicaps). The Soviet dictator Josef Stalin murdered on an even greater scale, killing some 30 million real and imagined enemies during his violent rule. Between 1975 and 1980, Pol Pot's Communist regime in Cambodia butchered all "capitalists," which included anyone able to speak a Western language. In all, some 2 million people (one-fourth of the population) perished in the Cambodian "killing fields" (Shawcross, 1979).

Tragically, genocide continues even today. Recent examples include Hutus killing Tutsis in the African nation of Rwanda and Serbs killing Bosnians in the Balkans of Eastern Europe.

These four patterns of minority-majority contact have all been played out in the United States. Although many people proudly point to patterns of pluralism and assimilation, it is also important to recognize the degree to which U.S. society has been built on segregation (of African Americans) and genocide (of Native Americans). The remainder of this chapter examines how these four patterns have

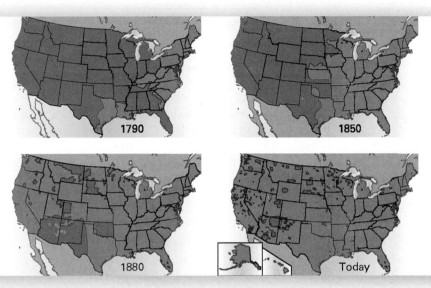

SEEING OURSELVES

NATIONAL MAP 11-2
Land Controlled by Native Americans,
1790 to Today

In 1790, Native Americans controlled three-fourths of the land that eventually became today's United States. Today, Native Americans control 314 reservations, scattered across the United States, that account for just 2 percent of the country's land area. How would you characterize these locations?

Source: Copyright © 1998 by The New York Times Co. Reprinted by permission. All rights reserved.

shaped the past and present social standing of major racial and ethnic categories in the United States.

Race and Ethnicity in the United States

> Give me your tired, your poor,
> Your huddled masses yearning to breathe free,
> The wretched refuse of your teeming shore,
> Send these, the homeless, tempest-tossed to me:
> I lift my lamp beside the golden door.

These words by Emma Lazarus, written on the Statue of Liberty, express cultural ideals of human dignity, personal freedom, and opportunity. Indeed, the United States has provided more of the "good life" to more immigrants than any other nation. But as the history of this country's minorities reveals, our golden door has opened more widely for some than for others.

NATIVE AMERICANS

The term "Native Americans" refers to the hundreds of societies—including Aleuts, Cherokee, Zuni, Sioux, Mohawk, Aztec, and Inca—who first settled the Western Hemisphere. Some 30,000 years before Christopher Columbus (1446–1506) happened upon the Americas, migrating peoples crossed a land bridge from Asia to North America where the Bering Strait (off the coast of Alaska) lies today. Gradually, they spread throughout North and South America.

When the first Europeans arrived late in the fifteenth century, Native Americans numbered in the millions. But by the beginning of the twentieth century, after continual oppression and even acts of genocide, the "vanishing Americans" numbered only 250,000 (Dobyns, 1966; Tyler, 1973). The land they controlled also shrank dramatically, as shown in National Map 11–2.

Columbus first referred to the Native Americans that he encountered as "Indians" because he mistakenly thought he had reached India, where he was hoping to end up. Columbus found the native people passive and peaceful, in stark contrast to the materialistic and competitive Europeans (Matthiessen, 1984; Sale, 1990). Yet even as Europeans seized the land of Native Americans, they justified their actions by calling their victims thieves and murderers (Unruh, 1979; Josephy, 1982).

After the Revolutionary War, the new U.S. government adopted a pluralist approach to Native American societies and tried to gain more land through treaties. Payment for land was far from fair, however, and when Native Americans resisted surrendering their homelands, the U.S. government simply used its superior military power to evict them. By the early 1800s, few Native Americans remained east of the Mississippi River.

In 1871, the United States declared Native Americans wards of the government and adopted a strategy of forced assimilation. Relocated to specific territories designated as "reservations," Native Americans continued to lose their land, and they were well on their way to losing their culture as well. Reservation life encouraged dependency, replacing

TABLE 11-2

The Social Standing of Native Americans, 2000

	Native Americans	Entire U.S. Population
Median family income	$33,144*	$50,891
Percentage in poverty	25.7%*	11.3%
Completion of four or more years of college (age 25 and over)	11.5%	25.6%

*Data are for 1999.

Sources: U.S. Census Bureau (2003, 2004).

ancestral languages with English and traditional religion with Christianity. Officials took many children from their parents and handed them over to boarding schools, where they were resocialized as "Americans." Authorities gave local control of reservations to the few Native Americans who supported government policies, and they distributed reservation land, traditionally held collectively, as private property to individual families (Tyler, 1973).

Not until 1924 were Native Americans entitled to U.S. citizenship. After that, many migrated from the reservations, adopting mainstream cultural patterns and marrying non–Native Americans. Today, four out of ten Native Americans consider themselves biracial or multiracial (Raymond, 2001; Wellner, 2001), and many large cities now contain sizable Native American populations. However, as Table 11–2 shows, the income of Native Americans is far below the U.S. average, and relatively few Native Americans earn a college degree.[2]

From in-depth interviews with Native Americans in a western city, Joan Albon (1971) concluded that their low social standing was a result of cultural factors, including their noncompetitive view of life and reluctance to pursue higher education. In addition, she noted, many Native Americans have dark skin, which makes them targets of prejudice and discrimination.

Members of the many American Indian nations have recently reclaimed pride in their cultural heritage. Traditional

cultural organizations report a surge in new membership applications, and many children can now speak native languages better than their parents. The legal right of Native Americans to govern their reservations has enabled some tribes to build highly profitable gaming casinos. But the wealth produced from gambling has enriched relatively few Native peoples, and most profits go to non-Indian investors (Bartlett & Steele, 2002). While some prosper, most Native Americans remain severely disadvantaged, with a profound sense of the injustice they have suffered at the hands of white people.

 For more information on Native Americans, visit this site: http://www.nativeweb.org

WHITE ANGLO-SAXON PROTESTANTS

White Anglo-Saxon Protestants (WASPs) were not the first people to inhabit the United States, but they came to dominate the nation once English settlement began. Most WASPs are of English ancestry, but this category also includes people from Scotland and Wales. With some 31 million people claiming English ancestry, 10 to 15 percent of our society has some WASP background. National Map 11–3 shows the highest concentrations of WASPs across the United States.

Historically, WASP immigrants were highly skilled and motivated to achieve by what we now call the Protestant work ethic. Because of their numbers and power, WASPs were not subject to the prejudice and discrimination experienced by other categories of immigrants. In fact, the historical dominance of WASPs has led others to want to become more like them.

WASPs were never one single group; especially during colonial times, hostility separated English Anglicans from Scots-Irish Presbyterians (Parrillo, 1994). But in the nineteenth century, most WASPs joined together to oppose the arrival of "undesirables" such as the Germans in the 1840s and Italians in the 1880s. Political movements managed to legally limit the flow of immigrants. Those who could afford it sheltered themselves in exclusive suburbs and restrictive clubs. Thus, the 1880s—the decade that first saw the Statue of Liberty welcome immigrants to the United States—also saw the founding of the first country club with only WASP members (Baltzell, 1964).

By the middle of the twentieth century, however, WASP wealth and power had peaked, as indicated by the 1960 election of John Fitzgerald Kennedy, the first Irish Catholic president. Yet the WASP cultural legacy remains. English is this country's dominant language and Protestantism the majority religion. Our legal system also reflects its English origins. But the historical dominance of WASPs

---

[2]In making comparisons of education and income, keep in mind that various categories of the U.S. population have different median ages. In 2000, the median age for all U.S. people was 35.3 years; for Native Americans, it was 28.0 years. Because people's schooling and income increase over time, this age difference accounts for some of the differences in Table 11–2.

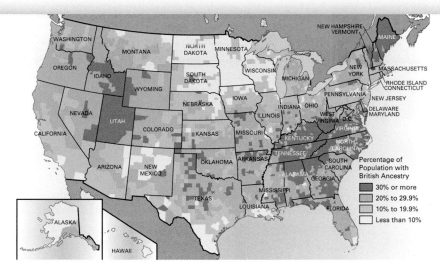

The Concentration of People of WASP Ancestry across the United States

Many people associate white Anglo-Saxon Protestants with elite communities along the eastern and western seaboards of the United States. But the highest concentrations of WASPs are in Utah (because of migrations of Mormons with English ancestry), Appalachia, and northern New England (because of historic immigration). Overall, however, WASPs form a large share of the U.S. population almost everywhere except Alaska, South Texas, Hawaii, and the upper Great Plains. Do you know why?

Source: From Rodger Doyle, *Atlas of Contemporary America*. Copyright © 1994 by Facts on File, Inc. Reprinted with permission of Facts on File, Inc.

Percentage of Population with British Ancestry
- 30% or more
- 20% to 29.9%
- 10% to 19.9%
- Less than 10%

---

is most evident in the widespread use of the terms "race" and "ethnicity" to describe everyone but them.

AFRICAN AMERICANS

Although Africans accompanied Spanish explorers to the New World in the fifteenth century, most accounts mark the beginning of black history in the United States as 1619, when a Dutch trading ship brought twenty Africans to Jamestown, Virginia. Whether these people arrived as slaves or as indentured servants who paid their passage by performing labor for a specified period, being of African descent on these shores soon became virtually synonymous with being a slave. In 1661, Virginia enacted the first law recognizing slavery (Sowell, 1981).

Slavery was the foundation of the southern colonies' plantation system. White people ran plantations using slave labor, and until 1808, some were also slave traders. Traders—including North Americans, Africans, and Europeans—forcibly transported some 10 million Africans to various countries in the Americas, including 400,000 to the United States. On small sailing ships, hundreds of slaves were chained for the several weeks it took to cross the Atlantic Ocean. Filth and disease killed many and drove others to suicide. Overall, perhaps half died en route (Franklin, 1967; Sowell, 1981).

Read personal accounts of slavery at http://lcweb2.loc.gov/ammem/snhtml/

Surviving the miserable journey was a mixed blessing, bringing with it a life of servitude. Although some slaves ended up working in cities at various trades, most labored in the fields, often from daybreak until sunset and even longer during the harvest. The law allowed owners to use whatever disciplinary measures they deemed necessary to ensure that slaves were obedient and productive. Even killing a slave rarely prompted legal action. Owners also broke up slave families at public auctions, where human beings were bought and sold as pieces of property. Unschooled and dependent on their owners for all their basic needs, slaves had little control over their lives (Franklin, 1967; Sowell, 1981).

Some free people of color lived in both the North and the South, laboring as small-scale farmers, skilled workers, and small business owners. But the lives of most African Americans stood in glaring contradiction to the principles of freedom on which the United States was founded. The Declaration of Independence states,

> We hold these Truths to be self-evident, that all Men are created equal, that they are endowed by their Creator with certain unalienable Rights, that among these are Life, Liberty, and the Pursuit of Happiness.

However, most white people did not apply these ideals to African Americans. In the *Dred Scott* case in 1857, the U.S. Supreme Court addressed the question, "Are blacks citizens?" by writing, "We think they are not, and that they are not included, and were not intended to be included, under

The efforts of these four women greatly advanced the social standing of African Americans in the United States. Pictured above, from left to right: Sojourner Truth (1797–1883), born a slave, became an influential preacher and outspoken abolitionist who was honored by President Lincoln at the White House. Harriet Tubman (1820–1913), after escaping from slavery herself, masterminded the flight from bondage of hundreds of African American men and women via the "Underground Railroad." Ida Wells-Barnett (1862–1931), born to slave parents, became a partner in a Memphis newspaper and served as a tireless crusader against the terror of lynching. Marian Anderson (1902–1993), an exceptional singer whose early career was restrained by racial prejudice, broke symbolic "color lines" by singing in the White House (1936) and on the steps of the Lincoln Memorial to a crowd of almost 100,000 people (1939).

the word 'citizens' in the Constitution, and can therefore claim none of the rights and privileges which that instrument provides for and secures for citizens of the United States" (quoted in Blaustein & Zangrando, 1968:160). Thus arose what the Swedish sociologist Gunnar Myrdal (1944) called the *American dilemma:* a democratic society's denial of basic rights and freedoms to an entire category of people. To resolve this dilemma, many white people simply defined African Americans as innately inferior and undeserving of equality (Leach, 2002).

In 1865, the Thirteenth Amendment to the Constitution outlawed slavery. Three years later, the Fourteenth Amendment reversed the *Dred Scott* ruling, granting citizenship to all people born in the United States. The Fifteenth Amendment, ratified in 1870, stated that neither race nor previous condition of servitude should deprive anyone of the right to vote. However, so-called *Jim Crow laws*—classic cases of institutionalized discrimination—segregated U.S. society into two racial castes. Especially in the South, white people beat and lynched black people (and some white people) who challenged the racial hierarchy.

The twentieth century brought dramatic changes for African Americans. After World War I, tens of thousands of women and men fled the rural South for jobs in northern factories. Although some did find more economic opportunity,

few escaped racial prejudice and discrimination, which placed them lower in the social hierarchy than white immigrants arriving from Europe.

In the 1950s and 1960s, a national civil rights movement grew out of landmark judicial decisions that outlawed segregated schools and overt discrimination in employment and public accommodations. In addition, the "black power" movement gave African Americans a renewed sense of pride and purpose.

Despite these gains, people of African descent continue to occupy a lower social position in the United States, as shown in Table 11–3. The median income of African American families in 2003 ($34,369) was only 57 percent of non-Hispanic white family income ($59,937), a ratio that has changed little in thirty years.[3] Black families remain three times as likely as white families to be poor.

---

[3]Here, again, a median age difference (non-Hispanic white people, 38.6; black people, 30.2) accounts for some of the income and educational disparities. More important is a higher proportion of one-parent families among blacks than whites. Comparing only married-couple families, African Americans (median income $52,556 in 2003) earned 79 percent as much as non-Hispanic whites ($66,572).

The number of African American families securely in the middle class rose by more than half between 1980 and 2003; 49 percent earn more than $35,000 a year, and 34 percent earn $50,000 or more. But most African Americans are still working-class or poor; indeed, for many African Americans, earnings have slipped in recent years as factory jobs, vital to residents of inner cities, have been lost to other countries where labor costs are lower. Consequently, black unemployment is more than twice as high as white unemployment; among African American teenagers in many cities, the figure exceeds 40 percent (Smith, 2002; U.S. Department of Labor, 2004).

Since 1980, African Americans have made remarkable educational progress. The share of adults completing high school rose from half to almost three-fourths, nearly closing the gap between whites and blacks. Between 1980 and 2003, the share of African American adults with at least a college degree rose from 8 percent to more than 17 percent. But as Table 11–3 shows, African Americans are still at only two-thirds the national standard when it comes to completing four years of college.

The political clout of African Americans has also increased. As a result of both black migration to the cities and white flight to the suburbs, half of this country's ten largest cities have elected African American mayors. Yet in 2004, African Americans accounted for just 38 members (including delegates) of the House of Representatives (8.7 percent of 435), no member (out of 100) in the Senate, and no state governors.

In sum, for nearly 400 years, people of African ancestry in the United States have struggled for social equality. As a nation, the United States has come far in this pursuit. Overt discrimination is now illegal, and research documents a long-term decline in prejudice against African Americans (Firebaugh & Davis, 1988; Wilson, 1992; NORC, 2003).

In 1913, fifty years after the abolition of slavery, W. E. B. Du Bois proudly noted the extent of black achievement. But Du Bois also cautioned that racial caste remained strong in the United States. Almost a century later, the racial hierarchy persists.

ASIAN AMERICANS

Although Asian Americans share some racial traits, enormous cultural diversity marks this category of people. In 2000, the total number of Asian Americans exceeded 10 million, approaching 4 percent of the U.S. population. The largest category of Asian Americans is people of Chinese ancestry (2.4 million), followed by those of Filipino (1.8 million), Asian Indian (1.7 million), Vietnamese (1.1 million), Korean (1 million), and Japanese (800,000)

TABLE 11–3

The Social Standing of African Americans, 2003

	African Americans	Entire U.S. Population
Median family income	$34,369*	$52,680
Percentage in poverty	24.4%*	12.5%
Completion of four or more years of college (age 25 and over)	17.3%*	27.2%

*For purposes of comparison with other tables in this chapter, 2000 data are as follows: median family income, $34,204; percentage in poverty, 22.1%; completion of four or more years of college, 16.6%.

Sources: U.S. Census Bureau (2000, 2001, 2004).

descent. More than one-third of Asian Americans live in California.

Young Asian Americans have commanded attention and respect as high achievers and are disproportionately represented at our country's best colleges and universities. Many of their elders also have made economic and social gains; most Asian Americans now live in middle class suburbs. Yet despite (and sometimes because of) their record of achievement, Asian Americans sometimes are avoided or treated with outright hostility (O'Hare, Frey, & Fost, 1994; Chua-Eoan, 2000).

At the same time, the "model minority" image of Asian Americans hides the poverty found among their ranks. We will focus on the history and current standing of Chinese Americans and Japanese Americans—the longest-established Asian American minorities—and conclude with a brief look at the most recent arrivals.

Chinese Americans. Chinese immigration to the United States began in 1849 with the economic boom of California's Gold Rush. New towns and businesses sprang up overnight, and the demand for cheap labor attracted some 100,000 Chinese immigrants. Most Chinese workers were young, hardworking men willing to take lower-status jobs rejected by whites. But the economy soured in the 1870s, and desperate whites began to compete with the Chinese for whatever jobs could be found. Suddenly the hardworking Chinese posed a threat. In short, economic hard times led to prejudice and discrimination (Ling, 1971; Boswell, 1986).

Soon whites acted to bar the Chinese from many occupations. Courts also withdrew legal protections, unleashing vicious campaigns against the "Yellow Peril." Everyone seemed to line up against the Chinese, as expressed in the popular phrase of the time that someone up against great

TABLE 11-4

The Social Standing of Asian Americans, 2003

	All Asian Americans	Chinese Americans	Japanese Americans	Korean Americans	Filipino Americans	Entire U.S. Population
Median family income	$63,251**	$62,000*	$77,000*	$51,000*	$70,000*	$52,680
Percentage in poverty	11.8%**	11.8%*	5.9%*	11.6%*	5.4%*	12.5%
Completion of four or more years of college (age 25 and over)	49.8%**	53.8%*	45.8%*	45.8%*	51.8%*	27.2%

*Author estimates based on latest available data.

**For purposes of comparison with other tables in this chapter, 2000 data for all Asians are as follows: median family income, $62,617; percentage in poverty, 10.8%; completion of four or more years of college, 43.9%.

Sources: U.S. Census Bureau (2000, 2001, 2004).

odds did not have "a Chinaman's chance" (Sung, 1967; Sowell, 1981).

In 1882, the U.S. government passed the first of several laws limiting Chinese immigration. This action created domestic hardship because in the United States, Chinese men outnumbered Chinese women by twenty to one. This sex imbalance drove the Chinese population down to only 60,000 by 1920. Because Chinese women already in the United States were in high demand, they soon lost much of their traditional submissiveness to men (Hsu, 1971; Lai, 1980; Sowell, 1981).

Responding to racial hostility, some Chinese moved east; many more sought the relative safety of urban Chinatowns. There Chinese traditions flourished, and kinship networks, called *clans,* offered financial assistance to individuals and represented the interests of all. At the same time, however, living in an all-Chinese community discouraged people from learning English, which limited their job opportunities (Wong, 1971).

A renewed need for labor during World War II prompted President Franklin Roosevelt to end the ban on Chinese immigration in 1943 and to extend the rights of citizenship to Chinese Americans born abroad. Many responded by moving out of Chinatowns and pursuing cultural assimilation. In turn-of-the-century Honolulu, for example, 70 percent of the Chinese people lived in Chinatown; today, the figure is below 20 percent.

By 1950, many Chinese Americans had experienced upward social mobility. Today, people of Chinese ancestry are no longer limited to self-employment in laundries and restaurants; many hold high-prestige positions, especially in fields related to science and new information technology.

As shown in Table 11–4, the median family income of Chinese Americans in 2003 ($62,000) stood above the national average ($52,680). However, the higher income of all Asian Americans reflects a larger number of family members in the labor force.[4] Chinese Americans also have an enviable record of educational achievement, with almost twice the national average of college graduates.

Despite their success, many Chinese Americans still deal with subtle (and sometimes overt) prejudice and discrimination. Such hostility is one reason that poverty among Chinese Americans stands near the national average. Poverty is higher still among those who remain in the socially isolated Chinatowns working in restaurants or other low-paying jobs. Sociologists debate whether racial and ethnic enclaves help their residents or exploit them (Portes & Jensen, 1989; Zhou & Logan, 1989; Kinkead, 1992; Gilbertson & Gurak, 1993).

Japanese Americans. Japanese immigration to the United States began slowly in the 1860s, reaching only 3,000 by 1890. Most of these immigrants came to the Hawaiian Islands (annexed by the United States in 1898 and made a state in 1959) to take low-paying jobs. After 1900, as the number of Japanese immigrants to California increased (reaching 140,000 by 1915), white hostility increased (Takaki, 1998). In 1907, the United States signed an agreement with Japan

---

[4]Median age for all Asian Americans in 2000 was 32.7 years, somewhat below the national median of 35.3 and the non-Hispanic white median of 38.6. But specific categories vary widely in median age: Japanese, 36.1; Chinese, 32.1; Filipino, 31.1; Korean, 29.1; Asian Indian, 28.9; Cambodian, 19.4; Hmong, 12.5.

limiting the entry of men—the chief economic threat—while allowing Japanese women to immigrate to ease the sex ratio imbalance. In the 1920s, state laws in California and dozens of other states mandated segregation and banned interracial marriage, virtually ending further Japanese immigration. Not until 1952 did the United States extend citizenship to foreign-born Japanese.

Japanese and Chinese immigrants differed in three ways. First, there were fewer Japanese immigrants, so they escaped some of the hostility directed at the more numerous Chinese. Second, the Japanese knew much more about the United States than the Chinese did, which helped them assimilate (Sowell, 1981). Third, Japanese immigrants favored rural farming to clustering together in cities. But many white people objected to Japanese ownership of farmland, so in 1913, California barred further purchases. Many foreign-born Japanese (called the *Issei*) responded by operating farms legally owned by their U.S.-born children (*Nisei*), who were constitutionally entitled to citizenship.

Japanese Americans faced their greatest crisis after Japan bombed the U.S. naval fleet at Pearl Harbor, Hawaii, on December 7, 1941. Rage toward Japan was directed at the Japanese living in the United States. Some people feared that the Japanese here would spy for Japan or commit acts of sabotage. Within a year, President Franklin Roosevelt signed Executive Order 9066, an unprecedented action intended to protect national security by detaining people of Japanese descent in military camps. Authorities soon relocated 110,000 people (90 percent of all U.S. Japanese) to remote inland reservations (Sun, 1998).

Concern about national security always rises in times of war, but Japanese internment was sharply criticized. First, it targeted an entire category of people, not one of whom was ever known to have committed a disloyal act. Second, roughly two-thirds of those imprisoned were *Nisei*, U.S. citizens by birth. Third, although the United States was also at war with Germany and Italy, no sweeping action of this kind was taken against people of German or Italian ancestry.

Relocation meant being forced to sell homes, furnishings, and businesses on short notice for pennies on the dollar. As a result, almost the entire Japanese American population was economically devastated. In military prisons—surrounded by barbed wire and guarded by armed soldiers—families crowded into single rooms, often in buildings that had previously sheltered livestock. The internment ended in 1944, when the Supreme Court declared the policy unconstitutional. In 1988, Congress awarded $20,000 to each victim as token compensation.

After World War II, Japanese Americans staged a dramatic recovery. Having lost their traditional businesses, many entered new occupations, and driven by cultural values

Although sometimes portrayed as a successful "model minority," Asian Americans are highly diverse and, like other categories of people, include both rich and poor. These young people contend with many of the same patterns of prejudice and discrimination familiar to members of other minorities.

stressing the importance of education and hard work, Japanese Americans have enjoyed remarkable success. In 2003, the median income of Japanese American households was almost 50 percent above the national average. The rate of poverty among Japanese Americans was less than half the national figure.

 To learn more about Japanese society, go to http://www.jinjapan.org

Upward social mobility has encouraged cultural assimilation and interracial marriage. Younger generations of Japanese Americans rarely live in residential enclaves, as many Chinese Americans still do, and a majority marry non-Japanese partners. In the process, many have abandoned their traditions, including the Japanese language. A high proportion of Japanese Americans belong to ethnic associations as a way of maintaining their ethnic identity (Fugita & O'Brien, 1985). Still, some appear to be caught between two worlds, no longer culturally Japanese yet, because of racial differences, not completely accepted in the larger society.

Recent Asian immigrants. More recent immigrants from Asia include Koreans, Filipinos, Indians, Vietnamese, Guamanians, and Samoans. Overall, the Asian American population increased by 48 percent between 1990 and 2000 and currently accounts for one-third of all immigration to the United States (U.S. Citizenship and Immigration Services, 2004).

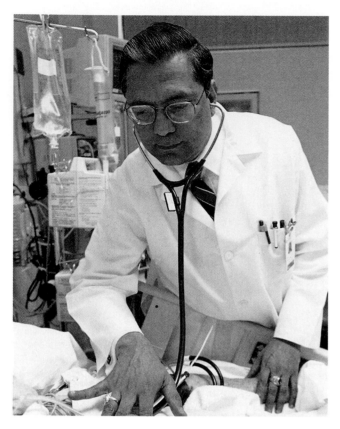

Of all ethnic minorities, people of Asian Indian descent are the most well off, with a large share working in medicine or holding other professional positions. How do you explain the pattern by which some ethnic categories, on average, have higher or lower social standing than others?

Generally speaking, the entrepreneurial spirit is strong among Asian immigrants. Asians are slightly more likely than Latinos, three times more likely than African Americans, and eight times more likely than Native Americans to own and operate small businesses (U.S. Small Business Administration, 2001a). Among all Asian Americans, Koreans are the most likely to own small businesses. For example, most small grocery stores in New York City are Korean-owned; in Los Angeles, Koreans operate a large share of liquor stores. Although many Koreans work long hours in businesses such as these, Korean American families earn slightly lower than average incomes, as shown in Table 11–4. To add to their burden, Korean Americans face limited social acceptance, even among other categories of Asian Americans.

The data in Table 11–4 show that Filipinos generally have fared well. But a closer look reveals a mixed pattern, with some Filipinos highly successful in the professions (especially in medicine) and others holding low-skill jobs (Parrillo, 1994).

For many Filipino families, the key to high income is working women. Almost three-fourths of Filipino American women are in the labor force, compared with just half of Korean American women. Moreover, many of these women are professionals, reflecting the fact that 42 percent of Filipino American women have a four-year college degree, compared with 26 percent of Korean American women.

In sum, a survey of Asian Americans presents a complex picture. The Japanese come closest to having achieved social acceptance, but some surveys reveal greater prejudice against Asian Americans than against African Americans (Parrillo, 2003a). Median income data suggest that many Asian Americans have prospered. But these numbers reflect the fact that many Asian Americans live in Hawaii, California, or New York, where incomes are high but so is the cost of living (Takaki, 1998). Then, too, many Asian Americans remain poor. One thing is clear—their high immigration rate means that people of Asian ancestry will play a central role in U.S. society in the decades to come.

HISPANIC AMERICANS

In 2000, the number of Hispanics in the United States topped 35 million (12.5 percent of the U.S. population), surpassing the number of African Americans (12.3 percent) and making Hispanics the largest racial or ethnic minority. Keep in mind that few who fall in this category describe themselves as "Hispanic" or "Latino." Like Asian Americans, Hispanics are really a cluster of distinct populations, each of which identifies with a particular ancestral nation (Marín & Marín, 1991). About two out of three Hispanics (some 20 million) are Mexican Americans, or "Chicanos." Puerto Ricans are next in number (3 million), followed by Cuban Americans (1.2 million). Many other nations of Latin America are represented by smaller numbers.

Although the Hispanic population is increasing all over the country, most Hispanic Americans live in the Southwest. One of four Californians is Latino (in greater Los Angeles, almost half the people are Latino). National Map 11–4 shows the distribution of the Hispanic, African American, and Asian American populations across the United States.

Median family income for all Hispanics—$34,272 in 2003—stands well below the national average.[5] As the

---

[5]The 2000 median age of the U.S. Hispanic population was 25.8 years, well below the national median of 35.3 years. This difference accounts for some of the disparity in income and education.

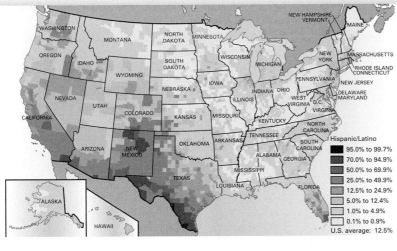

NATIONAL MAP 11–4

The Concentration of Hispanics or Latinos, African Americans, and Asian Americans, by County, 2000

In 2000, people of Hispanic or Latino descent represented 12.5 percent of the U.S. population, compared with 12.3 percent African Americans and 3.6 percent Asian Americans. These three maps show the geographic distribution of these categories of people in 2000. Comparing them, we see that the southern half of the United States is home to far more minorities than the northern half. But do the three concentrate in the same areas? What patterns do the maps reveal?

Source: U.S. Census Bureau (2001).

Hispanic/Latino
- 95.0% to 99.7%
- 70.0% to 94.9%
- 50.0% to 69.9%
- 25.0% to 49.9%
- 12.5% to 24.9%
- 5.0% to 12.4%
- 1.0% to 4.9%
- 0.1% to 0.9%

U.S. average: 12.5%

African American
- 70.0% to 86.5%
- 50.0% to 69.9%
- 25.0% to 49.9%
- 12.3% to 24.9%
- 5.0% to 12.2%
- 1.0% to 4.9%
- 0.0% to 0.9%

U.S. average: 12.3%

Asian American
- 25.0% to 46.0%
- 12.5% to 24.9%
- 3.6% to 12.4%
- 1.0% to 3.5%
- 0.0% to 0.9%

U.S. average: 3.6%

The strength of family bonds and neighborhood ties is evident in Carmen Lomas Garza's painting *Barbacoa para Cumpleanos* (Birthday Party Barbecue).

Carmen Lomas Garza, *Barbacoa para Cumpleanos* (Birthday Party Barbecue). Alkyds on canvas, 38 × 48 inches. (C) 1993 Carmen Lomas Garza (reg. 1994). Photo credit: M. Lee Fatherree. Collection of Federal Reserve Bank of Dallas.

following sections explain, however, some categories of Hispanics have fared better than others.

Mexican Americans.   Some Chicanos are descendants of people who lived in a part of Mexico annexed by the United States after the Mexican American War (1846–48). However, most Mexican Americans are recent immigrants. Indeed, more immigrants now come to the United States from Mexico than from any other country.

Like many other immigrants, many Mexican Americans have worked as low-wage laborers, on farms or elsewhere. Table 11–5 shows that the 2003 median family income for Mexican Americans was $33,533, about two-thirds the national average. Almost one-fourth of Chicano families are poor—nearly twice the national average. Finally, despite gains since 1980, Mexican Americans still have a high dropout rate and, on average, receive much less schooling than U.S. adults as a whole.

Puerto Ricans.   Puerto Rico (like the Philippines) became a possession of the United States when the Spanish-American War ended in 1898. In 1917, Puerto Ricans (but not Filipinos) became U.S. citizens.

New York City is home to about 1 million Puerto Ricans. However, about one-third of this community is severely disadvantaged. Adjusting to cultural patterns on the mainland—including, for many, learning English—is one major challenge; also, Puerto Ricans with darker skin

encounter much prejudice and discrimination. As a result, more people return to Puerto Rico each year than arrive: During the 1990s, the Puerto Rican population of New York actually fell by about 100,000 (Navarro, 2000).

This "revolving door" pattern makes assimilation more difficult. Three-fourths of Puerto Rican families in the United States speak Spanish at home, compared with about half of Mexican American families (Sowell, 1981; Stevens & Swicegood, 1987). Speaking only Spanish maintains a strong ethnic identity, but it also limits economic opportunity. Puerto Ricans also have a higher rate of women-headed households than other Hispanics, a pattern that puts families at greater risk of poverty. Table 11–5 shows that the 2003 median household income for Puerto Ricans was $30,095, a little more than half the national average. Although long-term mainland residents have made economic gains, more recent immigrants from Puerto Rico continue to struggle to find work. Overall, Puerto Ricans remain the most disadvantaged Hispanic minority.

Cuban Americans.   Within little more than a decade after the 1959 Marxist revolution led by Fidel Castro, 400,000 Cubans had fled to the United States. Most settled in Miami. Many immigrants were highly educated business and professional people who wasted little time becoming as successful in the United States as they had been in their homeland.

Table 11–5 shows that the median household income for Cuban Americans in 2003 was $35,217, above that of

TABLE 11-5

The Social Standing of Hispanic Americans, 2003

	All Hispanics	Mexican Americans	Puerto Ricans	Cuban Americans	Entire U.S. Population
Median family Income	$34,272*	$33,533	$30,095	$35,217	$52,680
Percentage in poverty	22.5%*	22.8%	26.1%	16.5%	12.5%
Completion of four or more years of college (age 25 and over)	11.4%*	7.5%	14.0%	18.6%	27.2%

*For purposes of comparison with other tables in this chapter, 2000 data for all Hispanics are as follows: median family income, $35,050; percentage in poverty, 21.2%; completion of four or more years of college, 10.6%.

Sources: U.S. Census Bureau (2000, 2001, 2003, 2004).

other Hispanics yet still well below the national average. The 1.2 million Cuban Americans living in the United States today have managed a delicate balancing act, achieving in the larger society while holding on to much of their traditional culture. Of all Hispanics, Cubans are the most likely to speak Spanish in their homes; eight out of ten families do so. However, cultural distinctiveness and living in highly visible communities such as Miami's Little Havana provoke hostility from some people.

WHITE ETHNIC AMERICANS

The term "white ethnics" recognizes the ethnic heritage and social disadvantages of many white people. White ethnics are non-WASPs whose ancestors lived in Ireland, Poland, Germany, Italy, or other European countries. More than half of the U.S. population falls into one or another white ethnic category.

Unprecedented emigration from Europe in the nineteenth century first brought Germans and Irish and then Italians and Jews to our shores. Despite cultural differences, all shared the hope that the United States would offer greater political freedom and economic opportunity than their homelands. Most did live better in this country, but the belief that "the streets of America are paved with gold" turned out to be a far cry from reality. Many immigrants found only hard labor for low wages.

White ethnics also endured their share of prejudice and discrimination. Many employers shut their doors to immigrants, posting signs such as "None need apply but Americans" (Handlin, 1941:67). By 1921, Congress enacted a quota system greatly limiting immigration, especially by southern and eastern Europeans, who were likely to have darker skin and to differ culturally from the dominant WASPs. This system remained in place until 1968 (Fallows, 1983).

In response to prejudice and discrimination, many white ethnics formed supportive residential enclaves. Some also gained footholds in certain businesses and trades: Italian Americans entered the construction industry, Irish Americans worked in construction and took civil service jobs, Jews predominated in the garment industry, and many Greeks (like the Chinese) worked in the retail food business (Newman, 1973).

Many white ethnics still live in traditional working-class neighborhoods, although those who prospered have gradually assimilated. Most descendants of immigrants who labored in sweatshops and lived in crowded tenements now make enough money to lead comfortable lives. As a result, their ethnic heritage is a source of pride.

Race and Ethnicity: Looking Ahead

The United States has been, and will remain, a land of immigrants. Immigration has brought striking cultural diversity and tales of success, hope, and struggle told in hundreds of languages.

Most immigrants arrived in a great wave that peaked about 1910. The next two generations brought economic gains and at least some cultural assimilation. The government also extended citizenship to Native Americans (1924), foreign-born Filipinos (1942), Chinese Americans (1943), and Japanese Americans (1952).

A second wave of immigration began after World War II and swelled as the government relaxed immigration laws in the 1960s. During the 1990s, nearly 1 million people came to the United States each year, more than twice the number that arrived during the "Great Immigration" a century ago

CONTROVERSY & DEBATE

Affirmative Action: Solution or Problem?

Barbara Gruttner, who is white, claimed that she was the victim of racial discrimination. She maintained that the University of Michigan Law School unfairly denied her application for admission while admitting many less qualified African American applicants. The basis of her claim was the fact that Michigan, a state university, admitted just 9 percent of white students with her grade point average and law school aptitude test scores, while admitting 100 percent of comparable African American applicants.

In 2003, the Supreme Court heard Gruttner's complaint in a review of the admissions policies of both the law school and the undergraduate program at the University of Michigan. In a 6–3 decision, the court ruled against Gruttner, claiming that the University of Michigan Law School could take account of the race of applicants in the interest of creating a socially diverse student body. At the same time, however, the court struck down the university's undergraduate admissions policy, a point system that took account of grades and college board scores but also gave underrepresented minorities a numerical bonus. The Court ruled that a point system of this kind is too close to the rigid quota systems rejected by the Court in the past.

With this ruling, the Supreme Court continued to oppose any quotalike systems while at the same time reaffirming the importance of racial diversity on campus. Thus, colleges and universities can take account of race in order to increase the number of traditionally underrepresented students, as long as race is treated as one variable in a process that evaluates each applicant as an individual (Stout, 2003).

How did the controversial policy of affirmative action begin? The answer

takes us back to the end of World War II, when the U.S. government funded higher education for veterans of all races. The G.I. Bill held special promise for African Americans, most of whom needed financial assistance to enroll in college. The program was so successful that by 1960, some 350,000 black men and women were on college campuses with government funding.

There was just one problem: These newly educated people were not finding the kinds of jobs for which they were qualified. In short, educational opportunity was not producing economic opportunity.

Thus, in the early 1960s, the Kennedy administration devised a program of "affirmative action" to provide broader opportunities to qualified minorities. Employers and educators were instructed to carefully monitor hiring, promotion, and admissions policies to eliminate discrimination—even if unintended—against minorities.

Defenders of affirmative action see it, first, as a sensible response to our nation's racial and ethnic history, especially for African Americans, who suffered through two centuries of slavery and a century of segregation under Jim Crow laws. Throughout our history, they claim, being white gave people a big advantage. Thus, minority preference

(although newcomers now enter a country that has five times as many people). Most of today's immigrants come not from Europe but from Latin America and Asia, with Mexicans, Asian Indians, and Filipinos arriving in the largest numbers.

Many new arrivals face much the same prejudice and discrimination as those who came before them. Indeed, recent years have witnessed rising hostility toward foreigners

(sometimes called *xenophobia,* with Greek roots meaning "fear of what is strange"). In 1994, California voters passed Proposition 187, cutting social services (including schooling) to illegal immigrants. Since then, voters there have mandated that all children learn English in school. In 2000, some landowners along the southwestern border of the United States took up arms to defend themselves against

today is fair compensation for unfair majority preference in the past.

Second, given our racial history, many analysts think it is unlikely that the United States will ever become a color-blind society. Prejudice and discrimination are woven deeply in the fabric of U.S. society; simply endorsing the principle of color blindness does not mean that everyone will compete fairly.

Third, supporters maintain that affirmative action has worked. Where would minorities be if our government had not enacted this policy three decades ago? Indeed, major employers, such as fire and police departments in large cities, began hiring minorities and women only because of affirmative action. Affirmative action has played an important part in expanding the African American middle class. Furthermore, affirmative action has increased interracial interaction on campus and advanced the careers of a generation of black students.

About 80 percent of African Americans claim that affirmative action is needed to secure equal opportunity. But affirmative action draws criticism from others. Indeed, a recent poll shows that 73 percent of white people and 56 percent of Hispanics oppose preferences for African Americans (NORC, 2003). As this opposition to affirmative action was building during the 1990s, courts began to trim back such policies. Critics argue, first, that affirmative action started out as a temporary remedy to ensure fair competition but became a system of "group preferences" and quotas. In other words, the policy did not remain true to the goal of promoting color blindness as set out in the 1964 Civil Rights Act. By the 1970s, it had become "reverse discrimination," favoring people not because of their performance but because of their race, ethnicity, or sex.

Second, critics argue that affirmative action divides society. If racial preferences were wrong in the past, they are wrong now. Why should whites today, many of whom are far from privileged, be penalized for past discrimination that was in no way their fault? Our society has undone most of the institutional prejudice and discrimination of earlier times, so that minorities can and do enjoy success according to their personal merit. Giving entire categories of people special treatment compromises standards of excellence, calls into question the real accomplishments of minorities, and offends public opinion.

A third argument is that affirmative action benefits those who need it least. Favoring minority-owned corporations or holding places in law school for minorities helps already privileged people. Affirmative action has done little for the African American underclass that most needs help.

In sum, there are good arguments both for and against affirmative action. Indeed, people who believe the ultimate goal is a society where no racial or ethnic category dominates fall on both sides of the debate. The disagreement is not whether people of all colors should have equal opportunity but whether the current policy of affirmative action is part of the solution or part of the problem.

CONTINUE THE DEBATE . . .

1. Because society historically has favored males over females and whites over people of color, would you agree that white males have received more "affirmative action" than anyone else? Why or why not?
2. Should affirmative action include only disadvantaged categories of minorities (say, African Americans and Native Americans) and exclude more affluent categories (such as Japanese Americans)? Why or why not?
3. Should state universities admit applicants with an eye toward advancing minorities and thereby reducing racial inequality? Do you think that goal is as important as the goal of admitting the most qualified individuals?

Sources: Bowen & Bok (1999), Fetto (2002c), Fineman & Lipper (2003), Kantrowitz & Wingert (2003), and NORC (2003).

large numbers of illegal immigrants coming in from Mexico, and some political candidates have called for drastic action to cut off further immigration. More broadly, as the Controversy & Debate box explains, the debate over affirmative action rages as hotly as ever.

Like those who came before, today's immigrants try to blend into U.S. society without completely giving up their traditional culture. Some still build racial and ethnic enclaves, so that in many cities across the country the Little Havanas and Koreatowns of today stand alongside the Little Italys and Chinatowns of the past. In addition, new arrivals still carry the traditional hope that their racial and ethnic diversity can be a source of pride, not a badge of inferiority.

Summary

1. Races are socially constructed categories by which societies set apart people with various physical traits. Although a century ago scientists assigned people to one of three broad categories—Caucasoids, Negroids, and Mongoloids—there are no pure races.

2. Ethnicity is based not on biology but on shared cultural heritage.

3. Minorities, including people of certain races and ethnicities, are categories of people society sets apart, making them both distinct and disadvantaged.

4. Prejudice is a rigid and unfair generalization about a category of people. Racism, a destructive type of prejudice, asserts that one race is innately superior or inferior to another.

5. Discrimination is a pattern of action by which a person treats various categories of people unequally.

6. Pluralism means that racial and ethnic categories, although distinct, have equal social standing. Assimilation is a process by which minorities gradually adopt the patterns of the dominant culture. Segregation is the physical and social separation of categories of people. Genocide is the extermination of a category of people.

7. Native Americans, the earliest human inhabitants of the Americas, have endured genocide, segregation, and forced assimilation. Today, Native American social standing is well below the national average.

8. WASPs predominated among the original European settlers of the United States, and many continue to enjoy high social standing today.

9. African Americans experienced two centuries of slavery. Emancipation in 1865 gave way to segregation by law. Today, despite legal equality, African Americans are still relatively disadvantaged.

10. Chinese and Japanese Americans have suffered from both prejudice and discrimination. Although some prejudice and discrimination continues, both categories now have above-average income and schooling. Recent Asian immigration, especially of Asian Indians and Filipinos, now accounts for one-third of all immigration to the United States.

11. Hispanics, the largest U.S. minority, include many ethnicities sharing a Spanish heritage. Mexican Americans, the largest Hispanic minority, are concentrated in the Southwest. Cubans, concentrated in Miami, are the wealthiest Hispanics; Puerto Ricans, most of whom live in New York, are the poorest.

12. White ethnics are non-WASPs of European ancestry. Although they made gains throughout the twentieth century, many white ethnics still struggle for economic security.

13. Immigration has increased in recent years. No longer primarily from Europe, most immigrants now arrive from Latin America and Asia.

Key Concepts

race (p. 280) a socially constructed category composed of people who share biologically transmitted traits that members of a society consider important

ethnicity (p. 282) a shared cultural heritage

minority (p. 283) any category of people distinguished by physical or cultural difference that a society sets apart and subordinates

prejudice (p. 284) a rigid and unfair generalization about an entire category of people

racism (p. 287) the belief that one racial category is innately superior or inferior to another

scapegoat (p. 287) a person or category of people, typically with little power, whom people unfairly blame for their own troubles

discrimination (p. 289) treating various categories of people unequally

institutional prejudice and discrimination (p. 290) bias built into the operation of society's institutions

pluralism (p. 290) a state in which people of all races and ethnicities are distinct but have equal social standing

assimilation (p. 291) the process by which minorities gradually adopt patterns of the dominant culture

miscegenation (p. 291) biological reproduction by partners of different racial categories

segregation (p. 291) the physical and social separation of categories of people

genocide (p. 292) the systematic killing of one category of people by another

CRITICAL-THINKING QUESTIONS

1. What is the difference between race and ethnicity? What does it mean to say that race and ethnicity are socially constructed?

2. Do you think all people of color, rich or poor, should be considered minorities? Why or why not?

3. Many historians claim the history of the United States is the history of immigrants. Do you agree with this statement? Is it as true today as it was in the past?

4. Many people assume that only white people display prejudice and engage in discrimination. To what extent do minorities exhibit prejudice and discrimination against whites? Against other minorities?

APPLICATIONS AND EXERCISES

1. Does your college or university take account of race and ethnicity in its admissions policies? Ask to speak with an admissions officer to see what you can learn about your school's use of race and ethnicity in admissions. Ask whether there is a "legacy" policy that favors children of parents who attended the school.

2. Give several of your friends or family members a quick quiz, asking them what share of the U.S. population is white, Hispanic, African American, and Asian (see Table 11–1 on page 283). If they are like most people, they will exaggerate the share of minorities and understate the white proportion (Labovitz, 1996). What do you make of the results?

3. Ask immigrants on your campus or in your local community about their homelands and their experiences since arriving in the United States, and compare what you learn from them with what you have read in this chapter.

4. Packaged in the back of this new textbook is an interactive CD-ROM that offers a variety of video and interactive review materials intended to help you better understand the material covered in this chapter. For this chapter, the CD-ROM contains a relevant clip from *ABC News*, an author's tip video, interactive map animations, an interactive timeline, and flashcards with audio pronunciations of the more difficult words.

SITES TO SEE

http://www.prenhall.com/macionis
Visit the interactive Companion Website™ that accompanies this text. Begin by clicking on the cover of your book. You will find a chapter-by-chapter study guide, practice tests, suggested Web links, and links to other relevant material.

http://www.naacp.org
http://www.adl.org/adl.asp
These two organizations—the National Association for the Advancement of Colored People and the Anti-Defamation League—are concerned with fighting prejudice and discrimination and advancing the social standing of minorities in the United States. Determine each organization's strategies and goals.

http://w3.access.gpo.gov/eop/ca/index.html
This useful data site, operated by the Council of Economic Advisers, provides an assessment of social and economic well-being of various racial and ethnic categories of the U.S. population.

http://www.collegeboard.com/repository/minorityhig_3948.pdf
Read the report of the College Board's National Task Force on Minority High Achievement, which analyzes racial and ethnic differences in higher education.

 INVESTIGATE WITH RESEARCH NAVIGATOR™

Follow the instructions found on page 32 of this textbook to access the features of **Research Navigator™**. Once at the Web site, enter your Login Name and Password. Then, to use the **Content Select™** database, enter keywords such as "race," "ethnicity," and "segregation" and the search engine will supply relevant and recent scholarly and popular press publications. Use the *New York Times* **Search-by-Subject Archive** to find recent news articles related to sociology and the **Links Library** feature to find relevant Web links organized by the key terms associated with this chapter.

CHAPTER TWELVE

Economics and Politics

What is a social institution?

How does change in the economy reshape society?

Why do some critics say that the United States
is not really a democracy?

Economics and politics are two social institutions that affect how wealth and power ▶ are distributed throughout a society's population. The expansion of international trade by the World Trade Organization has sparked opposition from some people, who fear it will harm working people living in low-income nations.

Here's a quick quiz about the U.S. economy. (Hint: All five questions have the same right answer.)

- Which business do 100 million people in the United States visit each week?

- Which U.S. company, on average, opens a new store every day?

- Which U.S. company is the largest employer in the country after the federal government?

- Which U.S. company will create nearly 800,000 new jobs over the next five years?

- Which single company accounted for 25 percent of all the growth in U.S. economic output during the second half of the 1990s?

You have probably guessed that the correct answer is Wal-Mart, the global discount store chain founded by Sam Walton, who opened his first store in Arkansas in 1962. By 2004, Wal-Mart was making $256 billion in sales through 3,600 stores in the United States and 1,500 stores in other countries from Brazil to China (Saporito, 2003).

But not everyone is happy with the expansion of Wal-Mart. Across the United States, people have formed a social movement to keep Wal-Mart out of their local communities, fearing the loss of local businesses and, in some cases, local culture. Critics claim that the merchandising giant pays low wages at home, keeps out unions, and sells many products made in sweatshops abroad (Rousseau, 2002).

This chapter explores the economy and the closely related institution of politics. A number of very large corporations, including Wal-Mart, are at the center of the U.S. economy, raising questions about just how the economy operates, whose interests it ought to serve, and to what extent big business shapes the political life of the United States.

Economics and politics are each a **social institution,** *a major sphere of social life, or societal subsystem, organized to meet human needs.* The two chapters that follow consider other social institutions: Chapter 13 focuses on the family and religion, and Chapter 14 highlights education and medicine. These discussions explain how social institutions have changed over the course of history, describe how they operate today, and point out controversies that are likely to shape them tomorrow.

The Economy: Historical Overview

The **economy** is *the social institution that organizes a society's production, distribution, and consumption of goods and services.* The economy operates—for better or worse—in a generally predictable manner. *Goods* are commodities ranging from necessities (such as food, clothing, and shelter) to luxury items (such as automobiles, swimming pools, and yachts). *Services* are activities that benefit others (including the work of priests, doctors, teachers, and computer software specialists).

THE AGRICULTURAL REVOLUTION

As Chapter 2 ("Culture") explained, the earliest societies were made up of hunters and gatherers living off the land.

As societies industrialize, a smaller and smaller share of the labor force works in agriculture. In the United States, much of what agricultural work remains is performed by immigrants from lower-income nations. This grape worker in southern California is a recent immigrant from Mexico.

In such societies, there was no distinct economy; producing and consuming were part of family life.

Harnessing animals to plows around 5,000 years ago permitted the development of agriculture, which was ten times as productive as hunting and gathering. The resulting surplus meant that not everyone had to produce food, so many people took on specialized work: making tools, raising animals, and building dwellings. Soon towns sprang up, linked by networks of traders. These four factors—agricultural technology, specialized work, permanent settlements, and trade—made the economy a distinct social institution.

THE INDUSTRIAL REVOLUTION

By the mid-eighteenth century, a second technological revolution was underway, starting in England and spreading to the United States. Industrialization changed the economy in five ways:

1. **New sources of energy.** Throughout history, "energy" had meant the muscle power of people or animals. Then, in 1765, the English inventor James Watt introduced the steam engine. A hundred times more powerful than muscle power, early steam engines soon drove heavy machinery.

2. **Centralization of work in factories.** Steam-powered machinery moved work from homes to factories, centralized workplaces that housed the machines.

3. **Manufacturing and mass production.** Before the Industrial Revolution, most people grew or gathered raw materials (such as grain, wood, or wool). In an industrial economy, people working in factories turn raw materials into finished products (such as furniture and clothing).

4. **Specialization.** Historically, artisans at home made products from beginning to end. In the factory, a laborer repeats a single task over and over, making only a small contribution to the finished product.

5. **Wage labor.** Instead of working for themselves, factory workers became wage laborers who sold their labor to strangers, who often cared less for them than for the machines they operated. (Recall the story at the start of Chapter 9, in which after a tragic fire, the manager of a Bangladesh sweatshop was more concerned about the harm to his factory than the death of his workers.)

The Industrial Revolution raised living standards as the production of countless new products fueled an expanding economy. However, the benefits of industrial technology were shared very unequally, especially at the beginning. Some factory owners made huge fortunes, but the majority of workers lived close to poverty. Children slaved in factories or deep in coal mines for pennies a day. With time, workers formed labor unions to collectively represent their interests to factory owners. Over the course of the twentieth century, new laws banned child labor, set minimum wage levels, improved workplace safety, and extended schooling and political rights to a larger segment of the population.

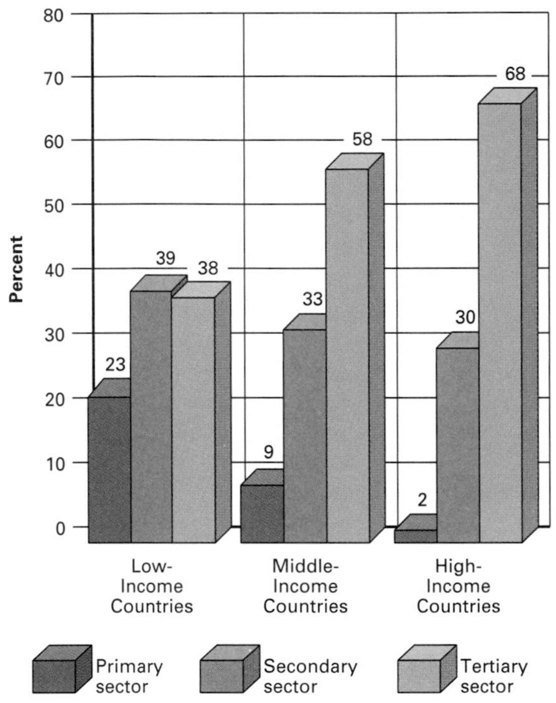

FIGURE 12–1 The Size of Economic Sectors by Income Level of Country

Source: Estimates based on United Nations Development Programme (2000) and World Bank (2000).

THE INFORMATION REVOLUTION AND POSTINDUSTRIAL SOCIETY

By about 1950, the nature of production was changing once again. The United States was creating a **postindustrial economy,** *a productive system based on service work and high technology.* Automated machinery (and more recently, robotics) reduced the role of human labor in production while expanding the ranks of clerical workers and managers. Service industries—including sales, health care, food service, and banking—currently employ most working people in this country. The postindustrial era, then, is marked by a shift from industrial work to service work.

Driving this economic change is a third technological breakthrough: the computer. Just as factories did two centuries ago, the Information Revolution, with new kinds of products and new forms of communication, has changed the character of work itself. In general, we see three changes:

1. **From tangible products to ideas.** The industrial era was defined by the production of goods; in the post-industrial era, work involves manipulating symbols. Computer programmers, writers, financial analysts, advertising executives, architects, editors, and various types of consultants make up the labor force of the information age.

2. **From mechanical skills to literacy skills.** The Industrial Revolution required mechanical skills, but the Information Revolution requires literacy skills: speaking and writing well and, of course, using computers. People able to communicate effectively enjoy new opportunities; people without these skills face declining prospects.

3. **From factories to almost anywhere.** Industrial technology drew workers to factories that were near power sources, but computer technology allows people to work almost anywhere. Laptop computers, cell phones, and portable fax machines can turn the home, car, or even an airplane into a "virtual office." In short, new information technology blurs the line between work and home life.

SECTORS OF THE ECONOMY

The three revolutions just described reflect a shifting balance among the three sectors of the economy. The **primary sector** is *the part of the economy that draws raw materials from the natural environment.* The primary sector—agriculture, ranching, fishing, forestry, and mining—is largest in low-income nations. Figure 12–1 shows that 23 percent of the economic output of low-income countries is in the primary sector, compared with 9 percent of economic activity among middle-income nations and just 2 percent in high-income countries like the United States.

The **secondary sector,** *the part of the economy that transforms raw materials into manufactured goods,* includes operations such as refining petroleum into gasoline and turning metals into automobiles. The globalization of industry means that just about all the world's countries derive a significant share of their economic output from the secondary sector. As Figure 12–1 shows, the secondary sector accounts for a greater share of economic output in low-income nations than it does in high-income countries.

The **tertiary sector** is *the part of the economy that involves services rather than goods.* Accounting for just 38 percent of economic output in low-income countries, the tertiary sector grows with industrialization and dominates the economies of middle-income countries (58 percent) and high-income, postindustrial nations (68 percent). Today, about 76 percent of the U.S. labor force does service work, including clerical

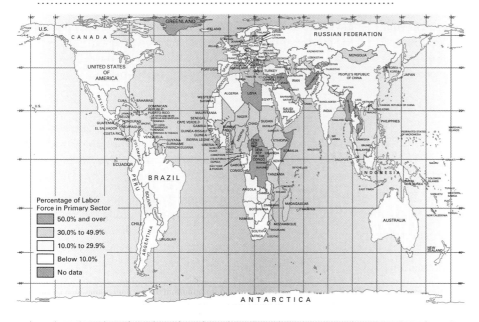

GLOBAL MAP 12–1

Agricultural Employment in Global Perspective

The primary sector of the economy is largest in the nations that are least developed. Thus, in the poor countries of Africa and Asia, up to half of all workers are farmers. This picture is altogether different in the world's most economically developed countries— including the United States, Canada, Great Britain, and Australia—which have 2 percent of their labor force in agriculture.

Percentage of Labor Force in Primary Sector

- 50.0% and over
- 30.0% to 49.9%
- 10.0% to 29.9%
- Below 10.0%
- No data

GLOBAL MAP 12–2

Service-Sector Employment in Global Perspective

The tertiary sector of the economy becomes ever larger as a nation's income level rises. In the United States, Canada, the countries of Western Europe, Australia, and Japan, about two-thirds of the labor force perform service work.

Sources: Data from United Nations Development Programme (2000) and World Bank (2000, 2001); map projection from *Peters Atlas of the World* (1990).

Percentage of Labor Force in Tertiary Sector

- 60.0% and over
- 50.0% to 59.9%
- 40.0% to 49.9%
- Below 40.0%
- No data

work and positions in food service, sales, law, health care, advertising, and teaching.

THE GLOBAL ECONOMY

New information technology is drawing nations of the world closer together, creating a **global economy,** *expanding economic activity that crosses national borders.* The development of a global economy has four major consequences. First, a global division of labor causes different regions of the world to specialize in different sectors of economic activity. As Global Map 12–1 shows, agriculture represents more than half of the total economic output in the world's poorest countries. Global Map 12–2 shows that most of the economic output in high-income countries, including the United States, is in the service sector.

Second, an increasing number of products pass through more than one nation. Look no further than your morning coffee: It may have been grown in Colombia and transported to New Orleans on a freighter that was registered in Liberia, made in Japan using steel from Korea, and fueled by oil from Venezuela.

Third, national governments no longer control economic activity within their borders. In fact, governments cannot even regulate the value of their national currencies because dollars, euros, pounds sterling, yen, and other currencies are traded around the clock in the financial centers of Tokyo, London, and New York, which are linked by satellite communications.

The fourth consequence of the global economy is that a small number of businesses, operating internationally, now control a vast share of the world's economic activity. According to one estimate, the 600 largest multinational companies account for half the world's economic output (Kidron & Segal, 1991; Gergen, 2002).

The planet is divided into 192 politically distinct nations. But the rising level of international trade makes nationhood less important than it was even a decade ago.

Economic Systems: Paths to Justice

October 20, Saigon, Vietnam. Sailing up the narrow Saigon River is an unsettling experience for anyone who came of age in the 1960s. We need to remember that Vietnam is a country, not a war, and that thirty years have passed since the last U.S. helicopter lifted off the rooftop of the U.S. embassy, ending our country's presence there.

Saigon is becoming a boomtown. Neon signs bathe the city's waterfront in color; hotels, bankrolled by Western corporations, push skyward from a dozen construction sites; taxi meters record fares in U.S. dollars, not Vietnamese dong; and Visa and American Express stickers decorate the doors of fashionable shops that cater to tourists from Japan, France, and the United States.

There is heavy irony here: After decades of fighting, millions of lives lost on both sides, and the victory of Communist forces, the Vietnamese are doing an about-face and turning toward capitalism. What we see today is what might well have happened had the U.S. and South Vietnamese forces won the war.

Every society's economy makes a statement about justice by determining who gets what. Two general economic models are capitalism and socialism. However, no nation anywhere in the world has an economy that is purely one or the other; capitalism and socialism are two ends of a spectrum along which the actual economies of the world fall. We will look, in turn, at each of these two models.

CAPITALISM

Capitalism is *an economic system in which natural resources and the means of producing goods and services are privately owned.* An ideal capitalist economy has three distinctive features:

1. **Private ownership of property.** In a capitalist economy, individuals can own almost anything. The more capitalist an economy, the more private ownership there is of wealth-producing property such as factories, real estate, and natural resources.

2. **Pursuit of personal profit.** A capitalist society tries to create profit and wealth. The profit motive is considered the natural way of doing business.

3. **Competition and consumer choice.** A purely capitalist economy is a free-market system with no government interference (sometimes called a *laissez-faire* economy, from French words meaning "to leave alone"). According to the Scottish economist Adam Smith (1723–1790), a freely competitive economy regulates itself by the "invisible hand" of the law of supply and demand (1937, orig. 1776).

   Consumers guide a market economy, Smith explained, by choosing goods and services offering the greatest value. Producers advertise their products, seeking the customer's business by providing higher-quality goods at lower prices. From narrow self-interest, as Smith put it, comes "the greatest good for the greatest number of people." Government control of an economy, on the other hand, distorts market forces, reduces producer motivation, lessens quality, and shortchanges consumers.

"Justice" in a capitalist system amounts to freedom of the marketplace, where anyone can produce, buy, and invest according to individual self-interest. The increasing popularity of Wal-Mart, described in the opening to this chapter, reflects the fact that the company offers a high level of value to customers who choose to shop there.

The United States is considered a capitalist nation because most businesses are privately owned. However, government plays a large role in U.S. economic affairs. The U.S. government owns and operates a number of businesses,

Capitalism still thrives in Hong Kong (left), evident in streets choked with advertising and shoppers. Socialism is more the rule in China's capital of Beijing (right), a city dominated by government buildings rather than a downtown business district.

including almost all of this country's schools, roads, parks, museums, the U.S. Postal Service, the Amtrak railroad system, and the entire U.S. military. The U.S. government also had a major hand in building the Internet. In addition, the government uses taxation and other forms of regulation to influence what companies produce, to control the quality and cost of merchandise, to regulate what businesses import and export, and to motivate consumers to conserve natural resources.

The U.S. government also sets minimum wage levels, enforces workplace safety standards, regulates corporate mergers, provides farm price supports, and gives income in the form of Social Security, public assistance, student loans, and veterans' benefits to a majority of its people. Local, state, and federal governments together are the nation's biggest employer, with 16 percent of the nonfarm labor force on their payrolls (U.S. Census Bureau, 2003).

SOCIALISM

Socialism is *an economic system in which natural resources and the means of producing goods and services are collectively owned.* In its ideal form, a socialist economy rejects each of the three characteristics of capitalism just described in favor of three opposite features:

1. **Collective ownership of property.** A socialist economy limits rights to private property, especially property

used to generate income. Government controls such property and makes housing and other goods available to all, not just to the people with the most money.

2. **Pursuit of collective goals.** The individualistic pursuit of profit goes against the collective orientation of socialism. What capitalism celebrates as the "entrepreneurial spirit," socialism condemns as greed; individuals are urged to work for the common good of all.

3. **Government control of the economy.** Socialism rejects capitalism's laissez-faire approach in favor of a *centrally controlled* or *command* economy operated by government. Commercial advertising thus plays little role in socialist economies.

"Justice" in a socialist context means not competing to gain wealth but meeting everyone's basic needs in a roughly equal manner. From a socialist point of view, a capitalist practice such as cutting back on workers' wages and benefits to boost company earnings puts profits before people and is thus an injustice.

The People's Republic of China and some two dozen other nations in Asia, Africa, and Latin America have socialist economies, with almost all wealth-generating property under state control (McColm et al., 1991; Freedom House, 2004). The extent of world socialism has declined in recent years as countries in Eastern Europe and the former Soviet Union have geared their economies toward a market system.

Global comparisons indicate that socialist economies generate greater economic equality although living standards remain relatively low. Capitalist economies, by contrast, generate more economic inequality although living standards are relatively high. As the Russian Federation has moved from socialism toward capitalism, there is widespread evidence of increasing economic inequality, including the building of large mansions by those who have become rich. This complex is being built by a business tycoon in the suburbs of the Russian capital, an area coming to be known as "the Beverly Hills of Moscow."

WELFARE CAPITALISM AND STATE CAPITALISM

Some nations in Western Europe, including Sweden and Italy, have market-based economies but also offer broad social welfare programs. Analysts call this third type of economic system **welfare capitalism,** *an economic and political system that combines a mostly market-based economy with extensive social welfare programs.*

Under welfare capitalism, the government owns some of the largest industries and services, such as transportation, the mass media, and health care. In Sweden and Italy, about 12 percent of economic production is "nationalized," or state-controlled. That leaves most industry in private hands but subject to extensive government regulation. High taxation (aimed especially at the rich) funds a wide range of social welfare programs, including universal health care and child care (Olsen, 1996).

Yet another alternative is **state capitalism,** *an economic and political system in which companies are privately owned but cooperate closely with the government.* State capitalism is the rule in the nations along the Pacific Rim. Japan, South Korea, and Singapore are all capitalist countries, but their governments work in partnership with large companies, supplying financial assistance and controlling foreign imports to help their businesses compete in world markets (Gerlach, 1992).

RELATIVE ADVANTAGES OF CAPITALISM AND SOCIALISM

Which economic system works best? Comparing economies is difficult because all countries mix capitalism and socialism to varying degrees. Nations also differ in cultural attitudes toward work, natural resources, technological development,

and patterns of trade. Despite such complicating factors, some crude comparisons are revealing.

Economic productivity. One key dimension of economic performance is productivity. A commonly used measure of economic output is *gross domestic product* (GDP), the total value of all goods and services produced annually. Per capita (per-person) GDP allows us to compare the economic performance of nations of different population sizes.

The output of mostly capitalist countries at the end of the 1980s varied somewhat, but averaging the figures for the United States, Canada, and the nations of Western Europe yielded a per capita GDP of about $13,500. The comparable figure for the former Soviet Union and the nations of Eastern Europe was about $5,000. This means that the capitalist countries outproduced the socialist nations by a ratio of 2.7 to 1 (United Nations Development Programme, 1990). A recent comparison of economic output found that (mostly capitalist) South Korea outproduced (mostly socialist) North Korea by about 18 to 1 (Omestad, 2003).

Economic equality. The distribution of resources within the population is another important measure of economic performance. A comparative study in the mid-1970s looked at income ratios based on the earnings of the richest 5 percent of the population and the poorest 5 percent (Wiles, 1977). Societies with mostly capitalist economies had an income ratio of about 10 to 1; the figure for socialist countries was 5 to 1. In other words, *capitalist economies support a higher overall standard of living but with greater income inequality.* Said another way, socialist economies create more economic equality but provide a lower overall living standard.

Personal freedom. One additional consideration in evaluating capitalism and socialism is the personal freedom each system gives its people. Capitalism emphasizes the *freedom to* pursue self-interest and depends on the freedom of producers and consumers to interact with little interference from the state. Socialism, by contrast, emphasizes *freedom from* basic want. The goal of equality requires the state to regulate the economy, which in turn limits personal choices and opportunities for citizens.

To date, no system has been able to offer both political freedom and economic equality. In the capitalist United States, our political system offers many personal freedoms, but they are not worth as much to a poor person as to a rich one. On the other side of the coin, China or North Korea has more economic equality, but people cannot speak out or travel inside and outside the country freely.

CHANGES IN SOCIALIST COUNTRIES

In 1989 and 1990, the nations of Eastern Europe, which had been seized by the former Soviet Union at the end of World War II, overthrew their socialist regimes. These nations—including the former German Democratic Republic, the Czech Republic, Slovakia, Hungary, Romania, and Bulgaria—are all moving toward capitalist market systems after decades of state-controlled socialist economies. At the end of 1991, the Soviet Union itself formally dissolved and has introduced some free-market principles. Ten years later, 75 percent of businesses were partly or entirely under private ownership (Montaigne, 2001).

There were many reasons for these sweeping changes. First, the capitalist economies far outproduced their socialist counterparts. The socialist economies were successful in achieving economic equality, but living standards were low compared with those of Western Europe. Second, Soviet socialism was heavy-handed, rigidly controlling the media and restricting individual freedoms. In other words, socialism did away with *economic* elites, as Karl Marx predicted, but as Max Weber foresaw, socialism increased the power of *political* elites.

So far, the market reforms in Eastern Europe are proceeding unevenly. Some nations (Czech Republic, Slovakia, Poland, and the Baltic states of Latvia, Estonia, and Lithuania) are doing pretty well. But other countries (Romania, Bulgaria, and the Russian Federation) have been hit by price increases and falling living standards. Officials hope that expanding production will gradually bring a turnaround. However, introducing a market economy has also brought more economic inequality—by 2000, economic inequality in Russia was greater than in the United States (Buraway, 1997; World Bank, 2004).

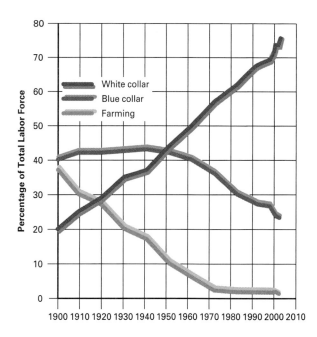

FIGURE 12-2 The Changing Pattern of Work in the United States, 1900–2003

Source: Estimates based on U.S. Department of Labor (2004).

Work in the Postindustrial Economy

Economic change is occurring not just in the socialist world but also in the United States. In 2003, a total of 138 million people—representing nearly two-thirds of those aged sixteen and over—were working for income. A larger share of men (68.9 percent) than women (56.1 percent) had jobs, although the gap is closing. Among men, 59.5 percent of African Americans were employed, compared with 70.1 percent of whites, 70.9 percent of Asians, and 74.3 percent of Hispanics. Among women, 55.6 percent of African Americans were employed, compared with 56.3 percent of whites, 54.9 percent of Asians, and 51.2 percent of Hispanics.

THE CHANGING WORKPLACE

In 1900, roughly 40 percent of U.S. workers were farmers. In 2003, just 1 percent were in agriculture. The family farm of yesterday has been replaced by *corporate agribusinesses.* Land is now more productive, but this change has caused painful adjustments across the country as a way of life is lost (Dudley, 2000). Figure 12–2 illustrates the shrinking role of the primary sector in the U.S. economy.

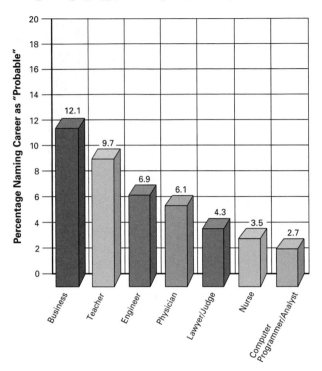

STUDENT SNAPSHOT

FIGURE 12-3 The Careers Most Commonly Named as Probable by First-Year College Students, 2003

Source: Sax et al. (2003).

A century ago, industrialization swelled the ranks of blue-collar workers. By 1950, however, a white-collar revolution had moved most workers from factories into service occupations. By 2003, 76 percent of the labor force worked in the service sector, and 92 percent of new jobs were being created in this sector (U.S. Department of Labor, 2004).

As Chapter 8 ("Social Stratification") explained, much service work—including sales, clerical positions, and work in hospitals and restaurants—pays much less than older factory jobs. This means that many jobs in this postindustrial era provide only a modest standard of living. Those affected the most by this shift are women and other minorities (Nelson, 1994; Kalleberg, Reskin, & Hudson, 2000).

LABOR UNIONS

The changing U.S. economy has seen a decline in *labor unions,* organizations that seek to improve wages and working conditions. Union membership increased rapidly after 1935, reaching more than one-third of nonfarm workers by 1950. By 1970, union rolls peaked at almost 25 million people. Since then, membership has declined to about 13 percent of nonfarm workers, or some 15.8 million men and women. Looking more closely, 37 percent of government workers are members of unions, compared with just 8 percent of private (nongovernment) workers (Clawson & Clawson, 1999; Goldfield, 2000).

The pattern of union decline holds in other high-income countries as well, yet unions claim a far smaller share of workers in the United States than elsewhere. From a low of 19 percent in Japan, union membership climbs to 31 percent in Canada, between 30 and 40 percent in much of Europe, to a high of 77 percent in Sweden (International Labour Organization, 2002).

The widespread decline in union membership follows the shrinking industrial sector of the economy; newer service jobs are less likely to be unionized. In recent years, however, decreased job security has given unions a short-term boost. Long-term gains probably depend on the ability of unions to adapt to the new global economy. Union members in the United States, used to seeing foreign workers as "the enemy," will have to build new international alliances (Church, 1994; Greenhouse, 2000).

PROFESSIONS

All kinds of jobs today are called *professional;* there are professional tennis players, professional house cleaners, and even professional exterminators. As distinct from an *amateur* (from the Latin for "lover," meaning one who acts out of love for the activity itself), a professional does some task to earn a living. But what exactly is a profession?

A **profession** is *a prestigious, white-collar occupation that requires extensive formal education.* People performing this kind of work make a *profession,* or public declaration, of their willingness to work according to certain principles. Professions include the ministry, medicine, law, academia, and fields such as architecture, accountancy, and social work. Occupations are professional to the extent that they demonstrate the following four characteristics (Goode, 1960; Ritzer & Walczak, 1990):

1. **Theoretical knowledge.** Professionals have theoretical knowledge of their field rather than simply technical training. Anyone can learn first-aid skills, for example, but doctors have a theoretical understanding of human health. This means that tennis players,

house cleaners, and exterminators do not really qualify as "professionals."

2. **Self-regulating practice.** The typical professional is self-employed, "in private practice" rather than working for a company. Professionals oversee their own work and observe a code of ethics.

3. **Authority over clients.** Because of their expertise, professionals are sought out by clients, who value their advice and follow their directions.

4. **Community orientation rather than self-interest.** The traditional professing of duty states an intention to serve the community rather than merely seek income.

In almost all cases, professional work requires a college degree and a graduate degree. Not surprisingly, professions are well represented among the jobs beginning college students say they hope to get after graduation, as shown in Figure 12–3.

Many new occupations in the postindustrial economy seek to *professionalize* their services. Claiming professional standing usually begins by renaming the work to suggest special, theoretical knowledge, moving the field away from its original, lesser reputation. Stockroom workers become "inventory supply managers," and exterminators are reborn as "insect control specialists."

Interested parties may also form a professional association that certifies their skills. The organization licenses its members, writes a code of ethics, and emphasizes the work's importance. To win public acceptance, a professional association may also establish schools or other training facilities and perhaps start a professional journal. Not all occupations try to claim professional status. Some *paraprofessionals*, including paralegals and medical technicians, possess specialized skills but lack the extensive theoretical education required of full professionals.

SELF-EMPLOYMENT

Self-employment—earning a living without working for a large organization—was once common in the United States. About 80 percent of the labor force was self-employed in 1800, compared with just 7.5 percent of workers today (9.5 percent of men and 6.0 percent of women) (U.S. Department of Labor, 2004).

Lawyers, doctors, and other professionals are well represented among the ranks of the self-employed. But most self-employed workers are small business owners (including people who buy and sell using the Internet), farmers, plumbers, carpenters, freelance writers and editors, artists, and long-distance

Visit the Web site of the Small Business Administration at http://www.sba.gov

Unemployment means not having a job and the income it provides. But it also means not having the respect that comes from being self-reliant in a society that expects people to take care of themselves. How does the sociological perspective help us to understand being out of work as more than a personal problem?

truck drivers. In all, more self-employed people have blue-collar than white-collar jobs.

Women own nearly 40 percent of this nation's small businesses, and the share is rising. The 9.1 million firms owned by U.S. women now employ almost 30 million people and generate close to $4 trillion in annual sales (U.S. Small Business Administration, 2001b).

UNEMPLOYMENT

Every society has some level of unemployment. Few young people entering the labor force find a job right away. Workers temporarily leave their jobs to seek new work or to stay at home raising children. Union members strike. Others suffer from long-term illnesses. Still others are illiterate or without the skills to perform useful work.

But unemployment is not just an individual situation; it is also caused by the economy. Jobs disappear as occupations

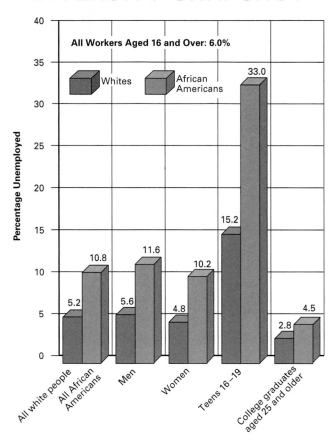

DIVERSITY SNAPSHOT

All Workers Aged 16 and Over: 6.0%

Whites | African Americans

Percentage Unemployed

Category	Whites	African Americans
All white people / All African Americans	5.2	10.8
Men	5.6	11.6
Women	4.8	10.2
Teens 16–19	15.2	33.0
College graduates aged 25 and older	2.8	4.5

FIGURE 12–4 Official U.S. Unemployment Rates for Various Categories of Adults, 2003

Source: U.S. Department of Labor (2004).

become obsolete, businesses close in the face of foreign competition or economic recession, and companies "downsize"

For more on minority unemployment, go to http://www.brookings.edu/es/urban/publications/offnerexsum.htm

to become more profitable. Since 1980, the 500 largest U.S. businesses have eliminated some 5 million jobs—one-fourth of the total. The economic slowdown that began in 2000 resulted in millions of lost jobs, especially among white-collar workers who had held on to their jobs during past downturns (Cullen, 2002).

In 2003, some 8.8 million people over the age of sixteen were unemployed—about 6.0 percent of the civilian labor force. Some regions of the United States, especially rural areas, have unemployment rates double the national average.

Figure 12–4 shows that unemployment among African Americans (10.8 percent) is more than twice the rate among white people (5.2 percent). For both races, women have lower rates of unemployment compared to men.

WORKPLACE DIVERSITY: RACE AND GENDER

Traditionally, white men have been the mainstay of the U.S. labor force. As explained in Chapter 11 ("Race and Ethnicity"), however, our country's proportion of minorities is rising rapidly. Between 1990 and 2000, the African American population increased by 16 percent, more than five times the 3 percent increase for non-Hispanic white people. The jump in the Hispanic population was even greater, at 58 percent, and the increase among Asian Americans was 48 percent. The Diversity box takes a closer look at how the increase of minority populations will affect the workplace.

NEW INFORMATION TECHNOLOGY AND WORK

July 2, Ticonderoga, New York. The manager of the local hardware store scans the bar codes of a bagful of items. "The computer not only totals the costs," she explains, "but it also keeps track of inventory, places orders with the warehouse, and decides which products to continue to sell and which to discontinue." "Sounds like what you used to do, Maureen," I respond with a smile. "Yep," she nods, with no smile at all.

Computers and new information technology play a central role in the twenty-first-century workplace. The Information Revolution is changing what people do in some basic ways (Rule & Brantley, 1992; Vallas & Beck, 1996):

1. **Computers are deskilling labor.** Just as industrial machines replaced the master craftsworkers of an earlier era, computers now threaten the skills of managers. More business operations are based not on executive decisions but on computer modeling. A machine, not a person, decides whether to place an order, resupply a client, or approve a loan application.

2. **Computers are making work more abstract.** Most industrial workers have a hands-on relationship with their product. Postindustrial workers manipulate symbols to perform abstract tasks, such as making a company more profitable or making software more user-friendly.

3. **Computers limit workplace interaction.** As workers spend more time at computer terminals, they become isolated from one another.

DIVERSITY: RACE, CLASS, & GENDER

Twenty-First-Century Diversity: Changes in the Workplace

An upward trend in the U.S. minority population is changing the face of the workplace. As the figure shows, the number of non-Hispanic white men in the U.S. labor force will rise by a modest 3 percent between 2002 and 2012, but the number of African American men will increase by 20 percent, the number of Hispanic men will increase by 29 percent, and the number of Asian men will increase by a much greater 54 percent. Among non-Hispanic white women, the projected rise is 3 percent, among African American women, 19 percent, and among Hispanic women, 38 percent. Asian women will show the greatest gains, estimated at 47 percent.

Within a decade, non-Hispanic white men will represent 35 percent of all workers, and that figure will continue to drop. Companies that welcome social diversity will tap the largest pool of talent and enjoy a competitive advantage.

Welcoming social diversity means, first, recruiting talented workers of both sexes and of all racial and cultural backgrounds. But developing the potential of all employees means seeing that the needs of women and other minorities may not be the same as those of white men. For example, child care at the workplace is a big issue for working mothers.

Second, businesses must develop effective ways to deal with tension that arises from social differences. They will have to work harder at treating workers equally and respectfully and show zero tolerance for racial or sexual harassment.

Third, companies will have to rethink current promotion practices. At present, only 8 percent of Fortune 500 top executives are women, and just 4 percent are other minorities. In a survey of U.S. companies, the U.S. Equal Employment Opportunity Commission confirmed that non-Hispanic white men, who are 35 percent of adults aged twenty to sixty-four, hold 56 percent of management jobs; the comparable figures are 35 and 28 percent, respectively, for non-Hispanic white women, 12 and 7 percent for non-Hispanic African Americans, and 13 and 5 percent for Hispanics.

WHAT DO YOU THINK?

1. Why is the U.S. workplace becoming more diverse?
2. In your opinion, what should businesses do to support minority workers?
3. How can the ideas discussed in the box be applied to other areas of U.S. life?

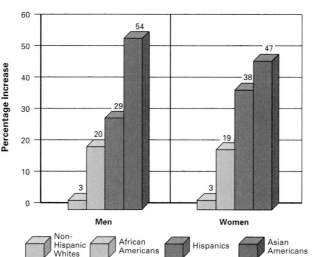

Projected Increase in the Numbers of People in the U.S. Labor Force, 2002–2012

Sources: Catalyst (2004), Toossi (2004), and U.S. Equal Employment Opportunity Commission (2004).

---

4. **Computers increase employers' control of workers.** Computers allow supervisors to check employees' output continuously, whether they work at keyboard terminals or on assembly lines.

Such changes remind us that technology is not socially neutral. Computers not only change the way we work but also give employers more power over employees. For this reason, people welcome some aspects of the Information Revolution more than others.

Corporations

At the core of today's capitalist economy is the **corporation,** *an organization with a legal existence, including rights and liabilities, apart from that of its members.* Incorporating makes an organization a legal entity, able to enter into contracts and own property. Of more than 24 million businesses in the United States, 5 million are incorporated (U.S. Census Bureau, 2003). Incorporating protects the wealth of owners from lawsuits that arise as a result of business debts

In today's corporate world, computers are changing the nature of work just as factories did more than a century ago. In what ways is computer-based work different from factory work? In what ways is it the same?

or harm to consumers; it can also mean a lower tax rate on the company's profits.

ECONOMIC CONCENTRATION

Most U.S. corporations are small, with assets of less than $500,000, so it is the largest corporations that dominate our nation's economy. In 2001, some 1,896 corporations had assets exceeding $2.5 billion, representing three-fourths of all corporate assets (Internal Revenue Service, 2004). For this reason, we can say that corporations concentrate economic output.

The largest U.S. corporation in terms of sales is Wal-Mart, with $104.9 billion in total assets. Wal-Mart employs more people than the state governments of California, Texas, Colorado, New York, and Florida combined. Its sales ($256 billion in 2004) equal the tax revenues of nearly half the states.

CORPORATE LINKAGES

Economic concentration creates *conglomerates,* giant corporations composed of many smaller corporations. Conglomerates form as corporations enter new markets, spin off new companies, or merge with other companies. For example, Altria is a conglomerate that includes Philip Morris (tobacco products), Nabisco and Post (food products), and Starbucks (coffee).

Many conglomerates are linked because they own each other's stock, the result being worldwide corporate alliances of staggering size. General Motors, for example, owns Opel (Germany), Vauxhall (Great Britain), and half of Saab (Sweden) and has partnerships with Suzuki, Isuzu, and Toyota (Japan). Similarly, Ford owns Jaguar and Aston Martin (Great Britain) and a share of Mazda (Japan), Kia (Korea), and Volvo (Sweden).

Another type of corporate linkage is the *interlocking directorate,* a social network of people who serve as directors of many corporations (Weidenbaum, 1995; Kono et al., 1998). These boardroom connections provide access to valuable information about other companies' products and marketing strategies. While perfectly legal, such linkages encourage illegal activity, such as price-fixing, as companies share information about their pricing policies.

CORPORATIONS: ARE THEY COMPETITIVE?

According to the capitalist model, businesses operate independently in a competitive market. But in light of the extensive linkages that exist between them, it is obvious that large corporations do not operate independently. Also, a few large corporations dominate many markets, so they are not truly competitive.

Law forbids a large company from establishing a **monopoly,** *the domination of a market by a single producer,* because a monopoly could simply dictate prices. But **oligopoly,** *the domination of a market by a few producers,* is both legal and common. This pattern results from the huge investment needed to enter a major market, such as the auto industry, which is beyond the reach of all but the biggest companies. In addition, true competition involves risk, which any company tries to avoid.

The federal government seeks to regulate corporations in order to protect the public interest. Yet as recent corporate scandals have shown, corporate wrongdoing harms millions of people, and regulation is often too little too late. The government is also the corporate world's single biggest customer and sometimes steps in to support struggling corporations with billion-dollar loan programs. In addition, as the Applying Sociology box explains, state governments' aid to corporations has drawn fire as "corporate welfare."

CORPORATIONS AND THE GLOBAL ECONOMY

Corporations have grown so large that they now account for most of the world's economic output. The biggest corporations, based in the United States, Japan, and Western

APPLYING SOCIOLOGY
Them That's Got, Gets: The Case of Corporate Welfare

Would you like the government to slash your income taxes and end sales tax on your purchases? What about offering you money to buy a new house at a below-market interest rate? Would you like the government to hook up all your utilities for free and pay your water and electric bills?

For an ordinary person, such deals sound too good to be true. But our tax money is doing exactly that—not for families but for big corporations. All a large company has to do is declare a willingness to relocate and then wait for the offers from state and local governments to come pouring in.

Supporters call government aid to corporations "public-private partnerships." They point to the jobs corporations create, sometimes in areas hard hit by earlier business closings. For a city or county with a high unemployment rate, the promise of a new factory is simply too good to pass up. If incentives in the form of tax relief or free utilities are needed to seal the deal, it is money well spent.

Critics call such arrangements "corporate welfare." They agree that companies create new jobs, but they point out that the corporations get much more than they give. In 1991, for example, the state of Indiana offered $451 million in incentives to lure United Airlines to build an aircraft maintenance facility there. United Airlines built the facility and hired 6,300 people. But some simple math shows that the cost to Indiana came out to be a whopping $72,000 per job. Much the same happened in 1993, when Alabama offered $253 million in incentives to Mercedes-Benz to build an automobile assembly plant in Tuscaloosa. The plant opened and 1,500 people were hired—at an average cost to Alabama of $169,000 for each worker. In 1997, Pennsylvania gave $307 million in incentives to a

Norwegian company to reopen part of Philadelphia's naval shipyard. Once the deal was signed, 950 people were hired, at a cost of $323,000 per job. In 2002, Georgia spent $67,000 per job to bring in a new DaimlerChrysler auto plant. Across the country, the pattern is much the same. Overall, government support to corporations exceeds $15 billion each year, far more than the total welfare dollars given to people who are poor.

Although new plants do create some jobs, most jobs are simply moved from one place to another. But not all jobs pay well. Nor is there any guarantee that once settled, a corporation will stay, since businesses are free to make a better deal and move to another location.

WHAT DO YOU THINK?

1. Why do governments give tax breaks to businesses?
2. Does this policy help local communities or corporations? Why?
3. Overall, do you support the tax breaks for business described here? Why or why not?

Sources: Bartlett & Steele (1998) and various news reports.

Europe, consider the entire world one huge marketplace. Many large companies, such as McDonald's, make most of their money outside the United States.

Global corporations know that poor countries contain most of the world's people and resources. In addition, as shown in Figure 12–5 on page 324, labor costs there are attractively low: A manufacturing worker in Mexico labors for almost two weeks to earn about what a German worker earns in a single day.

As Chapter 9 ("Global Stratification") explained, the impact of multinational corporations on low-income countries is controversial. Modernization theorists claim that multinational corporations, by unleashing the great productivity of capitalism, raise living standards in poor nations, offering them tax revenues, capital investment, new jobs, and advanced technology that together accelerate economic growth (Berger, 1986; Firebaugh & Beck, 1994; Firebaugh & Sandu, 1998).

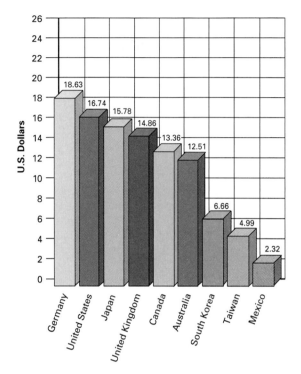

FIGURE 12-5 Average Hourly Wages for Workers in Manufacturing, 2002

Source: U.S. Department of Labor (2004).

1960; lower-paying service work, especially computer-related jobs, makes up the difference. For industrial workers, the postindustrial economy has brought unemployment and declining wages. Our society must face up to the challenge of providing millions of men and women with the language and computer skills needed in the new economy. Yet as the economic collapse of many dot-coms in 2001 and 2002 shows, even this new type of work can experience a downturn. In addition, there are regional differences in the economic outlook: National Map 12–1 shows which regions are projected to gain and which are expected to lose jobs in this decade.

A second transformation that will mark the new century is the expansion of the global economy. Two centuries ago, the ups and downs of a local economy reflected events and trends in a single town. One century ago, communities across the country became economically linked so that one town's prosperity depended on producing goods demanded by people elsewhere in the country. Today, it makes less sense to speak of a national economy because what people in a Kansas farm town produce and consume may be affected as much by what happens in the wheat-growing region of Russia as by events in their own state capital. In short, U.S. workers are not only creating new products and services but are also working in response to factors and forces that are distant and unseen.

Finally, analysts around the world are rethinking conventional economic models. The global economy shows that socialism is less productive than capitalism, one important reason for the collapse of socialist regimes in Eastern Europe and the former Soviet Union. But capitalism, too, is changing and now operates with significant government regulation, partly to address the economic inequality generated by market systems.

What will be the long-term effects of these changes? Two conclusions seem certain. First, the economic future of the United States and other nations will be played out in a global arena. The new postindustrial economy in the United States is inseparable from the increasing industrial production of other nations. Second, we must address the urgent challenges of global inequality and population increase. Whether the world economy reduces or enlarges the gap between rich and poor societies may end up steering our planet toward peace or war.

Dependency theorists respond that multinationals intensify global inequality, blocking the development of local industries and pushing poor countries to make goods for export rather than food and other products for local consumption. From this standpoint, multinationals make poor nations poorer and increasingly dependent on rich nations (Wallerstein, 1979; Delacroix & Ragin, 1981; Bergesen, 1983; Walton & Ragin, 1990).

LOOKING AHEAD: THE ECONOMY OF THE TWENTY-FIRST CENTURY

Social institutions are a society's ways of meeting people's needs. But as we have seen, the U.S. economy only partly succeeds in this respect. Although highly productive, our economy provides for some much better than for others. In addition, the Information Revolution continues to change our economy. First, the share of the U.S. labor force engaged in manufacturing is now half of what it was in

Politics: Historical Overview

There is a close link between economics and **politics** (or "the polity"), *the social institution that distributes power, sets a society's goals, and makes decisions.* Early in the twentieth century, Max Weber (1978, orig. 1921) defined **power** as *the*

The economic prospects of counties across the United States are not the same. Much of the midsection of the country is projected to lose jobs. By contrast, the coastal regions and most of the West are rapidly gaining jobs. What factors might account for this pattern?

Source: Used with permission of Woods & Poole Economics, Washington, D.C.

Employment Growth or Decline, Projections to 2010
- Big gain: 17% to 58%
- Moderate gain: 9% to 16%
- Small gain: 1% to 8%
- Job loss: −10% to 0%
- No data

ability to achieve desired ends despite resistance from others. To a large degree, the exercise of power is the business of **government,** *a formal organization that directs the political life of a society.*

Brute force is the most basic form of power. But no government that gets power *only* from sheer force lasts for long, and life in such a society would be a nightmare of terror. Social organization depends on creating agreement about goals and how to attain them. This brings us to the concept of **authority,** *power that people perceive as legitimate rather than coercive.*

A society's source of authority depends, in turn, on its economy. According to Max Weber, preindustrial societies rely on *traditional authority,* power legitimized by respect for long-established cultural patterns. Woven into a society's collective memory, traditional authority may seem almost sacred. Chinese emperors in centuries past were legitimized by tradition, as were the nobles in medieval Europe.

Traditional authority declines as societies industrialize. For example, royal families still exist in ten European nations, but the democratic cultures of countries such as the United Kingdom, Sweden, and Denmark have shifted power to commoners elected to office. Weber explained that the expansion of rational bureaucracy is the modern foundation of authority. *Rational-legal authority* (sometimes called *bureaucratic authority*) is power legitimized by rationally enacted law.

Traditional authority is tied to family; rational-legal authority flows from offices in governments. A traditional monarch passes power on to heirs; a modern president takes and gives up power according to law.

Weber described one additional type of authority that has surfaced throughout history. *Charismatic authority* is power legitimized by the extraordinary personal qualities—charisma—of a leader. Unlike its traditional and rational-legal counterparts, charismatic authority depends less on a person's ancestry or office and more on individual personality. Followers see in charismatic leaders some special, perhaps even divine power. Examples of charismatic leaders include Jesus of Nazareth, Nazi Germany's Adolf Hitler, the liberator of India Mahatma Gandhi, and the civil rights leader Martin Luther King Jr. All charismatic leaders aim to radically transform society, which makes them highly controversial (and explains why few charismatics die of old age).

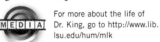

For more about the life of Dr. King, go to http://www.lib.lsu.edu/hum/mlk

Because charismatic authority flows from a single individual, the leader's death creates a crisis. The survival of a charismatic movement, Weber explained, requires the **routinization of charisma:** *the transformation of charismatic authority into some combination of traditional and bureaucratic authority.* After the death of Jesus, for example, followers institutionalized his teachings in a church, built on tradition and bureaucracy. Routinized in this way, the Roman Catholic Church has existed for nearly 2,000 years.

Global Political Systems

The world's political systems differ in countless ways. Generally, however, they fall into four categories: monarchy, democracy, authoritarianism, and totalitarianism.

In 2004, just 28 of the world's 192 nations were political monarchies where single families pass power from generation to generation. Here, the African nation of Swaziland celebrates the coronation of a young king.

MONARCHY

Monarchy (with Latin and Greek roots meaning "one ruler") is *a type of political system in which a single family rules from generation to generation.* Monarchy is commonly found in agrarian societies; for example, the Bible tells of great kings such as David and Solomon. In the world today, twenty-eight nations have royal families;[1] most trace their ancestry back for centuries. In Weber's analysis, then, monarchy is legitimized by tradition.

During the Middle Ages, *absolute monarchs* in much of the world claimed a monopoly of power based on divine right. In some nations—including Kuwait, Saudi Arabia, and Bahrain—monarchs still exercise virtually absolute control over their people.

With industrialization, however, monarchs gradually pass from the scene in favor of elected officials. All the European societies with royal families today are *constitutional monarchies,* meaning that their monarchs are little more than symbolic heads of state; actual governing is the responsibility of elected officials, led by a prime minister

[1]In Europe: Sweden, Norway, Denmark, Great Britain, the Netherlands, Liechtenstein, Luxembourg, Belgium, Spain, and Monaco; in the Middle East: Jordan, Saudi Arabia, Oman, Qatar, Bahrain, and Kuwait; in Africa: Lesotho, Swaziland, and Morocco; in Asia and the Pacific: Brunei, Samoa, Tonga, Thailand, Malaysia, Cambodia, Nepal, Bhutan, and Japan.

and guided by a constitution. In these countries, nobility formally reigns, but elected officials actually rule.

DEMOCRACY

The historical trend throughout most of the world is toward **democracy,** *a type of political system that gives power to the people as a whole.* More correctly, a system of *representative democracy* puts authority in the hands of leaders who, from time to time, compete for office in elections.

Most rich countries in the world claim to be democratic (including those that still have royal families). Industrialization and democracy often go together because both require a literate populace. Also, the traditional legitimization of power in a monarchy gives way, with industrialization, to rational-legal authority. Thus, democracy and rational-legal authority are linked in the same way as monarchy and traditional authority.

But high-income countries such as the United States are not truly democratic for two reasons. First, there is the problem of bureaucracy. The U.S. federal government has more than 3 million regular employees, 6 million contract workers, 1.4 million uniformed service personnel, and 2.4 million employees paid for by various grants and special funding—about 13 million workers in all. In addition, another 18 million people work in 88,000 local governments across the country. Most people who run the government are never elected by anyone and do not have to answer directly to the people.

The second problem involves economic inequality, because rich people have far more political power than poor people. Both George W. Bush and John Kerry, who ran for the presidency in 2004, are very wealthy men, and in the game of politics, "money talks." Given the even greater resources of billion-dollar corporations and labor unions, how can we think that our "democratic" system responds to—or even hears—the voices of "average people"?

Still, democratic nations do provide many rights and freedoms. Global Map 12–3 shows one assessment of political freedom around the world. According to Freedom House, an organization that tracks political trends, 88 of the world's 192 nations (with 44 percent of the global population) were "free," respecting many civil liberties, in 2004. This represents a gain for democracy: Just 76 nations were free a decade earlier (Freedom House, 2004).

AUTHORITARIANISM

Some governments actively resist involving their people in politics. **Authoritarianism** is *a political system that denies the people participation in government.* An authoritarian government is indifferent to people's needs and offers them

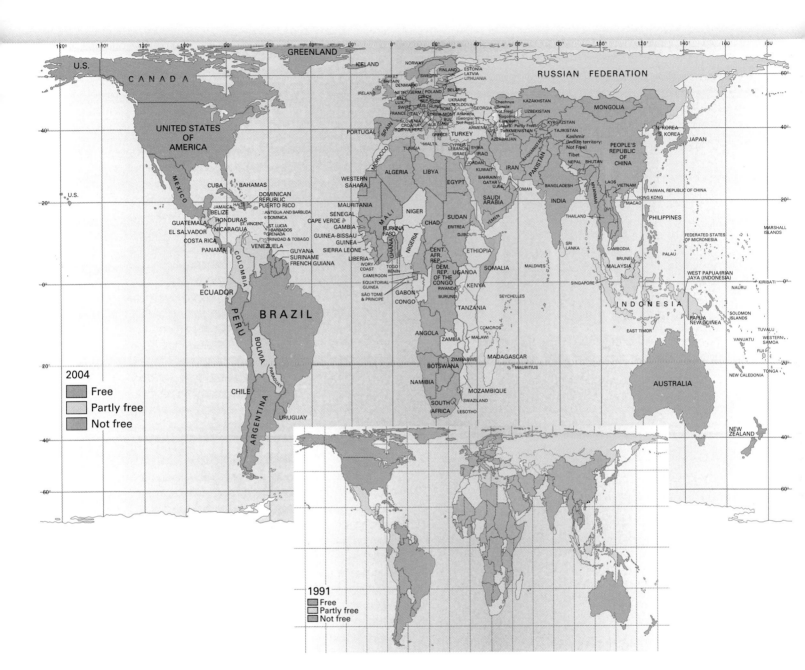

2004

- Free
- Partly free
- Not free

1991
- Free
- Partly free
- Not free

WINDOW ON THE WORLD

GLOBAL MAP 12-3 Political Freedom in Global Perspective

In 2004, a total of 88 of the world's nations, containing 44 percent of all people, were politically "free"; that is, they offered their citizens extensive political rights and civil liberties. Another 55 countries, which included 21 percent of the world's people, were "partly free," with more limited rights and liberties. The remaining 49 nations, home to 35 percent of humanity, fall into the category of "not free." In these countries, government sharply restricts individual initiative. Between 1980 and 2004, democracy made significant gains, largely in Latin America and Eastern Europe. In Asia, India (containing 1 billion people) returned to the "free" category in 1999. In 2000, Mexico joined the ranks of nations considered "free" for the first time.

Source: Freedom House (2004).

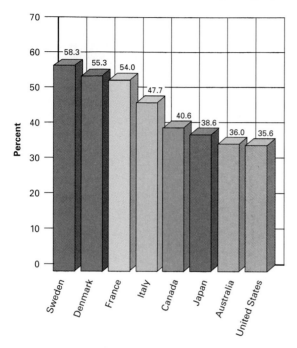

GLOBAL SNAPSHOT

FIGURE 12-6 The Size of Government:
Government Expenditures
as a Percentage of Gross Domestic
Product, 2002

Source: U.S. Census Bureau (2003).

closely monitors the activities not just of visitors but of all its citizens. Similarly, the government of North Korea uses surveillance equipment and powerful computers to collect information about its people and to control them.

Some totalitarian governments claim to represent the will of the people, but most seek to bend people to the will of the government. Such governments are *total* concentrations of power, allowing no organized opposition. Denying people the right to assemble and controlling access to information, these governments create an atmosphere of isolation and fear. In the former Soviet Union, for example, most citizens had no access to telephone directories, copying equipment, fax machines, or even accurate city maps.

Socialization in totalitarian societies is highly political, seeking obedience and commitment to the system. In North Korea, one of the world's most totalitarian nations, pictures of leaders and political messages are everywhere, reminding citizens that they owe total allegiance to the state. Government-controlled schools and mass media present only official versions of events.

Totalitarian governments span the political spectrum from fascist (including Nazi Germany) to communist (such as North Korea). In all cases, however, one party claims total control of the society and permits no opposition.

A GLOBAL POLITICAL SYSTEM?

Is globalization changing politics in the same way that it is changing the economy? On one level, the answer is no. Although most of today's economic activity is international, the world remains divided into nation-states just as it has been for centuries. The United Nations (founded in 1945) was a small step toward global government, but to date its political role in world affairs has been limited.

On another level, however, politics has become a global process. For some analysts, multinational corporations represent a new political order because of their enormous power to shape events throughout the world. In other words, politics is dissolving into business as corporations grow larger than governments.

Also, the Information Revolution has moved national politics onto the world stage. E-mail, cellular phones, satellite transmission systems, and fax machines mean that few countries can conduct their political affairs in complete privacy.

Finally, several thousand *nongovernmental organizations* (NGOs) seek to advance global issues, such as human rights (Amnesty International) and environmental protection (Greenpeace). NGOs will continue to play a key role in expanding the global political culture.

In sum, just as individual nations are losing control of their own economies, governments cannot fully manage the political events occurring within their borders.

no voice in selecting leaders. The absolute monarchies in Saudi Arabia and Bahrain are authoritarian, as is the military junta in Ethiopia.

TOTALITARIANISM

October 22, near Saigon, Vietnam. Six U.S. students have been arrested, allegedly for talking to Vietnamese students and taking pictures at the university. The Vietnamese minister of education has canceled the reception tonight, claiming that our students' meeting with their students threatens Vietnam's security.

The most intensely controlled political form is **totalitarianism,** *a highly centralized political system that extensively regulates people's lives.* Totalitarian systems emerged in the twentieth century as governments gained the ability to rigidly control a population. The Vietnamese government

Lower-income people have more pressing financial needs and so they tend to focus on economic issues, such as the level of the minimum wage. Higher-income people, by contrast, provide support for many social issues, such as animal rights.

Politics in the United States

After fighting a revolutionary war against Great Britain to gain political independence, the United States replaced the British monarchy with a representative democracy. Our nation's political development reflects its distinctive history, capitalist economy, and cultural heritage.

U.S. CULTURE AND THE RISE OF THE WELFARE STATE

The political culture of the United States can be summed up in one word: individualism. This emphasis is found in the Bill of Rights, which guarantees freedom from undue government interference. It was this individualism that the nineteenth-century poet and philosopher Ralph Waldo Emerson had in mind when he said, "The government that governs best is the government that governs least."

But most people stop short of Emerson's position, believing that government is necessary to defend the country, operate highway systems and schools, and maintain law and order. Furthermore, government has grown into a vast and complex **welfare state,** *government agencies and programs that provide benefits to the population.* Government benefits begin even before birth (through prenatal nutrition programs) and continue into old age (through Social Security and Medicare). Some programs are especially important to the poor, who are not well served by our capitalist economic system; nevertheless, students, farmers, homeowners, small business operators, veterans, performing artists, and even giant corporations also get various subsidies and supports. In fact, a majority of U.S. adults look to government for at least part of their income.

Today's welfare state is the result of a gradual increase in the size and scope of government. In 1789, when the presence of the federal government amounted to little more than a flag in most communities, the entire federal budget was a mere $4.5 million ($1.50 for every person in the nation). Since then, it has steadily risen, reaching $2.1 trillion in 2003 ($7,400 for every person in the country).

Similarly, when our nation was founded, one government employee served every 1,800 citizens. Today, about one in seven people in the United States is a government employee—more than are engaged in manufacturing (U.S. Census Bureau, 2003).

Despite its size, the U.S. welfare state is still smaller than in many other high-income nations. Figure 12–6 shows that government is larger in most of Europe, especially in Scandinavian countries such as Denmark and Sweden.

THE POLITICAL SPECTRUM

Who supports a bigger welfare state? Who wants to cut it back? Answers to such questions reveal attitudes that form the

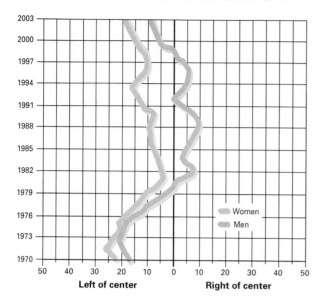

FIGURE 12-7 Left-Right Political Identification
of College Students, 1970–2003

Sources: Astin et al. (2002) and Sax et al. (2003).

political spectrum, which ranges from the extremely liberal on the left to the extremely conservative on the right. In the United States, about one-fourth of adults fall on the liberal or "left" side, one-third say they are on the conservative or "right" side, and 38 percent say they are "middle of the road" (the remainder say they are "not sure") (NORC, 2003:98).

The political spectrum helps us understand two types of issues: economic and social. With regard to economic issues, liberals support extensive government regulation of the economy in order to reduce income inequality. Economic conservatives want to limit the hand of government in the economy and allow market forces more freedom.

Social issues are moral questions, ranging from abortion and the death penalty to gay rights and the treatment of minorities. Social liberals support equal rights and opportunities for all categories of people, view abortion as a matter of individual choice, and oppose the death penalty because it has been unfairly applied to minorities. The "family values" agenda of social conservatives supports traditional gender roles and opposes gay families, affirmative action, and other "special programs" for minorities. Social conservatives condemn abortion as morally wrong and support the death penalty.

Of the two major political parties in the United States, the Republican party is more conservative on both economic and social issues and the Democratic party is more liberal. But most people mix conservative and liberal attitudes. With wealth to protect, many higher-income people hold conservative views on economic issues. Yet their extensive schooling and secure social standing lead most to be social liberals. Lower-income people show the opposite pattern, with most being liberal on economic issues but supporting a socially conservative agenda (Erikson, Luttbeg, & Tedin, 1980; McBroom & Reed, 1990). African Americans, both rich and poor, tend to be liberal (especially on economic issues) and for half a century have voted Democratic. Historically, Latinos, Asian Americans, and Jews also have supported the Democratic party.

Women tend to be somewhat more liberal than men. Among U.S. adults, more women lean toward the Democratic party, while more men vote for Republican candidates. Figure 12–7 shows how this pattern has changed over time among college students. Although there have been changes in student attitudes—they were more liberal in the 1970s, more conservative in the 1980s, and became a bit more liberal again in the 1990s—college women have remained consistently more liberal than college men (Astin et al., 2002; NORC, 2003).

PARTY IDENTIFICATION

Because many people hold mixed political attitudes, with liberal views on some issues and conservative stands on others, party identification in this country is weak. Surveys show that about 43 percent favor the Democratic party, and about 35 percent favor the Republican party; yet just 15 percent claim to be "strong Democrats" and 12 percent claim to be "strong Republicans." Almost 20 percent say they are "independent" (NORC, 2003). This lack of strong party identification is one reason each of the two major parties gains or loses power from election to election. Democrats held the White House in 1996 and gained ground in Congress in 1996, 1998, and 2000. In 2002 and 2004, the tide turned again as Republicans made gains in Congress and retained control of the White House.

 To learn more about how researchers conduct political polls, go to http://faculty.vassar.edu/lowry/polls.html

There is also a rural-urban divide in U.S. politics. People in urban areas typically vote Democratic, and those in rural areas vote Republican. National Map 12–2 shows the county-by-county results for the 2004 election. Republican George W. Bush won in about 2,500 counties, most of them rural. Democrat John Kerry won in about 700 counties, most of them urban with large populations.

SEEING OURSELVES

NATIONAL MAP 12-2

The Presidential Election, 2004:
Popular Vote by County

George W. Bush won the 2004 presidential election with 51 percent of the total popular vote, but he received a majority in about 80 percent of the nation's counties. John Kerry, who gained 48 percent of the popular vote, did well in more densely populated urban areas. What social differences do you think distinguish the areas that voted Republican and Democratic? Why are rural areas mostly Republican and urban areas mostly Democratic?

Source: Copyright © 2004 by *The New York Times*. Reprinted by permission. All rights reserved.

SPECIAL-INTEREST GROUPS

For years, a debate has raged across the United States about the private ownership of firearms. Organizations such as the Brady Campaign to Prevent Gun Violence support stricter gun laws; other organizations, including the National Rifle Association, strongly oppose them. Each is an example of a *special-interest group,* people organized to address some economic or social issue. Special-interest groups, which include associations of older adults, farmers, fireworks producers, and environmentalists, among others, are strong in nations where political parties tend to be weak. Many special-interest groups employ *lobbyists* to work on their behalf, trying to get members of Congress to support their goals. Washington, D.C., is home to more than 15,000 of them.

Political action committees (PACs) are formed by special-interest groups to raise and spend money in support of political aims. PACs channel most of their funds directly to candidates likely to support their interests. Since they were created in the 1970s, the number of PACs has grown rapidly to more than 4,000 (Federal Election Commission, 2004).

Because of the rising costs of campaigns, most candidates eagerly accept financial support from PACs. In the 2000 congressional elections, about 40 percent of all funding came from PACs, and senators seeking reelection received, on average, at least $1 million each in PAC contributions. Supporters maintain that PACs represent the interests of a vast array of businesses, unions, and church groups, thereby increasing political participation. Critics counter that organizations supplying cash to politicians expect to be treated favorably in return, so that in effect, PACs try to buy political influence (Cook, 1993; Center for Responsive Politics, 2002).

In 2000, the campaigns of presidential candidates cost a total of $3 billion, and another $3 billion was spent by congressional candidates and people running in state and local elections. Does having the most money matter? The answer is yes: Overall, 90 percent of the candidates with the most money won the election. Concerns about the power of money led to much discussion of campaign financing. In 2002, Congress passed a modest reform, limiting the amount of unregulated money that candidates can collect. Despite such attempts at reform, the 2004 presidential race became the most expensive in history.

VOTER APATHY

A disturbing fact of U.S. political life is that many people don't care enough about politics to vote. In fact, U.S. citizens are less likely to vote today than they were a century ago. In the 2000 presidential election, which turned on a few hundred votes, only half the registered voters went to the polls. In 2004, the share rose to 60 percent, still lower than in almost all other high-income countries.

Who is and is not likely to vote? Research shows that women and men are equally likely to cast a ballot. People over sixty-five, however, are twice as likely to vote as college-age

 Learn more about voting, public opinion, and political participation at this Web site: http://www.umrich.edu/~nes/

adults (half of whom have not even registered). Non-Hispanic whites are more likely to vote (62 percent voted in 2000) than African Americans (57 percent) and

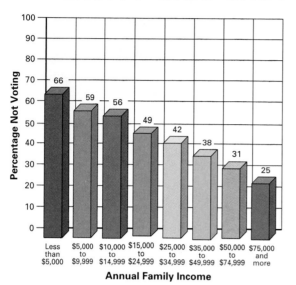

FIGURE 12–8 Political Apathy by Income Level

Percentage of adults who reported not voting in the 2000 presidential election, by annual family income.

Source: U.S. Census Bureau (2002).

Hispanics (45 percent). In general, people with a bigger stake in society—homeowners, parents with children at home, people with extensive schooling and good jobs—are more likely to vote. Income matters, too: People earning more than $75,000 a year are nearly twice as likely to vote (75 percent in 2000) as people earning $5,000 to $10,000 (41 percent) (U.S. Census Bureau, 2002).

Of course, we should expect some nonvoting because at any given time, millions of people are sick or disabled; millions more are away from home. Many more people move to a new neighborhood and forget to reregister. Finally, registering and voting depend on the ability to read and write, which discourages the tens of millions of U.S. adults who have limited literacy skills. Finally, people with physical disabilities that limit mobility have a lower turnout than the general population (Schur & Kruse, 2000; Brians & Grofman, 2001).

Conservatives suggest that apathy amounts to *indifference* to politics because most people are content with their lives. Liberals, and especially political radicals further to the left, counter that apathy reflects *alienation* from politics: People are so deeply dissatisfied with society that they

doubt elections will make any real difference. Figure 12–8 provides data that confirm the link between income and voting: Most high-income people *do,* and most low-income people *don't.* The fact that the disadvantaged and powerless are least likely to vote suggests that the liberal explanation for voter apathy probably is closer to the truth.

NONVOTING BY CONVICTED CRIMINALS

Although the right to vote is at the foundation of U.S. democracy, forty-eight of the fifty states (all except Vermont and Maine) have laws that bar felons—people in jail, on probation, or on parole after being convicted of a serious crime—from voting. Ten states go further and bar many or all ex-felons from ever voting again.

Do such laws make a difference in U.S. elections? The answer is yes: The number of people prevented from voting by these laws approaches 10 million. Because convicted felons show better than a two-to-one preference for Democratic over Republican candidates, and allowing for expected voter apathy, one recent study concluded that if these laws were not in force, Democrats would have won more congressional races and Al Gore would have defeated George W. Bush for the presidency in 2000 (Uggen & Manza, 2002).

Theoretical Analysis of Politics

Sociologists have long debated how power is spread throughout the U.S. population. Power is a very difficult topic to study because decision making is complex and often takes place behind closed doors. Despite this difficulty, researchers have developed three competing models of power in the United States.

THE PLURALIST MODEL: THE PEOPLE RULE

The **pluralist model,** closely linked to structural-functional theory, is *an analysis of politics that sees power as spread among many competing interest groups.* Pluralists claim, first, that politics is an arena of negotiation. With limited resources, no organization can expect to achieve all of its goals. Organizations therefore operate as *veto groups,* realizing some goals but mostly keeping opponents from achieving all of their ends. The political process relies heavily on creating alliances and compromises between numerous interest groups so that policies gain wide support. In short, pluralists see power as spread widely throughout society, with all people having at least some voice in the political system (Dahl, 1961, 1982; Rothman & Black, 1998).

APPLYING THEORY
POLITICS

	Pluralist Model	Power-Elite Model	Political-Economy Model
Which theoretical approach is applied?	Structural-functional approach	Social-conflict approach	Social-conflict approach
How is power spread throughout society?	Power is spread widely, so that all groups have some voice.	Power is concentrated in the hands of top business, political, and military leaders.	Power is directed by the operation of the capitalist economy.
Is the United States a democracy?	Yes. Power is spread widely enough to make the country a democracy.	No. Power is too concentrated for the country to be a democracy.	No. The capitalist economy sets political decision-making, so the country is not a democracy.

THE POWER-ELITE MODEL: A FEW PEOPLE RULE

The **power-elite model,** based on social-conflict theory, is *an analysis of politics that sees power as concentrated among the rich.* The term "power elite" was coined by C. Wright Mills (1956), a social-conflict theorist who argued that the upper class holds most of society's wealth, prestige, and power.

Mills claimed that members of the power elite are in charge of the three major sectors of U.S. society: the economy, government, and the military. Thus, the power elite is made up of the "super-rich" (corporate executives and major stockholders); top officials in Washington, D.C., and state capitals around the country; and the highest-ranking officers in the U.S. military.

Mills explained that these elites move from one sector to another, building power as they go. Vice President Dick Cheney, for example, has moved back and forth between powerful positions in the corporate world and the federal government. Colin Powell moved from a top position in the U.S. military to become secretary of state. More broadly, when President Bush took office, he assembled a cabinet in which all members but one were already millionaires.

Power-elite theorists say that the United States is not a democracy because the concentration of wealth and power is simply too great for the average person's voice to be heard. They reject the pluralist idea that various centers of power serve as checks and balances on one another; according to the power-elite model, those at the top face no real opposition (Bartlett & Steele, 2000; Moore et al., 2002).

THE MARXIST MODEL: BIAS IN THE SYSTEM ITSELF

A third approach to understanding U.S. politics is the **Marxist political-economy model,** *an analysis that explains politics in terms of the operation of a society's economic system.* Like the power-elite model, the Marxist approach is a social-conflict model that rejects the idea that the United States is a political democracy. But whereas the power-elite model focuses on the enormous wealth and power of certain individuals, the Marxist model looks to the bias rooted in this nation's institutions, especially its economy. Karl Marx believed that a society's economic system (capitalist or socialist) shapes its political system. Therefore, power elites do not simply appear on the scene; they are creations of capitalism.

From this point of view, reforming the political system—by, say, limiting the amount of money that rich people can contribute to political candidates—is unlikely to bring about true democracy. The problem does not lie in the *people* who exercise great power or the *people* who don't vote; the problem is the *system* itself—what Marxists call the "political economy of capitalism." In other words, as long as the United States has a predominantly capitalist economy, just as the majority of people are exploited in the workplace, they will also be shut out of politics.

Critical review. The Applying Theory table summarizes the three models of the U.S. political system. Which of the three models is correct? Over the years, research has shown support for each one. In the end, of course, how you think our political system ought to work is as much a matter of political values as it is of scientific fact.

Classic research by Nelson Polsby (1959) supports the pluralist model. Polsby studied the politics of New Haven, Connecticut, where he found that key decisions involving urban renewal, choosing political candidates, and running the city's schools were made by different groups. Polsby concluded that in New Haven, no one group—not even the upper class—ruled all the others.

Robert and Helen Lynd (1937) studied Muncie, Indiana (which they called "Middletown," to suggest it was a typical city), and documented the fortune amassed by a single family, the Balls, from its business producing glass canning jars. Their findings support the power-elite position. The Lynds showed how the Ball family dominated many aspects of the city's life, pointing to that family's name on a local bank, university, hospital, and department store. In Muncie, according to the Lynds, the power elite was more or less a single family.

From the Marxist perspective, the point is not which individuals make decisions. Rather, as Alexander Liazos (1982:13) explains, "The basic tenets of capitalist society shape everyone's life: the inequalities of social classes and the importance of profits over people." As long as the basic institutions of society are organized to meet the needs of the few rather than the many, Liazos concludes, a truly democratic society is impossible.

Clearly, the political system in the United States gives almost everyone the right to participate in politics through elections. But as the power-elite and Marxist models point out, the U.S. political system is, at the very least, far less democratic than most people think. Most citizens have the right to vote, but the major political parties and their candidates typically support only the positions that are acceptable to the most powerful segments of society and consistent with the operation of our capitalist economy.

Whatever the reasons, many people in the United States are losing confidence in their leaders. More than 80 percent of U.S. adults report having, at best, only "some confidence" that members of Congress and other government officials will do what is best for the country (NORC, 2003:977, 1132).

Power beyond the Rules

Politics is always a matter of disagreement over a society's goals and the means to achieve them. A political system tries to settle controversy within a system of rules. But political activity sometimes breaks the rules or even tries to do away with the entire system.

REVOLUTION

Political revolution is *the overthrow of one political system in order to establish another.* Revolution goes beyond *reform,* or change within a system, and even beyond a *coup d'état* (in French, literally "stroke of the state"), by which one leader topples another. Revolution involves change in the *type* of system itself.

No type of political system is immune to revolution, nor does revolution produce any one particular kind of government. Our country's Revolutionary War (1775–76) changed colonial rule by the British monarchy into a representative democracy. French revolutionaries in 1789 also overthrew a monarch, only to set the stage for the return of a monarchy in the person of Napoleon. In 1917, the Russian Revolution replaced a monarchy with a socialist government built on the ideas of Karl Marx. In 1991, a second Russian revolution dismantled the socialist Soviet Union, and the nation was reborn as the Russian Federation, moving toward a market system and a greater political voice for its people.

Despite their striking variety, revolutions share a number of traits (Tocqueville, 1955, orig. 1856; Skocpol, 1979; Lewis, 1984; Tilly, 1986):

1. **Rising expectations.** Common sense suggests that revolution is more likely when people are severely deprived, but history shows that most revolutions occur when people's lives are improving. Rising expectations, rather than bitterness and despair, make revolution more likely.

2. **Unresponsive government.** Revolution becomes more likely when a government is unwilling to reform itself, especially when demands for change being made by powerful segments of society are not heard.

3. **Radical leadership by intellectuals.** The English philosopher Thomas Hobbes (1588–1679) claimed that intellectuals provide the justification for revolution, and universities often are at the center of political change. For example, students played a key role in China's prodemocracy movement and in the uprisings in Eastern Europe.

4. **Establishing a new legitimacy.** Overthrowing a political system is not easy, but ensuring a revolution's long-term success is harder still. Some revolutionary movements are held together merely by hatred of the past regime and fall apart once new leaders are installed. Revolutionaries must also guard against counterrevolutionary drives led by overthrown leaders. This explains the speed and ruthlessness with which victorious revolutionaries typically dispose of former leaders.

Scientific research cannot say whether a revolution is good or bad. That judgment depends on personal values and in any case becomes clear only many years later. Fifteen years after its revolution, the future of the former Soviet Union remains uncertain.

Increasing security in a time of danger generally means reducing freedom. As part of the ongoing "war on terror," security teams are far more evident in public places. In what ways does increased police surveillance threaten our freedoms?

TERRORISM

On September 11, 2001, terrorists hijacked four commercial airliners; one crashed in a wooded area, but the other three crashed into public buildings full of people. The attack killed more than 3,000 innocent people (representing sixty-eight nations), injured many thousands more, completely destroyed the twin towers of the World Trade Center in New York City, and seriously damaged the Pentagon in Washington, D.C. Not since the attack on Pearl Harbor at the outbreak of World War II had the United States suffered such a blow. This event was the most serious terrorist act ever recorded.

Terrorism refers to *acts of violence or the threat of such violence used as a political strategy by an individual or a group.* Like revolution, terrorism is a political act beyond the rules of established political systems. According to Paul Johnson (1981), terrorism has four distinguishing characteristics.

First, terrorists try to paint violence as a legitimate political tactic, despite the fact that such acts are condemned by virtually every nation. Terrorists also bypass (or are excluded from) established channels of political negotiation. Therefore, terrorism is a weak organization's strategy against a stronger enemy. In recent decades, terrorism has become commonplace in international politics. In 2003, there were 208 acts of terrorism worldwide, which claimed 625 lives and injured 3,646 people. Of these, 60 (29 percent) were directed against the United States (U.S. Department of State, 2004).

 Read the U.S. State Department's annual report on global terrorism at http://www.state.gov/s/ct/rls/pgtrpt/2003/

Second, terrorism is used not just by groups but also by governments against their own people. *State terrorism* is the use of violence, generally without support of law, by government officials. State terrorism is lawful in some authoritarian and totalitarian states, which survive by creating widespread fear and intimidation. Saddam Hussein, for example, relied on secret police and state terror to protect his power in Iraq.

Third, democratic societies reject terrorism in principle, but they are especially vulnerable to terrorists because they give extensive civil liberties to their people and have less extensive police networks. In contrast, totalitarian regimes make widespread use of state terrorism, but their extensive police power minimizes opportunities for individual acts of terror.

Fourth, and finally, terrorism is always a matter of definition. Governments claim the right to maintain order, even by force, and may label opposition groups who use violence as "terrorists." Political differences may explain why one person's "terrorist" is another's "freedom fighter."

Hostage taking and outright killing provoke popular anger, but taking action against terrorists is difficult. Because most terrorist groups have no formal connection to any established state, identifying those responsible may be all but impossible, and a military response may risk confrontation with other governments. Yet as terrorism expert Brian Jenkins warns, the failure to respond "encourages other terrorist groups, who begin to realize that this can be a pretty cheap way to wage war" (quoted in Whitaker, 1985:29).

War and Peace

Perhaps the most critical political issue is **war,** *organized, armed conflict among the people of various nations, directed by their governments.* War is as old as humanity, of course,

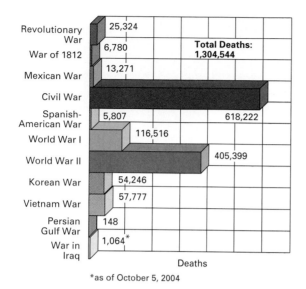

Revolutionary War	25,324				
War of 1812	6,780	Total Deaths: 1,304,544			
Mexican War	13,271				
Civil War					618,222
Spanish-American War	5,807				
World War I		116,516			
World War II			405,399		
Korean War		54,246			
Vietnam War		57,777			
Persian Gulf War	148				
War in Iraq	1,064*				

Deaths

*as of October 5, 2004

FIGURE 12-9   Deaths of Americans in Eleven U.S. Wars

Sources: Compiled from various sources by Maris A. Vinovskis (1989) and the author.

but understanding it is crucial today because humanity now has weapons that can destroy the entire planet.

At almost any moment during the twentieth century, nations somewhere in the world were engaged in violent conflict. In its short history, the United States has participated in eleven major wars. From the Revolutionary War to the War in Iraq, more than 1.3 million U.S. men and women have been killed in armed conflicts, as shown in Figure 12–9, and many times that number have been injured. Thousands more died in "undeclared wars" and limited military actions in the Dominican Republic, Lebanon, Grenada, Panama, Somalia, Haiti, Bosnia, and elsewhere.

THE CAUSES OF WAR

Wars occur so often that we might think that there is something "natural" about armed conflict. But there is no evidence that human beings must wage war under any particular circumstances. On the contrary, governments around the world usually have to force their people to go to war.

Like other forms of social behavior, warfare is a product of *society* that varies in purpose and intensity from place to place. The Semai of Malaysia, among the most peace-loving of the world's peoples, rarely resort to violence. In contrast, the Yąnomamö (see the box on page 39) are quick to wage war.

If society holds the key to war or peace, under what circumstances do humans go to war? Quincy Wright (1987) cites five factors that promote war:

1. **Perceived threats.** Nations mobilize in response to a perceived threat to their people, territory, or culture. Leaders justified the recent U.S.-led military campaign against Iraq, for example, by stressing the threat posed by Saddam Hussein to the United States.

2. **Social problems.** When internal problems cause widespread frustration at home, a nation's leaders may divert attention by attacking an external "enemy" as a form of scapegoating. While U.S. leaders defended the War in Iraq as a matter of national security, the start of the war shifted the nation's attention from the struggling national economy and boosted the popularity of President Bush.

3. **Political objectives.** Poor nations, such as Vietnam, have fought wars to end foreign domination. Powerful countries such as the United States use a periodic "show of force" (recall the recent deployments of troops in Somalia, Haiti, Bosnia, Afghanistan, and Iraq) to increase global political standing.

4. **Moral objectives.** Nations rarely claim that they are going to war to gain wealth and power. Instead, their leaders infuse military campaigns with moral urgency. By calling the 2003 War in Iraq "Operation Iraqi Freedom," U.S. leaders portrayed the mission as a morally justified war of liberation from an evil tyrant.

5. **The absence of alternatives.** A fifth factor promoting war is the lack of alternatives. Preventing war was one reason that the United Nations was created. Although it still tries to maintain international peace, the UN has had limited success in resolving tensions among nations and thus preventing war.

IS TERRORISM A NEW KIND OF WAR?

After the terrorist attacks of September 11, 2001, U.S. government officials spoke of terrorism as a new kind of war. War has historically followed certain patterns: It is played out according to at least some basic rules; the warring parties are known to each other; and the objectives of the warring parties—which generally involve control of territory—are clearly stated.

Terrorism breaks from these patterns. The identity of terrorist individuals and organizations may not be known, those responsible may deny their responsibility, and their goals may be unclear. The recent terrorist attacks against the United States were not attempts to defeat the nation militarily or to secure territory. They were carried out by people representing not a country but a cause, one that was not well understood in the United States. In short, they were expressions of anger and hate intended to create widespread fear.

Conventional warfare is symmetrical, with nations sending armies into battle. By contrast, terrorism is a new kind of war: an asymmetrical conflict in which a small number of attackers use terror and their own willingness to die as a means to level the playing field against a much more powerful enemy. Although the terrorists may be ruthless, the nation under attack must use caution in its response to terror because little may be known about the identity and location of those responsible. It is for this reason that U.S. officials maintain that the reaction to the September 11 attacks will unfold over a period of years.

THE COSTS AND CAUSES OF MILITARISM

The costs of war extend far beyond battlefield casualties. The world's nations spend almost $1 trillion annually (about $150 for every person on the planet) for military purposes. Such expenditures mean less money available to aid hundreds of millions of poor people in their struggle for survival.

Defense is the U.S. government's second biggest expenditure (after Social Security), accounting for 18 percent of all federal spending, or $376 billion, in 2003. The United States has emerged as the world's single military superpower, with more military might than the next nine countries combined (Gergen, 2002).

For decades, military spending went up because of the *arms race* between the United States and the former Soviet Union, which dropped out of the race after its collapse in 1991. But some analysts (who support power-elite theory) link high military spending to the domination of U.S. society by a **military-industrial complex,** *the close association of the federal government, the military, and defense industries.* The roots of militarism, then, lie not just in external threats but also in the institutional structures here at home (Marullo, 1987; Barnes, 2002b).

A final reason for continuing militarism is regional conflict. In the 1990s, localized wars broke out in Bosnia, Chechnya, and Zambia, and today tensions run high between Israel and the Palestinians, as well as between India and Pakistan. Even limited wars have the potential to grow and involve other countries, including the United States. India and Pakistan, both nuclear powers, moved to the brink of war in 2002. In 2003, the announcement by North Korea that it, too, had nuclear weapons raised tensions in Asia.

NUCLEAR WEAPONS

Despite the easing of superpower tensions, the world still contains 20,000 nuclear warheads, representing a destructive power equal to five tons of TNT for every person on the planet. If even a small fraction of this arsenal is used in war, life as we know it would end on much of the Earth. Albert

In the summer of 2004, Iyad Allawi became the prime minister of Iraq after the United States led a war to oust dictator Saddam Hussein. Here, Allawi looks on as outgoing U.S. administrator Paul Bremer shakes hands with Iraqi Chief Justice Midhat al-Mahmoudi. This war has been controversial in the United States and unpopular in much of the world. Do you think the War in Iraq was a necessary step to defending the United States from terror? Why or why not?

Einstein, whose genius contributed to the development of nuclear weapons, reflected, "The unleashed power of the atom has changed everything *save our modes of thinking,* and we thus drift toward unparalleled catastrophe." In short, nuclear weapons make full-scale war unthinkable in a world not yet capable of peace.

The United States, the Russian Federation, Great Britain, France, the People's Republic of China, Israel, India, Pakistan, and North Korea all have nuclear weapons. Although a few nations stopped the development of nuclear weapons—Argentina and Brazil halted work in 1990, and South Africa dismantled its arsenal in 1991—by 2010, as many as fifty countries could have the ability to fight a nuclear war. Such a trend makes any regional conflict far more dangerous.

MASS MEDIA AND WAR

The War in Iraq was the first war in which television crews traveled with U.S. troops, reporting as the campaign unfolded. The mass media provided ongoing and detailed reports of events; cable television made available live coverage of the war twenty-four hours a day, seven days a week.

Those media outlets critical of the war—especially the Arab news channel Al-Jazeera—tended to report the slow pace of the conflict, the casualties to the U.S. and allied forces, and the deaths and injuries suffered by Iraqi civilians, information that increased pressure to end the war. Media outlets supportive of the war—including most news organizations in the United States—tended to report the rapid pace of the war and the casualties to Iraqi forces and to downplay harm to Iraqi civilians as minimal and unintended. In sum, the power of the mass media to provide selective information to a worldwide audience means that television and other media are almost as important to the outcome of a conflict as the military who are doing the actual fighting.

PURSUING PEACE

How can the world reduce the dangers of war? Here are the most recent approaches to securing peace:

1. **Deterrence.** The logic of the arms race holds that security comes from a balance of terror between the superpowers. The principle of *mutual assured destruction* (MAD) means that a nation launching a first strike against another will face greater retaliation. This deterrence policy kept the peace for almost fifty years during the Cold War. Yet it encouraged an enormous arms race and cannot control nuclear proliferation, which poses a growing threat to peace. Deterrence also does little to stop terrorism or to prevent war started by a stronger nation (such as the United States) against a weaker foe (such as the Taliban government in Afghanistan or Saddam Hussein in Iraq).

2. **High-technology defense.** If technology created the weapons, perhaps it can also protect us from them; such is the claim of the *strategic defense initiative* (SDI). Under SDI, satellites and ground installations would destroy enemy missiles soon after they were launched. Partly in response to the September 11 attacks, two-thirds of U.S. adults now support SDI (Thompson & Waller, 2001; "Female Opinion," 2002). However, critics claim that the system, which they refer to as "Star Wars," would be, at best, a leaky umbrella. Others worry that building such a system will spark another massive arms race.

3. **Diplomacy and disarmament.** Some analysts believe that the best road to peace is diplomacy rather than technology (Dedrick & Yinger, 1990). Teams of diplomats working together can increase security by reducing, rather than building, weapon stockpiles.

   But disarmament has limitations. No nation wants to be weakened by eliminating its defenses. Successful diplomacy depends on everyone involved sharing responsibility for a common problem (Fisher & Ury, 1988). Although the United States and the Soviet Union succeeded in negotiating arms reduction agreements that remain in effect, the threat from other nations such as North Korea is increasing.

4. **Resolving underlying conflict.** In the end, reducing the dangers of war may depend on resolving the issues that have fueled the arms race. Even as the United States claims to be fighting in Iraq to spread the values of freedom and political democracy, many Islamic people see this country as fighting the entire Muslim world. Perhaps the world needs to ask whether it is wise to be spending thousands of times as much money on militarism as we spend on efforts to find peaceful solutions (Sivard, 1988; Kaplan & Schaffer, 2001).

LOOKING AHEAD: POLITICS IN THE TWENTY-FIRST CENTURY

Just as economies are changing, so are political systems. Several problems and trends are likely to be important as the twenty-first century unfolds.

One troublesome problem in the United States is inconsistency between our democratic ideals and our low turnout at the polls. Perhaps, as conservative pluralist theorists say, many people do not bother to vote because they are content with their lives. On the other hand, the liberal power-elite theorists may be right when they say that people withdraw from a system that concentrates wealth and power in the hands of so few people. Or perhaps, as radical Marxist critics claim, people find that our political system offers little real choice, limiting options and policies to those that support our capitalist economy. In any case, the current high level of apathy calls for significant political reform.

A second major trend is the global rethinking of political models. The Cold War cast political debate in the form of two opposing models, capitalism and socialism. Today, however, discussion includes a broader range of political systems that links government to the economy in a variety of ways. "Welfare capitalism," as found in Sweden, or "state capitalism," as found in South Korea and Japan, are just two possibilities. The Controversy & Debate box looks at the current lack of democratic governments among the world's Islamic countries.

Third, we still face the danger of war in many parts of the world. Even as the United States and the Russian Federation dismantle some warheads, vast stockpiles of nuclear weapons remain, and nuclear technology continues to spread around the world. In addition, new superpowers are likely to arise (the People's Republic of China and India are likely candidates), just as regional conflicts and terrorism are likely to continue. We can only hope (and vote!) for leaders who will find nonviolent solutions to the age-old problems that provoke war, putting us on the road to world peace.

CONTROVERSY & DEBATE

Islam and Freedom: A "Democracy Gap"?

As the United States and its allies launched the War in Iraq, President Bush spoke hopefully of liberating the Iraqi people and holding up a democratic Iraq as an example to the rest of the Islamic world. As a recent study by Freedom House shows, however, the president is up against some long odds.

Freedom House reports that 47 of the world's 192 nations have an Islamic majority population. As the figure shows, just 11 (23.4 percent) of these 47 countries have democratic governments, and Freedom House rates only one—Mali—as "free." Of the 145 nations without a majority Islamic population, 110 (75.9 percent) have democratic governments, and 84 are rated as "free." In other words, countries without Islamic majorities are three times more likely to have democratic governments than countries with Islamic majorities. Freedom House concludes that countries with Islamic majority populations display a disturbing "democracy gap."

This relative lack of democracy holds for all world regions that have Islamic-majority nations—Africa, Central Europe, the Middle East, and Asia. The pattern is especially strong among the sixteen Islamic majority states in the Middle East and North Africa that are ethnically Arabic—none is an electoral democracy.

What explains this "democracy gap"? Freedom House points to four factors. First, countries with Islamic-majority populations typically are less developed economically, with limited schooling for their people and widespread poverty. Second, these countries have cultural traditions that rigidly control the lives of women, providing them with few economic, educational, or political opportunities. Third, while most countries limit the power of religious elites in government, and some (including the United States) even require a "separation of church and state," Islamic-majority nations support involving Islamic leaders in government. In just two recent cases—Iran under the ayatollahs and Afghanistan under the Taliban—have Islamic leaders actually taken formal control of government; in many nations, however, they exert a considerable influence on politics.

Fourth, and finally, the enormous wealth that comes from Middle Eastern oil plays a part in preventing democratic government. In Iraq, Saudi Arabia, Kuwait, Qatar, and other nations, this resource has provided astounding riches to a small number of families, which they use to strengthen their political control. In addition, oil wealth permits elites to build airports and other modern facilities without encouraging broader economic development that would raise the living standards of the majority.

For all these reasons, Freedom House concludes that the road to democracy for Islamic-majority nations is likely to be long. Yet there are also reasons to think that change will come. In 1950, very few Catholic-majority countries (mostly in Europe and Latin America) had democratic governments. Today, however, most of these nations are democratic. Note, too, that a majority of the world's Muslim people—who live in Nigeria, Turkey, Bangladesh, India, Indonesia, and the United States—already live under democratic governments.

CONTINUE THE DEBATE . . .

1. Do you think the United States is right or wrong in seeking to bring about a democratic political system in Iraq? Why?
2. Do you expect to see greater democracy in Islamic-majority countries fifty years from now? Why or why not?
3. Can you point to several reasons that Muslim people might object to the kind of political system we call "democracy"?

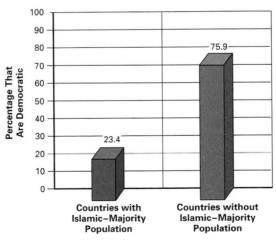

Democracy in Countries with and without Islamic-Majority Populations

Source: Karatnycky (2002).

Source: Based on Karatnycky (2002).

SUMMARY

Economics

1. The economy is the major social institution by which a society produces, distributes, and consumes goods and services.

2. The primary sector of the economy produces raw materials; the secondary sector produces manufactured goods; the tertiary sector involves services rather than goods.

3. Capitalism is based on private ownership of productive property and the pursuit of profit in a competitive marketplace. Socialism is based on collective ownership of productive property through government control of the economy.

4. Capitalism's great productivity provides a high overall standard of living but with high income inequality; socialism is less productive, generating lower living standards but with less economic inequality.

5. The emerging global economy links many nations across national boundaries.

6. The United States is a postindustrial nation with only a small percentage of workers holding agricultural jobs; just one-fourth have blue-collar, industrial jobs; 76 percent have white-collar, service jobs.

7. A profession is a special category of white-collar work based on theoretical knowledge, self-regulating practice, authority over clients, and emphasis on serving the community.

8. In 2003, some 6.0 percent of U.S. workers were unemployed, with young people and minorities most likely to be without jobs.

9. Women and other minorities represent an increasing share of all U.S. workers.

10. Corporations are the core of the U.S. economy. Most large conglomerates now operate in many countries.

Politics

1. Politics is the major social institution by which a society distributes power and organizes decision making. Max Weber claimed that power is legitimized by tradition, rationally enacted rules, or the personal charisma of a leader.

2. Monarchy is common to preindustrial societies; industrialization favors the development of democracy.

3. Authoritarian political systems deny the people participation in government. Totalitarian political systems go even further, tightly controlling people's everyday lives.

4. The political spectrum—from the liberal left to the conservative right—involves attitudes on economic issues (such as how much the government regulates the economy) and social issues (including the rights and opportunities of women and other minorities).

5. Special-interest groups tend to be strong in countries like the United States that have weak political parties. Only 50 to 60 percent of eligible U.S. voters cast ballots in national presidential elections.

6. The pluralist model of U.S. politics views power as spread widely among competing interest groups; the power-elite model believes that power is concentrated in a small, wealthy segment of society; the Marxist political-economy model says the capitalist economy makes true democracy impossible.

7. Revolution is the overthrow of one political system in order to establish another. Terrorism uses violence in pursuit of a political goal.

8. War is armed conflict between governments. The spread of nuclear weapons increases the threat of global catastrophe. Terrorism is a new form of asymmetrical conflict in which individuals or organizations use terror as a tactic against a more powerful enemy.

KEY CONCEPTS

Economics

social institution (p. 310) a major sphere of social life, or societal subsystem, organized to meet human needs

economy (p. 310) the social institution that organizes a society's production, distribution, and consumption of goods and services

postindustrial economy (p. 312) a productive system based on service work and high technology

primary sector (p. 312) the part of the economy that draws raw materials from the natural environment

secondary sector (p. 312) the part of the economy that transforms raw materials into manufactured goods

tertiary sector (p. 312) the part of the economy that involves services rather than goods

global economy (p. 313) expanding economic activity that crosses national borders

capitalism (p. 314) an economic system in which natural resources and the means of producing goods and services are privately owned

socialism (p. 315) an economic system in which natural resources and the means of producing goods and services are collectively owned

welfare capitalism (p. 316) an economic and political system that combines a mostly market-based economy with extensive social welfare programs

state capitalism (p. 316) an economic and political system in which companies are privately owned but cooperate closely with the government

profession (p. 318) a prestigious, white-collar occupation that requires extensive formal education

corporation (p. 321) an organization with a legal existence, including rights and liabilities, apart from that of its members

monopoly (p. 322) the domination of a market by a single producer

oligopoly (p. 322) the domination of a market by a few producers

Politics

politics (p. 324) the social institution that distributes power, sets a society's goals, and makes decisions

power (p. 324) the ability to achieve desired ends despite resistance from others

government (p. 325) a formal organization that directs the political life of a society

authority (p. 325) power that people perceive as legitimate rather than coercive

routinization of charisma (p. 325) the transformation of charismatic authority into some combination of traditional and bureaucratic authority

monarchy (p. 326) a type of political system in which a single family rules from generation to generation

democracy (p. 326) a type of political system that gives power to the people as a whole

authoritarianism (p. 326) a political system that denies the people participation in government

totalitarianism (p. 328) a highly centralized political system that extensively regulates people's lives

welfare state (p. 329) government agencies and programs that provide benefits to the population

pluralist model (p. 332) an analysis of politics that sees power as spread among many competing interest groups

power-elite model (p. 333) an analysis of politics that sees power as concentrated among the rich

Marxist political-economy model (p. 333) an analysis that explains politics in terms of the operation of a society's economic system

political revolution (p. 334) the overthrow of one political system in order to establish another

terrorism (p. 335) acts of violence or the threat of such violence used as a political strategy by an individual or a group

war (p. 335) organized, armed conflict among the people of various nations, directed by their governments

military-industrial complex (p. 337) the close association of the federal government, the military, and defense industries

CRITICAL-THINKING QUESTIONS

1. As social institutions, what are the economy and the political system supposed to do? How well, in your opinion, does each do its job?

2. In what specific ways did the Industrial Revolution change the economy of the United States? How is today's Information Revolution changing the economy once again?

3. Compare the pluralist, power-elite, and Marxist models of political power. Which do you think is most correct? Why?

4. How are both the economy and politics becoming global in scope? What changes in each would you expect by the end of the twenty-first century?

APPLICATIONS AND EXERCISES

1. General data on the U.S. economy—76 percent of output in the service sector, 23 percent in the industrial sector, and 1 percent in the primary sector—hide great variety within this country. Visit the library and locate data that profile your own city, county, or state.

2. Visit a discount store such as Wal-Mart or Kmart and select an area of the store of interest to you. Do a little "fieldwork," inspecting products to see where they are made. Does your research support the existence of a global economy?

3. Trace the growth in the size of the federal government over the past fifty years. Then try to discover how organizations at different points along the political spectrum (from socialist organizations on the left through the Democratic and Republican parties to right-wing militia groups) view the size of the current welfare state.

4. Freedom House, the organization that studies civil rights and political liberty around the world, publishes an annual report, *Freedom in the World*. Find a copy in the library or on the Freedom House Web site (http://www.freedomhouse.org), and examine the trends or political profiles of countries of interest to you.

5. Packaged in the back of this new textbook is an interactive CD-ROM that offers a variety of video and interactive review materials intended to help you better understand the material covered in this chapter. For this chapter, the CD-ROM contains a relevant clip from *ABC News,* an author's tip video, interactive map animations, an interactive timeline, and flashcards with audio pronunciations of the more difficult words.

 ## SITES TO SEE

http://www.prenhall.com/macionis

Visit the interactive Companion Website™ that accompanies this text. Begin by clicking on the cover of your book. You will find a chapter-by-chapter study guide, practice tests, suggested Web links, and links to other relevant material.

http://www.bls.gov

Visit the Web site operated by the Bureau of Labor Statistics, where you will find a wide range of interesting data and reports.

http://www.nber.org

Another worthwhile site, run by the National Bureau of Economic Research, explains the operation of the economy.

http://www2.kenyon.edu/Projects/FamFarm/

Several years ago, students at Kenyon College in Ohio prepared this Web site to study the economics of family farms in rural Knox County.

http://www.fao.org

The Food and Agriculture Organization is a part of the United Nations concerned with how well the global economy meets the needs of the world's people. From its home page, look for the FAO's annual report, titled *State of Food Insecurity in the World.*

http://www.amnesty.org

Amnesty International operates a useful Web site that offers information about the state of human rights around the world.

http://www.cawp.rutgers.edu/

The Center for American Women and Politics is a resource providing information on and analysis of women in politics and government.

http://www.coara.or.jp/~ryoji/abomb/e-index.html

Few of us have firsthand experience of the horrors of war. This Web site provides a survivor's personal account of the U.S. bombing of the Japanese city of Hiroshima, the first time the atomic bomb was used in warfare.

 ## INVESTIGATE WITH RESEARCH NAVIGATOR™

Follow the instructions found on page 32 of this textbook to access the features of **Research Navigator™.** Once at the Web site, enter your Login Name and Password. Then, to use the **Content Select™** database, enter keywords such as "corporations," "political economy," and "terrorism," and the search engine will supply relevant and recent scholarly and popular press publications. Use the *New York Times* **Search-by-Subject Archive** to find recent news articles related to sociology and the **Links Library** feature to find relevant Web links organized by the key terms associated with this chapter.

May 31, 2004

Rewards of a 90-Hour Week: Poverty and Dirty Laundry

By STEVEN GREENHOUSE

For the many New Yorkers who dread spending two hours in a noisy, often smelly laundry washing and drying their clothes, it is a godsend that most laundries will handle that unpleasant chore for them, and for as little as $5 a load.

But few customers pay attention to the thousands of "wash and fold" workers—most of them women from Mexico—who actually handle their laundry. . . . In humid basements and backrooms around the city, they shovel clothes in and out of washers and dryers, matching socks and folding hundreds of towels and undergarments each day.

Most laundry workers earn less, often far less, than the minimum wage of $5.15 an hour. Gabriela Mendez, a veteran of six Manhattan laundries, said one paid her $230, or $3.19 an hour, for a 72-hour week, while at another she earned $220, or $2.45 an hour, for a 90-hour week.

She and other workers boil over with tales of oppressive conditions or abusive bosses. . . .

In recent months, the wages and working conditions of laundry workers have begun to attract outside attention. The state attorney general, Eliot Spitzer, has begun cracking down on a handful of laundries, winning tens of thousands of dollars in back wages for the workers and pressuring some laundries to begin granting paid sick days and one-week vacations. Several immigrant advocacy groups have taken up the cause of laundry employees, and an effort has begun to unionize some workers. . . .

[A]t a majority of the laundries investigated by the office, there have been allegations of oppressive working conditions, including sexual harassment, physical and verbal abuse and poor environmental conditions, like the use of harsh chemicals. . . .

Ms. Mendez said she grew so fed up with the illegal wages she was paid at laundry after laundry that she complained to Casa Mexico, an immigrant advocacy group, and then to the attorney general. She, her husband and their 5-year-old son live with two other families in a bare-bones three-bedroom apartment in Corona, Queens. Her 12-year-old son lives with her mother back in Mexico.

"We came here because we were living in poverty," Ms. Mendez said. "We didn't have enough to buy shoes. All we ate was tortilla and beans, and we didn't have enough to buy fruit. I wanted something much better for the children."

She complained that one laundry did not give the workers gloves even though they handled sheets smeared with blood. Another, she said, prohibited them from drinking water from the tap, despite the sweltering heat. Ms. Mendez also said that one boss hit her because she took a 45-minute lunch, 15 minutes longer than usual. . . .

Many laundries have raised wages after seeing the attorney general's enforcement actions and after immigrant groups began fighting for laundry workers. During the past year, workers say, pay has climbed at many of them by $30 to $100 a week. Many laundries that paid $250 for a 72-hour-week now pay $300 or even $350, which still violates minimum wage and overtime laws. . . .

Piedad G., an illegal immigrant from Mexico City who also declined to give her last name, said Symphony Cleaners suddenly laid her off after she began complaining about conditions. She said she worked from 7 a.m. to 7 p.m. Mondays through Saturdays, leaving her apartment in Queens an hour before work and returning an hour after work.

"When you work 7 to 7, it's like you're only living to work," she said, adding that she received $300 for 66 hours' work, which translates to $4.55 an hour.

She said she received no vacation days, no paid sick days, no health insurance and only one paid holiday, Christmas. Last summer, she said, a co-worker fainted from the heat. . . .

Back in Mexico City, Piedad G. said, she was a dental receptionist. She said she and her husband each paid $3,000 to be smuggled into the United States, expecting to earn far more here to help pay their two sons' tuition for high school and eventually college. She burst into tears when she started talking about her children, whom she said she has not seen for three years.

"Life is a lot more difficult here than I thought," she said. "Sometimes I think I was crazy to come here. This is a country with a lot of opportunities, but in order to take advantage of those opportunities you have to suffer a lot."

WHAT DO YOU THINK?

1. In light of the low pay earned by many immigrant laundry workers, why have they come to the United States? Do you think they expected the life they have found? Why or why not?

2. Why have wages in the laundry industry been going up? Do you think these workers will eventually receive a decent, living wage? Explain your answer.

Adapted from the original article by Steven Greenhouse published in *The New York Times* on May 31, 2004. Copyright © 2004 by The New York Times Company. Reprinted with permission.

CHAPTER THIRTEEN

Family and Religion

How are families in the United States changing?

What is the role of religion in society today?

Why are the family and religion important
in today's world?

The family and religion are social institutions that shape people's behavior and beliefs. ▶
The two institutions often come together in ritual events,
such as this Jewish wedding ceremony.

Diane Carp had the career of her dreams: She worked as a nurse in a pediatric intensive care unit and found great satisfaction in helping children in need. Even with her long hours at the hospital, she saved time to teach nursing classes at the nearby university and also to work on several research projects. She is widely known and well respected in her northern New Jersey community.

With so many responsibilities at work, it may be no surprise to learn that Diane Carp never quite got around to marrying. She recalls, "I had always thought I had such a rewarding career. . . . Part of me kept saying that I did not need the other stuff, the husband and the kids. Then, suddenly I was forty and I realized that if I were going to do something, I had better do it now."

Carp decided she wanted a child and set out to adopt an infant girl from China, one of the few countries that permits adoption by foreigners who are single and over forty. She filled out volumes of paperwork and sent off her application. Fifteen months later, she was in China for the joyful first meeting with her daughter, Kai Li. This experience has been so wonderful for them that today, five years later, Carp is going through the process once again so that Kai Li will have a little sister.

"I have friends who say, 'Hey, I have someone I'd really like you to meet.' I reply, 'Well, thanks, but I really don't have time for another relationship.' I would rather devote the extra time to helping another child" (Padawer, 2001).

Diane Carp's story illustrates an important trend: Families in the United States do not conform to any one model and are more diverse than ever before. Families differ because people's desires and situations differ. But family diversity also sparks a good deal of debate. Because one child in three is born to an unmarried woman and our divorce rate is high, half of U.S. children live with just one parent for some time before the age of eighteen. Carp recently commented, "I would rather my daughter have a father. But that was not an option."

Some people claim the family is falling apart, but others think that families are merely changing. For better or worse, in fact, the family is changing faster than any other social institution (Bianchi & Spain, 1996). When Carp was born, the "ideal family" consisted of a working husband, a homemaker wife, and their young children. Today, just one in four U.S. households fits that description.

At the same time, religion is changing, too, as membership in long-established churches is declining and new sects are flourishing. This chapter examines the family and religion, which are closely linked as society's *symbolic institutions*. Both help establish morality, maintain traditions, and join people together. Focusing on the United States with comparisons to other countries, we will examine why many people consider the family and religion the foundations of society, while others predict—and may even encourage—the decline of both institutions.

The Family: Basic Concepts

The **family** is *a social institution that unites people in cooperative groups to oversee the bearing and raising of children.* Family ties are also called **kinship,** *a social bond based on blood, marriage, or adoption.* All societies have families, but exactly who people call their kin has varied through history and varies today from one culture to another. In the United States, most people regard a **family unit** as *a social group of two or more people, related by blood, marriage, or adoption, who usually live together.* In this country and throughout the

Families vary from culture to culture and also over time. But everywhere, people celebrate the ritual of marriage that extends kinship into a new generation. This idea is expressed clearly in David Botello's painting, *Wedding Photos at Hollenbeck Park.*

David Botello, *Wedding Photos at Hollenbeck Park*, 1990.

world, families form around **marriage,** *a legal relationship, usually involving economic cooperation as well as sexual activity and childbearing, that people expect to last.*

Today, some people object to defining only married couples and children as families because it endorses a single standard of behavior as moral. Because some business and government programs still use this conventional definition, many unmarried but committed partners of the same or opposite sex are excluded from family health care and other benefits. However, organizations are gradually coming to recognize *families of affinity:* people with or without legal or blood ties who feel they belong together and want to define themselves as a family.

Because the U.S. Census Bureau uses the conventional definition of family,[1] sociologists who use Census Bureau data describing "families" must accept it. But as noted, the national trend is toward a broader definition of family.

The Family: Global Variations

In preindustrial societies, people take a broad view of family ties, recognizing the **extended family,** *a family unit that includes parents and children as well as other kin.* This group is also called the *consanguine family* because it includes everyone

[1]According to the Census Bureau, there were 112 million U.S. households in 2003. Of these, 76.2 million (68 percent) were family households; the rest contained single people or unrelated people living together. In 1960, 85 percent of all households were families.

with "shared blood." With industrialization, however, increasing social mobility and geographic migration give rise to the **nuclear family,** *a family unit composed of one or two parents and their children.* The nuclear family is also called the *conjugal family,* meaning "based on marriage." Although many members of our society live in extended families, the nuclear family is the most common family form.

MARRIAGE PATTERNS

Cultural norms, and often laws, identify people as suitable or unsuitable marriage partners. Some norms promote **endogamy,** *marriage between people of the same social category.* Endogamy limits marriage prospects to others of the same age, village, race, religion, or social class. By contrast, **exogamy** is *marriage between people of different social categories.* In rural India, for example, a person is expected to marry someone from the same caste (endogamy) but from a different village (exogamy). The reason for endogamy is that people of similar position pass along their standing to their children, thereby maintaining the traditional social hierarchy. Exogamy, on the other hand, links communities and encourages the spread of culture.

In higher-income nations, laws permit only **monogamy** (from Greek, meaning "one union"), *marriage that unites two partners.* Global Map 13–1 on page 348 shows that monogamy is the rule throughout the Americas and Europe. But many lower-income countries—especially in Africa and southern Asia—permit **polygamy** (Greek, "many unions"), *marriage that unites three or more people.* Polygamy has two forms. By far the more common is *polygyny* (Greek, "many

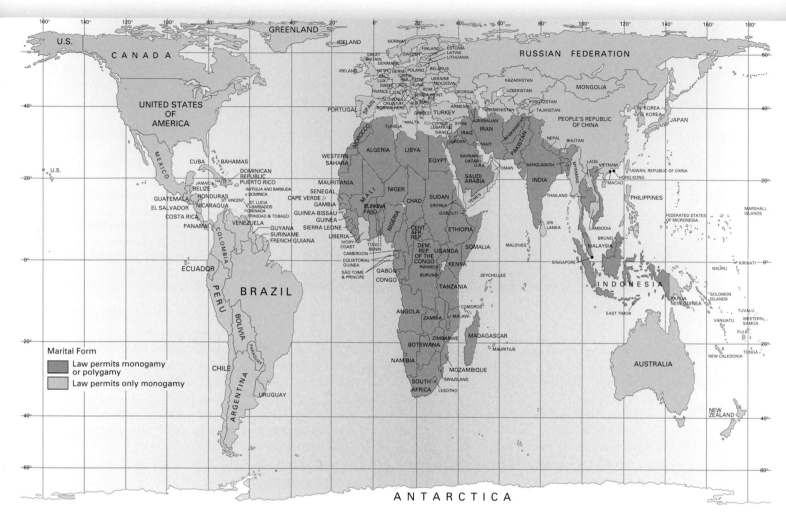

WINDOW ON THE WORLD

GLOBAL MAP 13-1   Marital Form in Global Perspective

Monogamy is the only legal form of marriage throughout the Western Hemisphere and in much of the rest of the world. In most African nations and in southern Asia, however, polygamy is permitted by law. In many cases, this practice reflects the historic influence of Islam, a religion that allows a man to have up to four wives. Even so, most marriages in these countries are monogamous, primarily for financial reasons.

Source: *Peters Atlas of the World* (1990).

women"), a form of marriage that unites one man and two or more women. For example, Islamic nations in the Middle East and Africa permit men up to four wives. Even so, most Islamic families are monogamous because few men can afford to support several wives and even more children. *Polyandry* (Greek, "many men") unites one woman and two or more men. This extremely rare pattern exists in Tibet, a

mountainous land where agriculture is difficult. There, polyandry discourages the division of land into parcels too small to support a family and divides the work of farming among many men.

Most of the world's societies at some time have permitted more than one marital pattern. Even so, as noted already, most marriages have been monogamous (Murdock,

1965, orig. 1949). The historical preference for monogamy reflects two facts of life: Supporting several spouses is a heavy financial burden, and the number of men and women in most societies is roughly the same.

RESIDENTIAL PATTERNS

Just as societies regulate mate selection, they also designate where a couple lives. In preindustrial societies, most newly-weds live with one set of parents who offer protection, support, and assistance. Most often, married couples live with or near the husband's family, an arrangement called *patrilocality* (Greek, "place of the father"). But in some societies (such as the North American Iroquois), couples live with or near the wife's family, which is called *matrilocality* ("place of the mother"). Societies that engage in frequent local warfare tend toward patrilocality, so sons are close to home to offer protection. Societies that engage in distant warfare may be patrilocal or matrilocal, depending on whether sons or daughters have greater economic value (Ember & Ember, 1971, 1991).

Industrial societies typically do not follow either of these patterns. Finances permitting, they favor *neolocality* (Greek, "new place"), in which a married couple lives apart from both sets of parents.

PATTERNS OF DESCENT

Descent refers to *the system by which members of a society trace kinship over generations.* Most preindustrial societies trace kinship through just the father's or the mother's side of the family. *Patrilineal descent,* the more common pattern, traces kinship through males, so that property flows from fathers to sons. Patrilineal descent characterizes most pastoral and agrarian societies, in which men produce the most valued resources. *Matrilineal descent,* by which people define only the mother's side as kin and property passes from mothers to daughters, is found in horticultural societies where women are the primary food producers.

Industrial societies with greater gender equality recognize *bilateral descent* ("two-sided descent"). That is, children recognize people on both the father's side and the mother's side of the family as relatives.

PATTERNS OF AUTHORITY

Worldwide, polygyny, patrilocality, and patrilineal descent are dominant and reflect the global pattern of patriarchy. Indeed, as Chapter 10 ("Gender Stratification") explains, no truly matriarchal society has ever existed.

In industrial societies such as the United States, more egalitarian families are evolving as the share of women in the labor force goes up. However, men are still typically heads of households, and most U.S. parents give children their father's last name.

Theoretical Analysis of the Family

As in earlier chapters, the various theoretical approaches offer a range of insights about the family.

FUNCTIONS OF THE FAMILY: STRUCTURAL-FUNCTIONAL ANALYSIS

According to the structural-functional approach, the family performs many vital tasks. In fact, the family operates as the backbone of society.

1. **Socialization.** As noted in Chapter 3 ("Socialization: From Infancy to Old Age"), the family is the first and most important setting for child rearing. Ideally, parents help children become well-integrated and contributing members of society (Parsons & Bales, 1955). Of course, family socialization continues throughout the life cycle, from childhood to old age. Nor is this process a one-way street: For example, as any parent knows, mothers and fathers learn as much from their children as the children learn from them.

2. **Regulation of sexual activity.** Every culture regulates sexual activity in the interest of maintaining kinship organization and property rights. As discussed in Chapter 6 ("Sexuality and Society"), the **incest taboo** is *a norm forbidding sexual relations or marriage between certain relatives.* Although the incest taboo exists in societies around the world, exactly which relatives cannot marry varies from one culture to another (Murdock, 1965, orig. 1949).

   Reproduction between close relatives can result in mental and physical damage to offspring. Yet only humans observe an incest taboo, suggesting that the key reason for controlling incest is social. Why? First, the incest taboo limits sexual competition in families by restricting sex to spouses. Second, because kinship defines people's rights and obligations toward one another, reproduction between close relatives would hopelessly confuse kinship ties and threaten the social order. Third, forcing people to marry beyond their immediate families integrates the larger society.

3. **Social placement.** Families are not needed for people to reproduce, but they help maintain social organization.

APPLYING THEORY
FAMILY

	Structural-Functional Approach	Social-Conflict Approach	Symbolic-Interaction Approach
What is the level of analysis?	Macro-level	Macro-level	Micro-level
What is the importance of the family for society?	The family performs vital tasks, including socializing the young and providing emotional and financial support for members. The family helps regulate sexual activity.	The family perpetuates social inequality by handing down wealth from one generation to the next. The family supports patriarchy as well as racial and ethnic inequality.	The reality of family life is constructed by members in their interaction. Courtship typically brings together people who offer the same level of advantages.

Parents pass on their own social identity—in terms of race, ethnicity, religion, and social class—to children at birth.

4. **Material and emotional security.** Many view the family as a "haven in a heartless world," offering physical protection, emotional support, and financial assistance. In support of this view, people living in families tend to be healthier than people living alone.

Critical review. Structural-functional analysis explains why society, at least as we know it, is built on families. But this approach glosses over the diversity of U.S. family life and ignores how other social institutions (such as government) could meet at least some of the same human needs. Finally, structural-functionalism overlooks the negative aspects of family life, including patriarchy and family violence.

INEQUALITY AND THE FAMILY: SOCIAL-CONFLICT ANALYSIS

Like the structural-functional approach, the social-conflict approach considers the family central to our way of life. But instead of focusing on ways in which kinship benefits society, conflict theorists point out how the family perpetuates social inequality.

1. **Property and inheritance.** Friedrich Engels (1902, orig. 1884) traced the origin of the family to men's need (especially in the higher classes) to identify heirs so that they could hand down property to their sons. Families thus concentrate wealth and reproduce the class structure in each new generation (Mare, 1991).
2. **Patriarchy.** To know their heirs, men must control the sexuality of women. Families therefore transform women into the sexual and economic property of men. A century ago in the United States, most wives' earnings belonged to their husbands. Today, women still bear most of the responsibility for child rearing and housework (Benokraitis & Feagin, 1995; Stapinski, 1998; England, 2001).
3. **Race and ethnicity.** Racial and ethnic categories persist over generations only to the degree that people marry others like themselves. Endogamous marriage supports racial and ethnic hierarchies.

Critical review. Social-conflict analysis shows another side of family life: its role in social stratification. Friedrich Engels criticized the family as part and parcel of capitalism. But noncapitalist societies also have families (and family problems). The family may be linked to social inequality, as Engels argued, but it carries out societal functions not easily accomplished by other means.

CONSTRUCTING FAMILY LIFE: MICRO-LEVEL ANALYSIS

Both the structural-functional and social-conflict approaches view the family as a structural system. By contrast, micro-level analysis explores how individuals shape and experience family life.

The symbolic-interaction approach. Ideally, family living offers an opportunity for *intimacy,* a word with Latin roots that mean "sharing fear." As family members share many activities over time, they build emotional bonds. Of course, the fact that parents act as authority figures often limits their closeness with younger children. Only as young people reach adulthood do kinship ties open up to include sharing confidences as well as turning to one another for help with daily tasks and responsibilities (Macionis, 1978).

People in every society recognize the reality of physical attraction. But the power of romantic love, captured in Christian Pierre's painting, *I Do,* holds surprisingly little importance in traditional societies. In much of the world, it would be less correct to say that individuals marry individuals and more true to say that families marry families. In other words, parents arrange marriages for their children with an eye to the social position of the kin groups involved.

The social-exchange approach. Social-exchange analysis, another micro-level approach, describes courtship and marriage as forms of negotiation (Blau, 1964). Dating allows each person to assess the advantages and disadvantages of a potential spouse. In essence, exchange analysts suggest, people "shop around" to make the best "deal" they can in a partner in light of what they have to offer.

In patriarchal societies, gender roles dictate the elements of exchange: Men bring wealth and power to the marriage marketplace, and women bring beauty. The importance of beauty explains women's traditional concern with their appearance and sensitivity about revealing their age. But as women have joined the labor force and have become less dependent on men to support them, the terms of exchange are becoming more similar for men and women.

Critical review. Micro-level analysis offers a useful balance to structural-functional and social-conflict visions of the family as an institutional system. Both the symbolic-interaction and social-exchange approaches focus on the individual experience of family life. However, micro-level analysis misses the bigger picture: Family life is similar for people in the same social and economic categories. The Applying Theory table summarizes what we learn from the three theoretical approaches to family life.

U.S. families vary in some predictable ways according to social class and ethnicity, and as the next section explains, they typically evolve through distinct stages linked to the life course.

Stages of Family Life

Members of our society recognize several distinct stages of family life across the life course.

COURTSHIP AND ROMANTIC LOVE

November 2, Kandy, Sri Lanka. Winding through the rain forest of this beautiful island, our van driver, Harry, recounts how he met his wife. Actually, it was more of an arrangement: The two families were Buddhist and of the same caste. "We got along well, right from the start," recalls Harry. "We had the same background. I suppose she or I could have said no. But 'love marriages' happen in the city, not in the village where I grew up."

In rural Sri Lanka, as in preindustrial societies throughout the world, most people consider courtship too important to be left to the young (Stone, 1977). *Arranged marriages* are alliances between two extended families of similar social standing and usually involve an exchange not just of children but also of wealth and favors. Romantic love has little to do with arranged marriages, and parents may make such arrangements when their children are very young. A century ago in Sri Lanka and India, half of all girls married before age fifteen (Mayo, 1927; Mace & Mace, 1960). As the Global Sociology box on page 352 explains, in some parts of rural India, child marriage is still found today.

GLOBAL SOCIOLOGY

Early to Wed: A Report from Rural India

Sumitra Jogi cries as her wedding is about to begin. Are they tears of joy? Not exactly. This "bride" is an eleven-month-old squirming in the arms of her mother. The groom? A boy of six.

In a remote village in India's western state of Rajasthan, the two families gather at midnight to celebrate a traditional wedding ritual. It is May 2, in Hindu tradition an especially good day to marry. Sumitra's father smiles as the ceremony begins; her mother cradles the infant, who has fallen asleep. The groom, wearing a special costume and a red and gold turban on his head, gently reaches up and grasps the baby's hand. Then, as the ceremony ends, the young boy leads the child and mother around the wedding fire three-and-one-half times while the audience beams at the couple's first steps together as husband and wife.

Child weddings are illegal in India, but traditions are strong in rural regions, and marriage laws are hard to enforce. As a result, thousands of children marry each year. "In rural Rajasthan," explains one social worker, "all the girls are married by age fourteen. These are poor, illiterate families, and they don't want to keep girls past their first menstrual cycle."

For a time, Sumitra Jogi will remain with her parents. But in eight or ten years, a second ceremony will send her to live with her husband's family, and her married life will begin.

If the reality of marriage is years in the future, why do families push their children to marry at such an early age? Parents of girls know that the younger the bride, the smaller the dowry offered to the groom's family. Also, when girls marry this young, there is no question about their virginity, which raises their value on the marriage market. No one in these situations thinks about love or the fact that the children are too young to understand what is taking place.

WHAT DO YOU THINK?

1. In traditional societies, why do parents arrange the marriages of their children?
2. What are some advantages and disadvantages of arranged marriages?
3. Can you point to specific social considerations that guide mate selection in the United States?

Source: Based on Anderson (1995).

Industrialization both erodes the importance of extended families and weakens traditions. Young people who choose their own mates delay marriage until they gain the experience needed to select a suitable partner. Dating sharpens courtship skills and allows sexual experimentation.

Our culture celebrates *romantic love*—affection and sexual passion toward another person—as the basis for marriage. We find it hard to imagine marriage without love, and our popular culture, from fairy tales such as "Cinderella" to today's paperback romance novels, portrays love as the key to a successful marriage. However, as Figure 13–1 shows, in many countries, romantic love plays a much smaller role in marriage.

Our society's emphasis on romantic love motivates young people to "leave the nest" to form families of their own; physical passion may also help a new couple through difficult adjustments in living together (Goode, 1959). On

 Check out how people use the Internet to find partners at http://www.loveme.com

the other hand, because feelings change over time, romantic love is a less stable foundation for marriage than social and economic considerations, one reason that the divorce rate is much higher in the United States than in nations where culture limits choices in partners.

But even in our country, sociologists point out, society aims Cupid's arrow more than we like to think. Most people fall in love with others of the same race, of comparable age, and of similar social class. Our society "arranges" marriages by encouraging **homogamy** (literally, "like marrying like"), *marriage between people with the same social characteristics.*

SETTLING IN: IDEAL AND REAL MARRIAGE

Our culture gives young people an idealized, "happily ever after" picture of marriage. Such optimism can lead to disappointment, especially for women, who are taught that marriage is the key to happiness. Also, romantic love involves a lot of fantasy: We fall in love with others not always as they are but as we want them to be.

Sexuality, too, can be a source of disappointment. In the romantic haze of falling in love, people may see marriage as an endless sexual honeymoon only to realize that sex becomes less than an all-consuming passion. Although the frequency of marital sex does decline over time, about two in three married people report that they are satisfied with the sexual dimension of their relationship. In general, couples with the best sexual relationships experience the most satisfaction in their marriages. Sex may not be the key to marital happiness, but good sex and good relationships often go together (Blumstein & Schwartz, 1983; Laumann et al., 1994).

Infidelity—sexual activity outside marriage—is another area where the reality of marriage does not match our cultural ideal. In a recent survey, 92 percent of U.S. adults said sex outside of marriage is "always wrong" or "almost always wrong." Even so, 21 percent of men and 13 percent of women indicated (in a private, written questionnaire) that they had been sexually unfaithful to their partners at least once (NORC, 2003:234, 1227).

CHILD REARING

Despite the demands children make on us, U.S. adults overwhelmingly identify raising children as one of life's great joys (NORC, 2003:1071). However, as Table 13–1 on page 354 shows, few people today want more than three children. Two centuries ago, *eight* children was the U.S. average.

Big families pay off in preindustrial societies because children supply needed labor. Thus, people regard having children as a wife's duty, and in the absence of effective birth control, childbearing is a regular event. Of course, a high death rate in preindustrial societies prevents many children from reaching adulthood; as late as 1900, one-third of children in the United States died by age ten.

Industrialization transforms children—economically speaking—from an asset to a liability. It now costs more than $200,000 to raise one child, including college tuition (Lino, 2004). No wonder the U.S. average steadily dropped during the twentieth century to one child per family today.[2]

---

[2]According to the U.S. Census Bureau, the mean number of children per family was 0.87 in 2003. For non-Hispanic white families, the mean was 0.79; for African Americans, 1.05; and for Hispanics, 1.18.

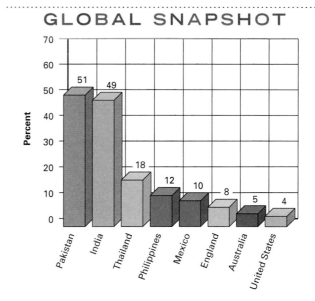

GLOBAL SNAPSHOT

FIGURE 13–1   Percentage of College Students Who Express a Willingness to Marry without Romantic Love

Source: Levine (1993).

The trend toward smaller families is most pronounced in high-income nations. The picture differs in lower-income countries in Latin America, Asia, and especially Africa, where many women have few alternatives to bearing children. In such societies, as a glance back at Global Map 1–1 on page 3 shows, four to six children is still the norm.

Parenting is a very expensive, long-term commitment. As our society has given people greater choice about family life, more U.S. adults have decided to delay childbirth or to remain childless. In 1960, almost 90 percent of women between the ages of twenty-five and twenty-nine who had ever married had at least one child; today, this proportion is just 69 percent (U.S. Census Bureau, 2003).

About two-thirds of parents in the United States claim they would like to devote more of their time to child rearing (Snell, 1990; Clark, 2002). But unless we accept a lower standard of living, the need for income demands that most parents pursue careers outside the home, even if that means giving less attention to their families.

Children of working parents spend most of the day at school. But after school, about 3.3 million youngsters (15 percent of six- to twelve-year-olds) are *latchkey kids* who fend for themselves (Vandivere et al., 2003). Traditionalists in the "family values" debate charge that many mothers work

TABLE 13-1

The Ideal Number of Children for U.S. Adults, 2002

Number of Children	Proportion of Respondents
0	1.4%
1	3.2
2	49.2
3	24.6
4	8.9
5	1.8
6 or more	0.7
"As many as you want"	8.7
No response	1.5

Source: *General Social Surveys, 1972–2002: Cumulative Codebook* (Chicago: National Opinion Research Center, 2003), p. 230.

at the expense of their children, who receive less parenting. Progressives reply that such criticism unfairly blames women for wanting the same opportunities men have long enjoyed.

Congress took a small step toward easing the conflict between family and job responsibilities by passing the Family and Medical Leave Act in 1993. This law allows up to ninety days' unpaid leave from work for a new child or a serious family emergency. But it has not put an end to the need to juggle parental and job responsibilities. When mothers work, who cares for the kids? More than half of children under age five receive care from a parent (27 percent) or a relative (26 percent). The remaining 47 percent of young children are cared for by a nonrelative: 29 percent attend day care or preschool, 13 percent are cared for in a nonrelative's home, and 5 percent are cared for in their own home by a nanny or babysitter (Urban Institute, 2004).

 A report on the quality of child care given by relatives can be found at http://www.urban.org/url.cfm?ID=310270

THE FAMILY IN LATER LIFE

Increasing life expectancy in the United States means that couples who stay married do so for a long time. By age sixty, most have completed the task of raising children. At this point, marriage brings a return to living with only a spouse.

Like the birth of children, their departure—the "empty nest"—requires adjustments, although a marriage often becomes closer and more satisfying. Years of living together may have lessened a couple's sexual passion, but understanding and commitment often increase.

Personal contact with children usually continues because most older adults live a short distance from at least one of their grown children. One-third of all U.S. adults (60 million) are grandparents, many of whom help with child care and other responsibilities. Among African Americans (who have a high rate of single parenting), grandmothers have an especially important position in family life (Clemetson, 2000; U.S. Census Bureau, 2003).

The other side of the coin is that adults in midlife now provide more care for aging parents. The "empty nest" may not be filled by a parent coming to live in the home, but many adults find that caring for parents living to eighty and beyond can be more taxing than raising young children. The oldest of the "baby boomers"—now sixty—are called the "sandwich generation" because many (especially women) will spend as many years caring for their aging parents as they did caring for their children (Lund, 1993).

The final, and surely the most difficult, transition in married life comes with the death of a spouse. Wives typically outlive husbands because of their greater life expectancy and the fact that women usually marry men several years older. Wives can thus expect to spend some years as widows. The challenge of living alone after the death of a spouse is especially great for men, who usually have fewer friends than widows and may lack housekeeping skills.

U.S. Families: Class, Race, and Gender

Dimensions of inequality—social class, ethnicity, race, and gender—are powerful forces that shape marriage and family life. This discussion addresses each of these factors in turn, but bear in mind that they overlap in our lives.

SOCIAL CLASS

Social class determines a family's financial security and range of opportunities. Interviewing working-class women, Lillian Rubin (1976) found that wives thought a good husband was a man who held a steady job, did not drink too much, and was not violent. Rubin's middle-class respondents, by contrast, never mentioned such things; these women simply *assumed* that a husband would provide a safe and secure home. Their ideal husband was a man with whom they could communicate easily and share feelings and experiences.

Clearly, what women (and men) hope for in marriage—and what they end up with—is linked to their social class. Much the same holds for children: Boys and girls lucky enough to be born into more affluent families enjoy better mental and physical health, develop more self-confidence,

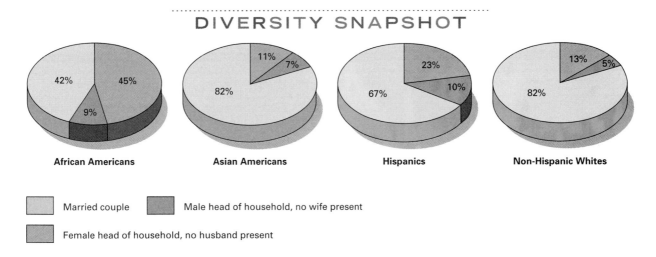

DIVERSITY SNAPSHOT

African Americans

Asian Americans

Hispanics

Non-Hispanic Whites

- Married couple
- Male head of household, no wife present
- Female head of household, no husband present

FIGURE 13-2 Family Form in the United States, 2003

Source: U.S. Census Bureau (2004).

and go on to greater achievement than children born to poor parents (McLeod & Shanahan, 1993; Duncan et al., 1998).

ETHNICITY AND RACE

Although ethnicity and race also shape families, American Indian, Latino, and African American families (like all families) do not fit any one stereotype (Allen, 1995).

American Indian families. People who migrate from tribal reservations to cities often seek out others—especially kin and members of the same tribe—for help in getting settled. One recent study tells the story of two women migrants to the San Francisco area who met at a meeting of an Indian organization and realized they were of the same tribe. The women and their children decided to share an apartment, and soon after, the children began to refer to one another as brothers, sisters, and cousins. As the months passed, the two mothers came to think of themselves as sisters (Lobo, 2002).

Migration also creates "fluid households" with changing membership. In another case from this same study, a woman, her aunt, and their children rented a large apartment in San Francisco. Over the course of several months, they welcomed into their home more than thirty other urban migrants, each of whom stayed for a short time while looking for housing of their own. Such patterns of mutual assistance, involving real or fictional kinship, are common among low-income people (Lobo, 2002).

Latino families. Many Latinos enjoy the loyalty and support of extended families. Traditionally, Hispanic parents exercise greater control over children's courtship, considering marriage an alliance of families and not just a bond based on romantic love. Some Hispanic families also follow conventional gender roles, prizing *machismo*—strength, daring, and sexual conquest—among men and treating women with respect but also close supervision.

Assimilation into the larger society is changing these traditional patterns. For example, many Puerto Ricans who migrate to New York lose their ties to the strong extended families they knew in Puerto Rico. Traditional male authority over women has also lessened, especially among wealthy Latino families, whose number has tripled in the past twenty years (O'Hare, 1990; Lach, 1999).

African American families. The U.S. Census Bureau reports that the typical African American family earned $34,369 in 2003, or 65 percent of the national average. People of African ancestry are three times as likely as non-Hispanic whites to be poor, and poverty means that families experience unemployment and underemployment and in some cases crime and drug abuse.

Under these circumstances, maintaining stable family ties is difficult. For example, 25 percent of African American women in their forties have never married, compared with about 10 percent of white women of the same age. This means that women of color—often with children—are more likely to be heads of households. Figure 13–2 shows that women headed 45 percent of African American

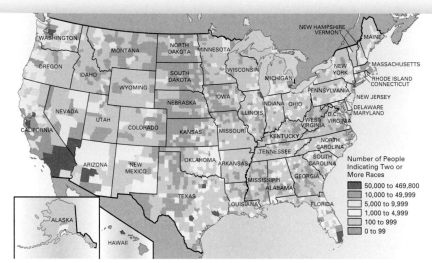

Racially Mixed People across the United States

Where are racially mixed marriages most common? No precise data of this kind are currently available, but the Census Bureau does publish the distribution of racially mixed people—those, presumably, who have parents of two different racial categories. This map shows the distribution of people who described themselves as racially mixed in the 2000 census. What can you say about where such people live and, thus, where racially mixed marriages are most common?

Source: U.S. Census Bureau (2001).

Number of People Indicating Two or More Races

- 50,000 to 469,800
- 10,000 to 49,999
- 5,000 to 9,999
- 1,000 to 4,999
- 100 to 999
- 0 to 99

families in 2003, compared with 23 percent of Hispanic families, 13 percent of non-Hispanic white families, and 11 percent of Asian and Pacific Islander families (U.S. Census Bureau, 2004).

Regardless of race, single-mother families are always at high risk of poverty. Twenty percent of U.S. families headed by non-Hispanic white women are poor. The higher poverty rate among families headed by African American women (37 percent) and Hispanic women (37 percent) is strong evidence of how the intersection of class, race, and gender can put women at a disadvantage. African American families with both wife and husband in the home, which represent almost half the total, are much stronger economically, earning 79 percent as much as comparable non-Hispanic white families. But 68 percent of African American children are born to single women, and 34 percent of African American boys and girls are growing up poor today, meaning that these families carry much of the burden of child poverty in the United States (Hogan & Kitagawa, 1985; Martin et al., 2003; U.S. Census Bureau, 2004).

Ethnically and racially mixed marriages. Most spouses have similar social backgrounds with regard to class, race, and ethnicity. But over the course of the twentieth century, ethnicity mattered less and less. A woman of German and French ancestry might readily marry a man of Irish and English background without disapproval from their families or from society in general.

Race has been a more powerful barrier. Before a 1967 Supreme Court decision (*Loving* v. *Virginia*), interracial marriage was illegal in sixteen states. Today, African, Asian, and Native Americans make up 17 percent of the U.S. population, so if people ignored race in choosing spouses, we would expect about the same share of marriages to be mixed. The actual proportion of mixed marriages is only 2.9 percent, showing that race still matters in social relations. Even so, most U.S. teens now claim they have dated someone of another race, and the number of racially mixed marriages is rising steadily.

Black-white marriages are most numerous, as the large African American population (12 percent of the U.S. total) would lead us to expect. In relation to population size, though, whites in racially mixed marriages are most likely to have partners of Asian ancestry (U.S. Census Bureau, 2001). National Map 13–1 shows the distribution of self-described multiracial people, one good indicator of the extent of racially mixed marriages.

GENDER

Jessie Bernard (1982, orig. 1973) says that every marriage is actually *two* different relationships: a woman's marriage and a man's marriage. The reason is that few marriages are composed of two equal partners. Although patriarchy has diminished, we still expect husbands to be older and taller than their wives and to have more important, better-paid careers.

Why, then, do many people think that marriage benefits women more than men? The positive stereotype of the carefree bachelor contrasts sharply with the negative image of the lonely spinster, suggesting that women are fulfilled only through being wives and mothers.

But according to Bernard, married women have poorer mental health, less happiness, and more passive attitudes toward life than single women do. Married men, on the other hand, generally live longer, are mentally better off, and report being happier than single men. These differences suggest why, after divorce, men are more eager than women to find a new partner.

Bernard concludes that there is no better assurance of long life, health, and happiness for a man than having a woman well socialized to devote her life to taking care of him and providing the security of a well-ordered home. She is quick to add that marriage *could* be healthful for women if husbands did not dominate wives and expect them to do almost all the housework.

Transitions and Problems in Family Life

The newspaper columnist Ann Landers once remarked that one marriage in twenty is wonderful, five in twenty are good, ten in twenty are tolerable, and the remaining four are "pure hell." Families can be a source of joy, but the reality of family life often falls short of the ideal.

DIVORCE

U.S. society strongly supports marriage, and about nine out of ten people at some point "tie the knot." But many of today's marriages unravel. Figure 13–3 shows the tenfold increase in the U.S. divorce rate over the past century. By 2003, almost four in ten marriages were ending in divorce (for African Americans, the rate was about six in ten). Ours is the highest divorce rate in the world: about one-and-one-half times as high as in Canada and Germany and nearly six times higher than in Italy (Japanese Ministry of Health, Labour, and Welfare, 2004).

Causes of divorce. The high U.S. divorce rate has many causes (Weitzman, 1985; Furstenberg & Cherlin, 1991; Etzioni, 1993; Popenoe, 1999; Greenspan, 2001):

1. **Individualism is on the rise.** Today's family members spend less time together. We have become more individualistic, more concerned with our own personal

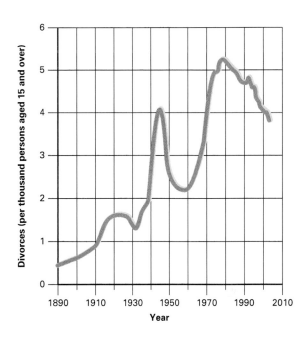

FIGURE 13-3 Divorce Rate for the United States, 1890–2003

Source: Munson & Sutton (2004).

happiness than with the well-being of our families and children.

2. **Romantic love often fades.** Because our culture bases marriage on romantic love, relationships may fail as sexual passion fades. Many people end a marriage in favor of a new relationship that promises renewed excitement and romance.

3. **Women are less dependent on men.** Women's increasing participation in the labor force has reduced wives' financial dependency on their husbands. Thus, women find it easier to leave unhappy marriages.

4. **Many of today's marriages are stressful.** With both partners working outside the home in most cases, jobs leave less time and energy for family life. This makes raising children harder than ever. Children do stabilize some marriages, but divorce is most common during the early years of marriage when many couples have young children.

5. **Divorce is socially acceptable.** Divorce no longer carries the powerful stigma it did a century ago. Family and friends are now less likely to discourage couples in conflict from divorcing.

Divorce may be a solution for a couple in an unhappy marriage, but it can be a problem for children who experience the withdrawal of a parent from their social world. In what ways can divorce be harmful to children? Is there a positive side to divorce? How might separating parents better prepare their children for the transition of parental divorce?

6. **Legally, a divorce is easier to get.** In the past, courts required divorcing couples to demonstrate that one or both were guilty of behavior such as adultery or physical abuse. Today, all states allow divorce if a couple simply thinks their marriage has failed. Concern about easy divorce, voiced by more than half of U.S. adults, has led some states to consider rewriting their marriage laws.

Who divorces? At greatest risk of divorce are young couples—especially those who marry after a brief courtship, have little money, and have yet to mature emotionally. The chance of divorce also rises if a couple marries after an unexpected pregnancy or if one or both partners have substance abuse problems. People whose parents divorced also have a higher divorce rate themselves. Researchers suggest a role-modeling effect: Children who see parents go through divorce are more likely to consider divorce themselves

(Amato, 2001). Finally, people who are not religious are more likely to divorce than those who have strong religious beliefs.

Divorce is also more common if both partners have successful careers, perhaps because of the strains of a two-career marriage but also because financially secure people may not feel they have to stay in an unhappy home. Finally, men and women who divorce once are more likely to divorce again, probably because high-risk factors follow them from one marriage to another (Glenn & Shelton, 1985).

Because mothers usually gain custody of children but fathers typically earn more income, the well-being of many children depends on fathers making court-ordered child support payments. Courts award child support in 59 percent of all divorces involving children. Yet in any given year, half of children legally entitled to support receive partial payments or no payments at all. Some 3.4 million "deadbeat dads" fail to support their youngsters. In response, federal legislation now requires employers to withhold money from the earnings of parents who fail to pay up, and in 1998, refusal to make child support payments or moving to another state to avoid making such payments became a felony (U.S. Census Bureau, 2003).

REMARRIAGE

Four out of five people who divorce remarry, most within five years. Nationwide, about half of all marriages are now remarriages for at least one partner. Men, who benefit more from wedlock, are more likely than women to remarry.

 Learn more about remarriage and other family issues at http://www.cdc.gov/nchs/data/series/sr_23/sr23_022.pdf

Remarriage often creates *blended families,* composed of children and some combination of biological parents and stepparents. Members of blended families thus have to define precisely who is part of the nuclear family. Adjustments are necessary; for example, a former "only child" may suddenly find that she now has two older brothers. At the same time, blended families offer both young and old the chance to relax rigid family roles.

FAMILY VIOLENCE

The ideal family is a source of pleasure and support. However, the disturbing reality of many homes is *family violence,* emotional, physical, or sexual abuse of one family member by another. The sociologist Richard J. Gelles calls the family "the most violent group in society with the exception of the police and the military" (quoted in Roesch, 1984:75).

Violence against women. Family brutality often goes unreported to police. Even so, the U.S. Bureau of Justice Statistics (2003) estimates that about 700,000 people are victims of domestic violence each year. Of this total, 85 percent of cases involve violence against women, and the remaining 15 percent involve violence against men. Fully 33 percent of women who are victims of homicide (but just 4 percent of men) are killed by spouses or, more often, ex-spouses. Nationwide, the death toll from family violence is about 1,247 women each year. Overall, women are more likely to be injured by a family member than to be mugged or raped by a stranger or hurt in an automobile accident (Shupe, Stacey, & Hazlewood, 1987; Blankenhorn, 1995).

Historically, the law defined wives as the property of their husbands, so no man could be charged with raping his wife. Today, however, all fifty states have *marital rape laws*. The law no longer regards domestic violence as a private, family matter and thus gives victims more options. Now, even without separation or divorce, a woman can obtain court protection from an abusive spouse, and all states have stalking laws that prohibit an ex-partner from following or otherwise threatening the former partner. Finally, communities across North America have established shelters to provide counseling and temporary housing for women and children driven from their homes by domestic violence.

Violence against children. Family violence also victimizes children. Each year, there are roughly 3 million reports of alleged child abuse or neglect, with about 1,400 of them involving a child's death. Child abuse involves more than physical injury; abusive adults can also misuse power and trust to damage a child's emotional well-being. Child abuse and neglect are most common among the youngest and most vulnerable children (Van Biema, 1994; Besharov & Laumann, 1996).

Learn more about child abuse at http://www.nncc.org

Although child abusers conform to no simple stereotype, they are more likely to be women (58 percent) than men (42 percent). But almost all abusers share one trait: having been abused themselves as children. Researchers have found that violent behavior in close relationships is learned; in families, violence begets violence (Browning & Laumann, 1997; Levine, 2001; National Clearinghouse on Child Abuse and Neglect Information, 2004).

Alternative Family Forms

Most families in the United States are still composed of a married couple who raise children. But in recent decades, our society has displayed increasing diversity in family life.

ONE-PARENT FAMILIES

Thirty-two percent of U.S. families with children under eighteen have only one parent in the household, a proportion that more than doubled during the past generation. Put another way, 28 percent of U.S. children now live with only one parent, and about half will do so before reaching eighteen. One-parent families, 82 percent of which are headed by a single mother, result from divorce, death, or an unmarried person's decision to have a child.

Single parenthood increases a woman's risk of poverty because it limits her ability to work and to further her education. The opposite is also true: Poverty raises the odds that a woman will become a single mother (Trent, 1994). But single parenthood goes well beyond the poor: One-third of women in the United States become pregnant as teenagers, and many decide to raise their children whether they marry or not. Looking back at Figure 13–2, note that 54 percent of African American families are headed by a single parent. Single parenthood is less common among Hispanics (33 percent), Asian Americans (18 percent), and non-Hispanic whites (18 percent). In many single-parent families, mothers turn to their own mothers for support. In the United States, then, the rise in single parenting is tied to a declining role for fathers and the growing importance of grandparenting.

Research indicates that growing up in a one-parent family usually disadvantages children. Some studies claim that because a father and a mother each make a distinctive contribution to a child's social development, it is unrealistic to expect a single parent to do as good a job. But the most serious problem for one-parent families, especially if that parent is a woman, is poverty. On average, children growing up in a single-parent family start out poorer, get less schooling, and end up with lower incomes as adults. Such children are also more likely to be single parents themselves (Popenoe, 1993a; Shapiro & Schrof, 1995; Webster, Orbuch, & House, 1995; Wu, 1996; Duncan et al., 1998; Kantrowitz & Wingert, 2001; McLanahan, 2002).

COHABITATION

Cohabitation is *the sharing of a household by an unmarried couple.* The number of cohabiting couples in the United States has increased from about 500,000 in 1970 to about 5.5 million today (almost 5 million heterosexual couples and 600,000 homosexual couples), or about 9 percent of all couples (U.S. Census Bureau, 2003).

In global perspective, cohabitation as a long-term form of family life, with or without children, is common in Sweden and other Scandinavian countries, but it is rare in more traditional (especially Roman Catholic) nations such as Italy. Cohabitation is gaining in popularity in the United

In recent years, the proportion of young people who cohabit—that is, live together without being married—has risen sharply. This trend contributes to the debate over what is and is not a family: Do you consider a cohabiting couple a family? Why or why not?

States, with almost half of people between twenty-five and forty-four years of age having cohabited at some point.

Cohabiting tends to appeal more to independent-minded people and those who favor gender equity (Brines & Joyner, 1999). Most couples cohabit for no more than a few years, with about half deciding to marry and half splitting up. Mounting evidence suggests that living together may actually discourage marriage because partners (especially men) become used to low-commitment relationships. For this reason, cohabiting couples who have children (currently representing one-eighth of all births) are not always long-term parents. Figure 13–4 shows that just 5 percent of children born to cohabiting couples will live until age eighteen with both biological parents, if the parents remain unmarried. The share rises to 36 percent among children whose parents marry at some point, but this is still half of the 70 percent

figure for children whose parents married before they were born. When cohabiting couples with children separate, the involvement of both parents, including financial support, is far from certain (Popenoe & Whitehead, 1999; Smock, 2000; Phillips, 2001; Scommegna, 2002).

GAY AND LESBIAN COUPLES

In 1989, Denmark became the first country to permit lawful homosexual marriages. This change extended social legitimacy to gay and lesbian couples and equalized advantages in inheritance, taxation, and joint property ownership. The Netherlands (2001), Belgium (2003), and Canada (2003) have followed suit. Fifteen other European countries now recognize gay civil partnerships (Knox, 2004).

Change came more slowly to the United States, where several states (Vermont and Hawaii), as well as a number of major cities (including San Francisco and New York), passed laws providing limited marital benefits for gay and lesbian couples. Still, the U.S. Congress passed a law in 1996 defining marriage as joining one man and one woman, and until 2004, gay marriage remained illegal in all fifty states.

Then the pace of change greatly increased. In 2004, the Supreme Court of Massachusetts ruled that gay couples had a right to marry, and legal marriages began in May of that year (subject to possible new legislation in the future). The Massachusetts court decision prompted officials in San Francisco and a number of other U.S. cities to perform thousands of marriages for gay couples, despite state laws that banned such unions. Courts are currently deciding whether these marriages will remain legal. In the November, 2004, elections, however, voters in eleven states passed ballot measures changing their state constitutions to recognize only marriages between one man and one woman.

Most gay couples with children in the United States are raising the offspring of previous, heterosexual unions; some couples have adopted children. But many gay parents are quiet about their sexual orientation, not wanting to draw unwelcome attention to their children or to themselves. In several widely publicized cases, courts have removed children from the custody of homosexual couples, citing the "best interests" of the children.

Gay parenting challenges many traditional ideas. But it also indicates that many gay and lesbian couples want to form families just as heterosexuals do.

SINGLEHOOD

Because nine out of ten people in the United States marry, we tend to see singlehood as a temporary stage of life. However, increasing numbers of people are choosing to live alone. In 1950, only one household in ten contained a single person. By 2003, this proportion had risen to one in four, a total of 52 million single adults (U.S. Census Bureau, 2004).

Most striking is the rising share of single young women. In 1960, some 28 percent of women aged twenty to twenty-four were single; by 2003, the proportion had soared to 75 percent. Underlying this trend is women's greater participation in the labor force. Women who are economically secure view a husband as a matter of choice rather than a financial necessity (Edwards, 2000).

By midlife, many unmarried women sense a lack of available men. Because our society expects women to "marry up," the older a woman is, the more education she has, and the better her job, the more difficulty she will have finding a suitable husband.

NEW REPRODUCTIVE TECHNOLOGY

Recent medical advances involving new reproductive technology are also changing families. A generation ago, England's Louise Brown became the world's first "test-tube baby"; since then, tens of thousands of children have been conceived this way. A decade from now, 2 or 3 percent of births in high-income nations may result from new reproductive technologies.

Test-tube babies are the product of *in vitro fertilization,* in which doctors unite a woman's egg and a man's sperm "in glass" (usually not a test tube but a shallow dish) rather than in a woman's body. Doctors then either implant the resulting embryo in the womb of the woman who is to bear the child or freeze it for use at a later time.

At present, new reproductive technologies help some couples who cannot conceive normally have children. Looking ahead, these techniques may also help reduce the incidence of birth defects. Genetic screening of sperm and eggs would allow medical specialists to increase the odds for the birth of a healthy baby. But new reproductive technology raises fascinating and troubling questions: When one woman carries an embryo developed from the egg of another, who is the mother? When a couple divorces, which spouse is entitled to use the frozen embryos? Can one partner have a child years later against the will of the other? Such questions remind us that technology changes faster than our capacity to understand the consequences of its use (Cohen, 1998; Nock, Wright, & Sanchez, 1999).

LOOKING AHEAD: THE FAMILY IN THE TWENTY-FIRST CENTURY

Without a doubt, family life in the United States will continue to change in years to come, and change often causes

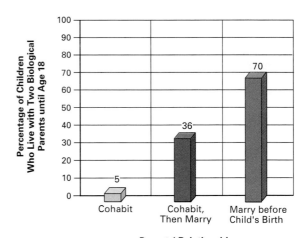

FIGURE 13-4 Parental Involvement in Children's Lives: Cohabiting and Married Parents

Source: Phillips (2001).

controversy. Advocates of "traditional family values" line up against those who support greater personal choice; the Critical Thinking box on pages 362–63 outlines some of the issues. Sociologists cannot predict the outcome of this debate, but we can suggest five likely future trends.

First, the divorce rate is likely to remain high, even in the face of evidence that marital breakups harm children. Today's marriages are about as durable as they were a century ago, when many were cut short by death. The difference is that now more couples *choose* to end marriages that fail to meet their expectations. Although the divorce rate declined slightly in the 1990s, it is unlikely that we will ever return to the low rates that marked the early decades of the twentieth century.

Second, family life in the future will be more diverse than ever. Cohabiting couples, one-parent families, gay and lesbian families, and blended families are all on the increase. Most families are still based on marriage, and most married couples still have children. But the diversity of family forms implies a trend toward more personal choice.

Third, men will play a limited role in child rearing. In the 1950s, a decade many people consider the "golden age" of families, men began to withdraw from active parenting (Snell, 1990; Stacey, 1990). In recent years, a countertrend has become evident, with some older, highly educated fathers staying at home with young

You can visit a Web site for stay-at-home fathers at http://www.slowlane.com

CRITICAL THINKING
Should We Save the Traditional Family?

What are "traditional families"? Are they vital to our way of life or a barrier to progress? People use the term "traditional family" to mean a married couple who, at some point in their lives, raise children. Statistically speaking, traditional families are less common than they used to be. In 1950, as the figure shows, 90 percent of U.S. households were families: two or more people related by blood, marriage, or adoption. By 2003, just 68 percent of households were families because of rising levels of divorce, cohabitation, and singlehood.

Of course, "traditional family" is more than just a term; it is also a moral statement. Support for the traditional family implies giving high value to becoming and remaining married, placing children ahead of careers, and favoring two-parent families over various "alternative lifestyles."

On one side of the debate, David Popenoe warns of the decline of the traditional family since 1960. Back then, married couples with children accounted for almost half of all households; today, the figure is 23 percent.

Singlehood is up, from 10 percent of households in 1960 to 26 percent now. And the divorce rate has risen by 60 percent since 1960, so that four in ten of today's marriages end in permanent separation. Moreover, because of both divorce and children born to single women, the share of youngsters who

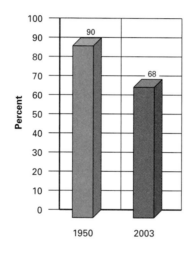

Share of U.S. Households That the Census Bureau Classifies as Families, 1950 and 2003

will live with just one parent before age eighteen has quadrupled since 1960 to 50 percent. In other words, just one in four of today's children will grow up with two parents and go on to maintain a stable marriage as an adult.

In light of such data, Popenoe concludes that the family is falling apart. He sees a fundamental shift from a "culture of marriage" to a "culture of divorce," where traditional vows of marital commitment—"'til death us do part"—now amount to little more than "as long as I am happy." Drawing on national survey data, Daniel Yankelovich (1994:20) sums it up this way:

> The quest for greater individual choice clashed directly with the obligations and social norms that held families and communities together in earlier years. People came to feel that questions of how to live and with whom to live were a matter of individual choice not to be governed by restrictive norms. As a nation, we came to experience the bonds to marriage, family, children, job, community, and country as constraints that

children, many using computer technology to continue their work. But the stay-at-home dad represents no more than 10 percent of fathers with young children (Gardner, 1996; U.S. Census Bureau, 2003). The bigger picture is that the high divorce rate in the United States and the increase in single motherhood are weakening children's ties to fathers and increasing children's risk of poverty.

Fourth, families will continue to feel the effects of economic change. In many homes, both household partners work, reducing marriage and family to the interaction of weary men and women trying to fit a little "quality time" with their children into an already full schedule. The long-term

effects of the two-career couple on families as we have known them are likely to be mixed.

Fifth and finally, the importance of new reproductive technology will increase. Ethical concerns about whether what *can* be done *should* be done will surely slow these developments, but new reproductive technology will continue to alter the traditional meaning of parenthood.

Despite the changes and controversies that have shaken the family in the United States, most people still report being happy as partners and parents. Marriage and family life will likely remain a foundation of our society for some time to come.

were no longer necessary. Commitments have loosened.

The negative consequences of the cultural trend toward weaker families, Popenoe continues, are obvious everywhere: As we pay less and less attention to children, the crime rate goes up along with a host of other problem behaviors, including underage smoking and drinking and premarital sex.

As Popenoe sees it, we must work hard and quickly to reverse current trends. Government cannot be the solution and may even be part of the problem: Since 1960, as families have weakened, government spending on social programs has soared fivefold. To save the traditional family, says Popenoe, we need a cultural turnaround, similar to what has happened with regard to cigarette smoking. In this case, we must replace our "me first" attitudes in favor of commitment to spouses and children and publicly endorse the two-parent family as best for the well-being of children.

But Judith Stacey provides a different viewpoint, saying "good riddance" to the traditional family (1993). In her view, the traditional family is more problem than solution (1990:269):

The family is not here to stay. Nor should we wish it were. On the contrary, I believe that all democratic people, whatever their kinship preferences, should work to hasten its demise.

The main reason for rejecting the traditional family, Stacey explains, is that it perpetuates social inequality. Families play a key role in maintaining the class hierarchy by transferring wealth as well as "cultural capital" from one generation to another. Feminists criticize the traditional family's patriarchal form, which subjects women to their husbands' authority and expects them to take most of the responsibility for housework and child care. From a gay rights perspective, Stacey adds, a society that values traditional families also denies homosexual men and women equal participation in social life.

Stacey thus applauds the breakdown of the traditional family as a measure of social progress. She does not consider the family a basic social institution but a political construction that elevates one category of people—affluent white men—at the expense of women, homosexuals, and poor people.

Stacey also claims that the concept of "traditional family" is increasingly irrelevant in a diverse society in which both men and women work for income. What our society needs, she concludes, is not a return to some golden age of the family but political and economic change, including income equality for women, universal health care, programs to reduce unemployment, and expanded sex education in the schools. Such measures not only help families but also ensure that people in diverse family forms receive the respect and dignity they deserve.

WHAT DO YOU THINK?

1. To strengthen families, Popenoe suggests that parents put children ahead of their own careers by limiting their joint workweek to sixty hours. Do you agree? Why or why not?
2. Judith Stacey thinks that marriage is weaker today because women are rejecting patriarchal relationships. What do you think about this argument?
3. Do we need to change family patterns for the well-being of our children? As you see it, what specific changes are called for?

Sources: Stacey (1990, 1993), Popenoe (1993a), Council on Families in America (1995), Sawhill (2002), and U.S. Census Bureau (2003, 2004).

Religion: Basic Concepts

Like the family, religion has played a central part in the drama of human history. Families have long used religious rituals to celebrate birth, recognize adulthood, and mourn the dead.

The French sociologist Emile Durkheim said religion involves "things that surpass the limits of our knowledge" (1965:62, orig. 1915). As human beings, we define most objects, events, and experiences as **profane** (from Latin, meaning "outside the temple"), *an ordinary element of everyday life.* But we also consider some things **sacred,** *set apart as extraordinary, inspiring awe and reverence.* Setting the sacred apart from the profane is the essence of all religious belief. **Religion,** then, is *a social institution involving beliefs and practices based on a conception of the sacred.*

A global perspective shows great variety in matters of faith, with no one thing sacred to everyone on Earth. Although people regard most books as profane, Jews believe the Torah (the first five books of the Hebrew Bible or the Old Testament) is sacred, in the same way that Christians revere the Old and New Testaments of the Bible and Muslims exalt the Qur'an (Koran).

But no matter how a community of believers draws religious lines, Durkheim (1965:62, orig. 1915) explained, people

Religion is founded on the concept of the sacred: that which is set apart as extraordinary and which demands our submission. Bowing, kneeling, or prostrating oneself are all ways of symbolically surrendering to a higher power. This monk is performing an act of prostration circumambulation, a complicated way of saying that he falls flat on the ground every few steps as he moves around a holy shrine. In this way, he expresses his complete surrender to his faith.

understand profane things in terms of everyday usefulness: We log on to the Internet with our computer or turn a key to start our car. What is sacred we reverently set apart from daily life, giving it a "forbidden" aura. For example, Muslims remove their shoes before entering a mosque to avoid defiling a sacred place with soles that have touched the profane ground outside.

The sacred is embodied in *ritual,* or formal ceremonial behavior. Holy Communion is the central ritual of Christianity; to the Christian faithful, the wafer and wine consumed during Communion are never treated in a profane way as food but as the sacred symbols of the body and blood of Jesus Christ.

Because religion deals with ideas that transcend everyday experience, neither common sense nor sociology can prove or disprove religious doctrine. Religion is a matter of **faith,** *belief based on conviction rather than scientific evidence.* The New Testament of the Bible defines faith as "the conviction of things not seen" (Hebrews 11:1) and urges Christians to "walk by faith, not by sight" (2 Corinthians 5:7).

Some people with strong religious beliefs may be disturbed by the thought of sociologists turning a scientific eye on what they hold sacred. However, sociological study is no threat to anyone's faith. Sociologists study religion just as they study the family, to understand religious experiences around the world and how religion is tied to other social institutions. They make no judgments about whether a specific religion is "right" or "wrong." Sociological analysis takes a more worldly approach, seeking to understand why religion takes a particular form in one society or another and how religious activity affects society as a whole.

Theoretical Analysis of Religion

Sociologists have applied the theoretical approaches to the study of religion. Each provides distinctive insights about religious life.

FUNCTIONS OF RELIGION: STRUCTURAL-FUNCTIONAL ANALYSIS

According to Emile Durkheim (1965, orig. 1915), society has a life and power of its own beyond the life of any individual. In other words, society itself is godlike, shaping the lives of its members and living on beyond them. Thus, in practicing religion, people celebrate the awesome power of their society.

No wonder people around the world transform everyday objects into sacred symbols of their collective life. Members of technologically simple societies do this with a **totem,** *an object in the natural world collectively defined as sacred.* The totem—perhaps an animal or an elaborate work of art—becomes the centerpiece of ritual and symbolizes the power of collective life over any individual. In our society, the flag is a quasi-religious totem that is not to be used in a profane way (say, as clothing) or allowed to touch the ground.

Durkheim identified three major functions of religion that contribute to the operation of society:

1. **Social cohesion.** Religion unites people through shared symbolism, values, and norms. Religious thought and ritual establish morality and rules of fair play that make organized social life possible.

2. **Social control.** Society uses religious ideas to promote conformity. In medieval Europe, for example,

monarchs claimed to rule by divine right. Even today, our leaders publicly ask for God's blessing, implying to audiences that their efforts are right and just.

3. **Providing meaning and purpose.** Religious belief offers the comforting sense that our brief lives serve some greater purpose. Strengthened by such beliefs, people are less likely to despair in the face of change or even tragedy. For this reason, we mark major life transitions— including birth, marriage, and death—with religious observances.

Critical review. In Durkheim's structural-functional analysis, religion represents the collective life of society. The major weakness of this approach is that it downplays religion's dysfunctions, especially the fact that strongly held beliefs can generate social conflict. Terrorists have claimed that God supports their actions, and nations march to war under the banner of their God. Especially in light of recent world events, few people would deny that religious beliefs have provoked more violence in the world than differences in social class have.

Regularly taking part in religious rituals sharpens the distinction between the sacred and the profane. The wafer used in the Christian ritual of holy communion is never thought of in the everyday sense of food; rather, it is a sacred symbol of the body of Christ.

CONSTRUCTING THE SACRED: SYMBOLIC-INTERACTION ANALYSIS

From a symbolic-interaction point of view, religion (like all of society) is socially constructed (although perhaps with divine inspiration). Through various rituals—from daily prayer to annual events such as Easter or Passover—people sharpen the distinction between sacred and profane. Furthermore, says Peter Berger (1967:35–36), placing our small, brief lives within some "cosmic frame of reference" gives us the appearance of "ultimate security and permanence."

Marriage is a good example. If two people look on marriage as a simple contract, they can walk away whenever they want. Their bond makes much stronger claims on them when it is defined as holy matrimony, surely one reason for the lower divorce rate among people with strong religious beliefs. More generally, whenever humans face uncertainty or life-threatening situations—such as illness, natural disaster, or terrorist attack—we turn to our sacred symbols.

Critical review. In the symbolic-interaction approach, religion gives everyday life sacred meaning. Berger adds that the sacred's ability to give meaning and stability to society depends on ignoring the fact that it is socially constructed. After all, how much strength could we gain from sacred beliefs if we saw them merely as a means of coping with tragedy? Also, this micro-level view ignores religion's link to social inequality, to which we now turn.

INEQUALITY AND RELIGION: SOCIAL-CONFLICT ANALYSIS

The social-conflict approach highlights religion's support of social inequality. Religion, proclaimed Karl Marx, serves elites by legitimizing the status quo and diverting people's attention from social inequities.

Even today, the British monarch is the formal head of the Church of England, illustrating the close alliance between religious and political elites. In practical terms, working for political change may mean opposing the church and, by implication, God. Religion also encourages people to accept the social problems of this world while they look hopefully to a "better world to come." In a well-known statement, Marx dismissed religion as "the sigh of the oppressed creature, the sentiment of a heartless world, and the soul of soulless conditions. It is the opium of the people" (1964:27, orig. 1848).

Religion and social inequality are also linked through gender, because virtually all the world's major religions are patriarchal. For example, the Qur'an, the sacred text of Islam, gives men social dominance over women:

> Men are in charge of women. . . . Hence good women are obedient. . . . As for those whose rebelliousness you fear, admonish them, banish them from your bed, and scourge them. (quoted in Kaufman, 1976:163)

Patriarchy is found in all the world's major religions, including Christianity, Judaism, and Islam. Male dominance can be seen in restrictions that limit religious leadership to men and also in regulations that prohibit women from worshipping along with men.

Christianity, the major religion in the Western Hemisphere, has also supported patriarchy. Although Christians revere Mary, the mother of Jesus, the New Testament instructs us:

> A man . . . is the image and glory of God; but woman is the glory of man. For man was not made from woman, but woman from man. Neither was man created for woman, but woman for man. (1 Corinthians 11:7–9)
>
> As in all the churches of the saints, the women should keep silence in the churches. For they are not permitted to speak, but should be subordinate, as even the law says. If there is anything they desire to know, let them ask their husbands at home. For it is shameful for a woman to speak in church. (1 Corinthians 14:33–35)
>
> Wives, be subject to your husbands, as to the Lord. For the husband is the head of the wife as Christ is the head of the church. . . . As the church is subject to Christ, so let wives also be subject in everything to their husbands. (Ephesians 5:22–24)

Judaism also has traditionally supported patriarchy. Male Orthodox Jews recite the following prayer each day:

> Blessed art thou, O Lord our God, King of the Universe, that I was not born a gentile.
> Blessed art thou, O Lord our God, King of the Universe, that I was not born a slave.
> Blessed art thou, O Lord our God, King of the Universe, that I was not born a woman.

Despite patriarchal traditions, most religions now have women in leadership roles, and many are introducing more gender-neutral language in hymnals and prayer books. Such changes involve not just organizational patterns but conceptions of God. Theologian Mary Daly puts the matter bluntly: "If God is male, then male is God" (cited in Woodward, 1989:58).

Critical review.   Social-conflict analysis emphasizes the power of religion to legitimize social inequality. Yet religion also promotes change toward equality. For example, nineteenth-century religious groups in the United States played an important role in the movement to abolish slavery. In the 1950s and 1960s, religious organizations and their leaders were at the core of the civil rights movement. In the 1960s and 1970s, many clergy actively opposed the Vietnam War, and today many support any number of progressive issues such as feminism and gay rights.

The Applying Theory table summarizes the three theoretical approaches to understanding religion.

Religion and Social Change

Religion is not just the conservative force portrayed by Karl Marx. In fact, at some points in history, as Max Weber (1958, orig. 1904–5) explained, religion has promoted dramatic social change.

MAX WEBER: PROTESTANTISM AND CAPITALISM

Weber believed that particular religious ideas set into motion a wave of change that brought about the industrialization of Western Europe. The rise of industrial capitalism

APPLYING THEORY

RELIGION

	Structural-Functional Approach	Symbolic-Interaction Approach	Social-Conflict Approach
What is the level of analysis?	Macro-level	Micro-level	Macro-level
What is the importance of religion for society?	Religion performs vital tasks, including uniting people and controlling behavior. Religion gives life meaning and purpose.	Religion strengthens marriage by giving it (and family life) sacred meaning. People often turn to sacred symbols for comfort when facing danger and uncertainty.	Religion supports social inequality by claiming that the social order is just. Religion turns attention from problems in this world to a "better world to come."

was encouraged by Calvinism, a movement within the Protestant Reformation.

Central to the religious thought of John Calvin (1509–1564) is the doctrine of *predestination:* An all-knowing, all-powerful God has selected some people for salvation while condemning most to eternal damnation. Each person's fate, sealed before birth and known only to God, is either eternal glory or endless hellfire.

Driven by anxiety over their fate, Calvinists understandably looked for signs of God's favor in this world and came to see prosperity as a sign of divine blessing. Religious conviction and a rigid devotion to duty thus led Calvinists to work hard, and many amassed great wealth. But money was not for selfish spending or for sharing with the poor, whose plight they saw as a mark of God's rejection. As agents for God's work on Earth, Calvinists believed that they could best fulfill their "calling" by reinvesting profits and achieving ever-greater success in the process.

All the while, the Calvinists lived thrifty lives and embraced technological advances, thereby laying the groundwork for the rise of industrial capitalism. In time, the religious fervor that motivated early Calvinists weakened, resulting in a profane "Protestant work ethic." To Max Weber, industrial capitalism itself was a "disenchanted" religion, further showing the power of religion to change the shape of society.

LIBERATION THEOLOGY

Historically, Christianity has reached out to suffering and oppressed people, urging all to strengthen their faith in a better life to come. In recent decades, however, some church leaders and theologians have taken a decidedly political approach and endorsed **liberation theology,** *the combining of Christian principles with political activism, often Marxist in character.*

This social movement started in the late 1960s in Latin America's Roman Catholic Church. Today, Christian activists continue to help people in poor nations liberate themselves from abysmal poverty. Their message is simple: Social oppression runs counter to Christian morality, so as a matter of faith and justice, Christians must promote greater social equality.

Despite its Roman Catholic beginnings, Pope John Paul II condemns liberation theology for distorting church doctrine with left-wing politics. Nevertheless, the liberation theology movement has grown in Latin America, where many people's Christian faith drives them to improve conditions for the world's poor (Neuhouser, 1989; J. Williams, 2002).

Church, Sect, and Cult

Sociologists categorize the hundreds of different religious organizations found in the United States along a continuum, with *churches* at one end and *sects* at the other. Drawing on the ideas of his teacher Max Weber, Ernst Troeltsch (1931) defined a **church** as *a type of religious organization that is well integrated into the larger society.* Churchlike organizations typically persist for centuries and include generations of the same families. Churches have well-established rules and regulations and expect leaders to be formally trained and ordained.

Though concerned with the sacred, a church accepts the ways of the profane world. Church members conceive of God in intellectual terms (say, as a force for good) and favor abstract moral standards ("Do unto others as you would have them do unto you"). By teaching morality in safely abstract terms, church leaders avoid social controversy. For example, many churches that celebrate the unity of all peoples have all-white memberships. Such duality minimizes conflict between the church and political life (Troeltsch, 1931).

In global perspective, the range of religious activity is truly astonishing. Members of this Southeast Asian cult show their devotion to God by suspending themselves in the air using ropes and sharp hooks that pierce their skin.

> December 11, Casablanca, Morocco. The waves of the Atlantic crash along the walls of Casablanca's magnificent coastline mosque, said to be the largest in the world. From the top of the towering structure, a green laser beam cuts through the sky pointing to Mecca, the holy city of Islam, toward which the faithful bow in prayer. To pay for this monumental house of worship, King Hassan II, Morocco's head of state and religious leader, levied a tax on every citizen in his realm. This example of government religion contrasts sharply with our ideas about the separation of church and state.

A church may operate as an arm of the state. A **state church** is *a church formally allied with the state,* as illustrated by Islam in Morocco. State churches have existed throughout human history; for centuries, Roman Catholicism was the official religion of the Roman Empire, as was Confucianism in China until early in the twentieth century. Today, the Anglican church is the official church of England, and Islam is the official religion of Pakistan and Iran. State churches count everyone in a society as a member, which sharply limits tolerance of religious differences.

A **denomination,** by contrast, is *a church, independent of the state, that recognizes religious pluralism.* Denominations exist in nations that formally separate church and state, such as the United States. This nation has dozens of Christian denominations, including Catholics, Baptists, Episcopalians, Methodists, and Lutherans—as well as various categories of Judaism and other traditions. Although members of any denomination hold to their own beliefs, they recognize the right of others to have alternative beliefs.

Unlike a church, which tries to fit into the larger society, a **sect** is *a type of religious organization that stands apart from the larger society.* Sect members have rigid religious convictions and deny the beliefs of others. In extreme cases, members of a sect may withdraw completely from society to practice their faith without interference. The Amish community is one example of a North American sect that isolates itself. Because U.S. culture generally considers religious tolerance a virtue, members of sects sometimes are accused of being narrow-minded in insisting that they alone follow the true religion (Kraybill, 1994; P. Williams, 2002).

In organizational terms, sects are less formal than churches. Sect members may be highly spontaneous and emotional in worship, whereas members of churches tend to listen passively to their leaders. Sects also reject the intellectualized religion of churches, stressing instead the personal experience of divine power. Rodney Stark (1985:314) contrasts a church's vision of a distant God—"Our Father, who art in Heaven"—with a sect's more immediate God—"Lord, bless this poor sinner kneeling before you now."

Churches and sects also have different patterns of leadership. The more churchlike an organization, the more likely that its leaders are formally trained and ordained. Sectlike organizations, which celebrate the personal presence of God, expect their leaders to show divine inspiration in the form of **charisma** (from Greek, meaning "divine favor"), *extraordinary personal qualities that can infuse people with emotion and turn them into followers.*

Sects generally form as breakaway groups from established religious organizations (Stark & Bainbridge, 1979).

Their psychic intensity and informal structure make them less stable than churches, and many sects blossom, only to disappear soon after. Over the long term, sects typically become more like churches, losing fervor as they become more bureaucratic.

To sustain their membership, many sects actively recruit, or *proselytize*, new members. Sects value highly the experience of *conversion*, or religious rebirth. For example, Jehovah's Witnesses visit door to door to share their faith with others in the hope of attracting new members.

Finally, churches and sects differ in their social composition. Because they are more closely tied to the world, well-established churches tend to include people of high social standing. Sects attract more disadvantaged people. A sect's openness to new members and promise of salvation and personal fulfillment appeal to people who see themselves as social outsiders.

A **cult** is *a religious organization that is largely outside a society's cultural traditions.* Most sects spin off from a conventional religious organization; by contrast, a cult typically forms around a highly charismatic leader who offers a compelling message of a new and very different way of life. As many as 5,000 cults exist in the United States (Marquand & Wood, 1997).

Because some cult principles or practices are unconventional, many people view cults as deviant or even evil. The suicides of thirty-nine members of California's Heaven's Gate cult in 1997—people who claimed that dying was the doorway to a higher existence, perhaps in the company of aliens from outer space—confirmed the negative image the public holds of many cults. In short, say some scholars, calling a religious community a "cult" amounts to dismissing its members as crazy (Shupe, 1995; Gleick, 1997).

There is nothing basically wrong with this kind of religious organization. Many religions—Christianity, Islam, and Judaism included—began as cults. Of course, few cults exist for very long. One reason is that they are even more at odds with the larger society than sects. Many cults demand that members not only accept their teaching but also embrace a radically new lifestyle. This is why people sometimes accuse cults of brainwashing their members, although research suggests that most people who join cults experience no psychological harm (Kilbourne, 1983; P. Williams, 2002).

Religion in History

Like the family, religion is a part of every known society. Also like the family, religion shows marked variation both historically and cross-culturally.

Early hunters and gatherers embraced **animism** (from Latin, meaning "the breath of life"), *the belief that elements of the natural world are conscious life forms that affect humanity.* Animistic people view forests, oceans, mountains, and even the wind as spiritual forces. Many Native American societies are animistic, which accounts for their reverence for the natural environment.

Belief in a single divine power responsible for creating the world arose with pastoral and horticultural societies. The conception of God as a "shepherd" arose because Christianity, Judaism, and Islam all had their beginnings among pastoral peoples.

Religion becomes more important in agrarian societies. The central role of religion in social life is seen in the huge cathedrals that dominated the towns of medieval Europe.

The Industrial Revolution introduced a growing emphasis on science. More and more, people looked to physicians and scientists for the guidance and comfort they  used to get from priests. However, religion persists in industrial societies because science is powerless to address issues of ultimate meaning in human life. In other words, *how* this world works is a matter for scientists, but *why* we and the rest of the universe exist is a question of faith.

To learn more about different religions, visit http://www.adherents.com

Religion in the United States

Just as people debate the health of family life in the United States, so analysts disagree about the strength of religion in our society. Research shows that changes are underway but also confirms the ongoing role of religion in social life (Greeley, 1989; Woodward, 1992a; Hadaway, Marler, & Chaves, 1993).

RELIGIOUS COMMITMENT

National surveys show that about 85 percent of adults in the United States claim a religious preference (NORC, 2003:131). More than half of U.S. adults consider themselves Protestants, one-fourth are Catholics, and 2 percent are Jews. Significant numbers of people also hold to dozens of other religions, from animism to Zen Buddhism, making our society as religiously diverse as any on Earth. Furthermore, as Figure 13–5 on page 370 shows, in few industrial societies do people claim to be as religious as in the United States.

The religious diversity of the United States stems from a constitutional ban on any government-sponsored religion and from our historically high numbers of immigrants

GLOBAL SNAPSHOT

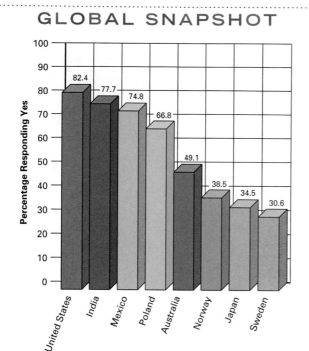

FIGURE 13-5   Religiosity in Global Perspective

Survey Question: "Do you gain comfort and strength from religion?"

Source: Inglehart et al. (2000).

from all over the world. National Map 13–2 shows the share of people who claim to belong to any church.

National Map 13–3 goes a step further, showing us that the religion most people identify with varies by region. New England and the Southwest are predominantly Catholic, the South is overwhelmingly Baptist, and Lutherans predominate in the northern Plains states. In and around Utah, there is a heavy concentration of members of the Church of Jesus Christ of Latter-Day Saints (Mormons).

Religiosity is *the importance of religion in a person's life.* However, exactly how religious we are depends on precisely how we operationalize this concept. For example, 86 percent of U.S. adults claim to believe in a divine power, although just 60 percent claim that they "know that God exists and have no doubts about it" (NORC, 2003:357). Fifty-six percent of adults say they pray at least once a day, but just 30 percent report attending religious services on a weekly or almost weekly basis (NORC, 2003:133, 140).

Clearly, the question "How religious are we?" has no easy answer, and it is likely that many people claim to be more

religious than they really are. Overall, although most people in the United States claim to be at least somewhat religious, probably no more than one-third actually are. Religiosity also

 Find online resources for the study of religion at http://www.princeton.edu/ ~csrelig/links/links.html

varies among denominations. Members of sects are the most religious of all, followed by Catholics and then Episcopalians and other "mainstream" Protestants (Hadaway, Marler, & Chaves, 1993; Sherkat & Ellison, 1999; Miller & Stark, 2002).

What are the consequences of greater religiosity? Researchers have linked a number of social patterns to strong religious beliefs, including low rates of delinquency among young people and low rates of divorce among adults. According to one recent study, religiosity helps bind children, parents, and local communities in ways that benefit young people, enhancing their educational achievement (Muller & Ellison, 2001).

RELIGION: CLASS, ETHNICITY, AND RACE

Religious affiliation is related to a number of other factors, including social class, ethnicity, and race.

Social class.   A study of *Who's Who in America,* which profiles U.S. high achievers, showed that 33 percent of the people who gave a religious affiliation were Episcopalians, Presbyterians, and United Church of Christ members, denominations that together account for less than 10 percent of the population. Jews also enjoy high social position, with this 2 percent of the population accounting for 12 percent of listings in *Who's Who.*

Research shows that on average, members of other denominations, including Methodists and Catholics, have moderate social standing. Lower social standing is typical of Baptists, Lutherans, and members of sects. Of course, there is considerable variation within all denominations (Davidson, Pyle, & Reyes, 1995; Waters, Heath, & Watson, 1995; Keister, 2003).

Ethnicity.   Throughout the world, religion is tied to ethnicity, largely because one religion often predominates in a single nation or geographic region. Islam predominates in the Arab societies of the Middle East, for example, just as Hinduism is fused with the culture of India. Christianity and Judaism do not follow this pattern; although these religions are mostly Western, Christians and Jews are found all over the world.

Religion and national identity are linked in the United States as well. For example, we have Anglo-Saxon

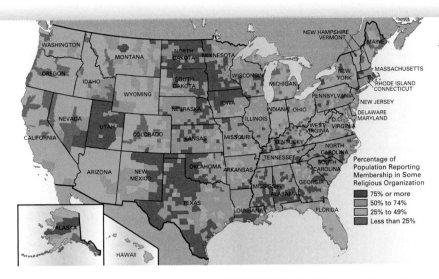

Religious Membership across the United States

In general, people in the United States are more religious than people in other high-income nations. Yet membership in a religious organization is more common in some parts of the country than in others. What pattern do you see in the map? Can you explain the pattern?

Source: From Rodger Doyle, *Atlas of Contemporary America.* Copyright © 1994 by Facts on File, Inc. Reprinted with the permission of Facts on File, Inc.

Percentage of Population Reporting Membership in Some Religious Organization
- 75% or more
- 50% to 74%
- 25% to 49%
- Less than 25%

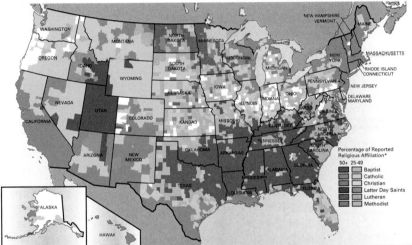

NATIONAL MAP 13-3
Religious Diversity across the United States

In most counties, at least 25 percent of people who report having an affiliation are members of the same religious organization. Thus, although the United States is religiously diverse at the national level, most people live in communities where one denomination predominates. What historical facts might account for this pattern?

When two or more churches have 25 to 49 percent of the membership in a county, the largest is shown. When no church has 25 percent of the membership, that county is left blank.

Source: Glenmary Research Center (2002).

Percentage of Reported Religious Affiliation*
50+ 25-49
- Baptist
- Catholic
- Christian
- Latter Day Saints
- Lutheran
- Methodist

Protestants, Irish Catholics, and Greek Orthodox. This linking of nation and religious belief results from the arrival of immigrants from nations with a single major religion. Still, nearly every ethnic category displays at least some religious diversity. For example, people of English ancestry may be Protestants, Roman Catholics, Jews, Hindus, or followers of other religions.

Race. Scholars claim that the church is both the oldest and the most important social institution within the African American community. Transported to the Western Hemisphere in slave ships, most Africans became Christians, the dominant religion in the Americas, but they blended Christian belief with elements of African religions. Guided by this religious mix, Christian people of color have developed rituals that are quite spontaneous and emotional by European standards (Frazier, 1965; Roberts, 1980).

When African Americans migrated from the rural South to the industrial cities of the North around 1940, the church played a major role in addressing problems of dislocation, poverty, and prejudice (Pattillo-McCoy, 1998). Black churches have also provided an important avenue of achievement for talented men and women. The Reverends Martin Luther King Jr. and Jesse Jackson have achieved world recognition for their work as religious leaders.

Recent years have witnessed an increasing number of non-Christian African Americans, especially in large U.S. cities. Among them, the most common non-Christian religion is Islam, with an estimated 1 million African American followers (Paris, 2000).

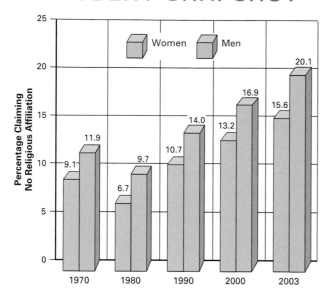

FIGURE 13-6 Religious Non-Affiliation among First-Year College Students, 1970–2003

Sources: Astin et al. (2002) and Sax et al. (2003).

Religion in a Changing Society

Like family life, religion is also changing in the United States. Sociologists focus on a major aspect of change: the process of secularization.

SECULARIZATION

Secularization is *the historical decline in the importance of the supernatural and the sacred.* Secularization (from Latin, meaning "the present age") is commonly associated with modern, technologically advanced societies in which science is the dominant mode of understanding.

Today, we are more likely to experience the transitions of birth, illness, and death in the presence of physicians (with scientific knowledge) than church leaders (whose knowledge is based on faith). This shift alone suggests that religion's importance for our everyday lives has declined. Harvey Cox explains:

> The world looks less and less to religious rules and rituals for its morality or its meanings. For some [people], religion provides a hobby, for others a mark of national or ethnic identification, for still others an aesthetic

delight. For fewer and fewer does it provide an inclusive and commanding system of personal and cosmic values and explanations. (1971:3; orig. 1965).

If Cox is right, should we expect religion to disappear someday? Most sociologists say no. The vast majority of people in the United States still profess a belief in God, and more people claim to pray each day than vote in national elections. In addition, religious affiliation today is higher than it was in 1850. Further, although affiliation in some religious organizations is declining, the numbers in others are increasing. Finally, although the share of new college students who say they have no religious preference almost doubled between 1970 and 2003, that share remains a clear minority, as shown in Figure 13–6 (Gorski, 2000; Stark & Finke, 2000; Hout & Fischer, 2002; Sax et al., 2003).

Secularization does not, then, signal the death of religion. More correctly, some dimensions of religion (such as belief in life after death) may have declined, but others (such as religious affiliation) have increased. Is secularization good or bad? Conservatives see any weakening of religion as a mark of moral decline. Progressives view secularization as liberation from the all-encompassing beliefs of the past, giving people greater choice about what to believe. Secularization has also brought many traditional religious practices (such as ordaining only men) into line with widespread social attitudes. Today, in many religions, ordination is open to women as well as men.

An important event in the trend toward secularization occurred in 1963 when the U.S. Supreme Court banned organized prayer in school as a violation of the constitutional separation of church and state. In recent years, however, religion has returned to many public schools. The Controversy & Debate box takes a closer look at the controversial issue of prayer in school.

CIVIL RELIGION

One dimension of secularization is what Robert Bellah (1975) calls **civil religion,** *a quasi-religious loyalty binding individuals in a basically secular society.* In other words, even in a mostly secular society, citizenship has religious qualities. Certainly, most people in the United States consider our way of life a force for moral good in the world. Many people also find religious qualities in political movements, whether liberal or conservative (Williams & Demerath, 1991).

Civil religion involves a range of rituals, from standing to sing the national anthem at sporting events to waving the flag at public parades. At all such events, the U.S. flag serves as a sacred symbol of our national identity, and we expect people to treat it with respect.

CONTROVERSY & DEBATE
Should Students Pray in School?

It is late afternoon on a cloudy spring day in Minneapolis, and two dozen teenagers have come together to pray. They share warm smiles as they enter the room. As soon as everyone is seated, the prayers begin, with one voice following another. One girl prays for her brother; a boy prays for the success of an upcoming food drive; another asks God to comfort a favorite teacher who is having a hard time. Then they join their voices to pray for all the teachers at their school who are not Christians. After the prayers, the young people sing Christian songs, discuss a scripture lesson, and bring their meeting to a close with a group hug.

What is so unusual about this prayer meeting is that it is taking place in room 133 of Patrick Henry High School, a *public* institution. Indeed, in public schools from coast to coast, something of a religious revival is taking place as more and more students hold meetings like this one.

You would have to be at least in your late forties to remember when it was routine for public school students to begin the day with Bible reading and prayer. In 1963, the Supreme Court ruled that doing so violated the separation of church and state mandated by the U.S. Constitution, making any religious activity anywhere in public schools illegal. But from the moment the ruling was announced, critics charged that by supporting a wide range of other activities and clubs while banning religious activity, schools were really being *antireligious*. In 1990, the Supreme Court handed down a new ruling, stating that religious groups can meet on school property as long as group membership is voluntary, the meetings are held outside regular class hours, and students rather than adults run them.

Today, student religious groups have formed in perhaps one-fourth of all public schools. Evangelical Christian organizations such as First Priority and National Network of Youth are using the Internet and word of mouth in an effort to expand the place of religion in every public school across the country. However, opponents of school prayer worry that religious enthusiasm may lead some students to pressure others to join their groups. Such disagreements ensure that the controversy over prayer in public schools will continue.

CONTINUE THE DEBATE . . .

1. Do you think that religious clubs should have the same freedom to operate on school grounds as other organizations? Why or why not?
2. The writers of our Constitution stated in the First Amendment that Congress should not establish any official religion and also pass no law that would interfere with the free practice of religion. How do you think this amendment applies to the issue of prayer in school?
3. In 1995, President Bill Clinton said, "Nothing in the First Amendment converts our public schools into religion-free zones." Do you think schools should support spiritual development as they would, say, athletic development? Why or why not?

Source: Based on Van Biema (1998, 1999).

"NEW AGE" SEEKERS: SPIRITUALITY WITHOUT FORMAL RELIGION

In recent decades, an increasing number of people are seeking spiritual development outside established religious organizations. This trend toward spirituality but away from established religious organizations has led some analysts to conclude that the United States is becoming a *postdenomination society*. In simple terms, more people seem to be spiritual seekers, believing in a vital spiritual dimension to human existence that they pursue more or less separately from any formal denomination.

What exactly is the difference between this "new age" focus on spirituality and a traditional concern with religion? As one analysis (Cimino & Lattin, 1999:62) puts it:

[Spirituality is] the search for . . . a religion of the heart, not the head. It . . . downplays doctrine and dogma, and revels in direct experience of the divine—whether it's called the "holy spirit" or "divine consciousness" or "true self." It's practical and personal, more about stress reduction than salvation, more therapeutic than theological. It's about feeling good rather than being good. It's as much about the body as the soul.

New Age "seekers" are people in pursuit of spiritual growth, often using the age-old technique of meditation. The goal of this activity is to quiet the mind so that, by moving away from everyday concerns, one can hear an inner, divine voice. Countless people attest to the spiritual value of meditation; it has also been linked to improved physical health.

From a traditional point of view, this concern with spirituality may seem more like psychology than religion. Yet like civil religion, it is a new form of religious interest in the modern world.

Finally, keep in mind the effect of high immigration on religious life in the United States. As people come from Latin America, Asia, and other regions and join the U.S. cultural mix, they are likely to fuse traditional religious ideas with ideas they encounter in their new land. The result is religious innovation (Yang & Ebaugh, 2001).

RELIGIOUS REVIVAL: "GOOD OL'-TIME RELIGION"

At the same time that "new age" spirituality is flourishing, a great deal of change has been going on in the world of organized religion. Membership in established, mainstream churches such as the Episcopalian and Presbyterian denominations has plummeted by almost 50 percent since 1960. During the same period, affiliation with other religious organizations (including the Mormons, Seventh-Day Adventists, and especially Christian sects) has risen just as dramatically. Secularization itself may be self-limiting, so that as churchlike organizations become more worldly, many people leave them in favor of sectlike communities that offer a more intense religious experience (Stark & Bainbridge, 1981; Roof & McKinney, 1987; Jacquet & Jones, 1991; Warner, 1993; Iannaccone, 1994; Hout, Greeley, & Wilde, 2001).

One striking religious trend today is the growth of **fundamentalism,** *a conservative religious doctrine that opposes intellectualism and worldly accommodation in favor of restoring traditional, otherworldly religion.* In the United States, fundamentalism has made the greatest gains among Protestants. Southern Baptists, for example, are the largest religious community in the United States. But fundamentalist groups have also grown among Roman Catholics and Jews.

In response to what they see as the growing influence of science and the weakening of the conventional family, religious fundamentalists defend what they call "traditional values." As they see it, liberal churches are simply too open to change. Religious fundamentalism is distinctive in five ways (Hunter, 1983, 1985, 1987):

1. **Fundamentalists take the words of sacred texts literally.** Fundamentalists insist on a literal reading of sacred texts such as the Bible to counter what they consider excessive intellectualism among more liberal Christian organizations. For example, fundamentalist Christians believe God created the world in seven days precisely as described in the Book of Genesis.

2. **Fundamentalists reject religious pluralism.** Fundamentalists believe that tolerance and relativism water down personal faith. Therefore, they maintain that their religious beliefs are true and other beliefs are not.

3. **Fundamentalists pursue the personal experience of God's presence.** In contrast to the worldliness and intellectualism of other religious organizations, fundamentalists encourage a return to "good old-time

In this outstanding example of U.S. folk art, Anna Bell Lee Washington's *Baptism 3* (1924) depicts the life-changing experience by which many people enter the Christian faith.

religion" and spiritual revival. Being "born again" and having a personal relationship with Jesus Christ should be evident in a person's everyday life.

4. **Fundamentalists oppose "secular humanism."** Fundamentalists think accommodation to the changing world undermines religious conviction. They reject "secular humanism," our society's tendency to look to scientific experts rather than God for guidance about how to live.

5. **Many fundamentalists endorse conservative political goals.** Although fundamentalism tends to back away from worldly concerns, some fundamentalist leaders (such as Ralph Reed, Pat Robertson, and Gary Bauer) have entered politics to oppose the "liberal agenda," which includes feminism and gay rights. Fundamentalists oppose abortion, gay marriage, and liberal bias in the media; they support the traditional two-parent family, seek a return of prayer in schools, and criticize the mass media for coloring stories with a liberal bias (Ellison & Sherkat, 1993; Green, 1993; Manza & Brooks, 1997; Thomma, 1997; Rozell, Wilcox, & Green, 1998).

Opponents regard fundamentalism as rigid and self-righteous. But many people find in fundamentalism, with its greater religious certainty and emphasis on experiencing God's presence, an appealing alternative to the more intellectual, tolerant, and worldly mainstream denominations (Marquand, 1997).

Which religious organizations are fundamentalist? In recent years, the world has become familiar with an extreme form of fundamentalist Islam that supports violent attacks against Western culture. In the United States, this term is most commonly applied to conservative Christian organizations in the evangelical tradition, including Pentecostals, Southern Baptists, Seventh-Day Adventists, and the Assemblies of God. Several national religious movements, including Promise Keepers (a men's organization) and Chosen Women, have a fundamentalist orientation. In national surveys, 30 percent of U.S. adults describe their upbringing as "fundamentalist," 40 percent claim a "moderate" religious upbringing, and 24 percent a "liberal" background (NORC, 2003:150).

In contrast to local congregations of years past, some religious organizations, especially fundamentalist ones, have become *electronic churches* dominated by "prime-time preachers" (Hadden & Swain, 1981). Electronic religion is found only in the United States. It has made people such as Oral Roberts, Pat Robertson, and Robert Schuller more famous than all but a few clergy in the past. Perhaps 5 percent of the national television audience (about 10 million people) are regular viewers of religious television, and 20 percent (about 40 million) watch some religious programming every week (NORC, 2003).

LOOKING AHEAD: RELIGION IN THE TWENTY-FIRST CENTURY

The popularity of media ministries, the growth of religious fundamentalism, and the connection of millions of people to mainstream churches show that religion will remain a major part of modern society. In fact, high levels of immigration from many religious countries (in Latin America and elsewhere) should intensify as well as diversify the religious character of U.S. society as the twenty-first century progresses.

The world is becoming more complex, and social change seems to move at a faster pace than our capacity to make sense of it all. But rather than weakening religion, this process fires the religious imagination. New technology that can alter, sustain, and even create life confronts us with difficult moral dilemmas. Against this backdrop of uncertainty, it is little wonder that many people look to their faith for assurance and hope.

SUMMARY

Family

1. Although families are found everywhere in the world, the definition of a family varies across cultures and over time.

2. In higher-income nations such as the United States, marriage is monogamous. Many lower-income countries permit polygamy, of which there are two types: polygyny and polyandry.

3. In global perspective, patrilocal residence is more common than matrilocal residence. Industrial societies favor neolocality. Descent in preindustrial societies tends to be either patrilineal or matrilineal; in industrial societies, descent is bilateral.

4. Structural-functional analysis identifies major family functions: socializing the young, regulating sexual activity, and providing social placement and emotional support. Social-conflict theory highlights how the family perpetuates inequality based on class, ethnicity, race, and gender. Symbolic-interaction analysis highlights the dynamic and changeable experience of family life.

5. In the United States and elsewhere, family life evolves over the life course, beginning with courtship, extending through child rearing, and ending with the death of a spouse, usually in old age.

6. Families in the United States are diverse, varying along with class position, ethnicity, race, gender, and personal preferences.

7. The divorce rate today is ten times higher than a century ago; almost four in ten current marriages will end in divorce. Most people who divorce, especially men, remarry.

8. Family violence is an important public issue.

9. Our society's family life is becoming more varied. Singlehood, cohabitation, one-parent families, and gay and lesbian families are on the rise.

Religion

1. Religion is a major social institution based on setting the sacred apart from the profane. Religion is grounded in faith, not scientific evidence. Sociologists study how religion affects society but make no claims as to the truth of any religious belief.

2. According to Durkheim, people celebrate the power of their society through religion. His structural-functional analysis suggests that religion promotes social cohesion and conformity and gives meaning and purpose to life.

3. Using the symbolic-interaction approach, Peter Berger explains that people socially construct religious beliefs as a response to life's uncertainties.

4. Social-conflict analyst Karl Marx claimed that religion supports inequality. By contrast, Max Weber's analysis showed how religious ideas can trigger societal change.

5. Churches, religious organizations that are well integrated into their societies, fall into two categories: state churches and denominations. Sects, the result of religious division, are marked by charismatic leadership and suspicion of the larger society. Cults represent new and unconventional religious beliefs and practices.

6. The religiosity of our society depends on how we operationalize the concept. Most people say they believe in God, but only about one-third of the U.S. population reports attending religious services regularly.

7. The concept of secularization refers to the diminishing importance of religion. Some measures of U.S. religiosity (including membership in mainstream churches) have declined; others (such as membership in sects and spiritual seeking) are on the rise. It is unlikely that religion will disappear.

8. Fundamentalism opposes religious accommodation to the world, advocates a literal reading of sacred texts, and pursues the personal experience of God's presence. Some fundamentalist Christians have become a conservative force in politics.

KEY CONCEPTS

Family

family (p. 346) a social institution that unites people in cooperative groups to oversee the bearing and raising of children

kinship (p. 346) a social bond based on blood, marriage, or adoption

family unit (p. 346) a social group of two or more people, related by blood, marriage, or adoption, who usually live together

marriage (p. 347) a legal relationship, usually involving economic cooperation as well as sexual activity and childbearing, that people expect to last

extended family (p. 347) a family unit that includes parents and children as well as other kin; also known as the *consanguine family*

nuclear family (p. 347) a family unit composed of one or two parents and their children; also known as the *conjugal family*

endogamy (p. 347) marriage between people of the same social category

exogamy (p. 347) marriage between people of different social categories

monogamy (p. 347) marriage that unites two partners

polygamy (p. 347) marriage that unites three or more people

descent (p. 349) the system by which members of a society trace kinship over generations

incest taboo (p. 349) a norm forbidding sexual relations or marriage between certain relatives

homogamy (p. 352) marriage between people with the same social characteristics

cohabitation (p. 359) the sharing of a household by an unmarried couple

Religion

profane (p. 363) an ordinary element of everyday life

sacred (p. 363) set apart as extraordinary, inspiring awe and reverence

religion (p. 363) a social institution involving beliefs and practices based on a conception of the sacred

faith (p. 364) belief based on conviction rather than scientific evidence

totem (p. 364) an object in the natural world collectively defined as sacred

liberation theology (p. 367) the combining of Christian principles with political activism, often Marxist in character

church (p. 367) a type of religious organization that is well integrated into the larger society

state church (p. 368) a church formally allied with the state

denomination (p. 368) a church, independent of the state, that recognizes religious pluralism

sect (p. 368) a type of religious organization that stands apart from the larger society

charisma (p. 368) extraordinary personal qualities that can infuse people with emotion and turn them into followers

cult (p. 369) a religious organization that is largely outside a society's cultural traditions

animism (p. 369) the belief that elements of the natural world are conscious life forms that affect humanity

religiosity (p. 370) the importance of religion in a person's life

secularization (p. 372) the historical decline in the importance of the supernatural and the sacred

civil religion (p. 372) a quasi-religious loyalty binding individuals in a basically secular society

fundamentalism (p. 374) a conservative religious doctrine that opposes intellectualism and worldly accommodation in favor of restoring traditional, otherworldly religion

CRITICAL-THINKING QUESTIONS

1. Identify important changes in U.S. families since 1960. What factors are responsible for these changes?

2. Are U.S. families becoming weaker or simply more diverse? What evidence supports your position?

3. Explain Karl Marx's claim that religion tends to support the status quo. Develop a counterargument, based on Max Weber's analysis of Calvinism, that religion is a major force for social change.

4. What evidence suggests that the importance of religion is declining in the United States? In what ways does religion seem to be getting stronger?

APPLICATIONS AND EXERCISES

1. Parents and grandparents can be a wonderful source of information about changes in marriage and the family. Spend an hour or two with married people of two different generations, and ask them at what ages they married, what their married lives have been like, and what changes in family life today stand out to them.

2. Relationships with various family members differ. With which family member—mother, father, brother, sister—do you most easily, and least easily, share confidences? Why? Which family member would you turn to first in a crisis? Why?

3. Some colleges are decidedly religious; others are passionately secular. Investigate the place of religion on your campus. Is your school affiliated with a religious organization? Was it ever? Is there a chaplain or other religious official? See whether you can learn from sources on campus what share of students regularly attend any religious service.

4. Is religion getting weaker? To test the secularization idea, go to the library or local newspaper office and find an issue of your local newspaper published fifty years ago and, if possible, another from 100 years ago. Compare attention to religious issues then and now.

5. Packaged in the back of this new textbook is an interactive CD-ROM that offers a variety of video and interactive review materials intended to help you better understand the material covered in this chapter. For this chapter, the CD-ROM contains a relevant clip from *ABC News,* an author's tip video, interactive map animations, an interactive timeline, and flashcards with audio pronunciations of the more difficult words.

 ## SITES TO SEE

http://www.prenhall.com/macionis

Visit the interactive Companion Website™ that accompanies this text. Begin by clicking on the cover of your book. You will find a chapter-by-chapter study guide, practice tests, suggested Web links, and links to other relevant material.

http://www.frc.org

This is the Web address for the Family Research Council, a conservative organization supporting what it calls "traditional family values." What does the council consider a "traditional family"? What values does it defend? Why? Are there family problems that it ignores?

http://www.polyamorysociety.org

Survey the increasing diversity of family life at the Web site for the Polyamory Society. What do you make of the society's views of family life?

http://www.bwanet.org
http://www.churchworldservice.org
http://www.catholicrelief.org
http://www.jdc.org

A number of religious organizations are involved in addressing hunger and other social problems. These Web sites describe the activities of the Baptist World Alliance, Church World Service, Catholic Relief Services, and American Jewish Joint Distribution Committee.

http://www.parishioners.org

This site offers information on a variety of religious issues, including cults and toleration of religious differences.

http://www.cair-net.org/mosquereport/

Read a report on Muslims in the United States by the Council on American-Islamic Relations.

http://www.beliefnet.com

Take the "What's your spiritual type" test and find out how religious you really are!

 ## INVESTIGATE WITH RESEARCH NAVIGATOR™

Follow the instructions found on page 32 of this textbook to access the features of **Research Navigator™**. Once at the Web site, enter your Login Name and Password. Then, to use the **Content Select™** database, enter keywords such as "family," "religion," and "cults," and the search engine will supply relevant and recent scholarly and popular press publications. Use the *New York Times* **Search-by-Subject Archive** to find recent news articles related to sociology and the **Links Library** feature to find relevant Web links organized by the key terms associated with this chapter.

September 7, 2003

Putting the American in "American Muslim"

By MUQTEDAR KHAN

WASHINGTON—Muslims in America. American Muslims. The difference between these two labels may seem a matter of semantics, but making the transition from the first to the second represents a profound, if somewhat silent, revolution that many of us in the Muslim community have been undergoing in the two years since Sept. 11.

On its face, this shift would seem to threaten the very core of Muslim identity and empowerment. After all, in the decade before the events of Sept. 11, Islam was one of the fastest-growing religions in North America. Mosques and Islamic schools were going up in every major city. Groups like the Council on American-Islamic Relations and the American Muslim Alliance established chapters in nearly every area with a Muslim population. . . .

At the time, the word that best summed up the Muslim sense of self was "fateh," a conqueror. Many religious and community leaders were convinced that Islam would not only manifest itself in its truest form in this country, but would also make America, already a great power, into a great society. Some even proclaimed that one day America would be an Islamic state.

On Sept. 11, of course, that dream evaporated. Today, the civil rights environment has declined drastically with the passage of the USA Patriot Act and other antiterrorism measures. Both sources of Islam's growth—immigration and conversion—are now in jeopardy, and we continue to face hostility and prejudice in many corners of society. There is no more talk of making America an Islamic state. Any reminder of this pre-9/11 vision generates sheepish giggles and snorts from Muslim audiences. . . .

Today, many Muslims realize that it is not their Islamic identity but their American citizenship that is fragile. Before Sept. 11, Muslims in America focused primarily on changing United States policy toward Palestine, Kashmir and Iraq. Since Sept. 11, the attempt to reconstitute our identity as American Muslims is making domestic relations and civil rights and interfaith relations more important.

Much of this is playing out at the local level. In Miami, for example, efforts are underway by a group of progressive Muslims to endow chairs in Islamic studies at American universities. In the Muslim community in Duluth, Minn., fund-raising has begun to support social services, including housing and health care initiatives for the poor. In Indianapolis, Muslim residents are opening soup kitchens. And think of the familiar advertising campaign by the Council on American-Islamic Relations in which Muslims announce, "We are American and we are Muslims." It is not without design that "American" is stated first.

Even more vital, many Muslims in this country have come to acutely understand the vulnerabilities of minorities and the importance of democracy and civil rights. Because we took our American citizenship for granted, we did not acknowledge its value and virtues. But now that it is imperiled, the overwhelming desire of many Muslims is that America remain true to its democratic and secular values. . . .

There is still much progress to be made. We need to continue to demonstrate that Muslims in this country constitute an ethical and philanthropic community that cares about humanitarian causes, about America and Americans and stands for justice and rights as embodied in the Constitution. Just like other ethnic groups before us, we have to pay our dues to this nation before we demand that they change themselves and the world for us.

But Americans, too, must play a role. They cannot allow events overseas to foster anti-Muslim sentiments and Islamophobia at home. They must recognize the insecurities and fears of their Muslim neighbors and extend a hand of friendship and support. The choices we face are tough, but Muslims must realize that the interests of our sons and daughters, who are American, must come before the interests of our brothers and sisters, whether they are Palestinian, Kashmiri or Iraqi. Only then will Muslims in America become American Muslims. . . .

WHAT DO YOU THINK?

1. What are the reasons for a rise in anti-Muslim attitudes in the United States since the Sept. 11 terrorist attacks? Is this a clear case of unfair prejudice or is some of this bias justified? Explain your position.

2. Considering that there are some 7 million Muslims in the United States—more than the membership of many Protestant denominations—should Islam play a greater role in this country's national life? Why or why not?

Adapted from the original article by Muqtedar Khan published in *The New York Times* on September 7, 2003. Copyright © 2003 by The New York Times Company. Reprinted with permission.

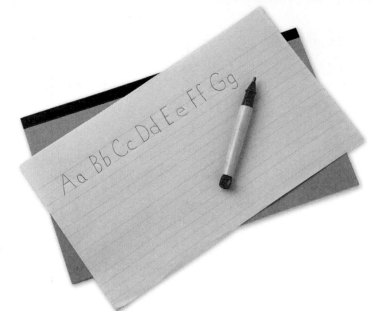

CHAPTER FOURTEEN

Education and Medicine

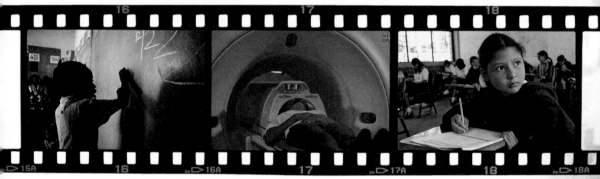

How are schooling and medical care linked
to social inequality in the United States?

In what ways did the Industrial Revolution make
both schooling and medical care widely available?

Why do people in poor nations have little access
to schooling and medical care?

14

Education and medicine are social institutions that gain great importance in the modern world. ▶
These young people in South Africa—all HIV positive—speak out in an effort
to teach others about the dangers of AIDS and to encourage those
already infected to receive new treatments.

The executives at J. C. Penney did not plan to get involved in a controversy over schooling in the United States. All they did was place on their clothing racks a T-shirt showing a trailer home and the words "HOME SKOOLED." Many customers were not amused. One week later, as angry letters poured in from parents across the country who had a much more positive view of home schooling, Penney removed the shirt from all its stores (Cloud & Morse, 2001).

If Penney had done a bit of sociological research, the company never would have considered selling the offending T-shirt. For one thing, home schooling is rapidly gaining in popularity—estimates place the number of children being schooled at home at 1.1 million. The number represents more than 2 percent of the K–12 population, or roughly the same as the total number of school-aged children living in Virginia. In addition to their large numbers, home-schooled children are commonly from families that are middle class or above in terms of social standing, and most have parents who are well educated. Most important of all, home-schooled children turn out to be pretty good students—on average, they academically outperform children who attend public schools.

This chapter begins by exploring *education,* a social institution that has particular importance in high-income nations, including the United States. You will learn *why* schooling is so important in these societies and *who* receives the most benefits from schooling. The second half of the chapter examines *medicine,* another social institution with great importance in the modern world. Good health, like good schooling, is distributed unequally throughout our society's population. In addition, like education, medicine reveals striking variation from society to society.

Education: A Global Survey

Education is *the social institution through which society provides its members with important knowledge, including basic facts, job skills, and cultural norms and values.* Education takes place in many ways, from informal family discussions around the dinner table to lectures and labs at large universities. In high-income nations, education is largely a matter of **schooling,** *formal instruction under the direction of specially trained teachers.*

SCHOOLING AND ECONOMIC DEVELOPMENT

The extent of schooling in any society is tied to its level of economic development. In countries with limited industrialization, which are home to most of the world's people, families and local communities teach young people important knowledge and skills. Formal schooling, and especially learning that is not directly linked to work, is available mainly to wealthy people. After all, the Greek root of the word *school* means "leisure." In ancient Greece, famous teachers such as Plato, Socrates, and Aristotle taught aristocratic, upper-class men; similarly, in ancient China, the famous philosopher K'ung Fu-tzu (Confucius) shared his wisdom with just a privileged few.

Today, schooling in low-income countries reflects the cultural diversity of each nation. In Iran, for example, schooling is closely tied to Islam. Similarly, schooling in Bangladesh (Asia), Zimbabwe (Africa), and Nicaragua (Latin America) has been shaped by the distinctive cultural traditions of these countries.

All low-income countries have one trait in common when it comes to schooling: There is not very much of it. In the poorest nations (including several in central Africa), only half of all children ever get to school; for the world as a whole, only half of all children ever get to the secondary grades. As a result, about one-third of people around the world cannot read or write. Global Map 14–1 shows the extent of illiteracy around the world, and the following national comparisons illustrate the link between schooling and economic development.

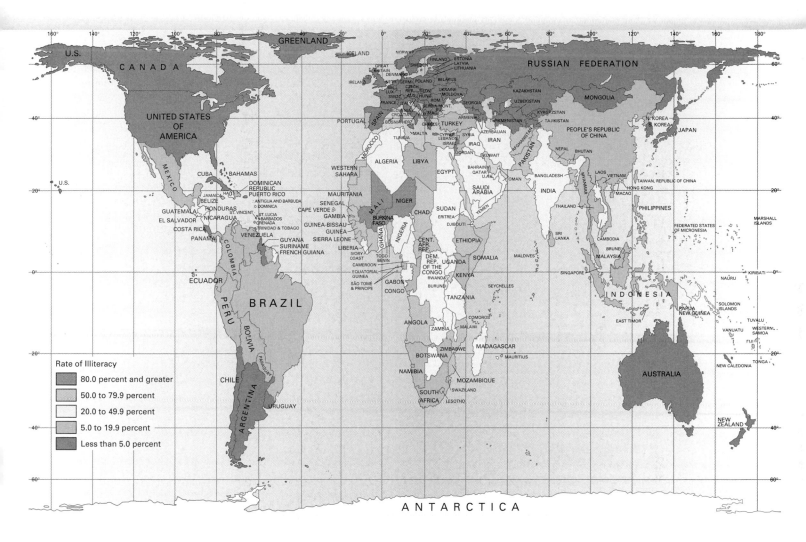

WINDOW ON THE WORLD

GLOBAL MAP 14–1   Illiteracy in Global Perspective

Reading and writing skills are widespread in high-income countries, where illiteracy rates generally are below 5 percent. In much of Latin America, however, illiteracy is more common, one consequence of limited economic development. In twenty-five nations—eighteen of them in Africa—illiteracy is the rule rather than the exception; there, people rely on the oral tradition of face-to-face communication rather than the written word.

Sources: United Nations Development Programme (2004) and World Bank (2004); map projection from *Peters Atlas of the World* (1990).

SCHOOLING IN INDIA

India is a middle-income country where people earn about 7 percent of the income of people in the United States, and most poor families depend on the earnings of children. Thus, even though India has outlawed child labor, many children continue to work in factories—weaving rugs or making handicrafts—for up to sixty hours a week, which greatly limits their chances for schooling.

Today, 77 percent of children in India complete primary school, typically in crowded schoolrooms where one teacher may face as many as sixty children. Less than half

TABLE 14-1

Educational Achievement in the United States, 1910–2003*

Year	High School Graduates	College Graduates	Median Years of Schooling
1910	13.5%	2.7%	8.1
1920	16.4	3.3	8.2
1930	19.1	3.9	8.4
1940	24.1	4.6	8.6
1950	33.4	6.0	9.3
1960	41.1	7.7	10.5
1970	55.2	11.0	12.2
1980	68.7	17.0	12.5
1990	77.6	21.3	12.4
2000	84.1	25.6	12.7
2003	84.6	27.2	n/a

*For people twenty-five years of age and over. Percentage of high school graduates includes those who go on to college. Percentage of high school dropouts can be calculated by subtracting percentage of high school graduates from 100 percent.

Source: U.S. Census Bureau (2004).

continue on to secondary education, and very few enter college. As a result, only about 60 percent of the people in this vast country are literate.

Patriarchy also shapes Indian education. Indian parents rejoice at the birth of a boy because he and his future wife both will contribute income to the family. But there are economic costs linked to raising a girl: Parents must provide a dowry at the time of her marriage, and after her marriage, a daughter's work benefits her husband's family. Therefore, many Indians see little reason to invest in the schooling of girls, which is why only 30 percent of girls (compared with 45 percent of boys) reach the secondary grades. So what do the girls do while the boys are in school? Most of the children working in Indian factories are girls—a family's way of benefiting from their daughters while they can (United Nations Development Programme, 1995).

SCHOOLING IN JAPAN

September 30, Kobe, Japan. Compared to people in the United States, the Japanese are particularly orderly. Young boys and girls on their way to school stand out with their uniforms, their arms filled with books, and a look of seriousness and purpose on their faces.

Schooling has not always been part of the Japanese way of life. Before industrialization brought mandatory education in 1872, only a privileged few attended school. Today, Japan's educational system is widely praised for producing some of the world's highest achievers.

The early grades concentrate on transmitting Japanese traditions, especially a sense of obligation to family. Starting in their early teens, students take a series of rigorous and highly competitive examinations. These written tests, which resemble the Scholastic Assessment Tests (SATs) used for college admissions in the United States, decide a Japanese student's future.

More men and women graduate from high school in Japan (96 percent) than in the United States (85 percent). But competitive examinations allow just 49 percent of high school graduates—compared to 62 percent in the United States—to enter college. Understandably, Japanese students take entrance examinations very seriously, and about half attend "cram schools" to prepare for them.

Japanese schooling produces impressive results. In a number of fields, notably mathematics and science, young Japanese students outperform students in every other high-income nation, including the United States (Brinton, 1988; Simons, 1989).

SCHOOLING IN THE UNITED STATES

The United States was among the first countries to set a goal of mass education. By 1850, about half the young people between the ages of five and nineteen were enrolled in school. By 1918, all states had passed *mandatory education laws* requiring children to attend school until the age of sixteen or completion of the eighth grade. Table 14–1 shows that this country reached a milestone in the mid-1960s, when for the first time a majority of U.S. adults had high school diplomas. Today, more than four out of five adults have a high school education, and more than one in four has a four-year college degree.

The U.S. educational system is shaped by both affluence and democratic principles. Thomas Jefferson thought the new nation could become democratic only if people "read and understand what is going on in the world" (quoted in Honeywell, 1931:13). As Figure 14–1 shows, the United States has an outstanding record of higher education for its people: No other country has as large a share of adults with a university degree (U.S. Census Bureau, 2003, 2004).

Schooling in the United States also tries to promote *equal opportunity.* National surveys show that most people think schooling is crucial to personal success, and a majority believe that everyone has the chance to get an education consistent with personal ability and talent (NORC, 2003). This

opinion expresses cultural ideals rather than actual reality. A century ago, for example, women were all but excluded from higher education; even today, most people who attend college come from families with above-average incomes.

In the United States, the educational system stresses the value of *practical* learning, knowledge that prepares people for their future jobs. This is in line with what the education philosopher John Dewey (1859–1952) called *progressive education,* by which schools in the United States generally try to make learning relevant to people's lives. In line with this philosophy, students seek out subjects of study that they believe will be important in their lives and to their prospects for future jobs. For example, as concerns about international terrorism have risen in recent years, so have the numbers of students choosing to study geography, international conflict, and Middle Eastern history and culture (Lord, 2001).

 Find a Census Bureau report on schooling and income at http://www.census.gov/population/www/socdemo/fld-of-trn.html

The Functions of Schooling

Structural-functional analysis focuses on ways in which schooling supports the operation and stability of society:

1. **Socialization.** Technologically simple societies look to families to transmit a way of life from one generation to the next. As societies gain complex technology, they turn to trained teachers to pass on specialized knowledge.

2. **Cultural innovation.** Schools invent new machines just as they create new ideas. Especially at centers of higher education, scholars conduct research that leads to discovery and changes our way of life.

3. **Social integration.** Schools mold a diverse population into one society sharing norms and values. This is one reason why states enacted mandatory education laws a century ago at a time when immigration was very high. In light of the ethnic diversity of many urban areas, schooling continues to serve the same purpose today.

4. **Social placement.** Schools identify talent and match instruction to ability. Schooling increases meritocracy by rewarding talent and hard work regardless of social background and provides a path to upward social mobility.

5. **Latent functions.** Schooling serves several less widely recognized functions. It provides child care for the growing number of one-parent and two-career families. In addition, it occupies thousands of young people in their twenties who would otherwise be

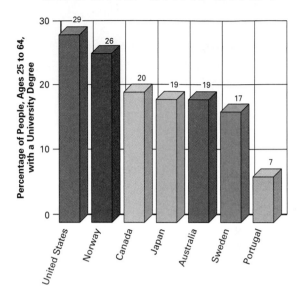

GLOBAL SNAPSHOT

FIGURE 14-1 College Degrees in Global Perspective

Source: U.S. Census Bureau (2003, 2004).

competing for a limited number of jobs. High schools, colleges, and universities also bring together people of marriageable age. Finally, school networks can be a valuable career resource throughout life.

Critical review. Structural-functional analysis stresses ways in which formal education supports the operation of a modern society. However, this approach overlooks the many problems of our educational system and how schooling helps reproduce the class structure in each generation.

Schooling and Social Inequality

Social-conflict analysis challenges the structural-functional idea that schooling develops everyone's talents and abilities. Instead, this approach emphasizes how schooling causes and perpetuates social inequality:

1. **Social control.** As Samuel Bowles and Herbert Gintis (1976) see it, the demand for public education in the late nineteenth century arose just as capitalists needed an obedient and disciplined workforce. Once in school, immigrants learned not only the English language but also the importance of following orders.

Sociological research has documented the fact that young people living in low-income communities suffer in school due to large class sizes, poor quality teaching, and insufficient budgets for technology and other instructional materials. In a nation where people believe that schools should give everyone a chance to develop talents and abilities, should such inequalities exist?

2. **Testing.** Critics claim that the aptitude tests widely used by schools reflect our society's dominant culture, placing minority students at a disadvantage. By defining majority students as smarter, standardized tests transform privilege into personal merit (Crouse & Trusheim, 1988; Putka, 1990).

3. **Tracking.** Despite controversy over standardized tests, most U.S. schools use them for **tracking,** *assigning students to different types of educational programs,* such as college preparatory classes, general education, and vocational and technical training. Tracking supposedly helps teachers meet a student's individual abilities and interests. However, education critic Jonathan Kozol (1992) considers tracking one of the "savage inequalities" in our school system. Most students from privileged backgrounds get into higher tracks, where they receive the best the school can offer. Students from disadvantaged backgrounds end up in lower tracks, where teachers stress memorization with little focus on creativity (Bowles & Gintis, 1976; Oakes, 1982, 1985; Kilgore, 1991; Gamoran, 1992).

PUBLIC AND PRIVATE EDUCATION

Across the United States, 89 percent of the 54 million primary and secondary school children attend state-funded public schools. The remainder go to private schools.

Most private school students attend one of the more than 8,000 *parochial* schools (from Latin, meaning "of

the parish") operated by the Roman Catholic Church. The Catholic school system grew rapidly a century ago as cities swelled with immigrants. Today, after decades of flight from the inner city by white people, many parochial schools enroll non-Catholics, including a growing number of African Americans whose families seek an alternative to the neighborhood public school.

Protestants also have private schools, often known as Christian academies. These schools are favored by parents who want religious instruction for their children, as well as parents of all backgrounds who seek higher academic and disciplinary standards.

Some 6,000 nonreligious private schools enroll young people, mostly from well-to-do families. Many of these are prestigious, expensive preparatory schools, modeled on British boarding schools, that not only provide strong academic programs but also teach the mannerisms, attitudes, and social graces of the upper class. Many "preppies" maintain lifelong school-based networks that provide numerous social advantages.

Are private schools better than public schools? Research shows that, holding social background constant, students in private schools do outperform those in public schools. The advantages of private schools include smaller classes, more demanding course work, and greater discipline (Coleman, Hoffer, & Kilgore, 1981; Coleman & Hoffer, 1987).

But even the public schools are not all the same. For example, Winnetka, Illinois, one of the richest suburbs in the country, spends more than $8,000 each year on each of its students, compared to less than $3,000 in poor areas such

as Socorro, Texas (Edwards, 1998). In response to such differences, Vermont recently passed Act 60, a law that distributes tax money equally across that state.

Funding is important because it allows schools in more affluent areas to offer better schooling than schools in poor communities. This difference also benefits whites over minorities, which is why some districts started a policy of *busing,* transporting students to achieve racial balance and equal opportunity in schools. Although only 5 percent of U.S. students are bused to schools outside their neighborhoods, this practice is controversial. Supporters claim that given the reality of racial segregation, the only way governments will adequately fund schools in poor, minority neighborhoods is if white children from richer areas attend. Critics respond that busing is expensive and undermines the concept of neighborhood schools. But almost everyone agrees on one thing: Given the racial imbalance of most urban areas, an effective busing policy would have to join inner cities and suburbs—a plan that has never been politically possible.

A classic report by a research team headed by James Coleman (1966) confirmed that schools with mostly minority populations suffer problems ranging from large class size to insufficient libraries and too few science labs. But the Coleman report cautioned that more money by itself will not magically ensure educational quality. More important are the cooperative efforts of teachers, parents, and the students themselves. In other words, even if school funding were exactly the same everywhere, students who benefit from more *social capital*—that is, those whose families value schooling, read to their children, and encourage the development of imagination—would still perform better. In short, we should not expect schools alone to overcome marked social inequality in the United States (Schneider et al., 1998; Israel, Beaulieu, & Hartless, 2001).

ACCESS TO HIGHER EDUCATION

Schooling is the main path to good jobs. But only 62 percent of U.S. high school graduates enroll in college immediately after graduation (National Center for Education Statistics, 2003). Among young people aged eighteen to twenty-four years, about 36 percent are enrolled in college.

The most important factor affecting access to higher education is money. College is expensive: Even at state-supported colleges and universities, tuition averages about $3,000 annually, and tuition at the most expensive private colleges and universities exceeds $40,000 a year. As shown in Figure 14–2, two-thirds of the children in families with incomes above $75,000 per year (roughly the richest 30 percent, who fall within the upper-middle class and upper

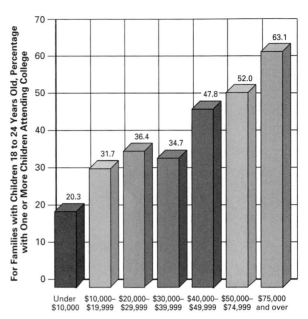

DIVERSITY SNAPSHOT

FIGURE 14-2   College Attendance and Family Income, 2002

Source: U.S. Census Bureau (2004).

class) attend college, but only 27 percent of children from families earning less than $20,000 a year go on to higher education (U.S. Census Bureau, 2004).

The cost of higher education prevents many minorities, typically those with below-average incomes, from attending college. As Figure 14–3 on page 388 shows, non-Hispanic whites are more likely than African Americans and Hispanics to complete high school, and this inequality appears on each step of the educational system ladder. For some, schooling is a path to social mobility, but it has not been able to overcome racial inequality in the United States.

Completing college brings many rewards, including higher earnings. Over a person's working lifetime, a college degree can add as much as $1 million to income. Table 14–2 on page 388 shows why. In 2002, men with an eighth-grade education typically earned $20,919; high school graduates averaged $33,206, and college graduates, $56,077. The ratios in parentheses show that a man with a bachelor's degree earns more than two-and-one-half times as much as a man with eight or fewer years of schooling. Across the board, women earn less than men, and added years of schooling

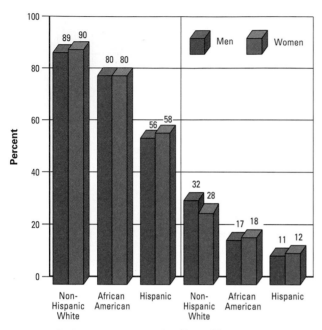

DIVERSITY SNAPSHOT

FIGURE 14–3 Educational Achievement for Various Categories of People, Aged 25 Years and Over, 2003

Source: U.S. Census Bureau (2004).

TABLE 14-2

Median Income by Sex and Educational Attainment*

Education	Men	Women
Professional degree	$100,000 (4.8)	$57,018 (3.5)
Doctorate	83,305 (4.0)	65,715 (4.0)
Master's	67,281 (3.2)	48,890 (3.0)
Bachelor's	56,077 (2.7)	40,853 (2.5)
1–3 years of college	40,851 (1.9)	29,400 (1.8)
4 years of high school	33,206 (1.6)	25,182 (1.5)
9–11 years of school	25,903 (1.2)	19,307 (1.2)
0–8 years of school	20,919 (1.0)	16,510 (1.0)

*Persons aged twenty-five years and over working full time, 2002. The earnings ratio, in parentheses, indicates how many times the lowest income level a person with additional schooling earns.

Source: U.S. Census Bureau (2004).

boosts their income more slowly. Keep in mind that for both men and women, some of the greater earnings that come with more schooling have to do with social background because the people with the most schooling are likely to come from well-off families to begin with.

GREATER OPPORTUNITY: EXPANDING HIGHER EDUCATION

With some 15.5 million people enrolled in colleges and universities, the United States is the world leader in providing a college education to its people. This country also enrolls more students from abroad than any other.

One reason for this achievement is that there are more than 4,000 colleges and universities in the United States. This number includes 2,364 four-year institutions (that award bachelor's degrees) and 1,833 two-year colleges (that award associate's degrees). Some two-year colleges are private, but most are publicly funded community colleges that serve a local area (usually a county) and charge low tuition (National Center for Education Statistics, 2003).

Historically, higher education has been a key path to better jobs and higher income. To offset the high cost of college, public funds have been used to allow many more people to enroll. After World War II, the GI Bill provided college funds to veterans; as a result, tens of thousands of men and women became the first generation in their families to attend college.

COMMUNITY COLLEGES

Since the 1960s, the expansion of state-funded community colleges has further increased access to higher education. According to the National Center for Education Statistics (2003), the 1,833 two-year colleges across the United States now enroll 39 percent of all college undergraduates.

Community colleges provide a number of specific benefits. First, their low cost places college courses and degrees within reach of millions of families who could not otherwise afford them. Put another way, many who enroll at community colleges today are the first members of their families to pursue a postsecondary degree. The low cost of community colleges is especially important during periods of economic recession, such as the slowdown that began in 2001. When the economy slumps and people lose their jobs, college enrollments—especially at low-cost community colleges—soar.

Second, community colleges have special importance to minorities. Currently, half of all African American and Hispanic undergraduates in the United States attend community colleges.

Third, although community colleges serve local populations, many attract students from around the world. Many

APPLYING THEORY

EDUCATION

	Structural-Functional Approach	Social-Conflict Approach
What is the level of analysis?	Macro-level	Macro-level
What is the importance of education for society?	Schooling performs many vital tasks for the operation of society, including socializing the young and encouraging discovery and invention to improve our lives. Schooling helps unite a diverse society by teaching shared norms and values.	Schooling maintains social inequality through unequal schooling for rich and poor. Within individual schools, tracking provides privileged children with better educations than poor children.

community colleges recruit students from abroad, and more than one-third of all foreign students enrolled on a U.S. campus are studying at community colleges (Briggs, 2002; Golden, 2002).

Finally, the highest priority of faculty who work at large universities is typically research, but the most important job for community college faculty is teaching. This means that although teaching loads are high (typically four or five classes each semester), community colleges appeal to faculty who find their greatest pleasure in the classroom. Community college students often get more attention from faculty than students at large universities (Jacobson, 2003).

PRIVILEGE AND PERSONAL MERIT

If attending college is a rite of passage for rich men and women, as social-conflict analysis suggests, then schooling transforms social privilege into personal merit. However, because of our cultural emphasis on individualism, we tend to see diplomas and degrees as badges of ability rather than as symbols of family wealth (Sennett & Cobb, 1973). When we congratulate the new graduate, we rarely recognize the resources—both financial and cultural—that made this achievement possible. Yet young people from families with incomes exceeding $100,000 a year average more than 200 points higher on the SAT college entrance examination than young people from families with $10,000 in annual income. The richer students are thus more likely to get into college; once there, they are also more likely to get a college degree. In a *credential society*—one that evaluates people based on their schooling—companies hire those with the best education. This process ends up harming those who are already disadvantaged (Collins, 1979).

Critical review. Social-conflict analysis links formal education to social inequality to show how schooling transforms

privilege into personal worthiness and disadvantage into personal deficiency. However, the social-conflict approach overlooks the extent to which schooling provides upward mobility for talented women and men from all backgrounds. In addition, despite claims that schooling supports the status quo, today's college curricula challenge social inequality on many fronts.

The Applying Theory table sums up what the theoretical approaches show us about education.

Problems in the Schools

An intense debate revolves around schooling in the United States. Because we expect schools to do so much—to equalize opportunity, teach discipline, and fire the imagination—few people think public schools are doing an excellent job. Although half of adults give our schools a grade of A or B, just as many give a grade of C or below (Phi Delta Kappa International, 2004).

DISCIPLINE AND VIOLENCE

When many of today's older teachers think back to their own student days, school "problems" consisted of talking out of turn, chewing gum, breaking the dress code, or cutting class. But today's schools are also dealing with drug and alcohol abuse, teenage pregnancy, and outright violence. Although almost everyone agrees schools should teach personal discipline, many think the job is no longer being done.

In recent years, violence has claimed the lives of students and teachers in schools across the United States. Moreover, in national surveys, about 25 percent of high school students and 11 percent of teachers report being victims of violence in and around schools in hundreds of thousands of cases that do not capture national headlines (Arnette & Walsleben, 1998).

DIVERSITY: RACE, CLASS, & GENDER
School Discipline: A Case of Racial Profiling?

Ken Russell was known as a troublemaker in his Modesto, California, high school. He doesn't deny it. But he also thinks he has been punished for more than his behavior. Why? Ken, who is African American, recently got into a scuffle with another boy, who is white. It started with name calling, Ken threw a punch, and there was a fistfight. Ken took some lumps, but the white boy required five stitches to close a wound over his left eye.

The school responded with suspensions: The white boy was sent home for three days, and Ken was suspended for more than a month. The school justified the difference by pointing to the white student's more serious injuries. But after hearing school officials describe the fight as "mutual," Ken's father thought his son's longer suspension was unfair. He filed a civil rights complaint, claiming that his son was punished more severely because he is black.

Records in the Modesto school district indicate a clear pattern: Black students are two-and-one-half times more likely than white students to be kicked out of school for misbehaving. Research confirms that this pattern holds nationwide, with African Americans more likely than whites to be suspended, expelled, or arrested at school.

Why? One Modesto school official claims the answer is simply that

black youngsters are more likely to misbehave. He points out that the school district also suspends far more males than females. "Does that mean," he asks, "that we discriminate against men?"

But others charge that racial bias is real. One recent study of school discipline in a large school district in Indiana concluded that black students were more likely than white students to be disciplined for the same behaviors,

Does race play a part in which students school officials charge with behavior problems? What about social class?

especially relatively minor issues such as making too much noise or acting disrespectfully. "You can choose not to use the word *racism*," the researcher concluded, "but districts need to look seriously at what is going on."

Perhaps both theories contain some truth. The National Association of Secondary School Principals confirms that blacks are more likely than whites to misbehave, but they claim the cause is not race but differences in social background. In other words, black children have more disciplinary problems in school because they are more likely to come from poor families where they are subject to disadvantages ranging from less parenting to exposure to lead-based paint. But if this is so, we are still left with the question, "Whose fault is that?"

WHAT DO YOU THINK?

1. Outline the arguments for and against the idea that school discipline unfairly targets African Americans. What is your position?
2. Do you think the fact that African American students are more likely to be disciplined than white students is a case of racial profiling? Why or why not?
3. What can schools do to ensure that all students are treated fairly?

Source: Morse (2002a).

Schools do not create the violence; in most cases, violence spills into schools from the surrounding community. Following the school shootings of the 1990s, many school districts adopted zero-tolerance policies that require suspension or expulsion for serious misbehavior. But such policies have become controversial because they often lead schools to suspend more African American students than white students. The Diversity box takes a closer look at this issue.

STUDENT PASSIVITY

If some schools are plagued by violence, many more are filled with bored students. Some of the blame for passivity can be placed on television (which now claims more of young people's time than school), parents (who are not involved enough with their children), and students themselves. But schools must share the blame (Coleman, Hoffer, & Kilgore, 1981).

Bureaucracy. The small, personal schools that served local communities a century ago have evolved into huge education factories. In a study of high schools across the United States, Theodore Sizer (1984:207–9) identified five ways in which large, bureaucratic schools undermine education:

1. **Rigid uniformity.** Bureaucratic schools run by outside specialists (such as state education officials) generally ignore the cultural character of local communities and the personal needs of their children.

2. **Numerical ratings.** School officials focus on attendance rates, dropout rates, and achievement test scores. They overlook dimensions of schooling that are difficult to quantify, such as creativity and enthusiasm.

3. **Rigid expectations.** Officials expect fifteen-year-olds to be in the tenth grade and eleventh graders to score at a certain level on a standardized verbal achievement test. Rarely are exceptionally bright and motivated students permitted to graduate early. Likewise, the system pushes poor performers on from grade to grade.

4. **Specialization.** High school students learn Spanish from one teacher, receive guidance from another, and are coached in sports by still others. Students experience this division of labor as a continual shuffling between fifty-minute periods throughout the school day. As a result, no school official comes to know the "complete" student.

5. **Little individual responsibility.** Highly bureaucratic schools do not empower students to learn on their own. Similarly, teachers have little say in how they teach their classes; they cannot accelerate learning without disrupting the system.

Of course, with 54 million schoolchildren in the United States, schools have to be bureaucratic to get the job done. But Sizer recommends that we "humanize" schools by eliminating rigid scheduling, reducing class size, and training teachers more broadly to make them more involved in the lives of their students. James Coleman (1993) adds that schools should be less "administratively driven" and more "output-driven." Perhaps this transformation could begin by ensuring that graduation from high school depends on what students have learned rather than how many years they have spent in the building.

The silent college classroom. Passivity is also common among college and university students (Gimenez, 1989). Sociologists rarely study the college classroom—a curious

For all categories of people in the United States, dropping out of school greatly reduces the chances to get a good job and earn a secure income. Why is the drop-out rate particularly high among Hispanic Americans?

fact considering how much time they spend there. A fascinating exception is a study of a coeducational university where David Karp and William Yoels (1976) found that even in small classes, only a few students speak up. Thus, passivity is a classroom norm, and students even become irritated if one of their number is especially talkative.

According to Karp and Yoels, most students think classroom passivity is their own fault. But as anyone who watches young people outside of class knows, they are usually active and vocal. Thus, it is schools that teach students to be passive, viewing instructors as experts who serve up "truth." Students see their proper role as quietly listening and taking notes. As a result, the researchers estimate, just 10 percent of college class time is used for discussion.

Faculty can bring students to life in their classrooms by making use of four teaching strategies: (1) calling on students by name when they volunteer, (2) positively reinforcing student participation, (3) asking analytical rather than factual questions and giving students time to answer, and (4) asking for student opinions even when no one volunteers a response (Auster & MacRone, 1994).

DROPPING OUT

If many students are passive in class, others are not there at all. The problem of *dropping out*—quitting before earning even a high school diploma—leaves young people (many of whom are disadvantaged to begin with) unprepared for the world of work and at high risk for poverty.

The dropout rate has declined slightly in recent decades; currently, 10.7 percent of people between the ages of sixteen and twenty-four are high school dropouts, a total of 3.8 million young women and men. Dropping out is least common among non-Hispanic whites (7.3 percent), more likely among non-Hispanic African Americans (10.9 percent), and most common among Hispanics (27.0 percent) (National Center for Education Statistics, 2004).

Some students drop out because of problems with the English language or because of pregnancy; others must work to support families. The dropout rate (10.7 percent) among children growing up in the poorest 20 percent of all households is more than six times as high as that (1.7 percent) for youngsters living in the richest 20 percent of households (National Center for Education Statistics, 2004). These data suggest that many dropouts are young people whose parents also have little schooling, revealing a multigenerational cycle of disadvantage.

ACADEMIC STANDARDS

Perhaps the most serious educational issue confronting our society is the quality of schooling. *A Nation at Risk,* a 1983 study of the quality of U.S. schools by the National Commission on Excellence in Education, begins with this alarming statement:

> If an unfriendly foreign power had attempted to impose on America the mediocre educational performance that exists today, we might well have viewed it as an act of war. As it stands, we have allowed this to happen to ourselves. (1983:5)

Supporting this claim, the report notes that "nearly 40 percent of seventeen-year-olds cannot draw inferences from written material; only one-fifth can write a persuasive essay; and only one-third can solve mathematical problems requiring several steps" (1983:9). Furthermore, scores on the Scholastic Assessment Test (SAT) show little improvement over time. In 1967, median scores were 516 on the mathematics test and 543 on the verbal test; by 2004, the average in mathematics had risen slightly to 518, and the verbal average had slipped to just 508. Nationwide, one-third of high school students—and more than half of those in urban schools—fail to master even the basics in reading, math, and science on the National Assessment of Education Progress examination (Marklein, 2000; Barnes, 2002a).

For many, even basic literacy is at issue. **Functional illiteracy,** *a lack of the reading and writing skills needed for everyday living,* is a problem for one in eight U.S. children who leave secondary school. For older people, the problem is even worse, with about 40 million U.S. adults (about 20 percent of the total) reading and writing at an eighth-grade level or below.

A Nation at Risk recommends drastic reform. First, it calls for schools to require *all* students to complete several years of English, mathematics, social studies, general science, and computer science. Second, schools should not promote students until they meet achievement standards. Third, teacher training must improve and teachers' salaries be raised to draw talent into the profession. *A Nation at Risk* concludes that schools must meet public expectations and that citizens must be prepared to pay for a job well done.

What has happened in the years since this report was issued? In some respects, schools have improved. A report by the Center on Education Policy (2000) noted the decline in the dropout rate, a trend toward schools offering more challenging courses, and a larger share of high school graduates going to college. Despite several tragic cases of shootings, school violence overall was down during the 1990s. At the same time, the evidence suggests that a majority of elementary school students are falling below standards in reading; in many cases, they can't read at all. In short, although some improvement is evident, much remains to be done.

The United States spends more on schooling its children than almost any other country. Even so, U.S. eighth graders lag behind their counterparts in other countries, placing seventeenth in the world in science achievement and twenty-eighth in mathematics (Bennett, 1997; Finn & Walberg, 1998). Cultural values play a big part in international comparisons. For example, U.S. students generally are less motivated and do less homework than students in Japan. Japanese young people also spend sixty more days in school each year than U.S. students. Perhaps one approach to improving schools is simply to have students spend more time there.

GRADE INFLATION

Academic standards depend on the use of grades that have clear meaning and are awarded for work of appropriate quality. Yet in recent decades, there has been a substantial amount of *grade inflation,* the awarding of higher and higher grades for average work. While not necessarily found in every school, grade inflation is evident in both high schools and colleges.

One recent study of high school grades shows how dramatic the change has been. In 1969, as Figure 14–4 shows, the high school records of students who had just entered college included more grades of C+ and below than grades of A–, A, and A+. By 2003, however, these A grades outnumbered grades of C+ and below by nine to one.

According to these researchers, there is no evidence that grade inflation will slow down anytime soon. As a result, the C grade (which used to mean "average") may all but disappear, making just about every student "above average."

What accounts for grade inflation? In part, teachers are clearly not as tough as they used to be. At the same time, the ever more competitive process of getting into college (and also graduate schools) puts pressure on schools to give high grades to make their graduates more successful (Astin et al., 2002).

Recent Issues in U.S. Education

Our society's schools continuously confront new challenges. Here we explore several recent and important educational issues.

SCHOOL CHOICE

Some analysts claim that our schools teach poorly because they have no competition. Thus, giving parents options about schooling their children might force all schools to do a better job. This is the essence of a policy called *school choice.*

The goal of school choice is to create a market for education so that parents and students can shop for the best value. According to one proposal, the government would provide vouchers to families with school-aged children and allow them to spend the money at public, private, or parochial schools. In recent years, major cities, including Indianapolis, Minneapolis, Milwaukee, Cleveland, Chicago, and Washington, D.C., as well as the states of Florida and Illinois, have experimented with choice plans designed to make public schools perform better in order to win the confidence of families. In addition, the Children's Scholarship Fund, a privately funded charity, has supported more than 40,000 children who want to attend nonpublic schools and has more than 1 million children on its waiting list (Lord, 2002).

Supporters claim that giving parents a choice about where to enroll their children is the only sure way to improve all schools. But critics (including teachers' unions) charge that school choice amounts to giving up on our nation's commitment to public education and that it will do little to improve schools in the central cities, where the need is greatest (Cohen, 1999; Morse, 2002b).

In 2002, President George W. Bush signed a new education bill that downplayed vouchers in favor of another approach to greater choice. Starting in the 2005–06 school year, all public schools must test every child in reading, mathematics, and science in grades three through eight. Although the federal government may provide more aid to

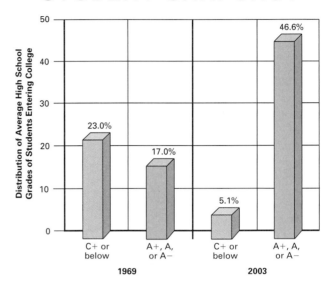

STUDENT SNAPSHOT

FIGURE 14-4   Grade Inflation in U.S. High Schools

Source: Sax et al. (2003).

schools with students who do not perform well, if those schools do not show improvements in test scores over time, low-income students will have the choice of special tutoring or transportation to another school (Lindlaw, 2002).

A more modest form of school choice involves *magnet schools,* 3,000 of which now exist across the country. Magnet schools offer special facilities and programs to promote educational excellence in a particular area, such as computer science, foreign languages, science and mathematics, or the arts. In school districts with magnet schools, parents can choose the one best suited to their child's particular talents and interests.

Another school choice strategy involves *charter schools,* public schools that are given more freedom to try new policies and programs. There are about 3,000 such schools in thirty-eight states, Washington, D.C., and Puerto Rico; they enroll about 700,000 students, about half of whom are minorities. In many of these schools, students have demonstrated high academic achievement, a requirement for renewal of the charter (U.S. Charter Schools, 2004).

A final development in the school choice movement is *schooling for profit.* Supporters of this plan say school systems can be operated more efficiently by private profit-making companies than by local governments. Private schooling is nothing new; across the United States, more

Educators have long debated the proper manner in which to school children with disabilities. On one hand, such children may benefit from distinctive facilities and specially trained teachers. On the other hand, they are less likely to be stigmatized as "different" if included in regular classroom settings. What does the debate over "special education" versus "inclusive education" mean for the classroom experience of all children, not only those who have disabilities?

than 25,000 schools are currently run by private organizations and religious groups. What is new is that hundreds of public schools, enrolling hundreds of thousands of students, are now run by private businesses for profit.

Research confirms that many public school systems suffer from bureaucratic bloat, spending far too much and teaching far too little. And our society has long looked to competition to improve quality. Evidence suggests that for-profit schools have greatly reduced administrative costs, but the educational results appear mixed. Although companies claim to improve student learning, some cities have cut back on business-run schooling. In recent years, school boards in Baltimore, Maryland; Miami, Florida; Hartford, Connecticut; and Boston, Massachusetts, have canceled the contracts of for-profit schooling corporations. But other cities are still willing to give for-profit schooling a try. For example, after Philadelphia's public school system failed to graduate one-third of its students, the state of Pennsylvania took over that city's schools and turned over many of them to for-profit companies. Emotions—both for and against privately run public schools—run high, and each side claims it speaks for the well-being of those caught in the middle: the school-children (Caruso, 2002; McGurn, 2002; Winters, 2002).

HOME SCHOOLING

Home schooling is gaining popularity across the United States. As noted in the opening to this chapter, about 1.1 million children (more than 2 percent of all school-aged children) have their formal schooling at home, and the number is increasing rapidly. This means that home schooling involves more school-age children than magnet schools, charter schools, and for-profit schools combined.

Why do parents undertake the enormous challenge of schooling their own children? Some twenty years ago, many of the parents who pioneered home schooling (which is now legal in every state) did not believe in public education, often because they wanted to give their children a strongly religious upbringing. Today, however, the majority are mothers and fathers who simply do not believe that public schools are doing a good job, and they think they can do better. To benefit their children, many parents are willing to change work schedules and to relearn algebra or other skills as necessary. Many belong to groups in which parents combine their efforts, specializing in what each knows best.

Supporters of home schooling point out that given the poor performance of many public schools, no one should be surprised that a growing number of parents are willing to step in to teach their own children. Furthermore, this system works—on average, students who learn at home outperform those who learn in school. Critics argue that home schooling reduces the amount of funding going to local public schools, which ends up hurting the majority of students. Moreover, as one critic points out, home schooling "takes some of the most affluent and articulate parents out of the system. These are the parents who know how to get things done with administrators" (Chris Lubienski, quoted in Cloud & Morse, 2001:48).

SCHOOLING PEOPLE WITH DISABILITIES

Many of the 5 million children with disabilities in the United States have difficulty getting to and from school; once there, many with crutches or wheelchairs cannot negotiate stairs and other obstacles in school buildings. Children with developmental disabilities such as mental retardation need extensive personal attention from specially trained teachers. As a result, many children with mental and physical disabilities have received a public education only after persistent efforts by parents and other concerned citizens (Horn & Tynan, 2001).

About one-half of children with disabilities are schooled in special facilities; the rest attend public schools, many joining regular classes. Including students with disabilities in the overall educational program is called *mainstreaming*. This form of *inclusive education* works best for physically impaired students who have no difficulty keeping up with the rest of the class. Another benefit is that mainstreaming allows all students to learn to interact with people different from themselves.

ADULT EDUCATION

In 2000, more than 88 million U.S. adults were enrolled in some type of schooling. These older students range in age from the mid-twenties to the seventies and beyond and make up 21 percent of students in degree-granting programs. Adults in school are more likely to be women than men, and most have above-average incomes.

Why do adults return to the classroom? The most common reasons given are to advance a career or train for a new job (66 percent), but many (43 percent) also point to the simple goal of personal enrichment (U.S. Census Bureau, 2003).

THE TEACHER SHORTAGE

A final challenge for U.S. schools is hiring enough teachers to fill the classrooms. A number of factors—including low salaries, frustration, and retirement, as well as rising enrollment and a reduction in class size—have combined to create more than 200,000 teaching vacancies in the United States each year.

How will these slots be filled? About the same number of people graduate with education degrees each year. Except for their education courses, most of them do not have a degree in a specific field (such as mathematics, biology, or English), and many have trouble passing state certification tests in the area they want to teach.

As a result, schools have adopted new recruitment strategies. Some analysts suggest that community colleges can play a larger role in teacher education. Others support using incentives such as higher salaries and signing bonuses to draw into teaching people who have already had successful careers. Another approach is for states to make teaching certification easier to get. Finally, many school districts are going global, actively recruiting in countries such as Spain, India, and the Philippines to bring talented women and men from around the world to U.S. classrooms (Lord, 2001; Philadelphia, 2001; Evelyn, 2002).

LOOKING AHEAD: SCHOOLING IN THE TWENTY-FIRST CENTURY

Despite the fact that the United States leads the world in sending people to college, the public school system struggles with serious problems, many of which have their roots in the larger society. We cannot expect schools by themselves to provide high-quality education. Schools will improve only if students, teachers, parents, and local communities commit themselves to educational excellence. In short, educational problems are *social* problems for which there is no quick fix.

For much of the twentieth century, there were just two models for education in the United States: public schools run by the government and private schools operated by nongovernment organizations. In recent decades, as we have noted, many new ideas about schooling have emerged, including schooling for profit and a wide range of choice programs. In the decades ahead, we will probably see some significant changes in mass education, guided in part by the results of social science research pointing out how various strategies work.

Another factor that will continue to shape schools is new information technology. Today, 97 percent of primary and secondary schools use computers for instruction. Computers prompt students to be more active and allow them to progress at their own pace. Computers do have limitations; they can never replace the personal insight or imagination of a motivated human teacher. Nor will technology ever solve all the problems that plague our schools, including violence and rigid bureaucracy. What we need is a broad plan for social change that refires this country's ambition to provide universal schooling of the highest quality—a goal that we have yet to achieve.

Medicine and Health

Another institution that expands greatly in modern societies is **medicine,** *the social institution that focuses on fighting disease and improving health.*

 Learn more about the World Health Organization at http://www.who.int/en/

In ideal terms, according to the World Health Organization (1946:3), **health** is *a state of complete physical, mental, and social well-being.* This definition emphasizes an important idea: *Health is as much a social as a biological issue.*

HEALTH AND SOCIETY

Society affects health in four basic ways:

1. **Cultural patterns define health.** Standards of health vary from culture to culture. A century ago, yaws, a contagious skin disease, was so common in tropical Africa that people there considered it normal (Dubos, 1980, orig. 1965). "Health," therefore, is sometimes a matter of having the same diseases as one's neighbors (Pinhey, Rubinstein, & Colfax, 1997).

   What people see as healthful also reflects what they think is morally good. People (especially men) in

TABLE 14-3

The Leading Causes of Death in the United States, 1900 and 2002

1900	2002
1. Influenza and pneumonia	1. Heart disease
2. Tuberculosis	2. Cancer
3. Stomach and intestinal disease	3. Stroke
4. Heart disease	4. Lung disease (noncancerous)
5. Cerebral hemorrhage	5. Accidents
6. Kidney disease	6. Diabetes
7. Accidents	7. Influenza and pneumonia
8. Cancer	8. Alzheimer's disease
9. Disease in early infancy	9. Kidney disease
10. Diphtheria	10. Blood disease

Sources: Information for 1900 is from William C. Cockerham, *Medical Sociology*, 2d ed. (Englewood Cliffs, N.J.: Prentice Hall, 1986), p. 24; information for 2002 is from Kenneth D. Kochanek & Betty L. Smith, *National Vital Statistics Reports*, vol. 52, no. 13 (Hyattsville, Md.: National Center for Health Statistics, 2004).

the United States think a competitive way of life is "healthy" because it fits our cultural mores, but stress contributes to heart disease and many other illnesses. On the other hand, people who object to homosexuality on moral grounds often call it "sick," even though it is natural from a biological point of view. Thus, ideas about health act as a form of social control, encouraging conformity to cultural norms.

2. **Cultural standards of health change over time.** Early in the twentieth century, some doctors warned women not to go to college because higher education strained the female brain. Others claimed that masturbation was a threat to health. We now know that both of these ideas are false. Fifty years ago, on the other hand, few doctors understood the dangers of cigarette smoking or too much sun exposure, practices that we now recognize as serious health risks. Even patterns of basic hygiene change over time. Today, 75 percent of U.S. adults report bathing every day; back in 1950, only 30 percent said the same (Gallup poll, cited in "Americans," 2000).

3. **A society's technology affects people's health.** In poor nations, infectious diseases are widespread because of malnutrition and poor sanitation. As industrialization raises living standards, people become healthier. But industrial technology also creates new

threats to health. As Chapter 15 ("Population, Urbanization, and Environment") explains, rich societies endanger health by encouraging overeating, overtaxing the world's resources, and creating pollution.

4. **Social inequality affects people's health.** All societies distribute resources unequally. Overall, the rich have far better physical, mental, and emotional health than the poor.

Health: A Global Survey

Because health is closely linked to social life, human well-being improved over the long course of history as societies developed more advanced technology. Differences in societal development are also the cause of striking differences in health around the world today.

HEALTH IN LOW-INCOME COUNTRIES

With only simple technology, our ancestors could do little to improve health. Hunters and gatherers faced frequent food shortages, which sometimes forced mothers to abandon their children. Those lucky enough to survive infancy were still vulnerable to injury and illness, so half died by age twenty and few lived to forty (Scupin, 2000; Nolan & Lenski, 2004).

As agricultural societies developed, food became more plentiful. Yet social inequality also increased, so that elites enjoyed better health than peasants and slaves, who lived in crowded, unsanitary shelters and often went hungry. In the growing cities of medieval Europe, human waste and refuse piled up in the streets, spreading infectious diseases, and plagues periodically wiped out entire towns (Mumford, 1961).

November 1, Central India. Poverty is not just a matter of what you have; it shapes what you are. Most of the people we see in the villages here have never had the benefit of a doctor or a dentist. The result is easy to see: People look old before their time.

In much of the world, poverty cuts decades off the life expectancy found in rich countries. A look back at Global Map 9–1 on page 233 shows that in the poorest countries of the world, most people die before reaching their teens. To make matters worse, medical personnel are few and far between, so that many of the world's poorest people never see a doctor.

The World Health Organization reports that 1 billion people around the world—one person in six—suffer from

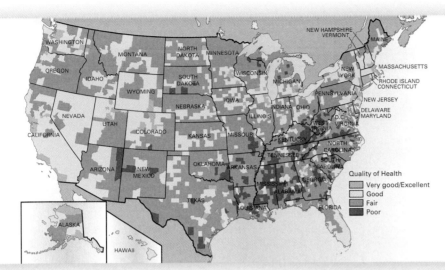

SEEING OURSELVES

NATIONAL MAP 14-1

Health across the United States

Average health varies from place to place throughout the United States. This map shows the results of a survey that asked people across the country about their personal health, including their smoking habits, nutritional diet, and frequency of illness. Looking at the map, what pattern do you see? Can you explain it?

Source: *American Demographics* magazine, October 2000, p. 50. Reprinted with permission from *American Demographics*. © 2000 by Intertec Publishing, a Primedia Company.

Quality of Health

Very good/Excellent
Good
Fair
Poor

serious illness due to poverty. Poor sanitation and malnutrition kill people of all ages. In a classic vicious circle, poverty breeds disease, which reduces people's ability to work, increasing poverty. When medical technology is used to control infectious disease, the populations of poor nations soar. But without enough resources to provide for the current population, poor societies can hardly afford population growth. Thus, programs to lower death rates in poor countries must be coupled with programs to reduce birth rates.

HEALTH IN HIGH-INCOME COUNTRIES

Industrialization dramatically changed patterns of health in Europe, although at first not for the better. By 1800, as the Industrial Revolution took hold, factory jobs drew people from all over the rural countryside. Cities became overcrowded, creating serious sanitation problems. Factories fouled the air with smoke, and workplace accidents were common.

However, as industrialization progressed, rising living standards translated into better nutrition and safer housing for most people, and health began to improve in Western Europe and North America. After 1850, medical advances also improved health, primarily by controlling infectious diseases. For example, in 1854, a researcher named John Snow mapped the street addresses of London's cholera victims and found that they had all drunk contaminated water from the same well (Rockett, 1994). Such discoveries by Snow and others led scientists to link cholera to specific bacteria and eventually to develop a

For information on nutrition and health, go to http://www.nal.usda.gov/fnic/etext/000056.html

vaccine against the deadly disease. Armed with scientific knowledge, early environmentalists campaigned against common practices such as dumping raw sewage into rivers used for drinking water. By the early twentieth century, death rates from infectious diseases had fallen sharply.

The leading killers in 1900—influenza and pneumonia—account for just a few percent of deaths in the United States today. As Table 14–3 shows, chronic illnesses, such as heart disease, cancer, and stroke, are now the leading killers in the United States. Industrialization delays death by shifting its primary causes from acute illnesses that strike at any age to the chronic illnesses of old age.

Health in the United States

Because the United States is a rich nation, its people are generally healthy by global standards. Still, some categories of people have much better health than others.

WHO IS HEALTHY? AGE, GENDER, CLASS, AND RACE

Social epidemiology is *the study of how health and disease are distributed throughout a society's population.* Social epidemiologists examine the origin and spread of epidemic diseases and show how people's health is tied to their physical and social environments. National Map 14–1 surveys the health of the population of the United States, where there is a twenty-year difference in average life expectancy between the richest and poorest communities. This difference can be viewed in terms of age, gender, social class, and race.

Masculinity: A Threat to Health?

Doctors call it "coronary-prone behavior." Psychologists call it "Type A personality." Sociologists recognize it as our culture's idea of masculinity. It is a combination of attitudes and behavior, common among men in our society, that includes chronic impatience ("C'mon! Get outta my way!"), uncontrolled ambition ("I've gotta have it. I *need* that!"), and free-floating hostility ("Why are so many people *such idiots*?").

This pattern, although normal from a cultural point of view, is one major reason that men who are driven to succeed are at high risk for heart disease. By acting out the Type A personality, we may get the job done, but we set in motion complex biochemical processes that are very hard on the human heart.

Here are a few questions to help you determine your own degree of risk (or that of someone important to you):

1. **Do you believe that you have to be aggressive to succeed? Do nice guys finish last?** For your heart's sake, try to remove hostility from your life. One starting point: Eliminate profanity from your speech. Try to replace aggression with compassion, which can be surprisingly effective in dealing with other people. Medically speaking, compassion and humor—rather than irritation and aggravation—will improve your health.

2. **How well do you handle uncertainty and opposition?** Do you have moments when you fume, "Why won't the waiter take my order?" or "This customer just doesn't get it!" We all like to know what's going on, and we want others to agree with us. But the world often doesn't work

this way. Accepting uncertainty and opposition makes us more mature and certainly healthier.

3. **Are you uncomfortable showing positive emotion?** Many men think giving and accepting love from women, from children, and from other men is a sign of weakness. But the medical truth is that love supports health and anger damages it.

As human beings, we have a great deal of choice about how we live. Think about the choices you make, and reflect on how our society's idea of masculinity often makes us hard on others (including those we love) and—just as important—hard on ourselves.

WHAT DO YOU THINK?

1. What about masculinity is harmful to health?
2. Why do you think so many people are unaware of how masculinity can be harmful to health?
3. How can sociology play a part in changing men's health for the better?

Sources: Based on Friedman & Rosenman (1974) and Levine (1990).

Age and gender. Death is now rare among young people. Still, young people do fall victim to accidents and, more recently, to acquired immune deficiency syndrome (AIDS).

Throughout the life course, women have better health than men. First, females are less likely than males to die before or immediately after birth. Then, as socialization into gender roles proceeds, males become more aggressive and individualistic, resulting in higher rates of accidents, violence, and suicide. As the Diversity box explains, the combination of chronic impatience, uncontrolled ambition, and outbursts of hostility that doctors call "coronary-prone behavior" is a fairly close match with our culture's definition of masculinity.

Social class and race. *Infant mortality*—the death rate among children under one year of age—is twice as high for disadvantaged children in the United States as for children born into privileged families. Although the health of the richest children in this country is the best in the world, our poorest children are as vulnerable to disease as those in low-income nations such as Nigeria and Vietnam.

Government researchers tell us that 72 percent of people in families with incomes over $35,000 think their health is excellent or very good, but only 44 percent of people in families earning less than $20,000 say the same. Conversely, only about 6 percent of higher-income people describe their health as fair or poor, compared with 25 percent of low-income people (Lethbridge-Cejku, Schiller, & Bernadel, 2004).

Poverty among African Americans—at three times the white rate—helps explain why black people are more likely to die in infancy and, as adults, suffer the effects of violence, drug abuse, and poor health (Hayward et al., 2000). Figure 14–5 shows that the life expectancy of white children born in 2001 is five years greater than for African American children (77.7 years compared with 72.2). Gender is an even stronger predictor of health than race: African American women outlive men of either race. From another angle, 80 percent of white men but just 66 percent of African American men will live to age sixty-five. The comparable figures for women are 88 percent for whites and 78 percent for African Americans.

CIGARETTE SMOKING

Cigarette smoking tops the list of preventable health hazards in the United States. Only after World War I did smoking become popular in this country. Despite growing evidence of its dangers, smoking remained fashionable even a generation ago. Today, however, an increasing number of people consider smoking a mild form of social deviance.

The popularity of cigarettes peaked in 1960, when 45 percent of U.S. adults smoked. By 2002, only 23 percent were lighting up (Centers for Disease Control and Prevention, 2004). Quitting is difficult because cigarette smoke contains nicotine, a physically addictive drug. Many people smoke to cope with stress: Divorced and separated people are likely to smoke, as are lower-income people, the unemployed, and people in the armed forces. Moreover, a slightly larger share of U.S. men (25 percent) than women (20 percent) smoke. But cigarettes, the only form of tobacco use popular among women, have taken a toll on women's health. By 1987, lung cancer surpassed breast cancer as a cause of death among U.S. women, who now account for 40 percent of all smoking-related deaths (Neergaard, 2001).

Some 440,000 men and women die prematurely each year as a direct result of cigarette smoking, a figure that exceeds the death toll from alcohol, cocaine, heroin, homicide, suicide, automobile accidents, and AIDS combined (Centers for Disease Control and Prevention, 2003). Smokers also suffer more often from minor illnesses such as the flu, and pregnant women who smoke increase the likelihood of spontaneous abortion, prenatal death, and low-birthweight babies. Even nonsmokers exposed to cigarette smoke have a high risk of smoking-related diseases.

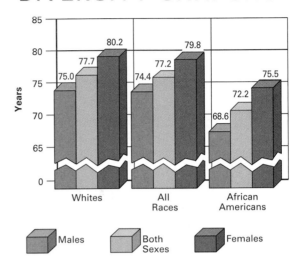

DIVERSITY SNAPSHOT

FIGURE 14-5 Life Expectancy of U.S. Children Born in 2001

Source: Arias (2004).

Tobacco is an $83 billion industry in the United States. In 1997, the tobacco industry admitted that cigarette smoking is harmful to health and agreed to stop marketing cigarettes to young people. Despite the antismoking trend in the United States, the percentage of college students who smoke has been creeping upward, to 29 percent in 2001 (Centers for Disease Control and Prevention, 2002). In addition, the use of chewing tobacco, also a threat to health, is increasing among the young.

The tobacco industry has increased marketing abroad, where there is less regulation of sales and advertising. Figure 14–6 on page 400 shows that in many countries (especially in Asia), a large majority of men smoke. Worldwide, more than 1 billion adults (about 30 percent of the total) smoke, consuming some 6 trillion cigarettes annually, and smoking is on the rise. The good news is that about ten years after quitting, an ex-smoker's health is about as good as that of someone who never smoked at all.

EATING DISORDERS

An *eating disorder* is an intense form of dieting or other unhealthy method of weight control. One eating disorder, *anorexia nervosa,* is characterized by dieting to the point of starvation; another is *bulimia,* which involves binge eating followed by induced vomiting to avoid weight gain.

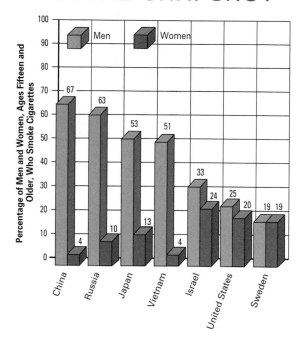

FIGURE 14-6 Cigarette Smoking in Selected Countries

Sources: Centers for Disease Control and Prevention (2004) and World Bank (2004).

Eating disorders have a significant cultural component; 95 percent of people who suffer from anorexia nervosa or bulimia are women, mostly from white, affluent families. For women, U.S. culture equates slenderness with being successful and attractive to men. Conversely, we tend to stereotype overweight women (and, to a lesser extent, men) as lazy, sloppy, and even stupid (Levine, 1987).

Research shows that most college-age women believe that "guys like thin girls," that being thin is crucial to physical attractiveness, and that they are not as thin as men would like. In fact, most college women actually want to be thinner than most college men want them to be. Most men express more satisfaction with their body shapes (Fallon & Rozin, 1985).

Because few women are able to meet our culture's unrealistic standards of beauty, many women develop a low self-image. It is our idealized image of beauty that leads many young women to diet to the point of risking their health and even their lives. The Global Sociology box explains how the introduction of U.S. culture to the island of Fiji soon resulted in a sharp increase in eating disorders among its women.

SEXUALLY TRANSMITTED DISEASES

Sexual activity, though both pleasurable and vital to the continuation of our species, can transmit more than fifty kinds of infection, or *venereal disease* (from Venus, the Roman goddess of love). Because U.S. culture associates sex with sin, some people regard sexually transmitted diseases (STDs) not only as illnesses but also as marks of immorality.

STDs grabbed national attention during the "sexual revolution" of the 1960s, when infection rates rose dramatically as people began sexual activity earlier and had a greater number of partners. This means that STDs are an exception to the general decline in infectious diseases over the course of the past century. By the late 1980s, the rising danger of STDs, especially AIDS, generated a sexual counterrevolution as people moved away from casual sex (Kain, 1987; Laumann et al., 1994). The following sections briefly describe several common STDs.

Gonorrhea and syphilis. Gonorrhea and syphilis, among the oldest known diseases, are caused by microscopic organisms that are almost always transmitted by sexual contact. Untreated, gonorrhea causes sterility, and syphilis can damage major organs and result in blindness, mental disorders, and death.

In 2002, some 352,000 cases of gonorrhea and 33,000 instances of syphilis were recorded in the United States, although the actual numbers may be several times higher. Most cases are contracted by non-Hispanic African Americans (73 percent), with lower numbers among non-Hispanic whites (17 percent), Latinos (8 percent), and Asian and Native Americans (almost 2 percent) (Centers for Disease Control and Prevention, 2003).

Both gonorrhea and syphilis can be cured easily with antibiotics such as penicillin. Thus, neither is a major health problem in the United States.

Genital herpes. Genital herpes is a virus that infects as many as 50 million adults in the United States (one in five). Though far less serious than gonorrhea and syphilis, herpes is incurable. People with genital herpes may not have any symptoms, or they may experience periodic, painful blisters on the genitals accompanied by fever and headache. Although it is not fatal to adults, women with active genital herpes can transmit the disease during a vaginal delivery, and it can be deadly to newborns. Therefore, infected women often give birth by cesarean section (Sobel, 2001).

AIDS. The most serious of all sexually transmitted diseases is acquired immune deficiency syndrome (AIDS). Identified in 1981, it is incurable and almost always fatal. AIDS is caused by the human immunodeficiency virus

GLOBAL SOCIOLOGY

Gender and Eating Disorders: A Report from Fiji

In 1995, television came to Fiji, a small group of islands in the South Pacific Ocean. A single cable channel carried programming from the United States, Great Britain, and Australia. Anne Becker, a Harvard researcher specializing in eating disorders, read the news with great interest, wondering what effect the new culture being poured in via television would have on young women there.

Traditionally, Fijian culture emphasizes good nutrition and looking strong and healthy. The idea of dieting to look very thin was almost unknown. So it is not surprising that in 1995, Becker found just 3 percent of teenage girls reported ever vomiting to control their weight. By 1998, however, a striking change had taken place, with 15 percent of teenage girls—a fivefold increase—reporting this practice. Becker also found that 62 percent of girls claimed they had dieted during the previous month and 74 percent reported feeling "too big" or "fat."

The rapid rise in eating disorders in Fiji, which Becker linked to the introduction of television, shows the power of culture to shape patterns of health. Eating disorders, including anorexia nervosa and bulimia, are even more common in the United States, where about half of college women report engaging in such behavior, even though most of these women, medically speaking, are not overweight. Indeed, Fijian women are now learning what many women in the United States already believe: "You are never too thin to feel fat."

WHAT DO YOU THINK?

1. How do we know that eating disorders are a social issue as well as a medical issue?
2. At what age do you think girls begin to learn that "you are never too thin to feel fat"?
3. What social changes might reduce the rate of eating disorders among U.S. women?

Source: Based on Becker (1999).

(HIV), which attacks white blood cells, weakening the immune system. AIDS thus makes a person vulnerable to a wide range of other diseases that eventually cause death.

AIDS deaths in the United States numbered 16,371 in 2002. But officials recorded some 26,000 new cases in the United States that year, raising the total number of cases on record to more than 877,000. Of these, about 502,000 have died (Centers for Disease Control and Prevention, 2002).

Globally, HIV infects some 40 million people—half of them under age twenty-five—and the number is rising rapidly. The global death toll now exceeds 20 million, with just 2 percent of all deaths in the United States. Global Map 14–2 on page 402 shows that Africa (more specifically, countries south of the Sahara) has the highest HIV infection rate and accounts for 66 percent of all world cases. A recent United Nations study found that across much of sub-Saharan Africa, fifteen-year-olds face a fifty-fifty chance of becoming infected with HIV. The risk is especially high for girls, not only because HIV is transmitted more easily from men to women but also because many African cultures encourage women to be submissive to men. According to some analysts, the AIDS crisis now threatens the political and economic security of Africa and, indeed, the entire world (Ashford, 2002; United Nations, 2002).

Upon infection, people with HIV display no symptoms at all, so most are unaware of their condition. Symptoms of AIDS may not appear for a year or longer, during which time an infected person may infect others. Within five years, one-third of infected people develop full-blown AIDS; half develop AIDS within ten years, and almost all become sick within twenty years.

HIV is infectious but not contagious. That is, HIV is transmitted from person to person through blood, semen, or breast milk but not through casual contact such as shaking hands, hugging, sharing towels or dishes, swimming together, or even coughing and sneezing. The risk of transmitting AIDS through saliva (as in kissing) is extremely low. The risk of transmitting HIV through sexual activity is greatly reduced by the use of latex condoms. However, abstinence or an exclusive relationship with an uninfected person is the only sure way to avoid infection.

Specific behaviors place people at high risk for HIV infection. The first is *anal sex,* which can cause rectal bleeding, allowing easy transmission of HIV from one person to another. The fact that many homosexual and bisexual men engage in anal sex helps explain why these categories of people account for 48 percent of AIDS cases in the United States.

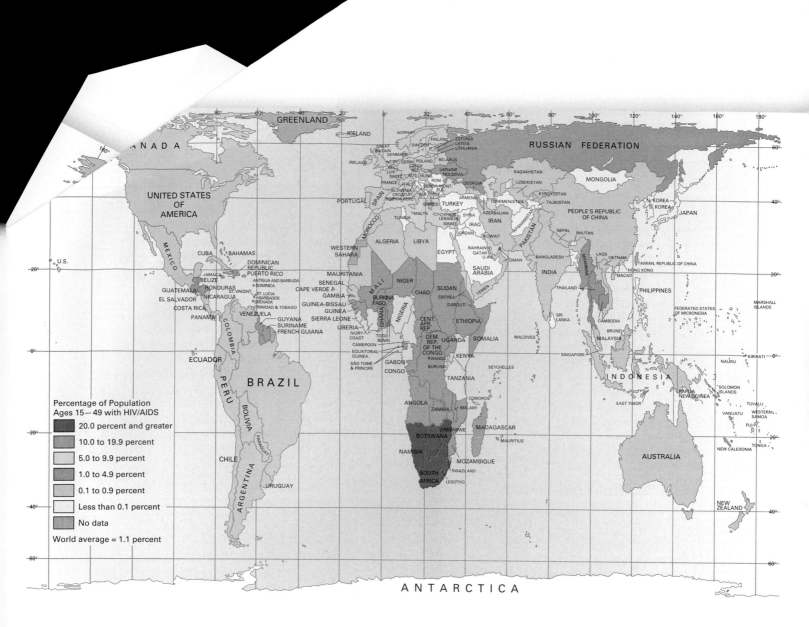

WINDOW ON THE WORLD

GLOBAL MAP 14-2 HIV/AIDS Infection of Adults in Global Perspective

Almost 70 percent of all global HIV infections are in sub-Saharan Africa. In countries such as Botswana and Swaziland, more than one-third of people between the ages of fifteen and forty-nine are infected with HIV/AIDS. This very high infection rate reflects the prevalence of other sexually transmitted diseases and infrequent use of condoms, two factors that promote heterosexual transmission of HIV. All of Southeast Asia accounts for about 17 percent of global HIV infections. In countries such as Cambodia and Thailand, 2 to 3 percent of people aged fifteen to forty-nine are now infected. All of North and South America taken together account for 8 percent of global HIV infections. In the United States, 0.6 percent of people aged fifteen to forty-nine are infected. The incidence of infection in Muslim nations is extremely low by world standards.

Source: Population Reference Bureau (2004); map projection from *Peters Atlas of the World* (1990).

Sharing needles used to inject drugs is a second high-risk behavior. At present, intravenous drug users account for 27 percent of people with AIDS, so sex with an intravenous drug user is also very risky. Because intravenous drug use is more common among poor people in the United States, AIDS is becoming a disease of the socially disadvantaged. Minorities make up a majority of all people with AIDS: Non-Hispanic African Americans (12 percent of the population) account for 42 percent of people with AIDS, and Latinos (13 percent of the population) represent 20 percent of all AIDS cases. Almost 80 percent of all women and children with the disease are African American or Latino. By contrast, Asian Americans and Native Americans together account for only about 1 percent of people with AIDS (Centers for Disease Control and Prevention, 2002).

Use of *any drug,* including alcohol, also increases the risk of being infected with HIV because it impairs judgment. In other words, even people who understand the risks may make bad choices once they are under the influence of alcohol, marijuana, or some other drug.

As Figure 14–7 shows, only 16 percent of people with AIDS in the United States became infected through heterosexual contact (although heterosexuals, infected in various ways, account for more than 30 percent of AIDS cases). But heterosexual activity does transmit HIV, and the danger rises with the number of sexual partners, especially if they fall into high-risk categories. Worldwide, heterosexual relations are the primary means of HIV transmission, accounting for two-thirds of all infections.

Treating just one person with AIDS costs hundreds of thousands of dollars, and this figure may rise as new therapies appear. At present, government health programs, private insurance, and personal savings rarely cover more than a fraction of the cost of treatment. In addition, there is the mounting cost of caring for at least 75,000 U.S. children orphaned by AIDS. Overall, there is little doubt that AIDS is both a medical and a social problem of monumental proportions.

The U.S. government responded slowly to the AIDS crisis, largely because gays and intravenous drug users are widely viewed as deviant. But funding for AIDS research has increased (now totaling some $11 billion annually), and researchers have identified some drugs, including protease inhibitors, that suppress the symptoms of the disease. But educational programs remain the most effective weapon against AIDS because prevention is the only way to stop a disease that has no cure.

ETHICAL ISSUES SURROUNDING DEATH

Now that technological advances have given human beings the power to draw the line separating life and death, people

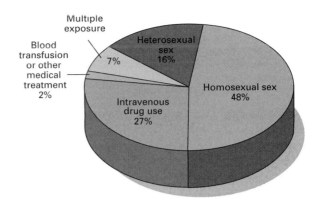

FIGURE 14-7   Types of Transmission for Reported U.S. AIDS Cases as of 2002

Source: Centers for Disease Control and Prevention (2002).

often must make the decision about how and when to do so. In other words, technology has added an ethical dimension to health and illness.

When does death occur?   Common sense suggests that life ends when breathing and heartbeat stop. But the ability to revive or replace a heart and artificially sustain respiration makes this definition of death obsolete. Thus, medical and legal experts in the United States define death as an *irreversible* state involving no response to stimulation, no movement or breathing, no reflexes, and no indication of brain activity (Ladd, 1979; Wall, 1980; Jones, 1998).

Do people have a right to die?   Today, medical personnel, family members, and patients themselves bear the agonizing burden of deciding when a terminally ill person should die. Among the most difficult cases are the 10,000 people in the United States in a permanent vegetative state who cannot express their own desires about life and death. Generally speaking, the first duty of doctors and hospitals is to protect a patient's life. Even so, a mentally competent person in the process of dying can refuse medical treatment or even nutrition (either at the time or, in advance, through a document called a "living will").

"Mercy killing" is the common term for **euthanasia,** *assisting in the death of a person suffering from an incurable disease.* Euthanasia (from Greek, meaning "a good death") poses an ethical dilemma, considered by some an act of kindness and by others a form of killing.

Whether there is a "right to die" is one of today's most difficult issues. All people with incurable diseases have a right to refuse treatment that might prolong their lives. But whether a doctor should be allowed to help bring about death is at the heart of today's debate. In 1994, three states—Washington, California, and Oregon—asked voters whether doctors should be able to help people who wanted to die. Only Oregon's proposition passed, and the law was quickly challenged and remained tied up in court until 1997, when voters again endorsed it. Since then, Oregon doctors have legally assisted in the death of terminally ill patients. In 1997, however, the U.S. Supreme Court decided that under the U.S. Constitution, there is no "right to die," a decision that has slowed the spread of such laws.

Supporters of *active* euthanasia—allowing a dying person to enlist the services of a doctor to bring on a quick death—argue that there are circumstances (such as when a dying person suffers from great pain) that make death preferable to life. Critics counter that permitting active euthanasia invites abuse. They fear that patients will feel pressure to end their lives to spare family members the burden of caring for them and the high costs of hospitalization. Research in the Netherlands, where physician-assisted suicide is legal, indicates that about one-fifth of all such deaths have occurred without a patient explicitly requesting to die (Gillon, 1999).

In the United States, a majority of adults express support for giving dying people the right to choose to die with a doctor's help (NORC, 2003). Therefore, the right-to-die debate is sure to continue.

The Medical Establishment

Throughout most of human history, health care was the responsibility of individuals and their families. Medicine emerges as a social institution only as societies become more productive and people take on specialized work.

Members of agrarian societies today still turn to various traditional health practitioners, including acupuncturists and herbalists. In industrial societies, medical care falls to specially trained and licensed professionals, from anesthesiologists to X-ray technicians. The medical establishment of modern, industrial societies took form over the last 150 years.

THE RISE OF SCIENTIFIC MEDICINE

In colonial times, herbalists, druggists, barbers, midwives, and ministers practiced the healing arts. But not all were effective. Unsanitary instruments, lack of anesthesia, and simple ignorance made surgery a terrible ordeal, and doctors probably killed as many people as they saved.

Doctors made medicine into a science by following scientific procedures to study the human body and how it works, emphasizing surgery and the use of drugs to fight

disease. Pointing to their specialized knowledge, doctors gradually established themselves as self-regulating professionals with medical degrees. The American Medical Association (AMA), founded in 1847, symbolized the growing acceptance of a scientific model of medicine.

Still, traditional practitioners of health care had their supporters. The AMA opposed them by seeking control of the certification process. In the early 1900s, state licensing boards agreed to certify only doctors trained in the scientific programs approved by the AMA. As a result, schools teaching other healing skills began to close, which soon limited the practice of medicine to individuals holding an M.D. degree. Accordingly, the prestige and income of doctors rose dramatically; today, men and women with M.D. degrees earn, on average, $250,000 annually.

Practitioners who did things differently, such as osteopathic physicians, concluded that they had no choice but to fall in line and follow AMA standards. Thus osteopaths (with D.O. degrees), originally concerned with treating illness by manipulating the skeleton and muscles, today treat illness with drugs in much the same way as medical doctors (with M.D. degrees). Chiropractors, herbal healers, and midwives still practice but have lower standing within the medical profession.

Scientific medicine, taught in expensive, urban medical schools, also changed the social profile of doctors so that most physicians came from privileged backgrounds and practiced in cities. Women, who had played a large part in many fields of healing, were scorned by the AMA. Some early medical schools did train women and African Americans, but with few financial resources, most of these schools eventually closed. Only in recent decades has the social diversity of the medical profession increased, with women and African Americans representing 30 percent and 5 percent of physicians, respectively (U.S. Department of Labor, 2004).

HOLISTIC MEDICINE

Recently, the scientific model of medicine has been tempered by the introduction of **holistic medicine,** *an approach to health care that emphasizes prevention of illness and takes into account a person's entire physical and social environment.* Holistic practitioners agree on the need for drugs, surgery, artificial organs, and high technology, but they emphasize treatment of the whole person instead of symptoms, and health rather than disease. There are three foundations of holistic health care (Gordon, 1980; Patterson, 1998):

1. **Patients are people.** Holistic practitioners are concerned not only with symptoms but also with how people's environment and lifestyle affect health. Holistic practitioners extend the bounds of

The profession of surgery has existed only for several centuries. Before that, barbers offered their services to the very sick, often cutting the skin to "bleed" a patient. Of course, this "treatment" was rarely effective, but it did produce plenty of bloody bandages, which practitioners hung out to dry. This practice identifies the origin of the red and white barber poles we see today.

Jan Sanders von Hemessen (c. 1504–1566), *The Surgeon,* oil on panel. Prado, Madrid, Spain/Giraudon/Bridgeman Art Library.

conventional medicine, taking an active role in fighting poverty, environmental pollution, and other dangers to public health.

2. **Responsibility, not dependency.** A scientific approach to medicine puts doctors in charge of health, and patients are to follow doctors' orders. Holistic medicine tries to shift some responsibility for health from doctor to patient by emphasizing health-promoting behavior. Holistic medicine favors an *active* approach to *health* rather than a *reactive* approach to *illness.*

3. **Personal treatment.** Scientific medicine treats patients in impersonal offices and hospitals, both disease-centered settings. Holistic practitioners favor, as much as possible, a personal and relaxed environment such as the home.

In sum, holistic care does not oppose scientific medicine but shifts the emphasis from treating disease to achieving the greatest well-being for everyone. Considering that the AMA certifies more than fifty medical specialties, there is a need for practitioners concerned with the whole patient.

PAYING FOR MEDICAL CARE: A GLOBAL SURVEY

As medicine has come to rely on high technology, the costs of medical care in industrial societies have skyrocketed. Countries throughout the world have adopted different strategies to meet these costs.

People's Republic of China. A poor, agrarian society in the process of industrializing, the People's Republic of China faces the immense task of providing for the health of more than 1 billion people. China has experimented with private medicine, but the government controls most health care.

China's "barefoot doctors," roughly comparable to U.S. paramedics, bring some modern methods of medical care to peasants in rural villages. Traditional healing arts, involving acupuncture and medicinal herbs, are still widely practiced. The Chinese approach to health is based on a holistic concern for the interplay of mind and body (Kaptchuk, 1985).

Russian Federation. The Russian Federation is struggling to transform a state-dominated economy into more of a market system. For this reason, medical care in this country is in transition. Nevertheless, the idea that everyone has a right to basic medical care remains widespread.

As in China, people in the Russian Federation do not choose a doctor but report to a local government health facility. Physicians have much lower incomes than medical doctors in the United States, earning about the same salary as skilled industrial workers (U.S. doctors earn roughly five times as much as U.S. industrial workers). Also, about 70 percent of Russia's doctors are women, compared to 30 percent in the United States. As in our society, occupations dominated by women offer fewer financial rewards in the Russian Federation.

Funded by government taxes, health care in Russia has suffered setbacks in recent years, partly due to a falling standard of living. A rising demand for medical care has strained a bureaucratic system that at best provides highly standardized and impersonal care. The optimistic view is that as market reforms proceed, both living standards and the quality of medical service will improve. In any case,

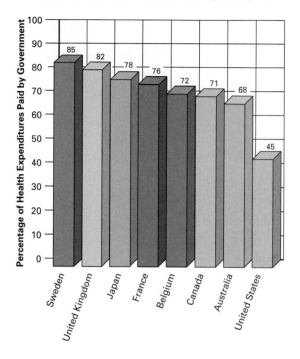

FIGURE 14–8 Extent of Socialized Medicine in Selected Countries

Sources: U.S. Census Bureau (2003) and World Bank (2004).

what does seem certain is that inequalities in medical care will increase (Specter, 1995; Landsberg, 1998).

Sweden. In 1891, Sweden began a mandatory, comprehensive system of government medical care. Citizens pay for this program with their taxes, which are among the highest in the world. Typically, doctors are government employees and most hospitals are government-managed. Sweden's system is called **socialized medicine,** *a medical care system in which the government owns and operates most medical facilities and employs most doctors.*

Great Britain. In 1948, Great Britain also established socialized medicine by creating a dual system of medical services. All British citizens are entitled to medical care provided by the National Health Service, but those who can afford it can also go to doctors and hospitals that operate privately.

Canada. Since 1972, Canada has had a single-payer model of medical care that provides care to all Canadians. Like a vast insurance company, the Canadian government pays

doctors and hospitals according to a set schedule of fees. But Canada's system, like Great Britain's, has two tiers, with some doctors working outside the government-funded system and setting their own fees.

Canada boasts of providing care for everyone at a lower cost than the (nonuniversal) medical system in the United States. However, the Canadian system uses less state-of-the-art technology and responds more slowly to people's needs, so that people may wait months to have major surgery. The Canadian system provides care for all its citizens, regardless of income, unlike the United States, in which lower-income people are often denied medical care (Rosenthal, 1991; Macionis & Gerber, 2005).

Japan. Physicians in Japan operate privately, but a combination of government programs and private insurance pays medical costs. As shown in Figure 14–8, the Japanese approach medical care much like the Europeans, with most medical expenses paid through the government.

PAYING FOR MEDICAL CARE: THE UNITED STATES

The United States stands alone among high-income nations in having no universal, government-operated program of medical care. Ours is a **direct-fee system,** *a medical care system in which patients pay directly for the services of doctors and* *hospitals.* Thus, whereas Europeans look to government to fund 80 percent of medical costs (paid for through taxation), the U.S. government pays less than half of this country's medical costs (U.S. Census Bureau, 2004).

Read the government report *Healthy People 2010* at http://www.cdc.gov/nchs/hphome.htm

In the United States, rich people can buy the best medical care in the world, but poor people are worse off than their counterparts in Europe. This difference translates into relatively high death rates among both infants and adults in the United States compared with many European countries (United Nations Development Programme, 2004).

Why does the United States have no national medical care program? First, because our culture stresses self-reliance, our society has limited government. Second, political support for a national medical program has not been strong, even among labor unions, which have concentrated on winning medical care benefits from employers. Third, the AMA and the insurance industry have strongly and consistently opposed national medical care (Starr, 1982).

Medical expenditures in the United States have increased dramatically, from $12 billion in 1950 to more than $1.4 trillion in 2002. This amounts to more than $4,000 per person, more than any other nation spends for medical care. Who pays the medical bills?

Private insurance programs. In 2003, some 174 million people in the United States (60 percent) received medical care benefits from a family member's employer or labor union. Another 26 million people (9 percent) purchased some private coverage on their own. Combining these figures, 69 percent of the U.S. population has private insurance, although few such programs pay all medical costs (U.S. Census Bureau, 2004).

Public insurance programs. In 1965, Congress created Medicare and Medicaid. Medicare pays some of the medical costs for people over age sixty-five; in 2003, it covered 39 million men and women, 14 percent of the population. In the same year, Medicaid, a medical insurance program for the poor, provided benefits to 36 million people, about 12 percent of the population. An additional 10 million veterans (4 percent) can obtain free care in government-operated hospitals. In all, 27 percent of this country's people get medical benefits from the government, but most also have private insurance.

Health maintenance organizations. About 76 million people (26 percent) in the United States belong to a **health maintenance organization** (HMO), *an organization that provides comprehensive medical care to subscribers for a fixed fee.* HMOs vary in cost and benefits, but none provides full coverage. Fixed fees make these organizations profitable if subscribers stay healthy; therefore, many take a preventive approach to health. However, HMOs have been criticized for refusing to pay for medical procedures that they consider unnecessary. Congress is currently debating the extent to which patients can sue HMOs to obtain better care.

In all, 84 percent of the U.S. population has some medical care coverage, either private or public. Yet most plans do not provide full coverage, so serious illness threatens even middle-class people with financial hardship. Most programs also exclude many medical services, such as dental care and treatment for mental health and substance abuse problems. Worse, 45 million people (almost 16 percent of the population) have no medical insurance at all, even though 74 percent of these people are working. Almost as many lose their coverage temporarily each year because of layoffs or job changes. Caught in the medical care bind are mostly low- to moderate-income people who cannot afford to pay for the medical care they need to stay healthy (Brink, 2002; U.S. Census Bureau, 2004).

THE NURSING SHORTAGE

Another issue in medical care is the shortage of nurses across the United States. In 2003, there were some 2.4 million nurses (people with the degree of R.N., registered

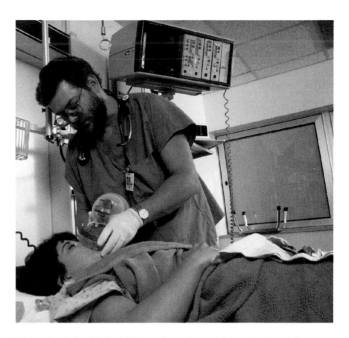

Throughout the United States, there is a serious shortage of nurses. One strategy for filling the need is for nursing programs to recruit more men into this profession; currently, men account for only 8 percent of nurses with R.N. degrees.

nurse), but about 11 percent of the available jobs (roughly 200,000 positions) are currently unfilled.

The immediate cause of the shortage is that fewer people are entering the nursing profession. During the last decade, enrollments in nursing programs have dropped by one-third, even as the need for nurses (driven by the aging of the U.S. population) goes up. Why this decline? One factor is that today's young women have a wide range of job choices, and fewer are drawn to the traditionally female occupation of nursing. This fact is evident in the rising median age of working nurses, which is now forty-three. Another is that many of today's nurses are unhappy with their working conditions, citing heavy patient loads, too much required overtime, a stressful working environment, and a lack of recognition and respect from supervisors, doctors, and hospital managers. In fact, one recent survey found that a majority of working nurses say they would not recommend the field to others, and more R.N.s are leaving the field for other jobs.

A hopeful sign is that the nursing shortage is bringing change to this profession. Salaries, which range from about $45,000 for general-duty nurses to $100,000 for certified nurse anesthetists, are rising, although slowly. Some hospitals and doctors are also offering signing bonuses in efforts to

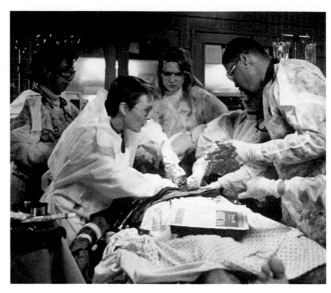

Our national view of medicine has changed during the last several decades. Television viewers in the 1970s watched doctors like Marcus Welby, M.D., confidently take charge of situations in a fatherly—and almost godlike—manner. By the 1990s, programs like "E.R." gave a more realistic view of the limitations of medicine to address illness, as well as the violence that wracks our society.

attract new nurses. In addition, nursing programs are trying harder to recruit a more diverse population, seeking more minorities (which are currently underrepresented) and, especially, more men (who now make up only 8 percent of R.N.s) (DeFrancis, 2002a, 2002b; Dworkin, 2002; Yin, 2002).

Theoretical Analysis of Medicine

Each of the theoretical approaches in sociology helps us organize and understand facts and issues concerning human health.

STRUCTURAL-FUNCTIONAL ANALYSIS

Talcott Parsons (1951) viewed medicine as society's strategy to keep its members healthy. Parsons considered illness to be dysfunctional because it reduces people's abilities to perform their roles.

The sick role. Society responds to illness not only by providing medical care but also by allowing people a **sick role,** *patterns of behavior defined as appropriate for people who are ill.* According to Parsons, the sick role releases people from everyday responsibilities. However, people cannot simply claim to be ill; they must "look the part" and, in serious cases, get the help of a medical expert. After assuming the sick role, the patient must do whatever is needed to regain good health, including cooperating with health professionals.

The physician's role. Physicians evaluate people's claims of sickness and help restore the sick to normal routines. Because of their specialized knowledge, physicians expect patients to follow "doctor's orders" in order to complete treatment.

Critical review. Parsons's analysis links illness and medicine to the broader organization of society. Others have extended the concept of the sick role to some nonillness situations such as pregnancy (Myers & Grasmick, 1989).

One limitation of the sick-role concept is that it applies to acute conditions (like the flu) better than to chronic illnesses (such as heart disease), which may not be reversible. In addition, a sick person's ability to assume the sick role (take time off from work to regain health) depends on the person's resources. Finally, illness is not completely dysfunctional; it can have some positive consequences. Many people who experience a serious illness consider it an opportunity to reevaluate their lives and gain a better sense of what is truly important to them (Myers, 2000).

SYMBOLIC-INTERACTION ANALYSIS

Using the symbolic-interaction approach, society is less a grand system than a complex and changing reality. In this view, health and medical care are socially constructed by people in everyday interaction.

Socially constructing illness. If both health and illness are socially constructed, people in a poor society may view malnutrition as normal. Similarly, many members of our own society give little thought to the harmful effects of a rich diet.

Our response to illness also is based on social definitions that may or may not square with medical facts. People with AIDS may be forced to deal with prejudice that has no medical basis. Students may pay no attention to symptoms of illness on the eve of vacation but head for the infirmary hours before a midterm examination. In short, health is less an objective fact than a negotiated outcome.

How people define a medical situation may actually affect how they feel. Medical experts marvel at *psychosomatic* disorders (a fusion of the Greek words for "mind" and "body"), when state of mind guides physical sensations (Hamrick, Anspaugh, & Ezell, 1986). Applying sociologist W. I. Thomas's theorem (presented in Chapter 4, "Social Interaction in Everyday Life"), we can say that once health or illness is defined as real, it can become real in its consequences.

Socially constructing treatment. Also in Chapter 4 we used Erving Goffman's dramaturgical approach to explain how doctors tailor their physical surroundings (their office) and their behavior (the "presentation of self") so that others see them as competent and in charge.

The sociologist Joan Emerson (1970) further illustrates this process of reality construction in her analysis of the gynecological examination carried out by a male doctor. The situation could be seriously misinterpreted because a man touching a woman's genitals is conventionally viewed as a sexual act and possibly an assault. To ensure that the situation is defined as impersonal and professional, medical personnel wear uniforms, and the examination room is furnished with nothing but medical equipment. The doctor's manner is designed to make the patient feel that to him, examining the genital area is no different from treating any other part of the body. A female nurse usually is present during the examination, not only to assist the physician but also to avoid any impression that a man and woman are "alone together."

Managing situational definitions is rarely taught in medical schools. This is unfortunate, because as Emerson's analysis shows, understanding how medical personnel construct reality in the examination room is as important as mastering the medical skills needed for treatment.

Critical review. The symbolic-interaction approach reveals that what people view as healthful or harmful depends on a host of factors that are not, strictly speaking, medical. This approach also shows that in any medical

STUDENT SNAPSHOT

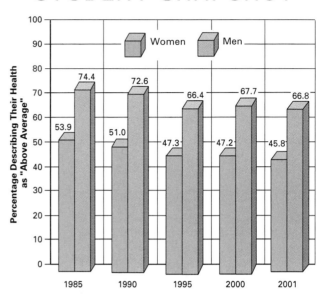

FIGURE 14-9 Self-Assessment of Physical Health by First-Year College Students, 1985–2001

Source: Astin et al. (2002).

procedure, both patient and medical staff engage in a subtle process of reality construction.

Critics fault the symbolic-interaction approach for implying that there are no objective standards of well-being. Certain physical conditions do indeed cause specific changes in people, regardless of how we may view those conditions. For example, people who lack sufficient nutrition and safe water suffer from their unhealthy environment, whether they define their surroundings as normal or not.

Figure 14–9 shows that since 1985, the share of beginning college students in the United States who describe their physical health as "above average" has been dropping. Do you think this trend reflects changing perceptions or a real decline in health (due, say, to eating more unhealthy food)? Why do you think more men than women see their health as above average?

SOCIAL-CONFLICT ANALYSIS

Social-conflict analysis points out the connection between health and social inequality and, taking the lead from Karl Marx, ties medicine to the operation of capitalism. Researchers have focused on three main issues: access to

APPLYING THEORY

HEALTH

	Structural-Functional Approach	Symbolic-Interaction Approach	Social-Conflict Approach
What is the level of analysis?	Macro-level	Micro-level	Macro-level
How does each approach relate health to society?	Illness is dysfunctional for society because it prevents people from carrying out their daily roles. The sick role releases people who are ill from responsibilities while they try to get well.	Societies define "health" and "illness" differently according to their living standards. How people define their own health affects how they actually feel (psychosomatic conditions).	Health is linked to social inequality, with rich people having more access to care than poor people. Capitalist health care places the drive for profits over the needs of people, treating symptoms rather than addressing poverty as a cause of illness.

medical care, the effects of the profit motive, and the politics of medicine.

Access to care. Health is important to everyone. But by requiring individuals to pay for health, capitalist societies allow the richest people to have the best health. The access problem is more serious in the United States than in most other high-income nations because we do not have a universal medical care system.

Conflict theorists argue that capitalism provides excellent health care for the rich but not for the rest of the population. Most of the 45 million people in the United States who lack any medical care coverage at present have low incomes.

The profit motive. Some social-conflict analysts go further, arguing that the real problem is not access to medical care but the character of capitalist medicine itself. The profit motive turns doctors, hospitals, and the pharmaceutical industry into multibillion-dollar corporations. The drive for higher profits encourages unnecessary tests and surgery and overreliance on expensive drugs rather than improving people's living conditions.

Of some 24 million surgical operations performed in the United States each year, three-fourths are elective, meaning that they are intended to promote long-term health and are not prompted by a medical emergency. Of course, any medical procedure or use of drugs is risky and harms between 5 and 10 percent of patients. Therefore, social-conflict theorists argue that surgery reflects the financial interests of surgeons and hospitals as well as the medical needs of patients (Cowley, 1995; Nuland, 1999).

Finally, say conflict theorists, our society is all too tolerant of doctors having a direct financial interest in the tests and procedures they order for their patients (Pear & Eckholm, 1991). In short, medical care should be motivated by a concern for people, not profits.

Medicine as politics. Although science declares itself to be politically neutral, scientific medicine often takes sides on significant social issues. For example, the medical establishment has always strongly opposed government medical care programs. The history of medicine shows that racial and sexual discrimination have been supported by "scientific" opinions about, say, the inferiority of women (Leavitt, 1984). Consider the diagnosis of "hysteria," a term that has its origins in the Greek word *hyster,* meaning "uterus." In choosing this word to describe a wild, emotional state, the medical profession suggested that being a woman is somehow the same as being irrational.

Even today, according to conflict theory, scientific medicine explains illness in terms of bacteria and viruses, ignoring the damaging effects of poverty. In effect, scientific medicine hides the bias in our medical system by transforming this social issue into simple biology.

Critical review. Social-conflict analysis provides still another view of the relationships between health, medicine, and society. According to this approach, social inequality is the reason some people have better health than others.

The most common objection to the conflict approach is that it minimizes the advances in U.S. health that can be credited to scientific medicine and higher living standards. Although there is plenty of room for improvement, health indicators for our population as a whole rose steadily over the course of the twentieth century, and they compare well with those in other high-income nations.

In sum, sociology's three major theoretical approaches explain why health and medicine are social issues. The Applying Theory table sums up what they teach us.

But advancing technology will not solve every health problem. On the contrary, as the Controversy & Debate box explains, today's advancing technology is raising new questions and concerns.

CONTROVERSY & DEBATE

The Genetic Crystal Ball: Do We Really Want to Look?

The liquid in the laboratory test tube seems ordinary enough, like a syrupy form of water. But this liquid is one of the greatest medical breakthroughs of all time; it may even hold the key to life itself. The liquid is deoxyribonucleic acid, or DNA, the spiraling molecule found in every cell of the human body that contains the blueprint for making each one of us human as well as different from every other person.

The human body is composed of some 100 trillion cells, most of which contain a nucleus of twenty-three pairs of chromosomes (one of each pair comes from each parent). Each chromosome is packed with DNA in segments called genes. Genes guide the production of protein, the building block of the human body.

If genetics sounds complicated (and it is), the social implications of genetic knowledge are even more complex. Scientists discovered the structure of the DNA molecule in 1952, but it wasn't until 2000 that scientists neared the goal of mapping the human genome. Charting our genetic landscape may lead to understanding how each bit of DNA shapes our being. But do we really want to turn the key to understand life itself? And what do we do with this knowledge once we have it?

In the Human Genome Project, many scientists see the opportunity to stop certain illnesses dead in their tracks. Research has already identified genetic abnormalities that cause some forms of cancer, sickle-cell anemia, muscular dystrophy,

Huntington's disease, cystic fibrosis, and other crippling and deadly afflictions. In the future, genetic screening—a scientific "crystal ball"—could tell people their medical destiny and allow doctors to manipulate segments of DNA to prevent diseases before symptoms appear.

But many people urge caution in such research, warning that genetic information can easily be abused. At its worst, genetic mapping opens the door to Nazi-like efforts to breed a "super race." Indeed, in 1994, the People's Republic of China began to regulate marriage and childbirth with the purpose of avoiding "new births of inferior quality."

It seems inevitable that some parents will want to use genetic testing to predict the health (or even the eye color) of their future children. What if they want to abort a fetus because it falls short of their standards? When

genetic manipulations become possible, should parents be able to create "designer children"?

Then there is the issue of "genetic privacy." Can a bride-to-be request a genetic evaluation of her fiancé before agreeing to marry? Can life insurance companies demand genetic testing before issuing policies? Should employers be allowed to screen job applicants to weed out those whose future illnesses might drain their health care funds? Clearly, what is scientifically possible is not always morally desirable. Society is already struggling with questions about the proper use of our expanding knowledge of human genetics. Such ethical dilemmas will only multiply as genetic research moves forward in the years to come.

CONTINUE THE DEBATE . . .

1. Traditional wedding vows join couples "in sickness and in health." Do you think people have a right to know the future health prospects of their potential partner before tying the knot?
2. What do you think about the possibility of parents genetically designing their children?
3. Should private companies doing genetic research be allowed to patent their discoveries so that they alone can profit from the results, or should this valuable information be made available to all companies? Why?

Scientists are learning more and more about the genetic factors that prompt the eventual development of serious diseases. If offered the opportunity, would you want to undergo a genetic screening that would predict the future of your own health?

Sources: Nash (1995), Thompson (1999), and Golden & Lemonick (2000).

The famous French scientist Louis Pasteur (1822–1895), who spent much of his life studying how bacteria cause disease, said just before he died that health depends less on bacteria than on the social environment in which bacteria operate (Gordon, 1980:7). Explaining Pasteur's insight is sociology's contribution to human health.

LOOKING AHEAD: HEALTH IN THE TWENTY-FIRST CENTURY

In the early 1900s, deaths from infectious diseases such as diphtheria and measles were widespread. Because scientists had not yet developed penicillin and other antibiotics, even a simple infection from a minor wound was sometimes life-threatening. Today, a century later, most members of our society take good health and long life for granted. It seems reasonable to expect improvements in U.S. health to continue throughout the twenty-first century.

Another encouraging trend is that more people are taking responsibility for their own health (Caplow et al., 1991). Every one of us can live better and longer if we avoid tobacco, eat sensibly and in moderation, and exercise regularly.

Yet health problems will continue to plague U.S. society in the decades to come. The biggest problem, discussed throughout this chapter, is this nation's double standard in health: well-being for the rich but higher rates of disease for the poor. International comparisons reveal that the United States lags in some measures of human health because we neglect the people at the margins of our society. An important question for this new century, then, is how a rich society can afford to let millions of people live without the security of medical care.

Finally, we find that health problems are far greater in low-income nations than in the United States. The good news is that life expectancy for the world as a whole has been rising—from forty-eight years in 1950 to sixty-seven years today—and the biggest gains have been in poor countries (Population Reference Bureau, 2004). But in much of Latin America, Asia, and especially Africa, hundreds of millions of adults and children lack not only medical attention but adequate food and safe water as well. Improving the health of the world's poorest people is a critical challenge in the twenty-first century.

SUMMARY

Education

1. Education is a major social institution for transmitting knowledge and skills as well as passing on norms and values. In preindustrial societies, education occurs informally within the family; industrial societies develop formal systems of schooling.

2. The United States was among the first countries to require mass public education, reflecting both democratic political ideals and the need for a trained industrial workforce.

3. The structural-functional approach highlights the functions of schooling, including socialization, social placement, social integration, and innovation. Latent functions include child care and building social networks.

4. Social-conflict analysis links schooling to social hierarchies involving class, race, and gender. Formal education is seen as generating conformity in order to produce obedient adult workers.

5. Most young people in the United States attend state-funded public schools. Most privately funded schools are affiliated with religious organizations.

6. Almost 85 percent of U.S. adults over age twenty-five are high school graduates, and more than 27 percent have a four-year college degree.

7. National opinion is critical of public schools. Violence is a problem in many U.S. schools, and educational bureaucracy fosters high dropout rates and widespread student passivity.

8. Declining academic standards are reflected in today's lower average scores on achievement tests, the functional illiteracy of a significant share of high school graduates, and grade inflation in high school and college.

9. The school choice movement seeks to make educational systems more responsive to the public through the use of magnet schools, charter schools, and for-profit schooling, all of which remain controversial.

10. Some 1.1 million U.S. children are home-schooled. Many parents home-school in the belief that they can do a better job than their local public schools.

11. Historically, children with mental or physical disabilities have been schooled in special classes or not at all. Mainstreaming is an attempt to give them broader opportunities.

Medicine

1. Health is a social issue because well-being depends on a society's technology and distribution of resources. Culture shapes definitions of health and patterns of health care.

2. Poor nations suffer from inadequate sanitation, hunger, and other problems linked to poverty. Life expectancy is about

twenty years less than in the United States; in the poorest nations, half the children do not survive to adulthood.

3. Health improved dramatically in Western Europe and North America in the nineteenth century, first because of industrialization and later because of medical advances.

4. Infectious diseases were leading killers a century ago. Today, most people in the United States die in old age of chronic illnesses such as heart disease, cancer, or stroke.

5. More than three-fourths of U.S. children born today can expect to reach age sixty-five. Throughout the life course, women have better health than men, and people of high social position enjoy better health than others.

6. Cigarette smoking is the greatest preventable cause of death in the United States.

7. The incidence of sexually transmitted diseases has risen since 1960, an exception to the general decline in infectious disease.

8. Advancing medical technology presents ethical dilemmas concerning how and when death should occur.

9. Historically a family concern, medical care is now the responsibility of trained specialists. The model of scientific medicine underlies the U.S. medical establishment. The holistic approach seeks to give people greater responsibility for their own health.

10. Socialist societies define government medical care as a basic right. Capitalist societies view medical care as a commodity to be purchased, although most capitalist governments (the United States being a significant exception) help pay for medical care through socialized medicine or national health insurance.

11. Central to the structural-functional analysis of health is the concept of the sick role, which releases sick people from routine responsibilities. The symbolic-interaction approach investigates the social construction of both health and medical treatment. Social-conflict analysis focuses on unequal access to health care and criticizes our medical system for its profit orientation.

Key Concepts

Education

education (p. 382) the social institution through which society provides its members with important knowledge, including basic facts, job skills, and cultural norms and values

schooling (p. 382) formal instruction under the direction of specially trained teachers

tracking (p. 386) assigning students to different types of educational programs

functional illiteracy (p. 392) a lack of the reading and writing skills needed for everyday living

Medicine

medicine (p. 395) the social institution that focuses on fighting disease and improving health

health (p. 395) a state of complete physical, mental, and social well-being

social epidemiology (p. 397) the study of how health and disease are distributed throughout a society's population

euthanasia (p. 403) assisting in the death of a person suffering from an incurable disease; also known as *mercy killing*

holistic medicine (p. 404) an approach to health care that emphasizes prevention of illness and takes into account a person's entire physical and social environment

socialized medicine (p. 406) a medical care system in which the government owns and operates most medical facilities and employs most doctors

direct-fee system (p. 406) a medical care system in which patients pay directly for the services of doctors and hospitals

health maintenance organization (HMO) (p. 407) an organization that provides comprehensive medical care to subscribers for a fixed fee

sick role (p. 408) patterns of behavior defined as appropriate for people who are ill

Critical-Thinking Questions

1. Why does industrialization lead societies to expand their system of schooling?

2. In what ways is schooling in the United States shaped by our economic system? By our cultural values? By social inequality?

3. Why is health as much a social as a biological issue?

4. Can you point to ways in which people can take responsibility for their own health? What traits of society as a whole shape patterns of health?

APPLICATIONS AND EXERCISES

1. Arrange to visit a secondary school near your college or home. Does it have a tracking policy? If so, find out how it works. If not, find out why. How much importance does a student's family background have in classroom placement?

2. Most people agree that teaching our children is a vital task. Yet most teachers earn relatively low salaries. Check the prestige ranking for teachers back in Table 8–2 on page 207. What can you find out at the library about the average salaries of teachers compared with other workers? Can you explain this pattern?

3. Since 1975, the federal government and all fifty states have passed special-education laws providing for children with physical disabilities. After the passage of the Americans with Disabilities Act in 1990, schools have sought to teach students with a broader range of physical and mental disabilities. Do some library research or contact officials on your campus to learn more about how these laws are changing education.

4. Arrange to speak with a midwife about her work helping women give birth. How do midwives differ in approach from obstetricians?

5. In most communities, a trip to the local courthouse is all it takes to find public records showing people's cause of death. Take a look at such records for people who lived in your community a century ago and for more recent residents. What patterns in life expectancy emerge? How do causes of death differ?

6. Packaged in the back of this new textbook is an interactive CD-ROM that offers a variety of video and interactive review materials intended to help you better understand the material covered in this chapter. For this chapter, the CD-ROM contains a relevant clip from *ABC News,* an author's tip video, interactive map animations, an interactive timeline, and flashcards with audio pronunciations of the more difficult words.

 ## SITES TO SEE

http://www.prenhall.com/macionis

View the interactive Companion Website™ that accompanies this text. Begin by clicking on the cover of your book. You will find a chapter-by-chapter study guide, practice tests, suggested Web links, and links to other relevant material.

http://www.acpe.asu.edu/VirtualU

To explore how new information technology is reshaping education, read about the founding of Western Virtual University, this country's first "cyber-college." What are the advantages and disadvantages of this type of schooling?

http://www2.kenyon.edu/Projects/Famfarm/

Visit the Family Farm Web site at Kenyon College. This site was created by students to share what they have learned about farming and life in a rural county in central Ohio.

http://nces.ed.gov/pubsearch/pubsinfo.asp?pubid=2004004

Read this government report on crime and safety in public schools. Is the problem getting better or worse?

http://chronicle.com

This site provides general news and information about higher education.

http://www.cdc.gov

The Web site for the Centers for Disease Control and Prevention provides health news, statistical data, and even traveler's health advisories.

http://www3.who.int/whosis/menu.cfm

Visit the World Health Organization's Statistical Information System to find basic health indicators for many of the world's nations, as well as data profiling the health of the U.S. population.

http://www.doctorsoftheworld.org
http://www.imc-la.org
http://www.dwb.org

Can people make a difference? Here are Web sites for several organizations of physicians that are involved in improving health around the world. The first is operated by Doctors of the World, the second by the International Medical Corps, and the third by Doctors without Borders.

 ## INVESTIGATE WITH RESEARCH NAVIGATOR™

Follow the instructions found on page 32 of this textbook to access the features of **Research Navigator™.** Once at the Web site, enter your Login Name and Password. Then, to use the **Content Select™** database, enter keywords such as "testing," "school violence," "euthanasia," and "AIDS," and the search engine will supply relevant

and recent scholarly and popular press publications. Use the *New York Times* **Search-by-Subject Archive** to find recent news articles related to sociology and the **Links Library** feature to find relevant Web links organized by the key terms associated with this chapter.

October 22, 2002

Good and Bad Marriage, Boon and Bane to Health

By SHARON LERNER

In the early 1970's, demographers began to notice a strange pattern in life span data: Married people tended to live longer than their single, divorced and widowed counterparts.

The so-called marriage benefit persists today, with married people generally less likely to have surgery and to die from all causes, including stroke, pneumonia and accidents. At its widest, the gap is striking, with middle-aged men in most developed countries about twice as likely to die if they are unmarried.

Many have argued that the difference in life expectancy is . . . because healthier people are more likely to marry. But an emerging group of marriage advocates has put a spotlight on the medical potential of the institution. . . .

But even as marriage is being packaged as a boon to health, there is a new caveat. While people in good, stable partnerships do, on average, have less disease and later death, mounting evidence suggests that those in strained and unhappy relationships tend to fare worse medically. . . .

Men and women who reported low-quality marriages had more gum disease and cavities than happily married people. Two studies found marital strain to be linked to ulcers in the stomach and intestine. And people's satisfaction with their relationships appears to alter how they experience pain.

Some of these physical effects seem to be direct results of behavior. . . . [A]ccording to Dr. James Coyne, a professor of psychiatry at the University of Pennsylvania, who has studied the effects of marital quality on recovery from congestive heart failure, a good marriage can give a person a reason to stay alive. . . .

In contrast, he said, a bad marriage can be worse than none at all. . . .

[A]ccording to Dr. Coyne's study, published last year in *The American Journal of Cardiology* . . . the quality of patients' marriages predicted their recoveries as well as the pumping ability of their hearts.

According to Dr. Janice Kiecolt-Glaser, a professor of psychiatry at Ohio State University, and her husband, Dr. Ronald Glaser, an immunologist, marital arguments cause changes in the endocrine and immune systems.

During and after stressful conversations, levels of the hormones epinephrine and cortisol rise and can stay elevated for more than 22 hours afterward. Blood pressure and heart rate also tend to go up with relationship stress. . . .

. . . [I]n what may be the oddest study in the field, Dr. Kiecolt-Glaser and Dr. Glaser are now researching how the quality of a marriage affects the body's ability to repair itself.

In the continuing study, the scientists admit subjects to a hospital, inflict minor wounds on their arms, and then chart their interactions with their spouses and their progress in healing.

As with the overall "marriage benefit," which for women is smaller than for men and possibly even nonexistent, according to some researchers, women are more vulnerable to relationship-related health problems.

. . . [A] 15-year study of members of a large health maintenance organization in Oregon found that having unequal decision making power in marriage was associated with a higher risk of death for women, though not for men.

In Dr. Coyne's study of congestive heart failure, there was a stronger association between marital discord and death among women. Seven of the eight women with the poorest marital quality died within two years of the first assessment. . . .

For Dr. Alex Zautra, a professor of psychology at Arizona State University in Tempe, who has shown an association between criticism from intimate partners and joint pain in women with rheumatoid arthritis, the lesson from this growing literature is not to think of interpersonal ties as either all positive or negative.

"In truth, all relationships have both good and bad aspects to them," Dr. Zautra said. The point, he said, is that, in all their complexity, they matter. "At the heart of this is how people's emotions affect their health. People need to start thinking about that."

WHAT DO YOU THINK?

1. Recalling Durkheim's study of suicide described in Chapter 1 ("The Sociological Perspective"), how might Durkheim respond to this article?

2. Would you expect the "marriage benefit" to extend to members of same-sex couples? Why or why not?

Adapted from the original article by Sharon Lerner published in *The New York Times* on October 22, 2002. Copyright © 2002 by The New York Times Company. Reprinted with permission.

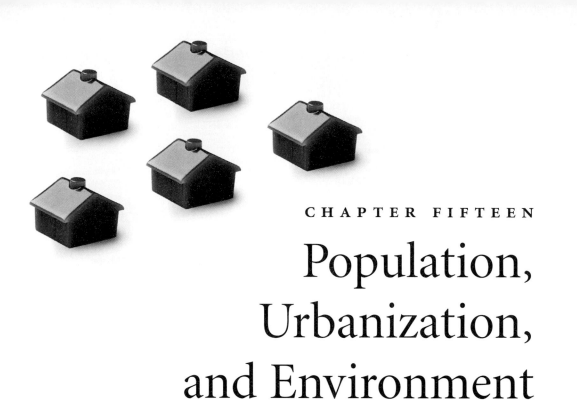

CHAPTER FIFTEEN

Population, Urbanization, and Environment

Why do many people worry about the rapid rate
of global population increase?

What are the special experiences of city living?

How is the state of the natural environment
a social issue?

Societies with more people and ever-larger cities challenge the natural environment ▶ as never before. To protect herself from air pollution in an industrial area of Chekka, Lebanon, this girl carries a face mask on her way to school.

There's not much choice when people decide to eat out in Bisbee, North Dakota: The Chocolate Shop is the only place in town. Sylvia Schmidt, who has lived in Bisbee all her life, owns the small eatery. Shaking her head, she explains that she loses money every day she serves hot food to the small number of locals and an occasional visitor who passes through town. But she has enough saved to get by, and so although she's past what most folks call retirement age, she keeps the business going if only because she can't bear the thought of her town folding up. Thinking back, she says with a smile, "You can't imagine what it used to be like."

Bisbee is indeed in decline. The town now has just 227 people, down from about 300 ten years ago, making the population lower than when Bisbee was a frontier town in the mid-1800s. Pettsinger's movie house closed long ago, Brannon's Drug Store is gone, and Dick's Red Owl no longer sells groceries. The local church can no longer afford the salary of a priest. The local high school has just sixty-nine students; the elementary school, thirty-one. Houses in Bisbee sell for as little as $2,000, yet no one is moving in.

Bob Weltin also grew up in Bisbee and at forty-three is now the town's mayor. But as he sips a cup of Sylvia's coffee at the Chocolate Shop, he says that he has decided to call it quits, stepping down as mayor and moving to a larger community (Johnson, 2001).

There are hundreds of towns like Bisbee on the Great Plains that are hanging on by a thread. This chapter investigates population patterns, explaining why people move from place to place, why cities get so large, and why small towns sometimes die. We shall also look at how populations change and how our way of life affects the physical environment.

Demography: The Study of Population

When humans first began to cultivate plants some 12,000 years ago, the Earth's entire population was about 5 million, or about the population of Minnesota today. Very slow growth pushed the total in 1 B.C.E. to perhaps 300 million, or a bit more than the population of today's United States (Haub, 2002a).

About 1750, world population began to spike upward. We now add 73 million people to the planet each year, for a total of 6.4 billion in 2005.

The causes and consequences of this drama are the focus of **demography,** *the study of human population.* Demography (from Greek, meaning "description of people") is a cousin of sociology that analyzes the size and composition of a population and studies how people move from place to place. Demographers not only collect statistics but also pose important questions about the effects of population growth and suggest how it might be controlled. The following sections present basic demographic concepts.

FERTILITY

The study of human population begins with how many people are born. **Fertility** is *the incidence of childbearing in a country's population.* During her childbearing years, from the onset of menstruation (typically in the early teens) to menopause (usually in the late forties), a woman is capable of bearing more than twenty children. But *fecundity,* or maximum possible childbearing, is sharply reduced by cultural norms, finances, and personal choice.

Demographers describe fertility using the **crude birth rate,** *the number of live births in a given year for every 1,000 people in a population.* To calculate a crude birth rate, divide the number of live births in a year by the society's total population and multiply the result by 1,000. In the United

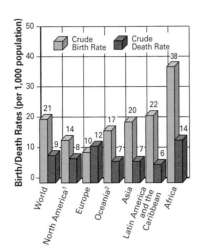

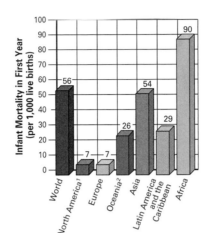

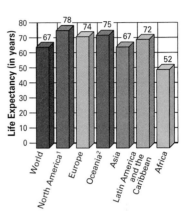

FIGURE 15–1   (a) Crude Birth Rates and Crude Death Rates,
                (b) Infant Mortality Rates, and (c) Life Expectancy, 2003

[1]United States and Canada.

[2]Australia, New Zealand, and South Pacific Islands.

Source: Population Reference Bureau (2004).

States in 2002, there were 4.0 million live births in a population of 288 million, yielding a crude birth rate of 13.9 (Martin et al., 2003).

> January 18, Coshocton County, Ohio. Having just finished off the mountains of meat and potatoes that make up a typical Amish meal, we have gathered in the living room of Jacob Raber, a member of this rural Amish community. Mrs. Raber, a mother of four, is telling us about Amish life. "Most of the women I know have five or six children," she says with a smile, "but certainly not everybody. Some have eleven or twelve!"

A country's birth rate is described as "crude" because it is based on the entire population, not just women in their childbearing years. Furthermore, this measure ignores differences among various categories of the population: Fertility among the Amish, for example, is quite high, and fertility among Asian Americans is low. But this measure is easy to calculate and allows rough comparisons of the fertility of one country or region in relation to others. Figure 15–1 shows that in global perspective, the crude birth rate of North Americans is low.

MORTALITY

Population size also reflects **mortality,** *the incidence of death in a country's population.* To measure mortality, demographers use a **crude death rate,** *the number of deaths in a given year for every 1,000 people in a population.* This time, we take the number of deaths in a year, divide by the total population, and multiply the result by 1,000. In 2002, there were 2.45 million deaths in the U.S. population of 288 million, yielding a crude death rate of 8.5 (Kochanek et al., 2004). As Figure 15–1 shows, in global context, this rate is about average.

A third useful demographic measure is the **infant mortality rate,** *the number of deaths among infants under one year of age for each 1,000 live births in a given year.* To compute infant mortality, divide the number of deaths of children under one year of age by the number of live births during the same year and multiply the result by 1,000. In 2002, there were 28,000 infant deaths and 4.0 million live births in the United States. Dividing the first number by the second and multiplying the result by 1,000 yields an infant mortality rate of 7.0. The second part of Figure 15–1 indicates that by world standards, North American infant mortality is low.

But remember the differences among various categories of people. For example, African Americans, with nearly three times the burden of poverty as whites, have an infant mortality rate of 14.4—more than twice the white rate of 5.8.

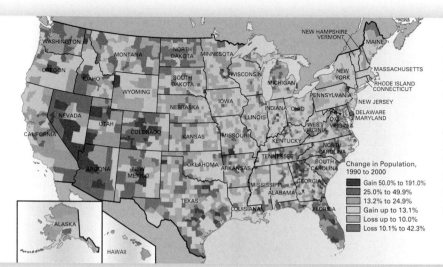

This map, based on results of the 2000 census, shows that population is moving from the heartland of the United States toward the coasts. What do you think is causing this internal migration? What types of people do you think remain in counties that are losing population?

Source: U.S. Census Bureau (2001).

Change in Population, 1990 to 2000

- Gain 50.0% to 191.0%
- 25.0% to 49.9%
- 13.2% to 24.9%
- Gain up to 13.1%
- Loss up to 10.0%
- Loss 10.1% to 42.3%

Low infant mortality greatly raises **life expectancy,** *the average life span of a country's population.* U.S. males born in 2002 can expect to live 74.5 years, and females can look forward to 79.9 years. As the third part of Figure 15–1 shows, life expectancy for North Americans is twenty-five years greater than that typical of low-income countries of Africa.

MIGRATION

Population size is also affected by **migration,** *the movement of people into and out of a specified territory.* Movement into a territory, or *immigration,* is measured as an *in-migration rate,* calculated as the number of people entering an area for every 1,000 people in the population. Movement out of a territory, or *emigration,* is measured in terms of an *out-migration rate,* the number leaving for every 1,000 people. Both types of migration usually occur at the same time, of course, and the difference between the in-migration rate and the out-migration rate is called the *net migration rate.*

All nations experience some degree of internal migration, that is, movement within their borders, from one region to another. National Map 15–1 shows where the U.S. population is moving and the places being left behind (notice the heavy losses in North Dakota, as suggested in the opening story for this chapter).

Migration is sometimes voluntary, as when people leave a dying town to move to a large city. In such cases, "push-pull" factors are usually at work, as a lack of jobs "pushes" people to move from one area as they are "pulled"

to another place with more opportunities. Migration can also be involuntary, such as the forced transport of 10 million Africans to the Western Hemisphere as slaves.

POPULATION GROWTH

Fertility, mortality, and migration all affect the size of a society's population. In general, rich nations (such as the United States) grow almost as much from immigration as natural increase; poorer nations (such as India) grow almost entirely from natural increase.

To calculate a population's *natural growth rate,* demographers subtract the crude death rate from the crude birth rate. The natural growth rate of the U.S. population in 2002 was 5.4 per 1,000 (the crude birth rate of 13.9 minus the crude death rate of 8.5), or about 0.5 percent annual growth.

Global Map 15–1 shows that population growth in the United States and other high-income nations is well below the world average of 1.3 percent. The Earth's low-growth continents are Europe (currently posting a slight decline, expressed as −0.2 percent annual growth), North America (0.5 percent), and Oceania (1.0 percent). At the global average is Asia (1.3 percent), with Latin America (1.6 percent) slightly higher. The highest-growth region of the world is Africa (2.4 percent).

A handy rule for estimating population growth is to divide 70 by a society's population growth rate to calculate the *doubling time* in years. Thus, an annual growth rate of 2 percent (found in parts of Latin America) doubles a

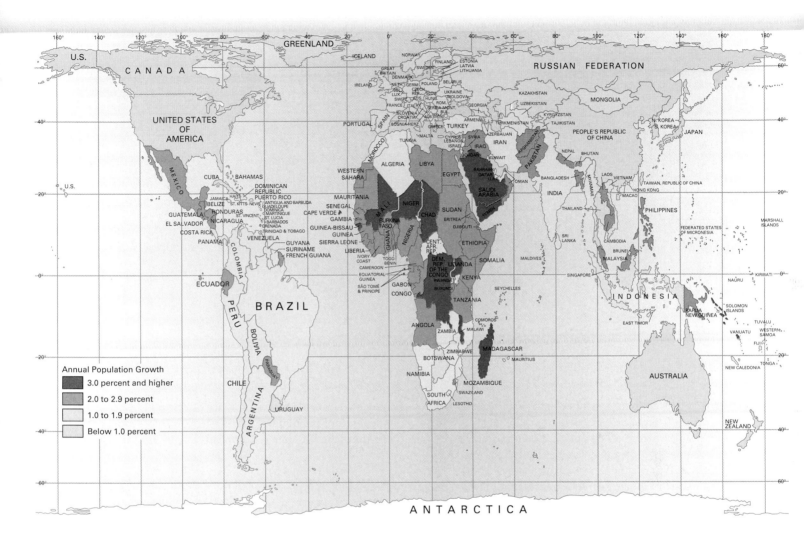

WINDOW ON THE WORLD

GLOBAL MAP 15-1   Population Growth in Global Perspective

The richest countries of the world—including the United States, Canada, and the nations of Europe—have growth rates below 1 percent. The nations of Latin America and Asia typically have growth rates around 1.6 percent, which double a population in forty-four years. Africa has an overall growth rate of 2.4 percent (despite only small increases in countries with a high rate of AIDS), which cuts the doubling time to twenty-nine years. In global perspective, we see that a society's standard of living is closely related to its rate of population growth: Population is rising fastest in the world regions that can least afford to support more people.

Source: Population Reference Bureau (2004); map projection from *Peters Atlas of the World* (1990).

population in thirty-five years, and a 3 percent growth rate (found in some countries in Africa) drops the doubling time to just twenty-four years. The rapid population growth of the poorest countries is deeply troubling because these countries can barely support the populations they have now.

POPULATION COMPOSITION

Demographers also study the makeup of a society's population at a given point in time. One variable is the **sex ratio,** *the number of males for every 100 females in a nation's population.*

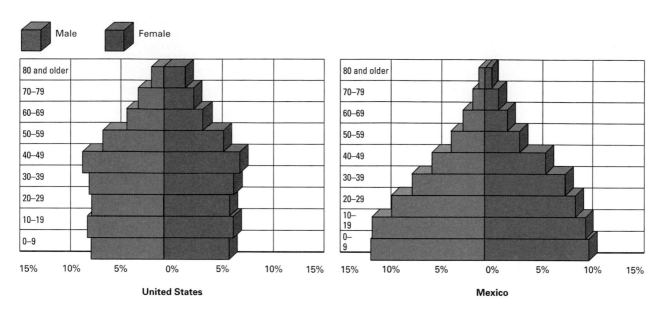

FIGURE 15-2   Age-Sex Population Pyramids for the United States and Mexico, 2003

Source: U.S. Census Bureau (2004).

In 2002, the sex ratio in the United States was 96, or 96 males for every 100 females. Sex ratios usually are below 100 because, on average, women outlive men. In India, however, the sex ratio is 107 because parents value sons more than daughters and may either abort a female fetus or, after birth, give more care to a male infant, raising the odds that a female child will die.

A more complex measure is the **age-sex pyramid,** *a graphic representation of the age and sex of a population.* Figure 15–2 presents the age-sex pyramids for the United States and Mexico. Higher death rates as people age give these figures a rough pyramid shape. In the U.S. pyramid, the bulge corresponding to ages forty through forty-nine reflects high birth rates during the *baby boom.* The contraction just below—that is, people in their thirties—reflects the subsequent *baby bust.* The birth rate has continued to decline from its high of 25.3 in 1957 to 13.9 in 2002.

Comparing the U.S. and Mexican age-sex pyramids shows different demographic trends. The age-sex pyramid for Mexico, like that of other lower-income nations, is wide at the bottom (reflecting higher birth rates) and narrows quickly by what we would call middle age (due to higher mortality). In short, Mexico is a much younger society, with a median age of twenty-four, compared to thirty-five in the United States. With a larger share of women still in their childbearing years, therefore, Mexico's

 To find out more about U.S. demography, go to http:// www.census.gov

crude birth rate (25) is nearly twice our own (13.9), and its annual rate of population growth (2.1 percent) is more than four times the U.S. rate (0.5 percent).

History and Theory of Population Growth

In the past, people wanted large families because human labor was the key to productivity. Moreover, until rubber condoms appeared 150 years ago, preventing pregnancy was uncertain at best. But high death rates from infectious diseases put a constant brake on population growth.

A major demographic shift, shown in Figure 15–3, began about 1750 as the world's population turned upward, reaching the 1 billion mark by 1800. This milestone (which took all of human history to reach) was matched barely a century later in 1930, when a second billion people were added to the planet. In other words, not only was population increasing, but the *rate* of growth was accelerating. Global population reached 3 billion by 1962 (just thirty-two years later) and 4 billion by 1974 (only twelve years later). The rate of world population increase has slowed recently, but the planet passed the 5 billion mark in 1987 and the 6 billion mark late in 1999. In no previous century did the world's population even double. In the twentieth century, it quadrupled.

Currently, the world is gaining 73 million people each year, with 96 percent of this increase in poor countries.

Experts predict that the Earth's population will be between 8 and 9 billion in 2050 (O'Neill & Balk, 2001). Given the world's troubles feeding its present population, such an increase is a matter of urgent concern.

MALTHUSIAN THEORY

The sudden population growth 250 years ago sparked the development of demography. Thomas Robert Malthus (1766–1834), an English economist and clergyman, warned that rapid population increase would lead to social chaos. Malthus (1926, orig. 1798) calculated that population would increase by what mathematicians call *geometric progression,* illustrated by the series of numbers 2, 4, 8, 16, 32, and so on. At such a rate, Malthus concluded, world population would soon soar out of control.

Food production would also increase, Malthus explained, but only in *arithmetic progression* (as in the series 2, 3, 4, 5, 6, etc.) because even with new agricultural technology, farmland is limited. Thus, Malthus presented a troubling vision of the future: people reproducing beyond what the planet could feed, leading ultimately to widespread starvation and war over what resources were left.

Malthus recognized that artificial birth control or abstaining from sex might change his prediction. But he found one morally wrong and the other quite impractical. Thus, famine and war stalked humanity in Malthus's mind, and he was justly known as "the dismal parson."

Critical review. Fortunately, Malthus's prediction was flawed. First, by 1850, the European birth rate began to drop, partly because with industrialization, children were becoming an economic liability rather than an asset and partly because people began using artificial birth control. Second, Malthus underestimated human ingenuity: Modern irrigation techniques, fertilizers, and pesticides have increased farm production far more than he could have imagined.

Some criticized Malthus for ignoring the role of social inequality in world abundance and famine. For example, Karl Marx (1967, orig. 1867) objected to his view of suffering as a "law of nature" rather than the curse of capitalism. More recently, "critical demographers" claim that saying poverty is caused by a high birth rate in low-income countries amounts to blaming the victims. On the contrary, they see global inequality as the real issue (Horton, 1999; Kuumba, 1999).

Still, Malthus offers an important lesson. Habitable land, clean water, and fresh air are limited resources, and increased economic productivity has taken a heavy toll on the natural environment. In addition, medical advances

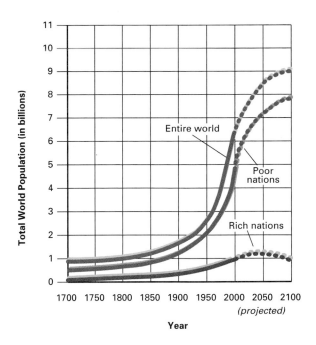

FIGURE 15-3   The Increase in World Population, 1700–2100

have lowered death rates, pushing up world population. In principle, of course, no level of population growth can go on forever. Thus, people everywhere must become aware of the dangers of population increase.

DEMOGRAPHIC TRANSITION THEORY

A more complex analysis of population change is **demographic transition theory,** *the thesis that population patterns reflect a society's level of technological development.* Figure 15–4 on page 424 shows the demographic consequences at four levels of technological development. Preindustrial, agrarian societies (Stage 1) have high birth rates because of the economic value of children and the absence of birth control. Death rates are also high due to low living standards and limited medical technology. Outbreaks of disease neutralize births, so population rises and falls with only a modest overall increase. This was the case for thousands of years in Europe before the Industrial Revolution.

Stage 2, the onset of industrialization, brings a demographic transition as death rates fall due to greater food supplies and scientific medicine. But birth rates remain high, resulting in rapid population growth. It was during Europe's Stage 2 that Malthus formulated his ideas, which

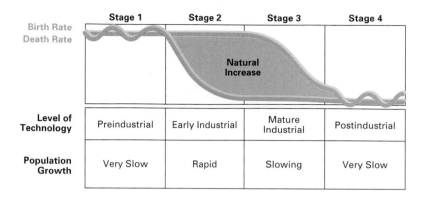

	Stage 1	Stage 2	Stage 3	Stage 4
Birth Rate Death Rate		Natural Increase		
Level of Technology	Preindustrial	Early Industrial	Mature Industrial	Postindustrial
Population Growth	Very Slow	Rapid	Slowing	Very Slow

FIGURE 15–4

Demographic Transition Theory

accounts for his pessimistic view of the future. The world's poorest countries today are in this high-growth stage.

In Stage 3, a mature industrial economy, the birth rate drops, curbing population growth once again. Fertility falls because most children survive to adulthood and because high living standards make raising children expensive. In short, affluence transforms children from economic assets into economic liabilities. Smaller families, made possible by effective birth control, are also favored by women working outside the home. As birth rates follow death rates downward, population growth slows further.

Stage 4 corresponds to a postindustrial economy in which the demographic transition is complete. The birth rate remains low, partly because two-income couples gradually become the norm and partly because the cost of raising children continues to increase. This trend, coupled with steady death rates, means that population grows only very slowly or even decreases. This is the case today in Japan, Europe, and the United States.

Critical review. Demographic transition theory suggests that the key to population control lies in technology. Instead of the runaway population increase feared by Malthus, this theory sees technology slowing growth and spreading material plenty.

Demographic transition theory is linked to modernization theory, one approach to global development discussed in Chapter 9 ("Global Stratification"). Modernization theorists are optimistic that poor countries will solve their population problems as they industrialize. But critics, notably dependency theorists, strongly disagree. Without a significant redistribution of global resources, they maintain, our planet will become increasingly divided into industrialized "haves," enjoying low population growth, and nonindustrialized "have-nots," struggling in vain to feed more and more people.

GLOBAL POPULATION TODAY: A BRIEF SURVEY

What can we say about population in today's world? Drawing on the discussion so far, we can identify important patterns and reach several conclusions.

The low-growth North. When the Industrial Revolution began in the Northern Hemisphere, population growth in Western Europe and North America was a high 3 percent annually. But in the centuries since, the growth rate steadily declined and in 1970 fell below 1 percent. As our postindustrial society settles into Stage 4, the U.S. birth rate is less than the replacement level of 2.1 children per woman, a point demographers call **zero population growth,** *the level of reproduction that maintains population at a steady state.* More than sixty nations, almost all of them rich, are at or below the point of zero population growth.

To find out more about population growth, go to http://www.populationconnection.org

Factors holding down population in these postindustrial societies include a high proportion of men and women in the labor force, rising costs of raising children, trends toward later marriage and singlehood, and widespread use of contraceptives and abortion.

In high-income nations, then, population increase is not the problem that it is in poor countries. Indeed, many governments in high-income countries are concerned about a future problem of *underpopulation,* because declining population size may be difficult to reverse and because the swelling ranks of the elderly have fewer and fewer young people to look to for support in old age (McDonald, 2001; Kent & Mather, 2002).

The high-growth South. Population is a critical problem in poor nations of the Southern Hemisphere. No nation in the world lacks industrial technology entirely; demographic

Fertility in the United States has fallen during the past century and is now quite low. But some categories of the U.S. population have much higher fertility rates. One example is the Amish, a religious society living in rural areas of Ohio, Pennsylvania, and other states. It is common for Amish couples to have five, six, or more children. Why do you think the Amish favor large families?

transition theory's Stage 1 applies just to remote rural areas of low-income nations. But much of Latin America, Africa, and Asia is at Stage 2, with a mix of agrarian and industrial economies. Advanced medical technology, supplied by rich societies, has sharply reduced death rates, but birth rates remain high. This is why poor societies now account for two-thirds of the Earth's people and 96 percent of global population increase.

In poor countries throughout the world, birth rates have fallen from an average of about six children per woman in 1950 to about four today. But fertility this high will only intensify global poverty. At a 1994 global population conference in Cairo, delegates from 180 nations agreed that a key element in controlling world population growth is to raise the status of women. The Diversity box on page 426 takes a closer look.

In recent decades, the world has made significant progress in lowering fertility. Mortality also has come down. Although few people would oppose medical programs that save lives—most of them children's—lower death rates mean rising population. In fact, population growth in most low-income regions of the world results *mostly* from falling death rates. Around 1920, Europe and North America began taking steps to spread scientific medicine and better nutrition around the world. Since then, inoculations against infectious diseases and the use of antibiotics and insecticides have pushed down death rates with stunning effectiveness. For example, in Sri Lanka, malaria caused half of all deaths in the 1930s; a decade later, use of insecticides to kill malaria-carrying mosquitoes cut

Read about population control in South Asia at http://www.asia-initiative.org/

the death toll from this disease in half. Although this is a great medical achievement, Sri Lanka's population began to soar. Similarly, India's infant mortality rate slid from 130 in 1975 to 64 in 2003, boosting that nation's population over the 1 billion mark.

In short, in much of the world, mortality is falling, especially among children. In order to limit population growth, the world—especially poor countries—must control births as successfully as it is fending off death.

Urbanization: The Growth of Cities

October 8, Hong Kong. The cable train grinds to the top of Victoria Peak, where we behold one of the world's most spectacular vistas: the city of Hong Kong at night. A million bright, colorful lights ring the harbor as ships, ferries, and traditional Chinese junks churn by. Few cities match Hong Kong for sheer energy: This small city is as economically productive as the state of Wisconsin or the nation of Finland. We could sit here for hours entranced by the spectacle of Hong Kong.

Throughout most of human history, the sights and sounds of great cities such as Hong Kong, New York, and Los Angeles were simply unimaginable. Our distant ancestors lived in small, nomadic groups, moving from place to place as they depleted vegetation or hunted migratory game. The small settlements that marked the emergence of civilization in the Middle East some 12,000 years ago held

DIVERSITY: RACE, CLASS, & GENDER

Empowering Women: The Key to Controlling Population Growth

Sohad Ahmad lives with her husband in a farming village 50 miles south of Cairo, Egypt's capital city. Ahmad lives a poor life, like hundreds of millions of other women in the world. Yet her situation differs in an important respect: She has had only two children and will have no more.

Why do Ahmad and her husband reject the conventional wisdom that children are an economic asset? One part of the answer is that Egypt's growing population has already created such a demand for land that Ahmad's family could not afford more even if they had the children to farm it. But the main reason is that she does not want her life defined only by childbearing.

Like Ahmad, more women in Egypt are taking control of their fertility and seeking educational and economic opportunities. Indeed, this country has made great progress in reducing its annual population growth from 3.0 percent just ten years ago to 2.0 percent today.

With its focus on raising the standing of women, the 1994 Cairo conference on global population broke new ground. Past population control programs simply tried to make birth control technology available to women, a vital effort because only half of the world's married women use effective birth control. But even with available birth control, population continues to swell in societies that define women's primary responsibility as raising children.

Dr. Nafis Sadik, an Egyptian woman who heads the United Nations' efforts at population control, sums up the new approach to lowering birth rates this way: *Give women more life choices, and they will have fewer children.* In other words, women with access to schooling and jobs, who can decide when and whether to marry, and who bear children as a matter of choice will limit their own fertility. Schooling must be available to older women, too, Sadik adds, because elders exercise great influence in local communities.

Evidence from countries around the world supports the idea that controlling population and raising the social standing of women are one and the same.

A simple truth: Women who have more opportunity for schooling and paid work have fewer children. As more women attend school in traditional societies, the fertility rate in these countries is falling.

WHAT DO YOU THINK?

1. Why do many analysts claim that controlling population depends on expanding women's choices?
2. What specific laws or programs can you think of that might reduce women's childbearing?
3. Is population control an issue for people in both rich and poor countries? Explain your view.

Sources: Ashford (1995), Axinn & Barber (2001), and Population Reference Bureau (2004).

---

only a small fraction of the Earth's people. Today, the largest three or four cities of the world hold as many people as the entire planet did back then.

Urbanization is *the concentration of humanity into cities.* Urbanization both redistributes population within a society and transforms many patterns of social life. We will trace these changes in terms of three urban revolutions: the emergence of cities beginning 10,000 years ago, the development of industrial cities after 1750, and the explosive growth of cities in poor countries today.

THE EVOLUTION OF CITIES

Cities are a relatively new development in human history. Only about 12,000 years ago did our ancestors begin founding permanent settlements, which paved the way for the *first urban revolution.*

The first cities. Hunting and gathering forced people to move all the time; however, once our ancestors discovered how to domesticate animals and cultivate crops, they were able to stay in one place. Raising their own food also created a material surplus, which freed some people from food production and allowed them to build shelters, make tools, weave cloth, and take part in religious rituals. The emergence of cities led to both specialization and higher living standards.

The first city was Jericho, which lies to the north of the Dead Sea in what is now the West Bank. Dating back 10,000 years, it was home to only 600 people. But as the centuries passed, cities grew to tens of thousands of people and became the centers of vast empires. By 3000 B.C.E., Egyptian cities flourished, as did cities in China about 2000 B.C.E. and in Central and South America about 1500 B.C.E. In North America, however, only a few Native American societies formed settlements; widespread urbanization did not take place until the arrival of European settlers in the seventeenth century.

Preindustrial European cities. European cities date back some 5,000 years to the Greeks and, later, the Romans, both of whom formed great empires and founded cities across Europe, including Vienna, Paris, and London. With the fall of the Roman Empire, the so-called Dark Ages began as people withdrew within defensive walled settlements and warlords battled for territory. Only in the eleventh century did Europe become more peaceful; trade flourished once again, allowing cities to grow.

Medieval cities were quite different from those familiar to us today. Beneath towering cathedrals, the narrow, winding streets of London, Brussels, and Florence teemed with merchants, artisans, priests, peddlers, jugglers, nobles, and servants. Occupational groups such as bakers, carpenters, and metalworkers clustered in distinct sections or "quarters." Ethnicity also defined communities as people sought to keep out those who differed from themselves. The term "ghetto" (from the Italian word *borghetto,* meaning "outside the city walls") was first used to describe the neighborhood into which the Jews of Venice were segregated.

Industrial European cities. As the Middle Ages came to a close, steadily increasing commerce enriched a new urban middle class called the *bourgeoisie* (French, meaning "townspeople"). With more and more money, the bourgeoisie soon rivaled the hereditary nobility.

By about 1750, the Industrial Revolution triggered a *second urban revolution,* first in Europe and then in North America. The tremendous productive power of factories caused cities to grow bigger than ever before. London, the largest European city, reached 550,000 people by 1700 and exploded to 6.5 million by 1900 (Weber, 1963, orig. 1899; Chandler & Fox, 1974).

Cities not only grew but changed shape as well. Older winding streets gave way to broad, straight boulevards to

In the cities of the early industrial era, life was lived on the streets. This street scene in New York City almost a century ago is quite different from urban life in most cities today, where life has moved into restricted spaces, such as malls, apartment complexes, and private homes. Can you think of reasons for this change?

handle the increasing flow of commercial traffic. Steam and electric trolleys soon crisscrossed the expanding cities. Because land was now a commodity to be bought and sold, developers divided cities into regular-sized lots (Mumford, 1961). The center of the city was no longer the cathedral but a bustling central business district filled with banks, retail stores, and tall office buildings.

With a new focus on business, cities became ever more crowded and impersonal. Crime rates rose. Especially at the outset, a few industrialists lived in grand style, but most men, women, and children barely survived by working in factories.

Organized efforts by workers eventually brought improvements to the workplace, better housing, and the right to vote. Public services such as water, sewer systems, and electricity further improved urban living. Today, some

TABLE 15-1

The Urban Population of the United States, 1790–2000

Year	Population (in millions)	Percentage Urban
1790	3.9	5.1%
1800	5.3	6.1
1820	9.6	7.3
1840	17.1	10.5
1860	31.4	19.7
1880	50.2	28.1
1900	76.0	39.7
1920	105.7	51.3
1940	131.7	56.5
1960	179.3	69.9
1980	226.5	73.7
2000	281.4	80.3

Source: U.S. Census Bureau (2001).

urbanites still live in poverty, but a rising standard of living has partly fulfilled the city's historical promise of a better life.

THE GROWTH OF U.S. CITIES

As noted, most of the Native Americans who inhabited North America for thousands of years before the arrival of Europeans were migratory people who formed few permanent settlements. The spread of villages and towns came after European colonization.

Colonial settlement: 1565–1800. In 1565, the Spanish built a settlement at St. Augustine, Florida, and in 1607, the English founded Jamestown, Virginia. However, the first lasting settlement came in 1624 when the Dutch established New Amsterdam, later renamed New York.

New York and Boston (founded by the English in 1630) started out as tiny villages in a vast wilderness. They resembled medieval towns in Europe, with narrow, winding streets that still curve through lower Manhattan and downtown Boston.

But economic growth soon transformed these villages into thriving towns with wide streets usually laid out in a grid pattern. Even so, when the first census was completed in 1790, as Table 15–1 shows, just 5 percent of the nation's people lived in cities.

Urban expansion: 1800–1860. Early in the nineteenth century, towns sprang up along the transportation routes that opened the American West. By 1860, Buffalo, Cleveland, Detroit, and Chicago were all changing the face of the Midwest, and about one-fifth of the U.S. population lived in cities.

Urban expansion was greatest in the northern states; New York City, for example, had ten times the population of Charleston, South Carolina. The division of the United States into the industrial-urban North and the agrarian-rural South was one major cause of the Civil War (Schlesinger, 1969).

The metropolitan era: 1860–1950. The Civil War (1861–1865) gave an enormous boost to urbanization as factories strained to produce weapons. Waves of people deserted the countryside for cities in hopes of finding better jobs. Joining them were tens of millions of immigrants, most from Europe, forming a culturally diverse urban mix.

In 1900, New York's population soared passed the 4 million mark, and Chicago, a city of scarcely 100,000 people in 1860, was closing in on 2 million. Such growth marked the era of the **metropolis** (from Greek words meaning "mother city"), *a large city that socially and economically dominates an urban area*. Metropolises became the economic centers of the United States. By 1920, urban areas were home to a majority of the U.S. population.

Industrial technology pushed city populations higher and higher. In the 1880s, steel girders and mechanical elevators permitted the construction of buildings over ten stories high. In 1930, New York's Empire State Building was hailed as an urban wonder; this early skyscraper was the highest point in the New York skyline, stretching 102 stories into the clouds.

Urban decentralization: 1950–present. The industrial metropolis reached its peak about 1950. Since then, something of a turnaround, called *urban decentralization*, has occurred as people have left downtown areas for outlying **suburbs**, *urban areas beyond the political boundaries of a city*. The old industrial cities of the Northeast and Midwest stopped growing, and some lost considerable population, in the decades after 1950. The urban landscape of densely packed central cities evolved into sprawling suburban regions.

SUBURBS AND URBAN DECLINE

Imitating European nobility, some of the rich in the United States had town houses in the city as well as country homes beyond the city limits. But not until after World War II did ordinary people find a suburban home within their reach. With more and more cars, new four-lane highways, government-backed mortgages, and inexpensive tract homes, suburbs grew as never before. By 1999, most of the U.S. population lived in suburbs, where they frequented nearby shopping malls rather than the older downtown shopping districts (Pederson, Smith, & Adler, 1999; Macionis & Parrillo, 2004).

As many older cities of the Snowbelt—the Northeast and Midwest—lost higher-income taxpayers to the suburbs, they struggled to pay for expensive social programs for the poor who remained. Many cities fell into financial crisis, and inner-city decay became severe. Especially to white people, the inner cities became synonymous with slum housing, crime, drugs, unemployment, the poor, and minorities (Stahura, 1986; Galster, 1991).

Urban critic Paul Goldberger (2002) points out that the decline of central cities also has led to a decline in the importance of public space. Historically, the heart of city life was played out on public streets. The French word for a sophisticated person is *boulevardier,* which literally means "street person." However, this same term has a negative meaning in the United States today. The active life that once took place on public streets and in public squares now takes place in shopping malls, cineplex lobbies, and gated communities—all private spaces. Further reducing the vitality of today's urban places is the spread of television, the Internet, and other media that people use inside their private homes.

POSTINDUSTRIAL SUNBELT CITIES

As the older Snowbelt cities fell into decline, Sunbelt cities in the South and West grew rapidly. The soaring populations of cities such as Los Angeles and Houston reflect a population shift to the Sunbelt, where 60 percent of U.S. people now live. In addition, most of today's immigrants enter the country in the Sunbelt region. The result: Back in 1950, nine of the ten largest U.S. cities were in the Snowbelt; by 2000, six of the top ten were in the Sunbelt (U.S. Census Bureau, 2001).

Unlike their colder counterparts, these cities came of age *after* urban decentralization began. So while Snowbelt cities have long been enclosed by a ring of politically independent suburbs, Sunbelt cities have pushed their boundaries outward along with the population flow. Chicago covers 227 square miles; Houston covers more than 550 square miles, and the greater Houston metropolitan region covers almost 9,000 square miles—an area the size of New Jersey.

The great sprawl of Sunbelt cities has its drawbacks. Many people in cities such as Atlanta, Dallas, Phoenix, and Los Angeles argue that the growth follows no plan and

results in traffic-clogged roads leading to poorly planned developments. As a result, voters in many communities across the United States have passed ballot initiatives seeking to limit urban sprawl (Lacayo, 1999; Romero & Liserio, 2002).

MEGALOPOLIS: THE REGIONAL CITY

Another result of urban decentralization is urban regions, or regional cities. The U.S. Census Bureau (2003) recognizes 362 *metropolitan statistical areas.* These areas include at least one city with 50,000 or more people. The bureau also recognizes 560 *micropolitan statistical areas,* urban areas with at least one city of 10,000 to 50,000 people. *Core based statistical areas* (CBSAs) include both metropolitan and micropolitan statistical areas.

The biggest CBSAs contain millions of people and cover areas that extend into several states. In 2000, the biggest CBSA was New York and its adjacent urban areas in Long Island, western Connecticut, and northern New Jersey and Pennsylvania, with a total population of more than 21 million. Next in size is the CBSA in southern California that includes Los Angeles, Riverside, and Long Beach, with a population of more than 16 million.

As regional cities grow, they begin to overlap. For example, along the East Coast, a 400-mile supercity stretches all the way from New England to Virginia. In the early 1960s, the French geographer Jean Gottmann (1961) coined the term **megalopolis** to designate *a vast urban region containing a number of cities and their surrounding suburbs.* Other supercities cover the eastern coast of Florida and stretch from Cleveland west to Chicago.

EDGE CITIES

Urban decentralization has also created *edge cities,* business centers some distance from the old downtowns. Edge cities—a mix of corporate office buildings, shopping malls, hotels, and entertainment complexes—differ from suburbs, which contain mostly homes. The population of suburbs peaks at night, but the population of edge cities peaks during the workday.

As part of expanding urban regions, most edge cities have no clear physical boundaries. Some do have names, including Las Colinas (near the Dallas–Fort Worth airport), Tyson's Corner (in Virginia, near Washington, D.C.), and King of Prussia (northwest of Philadelphia). Other edge cities are known only by the major highways that flow through them, including Route 1 in Princeton, New Jersey, and Route 128 near Boston (Garreau, 1991; Macionis & Parrillo, 2004).

The rural rebound has been most pronounced in towns that offer spectacular natural beauty. There are times when people living in the scenic town of Park City, Utah, cannot even find a parking space.

THE RURAL REBOUND

Over the course of U.S. history, as shown by the data in Table 15–1, the urban population of the nation has increased steadily. Immigration has played a part in this increase because most newcomers to this country settle in cities. There has also been considerable migration from rural areas to urban places, typically by people seeking greater economic opportunity.

However, in the 1990s, three-fourths of the rural counties across the United States gained population, a trend analysts have called the "rural rebound." Most of this gain resulted from migration of people from urban areas. This trend has not affected all rural places: As the opening to this chapter explains, many small towns in rural areas (especially in the midsection of the country from North Dakota down to Texas, as shown on National Map 15–1 on page 420) are struggling simply to stay alive. But even in these areas, the losses slowed during the 1990s (Johnson, 1999, 2001).

The greatest gains have come to rural communities that offer scenic and recreational attractions, such as lakes, mountains, and ski areas. People are drawn not only to the natural beauty of rural communities but also to their slower pace: less traffic, a lower crime rate, and cleaner air. A number of companies have relocated to rural counties as well, which has increased economic opportunity for the rural population (Johnson, 1999; Johnson & Fuguitt, 2000).

Urbanism as a Way of Life

Early sociologists in Europe and the United States focused their attention on the rise of cities. We briefly present their accounts of urbanism as a way of life.

FERDINAND TÖNNIES: *GEMEINSCHAFT* AND *GESELLSCHAFT*

In the nineteenth century, the German sociologist Ferdinand Tönnies (1855–1937) studied how life in the new industrial metropolis differed from life in rural villages. From this contrast, he developed two concepts that have become a lasting part of sociology's terminology.

Tönnies (1963, orig. 1887) used the German word **Gemeinschaft** (meaning roughly "community") to refer to *a type of social organization in which people are closely linked by kinship and tradition.* The *Gemeinschaft* of the rural village, Tönnies explained, joins people in what amounts to a single primary group.

By and large, argued Tönnies, *Gemeinschaft* does not exist in the modern city. On the contrary, urbanization creates **Gesellschaft** (a German word, meaning roughly "association"), *a type of social organization in which people come together only on the basis of individual self-interest.* In the *Gesellschaft* way of life, individuals are motivated by their own needs rather than by a desire to help improve the well-being of everyone. By and large, city dwellers have little sense of community or common identity and look to other people mainly when they need something. Tönnies saw in urbanization the weakening of close, long-lasting social relations in favor of the brief and impersonal ties—or secondary relationships—typical of business.

EMILE DURKHEIM: MECHANICAL AND ORGANIC SOLIDARITY

The French sociologist Emile Durkheim agreed with much of Tönnies's thinking about cities. However, Durkheim countered that urbanites do not lack social bonds; they simply organize social life differently than rural people.

Durkheim described traditional, rural life as *mechanical solidarity,* social bonds based on common sentiments and shared moral values. With its emphasis on tradition, Durkheim's concept of mechanical solidarity bears a striking

Peasant Dance (above, c. 1565), by Pieter Breughel the Elder, conveys the essential unity of rural life forged by generations of kinship and neighborhood. By contrast, Ernest Fiene's *Nocturne* (left) communicates the impersonality common to urban areas. Taken together, these paintings capture Tönnies's distinction between *Gemeinschaft* and *Gesellschaft*.

Pieter Breughel the Elder (c. 1525/30–1569), *Peasant Dance*, c. 1565, Kunsthistorisches Museum, Vienna/Superstock. Ernest Fiene (1894–1965), *Nocturne*. Photograph © Christie's Images.

similarity to Tönnies's *Gemeinschaft*. Urbanization erodes mechanical solidarity, Durkheim explained, but it also generates a new type of bonding, which he called *organic solidarity*, social bonds based on specialization and interdependence. This concept, which parallels Tönnies's *Gesellschaft*, reveals an important difference between the two thinkers. Both thought the growth of industrial cities weakened tradition, but Durkheim optimistically pointed to a new kind of solidarity. Where societies had been built on *likeness*, Durkheim now saw social life based on *difference*.

For Durkheim, urban society offers more individual choice, moral tolerance, and personal privacy than people find in rural villages. In sum, Durkheim thought that something is lost in the process of urbanization, but much is gained.

GEORG SIMMEL: THE BLASÉ URBANITE

The German sociologist Georg Simmel (1858–1918) offered a microanalysis of cities, studying how urban life shapes individual experience. According to Simmel, individuals see the city as a crush of people, objects, and events. To prevent being overwhelmed by all this stimulation, urbanites develop a *blasé attitude*, tuning out much of what goes on around them. Such detachment does not mean that city dwellers lack compassion for others; they simply keep

their distance as a survival strategy so they can focus their time and energy on those who really matter to them.

THE CHICAGO SCHOOL: ROBERT PARK AND LOUIS WIRTH

Sociologists in the United States soon joined the study of rapidly growing cities. Robert Park (1864–1944), a leader of the first U.S. sociology program at the University of Chicago, sought to add a street-level perspective by getting out and studying real cities. As he said of himself, "I suspect that I have actually covered more ground, tramping about in cities in different parts of the world, than any other living man" (1950:viii). Walking the streets, Park found the city to be an organized mosaic of distinctive ethnic communities, commercial centers, and industrial districts. Over time, he observed these "natural areas" develop and change in relation to one another. To Park, the city was a living organism—a human kaleidoscope.

Another major figure in the Chicago School of urban sociology was Louis Wirth (1897–1952). Wirth (1938) is best known for blending the ideas of Tönnies, Durkheim, Simmel, and Park into a comprehensive theory of urban life.

Wirth began by defining the city as a setting with a large, dense, and socially diverse population. These traits result in an impersonal, superficial, and transitory way of life. Living among millions of others, urbanites come into contact with many more people than residents of rural areas. Thus, when city people notice others at all, they usually know them not in terms of *who they are* but *what they do*— as, for instance, the bus driver, the florist, or the grocery store clerk. Specialized, urban relationships sometimes are pleasant for all concerned. But we should remember that self-interest rather than friendship is the main reason for the interaction.

Finally, the impersonal nature of urban relationships, together with the great social diversity found in cities today, makes city dwellers more tolerant than rural villagers. Rural communities often jealously enforce their narrow traditions, but the heterogeneous population of a city rarely shares any single code of moral conduct (Wilson, 1985, 1995).

Critical review. In both Europe and the United States, early sociologists presented a mixed view of urban living. Rapid urbanization troubled Tönnies and Wirth, who saw personal ties and traditional morality lost in the anonymous rush of the city. Durkheim and Park emphasized urbanism's positive face, pointing to more personal freedom and greater personal choice.

One problem with all of these views is that they paint urbanism in broad strokes that overlook the effects of class, race, and gender. There are many kinds of urbanites—rich and poor, black and white, Anglo and Latino, women and men—all leading distinctive lives (Gans, 1968). Indeed, as the Diversity box explains, the share of racial and ethnic minorities in the largest U.S. cities increased sharply during the 1990s. We see social diversity most clearly in cities, where various categories of people are large enough to form visible communities (Macionis & Parrillo, 2004).

URBAN ECOLOGY

Sociologists (especially members of the Chicago School) developed **urban ecology,** *the study of the link between the physical and social dimensions of cities.* For example, why are cities located where they are? The first cities emerged in fertile regions where the ecology favored raising crops. Pre-industrial people, concerned with defense, built their cities on mountains (ancient Athens was perched on an outcropping of rock) or surrounded by water (Paris and Mexico City were built on islands). With the Industrial Revolution, economic considerations situated all major U.S. cities near rivers and natural harbors that facilitated trade.

Urban ecologists also study the physical design of cities. In 1925, Ernest W. Burgess, a student and colleague of Robert Park's, described land use in Chicago in terms of *concentric zones.* City centers, Burgess observed, are business districts bordered by a ring of factories, followed by residential rings with housing that becomes more expensive the farther it is from the noise and pollution of the city's center.

Homer Hoyt (1939) refined Burgess's observations, noting that distinctive districts sometimes form *wedge-shaped sectors.* For example, one fashionable area may develop next to another, or an industrial district may extend outward from a city's center along a train or trolley line.

Chauncy Harris and Edward Ullman (1945) added yet another insight: As cities decentralize, they lose their single-center form in favor of a *multicentered model.* As cities grow, residential areas, industrial parks, and shopping districts typically push away from one another. Few people want to live close to industrial areas, for example, so the city becomes a mosaic of distinct districts.

Social area analysis investigates what people in particular neighborhoods have in common. Three factors seem to explain most of the variation in neighborhood types: family patterns, social class, and race and ethnicity (Shevky & Bell, 1955; Johnston, 1976). Families with children look for areas with large apartments or single-family homes and good schools. The rich seek high-prestige neighborhoods, often in the central city near cultural attractions. People with a common ethnic heritage cluster in distinctive communities.

Finally, Brian Berry and Philip Rees (1969) tied together many of these insights. They explained that distinct family types tend to settle in the concentric zones described by Ernest Burgess. Specifically, households with few children tend to cluster toward the city's center, and those with more children live farther away. Social class differences are primarily responsible for the sector-shaped districts described by Homer Hoyt; the rich occupy one "side of the tracks" and the poor the other. And racial and ethnic neighborhoods are found at various places throughout the city, consistent with Harris and Ullman's multicentered model.

URBAN POLITICAL ECONOMY

In the late 1960s, many large U.S. cities were rocked by major riots. In the wake of this unrest, some analysts turned away from the ecological approach to a social-conflict understanding of city life. The *urban political-economy model* applies Karl Marx's analysis of conflict in the workplace to conflict in the city (Lindstrom, 1995).

Political economists disagree with the ecological approach, which sees the city as a natural organism with particular districts and neighborhoods developing according to an internal logic. They claim that city life is defined by people with power: corporate leaders and political officials. Capitalism, which transforms the city into real estate traded for profit and concentrates wealth in the hands of the

Census 2000: Minorities Now a Majority in the Largest U.S. Cities

According to the results of the 2000 U.S. Census, minorities— Hispanics, African Americans, and Asians—are now a majority of the population in 48 of the 100 largest U.S. cities, up from 30 in 1990.

Why the change? One reason is that large cities have been losing their non-Hispanic white populations. For example, by 2000, Santa Ana, California, had lost 38 percent of the white population it had in 1990; the drop was 40 percent in Birmingham, Alabama, and a whopping 53 percent in Detroit, Michigan. The white share of the population of all 100 of the largest cities fell from 52 percent in 1990 to 44 percent in 2000.

But perhaps the biggest reason for the minority-majority trend is the increase in immigration. Immigration, coupled with higher birth rates among new immigrants, resulted in a 43 percent gain in the Hispanic population (almost 4 million people) of the largest 100 cities between 1990 and 2000. The Asian population also surged by 40 percent (more than 1.1 million people). The African

American population was about steady over the course of the past decade.

Political officials and other policy makers are examining these figures closely. Clearly, the future vitality of the largest U.S. cities depends on meeting the needs and taking advantage of the contributions of their swelling minority populations.

WHAT DO YOU THINK?
1. Why are the minority populations of large U.S. cities increasing?
2. What positive changes does a minority-majority bring to a city?
3. What challenges does a minority-majority bring to a city?

Sources: Based on Schmitt (2001) and U.S. Census Bureau (2001).

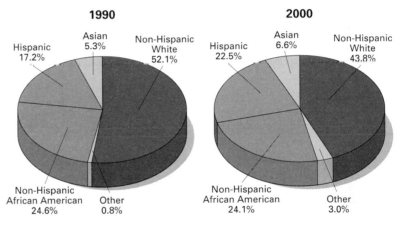

1990

Hispanic 17.2%
Asian 5.3%
Non-Hispanic White 52.1%
Non-Hispanic African American 24.6%
Other 0.8%

Total population: 51,765,000

2000

Hispanic 22.5%
Asian 6.6%
Non-Hispanic White 43.8%
Non-Hispanic African American 24.1%
Other 3.0%

Total population: 58,442,000

Minority Population Change in the 100 Largest U.S. Cities

---

few, is the key to understanding city life. From this point of view, the decline in industrial Snowbelt cities after 1950 was the result of deliberate decisions by the corporate elite to move their production facilities to the Sunbelt (where labor is cheaper and less likely to be unionized) or move them out of the country entirely to low-income nations (Molotch, 1976; Castells, 1977, 1983; Feagin, 1983; Lefebvre, 1991; Jones & Wilson, 1999).

Critical review. The fact that many U.S. cities are in crisis, with widespread poverty, high crime, and barely functioning schools, seems to favor the political-economy view over the urban ecology approach. But one criticism applies to both: They focus on U.S. cities during a limited period of history.

Much of what we know about industrial cities does not apply to preindustrial towns in our own past or the rapidly growing cities in many poor nations today. It is unlikely that any single model of cities can account for the full range of urban diversity found in the world today.

Urbanization in Poor Societies

November 16, Cairo, Egypt. People call the vast Muslim cemetery in Old Cairo the "City of the Dead." In truth, it is very much alive: Tens of thousands of squatters have moved into the mausoleums, making this place an eerie mix of life and death. Children run across the stone floors, clotheslines stretch between the monuments, and an occasional television antenna protrudes from a tomb roof. With Cairo gaining 1,000 people a day, families live where they can.

Twice in its history, the world has experienced a revolutionary expansion of cities. The first urban revolution began about 8000 B.C.E. with the first urban settlements and continued until permanent settlements were in place on several continents. About 1750, the second urban revolution took off; it lasted for two centuries as the Industrial Revolution spurred rapid growth of cities in Europe and North America.

A *third urban revolution* is now underway. Today, 75 percent of people in high-income countries are already city dwellers. But extraordinary urban growth is occurring in poor nations. In 1950, about 25 percent of the people in low-income countries lived in cities; in 2005, the figure is close to 50 percent. In addition, in 1950, only seven cities in the world had populations over 5 million, and only two of these were in low-income countries. By 2004, fifty-five urban areas had passed this mark, and thirty-eight of them were in less developed nations (Brockerhoff, 2000; World Gazetteer, 2004).

This third urban revolution is taking place because many poor nations have entered the high-growth Stage 2 of demographic transition theory. Falling death rates have fueled population increase in Latin America, Asia, and especially Africa. For urban areas, the rate of increase is *twice* as high because, in addition to natural increase, millions of people leave the countryside each year in search of jobs, health care, education, and conveniences such as running water and electricity.

Cities do offer more opportunities than rural areas, but they provide no quick fix for the problems of escalating population and grinding poverty. Many cities in less developed nations—including Mexico City, Egypt's Cairo, India's Calcutta, and Manila in the Philippines—are simply unable to meet the basic needs of much of their population. All these cities are surrounded by wretched shantytowns, settlements of makeshift homes built from discarded materials. As noted in Chapter 9 ("Global Stratification"), even city dumps are home to thousands of poor people, who pick through the waste hoping to find enough to make it through another day.

Environment and Society

The human species has prospered, rapidly increasing in population over the entire the planet. An increasing share of the global population now lives in large, complex settlements that offer the promise of a better life than that found in rural villages.

But these advances have come at a high price. Never before in history have human beings placed such demands on the Earth. This disturbing development brings us to the final section of this chapter: a look at the interplay of the natural environment and society. Like demography, **ecology** is another cousin of sociology, formally defined as *the study of the interaction of living organisms and the natural environment.* Ecology rests on the research of natural scientists as well as social scientists. In this text, we focus on the aspects of ecology that involve familiar sociological concepts and issues.

The **natural environment** is *the Earth's surface and atmosphere, including living organisms, air, water, soil, and other resources necessary to sustain life.* Like every other species, humans depend on the natural environment to survive. Yet with our capacity for culture, humans stand apart from other species; we alone take deliberate action to remake the world according to our own interests and desires, for better and for worse.

Why is the environment of interest to sociologists? Environmental problems—from pollution to global warming—do not arise from the natural world operating on its own. Such problems result from the specific actions of human beings, making them *social* problems (Marx, 1994).

THE GLOBAL DIMENSION

The study of the natural environment must be approached from a global perspective. Regardless of political divisions between nations, the planet is a single **ecosystem,** *a system composed of the interaction of all living organisms and their natural environment.*

The Greek meaning of *eco* is "house," reminding us that this planet is our home and that all living things and their natural environment are interrelated. A change in any part of the natural environment sends ripples through the entire global ecosystem.

Consider, from an ecological point of view, our national love of eating hamburgers. People in North America (and, increasingly, around the world) have created a huge demand for beef, which has greatly expanded ranching in Brazil, Costa Rica, and other Latin American nations. To produce the lean meat sought by fast-food corporations, cattle in Latin America feed on grass, which uses a great deal of land. Latin American ranchers clear the land for grazing by destroying thousands of square miles of forests each year. These tropical forests are vital to maintaining the Earth's atmosphere. Deforestation ends up threatening everyone, including those people back in the United States enjoying their hamburgers (Myers, 1984b).

The most important insight sociology offers about our physical world is that environmental problems do not simply "happen." Rather, the state of the natural environment reflects the ways in which social life is organized—how people live and what they think is important. Moreover, the greater the technological power of a society, the greater that society's ability to threaten the natural environment.

TECHNOLOGY AND THE ENVIRONMENTAL DEFICIT

Sociologists point to a simple formula: $I = PAT$, where environmental impact (I) reflects a society's population (P), its level of affluence (A), and its level of technology (T). Members of societies with simple technology—the hunters and gatherers described in Chapter 2 ("Culture")—hardly affect the environment because they are small in number, poor, and have only simple technology. On the contrary, nature affects their lives as they follow the migration of game, watch the rhythm of the seasons, and suffer from natural catastrophes, such as fires, floods, droughts, and storms.

Societies at intermediate stages of sociocultural evolution have a somewhat greater capacity to affect the environment. But the environmental impact of horticulture (small-scale farming), pastoralism (the herding of animals), and even agriculture (the use of animal-drawn plows) is limited because people still rely on muscle power for producing food and other goods.

Human control of the natural environment increased dramatically with the Industrial Revolution. Muscle power gave way to engines that burn fossil fuels: coal at first and then oil. Such machinery affects the environment in two ways: by consuming natural resources and by releasing pollutants into the atmosphere. Even more important, humans armed with industrial technology are able to bend nature to their will, tunneling through mountains, damming rivers, irrigating deserts, and drilling for oil on the ocean floor. This explains why people in rich nations, who represent just 18 percent of humanity, use 80 percent of the world's energy (Miller, 1992; York, Rosa, & Deitz, 2002).

The environmental impact of industrial technology goes beyond energy consumption. Just as important is the fact that members of industrial societies produce 100 times more goods than people in agrarian societies. Higher living standards, in turn, increase the problems of solid waste (because people ultimately throw away most of what they produce) and pollution (industrial production generates smoke and other toxic substances).

Right from the start, people recognized the material benefits of industrial technology. But only a century later did they begin to see its long-term effects on the natural environment, which set the stage for the growth of the environmental movement. Today, we realize that the technological power to make our lives better can also put the lives of future generations at risk, and there is a national debate about how to address this issue.

Evidence is mounting that we are running up an **environmental deficit,** *profound and long-term harm to the natural environment caused by humanity's focus on short-term material affluence* (Bormann, 1990). The concept of environmental deficit is important for three reasons. First, it reminds us that the state of the environment is a *social issue,* reflecting choices people make about how to live. Second, it suggests that much environmental damage—to the air, land, or water—is *unintended.* By focusing on the short-term benefits of, say, cutting down forests, strip mining, or using throwaway packaging, we fail to see their long-term environmental effects. Third, in some respects, the environmental deficit is *reversible.* Inasmuch as societies have created environmental problems, societies can undo many of them.

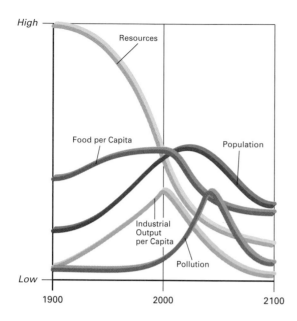

High

Resources

Food per Capita

Population

Industrial
Output
per Capita

Pollution

Low

1900   2000   2100

FIGURE 15-5 The Limits to Growth: Projections

Source: Based on Meadows et al. (1972).

CULTURE: GROWTH AND LIMITS

Whether we recognize environmental dangers and decide to do something about them is a cultural matter. Thus, along with technology, culture has powerful environmental consequences.

The logic of growth.   One of the core values that underlie social life in the United States is *material comfort,* the belief that money and the things it buys enrich our lives. We also believe in the idea of *progress,* thinking that the future will be better than the present. In addition, we look to *science* to make our lives easier and more rewarding. In simpler terms, "having things is good," "life gets better," and "people are clever." Taken together, such cultural values form the *logic of growth.*

An optimistic view of the world, the logic of growth holds that more powerful technology has improved our lives and that new discoveries will continue to do so into the future. Throughout the history of the United States and other high-income nations, the logic of growth has been the driving force behind settling the wilderness, building towns and roads, and the pursuit of material affluence.

However, "progress" can lead to unexpected problems, including strain on the environment. The logic of growth responds by arguing that people (especially scientists and other technology experts) will find a way out of any problem placed in our path. If, for example, the world runs short of oil, scientists will come up with electric, solar, or nuclear engines or some as yet unknown technology to meet the world's energy needs.

Environmentalists counter that the logic of growth is flawed because it assumes that natural resources such as clean air, fresh water, and the Earth's topsoil will always be plentiful. We can and will exhaust these *finite* resources if we continue to pursue growth at any cost. Echoing Malthus, environmentalists warn that if we call on the Earth to support increasing numbers of people, we will surely destroy the environment—and ourselves—in the process.

The limits to growth.   If we cannot invent our way out of the problems created by the logic of growth, perhaps we need another way of thinking about the world. Environmentalists claim that growth must have limits. Stated simply, the *limits to growth* thesis is that humanity must put in place policies to control population increase, pollution, and the use of resources in order to avoid environmental collapse.

In *The Limits to Growth,* a controversial book that had a large hand in launching the environmental movement, Donella Meadows and her colleagues (1972) used a computer model to calculate the planet's available resources, rates of population growth, amount of land available for cultivation, levels of industrial and food production, and amount of pollutants released into the atmosphere. The model reflects changes that have occurred since 1900 and projects forward to the end of the twenty-first century. The authors concede that such long-range predictions are speculative, and some critics think they are plain wrong (Simon, 1981). But right or wrong, the general conclusions of the study, shown in Figure 15–5, call for serious consideration.

According to the limits to growth thesis, we are quickly using up the Earth's finite resources. Supplies of oil, natural gas, and other energy sources are already falling sharply and will continue to drop, a little faster or more slowly depending on conservation policies in rich nations and how fast other nations industrialize. Although food production per person will continue to rise during this century, world hunger will persist because existing food supplies are distributed so unequally. By 2050, the model predicts that hunger will reach a crisis level, first stabilizing population and then sending it back downward. Sooner or later, resource depletion will cripple industrial output as well. Only then will pollution rates fall.

Limits to growth theorists are also known as neo-Malthusians because they share Malthus's pessimism about the future. They doubt that current patterns of life are sustainable for even another century. If so, we face a fundamental choice: Either we make deliberate changes in how we live, or widespread calamity will force change on us.

SOLID WASTE: THE DISPOSABLE SOCIETY

Across the United States, people generate a massive amount of solid waste–about 1.5 billion pounds *each and every day.* Figure 15–6 shows the composition of a typical community's trash.

As a rich nation containing people who value convenience, the United States has become a *disposable society.* We consume more products than virtually any other nation on Earth, many of which have throwaway packaging. For example, fast food is served in cardboard, plastic, and Styrofoam containers that we throw away within minutes. But countless other products—from film to fishhooks—are elaborately packaged to make them more attractive to the customer and to discourage tampering and theft.

Manufacturers market soft drinks, beer, and fruit juices in aluminum cans, glass jars, and plastic containers, which not only use up finite resources but also create mountains of solid waste. Countless items are intentionally designed to be disposable: pens, razors, flashlights, batteries, even cameras. Other goods, from light bulbs to automobiles, are designed to have a limited useful life after which they become unwanted junk. As Paul H. Connett (1991) points out, even the words we use to describe what we throw away—"waste," "trash," "refuse," "garbage," "rubbish"—show how little we value what we cannot immediately use. But this was not always the case, as the Applying Sociology box on page 438 explains.

Living in a rich society, the average person in the United States consumes 50 times more steel, 170 times more newspaper, 250 times more gasoline, and 300 times more plastic each year than the typical person in a low-income country such as Haiti (Miller, 1992). This high level of consumption means that we in the United States not only use a disproportionate share of the planet's natural resources but also generate most of the world's refuse.

We like to say that we "throw things away." But 80 percent of our solid waste never "goes away." Rather, it ends up in landfills, which are, literally, filling up. Material in landfills also can pollute groundwater. Although in most places laws now regulate what can be discarded in a landfill, the Environmental Protection Agency has identified 30,000 dump sites across the United States containing hazardous materials that are polluting water both above and below the ground. In addition, what goes into landfills all too often stays there, sometimes for centuries. Tens of millions of tires, diapers, and other items that we bury in landfills each year do not decompose and will be an unwelcome legacy for future generations.

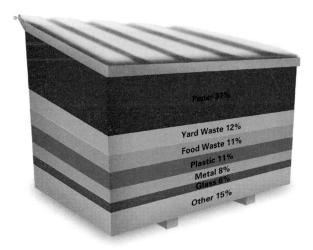

FIGURE 15-6 Composition of Community Trash

Source: U.S. Environmental Protection Agency (2003).

Environmentalists argue that we should address the problem of solid waste by doing what many of our ancestors did: Turn "waste" into a resource. One way to do this is through *recycling*, reusing resources we would otherwise throw away. Recycling is an accepted practice in Japan and many other nations, and it is becoming more common in the United States, where we now reuse about 30 percent of waste materials. The share is increasing as laws mandate reuse of certain materials such as glass bottles and aluminum cans. Because of our nation's market-based economy, recycling will also increase as it becomes more profitable.

WATER AND AIR

Oceans, lakes, and streams are the lifeblood of the global ecosystem. Humans depend on water for drinking, bathing, cooling, cooking, recreation, and a host of other activities.

According to what scientists call the *hydrologic cycle*, the Earth naturally recycles water and refreshes the land. The process begins as heat from the sun causes the Earth's water, 97 percent of which is in the oceans, to evaporate and form clouds. Because water evaporates at lower temperatures than most pollutants, the water vapor that rises from the seas is relatively pure, leaving various contaminants behind. Water then falls to the Earth as rain, which drains into streams and rivers and, finally, returns to the sea. Two major concerns about water, then, are supply and pollution.

Water supply.   Only about 1 percent of the Earth's water is suitable for drinking. It is not surprising, then, that for

APPLYING SOCIOLOGY

Why Grandmother Had No Trash

Grandma Macionis, we always used to say, never threw away anything. She was born and raised in Lithuania—the "old country"—where life in a poor village shaped her in ways that never changed, even after she came to the United States as a young woman and settled in Philadelphia.

After opening a birthday present, she would carefully save the box, wrapping paper, and ribbon, which meant as much to her as the gift they contained. Grandma never wore new clothes, her kitchen knives were worn thin from decades of sharpening, and all her garbage was recycled as compost for her vegetable garden.

As strange as Grandma seemed to her grandchildren, she was a product of her culture. A century ago, there was little "trash." If a pair of socks wore thin, Grandma mended them,

probably more than once. When they were beyond repair, she used them as a rag for cleaning or sewed them (with other old clothing) into a quilt. For her, everything had value, if not in one way, then in another.

During the twentieth century, as women joined men working outside of the home, income went up and people spent less time at home. Families began buying more and more "time-saving" products. Before long, few people cared about the home recycling that Grandma practiced. Soon cities sent crews from block to block to pick up truckloads of discarded material. The era of "trash" had begun.

WHAT DO YOU THINK?

1. Just as Grandma Macionis was a product of her culture, so are we. What cultural values make people today demand "time-saving" products and "convenience" packaging?
2. What do you think are the prospects for expanding recycling of materials in the near future?
3. Would you support laws that limited people's trash? Why or why not?

---

thousands of years, water rights have figured prominently in laws around the world. Today, as Global Map 15–2 shows, some regions of the world, especially the tropics, enjoy plentiful fresh water, using only a small share of the available supply. High demand, coupled with modest reserves, make water supply a matter of concern in much of North America and Asia, where people look to rivers rather than rainfall for their water. In China, deep aquifers are dropping rapidly. In the Middle East, water supply is reaching a critical level. Iran is rationing water in its capital city. In Egypt, people can consume just one-sixth as much water from the Nile River today as in 1900. Across northern Africa and the Middle East, experts predict, as many as 1 billion people may lack the water they need for irrigation and drinking by 2025 (Postel, 1993; "China Faces Water Shortage," 2001).

Rising population and the development of more complex technology have greatly increased the world's appetite for water. The global consumption of water (now estimated at 4 billion cubic feet per year) has doubled since 1950 and

is rising steadily. As a result, even in parts of the world that receive plenty of rainfall, people are using groundwater faster than it can be replenished naturally. In the Tamil Nadu region of southern India, for example, people are drawing so much groundwater that the local water table has fallen 100 feet over the last several decades. Mexico City—which has sprawled to some 1,400 square miles—has pumped so much water from its underground aquifer that the city has sunk 30 feet in the past century and continues to drop about 2 inches per year. Farther north in the United States, the Ogallala aquifer, which lies below seven states from South Dakota to Texas, is now being pumped so rapidly that some experts fear it could run dry within several decades.

In light of such developments, we must face the reality that water is a valuable and finite resource. Greater conservation of water by individuals (the average person consumes 10 million gallons in a lifetime) is part of the answer. However, households around the world account for just 10 percent of

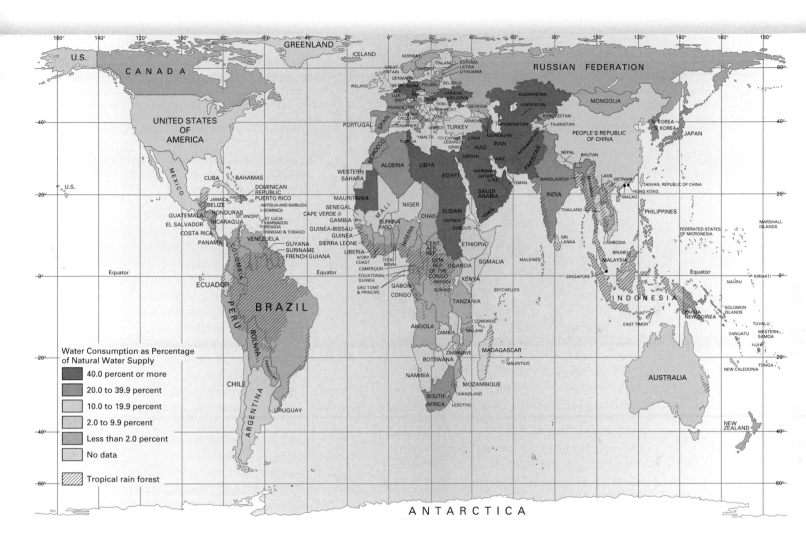

WINDOW ON THE WORLD

GLOBAL MAP 15-2 Water Consumption in Global Perspective

This map shows water consumption as a percentage of each country's renewable water resources. Nations near the equator use only a tiny share of their available resources; indeed, much of this region is covered with rain forest. Northern Africa and the Middle East are a different story, however, with dense populations drawing on very limited water resources. As a result, in countries such as Libya, Egypt, and Saudi Arabia, people (especially the poor) do not have as much water as they would like or, often, as they need.

Source: United Nations Development Programme (2000).

water use. We need to curb water consumption by industry, which uses 25 percent of the global total, and farming, which consumes two-thirds of the total for irrigation.

New irrigation technology may reduce the demand for water in the future. But here again, we see how population increase, as well as economic growth, strains our ecosystem (Postel, 1993; Population Action International, 2000).

Water pollution. In large cities—from Mexico City to Cairo to Shanghai—many people have no choice but to

Water is vital to life, and it is also in short supply. The state of Gujarat, in western India, has experienced a decade-long drought. In the village of Natwarghad, people crowd together, lowering pots into the local well, taking what little water is left.

contaminating water (in lakes and streams that collect acid rain). Acid rain is truly a global phenomenon because the regions that suffer the harmful effects may be thousands of miles from the source of the pollution. For instance, British power plants have caused acid rain that has devastated forests and fish in Norway and Sweden, 1,000 miles to the northeast. In the United States, we see a similar pattern as midwestern smokestacks have harmed the natural environment of upstate New York and New England.

Air pollution. Because we are surrounded by air, most people in the United States are more aware of air pollution than contaminated water. One of the unexpected consequences of industrial technology—especially the factory and the motor vehicle—has been a decline in air quality. In 1950, exhaust fumes from automobiles shrouded cities such as Los Angeles. In London, factory smokestacks, automobiles, and coal fires used to heat households all added up to what was probably the worst urban air quality of the last century. What some British jokingly called "pea soup" was in reality a deadly mix of pollution: During five days in 1952, an especially thick haze that hung over London killed 4,000 people.

Air quality improved in the final decades of the twentieth century. Rich nations passed laws that banned high-pollution heating, including the coal fires that choked London fifty years ago. In addition, scientists devised ways to make factories as well as automobiles and trucks operate much more cleanly.

If high-income countries can breathe a bit more easily than they once did, the problem of air pollution in poor societies is becoming more serious. One reason is that people in low-income countries still rely on wood, coal, peat, or other "dirty" fuels to cook their food and heat their homes. In addition, nations eager to encourage short-term industrial development may pay little attention to the longer-term dangers of air pollution. As a result, many cities in Latin America, Eastern Europe, and Asia are plagued by air pollution as bad as London's pea soup fifty years ago.

drink contaminated water. Infectious diseases such as typhoid, cholera, and dysentery, all caused by waterborne microorganisms, spread rapidly through these populations. In addition to ensuring ample *supplies* of water, we must protect the *quality* of water.

Water quality in the United States is generally good by global standards. However, even here the problem of water pollution is steadily growing. According to the Sierra Club, an environmental activist organization, rivers and streams across the United States absorb some 500 million pounds of toxic waste each year. This pollution results not just from intentional dumping but also from the runoff of agricultural fertilizers and lawn chemicals.

A special problem is *acid rain*—rain made acidic by air pollution—that destroys plant and animal life. Acid rain (or snow) begins with power plants burning fossil fuels (oil and coal) to generate electricity; this burning process releases sulfuric and nitrous oxides into the air. As the wind sweeps these gases into the atmosphere, they react with the air to form sulfuric and nitric acids, which turn atmospheric moisture acidic.

This is a clear case of one type of pollution causing another: Air pollution (from smokestacks) ends up

THE RAIN FORESTS

Rain forests are *regions of dense forestation, most of which circle the globe close to the equator.* A glance back at Global Map 15–2 on page 439 shows that the largest tropical rain forests are in South America (notably Brazil), west-central Africa, and Southeast Asia. In all, the world's rain forests cover some 2 billion acres, or 7 percent of the Earth's total land surface.

Like other global resources, rain forests are falling victim to the needs and appetites of the surging world population. As noted earlier, to meet the demand for beef, ranchers in Latin America burn forested areas to increase their supply of grazing land. We are also losing rain forests to the hardwood trade. People in rich nations pay high prices for mahogany and other woods because, as environmentalist Norman Myers (1984c:88) puts it, they have "a penchant for parquet floors, fine furniture, fancy paneling, weekend yachts, and high-grade coffins." Under such economic pressure, the world's rain forests are now just half their original size, and they continue to shrink by about 1 percent (65,000 square miles) annually. Unless we stop this loss, the rain forests will vanish before the end of the twenty-first century and with them protection for the Earth's biodiversity and climate.

 For more information about rain forests, visit http://www.rainforestweb.org

Global warming. Why are rain forests so important? One reason is that they cleanse the atmosphere of carbon dioxide (CO_2). Since the beginning of the Industrial Revolution, the amount of carbon dioxide produced by humans (mostly from factories and automobiles) has risen sharply. Much of this CO_2 is absorbed by the oceans. But plants take in carbon dioxide and expel oxygen. This is why the rain forests are vital to maintaining the chemical balance of the atmosphere.

The problem is that production of carbon dioxide is rising while the amount of plant life on the Earth is shrinking. To make matters worse, rain forests are being destroyed mostly by burning, which releases even more carbon dioxide into the atmosphere. Experts estimate that the atmospheric concentration of carbon dioxide is now 20 to 30 percent higher than it was 150 years ago (Revkin, 2002).

 The Heinz Center publishes analyses of society's effect on the natural environment at http://www.heinzctr.org/publications.htm

High above the Earth, carbon dioxide acts like the glass roof of a greenhouse, letting heat from the sun pass through to the Earth while preventing much of it from radiating back away from the planet, a mechanism called the *greenhouse effect.* The result, say ecologists, is **global warming,** *a rise in the Earth's average temperature due to an increasing concentration of carbon dioxide in the atmosphere.* Over the past century, the global temperature has risen about 1 degree Fahrenheit (to an average of 58° F). Scientists warn that it

The world's rain forests continue to shrink by about 1 percent each year. The Amazon Highway, being built through the Brazilian rain forest, is to many people a welcome source of economic development. But what effect will such development have on the local environment? What difference does this make for us here in the United States?

could rise by 5° F to 10° F during this century, which would melt vast areas of the polar ice caps and raise the sea level to cover low-lying land around the world. Were this to happen, water would cover all of Bangladesh, for example, and much of the coastal United States, including Washington, D.C., right up to the steps of the White House. On the other hand, the U.S. Midwest, currently one of the most productive agricultural regions in the world, probably would become arid.

Not all scientists share this gloomy outlook. Some point out that global temperature changes have been taking place throughout history, apparently having little or nothing to do with rain forests. Higher concentrations of carbon dioxide in the atmosphere might speed up plant growth (because plants thrive on this gas), which would correct the imbalance and nudge the Earth's temperature downward once again. But a consensus is building that global warming is a problem that threatens the future for all of us (Begley, 1997; McDonald, 1999).

Members of small, simple societies, such as the Tan't Batu, who thrive in the Philippines, live in harmony with nature; such people do not have the technological means to greatly affect the natural world. Although we in complex societies like to think of ourselves as superior to such people, the truth is that there is much we can—and must—learn from them.

Declining biodiversity. Clearing rain forests also reduces the Earth's *biodiversity*. This is because rain forests are home to almost half of the planet's living species.

On Earth, there are as many as 30 million species of animals, plants, and microorganisms. Several dozen unique species of plants and animals cease to exist each day. But given the vast number of living species, why should we be concerned? Environmentalists give three reasons. First, our planet's biodiversity provides a varied source of human food. Using agricultural high technology, scientists can "splice" familiar crops with more exotic plant life, making food more bountiful and more resistant to insects and disease. Thus, biodiversity helps feed our planet's rapidly increasing population.

Second, animal and plant biodiversity is a vital genetic resource. Medical and pharmaceutical researchers rely on it to provide hundreds of new compounds each year that cure disease and improve our lives. For example, children in the United States now have a good chance of surviving leukemia, a disease that was almost a sure killer two generations ago, because of a compound derived from a pretty tropical flower called the rosy periwinkle. The oral birth control pill, used by tens of millions of women in this country, is another product of plant research, this one involving the Mexican forest yam.

Third, with the loss of any species of life—whether it is the magnificent California condor, the famed Chinese panda, the spotted owl, or even a single species of ant—the beauty and complexity of our natural environment are diminished. And there are clear warning signs: Three-fourths of the world's 9,000 bird species are declining in number.

Finally, unlike pollution, the extinction of any species is irreversible and final. An important ethical question is whether people living today have the right to impoverish the world for those who will live tomorrow (Myers, 1991; Wilson, 1991; Brown et al., 1993).

ENVIRONMENTAL RACISM

Conflict theory has given birth to the concept of **environmental racism,** *the pattern by which environmental hazards are greatest for poor people, especially minorities.* Historically, factories that spew pollution have stood near neighborhoods housing the poor and people of color. Why? In part, the poor themselves were drawn to factories in search of work, and their low incomes often meant they could afford housing only in undesirable neighborhoods. Sometimes the only housing that fit their budgets stood in the very shadow of the plants and mills where they worked.

Nobody wants a factory or dump nearby, of course, but the poor have little power to resist. Through the years, the most serious environmental hazards have been placed near Newark, New Jersey (not in upscale Bergen County), in southside Chicago (not wealthy Lake Forest), or on Native American reservations in the West (not in affluent suburbs of Denver or Phoenix) (Commission for Racial Justice, 1994; Bohon & Humphrey, 2000).

CONTROVERSY & DEBATE
Apocalypse: Will People Overwhelm the Earth?

Are you worried about the world's increasing population? Think about this: By the time you finish reading this box, more than 1,000 people will be added to our planet. By this time tomorrow, global population will rise by about 200,000. Currently, as the table shows, there are about four births for every two deaths on the planet, pushing the world's population upward by 73 million annually. Global population growth amounts to adding another Egypt to the world every year.

It is no wonder that many demographers and environmentalists are deeply concerned about the future. The Earth has an unprecedented population: The 2 billion people we have added since 1974 alone exceeds the planet's total in 1900. Might Thomas Malthus—who predicted that overpopulation would use up the Earth's resources and plunge humanity into war and suffering—be right after all? Lester Brown and other *neo-Malthusians* predict a coming apocalypse if we do not change our ways. Brown admits that Malthus failed to imagine how much technology (especially fertilizers and altering plant genetics) could boost the planet's agricultural output. But he maintains that the Earth's rising population is nevertheless rapidly outstripping its finite resources. Families in many poor countries can find little firewood, members of rich societies are depleting worldwide oil reserves, and everyone is draining our supply of clean water and poisoning the planet with waste. Some analysts argue that we have already passed the Earth's "carrying capacity" for population and we need to hold the line or even reduce population to ensure our long-term survival.

But other analysts, the *anti-Malthusians,* sharply disagree. Julian Simon points out that centuries after Malthus predicted catastrophe, the Earth supports almost six times as many people who, on average, live longer, healthier lives than ever before. With more advanced technology, people have devised ways to increase productivity and limit population increase. As Simon sees it, this is cause for celebration. Human ingenuity has consistently proven the doomsayers wrong, and Simon is betting it will continue to do so.

CONTINUE THE DEBATE . . .

1. Where do you place your bet? Do you think the Earth can support 4, 6, 8, or 10 billion people? Why?
2. Ninety-six percent of current population growth is in poor countries. What does this mean for the future of rich nations? For the future of poor ones?
3. What should people in rich countries do to ensure their children's future?

Global Population Increase

	Births	Deaths	Net Increase
Per year	129,108,390	56,540,896	72,567,494
Per month	10,759,033	4,711,741	6,047,291
Per day	352,755	154,483	198,272
Per hour	14,698	6,437	8,261
Per minute	245	107	138
Per second	4.1	1.8	2.3

Sources: Based in part on Brown (1995), Simon (1995), Scanlon (2001), and Smail (2004).

Looking Ahead: Toward a Sustainable Society and World

The demographic analysis presented in this chapter points to some disturbing trends. First, the Earth's population has reached record levels because birth rates remain high in poor nations and death rates have fallen just about everywhere. Reducing fertility will remain a pressing issue throughout this century. Even with some recent decline in population increase, the nightmare of Thomas Malthus is still a real possibility, as the Controversy & Debate box explains.

Furthermore, population growth remains greatest in the poorest countries of the world, which lack the means to support their present populations, much less their future ones. Supporting 73 million additional people on our planet each year, 70 million of whom are in poor societies, will take a global commitment to provide not only food but also housing, schools, and employment. The well-being of the entire world may ultimately depend on resolving the economic and social problems of poor, overly populated countries and bridging the widening gulf between "have" and "have-not" societies.

Urbanization is continuing, especially in poor countries. People have always sought out cities in the hope of finding a better life. But the sheer numbers of people who live in the emerging global supercities, including Mexico City, São Paulo (Brazil), Kinshasa (Democratic Republic of the Congo), Bombay (India), and Manila (the Philippines), have created urban problems on a massive scale.

Throughout the world, humanity is facing a serious environmental challenge. Part of this problem is population increase, which is greatest in poor societies. But high levels of consumption, which mark rich nations such as ours, also play a role. By increasing the planet's environmental deficit, our present way of life is borrowing against the well-being of our children and their children. Globally, members of rich societies, who currently consume so much of the Earth's resources, are mortgaging the future security of the poor countries of the world.

The answer, in principle, is to create an **ecologically sustainable culture,** *a way of life that meets the needs of the present generation without threatening the environmental legacy of future generations.* Sustainable living depends on three strategies.

First, the world needs to *bring population growth under control.* The current population of 6.4 billion is already straining the natural environment. Clearly, the higher world population climbs, the more difficult environmental problems will become. Even if the recent slowing of population growth continues, the world will have 8 billion people by 2050. Few analysts think that the Earth

 To read more about population increase, the environment, and global inequality, go to http://www.peopleandplanet.net

can support this many people; most argue that we must hold the line at about 7 billion, and some argue that we must *decrease* population in the coming decades (Smail, 2004).

A second strategy is to *conserve finite resources.* This means meeting our needs with a responsible eye toward the future by using resources efficiently, seeking alternative sources of energy, and in some cases, learning to live with less.

A third strategy is to *reduce waste.* Whenever possible, simply using less is the best way to do this. But recycling programs are also part of the answer.

In the end, making all three of these strategies work depends on a more basic change in the way we think about ourselves and our world. Our *egocentric* outlook sets our own interests as standards for how to live; a sustainable environment demands an *ecocentric* outlook that helps us see that the present is tied to the future and that everyone must work together. Most nations in the southern half of the world are *underdeveloped,* unable to meet the basic needs of their people. At the same time, most countries in the northern half of the world are *overdeveloped,* using more resources than the Earth can sustain over time. Changes needed to create a sustainable ecosystem will not come easily. But the price of not responding to the growing environmental deficit will certainly be greater (Kellert & Bormann, 1991; Brown et al., 1993; Population Action International, 2000).

Finally, consider that the great dinosaurs dominated this planet for some 160 million years and then perished forever. Humanity is far younger, having existed for a mere 250,000 years. Compared to the rather dimwitted dinosaurs, our species has the gift of great intelligence. But how will we use this ability? What are the chances that humans will continue to flourish 160 million years—or even 1,000 years—from now? The answer depends on the choices made by one of the 30 million species living on Earth: human beings.

Summary

Population

1. Fertility and mortality, measured as crude birth rates and crude death rates, are major factors affecting population size. In global terms, U.S. population growth is low.

2. Migration, another key demographic concept, has special importance to population increase in the United States and to the growth of cities everywhere.

3. Demographers use age-sex pyramids to graphically show the composition of a population and to project population trends. Sex ratio is a society's balance of females and males.

4. Historically, world population grew slowly because high birth rates were largely offset by high death rates. About 1750, a demographic transition began as world population rose sharply, mostly because of falling death rates.

5. Thomas Robert Malthus warned that population growth would outpace food production, resulting in social calamity. Demographic transition theory, however, contends that technological advances gradually slow population increase.

6. World population is expected to reach between 8 and 9 billion by 2050. Such an increase will likely overwhelm many poor societies, where most of the increase will take place.

Urbanization

1. The first urban revolution began with the appearance of cities about 8000 B.C.E. By the start of the common era, cities had emerged in most regions of the world except for North America.

2. Preindustrial cities have low-rise buildings, narrow, winding streets, and personal social ties.

3. A second urban revolution began about 1750 as the Industrial Revolution propelled rapid urban growth in Europe. The physical form of cities changed as planners created wide, regular streets to facilitate trade. The focus on commerce, as well as swelling population, made urban life more anonymous.

4. Urbanism came to North America with Europeans, who settled in a string of colonial towns dotting the Atlantic coastline. By 1850, hundreds of new cities had been founded from coast to coast.

5. By 1920, a majority of the U.S. population lived in urban areas, and the largest metropolises were home to millions of people.

6. About 1950, cities began to decentralize with the growth of suburbs and edge cities. Nationally, Sunbelt cities—but not most older Snowbelt cities—are increasing in size and population.

7. Rapid urbanization in Europe during the nineteenth century led early sociologists to contrast rural and urban life. Ferdinand Tönnies built his analysis on the concepts of *Gemeinschaft* and *Gesellschaft,* and Emile Durkheim devised parallel concepts of mechanical solidarity and organic solidarity. Georg Simmel claimed that the overstimulation of city life produced a blasé attitude in urbanites.

8. At the University of Chicago, Robert Park believed that cities permit greater social freedom. Louis Wirth saw large, dense, heterogeneous populations creating an impersonal and self-interested but tolerant way of life. Other researchers have explored urban ecology and urban political economy.

9. A third urban revolution is now occurring in poor countries, where most of the world's largest cities will soon be found.

Environment

1. A key factor affecting the natural environment is how human beings organize social life. Therefore, ecologists study how living organisms interact with their environment.

2. Societies increase the environmental deficit by focusing on short-term benefits and ignoring the long-term consequences of their way of life.

3. Our ability to alter the natural world lies in our capacity for culture. Humanity's effect on the environment has increased along with the development of complex technology.

4. The "logic of growth" thesis supports economic development, claiming that people can solve environmental problems as they arise. The opposing "limits to growth" thesis states that societies must curb development to prevent eventual environmental collapse.

5. Environmental issues include disposing of solid waste and protecting the quality of air and water. The supply of clean water is already low in some parts of the world.

6. Rain forests help remove carbon dioxide from the atmosphere and are home to a large share of this planet's living species. Under pressure from commercial interests, the world's rain forests are now half their original size and are shrinking by about 1 percent annually.

7. Environmental racism is the pattern by which the poor, especially minorities, suffer most from environmental hazards.

8. A sustainable environment does not threaten the well-being of future generations. Achieving this goal requires controlling world population, conserving finite resources, and reducing waste and pollution.

KEY CONCEPTS

Population

demography (p. 418) the study of human population

fertility (p. 418) the incidence of childbearing in a country's population

crude birth rate (p. 418) the number of live births in a given year for every 1,000 people in a population

mortality (p. 419) the incidence of death in a country's population

crude death rate (p. 419) the number of deaths in a given year for every 1,000 people in a population

infant mortality rate (p. 419) the number of deaths among infants under one year of age for each 1,000 live births in a given year

life expectancy (p. 420) the average life span of a country's population

migration (p. 420) the movement of people into and out of a specified territory

sex ratio (p. 421) the number of males for every 100 females in a nation's population

age-sex pyramid (p. 422) a graphic representation of the age and sex of a population

demographic transition theory (p.423) the thesis that population patterns reflect a society's level of technological development

zero population growth (p. 424) the level of reproduction that maintains population at a steady state

Urbanization

urbanization (p. 426) the concentration of humanity into cities

metropolis (p. 428) a large city that socially and economically dominates an urban area

suburbs (p. 428) urban areas beyond the political boundaries of a city

megalopolis (p. 429) a vast urban region containing a number of cities and their surrounding suburbs

Gemeinschaft (p. 430) a type of social organization in which people are closely linked by kinship and tradition

Gesellschaft (p. 430) a type of social organization in which people come together only on the basis of individual self-interest

urban ecology (p. 432) the study of the link between the physical and social dimensions of cities

Environment

ecology (p. 434) the study of the interaction of living organisms and the natural environment

natural environment (p. 434) the Earth's surface and atmosphere, including living organisms, air, water, soil, and other resources necessary to sustain life

ecosystem (p. 434) a system composed of the interaction of all living organisms and their natural environment

environmental deficit (p. 435) profound and long-term harm to the natural environment caused by humanity's focus on short-term material affluence

rain forests (p. 440) regions of dense forestation, most of which circle the globe close to the equator

global warming (p. 441) a rise in the Earth's average temperature due to an increasing concentration of carbon dioxide in the atmosphere

environmental racism (p. 442) the pattern by which environmental hazards are greatest for poor people, especially minorities

ecologically sustainable culture (p. 444) a way of life that meets the needs of the present generation without threatening the environmental legacy of future generations

CRITICAL-THINKING QUESTIONS

1. What are fertility and mortality rates? Which one has been more important in increasing global population?

2. Evaluate the environmental prediction of Thomas Robert Malthus. On balance, do you think he was more wrong or more right? Why?

3. According to demographic transition theory, how does economic development affect population patterns?

4. According to Ferdinand Tönnies, Emile Durkheim, Georg Simmel, and Louis Wirth, what characterizes urbanism as a way of life? Note several differences in the ideas of these thinkers.

APPLICATIONS AND EXERCISES

1. Here is an illustration of the problem of runaway growth (Milbrath, 1989:10): *A pond has a single water lily growing on it. The lily doubles in size each day. In thirty days, it covers the entire pond. On which day does it cover half the pond?* Discuss the implications of your answer for population increase.

2. Draw a mental map of a city familiar to you with as much detail of specific places, districts, roads, and transportation facilities as you can. Compare your map with a published one or, better yet, a map drawn by someone you know. Try to account for the differences.

3. Get a plastic trash bag, and carry it around with you for one full day. Put everything you throw away in the bag. Afterward, weigh what you have; multiply this amount by 365 to estimate your yearly "trash factor." Multiply this amount by 294 million to estimate the annual waste of the entire U.S. population.

4. Packaged in the back of this new textbook is an interactive CD-ROM that offers a variety of video and interactive review materials intended to help you better understand the material covered in this chapter. For this chapter, the CD-ROM contains a relevant clip from *ABC News,* an author's tip video, interactive map animations, an interactive timeline, and flashcards with audio pronunciations of the more difficult words.

 SITES TO SEE

http://www.prenhall.com/macionis

Visit the interactive Companion Website™ that accompanies this text. Begin by clicking on the cover of your book. You will find a chapter-by-chapter study guide, practice tests, suggested Web links, and links to other relevant material.

http://www.eclac.org

This site, created by the Economic Commission for Latin America and the Caribbean (part of the United Nations), provides statistics on population patterns for this region of the world. Most of the site is available in both English and Spanish.

http://www.un.org/popin/wdtrends.htm

Want to learn more about global population trends? Read this report from the United Nations.

http://www.riotmanhattan.com/riotmanhattan/webcam.html

Watch big-city life from the comfort of your own home: This site uses a Web camera showing the action on New York City's Fifth Avenue and Forty-Fifth Street. What can you learn from "people

watching" in this way? What does this observation *not* tell you about urban life?

http://www.hud.gov

This is the Web site for the government's Department of Housing and Urban Development.

http://www.sierraclub.org
http://www.greenpeace.org

Here are two environmental sites, maintained by the Sierra Club and Greenpeace, respectively. Visit the sites and see how these two organizations are similar to one another and how they differ.

http://www.urban.nyu.edu

New York University's Taub Urban Research Center is on the Internet. Visit this site to survey recent research on urban issues.

http://www.wri.org/

The World Resources Institute provides information on the state of the planet's environment.

 INVESTIGATE WITH RESEARCH NAVIGATOR™

Follow the instructions on page 32 of this textbook to access the features of **Research Navigator™**. Once at the Web site, enter your Login Name and Password. Then, to use the **Content Select™** database, enter keywords such as "demography," "urbanism," and "global warming," and the search engine will supply relevant and recent scholarly and popular press publications. Use the *New York Times* **Search-by-Subject Archive** to find recent news articles related to sociology and the **Link Library** feature to find relevant Web links organized by the key terms associated with this chapter.

CHAPTER SIXTEEN

Social Change: Modern and Postmodern Societies

Why do societies change?

How do social movements both encourage
and resist social change?

What have important sociologists said is good and bad
about modern society?

Social change often brings together traditional and modern ways of life. ►
These Aboriginal boys in Australia are discovering the world
of the Internet.

The five-story red brick apartment building at 253 East Tenth Street in New York has been standing for more than a century. In 1900, one of the twenty small apartments in the building was occupied by thirty-nine-year-old Julius Streicher, Christine Streicher, age thirty-three, and their four young children. The Streichers were immigrants, both having come in 1885 from their native Germany to New York, where they met and soon married.

The Streichers probably considered themselves successful. Julius operated a small clothing shop a few blocks from his apartment; Christine stayed at home, raised the children, and did housework. Like most people in the country at that time, neither Julius nor Christine had graduated from high school, and they worked for ten to twelve hours a day, six days a week. Their income—average for that time—was about $35 a month, or about $425 per year. (In today's dollars, that would be slightly more than $8,000, which would put the family well below today's poverty line.) They spent almost half of their income for food; most of the rest went for rent.

Today, Dorothy Sabo resides at 253 East Tenth Street, living alone in the same apartment where the Streichers spent much of their lives. Now eighty-seven, she is retired from a career teaching art at a nearby museum. In many respects, Sabo's life has been far easier than the life the Streichers knew. For one thing, when the Streichers lived there, the building had no electricity (people used kerosene lamps and candles) and no running water (Christine Streicher spent most of every Monday doing laundry using water she carried from a public fountain at the end of the block). There were no telephones, no television, and, of course, no computers. Today, Dorothy Sabo takes such conveniences for granted. Although she is hardly rich, her pension and Social Security amount to several times as much (in constant dollars) as the Streichers earned.

Sabo has her own worries. She is concerned about the environment and often speaks out about global warming. But here again, a look back in time is instructive. A century ago, if the Streichers and their neighbors thought about "the environment," they probably would have winced at the smell coming up from the street. At a time when motor vehicles were just beginning to appear in New York City, carriages, trucks, and trolleys were all pulled by horses—thousands of them. These animals dumped 60,000 gallons of urine and 2.5 million pounds of manure on the streets every day (based on Simon & Cannon, 2001).

It is difficult for us to imagine how different life was a century ago. Not only was life much harder back then, it was also much shorter. Statistical records show that life expectancy was just forty-six years for men and forty-eight years for women (compared to seventy-four and eighty years today).

 Learn about the lives of men and women, black and white, living in New York City a century ago at http://www.albany.edu/mumford/1920/groups.html

Over the course of the past century, much has changed for the better. Yet as this chapter explains, social change is not all positive. On the contrary, change has negative consequences, too, creating unexpected new problems. Early sociologists were mixed in their assessment of *modernity*, changes brought about by the Industrial Revolution. In the same way, today's sociologists point to both good and bad aspects of *postmodernity*, the recent transformations caused by the Information Revolution and the postindustrial economy. One thing is clear: For better or worse, the rate of change has never been faster than it is now.

What Is Social Change?

In earlier chapters, we examined relatively fixed or *static* social patterns, including status and role, social stratification, and social institutions. We also looked at the *dynamic* forces that have shaped our way of life, ranging from innovations in technology to the growth of bureaucracy and the expansion of cities. All these trends are dimensions of **social change,** *the transformation of culture and social institutions over time.* This complex process has four major characteristics:

1. **Social change happens all the time.** "Nothing is certain except death and taxes," goes the old saying. Yet our thoughts about death have changed dramatically as life expectancy in the United States has nearly doubled, as indicated in the opening to this chapter. Back in 1900, the Streichers and almost all other people in the United States paid little or no taxes on their earnings; taxes increased dramatically over the course of the twentieth century, along with the size and scope of government. In short, virtually everything is subject to the twists and turns of change.

    Still, some societies change faster than others. As Chapter 2 ("Culture") explained, hunting and gathering societies change quite slowly; members of technologically complex societies, on the other hand, can witness significant change within a single lifetime.

    It is also true that in a given society, some cultural elements change faster than others. William Ogburn's

    For an introduction to the recent controversy over stem cell research, visit http://stemcells.nih.gov/index.asp

    theory of *cultural lag* (see Chapter 2) asserts that material culture (that is, things) usually changes faster than nonmaterial culture (ideas and attitudes). For example, genetic technology that allows scientists to alter and perhaps even create life has developed more rapidly than have our ethical standards for deciding when and how to use it.

2. **Social change is sometimes intentional but often unplanned.** Industrial societies actively promote many types of change. Scientists seek more efficient forms of energy, and advertisers try to convince us that life is incomplete without this or that new gadget. Yet rarely can anyone envision all the consequences of changes as they are set in motion.

Today, most of the people with access to computers live in rich countries such as the United States. But the number of people in low-income nations going "online" is on the rise. How do you think the introduction of new information technology will change more traditional societies? Are all the changes likely to be for the good?

Back in 1900, when the country still relied on horses for transportation, people looked ahead to motor vehicles that would take a single day to carry them distances that used to take weeks or months. But no one could see how much the mobility provided by automobiles would alter life in the United States, scattering family members, threatening the environment, and reshaping cities and suburbs. Nor could automotive pioneers have predicted the more than 42,000 deaths that occur in car accidents each year in the United States alone.

3. **Social change is controversial.** The history of the automobile shows that social change brings both good and bad consequences. Capitalists welcomed the Industrial Revolution because advancing technology increased productivity and swelled profits. However, workers feared that machines would make their skills obsolete and resisted the push toward "progress."

    Today, as in the past, people disagree about how we ought to live. As a result, the changing patterns of social interaction between black people and white

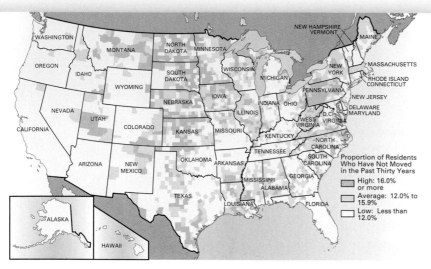

Who Stays Put? Residential Stability across the United States

Overall, only about 9 percent of U.S. residents have not moved during the last thirty years. Counties with a higher proportion of "long-termers" typically have experienced less change over recent decades: Many neighborhoods have been in place since before World War II, and many of the same families live in them. As you look at the map, what can you say about these stable areas? Why are most of these counties rural and at some distance from the coasts?

Source: U.S. Census Bureau (1996).

people, women and men, and gays and heterosexuals are welcomed by some people but opposed by others.

4. **Some changes matter more than others.** Some changes (such as clothing fads) have only passing significance; other changes (like computers) last a long time and may change the entire world. Will the Information Revolution turn out to be as important as the Industrial Revolution? Like the automobile and television, computers have both positive and negative effects, providing new kinds of jobs while eliminating old ones, isolating people in offices while linking people in global electronic networks, offering vast amounts of information while threatening personal privacy.

Causes of Social Change

Social change has many causes. In a world linked by sophisticated communication and transportation technology, change in one place often sets off change elsewhere.

CULTURE AND CHANGE

Chapter 2 ("Culture") identified three important sources of cultural change. First, *invention* produces new objects, ideas, and social patterns. Rocket propulsion research, which began in the 1940s, has produced sophisticated spacecraft that can reach toward the stars. Today we take such technology for granted; during the present century, a

significant number of people will probably experience space travel.

Second, *discovery* occurs as people take notice of existing elements of the world. For example, medical advances offer a growing understanding of the human body. Beyond their direct effects on human health, medical discoveries have extended life expectancy, setting in motion the "graying" of U.S. society (see Chapter 3, "Socialization: From Infancy to Old Age").

Third, *diffusion* creates change as products, people, and information spread from one society to another. Ralph Linton (1937a) recognized that many familiar aspects of our culture came from other lands. For example, the cloth used to make our clothing was developed in Asia, the clocks we see all around us were invented in Europe, and coins we carry in our pockets were devised in Turkey.

In general, material things diffuse more easily than cultural ideas. That is, new breakthroughs such as the science of cloning occur faster than our understanding of when—and even whether—they are morally desirable.

CONFLICT AND CHANGE

Tension and conflict within a society also produce change. Karl Marx saw class conflict as the engine that drives societies from one historical era to another. In industrial-capitalist societies, he maintained, the struggle between capitalists and workers pushes society toward a socialist system of production.

In more than a century since Marx's death, this model has proven simplistic. Yet Marx correctly foresaw that social conflict arising from inequality (involving not just class but race and gender as well) would force changes in every society, including our own.

IDEAS AND CHANGE

Max Weber also contributed to our understanding of social change. Although Weber acknowledged that conflict could bring about change, he traced the roots of most social changes to ideas. For example, people with charisma (Martin Luther King Jr. was one example) can carry a message that sometimes changes the world.

Weber highlighted the importance of ideas by revealing how the religious beliefs of early Protestants set the stage for the spread of industrial capitalism (see Chapter 13, "Family and Religion"). The fact that industrial capitalism developed primarily in areas of Western Europe where the Protestant work ethic was strong proved to Weber (1958, orig. 1904 5) the power of ideas to bring about change.

DEMOGRAPHIC CHANGE

Population patterns can also transform a society. The typical U.S. household (4.8 people) was almost twice as large in 1900 as it is today (2.6 people). Women are having fewer children, and more people are living alone. Change is also taking place as our population grows older. As Chapter 3 ("Socialization: From Infancy to Old Age") explained, 12 percent of the U.S. population was over age sixty-five in 2000, three times the proportion back in 1900. By the year 2030, seniors will account for 20 percent of the total (U.S. Census Bureau, 2003). Medical research and health care services already focus extensively on the elderly, and life will change in countless other ways as homes and household products are redesigned to meet the needs of growing numbers of older consumers.

Migration within and between societies is another demographic factor that promotes change. Between 1870 and 1930, tens of millions of immigrants entered the industrial cities in the United States. Millions more from rural areas joined the rush. As a result, farm communities declined, metropolises expanded, and by 1920 the United States for the first time became a mostly urban nation. Similar changes are taking place today as people moving from the Snowbelt to the Sunbelt mix with new immigrants from Latin America and Asia.

Where in the United States have demographic changes been greatest? National Map 16–1 provides one answer, showing counties where the largest share of people have lived in their present homes for thirty years or more.

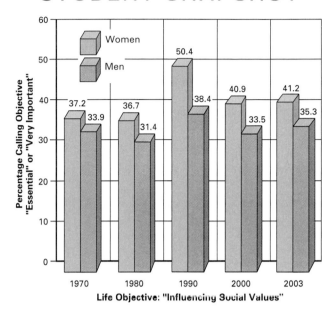

STUDENT SNAPSHOT

FIGURE 16-1 First-Year College Students' Desire to Influence Social Values, 1970–2003

Source: Sax et al. (2003).

SOCIAL MOVEMENTS AND CHANGE

A final cause of social change lies in our own efforts. People commonly band together to form a **social movement,** *an organized activity that encourages or discourages social change.* Our nation's history includes all kinds of social movements, from the colonial drive for independence to today's organizations supporting or opposing abortion, gay rights, and the death penalty. As Figure 16–1 shows, many—but not most—students consider influencing society to be an important goal during their college years, with the exact share rising and falling over time. Even so, this priority remains somewhat stronger among college women than among college men.

Types of social movements. Researchers classify social movements according to the type of change they seek (Aberle, 1966; Cameron, 1966; Blumer, 1969). One variable asks, *Who is changed?* Some movements target selected people, and others try to change everyone. A second variable asks, *How much change?* Some movements attempt only superficial change; others pursue a radical transformation of society. Combining these variables results in four types of social movements, shown in Figure 16–2 on page 454.

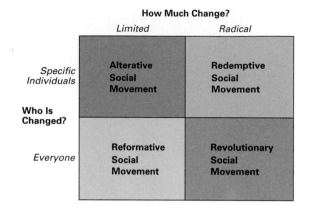

How Much Change?

	Limited	Radical
Specific Individuals	Alterative Social Movement	Redemptive Social Movement
Everyone	Reformative Social Movement	Revolutionary Social Movement

Who Is Changed?

FIGURE 16-2 Four Types of Social Movements

Source: Based on Aberle (1966).

Alterative social movements are the least threatening to the status quo because they seek limited change in only part of the population. Their aim is to help certain people *alter* their lives. Promise Keepers is one example of an alterative social movement; it encourages Christian men to be more spiritual and supportive of their families.

 Visit the Promise Keepers Web site at http://www. promisekeepers.org

Redemptive social movements also target specific individuals, but they seek more radical change. Their aim is to help certain people *redeem* their lives. For example, Alcoholics Anonymous is an organization that helps people with an alcohol addiction achieve a sober life.

Reformative social movements aim for only limited change but target everyone. The environmental movement seeks to interest everyone in protecting the natural environment.

Revolutionary social movements are the most extreme of all, striving for major transformation of an entire society. Sometimes pursuing specific goals, sometimes spinning utopian dreams, these social movements, including both the left-wing Communist party (seeking government control of the economy) and right-wing militia groups (seeking the destruction of "big government") attempt to radically change major social institutions.

Explaining social movements. Sociologists have developed several explanations of social movements. *Deprivation theory* holds that social movements arise among people who feel deprived of something, such as income, safe working conditions, or political rights. Whether you feel deprived or not, of course, depends on your expectations. Thus, people band together in response to **relative deprivation,** *a perceived*

disadvantage arising from a specific comparison. This concept helps explain why movements for change surface in both good and bad times: It is not people's absolute standing that counts but how they perceive their own situation in relation to the situations of others (Davies, 1962; Merton, 1968).

Mass-society theory, a second explanation, argues that social movements attract socially isolated people who seek a sense of identity and purpose through their membership. From this point of view, social movements have a personal as well as a political agenda (Melucci, 1989).

Resource mobilization theory, a third theoretical scheme, links the success of any social movement to available resources, including money, human labor, and the mass media. Because most social movements begin small, they must look beyond themselves to mobilize the resources required for success (Meyer & Whittier, 1994; Valocchi, 1996; Zhao, 1998).

Fourth, *culture theory* points out that social movements depend not only on material resources but also on cultural symbols. People must have a shared understanding of injustice in the world before they can mobilize to bring about change. In addition, specific symbols (such as photographs of the burning World Trade Center after the September 11 attacks, a site later referred to simply as "ground zero") help mobilize people to act (supporting the military campaigns in Afghanistan and Iraq) (McCarthy & Zald, 1996; J. Williams, 2002).

Fifth, *new social movements theory* points out the distinctive character of recent social movements in postindustrial societies. Not only are these movements typically national or international in scope, but most focus on quality-of-life issues—including the natural environment, world peace, or animal rights—rather than more traditional economic issues.

 For information on laws involving animal rights, see http://www.animal-law.org

This broader scope of contemporary social movements results from closer ties between governments and between ordinary people around the world, who are now linked by the mass media and new information technology (McAdam, McCarthy, & Zald, 1988; Kriesi, 1989; Pakulski, 1993; Jenkins & Wallace, 1996).

Sixth, and finally, *political economy theory* is a Marxist approach that claims that social movements arise within capitalist societies because the capitalist economic system fails to meet the needs of the majority of people. Despite great economic productivity, U.S. society is in crisis, with millions of people unable to find good jobs, living below the poverty line, and surviving without health insurance. Social movements arise as a response to such conditions. Workers organize to demand higher wages, citizens rally for a health policy that protects everyone, and people

Social movements are often given great energy by powerful visual images, which is one key idea of culture theory. During World War II, this photo of six soldiers raising the U.S. flag on the tiny Pacific island of Iwo Jima increased morale at home and, later, was the inspiration for a memorial sculpture. Some twenty-five years later, the news included the photo on the right, showing children running from a napalm strike by U.S. planes in South Vietnam. The girl in the middle of the picture had ripped the flaming clothes from her body. This photo increased the strength of the social movement against the war in Vietnam.

march in opposition to spending billions to fund wars while ignoring basic needs at home (Buechler, 2000).

Stages in social movements. Social movements typically unfold in stages. The *emergence* of social movements occurs as people think that all is not well. Some, such as the civil rights and women's movements, are born of widespread dissatisfaction. Others emerge as a small group tries to mobilize the population, as when gay activists raised public concern about AIDS.

Coalescence takes place when a social movement defines itself and develops a strategy for attracting new members and "going public." Leaders determine policies and decide on tactics, which may include demonstrations or rallies to attract media attention.

As it gains members and resources, a social movement may undergo *bureaucratization*. As a movement becomes established, it depends less on the charisma and talents of a few leaders and more on a professional staff, which increases the chances for the movement's long-term survival.

Finally, social movements *decline* as resources dry up, the group faces overwhelming opposition, or members achieve their goals and lose interest. Some well-established organizations outlive their original causes and move on to new crusades; others lose touch with the idea of changing society and choose, instead, to become part of the "system" (Piven & Cloward, 1977; Miller, 1983).

Modernity

A central concept in the study of social change is **modernity,** *social patterns resulting from industrialization.* In everyday terms, modernity (its Latin root means "lately") refers to the present in relation to the past. Sociologists use this catch-all concept to describe the many social patterns set in motion by the Industrial Revolution beginning in Western Europe in the mid-eighteenth century. **Modernization,** then, is *the process of social change begun by industrialization.* The timeline inside the front cover of this book highlights important events that mark the emergence of modernity. Table 16–1 on page 456 provides a summary of change in the United States over the course of the twentieth century.

Peter Berger (1977) identified four major characteristics of modernization:

1. **The decline of small, traditional communities.**
   Modernity involves "the progressive weakening, if not destruction, of the . . . relatively cohesive communities in which human beings have found solidarity and meaning throughout most of history" (Berger, 1977:72). For thousands of years, in the camps of hunters and gatherers and in the rural villages of Europe and North America, people lived in small communities where life revolved around family and neighborhood. Such traditional worlds give each

TABLE 16-1

The United States: A Century of Change

	1900	2000
National population	76,000,000	281,000,000
Percentage urban	40%	80%
Life expectancy	46 years (men), 48 years (women)	74 years (men), 79 years (women)
Median age	22.9 years	35.3 years
Average household income	$8,000 (in 2000 dollars)	$40,000 (in 2000 dollars)
Share of income spent on food	43%	15%
Share of homes with flush toilets	10%	98%
Average number of cars	1 car for every 2,000 households	1.3 cars for every household
Divorce rate	About 1 in 20 marriages ends in divorce	About 8 in 20 marriages end in divorce
Average gallons of petroleum products consumed per person per year	34	1,100

person a well-defined place that, while limiting choice, offers a strong sense of identity, belonging, and purpose.

Small, isolated communities still exist in the United States, of course, but they are home to only a tiny percentage of our nation's people. These days, their isolation is only geographic: Cars, telephones, television, and computers give most rural families the pulse of the larger society and connect them to the entire world.

2. **The expansion of personal choice.** People in traditional, preindustrial societies view their lives as shaped by forces—gods, spirits, or simply fate—beyond human control. As the power of tradition weakens, people come to see their lives as an unending series of options, a process Berger calls *individualization*. For instance, many people in the United States choose a particular "lifestyle" (sometimes adopting one after another), showing an openness to change. Indeed, it is a common belief that people *should* take control of their lives.

3. **Increasing social diversity.** In preindustrial societies, strong family ties and powerful religious beliefs enforce conformity and discourage diversity and change. Modernization promotes a more rational, scientific worldview as tradition loses its hold and people gain more and more individual choice. The growth of cities, the expansion of impersonal bureaucracy, and the social mix of people from various backgrounds combine to encourage diverse beliefs and behavior.

4. **Orientation toward the future and a growing awareness of time.** Premodern people focus on the past;

people in modern societies think more about the future. Modern people are not only forward-looking but also optimistic that new inventions and discoveries will improve their lives.

Modern people organize daily routines down to the very minute. With the introduction of clocks in the late Middle Ages, Europeans began to think not in terms of sunlight and seasons but in terms of hours and minutes. Focused on personal gain, modern people demand precise measurement of time and are likely to agree that "time is money." According to Berger, one indicator of a society's degree of industrialization is the share of people wearing wristwatches.

Finally, recall that modernization touched off the development of sociology itself. As Chapter 1 ("Sociology: Perspective, Theory, and Method") explained, the discipline originated in the wake of the Industrial Revolution in Western Europe, at a point when social change was proceeding rapidly. Early European and U.S. sociologists tried to analyze the rise of modern society and its consequences, both good and bad, for human beings.

FERDINAND TÖNNIES: THE LOSS OF COMMUNITY

The German sociologist Ferdinand Tönnies (1855–1937) produced a lasting account of modernization in his theory of *Gemeinschaft* and *Gesellschaft* (see Chapter 15, "Population, Urbanization, and Environment"). Like Peter Berger, whose work he influenced, Tönnies (1963, orig. 1887) viewed modernization as the progressive

 For a short biography of Ferdinand Tönnies, visit the Gallery of Sociologists at http://www.TheSociologyPage.com

George Tooker's 1950 painting *The Subway* depicts a common problem of modern life: Weakening social ties and eroding traditions create a generic humanity in which everyone is alike yet each person is an anxious stranger in the midst of others.

George Tooker, *The Subway,* 1950, egg tempera on gesso panel, 18 1/8 × 36 1/8", Whitney Museum of American Art, New York. Purchased with funds from the Juliana Force Purchase Award, 50.23. Photograph © 2000 Whitney Museum of American Art.

loss of *Gemeinschaft,* or human community. As Tönnies saw it, the Industrial Revolution weakened the social fabric of family and tradition by introducing a businesslike emphasis on facts, efficiency, and money. European and North American societies gradually became rootless and impersonal as people came to associate with one another mostly on the basis of self-interest, the state Tönnies termed *Gesellschaft.*

Early in the twentieth century, at least some parts of the United States could be described using Tönnies's concept of *Gemeinschaft.* Families that had lived for many generations in small villages and towns were bound together into a hardworking, slow-moving way of life. Telephones (invented in 1876) were rare; it wasn't until 1915 that someone placed the first coast-to-coast call (see the timeline inside the front cover of this book). Living without television (introduced in 1933 and widespread after 1950), families entertained themselves, often gathering with friends in the evening to share stories, sorrows, or song. Without rapid transportation (Henry Ford's assembly line began in 1908, but cars became common only after World War II), for many people, the town in which they lived was their entire world.

Inevitable tensions and conflicts divided these communities of the past. But according to Tönnies, the traditional spirit of *Gemeinschaft* meant that people were "essentially united in spite of all separating factors" (1963:65, orig. 1887).

Modernity turns society inside out so that, as Tönnies put it, people are "essentially separated in spite of uniting factors" (1963:65, orig. 1887). This is the world of *Gesellschaft,* where, especially in large cities, most people live among strangers and ignore the people they pass on the street. Trust is hard to come by in a mobile and anonymous society in which, according to researchers, people tend to put their personal needs ahead of group loyalty and an increasing majority of adults believe "you can't be too careful" in

dealing with people (NORC, 2003:181). No wonder researchers conclude that even as we have become more affluent, the social health of modern societies has declined (Myers, 2000).

Critical review. Tönnies's theory of *Gemeinschaft* and *Gesellschaft* is widely used to describe modernization. The theory's strength lies in its synthesis of various dimensions of change: growing population, the rise of cities, and increasingly impersonal interaction. But modern life, though often impersonal, still has some degree of *Gemeinschaft.* Even in a world of strangers, modern friendships can be strong and lasting. In addition, some analysts think that Tönnies favored—perhaps even romanticized—traditional societies while overlooking bonds of family and friendship that continue to flourish in modern societies.

EMILE DURKHEIM: THE DIVISION OF LABOR

The French sociologist Emile Durkheim shared Tönnies's interest in the important social changes that resulted from the Industrial Revolution. For Durkheim (1964a, orig. 1893), modernization was marked by an increasing **division of labor,** or *specialized economic activity.* Every member of a traditional society performs more or less the same activities; modern societies function by having people perform highly specialized roles.

Durkheim explained that preindustrial societies are held together by *mechanical solidarity,* or shared moral sentiments (see Chapter 15). Thus, members of such societies view everyone as basically alike, doing the same work and belonging together. Durkheim's concept of mechanical solidarity is virtually the same as Tönnies's *Gemeinschaft.*

With modernization, the division of labor becomes more and more pronounced. To Durkheim, this change

Max Weber maintained that the distinctive character of modern society was its rational worldview. Virtually all of Weber's work on modernity centered on types of people he considered typical of their age: the scientist, the capitalist, and the bureaucrat. Each is rational to the core: The scientist is committed to the orderly discovery of truth, the capitalist to the orderly pursuit of profit, and the bureaucrat to orderly conformity to a system of rules.

means less mechanical solidarity but more of another kind of tie: *organic solidarity,* or the mutual dependency between people engaged in specialized work. Put simply, modern societies are held together not by likeness but by difference: All of us must depend on others to meet most of our needs. Organic solidarity corresponds to Tönnies's concept of *Gesellschaft.*

Despite obvious similarities in their thinking, Durkheim and Tönnies viewed modernity somewhat differently. To Tönnies, modern *Gesellschaft* amounted to the loss of social solidarity because people lose the "natural" and "organic" bonds of the rural village, leaving only the "artificial" and "mechanical" ties of the big city. Durkheim had a different view of modernity, even reversing Tönnies's language to bring home the point. Durkheim labeled modern society "organic," arguing that modern society is no less natural than any other, and he described traditional societies as "mechanical" because they are so regimented. Durkheim viewed modernization not so much as a loss of community as a change from community based on bonds of likeness (kinship and neighborhood) to community based on economic interdependence (the division of labor). Durkheim's view of modernity is thus both more complex and more positive than Tönnies's view.

Critical review. Durkheim's work, which resembles that of Tönnies, is a highly influential analysis of modernity. Of the two, Durkheim was the more optimistic; still, he feared

that modern societies might become so diverse that they would collapse into **anomie,** *a condition in which society provides little moral guidance to individuals.* Living with weak moral norms, modern people can become egocentric, placing their own needs above those of others and finding little purpose in life.

The suicide rate, which Durkheim considered a good index of anomie, did in fact increase in the United States over the course of the twentieth century. The vast majority of U.S. adults report that they see moral questions not in clear terms of right and wrong but as confusing "shades of gray," also supporting Durkheim's view (NORC, 2003:359). Yet shared norms and values seem strong enough to give most people a sense of meaning and purpose. Whatever the hazards of anomie, most people value the personal freedom modern society gives us.

MAX WEBER: RATIONALIZATION

For Max Weber, modernity meant replacing a traditional worldview with a rational way of thinking. In preindustrial societies, tradition acts as a constant brake on social change. To traditional people, "truth" is roughly the same as "what has always been" (1978:36, orig. 1921). To modern people, by contrast, truth is the result of rational calculation. Because they value efficiency and have little reverence for the past, modern people will adopt whatever social patterns allow them to achieve their goals.

Echoing Tönnies's and Durkheim's claim that industrialization weakens tradition, Weber declared modern society to be "disenchanted." The unquestioned truths of an earlier time had been challenged by rational thinking. In short, said Weber, modern society turns away from the gods. Throughout his life, Weber studied various modern "types"—the scientist, the capitalist, the bureaucrat—all of whom share the detached worldview that he believed was coming to dominate humanity.

Critical review. Compared with Tönnies and especially Durkheim, Weber was very critical of modern society. He knew that science could produce technological and organizational wonders, yet he worried that science was carrying us away from more basic questions about the meaning and purpose of human existence. Weber feared that rationalization, especially in bureaucracies, would erode the human spirit with endless rules and regulations.

Some of Weber's critics think that the alienation Weber attributed to bureaucracy actually stemmed from social inequality. This issue leads us to the ideas of Karl Marx.

KARL MARX: CAPITALISM

For Karl Marx, modern society was synonymous with capitalism; he saw the Industrial Revolution primarily as a *capitalist revolution*. Marx traced the emergence of the bourgeoisie in medieval Europe to the expansion of commerce. The bourgeoisie

 For more on Durkheim, Weber, and Marx, visit the Gallery of Sociologists at http://www. TheSociologyPage.com

gradually displaced a feudal aristocracy as the Industrial Revolution gave it control of a powerful new productive system.

Marx agreed that modernity weakened small communities (as described by Tönnies), increased the division of labor (as noted by Durkheim), and encouraged a rational worldview (as Weber claimed). But he saw these simply as conditions necessary for capitalism to flourish. According to Marx, capitalism draws population from farms and small towns into an ever-expanding market system centered in the cities; specialization is needed for efficient factories, and rationality is illustrated by the capitalists' endless pursuit of profit.

Earlier chapters have painted Marx as a spirited critic of capitalist society, but his vision of modernity also incorporates a considerable measure of optimism. Unlike Weber, who viewed modern society as an "iron cage" of bureaucracy, Marx believed that social conflict in capitalist societies would sow the seeds of revolutionary change, leading to an egalitarian socialism. Such a society, as he saw it, would harness the wonders of industrial technology to enrich people's lives and rid the world of classes, the source of social conflict

and so much suffering. Although Marx's evaluation of modern capitalist society was highly negative, he imagined a future of human freedom, creativity, and community.

Critical review. Marx's theory of modernization is a complex theory of capitalism. But he underestimated the dominance of bureaucracy in shaping modern societies. In socialist societies, in particular, the stifling effects of bureaucracy have turned out to be as bad as, or even worse than, the dehumanizing aspects of capitalism. The upheavals in Eastern Europe and the former Soviet Union in the 1990s reveal the depth of popular opposition to oppressive state bureaucracies.

Structural-Functional Analysis: The Theory of Mass Society

> November 11, on Interstate 275. From the car window, we see BP and Sunoco gas stations, a Kmart and a Wal-Mart, an AmeriSuites hotel, a Bob Evans, a Chi-Chi's Mexican restaurant, and a McDonald's. This road happens to circle Cincinnati, Ohio. But it could be just about anywhere in the United States.

The rise of modernity is a complex process involving many dimensions of change, described in previous chapters and reviewed in the Summing Up table on page 460. How can we make sense of so many changes going on at once? Sociologists have two broad explanations of modern society, one guided by the structural-functional approach and the other based on social-conflict theory.

The first explanation—guided by the structural-functional approach and drawing on the ideas of Tönnies, Durkheim, and Weber—understands modernity as the emergence of *mass society* (Kornhauser, 1959; Nisbet, 1969; Berger, Berger, & Kellner, 1974; Pearson, 1993). A **mass society** is *a society in which prosperity and bureaucracy have weakened traditional social ties.* A mass society is productive; on average, people have more income than ever. At the same time, it is marked by weak kinship and impersonal neighborhoods, so individuals often feel socially isolated. Although many people have material plenty, they are spiritually weak and often experience more uncertainty about how to live.

THE MASS SCALE OF MODERN LIFE

Mass-society theory argues, first, that the scale of modern life has greatly increased. Before the Industrial Revolution,

SUMMING UP

Traditional and Modern Societies: The Big Picture

Elements of Society	Traditional Societies	Modern Societies
Cultural Patterns		
Values	Homogeneous; sacred character; few subcultures and countercultures	Heterogeneous; secular character; many subcultures and countercultures
Norms	Great moral significance; little tolerance of diversity	Variable moral significance; high tolerance of diversity
Time orientation	Present linked to past	Present linked to future
Technology	Preindustrial; human and animal energy	Industrial; advanced energy sources
Social Structure		
Status and role	Few statuses, most ascribed; few specialized roles	Many statuses, some ascribed and some achieved; many specialized roles
Relationships	Typically primary; little anonymity or privacy	Typically secondary; much anonymity and privacy
Communication	Face to face	Face-to-face communication supplemented by mass media
Social control	Informal gossip	Formal police and legal system
Social stratification	Rigid patterns of social inequality; little mobility	Fluid patterns of social inequality; high mobility
Gender patterns	Pronounced patriarchy; women's lives centered on the home	Declining patriarchy; increasing number of women in the paid labor force
Settlement patterns	Small-scale; population typically small and widely dispersed in rural villages and small towns	Large-scale; population typically large and concentrated in cities
Social Institutions		
Economy	Based on agriculture; much manufacturing in the home; little white-collar work	Based on industrial mass production; factories become centers of production; increasing white-collar work
State	Small-scale government; little state intervention in society	Large-scale government; much state intervention in society
Family	Extended family as the primary means of socialization and economic production	Nuclear family retains some socialization functions but is more a unit of consumption than of production
Religion	Religion guides worldview; little religious pluralism	Religion weakens with the rise of science; extensive religious pluralism
Education	Formal schooling limited to elites	Basic schooling becomes universal, with growing proportion receiving advanced education
Health	High birth and death rates; short life expectancy because of low standard of living and simple medical technology	Low birth and death rates; longer life expectancy because of higher standard of living and sophisticated medical technology
Social Change	Slow; change evident over many generations	Rapid; change evident within a single generation

Europe and North America formed a mosaic of countless rural villages and small towns. In these local communities, which inspired Tönnies's concept of *Gemeinschaft*, people lived out their lives surrounded by kin and guided by a shared heritage. Gossip was an informal yet highly effective way of ensuring conformity to community standards. Such small communities tolerated little social diversity—the state of mechanical solidarity described by Durkheim.

For example, before 1690, English law demanded that everyone participate regularly in the Christian ritual of Holy Communion (Laslett, 1984). On the North American continent, only Rhode Island among the New England colonies tolerated any religious dissent. Because social differences were repressed in favor of conformity to established norms, subcultures and countercultures were few, and change proceeded slowly.

Increasing population, the growth of cities, and specialized economic activity driven by the Industrial Revolution gradually altered this pattern. People came to know one another by their jobs (for example, as "the doctor" or "the bank clerk") rather than by their kinship group or hometown. People looked on most others simply as strangers. The face-to-face communication of the village was eventually replaced by the impersonal mass media: newspapers, radio, television, and more recently, computer networks. Large organizations steadily assumed more and more responsibility for the daily needs that had once been fulfilled by family, friends, and neighbors; public education drew more and more people to schools; police, lawyers, and courts supervised a formal criminal justice system. Even charity became the work of faceless bureaucrats working for various social welfare agencies.

Geographic mobility, mass communication, and exposure to diverse ways of life all weaken traditional values. People become more tolerant of social diversity, defending individual rights and freedom of choice. Treating people differently because of their race, sex, or religion comes to be defined as backward and unjust. In the process, minorities at the margins of society gain greater power and broader participation in public life.

The mass media give rise to a national culture that washes over the traditional differences that used to set off one region from another. As one analyst put it, "Even in Baton Rouge, La., the local kids don't say 'y'all' anymore; they say 'you guys' just like on TV" (Gibbs, 2000:42). Mass-society theorists fear that the transformation of people of various backgrounds into a generic mass may end up dehumanizing everyone.

THE EVER-EXPANDING STATE

In the small-scale preindustrial societies of Europe, government amounted to little more than a local noble. A royal family formally reigned over an entire nation, but in the absence of swift transportation and efficient communication, even the power of absolute monarchs fell far short of that wielded by today's political leaders.

As technological innovation allowed government to expand, the centralized state grew in size and importance. At the time the United States gained independence from Great Britain, the federal government was a tiny organization with the primary function of providing national defense. Since then, government has assumed responsibility for more and more areas of social life: schooling the population, regulating wages and working conditions, establishing standards for products of all sorts, and providing financial assistance to the ill and the unemployed. To pay for

such programs, taxes have soared: Today's average worker labors more than four months each year just to pay for the broad array of services the government provides.

In a mass society, power resides in large bureaucracies, leaving people in local communities with little control over their lives. For example, state officials mandate that local schools must meet educational standards, local products must be government-certified, and every citizen must maintain extensive tax records. Although such regulations may protect people and enhance social equality, they also force us to deal more and more with nameless officials in distant and often unresponsive bureaucracies, and they undermine the autonomy of families and local communities.

Critical review. The growing scale of modern life may have positive aspects, but only at the cost of our cultural heritage. Modern societies increase individual rights, have greater tolerance of social differences, and raise living standards (Inglehart & Baker, 2000). But they are prone to what Weber feared most—excessive bureaucracy—as well as to Tönnies's self-centeredness and Durkheim's anomie. The size, complexity, and tolerance of diversity of modern societies all but doom traditional values and family patterns, leaving individuals isolated, powerless, and materialistic. As Chapter 12 ("Economics and Politics") noted, voter apathy is a serious problem in the United States. But should we be surprised that individuals in vast, impersonal societies such as ours end up thinking that no one person can make much of a difference?

Critics sometimes say that mass-society theory romanticizes the past. They remind us that many people in the small towns of our past were eager to set out for a better standard of living in cities. This approach also ignores problems of social inequality. Critics say mass-society theory attracts social and economic conservatives who defend conventional morality and are indifferent to the historical inequality of women and other minorities.

Social-Conflict Analysis: The Theory of Class Society

The second explanation of modernity derives mostly from the ideas of Karl Marx. From a social-conflict perspective, modernity takes the form of a **class society**, *a capitalist society with pronounced social stratification.* While agreeing that modern societies have expanded to a mass scale, this approach views the heart of modernization as an expanding capitalist economy, marked with inequality (Habermas, 1970; Polenberg, 1980; Blumberg, 1981; Harrington, 1984).

Many people marveled at the industrial technology that was changing the world a century ago. But some critics pointed out that the social consequences of the Industrial Revolution were not all positive. The painting *Trabajadores* (Workers) by Mirta Cerra portrays the exhausting and mind-numbing routines of manual workers.

Mirta Cerra (1904–1986), *Trabajadores*, oil on canvas laid down on panel, 46 × 62 in. (107.3 × 157.5 cm). © Christie's Images.

CAPITALISM

Class-society theory follows Marx in claiming that the increasing scale of social life in modern times has resulted from the growth and greed unleashed by capitalism. Because a capitalist economy pursues ever-greater profits, both production and consumption steadily increase.

According to Marx, capitalism rests on "naked self-interest" (Marx & Engels, 1972:337, orig. 1848). This self-centeredness weakens the social ties that once united small-scale communities. Capitalism also treats people as commodities: a source of labor and a market for capitalist products.

Capitalism supports science not just as the key to greater productivity but as an ideology that justifies the status quo. Modern societies encourage people to view human well-being as a technical puzzle that can be solved by engineers and other experts rather than through the pursuit of social justice. For example, a capitalist culture seeks to improve health through advances in scientific medicine rather than by eliminating poverty, which is a core cause of poor health.

Businesses also raise the banner of scientific logic, trying to increase profits through greater efficiency. As Chapter 12 ("Economics and Politics") explained, capitalist corporations have reached enormous size and control unimaginable wealth by "going global" as multinationals. From the class-society point of view, the expanding scale of life is less a function of *Gesellschaft* than the expected and destructive consequence of capitalism.

PERSISTENT INEQUALITY

Modernity has gradually worn away some of the rigid categories that divided preindustrial societies. But class-society theory maintains that elites persist as capitalist millionaires rather than nobles born to wealth and power. In the United States, we may have no hereditary monarchy, but the richest 5 percent of the population controls about 60 percent of all privately held property.

What of the state? Mass-society theorists argue that the state works to increase equality and fight social problems. Marx disagreed; he doubted that the state could accomplish more than minor reforms because, as he saw it, real power lies in the hands of capitalists who control the economy. Other class-society theorists add that to the extent that working people and minorities do enjoy greater political rights and a higher standard of living today, these changes came about because of political struggle, not government goodwill. They conclude that despite our pretensions of democracy, most people are still powerless in the face of wealthy elites.

Critical review. Class-society theory dismisses Durkheim's argument that people in modern societies suffer from anomie, claiming instead that most people deal with alienation and powerlessness. Not surprisingly, the class-society interpretation of modernity enjoys widespread support among liberals (and radicals) who favor greater equality and seek extensive regulation (or abolition) of the capitalist marketplace.

SUMMING UP

Two Interpretations of Modernity

	Mass Society	Class Society
Process of modernization	Industrialization; growth of bureaucracy	Rise of capitalism
Effects of modernization	Increasing scale of life; rise of the state and other formal organizations	Expansion of the capitalist economy; persistence of social inequality

A basic criticism of class-society theory is that it overlooks the increasing prosperity of modern societies and the fact that discrimination based on race, ethnicity, religion, and gender is now illegal and is widely regarded as a social problem. Furthermore, most people in the United States do not want an egalitarian society; they prefer a system of unequal rewards that reflects personal differences in talent and effort.

Based on socialism's failure to generate a high overall standard of living, few observers think that a centralized economy would cure the ills of modernity. Many other problems in the United States—from unemployment, homelessness, and industrial pollution to unresponsive government—are also found in socialist nations such as the former Soviet Union.

The Summing Up table compares views of modern society offered by mass-society theory and class-society theory. Mass-society theory focuses on the increasing impersonality of social life and the growth of government; class-society theory stresses the expansion of capitalism and the persistence of inequality.

Modernity and the Individual

Both mass- and class-society theories look at the broad patterns of change since the Industrial Revolution. From these macro-level approaches, we can also draw micro-level insights into how modernity shapes individual lives.

MASS SOCIETY: PROBLEMS OF IDENTITY

Modernity liberated individuals from the small, tightly knit communities of the past. Most members of modern societies have privacy and freedom to express their individuality. However, mass-society theory suggests that extensive social diversity, isolation, and rapid social change make it difficult for many people to establish any coherent identity at all (Wheelis, 1958; Berger, Berger, & Kellner, 1974).

Chapter 3 ("Socialization: From Infancy to Old Age") explained that people's personalities are mostly a product of their social experiences. The small, homogeneous, and slowly changing societies of the past provided a firm (if narrow) foundation for building a personal identity. Even today, Amish communities that flourish in the United States teach young men and women "correct" ways to think and behave. Not everyone born into an Amish community can tolerate such rigid demands for conformity, but most members establish a well-integrated and satisfying personal identity (Hostetler, 1980; Kraybill & Olshan, 1994).

Mass societies are quite another story. Socially diverse and rapidly changing, they offer only shifting sands on which to build a personal identity. Left to make many life decisions on their own, people—especially those with greater wealth—face a confusing range of options. The freedom to choose has little value without standards to guide the selection process; in a tolerant mass society, people may find little reason to choose one path over another. As a result, many people shuttle from one identity to another, changing their lifestyles, relationships, and even religions in search of an elusive "true self." Given the widespread relativism of modern societies, people without a moral compass lack the security and certainty once provided by tradition.

To David Riesman (1970, orig. 1950), modernization brings changes in **social character,** *personality patterns common to members of a particular society.* Preindustrial societies promote what Riesman calls **tradition-directedness,** *rigid conformity to time-honored ways of living.* Members of such societies model their lives on those of their ancestors, so that "living the good life" amounts to "doing what people have always done."

Tradition-directedness corresponds to Tönnies's *Gemeinschaft* and Durkheim's mechanical solidarity. Culturally conservative, tradition-directed people think and act alike. Unlike the conformity often found in modern societies, the uniformity of tradition-directedness is not an effort to imitate a popular celebrity or follow the latest

Mass-society theory relates feelings of anxiety and lack of meaning in the modern world to rapid social change that washes away tradition. This notion of modern emptiness is captured in the photo at the left. Class-society theory, by contrast, ties such feelings to social inequality, by which some categories of people are made into second-class citizens (or not made citizens at all), an idea expressed in the photo at the right.

trend. Instead, people are alike because they all draw on the same solid cultural foundation. Amish women and men exemplify tradition-directedness; in the Amish culture, tradition ties everyone to ancestors and descendants in an unbroken chain of righteous living.

Members of diverse and rapidly changing societies define a tradition-directed personality as deviant because it seems so rigid. Modern people prize personal flexibility, the capacity to adapt, and sensitivity to others. Riesman calls this type of social character **other-directedness,** *openness to the latest trends and fashions, often expressed by imitating others.* Because their socialization occurs within societies that are continuously in flux, other-directed people develop fluid identities marked by superficiality, inconsistency, and change. They try on different "selves" almost like new clothing, seek out role models, and engage in varied performances as they move from setting to setting (Goffman, 1959). In a traditional society, such "shiftiness" marks a person as untrustworthy, but in a changing, modern society, the chameleonlike ability to fit in virtually anywhere is very useful.

In societies that value the up-to-date rather than the traditional, people anxiously look to others for approval, using members of their own generation rather than elders

as role models. Peer pressure can be irresistible to people without strong standards to guide them. Our society urges people to be true to themselves, but when social surroundings change so rapidly, how can people develop the self to which they should be true? This problem lies at the root of the identity crisis so widespread in industrial societies today. *Who am I?* and *What is right?* are nagging questions that many of us struggle to answer. In truth, this problem is not so much us as the inherently unstable mass society in which we live.

CLASS SOCIETY: PROBLEMS OF POWERLESSNESS

Class-society theory paints a different picture of modernity's effects on individuals. This approach maintains that persistent inequality undermines modern society's promise of individual freedom. For some, modernity serves up great privilege, but for many, everyday life means coping with economic uncertainty and a gnawing sense of powerlessness (Newman, 1993; Ehrenreich, 2001).

For racial and ethnic minorities, the problem of relative disadvantage looms even larger. Similarly, although women participate more broadly in modern societies, they continue to run up against traditional barriers of sexism. This approach rejects mass-society theory's claim that people suffer from too much freedom; according to class-society theory, our society still denies a majority of people full participation in social life.

As Chapter 9 ("Global Stratification") explained, the expanding scope of world capitalism has placed more of the Earth's population under the influence of multinational corporations. As a result, more than three-fourths of the world's income is concentrated in high-income nations, where just 18 percent of its people live. Is it any wonder, class-society theorists ask, that people in poor nations seek greater power to shape their own lives?

The problem of widespread powerlessness led Herbert Marcuse (1964) to challenge Max Weber's claim that modern society is rational. Marcuse condemned modern society as irrational for failing to meet the needs of so many people. Although modern capitalist societies produce unparalleled wealth, poverty remains the daily plight of more than 1 billion people. Marcuse added that technological advances further reduce people's control over their own lives. The advent of high technology has generally conferred a great deal of power on a core of specialists—not the majority of people—who now dominate discussion of events such as computing, energy production, and health care. Countering the popular view that technology *solves* the world's problems, Marcuse suggested that it is more accurate to say that science *causes* them. In sum, class-society theory asserts that people suffer because modern societies have concentrated both wealth and power in the hands of a privileged few.

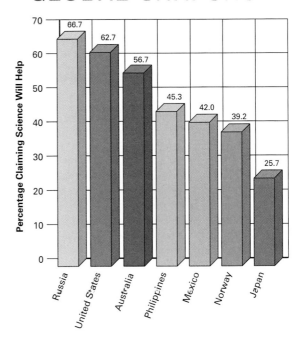

GLOBAL SNAPSHOT

FIGURE 16-3 Support for Science: A Global Survey

Survey Question: "In the long run, do you think the scientific advances we are making will help or harm humankind?"

Source: Inglehart et al. (2000).

Modernity and Progress

In modern societies, most people expect—and applaud—social change. We link modernity to the idea of *progress* (from Latin, meaning "moving forward"), a state of continual improvement. By contrast, we see stability as stagnation.

Given our bias in favor of change, members of our society tend to regard traditional cultures as backward. But change, particularly toward material affluence, is a mixed blessing. As the Critical Thinking box on pages 466–67 shows, social change is too complex simply to equate with progress.

Even getting rich has both advantages and disadvantages, as the cases of the Kaiapo and Gullah show. Historically, among people in the United States, a rising standard of living has made lives longer and materially more comfortable. At the same time, many people wonder whether today's routines are too stressful, with families often having little time to relax or simply spend time together.

Indeed, in most high-income countries, measures of happiness show a decline over the course of recent decades (Myers, 2000).

Science, too, has its pluses and minuses. As Figure 16–3 shows, people in the United States are confident—more than those in most other industrial societies—that science improves our lives. But surveys also show that many adults in the United States feel that science "makes our way of life change too fast" (NORC, 2003:346).

New technology has always sparked controversy. A century ago, the introduction of automobiles and telephones allowed more rapid transportation and more efficient communication. At the same time, such technology also weakened traditional attachments to hometowns and even to families. Today, people might wonder whether computer technology will do the same thing: giving us access to people around the world but shielding us from the community right outside our doors; providing more information than ever before but in the process threatening personal privacy.

Does "Modern" Mean "Progress"? Brazil's Kaiapo and Georgia's Gullah Community

The firelight flickers in the gathering darkness. Chief Kanhonk sits, as he has done at the end of the day for many years, ready to begin an evening of animated talk and storytelling (Simons, 2004). This is the hour when the Kaiapo, a small society in Brazil's lush Amazon region, celebrate their heritage. Because the Kaiapo are a traditional people with no written language, the elders rely on evenings by the fire to pass along their culture to their children and grandchildren. In the past, evenings like this have been filled with tales of brave Kaiapo warriors fighting off Portuguese traders in pursuit of slaves and gold.

But as the minutes pass, only a few older villagers assemble for the evening ritual. "It is the Big Ghost," one man grumbles, explaining the poor turnout. The "Big Ghost" has indeed descended on them; its bluish glow spills from windows throughout the village. The Kaiapo children—and many adults as well—are watching sitcoms on television.

Buying a television several years ago has had consequences far greater than anyone imagined. In the end, what their enemies failed to do with guns, the Kaiapo may well do to themselves with prime-time programming.

The Kaiapo are among the 230,000 native peoples who inhabit Brazil. They stand out because of their striking body paint and ornate ceremonial dress. During the 1980s, they became rich from gold mining and harvesting mahogany trees. Now they must decide if their newfound fortune is a blessing or a curse.

To some, affluence means the opportunity to learn about the outside world through travel and television. Others, like Chief Kanhonk, are not so

 To see pictures of Brazil's Kaiapo, go to http://www. ddbstock.com/largeimage/ amindns.html

sure. Sitting by the fire, he thinks aloud, "I have been saying that people must buy useful things like knives and fishing hooks. Television does not fill the stomach. It only shows our children and grandchildren white people's things." Bebtopup, the oldest priest, nods in agreement: "The night is the time the old people teach the young people. Television has stolen the night" (Simons, 2004:494).

Far to the north, half an hour by ferry from the coast of Georgia, lies the swampy island community of Hog Hammock. The seventy African American residents of the island today trace their

---

In short, we all realize that social change comes faster all the time, but we may disagree about whether a particular change is good or bad for society.

Modernity: Global Variation

 October 1, Kobe, Japan. Riding the computer-controlled monorail high above the streets of Kobe or the

200-mile-per-hour bullet train to Tokyo, we see Japan as the society of the future, in love with high technology. Yet the Japanese remain strikingly traditional in other respects: Few corporate executives and almost no politicians are women, young people still show seniors great respect, and public orderliness contrasts with the chaos of cities in the United States.

Japan is a nation at once traditional and modern. This contradiction reminds us that although it is useful to

ancestry back to the first slaves who settled here in 1802.

Walking past the brightly painted houses that stand among yellow pine trees draped with Spanish moss, a visitor can easily feel transported back in time. The local people, known as Gullahs (or, in some places, Geechees), speak a mixture of English and West African languages. They fish, living much the same as they have for hundreds of years.

But the future of this way of life is now in doubt. Few young people who are raised in Hog Hammock can find work; beyond fishing and making traditional crafts, there are simply no jobs to do. "We have been here nine generations and we are still here," says one local. Then, referring to the nineteen children who now live on the island, she adds, "It's not that they don't want to be here; it's that there's nothing here for them—they need to have jobs" (Curry, 2001:41).

Just as important, with people on the mainland looking for waterside homes for vacations or year-round living, the island is now becoming prime real estate. Not long ago, one larger house went up for sale and the community was shocked to learn of an asking price over $1 million. The locals know only too well that higher property values will mean high taxes that few

can afford to pay. In short, Hog Hammock is likely to become another Hilton Head, once a Gullah community on the South Carolina coast that is now home to well-to-do people from the mainland.

The odds are that before long, the people of Hog Hammock will be selling their homes and moving inland. But

 Learn more about Gullah culture at http://www.knowitall. org/gullahnet

few people are happy about selling out, even for a good price. On the

contrary, moving away will mean the end of their cultural heritage.

The stories of both the Kaiapo and the people of Hog Hammock show us that change is not a simple path toward "progress." These people may be moving toward modernity, but this process will have both positive and negative consequences. In the end, both groups of people may enjoy a higher standard of living with better shelter, more clothing, and new technology. On the other hand, their new affluence will come at the price of their traditions. The drama of these people is now being played out around the world as more and more traditional cultures are being lured away from their heritage by the affluence and materialism of rich societies.

WHAT DO YOU THINK?

1. Why is social change both a winning and a losing proposition for traditional people?
2. Do the changes described here improve the lives of the Kaiapo? What about the Gullah community?
3. Do traditional people have any choice about becoming more modern? Explain your view.

Sources: Based on Curry (2001) and Simons (2004).

contrast traditional and modern social patterns, the old and the new often coexist in unexpected ways. In the People's Republic of China, ancient Confucian principles are mixed with contemporary socialist thinking. In Saudi Arabia and Qatar, a love of the latest modern technology is mixed with respect for the ancient principles of Islam. Likewise, in Mexico and much of Latin America, people observe centuries-old Christian rituals even as they struggle to move ahead economically. In short, combinations of traditional and modern are far from unusual—rather, they are found throughout the world.

Postmodernity

If modernity was the product of the Industrial Revolution, is the Information Revolution creating a postmodern era? A number of scholars use the term **postmodernity** to refer to *social patterns characteristic of postindustrial societies.*

The term "postmodernism" has been used for decades in literary, philosophical, and even architectural circles. It has moved into sociology on a wave of social criticism that has been building since the spread of left-leaning politics in the 1960s. Although there are many variations of postmodern

APPLYING SOCIOLOGY

Tracking Change: Is Life in the United States Getting Better or Worse?

We began this chapter with a look at what life was like in 1900, more than a century ago. It is easy to see that in many ways, life is far better today than it was for our grandparents and great-grandparents. But especially in recent decades, the indicators are not so clear-cut: Life may be improving in some ways, but in others, it is getting worse. Here is a look at some trends shaping the United States since 1970.

First, the good news: By some measures, shown in the first set of figures, life in this country is clearly improving. Infant mortality has fallen steadily, meaning that fewer and fewer children die soon after birth. In addition, an increasing share of people are reaching old age, and after reaching sixty-five, they are living longer than ever. More good news: The poverty rate among the elderly is well below what it was in 1970. Schooling is another area of improvement: The share of people dropping out of high school is down, and the share completing college is up.

Second, some "no news" results: A number of indicators show that life is about the same as it was in the 1970s. For example, teenage drug use was about the same in 2002 as a generation

The good news ...

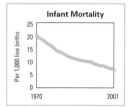

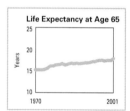

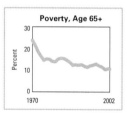

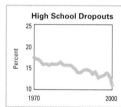

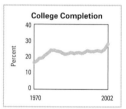

No news ...

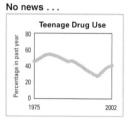

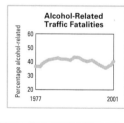

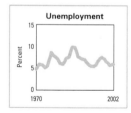

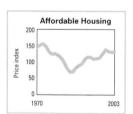

thinking, all share the following five themes (Hall & Neitz, 1993; Inglehart, 1997; Rudel & Gerson, 1999):

1. **In important respects, modernity has failed.** The promise of modernity was a life free from want. As many postmodernist critics see it, however, the twentieth century was unsuccessful in solving social problems such as poverty, evidenced by the fact that many people still lack financial security.

2. **The bright light of "progress" is fading.** Modern people look to the future expecting that their lives will improve in significant ways. Members (and even leaders) of a postmodern society have less confidence about what the future holds. The strong optimism that carried society

into the modern era more than a century ago has given way to widespread pessimism: Most U.S. adults believe that life is getting worse (NORC, 2003:208).

3. **Science no longer holds the answers.** The defining trait of the modern era was a scientific outlook and a confident belief that technology would make life better. But postmodern critics argue that science has failed to solve many old problems (such as poor health) and has even created new problems (such as pollution and resource depletion).

   Postmodernist thinkers discredit science for implying a singular truth. On the contrary, they maintain, there is no one Truth. This means that objective

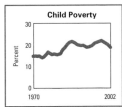

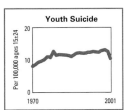

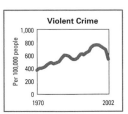

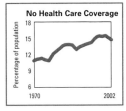

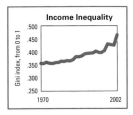

before. Likewise, alcohol-related traffic deaths number about the same. Unemployment has had its ups and downs, but the overall level has stayed about the same. Finally, there was about the same amount of affordable housing in the United States in 2003 as in 1970.

Then there's the bad news: By some measures, several having to do with children, the quality of life in the United States has actually fallen. The official rate of child abuse is up, as is the level of child poverty and the rate of suicide among youths. Although the level of violent crime fell through most of the 1990s, it still remains above

the 1970 level. Average weekly wages, one measure of basic economic security, show a downward trend, meaning that more families have had to rely on two or more wage earners to maintain family income. The number of people without health insurance is also on the rise. Finally, economic inequality in this country has been increasing.

Overall, the evidence does not support any simple ideas about "progress over time." Social change has been, and probably will continue to be, a complex process that reflects the priorities we set for this nation as well as our will to achieve them.

WHAT DO YOU THINK?

1. Some analysts claim that U.S. society contains a contradiction: Over recent decades, we see increasing economic health but declining social health. Based on the data presented here, do you agree? Why or why not?

2. Which of these trends do you find most important? Why?

3. Overall, do you think the quality of life in the United States is improving or not? Why?

Sources: Miringoff & Miringoff (1999) and Myers (2000).

reality does not exist; rather, many realities result from "social construction."

4. **Cultural debates are intensifying.** Now that more people have all the material things they really need, ideas are taking on more importance. In this sense, postmodernity is also a postmaterialist era, in which issues such as social justice, the environment, and animal rights command more and more public attention.

5. **Social institutions are changing.** Just as industrialization brought sweeping transformation to social institutions, the rise of a postindustrial society is remaking society all over again. For example, the Industrial Revolution placed *material things* at the

center of productive life; the Information Revolution emphasizes *ideas*. Similarly, the postmodern family no longer conforms to any one pattern; on the contrary, individuals are choosing between many family forms.

Critical review. Analysts who claim that the United States and other high-income nations are entering a postmodern era criticize modernity for failing to meet human needs. In defense of modernity, there have been marked increases in longevity and living standards over the past century. Even if we were to accept postmodernist views that science is bankrupt and progress is a sham, what are the alternatives?

The Applying Sociology box offers evidence suggesting life in the United States is and is not getting better.

Many people see modernity as a mix of promise and danger. The mural *Read between the Lines* by Mexican American artist David Botello (1975), found in East Los Angeles, contains the words, "Cuisense Amigos" ("Be careful, friends"). Looking at the mural, what about the modern U.S. way of life is Botello worried about? (In what ways is the heritage of Mexican Americans threatened in the United States?)

David Botello, *Read between the Lines,* 1975, mural on Ford and Olympic Boulevards, East Los Angeles, acrylic on stucco, 10 × 20 ft.

Looking Ahead: Modernization and Our Global Future

Imagine the entire world's population reduced to a single village of 1,000 people. About 180 residents of this "global village" come from high-income countries. Another 180 people are so poor that their lives are at risk.

The tragic plight of the world's poor shows that some desperately needed change has not yet occurred. Chapter 9 ("Global Stratification") presented two competing views of why 1 billion people the world over are poor. *Modernization theory* claims that in the past, the entire world was poor and technological change, especially the Industrial Revolution, enhanced human productivity and raised living standards in many nations. From this point of view, the solution to global poverty is to promote technological development around the world.

For reasons suggested earlier, however, global modernization may be difficult. Recall that David Riesman portrayed preindustrial people as *tradition-directed* and likely to resist change. So modernization theorists urge the world's rich nations to help poor countries grow economically. Industrial nations can speed development by exporting technology to poor regions, welcoming students from these countries, and providing foreign aid to stimulate economic growth.

The review of modernization theory in Chapter 9 points to some success for these policies in Latin America and more dramatic results in the small Asian countries of Taiwan, South Korea, Singapore, and Hong Kong. But

jump-starting development in the poorest countries of the world poses greater challenges. Even where dramatic change has occurred, modernization involves a trade-off. Traditional people, such as Brazil's Kaiapo, may gain wealth through economic development, but only at the cost of losing their traditional identity and values as they are drawn into a global "McCulture" based on Western materialism, pop music, trendy clothes, and fast food. One Brazilian anthropologist expressed optimism about the future of the Kaiapo: "At least they quickly understood the consequences of watching television. . . . Now [they] can make a choice" (Simons, 2004:495).

Not everyone thinks that modernization is really an option. According to *dependency theory,* a second approach to global stratification presented in Chapter 9, today's poor societies struggle to modernize, even if they want to. From this point of view, the major barrier to economic development is not traditionalism but global domination by rich capitalist societies.

In effect, dependency theory asserts that rich nations achieved their modernization at the expense of poor ones, which provided them with valuable natural resources and human labor. Even today, the world's poorest countries remain locked in a disadvantageous economic relationship with rich nations, dependent on wealthy countries to buy their raw materials and in return provide them with whatever manufactured products they can afford. According to this view, continuing ties with rich societies will only perpetuate current patterns of global inequality.

Whichever approach one finds more convincing, we can no longer isolate the study of the United States from the rest of the world. At the beginning of the twentieth century, a majority of people in even the richest nations lived in relatively small settlements with limited awareness of the larger world. Now, with advancing communications technology, the entire world has become one human village because the lives of all people are increasingly linked.

The last century witnessed unprecedented human achievement. Yet solutions to many problems of human existence—including finding meaning in life, resolving conflicts between societies, and eliminating poverty— have eluded us. The Controversy & Debate box on pages 472–73 examines one dilemma of our postindustrial society: balancing individual freedom and personal responsibility. To the list of pressing matters new concerns have been added, such as controlling population growth and establishing a sustainable natural environment. In the future, we must be prepared to tackle such problems with imagination, compassion, and determination. Our growing understanding of human society gives us reason to look to the task with optimism.

SUMMARY

1. All societies change, some more quickly than others. Social change often generates controversy.

2. Social change is the result of invention, discovery, and cultural diffusion as well as social conflict.

3. Social movements are deliberate efforts to promote or resist change. Analysts link social movements to relative deprivation, the rootlessness of mass society, an organization's ability to obtain resources, cultural symbols that encourage change, and the operation of the capitalist economy.

4. Modernity results from the process of industrialization, which, according to Peter Berger, includes the weakening of traditional communities, expansion of personal choice, increasingly diverse beliefs, and a keen awareness of the future.

5. Ferdinand Tönnies described modernization as the transition from *Gemeinschaft* to *Gesellschaft*, which signifies the progressive loss of community amid growing individualism.

6. Emile Durkheim saw modernization as a function of society's expanding division of labor. Mechanical solidarity, based on shared activities and beliefs, gradually gives way to organic solidarity, in which specialization makes people interdependent.

7. According to Max Weber, modernity replaces traditional thinking with rationality. Weber feared the dehumanizing effects of rational organization.

8. Karl Marx saw modernity as the triumph of capitalism over feudalism. Viewing capitalist societies as arenas of conflict, Marx spoke out for revolutionary change to achieve a more egalitarian socialist society.

9. According to mass-society theory, modernity increases the scale of life, enlarging the role of government and other formal organizations in carrying out tasks previously performed by family members and neighbors. Cultural diversity and rapid social change make it difficult for people in modern societies to define what is morally good, develop stable identities, and find meaning in their lives.

10. According to class-society theory, capitalism is central to Western modernization. This approach charges that by concentrating wealth in the hands of a few, capitalism generates widespread feelings of powerlessness.

11. Social change is too complex and controversial to be equated simply with progress.

12. "Postmodernity" refers to cultural traits typical of postindustrial societies. Postmodern criticism of society centers on the failure of modernity, especially science, to fulfill its promise of prosperity and well-being.

13. In a global context, modernization theory links global poverty to the power of tradition. Some modernization theorists support policies by rich societies to assist the economic development of poor nations.

14. Dependency theory explains global poverty as the product of the world economic system. The operation of multinational corporations ensures that poor nations will remain economically dependent on rich nations.

KEY CONCEPTS

social change (p. 451) the transformation of culture and social institutions over time

social movement (p. 453) an organized activity that encourages or discourages social change

relative deprivation (p. 454) a perceived disadvantage arising from a specific comparison

modernity (p. 455) social patterns resulting from industrialization

Personal Freedom and Social Responsibility: Can We Have It Both Ways?

Shortly after midnight on a crisp March evening in 1964, Kitty Genovese drove into the parking lot of her New York apartment complex. She turned off the headlights, locked the car doors, and headed across the blacktop toward the entrance to her building. Out of nowhere, a man holding a knife lunged at her, and as she shrieked in terror, he stabbed her repeatedly. Windows opened above as curious neighbors looked down to see what was going on. The attacker stopped for a moment, but when the windows closed, he went back to his deadly business. The attack continued for more than thirty minutes until Genovese lay dead in her doorway. A follow-up investigation failed to identify the assailant but did confirm a stunning fact: *Dozens of neighbors had witnessed the attack on Kitty Genovese, but not one helped her or even called the police.*

Decades later, people still recall the Genovese tragedy in discussions of what we owe one another. As members of a modern, postindustrial society, we prize our individual rights and personal privacy, but we sometimes withdraw from public responsibility and turn a cold shoulder to people in need. When a cry for help is met by indifference, have we pushed our modern idea of personal freedom too far? How can "free" individuals keep a sense of human community?

These questions highlight the tension between traditional and modern social systems, which is evident in the writings of all the sociologists discussed in this chapter. Tönnies, Durkheim, and others concluded that in some respects, traditional community and modern individualism don't go together. Society can unite its members as a moral community only by limiting their range of personal choices about how to live. In short, although we value both community and freedom, we can't have it both ways.

The sociologist Amitai Etzioni (1993, 1996, 2003) has tried to strike a middle ground. The communitarian movement rests on the simple idea that "strong rights presume strong responsibilities." Put another way, an individual's pursuit of self-interest must be balanced by a commitment to the larger community.

Etzioni claims that modern people have become too focused on individual rights. People expect the system to provide for them, but they are reluctant to support the system. Although most of us believe in the principle of trial by a jury of one's peers, fewer and fewer people today are willing to perform jury duty. Similarly, the public is quick to accept government services but increasingly reluctant to pay for these services through taxes.

Communitarians advance four proposals toward balancing individual rights with public responsibilities. First, our society should stop the expanding "culture of rights" by which people place their own interests ahead of social involvement. After all, the Constitution allows us many rights, but there is nothing in it about doing whatever we want. Second, communitarians remind us that all rights involve responsibilities. We cannot simply take from society without giving something back. Third, some responsibilities, such as upholding the law or protecting the natural environment, are too important for anyone to ignore. Fourth, defending legitimate community interests may mean limiting individual rights. For example, protecting public safety might

modernization (p. 455) the process of social change begun by industrialization

division of labor (p. 457) specialized economic activity

anomie (p. 458) Durkheim's term for a condition in which society provides little moral guidance to individuals

mass society (p. 459) a society in which prosperity and bureaucracy have weakened traditional social ties

class society (p. 461) a capitalist society with pronounced social stratification

social character (p. 463) personality patterns common to members of a particular society

tradition-directedness (p. 463) rigid conformity to time-honored ways of living

other-directedness (p. 464) openness to the latest trends and fashions, often expressed by imitating others

postmodernity (p. 467) social patterns characteristic of postindustrial societies

mean subjecting some workers to drug tests.

The communitarian movement appeals to many people who, along with Etzioni, seek to balance personal freedom with social responsibility. But critics from both ends of the political spectrum have attacked this initiative. To those on the left, problems ranging from voter apathy to street crime cannot be solved by some vague idea of "social reintegration." Instead, we need expanded government programs to increase social equality. Specifically, these critics say, we must curb the political influence of the rich and actively fight racism and sexism.

Conservatives on the political right find fault with Etzioni's proposals for different reasons (Pearson, 1995). To them, the communitarian movement amounts to little more than a rerun of the 1960s leftist agenda. The communitarian vision of a good society favors liberal goals (such as protecting the environment) but says little about conservative goals such as allowing organized prayer in school or restoring the strength of traditional families. Conservatives ask whether a free society should permit the kind of social engineering that Etzioni advocates, such as instituting antiprejudice programs in schools and requiring people to perform a year of national service.

Perhaps, as Etzioni himself has suggested, the fact that both the left and the right find fault with his views indicates that he has identified a moderate, sensible answer to a serious problem. But it may also be that people in a society as diverse as the United States will not easily agree about what they owe to themselves and to one another.

CONTINUE THE DEBATE . . .

1. Have you ever chosen not to come to the aid of someone in need or danger? Why?
2. President Kennedy admonished us, "Ask not what your country can do for you; ask what you can do for your country." Do you think people today support this idea? What makes you think so?
3. Does our society need to balance rights with increased responsibility? Explain your position.

In today's world, people can find new ways to express age-old virtues such as concern for their neighbors and extending a hand to those in need. Habitat for Humanity, an organization with chapters in cities and towns across the United States, is made up of people who want to help local families realize their dream of owning a home.

CRITICAL-THINKING QUESTIONS

1. How well do you think Tönnies, Durkheim, Weber, and Marx predicted the character of modern society? How are their visions of modernity the same? How do they differ?

2. What traits lead some to call the United States a "mass society"? Why do other analysts describe the United States as a "class society"?

3. What is the difference between *anomie* (a trait of mass society) and *alienation* (a characteristic of class society)? Among which categories of the U.S. population would you expect each to be more pronounced?

4. Why do some analysts believe the United States has become a postmodern society? Do you agree? Why or why not?

APPLICATIONS AND EXERCISES

1. Do you have an elderly relative or friend? Most older people will be happy to tell you about the social changes they have seen in their lifetimes.

2. Ask people in your class or friendship group to make five predictions about U.S. society in the year 2050, when today's twenty-year-olds will be senior citizens. On what issues do you agree? Disagree?

3. Has the rate of social change been increasing? Do some research about inventions over time to answer this question. For example, consider modes of travel, including walking, riding animals, trains, cars, airplanes, and rockets in space.

The first two characterized society for tens of thousands of years; the last four emerged in barely two centuries.

4. Packaged in the back of this new textbook is an interactive CD-ROM that offers a variety of video and interactive review materials intended to help you better understand the material covered in this chapter. For this chapter, the CD-ROM contains a relevant clip from *ABC News,* an author's tip video, interactive map animations, an interactive timeline, and flashcards with audio pronunciations of the more difficult words.

 ## SITES TO SEE

http://www.prenhall.com/macionis

Visit the interactive Companion Website™ that accompanies this text. Begin by clicking on the cover of your book. You will find a chapter-by-chapter study guide, practice tests, suggested Web links, and links to other relevant material.

http://www.gwu.edu/~ccps/

Want to learn more about the Communitarian Network? This site tells about its goals.

http://www.utoronto.ca/utopia/

Deliberate change sometimes is inspired by visions of *utopia,* an ideal society that exists nowhere. Read about the Society for Utopian Studies at this Web site.

http://www.TheSociologyPage.com or **http://www.macionis.com**

Finally, on a personal note, I hope this book has helped you and will be a useful resource to keep for courses later on. Please visit my Web page and send an e-mail message (macionis@kenyon.edu) with your thoughts and suggestions. And, yes, I *will* write back!

John J. Macionis

 ## INVESTIGATE WITH RESEARCH NAVIGATOR™

Follow the instructions found on page 32 of this textbook to access the features of **Research Navigator™.** Once at the Web site, enter your Login Name and Password. Then, to use the **Content Select™** database, enter keywords such as "social change," "modernity," and "postmodernity," and the search engine will supply relevant and recent scholarly and popular press publications. Use the *New York Times* **Search-by-Subject Archive** to find recent news articles and the **Links Library** feature to find relevant Web links organized by the key terms associated with this chapter.

January 1, 2004

Indian Soybean Farmers Join the Global Village

By AMY WALDMAN

TIHI, India—At least once a day in this village of 2,500 people, Ravi Sham Choudhry turns on the computer in his front room and logs in to the Web site of the Chicago Board of Trade.

He has the dirt of a farmer under his fingernails and pecks slowly at the keys. But he knows what he wants: the prices for soybean commodity futures.

A drop in prices on the Chicago Board . . . could augur a drop in prices here, meaning that he and fellow soybean farmers should sell their crop now. An increase there argues that the farmers should wait for prices to rise. . . .

The correlation is rough but real. Real, too, is the link between farmers in rural central India and around the globe, thanks to a company's innovation.

The concept is the e-choupal, taken from the Hindi word for village square, or gathering place. The twist is the "e": providing a computer and Internet connections for farmers to gather around. . . .

E-choupal [also] . . . gives them access to local weather conditions, soil-testing techniques and other expert knowledge that will increase their productivity. . . .

There are now . . . 3,000 . . . [e-choupals] in India. They are serving 18,000 villages, reaching up to 1.8 million farmers. . . .

[T]he company behind e-choupals, ITC Ltd., has done as much as anyone to bridge India's vast digital divide: most of its one billion people have no access to the technology developed by some of their fellow Indians, whether in Bangalore or Silicon Valley. . . .

ITC's chairman, Y. C. Deveshwar . . . [said] "We are laying infrastructure in a sense." . . . Sixty companies have already taken part in a pilot project to sell services and goods, from insurance to seeds to motorbikes to biscuits, through ITC. . . .

E-choupals were born in 2000 from ITC's determination to capture more of the soybean crop, which it turns into oil to sell in India and into animal feed to export. In purchasing soya, it has long been dependent on a static, archaic system: Farmers sold to village traders or went to government markets, settling for whatever price was offered. ITC then had to buy from the traders or markets, with little quality control and high transaction costs.

The idea of the e-choupals was to allow the company to buy more directly from farmers. . . .

S. Shivakumar, 43, the head of the company's international business division and the originator of e-choupals, said he had long been frustrated by how a lack of opportunity limited the ambitions and achievements of Indian farmers.

"This has been a clear commercial initiative with social good in mind," he said.

Mr. Deveshwar agreed, saying he found it hard to become enthusiastic about making a rich man richer, but felt very motivated to make a poor farmer less so. . . .

ITC selects a lead farmer, or sanchalak, to run each e-choupal, which serves three to four villages. He is meant to be literate, progressive, young, with an entrepreneurial spark and a good reputation.

Mr. Choudhry, the lead farmer here, said he took an oath in front of the whole village to "work for the welfare of farmers with honesty and integrity." Farmers from his and nearby villages call or stop by to check prices or exchange information. For his efforts, he gets one-half of 1 percent commission on whatever farmers in his area sell to ITC.

Last year, Mr. Choudhry earned 14,000 rupees, about $300, in commission. This year, he has earned that much in one month.

"Our underlying assumption that farmers are entrepreneurial has proved true," Mr. Shivakumar said. . . .

[E]-choupals seem to be reducing inequality of access to information between some rural poor and the urban middle class. Monitoring data show that 70 percent of the activity on the ITC computers does not involve the choupal, . . . and exploration of the Internet has just begun.

In this village, schoolchildren have already discovered they can check examination results online, and Mr. Choudhry's father and son have found Web versions of Hindi newspapers. . . .

In Chapra village, Atul Singh, 17, the son of the sanchalak, has learned how to download music from indiafm.com and to chat on Yahoo.

"How r u?" he typed, as his screen informed him that "asian-honeypie has joined the room." A flood of obscenities from a hacker then filled the screen, as the mellifluous cooing of a Hindi song, "How Unfaithful You Are, My Dear Friend," filled the room.

WHAT DO YOU THINK?

1. In India, a nation where two-thirds of the people still work in agriculture, how is the e-choupal a mix of both tradition and modernity?

2. In what ways are village people in India making use of the computer? How is this likely to change their lives?

Adapted from the original article by Amy Waldman published in *The New York Times* on January 1, 2004. Copyright © 2004 by The New York Times Company. Reprinted with permission.

GLOSSARY

abortion   the deliberate termination of a pregnancy

absolute poverty   a deprivation of resources that is life-threatening

achieved status   a social position a person takes on voluntarily that reflects personal ability and effort

Afrocentrism   emphasizing and promoting African cultural patterns

ageism   prejudice and discrimination against older people

age-sex pyramid   a graphic representation of the age and sex of a population

agriculture   large-scale cultivation using plows harnessed to animals or more powerful energy sources

alienation   the experience of isolation and misery resulting from powerlessness

animism   the belief that elements of the natural world are conscious life forms that affect humanity

anomie   Durkheim's term for a condition in which society provides little moral guidance to individuals

anticipatory socialization   learning that helps a person achieve a desired position

ascribed status   a social position a person receives at birth or takes on involuntarily later in life

asexuality   no sexual attraction to people of either sex

assimilation   the process by which minorities gradually adopt patterns of the dominant culture

authoritarianism   a political system that denies the people participation in government

authority   power that people perceive as legitimate rather than coercive

beliefs   specific statements that people hold to be true

bisexuality   sexual attraction to people of both sexes

blue-collar occupations   lower-prestige jobs that involve mostly manual labor

bureaucracy   an organizational model rationally designed to perform tasks efficiently

bureaucratic inertia   the tendency of bureaucratic organizations to perpetuate themselves

bureaucratic ritualism   a focus on rules and regulations to the point of undermining an organization's goals

capitalism   an economic system in which natural resources and the means of producing goods and services are privately owned

capitalists   people who own and operate factories and other businesses in pursuit of profits

caste system   social stratification based on ascription, or birth

cause and effect   a relationship in which change in one variable (the independent variable) causes change in another (the dependent variable)

charisma   extraordinary personal qualities that can infuse people with emotion and turn them into followers

church   a type of religious organization that is well integrated into the larger society

civil religion   a quasi-religious loyalty binding citizens in a basically secular society

class society   a capitalist society with pronounced social stratification

class system   social stratification based on both birth and individual achievement

cohabitation   the sharing of a household by an unmarried couple

cohort   a category of people with a common characteristic, usually their age

colonialism   the process by which some nations enrich themselves through political and economic control of other nations

community-based corrections   correctional programs operating within society at large rather than behind prison walls

concept   a mental construct that represents some part of the world in a simplified form

concrete operational stage   Piaget's term for the level of human development at which individuals first see causal connections in their surroundings

corporate crime   the illegal actions of a corporation or people acting on its behalf

corporation   an organization with a legal existence, including rights and liabilities, apart from that of its members

correlation   a relationship in which two (or more) variables change together

counterculture   cultural patterns that strongly oppose those widely accepted within a society

crime   the violation of a society's formally enacted criminal law

crimes against the person (**violent crimes**)   crimes that direct violence or the threat of violence against others

crimes against property (**property crimes**)   crimes that involve theft of property belonging to others

criminal justice system   a formal response by police, courts, and prison officials to alleged violations of the law

criminal recidivism   later offenses by people previously convicted of crimes

critical sociology   the study of society that focuses on the need for social change

crude birth rate   the number of live births in a given year for every 1,000 people in a population

crude death rate   the number of deaths in a given year for every 1,000 people in a population

cult   a religious organization that is largely outside a society's cultural traditions

cultural integration   the close relationships among various elements of a cultural system

cultural lag   the fact that some cultural elements change more quickly than others, disrupting a cultural system

cultural relativism   the practice of evaluating a culture by its own standards

cultural transmission   the process by which one generation passes culture to the next

cultural universals   traits that are part of every known culture

culture   the values, beliefs, behavior, and material objects that together form a people's way of life

culture shock   personal disorientation when experiencing an unfamiliar way of life

Davis-Moore thesis   the assertion that social stratification exists in every society because it has beneficial consequences for the operation of society

democracy   a type of political system that gives power to the people as a whole

demographic transition theory   the thesis that population patterns reflect a society's level of technological development

demography the study of human population

denomination a church, independent of the state, that recognizes religious pluralism

dependency theory a model of economic and social development that explains global inequality in terms of the historical exploitation of poor nations by rich ones

descent the system by which members of a society trace kinship over generations

deterrence the attempt to discourage criminality through the use of punishment

deviance the recognized violation of cultural norms

direct-fee system a medical care system in which patients pay directly for the services of doctors and hospitals

discrimination treating various categories of people unequally

division of labor specialized economic activity

dramaturgical analysis Erving Goffman's term for the study of social interaction in terms of theatrical performance

dyad a social group with two members

dysfunction (*see* social dysfunction)

ecologically sustainable culture a way of life that meets the needs of the present generation without threatening the environmental legacy of future generations

ecology the study of the interaction of living organisms and the natural environment

economy the social institution that organizes a society's production, distribution, and consumption of goods and services

ecosystem a system composed of the interaction of all living organisms and their natural environment

education the social institution through which society provides its members with important knowledge, including basic facts, job skills, and cultural norms and values

ego Freud's term for a person's conscious efforts to balance innate pleasure-seeking drives with the demands of society

endogamy marriage between people of the same social category

environmental deficit profound and long-term harm to the natural environment caused by humanity's focus on short-term material affluence

environmental racism the pattern by which environmental hazards are greatest for poor people, especially minorities

ethnicity a shared cultural heritage

ethnocentrism the practice of judging another culture by the standards of one's own culture

ethnomethodology Harold Garfinkel's term for the study of the way people make sense of their everyday surroundings

Eurocentrism the dominance of European (especially English) cultural patterns

euthanasia assisting in the death of a person suffering from an incurable disease; also known as *mercy killing*

exogamy marriage between people of different social categories

experiment a research method for investigating cause and effect under highly controlled conditions

expressive leadership group leadership that focuses on the group's well-being

extended family a family unit that includes parents and children as well as other kin; also known as the *consanguine family*

faith belief based on conviction rather than scientific evidence

family a social institution that unites people in cooperative groups to oversee the bearing and raising of children

family unit a social group of two or more people, related by blood, marriage, or adoption, who usually live together

feminism the advocacy of social equality for men and women, in opposition to patriarchy and sexism

feminization of poverty the trend of women making up an increasing proportion of the poor

fertility the incidence of childbearing in a country's population

folkways norms for routine or casual interaction

formal operational stage Piaget's term for the level of human development at which individuals think abstractly and critically

formal organization a large secondary group organized to achieve its goals efficiently

functional illiteracy a lack of the reading and writing skills needed for everyday living

fundamentalism a conservative religious doctrine that opposes intellectualism and worldly accommodation in favor of restoring traditional, otherworldly religion

Gemeinschaft a type of social organization in which people are closely tied by kinship and tradition

gender the personal traits and social positions that members of a society attach to being female or male

gender roles (sex roles) attitudes and activities that a society links to each sex

gender stratification the unequal distribution of wealth, power, and privilege between men and women

generalized other Mead's term for widespread cultural norms and values we use as a reference in evaluating ourselves

genocide the systematic killing of one category of people by another

gerontocracy a form of social organization in which the elderly have the most wealth, power, and prestige

gerontology the study of aging and the elderly

Gesellschaft a type of social organization in which people come together only on the basis of individual self-interest

global economy expanding economic activity that crosses national borders

global perspective the study of the larger world and our society's place in it

global stratification patterns of social inequality in the world as a whole

global warming a rise in the Earth's average temperature due to an increasing concentration of carbon dioxide in the atmosphere

government a formal organization that directs the political life of a society

groupthink the tendency of group members to conform, resulting in a narrow view of some issue

hate crime a criminal act against a person or a person's property by an offender motivated by racial or other bias

health a state of complete physical, mental, and social well-being

health maintenance organization (HMO) an organization that provides comprehensive medical care to subscribers for a fixed fee

heterosexism a view that labels anyone who is not heterosexual as "queer"

heterosexuality sexual attraction to someone of the other sex

high culture cultural patterns that distinguish a society's elite

high-income countries the richest nations with the highest overall standards of living

holistic medicine an approach to health care that emphasizes prevention of illness and takes into account a person's entire physical and social environment

homogamy marriage between people with the same social characteristics

homophobia discomfort over close personal interaction with people thought to be gay, lesbian, or bisexual

homosexuality sexual attraction to someone of the same sex

horticulture the use of hand tools to raise crops

hunting and gathering the use of simple tools to hunt animals and gather vegetation for food

id Freud's term for the human being's basic drives

ideology cultural beliefs that justify particular social arrangements, including patterns of inequality

incest taboo a norm forbidding sexual relations or marriage between certain relatives

income wages or salary from work and earnings from investments

industry the production of goods using advanced sources of energy to drive large machinery

infant mortality rate the number of deaths among infants under one year of age for each 1,000 live births in a given year

in-group a social group toward which a member feels respect and commitment

institutional prejudice and discrimination bias built into the operation of society's institutions

instrumental leadership group leadership that focuses on the completion of tasks

intergenerational social mobility upward or downward social mobility of children in relation to their parents

interpretive sociology the study of society that focuses on the meanings people attach to their social world

intersection theory the investigation of the interplay of race, class, and gender, often resulting in multiple dimensions of disadvantage

intersexual people people whose bodies (including genitals) have both female and male characteristics

intragenerational social mobility a change in social position occurring during a person's lifetime

kinship a social bond based on blood, marriage, or adoption

labeling theory the assertion that deviance and conformity result not so much from what people do as from how others respond to those actions

language a system of symbols that allows people to communicate with one another

latent functions the unrecognized and unintended consequences of any social pattern

liberation theology the combining of Christian principles with political activism, often Marxist in character

life expectancy the average life span of a country's population

looking-glass self Charles Horton Cooley's term for a self-image based on how we think others see us

low-income countries nations with a low standard of living in which most people are poor

macro-level orientation a broad focus on social structures that shape society as a whole

manifest functions the recognized and intended consequences of any social pattern

marriage a legal relationship, usually involving economic cooperation as well as sexual activity and childbearing, that people expect to last

Marxist political-economy model an analysis that explains politics in terms of the operation of a society's economic system

mass media the means for delivering impersonal communications to a vast audience

mass society a society in which prosperity and bureaucracy have weakened traditional social ties

master status a status that has special importance for social identity, often shaping a person's entire life

matriarchy a form of social organization in which females dominate males

measurement a procedure for determining the value of a variable in a specific case

medicalization of deviance the transformation of moral and legal deviance into a medical condition

medicine the social institution that focuses on fighting disease and improving health

megalopolis a vast urban region containing a number of cities and their surrounding suburbs

meritocracy social stratification based on personal merit

metropolis a large city that socially and economically dominates an urban area

micro-level orientation a close-up focus on social interaction in specific situations

middle-income countries nations with a standard of living about average for the world as a whole

migration the movement of people into and out of a specified territory

military-industrial complex the close association of the federal government, the military, and defense industries

minority any category of people distinguished by physical or cultural difference that a society sets apart and subordinates

miscegenation biological reproduction by partners of different racial categories

modernity social patterns resulting from industrialization

modernization the process of social change begun by industrialization

modernization theory a model of economic and social development that explains global inequality in terms of technological and cultural differences between nations

monarchy a type of political system in which a single family rules from generation to generation

monogamy marriage that unites two partners

monopoly the domination of a market by a single producer

mores norms that are widely observed and have great moral significance

mortality the incidence of death in a country's population

multiculturalism an educational program recognizing the cultural diversity of the United States and promoting the equality of all cultural traditions

multinational corporation a large business that operates in many countries

natural environment the Earth's surface and atmosphere, including living organisms, air, water, soil, and other resources necessary to sustain life

neocolonialism a new form of global power relationships that involves not direct political control but economic exploitation by multinational corporations

network a web of weak social ties

nonverbal communication communication using body movements, gestures, and facial expressions rather than speech

norms rules and expectations by which a society guides the behavior of its members

nuclear family a family unit composed of one or two parents and their children; also known as the *conjugal family*

oligarchy the rule of the many by the few

oligopoly the domination of a market by a few producers

organizational environment factors outside an organization that affect its operation

organized crime a business supplying illegal goods or services

other-directedness openness to the latest trends and fashions, often expressed by imitating others

out-group a social group toward which a person feels a sense of competition or opposition

paradigm (see theoretical approach)

participant observation a research method in which investigators systematically observe people while joining them in their routine activities

pastoralism the domestication of animals

patriarchy a form of social organization in which males dominate females

peer group a social group whose members have interests, social position, and age in common

personality a person's fairly consistent patterns of acting, thinking, and feeling

personal space the surrounding area over which a person makes some claim to privacy

plea bargaining a legal negotiation in which a prosecutor reduces a charge in exchange for a defendant's guilty plea

pluralism a state in which people of all races and ethnicities are distinct but have equal social standing

pluralist model an analysis of politics that sees power as spread among many competing interest groups

political revolution the overthrow of one political system in order to establish another

politics the social institution that distributes power, sets a society's goals, and makes decisions

polygamy marriage that unites three or more people

popular culture cultural patterns that are widespread among a society's population

pornography sexually explicit material intended to cause sexual arousal

positivism a way of understanding based on science

postindustrial economy a productive system based on service work and high technology

postmodernity social patterns characteristic of postindustrial societies

power the ability to achieve desired ends despite resistance from others

power-elite model an analysis of politics that sees power as concentrated among the rich

prejudice a rigid and unfair generalization about an entire category of people

preoperational stage Piaget's term for the level of human development at which individuals first use language and other symbols

presentation of self Erving Goffman's term for a person's efforts to create specific impressions in the minds of others

primary group a small social group whose members share personal and lasting relationships

primary sector the part of the economy that draws raw materials from the natural environment

primary sex characteristics the genitals, organs used for reproduction

profane an ordinary element of everyday life

profession a prestigious, white-collar occupation that requires extensive formal education

proletarians people who sell their productive labor for wages

prostitution the selling of sexual services

queer theory a growing body of research findings that challenges the heterosexual bias in U.S. society

race a socially constructed category composed of people who share biologically transmitted traits that members of a society consider important

racism the belief that one racial category is innately superior or inferior to another

rain forests regions of dense forestation, most of which circle the globe close to the equator

rationality a way of thinking that emphasizes deliberate, matter-of-fact calculation of the most efficient means to accomplish a particular task

rationalization of society Weber's term for the historical change from tradition to rationality as the dominant mode of human thought

reference group a social group that serves as a point of reference in making evaluations and decisions

rehabilitation a program for reforming the offender to prevent later offenses

relative deprivation a perceived disadvantage arising from a specific comparison

relative poverty the deprivation of some people in relation to those who have more

reliability consistency in measurement

religion a social institution involving beliefs and practices based on a conception of the sacred

religiosity the importance of religion in a person's life

research method a systematic plan for doing research

resocialization radically changing an inmate's personality by carefully controlling the environment

retribution an act of moral vengeance by which society makes the offender suffer as much as the suffering caused by the crime

role behavior expected of someone who holds a particular status

role conflict conflict among the roles corresponding to two or more statuses

role set a number of roles attached to a single status

role strain tension among the roles connected to a single status

routinization of charisma the transformation of charismatic authority into some combination of traditional and bureaucratic authority

sacred set apart as extraordinary, inspiring awe and reverence

Sapir-Whorf thesis the idea that people perceive the world through the cultural lens of language

scapegoat a person or category of people, typically with little power, whom people unfairly blame for their own troubles

schooling formal instruction under the direction of specially trained teachers

science a logical system that bases knowledge on direct, systematic observation

scientific management Frederick Taylor's term for the application of scientific principles to the operation of a business or other large organization

secondary group a large and impersonal social group whose members pursue a specific goal or activity

secondary sector the part of the economy that transforms raw materials into manufactured goods

secondary sex characteristics bodily development, apart from the genitals, that distinguishes biologically mature females and males

sect a type of religious organization that stands apart from the larger society

secularization the historical decline in the importance of the supernatural and the sacred

segregation the physical and social separation of categories of people

self George Herbert Mead's term for the part of an individual's personality composed of self-awareness and self-image

sensorimotor stage Piaget's term for the level of human development at which individuals experience the world only through their senses

sex the biological distinction between females and males

sexism the belief that one sex is innately superior to the other

sex ratio the number of males for every 100 females in a nation's population

sexual harassment comments, gestures, or physical contact of a sexual nature that are deliberate, repeated, and unwelcome

sexual orientation a person's romantic and emotional attraction to another person

sick role patterns of behavior defined as appropriate for people who are ill

significant others people—such as parents—who have special importance for socialization

social change the transformation of culture and social institutions over time

social character personality patterns common to members of a particular society

social-conflict approach a framework for building theory that sees society as an arena of inequality that generates conflict and change

social construction of reality the process by which people creatively shape reality through social interaction

social control attempts by society to regulate people's thoughts and behavior

social dysfunction any social pattern that may disrupt the operation of society

social epidemiology the study of how health and disease are distributed throughout a society's population

social functions the consequences of any social pattern for the operation of society as a whole

social group two or more people who identify and interact with one another

social institution a major sphere of social life, or societal subsystem, organized to meet human needs

social interaction the process by which people act and react in relation to others

socialism an economic system in which natural resources and the means of producing goods and services are collectively owned

socialization the lifelong social experience by which individuals develop their human potential and learn culture

socialized medicine a medical care system in which the government owns and operates most medical facilities and employs most doctors

social mobility a change in position within the social hierarchy

social movement an organized activity that encourages or discourages social change

social stratification a system by which a society ranks categories of people in a hierarchy

social structure any relatively stable pattern of social behavior

societal protection rendering an offender incapable of further offenses temporarily through imprisonment or permanently by execution

society people who interact in a defined territory and share a culture

sociobiology a theoretical approach that explores ways in which human biology affects how we create culture

socioeconomic status (SES) a composite ranking based on various dimensions of social inequality

sociology the systematic study of human society

state capitalism an economic and political system in which companies are privately owned but cooperate closely with the government

state church a church formally allied with the state

status a social position that a person holds

status consistency the degree of consistency in a person's social standing across various dimensions of social inequality

status set all the statuses a person holds at a given time

stereotype an exaggerated description applied to every person in some category

stigma a powerfully negative label that greatly changes a person's self-concept and social identity

structural-functional approach a framework for building theory that sees society as a complex system whose parts work together to promote solidarity and stability

structural social mobility a shift in the social position of large numbers of people due more to changes in society than to individual efforts

subculture cultural patterns that set apart some segment of a society's population

suburbs urban areas beyond the political boundaries of a city

superego Freud's term for the cultural values and norms internalized by an individual

survey a research method in which subjects respond to a series of statements or questions in a questionnaire or an interview

symbol anything that carries a particular meaning recognized by people who share a culture

symbolic-interaction approach a framework for building theory that sees society as the product of the everyday interactions of individuals

technology knowledge that people use to make a way of life in their surroundings

terrorism acts of violence or the threat of such violence used as a political strategy by an individual or a group

tertiary sector the part of the economy that involves services rather than goods

theoretical approach a basic image of society that guides thinking and research

theory a statement of how and why specific facts are related

Thomas theorem W. I. Thomas's statement that situations defined as real are real in their consequences

total institution a setting in which people are isolated from the rest of society and manipulated by an administrative staff

totalitarianism a highly centralized political system that extensively regulates people's lives

totem an object in the natural world collectively defined as sacred

tracking assigning students to different types of educational programs

tradition values and beliefs passed from generation to generation

tradition-directedness rigid conformity to time-honored ways of living

transsexuals people who feel they are one sex even though biologically they are the other

triad a social group with three members

urban ecology the study of the link between the physical and social dimensions of cities

urbanization the concentration of humanity into cities

validity actually measuring exactly what you intend to measure

values culturally defined standards that people use to assess desirability, goodness, and beauty and that serve as broad guidelines for social living

variable a concept whose value changes from case to case

victimless crimes (crimes without complaint) violations of law in which there are no obvious victims

war organized, armed conflict among the people of various nations, directed by their governments

wealth the total value of money and other assets, minus outstanding debts

welfare capitalism an economic and political system that combines a mostly market-based economy with extensive social welfare programs

welfare state government agencies and programs that provide benefits to the population

white-collar crime crime committed by people of high social position in the course of their occupations

white-collar occupations higher-prestige jobs that involve mostly mental activity

zero population growth the level of reproduction that maintains population at a steady state

REFERENCES

ABERLE, DAVID F. *The Peyote Religion among the Navaho.* Chicago: Aldine, 1966.

ADLER, JERRY. "When Harry Called Sally . . ." *Newsweek* (October 1, 1990):74.

ADORNO, THEODOR W., et al. *The Authoritarian Personality.* New York: Harper, 1950.

AIZCORBE, ANA M., ARTHUR B. KENNICKELL, and KEVIN B. MOORE. "Recent Changes in U.S. Family Finances: Evidence from the 1998 and 2001 Survey of Consumer Finances." *Federal Reserve Bulletin.* Vol. 89, No. 1 (January 2003):1–32. [Online] Available September 25, 2003, at http://www.federalreserve.gov/pubs/bulletin/2003/0103lead.pdf

AKERS, RONALD L., MARVIN D. KROHN, LONN LANZA-KADUCE, and MARCIA RADOSEVICH. "Social Learning and Deviant Behavior." *American Sociological Review.* Vol. 44, No. 4 (August 1979):636–55.

ALAN GUTTMACHER INSTITUTE. "Can More Progress Be Made? Teenage Sexual and Reproductive Behavior in Developed Countries." 2001. [Online] Available August 14, 2002, at http://www.agi-usa.org/pubs/euroteens_summ.pdf

———. "Teen Pregnancy: Trends and Lessons Learned." Issues in Brief. 2002 Series, No. 1. 2002. [Online] Available September 28, 2004, at http://www.agi-usa.org/pubs/ib_1-02.pdf

———. "U.S. Teenage Pregnancy Statistics: Overall Trends, Trends by Race and Ethnicity and State-by-State Information." Updated February 19, 2004. [Online] Available September 28, 2004, at http://www.agi-usa.org/pubs/state_pregnancy_trends.pdf

ALBON, JOAN. "Retention of Cultural Values and Differential Urban Adaptation: Samoans and American Indians in a West Coast City." *Social Forces.* Vol. 49, No. 3 (March 1971):385–93.

ALFORD, RICHARD. "The Structure of Human Experience: Expectancy and Affect: The Case of Humor." Unpublished paper, Department of Sociology, University of Wyoming, 1979.

ALLAN, EMILIE ANDERSEN, and DARRELL J. STEFFENSMEIER. "Youth, Underemployment, and Property Crime: Differential Effects of Job Availability and Job Quality on Juvenile and Young Adult Arrest Rates." *American Sociological Review.* Vol. 54, No. 1 (February 1989):107–23.

ALLEN, THOMAS B., and CHARLES O. HYMAN. *We Americans: Celebrating a Nation, Its People, and Its Past.* Washington, D.C.: National Geographic, 1999.

ALLEN, WALTER R. "African American Family Life in Social Context: Crisis and Hope." *Sociological Forum.* Vol. 10, No. 4 (December 1995):569–92.

ALTER, JONATHAN. "Down to Business." *Newsweek* (May 12, 1997): 58–60.

ALTONJI, JOSEPH G., ULRICH DORASZELSKI, and LEWIS SEGAL. "Black/White Differences in Wealth." *Economic Perspectives.* Vol. 24, No. 1 (First Quarter 2000):38–50.

ALVERSON, HOYT. *Mind in the Heart of Darkness.* New Haven, Conn.: Yale University Press, 1978.

AMATO, PAUL R. "What Children Learn from Divorce." *Population Today.* Vol. 29, No. 1 (January 2001):1, 4.

AMERICAN BAR ASSOCIATION. "First-Year Enrollment in ABA-Approved Law Schools, 1947–2002 (Percentage of Women)." [Online] Available October 6, 2004, at http://www.abanet.org/legaled/statistics/femstats.html

American Demographics. Zandi Group survey. Vol. 20 (March 3, 1998):38.

———. (April 2002):6.

AMERICAN PSYCHOLOGICAL ASSOCIATION. *Violence and Youth: Psychology's Response.* Washington, D.C.: American Psychological Association, 1993.

AMERICAN SOCIOLOGICAL ASSOCIATION. "Code of Ethics." Washington, D.C.: American Sociological Association, 1997.

"Americans and Homosexual Civil Unions." *Society.* Vol. 40, No. 1 (December 2002):2.

AMNESTY INTERNATIONAL. "Website against the Death Penalty." [Online] Available August 27, 2003, at http://web.amnesty.org/pages/deathpenalty-countries-eng

———. "Abolitionist and Retentionist Countries." [Online] Available June 26, 2004, at http://web.amnesty.org/web/web.nsf/print/deathpenalty-countries-eng

ANDERSON, ELIJAH. "The Code of the Streets." *Atlantic Monthly.* Vol. 273 (May 1994):81–94.

———. "The Ideologically Driven Critique." *American Journal of Sociology.* Vol. 197, No. 6 (May 2002):1533–50.

ANDERSON, JOHN WARD. "Early to Wed: The Child Brides of India." *Washington Post* (May 24, 1995):A27, A30.

ANNAN, KOFI. "Astonishing Facts." *New York Times* (September 27, 1998):16.

ARIAS, ELIZABETH. "United States Life Tables, 2001." *National Vital Statistics Report.* Vol. 52, No. 14 (February 18, 2004). Hyattsville, Md.: National Center for Health Statistics, 2004.

ARIAS, ELIZABETH, ROBERT N. ANDERSON, HSIANG-CHING KUNG, SHERRY L. MURPHY, and KENNETH D. KOCHANEK. "Deaths: Final Data for 2001." *National Vital Statistics Reports.* Vol. 52, No. 3. Hyattsville, Md.: National Center for Health Statistics, 2003.

ARIÈS, PHILIPPE. *Centuries of Childhood: A Social History of Family Life.* New York: Vintage Books, 1965.

———. *Western Attitudes toward Death: From the Middle Ages to the Present.* Baltimore: Johns Hopkins University Press, 1974.

ARMSTRONG, ELISABETH. *The Retreat from Organization: U.S. Feminism Reconceptualized.* Albany: State University of New York Press, 2002.

ARNETTE, JUNE L., and MARJORIE C. WALSLEBEN. "Combating Fear and Restoring Safety in Schools." *Juvenile Justice Bulletin* (April 1998).

ARONOWITZ, STANLEY. *The Politics of Identity: Class, Culture, and Social Movements.* New York: Routledge, 1992.

ASANTE, MOLEFI KETE. *Afrocentricity.* Trenton, N.J.: Africa World Press, 1988.

ASCH, SOLOMON. *Social Psychology.* Englewood Cliffs, N.J.: Prentice Hall, 1952.

ASHFORD, LORI S. "New Perspectives on Population: Lessons from Cairo." *Population Bulletin.* Vol. 50, No. 1 (March 1995).

———. "Young Women in Sub-Saharan Africa Face a High Risk of HIV Infection." *Population Today.* Vol. 30, No. 2 (February/March 2002):3, 6.

ASTIN, ALEXANDER W., LETICIA OSEGUERA, LINDA J. SAX, and WILLIAM S. KORN. *The American Freshman: Thirty-Five-Year Trends.* Los Angeles: University of California Higher Education Research Institute, 2002.

AUSTER, CAROL J., and MINDY MACRONE. "The Classroom as a Negotiated Social Setting: An Empirical Study of the Effects of Faculty Members' Behavior on Students' Participation." *Teaching Sociology.* Vol. 22, No. 4 (October 1994):289–300.

AXINN, WILLIAM G., and JENNIFER S. BARBER. "Mass Education and Fertility Transition." *American Sociological Review.* Vol. 66, No. 4 (August 2001):481–505.

BACKMAN, CARL B., and MURRAY C. ADAMS. "Self-Perceived Physical Attractiveness, Self-Esteem, Race, and Gender." *Sociological Focus.* Vol. 24, No. 4 (October 1991):283–90.

BAKER, MARY ANNE, et al. *Women Today: A Multidisciplinary Approach to Women's Studies.* Monterey, Calif.: Brooks/Cole, 1980.

BAKER, PATRICIA S., WILLIAM C. YOELS, JEFFREY M. CLAIR, and RICHARD M. ALLMAN. "Laughter in the Triadic Geriatric Encounters: A Transcript-Based Analysis." In REBECCA J. ERIKSON and BEVERLY CUTHBERTSON-JOHNSON, eds., *Social Perspectives on Emotion.* Vol. 4. Greenwich, Conn.: JAI Press, 1997:179–207.

BAKER, ROSS. "Business as Usual." *American Demographics.* Vol. 19, No. 4 (April 1997):28.

BALTZELL, E. DIGBY. *The Protestant Establishment: Aristocracy and Caste in America.* New York: Vintage Books, 1964.

———. "The Protestant Establishment Revisited." *American Scholar.* Vol. 45, No. 4 (Autumn 1976):499–518.

———. *Philadelphia Gentlemen: The Making of a National Upper Class.* Philadelphia: University of Pennsylvania Press, 1979a; orig. 1958.

———. *Puritan Boston and Quaker Philadelphia.* New York: Free Press, 1979b.

———. "The WASP's Last Gasp." *Philadelphia Magazine* (September 1988):104–07, 184–88.

———. *Sporting Gentlemen: From the Age of Honor to the Cult of the Superstar.* New York: Free Press, 1995.

BANFIELD, EDWARD C. *The Unheavenly City Revisited.* Boston: Little, Brown, 1974.

BARASH, DAVID P. *The Whisperings Within.* New York: Penguin Books, 1981.

BARNES, JULIAN E. "Wanted: Readers." *U.S. News & World Report* (September 9, 2002a):44–45.

———. "War Profiteering." *U.S. News & World Report* (May 13, 2002b):20–24.

———. "Unequal Education." *U.S. News & World Report* (March 22, 2004):66–75.

BARON, JAMES N., MICHAEL T. HANNAN, and M. DIANE BURTON. "Building the Iron Cage: Determinants of Managerial Intensity in the Early Years of Organizations." *American Sociological Review.* Vol. 64, No. 4 (August 1999):527–47.

BARONE, MICHAEL. "Lessons of History." *U.S. News & World Report* (May 20, 2002):24.

BARR, ROBERT. "Archbishop of Canterbury Is Enthroned." [Online] Available February 27, 2003, at http://news.yahoo.com

BARTLETT, DONALD L., and JAMES B. STEELE. "Corporate Welfare." *Time* (November 9, 1998):36–54.

———. "How the Little Guy Gets Crunched." *Time* (February 7, 2000):38–41.

———. "Wheel of Misfortune." *Time* (December 16, 2002):44–58.

BASSUK, ELLEN J. "The Homelessness Problem." *Scientific American.* Vol. 251, No. 1 (July 1984):40–45.

BAUER, P. T. *Equality, the Third World, and Economic Delusion.* Cambridge, Mass.: Harvard University Press, 1981.

BAYDAR, NAZLI, and JEANNE BROOKS-GUNN. "Effect of Maternal Employment and Child-Care Arrangements on Preschoolers' Cognitive and Behavioral Outcomes:

Evidence from Children from the National Longitudinal Survey of Youth." *Developmental Psychology.* Vol. 27 (1991):932–35.

BEARAK, BARRY. "Lives Held Cheap in Bangladesh Sweatshops." *New York Times* (April 15, 2001):A1, A12.

BECKER, ANNE E. "The Association of Television Exposure with Disordered Eating Among Ethnic Fijian Adolescent Girls." Paper presented at the annual meeting of the American Psychiatric Association, Washington, D.C., May 19, 1999.

BECKER, HOWARD S. *Outside: Studies in the Sociology of Deviance.* New York: Free Press, 1966.

BEDARD, PAUL. "Washington Whispers." *U.S. News & World Report* (March 25, 2002):2.

BEEGHLEY, LEONARD. *The Structure of Social Stratification in the United States.* Needham Heights, Mass.: Allyn & Bacon, 1989.

BEGLEY, SHARON. "Gray Matters." *Newsweek* (March 7, 1995):48–54.

———. "How to Beat the Heat." *Newsweek* (December 8, 1997):34–38.

BELLAH, ROBERT N. *The Broken Covenant.* New York: Seabury Press, 1975.

BELLAH, ROBERT N., RICHARD MADSEN, WILLIAM M. SULLIVAN, ANN SWIDLER, and STEVEN M. TIPTON. *Habits of the Heart: Individualism and Commitment in American Life.* New York: Harper & Row, 1985.

BELLUCK, PAM. "Black Youths' Rate of Suicide Rising Sharply." *New York Times* (March 20, 1998):A1, A18.

BEM, SANDRA LIPSITZ. *The Lenses of Gender: Transforming the Debate on Sexual Inequality.* New Haven, Conn.: Yale University Press, 1993.

BENEDICT, RUTH. "Continuities and Discontinuities in Cultural Conditioning." *Psychiatry.* Vol. 1 (May 1938):161–67.

BENJAMIN, LOIS. *The Black Elite: Facing the Color Line in the Twilight of the Twentieth Century.* Chicago: Nelson-Hall, 1991.

BENJAMIN, MATTHEW. "Suite Deals." *U.S. News & World Report* (April 29, 2002):32–34.

BENNETT, WILLIAM J. "School Reform: What Remains to Be Done." *Wall Street Journal* (September 2, 1997):A18.

BENOKRAITIS, NIJOLE, and JOE FEAGIN. *Modern Sexism: Blatant, Subtle, and Overt Discrimination.* 2d ed. Upper Saddle River, N.J.: Prentice Hall, 1995.

BENSON, MICHAEL L., and FRANCIS T. CULLEN. *Combating Corporate Crime.* Boston: Northeastern University Press, 1998.

BERGAMO, MONICA, and GERSON CAMAROTTI. "Brazil's Landless Millions." *World Press Review.* Vol. 43, No. 7 (July 1996):46–47.

BERGER, PETER L. *Invitation to Sociology.* New York: Anchor Books, 1963.

———. *The Sacred Canopy: Elements of a Sociological Theory of Religion.* Garden City, N.Y.: Doubleday, 1967.

———. *Facing Up to Modernity: Excursions in Society, Politics, and Religion.* New York: Basic Books, 1977.

———. *The Capitalist Revolution: Fifty Propositions about Prosperity, Equality, and Liberty.* New York: Basic Books, 1986.

———. "Sociology: A Disinvitation?" *Society.* Vol. 30, No. 1 (November/December 1992):12–18.

BERGER, PETER L., BRIGITTE BERGER, and HANSFRIED KELLNER. *The Homeless Mind: Modernization and Consciousness.* New York: Vintage Books, 1974.

BERGESEN, ALBERT, ed. *Crises in the World-System.* Beverly Hills, Calif.: Sage, 1983.

BERNARD, JESSIE. *The Female World.* New York: Free Press, 1981.

———. *The Future of Marriage.* New Haven, Conn.: Yale University Press, 1982, orig. 1973.

BERNSTEIN, NINA. "On Frontier of Cyberspace, Data Is Money, and a Threat." *New York Times* (June 12, 1997):A1, B14–15.

BERRILL, KEVIN T. "Anti-Gay Violence and Victimization in the United States: An Overview." In GREGORY M. HEREK and KEVIN T. BERRILL, eds., *Hate Crimes: Confronting Violence against Lesbians and Gay Men.* Newbury Park, Calif.: Sage, 1992:19–45.

BERRY, BRIAN L., and PHILIP H. REES. "The Factorial Ecology of Calcutta." *American Journal of Sociology.* Vol. 74, No. 5 (March 1969):445–91.

BESHAROV, DOUGLAS J., and LISA A. LAUMANN. "Child Abuse Reporting." *Society.* Vol. 34, No. 4 (May/June 1996):40–46.

BEST, RAPHAELA. *We've All Got Scars: What Boys and Girls Learn in Elementary School.* Bloomington: Indiana University Press, 1983.

BEUTEL, ANN M., and MARGARET MOONEY MARINI. "Gender and Values." *American Sociological Review.* Vol. 60 (June 1995):436–48.

BIAN, YANJIE. "Chinese Social Stratification and Social Mobility." *Annual Review of Sociology.* Vol. 28 (2002):91–116.

BIANCHI, SUZANNE M., and LYNNE M. CASPER. "American Families." *Population Bulletin.* Vol. 55, No. 4 (December 2000).

BIANCHI, SUZANNE M., and DAPHNE SPAIN. "Women, Work, and Family in America." *Population Bulletin.* Vol. 51, No. 3 (December 1996).

BLACKWOOD, EVELYN, and SASKIA WIERINGA, eds. *Female Desires: Same-Sex Relations and Transgender Practices across Cultures.* New York: Columbia University Press, 1999.

BLANKENHORN, DAVID. *Fatherless America: Confronting Our Most Urgent Social Problem.* New York: HarperCollins, 1995.

BLAU, JUDITH R., and PETER M. BLAU. "The Cost of Inequality: Metropolitan Structure and Violent Crime." *American Sociological Review.* Vol. 47, No. 1 (February 1982):114–29.

BLAU, PETER M. *Exchange and Power in Social Life.* New York: Wiley, 1964.

———. *Inequality and Heterogeneity: A Primitive Theory of Social Structure.* New York: Free Press, 1977.

BLAU, PETER M., TERRY C. BLUM, and JOSEPH E. SCHWARTZ. "Heterogeneity and Intermarriage." *American Sociological Review.* Vol. 47, No. 1 (February 1982):45–62.

BLAU, PETER M., and OTIS DUDLEY DUNCAN. *The American Occupational Structure.* New York: Wiley, 1967.

BLAUSTEIN, ALBERT P., and ROBERT L. ZANGRANDO. *Civil Rights and the Black American.* New York: Washington Square Press, 1968.

BLUMBERG, PAUL. *Inequality in an Age of Decline.* New York: Oxford University Press, 1981.

BLUMER, HERBERT G. "Collective Behavior." In ALFRED MCCLUNG LEE, ed., *Principles of Sociology.* 3d ed. New York: Barnes & Noble Books, 1969:65–121.

BLUMSTEIN, PHILIP, and PEPPER SCHWARTZ. *American Couples.* New York: Morrow, 1983.

BOBO, LAWRENCE D., and VINCENT L. HUTCHINGS. "Perceptions of Racial Group Competition: Extending Blumer's Theory of Group Position to a Multiracial Social Context." *American Sociological Review.* Vol. 61, No. 6 (December 1996):951–72.

BOERNER, CHRISTOPHER, and THOMAS LAMBERT. "Environmental Injustice." *Public Interest* (Winter 1995):61–82.

BOGARDUS, EMORY S. "Social Distance and Its Origins." *Sociology and Social Research.* Vol. 9 (July/August 1925):216–25.

———. *A Forty-Year Racial Distance Study.* Los Angeles: University of Southern California Press, 1967.

BOHANNAN, CECIL. "The Economic Correlates of Homelessness in Sixty Cities." *Social Science Quarterly.* Vol. 72, No. 4 (December 1991):817–25.

BOHLEN, CELESTINE. "Facing Oblivion, Rust-Belt Giants Top Russian List of Vexing Crises." *New York Times* (November 8, 1998):1, 6.

BOHON, STEPHANIE A., and CRAIG R. HUMPHREY. "Courting LULUs: Characteristic of Suitor and Objector Communities." *Rural Sociology.* Vol. 65, No. 3 (September 2000):376–95.

BONNER, JANE. Research presented in *The Two Brains.* Public Broadcasting System telecast, 1984.

BOOTH, ALAN, and JAMES DABBS. "Male Hormone is Linked to Marital Problems." *Wall Street Journal* (August 19, 1992):B1.

BOOTH, WILLIAM. "By the Sweat of Their Brows: A New Economy." *Washington Post* (July 13, 1998):A1, A10–A11.

BORMANN, F. HERBERT. "The Global Environmental Deficit." *BioScience.* Vol. 40 (1990):74.

BOSWELL, TERRY E. "A Split Labor Market Analysis of Discrimination against Chinese Immigrants, 1850–1882." *American Sociological Review.* Vol. 51, No. 3 (June 1986):352–71.

BOSWELL, TERRY E., and WILLIAM J. DIXON. "Marx's Theory of Rebellion: A Cross-National Analysis of Class Exploitation, Economic Development, and Violent Revolt." *American Sociological Review.* Vol. 58, No. 5 (October 1993):681–702.

BOTT, ELIZABETH. *Family and Social Network.* New York: Free Press, 1971, orig. 1957.

BOWEN, WILLIAM G., and DEREK K. BOK. *The Shape of the River: Long-Term Consequences of Considering Race in College and University Admissions.* Princeton, N.J.: Princeton University Press, 1999.

BOWLES, SAMUEL, and HERBERT GINTIS. *Schooling in Capitalist America: Educational Reform and the Contradictions of Economic Life.* New York: Basic Books, 1976.

BOYER, DEBRA. "Male Prostitution and Homosexual Identity." *Journal of Homosexuality.* Vol. 17, Nos. 1–2 (Fall/Winter 1989):151–84.

BOYLE, ELIZABETH HEGER, FORTUNATA SONGORA, and GAIL FOSS. "International Discourse and Local Politics: Anti-Female-Genital-Cutting Laws in Egypt, Tanzania, and the United States." *Social Problems.* Vol. 48, No. 4 (November 2001):524–44.

BOZA, TANYA GOLASH. "Proposed American Sociological Association Statement on Race." [Online] Available October 24, 2002, at http://www.unc.edu/~tatiana

BRAITHWAITE, JOHN. "The Myth of Social Class and Criminality Reconsidered." *American Sociological Review.* Vol. 46, No. 1 (February 1981):36–57.

BRECHIN, STEVEN R., and WILLETT KEMPTON. "Global Environmentalism: A Challenge to the Postmaterialism Thesis." *Social Science Quarterly*. Vol. 75, No. 2 (June 1994):245–69.

BRIANS, CRAIG LEONARD, and BERNARD GROFMAN. "Election Day Registration's Effect on U.S. Voter Turnout." *Social Science Quarterly*. Vol. 82, No. 1 (March 2001):170–83.

BRIGGS, TRACEY WONG. "Two Years, Changed Lives." *USA Today* (April 22, 2002):D1–D2.

BRINES, JULIE, and KARA JOYNER. "The Ties That Bind: Principles of Cohesion in Cohabitation and Marriage." *American Sociological Review*. Vol. 64, No. 3 (June 1999):333–55.

BRINK, SUSAN. "Living on the Edge." *U.S. News & World Report* (October 14, 2002):58–64.

BRINTON, MARY C. "The Social-Institutional Bases of Gender Stratification: Japan as an Illustrative Case." *American Journal of Sociology*. Vol. 94, No. 2 (September 1988):300–34.

BROCKERHOFF, MARTIN P. "An Urbanizing World." *Population Bulletin*. Vol. 55, No. 3 (September 2000).

BRODER, DAVID S. "Stock Options Belong in the Line of Fire." *Columbus Dispatch* (April 21, 2002):G3.

BRODKIN, KAREN. "How Jews Became White Folks." In PAULA S. ROTHENBERG, ed., *White Privilege*. New York: Worth, 2001.

BROOKS, DAVID. *Bobos in Paradise: The New Upper Class and How They Got There*. New York: Simon & Schuster, 2000.

BROWN, LESTER R. "Reassessing the Earth's Population." *Society*. Vol. 32, No. 4 (May/June 1995):7–10.

BROWN, LESTER R., et al., eds. *State of the World, 1993: A Worldwatch Institute Report on Progress toward a Sustainable Society*. New York: Norton, 1993.

BROWNING, CHRISTOPHER R., and EDWARD O. LAUMANN. "Sexual Contact between Children and Adults: A Life Course Perspective." *American Sociological Review*. Vol. 62, No. 5 (August 1997):540–60.

BUECHLER, STEVEN M. *Social Movements in Advanced Capitalism: The Political Economy and Cultural Construction of Social Activism*. New York: Oxford University Press, 2000.

Bulletin of the Atomic Scientists. "Current Time." November 4, 2002. [Online] Available November 4, 2004, at http://www.thebulletin.org

BURAWAY, MICHAEL. "Review Essay: The Soviet Descent into Capitalism." *American Journal of Sociology*. Vol. 102, No. 5 (March 1997):1430–44.

BURCH, ROBERT. Testimony to House of Representatives Hearing in "Review: The World Hunger Problem." October 25, 1983, Serial 98-38.

BURKETT, ELINOR. "God Created Me to Be a Slave." *New York Times Sunday Magazine* (October 12, 1997):56–60.

CABLE NEWS NETWORK. 2004. [Online] Available Sept. 27, 2004 at www.cnn.com/SPECIALS/2003/iraq/forces/casualties.

CAMARA, EVANDRO. Personal communication, 2000.

CAMERON, WILLIAM BRUCE. *Modern Social Movements: A Sociological Outline*. New York: Random House, 1966.

CAMPO-FLORES, ARIAN. "'Macho' or 'Sweetness'?" *Newsweek* (July 1, 2002).

CAPEK, STELLA A. "The 'Environmental Justice' Frame: A Conceptual Discussion and an Application." *Social Problems*. Vol. 40, No. 1 (February 1993):5–24.

CAPLOW, THEODORE, HOWARD M. BAHR, JOHN MODELL, and BRUCE A. CHADWICK. *Recent Social Trends in the United States, 1960–1990*. Montreal: McGill-Queen's University Press, 1991.

CARLEY, KATHLEEN. "A Theory of Group Stability." *American Sociological Review*. Vol. 56, No. 3 (June 1991):331–54.

CARLSON, NORMAN A. "Corrections in the United States Today: A Balance Has Been Struck." *American Criminal Law Review*. Vol. 13, No. 4 (Spring 1976):615–47.

CARMICHAEL, STOKELY, and CHARLES V. HAMILTON. *Black Power: The Politics of Liberation in America*. New York: Vintage Books, 1967.

CARROLL, JAMES R. "Congress Is Told of Coal-Dust Fraud; Senator from Minnesota Rebukes Industry." *Louisville Courier Journal* (May 27, 1999):1A.

CARSON, RACHEL. *Silent Spring*. Boston: Houghton Mifflin, 1962.

CARUSO, DAVID B. "42 Philadelphia Schools Privatized." [Online] Available April 18, 2002, at http://news.yahoo.com

CASTELLS, MANUEL. *The Urban Question*. Cambridge, Mass.: MIT Press, 1977.

———. *The City and the Grass Roots*. Berkeley: University of California Press, 1983.

CATALYST. *Women CEOs*. October 2003. [Online] Available July 25, 2004, at http://www.catalystwomen.org/press_room/factsheets/fact_women_ceos.htm

———. *2002 Catalyst Census of Women Corporate Officers and Top Earners in the Fortune 500*. [Online] Available July 25, 2004, at http://www.catalystwomen.org/press_room/factsheets/COTE%20Factsheet%202002.pdf

CBS NEWS. Report on Female Achievement in U.S. Schools. November 1, 2002.

CENTER FOR AMERICAN WOMEN AND POLITICS. EAGLETON INSTITUTE OF POLITICS, RUTGERS UNIVERSITY. "Women in State Legislatures, 2004." July 2004. [Online] Available October 6, 2004, at http://www.cawp.rutgers.edu/Facts/Officeholders/stleg.pdf

CENTER FOR RESPONSIVE POLITICS. Election Overview, 2000 Cycle: Fundraising at a Glance. [Online] Available November 1, 2002, at http://www.opensecrets.org/overview/index.asp

———. The Big Picture: 2002 Cycle: Totals by Sector. [Online] Available December 28, 2003, at http://www.opensecrets.org/bigpicture/sectors.asp?cycle=2002

———. The Big Picture: 2002 Cycle: Where the Money Came From. [Online] Available December 28, 2003, at http://www.opensecrets.org/bigpicture/sherefrom.asp?cycle=2002

CENTER ON EDUCATION POLICY AND AMERICAN YOUTH POLICY FORUM. *Do You Know . . . the Good News about American Education?* Washington, D.C.: Center on Education Policy and American Youth Policy Forum, 2000. [Online] Available on October 8, 2004, at http://www.aypf.org/publicatons/Good_News.pdf

CENTERS FOR DISEASE CONTROL AND PREVENTION. *HIV/AIDS Surveillance Report*. Vol. 14. 2002. [Online] Available November 7, 2004, at http://www.cdc.gov/hiv/stats/hasr1402.htm

———. "Trends in Cigarette Smoking among High School Students—United States, 1991–2001." *Morbidity and Mortality Weekly Report*. Vol. 51, No. 19 (May 17, 2002):409–12.

———. "Cigarette Smoking-Attributable Morbidity—United States, 2000." *Morbidity and Mortality Weekly Report*. Vol. 52, No. 35 (September 5, 2003):842–44.

———. *Sexually Transmitted Disease Surveillance, 2002*. September, 2003. [Online] Available November 6, 2004, at http://www.cdc.gov/std/stats/

———. "Cigarette Smoking among Adults—United States, 2002." *Morbidity and Mortality Weekly Report*. Vol. 53, No. 20 (May 28, 2004):427–31.

CHAGNON, NAPOLEON A. *Yąnomamö: The Fierce People*. 4th ed. Austin, Tex.: Holt, Rinehart and Winston, 1992.

CHANDLER, TERTIUS, and GERALD FOX. *3000 Years of Urban History*. New York: Academic Press, 1974.

CHANDLER, TIMOTHY D., YOSHINORI KAMO, and JAMES D. WERBEL. "Do Delays in Marriage and Childbirth Affect Earnings?" *Social Science Quarterly*. Vol. 75, No. 4 (December 1994):838–53.

CHAVES, MARK. "Ordaining Women: The Diffusion of an Organizational Innovation." *American Journal of Sociology*. Vol. 101, No. 4 (January 1996):840–73.

CHAVEZ, LINDA. "Promoting Racial Harmony." In GEORGE E. CURRY, ed., *The Affirmative Action Debate*. Reading, Mass.: Addison-Wesley, 1996.

"China Faces Water Shortage." *Popline*. Vol. 23 (December 2001):1–4.

CHIRICOS, TED, RANEE McENTIRE, and MARC GERTZ. "Perceived Racial and Ethnic Composition of Neighborhood and Perceived Risk of Crime." *Social Problems*. Vol. 48, No. 3 (August 2001):322–40.

CHOLDIN, HARVEY M. "How Sampling Will Help Defeat the Undercount." *Society*. Vol. 34, No. 3 (March/April 1997):27–30.

CHRONICLE OF HIGHER EDUCATION. 2004–5 Almanac. 2004. [Online] Available October 7, 2004, at http://chronicle.com/free/almanac/2004/index.htm

CHUA-EOAN, HOWARD. "Profiles in Outrage." *Time* (September 25, 2000):38–39.

CHURCH, GEORGE J. "Unions Arise—with New Tricks." *Time* (June 13, 1994):56–58.

———. "Ripping Up Welfare." *Time* (August 12, 1996):18–22.

CIMINO, RICHARD, and DON LATTIN. "Choosing My Religion." *American Demographics*. Vol. 21, No. 4 (April 1999):60–65.

CLARK, J. R., and DWIGHT R. LEE. "Sentencing Laffer Curves, Political Myopia, and Prison Space." *Social Science Quarterly*. Vol. 77, No. 2 (June 1996):245–72.

CLARK, KIM. "Bankrupt Lives." *U.S. News & World Report* (September 16, 2002):52–54.

CLARK, MARGARET S., ed. *Prosocial Behavior*. Newbury Park, Calif.: Sage, 1991.

CLAWSON, DAN, and MARY ANN CLAWSON. "What Has Happened to the U.S. Labor Movement? Union Decline and Renewal." *Annual Review of Sociology*. Vol. 25 (1999):95–119.

CLEMETSON, LYNETTE. "Grandma Knows Best." *Newsweek* (June 12, 2000):60–61.

CLOUD, JOHN. "What Can the Schools Do?" *Time* (May 3, 1999):38–40.

CLOUD, JOHN, and JODIE MORSE. "Home Sweet School." *Time* (August 27, 2001):46–54.

CLOWARD, RICHARD A., and LLOYD E. OHLIN. *Delinquency and Opportunity: A Theory of Delinquent Gangs*. New York: Free Press, 1966.

COAKLEY, JAY J. *Sport in Society: Issues and Controversies*. 4th ed. St. Louis, Mo.: Mosby, 1990.

COHEN, ADAM. "Test-Tube Tug-of-War." *Time* (April 6, 1998):65.

———. "A First Report Card on Vouchers." *Time* (April 26, 1999):36–38.

COHEN, ALBERT K. *Delinquent Boys: The Culture of the Gang.* New York: Free Press, 1971, orig. 1955.

COHEN, LLOYD R. "Sexual Harassment and the Law." *Society.* Vol. 28, No. 4 (May/June 1991):8–13.

COLE, GEORGE F., and CHRISTOPHER E. SMITH. *Criminal Justice in America.* 3d ed. Belmont, Calif.: Wadsworth, 2002.

COLEMAN, JAMES S. "The Design of Organizations and the Right to Act." *Sociological Forum.* Vol. 8, No. 4 (December 1993):527–46.

COLEMAN, JAMES S., et al. *Equality of Educational Opportunity.* Washington, D.C.: U.S. Government Printing Office, 1966.

COLEMAN, JAMES S., and THOMAS HOFFER. *Public and Private High Schools: The Impact of Communities.* New York: Basic Books, 1987.

COLEMAN, JAMES, THOMAS HOFFER, and SALLY KILGORE. *Public and Private Schools: An Analysis of Public Schools and Beyond.* Washington, D.C.: National Center for Education Statistics, 1981.

COLEMAN, RICHARD P., and BERNICE L. NEUGARTEN. *Social Status in the City.* San Francisco: Jossey-Bass, 1971.

COLEMAN, RICHARD P., and LEE RAINWATER. *Social Standing in America.* New York: Basic Books, 1978.

COLLEGE BOARD. 2004 College-Bound Seniors Tables and Related Items. "Table 7: SAT Score Gains—Especially in Math—for Most Racial/Ethnic Groups between 1994 and 2004." [Online] Available November 1, 2004 at http://www.collegeboard.com/prod_downloads/about/news_info/cbsenior/yr2004/links.html

COLLINS, RANDALL. *The Credential Society: A Historical Sociology of Education and Stratification.* New York: Academic Press, 1979.

COLLYMORE, YVETTE. "Migrant Street Children on the Rise in Central America." *Population Today.* Vol. 30, No. 2 (February/March 2002):1, 4.

COLTON, HELEN. *The Gift of Touch: How Physical Contact Improves Communication, Pleasure, and Health.* New York: Seaview/Putnam, 1983.

COMMISSION FOR RACIAL JUSTICE AND UNITED CHURCH OF CHRIST. *CRJ Reporter.* New York: Commission for Racial Justice and United Church of Christ, 1994.

COMTE, AUGUSTE. *Auguste Comte and Positivism: The Essential Writings.* GERTRUD LENZER, ed. New York: Harper Torchbooks, 1975, orig. 1851–54.

CONNETT, PAUL H. "The Disposable Society." In F. HERBERT BORMANN and STEPHEN R. KELLERT, eds., *Ecology, Economics, and Ethics: The Broken Circle.* New Haven, Conn.: Yale University Press, 1991:99–122.

COOK, RHODES. "House Republicans Scored a Quiet Victory in '92." *Congressional Quarterly Weekly Report.* Vol. 51, No. 16 (April 17, 1993):965–68.

COOLEY, CHARLES HORTON. *Social Organization.* New York: Schocken Books, 1962, orig. 1909.

———. *Human Nature and the Social Order.* New York: Schocken Books, 1964, orig. 1902.

COONEY, MARK. "From Warfare to Tyranny: Lethal Conflict and the State." *American Sociological Review.* Vol. 62, No. 2 (April 1997):316–38.

CORCORAN, MARY, SANDRA K. DANZIGER, ARIEL KALIL, and KRISTIN S. SEEFELDT. "How Welfare Reform Is Affecting Women's Work." *Annual Review of Sociology.* Vol. 26 (2000):241–69.

CORNELL, BARBARA. "Pulling the Plug on TV." *Time* (October 16, 2000):F16.

CORRELL, SHELLEY J. "Gender and the Career Choice Process: The Role of Biased Self-Assessment." *American Journal of Sociology.* Vol. 106, No. 6 (May 2001):1691–1730.

CORTESE, ANTHONY J. *Provocateur: Images of Women and Minorities in Advertising.* Lanham, Md.: Rowman & Littlefield, 1999.

COSE, ELLIS. "The Good News about Black America." *Newsweek* (June 7, 1999):28–40.

COSER, LEWIS. *The Functions of Social Conflict.* New York: Free Press, 1956.

COUNCIL ON FAMILIES IN AMERICA. *Marriage in America: A Report to the Nation.* New York: Institute for American Values, 1995.

COUNTS, G. S. "The Social Status of Occupations: A Problem in Vocational Guidance." *School Review.* Vol. 33, No. X (January 1925):16–27.

COURTWRIGHT, DAVID T. *Violent Land: Single Men and Social Disorder from the Frontier to the Inner City.* Cambridge, Mass.: Harvard University Press, 1996.

"Cousin Couples." [Online] Available June 21, 2004, at http://www.CousinCouples.com

COVINGTON, JEANETTE. "Racial Classification in Criminology: The Reproduction of Racialized Crime." *Sociological Forum.* Vol. 10, No. 4 (December 1995):547–68.

COWLEY, GEOFFREY. "The Prescription That Kills." *Newsweek* (July 17, 1995):54.

COX, HARVEY. "Church and Believers: Always Strangers?" In THOMAS ROBBINS and DICK ANTHONY, eds. *In Gods We Trust: New Patterns of Religious Pluralism in America.* 2d ed. New Brunswick, N.J.: Transaction, 1990:449–62.

COYOTE (Call Off Your Old Tired Ethics). [Online] Available April 2, 2000, at http://www.freedomusa.org/coyotela/what-is.html

CROOK, STEPHAN, JAN PAKULSKI, and MALCOLM WATERS. *Postmodernization: Change in Advanced Society.* Newbury Park, Calif.: Sage, 1992.

CROSSEN, CYNTHIA, and ELLEN GRAHAM. "Good News—and Bad—about America's Health." *Wall Street Journal* (June 28, 1996):R1.

CROSSETTE, BARBARA. "Female Genital Mutilation by Immigrants Is Becoming Cause for Concern in the U.S." *New York Times International* (December 10, 1995):11.

CROUSE, JAMES, and DALE TRUSHEIM. *The Case against the SAT.* Chicago: University of Chicago Press, 1988.

CULLEN, LISA TAKEUCHI. "Will Manage for Food." *Time* (October 14, 2002):52–56.

CUMMINGS, SCOTT, and THOMAS LAMBERT. "Anti-Hispanic and Anti-Asian Sentiments among African Americans." *Social Science Quarterly.* Vol. 78, No. 2 (June 1997):338–53.

CURRIE, ELLIOTT. *Confronting Crime: An American Challenge.* New York: Pantheon Books, 1985.

CURRY, ANDREW. "The Gullahs' Last Stand?" *U.S. News & World Report* (June 18, 2001):40–41.

CURTIS, JAMES E., DOUGLAS E. BAER, and EDWARD G. GRABB. "Nations of Joiners: Explaining Voluntary Association Membership in Democratic Societies." *American Sociological Review.* Vol. 66, No. 6 (December 2001):783–805.

CURTIS, JAMES E., EDWARD G. GRABB, and DOUGLAS E. BAER. "Voluntary Association Membership in Fifteen Countries: A Comparative Analysis." *American Sociological Review.* Vol. 57, No. 2 (April 1992):139–52.

CURTISS, SUSAN. *Genie: A Psycholinguistic Study of a Modern-Day "Wild Child."* New York: Academic Press, 1977.

DAHL, ROBERT A. *Who Governs?* New Haven, Conn.: Yale University Press, 1961.

———. *Dilemmas of Pluralist Democracy: Autonomy vs. Control.* New Haven, Conn.: Yale University Press, 1982.

DAHRENDORF, RALF. *Class and Class Conflict in Industrial Society.* Stanford, Calif.: Stanford University Press, 1959.

DALY, MARTIN, and MARGO WILSON. *Homicide.* New York: Aldine, 1988.

DARROCH, JACQUELINE E., JENNIFER J. FROST, SUSHEELA SINGH, and the Study Team. "Teenage Sexual and Reproductive Behavior in Developed Countries: Can More Progress Be Made?" Alan Guttmacher Institute (November 2001). [Online] Available August 14, 2002, at http://www.agi-usa

DAVIDSON, JAMES D., RALPH E. PYLE, and DAVID V. REYES. "Persistence and Change in the Protestant Establishment, 1930–1992." *Social Forces.* Vol. 74, No. 1 (September 1995):157–75.

DAVIDSON, JULIA O'CONNELL. *Prostitution, Power, and Freedom.* Ann Arbor: University of Michigan Press, 1998.

DAVIES, CHRISTIE. *Ethnic Humor around the World: A Comparative Analysis.* Bloomington: Indiana University Press, 1990.

DAVIES, JAMES C. "Toward a Theory of Revolution." *American Sociological Review.* Vol. 27, No. 1 (February 1962):5–19.

DAVIES, MARK, and DENISE B. KANDEL. "Parental and Peer Influences on Adolescents' Educational Plans: Some Further Evidence." *American Journal of Sociology.* Vol. 87, No. 2 (September 1981):363–87.

DAVIS, BYRON BRADLEY. "Sports World." *Christian Science Monitor* (September 9, 1997):11.

DAVIS, DONALD M., cited in "TV Is a Blonde, Blonde World." *American Demographics* (special issue): "Women Change Places" (1993).

DAVIS, KINGSLEY. "Extreme Social Isolation of a Child." *American Journal of Sociology.* Vol. 45, No. 4 (January 1940):554–65.

———. "Final Note on a Case of Extreme Isolation." *American Journal of Sociology.* Vol. 52, No. 5 (March 1947):432–37.

———. "The Myth of Functional Analysis as a Special Method in Sociology and Anthropology." *American Sociological Review.* Vol. 24, No. 1 (February 1959):75ff.

———. "Sexual Behavior." In ROBERT K. MERTON and ROBERT NISBET, eds., *Contemporary Social Problems.* 3d ed. New York: Harcourt Brace Jovanovich, 1971:313–60.

DAVIS, KINGSLEY, and WILBERT MOORE. "Some Principles of Stratification." *American Sociological Review.* Vol. 10, No. 2 (April 1945):242–49.

DEDRICK, DENNIS K., and RICHARD E. YINGER. "MAD, SDI, and the Nuclear Arms Race." Unpublished manuscript. Georgetown College, Georgetown, Ky., 1990.

DE FINA, ROBERT H., and THOMAS M. ARVANITES. "The Weak Effect of Imprisonment on Crime, 1971–1998." *Social Science Quarterly.* Vol. 83, No. 3 (September 2002):635–53.

DEFRANCIS, MARC. "U.S. Elder Care Is in a Fragile State." *Population Today.* Vol. 30, No. 1 (January 2002a):1–3.

———. "A Spiraling Shortage of Nurses." *Population Today.* Vol. 30, No. 2 (February/March 2002b):8–9.

DELACROIX, JACQUES, and CHARLES C. RAGIN. "Structural Blockage: A Cross-National Study of Economic Dependency, State Efficacy, and Underdevelopment." *American Journal of Sociology.* Vol. 86, No. 6 (May 1981):1311–47.

DEMERATH, N. J., III. "Who Now Debates Functionalism? From *System, Change, and Conflict* to 'Culture, Choice, and Praxis.'" *Sociological Forum.* Vol. 11, No. 2 (June 1996):333–45.

DICKINSON, AMY. "When Dating Is Dangerous." *Time* (August 27, 2001):76.

DI IULIO, JOHN J., JR. "Broken Streets, Broken Lives." *Public Interest* (Spring 2000):106–10.

DIXON, WILLIAM J., and TERRY BOSWELL. "Dependency, Disarticulation, and Denominator Effects: Another Look at Foreign Capital Penetration." *American Journal of Sociology.* Vol. 102, No. 2 (September 1996):543–62.

DOBYNS, HENRY F. "An Appraisal of Techniques with a New Hemispheric Estimate." *Current Anthropology.* Vol. 7, No. 4 (October 1966):395–446.

DOLLARD, JOHN, et al. *Frustration and Aggression.* New Haven, Conn.: Yale University Press, 1939.

DOMHOFF, G. WILLIAM. *Who Rules America Now? A View of the '80s.* Englewood Cliffs, N.J.: Prentice Hall, 1983.

DONAHUE, JOHN J., III, and STEVEN D. LEAVITT. Research cited in "New Study Claims Abortion Is Behind Decrease in Crime." *Population Today.* Vol. 28, No. 1 (January 2000):1, 4.

DONOVAN, VIRGINIA K., and RONNIE LITTENBERG. "Psychology of Women: Feminist Therapy." In BARBARA HABER, ed., *The Women's Annual, 1981: The Year in Review.* Boston: Hall, 1982:211–35.

DOYLE, JAMES A. *The Male Experience.* Dubuque, Iowa: Brown, 1983.

D'SOUZA, DINESH. "The Billionaire Next Door." *Forbes* (October 11, 1999):50–62.

DU BOIS, W. E. B. *The Philadelphia Negro: A Social Study.* New York: Schocken Books, 1967; orig. 1899.

DUBOS, RENÉ. *Man Adapting.* New Haven, Conn.: Yale University Press, 1980; orig. 1965.

DUDLEY, KATHRYN MARIE. *Debt and Dispossession: Farm Loss in America's Heartland.* Chicago: University of Chicago Press, 2000.

DUNCAN, CYNTHIA M. *Worlds Apart: Why Poverty Persists in Rural America.* New Haven, Conn.: Yale University Press, 1999.

DUNCAN, GREG J., W. JEAN YEUNG, JEANNE BROOKS-GUNN, and JUDITH R. SMITH. "How Much Does Childhood Poverty Affect the Life Chances of Children?" *American Sociological Review.* Vol. 63, No. 3 (June 1998):406–23.

DUREX GLOBAL SEX SURVEY. Reported in *Time* (October 30, 2000):31.

DURKHEIM, EMILE. *The Division of Labor in Society.* New York: Free Press, 1964a, orig. 1893.

———. *The Rules of Sociological Method.* New York: Free Press, 1964b, orig. 1895.

———. *The Elementary Forms of Religious Life.* New York: Free Press, 1965, orig. 1915.

———. *Suicide.* New York: Free Press, 1966, orig. 1897.

DWORKIN, ANDREA. *Intercourse.* New York: Free Press, 1987.

DWORKIN, RONALD W. "Where Have All the Nurses Gone?" *Public Interest.* Vol. 148 (Summer 2002):23–36.

EBAUGH, HELEN ROSE FUCHS. *Becoming an Ex: The Process of Role Exit.* Chicago: University of Chicago Press, 1988.

EBOH, CAMILLUS. "Nigerian Woman Loses Appeal against Stoning Death." [Online] Available August 19, 2002, at http://news.yahoo.com

EDIN, KATHRYN, and LAURA LEIN. "Work, Welfare, and Single Mothers' Economic Survival Strategies." *American Sociological Review.* Vol. 62, No. 2 (April 1996):253–66.

EDWARDS, TAMALA M. "Revolt of the Gentry." *Time* (June 15, 1998):34–35.

———. "Flying Solo." *Time* (August 28, 2000):47–55.

EHRENREICH, BARBARA. *The Hearts of Men: American Dreams and the Flight from Commitment.* Garden City, N.Y.: Anchor Books, 1983.

———. "The Real Truth about the Female Body." *Time* (March 15, 1999):56–65.

———. *Nickel and Dimed: On (Not) Getting By in America.* New York: Holt, 2001.

EICHLER, MARGRIT. *Nonsexist Research Methods: A Practical Guide.* Winchester, Mass.: Unwin Hyman, 1988.

EKMAN, PAUL. "Biological and Cultural Contributions to Body and Facial Movements in the Expression of Emotions." In AMELIE OKSENBURG RORTY, ed., *Explaining Emotions.* Berkeley: University of California Press, 1980a:73–101.

———. *Face of Man: Universal Expression in a New Guinea Village.* New York: Garland Press, 1980b.

———. *Telling Lies: Clues to Deceit in the Marketplace, Politics, and Marriage.* New York: Norton, 1985.

ELIAS, ROBERT. *The Politics of Victimization: Victims, Victimology and Human Rights.* New York: Oxford University Press, 1986.

ELLIOT, DELBERT S., and SUZANNE S. AGETON. "Reconciling Race and Class Differences in Self-Reported and Official Estimates of Delinquency." *American Sociological Review.* Vol. 45, No. 1 (February 1980):95–110.

ELLISON, CHRISTOPHER G., JOHN P. BARTKOWSKI, and MICHELLE L. SEGAL. "Do Conservative Protestant Parents Spank More Often? Further Evidence from the National Survey of Families and Households." *Social Science Quarterly.* Vol. 77, No. 3 (September 1996):663–73.

ELLISON, CHRISTOPHER G., and DARREN E. SHERKAT. "Conservative Protestantism and Support for Corporal Punishment." *American Sociological Review.* Vol. 58, No. 1 (February 1993):131–44.

ELMER-DEWITT, PHILIP. "Now for the Truth about Americans and Sex." *Time* (October 17, 1994):62–70.

EMBER, MELVIN, and CAROL R. EMBER. "The Conditions Favoring Matrilocal versus Patrilocal Residence." *American Anthropologist.* Vol. 73, No. 3 (June 1971):571–94.

———. *Anthropology.* 6th ed. Englewood Cliffs, N.J.: Prentice Hall, 1991.

EMERSON, JOAN P. "Behavior in Private Places: Sustaining Definitions of Reality in Gynecological Examinations." In HANS PETER DREITZEL, ed., *Recent Sociology.* Vol. 2. New York: Collier, 1970:74–97.

EMERSON, MICHAEL O., GEORGE YANCEY, and KAREN J. CHAI. "Does Race Matter in Residential Segregation? Exploring the Preferences of White Americans." *American Sociological Review.* Vol. 66, No. 6 (December 2001):922–35.

ENGELS, FRIEDRICH. *The Origin of the Family.* Chicago: Kerr, 1902, orig. 1884.

ENGLAND, PAULA. *Comparable Worth: Theories and Evidence.* Hawthorne, N.Y.: Aldine, 1992.

———. "Three Reviews on Marriage." *Contemporary Sociology.* Vol. 30, No. 6 (November 2001):564–65.

ENGLAND, PAULA, JOAN M. HERMSEN, and DAVID A. COTTER. "The Devaluation of Women's Work: A Comment on Tam." *American Journal of Sociology.* Vol. 105, No. 6 (May 2000):1741–60.

ERIKSON, ERIK H. *Childhood and Society.* New York: Norton, 1963, orig. 1950.

ERIKSON, ROBERT S., NORMAN R. LUTTBEG, and KENT L. TEDIN. *American Public Opinion: Its Origins, Content, and Impact.* 2d ed. New York: Wiley, 1980.

ESTES, RICHARD J., and NEIL ALAN WEINER. "The Commercial Sexual Exploitation of Children in the U.S., Canada, and Mexico." University of Pennsylvania School of Social Work, revised April 2002. [Online] Available October 9, 2004, at http://caster.ssw.upenn.edu/~restes/CSEC_Files/Abstract_010918.pdf

ETZIONI, AMITAI. *A Comparative Analysis of Complex Organization: On Power, Involvement, and Their Correlates.* Rev. and enlarged ed. New York: Free Press, 1975.

———. "How to Make Marriage Matter." *Time* (September 6, 1993):76.

———. "The Responsive Community: A Communitarian Perspective." *American Sociological Review.* Vol. 61, No. 1 (February 1996):1–11.

———. *My Brother's Keeper: A Memoir and a Message.* Lanham, Md.: Rowman & Littlefield, 2003.

EVELYN, JAMILAH. "Community Colleges Play Too Small a Role in Teacher Education, Report Concludes." *Chronicle of Higher Education Online.* [Online] Available October 24, 2002, at http://chronicle.com/daily/2002/10/2002102403n.htm

FAGAN, JEFFREY, FRANKLIN E. ZIMRING, and JUNE KIM. "Declining Homicide in New York City: A Tale of Two Trends." *National Institute of Justice Journal.* Vol. 237 (October 1998):12–13.

FALK, GERHARD. Personal communication, 1987.

FALLON, A. E., and P. ROZIN. "Sex Differences in Perception of Desirable Body Shape." *Journal of Abnormal Psychology.* Vol. 94, No. 1 (1985):100–05.

FALLOWS, JAMES. "Immigration: How It's Affecting Us." *Atlantic Monthly* (November 1983):45 ff.

FARLEY, CHRISTOPHER JOHN. "Winning the Right to Fly." *Time* (August 28, 1995):62–64.

FATTAH, HASSAN. "A More Diverse Community." *American Demographics.* Vol. 24, No. 7 (July/August 2002):39–43.

FEAGIN, JOE R. *The Urban Real Estate Game.* Englewood Cliffs, N.J.: Prentice Hall, 1983.

FEATHERMAN, DAVID L., and ROBERT M. HAUSER. *Opportunity and Change.* New York: Academic Press, 1978.

FEDARKO, KEVIN. "Land Mines: Cheap, Deadly, and Cruel." *Time* (May 13, 1996):54–55.

FEDERAL BUREAU OF INVESTIGATION. *Crime in the United States, 2002.* Washington, D.C.: Federal Bureau of Investigation, 2003. [Online] Available September 28, 2004, at http://www.fbi.gov/ucr/ucr.htm#cius

FEDERAL ELECTION COMMISSION. "FEC Issues Semi-Annual Federal PAC Count." September 1, 2004. [Online] Available October 10, 2004, at http://www.fec.gov/press/press2004/20040901paccount.html

FELLMAN, BRUCE. "Taking the Measure of Children's TV." *Yale Alumni Magazine* (April 1995):46–51.

"Female Opinion and Defense since September 11th." *Society.* Vol. 39, No. 3 (March/April 2002):2.

FENYVESI, CHARLES. "Walled Streets." *U.S. News & World Report* (March 25, 2002):57.

FERNANDEZ, ROBERTO M., and NANCY WEINBERG. "Sifting and Sorting: Personal Contacts and Hiring in a Retail Bank." *American Sociological Review.* Vol. 62, No. 6 (December 1997):883–902.

FERREE, MYRA MARX, and BETH B. HESS. *Controversy and Coalition: The New Feminist Movement across Four Decades of Change.* 3d ed. New York: Routledge, 1995.

FETTO, JOHN. "Down for the Count." *American Demographics.* Vol. 21, No. 11 (November 1999):46–47.

————. "Lean on Me." *American Demographics.* Vol. 22, No. 12 (December 2000):16–17.

————. "Gay Friendly?" *American Demographics.* Vol. 24, No. 5 (May 2002a):16.

————. "Roomier Rentals" *American Demographics.* Vol. 24, No. 5 (May 2002b):17.

————. "A View from the Top?" *American Demographics.* Vol. 24, No. 7 (July/August 2002c):14.

————. "Me Gusta TV." *American Demographics.* Vol. 24, No. 11 (January 2003):14–15.

FINE, GARY ALAN. "Nature and the Taming of the Wild: The Problem of 'Overpick' in the Culture of Mushroomers." *Social Problems.* Vol. 44, No. 1 (February 1997):68–88.

FINEMAN, HOWARD, and TAMARA LIPPER. "Spinning Race." *Newsweek* (January 27, 2003):26–29.

FINN, CHESTER E., JR., and REBECCA L. GAU. "New Ways of Education." *Public Interest* (Winter 1998):79–92.

FINN, CHESTER E., JR., and HERBERT J. WALBERG. "The World's Least Efficient Schools." *Wall Street Journal* (June 22, 1998):A22.

FIREBAUGH, GLENN. "Growth Effects of Foreign and Domestic Investment." *American Journal of Sociology.* Vol. 98, No. 1 (July 1992):105–30.

————. "Does Foreign Capital Harm Poor Nations? New Estimates Based on Dixon and Boswell's Measures of Capital Penetration." *American Journal of Sociology.* Vol. 102, No. 2 (September 1996):563–75.

————. "Empirics of World Income Inequality." *American Journal of Sociology.* Vol. 104, No. 6 (May 1999):1597–1630.

————. "The Trend in Between-Nation Income Inequality." *Annual Review of Sociology.* Vol. 26 (2000):323–39.

FIREBAUGH, GLENN, and FRANK D. BECK. "Does Economic Growth Benefit the Masses? Growth, Dependence, and Welfare in the Third World." *American Sociological Review.* Vol. 59, No. 5 (October 1994):631–53.

FIREBAUGH, GLENN, and KENNETH E. DAVIS. "Trends in Antiblack Prejudice, 1972–1984: Region and Cohort Effects." *American Journal of Sociology.* Vol. 94, No. 2 (September 1988):251–72.

FIREBAUGH, GLENN, and DUMITRU SANDU. "Who Supports Marketization and Democratization in Post-Communist Romania?" *Sociological Forum.* Vol. 13, No. 3 (September 1998):521–41.

FISHER, ELIZABETH. *Woman's Creation: Sexual Evolution and the Shaping of Society.* Garden City, N.Y.: Anchor/Doubleday, 1979.

FISHER, ROGER, and WILLIAM URY. "Getting to Yes." In WILLIAM M. EVAN and STEPHEN HILGARTNER, eds., *The Arms Race and Nuclear War.* Englewood Cliffs, N.J.: Prentice Hall, 1988:261–68.

FISKE, ALAN PAIGE. "The Cultural Relativity of Selfish Individualism: Anthropological Evidence That Humans Are Inherently Sociable." In MARGARET S. CLARK, ed., *Prosocial Behavior.* Newbury Park, Calif.: Sage, 1991:176–214.

FLAHERTY, MICHAEL G. "A Formal Approach to the Study of Amusement in Social Interaction." *Studies in Symbolic Interaction.* Vol. 5. New York: JAI Press, 1984:71–82.

————. "Two Conceptions of the Social Situation: Some Implications of Humor." *Sociological Quarterly.* Vol. 31, No. 1 (Spring 1990).

FOBES, RICHARD. "Creative Problem Solving." *Futurist.* Vol. 30, No. 1 (January/February 1996):19–22.

FONDA, DAREN. "Selling in Tongues." *Time* (Global Business edition, November 2001):B12–B16.

FORD, CLELLAN S., and FRANK A. BEACH. *Patterns of Sexual Behavior.* New York: Harper Bros., 1951.

FORNOS, WERNER. "Our Struggle Continues." *Popline* (November/December 1997):1.

FOUCAULT, MICHEL. *The History of Sexuality: An Introduction.* Vol. 1. Robert Hurley, trans. New York: Vintage Books, 1990, orig. 1978.

FRANK, ANDRÉ GUNDER. *On Capitalist Underdevelopment.* Bombay: Oxford University Press, 1975.

————. *Crisis in the World Economy.* New York: Holmes & Meier, 1980.

————. *Reflections on the World Economic Crisis.* New York: Monthly Review Press, 1981.

FRANK, JOHN DAVID, JOHN W. MEYER, and DAVID MIYAHARA. "The Individualist Polity and the Prevalence of a Professionalized Psychology: A Cross-National Study." *American Sociological Review.* Vol. 60, No. 3 (June 1995):360–77.

FRANKLIN, JOHN HOPE. *From Slavery to Freedom: A History of Negro Americans.* 3d ed. New York: Vintage Books, 1967.

FRAZIER, E. FRANKLIN. *Black Bourgeoisie: The Rise of a New Middle Class.* New York: Free Press, 1965.

FREDRICKSON, GEORGE M. *White Supremacy: A Comparative Study in American and South African History.* New York: Oxford University Press, 1981.

FREE, MARVIN D. "Religious Affiliation, Religiosity, and Impulsive and Intentional Deviance." *Sociological Focus.* Vol. 25, No. 1 (February 1992):77–91.

FREEDMAN, ESTELLE B. *No Turning Back: The History of Feminism and the Future of Women.* New York: Ballantine Books, 2002.

FREEDOM HOUSE. *Freedom in the World, 2004.* Lanham, Md.: Rowman & Littlefield, 2004. [Online] Available October 10, 2004, at http://www.freedomhouse.org/research/index.htm

FRENCH, MARILYN. *Beyond Power: On Women, Men, and Morals.* New York: Summit Books, 1985.

FRIEDMAN, MEYER, and RAY II. ROSENMAN. *Type A Behavior and Your Heart.* New York: Fawcett Crest, 1974.

FUGITA, STEPHEN S., and DAVID J. O'BRIEN. "Structural Assimilation, Ethnic Group Membership, and Political Participation among Japanese Americans: A Research Note." *Social Forces.* Vol. 63, No. 4 (June 1985):986–95.

FULKERSON, JENNIFER. "When Lawyers Advertise." *American Demographics.* Vol. 17, No. 6 (June 1995):54–55.

FULLER, REX, and RICHARD SCHOENBERGER. "The Gender Salary Gap: Do Academic Achievement, Intern Experience, and College Major Make a Difference?" *Social Science Quarterly.* Vol. 72, No. 4 (December 1991):715–26.

FURSTENBERG, FRANK F., JR., and ANDREW CHERLIN. *Divided Families: What Happens to Children When Parents Part.* Cambridge, Mass.: Harvard University Press, 1991.

GAGNÉ, PATRICIA, and RICHARD TEWKSBURY. "Conformity Pressures and Gender Resistance among Transgendered Individuals." *Social Problems.* Vol. 45, No. 1 (February 1998):81–101.

GAGNÉ, PATRICIA, RICHARD TEWKSBURY, and DEANNA MCGAUGHEY. "Coming Out and Crossing Over: Identity Formation and Proclamation in a Transgender Community." *Gender and Society.* Vol. 11, No. 4 (August 1997):478–508.

GALLAGHER, MAGGIE. "Does Bradley Know What Poverty Is?" *New York Post* (October 28, 1999):37.

GALSTER, GEORGE. "Black Suburbanization: Has It Changed the Relative Location of Races?" *Urban Affairs Quarterly.* Vol. 26, No. 4 (June 1991):621–28.

GAMORAN, ADAM. "The Variable Effects of High-School Tracking." *American Sociological Review.* Vol. 57, No. 6 (December 1992):812–28.

GANS, HERBERT J. *People and Plans: Essays on Urban Problems and Solutions.* New York: Basic Books, 1968.

GARDNER, MARILYN. "At-Home Dads Give Their New Career High Marks." *Christian Science Monitor* (May 30, 1996):1, 12.

GARDYN, REBECCA. "The Mating Game." *American Demographics.* Vol. 24, No. 7 (July/August 2002):33–37.

GARFINKEL, HAROLD. "Conditions of Successful Degradation Ceremonies." *American Journal of Sociology.* Vol. 61, No. 2 (March 1956):420–24.

————. *Studies in Ethnomethodology.* Cambridge, Mass.: Polity Press, 1967.

GARREAU, JOEL. *Edge City.* New York: Doubleday, 1991.

GEERTZ, CLIFFORD. "Common Sense as a Cultural System." *Antioch Review.* Vol. 33, No. 1 (Spring 1975):5–26.

GELLES, RICHARD J., and CLAIRE PEDRICK CORNELL. *Intimate Violence in Families.* 2d ed. Newbury Park, Calif.: Sage, 1990.

GERBER, THEODORE P., and MICHAEL HOUT. "More Shock than Therapy: Market Transition, Employment, and Income in Russia, 1991–1995." *American Journal of Sociology.* Vol. 104, No. 1 (July 1998):1–50.

GERGEN, DAVID. "King of the World." *U.S. News & World Report* (February 25, 2002):84.

GERLACH, MICHAEL L. *The Social Organization of Japanese Business.* Berkeley: University of California Press, 1992.

GESCHWENDER, JAMES A. *Racial Stratification in America.* Dubuque, Iowa: Brown, 1978.

GEWERTZ, DEBORAH. "A Historical Reconsideration of Female Dominance among the Chambri of Papua New Guinea." *American Ethnologist.* Vol. 8, No. 1 (1981):94–106.

GIBBS, NANCY. "The Pulse of America along the River." *Time* (July 10, 2000):42–46.
———. "What Kids (Really) Need." *Time* (April 30, 2001):48–49.

GIDDENS, ANTHONY. *The Transformation of Intimacy.* Cambridge: Polity Press, 1992.

GIGLIOTTI, RICHARD J., and HEATHER K. HUFF. "Role-Related Conflicts, Strains, and Stresses of Older-Adult College Students." *Sociological Focus.* Vol. 28, No. 3 (August 1995):329–42.

GILBERTSON, GRETA A., and DOUGLAS T. GURAK. "Broadening the Enclave Debate: The Dual Labor Market Experiences of Dominican and Colombian Men in New York City." *Sociological Forum.* Vol. 8, No. 2 (June 1993):205–20.

GILLIGAN, CAROL. *In a Different Voice: Psychological Theory and Women's Development.* Cambridge, Mass.: Harvard University Press, 1982.
———. *Making Connections: The Relational Worlds of Adolescent Girls at Emma Willard School.* Cambridge, Mass.: Harvard University Press, 1990.

GILLON, RAANAN. "Euthanasia in the Netherlands: Down the Slippery Slope?" *Journal of Medical Ethics.* Vol. 25, No. 1 (February 1999):3–4.

GIMENEZ, MARTHA E. "Silence in the Classroom: Some Thoughts about Teaching in the 1980s." *Teaching Sociology.* Vol. 17, No. 2 (April 1989):184–91.

GIOVANNINI, MAUREEN. "Female Anthropologist and Male Informant: Gender Conflict in a Sicilian Town." In JOHN J. MACIONIS and NIJOLE V. BENOKRAITIS, eds., *Seeing Ourselves: Classic, Contemporary, and Cross-Cultural Readings in Sociology.* 2d ed. Englewood Cliffs, N.J.: Prentice Hall, 1992:27–32.

GIROUX, GREGORY L. "GOP Maintains Thin Edge." *CQ Weekly.* Vol. 58, No. 44 (November 11, 2000):2652.

GITLIN, TODD. "Postmodernism: Roots and Politics." *Dissent* (Winter 1989):100–08.

GLEICK, ELIZABETH. "The Marker We've Been Waiting For." *Time* (April 7, 1997):28–42.

GLENMARY RESEARCH CENTER. *Major Religious Families by Counties of the United States: 2000* (map). Nashville, Tenn.: Glenmary Research Center, 2002.

GLENN, NORVAL D., and BETH ANN SHELTON. "Regional Differences in Divorce in the United States." *Journal of Marriage and the Family.* Vol. 47, No. 3 (August 1985):641–52.

GLUECK, SHELDON, and ELEANOR GLUECK. *Unraveling Juvenile Delinquency.* New York: Commonwealth Fund, 1950.

GOESLING, BRIAN. "Changing Income Inequalities within and between Nations: New Evidence." *American Sociological Review.* Vol. 66, No. 5 (October 2001):745–61.

GOETTING, ANN. *Getting Out: Life Stories of Women Who Left Abusive Men.* New York: Columbia University Press, 1999.

GOFFMAN, ERVING. *The Presentation of Self in Everyday Life.* Garden City, N.Y.: Anchor Books, 1959.
———. *Asylums: Essays on the Social Situation of Mental Patients and Other Inmates.* Garden City, N.Y.: Anchor Books, 1961.
———. *Stigma: Notes on the Management of Spoiled Identity.* Englewood Cliffs, N.J.: Prentice Hall, 1963.
———. *Interactional Ritual: Essays on Face-to-Face Behavior.* Garden City, N.Y.: Anchor Books, 1967.
———. *Gender Advertisements.* New York: Harper Colophon, 1979.

GOLDBERG, BERNARD. *Bias: A CBS Insider Exposes How the Media Distort the News.* Washington, D.C.: Regnery, 2002.

GOLDBERG, STEVEN. *The Inevitability of Patriarchy.* New York: Morrow, 1974.

GOLDBERGER, PAUL. Lecture delivered at Kenyon College, Gambier, Ohio, September 22, 2002.

GOLDEN, DANIEL. "Some Community Colleges Fudge the Facts to Attract Foreign Students." *Wall Street Journal* (April 2, 2002):B1, B4.

GOLDEN, FREDERIC. "Lying Faces Unmasked." *Time* (April 5, 1999):52.

GOLDEN, FREDERIC, and MICHAEL D. LEMONICK. "The Race Is Over." *Time* (July 3, 2000):18–23.

GOLDFIELD, MICHAEL. "Rebounding Unions Target Service Sector." *Population Today.* Vol. 28, No. 7 (October 2000):3, 10.

GOLDSMITH, H. H. "Genetic Influences on Personality from Infancy." *Child Development.* Vol. 54, No. 2 (April 1983):331–35.

GOODE, WILLIAM J. "The Theoretical Importance of Love." *American Sociological Review.* Vol. 24, No. 1 (February 1959):38–47.

———. "Encroachment, Charlatanism, and the Emerging Profession: Psychology, Sociology and Medicine." *American Sociological Review.* Vol. 25, No. 6 (December 1960):902–14.

GORDON, JAMES S. "The Paradigm of Holistic Medicine." In ARTHUR C. HASTINGS et al., eds., *Health for the Whole Person: The Complete Guide to Holistic Medicine.* Boulder, Colo.: Westview Press, 1980:3–27.

GORING, CHARLES BUCKMAN. *The English Convict: A Statistical Study.* Montclair, N.J.: Patterson Smith, 1972, orig. 1913.

GORSKI, PHILIP S. "Historicizing the Secularization Debate: Church, State, and Society in Late Medieval and Early Modern Europe, ca. 1300 to 1700." *American Sociological Review.* Vol. 65, No. 1 (February 2000):138–67.

GOTHAM, KEVIN FOX. "Race, Mortgage Lending, and Loan Rejections in a U.S. City." *Sociological Focus.* Vol. 31, No. 4 (October 1998):391–405.

GOTTFREDSON, MICHAEL R., and TRAVIS HIRSCHI. "National Crime Control Policies." *Society.* Vol. 32, No. 2 (January/February 1995):30–36.

GOTTMANN, JEAN. *Megalopolis.* New York: Twentieth Century Fund, 1961.

GOUGH, KATHLEEN. "The Origin of the Family." *Journal of Marriage and the Family.* Vol. 33, No. 4 (November 1971):760–71.
———. "The Origin of the Family." In JOHN J. MACIONIS and NIJOLE V. BENOKRAITIS, eds., *Seeing Ourselves: Classic, Contemporary, and Cross-Cultural Readings in Sociology.* Englewood Cliffs, N.J.: Prentice Hall, 1989.

GRATTET, RYKEN. "Hate Crimes: Better Data or Increasing Frequency?" *Population Today.* Vol. 28, No. 5 (July 2000):1, 4.

GREELEY, ANDREW M. *Religious Change in America.* Cambridge, Mass.: Harvard University Press, 1989.
———. "Religious Revival in Eastern Europe." *Society.* Vol. 39, No. 2 (January/February 2002):76–77.

GREEN, GARY PAUL, LEANN M. TIGGES, and DANIEL DIAZ. "Racial and Ethnic Differences in Job-Search Strategies in Atlanta, Boston, and Los Angeles." *Social Science Quarterly.* Vol. 80, No. 2 (June 1999):263–90.

GREENBERG, DAVID F. *The Construction of Homosexuality.* Chicago: University of Chicago Press, 1988.

GREENFIELD, LAWRENCE A. *Child Victimizers: Violent Offenders and Their Victims.* Washington, D.C.: U.S. Bureau of Justice Statistics, 1996.

GREENHOUSE, STEVEN. "Despite Defeat on China Bill, Labor Is on the Rise." *New York Times* (May 20, 2000): A1, A18.

GREENSPAN, STANLEY I. *The Four-Thirds Solution: Solving the Child-Care Crisis in America.* Cambridge, Mass.: Perseus, 2001.

GURAK, DOUGLAS T., and JOSEPH P. FITZPATRICK. "Intermarriage among Hispanic Ethnic Groups in New York City." *American Journal of Sociology.* Vol. 87, No. 4 (January 1982):921–34.

GURNETT, KATE. "On the Forefront of Feminism." *Albany Times Union* (July 5, 1998):G1, G6.

GWYNNE, S. C., and JOHN F. DICKERSON. "Lost in the E-Mail." *Time* (April 21, 1997):88–90.

HABERMAS, JÜRGEN. *Toward a Rational Society: Student Protest, Science, and Politics.* JEREMY J. SHAPIRO, trans. Boston: Beacon Press, 1970.

HACKER, HELEN MAYER. "Women as a Minority Group." *Social Forces.* Vol. 30 (October 1951):60–69.

HADAWAY, C. KIRK, PENNY LONG MARLER, and MARK CHAVES. "What the Polls Don't Show: A Closer Look at U.S. Church Attendance." *American Sociological Review.* Vol. 58, No. 6 (December 1993):741–52.

HADDEN, JEFFREY K., and CHARLES E. SWAIN. *Prime Time Preachers: The Rising Power of Televangelism.* Reading, Mass.: Addison-Wesley, 1981.

HAFNER, KATIE. "Making Sense of the Internet." *Newsweek* (October 24, 1994):46–48.

HAGAN, JACQUELINE MARIA. "Social Networks, Gender, and Immigrant Incorporation: Resources and Restraints." *American Sociological Review.* Vol. 63, No. 1 (February 1998):55–67.

HAGAN, JOHN, and PATRICIA PARKER. "White-Collar Crime and Punishment: The Class Structure and Legal Sanctioning of Securities Violations." *American Sociological Review.* Vol. 50, No. 3 (June 1985):302–16.

HAIG, ROBIN ANDREW. *The Anatomy of Humor: Biopsychosocial and Therapeutic Perspectives.* Springfield, Ill.: Thomas, 1988.

HALBERSTAM, DAVID. *The Reckoning.* New York: Avon Books, 1986.

HALEDJIAN, DEAN. *How to Tell a Businessman from a Businesswoman.* Annandale, Va.: Northern Virginia Community College, 1997.

HALL, JOHN R., and MARY JO NEITZ. *Culture: Sociological Perspectives.* Englewood Cliffs, N.J.: Prentice Hall, 1993.

HALL, KELLEY J., and BETSY LUCAL. "Tapping in Parallel Universes: Using Superhero Comic Books in Sociology Courses." *Teaching Sociology.* Vol. 27, No. 1 (January 1999):60–66.

HALLINAN, MAUREEN T. "The Sociological Study of Social Change." *American Sociological Review.* Vol. 62, No. 1 (February 1997):1–11.

HAMER, DEAN, and PETER COPELAND. *The Science of Desire: The Search for the Gay Gene and the Biology of Behavior.* New York: Simon & Schuster, 1994.

HAMILTON, ANITA. "Speeders, Say Cheese." *Time* (September 17, 2001):32.

HAMMOND, PHILIP E. "Introduction." In PHILIP E. HAMMOND, ed., *The Sacred in a Secular Age: Toward Revision in the Scientific Study of Religion.* Berkeley: University of California Press, 1985:1–6.

HAMRICK, MICHAEL H., DAVID J. ANSPAUGH, and GENE EZELL. *Health.* Columbus, Ohio: Merrill, 1986.

HAN, WENJUI, and JANE WALDFOGEL. "Child Care Costs and Women's Employment: A Comparison of Single and Married Mothers with Preschool-Aged Children." *Social Science Quarterly.* Vol. 83, No. 5 (September 2001):552–68.

HANDLIN, OSCAR. *Boston's Immigrants, 1790–1865: A Study in Acculturation.* Cambridge, Mass.: Harvard University Press, 1941.

HANEY, CRAIG, CURTIS BANKS, and PHILIP ZIMBARDO. "Interpersonal Dynamics in a Simulated Prison." *International Journal of Criminology and Penology.* Vol. 1 (1973):69–97.

HANEY, LYNNE. "After the Fall: East European Women since the Collapse of State Socialism." *Contexts.* Vol. 1, No. 3 (Fall 2002):27–36.

HARLOW, HARRY F., and MARGARET KUENNE HARLOW. "Social Deprivation in Monkeys." *Scientific American* (November 1962):137–46.

HARPSTER, PAULA, and ELIZABETH MONK-TURNER. "Why Men Do Housework: A Test of Gender Production and the Relative Resources Model." *Sociological Focus.* Vol. 31, No. 1 (February 1998):45–59.

HARRIES, KEITH D. *Serious Violence: Patterns of Homicide and Assault in America.* Springfield, Ill.: Thomas, 1990.

HARRINGTON, MICHAEL. *The New American Poverty.* New York: Penguin, 1984.

HARRIS, CHAUNCY D., and EDWARD L. ULLMAN. "The Nature of Cities." *Annals.* Vol. 242 (November 1945):7–17.

HARRIS, DAVID R., and JEREMIAH JOSEPH SIM. "Who Is Multiracial? Assessing the Complexity of Lived Race." *American Sociological Review.* Vol. 67, No. 4 (August 2002):614–27.

HARRIS, MARVIN. "Why Men Dominate Women." *New York Times Magazine* (November 13, 1977):46, 115–23.

———. *Cultural Anthropology.* 2d ed. New York: Harper & Row, 1987.

HAUB, CARL. "Has Global Growth Reached Its Peak?" *Population Today.* Vol. 30, No. 6 (August/September 2002a):6.

———. "How Many People Have Ever Lived on Earth?" *Population Today.* Vol. 30, No. 8 (November/December 2002b):3–4.

HAWTHORNE, PETER. "South Africa's Makeover." *Time* (July 12, 1999).

HAYWARD, MARK D., EILEEN M. CRIMMINS, TONI P. MILES, and YU YANG. "The Significance of Socioeconomic Status in Explaining the Racial Gap in Chronic Health Conditions." *American Sociological Review.* Vol. 65, No. 6 (December 2000):910–30.

HEATH, JULIA A., and W. DAVID BOURNE. "Husbands and Housework: Parity or Parody?" *Social Science Quarterly.* Vol. 76, No. 1 (March 1995):195–202.

HELGESEN, SALLY. *The Female Advantage: Women's Ways of Leadership.* New York: Doubleday, 1990.

HELIN, DAVID W. "When Slogans Go Wrong." *American Demographics.* Vol. 14, No. 2 (February 1992):14.

HENLEY, NANCY, MYKOL HAMILTON, and BARRIE THORNE. "Womanspeak and Manspeak: Sex Differences in Communication, Verbal and Nonverbal." In JOHN J. MACIONIS and NIJOLE V. BENOKRAITIS, eds., *Seeing Ourselves: Classic, Contemporary, and Cross-Cultural Readings in Sociology.* 2d ed. Englewood Cliffs, N.J.: Prentice Hall, 1992:10–15.

HERDT, GILBERT H. "Semen Transactions in Sambian Culture." In DAVID N. SUGGS and ANDREW W. MIRACLE, eds., *Culture and Human Sexuality.* Pacific Grove, Calif.: Brooks/Cole, 1993:298–327.

HEREK, GREGORY M. "Myths about Sexual Orientation: A Lawyer's Guide to Social Science Research." *Law and Sexuality.* Vol. 1 (1991):133–72.

HERMAN, DIANNE. "The Rape Culture." In JOHN J. MACIONIS and NIJOLE V. BENOKRAITIS, eds., *Seeing Ourselves: Classic, Contemporary, and Cross-Cultural Readings in Sociology.* 5th ed. Upper Saddle River, N.J.: Prentice Hall, 2001.

HERRNSTEIN, RICHARD J., and CHARLES MURRAY. *The Bell Curve: Intelligence and Class Structure in American Life.* New York: Free Press, 1994.

HESS, BETH B. "Breaking and Entering the Establishment: Committing Social Change and Confronting the Backlash." *Social Problems.* Vol. 46, No. 1 (February 1999):1–12.

HESS, STEPHEN. "Reporters Who Cover Congress." *Society.* Vol. 28, No. 2 (January/February 1991):60–65.

HEYMANN, PHILIP B. "Civil Liberties and Human Rights in the Aftermath of September 11." *Harvard Journal of Law and Public Policy.* Vol. 25, No. 2 (Spring 2002):441–57.

HIGHTOWER, JIM. *Eat Your Heart Out: Food Profiteering in America.* New York: Crown, 1975.

HILL, MARK E. "Race of the Interviewer and Perception of Skin Color: Evidence from the Multi-City Study of Urban Inequality." *American Sociological Review.* Vol. 67, No. 1 (February 2002):99–108.

HIRSCHI, TRAVIS. *Causes of Delinquency.* Berkeley: University of California Press, 1969.

HOBSON, KATHERINE. "Kissing Cousins." *U.S. News & World Report* (April 15, 2002):77.

HOCHSCHILD, ARLIE RUSSELL. "Emotion Work, Feeling Rules, and Social Structure." *American Journal of Sociology.* Vol. 85, No. 3 (November 1979):551–75.

———. *The Managed Heart.* Berkeley: University of California Press, 1983.

HODGE, ROBERT W., DONALD J. TREIMAN, and PETER H. ROSSI. "A Comparative Study of Occupational Prestige." In REINHARD BENDIX and SEYMOUR MARTIN LIPSET, eds., *Class, Status, and Power: Social Stratification in Comparative Perspective.* 2d ed. New York: Free Press, 1966:309–21.

HOGAN, DENNIS P., and EVELYN M. KITAGAWA. "The Impact of Social Status and Neighborhood on the Fertility of Black Adolescents." *American Journal of Sociology.* Vol. 90, No. 4 (January 1985):825–55.

HOGAN, RICHARD, and CAROLYN C. PERRUCCI. "Producing and Reproducing the Class and Status Differences: Racial and Gender Gaps in U.S. Employment and Retirement Income." *Social Problems.* Vol. 45, No. 4 (November 1998):528–49.

HOLMES, THOMAS H., and RICHARD H. RAHE. "The Social Readjustment Rating Scale." *Journal of Psychosomatic Research.* Vol. 11 (1967):213–18.

HONEYWELL, ROY J. *The Educational Work of Thomas Jefferson.* Cambridge, Mass.: Harvard University Press, 1931.

HORN, WADE F., and DOUGLAS TYNAN. "Revamping Special Education." *Public Interest* (Summer 2001):36–53.

HORTON, HAYWARD DERRICK. "Critical Demography: The Paradigm of the Future?" *Sociological Forum.* Vol. 14, No. 3 (September 1999):363–67.

HOSTETLER, JOHN A. *Amish Society.* 3d ed. Baltimore: Johns Hopkins University Press, 1980.

HOUT, MICHAEL. "More Universalism, Less Structural Mobility: The American Occupational Structure in the 1980s." *American Journal of Sociology.* Vol. 95, No. 6 (May 1998):1358–400.

HOUT, MICHAEL, CLEM BROOKS, and JEFF MANZA. "The Persistence of Classes in Post-Industrial Societies." *International Sociology.* Vol. 8, No. 3 (September 1993):259–77.

HOUT, MICHAEL, and CLAUDE S. FISHER. "Why More Americans Have No Religious Preference: Politics and Generations." *American Sociological Review.* Vol. 67, No. 2 (April 2002):165–90.

HOUT, MICHAEL, and ANDREW M. GREELEY. "The Center Doesn't Hold: Church Attendance in the United States, 1940–1984." *American Sociological Review.* Vol. 52, No. 3 (June 1987):325–45.

HOUT, MICHAEL, ANDREW M. GREELEY, and MELISSA J. WILDE. "The Demographic Imperative in Religious Change in the United States." *American Journal of Sociology.* Vol. 107, No. 2 (September 2001):468–500.

HOYT, HOMER. *The Structure and Growth of Residential Neighborhoods in American Cities.* Washington, D.C.: Federal Housing Administration, 1939.

HSU, FRANCIS L. K. *The Challenge of the American Dream: The Chinese in the United States.* Belmont, Calif.: Wadsworth, 1971.

HUFFMAN, KAREN. *Psychology in Action.* New York: Wiley, 2000.

HUFFMAN, MATT L., STEVEN C. VELASCO, and WILLIAM T. BIELBY. "Where Sex Composition Matters Most: Comparing the Effects of Job versus Occupational Sex Composition of Earnings." *Sociological Focus.* Vol. 29, No. 3 (August 1996):189–207.

HUGHES, MICHAEL, and MELVIN E. THOMAS. "The Continuing Significance of Race Revisited: A Study of Race, Class, and Quality of Life in America, 1972 to 1996." *American Sociological Review.* Vol. 63, No. 6 (December 1998):785–95.

HUMAN RIGHTS WATCH. "Children's Rights: Child Labor." 2004. [Online] Available September 22, 2004, at http://www.hrw.org/children/labor.htm

HUMMER, ROBERT A., RICHARD G. ROGERS, CHARLES B. NAM, and FELICIA B. LE CLERE. "Race/Ethnicity, Nativity, and U.S. Adult Mortality." *Social Science Quarterly.* Vol. 80, No. 1 (March 1999):136–53.

HUNTER, JAMES DAVISON. *American Evangelicalism: Conservative Religion and the Quandary of Modernity.* New Brunswick, N.J.: Rutgers University Press, 1983.

———. "Conservative Protestantism." In PHILIP E. HAMMOND, ed., *The Sacred in a Secular Age.* Berkeley: University of California Press, 1985:50–66.

———. *Evangelicalism: The Coming Generation.* Chicago: University of Chicago Press, 1987.

HURLEY, ANDREW. *Environmental Inequalities: Class, Race, and Industrial Pollution in Gary, Indiana, 1945–1980*. Chapel Hill: University of North Carolina Press, 1995.

HYMOWITZ, CAROL. "World's Poorest Women Advance by Entrepreneurship." *Wall Street Journal* (September 9, 1995):B1.

IANNACCONE, LAURENCE R. "Why Strict Churches Are Strong." *American Journal of Sociology*. Vol. 99, No. 5 (March 1994):1180–211.

IDE, THOMAS R., and ARTHUR J. CORDELL. "Automating Work." *Society*. Vol. 31, No. 6 (September/October 1994):65–71.

INCIARDI, JAMES A. *Elements of Criminal Justice*. 2d ed. New York: Oxford University Press, 2000.

INCIARDI, JAMES A., HILARY L. SURRATT, and PAULO R. TELLES. *Sex, Drugs, and HIV/AIDS in Brazil*. Boulder, Colo.: Westview Press, 2000.

INGLEHART, RONALD. *Modernization and Postmodernization: Cultural, Economic, and Political Change in 43 Societies*. Princeton, N.J.: Princeton University Press, 1997.

INGLEHART, RONALD, and WAYNE E. BAKER. "Modernization, Cultural Change, and the Persistence of Traditional Values." *American Sociological Review*. Vol. 65, No. 1 (February 2000):19–51.

INGLEHART, RONALD, et al. *World Values Surveys and European Values Surveys, 1981–1984, 1990–1993, and 1995–1997*. [Computer file] ICPSR version. Ann Arbor, Mich. Interuniversity Consortium for Political and Social Research, 2000.

INTERNAL REVENUE SERVICE. "Personal Wealth, 1998." *Statistics of Income Bulletin* (April 2003):88.

———. "Corporation Income Tax Returns, 2001." *Statistics of Income Bulletin, Summer 2004*. September, 2004. [Online] Available November 3, 2004, at http://www.irs.gov/pub/irs-soi/01corart.pdf

INTERNATIONAL LABOUR ORGANIZATION. *World Labour Report, 1997–98*. "Table 1.2. Trade Union Density." Rev. November 1, 2002. [Online] Available October 9, 2004, at http://www.ilo.org/public/english/dialogue/ifpdial/publ/wlr97/annex/tab12.htm

INTERNATIONAL MONETARY FUND. *World Economic Outlook: Asset Prices and the Business Cycle*. May 2000. [Online] Available October 9, 2004, at http://www.imf.org/external/pubs/ft/weo/2000/01/index.htm

INTERNATIONAL TELECOMMUNICATION UNION. *World Telecommunication Development Report, 2003*. Data cited in World Bank, *2004 World Development Indicators*. Washington, D.C.: World Bank, 2004.

INTER-PARLIAMENTARY UNION. "Women in National Parliaments." [Online] Available July 25, 2004, at http://www.ipu.org/wmn-e/classif.htm and http://www.ipu.org/wmn-e/world.htm

ISRAEL, GLENN D., LIONEL J. BEAULIEU, and GLEN HARTLESS. "The Influence of Family and Community Social Capital on Educational Achievement." *Rural Sociology*. Vol. 66, No. 1 (March 2001):43–68.

JACOBS, DAVID, and JASON T. CARMICHAEL. "The Political Sociology of the Death Penalty: A Pooled Time-Series Analysis." *American Sociological Review*. Vol. 67, No. 1 (February 2002):109–31.

JACOBS, DAVID, and RONALD E. HELMS. "Toward a Political Model of Incarceration: A Time-Series Examination of Multiple Explanations for Prison Admission Rates." *American Journal of Sociology*. Vol. 102, No. 2 (September 1996):323–57.

JACOBSON, JENNIFER. "Professors Are Finding Better Pay and More Freedom at Community Colleges." *Chronicle of Higher Education Online* (March 7, 2003). [Online] Available March 7, 2003, at http://www.chronicle.com

JACQUET, CONSTANT H., and ALICE M. JONES. *Yearbook of American and Canadian Churches, 1991*. Nashville, Tenn.: Abingdon Press, 1991.

JAGGER, ALISON. "Political Philosophies of Women's Liberation." In LAUREL RICHARDSON and VERTA TAYLOR, eds., *Feminist Frontiers: Rethinking Sex, Gender, and Society*. Reading, Mass.: Addison-Wesley, 1983.

JANIS, IRVING L. *Victims of Groupthink*. Boston: Houghton Mifflin, 1972.

———. *Crucial Decisions: Leadership in Policymaking and Crisis Management*. New York: Free Press, 1989.

JAPANESE MINISTRY OF HEALTH, LABOUR, AND WELFARE. STATISTICS AND INFORMATION DEPARTMENT. *International Comparisons of Divorce Rates*. [Online] Available November 4, 2004, at http://web-jpn.org/stat/stats/02VIT33.html

JENCKS, CHRISTOPHER. "Genes and Crime." *New York Review* (February 12, 1987):33–41.

JENKINS, J. CRAIG, and MICHAEL WALLACE. "The Generalized Action Potential of Protest Movements: The New Class, Social Trends, and Political Exclusion Explanations." *Sociological Forum*. Vol. 11, No. 2 (June 1996):183–207.

JENNESS, VALERIE, and RYKEN GRATTET. *Making a Hate Crime: From Movement to Law Enforcement*. New York: Russell Sage Foundation, 2001.

JOHNSON, DIRK. "Death of a Small Town." *Newsweek* (September 10, 2001):30–31.

JOHNSON, KENNETH M. "The Rural Rebound." *Population Reference Bureau Reports on America*. Vol. 1, No. 3 (September 1999). [Online] Available October 9, 2004, at http://www.prb.org/Content/NavigationMenu/PRB/AboutPRB/Reports_on_America/ReportonAmericaRuralRebound.pdf

JOHNSON, KENNETH M., and GLENN V. FUGUITT. "Continuity and Change in Rural Migration Patterns, 1950–1995." *Rural Sociology*. Vol. 65, No. 1 (March 2000):27–49.

JOHNSON, PAUL. "The Seven Deadly Sins of Terrorism." In BENJAMIN NETANYAHU, ed., *International Terrorism*. New Brunswick, N.J.: Transaction Books, 1981:12–22.

JOHNSTON, DAVID CAY. "Voting, America's Not Keen On. Coffee Is Another Matter." *New York Times* (November 10, 1996):sec.4, p. 2.

JOHNSTON, R. J. "Residential Area Characteristics." In DAVID T. HERBERT and R. J. JOHNSTON, eds., *Social Areas in Cities*. Vol. 1: *Spatial Processes and Form*. New York: Wiley, 1976:193–235.

JONES, ANDREW E. G., and DAVID WILSON. *The Urban Growth Machine: Critical Perspectives*. Albany: State University of New York Press, 1999.

JONES, D. GARETH. "Brain Death." *Journal of Medical Ethics*. Vol. 24, No. 4 (August 1998):237–43.

JONES, JUDY. "More Miners Will Be Offered Free X-Rays; Federal Agency Wants to Monitor Black-Lung Cases." *Louisville Courier Journal* (May 13, 1999):1A.

JONES, ROBERT EMMET, and LEWIS F. CARTER. "Concern for the Environment among Black Americans: An Assessment of Common Assumptions." *Social Science Quarterly*. Vol. 75, No. 3 (September 1994):560–79.

JORDAN, ELLEN, and ANGELA COWAN. "Warrior Narratives in the Kindergarten Classroom: Renegotiating the Social Contract?" *Gender and Society*. Vol. 9, No. 6 (December 1995):727–43.

JOSEPHY, ALVIN M., JR. *Now That the Buffalo's Gone: A Study of Today's American Indians*. New York: Knopf, 1982.

JOYNSON, ROBERT B. "Fallible Judgments." *Society*. Vol. 31, No. 3 (March/April 1994):45–52.

KAIN, EDWARD L. "A Note on the Integration of AIDS into the Sociology of Human Sexuality." *Teaching Sociology*. Vol. 15, No. 4 (July 1987):320–23.

———. *The Myth of Family Decline: Understanding Families in a World of Rapid Social Change*. Lexington, Mass.: Lexington Books, 1990.

KALLEBERG, ARNE L., BARBARA F. RESKIN, and KEN HUDSON. "Bad Jobs in America: Standard and Nonstandard Employment Relations and Job Quality in the United States." *American Sociological Review*. Vol. 65, No 2 (April 2000):256–78.

KALLEBERG, ARNE L., and MARK E. VAN BUREN. "Is Bigger Better? Explaining the Relationship between Organization Size and Job Rewards." *American Sociological Review*. Vol. 61, No. 1 (February 1996):47–66.

KAMINER, WENDY. "Volunteers: Who Knows What's in It for Them?" *Ms.* (December 1984):93–96, 126–28.

———. "Demasculinizing the Army." *New York Times Review of Books* (June 15, 1997):7.

KANE, EMILY W. "Racial and Ethnic Variations in Gender-Related Attitudes." *Annual Review of Sociology*. Vol. 26 (2000):419–39.

KANN, LAURA, et al. "Youth Risk Behavior Surveillance: United States, 1993." *Morbidity and Mortality Weekly Report*. Vol. 44 (March 24, 1995):S-1.

KANTER, ROSABETH MOSS. *Men and Women of the Corporation*. New York: Basic Books, 1977.

KANTER, ROSABETH MOSS, and BARRY A. STEIN. "The Gender Pioneers: Women in an Industrial Sales Force." In ROSABETH MOSS KANTER and BARRY A. STEIN, eds., *Life in Organizations*. New York: Basic Books, 1979:134–60.

KANTROWITZ, BARBARA, and PAT WINGERT. "Unmarried with Children." *Newsweek* (May 28, 2001):46–52.

———. "What's at Stake." *Newsweek* (January 27, 2003):30–37.

KAO, GRACE. "Group Images and Possible Selves among Adolescents: Linking Stereotypes to Expectations by Race and Ethnicity." *Sociological Forum*. Vol. 15, No. 3 (September 2000):407–30.

KAPLAN, DAVID E., and MICHAEL SCHAFFER. "Losing the Psywar." *U.S. News & World Report* (October 8, 2001):46.

KAPLAN, ELAINE BELL. "Black Teenage Mothers and Their Mothers: The Impact of Adolescent Childbearing on Daughters' Relations with Mothers." *Social Problems*. Vol. 43, No. 4 (November 1996):427–43.

KAPTCHUK, TED. "The Holistic Logic of Chinese Medicine." In SHEPARD BLISS et al., eds., *The New Holistic Health Handbook*. Lexington, Mass.: Steven Greene Press/Penguin, 1985:41.

KARATNYCKY, ADRIAN. "The 2001–2002 Freedom House Survey of Freedom: The Democracy Gap." In *Freedom in the World, 2001–2002*. New York: Freedom House, 2002:7–18.

KARP, DAVID A., and WILLIAM C. YOELS. "The College Classroom: Some Observations on the Meaning of Student Participation." *Sociology and Social Research.* Vol. 60, No. 4 (July 1976):421–39.

KARRFALT, WAYNE. "A Multicultural Mecca." "*American Demographics.* Vol. 25, No. 4 (May 2003):54–55.

KATES, ROBERT W. "Ending Hunger: Current Status and Future Prospects." *Consequences.* Vol. 2, No. 2 (Summer 1996):3–11.

KAUFMAN, MICHAEL T. "Face It: Your Looks Are Revealing." *New York Times* (2002).

KAUFMAN, ROBERT L. "Assessing Alternative Perspectives on Race and Sex Employment Segregation." *American Sociological Review.* Vol. 67, No. 4 (August 2002):547–72.

KAUFMAN, WALTER. *Religions in Four Dimensions: Existential, Aesthetic, Historical, and Comparative.* New York: Reader's Digest Press, 1976.

KAY, PAUL, and WILLETT KEMPTON. "What Is the Sapir-Whorf Hypothesis?" *American Anthropologist.* Vol. 86, No. 1 (March 1984):65–79.

KEISTER, LISA A. *Wealth in America: Trends in Wealth Inequality.* New York: Cambridge University Press, 2000.

———. "Religion and Wealth: The Role of Religious Affiliation and Participation in Early Adult Asset Accumulation." *Social Forces,* Vol. 82, No. 1 (September 2003):173–205.

KEISTER, LISA A., and STEPHANIE MOLLER. "Wealth Inequality in the United States." *Annual Review of Sociology.* Vol. 26 (2000):63–81.

KELLER, HELEN. *The Story of My Life.* New York: Doubleday, 1903.

KELLERT, STEPHEN R., and F. HERBERT BORMANN. "Closing the Circle: Weaving Strands among Ecology, Economics, and Ethics." In F. HERBERT BORMANN and STEPHEN R. KELLERT, eds., *Ecology, Economics, and Ethics: The Broken Circle.* New Haven, Conn.: Yale University Press, 1991:205–10.

KEMP, DOMINIC. "Deaths, Diseases Traced to Environment." *Popline* (May/June 1998):3.

KENT, MARY M., and MARK MATHER. "What Drives U.S. Population Growth?" *Population Bulletin.* Vol. 57, No. 4 (December 2002):3–40.

KENTOR, JEFFREY. "The Long-Term Effects of Foreign Investment Dependence on Economic Growth, 1940–1990." *American Journal of Sociology.* Vol. 103, No. 4 (January 1998):1024–46.

———. "The Long-Term Effects of Globalization on Income Inequality, Population Growth, and Economic Development." *Social Problems.* Vol. 48, No. 4 (November 2001):435–55.

KERCKHOFF, ALAN C., RICHARD T. CAMPBELL, and IDEE WINFIELD-LAIRD. "Social Mobility in Great Britain and the United States." *American Journal of Sociology.* Vol. 91, No. 2 (September 1985):281–308.

KEYS, JENNIFER. "Feeling Rules That Script the Abortion Experience." Paper presented at the annual meeting of the American Sociological Association, Chicago, August 2002.

KIDRON, MICHAEL, and RONALD SEGAL. *The New State of the World Atlas.* New York: Simon & Schuster, 1991.

KILBOURNE, BROCK K. "The Conway and Siegelman Claims against Religious Cults: An Assessment of Their Data." *Journal for the Scientific Study of Religion.* Vol. 22, No. 4 (December 1983):380–85.

KILGORE, SALLY B. "The Organizational Context of Tracking in Schools." *American Sociological Review.* Vol. 56, No. 2 (April 1991):189–203.

KING, KATHLEEN PIKER, and DENNIS E. CLAYSON. "The Differential Perceptions of Male and Female Deviants." *Sociological Focus.* Vol. 21, No. 2 (April 1988):153–64.

KINKEAD, GWEN. *Chinatown: A Portrait of a Closed Society.* New York: Harper-Collins, 1992.

KINSEY, ALFRED C., WARDELL B. POMEROY, and CLYDE E. MARTIN. *Sexual Behavior in the Human Male.* Philadelphia: Saunders, 1948.

KINSEY, ALFRED C., WARDELL B. POMEROY, CLYDE E. MARTIN, and PAUL H. GEBHARD. *Sexual Behavior in the Human Female.* Philadelphia: Saunders, 1953.

KITTRIE, NICHOLAS N. *The Right to Be Different: Deviance and Enforced Therapy.* Baltimore: Johns Hopkins University Press, 1971.

KLEIN, J. D. "The National Longitudinal Study on Adolescent Health: Preliminary Results: Great Expectations." *Journal of the American Medical Association.* Vol. 278, No. 10 (September 10, 1997):864–865.

KLEINFELD, JUDITH. "Student Performance: Males versus Females." *Public Interest* (Winter 1999):3–20.

KLUCKHOHN, CLYDE. "As an Anthropologist Views It." In ALBERT DEUTH, ed., *Sex Habits of American Men.* New York: Prentice Hall, 1948.

KNOX, NOELLE. "European Gay Union Trends Influence U.S. Debate." *USA Today* (July 14, 2004):5A.

KOCHANEK, KENNETH D., SHERRY L. MURPHY, ROBERT N. ANDERSON, and CHESTER SCOTT. "Deaths: Final Data for 2002." *National Vital Statistics Report.* Vol. 53,

No. 5 (October 12, 2004). Hyattsville, Md.: National Center for Health Statistics, 2004.

KOHLBERG, LAWRENCE. *The Psychology of Moral Development: The Nature and Validity of Moral Stages.* New York: Harper & Row, 1981.

KOHLBERG, LAWRENCE, and CAROL GILLIGAN. "The Adolescent as Philosopher: The Discovery of Self in a Postconventional World." *Daedalus.* Vol. 100 (Fall 1971):1051–86.

KOHN, MELVIN L. *Class and Conformity: A Study in Values.* 2d ed. Homewood, Ill.: Dorsey Press, 1977.

KONO, CLIFFORD, DONALD PALMER, ROGER FRIEDLAND, and MATTHEW ZAFONTE. "Lost in Space: The Geography of Corporate Interlocking Directorates." *American Journal of Sociology.* Vol. 103, No. 4 (January 1998):863–911.

KOONTZ, STEPHANIE. *The Way We Never Were: American Families and the Nostalgia Trap.* New York: Basic Books, 1992.

KORNHAUSER, WILLIAM. *The Politics of Mass Society.* New York: Free Press, 1959.

KORPI, WALTER, and JOAKIM PALME. "The Paradox of Redistribution and Strategies of Equality: Welfare State Institutions, Inequality, and Poverty in the Western Countries." *American Sociological Review.* Vol. 65, No. 5 (October 1998):661–87.

KOUSHA, MAHNAZ. "Review of *Modernizing Women* by Valentine M. Moghadam." In *Gender and Society.* Vol. 8 (December 1994):624–26.

KOZOL, JONATHAN. *Rachel and Her Children: Homeless Families in America.* New York: Crown, 1988.

———. *Savage Inequalities: Children in America's Schools.* New York: Harper Perennial, 1992.

KRANTZ, MICHAEL. "Say It with a :-)." *Time* (1997):29.

KRAYBILL, DONALD B. *The Riddle of Amish Culture.* Baltimore: Johns Hopkins University Press, 1989.

———. "The Amish Encounter with Modernity." In DONALD B. KRAYBILL and MARC A. OLSHAN, eds., *The Amish Struggle with Modernity.* Hanover, N.H.: University Press of New England, 1994:21–33.

KRAYBILL, DONALD B., and MARC A. OLSHAN, eds. *The Amish Struggle with Modernity.* Hanover, N.H.: University Press of New England, 1994.

KRIESI, HANSPETER. "New Social Movements and the New Class in the Netherlands." *American Journal of Sociology.* Vol. 94, No. 5 (March 1989):1078–116.

KRISTOL, IRVING. "Life without Father." *Wall Street Journal* (November 3, 1994):A18.

KROLL, LUISA, and LEA GOLDMAN, eds. "Billionaires." *Forbes.* Vol. 173, No. 5 (March 15, 2004):91–154.

KRUGMAN, PAUL. "For Richer: How the Permissive Capitalism of the Boom Destroyed American Equality." *New York Times Magazine* (September 20, 2002):62 ff.

KRUKS, GABRIEL N. "Gay and Lesbian Homeless/Street Youth: Special Issues and Concerns." *Journal of Adolescent Health.* Special Issue No. 12 (1991):515–18.

KRYSAN, MARIA. "Community Undesirability in Black and White: Examining Racial Residential Preferences through Community Perceptions." *Social Problems.* Vol. 49, No. 4 (November 2002):521–43.

KÜBLER-ROSS, ELISABETH. *On Death and Dying.* New York: Macmillan, 1969.

KUUMBA, M. BAHATI. "A Cross-Cultural Race/Class/Gender Critique of Contemporary Population Policy: The Impact of Globalization." *Sociological Forum.* Vol. 14, No. 3 (March 1999):447–63.

KUZNETS, SIMON. "Economic Growth and Income Inequality." *American Economic Review.* Vol. 14, No. 1 (March 1955):1–28.

———. *Modern Economic Growth: Rate, Structure, and Spread.* New Haven, Conn.: Yale University Press, 1966.

LABOVITZ, PRICISSA. "Immigration: Just the Facts." *New York Times* (March 25, 1996).

LACAYO, RICHARD. "The Brawl over Sprawl." *Time* (March 22, 1999):44–48.

———. "Blood at the Root." *Time* (April 10, 2000):122–23.

LACH, JENNIFER. "The Color of Money." *American Demographics.* Vol. 21, No. 2 (February 1999):59–60.

LADD, JOHN. "The Definition of Death and the Right to Die." In JOHN LADD, ed., *Ethical Issues Relating to Life and Death.* New York: Oxford University Press, 1979:118–45.

LAI, H. M. "Chinese." In *Harvard Encyclopedia of American Ethnic Groups.* Cambridge, Mass.: Harvard University Press, 1980:217–33.

LANDSBERG, MITCHELL. "Health Disaster Brings Early Death in Russia." *Washington Times* (March 15, 1998):A8.

LANGBEIN, LAURA I. "Politics, Rules, and Death Row: Why States Eschew or Execute Executions." *Social Science Quarterly.* Vol. 80, No. 4 (December 1999):629–47.

LANGBEIN, LAURA I., and ROSEANA BESS. "Sports in School: Source of Amity or Antipathy?" *Social Science Quarterly.* Vol. 83, No. 2 (June 2002):436–54.

LAPCHICK, RICHARD. *2003 Racial and Gender Report Card*. Institute for Diversity and Ethics in Sport, University of Central Florida. 2003. [Online] Available April 14, 2004, at http://www.bus.ucf.edu/sport/public/downloads/media/ides/release_05.pdf

LAPPÉ, FRANCES MOORE, and JOSEPH COLLINS. *World Hunger: Twelve Myths*. New York: Grove Press/Food First Books, 1986.

LAREAU, ANNETTE. "Invisible Inequality: Social Class and Childrearing in Black Families and White Families." *American Sociological Review*. Vol. 67, No. 5 (October 2002):747–76.

LA ROSSA, RALPH, and DONALD C. REITZES. "Two? Two and One-Half? Thirty Months? Chronometrical Childhood in Early Twentieth-Century America." *Sociological Forum*. Vol. 166, No. 3 (September 2001):385–407.

LASLETT, BARBARA. "Family Membership, Past and Present." *Social Problems*. Vol. 25, No. 5 (June 1978):476–90.

LASLETT, PETER. *The World We Have Lost: England before the Industrial Age*. 3d ed. New York: Scribner, 1984.

LASSWELL, MARK. "A Tribe at War: Not the Yąnomami, the Anthropologists." *Wall Street Journal* (November 17, 2000):A17.

LAUMANN, EDWARD O., JOHN H. GAGNON, ROBERT T. MICHAEL, and STUART MICHAELS. *The Social Organization of Sexuality: Sexual Practices in the United States*. Chicago: University of Chicago Press, 1994.

LAVELLE, MARIANNE. "Payback Time." *U.S. News & World Report* (March 11, 2002):36–40.

———. "Rogue of the Year." *U.S. News & World Report* (December 30, 2002–January 6, 2003):32–45.

LEACH, COLIN WAYNE. "Democracy's Dilemma: Explaining Racial Inequality in Egalitarian Societies." *Sociological Forum*. Vol. 17, No. 4 (December 2002):681–96.

LEACOCK, ELEANOR. "Women's Status in Egalitarian Societies: Implications for Social Evolution." *Current Anthropology*. Vol. 19, No. 2 (June 1978):247–75.

LEAVITT, JUDITH WALZER. "Women and Health in America: An Overview." In JUDITH WALZER LEAVITT, ed., *Women and Health in America*. Madison: University of Wisconsin Press, 1984:3–7.

LEFEBVRE, HENRI. *The Production of Space*. Oxford: Blackwell, 1991.

LELAND, JOHN. "Bisexuality." *Newsweek* (July 17, 1995):44–49.

LEMERT, EDWIN M. *Social Pathology*. New York: McGraw-Hill, 1951.

———. *Human Deviance, Social Problems, and Social Control*. 2d ed. Englewood Cliffs, N.J.: Prentice Hall, 1972.

LENGERMANN, PATRICIA MADOO, and RUTH A. WALLACE. *Gender in America: Social Control and Social Change*. Englewood Cliffs, N.J.: Prentice Hall, 1985.

LENNON, MARY CLARE, and SARAH ROSENFELD. "Relative Fairness and the Doctrine of Housework: The Importance of Options." *American Journal of Sociology*. Vol. 100, No. 2 (September 1994):506–31.

LENSKI, GERHARD E. *Power and Privilege: A Theory of Social Stratification*. New York: McGraw-Hill, 1966.

LEONARD, EILEEN B. *Women, Crime, and Society: A Critique of Theoretical Criminology*. White Plains, N.Y.: Longman, 1982.

LERNER, DANIEL. *The Passing of Traditional Society: Modernizing the Middle East*. New York: Free Press, 1958.

LETHBRIDGE-CEJKU, MARGARET, JEANNINE S. SCHILLER, and LUTHER BERNADEL. *Summary Health Statistics for U.S. Adults: National Health Interview Survey, 2002*. Vital and Health Statistics, Series 10, No. 222. Washington, D.C.: National Center for Health Statistics, 2004.

LE VAY, SIMON. *The Sexual Brain*. Cambridge, Mass.: MIT Press, 1993.

LEVER, JANET. "Sex Differences in the Complexity of Children's Play and Games." *American Sociological Review*. Vol. 43, No. 4 (August 1978):471–83.

LEVINE, MICHAEL P. *Student Eating Disorders: Anorexia Nervosa and Bulimia*. Washington, D.C.: National Educational Association, 1987.

———. "Reducing Hostility Can Prevent Heart Disease." *Mount Vernon News* (August 9, 1990):4A.

LEVINE, ROBERT V. "Is Love a Luxury?" *American Demographics*. Vol. 15, No. 2 (February 1993):27–28.

LEVINE, SAMANTHA. "The Price of Child Abuse." *U.S. News & World Report* (April 9, 2001):58.

———. "Playing God in Illinois." *U.S. News & World Report* (January 13, 2003):13.

LEWIS, FLORA. "The Roots of Revolution." *New York Times Magazine* (November 11, 1984):70–86.

LEWIS, OSCAR. *The Children of Sanchez*. New York: Random House, 1961.

LIAZOS, ALEXANDER. "The Poverty of the Sociology of Deviance: Nuts, Sluts, and Preverts." *Social Problems*. Vol. 20, No. 1 (Summer 1972):103–20.

———. *People First: An Introduction to Social Problems*. Needham Heights, Mass.: Allyn & Bacon, 1982.

LICHTER, DANIEL T., and MARTHA L. CROWLEY. "Poverty in America: Beyond Welfare Reform." *Population Bulletin*. Vol. 57, No. 2 (June 2002):3–34.

LICHTER, DANIEL T., and RUKMALIE JAYAKODY. "Welfare Reform: How Do We Measure Success?" *Annual Review of Sociology*. Vol. 28 (2002):117–41.

LICHTER, S. ROBERT, and DANIEL R. AMUNDSON. "Distorted Reality: Hispanic Characters in TV Entertainment." In CLARA E. RODRIGUEZ, ed., *Latin Looks: Images of Latinas and Latinos in the U.S. Media*. Boulder, Colo.: Westview Press, 1997:57–79.

LIN, NAN, KAREN COOK, and RONALD S. BURT, eds. *Social Capital: Theory and Research*. Hawthorne, N.Y.: Aldine de Gruyter, 2001.

LIN, NAN, and WEN XIE. "Occupational Prestige in Urban China." *American Journal of Sociology*. Vol. 93, No. 4 (January 1988):793–832.

LINDLAW, SCOTT. "President Signs Education Bill." [Online] Available January 8, 2002, at http://news.yahoo.com

LINDSTROM, BONNIE. "Chicago's Post-Industrial Suburbs." *Sociological Focus*. Vol. 28, No. 4 (October 1995):399–412.

LING, PYAU. "Causes of Chinese Emigration." In AMY TACHIKI, ed., *Roots: An Asian American Reader*. Los Angeles: UCLA Asian American Studies Center, 1971:134–38.

LINN, MICHAEL. "Class Notes 1970." *Cornell Alumni News*. Vol. 99, No. 2 (September 1996):25.

LINO, MARK. *Expenditures on Children by Families, 2003*. U.S. Department of Agriculture, Center for Nutrition Policy and Promotion. Miscellaneous Publication No. 1528-2003. Washington, D.C.: U.S. Government Printing Office, 2004.

LINTON, RALPH. "One Hundred Percent American." *American Mercury*. Vol. 40, No. 160 (April 1937a):427–29.

———. *The Study of Man*. New York: Appleton-Century, 1937b.

LIPSET, SEYMOUR MARTIN. *Canada and the United States*. CHARLES F. DONAN and JOHN H. SIGLER, eds. Englewood Cliffs, N.J.: Prentice Hall, 1985.

LISKA, ALLEN E., and BARBARA D. WARNER. "Functions of Crime: A Paradoxical Process." *American Journal of Sociology*. Vol. 96, No. 6 (May 1991):1441–63.

LITTLE, CRAIG, and ANDREA RANKIN. "Why Do They Start It? Explaining Reported Early Teen Sexual Activity." *Sociological Forum*. Vol. 16, No. 4 (December 2001):703–29.

LOBO, SUSAN. "Census-Taking and the Invisibility of Urban American Indians." *Population Today*. Vol. 30, No. 4 (May/June 2002):3–4.

LOGAN, JOHN R., RICHARD D. ALBA, and WENQUAN ZHANG. "Immigrant Enclaves and Ethnic Communities in New York and Los Angeles." *American Sociological Review*. Vol. 67, No. 2 (April 2002):299–322.

LORD, MARY. "Good Teachers, the Newest Imports." *U.S. News & World Report* (April 9, 2001):54.

———. "A Battle for Children's Futures." *U.S. News & World Report* (March 4, 2002):35–6.

LORD, WALTER. *A Night to Remember*. Rev. ed. New York: Holt, Rinehart and Winston, 1976.

LOVEMAN, MARA. "Is 'Race' Essential?" *American Sociological Review*. Vol. 64, No. 6 (December 1999):890–98.

LUND, DALE A. "Caregiving." In *Encyclopedia of Adult Development*. Phoenix, Ariz.: Oryx Press, 1993:57–63.

LUNDMAN, RICHARD L. Correspondence with author, 1999.

LUO, JAR-DER. "The Significance of Networks in the Initiation of Small Businesses in Taiwan." *Sociological Focus*. Vol. 12, No. 2 (June 1997):297–317.

LUTZ, CATHERINE A. *Unnatural Emotions: Everyday Sentiments on a Micronesia Atoll and Their Challenge to Western Theory*. Chicago: University of Chicago Press, 1988.

LUTZ, CATHERINE A., and GEOFFREY M. WHITE. "The Anthropology of Emotions." In BERNARD J. SIEGEL, ALAN R. BEALS, and STEPHEN A. TYLER, eds., *Annual Review of Anthropology*. Vol. 15. Palo Alto, Calif.: Annual Reviews, 1986:405–36.

LYNCH, MICHAEL, and DAVID BOGEN. "Sociology's Asociological 'Core': An Examination of Textbook Sociology in Light of the Sociology of Scientific Knowledge." *American Sociological Review*. Vol. 62, No. 3 (June 1997):481–93.

LYND, ROBERT S., and HELEN MERRELL LYND. *Middletown in Transition*. New York: Harcourt, Brace & World, 1937.

LYNOTT, PATRICIA PASSUTH, and BARBARA J. LOGUE. "The 'Hurried Child': The Myth of Lost Childhood in Contemporary American Society." *Sociological Forum*. Vol. 8, No. 3 (September 1993):471–91.

MABRY, MARCUS, and TOM MASLAND. "The Man after Mandela." *Newsweek* (June 7, 1999):54–55.

MACCOBY, ELEANOR EMMONS, and CAROL NAGY JACKLIN. *The Psychology of Sex Differences*. Stanford, Calif.: Stanford University Press, 1974.

MACE, DAVID, and VERA MACE. *Marriage East and West*. Garden City, N.Y.: Double-day/Dolphin, 1960.

MACIONIS, JOHN J. "Intimacy: Structure and Process in Interpersonal Relationships." *Alternative Lifestyles*. Vol. 1, No. 1 (February 1978):113–30.

———. "A Sociological Analysis of Humor." Presentation to the Texas Junior College Teachers Association, Houston, 1987.

MACIONIS, JOHN J., and LINDA M. GERBER. *Sociology*. 5th Canadian ed. Toronto: Pearson Prentice Hall, 2005.

MACIONIS, JOHN J., and VINCENT R. PARRILLO. *Cities and Urban Life*. 3d ed. Upper Saddle River, N.J.: Prentice Hall, 2004.

MACKAY, JUDITH. *The Penguin Atlas of Human Sexual Behavior*. New York: Penguin, 2000.

MACPHERSON, KAREN. "Children Have a Full-Time Media Habit, Study Says." *Toledo Blade* (November 18, 1999):3.

MADDOX, SETMA. "Organizational Culture and Leadership Style: Factors Affecting Self-Managed Work Team Performance." Paper presented at the annual meeting of the Southwest Social Science Association, Dallas, February 1994.

MALTHUS, THOMAS ROBERT. *First Essay on Population, 1798*. London: Macmillan, 1926; orig. 1798.

MANZA, JEFF, and CLEM BROOKS. "The Religious Factor in U.S. Presidential Elections, 1960–1992." *American Journal of Sociology*. Vol. 103, No. 1 (July 1997):38–81.

Marathonguide.com. "Marathon Records." 2004. [Online] Available October 6, 2004, at http://www.marathonguide.com/history/index.cfm

MARCUSE, HERBERT. *One-Dimensional Man*. Boston: Beacon Press, 1964.

MARE, ROBERT D. "Five Decades of Educational Assortative Mating." *American Sociological Review*. Vol. 56, No. 1 (February 1991):15–32.

MARÍN, GERARDO, and BARBARA VAN OSS MARÍN. *Research with Hispanic Populations*. Newbury Park, Calif.: Sage, 1991.

MARKLEIN, MARY BETH. "Optimism Rises as SAT Math Scores Hit 30-Year High." *USA Today* (August 30, 2000):1A.

MARKOFF, JOHN. "Remember Big Brother? Now He's a Company Man." *New York Times* (March 31, 1991):7.

MARKS, ALEXANDRA. "U.S. Shelters Swell—with Families." *Christian Science Monitor*. [Online] Available December 4, 2001, at http://www.csmonitor.com

MARQUAND, ROBERT. "Worship Shift: Americans Seek Feeling of 'Awe.'" *Christian Science Monitor* (May 28, 1997):1, 8.

MARQUAND, ROBERT, and DANIEL B. WOOD. "Rise in Cults as Millennium Approaches." *Christian Science Monitor* (March 28, 1997):1, 18.

MARQUARDT, ELIZABETH, and NORVAL GLENN. *Hooking Up, Hanging Out, and Hoping for Mr. Right*. New York: Institute for American Values, 2001.

MARSHALL, SUSAN E. "Ladies against Women: Mobilization Dilemmas of Antifeminist Movements." *Social Problems*. Vol. 32, No. 4 (April 1985):348–62.

MARTIN, CAROL LYNN, and RICHARD A. FABES. "The Stability and Consequences of Young Children's Same-Sex Peer Interactions. *Developmental Psychology*. Vol. 37, No. 3 (May 2001):431–46.

MARTIN, JOHN M., and ANNE T. ROMANO. *Multinational Crime: Terrorism, Espionage, Drug and Arms Trafficking*. Newbury Park, Calif.: Sage, 1992.

MARTIN, JOYCE A., BRADY E. HAMILTON, PAUL D. SUTTON, STEPHANIE J. VENTURA, FAY MENACKER, and MARTHA L. MUNSON. "Births: Final Data for 2002." *National Vital Statistics Report*. Vol. 52, No. 10 (December 17, 2003). Hyattsville, Md.: National Center for Health Statistics, 2004.

MARTINEZ, RAMIRO, JR. "Latinos and Lethal Violence: The Impact of Poverty and Inequality." *Social Problems*. Vol. 43, No. 2 (May 1996):131–46.

MARULLO, SAM. "The Functions and Dysfunctions of Preparations for Fighting Nuclear War." *Sociological Focus*. Vol. 20, No. 2 (April 1987):135–53.

MARX, KARL. *Karl Marx: Selected Writings in Sociology and Social Philosophy*. T. B. Bottomore, trans. New York: McGraw-Hill, 1964.

———. *Capital*. FRIEDRICH ENGELS, ed. New York: International Publishers, 1967, orig. 1867.

———. "Theses on Feuer." In ROBERT C. TUCKER, ed., *The Marx-Engels Reader*. New York: Norton, 1972:107–09, orig. 1845.

MARX, KARL, and FRIEDRICH ENGELS. "Manifesto of the Communist Party." In ROBERT C. TUCKER, ed., *The Marx-Engels Reader*. New York: Norton, 1972:331–62, orig. 1848.

———. *The Marx-Engels Reader*. 2d ed. ROBERT C. TUCKER, ed. New York: Norton, 1978.

MARX, LEO. "The Environment and the 'Two Cultures' Divide." In JAMES RODGER FLEMING and HENRY A. GEMERY, eds., *Science, Technology, and the Environment: Multidisciplinary Perspectives*. Akron, Ohio: University of Akron Press, 1994:3–21.

MASSEY, DOUGLAS S. "Housing Discrimination 101." *Population Today*. Vol. 28, No. 6 (August/September 2000):1, 4.

MASSEY, DOUGLAS S., and NANCY A. DENTON. "Hypersegregation in U.S. Metropolitan Areas: Black and Hispanic Segregation along Five Dimensions." *Demography*. Vol. 26, No. 3 (August 1989):373–91.

MATTHIESSEN, PETER. *Indian Country*. New York: Viking Press, 1984.

MAUER, MARC. *The Crisis of the Young African American Male and the Criminal Justice System*. Report prepared for U.S. Commission on Civil Rights. Washington, D.C., April 15–16, 1999. [Online] Available October 1, 2004, at http://www.sentencingproject.org/pdfs/5022.pdf

MAYO, KATHERINE. *Mother India*. New York: Harcourt, Brace, 1927.

MCADAM, DOUG, JOHN D. MCCARTHY, and MAYER N. ZALD. "Social Movements." In NEIL J. SMELSER, ed., *Handbook of Sociology*. Newbury Park, Calif.: Sage, 1988:695–737.

MCALLISTER, J. F. O. "Cinderella, Career Gal." *Time* (April 23, 2001):8.

MCBROOM, WILLIAM H., and FRED W. REED. "Recent Trends in Conservatism: Evidence of Non-Unitary Patterns." *Sociological Focus*. Vol. 23, No. 4 (October 1990):355–65.

MCCAFFREY, DAWN, and JENNIFER KEYS. "Competitive Framing Processes in the Abortion Debate: Polarization-Vilification, Frame Saving, and Frame Debunking." *Sociological Quarterly*. Vol. 41, No. 1 (Winter 2000):41–61.

MCCARTHY, JOHN D., and MAYER N. ZALD. "Resource Mobilization and Social Movements: A Partial Theory." *American Journal of Sociology*. Vol. 82, No. 6 (May 1977):1212–41.

MCCOLM, R. BRUCE, et al. *Freedom in the World: Political Rights and Civil Liberties, 1990–1991*. New York: Freedom House, 1991.

MCDONALD, KIM A. "Debate over How to Gauge Global Warming Heats Up Meeting of Climatologists." *Chronicle of Higher Education*. Vol. 45, No. 22 (February 5, 1999):A17.

MCDONALD, PETER. "Low Fertility Not Politically Sustainable." *Population Today*. Vol. 29, No. 6 (August/September 2001):3, 8.

MCGURN, WILLIAM. "Philadelphia Dims Edison's Light." *Wall Street Journal* (March 20, 2002):A22.

MCKEE, VICTORIA. "Blue Blood and the Color of Money." *New York Times* (June 9, 1996):49–50.

MCLANAHAN, SARA. "Life without Father: What Happens to the Children?" *Contexts*. Vol. 1, No. 1 (Spring 2002):35–44.

MCLEOD, JANE D., and MICHAEL J. SHANAHAN. "Poverty, Parenting, and Children's Mental Health." *American Sociological Review*. Vol. 58, No. 3 (June 1993):351–66.

MCLEOD, JAY. *Ain't No Makin' It: Aspirations and Attainment in a Low-Income Neighborhood*. Boulder, Colo.: Westview Press, 1995.

MEAD, GEORGE HERBERT. *Mind, Self, and Society*. CHARLES W. MORRIS, ed. Chicago: University of Chicago Press, 1962; orig. 1934.

MEAD, MARGARET. *Sex and Temperament in Three Primitive Societies*. New York: Morrow, 1963, orig. 1935.

MEADOWS, DONELLA H., DENNIS L. MEADOWS, JORGAN RANDERS, and WILLIAM W. BEHRENS III. *The Limits to Growth: A Report on the Club of Rome's Project on the Predicament of Mankind*. New York: Universe, 1972.

MELTZER, BERNARD N. "Mead's Social Psychology." In JEROME G. MANIS and BERNARD N. MELTZER, eds., *Symbolic Interaction: A Reader in Social Psychology*. 3d ed. Needham Heights, Mass.: Allyn & Bacon, 1978.

MELUCCI, ALBERTO. *Nomads of the Present: Social Movements and Individual Needs in Contemporary Society*. Philadelphia: Temple University Press, 1989.

MENCKEN, F. CARSON, and IDEE WINFIELD. "Employer Recruiting and the Gender Composition of Jobs." *Sociological Focus*. Vol. 32, No. 2 (May 1999):210–20.

MENJIVAR, CECILIA. "Immigrant Kinship Networks and the Impact of the Receiving Context: Salvadorans in San Francisco in the Early 1990s." *Social Problems*. Vol. 44, No. 1 (February 1997):104–23.

MERTON, ROBERT K. "Social Structure and Anomie." *American Sociological Review*. Vol. 3, No. 6 (October 1938):672–82.

———. *Social Theory and Social Structure*. New York: Free Press, 1968.

METZ, MICHAEL E., and MICHAEL H. MINER. "Psychosexual and Psychosocial Aspects of Male Aging and Sexual Health." *Canadian Journal of Human Sexuality*. Vol. 7, No. 3 (Summer 1998):245–60.

METZGER, KURT. "Cities and Race." *Society*. Vol. 39, No. 1 (December 2001):2.

MEYER, DAVIS S., and NANCY WHITTIER. "Social Movement Spillover." *Social Problems*. Vol. 41, No. 2 (May 1994):277–98.

MICHELS, ROBERT. *Political Parties*. Glencoe, Ill.: Free Press, 1949; orig. 1911.

MILBRATH, LESTER W. *Envisioning a Sustainable Society: Learning Our Way Out*. Albany: State University of New York Press, 1989.

MILGRAM, STANLEY. "Behavioral Study of Obedience." *Journal of Abnormal and Social Psychology*. Vol. 67, No. 4 (1963):371–78.

———. "Group Pressure and Action against a Person." *Journal of Abnormal and Social Psychology*. Vol. 69, No. 2 (August 1964):137–43.

———. "Some Conditions of Obedience and Disobedience to Authority." *Human Relations.* Vol. 18 (February 1965):57–76.

MILLER, ALAN S., and RODNEY STARK. "Gender and Religiousness: Can Socialization Explanations Be Saved?" *American Journal of Sociology.* Vol. 107, No. 6 (May 2002):1399–423.

MILLER, ARTHUR G. *The Obedience Experiments: A Case of Controversy in Social Science.* New York: Praeger, 1986.

MILLER, FREDERICK D. "The End of SDS and the Emergence of Weatherman: Demise through Success." In JO FREEMAN, ed., *Social Movements of the Sixties and Seventies.* White Plains, N.Y.: Longman, 1983:279–97.

MILLER, G. TYLER, JR. *Living in the Environment: An Introduction to Environmental Science.* Belmont, Calif.: Wadsworth, 1992.

MILLER, WALTER B. "Lower-Class Culture as a Generating Milieu of Gang Delinquency." In MARVIN E. WOLFGANG, LEONARD SAVITZ, and NORMAN JOHNSTON, eds., *The Sociology of Crime and Delinquency.* 2d ed. New York: Wiley, 1970:351–63; orig. 1958.

MILLER, WILLIAM J., and RICK A. MATTHEWS. "Youth Employment, Differential Association, and Juvenile Delinquency." *Sociological Focus.* Vol. 34, No. 3 (August 2001):251–68.

MILLS, C. WRIGHT. *The Power Elite.* New York: Oxford University Press, 1956.

———. *The Sociological Imagination.* New York: Oxford University Press, 1959.

MIRACLE, TINA S., ANDREW W. MIRACLE, and ROY F. BAUMEISTER. *Human Sexuality: Meeting Your Basic Needs.* Upper Saddle River, N.J.: Prentice Hall, 2003.

MIRINGOFF, MARC, and MARQUE-LUISA MIRINGOFF. "The Social Health of the Nation." *Economist.* Vol. 352, No. 8128 (July 17, 1999):suppl. 6–7.

MIROWSKY, JOHN. "The Psycho-Economics of Feeling Underpaid: Distributive Justice and the Earnings of Husbands and Wives." *American Journal of Sociology.* Vol. 92, No. 6 (May 1987):1404–34.

MITCHELL, ALISON. "Give Me a Home Where the Buffalo Roam Less." *New York Times* (January 20, 2002):sec. 4, p. 5.

MOGELONSKY, MARCIA. "Reconfiguring the American Dream (House)." *American Demographics.* Vol. 19, No. 1 (January 1997):31–35.

MOLOTCH, HARVEY. "The City as a Growth Machine." *American Journal of Sociology.* Vol. 82, No. 2 (September 1976):309–33.

MONTAIGNE, FEN. "Russia Rising." *National Geographic* (September 2001):2–31.

MOORE, GWEN. "Gender and Informal Networks in State Government." *Social Science Quarterly.* Vol. 73, No. 1 (March 1992):46–61.

MOORE, GWEN, SARAH SOBIERAJ, J. ALLEN WHITT, OLGA MAYOROVA, and DANIEL BEAULIEU. "Elite Interlocks in Three U.S. Sectors: Nonprofit, Corporate, and Government." *Social Science Quarterly.* Vol. 83, No. 3 (September 2002):726–44.

MOORE, WILBERT E. "Modernization as Rationalization: Processes and Restraints." In MANNING NASH, ed., *Essays on Economic Development and Cultural Change in Honor of Bert F. Hoselitz.* Chicago: University of Chicago Press, 1977:29–42.

———. *World Modernization: The Limits of Convergence.* New York: Elsevier, 1979.

MORGAN, LAURIE A. "Glass Ceiling or Cohort Effect? A Longitudinal Study of the Gender Earnings Gap for Engineers, 1982 to 1989." *American Sociological Review.* Vol. 63, No. 4 (August 1998):479–93.

MORSE, JODIE. "Learning while Black." *Time* (May 27, 2002a):50–52.

———. "A Victory for Vouchers." *Time* (July 8, 2002b):32–34.

MULLER, CHANDRA, and CHRISTOPHER G. ELLISON. "Religious Involvement, Social Capital, and Adolescents' Academic Progress: Evidence from the National Education Longitudinal Study of 1988." *Sociological Focus.* Vol. 34, No. 2 (May 2001):155–83.

MULRINE, ANNA. "Risky Business." *U.S. News & World Report* (May 27, 2002):42–49.

MUMFORD, LEWIS. *The City in History: Its Origins, Its Transformations, and Its Prospects.* New York: Harcourt, Brace & World, 1961.

MUNSON, MARTHA L., and PAUL D. SUTTON. "Births, Marriages, Divorces, and Deaths: Provisional Data for 2003. *National Vital Statistics Report.* Vol. 52, No. 22 (June 10, 2004). Hyattsville, Md.: National Center for Health Statistics, 2004.

MURDOCK, GEORGE PETER. "Comparative Data on the Division of Labor by Sex." *Social Forces.* Vol. 15, No. 4 (May 1937):551–53.

———. "The Common Denominator of Cultures." In RALPH LINTON, ed., *The Science of Man in World Crisis.* New York: Columbia University Press, 1945:123–42.

———. *Social Structure.* New York: Free Press, 1965, orig. 1949.

MURPHY, SHERRY L. "Death: Final Data for 1998." *National Vital Statistics Report.* Vol. 48, No. 11 (November 2000):1–105.

MURRAY, STEPHEN O., and WILL ROSCOE, eds. *Studies of African Homosexualities.* New York: St. Martin's Press, 1998.

MYERS, DAVID G. *The American Paradox: Spiritual Hunger in an Age of Plenty.* New Haven, Conn.: Yale University Press, 2000.

MYERS, NORMAN. "Disappearing Cultures." In SIR EDMUND HILLARY, ed., *Ecology 2000: The Changing Face of the Earth.* New York: Beaufort Books, 1984a:162–69.

———. "Humanity's Growth." In SIR EDMUND HILLARY, ed., *Ecology 2000: The Changing Face of the Earth.* New York: Beaufort Books, 1984b:16–35.

———. "The Mega-Extinction of Animals and Plants." In SIR EDMUND HILLARY, ed., *Ecology 2000: The Changing Face of the Earth.* New York: Beaufort Books, 1984c:82–107.

———. "Biological Diversity and Global Security." In F. HERBERT BORMANN and STEPHEN R. KELLERT, eds., *Ecology, Economics, and Ethics: The Broken Circle.* New Haven, Conn.: Yale University Press, 1991:11–25.

MYERS, SHEILA, and HAROLD G. GRASMICK. "The Social Rights and Responsibilities of Pregnant Women: An Application of Parsons's Sick Role Model." Paper presented to the Southwestern Sociological Association, Little Rock, Arkansas, March 1989.

MYRDAL, GUNNAR. *An American Dilemma: The Negro Problem and Modern Democracy.* New York: Harper Bros., 1944.

NASH, J. MADELEINE. "To Know Your Own Fate." *Time* (April 3, 1995):62.

NATIONAL CENER FOR EDUCATION STATISTICS. *Digest of Education Statistics, 2002.* Washington, D.C.: U.S. Government Printing Office, 2003.

———. *Dropout Rates in the United States: 2001.* Washington, D.C.: U.S. Government Printing Office, 2004. [Online] Available November 6, 2004, at http://www.nces.ed.gov/pubs2005/2005046.pdf

NATIONAL CLEARINGHOUSE ON CHILD ABUSE AND NEGLECT INFORMATION. "Child Maltreatment 2002: Summary of Key Findings." 2004. [Online] Available November 4, 2004, at http://nccanch.acf.hhs.gov/pubs/factsheets/canstats.cfm

NATIONAL COMMISSION ON EXCELLENCE IN EDUCATION. *A Nation at Risk.* Washington, D.C.: U.S. Government Printing Office, 1983.

NAVARRO, MIREYA. "Puerto Rican Presence Wanes in New York." *New York Times* (February 28, 2000):A1, A20.

NEERGAARD, LAURAN. "Tobacco Devastating Women's Health." Yahoo! News. [Online] Available March 28, 2001, at http://www.yahoo.com

NELSON, AMY L. "The Effect of Economic Restructuring on Family Poverty in the Industrial Heartland, 1970–1990." *Sociological Focus.* Vol. 31, No. 2 (May 1998):201–16.

NELSON, JOEL I. "Work and Benefits: The Multiple Problems of Service Sector Employment." *Social Problems.* Vol. 42, No. 2 (May 1994):240–55.

NEUHOUSER, KEVIN. "The Radicalization of the Brazilian Catholic Church in Comparative Perspective." *American Sociological Review.* Vol. 54, No. 2 (April 1989):233–44.

NEUMAN, W. LAURENCE. *Social Research Methods: Qualitative and Quantitative Approaches.* 4th ed. Boston: Allyn & Bacon, 2000.

NEWMAN, KATHERINE S. *Declining Fortunes: The Withering of the American Dream.* New York: Basic Books, 1993.

NEWMAN, WILLIAM M. *American Pluralism: A Study of Minority Groups and Social Theory.* New York: Harper & Row, 1973.

NIELSEN, FRANÇOIS, and ARTHUR S. ALDERSON. "The Kuznets Curve: The Great U-Turn: Income Inequality in U.S. Counties, 1970 to 1990." *American Sociological Review.* Vol. 62, No. 1 (February 1997):12–33.

NIELSEN, JOYCE MCCARL, ed. *Feminist Research Methods: Exemplary Readings in the Social Sciences.* Boulder, Colo.: Westview Press, 1990.

NISBET, ROBERT A. *The Quest for Community.* New York: Oxford University Press, 1969.

NOCK, STEVEN L., JAMES D. WRIGHT, and LAURA SANCHEZ. "America's Divorce Problem." *Society.* Vol. 36, No. 4 (May/June 1999):43–52.

NOLAN, PATRICK, and GERHARD LENSKI. *Human Societies.* 9th ed. Boulder, Colo.: Paradigm, 2004.

NORC. *General Social Surveys, 1972–1991: Cumulative Codebook.* Chicago: National Opinion Research Center, 1991.

———. *General Social Surveys, 1972–2002: Cumulative Codebook.* Chicago: National Opinion Research Center, 2003.

NORD, MARK. "Does It Cost Less to Live in Rural Areas? Evidence from New Data on Food Scarcity and Hunger." *Rural Sociology.* Vol. 65, No. 1 (March 2000):104–25.

NOVAK, VIVECA. "The Cost of Poor Advice." *Time* (July 5, 1999):38.

NULAND, SHERWIN B. "The Hazards of Hospitalization." *Wall Street Journal* (December 2, 1999):A22.

OAKES, JEANNIE. "Classroom Social Relationships: Exploring the Bowles and Gintis Hypothesis." *Sociology of Education.* Vol. 55, No. 4 (October 1982):197–212.

———. *Keeping Track: How High Schools Structure Inequality.* New Haven, Conn.: Yale University Press, 1985.

O'CONNOR, RORY J. "Internet Declared Protected Speech." *Glens Falls* (N.Y.) *Post-Star* (June 27, 1997):A1–A2.

OGBURN, WILLIAM F. *On Culture and Social Change.* Chicago: University of Chicago Press, 1964.

O'HARE, WILLIAM P. "The Rise of Hispanic Affluence." *American Demographics.* Vol. 12, No. 8 (August 1990):40–43.

O'HARE, WILLIAM P., WILLIAM H. FREY, and DAN FOST. "Asians in the Suburbs." *American Demographics.* Vol. 16, No. 9 (May 1994):32–38.

OKRENT, DANIEL. "Raising Kids Online: What Can Parents Do?" *Time* (May 10, 1999):38–43.

OLSEN, GREGG M. "Re-Modeling Sweden: The Rise and Demise of the Compromise in a Global Economy." *Social Problems.* Vol. 43, No. 1 (February 1996):1–20.

OLZAK, SUSAN. "Labor Unrest, Immigration, and Ethnic Conflict in Urban America, 1880–1914." *American Journal of Sociology.* Vol. 94, No. 6 (May 1989):1303–33.

O'NEILL, BRIAN, and DEBORAH BALK. "World Population Futures." *Population Bulletin.* Vol. 56, No. 3 (September 2001):3–40.

"Online Privacy: It's Time for Rules in Wonderland." *Business Week* (March 20, 2000):82–96.

ORECKLIN, MICHELLE. "Earnings Report: J.K. and Judy." *Time* (January 13, 2003):72.

ORHANT, MELANIE. "Human Trafficking Exposed." *Population Today.* Vol. 30, No. 1 (January 2002):1, 4.

ORLANSKY, MICHAEL D., and WILLIAM L. HEWARD. *Voices: Interviews with Handicapped People.* Columbus, Ohio: Merrill, 1981.

ORWIN, CLIFFORD. "All Quiet on the Western Front?" *Public Interest* (Spring 1996): 3–9.

OSTRANDER, SUSAN A. "Upper-Class Women: The Feminine Side of Privilege." *Qualitative Sociology.* Vol. 3, No. 1 (Spring 1980):23–44.

———. *Women of the Upper Class.* Philadelphia: Temple University Press, 1984.

OUCHI, WILLIAM. *Theory Z: How American Business Can Meet the Japanese Challenge.* Reading, Mass.: Addison-Wesley, 1981.

"Our Cheating Hearts." Editorial. *U.S. News & World Report* (May 6, 2002):4.

OVADIA, SETH. "Race, Class, and Gender Differences in High School Seniors' Values: Applying Intersection Theory in Empirical Analysis." *Social Science Quarterly.* Vol. 82, No. 2 (June 2001):341–56.

OWEN, CAROLYN A., HOWARD C. ELSNER, and THOMAS R. MCFAUL. "A Half-Century of Social Distance Research: National Replication of the Bogardus Studies." *Sociology and Social Research.* Vol. 66 (1977):80–98.

PACKARD, MARK. Personal communication, 2002.

PADAWER, RUTH. "Striking Transformations for Nation's Families, Seniors." *Bergen* (Co. N.J.) *Record* (May 15, 2001):A1, A13.

PAKULSKI, JAN. "Mass Social Movements and Social Class." *International Sociology.* Vol. 8, No. 2 (June 1993):131–58.

PALLONE, NATHANIEL J., and JAMES J. HENNESSY. "Brain Dysfunction and Criminal Violence." *Society.* Vol. 35, No. 6 (September/October 1998):20–27.

PARIS, PETER J. "The Religious World of African Americans." In Jacob Neusner, ed. *World Religions in America: An Introduction.* Rev. and exp. ed. Louisville, Ky.: Westminster John Knox Press, 2000:48–65.

PARK, ROBERT E. *Race and Culture.* Glencoe, Ill.: Free Press, 1950.

PARRILLO, VINCENT N. "Diversity in America: A Sociohistorical Analysis." *Sociological Forum.* Vol. 9, No. 4 (December 1994):42–45.

———. *Strangers to These Shores.* 7th ed. Boston: Allyn & Bacon, 2003a.

———. "Updating the Bogardus Social Distance Studies: A New National Survey." Revised version of a paper presented at the annual meeting of the American Sociological Association, August 17, 2002. Provided by the author, 2003b.

PARSONS, TALCOTT. "Age and Sex in the Social Structure of the United States." *American Sociological Review.* Vol. 7, No. 4 (August 1942):604–16.

———. *The Social System.* Glencoe, Ill.: Free Press, 1951.

———. *Essays in Sociological Theory.* Glencoe, Ill.: Free Press, 1954.

———. *Societies: Evolutionary and Comparative Perspectives.* Englewood Cliffs, N.J.: Prentice Hall, 1966.

PARSONS, TALCOTT, and ROBERT F. BALES, eds. *Family, Socialization and Interaction Process.* Glencoe, Ill.: Free Press, 1955.

PATTERSON, ELISSA F. "The Philosophy and Physical of Holistic Health Care: Spiritual Healing as a Workable Interpretation." *Journal of Advanced Nursing.* Vol. 27, No. 2 (February 1998):287–94.

PATTILLO-MCCOY, MARY. "Church Culture as a Strategy of Action in the Black Community." *American Sociological Review.* Vol. 63, No. 6 (December 1998):767–84.

PAUL, ELLEN FRANKEL. "Bared Buttocks and Federal Cases." *Society.* Vol. 28, No. 4 (May/June, 1991):4–7.

PAUL, PAMELA. "News, Noticias, Nouvelles." *American Demographics.* Vol. 23, No. 11 (November 2001):26–31.

PEAR, ROBERT, and ERIK ECKHOLM. "When Healers Are Entrepreneurs: A Debate over Costs and Ethics." *New York Times* (June 2, 1991):1, 17.

PEARSON, DAVID E. "Post-Mass Culture." *Society.* Vol. 30, No. 5 (July/August 1993):17–22.

———. "Community and Sociology." *Society.* Vol. 32, No. 5 (July/August 1995):44–50.

PEASE, JOHN, and LEE MARTIN. "Want Ads and Jobs for the Poor: A Glaring Mismatch." *Sociological Forum.* Vol. 12, No. 4 (December 1997):545–64.

PEDERSON, DANIEL, VERN E. SMITH, and JERRY ADLER. "Sprawling, Sprawling. . . ." *Newsweek* (July 19, 1999):23–27.

PERLMUTTER, PHILIP. "Minority Group Prejudice." *Society.* Vol. 39, No. 3 (March/April 2002):59–65.

PESSEN, EDWARD. *Riches, Class, and Power: America before the Civil War.* New Brunswick, N.J.: Transaction, 1990.

Peters Atlas of the World. New York: HarperCollins, 1990.

PETERSEN, TROND, ISHAK SAPORTA, and MARC-DAVID L. SEIDEL. "Offering a Job: Meritocracy and Social Networks." *American Journal of Sociology.* Vol. 106, No. 3 (November 2000):763–816.

PETERSILIA, JOAN. "Probation in the United States: Practices and Challenges." *National Institute of Justice Journal.* No. 233 (September 1997):4.

PHI DELTA KAPPA INTERNATIONAL. *The 36th Annual Phi Delta Kappa/Gallup Poll of the Public's Attitudes toward the Public Schools.* [Online] Available November 6, 2004, at http://www.pdkintl.org/kappan/k0409pol.htm

PHILADELPHIA, DESA. "Rookie Teacher, Age 50." *Time* (April 9, 2001):66–68.

———. "Tastier, Plusher—and Fast." *Time* (September 30, 2002):57.

PHILLIPS, MELANIE. "What about the Overclass?" *Public Interest* (Fall 2001):38–43.

PIERCE, EMILY. "Momentum Swing." *CQ Weekly.* Vol. 58, No. 44 (November 11, 2000):26–46.

PINCHOT, GIFFORD, and ELIZABETH PINCHOT. *The End of Bureaucracy and the Rise of the Intelligent Organization.* San Francisco: Berrett-Koehler, 1993.

PINHEY, THOMAS K., DONALD H. RUBINSTEIN, and RICHARD S. COLFAX. "Overweight and Happiness: The Reflected Self-Appraisal Hypothesis Reconsidered." *Social Science Quarterly.* Vol. 78, No. 3 (September 1997):747–55.

PINKER, STEVEN. *The Language Instinct.* New York: Morrow, 1994.

PIRANDELLO, LUIGI. "The Pleasure of Honesty." In *To Clothe the Naked and Two Other Plays.* New York: Dutton, 1962:143–98.

PITNEY, JOHN J., JR. "What Scholars Don't Know about Term Limits." *Chronicle of Higher Education.* Vol. 41, No. 33 (April 28, 1995):A76.

PIVEN, FRANCES FOX, and RICHARD A. CLOWARD. *Poor People's Movements: Why They Succeed, How They Fail.* New York: Pantheon Books, 1977.

PODOLNY, JOEL M., and JAMES N. BARON. "Resources and Relationships: Social Networks and Mobility in the Workplace." *American Sociological Review.* Vol. 62, No. 5 (October 1997):673–93.

POLENBERG, RICHARD. *One Nation Divisible: Class, Race, and Ethnicity in the United States since 1938.* New York: Pelican Books, 1980.

POLLACK, ANDREW. "Happy in the East (^-^) or Smiling :-) in the West." *New York Times* (August 12, 1996).

POLLARD, KELVIN. "Play Ball! Demographics and Major League Baseball." *Population Today.* Vol. 24, No. 4 (April 1996):3.

POLSBY, NELSON W. "Three Problems in the Analysis of Community Power." *American Sociological Review.* Vol. 24, No. 6 (December 1959):796–803.

POMER, MARSHALL I. "Labor Market Structure, Intragenerational Mobility, and Discrimination: Black Male Advancement out of Low-Paying Occupations, 1962–1973." *American Sociological Review.* Vol. 51, No. 5 (October 1986):650–59.

PONIEWOZIK, JAMES. "Postnuclear Explosion." *Time* (November 6, 2000):110–11.

POPENOE, DAVID. "American Family Decline, 1960–1990: A Review and Appraisal." *Journal of Marriage and the Family.* Vol. 55, No. 3 (August 1993a):527–55.

———. "Parental Androgyny." *Society.* Vol. 30, No. 6 (September/October 1993b):5–11.

———. "Can the Nuclear Family Be Revived?" *Society.* Vol. 36, No. 5 (July/August 1999):28–30.

POPENOE, DAVID, and BARBARA DAFOE WHITEHEAD. *Should We Live Together? What Young Adults Need to Know about Cohabitation before Marriage.* New Brunswick, N.J.: National Marriage Project, 1999.

POPULATION ACTION INTERNATIONAL. *People in the Balance: Population and Resources at the Turn of the Millennium.* Washington, D.C.: Population Action International, 2000.

POPULATION REFERENCE BUREAU. *2004 World Population Data Sheet.* Washington, D.C.: Population Reference Bureau, 2004.

PORTER, EDUARDO. "Even 126 Sizes Do Not Fit All." *Wall Street Journal* (March 2, 2001):B1.

PORTES, ALEJANDRO, and LEIF JENSEN. "The Enclave and the Entrants: Patterns of Ethnic Enterprise in Miami before and after Mariel." *American Sociological Review.* Vol. 54, No. 6 (December 1989):929–49.

POSTEL, SANDRA. "Facing Water Scarcity." In LESTER R. BROWN et al., eds., *State of the World 1993: A Worldwatch Institute Report on Progress toward a Sustainable Society.* New York: Norton, 1993:22–41.

POWELL, CHRIS, and GEORGE E. C. PATON, eds. *Humor in Society: Resistance and Control.* New York: St. Martin's Press, 1988.

PRESTON, LEE E. "Corporate Boards and Corporate Governance." *Society.* Vol. 32, No. 3 (March/April 1995):17–20.

PRIMEGGIA, SALVATORE, and JOSEPH A. VARACALLI. "Southern Italian Comedy: Old to New World." In JOSEPH V. SCELSA, SALVATORE J. LA GUMINA, and LYDIO TOMASI, eds., *Italian Americans in Transition.* New York: American Italian Historical Association, 1990:241–52.

PUTKA, GARY. "SAT to Become a Better Gauge." *Wall Street Journal* (November 1, 1990):B1.

QUILLIAN, LINCOLN, and DEVAH PAGER. "Black Neighbors, Higher Crime? The Role of Racial Stereotypes in Evaluations of Neighborhood Crime." *American Journal of Sociology.* Vol. 107, No. 3 (November 2001):717–67.

QUINNEY, RICHARD. *Class, State and Crime: On the Theory and Practice of Criminal Justice.* New York: McKay, 1977.

RABKIN, JEREMY. "The Supreme Court in the Culture Wars." *Public Interest* (Fall 1996):3–26.

RALEY, R. KELLY. "A Shortage of Marriageable Men? A Note on the Role of Cohabitation in Black-White Differences in Marriage Rates." *American Journal of Sociology.* Vol. 61, No. 6 (December 1996):973–83.

RANK, MARK R., and THOMAS A. HIRSCHL. "Rags or Riches? Estimating the Probabilities of Poverty and Affluence across the Adult American Life Span." *Social Science Quarterly.* Vol. 82, No. 4 (December 2001):651–69.

RAPHAEL, RAY. *The Men from the Boys: Rites of Passage in Male America.* Lincoln: University of Nebraska Press, 1988.

RATNESAR, ROMESH. "Lost in the Middle." *Time* (September 14, 1998):60–62.

RAY, VERONICA. *Choosing Happiness: The Art of Living Unconditionally.* Center City, Minn.: Hazelden Foundation, 1991.

RAYMOND, JOAN. "The Multicultural Report." *American Demographics.* Vol. 23, No. 11 (November 2001):S1–S6.

RECKLESS, WALTER C., and SIMON DINITZ. "Pioneering with Self-Concept as a Vulnerability Factor in Delinquency." *Journal of Criminal Law, Criminology, and Police Science.* Vol. 58, No. 4 (December 1967):515–23.

RECTOR, ROBERT. "America Has the World's Richest Poor People." *Wall Street Journal* (September 24, 1998):A18.

REINHARZ, SHULAMIT. *Feminist Methods in Social Research.* New York: Oxford University Press, 1992.

REMOFF, HEATHER TREXLER. *Sexual Choice: A Woman's Decision.* New York: Dutton/Lewis, 1984.

RESKIN, BARBARA F., and DEBRA BRANCH MCBRIER. "Why Not Ascription? Organizations' Employment of Male and Female Managers." *American Sociological Review.* Vol. 65, No. 2 (April 2000):210–33.

REVKIN, ANDREW C. "Can Global Warming Be Studied Too Much?" *New York Times* (December 3, 2002):D1, D4.

RHODES, STEVE. "The Luck of the Draw." *Newsweek* (April 26, 1999):41.

RIDDLE, JOHN M., J. WORTH ESTES, and JOSIAH C. RUSSELL. "Ever since Eve: Birth Control in the Ancient World." *Archaeology.* Vol. 47, No. 2 (March/April 1994):29–35.

RIDGEWAY, CECILIA L. *The Dynamics of Small Groups.* New York: St. Martin's Press, 1983.

RIESMAN, DAVID. *The Lonely Crowd: A Study of the Changing American Character.* New Haven, Conn.: Yale University Press, 1970; orig. 1950.

RITZER, GEORGE. *The McDonaldization of Society: An Investigation into the Changing Character of Contemporary Social Life.* Thousand Oaks, Calif.: Pine Forge Press, 1993.

———. *The McDonaldization Thesis: Explorations and Extensions.* Thousand Oaks, Calif.: Sage, 1998.

———. "The Globalization of McDonaldization." *Spark* (February 2000):8–9.

RITZER, GEORGE, and DAVID WALCZAK. *Working: Conflict and Change.* 4th ed. Englewood Cliffs, N.J.: Prentice Hall, 1990.

ROBERTS, J. DEOTIS. *Roots of a Black Future: Family and Church.* Philadelphia: Westminster Press, 1980.

ROBINSON, LINDA. "A Timeworn Terrorism List." *U.S. News & World Report* (May 20, 2002):18, 21.

ROBINSON, THOMAS N., MARTA L. WILDE, LISA C. NAVRACRUZ, K. FARISH HAYDEL, and ANN VARADY. "Effects of Reducing Children's Television and Video Game Use on Aggressive Behavior." *Archives of Pediatrics and Adolescent Medicine.* Vol. 155, No. 1 (January 2001):17–23.

ROBINSON, VERA M. "Humor and Health." In PAUL E. MCGHEE and JEFFREY H. GOLDSTEIN, eds., *Handbook of Humor Research.* Vol. 2: *Applied Studies.* New York: Springer-Verlag, 1983:109–28.

ROCKETT, IAN R. H. "Population and Health: An Introduction to Epidemiology." *Population Bulletin.* Vol. 49, No. 3 (November 1994).

RODGERS, JOAN R. "An Empirical Study of Intergenerational Transmission of Poverty in the United States." *Social Science Quarterly.* Vol. 76, No. 1 (March 1995):178–94.

ROESCH, ROBERTA. "Violent Families." *Parents* (September 1984):74–76, 150–52.

ROGERS, RICHARD G., REBECCA ROSENBLATT, ROBERT A. HUMMER, and PATRICK M. KRUEGER. "Black-White Differentials in Adult Homicide Mortality in the United States." *Social Science Quarterly.* Vol. 82, No. 3 (September 2001):435–52.

ROGERS-DILLON, ROBIN H. "What Do We Really Know about Welfare Reform?" *Society.* Vol. 38, No. 2 (January/February 2001):7–15.

ROMERO, FRANCINE SANDERS, and ADRIAN LISERIO. "Saving Open Spaces: Determinants of 1998 and 1999 'Antisprawl' Ballot Measures." *Social Science Quarterly.* Vol. 83, No. 1 (March 2002):341–52.

ROOF, WADE CLARK, and WILLIAM MCKINNEY. *American Mainline Religion: Its Changing Shape and Future.* New Brunswick, N.J.: Rutgers University Press, 1987.

ROSEN, JEFFREY. *The Unwanted Gaze.* New York: Random House, 2000.

ROSENDAHL, MONA. *Inside the Revolution: Everyday Life in Socialist Cuba.* Ithaca, N.Y.: Cornell University Press, 1997.

ROSENFELD, MEGAN. "Little Boys Blue: Reexamining the Plight of Young Males." *Washington Post* (March 26, 1998):A1, A17–A18.

ROSENFELD, RICHARD. "Crime Decline in Context." *Contexts.* Vol. 1, No. 1 (Spring 2002):20–34.

ROSENTHAL, ELIZABETH. "Canada's National Health Plan Gives Care to All, with Limits." *New York Times* (April 30, 1991):A1, A16.

ROSS, JOHN. "To Die in the Street: Mexico City's Homeless Population Boom as Economic Crisis Shakes Social Protections." *SSSP Newsletter.* Vol. 27, No. 2 (Summer 1996):14–15.

ROSSI, ALICE S. "Gender and Parenthood." In ALICE S. ROSSI, ed., *Gender and the Life Course.* New York: Aldine, 1985:161–91.

ROSTOW, WALT W. *The Stages of Economic Growth: A Non-Communist Manifesto.* Cambridge: Cambridge University Press, 1960.

———. *The World Economy: History and Prospect.* Austin: University of Texas Press, 1978.

ROTHMAN, BARBARA KATZ. "Of Maps and Imaginations: Sociology Confronts the Genome." *Social Problems.* Vol. 42, No. 1 (February 1995):1–10.

ROTHMAN, STANLEY, and AMY E. BLACK. "Who Rules Now? American Elites in the 1990s." *Society.* Vol. 35, No. 6 (September/October 1998):17–20.

ROTHMAN, STANLEY, STEPHEN POWERS, and DAVID ROTHMAN. "Feminism in Films." *Society.* Vol. 30, No. 3 (March/April 1993):66–72.

ROUSSEAU, CARYN. "Unions Rally at Wal-Mart Stores." Yahoo! News. [Online] Available November 22, 2002, at http://dailynews.yahoo.com

ROZELL, MARK J., CLYDE WILCOX, and JOHN C. GREEN. "Religious Constituencies and Support for the Christian Right in the 1990s." *Social Science Quarterly.* Vol. 79, No. 4 (December 1998):815–27.

RUBIN, LILLIAN BRESLOW. *Worlds of Pain: Life in the Working-Class Family.* New York: Basic Books, 1976.

RUDEL, THOMAS K., and JUDITH M. GERSON. "Postmodernism, Institutional Change, and Academic Workers: A Sociology of Knowledge." *Social Science Quarterly.* Vol. 80, No. 2 (June 1999):213–28.

RUDOLPH, ELLEN. "Women's Talk: Japanese Women." *New York Times Magazine* (September 1, 1991).

RUGGLES, STEVEN. "The Origins of African-American Family Structure." *American Sociological Review.* Vol. 59, No. 1 (February 1994):136–51.

RULE, JAMES, and PETER BRANTLEY. "Computerized Surveillance in the Workplace: Forms and Delusions." *Sociological Forum.* Vol. 7, No. 3 (September 1992):405–23.

RUSSELL, CHERYL. "Are We in the Dumps?" *American Demographics.* Vol. 17, No. 1 (January 1995a):6.

———. "True Crime." *American Demographics.* Vol. 17, No. 8 (August 1995b):22–31.

RUSSELL, CHERYL, and MARCIA MOGELONSKY. "Riding High on the Market." *American Demographics.* Vol. 22, No. 4 (April 2000):44–54.

RYAN, WILLIAM. *Blaming the Victim.* Rev. ed. New York: Vintage Books, 1976.

RYMER, RUSS. *Genie*. New York: Harper Perennial, 1994.

RYTINA, JOAN HUBER, WILLIAM H. FORM, and JOHN PEASE. "Income and Stratification Ideology: Beliefs about the American Opportunity Structure" *American Journal of Sociology*. Vol. 75, No. 4 (January 1970):703–16.

SACHS, JEFFREY. "The Real Causes of Famine." *Time* (October 26, 1998):69.

SAINT JEAN, YANICK, and JOE R. FEAGIN. *Double Burden: Black Women and Everyday Racism*. Armonk, N.Y.: Sharpe, 1998.

SALA-I-MARTIN, XAVIER. "The World Distribution of Income." Working Paper No. 8933. Cambridge, Mass.: National Bureau of Economic Research, 2002.

SALE, KIRKPATRICK. *The Conquest of Paradise: Christopher Columbus and the Columbian Legacy*. New York: Knopf, 1990.

SAMPSON, ROBERT J., and JOHN H. LAUB. "Crime and Deviance over the Life Course: The Salience of Adult Social Bonds." *American Sociological Review*. Vol. 55, No. 5 (October 1990):609–27.

SAMUELSON, ROBERT J. "The Rich and Everyone Else." *Newsweek* (January 27, 2003):57.

SAPIR, EDWARD. "The Status of Linguistics as a Science." *Language*. Vol. 5 (1929):207–14.

———. *Selected Writings of Edward Sapir in Language, Culture, and Personality*. DAVID G. MANDELBAUM, ed. Berkeley: University of California Press, 1949.

SAPORITO, BILL. "Can Wal-Mart Get Any Bigger?" *Time* (January 13, 2003):38–43.

SAWHILL, ISABELL V. "The Perils of Early Motherhood." *Public Interest* (Winter 2002):74–84.

SAX, LINDA J., et al. *The American Freshman: National Norms for Fall 2003*. Los Angeles: UCLA Higher Education Research Institute, 2003.

SCANLON, JAMES P. "The Curious Case of Affirmative Action for Women." *Society*. Vol. 29, No. 2 (January/February 1992):36–42.

SCANLON, STEPHAN J. "Food Availability and Access in Less-Industrialized Societies: A Test and Interpretation of Neo-Malthusian and Technoecological Theories." *Sociological Forum*. Vol. 16, No. 2 (June 2001):231–62.

SCHAFFER, MICHAEL. "American Dreamers." *U.S. News & World Report* (August 26, 2002):12–16.

SCHAUB, DIANA. "From Boys to Men." *Public Interest* (Spring 1997):108–14.

SCHEFF, THOMAS J. *Being Mentally Ill: A Sociological Theory*. 2d ed. New York: Aldine, 1984.

SCHLESINGER, ARTHUR M., JR. "The City in American Civilization." In ALEXANDER B. CALLOW JR., ed., *American Urban History*. New York: Oxford University Press, 1969:25–41.

SCHLESINGER, JACOB M. "Finally, U.S. Median Income Approaches Old Heights." *Wall Street Journal* (September 25, 1998):B1.

SCHLOSSER, ERIC. *Fast Food Nation: The Dark Side of the All-American Meal*. New York: Perennial, 2002.

SCHMITT, ERIC. "Whites in Minority in Largest Cities, the Census Shows." *New York Times* (April 30, 2001):A1, A12.

SCHNAIBERG, ALLAN, and KENNETH ALAN GOULD. *Environment and Society: The Enduring Conflict*. New York: St. Martin's Press, 1994.

SCHNEIDER, MARK, MELISSA MARSCHALL, PAUL TESKE, and CHRISTINE ROCH. "School Choice and Culture Wars in the Classroom: What Different Parents Seek from Education." *Social Science Quarterly*. Vol. 79, No. 3 (September 1998):489–501.

SCHOFER, EVAN, and MARION FOURCADE-GOURINCHAS. "The Structural Contexts of Civil Engagement: Voluntary Association Membership in Comparative Perspective." *American Sociological Review*. Vol. 66, No. 6 (December 2001):806–28.

SCHULTZ, T. PAUL. "Inequality in the Distribution of Personal Income in the World: How It Is Changing and Why." *Journal of Population Economics*. Vol. 11, No. 2 (1998):307–44.

SCHUR, LISA A., and DOUGLAS L. KRUSE. "What Determines Voter Turnout? Lessons from Citizens with Disabilities." *Social Science Quarterly*. Vol. 81, No. 2 (June 2000): 571–87.

SCHUTT, RUSSELL K. "Objectivity versus Outrage." *Society*. Vol. 26, No. 4 (May/June 1989):14–16.

SCHWARTZ, BARRY. "Memory as a Cultural System: Abraham Lincoln in World War II." *American Sociological Review*. Vol. 61, No. 5 (October 1996):908–27.

SCHWARTZ, FELICE N. "Management, Women, and the New Facts of Life." *Harvard Business Review*. Vol. 89, No. 1 (January/February 1989):65–76.

SCHWARTZ, JOHN. "Simulated Prison in '71 Showed a Fine Line between 'Normal' and 'Monster.'" *New York Times* (May 6, 2004):A20.

SCOMMEGNA, PAOLA. "Increased Cohabitation Changing Children's Family Settings." *Population Today*. Vol. 30, No. 7 (July 2002):3, 6.

SCOTT, JOSEPH E., and J. CUVELIER. "Violence in *Playboy* Magazine: A Longitudinal Analysis." *Archives of Sexual Behavior*. Vol. 16 (1987):279–88.

SCOTT, W. RICHARD. *Organizations: Rational, Natural, and Open Systems*. Englewood Cliffs, N.J.: Prentice Hall, 1981.

SEAGER, JONI. *The Penguin Atlas of Women in the World*. 3d ed. New York: Penguin Putnam, 2003.

SEGAL, MADY WECHSLER, and AMANDA FAITH HANSEN. "Value Rationales in Policy Debates on Women in the Military: A Content Analysis of Congressional Testimony, 1941–1985." *Social Science Quarterly*. Vol. 73, No. 2 (June 1992):296–309.

SEIDMAN, STEVEN. *Queer Theory/Sociology*. Oxford: Blackwell, 1996.

SENNETT, RICHARD. *The Corrosion of Character: The Personal Consequences of Work in the New Capitalism*. New York: Norton, 1998.

SENNETT, RICHARD, and JONATHAN COBB. *The Hidden Injuries of Class*. New York: Vintage Books, 1973.

SENTENCING PROJECT. "Facts about Prisons and Prisoners." May 2004. [Online] Available September 30, 2004, at http://www.sentencingproject.org/pdfs/1035.pdf

SHAPIRO, JOSEPH P., and JOANNIE M. SCHROF. "Honor Thy Children." *U.S. News & World Report* (February 27, 1995):39–49.

SHARPE, ANITA. "The Rich Aren't So Different After All." *Wall Street Journal* (November 12, 1996):B1, B10.

SHAWCROSS, WILLIAM. *Sideshow: Kissinger, Nixon and the Destruction of Cambodia*. New York: Pocket Books, 1979.

SHEA, RACHEL HARTIGAN. "The New Insecurity." *U.S. News & World Report* (March 25, 2002):40.

SHELDON, WILLIAM H., EMIL M. HARTL, and EUGENE MCDERMOTT. *Varieties of Delinquent Youth*. New York: Harper Bros., 1949.

SHERKAT, DARREN E., and CHRISTOPHER G. ELLISON. "Recent Developments and Current Controversies in the Sociology of Religion." *Annual Review of Sociology*. Vol. 25 (1999):363–94.

SHERMAN, LAWRENCE W., and DOUGLAS A. SMITH. "Crime, Punishment, and Stake in Conformity: Legal and Informal Control of Domestic Violence." *American Sociological Review*. Vol. 57, No. 5 (October 1992):680–90.

SHEVKY, ESHREF, and WENDELL BELL. *Social Area Analysis*. Palo Alto, Calif.: Stanford University Press, 1955.

SHIPLEY, JOSEPH T. *Dictionary of Word Origins*. Totowa, N.J.: Roman & Allanheld, 1985.

SHIVELY, JOELLEN. "Cowboys and Indians: Perceptions of Western Films among American Indians and Anglos." *American Sociological Review*. Vol. 57, No. 6 (December 1992):725–34.

SHUPE, ANSON. *In the Name of All That's Holy: A Theory of Clergy Malfeasance*. Westport, Conn.: Praeger, 1995.

SHUPE, ANSON, WILLIAM A. STACEY, and LONNIE R. HAZLEWOOD. *Violent Men, Violent Couples: The Dynamics of Domestic Violence*. Lexington, Mass.: Lexington Books, 1987.

SIMMEL, GEORG. *The Sociology of Georg Simmel*. KURT WOLFF, ed. New York: Free Press, 1950:118–69, orig. 1902.

SIMON, JULIAN. *The Ultimate Resource*. Princeton, N.J.: Princeton University Press, 1981.

———. "More People, Greater Wealth, More Resources, Healthier Environment." In THEODORE D. GOLDFARB, ed., *Taking Sides: Clashing Views on Controversial Environmental Issues*. 6th ed. Guilford, Conn.: Dushkin, 1995.

SIMON, ROGER, and ANGIE CANNON. "An Amazing Journey." *U.S. News & World Report* (August 6, 2001):10–19.

SIMONS, CAROL. "Japan's *Kyoiku* Mamas." In JOHN J. MACIONIS and NIJOLE V. BENOKRAITIS, eds., *Seeing Ourselves: Classic, Contemporary, and Cross-Cultural Readings in Sociology*. Englewood Cliffs, N.J.: Prentice Hall, 1989:281–86.

SIMONS, MARLISE. "The Price of Modernization: The Case of Brazil's Kaiapo Indians." In JOHN J. MACIONIS and NIJOLE V. BENOKRAITIS, eds., *Seeing Ourselves: Classic, Contemporary, and Cross-Cultural Readings in Sociology*. 6th ed. Upper Saddle River, N.J.: Prentice Hall, 2004:494–500.

SIMPSON, GEORGE EATON, and J. MILTON YINGER. *Racial and Cultural Minorities: An Analysis of Prejudice and Discrimination*. 4th ed. New York: Harper & Row, 1972.

SIPES, RICHARD G. "War, Sports, and Aggression: An Empirical Test of Two Rival Theories." *American Anthropologist*. Vol. 75, No. 1 (January 1973):64–86.

SIVARD, RUTH LEGER. *World Military and Social Expenditures, 1987–88*. 12th ed. Washington, D.C.: World Priorities, 1988.

SIZER, THEODORE R. *Horace's Compromise: The Dilemma of the American High School*. Boston: Houghton Mifflin, 1984.

SKOCPOL, THEDA. *States and Social Revolutions: A Comparative Analysis of France, Russia, and China*. Cambridge: Cambridge University Press, 1979.

SLOAN, ALLAN. "Bad Boys Club." *Newsweek* (July 1, 2002):44–46.

SMAIL, J. KENNETH. "Let's Reduce Global Population!" In JOHN J. MACIONIS and NIJOLE V. BENOKRAITIS, eds., *Seeing Ourselves: Classic, Contemporary, and

Cross-Cultural Readings in Sociology. 6th ed. Upper Saddle River, N.J.: Prentice Hall, 2004:422–26.

SMART, TIM. ". . . and Those Who Came When I Called." *U.S. News & World Report* (December 30, 2002–January 6, 2003):48.

SMITH, ADAM. *An Inquiry into the Nature and Causes of the Wealth of Nations.* New York: Modern Library, 1937; orig. 1776.

SMITH, CRAIG S. "Authorities Took Victim's Organs, His Brother Says." *Columbus Dispatch* (March 11, 2001):A3.

SMITH, DOUGLAS A. "Police Response to Interpersonal Violence: Defining the Parameters of Legal Control." *Social Forces.* Vol. 65, No. 3 (March 1987):767–82.

SMITH, DOUGLAS A., and PATRICK R. GARTIN. "Specifying Specific Deterrence: The Influence of Arrest on Future Criminal Activity." *American Sociological Review.* Vol. 54, No. 1 (February 1989):94–105.

SMITH, DOUGLAS A., and CHRISTY A. VISHER. "Street-Level Justice: Situational Determinants of Police Arrest Decisions." *Social Problems.* Vol. 29, No. 2 (December 1981):167–77.

SMITH, RYAN A. "Race, Gender, and Authority in the Workplace: Theory and Research." *Annual Review of Sociology.* Vol. 28 (2002):509–42.

SMITH, TOM W. "Anti-Semitism Decreases but Persists." *Society.* Vol. 33, No. 3 (March/April 1996):2.

———. "Are We Grown Up Yet? U.S. Study Says Not 'til 26." [Online] Available May 23, 2003, at http://news.yahoo.com

SMITH-LOVIN, LYNN, and CHARLES BRODY. "Interruptions in Group Discussions: The Effects of Gender and Group Composition." *American Journal of Sociology.* Vol. 54, No. 3 (June 1989):424–35.

SMOCK, PAMELA J. "Cohabitation in the United States: An Appraisal of Research Themes, Findings, and Implications." *Annual Review of Sociology.* Vol. 26 (2000):1–20.

SMOLOWE, JILL. "When Violence Hits Home." *Time* (July 4, 1994):18–25.

SNELL, MARILYN BERLIN. "The Purge of Nurture." *New Perspectives Quarterly.* Vol. 7, No. 1 (Winter 1990):1–2.

SOBEL, RACHEL K. "Herpes Tests Give Answers You Might Need to Know." *U.S. News & World Report* (June 18, 2001):53.

SOUTH, SCOTT J., and KIM L. LLOYD. "Spousal Alternatives and Marital Dissolution." *American Sociological Review.* Vol. 60, No. 1 (February 1995):21–35.

SOUTH, SCOTT J., and STEVEN F. MESSNER. "Structural Determinants of Intergroup Association: Interracial Marriage and Crime." *American Journal of Sociology.* Vol. 91, No. 6 (May 1986):1409–30.

SOWELL, THOMAS. *Ethnic America.* New York: Basic Books, 1981.

———. *Race and Culture.* New York: Basic Books, 1994.

———. "Ethnicity and IQ." In STEVEN FRASER, ed., *The Bell Curve Wars: Race, Intelligence, and the Future of America.* New York: Basic Books, 1995:70–79.

SPATES, JAMES L. "Counterculture and Dominant Culture Values: A Cross-National Analysis of the Underground Press and Dominant Culture Magazines." *American Sociological Review.* Vol. 41, No. 5 (October 1976):868–83.

———. "The Sociology of Values." In RALPH TURNER, ed., *Annual Review of Sociology.* Vol. 9. (1983):27–49.

SPATES, JAMES L., and H. WESLEY PERKINS. "American and English Student Values." *Comparative Social Research.* Vol. 5. Greenwich, Conn.: JAI Press, 1982:245–68.

SPECTER, MICHAEL. "Plunging Life Expectancy Puzzles Russia." *New York Times* (August 2, 1995):A1, A2.

SPEIER, HANS. "Wit and Politics: An Essay on Laughter and Power." ROBERT JACKALL, ed. and trans. *American Journal of Sociology.* Vol. 103, No. 5 (March 1998):1352–401.

SPITZER, STEVEN. "Toward a Marxian Theory of Deviance." In DELOS H. KELLY, ed., *Criminal Behavior: Readings in Criminology.* New York: St. Martin's Press, 1980:175–91.

STACEY, JUDITH. *Patriarchy and Socialist Revolution in China.* Berkeley: University of California Press, 1983.

———. *Brave New Families: Stories of Domestic Upheaval in Late-Twentieth-Century America.* New York: Basic Books, 1990.

———. "Good Riddance to 'The Family': A Response to David Popenoe." *Journal of Marriage and the Family.* Vol. 55, No. 3 (August 1993):545–47.

STACK, STEVEN. "Occupation and Suicide." *Social Science Quarterly.* Vol. 82, No. 2 (June 2001):384–96.

STACK, STEVEN, IRA WASSERMAN, and ROGER KERN. "Adult Social Bonds and the Use of Internet Pornography." *Social Science Quarterly.* Vol. 85, No. 1 (March 2004):75–88.

STAHURA, JOHN M. "Suburban Development, Black Suburbanization, and the Black Civil Rights Movement since World War II." *American Sociological Review.* Vol. 51, No. 1 (February 1986):131–44.

STANLEY, LIZ, ed. *Feminist Praxis: Research, Theory, and Epistemology in Feminist Sociology.* London: Routledge, 1990.

STAPINSKI, HELENE. "Let's Talk Dirty." *American Demographics.* Vol. 20, No. 11 (November 1998):50–56.

STARK, RODNEY. *Sociology.* Belmont, Calif.: Wadsworth, 1985.

STARK, RODNEY, and WILLIAM SIMS BAINBRIDGE. "Of Churches, Sects, and Cults: Preliminary Concepts for a Theory of Religious Movements." *Journal for the Scientific Study of Religion.* Vol. 18, No. 2 (June 1979):117–31.

———. "Secularization and Cult Formation in the Jazz Age." *Journal for the Scientific Study of Religion.* Vol. 20, No. 4 (December 1981):360–73.

STARK, RODNEY, and ROGER FINKE. *Acts of Faith: Explaining the Human Side of Religion.* Berkeley: University of California Press, 2000.

STARR, PAUL. *The Social Transformation of American Medicine.* New York: Basic Books, 1982.

STARR, ROGER. "Recycling: Myths and Realities." *Public Interest.* No. 119 (Spring 1995):28–41.

STEELE, RANDY. "Awful but Lawful." *Boating* (June 2000):36.

STEELE, SHELBY. *The Content of Our Character: A New Vision of Race in America.* New York: St. Martin's Press, 1990.

STEIN, LISA. "Death Penalty." *U.S. News & World Report* (July 1, 2002):12–13.

STEINBERG, LAURENCE. "Failure outside the Classroom." *Wall Street Journal* (July 11, 1996):A14.

STEPHENS, JOHN D. *The Transition from Capitalism to Socialism.* Urbana: University of Illinois Press, 1986.

STERKE, CLAIRE E. *Tricking and Tripping: Prostitution in the Era of AIDS.* Putnam Valley, N.Y.: Social Change Press, 2000.

STERN, SOL. "Why the Catholic School Model Is Taboo." *Wall Street Journal* (July 17, 1996):A14.

STEVENS, GILLIAN, and GRAY SWICEGOOD. "The Linguistic Context of Ethnic Endogamy." *American Sociological Review.* Vol. 52, No. 1 (February 1987):73–82.

STIER, HAYA. "Continuity and Change in Women's Occupations following First Childbirth." *Social Science Quarterly.* Vol. 77, No. 1 (March 1996):60–75.

STODGHILL, RON, II. "Where'd You Learn That?" *Time* (June 15, 1998): 52–59.

STODGHILL, RON, II and AMANDA BOWER. "Where Everyone's a Minority." *Time* (September 2, 2002):25–30.

STOHL, MICHAEL, and GEORGE A. LOPEZ. *The State as Terrorist: The Dynamics of Government Violence and Repression.* Westport, Conn.: Greenwood Press, 1984.

STONE, LAWRENCE. *The Family, Sex, and Marriage in England, 1500–1800.* New York: Harper & Row, 1977.

STORMS, MICHAEL D. "Theories of Sexual Orientation." *Journal of Personality and Social Psychology.* Vol. 38, No. 5 (May 1980):783–92.

STOUFFER, SAMUEL A., EDWARD A. SUCHMAN, LELAND C. DE VINNEY, SHIRLEY A. STAR, and ROBIN M. WILLIAMS JR. *The American Soldier: Adjustment during Army Life.* Vol. 1. Princeton, N.J.: Princeton University Press, 1949.

STOUT, DAVID. "Supreme Court Splits on Diversity Efforts at University of Michigan." [Online] Available June 23, 2003, at http://news.yahoo.com

STRATTON, LESLIE S. "Why Does More Housework Lower Women's Wages? Testing Hypotheses Involving Job Effort and Hours Flexibility." *Social Sciences Quarterly.* Vol. 82, No. 1 (March 2001):67–76.

STROSS, RANDALL E. "The McPeace Dividend." *U.S. News & World Report* (April 1, 2002):36.

SULLIVAN, ANDREW. Lecture delivered at Kenyon College, Gambier, Ohio, April 4, 2002.

SULLIVAN, BARBARA. "McDonald's Sees India as Golden Opportunity." *Chicago Tribune* (April 5, 1995):B1.

SUMNER, WILLIAM GRAHAM. *Folkways.* New York: Dover, 1959, orig. 1906.

SUN, LENA H. "WWII's Forgotten Internees Await Apology." *Washington Post* (March 9, 1998):A1, A5, A6.

SUNG, BETTY LEE. *Mountains of Gold: The Story of the Chinese in America.* New York: Macmillan, 1967.

SUTHERLAND, EDWIN H. "White-Collar Criminality." *American Sociological Review.* Vol. 5, No. 1 (February 1940):1–12.

SUTTON, JOHN R. "Imprisonment and Social Classification in Five Common-Law Democracies, 1955–1985." *American Journal of Sociology.* Vol. 106, No. 2 (September 2000):350–86.

SWARTZ, STEVE. "Why Michael Milken Stands to Qualify for Guinness Book." *Wall Street Journal.* Vol. 70, No. 117 (March 31, 1989):1, 4.

SZASZ, THOMAS S. *The Myth of Mental Illness: Foundations of a Theory of Personal Conduct.* New York: Dell, 1961.

———. *The Manufacturer of Madness: A Comparative Study of the Inquisition and the Mental Health Movement.* New York: Harper & Row, 1970.

———. "Mental Illness Is Still a Myth." *Society*. Vol. 31, No. 4 (May/June 1994):34–39.

———. "Idleness and Lawlessness in the Therapeutic State." *Society*. Vol. 32, No. 4 (May/June 1995):30–35.

TAJFEL, HENRI. "Social Psychology of Intergroup Relations." *Annual Review of Psychology*. Palo Alto, Calif.: Annual Reviews, 1982:1–39.

TAKAKI, RONALD. *Strangers from a Different Shore*. Boston: Back Bay Books, 1998.

TALLICHET, SUZANNE E. "Barriers to Women's Advancement in Underground Coal Mining." *Rural Sociology*. Vol. 65, No. 2 (June 2000):234–52.

TANNAHILL, REAY. *Sex in History*. Chelsea, Mich.: Scarborough House, 1992.

TANNEN, DEBORAH. *You Just Don't Understand: Women and Men in Conversation*. New York: Morrow, 1990.

———. *Talking from 9 to 5: How Women's and Men's Conversational Styles Affect Who Gets Heard, Who Gets Credit, and What Gets Done at Work*. New York: Morrow, 1994.

TANNENBAUM, FRANK. *Crime and the Community*. New York: Columbia University Press, 1938.

TAVRIS, CAROL, and CAROL WADE. *Psychology in Perspective*. 3d ed. Upper Saddle River, N.J.: Prentice Hall, 2001.

TAX FOUNDATION. [Online] Available June 15, 2000, at http://www.taxfoundation.org

TAYLOR, FREDERICK WINSLOW. *The Principles of Scientific Management*. New York. Harper Bros., 1911.

"Terrorist Attacks Spur Unseen Human Toll." *Popline* (December 2001):1–2.

TERRY, DON. "In Crackdown on Bias, A New Tool." *New York Times* (June 12, 1993):8.

TEWKSBURY, RICHARD, and PATRICIA GAGNÉ. "Transgenderists: Products of Non-Normative Intersections of Sex, Gender, and Sexuality." *Journal of Men's Studies*. Vol. 5, No. 2 (November 1996):105–29.

THOMAS, PAULETTE. "Success at a Huge Personal Cost." *Wall Street Journal* (July 26, 1995):B1, B6.

THOMAS, PIRI. *Down These Mean Streets*. New York: Signet, 1967.

THOMAS, W. I. "The Relation of Research to the Social Process." In MORRIS JANOWITZ, ed., *W. I. Thomas on Social Organization and Social Personality*. Chicago: University of Chicago Press, 1966:289–305; orig. 1931.

THOMMA, STEVEN. "Christian Coalition Demands Action from GOP." *Philadelphia Inquirer* (September 14, 1997):A2.

THOMPSON, DICK. "Gene Maverick." *Time* (January 11, 1999):54–55.

THOMPSON, MARK, and DOUGLAS WALLER. "Shield of Dreams." *Time* (May 8, 2001):45–47.

THORNBERRY, TERRANCE P., and MARGARET FARNSWORTH. "Social Correlates of Criminal Involvement: Further Evidence on the Relationship between Social Status and Criminal Behavior." *American Sociological Review*. Vol. 47, No. 4 (August 1982):505–18.

THORNE, BARRIE, CHERIS KRAMARAE, and NANCY HENLEY, eds. *Language, Gender, and Society*. Rowley, Mass.: Newbury House, 1983.

THORNTON, ARLAND, WILLIAM G. AXINN, and DANIEL H. HILL. "Reciprocal Effects of Religiosity, Cohabitation, and Marriage." *American Journal of Sociology*. Vol. 98, No. 3 (November 1992):628–51.

TILLY, CHARLES. "Does Modernization Breed Revolution?" In JACK A. GOLDSTONE, ed., *Revolutions: Theoretical, Comparative, and Historical Studies*. New York: Harcourt Brace Jovanovich, 1986:47–57.

TITTLE, CHARLES R., WAYNE J. VILLEMEZ, and DOUGLAS A. SMITH. "The Myth of Social Class and Criminality: An Empirical Assessment of the Empirical Evidence." *American Sociological Review*. Vol. 43, No. 5 (October 1978):643–56.

TOCQUEVILLE, ALEXIS DE. *The Old Regime and the French Revolution*. STUART GILBERT, trans. Garden City, N.Y.: Anchor/Doubleday, 1955; orig. 1856.

TOLSON, JAY. "The Trouble with Elites." *Wilson Quarterly*. Vol. 19, No. 1 (Winter 1995):6–8.

TÖNNIES, FERDINAND. *Community and Society (Gemeinschaft und Gesellschaft)*. New York: Harper & Row, 1963; orig. 1887.

TOOSSI, MITRA. "Labor Force Projections to 2012: The Graying of the U.S. Workforce." *Monthly Labor Review*. Vol. 127, No. 2 (February 2004):37–57. [Online] Available July 30, 2004, at http://www.bls.gov/opub/mlr/2004/02/art3full.pdf

TORRES, LISA, and MATT L. HUFFMAN. "Social Networks and Job Search Outcomes among Male and Female Professional, Technical, and Managerial Workers." *Sociological Focus*. Vol. 35, No. 1 (February 2002):25–42.

TREAS, JUDITH. "Older Americans in the 1990s and Beyond." *Population Bulletin*. Vol. 50, No. 2 (May 1995).

TRENT, KATHERINE. "Family Context and Adolescents' Expectations about Marriage, Fertility, and Nonmarital Childbearing." *Social Science Quarterly*. Vol. 75, No. 2 (June 1994):319–39.

TROELTSCH, ERNST. *The Social Teaching of the Christian Churches*. New York: Macmillan, 1931.

TUMIN, MELVIN M. "Some Principles of Stratification: A Critical Analysis." *American Sociological Review*. Vol. 18, No. 4 (August 1953):387–94.

———. *Social Stratification: The Forms and Functions of Inequality*. 2d ed. Englewood Cliffs, N.J.: Prentice Hall, 1985.

TURNER, JONATHAN. *On the Origins of Human Emotions: A Sociological Inquiry into the Evolution of Human Emotions*. Stanford, Calif.: Stanford University Press, 2000.

TYLER, S. LYMAN. *A History of Indian Policy*. Washington, D.C.: U.S. Department of the Interior, Bureau of Indian Affairs, 1973.

UDRY, J. RICHARD. "Biological Limitations of Gender Construction." *American Sociological Review*. Vol. 65, No. 3 (June 2000):443–57.

UGGEN, CHRISTOPHER. "Ex-Offenders and the Conformist Alternative: A Job-Quality Model of Work and Crime." *Social Problems*. Vol. 46, No. 1 (February 1999):127–51.

UGGEN, CHRISTOPHER, and JEFF MANZA. "Democratic Contraction? Political Consequences of Felon Disenfranchisement in the United States." *American Sociological Review*. Vol. 67, No. 6 (December 2002):777–803.

UNITED NATIONS. *AIDS Epidemic Update*. Joint United Nations Programme on HIV/AIDS (UNAIDS) and World Health Organization. December, 2002. [Online] Available November 7, 2004, at http://www.unaids.org/

UNITED NATIONS DEVELOPMENT PROGRAMME. *Human Development Report, 1990*. New York: Oxford University Press, 1990.

———. *Human Development Report, 1995*. New York: Oxford University Press, 1995.

———. *Human Development Report, 1996*. New York: Oxford University Press, 1996.

———. *Human Development Report, 2000*. New York: Oxford University Press, 2000.

———. *Human Development Report, 2001*. New York: Oxford University Press, 2001.

———. *Human Development Report, 2002*. New York: Oxford University Press, 2002.

———. *Human Development Report, 2003*. New York: Oxford University Press, 2003.

———. *Human Development Report, 2004*. New York: Oxford University Press, 2004.

UNRUH, JOHN D., JR. *The Plains Across*. Urbana: University of Illinois Press, 1979.

URBAN INSTITUTE. "Nearly 3 Out of 4 Young Children with Employed Mothers Are Regularly in Child Care." April 28, 2004. [Online] Available October 12, 2004, at http://www.urban.org/UploadedPDF/900706.pdf

U.S. BUREAU OF ECONOMIC ANALYSIS. "Foreign Direct Investment in the United States: Country Detail for Selected Items." [Online] Available November 4, 2004, at http://www.bea.doc.gov/bea/di/fdilongcty.htm

U.S. BUREAU OF JUSTICE STATISTICS. *Violence against Women*. August, 1995. [Online] Available October 25, 2004, at http://www.ojp.usdoj.gov/bjs/pub/pdf/femvied.pdf

———. *Capital Punishment, 2002*. Washington, D.C.: U.S. Government Printing Office, 2003. [Online] Available July 5, 2004, at http://www.ojp.usdoj.gov/bjs/pub/pdf/cp02.pdf

———. *Criminal Victimization, 2002*. August, 2003. [Online] Available October 2, 2004, at http://www.ojp.usdoj.gov/bjs/pub/pdf/cv02.pdf

———. *Intimate Partner Violence, 1993–2001*. February, 2003. [Online] Available November 4, 2004, at http://www.ojp.usdoj.gov/bjs/pub/pdf/ipv01.pdf

———. "Corrections Statistics." [Online] Available October 2, 2004, at http://www.ojp.usdoj.gov/bjs/correct.htm

———. *Criminal Victimization, 2003*. September, 2004. [Online] Available October 2, 2004, at http://www.ojp.usdoj.gov/bjs/pub/pdf/cv03.pdf

———. *Prison and Jail Inmates at Midyear 2003*. May, 2004. [Online] Available October 2, 2004, at http://www.ojp.usdoj.gov/bjs/pub/pdf/pjim03.pdf

———. *Sourcebook of Criminal Justice Statistics, 2002*. [Online] Available September 29, 2004, at http://www.albany.edu/sourcebook

U.S. CENSUS BUREAU. *School Enrollment: Social and Economic Characteristics of Students: October 1995 (Update)*. PPL-55. Washington, D.C.: U.S. Government Printing Office, 1997.

———. "Census Bureau Counts 170,000 at Homeless Shelters." News release, October 31, 2000.

———. *Educational Attainment in the United States*, March 2000 (Update). Current Population Reports, P20-536. Washington, D.C.: U.S. Government Printing Office, 2000.

———. *The Black Population, 2000*. Census 2000 Brief, C2KBR/01-5. Washington, D.C.: U.S. Government Printing Office, 2001.

———. Census 2000, Summary File 1. "(Table) GCT-P6. Metropolitan Area, in Central City, not in Central City, County, and County Subdivision: 100 Percent Data by Race and Hispanic or Latino: 2000." 2001. [Online] Available November 10, 2004, at http://factfinder.census.gov/servlet/DatasetMainPageServlet?_program=DEC&_lang=en&_ts=

———. *The Hispanic Population, 2000.* Census 2000 Brief, C2KBR/01-3. Washington, D.C.: U.S. Government Printing Office, 2001.

———. *Mapping Census 2000: The Geography of U.S. Diversity.* Census Special Reports, Series CENSR/01-1. Washington, D.C.: U.S. Government Printing Office, 2001.

———. *Money Income in the United States, 2000.* Current Population Reports, P60-213. Washington, D.C.: U.S. Government Printing Office, 2001.

———. *The Native Hawaiian and Other Pacific Islander Population, 2000.* Census 2000 Brief, C2KBR/01-14. Washington, D.C.: U.S. Government Printing Office, 2001.

———. *Population Change and Distribution: 1990 to 2000.* Census 2000 Brief, C2KBR/01-2. Washington, D.C.: U.S. Government Printing Office, 2001.

———. *Poverty in the United States, 2000.* Current Population Reports, P60-214. Washington, D.C.: U.S. Government Printing Office, 2001.

———. *The 65 Years and Over Population, 2000.* Census 2000 Brief, C2KBR/01-10. Washington, D.C.: U.S. Government Printing Office, 2001.

———. *The Two or More Races Population, 2000.* Census 2000 Brief, C2KBR/01-6. Washington, D.C.: U.S. Government Printing Office, 2001.

———. *The White Population, 2000.* Census 2000 Brief, C2KBR/01-4. Washington, D.C.: U.S. Government Printing Office, 2001.

———. *The American Indian and Alaska Native Population, 2000.* Census 2000 Brief, C2KBR/01-15. Washington, D.C.: U.S. Government Printing Office, 2002.

———. *The Asian Population, 2000.* Census 2000 Brief, C2KBR/01-16. Washington, D.C.: U.S. Government Printing Office, 2002.

———. "Sex by Age. Summary File 1 Tables." [Online] Available September 26, 2002, at http://www.census.gov

———. *Voting and Registration in the Election of November 2000.* Current Population Reports, P20-542. Washington, D.C.: U.S. Government Printing Office, 2002. [Online] Available October 10, 2004, at http://www.census.gov/population/www/socdemo/voting.html

———. *Custodial Mothers and Fathers and Their Child Support: 2001.* Current Population Reports, P60-225. October, 2003. [Online] Available November 4, 2004, at http://www.census.gov/prod/2003pubs/p60-225.pdf

———. *Fertility of American Women: June 2002.* Current Population Reports (P20-548). "(Table) 1. Distribution of Women by Average Number of Children Ever Born, by Race, Marital Status, and Age: June 2002." October 23, 2003. [Online] Available October 12, 2004, at http://www.census.gov/population/socdemo/fertility/cps2002/tab01.pdf

———. *Grandparents Living with Grandchildren: 2000.* Census 2000 Brief, C2KBR-31. Washington, D.C.: U.S. Government Printing Office, 2003.

———. *The Hispanic Population in the United States, March 2002.* Current Population Reports (P20-545). Washington, D.C.: U.S. Government Printing Office, 2003.

———. *Married-Couple and Unmarried-Partner Households, 2000.* Washington, D.C.: U.S. Government Printing Office, 2003.

———. Metropolitan and Micropolitan Statistical Areas. "(Table) 7. Population in Combined Statistical Areas (CBSAs) and Their Component Metropolitan and Micropolitan Statistical Areas in Alphabetical Order and Numerical and Percent Change for the United States and Puerto Rico: 1990 and 2000." Rev. December 30, 2003. [Online] Available November 8, 2004, at http://www.census.gov/population/www/cen2000/phc-t29.html

———. *Statistical Abstract of the United States, 2003.* Washington, D.C.: U.S. Government Printing Office, 2003.

———. *America's Families and Living Arrangements: 2003.* "(Table) A2, F1." September 15, 2004. [Online] Available November 5, 2004, at http://www.census.gov/population/www/socdemo/hh-fam/cps2003.html

———. Census 2000 American Indian and Alaska Native Summary File (AIANSF). "(Table) DP-3. Profile of Selected Economic Characteristics, 2000." [Online] Available October 8, 2004, at http://factfinder.census.gov

———. Census 2000 Summary File 3. "(Table) QT-P13. Ancestry, 2000." [Online] Available October 7, 2004, at http://factfinder.census.gov

———. Current Population Survey, 2004 Annual Social and Economic Supplement. "(Table) FINC-01, FINC-02, FINC-06." Rev. June 25, 2004. [Online] Available October 3, 2004, at http://ferret.bls.census.gov/macro/032004/faminc/toc.htm

———. Current Population Survey, 2004 Annual Social and Economic Supplement. "(Table) PINC-01, PINC-03, PINC-05." Rev. June 25, 2004. [Online] Available September 23, 2004, at http://ferret.bls.census.gov/macro/032004/perinc/htm

———. Current Population Survey, 2004 Annual Social and Economic Supplement. "(Table) POV01, POV04, POV06." Rev. July 9, 2004. [Online] Available September 30, 2004, at http://ferret.bls.census.gov/macro/032004/pov/toc.htm

———. *Educational Attainment in the United States, 2003.* "(Table) 1, 1a." June 29, 2004. [Online] Available October 8, 2004, at http://www.census.gov/population/socdemo/education/cps2003.html

———. *Historical Income Tables—Families.* "(Table) F-2, F-3, F-5, F-23." Rev. July 8, 2004. [Online] Available October 3, 2004, at http://www.census.gov/hhes/income/histinc/incfamdet.html

———. *Historical Income Tables—People.* "(Table) P-10, P-36." Rev. May 13, 2004. [Online] Available September 22, 2004, at http://www.census.gov/hhes/income/hsitinc/p10.html

———. *Housing Vacancies and Homeownership Annual Statistics, 2003.* "(Table) 20. Homeownership Rates by Race and Ethnicity of Householder, 1994 to 2003." Rev. February 26, 2004. [Online] Available October 3, 2004, at http://www.census.gov/hhes/www/housing/hvs/annual03/ann03t20.html

———. *Income, Poverty, and Health Insurance Coverage in the United States, 2003.* Current Population Reports (P60-226). Washington, D.C.: U.S. Government Printing Office, 2004.

———. International Database. IDB Population Pyramids. September 30, 2004. [Online] Available October 14, 2004, at http://www.census.gov/ipc/www/idbnew.html

———. *Interracial Tables.* Table 2, "Race of Couples: 1990." [Online] Available October 12, 2004, at http://www.census.gov/population/socdemo/race/interractab2.txt

———. *School Enrollment—Social and Economic Characteristics of Students: October 2002.* "(Table) 15." Rev. January 8, 2004. [Online] Available August 16, 2004, at http://www.census.gov/population/socdemo/school/cps2002.html

———. "(Table) MS-3. Interracial Married Couples, 1980 to 2002." September 15, 2004. [Online] Available October 8, 2004, at http://www.census.gov/population/socdemo/hh-fam/tabMS-3.pdf

U.S. Charter Schools. "Answers to Frequently Asked Questions." [Online] Available November 6, 2004, at http://www.uscharterschools.org/pub/uscs_docs/o/faq.html

U.S. Citizenship and Immigration Services. *2003 Yearbook of Immigration Statistics.* September 2004. [Online] Available September 16, 2004, at http://uscis.gov/graphics/shared/aboutus/statistics/2003Yearbook.pdf

U.S. Department of Commerce. *Statistical Abstract of the United States, 1930.* Washington, D.C.: U.S. Government Printing Office, 1930.

U.S. Department of Education. *The State of Charter Schools, 2000.* [Online] Available July 16, 2001, at http://www.ed.gov/PDFDocs/4yrrpt.pdf

U.S. Department of Health and Human Services, Administration for Children and Families. *Temporary Assistance for Needy Families (TANF) Program.* Third Annual Report to Congress, August 2000. Washington, D.C.: U.S. Government Printing Office, 2000.

U.S. Department of Housing and Urban Development. "The Forgotten Americans: Homelessness—Programs and the People They Serve." December 1999. [Online] Available October 4, 2004, at http://www.huduser.org/publications/homeless/homelessness/contents.html

U.S. Department of Justice. *The Sexual Victimization of College Women.* December 2000. [Online] Available October 6, 2004, at http://www.ncjrs.org/pdffiles1/nij/182369.pdf

———. "Nearly Three Percent of College Women Experienced a Completed Rape or Attempted Rape During the College Year, According to a New Justice Department Report." [Online]. Accessed February 15, 2001, at http://www.ojp.usdoj.gov/bjs/pub/press/svcw.pr

U.S. Department of Labor, Bureau of Labor Statistics. "International Comparisons of Hourly Compensation Costs: Supplementary Tables, 1975–2002." Rev. May 21, 2004. [Online] Available August 1, 2004, at http://www.bls.gov/fls/hcompsupptabtoc.htm

———. Tables from *Employment and Earnings.* 2004b. [Online] Available October 6, 2004, at http://www.bls.gov/cps/#annual

U.S. Department of State. "World Military Expenditures and Arms Transfers, 1999–2000." June, 2002. [Online] Available November 4, 2004, at http://www.state.gov/documents/organization/18745.pdf

———. "Patterns of Global Terrorism, 2003." April 2004. [Online] Available October 10, 2004, at http://www.state.gov/s/ct/rls/pgtrpt/2003

USEEM, BERT. "Disorganization and the New Mexico Prison Riot of 1980." *American Sociological Review.* Vol. 50, No. 5 (October 1985):677–88.

U.S. ENVIRONMENTAL PROTECTION AGENCY. *Municipal Solid Waste in the United States: 2001 Facts and Figures.* Washington, D.C.: U.S. Government Printing Office, 2003.

U.S. EQUAL EMPLOYMENT OPPORTUNITY COMMISSION. "Occupational Employment in Private Industry by Race/Ethnic Group/Sex, and by Industry, United States, 2002." Rev. March 17, 2004. [Online] Available September 26, 2004, at http://www.eeoc.gov/stats/jobpat/2002/us.html

U.S. HOUSE OF REPRESENTATIVES. *1991 Green Book.* Washington, D.C.: U.S. Government Printing Office, 1991.

U.S. SMALL BUSINESS ADMINISTRATION. *Minorities in Business, 2001.* November 2001a. [Online] Available October 8, 2004, at http://www.sba.gov/advo/stats/stats_min.html

———. *Women in Business, 2001.* October 2001b. [Online] Available October 8, 2004, at http://www.sba.gov/advo/stats/stats_wib.html

VALDEZ, A. "In the Hood: Street Gangs Discover White-Collar Crime." *Police.* Vol. 21, No. 5 (May 1997):49–50, 56.

VALLAS, STEPHEN P., and JOHN P. BECK. "The Transformation of Work Revisited: The Limits of Flexibility in American Manufacturing." *Social Problems.* Vol. 43, No. 3 (August 1996):339–61.

VALOCCHI, STEVE. "The Emergence of the Integrationist Ideology in the Civil Rights Movement." *Social Problems.* Vol. 43, No. 1 (February 1996):116–30.

VAN BIEMA, DAVID. "Parents Who Kill." *Time* (November 14, 1994):50–51.

———. "Spiriting Prayer into School." *Time* (April 27, 1998):38–41.

———. "A Surge of Teen Spirit." *Time* (May 31, 1999):58–59.

VANDIVERE, SHARON, KATHRYN TOUT, MARTHA ZASLOW, JULIA CALKINS, and JEFFREY CAPIZZANO. *Unsupervised Time: Factors Associated with Self-Care.* Washington, D.C.: The Urban Institute, 2003. [Online] Available November 4, 2004, at http://www.urban.org/UploadedPDF/310894_OP71.pdf

VEDDER, RICHARD, and LOWELL GALLAWAY. "Declining Black Employment." *Society.* Vol. 30, No. 5 (July/August 1993):56–63.

VINOVSKIS, MARIS A. "Have Social Historians Lost the Civil War? Some Preliminary Demographic Speculations." *Journal of American History.* Vol. 76, No. 1 (June 1989):34–58.

VOGEL, EZRA F. *The Four Little Dragons: The Spread of Industrialization in East Asia.* Cambridge, Mass.: Harvard University Press, 1991.

VOGEL, LISE. *Marxism and the Oppression of Women: Toward a Unitary Theory.* New Brunswick, N.J.: Rutgers University Press, 1983.

VOLD, GEORGE B., and THOMAS J. BERNARD. *Theoretical Criminology.* 3d ed. New York: Oxford University Press, 1986.

VOSS, JACQUELINE, and LORI KOGAN. "Behavioral Impact of a Human Sexuality Course." Paper presented at the Western Region Annual Conference of the Society for the Scientific Study of Sexuality, Newport Beach, Calif., April 19–22, 2001.

WALDER, ANDREW G. "Career Mobility and the Communist Political Order." *American Sociological Review.* Vol. 60, No. 3 (June 1995):309–28.

WALDFOGEL, JANE. "The Effect of Children on Women's Wages." *American Sociological Review.* Vol. 62, No. 2 (April 1997):209–17.

WALKER, KAREN. "'Always There for Me': Friendship Patterns and Expectations among Middle- and Working-Class Men and Women." *Sociological Forum.* Vol. 10, No. 2 (June 1995):273–96.

WALL, THOMAS F. *Medical Ethics: Basic Moral Issues.* Washington, D.C.: University Press of America, 1980.

WALLERSTEIN, IMMANUEL. *The Modern World-System: Capitalist Agriculture and the Origins of the European World-Economy in the Sixteenth Century.* New York: Academic Press, 1974.

———. *The Capitalist World Economy.* New York: Cambridge University Press, 1979.

———. "Crises: The World Economy, the Movements, and the Ideologies." In ALBERT BERGESEN, ed., *Crises in the World System.* Beverly Hills, Calif.: Sage, 1983:21–36.

———. *The Politics of the World Economy: The States, the Movements, and the Civilizations.* Cambridge: Cambridge University Press, 1984.

WALLERSTEIN, JUDITH S., and SANDRA BLAKESLEE. *Second Chances: Men, Women, and Children a Decade after Divorce.* New York: Ticknor & Fields, 1989.

WALTON, JOHN, and CHARLES RAGIN. "Global and National Sources of Political Protest: Third World Responses to the Debt Crisis." *American Sociological Review.* Vol. 55, No. 6 (December 1990):876–90.

WARNER, R. STEPHEN. "Work in Progress toward a New Paradigm for the Sociological Study of Religion in the United States." *American Journal of Sociology.* Vol. 98, No. 5 (March 1993):1044–93.

WARNER, W. LLOYD, and PAUL S. LUNT. *The Social Life of a Modern Community.* New Haven, Conn.: Yale University Press, 1941.

WARR, MARK, and CHRISTOPHER G. ELLISON. "Rethinking Social Reactions to Crime: Personal and Altruistic Fear in Family Households." *American Journal of Sociology.* Vol. 106, No. 3 (November 2000):551–78.

WATERS, MELISSA S., WILL CARRINGTON HEATH, and JOHN KEITH WATSON. "A Positive Model of the Determination of Religious Affiliation." *Social Science Quarterly.* Vol. 76, No. 1 (March 1995):105–23.

WEBER, ADNA FERRIN. *The Growth of Cities.* New York: Columbia University Press, 1963; orig. 1899.

WEBER, MAX. *The Protestant Ethic and the Spirit of Capitalism.* New York: Scribner, 1958, orig. 1904–05.

———. *Economy and Society.* GÜNTER ROTH and CLAUS WITTICH, eds. Berkeley: University of California Press, 1978, orig. 1921.

WEBSTER, ANDREW. *Introduction to the Sociology of Development.* London: Macmillan, 1984.

WEBSTER, MURRAY, JR., and STUART J. HYSOM. "Creating Status Characteristics." *American Sociological Review.* Vol. 63, No. 3 (June 1998):351–78.

WEBSTER, PAMELA S., TERRI ORBUCH, and JAMES S. HOUSE. "Effects of Childhood Family Background on Adult Marital Quality and Perceived Stability." *American Journal of Sociology.* Vol. 101, No. 2 (September 1995):404–32.

WEIDENBAUM, MURRAY. "The Evolving Corporate Board." *Society.* Vol. 32, No. 3 (March/April 1995):9–20.

WEINBERG, GEORGE. *Society and the Healthy Homosexual.* Garden City, N.Y.: Anchor Books, 1973.

WEISBERG, D. KELLY. *Children of the Night: A Study of Adolescent Prostitution.* Lexington, Mass.: Heath, 1985.

WEITZMAN, LENORE J. *The Divorce Revolution: The Unexpected Social and Economic Consequences for Women and Children in America.* New York: Free Press, 1985.

———. "The Economic Consequences of Divorce Are Still Unequal: Comment on Peterson." *American Sociological Review.* Vol. 61, No. 3 (June 1996):537–38.

WELLNER, ALISON STEIN. "Discovering Native America." *American Demographics.* Vol. 23, No. 8 (August 2001):21.

———. "The Power of the Purse." *American Demographics.* Vol. 24, No. 7 (January/February 2002):S3–S10.

WESTERN, BRUCE. "The Impact of Incarceration on Wage Mobility and Inequality." *American Sociological Review.* Vol. 67, No. 4 (August 2002):526–46.

WHEELIS, ALLEN. *The Quest for Identity.* New York: Norton, 1958.

WHITAKER, MARK. "Ten Ways to Fight Terrorism." *Newsweek* (July 1, 1985):26–29.

WHITE, JACK E. "I'm Just Who I Am." *Time.* Vol. 149, No. 18 (May 5, 1997):32–36.

WHITE, RALPH, and RONALD LIPPITT. "Leader Behavior and Member Reaction in Three 'Social Climates.'" In DORWIN CARTWRIGHT and ALVIN ZANDER, eds., *Group Dynamics.* Evanston, Ill.: Row & Peterson, 1953:586–611.

WHITMAN, DAVID. "Shattering Myths about the Homeless." *U.S. News & World Report* (March 20, 1989):26, 28.

WHORF, BENJAMIN LEE. "The Relation of Habitual Thought and Behavior to Language." In *Language, Thought, and Reality: Selected Writings of Benjamin Lee Whorf.* JOHN B. CARROLL, ed. Cambridge, Mass.: MIT Press, 1956:134–59; orig. 1941.

WHYTE, WILLIAM FOOTE. *Street Corner Society.* Chicago: University of Chicago Press, 1981, orig. 1943.

WICKHAM, DE WAYNE. "Homeless Receive Little Attention from Candidates." *USA Today Online.* [Online] Available October 24, 2000, at http://www.usatoday.com/usatonline

WILCOX, CLYDE. "Race, Gender, and Support for Women in the Military." *Social Science Quarterly.* Vol. 73, No. 2 (June 1992):310–23.

WILES, P. J. D. *Economic Institutions Compared.* New York: Halsted Press, 1977.

WILKINSON, DORIS. "Transforming the Social Order: The Role of the University in Social Change." *Sociological Forum.* Vol. 9, No. 3 (September 1994):325–41.

WILLIAMS, JOHNNY E. "Linking Beliefs to Collective Action: Politicized Religious Beliefs and the Civil Rights Movement." *Sociological Forum.* Vol. 17, No. 2 (June 2002):203–22.

WILLIAMS, PETER W. *America's Religions: From Their Origins to the Twenty-First Century.* Urbana: University of Illinois Press, 2002.

WILLIAMS, RHYS H., and N. J. DEMERATH III. "Religion and Political Process in an American City." *American Sociological Review.* Vol. 56, No. 4 (August 1991):417–31.

WILLIAMS, ROBIN M., JR. *American Society: A Sociological Interpretation.* 3d ed. New York: Knopf, 1970.

WILLIAMSON, JEFFREY G., and PETER H. LINDERT. *American Inequality: A Macroeconomic History.* New York: Academic Press, 1980.

WILSON, BARBARA J. "National Television Violence Study." Reported by JULIA DUIN, "Study Finds Cartoon Heroes Initiate Too Much Violence." *Washington Times* (April 17, 1998):A4.

WILSON, EDWARD O. "Biodiversity, Prosperity, and Value." In F. HERBERT BORMANN and STEPHEN R. KELLERT, eds., *Ecology, Economics, and Ethics: The Broken Circle.* New Haven, Conn.: Yale University Press, 1991:3–10.

WILSON, JAMES Q., and RICHARD J. HERRNSTEIN. *Crime and Human Nature.* New York: Simon & Schuster, 1985.

WILSON, LOGAN. *American Academics Then and Now.* New York: Oxford University Press, 1979.

WILSON, THOMAS C. "Urbanism and Tolerance: A Test of Some Hypotheses Drawn from Wirth and Stouffer." *American Sociological Review.* Vol. 50, No. 1 (February 1985):117–23.

———. "Urbanism and Unconventionality: The Case of Sexual Behavior." *Social Science Quarterly.* Vol. 76, No. 2 (June 1995):346–63.

WILSON, WILLIAM JULIUS. *When Work Disappears: The World of the New Urban Poor.* New York: Knopf, 1996a.

———. "Work." *New York Times Magazine* (August 18, 1996b):26 ff.

WINNICK, LOUIS. "America's 'Model Minority.'" *Commentary.* Vol. 90, No. 2 (August 1990):22–29.

WINSHIP, CHRISTOPHER, and JENNY BERRIEN. "Boston Cops and Black Churches." *Public Interest* (Summer 1999):52–68.

WINTERS, REBECCA. "Trouble for School Inc." *Time* (May 27, 2002):53.

WIRTH, LOUIS. "Urbanism as a Way of Life." *American Journal of Sociology.* Vol. 44, No. 1 (July 1938):1–24.

WITKIN, GORDON. "The Crime Bust." *U.S. News & World Report* (May 25, 1998):28–40.

WITKIN-LANOIL, GEORGIA. *The Female Stress Syndrome: How to Recognize and Live with It.* New York: Newmarket Press, 1984.

WOLF, DIANE L., ed. *Feminist Dilemma of Fieldwork.* Boulder, Colo.: Westview Press, 1996.

WOLF, NAOMI. *The Beauty Myth: How Images of Beauty Are Used against Women.* New York: Morrow, 1990.

WOLFGANG, MARVIN E., ROBERT M. FIGLIO, and THORSTEN SELLIN. *Delinquency in a Birth Cohort.* Chicago: University of Chicago Press, 1972.

WOLFGANG, MARVIN E., TERRENCE P. THORNBERRY, and ROBERT M. FIGLIO. *From Boy to Man, from Delinquency to Crime.* Chicago: University of Chicago Press, 1987.

"Women and Power." *Christian Science Monitor* (September 6, 1995):1, 9–11.

WONDERS, NANCY A., and RAYMOND MICHALOWSKI. "Bodies, Borders, and Sex Tourism in a Globalized World: A Tale of Two Cities—Amsterdam and Havana." *Social Problems.* Vol. 48, No. 4 (November 2001):545–71.

WONG, BUCK. "Need for Awareness: An Essay on Chinatown, San Francisco." In AMY TACHIKI et al., eds., *Roots: An Asian American Reader.* Los Angeles: UCLA Asian American Studies Center, 1971:265–73.

WOODBERRY, ROBERT D. "When Surveys Lie and People Tell the Truth: Church Attenders." *American Sociological Review.* Vol. 63, No. 1 (February 1998):119–22.

WOODWARD, KENNETH L. "Feminism and the Churches." *Newsweek* (February 13, 1989):58–61.

———. "Talking to God." *Newsweek* (January 6, 1992):38–44.

WORLD BANK. *World Development Report, 1993.* New York: Oxford University Press, 1993.

———. *Entering the 21st Century: World Development Report, 1999/2000.* Washington, D.C.: World Bank, 2000.

———. *World Development Report, 2000/2001.* Washington, D.C.: World Bank, 2001.

———. *2003 World Development Indicators.* Washington, D.C.: World Bank, 2003.

———. *2004 World Development Indicators.* Washington, D.C.: World Bank, 2004.

WORLD GAZETTER. "(Table). Metropolitan Areas with More Than 500,000 Inhabitants." [Online] Available November 8, 2004, at http://www.world-gazetteer.com/home.htm

WORLD HEALTH ORGANIZATION. *Constitution of the World Health Organization.* New York: World Health Organization Interim Commission, 1946.

WORSLEY, PETER. "Models of the World System." In MIKE FEATHERSTONE, ed., *Global Culture: Nationalism, Globalization, and Modernity.* Newbury Park, Calif.: Sage, 1990:83–95.

WREN, CHRISTOPHER S. "In Soweto-by-the-Sea, Misery Lives on as Apartheid Fades." *New York Times* (June 9, 1991):1, 7.

WRIGHT, JAMES D. "Ten Essential Observations on Guns in America." *Society.* Vol. 32, No. 3 (March/April 1995):63–68.

WRIGHT, QUINCY. "Causes of War in the Atomic Age." In WILLIAM M. EVAN and STEPHEN HILGARTNER, eds., *The Arms Race and Nuclear War.* Englewood Cliffs, N.J.: Prentice Hall, 1987:7–10.

WRIGHT, RICHARD A. *In Defense of Prisons.* Westport, Conn.: Greenwood Press, 1994.

WRIGHT, ROBERT. "Sin in the Global Village." *Time* (October 19, 1998):130.

WU, LAWRENCE L. "Effects of Family Instability, Income, and Income Instability on the Risk of a Premarital Birth." *American Sociological Review.* Vol. 61, No. 3 (June 1996):386–406.

YAMAGATA, HISASHI, KUANG S. YEH, SHELBY STEWMAN, and HIROKO DODGE. "Sex Segregation and Glass Ceilings: A Comparative Static Model of Women's Career Opportunities in the Federal Government over a Quarter Century." *American Journal of Sociology.* Vol. 103, No. 3 (November 1997):566–632.

YANG, FENGGANG, and HELEN ROSE EBAUGH. "Transformations in New Immigrant Religions and Their Global Implications." *American Sociological Review.* Vol. 66, No. 2 (April 2001):269–88.

YANKELOVICH, DANIEL. "How Changes in the Economy Are Reshaping American Values." In HENRY J. AARON, THOMAS E. MANN, and TIMOTHY TAYLOR, eds., *Values and Public Policy.* Washington, D.C.: Brookings Institution, 1994.

YEATTS, DALE E. "Creating the High-Performance Self-Managed Work Team: A Review of Theoretical Perspectives." Paper presented at the annual meeting of the Southwest Social Science Association, Dallas, Tex., February 1994.

YIN, SANDRA. "Wanted: One Million Nurses." *American Demographics.* Vol. 24, No. 8 (September 2002):63–65.

YOELS, WILLIAM C., and JEFFREY MICHAEL CLAIR. "Laughter in the Clinic: Humor in Social Organization." *Symbolic Interaction.* Vol. 18, No. 1 (1995):39–58.

YORK, RICHARD, EUGENE A. ROSA, and THOMAS DEITZ. "Bridging Environmental Science with Environmental Policy: Plasticity of Population, Affluence, and Technology." *Social Science Quarterly.* Vol. 83, No. 1 (March 2002):18–34.

ZAKARIA, FAREED. "How to Wage the Peace." *Newsweek* (April 21, 2003):38–48.

ZHAO, DINGXIN. "Ecologies of Social Movements: Student Mobilization during the 1989 Prodemocracy Movement in Beijing." *American Journal of Sociology.* Vol. 103, No. 6 (May 1998):1493–529.

ZHOU, MIN, and JOHN R. LOGAN. "Returns of Human Capital in Ethnic Enclaves: New York City's Chinatown." *American Sociological Review.* Vol. 54, No. 5 (October 1989):809–20.

ZHOU, XUEGUANG, and LIREN HOU. "Children of the Cultural Revolution: The State and the Life Course in the People's Republic of China." *American Sociological Review.* Vol. 64, No. 1 (February 1999):12–36.

ZICKLIN, G. "Re-Biologizing Sexual Orientation: A Critique." Paper presented at the annual meeting of the Society for the Study of Social Problems, Pittsburgh, 1992.

ZIMBARDO, PHILIP G. "Pathology of Imprisonment." *Society.* Vol. 9 (April 1972):4–8.

ZIPP, JOHN F. "The Impact of Social Structure on Mate Selection: An Empirical Evaluation of an Active-Learning Exercise." *Teaching Sociology.* Vol. 30, No. 2 (April 2002):174–84.

ZOGBY INTERNATIONAL. Poll, reported in SANDRA YIN, "Race and Politics." *American Demographics.* Vol. 23, No. 8 (August 2001):11–13.

PHOTO CREDITS

Paul W. Liebhardt, ii. Larry Hamill Photography, xxxi.

CHAPTER 1: Spencer Grant/PhotoEdit, xxxiv (top); Library of Congress, xxxiv (left); The Granger Collection, xxxiv (middle); Corbis/Bettmann, xxxiv (right); Reuters/Corbis/Bettmann, 1; EyeWire Collection/Getty Images–Photodisc, 2; Caroline Penn/Corbis/Bettmann, 4 (top left); Minh-Thu Pham, 4 (top middle); Graham, Neal/Omni-Photo Communications, Inc., 4 (top right); Paul W. Liebhardt, 4 (bottom left); Alan Evrard/Robert Harding World Imagery, 4 (bottom middle); Paul W. Liebhardt, 4 (bottom right); Lineair/Peter Arnold, Inc., 6; North Wind Picture Archives, 9; Corbis/Bettmann, 10 (left); Brown Brothers, 10 (middle); Brown Brothers, 10 (right); Paul Marcus/Studio SPM, Inc., 12; Lisa Harris Gallery, 13; Museum of New Mexico, 18; New York Times Pictures, 22; Reuben Burrell/Hampton University/Lois Benjamin, 23; Cheryl Gerber/AP Wide World Photos, 27

CHAPTER 2: The Coca-Cola Company. Coca-Cola is a trademark of The Coca-Cola Company and used with its express permission, 34 (top); Anthony Bannister/Gallo Images/Corbis/Bettmann, 34 (left); Darren Staples/Reuters/Corbis/Bettmann, 34 (middle); Margaret Courtney-Clarke/Corbis/Bettmann, 34 (right); Michael Busselle/Corbis/Bettmann, 35; Charles Schwab & Company, Inc., 36; Paul W. Liebhardt, 37 (top left); Carlos Humberto/TDC/Contact/Corbis/Stock Market, 37 (top middle); © Doranne Jacobson/International Images, 37 (top right); Paul W. Liebhardt, 37 (center left); David Austen/Stock Boston, 37 (center middle); Hubertus Kanus/Photo Researchers, Inc., (37 center right); © Doranne Jacobson/International Images, 37 (bottom left); Art Wolfe/Getty Images Inc. – Stone Allstock, 37 (bottom right); Dimitri Lovetsky/AP Wide World Photos, 38; Herve Collart Odinetz/Corbis/Sygma, 39; Pearson Education/PH College, 40; Penguin Books USA, Inc., 43; SuperStock, Inc., 47; Shehzad Nooran/Still Pictures/Peter Arnold, Inc., 52; Paul Soloman/Woodfin Camp & Associates, 55; Ruth Orkin/Estate of Ruth Orkin Photo Archive, 56.

CHAPTER 3: Anthony Redpath/Corbis/Bettmann, 62 (top); Pete Saloutos/Corbis/Bettmann, 62 (left); Corbis Royalty Free, 62 (middle); Corbis Royalty Free, 62 (right); Paul Chesley/Getty Images Inc.—Stone Allstock, 63; Jose Luis Pelaez/Corbis Bettmann, 64; Isaacs Gallery Toronto, 65; Gareth Brown/Corbis/Bettmann, 67; Rimma Gerlovina and Valeriy Gerlovin, 69; Hampton University Museum, 72; 20th Century Fox/The Kobal Collection/Brandy Eve Allen, 76; Michael Newman/PhotoEdit, 79 (left); © John Garrett/Corbis, 79 (right); Eastcott/Momatiuk/The Image Works, 81.

CHAPTER 4: © Dorling Kindersley, 86 (top); Corbis Royalty Free, 86 (left, middle, and right);Wolfgang Kaehler/Corbis/Bettmann, 87; © www.franksiteman.com, 88; Gunnery Sgt. Blair A. McClellan, U.S. Marine Corps/US Department of Defense, 89; Ron Chapple/Getty Images, Inc. – Taxi, 92; Staton R. Winter/New York Times Pictures, 94; The Cartoon Bank, 96; Paul Ekman, Ph.D., 97 (left, right); Paul W. Liebhardt, 99 (left, middle, right); Barbara Penoya/Getty Images, Inc.- Photodisc., 100 (top left); Alan S. Weiner, 100 (top middle); Andy Crawford/© Dorling Kindersley, 100 (top right); © Guido Alberto Rossi/TIPS Images, 100 (bottom left); Chris Carroll/Corbis/Bettmann, 100 (bottom middle); Costa Manos/Magnum Photos, Inc., 100 (bottom right); Najlah Feanny/Stock Boston, 101; Martin, Inc., Butch/Getty Images Inc.—Image Bank, 104

CHAPTER 5: Janet Reilly, 108 (top); Annie Griffiths Belt/Corbis/Bettmann, 108 (left); Richard Cummins/Corbis/Bettmann, 108 (middle); David Joel/Getty Images, Inc., 108 (right); Jerry Lampen/Reuters/Corbis/Bettmann, 109; Robert Landau/Corbis/Bettmann, 110; Aaron J.H. Walker/Getty Images, Inc., 111; Spencer Grant/PhotoEdit, 114; Jonathan Green Studios, Inc., 116; Cliché Bibliothèque nationale de France, Paris. From The Horizon History of China by the editors of Horizon Magazine, The Horizon Publishing Co., Inc., 551 5th Avenue, New York, NY 10017. (C)1969. Bibliothèque nationale de France., 120; The Metropolitan Museum of Art , 122; Paul W.Liebhardt, 123; © Hulton Getty/Archive Photos, 124Courtesy: Google, 127 (left); Michael Newman/PhotoEdit, 127 (right).

CHAPTER 6: Davies & Starr/Getty Images Inc.—Stone Allstock, 134 (top); Patrik Giardino/Corbis/Bettmann, 134 (left); © Judith Miller/Dorling Kindersley/VinMagCo, 134 (middle); Maggie Hallahan/Corbis/Bettmann, 134 (right); Tony West/PICIMPACT/Corbis/Bettmann, 135; Paul Solomon/Woodfin Camp & Associates, 136; Andre Gallant/Getty Images Inc.—Image Bank, 137 (top left); Pete Turner, 137 (top middle); Brun/Photo Researchers, Inc., 137 (top right); Bruno Hadjih/Getty Images, Inc – Liaison, 137 (bottom left); Elliot Erwitt/Magnum Photos, Inc., 137 (bottom middle); George Holton/Photo Researchers, Inc., 137 (bottom right); Dominic Harcourt-Webster/Robert Harding World Imagery, 138; Corbis/Bettmann, 140; Bill Aron/PhotoEdit, 150; AKG London Ltd, 153.

CHAPTER 7: C Squared Studios/Getty Images, Inc.- Photodisc, 160 (top); Tom and Dee Ann McCarthy/Corbis/Bettmann, 160 (left); Bill Varie/Corbis/Bettmann, 160 (middle); Jack Star/Getty Images, Inc.- PhotoDisc, 160 (right); Tore Bergsaker/Corbis/Sygma, 161; Tony Freeman/PhotoEdit, 162; Melissa Moore/The Image Works, 163; Smithsonian American Art Museum/Art Resource/Smithsonian American Art Museum, 164; Robert Yager/Getty Images Inc.—Stone Allstock, 167; SW Production/Index Stock Imagery, Inc., 168; Andrew Lichtenstein/The Image Works, 170; AP Wide World Photos, 172; AP Wide World Photos, 177; The Cartoon Bank, 178; A. Ramey/Woodfin Camp & Associates, 181; U.S. Information Agency, 183; A. Ramey/PhotoEdit, 186.

CHAPTER 8: Tim Graham/Corbis/Sygma, 190 (top); Kevin Fleming/Corbis/Bettmann, 190 (left); Cydney Conger/Corbis/Bettmann, 190 (middle); Ralf-Finn Hestoft/Corbis/Bettmann, 190 (right); Antoine Serra/In Visu/Corbis/Bettmann, 191; Illustration by Ken Marschall (C)1992 from Titanic: An Illustrated History, a Viking Studio/Madison Press Book, 192; Sebastiao Salgado/Contact Press Images Inc., 193; Abbas/Magnum Photos, Inc., 194; AP Wide World Photos. 196; Julia Calfee/Polaris Images, 198; © Doranne Jacobson/International Images, 202; Ed Bock/Corbis/Stock Market, 209; Russell Lee/Corbis/Bettmann, 210; The Cartoon Bank, 211; Richard Pasley/Stock Boston, 213; Julia Calfee/Polaris Images, 214; North Wind Picture Archives. 216.

CHAPTER 9: Jeremy Horner/Corbis/Bettmann, 224 (left); Daniel Laine/Corbis/Bettmann, 224 (middle); James Sparshatt/Corbis/Bettmann, 224 (right); Les Stone/Corbis/Bettmann, 225; Getty Images, Inc.—Agence France Presse, 226; Martin Benjamin/The Image Works, 228 (top left); Peter Turnley/Corbis/Bettmann, 228 (top right); Pablo Bartholomew/Getty Images, Inc – Liaison, 228 (bottom); Reuters NewMedia Inc./Corbis/Bettmann, 229 (left); Chip Hires/Gamma Press USA, Inc., 229 (right); David Butow/Redux Pictures, 230; Yuri Cortez/Agence France Presse/Getty Images, 234; Malcolm Linton/Getty Images, Inc – Liaison, 235; Steve Maines/Stock Boston, 237; Joe McDonald/Corbis/Bettmann, 239 (left); Robert van der Hilst/Corbis/Bettmann, 239 (middle); Wolfgang Kaehler/Corbis/Bettmann, 239 (right); Mark Edwards/Still Pictures/Peter Arnold, Inc., 240.

CHAPTER 10: © Judith Miller/Dorling Kindersley/The Doll Express, 250 (top); Javier Pierini/Corbis/Bettmann, 250 (left); Jim Zuckerman/Corbis/Bettmann, 250 (middle); Digital Vision/Getty Images, Inc–Liaison, 250 (right); Gideon Mendel/Corbis/Bettmann, 251; Getty Images Inc.—Hulton Archive Photos, 252; Andy Cox/Getty Images Inc.—Stone Allstock, 253; Angela Fisher/Carol Beckwith/Robert Estall Photo Agency, 256; Tony Freeman/PhotoEdit, 258; Sonda Dawes/The Image Works, 264; Kuenzig/laif/Aurora Photos, 267; Getty Images Inc.—Hulton Archive Photos, 268; Richard B. Levine/Frances M. Roberts, 273; Carol Beckwith/Angela Fisher/Robert Estall Photo Agency, 274.

CHAPTER 11: Courtesy of the Library of Congress, 278 (top); Kevin Fleming/Corbis/Bettmann, 278, (left); Marcia Keegan/Corbis/Bettmann, 278 (middle); Sandy Huffacker/Zuma/Corbis/Bettmann, 278 (right); Gideon Mendel/Corbis/Bettmann, 279; Myrleen Ferguson Cate/PhotoEdit, 280; Joel Gordon/Joel Gordon Photography, 281 (top left); Leong Ka Tai, 281 (top middle); Owen Franken/Corbis/Bettmann, 281 (top right); Charles O'Rear/Corbis/Bettmann, 281 (bottom left); Paul W. Liebhardt, 281 (bottom middle); Lisi Dennis/Lisl Dennis, 281 (bottom right); Joel Gordon Photography, 282; Bob Daemmrich Photography, Inc., 285; Sean Sprague/Stock Boston, 287; Western History Collections, University of Oklahoma Libraries, 291; AP Wide World Photos, 292; Corbis/Bettmann, 296 (left); Culver Pictures, Inc.,

296 (middle left); Photographs and Prints Division, Schomburg Center for Research in Black Culture/The New York Public Library/Astor, Lenox, and Tilden Foundations, 296 (middle right); UPI/Corbis/Bettmann, 296 (right); A. Ramey/Woodfin Camp & Associates, 299; Jim West, 300; M. Lee Father-ree/Carmen Lomas Garza, 302; Carl D. Walsh/Aurora & Quanta Productions Inc., 304.

CHAPTER 12: Comstock Images/Getty Images, Inc—Comstock Images, 308 (top); Steve Kaufman/Corbis/Bettmann, 308 (left); Matthew McVay/Corbis/Bettmann, 308 (middle); Bernd Obermann/Corbis/Bettmann, 308 (right); Serra Antoine/Corbis/Bettmann, 309; AP Wide World Photos, 310; Catherine Karnow/Woodfin Camp & Associates, 311; Bellavia/REA/Corbis/SABA Press Photos, Inc., 315 (left); John Bryson/Corbis/Sygma, 315 (right); Gamma Press USA, Inc., 316; Chien-Chi Chang/Magnum Photos, Inc., 319; Matthew Borkoski/Index Stock Imagery, Inc., 322; AP Wide World Photos, 323; Durand/SIPA Press, 326; Timothy Fadek/Gamma Press USA, Inc., 329 (left); Joel Gordon Photography, 329 (right); Paul Fusco/Magnum Photos, Inc., 335; Polaris Images, 337.

CHAPTER 13: Getty Images – Photodisc, 344 (top); Tom & Dee Ann McCarthy/Corbis/Bettmann, 344 (left); Reuters/Bazuki Muhammad/Corbis/Bettmann, 344 (middle); Corbis Royalty Free, 344 (right); Owen Franken/Corbis/Bettmann, 355; Beth Balbierz/The Record, 346; David Botello, 347; Christian Pierre, B. 1962, I Do, American Private Collection, SuperStock, Inc., 351; AP Wide World Photos, 352; Mark J. Barrett/Creative Eye/MIRA.com, 358; Bill Bachmann/The Image Works, 360; Michael Freeman/Corbis/Bettmann, 364; Michael Newman/PhotoEdit, 365; David G. Wells/Corbis Digital Stock, 366; © Doranne Jacobson/International Images, 368; Philip North-Coombes/Getty Images Inc.—Stone Allstock, 374; Anna Belle Lee Washington/SuperStock, Inc., 375.

CHAPTER 14: Getty Images, Inc.- Photodisc, 380 (top); Louise Gubb/Corbis/SABA Press Photos, Inc., 380 (left); Richard T. Nowitz/Corbis/Bettmann, 380 (middle); Lynsey Addario/Corbis/Bettmann, 380 (right); Gideon Mendel/Corbis/Bettmann, 381; Getty Images, Inc., 382; Mary Kate Denny/PhotoEdit, 386 (left); Getty Images, Inc., 386 (right); Will & Deni McIntyre/Corbis/Bettmann, 390; Lawrence Migdale/Lawrence Migdale/Pix, 391; Mugshots/Corbis/Stock Market, 394; Steve Prezant/Corbis/Stock Market, 398; The Bridgeman Art Library International Ltd., 405Billy E. Barnes/PhotoEdit, 407;

ABC Television/Globe Photos, Inc., 408 (left); Globe Photos, Inc., 408 (right); Steve Murez/Black Star, 412.

CHAPTER 15: Jonathan Nourok/PhotoEdit, 416 (top); Gustavo Gilabert/Corbis/SABA Press Photos, Inc., 416 (left); Sheldon Collins/Corbis/Bettmann, 416 (middle); Robert Landau/Corbis/Bettmann, 416 (right); MUNIR NASA/UNEP/Peter Arnold, Inc., 417; David Butow/Corbis/Bettmann, 418; David and Peter Turnley/Corbis/Bettmann, 425; Lauren Goodsmith/The Image Works, 426; © Bettmann/Corbis, 427; Steve C. Wilson/Online USA, Inc./Getty Images Inc.—Hulton Archive Photos, 430; SuperStock, Inc., 431 (left); Christie's Images Inc., 431 (right); James King-Holmes/Science Photo Library/Photo Researchers, Inc., 435; Culver Pictures, Inc., 438; Dave Amit/Reuters/Landov LLC, 440; SuperStock, Inc., 441; Eric Pasquier/Corbis/Sygma, 442.

CHAPTER 16: Ryan McVay/Getty Images – Photodisc, 448 (top); Reuters/Corbis/Bettmann, 448 (left); Kevin Fleming/Corbis/Bettmann, 448 (middle); Corbis Royalty Free, 448 (right); Robert Essel NYC/Corbis/Bettmann, 449; Culver Pictures, Inc., 450; Mark Peters, 451; Corbis/Bettmann, 455 (left); Huynh Cong "Nick" Ut/AP Wide World Photos, 455 (right); Whitney Museum of American Art, 457; Pearson Education/PH College, 458; Christie's Images Inc., 462; Ed Pritchard/Getty Images Inc.—Stone Allstock, 463 (left); Mark Richards/PhotoEdit, 463 (right); Mauri Rautkari/WWF UK (World Wide Fund For Nature), 466; Kelly-Mooney Photography/Corbis/Bettmann, 467; David Botello, 470; Paul Howell/Getty Images, Inc – Liaison, 473.

TIMELINE: Association of American Railroads; Getty Images Inc.—Hulton Archive Photos; AT&T Archives; Library of Congress; Corbis/Bettmann; North Carolina Museum of History; Irene Springer/Pearson Education/PH College; Wilton, Chris Alan/Getty Images Inc.—Image Bank; Tim Ridley/Dorling Kindersley Media Library; Getty Images, Inc.—Hulton Archive Photos; Texas State Library and Archives Commission; AP Wide World Photos; Bettmann/Corbis/Bettmann; © Corbis/Bettman; Corbis Bettman; Getty Images, Inc.—Hulton Archive Photos; NASA/Johnson Space Center; Jason Laure/Woodfin Camp & Associates; Laima Druskis/Pearson Education/PH College; John Serafin; Brady/Pearson Education/PH College; Jan Butchofsky-Houser/Corbis/Bettmann; Robert F. Bukaty/AP Wide World Photos; Library of Congress; Library of Congress; Gerald Lopez © Dorling Kindersley; U.S. Air Force; © Dorling Kindersley; Unisys Corporation; The Coca-Cola Company. "Coca-Cola" is a registered trademark of The Coca-Cola Company and is registered with kind permission from The Coca-Cola Company.

NAME INDEX

SUBJECT INDEX

and economic inequality, 326
and free enterprise, 44
political freedom, political map of, 327
true democracy, restricting factors, 326
as U.S. value, 44
Democracy gap, and Islamic nations, 339
Democratic leadership, 112, 121
Democratic Party, 330
Democratic Republic of the Congo, as low-income nation, 229, 232
Demographic transition theory, 423–25
Demography, 418–24 (*see also* Population; Population growth)
defined, 418
fertility, 418
migration, 420
mortality, 419
and social change, 453
Denial of death, 79
Denmark, women's status, 264
Denomination, religious, 368
Dependency theory of development, 241–44, 470
colonialism, 241–42
and global inequality, 241–44
high-income countries, role of, 241–44
on modernization, 243–44
and multinationals, 324
Dependent variable, 16, 18, 21
Deprivation theory, of social movements, 454
Descent, kinship patterns, 348–49
Descriptive statistics, 15
Desegregation, of schools, 290–91
Deterrence
of criminals, 182–84
and war, 338
Development, human (*see* Human development)
Deviance, 162–78
and biology, 163–64
and capitalism, 171–72
control theory, 170–71
and criminality (*see* Crime)
and culture, 164
defined, 162
differential association theory, 170
functions of, 164–67
and gender, 174–75
labeling theory of, 167–71
medicalization of, 169
and personality traits, 164
and power, 171
primary and secondary, 167–68
social-conflict analysis, 171–73
and social diversity, 173–79
social foundations, 164
strain theory, 165–66
structural-functional analysis, 164–67, 173
subcultures, 48–49
symbolic-interaction analysis, 167–71, 173
Dharma, 237
Differential association theory, 170
Diffusion
of culture, 52
and social change, 452
Diplomacy, and peace, 338
Direct-fee system, health care, 406
Disability (*see* People with disabilities)
Disarmament, and peace, 338
Discipline, school problems, 389–90
Discovery (*see* Innovation and discovery)

Discrimination, 289–90 (*see also* Gender discrimination; Racial discrimination)
ageism, 78
and Asian Americans, 284, 297–99
defined, 289
institutional, 290–91
race/class/gender intersection, 264–65
relationship to prejudice, 290
reverse discrimination, 305
Disease (*see also* Health problems)
as master status, 89
Diversity (*see also* Cultural diversity; Multiculturalism; Social diversity)
and group dynamics, 116
and physical appearance, 37
religious, 369–71
and sociological perspective, 5–6
Divine right, 326
Division of labor, and modernization, 457–58
Divorce, 357–59
child custody, 272–73, 358
child support, 358
effects on children, 358, 361
frequency, reasons for, 357–58
increase in rate, 357, 361
and religious beliefs, 365
risk factors for, 358
women's financial decline, 6, 76–77, 359
Djibouti, women's status, 254
DNA (deoxyribonucleic acid), genetic research, 411
Doe v. Bolton, 155
Domestication, of animals, 45–46
Domestic violence (*see* Family violence)
Double standard
and biology, 57
defined, 20
and research, 20
sexual, 141
Downsizing, 215, 320
impact on workers, 130
Downward social mobility, 211, 215
Dramaturgical analysis, 95–99
elements of, 14
embarrassment and tact, 98–99
and gender, 97–98
idealization, 98
nonverbal communication, 96–97
patients and physicians, 95–96, 409
performances, 95–96
Dred Scott decision (1857), 295–96
Dropping out, 391–92
Drug trade
decline in, 187
as global issue, 179
Drug use
as deviant, 169, 171
and HIV/AIDS risk, 403
and homeless, 220
medicalization of, 169
as victimless crime, 176
Due process, 180–81
Dyads, 115–16

Earnings (*see* Income; Income level)
Eastern Europe (*see also* specific countries)
and communism, 196–97, 202
genocide in, 292
as middle-income area, 7, 229, 232
popular uprisings in, 202, 334
socialism, end of, 317
Eastern Orthodox Church, ethnicity of members, 282

Eating disorders, 399–401
E-choupal, 475
Ecologically sustainable culture, 444
Ecology (*see also* Natural environment)
defined, 434
urban ecology, 432
Economic development (*see also* Global stratification; Industrialization)
global map of, 7
high-income countries, 228–29
income level by, 231
low-income countries, 229–30
middle-income countries, 229
productivity measure, 316
and schooling, 382
Economic inequality (*see* Income inequality; Poverty; Wealth)
Economic systems, 314–17
capitalism, 314–15
socialism, 315–17
state capitalism, 316, 338
welfare capitalism, 316, 338
Economy, 310–16
agricultural, 310–11, 313
corporations, 321–24
and crime rate, 187
future view, 324
global (*see* Global economy)
government regulation, 304–8
and Industrial Revolution, 311
and Information Revolution, 46
and politics, 329
postindustrial (*see* Postindustrial economy)
primary/secondary/tertiary sectors, 312
service-sector employment, global map of, 313
and U.S. class structure, 215
Ecosystem, defined, 434
Ecuador, beauty in, 137
Edge cities, 429
Education, 382–95 (*see also* Schooling; Schools)
adult education, 395
and affirmative action, 304–5
and African Americans, 279–80, 290–91, 297, 386–89, 392
Afrocentric focus, 50
and Asian Americans, 297, 298, 388
defined, 382
and gender stratification, 263, 384–85
and Hispanic Americans (Latinos), 386–89, 392
home schooling, 394
illiteracy, global map of, 383
inclusive education, 394–95
and industrialization, 46
level of achievement (*see* Educational attainment)
mandatory, 384
and multiculturalism, 50
problems in schools (*see* School problems)
progressive, 385
and racial and ethnic minorities, 297, 386–89
school choice, 393–94
school segregation, 290–91
sex education, 148
social-conflict analysis, 385–89
and social stratification, 385–89
structural-functional analysis, 384
teacher shortage, 395
in U.S., 384–85

Educational attainment (*see also* College attendance)
African Americans, 23–24, 297, 388
Asian Americans, 178, 297–98
and future income, 387–88
gender stratification, 208
Hispanic Americans, 388
levels of achievement in U.S., 384
of men, 208, 388
professions, 318–19
and religiosity, 27, 370
and social prestige, 206–7
in U.S., 206–7, 384
and voter participation, 332
of women, 208, 263
Efficiency, as U.S. value, 43, 128
Ego, 66
Egypt
female genital mutilation, 267
population control, 426
water supply deficit, 438–39
Egypt, ancient, sibling marriages, 139
Elderly
and ageism, 78
biological changes, 77–78
caregivers of, 354
culture and view of, 78–79
family life, 354
graying of U.S., 77
health issues, 77–78
income of, 79
and industrialization, 78
as life stage, 77–79
nursing home residents, 85
and poverty, 79, 216
in preindustrial society, 78
retirement, 77, 79
and socialization process, 77–79
Elections (*see* Voting)
Electronic church, 375
Electronic mail (*see* E-mail)
El Salvador, as middle-income nation, 229
E-mail
effects on organizational structure, 121–22
emoticons, 41
and global networking, 117–18
privacy issues, 128
Embarrassment, and social interaction, 98–99
Emigration, meaning of, 420
Emoticons, 41
Emotions, 99–101
Empirical evidence, meaning of, 15
Employment (*see* Labor force; Occupations; Unemployment; Work; Women and workplace)
Empty nest, 354
Enclosure movement, 9
Endogamy, 193, 347
Energy sources, and industrialization, 9, 311, 435
England (*see* Great Britain)
English language
as global language, 8, 42
and multicultural U.S., 50
Enron Corporation, 172, 214
Entrepreneurs
Korean Americans, 300
women as, 261, 319
Environment
natural (*see* Natural environment)
organizational, 120–21
Environmental deficit, 435
Environmental movement, as social movement, 454

Leadership
   group leadership, 112–13
   instrumental and expressive leaders, 112
   styles of, 112–13
   women as leaders, 124–25
Learning
   cognitive development, 67–68
   by imitation, 69
Left-wing activities, as social movement, 454
Lesbians (*see also* Homosexuality)
   and heterosexism, 155–56
   as parents, 360
   same-sex marriage, 360
Liberal feminism, 271
Liberal politics
   and Democratic Party, 329
   on free society, 82
   fundamentalist opposition to, 375
   and mass media, 74
   and social class, 330
   on voter apathy, 332
   on welfare, 218–19
Liberation theology, 367
Liberty
   and democracy, 326
   Enlightenment views, 9
   in global perspective, 327
   as U.S. value, 44, 126
Libya, water supply deficit, 439
Life course (*see also* Human development)
   and family, 351–54
   patterns/variations, 80–81
   and socialization, 75–81
Life expectancy
   children in U.S., 399
   defined, 420
   gender differences, 253, 398
   global views, 233, 419
   increase in, 412
   married persons, 357
   racial/ethnic categories, 399
   and social class, 210
   in U.S., 420
Life instinct, 66
Limits to growth thesis, 436
Literacy
   and postindustrial society, 312
   and social equality, 203
   and voting, 332
Lithuania, as middle-income nation, 232
Lobbyists, 331
Logic of growth concept, 436
Looking-glass self, meaning of, 69
Love, courtship, 351–52
Loving v. Virginia, 356
Lower class, 210
Lower-middle class, 209–10
Lower-upper class, 209
Low-income countries (*see also* Global poverty; specific countries)
   air pollution problem, 231
   childbearing, global map, 3
   child labor, 52, 75, 384
   death, median age, 233
   defined, 7, 8, 227
   division of population and global income, 232
   economic development of, 7, 229–30
   family size, 3
   foreign debt of, 242
   global map of, 7
   gross domestic product (GDP), 7, 232
   health status, 396–97
   and modernization theory, 238–39

multinational corporations in, 238, 323–24
   natural disaster, effects of, 229
   per capita annual income of, 228n
   population growth, 229, 246, 424–25
   poverty in, 229–30, 236–38
   quality-of-life index, 232
   schooling in, 383–84
   urbanization in, 433–34
Low-income earners, 213
Lutherans, 368, 370
Lying, detection of, 97
Lynching, African Americans, 297

Macao, descriptions of, 127
McCulture, 470
McDonaldization of society, 127–30
Machismo, 355
McJobs, 130
Macro-level orientation, 13
Mafia, 173
Magnet schools, 393
Mainstreaming, students with disabilities, 394
Malaysia
   exports of, 242
   as middle-income nation, 229, 232
Male traits (*see* Masculine traits)
Malnutrition (*see* Starvation)
Malthusian theory, 423, 436, 443
Management, scientific management, 123–26
Mandatory education law, 384
Manifest function, defined, 12
Manila
   descriptions of, 231
   poverty of, 434
Mansions, building by wealthy, 214
Manufacturing (*see also* Industrialization; Industrial Revolution)
   development of, 9
   factories, 9, 46, 311
   and global economy, 215
   hourly wages, 324
   and Industrial Revolution, 311
   job decline in U.S., 215, 220
   Middle Ages, 9
Maoris (New Zealand), display of affection, 139
Marginality, social, 5
Marital forms
   descent patterns, 348–49
   endogamy, 193, 347
   exogamy, 347
   global map, 348
   monogamy, 347
   polyandry, 348
   polygamy, 347–48
   residence patterns, 349
Marital rape, 359
Market economy, capitalism, 314–15
Marriage
   arranged, 351–52
   child weddings, 351–52
   college student attitudes, 353
   courtship, 351–52
   death of spouse, 354
   defined, 347
   divorce, 342, 357–58, 361
   extramarital sex, 44, 143, 353
   forms of (*see* Marital forms)
   global variations, 347–48
   and health status, 357, 415
   and homogamy, 352
   incest taboo, 139–40, 152
   interracial marriage, 356
   mate selection, 351–52

religious construction of, 365
   remarriage, 358
   same-sex marriage, 360
   servile forms of, 236
   sexual satisfaction in, 353
   sibling marriages, 139
   societal norms, 2
   violence in, 358–59
Marxist revolutions, 203
Marxist theory
   on capitalism, 55, 198, 200, 432–33, 459, 461–63
   on class conflict, 452–53
   class-society theory, 461–63
   and communism, 196
   criticism of, 200–201
   on deviance, 171
   foundation of, 10, 55
   on functions of laws, 164, 171
   on gender stratification, 267–68
   on Industrial Revolution, 200
   on interests of rich and laws, 164, 170
   on materialism, 55
   on medical care, 409–10
   on modernity, 459, 461–63
   political-economy model, 333–34, 454
   on religion, 365
   on social change, 452–53
   on social conflict, 55, 200–201, 453–54
   and socialism, 198
   and socialist feminism, 271
   on social movements, 454
   on social stratification, 200–201
   on urban political-economy, 432–33
   of wealthy, 208
   of worker alienation, 122, 200
   of working class, 209
   world economy model, 243–44
Masai, 40
Masculine traits
   aggression, 256, 398
   and body language, 98
   as health threat, 398
   impersonal rules emphasis, 68
   justice perspective, 68
   negative aspects of, 255–56, 398
   and personal space, 98
   type A personality, 256, 398
   types of, 257, 269
Massage parlors, 148
Mass behavior (*see* Social movements)
Mass consumption, 239
Mass media (*see also* Television)
   advertising, 257–58
   and clothing styles, 159
   defined, 73
   and eating disorders, 401
   and gender socialization, 257–58
   Iraq War coverage, 337–38
   and liberal/conservative views, 74
   popular use, national map, 73
   as socialization agent, 72–74
   and violence, 74
Mass production, 311
Mass society, defined, 459
Mass-society theory
   identity problems in, 463–64
   of modernity, 459–61
   of social movements, 454
Master status
   defined, 89
   disability as, 89
   gender as, 89
   race and ethnicity as, 283
   stigma as, 169
Material culture, defined, 36

Materialism
   Marxist view, 55
   and social conflict, 55
   as U.S. value, 43
Mathematical ability, gender differences, 253
Matriarchy, defined, 254
Matrilineal descent, 349
Matrilocality, 349
Matrimony (*see* Marriage)
Mauritania, female slavery in, 235
Mauritius, as middle-income nation, 229
"Me" (Mead), 69
Mean, 15
Meaning, focus of sociology, 18
Measurement, of variables, 15
Mecca, 368
Mechanical solidarity, 430–31, 457–58
Media (*see* Mass media)
Median, 15
Medicaid, 407
Medical care, 404–12
   and capitalism, 409–10
   genetic research, 411
   in global perspective, 405–6
   health insurance, 406–7
   holistic care, 404–5
   in Japan, 406
   nursing shortage, 407–8
   physicians, 95–96, 98, 408
   and politics, 410
   in Russia, 405–6
   social-conflict analysis, 409–10
   social construction of, 409
   in socialist societies, 405–6
   socialized, global view, 406
   structural-functional analysis, 409–10
   symbolic-interaction analysis, 408–9
   in U.S., 406–8
Medicalization of deviance, 169
Medical technology
   genetic research, 411
   new reproductive technology, 361
   oral contraceptives, 141
Medicare, 407
Medicine (*see also* Medical care)
   defined, 395
   holistic, 404–5
   scientific medicine, 404
Megalopolis, 429
Melanesians, and sexuality, 153
Melting pot concept, 49–50, 291
Men
   aggression of, 256, 398
   arrest data, 177, 272
   deadbeat dads, 358
   educational attainment, 208, 388
   extramarital sex, 143
   fathers, stay at home, 359–60
   gender socialization, 256–58
   homosexual (*see* Gay people)
   life expectancy, 253, 357, 398
   male-female differences (*see* Feminine traits; Gender differences; Gender roles; Masculine traits)
   male rape, 150
   masculinity, negative aspects of, 255–56, 398
   men's rights movement, 272–73
   at midlife, 77
   networks of, 117
   occupations of, 206–7, 259
   opposition to feminism, 272
   patriarchy, 254–56
   patrilineal descent, 349
   patrilocality, 369

low-income countries, 229, 246, 424–25
Malthusian theory, 423, 443
and natural environment, 443
and sociocultural evolution, 423–24
world population increase (1700–2100), 423
zero population growth, 424
Pornography
opponent and proponent views, 147–48
as power issue, 155
and sexual violence, 267–68
Portugal, African colonies, 241
Positivism, Comte's view, 10
Postconventional level of moral development (Kohlberg), 68
Postdenomination society, 373
Postindustrial economy, 317–21
computers and nature of work, 320–21
future view, 130
and Information Revolution, 46
Kuznets curve, 204
organizations in, 130, 136, 320–21
professions in, 318–19
self-employment, 319
and service industries, 312
Postindustrial society
cities of, 429
and new social movements, 454
Postmodernity
defined, 450–51, 467
future view, 470–71
intellectual themes of, 468–69
Poverty, 215–20
absolute poverty, 216
and African Americans, 216, 399
and AIDS risk, 403
and Asian Americans, 216, 298
blaming society for, 219
blaming the victim of, 218–19, 241, 423
causes of, 217–18
and children, 216, 239
culture of, 217
and elderly, 79, 216
and environmental racism, 442
and families, 216–19, 356, 359
feminization of, 217
and gender, 216–18
global (see Global poverty)
and health status, 396–97
and Hispanic Americans, 208, 216, 302
homelessness, 220
of immigrant workers, 343
and Native Americans, 294
negative stigma of, 219
poverty line, 216
and racial and ethnic minorities, 216
relative poverty, 216
in rural areas, 217
shantytowns in U.S., 230
in U.S., 215–20, 230–31
and welfare reform, 218–19
and women, 213, 216–18, 356, 359
working poor, 210, 216, 219–20
Power
and authority, 325
defined, 324–25
and deviance, 171
global power relationships, 237–38
and heterosexual relations, 154–55
and in-groups, 115
intergroup relations, 114

and language use, 101
political (see Politics)
and sexual violence, 265
in social interaction, 95–96, 101
and wealth, 206, 326
of women, global map, 255
Power-elite model, 333
Powerlessness
as deviant, 171
and modernity, 464–65
Practicality, as U.S. value, 43
Preconventional level of moral development (Kohlberg), 68
Predestination, 367
Pregnancy (see also Reproduction)
abortion, 154–56
teenagers, 146–47, 359
Preindustrial societies (see also Agrarian societies; Horticultural societies; Hunting and gathering societies; Pastoral societies)
gender roles, 254
Prejudice, 284–87
ageism, 78–79
authoritarian personality theory, 288
conflict theory, 289
culture theory, 288
defined, 284
ethnocentrism, 52–53
measurement of, 284–86
racism, 287
relationship to discrimination, 290
scapegoat theory, 287–88
and stereotyping, 284, 290
Premarital sex, 143
Preoperational stage (Piaget), 67
Preparatory schools, 386
Presbyterians, 294
social class of, 370
Presentation of self, elements of, 95–99, 409
Presidential election (2000)
popular vote by county, national map, 331
voter income level, 211
Prestige
power-elite, 333
social, 205–8
and work (see Occupational prestige)
Primary deviance, 168
Primary economic sector, 312
Primary groups, 111–12, 114
Primary sex characteristics, 137
Primates
intelligence of, 38
social isolation study, 65–66
Primogeniture, 195
Prisons
versus community-based correction, 184–85
imprisonment, justification for, 182–83
inmate increase, 187
inmates voting prohibition, 332
and resocialization, 81
Stanford County Prison study, 21–22
Privacy
legislation related to, 129
snoop software, 133
surveillance methods, 129
technology and erosion of, 128–29
Privacy Act of 1974, 129
Private schools, 386, 393–94
Probation, 185
Pro-choice abortion position, 102, 155–56
Productivity, economic, measurement of, 316

Profane, defined, 363
Professions
defined, 318
men versus women in, 263
work characteristics of, 318–19
Profit motive
and capitalism, 314
in medical care, 410
Progress
and modernity, 465–66
and social change, 465–66
as U.S. value, 43
Progressive education, 385
Prohibition, 166, 173
Projective labeling, 169
Proletariat, defined, 200
Pro-life abortion position, 102, 155–56
Promise Keepers, 375, 454
Promotion practices, glass ceiling, 25, 262, 321
Property crime, 175–76
Property ownership
and capitalism, 314
collective, 315
and estate system, 195
inheritance rules, 349
Proposition 187, 304
Proselytize, 369
Prostitution, 148–50
global map of, 149
latent functions, 152
sexual slavery, 154
and social inequality, 154
as victimless crime, 149–50, 176
Protestant Church, schools of, 386
Protestantism (see also White Anglo-Saxon Protestants [WASPs])
denominations, 370
fundamentalist, 374–75
practice in U.S., 369–71
and social class, 370
Protestant Reformation, Calvinism, 366–67
Protestant work ethic
and capitalism, 366–67, 453
and white Anglo-Saxon Protestants (WASPs), 294
Psychoanalysis, 66
Psychosomatic disorders, 409
Puberty, sexual maturity, 137–38
Public-private partnerships, 323
Public schools, 386–87
Puerto Ricans
family life, 355
income of, 302–3
revolving door pattern, 302
social standing of, 303
Spanish language speakers, 302
Puerto Rico
and modernization, 239
U.S. control, 241
Punishment of criminals (see Corrections system)
Pygmies (Africa), 45

Qualitative data, 18
Quality circles, 125
Quality of life
global perspective, 232
new social movements theory, 454
U.S., 468–69
Quantitative data, 18
Queer theory, 155–56
Questionnaires, survey research, 23
Quid pro quo sexual harassment, 265
Qur'an (Koran), 363, 365

Race (see also Racial and ethnic minorities)
defined, 280
intelligence issue, 288–89
racial categories, 281
as social construction, 280–81
Race consciousness, meaning of, 289
Racial discrimination, 290–91
and accomplished African Americans, 23–25
civil rights movement, 56, 290–91, 296, 366
Du Bois on, 13, 297
institutional, 290–91
Jim Crow, 296, 304
and prejudice, 284–87
in professional sports, 16, 292
race/class/gender intersection, 264–65
racial profiling in schools, 390
segregation as (see Racial segregation)
and stereotyping, 74, 284, 290
and voting rights, 296
Racial and ethnic minorities, 280–305 (see also Ethnicity; Minorities; Multiculturalism; specific racial and ethnic categories)
African Americans, 295–97
arrest data, 178
Asian Americans, 297–300
bilingualism of, 282
composition in U.S., 283, 293–303
and discrimination, 289–90
and education, 297, 386–89
family life, 354–56
glass ceiling, 25, 321
and group dynamics, 116
and hate crimes, 174
health status, 399
Hispanic Americans, 300–303
income inequality, 265
in-group versus out-group, 114
interracial marriage, 356
intersection theory, 264–65
in labor force, 321
minority/majority interaction, 290–92
multiracial trend, 282
Native Americans, 293–94
negative views of (see Discrimination; Prejudice; Racial discrimination; Racism)
in nursing homes, 85
and organized crime, 173
political affiliation of, 330
and poverty, 216
and prejudice, 284–87
and racism, 287
and religion, 370–71
and sexually transmitted disease (STD), 400, 403
single-parent families, 359
and social inequality, 207–8
and social marginality, 5
social mobility of, 212–13
and social stratification, 207–8
stereotyping of, 74, 284, 290
and suicide rates, 4–5
and television programming, 74
and unemployment, 297, 320
in U.S., 293–303
in U.S. cities, 433
and voter participation, 331–32
white ethnic Americans, 303
and workplace discrimination, 124
and workplace diversity, 321

Suicide
  Durkheim's study, 4–5, 11, 458
  and gender, 4–5
  historical increase in, 458
  and modernity, 458
  national map of, 11
  and racial/ethnic minorities, 4–5
  and social integration, 4
  U.S. rates, 5, 11
Sunbelt cities, 429, 432
Superego, 66, 70, 164
Supply and demand, and capitalism, 314
Surrogate motherhood, 361
Survey research, 22–25
  African American elite study, 23–25
  elements of, 22–23
  interviews, 21–22
  population in, 23
  questionnaires, 23
  sampling in, 23
Survival of the fittest, 199
Sustainable living, 444
Sweatshops, 236
Sweden
  cohabitation, 359
  health care system in, 406
  as high-income nation, 232
  welfare capitalism, 316, 338
  women's status, 254, 264
Symbolic institutions, family and
    religion as, 346
Symbolic-interaction approach (see
    also individual topics)
  elements of, 13–14
  evaluation of, 14
Symbols
  cultural, 40
  cyber-symbols, 41
  defined, 40
  and group bonding, 454
  and social experience, 69
  written language as, 40
Syphilis, 400
Syria, as middle-income nation, 232

Tables, reading data of, 24
Taboos, incest taboo, 139–40, 152
Tact, and social interaction, 98–99
Taiwan, modernization of, 240
Taliban, 243, 254, 339
Tan't Batu people (Philippines), 442
Taxpayer cheating, 168
Tchambuli peoples (New Guinea),
    Mead's gender study, 253
Teacher shortage, 395
Technology
  computer use, 320–21, 395
  and culture, 44–46
  defined, 44
  and globalization, 8
  and industrial society (see
    Industrialization; Industrial
    revolution)
  information technology (see
    Computers; Information
    Revolution; Internet)
  Kuznets curve, 203–4
  in medicine (see Medical technology)
  military technology, 337
  and modernization, 461
  and organizations, 120–21
  and population growth, 424
  primitive and global poverty, 236
  and social change, 8–9
  and social stratification, 203–4
  sociocultural evolution, 45–46
  and workplace, 320–21
Teenagers (see Adolescents)

Telephones, and modernization, 457
Television (see also Mass media)
  electronic church, 375
  gender role stereotyping, 257–58
  minority characters, 74
  national map of, 73
  ownership, global view, 74
  pre-TV society, 457
  racial stereotyping, 74
  viewing habits, 73–74
  violence on, 74
Temporary Assistance for Needy
    Families (TANF), 219
Terminal illness, right-to-die, 403–4
Terrorism, 335–37 (see also
    September 11 attacks)
  versus conventional warfare, 336–37
  defined, 335
  features of, 335
  as global issue, 179
  state-sponsored, 335
  war on terror, 335
Tertiary economic sector, 312
Testing, standardized tests, 386, 392
Test-tube babies, 361
Thailand
  as middle-income nation, 232
  modernization of, 239
  prostitution, 150
  servile marriage in, 236
Thanatos (death instinct), 66
Theological stage of society (Comte),
    10
Theoretical approach, defined, 11
Theoretical paradigm (see Sociological
    theories)
Theory, defined, 11
Third estate, 195
Third World, 227 (see also Global
    poverty; Low-income countries)
Thirteenth Amendment, 296
Thomas theorem, 93
Three Worlds model, 227–28 (see also
    High-income countries; Low-
    income countries; Middle-income
    countries)
Tibet, polyandry, 348
Time, awareness of and modernity, 456
Titanic, 192, 200
Tobacco industry, 399
Togo, female genital mutilation, 267
Tool use, and sociocultural evolution,
    45
Torah, 363
Total institutions, 81 (see also
    Corrections system)
Totalitarianism, features of, 328
Totem, 364
Touching, as nonverbal
    communication, 98
Tracking in schools
  defined, 386
  social-conflict view, 13, 386
Trade, foreign exports, 242
Tradition
  defined, 119
  Gemeinschaft and community, 430,
    456–57, 460
  versus modernization, 238–39,
    455–56
  traditional authority, 325
  traditional societies (see Agrarian
    societies)
  tradition-directedness, 463–64, 470
Transnational corporation (see
    Multinational corporation)
Transportation (see Automobiles)
Transsexuals, 138, 156

Triads, 116
Trust
  and adolescents, 71
  Erikson's stage, 70
Turkey, descriptions of, 38
Tutsis, 292
Tyco International, 162, 172
Type A personality, 256, 398

Ukraine, as middle-income nation, 232
Underground Railroad, 298
Unemployment
  and African Americans, 296, 320
  causes of, 320
  and crime rate, 187
  Great Depression, 5
  rates in U.S., 320
United Church of Christ, social class
    of, 370
United Kingdom (see Great Britain)
United Nations
  as data source, 26
  and prevention of war, 336
  Universal Declaration of Human
    Rights, 236
United States (see also national maps
    list in table of contents; individual
    topics)
  age-sex population pyramid, 422
  aging in, 77–79
  arms race, 337
  automobile ownership, 45
  birth rate, 418–19
  capital punishment, 184–85
  constitution of (see Constitution of
    United States)
  core U.S. values, 43–44
  crime rates, 176
  culture compared to Canada, 58
  death, leading causes, 396
  death rate, 419
  display of affection, 139
  divorce rate in, 357
  economy (see Economy)
  education in, 384–85
  ethnic minority demographics, 301
  family income, 205, 206, 212, 215
  family size, 3
  family size ideal, 354
  gay people in population, 145
  gender equality ranking, 254
  government and politics (see Federal
    government; Politics, U.S.)
  graying of population (1900–2050),
    78
  health status, 383–90
  as high-income nation, 7, 228, 232
  high versus popular culture, 47–48
  housework and women, 91
  income distribution, 205
  individualism as value, 126
  infant mortality rate, 419
  job projections to 2010, 325
  labor force, 259
  language diversity, 50
  las colonias, 230
  life expectancy, 420
  McDonaldization concept, 127–30
  marriage laws, first cousins, 139
  and mass consumption, 239
  medical care programs, 406–8
  migration in, 420
  military spending, 337
  minorities in cities, 433
  minority-majority, 284
  as multicultural society, 36, 46, 58
  Native American reservations, 293–94
  occupational prestige in, 206

population change, 420
population growth, 421
postindustrial workplace, 317–21
poverty in, 215–20, 230–31
presidential election (2000), popular
    vote, 331
privacy issue, 128–29
quality of life in, 232, 468–69
racial and ethnic minorities, 280–305
religion in, 369–76
religious diversity, 371
schooling in, 384–95
sexual attitudes, 140–43
sexual orientation in, 145
shantytowns in, 230
slavery issue, 295–96
social classes, 208–10
social class inequality, 205–8
social mobility, 211–12
suicide rates, 5, 11
teenage pregnancy rates, 147
television ownership, 74
television viewing habits, 73–74
urbanization of, 428–29
urban population (1790–2000), 428
values of, 43–44
violent crime risk, 175
war casualties, historical view, 336
water supply deficit, 438
welfare state, 329
women in politics, 262–64
work, changing pattern, 317
Universal Declaration of Human
    Rights, 236
Upper class, 208–9
Upper-middle class, 209
Upper-upper class, 209
Upward social mobility, 211
Urban ecology, 432
Urbanism, 430–33
  blasé urbanite, 431
  Chicago school theories, 431–32
  and Gesellschaft, 430, 456–58, 462
  mechanical versus organic solidarity,
    430–31
  urban ecology, 432
  urban political economy, 432–33
Urbanization, 425–34 (see also Cities)
  cities, evolution of, 426–28
  defined, 426
  in low-income countries, 433–34
  urban revolution, 343
  in U.S., historical view, 428–29
USA PATRIOT Act, 129
USSR (see Soviet Union)
Utilitarian organizations, 119

Validity of measurement, 15
Value-free research, 18
Values
  and concept of deviance, 165
  contradictory values, 44
  defined, 43
  and language use, 101–3
  and social class, 210
  U.S. culture, 43–44
Variables
  correlation of, 15–18
  defined, 15
  dependent and independent, 16
  operationalizing, 15
  relationships between, 15, 16–18
  in sociological research, 15, 17–18
Venereal disease (see Sexually
    transmitted disease [STD])
Venezuela, as middle-income nation,
    232
Verstehen (understanding), 18

SINGLE PC LICENSE AGREEMENT AND LIMITED WARRANTY

READ THIS LICENSE CAREFULLY BEFORE OPENING THIS PACKAGE. BY OPENING THIS PACKAGE, YOU ARE AGREEING TO THE TERMS AND CONDITIONS OF THIS LICENSE. IF YOU DO NOT AGREE, DO NOT OPEN THE PACKAGE. PROMPTLY RETURN THE UNOPENED PACKAGE AND ALL ACCOMPANYING ITEMS TO THE PLACE YOU OBTAINED THEM [[FOR A FULL REFUND OF ANY SUMS YOU HAVE PAID FOR THE SOFT-WARE]]. *THESE TERMS APPLY TO ALL LICENSED SOFTWARE ON THE DISK EXCEPT THAT THE TERMS FOR USE OF ANY SHAREWARE OR FREEWARE ON THE DISKETTES ARE AS SET FORTH IN THE ELECTRONIC LICENSE LOCATED ON THE DISK:*

1. **GRANT OF LICENSE and OWNERSHIP:** The enclosed computer programs <<and data>> ("Software") are licensed, not sold, to you by Pearson Education, Inc. publishing as Prentice Hall ("We" or the "Company") and in consideration [[of your payment of the license fee, which is part of the price you paid]] [[of your purchase or adoption of the accompanying Company textbooks and/or other materials,]] and your agreement to these terms. We reserve any rights not granted to you. You own only the disk(s) but we and/or our licensors own the Software itself. This license allows you to use and display your copy of the Software on a single computer (i.e., with a single CPU) at a single location for <u>academic</u> use only, so long as you comply with the terms of this Agreement. You may make one copy for back up, or transfer your copy to another CPU, provided that the Software is usable on only one computer.

2. **RESTRICTIONS:** You may <u>not</u> transfer or distribute the Software or documentation to anyone else. Except for backup, you may <u>not</u> copy the documentation or the Software. You may <u>not</u> network the Software or otherwise use it on more than one computer or computer terminal at the same time. You may <u>not</u> reverse engineer, disassemble, decompile, modify, adapt, translate, or create derivative works based on the Software or the Documentation. You may be held legally responsible for any copying or copyright infringement that is caused by your failure to abide by the terms of these restrictions.

3. **TERMINATION:** This license is effective until terminated. This license will terminate automatically without notice from the Company if you fail to comply with any provisions or limitations of this license. Upon termination, you shall destroy the Documentation and all copies of the Software. All provisions of this Agreement as to limitation and disclaimer of warranties, limitation of liability, remedies or damages, and our ownership rights shall survive termination.

4. **LIMITED WARRANTY AND DISCLAIMER OF WARRANTY:** Company warrants that for a period of 60 days from the date you purchase this SOFTWARE (or purchase or adopt the accompanying textbook), the Software, when properly installed and used in accordance with the Documentation, will operate in substantial conformity with the description of the Software set forth in the Documentation, and that for a period of 30 days the disk(s) on which the Software is delivered shall be free from defects in materials and workmanship under normal use. The Company does <u>not</u> warrant that the Software will meet your requirements or that the operation of the Software will be uninterrupted or error-free. Your only remedy and the Company's only obligation under these limited warranties is, at the Company's option, return of the disk for a refund of any amounts paid for it by you or replacement of the disk. THIS LIMITED WARRANTY IS THE ONLY WARRANTY PROVIDED BY THE COMPANY AND ITS LICENSORS, AND THE COMPANY AND ITS LICENSORS DISCLAIM ALL OTHER WARRANTIES, EXPRESS OR IMPLIED, INCLUDING WITHOUT LIMITATION, THE IMPLIED WARRANTIES OF MERCHANTABILITY AND FITNESS FOR A PARTICULAR PURPOSE. THE COMPANY DOES NOT WARRANT, GUARANTEE OR MAKE ANY REPRESENTATION REGARDING THE ACCURACY, RELIABILITY, CURRENTNESS, USE, OR RESULTS OF USE, OF THE SOFTWARE.

5. **LIMITATION OF REMEDIES AND DAMAGES:**   IN NO EVENT, SHALL THE COMPANY OR ITS EMPLOYEES, AGENTS, LICENSORS, OR CONTRACTORS BE LIABLE FOR ANY INCIDENTAL, INDIRECT, SPECIAL, OR CONSEQUENTIAL DAMAGES ARISING OUT OF OR IN CONNECTION WITH THIS LICENSE OR THE SOFTWARE, INCLUDING FOR LOSS OF USE, LOSS OF DATA, LOSS OF INCOME OR PROFIT, OR OTHER LOSSES, SUSTAINED AS A RESULT OF INJURY TO ANY PERSON, OR LOSS OF OR DAMAGE TO PROPERTY, OR CLAIMS OF THIRD PARTIES, EVEN IF THE COMPANY OR AN AUTHORIZED REPRESENTATIVE OF THE COMPANY HAS BEEN ADVISED OF THE POSSIBILITY OF SUCH DAMAGES. IN NO EVENT SHALL THE LIABILITY OF THE COMPANY FOR DAMAGES WITH RESPECT TO THE SOFTWARE EXCEED THE AMOUNTS ACTUALLY PAID BY YOU, IF ANY, FOR THE SOFTWARE OR THE ACCOMPANYING TEXTBOOK. BECAUSE SOME JURISDICTIONS DO NOT ALLOW THE LIMITATION OF LIABILITY IN CERTAIN CIRCUMSTANCES, THE ABOVE LIMITATIONS MAY NOT ALWAYS APPLY TO YOU.

6. **GENERAL:** THIS AGREEMENT SHALL BE CONSTRUED IN ACCORDANCE WITH THE LAWS OF THE UNITED STATES OF AMERICA AND THE STATE OF NEW YORK, APPLICABLE TO CONTRACTS MADE IN NEW YORK, AND SHALL BENEFIT THE COMPANY, ITS AFFILIATES AND ASSIGNEES. HIS AGREEMENT IS THE COMPLETE AND EXCLUSIVE STATEMENT OF THE AGREEMENT BETWEEN YOU AND THE COMPANY AND SUPERSEDES ALL PROPOSALS OR PRIOR AGREEMENTS, ORAL, OR WRITTEN, AND ANY OTHER COMMUNICATIONS BETWEEN YOU AND THE COMPANY OR ANY REPRESENTATIVE OF THE COMPANY RELATING TO THE SUBJECT MATTER OF THIS AGREEMENT. If you are a U.S. Government user, this Software is licensed with "restricted rights" as set forth in subparagraphs (a)-(d) of the Commercial Computer-Restricted Rights clause at FAR 52.227-19 or in subparagraphs (c)(1)(ii) of the Rights in Technical Data and Computer Software clause at DFARS 252.227-7013, and similar clauses, as applicable.

Should you have any questions concerning this agreement or if you wish to contact the Company for any reason, please contact in writing:
Social Sciences Media Editor, Prentice Hall, One Lake Street Upper Saddle River, NJ 07458.